Anthony & B
Magistrates'

2020

Whilst care has been taken to ensure the accuracy of the contents of this book, no responsibility for loss occasioned to any person acting or refraining from action as a result of any statement in it can be accepted by the author or the publisher. Readers should take specialist professional advice before entering into any specific transaction.

Anthony & Berryman's Magistrates' Court Guide

2020

A J Turner

Barrister, Chambers of Adrian Turner, Eastbourne

LexisNexis®

LexisNexis® UK & Worldwide

United Kingdom	RELX (UK) Limited trading as LexisNexis®, 1–3 Strand, London WC2N 5JR and 9–10 St Andrew Square, Edinburgh EH2 2AF
LNUK Global Partners	LexisNexis® encompasses authoritative legal publishing brands dating back to the 19th century including: Butterworths® in the United Kingdom, Canada and the Asia-Pacific region; Les Editions du Juris Classeur in France; and Matthew Bender® worldwide. Details of LexisNexis® locations worldwide can be found at www.lexisnexis.com

Published by LexisNexis®

A CIP Catalogue record for this book is available from the British Library.

ISBN for this volume: 9781474311021

Printed and bound by CPI Group (UK) Ltd, Croydon, CR0 4YY

Visit LexisNexis UK at www.lexisnexis.co.uk

Comment

The HMCTS Reform Update – Crime states in its introduction 'Our ambition is to provide smarter, more joined-up and streamlined processes to deliver better criminal justice for all'.

In the list of reforms delivered so far, we then read:

- a digital case management system to support the Single Justice Procedure (SJP) for summary offences has handled over 31,000 Transport for London cases, cutting delays and waste;
- the make a plea online service for summary traffic offences has been rolled out to all police forces with more than 236,000 people entering a plea online since 2015;
- a magistrates' court rota is in use nationally, matching nearly 13,000 magistrates with court sittings;
- digital mark up is in use across all magistrates' courts, enabling the legal advisors in court to record the case outcome instantly;
- jurors can now reply to a jury summons online; and
- the common platform is handling real cases in a pilot in the Crown Court in Liverpool, and pilots have begun in SJP cases too.

Then, as to what will be delivered by the end of the year, we are informed HMCTS will have:

- completed a nationwide roll out so that all TV Licensing and DVLA prosecutions within the SJP are handled by the new digital case management system, with defendants able to plead online;
- published online listings of all SJP cases being heard as a result of prosecutions by Transport for London (TfL)and TV Licensing (TVL);
- started to pilot new proof of concept technology in video remand hearings;
- introduced additional functionality within the common platform pilot in Liverpool, in advance of a roll-out to other Crown Courts (the main roll-out taking place during 2020);
- expanded the use of common platform in magistrates' courts, starting with other SJP referrals and then widening out to cover other case types (with fuller roll-out during 2020).

On the face of it, there does not appear to be anything remarkable or controversial about any of this. It looks like management trying to maximise the benefits of IT, and that is no doubt what is intended. A close inspection of what is actually happening on the ground, however, suggests there should be concerns. Here are some examples.

Digital mark up

This means the immediate recording of court adjudications. It is fine in principle, but the current structure of DMU result entry means it often takes a long time, with one screen after another needing to be completed. Meanwhile, the court cannot be getting on with anything else, since the person doing the inputting is the bench legal advisor (or court associate). The system wastes a significant amount of court time, and can be very frustrating for BLAs who would rather be focusing on law and procedure than carrying out clerical tasks.

Video links

A great deal of time, money, travel and administration can be saved by using video link to conduct routine hearings with defendants who are in prison, and video conferencing has been around for a long time and works perfectly well in, for example, the commercial sector. However, CJS practitioners experience problems with it all too frequently. Serving prisoners are often moved around without being checked and, consequently, are not where they are 'supposed to be' at the time of the link; prison staff shortages, or prisoner refusal to leave the cell, can result in a 'no show'; or the equipment simply fails.

Single justice procedure

It is important to remember what this is, namely, in reality, an extension of the fixed penalty system. If the defendant signs the guilty plea section, even without a word of mitigation s/he will get a reduction of one-third of the fine (just as paying a fixed penalty promptly attracts a discount). Failure to do this will result in the statements accompanying the summons/requisition being read, leading almost inevitably to a conviction. This only takes seconds, but pushes the fine up by 50%. As to the level of the fine, this will be based on the defendant's means, as known or assumed. If these are not stated, an assumption of average net weekly pay will be made. So, those who are earning above that level profit by leaving the means section blank. Those who are worse off should, of course, fill it in. However, this assumes that they have the language and skills to do so, and appreciate the benefits. Many do not. Indeed, this is often what got them into trouble in the first place. Assuming that such people enjoy 'average net weekly pay', where the offence is economic, such as using a TV without a licence, it is simply unrealistic. Consequently, fines (with the accompanying 10% surcharges) are not paid and the bailiffs come calling to compound the misery. It flies in the face of this reality to think that putting the procedure on-line will improve the quality and outcomes of the single justice procedure. It will simply increase the discrimination against those who, through no fault of their own, lack access to a computer or the necessary literacy skills.

More fundamental issues

So much money going towards IT and video links means less money is available for other purposes, such as repairing buildings and recruiting more staff.

During the last decade or so, the criminal justice system has borne disproportionately large cuts in its budgets. This has caused dramatic falls in policing and prosecutions, under-funded public representation and dire conditions in our prisons.

I do not agree with many of the views expressed by the author of 'The Secret Barrister'. But I have no reason to doubt the accuracy of the many, lamentable failures the author relates. Not all were the result of under-funding, but most clearly were.

More court rooms, judges and case workers to ensure trials take place quickly should surely come before expensive IT solutions to 'improve' case management.

New material

The Courts and Tribunals (Judiciary and Functions of Staff) Act 2018 continues to wait in the wings, so 'justices' clerks' and 'clerks of the court' are yet to become 'designated officers' and 'persons authorised'.

The Offensive Weapons Act 2019 is the most significant piece of criminal justice litigation to be enacted since the last edition of this publication, but this, too, awaits implementation and, without any indication as to when this will happen, I have decided not to include in this edition the offences and the knife crime prevention orders it creates.

There is, nevertheless, a great deal of new material in *Anthony & Berryman 2020*. A full list appears below.

Criminal offences dealt with in magistrates' courts

A[8.20]	Householder defence where defendant became a trespasser after entering the premises	*R v Cheeseman*
A[9.5]	Resist PC where other officers were not acting in the execution of their duty	*Dixon v CPS*
A[9A]	New narrative on assaults on emergency workers	
A[11.13]	Offensive weapons and 'reasonable excuse'	*Garry v CPS*
A[15.11]	Assault – when deception as to medical qualifications can vitiate consent to a medical procedure	*R v Melin*
A[26.4A]	Supplying controlled drugs – number of offences created by s 4(3) of the MDA 1971	*R v Coker*
A[36.8]	Fraud – failure to disclose information – meaning of 'legal duty to disclose' and whether this embraces liability to disclose residence for council tax purposes	*R v D*
A[43.3]	Possession of indecent images and proof of knowledge	*R v Okoro*

A[43.8]	Indecent photographs of children – availability of the defence under s 160(1) of the Criminal Justice Act 1988 where the defendant had reasonable cause to suspect the image was indecent but not that it was an indecent image of a child	*R v Collier*
A[45.6]	When a service is performed for the purposes of the offence of making off without payment	*R v Wilkinson*
A[47.12]	Availability of self defence to a charge of obstructing a PC	*Oraki v CPS*
A[52.4]	Sexual touching – when purpose is relevant	*R v DJ*
A[52.6]	A link is required between 'for the purposes of sexual gratification' and the presence or observation of a child for the offence under s 11(1)(c) of the Sexual Offences Act 2003	*R v B and L*
A[56.2]	Plying for hire – bookings through the Uber app	*Reading Borough Council v Ali*
A[57.18]	The power of attorney exception where land can be stolen requires a valid power of attorney	*R v Gimbert*
A[68]	New offences added to 'voyeurism'	
A[72.14]	Persons who have standing in applications under s 4B(1) of the of the Dangerous Dogs Act 1991	*Henderson v Commissioner of Police for the Metropolis*
A[72.15]	Variation or enforcement of contingent destruction orders	*Chief Constable of Merseyside Police v Doyle*
A[72.20]	Fighting dogs – matters to be considered for the making of destruction orders other than on conviction	*R (Golding) v Crown Court at Maidstone*
A[85.3A]	Obstructing the highway – the relevance of arts 10 and 11 of the ECHR to the defence of 'lawful excuse'	*DPP v Zeigler*
A[87.4]	Psychoactive substances – the psychoactive effect may be produced directly or indirectly	*R v Rochester*

Sentencing and orders

B[8.16]	New narrative on ordering pre-sentence reports on committal for sentence	
B[8A]	New narrative on community protection notes and public spaces protection orders	
B[9.9]	New narrative on electronic monitoring as a stand-alone requirement in a community order or to monitor compliance with other requirements	
B[9.23]	New narrative on electronic monitoring of the offender's whereabouts otherwise than for the purpose of securing compliance with other requirements	
B[9.10]	Extension of community orders with an unpaid work requirement	*National Probation Service v Blackfriars Crown Court*
B[11.1]	Committal to prison for non-payment of confiscation orders	*R (on the application of Beach) v Folkestone Magistrates' Court*
B[12.20]	Wasted costs – parties to criminal proceedings	*Re Soni (Appeal against wasted costs order)*
B[13.6]	Inability of Crown Court to vary a CBO	*R v Potter*
B[15.17]	Pre-sentence reports and suspended sentences	*R v Ebbs*
B[19.10]	Where a detention and training order is imposed on a person in breach of an earlier DTO the new sentence must have immediate effect	*R v McGeechan*
B[34.24]	New narrative as to whether a custodial sentence may exceed six months where the terms imposed for the either way offence are in total less than six months	
B[34.31]	Consecutive sentences where an offence of possession of an offensive weapon is an aggravating feature of an offence of affray	*R v Birchall (Leevon)*

B[35.2]	Proceedings for gang/drug dealing-related injunctions are civil in nature	*Jones v Birmingham City Council*
B[38.2]	Variation of sentence to impose points disqualification must be dealt with in open court	*R v Cox*
B[38.5]	Proceeding in absence and re-opening convictions	*R (Rathor) v Southampton Magistrates' Court*
B[40.3]	The Crown Court cannot make a referral order	*R v Koffi*
B[44.3]	Indefinite sexual harm prevention orders	*R v Al Mahmood*
B[44.3]	Sexual harm prevention orders – indefinite ban on internet access impermissible	*R v Connor; R v Hewitt*
B[50.2]	New surcharge levels	

Road Traffic

C[5.45]	Purpose of the power to disqualify from driving under s 146 of the PCC(S)A 2000	*R v Griffin*
C[8.9]	Addition of new fixed penalty offences	
C[16.6]	Dangerous driving and joint enterprise	*Clarke v Farley*
C[16B.5A]	Causing death offences – causation is to be considered in the context of causing death and not causing the accident which led to death	*R v Wilson*
C[20.7]	When car parks are 'other public places'	*Richardson v DPP*
C[33.9]	Scope of mandatory insurance requirements under s 145(3) of the RTA 1988	

Procedure

D[1B.7]	Guidance on the procedure and exercise of power to postpone reporting of proceedings	*R v Sarker*
D[1B.12]	Abuse of process – same principles apply to private prosecution	*D Ltd v A*

D[4.3]	Need for strict compliance with mode of trial procedures	*R (Bahbahani) v Ealing Magistrates' Court*
D[5.1]	Bail Act offences cannot be committed to the Crown court otherwise than for sentence	*R v Osman*
D[6.4AA]	An unscheduled trial should not take place where the prosecutor is an associate prosecutor	*DPP v Berry*
D[6.17A]	Vacating trials where defence expert is unavailable	*R (Parashar) v Sunderland Magistrates' Court*
D[6.17B]	No power to prevent prosecution from proceeding where there has been a failure to comply with disclosure requirements, save as an abuse of process	
D[6.19A]	Absent defendants and sick certificates	*R (Rathor) v Southampton Magistrates' Court*
D[6.24]	Need for Newton hearing where homophobic aggravation is disputed	*DPP v Giles*
D[6.44A]	A failure to issue a requisition or single justice procedure notice at the same time as the charge may be a procedural error but it does not render the proceedings a nullity	*DPP v McFarlane*
D[6.48]	Procedure where justices refuse to state a case	*R (Arthur) v Crown Court at Blackfriars*

Civil and miscellaneous matters

F[5.5]	Issue of search warrants where post-arrest search powers are available	*R (Singh) v National Crime Agency*

Appreciation

I am very grateful indeed to the LexisNexis Commissioning Editor, Amy, and the Senior House Editor, Robin, for their great help, support and skill in taking in my, not always perfectly clear, instructions. I am also very grateful to my wife, Yelena, for checking my manuscript and for her patience generally.

ADRIAN TURNER

Barrister, Chambers of Adrian Turner, Eastbourne

Contents

Preface **v**

Table of statutes **xv**

Table of statutory instruments **xxxix**

Table of cases **xlv**

A CRIMINAL OFFENCES DEALT WITH IN MAGISTRATES' COURTS **1**

Index to criminal offences and table of maximum penalties **2**

B SENTENCING AND ORDERS **503**

Index to sentencing **504**

C ROAD TRAFFIC OFFENCES **735**

Index and penalties for road traffic offences **736**

Speed and distance chart **744**

Braking distances **745**

Shortest stopping distances **746**

Endorsement and disqualification **747**

D PROCEDURE **901**

E THE YOUTH COURT **983**

F CIVIL AND MISCELLANEOUS MATTERS **1031**

General index **1063**

Table of Statutes

Paragraph references printed in **bold** type indicate where the Statute is set out in part or in full.

A

Access to Justice Act 1999 .... D9.19
Administration of Justice Act 1970
s 41(1)(b) B50.4
Sch 9
para 13 .... B50.4
Pt 1
para 9A .... B 14.3
Administration of Justice Act (Miscellaneous Provisions) Act 1933
s 2(2)(b) B12.16A
Animal Welfare Act 2006
s 1 .... A 5.2
2 .... A 5.2
4 .... A5.3
(1) .... A 5.1, A 5.2
(2) .... A 5.1, A5.2
5 .... A 5.2
6 .... A 5.2
8 .... A5.3
(1) .... A 5.1
(7) .... A 5.2
9 .... A 5.1, A5.3
(1) .... A 5.2
31(1)(b) A5.2
(2) .... A 5.2
32 .... A5.5
33 .... A 5.4
34(5) A5.5
37 .... A 5.4
43 .... A 5.4
Anti-Social Behaviour Act 2003
s 1 .... A26.12
2 .... B 12.31
(3)(a), (b) A26.12
(6) A26.12
4 .... A26.12
Anti-Social Behaviour Act 2003 – *cont.*
s 5(4), (5) A26.12
6(1), (2) A26.12
Pt 1A (ss 11A–11I) A26.12
s 19 .... B37
20 .... A.1; B37
(2) .... B 37.6
(4) .... B 37.5
21 .... B37
(1), (1A) .... B 37.3
(3) .... B 37.7, B 37.9, B 37.10
22 .... B37, B 37.1, B 37.12
26 .... B37, B 37.4
(4) .... B 37.5
(6)–(8) .... B 37.5
26A(2) .... B 37.4
(8) .... B 37.11
26B(2) .... B 37.4
(3) .... B 37.5
(9) .... B 37.11
27 .... B37
(2) .... B 37.6
(3) .... B 37.7, B 37.9, B 37.10
28 .... B37, B 37.12
39(4) A76.7, A76A.4
40 .... A26.12
76–91 .... A26.12
Anti-social Behaviour, Crime and Policing Act 2014 .... B 13.1, B 44.1
s 1 .... B 37.1, B 37.2
(1)–(3) .... B 48.2
(4)–(7) .... B 48.3
2(1)(a)–(c) .... B 48.2
(3) .... B 48.2
3(1), (2) .... B 48.3
(6) .... B 48.3
4(1), (2) .... B 48.4

Anti-social Behaviour, Crime and Policing Act 2014 – *cont.*
s 5 .... B 49.2
6 .... B 48.6
7(1)–(4) .... B 48.7
8(1)–(3) .... B 48.8
9(1), (2) .... B 48.4
(3) .... B 48.1, B 48.4
(4)–(6) .... B 48.4
10(1) .... B 48.5
(2) .... B 48.1, B 48.5
(3) .... B 48.5
(5)–(8) .... B 48.5
13(1) .... B 48.3
14 .... B 48.2
(1), (2) .... B 48.6
(3) .... B 48.8
15–17 .... B 48.11
21 .... B 2.2, B 48.12
(2) .... B 25.1
(4), (5) .... B 25.1
22 .... B 13.5, B 37.2
(3), (4) .... B 13.2
(6) .... B 13.2
(8) .... B 13.2
23 .... B 13.4
(6) .... B 13.3
24(1), (2) .... B 13.5
25 .... B 13.6
26 .... B 13.6
(3) .... B 13.3
27, 28 .... B 13.6
30 .... B 13.7
33 .... B 2.3
(2)–(4) .... B 25.1
43(1) B8A.2
(3), (4) B8A.3
(5) B8A.2
(8) B8A.3
46 .... B8A.3, B8A.5
47 .... B8A.3, B8A.4
48, 49 .... B8A.3, B8A.5
50, 51 .... B8A.3
59(1)–(3) B8A.6
(4)–(7) B8A.7
61 .... B8A.9
63 .... B8A.10
64 .... B8A.7
66 .... B8A.11
67 .... B8A.12
Pt 4, Ch 3 (ss 76–93) B6. B8A.1

Anti-social Behaviour, Crime and Policing Act 2014 – *cont.*
s 76, 77 .... B 6.1
79 .... B 6.3
80(1) .... B 6.1
(4) .... B 6.2
(6), (7) .... B 6.2
81–84 .... B 6.2
85(1) .... B 6.3
88 .... B 6.2
90 .... B 6.2
92(1) .... B 6.2
116, 117 .... B 7.1
179 .... B 28.49
Sch 1 .... B 48.4, B 48.5
Pt 1 .... B 48.1
para 2(3)........... B 48.9
3................ B 48.9
4–7.............. B 48.9
9................ B 48.9
Sch 2
Pt 1 .... B 48.1
para 1(1)–(6)....... B 48.10
2(1)............. B 48.10
(5–(7)......... B 48.10
3................ B 48.10
4(12), (13)...... B 48.10
5–10............. B 48.10
12(3)–(6)........ B 48.10
14(1)............ B 48.10
15............... B 48.10

Anti-terrorism, Crime and Security Act 2001
s 108(1), (2) .... A 89.7

Assaults on Emergency Workers (Offences) Act 2018
s 1(2) A9A.1, A9A.2
(3) A9A.2
2 .... A9A.5
3(1), (2) A9A.3

Asylum and Immigration Treatment of Claimants, etc Act 2004
s 4 .... D 6.13A

B

Bail Act 1976 ...... A81.17; B 17.13; E 3.4; D8.26
s 3(6) .... E 3.5
3AA D8.65

Bail Act 1976 – *cont.*
s 6 .... A10.3
(1), (2) A10; D8.84
(6) ... A10.2; B 8.15; D4.2
(a) A10.3
(b) D5.1
(10)–(14) .... D 8.84
7 ..... D8.27, D8.28, D8.29
(2) A10.2; D8.85
(4), (5) D8.92
Sch 1
Pt I D8.27
para 6 .... D8.2
Pt IA D8.28
II D8.29
Bail Act 1996
s 3(6) D8.76
Bail (Amendment) Act 1993
.... D8.33
Banking and Financial Dealings Act 1971..... B 23.3, B 24.3
Betting, Gaming and Lotteries Act 1963.............. F3.1
Bribery Act 2010
.... A 89.4
s 1 .. A 89.1, A 89.5, A 89.7, A 89.10, A 89.11
2 . A 89.1, A 89.7, A 89.11
(2)–(8) .... A 89.6
3 .... A 89.6, A89.9
(3), (4) .... A 89.8
4 ... A 89.6, A 89.8, A 89.9
5 ....A 89.5
(2), (3) .... A 89.9
6 .... A 89.1, A 89.10, A 89.11
7 .... A 89.1, A 89.10

C

Care Standards Act 2000
.... B9.17, B49.17
Children Act 1989
.... D9.19
s 23(2)(a) B49.16
25(1) E3.8
(4) E3.7
(6) E3.8
105(1) E3.7
Children Act 2004
s 58 .... A15.18A, A19.5
Children and Young Persons Act 1933..................... E1
s 1 . A15.18A, A19.1, A19.6, A19.22
(1) A19.8, A19.32
(a) A43.7
18 .... E 1.3
37 .... A52.10; D 1B.3
39 ..... A52.11; B 48.11; D 1B.7; E2.4
30 .... E2.4
34A E5.1
44(1) E5.1
46 .... E 3.4
(1), (2) .... E 1.3
48(2) .... E 1.2
49 .... B 48.11; D 1B.7
50 .... E3.2; E5.1
99 .... E1.2
Sch 1A .... D 1B.7
Children and Young Persons Act 1963.................... E1
s 28 .... E3.22
29 .... E 1.2
Children and Young Persons Act 1969............. E1, E 3.7
Chronically Sick and Disabled Persons Act 1970
s 20 .... C9.7
Civil Evidence Act 1995
.... F4.7
Civil Partnership Act 2004
s 73 .... A17A.2
Clean Neighbourhoods and Environment Act 2005
s 84 .... A84.33
Sch 1
Para 4A A84.33
Communications Act 2003
s 126 .... A39.3
127(1) A16.7
(a) A16.2
(2) A16.7
363 .... A61.15
(2), (3) A61.1
Contempt of Court Act 1981
......................D 3.6
s 1, 2 .... D1B.8
4 ....D1B.8
(1), (2) D1B.7
9(1) .... **D 1B.10**

Contempt of Court Act 1981 – *cont.*
s 9(3), (4) D1B.10
11 .... 1B.7
12 .... D3.1, D 3.4, 3.5
(5) D3.16
Control of Pollution Act 1974
s 62 .... A74.2, A74.6
Copyright, Designs and Patents Act 1988
s 297 .... F2.27
(1) F2.28
Coroners and Justice Act 2009
.... D6.13A
s 62 .... A 43.1, A43.4
63–69 .... A43.4
Pt 3, Ch 2 (ss 86–97)
.... D 1B.7
s 115 .... E3.4
120 .... A 57.37; B45.46
122 .... D 4.4
(2) .... D 4.12
125 .... B 45.61
(1) .... A 57.37, A87.6; B45.46
(3), (4) .... A 57.37
137 .... C 5.7
162(2), (3) A43.4A
(6), (7) A43.4A
Sch 2 .... C 5.7
22
para 29 .... C 5.7
Counter-Terrorism Act 2008
s 41–45 .... B30.1
Sch 4 .... B30.1
5
para 2(3) .... B 30.1
7(1) .... B 30.1
8 .... B 30.1
15(2) B30.1
(4)(a)
.... B30.1
Courts Act 1971
s 52(3) .... F 5.47
Courts Act 2003
.... A72.21; D9.3
Pt 1 (ss 1–6) B50.2
s 29 .... D9.4, D9.5
30(3) B46.1
46 .... B46.1
50 .... E2.1
Courts Act 2003 – *cont.*
s 51 .... A9.4
(3) A9.6
53 .... D1B.2
57 .... A9.1, A47.5
66 .... B8.12, B40.3, B50.4
95 .... B28.18
98 .... B28.38
300 .... B28.83
Sch 5
para 2 .... B50.2
26(1), (2)
.... B 28.38
31(1)–(4)
.... B 28.38
32 .... B 28.38
37 .... B 28.38
38(3) .... B 28.38
40 .... B 28.38
42 .... B 28.38
42A .... B 28.63
Sch 37
Pt 7 .... B 28.83
Courts and Legal Services Act 1990 .... F2.16
s 56(2), (3) .... F 5.70
Crime and Courts Act 2013
.... C22A.7
s 44 .... B9.23
Sch 15 .... B9.23
Crime and Disorder Act 1998
s 1 .... B2
(8) B2.2
(10) B2.4
1A B2
1B B2
1C .... B2, B13.6; E 4.2
2, 3 .... B2
4 .... B2
5 .... A 20.6
(2)(b) A18.19
8 .... B37; E5.1
(2) .... B 2.4
(4) B37.5
(a) B37.8
(6) B37.1
(7A) B37.5
(8) B37.11
9 .... B37
(1) .... B37.2; E 3.18E
(1A) B37.2; E5.1
(4) B37.8

Crime and Disorder Act 1998 – *cont.*
s 9(5), (6) B37.9
(7) .... B37.7, B 37.10
10 .... B37
(1) .... A18.21; B 37.12
(2) .... A18.23; B 37.12
(3) A18.24
(4), (5) .... B 37.12
12(6) B37.1
28 .... B 45.2B
(1)(a) A8.16, A20.6
(b) A20.6
(3)(b) A8.16
(4) A8.17
29 ... A8.2, A 8.31, A15.2, A15.33, A70.1, A70.20; B 45.2B
30 ...... A18.16, A18.33; B 45.2B
31 . A20.2, A21.3, A21.4; B 45.2B
32 .. A41.2, A41.4; B 45.2B
(1)(a) A41.12
(b) A41.11A
34 .... E3.2
37(1) E5.1
49 .... D6.3
50A .... D 4.2
51 ... A12.2, A12.3, A12.4, A12.5, A13.2, A13.3, A13.4; D 4.2, D 4.11, D 5.1; E 3.18E
(1) .... D 4.5, D 4.6
(3) D5.2
(13) .... D 6.3
51A .... D 4.2, D 5.1; E3.18C, E 3.18E
(11) .... D 6.3
(12) . E 3.18A, E 3.18B
51B, 51C .. D 4.2, D 4.4; E 3.18, E 3.18D, E5.1
51D .... D 5.1
51E .... E 3.18A
(c), (d) D4.2
57 .... D8.22A
66(4) B22.2
Sch 3 .... D 4.12, D 5.1
para 13 .... B40.5
Crime and Security Act 2010
s 24–26 ...... B 23.1, B 24.1
Crime and Security Act 2010 – *cont.*
s 27 . B 23.1, B 23.2, B 23.3, B 24.1
28 .... B 23.1, B 24.1
(9) .... B 24.3
29 .... B 23.1, B 24.1
30 .. B 23.1, B 24.1, B 24.3
Crime (Sentences) Act 1997
s 35 .... B 28.83
Criminal Appeal Act 1968
s 9 .... A46.5
16A B12.16A
Criminal Attempts Act 1981
.... A57.2; D 4.9A
s 9 .... A63.6
(1) A63.1
Criminal Damage Act 1971
s 1 .... A18.1, A18.32
(1) A18.33, A18.34
(2), (3) A18.2
2 .... A18A.2
(a) A18A.1
3(a) A18B.1
6 .... F 1.19
Criminal Defence Service Act 2006.......... D9.19
Criminal Finances Act 2017
.... E5.46A
Criminal Justice Act 1925
s 41 .... D1B.8, D1B.9
Criminal Justice Act 1967
s 3 .... A 9.8
9 .... B45.55; D6.13
91 .... A28.2, A28.9
Criminal Justice Act 1971
s 1 .... A18.1
Criminal Justice Act 1972
s 24 .... C6.2
Criminal Justice Act 1982
.... C1.1
Criminal Justice Act 1987
s 2 .... F 5.17A
Criminal Justice Act 1988
.. A11.1, A11.4; D 6.17C
s 27 .... C32A.6
39 .... A15.1, A 15.33, A41.8B
40 .... D 5.2

Criminal Justice Act 1988 – *cont.*
s 139 ...... A11.1, A11.15, B 13.6, B45.46; E5.1
(1), (2) A11.6
(3), (4) . A11.6, A11.15
139A A11.1, A11.15; B45.46; E5.1
(1), (2) A11.15
139AA A11.15; B45.46; E5.1
160 .... A43.1
(1), (2) ... A43.3, A43.8
160A A43.4

Criminal Justice Act 1991
s 20A B28.18
(1A) B10.6
78 .... A9.1

Criminal Justice Act 2003
... A2.15, A14.6, A15.33, A18.32, A19.32; A30.3, A36.4, A37.1, A38.1, A39.1, A52.12; B 9.1, B 15.1, B 45.4, B 45.23, B 45.33, B 49.1; E5.1; SCH 21
s 29(2) D6.44A
(2B) D6.44A
(3B) D6.44A
51, 52 .... D8.22C
98 .... D6.14
100 .... D6.15
101(1)(d) D6.14
(g) D6.14
114 ...... A18.32; D6.4AA
(2) D6.16
142(1) C16A.10
142A A11.15, E5.1
143(1) B45.2, E5.1
(2) ... A5.4; B 34.B45.2, 47

Criminal Justice Act 2003 – *cont.*
s 144 ...... A3.5, A5.3, A5.5, A7.4, A8.31, A9.10, A10.3, A11.15, A12.20, A13.19, A14.6, A15.33, A16.7, A17A.4, A18.33; A19.32, A19A.4, A23.3, A24.2, A25.16, A 26.5, A 27.3, A27A.4, A 27B.4, A28.9, A29.4, A30.3, A34.15, A36.10, A38.4, A40.12, A41.11A, A41.12, A43.9, A44.4, A46.4, A47.15, A45.8, A49.4, A50.4, A51.3, A52.12, A54.6, A56.7, A 57.37, A57.37A, A58.8, A59.5, A61.15, A63.6, A65.18;A70.20, A 72.8, A 72.8A, A 80.20, A 89.11; B2.5, B45.2A, B45.46; C19.8, C20.19, C21.5, C22.32, C22.65, C 23.8, C 23.9, C25.20, C31.17, C33.23, C49.36
(1) .... B 45.61
(2), (3) B45.46
145 .... B 45.2B
146 .... B 45.2B; D6.24
147 .... B9.8
148 .... B9.8
(1) ... B28.16, B 45.61
(5) B9.2
149 .... B9.8
150 .... B9.8
150A .... B 9.2
152 .... B19.3
(2) ...... B9.21, B19.11, B28.16, B 45.61
153 .... B34.6

Criminal Justice Act 2003 – *cont.*
s 153(2) B15.17
156 .... B34.17
157 .... B34.18
161 .... D8.30
(2) .... B15.9, B 49.4, B 49.5
161A .... B 10.1, B50.3
162 .... B10.6, B45.2A
164 .... A80.20; B45.2A
(1), (2) B28.16
(4) B28.16
(5) B28.18
165 .... B50.4
(2) B28.18
172 .... B 8.7, B 45.2
(1)(b) D6.33
174 ... A3.5, A5.3, A5.5, A 7.4, A 8.31, A 9.10, A 10.3, A11.15, A12.20, A13.19, A14.6, A15.33, A17A.4, A18.32, A18.33, A18.34, A19.32, A19A.4, A41.12, A23.3, A24.2, A25.16, A 26.5, A 27.3, A27A.4, A 27B.4, A28.9, A29.4, A30.3, A34.15, A36.10, A38.4, A40.12, A43.9, A44.4, A45.8, A46.4, A47.15, A48.9, A49.4, A50.4, A51.3, A52.12, A53.10A, A54.6, A56.7, A 57.37, A57.37A, A58.8, A59.5, A61.15, A63.6, A65.18, A68.6, A70.20, A 72.8, A 72.8A, A 80.20, A 89.11; B2.5, B44.8, B45.2A, B45.53, B45.61; C 19.8, C20.19, C21.5, C22.32, C22.65, C23.8, C23.9, C25.20, C31.17, C33.23, C49.36
(1) ..... A 41.13; B45.2
(2)(a) B45.2
(d) B45.2
177 .... B4
(2A), (2B) B9.9
(3) B9.9
(5) B9.23A
Ch 3 (ss 181–195) B21.0
s 189 .... B 34.40

Criminal Justice Act 2003 – *cont.*
s 191 .... B 34.50
200(3) B9.23A
202 .. A29.4, A30.3, A43.9, A52.12, A53.10A, A68.6; B9.12
(2) B9.11A
204(3) .... B 16.18
207 .... A18.32, A18.33, A18.34, A 57.37, A57.37A
209 .... A18.33, A18.34, A 25.16, A 26.5, A 27.3, A27A.4, A 27B.4, A 57.37, A57.37A
212 .... A18.32, A18.33, A18.34, A 57.37, A57.37A
212A .... B 9.22
215(1)(a) B9.9
(b) B9.23
(2) B9.9
(4A) B9.9
(5), (6) B9.9
218(9) B9.23
224 .... A 7.4, A 8.31, A12.20, A13.19, A15.33, A18.32, A70.20; B 8.1; E 3.18, E 3.18C, E 3.18D
224A A14.6, A43.9, A52.12; B45.2A
225 .... A18.32; B45.2A
226(2) .... E 3.18C
226A .... A14.6, A19.32, A29.4, A30.3, A41.11A, A43.9, A52.12, A53.10A, A59.5, A68.6; B 8.1; B45.2A
226B ... E 3.18, E 3.18C, E 3.18D
229 .... A12.20, A13.19
240 ..... A 8.31, A 9.10; B 15.20, B 34.39
240A .... A 5.5, A10.3, A11.15, A17A.4, A18.32, A18.33, A18.34, A19.32, A19A.4, A41.11A, A41.12, A46.4, A50.4, A59.5; B2.5, B44.8, B45.2A
240ZA ... B 15.20, B 34.39

Criminal Justice Act 2003 – *cont.*
s 240A ...... A5.3, A 8.31, A 9.10, A14.6, A16.7, A29.4, A30.3, A36.10, A38.4, A40.12, A44.4, A45.8, A52.12, A53.10A, A54.6, A 57.37, A57.37A, A58.8, A63.6, A65.18, A68.6, A 89.11; C19.8, C20.19, C21.5, C22.32, C22.65, C23.8, C23.9, C25.20, C31.17
243(1), (1A) B15.22A, B34.53
244 .... B21.37
246 .... B34.54
255B ..... B 15.20, B 34.39
256AA .... B14.2, B 21.37, B34.53
256AB .... B 21.37, B34.532005
256AC B21.38
256B B21.37
256C(4) B21.38
258 .... D3.7
264B B21.37, B34.53
280(2) A41.5
Sch 3 .... D 4.1, D 4.7
8 .. A17.1; B 9.24, B9.26
Pt 2 .... B9.24
para 9(1)(c) A17.3
Sch 12 .... A17.1; B34.54
para 6 .... B34.46
8 .... B34.46
11 .... B 8.14
Sch 15 .... E5.1
Pt 1 ..... A2.1, A7.1, A8.1, A8.2, A12.1, A13.1, A15.2, A18.2, A19.1, A21.4, A41.1, A41.2, A41.3A, A46.1, A59.1, A66.1, A67.1, A70.2
2 . A14.1, A29.1, A29.2, A30.1, A43.1, A44.1, A52.1, A52.2, A53.1, A68.1
Sch 15B .... B 8.1
Pt 1 .... A43.9, A52.12
Sch 18A B45.2A
21 .... E5.1
25 .... A79.1

Criminal Justice Act 2003 – *cont.*
Sch 37
Pt 9 .... A79.1

Criminal Justice Act 2009
s 139(1) C22.23A

Criminal Justice and Courts Act 2015
s 33 .... A19A.1, A19A.4
(2) A19A.2
(3)–(6) A19A.3
(7)(a) A19A.2
(b) A19A.3
(8) A19A.2
34(2)–(7) A19A.2
35(2), (3) A19A.2
(5) A19A.2
84, 85 .... D6.48

Criminal Justice and Immigration Act 2008 A43.3; B 49.1
s 1 .... E 4.2
(3), (4) B49.4
(4)(a)–(c) .. B 45.61, B49.6
2–7 .... E 4.2
21, 22 ... B15.20, B 34.39A
38 .... A17.3
63–66 .... A14.1A
76(1)–(7) **A8.20**
(8), (8A) **A8.20**
(8B)–(8F) . **A8.20**, A 72.4
(9), (10) **A8.20**
80 .... B28.38
98(1)(b) B47.1
99(4) B47.2
100, 101 .... B47.3
102 .... B47.4
103 .... B47.5
104 .... B47.6
105, 106 .... B47.7
107–112 .... B47.4
113(8) B47.8
119, 120 .... A74.1
Sch 1 .... E 4.2
Pt 1
para.2................ B 49.3
3,.4............ B 49.4
29.............. B 49.4
30............ B 49.4A
32............ B 49.4A
Pt 2
para.7................ B49.23
.8................ B49.16

Criminal Justice and Immigration Act 2008 – *cont.*
para 11(7) B49.25
16 .... B49.16
18 .... B49.15
26 .... B49.12, B49.13
Pt 4
para 36 .... B49.23
Pt 5 .... B49.25
Sch 2 .... E 4.2
Pt 3
para 11(7) B49.25
12 .... B49.23
Pt 4
para 13, 14 .... B49.23
Sch 3 .... E 4.2
4 .... E 4.2
12
para 24 .... B49.5
Criminal Justice and Police Act 2001
s 39, 40 .... A69.2
42A A41.5
50 .... F5.16, F 5.20A
Criminal Justice and Public Order Act 1994 .... A34.6
s 25 .... D8.32
34–37 .... D6.22
38(3) .... D 6.22
51 .... A69.2
(1) A69.1
(2) A69.2
(7) A69.7
166 .... A34.4, A34.15
167 .... A56.1, A56.7
(5) A56.2
Criminal Justice (International Co-operation) Act 1990
Criminal Law Act 1967
s 3 .... A8.20, A18.19
(1) A20A; B16.17
(2) A20A
Criminal Law Act 1977
s 1, 1A .... A 81.5
Criminal Procedure (Attendance of Witnesses) Act 1965
s 2c .... B 12.20
Criminal Procedure and Investigations Act 1996
s 3 .... C22.23; D 6.12
Criminal Procedure and Investigations Act 1996 – *cont.*
s 6A .... D 6.12
6C D6.4AA
8 .... D 6.12
7A C22.23
8(3)(a), (b) C22.23
(4) C22.23
17 .... D 3.8
23(1) C22.23
Criminal Procedure (Insanity) Act 1964 .. B12.16A, B47.2; D6.4C
Crossbows Act 1987
.... A64.3
Customs and Excise Management Act 1979 .... B18.19
s 1(1) .... F 5.27
8(2) .... F 5.27
50 .... A36.10
102 .... C47.16, C47.21
161A .... F 5.27
170 .... A 4.1, A 27B.1, A36.10
(1) A4.1
(a) B31.2
(2) A4.1, A4.7, A27B.4
170B A36.10

D

Dangerous Dogs Act 1991
.... A 72.20, A72.21
s 1 .... A 72.10
(2) .... A 72.8A
(3) .... A 72.8A, A 72.20
3 .... A72.1, A72.20
(1) . A72.2, A72.3, A72.4, A72.8, A 72.8A, A72.10, A72.16
(1B) A72.4
(2) A72.2, A72.3
(3) .... A 72.8A, A72.10
(a) A72.8
4 .... A 72.20
(1)(a) .... A72.8, A 72.8A
(b) .... A72.8, A 72.8A, A72.17
(4)(b) .... A72.8, A 72.8A
(1A) A72.15
(a) A72.10

Dangerous Dogs Act 1991 – *cont.*
s 4(1B) A72.10
4A .... A72.15, A 72.20
(4), (5) .... A72.8, A 72.8A, A72.10
4B A72.20
(1) A72.10
(2A) A72.10, A72.20
(b) A72.10
10(3) A72.5
63 .... A72.15
Dogs Act 1871 .... A72.21
Dogs (Protection of Livestock) Act 1953
s 1 .... A73.1
3 .... A73.3
Domestic Violence, Crime and Victims Act 2004
s10 .... A15.1
s 12 .... A41.13
Drug Trafficking Act 1994
s 10(1) B11.2
42(1)(a), (b) F5.47
(2) F5.47
Drugs Act 2005 .... A23.1, A26.4A
s 9(2) A23.1
10(2) A23.2
12 .... A23.1, A23.3

E

Education Act 1996
s 8 .... A 49.3
434 .... A 49.3
443 .... B 37.1, B 37.12
444 .... B 37.1, B 37.12
(1) .. A 49.1, A 49.3, A 49.4
(1A) . A 49.2, A 49.3A, A 49.4
(1B) .... A 49.4
(2A) .... A 49.4
(8B) .... A 49.3A
566 .... A 49.3
576 .... A 49.3
Environmental Protection Act 1990
s 77 .... A 84.7
79 .... A84.7, A84.19
(1)(a) A84.3
Environmental Protection Act 1990 – *cont.*
s 79(1)(ga) A84.3
(6A) A84.3
(7) A84.4
80(4) A84.4, A84.17
(5) A84.4
(6) A84.17
82 .... A84.7, A84.19
(2) A84.31
86 .... A 84.7
87 .... A83.18
89(1)(a) C49.35A
(2) C49.35A
Equality Act 2010
s 173(1) A72.5
Extradition Act 2003
.... D7.10
s 62A(4) ... B12.16, B12.16A
135A(4) .. B12.16, B12.16A

F

Family Law Act 1996
s 42A A46.4
(1)–(3) .... A 46.1
62 ... D8.27, D8.28, D8.29
63(1) A17A.2
Finance Act 2000
s 144 .... A42.1
Firearms Act 1968
. A11.3, A33.4, A 33.9; B 9.13, B 31.2, B 49.11; E 3.18C
s 1 . A76.1, A 76.7, A 76.8A, A76A.4
(1)(a) D1B.12
(4) A76.8
2(1) A88.1
(2) A88.5
5(1) **A76A.3**
(a) A76A.1, D1B.12
(ab) A76A.1
(aba) . A76A.1, D1B.12
(ac)–(ae) A76A.1
(af) A76.7, A76A.1, A76A.4
(b) ... A76A.1, A76A.4
(c) A76A.1
(1A) **A76A.3**
(a) A76A.1
(7)–(9) **A76A.3**

Firearms Act 1968 – *cont.*
s 8–10 .... A76.10
11(1) A76.10
(2)–(5) A76.10
12 .... A76.10
13 .... A76.10
17(2) ... A 33.9A, A 77.9A
18 .... A77.6
19 .... A33.1, A33.4
20(1) A77.1
(2) A77.2
21(3) B5.16
22(4) A71.1, A71.5
23 .... A71A.1
(1), (1A) A71.5
(2) A71.6
(4) A71.5
24ZA A71A.1
46 .... F5.4
51A .... A 33.1, A76A.1; B45.46; E5.1
(1) ..... E3.18, E 3.18D
57(1) .... A 33.8
(b) .... A 76.6, A 77.8
(4) .. A 33.3, A 33.9A, A 77.9A
58(1) A76.7
(2) A76.17
(4) A76.3
Firearms Act 1982
.... A76.6, A77.8
Firearms Amendment Act 1988
s 15–18 .... A76.10
Schedule
para 1 .... A76.10
Firearms (Amendment) Act 1997
s 48 .... A76.7
Football (Disorder) Act 2000
.... B29
Football (Offences) Act 1991
.... A 34.6; B29.4
s 2 .... A34.1, A34.15
3 .... A34.2, A34.15
4 .... A34.3, A34.15
Football Spectators Act 1989
.... B29
Pt II (ss 14–22A)
.... B29.1
s 14 .... B29
14A B29.7, B29.18, B29.19
(5A) B29.32
Football Spectators Act 1989 – *cont.*
s 14B B29.5, B29.10, B29.33, B29.34
14D B29.35
19 .... B29.22A
21A B29.33
22 .... B29, B29.10
Sch 1 .. B29.4, B29.7, B29.32
Forgery and Counterfeiting Act 1981
Pt 1 (ss 1–13) A81.8A
s 1 .... A 64.3, A78.1
3 .... A78.2, A78.8
4 .... A78.3
9 .... D1B.8
(1)(g), (h) A78.6
10(2) A78.9
Fraud Act 2006 .... A39.3, A54.2, A55.2, A58.4
s 1 .... A36.4, A36.10
(2)(a) ... A36.1, A 36.6, A 36.8
(b) .... A36.1, A36.2, A 36.8
(c) .... A36.1, A36.3, A 36.9
2 .... A 36.6, A 36.7
(5) .... A 36.7
3 .... A36.8
4 .... A 36.9
5 .... A 36.7
6 .... A38.1, A38.3
7 ..... A38.4, A39.1, A39.4
(1)(a), (b) .... A 39.3
8 .... A38.3, A39.4
11 .... A37.1
31–35 .... A55.3

G

Gambling Act 2005
.... F3.1, F3.2
Pt 7 (ss 140–149)
.... F3.3
8 (ss 150–213)
.... F3.3
s 206 .... F3.3, F3.4
207 .... F3.3
(3) F3.4
208 .... F3.4

Game Act 1831 .... A86.31
s 2 .... A86.6
30 .... A86.1
34 .... A86.5
35 .... A86.8
41 .... A86.2
Game Laws Amendment Act 1960
s 4 .... A86.32
Gaming Act 1968
.... F3.1

H

Health and Safety at Work Act 1974
s 2 .. A80.3, A80.7, A 80.19, A 80.20
3 .. A80.3, A80.7, A 80.19, A 80.20
(1) A80.3
4–6 .... A80.3, A80.7
33 .... A80.8
(1)(a) .... A 80.20
(c) .... A 80.20
(g) A80.1
(o) A80.2
(1A) A80.3
42 .... A80.16
(1) .... A 80.20
(4) .... A 80.20
Sch 3A A80.4
Highway Act 1835
s 72 .... C1.6
Highways Act 1980
s 137 .... A85.1, A85.3A; C36.1A, C36.9
Human Rights Act 1998
.... D 1.1
s 3 .... A5.4
6(3)(b) A89.7
(4)–(6) A89.7
Sch 1 ... D 1.1, D 1.2, D 1.3, D 1.4, D9.2
art 2 .... D 1.5
3 .... D 1.5
4(1), (2) .... D 1.5
5 ... D 1.5, D 1.7, D8.2
6 . D 1.8, D 1B.1, D6.6
(1) . D 1.5, D 1A.1, D 1A.3, D 1B.2

Human Rights Act 1998 – *cont.*
art 6(3) .... D 1.5
7 .... D 1.5
8 .... D 1.5, D 1B.7
9 .... D 1.5
10 ..... D 1.5, D 1.7, D 1B.7
11 .... D 1.5
Hunting Act 2004
.... A 5.2
s 1–5 .... A86.1
Sch 3 .... A86.8

I

Identity Cards Act 2006
s 25(1) A32.2A
Identity Documents Act 2010
s 4 .... A32.2A
(1) A32.3
6(1) A32.1, A32.2A
Immigration Act 1971
.... B17.3
s 3(6) A81.17; B17.1
24 .... A81.1
(1)(a), (aa) A81.7
(b) A81.7
(i) A81.5
24A A81.8A
25 .... A81.2
(1)(a), (b) A81.5
25A, 25B A81.2
26 .... A81.3
(1) A81.8A
(c), (d) A81.6
26A A81.3
28(1)(a) A81.6
(c) A81.6
28D(4) F5.8
Sch 3
para 2 .... B 17.13
4 .... B 17.13
Immigration and Asylum Act 1999
s 7 .... A81.7
31(1) .... A32.2A, A 81.8A
32(2) .... A32.2A, A 81.8A
Industrial Relations Act 1971
s 134 .... A 85.3
Insolvency Act 1986
.... B28.31

Interpretation Act 1978
s 5 .... A41.13
7 .... C32A.4
32 .... C1.1
Sch 1 .... A41.2; C1.1

J

Justices of the Peace Act 1361
.... B5.20
Justices of the Peace Act 1968
s 1(7) B5.20

L

Legal Aid, Sentencing and Punishment of Offenders Act 2012................ B 34.40
Pt 1 (ss 1–43) .. B 15.8; D7.1
s 10 .... D7.1
13, 14 .... D7.4
17(1), (2) D7.5
20 .... D7.2
85 .. A 80.5; B 28.3, C 1.1, C 8.9, C 9.1, C 10.1, C 16.1, C 16A.1, C 16B.1, C 16C.1, C 16D.1, C 19.1, C 20.1, C 22.1, C 23.1, C25.1, C 31.1, C 32.1, C 33.1, C 38.1, C 46.1
76 .... B 9.22
86 .... B 28.3
Pt 3, Ch 3 (ss 91–107)
.... E 3.5
s 91 .... E 3.5
(3) .... E 3.17
92–94 .... E 3.5
97 .... E 3.5
98, 99 .... E 3.6
109 ..... B 15.20, B 34.39A
142 .... A 11.15
Sch 1 .... D7.1
3 .... D7.2
Licensed Premises (Exclusion of Certain Persons) Act 1980
.... B27
Licensing Act 1872
s 12 .... A28.1
Licensing Act 2002
s 2(1) .... D 1B.7
Licensing Act 2003
...... A28.7; B31.2; F 2.1
s 1 .... F2.4
7 .... F2.19
10 .... F2.19
11 .... F2.3
14 .... B27.1
29 .... F2.19
41 .... A3.5
46, 47 .... A3.5
51 .... F2.18
111 .... F2.2
120 .... F2.5
128(1) F2.28
129 .... B31; F2.28
(2), (3) B31.1
131(2)(a) F2.28
141 .... A 3.1, A 3.3
(2) .... A 3.4
146 .... A 3.2, A 3.3
147 .... A 3.3
147A A3.5; F2.27
161 .... F2.25
164, 165 .... F2.24
166 .... F2.26
167 .... F2.25
169A F2.27
181 .... F2.15, F2.20
(2)(b) F2.18
182 .... F2.19
193 .... A 28.7
Sch 4 .... B31.1; F2.28
5 .... F2.6
Lotteries and Amusements Act 1976.................... F3.1

M

Magistrates' Courts Act 1980
.... C1.1
s 8A, 8B D6.13
9(1) .... E 3.18F
10(1) .... D 6.17A
11 .... D 6.17A
(1)–(2A) D6.19
(3), (3A) . B 15.7, B 34.2; D6.19
(5) .... B 15.7, B 34.2; D6.19
(6), (7) D6.19
12 .. A57.2; D 4.9A, D6.26
15(1) .... D 6.17E

Magistrates' Courts Act 1980 – *cont.*
s 16A(1)(d) .... D 6.44A
(2), (3) .... D 6.44A
(6), (7) .... D 6.44A
16B(3) .... D 6.44A
16C–16E .... D 6.44A
17A D4.3
(6) .... B 8.5; D 4.2
17B(2) .... D 4.2
17E D6.3
18 .... D 4.2
(5) D6.3
19 .... D 4.2, D 4.6
(3) .... B 8.6
20 ... B 32.1, B 32.1; D4.3, D 4.6
(7)–(9) .... D 4.2
21 .... D 4.2; D 4.6
22 .... D 4.2; D 4.6
22A ... A57.2, A57.37A; D 4.9A
(1A) .... A57.2; D 4.9A
23 .... D 4.2
24 . B 38.5;D8.51; E 3.18C, E5.1
24A .... E 3.18, E 3.18A, E 3.18B, E 3.18D, E 3.18F
24B .... E 3.18, E 3.18A, E 3.18D, E 3.18F
24D D6.3
25 .... D4.10
27A B46.1, B46.2
29(2) .... B 40.5
32(9) C1.1
33(1) .... B 8.5
50 .... A84.31
51–53 .... B5.20
54 .... B5.20,B 7.1
55–57 .... B5.20
63 .... B 23.3, B 24.3
64 .... A26.17, A84.31;B12.24, B 12.31;F2.20
(1) .... F 5.47
79(2) B11.2
82(1)(c) B28.49, B50.4
(1A) B20.2, B28.49, B50.4
(4) .... B 28.76
85 .... B50.4
87(1) B28.38
s 87(3a) B28.38
88 .... B20.2
97 .... D 6.4A
101 .... A61.5
108 .... D3.16, D6.46
111 .... D6.47
115(3) B5.20
121 .... D 1B.1
(5A) D6.44A
123(2) D6.23
127 ... A 5.2; D6.23, D8.84
(1) F4.2
128 .... D8.33
(7) .... E 3.4
128A D8.33
133 .... B19.8
(1), (2) B34.23
135 .... B14.4, B20.2, B20, B28.49, B50.4
142 .... B38, B38.1, B38.4, B38.5; D6.19A; F4.6
(2) .... B38.2, B 38.5
150(1) B50.4
(3) B14.4
Sch 2 .... D 4.6
Mental Health Act 1983 .... B8.5, B 9.17, B15.23, B19.6A, B21.20, B34.18, B 39.7, B49.17; D6.13A, D6.37; E5.1; F 5.65, F 5.66
s 8 .... B32.17
35 .... B33.21
37 .... B12.21, B14.2, B32, B33, B33.2; D6.4C
(2)(a)(i) B33.1
(3) B32.1
(4) B33.1
(6) B32.4
38 .... B 33.22
39A B32.4
41 .... B33.10
135 .... F 5.64
Misuse of Drugs Act 1971 ... A22.1, A25.10, A38.3, A39.4
s 3 .... A27B.1, A 27B.4
4(1) ..... A 26.4A, A27A.1
(2) B31.2
(a) ... A 26.4A, A 27.1, A 27.3

Misuse of Drugs Act 1971 – *cont.*
s 4(2)(b) ..... A 27.1, A 27.3
(3) A26.1, A26.5, A26.4C; B31.2
(b), (c) A26.4A
4A A26.4C
5(2) A22.2, A25.1, A25.16; D8.30
(3) . A22.2, A26.1, A26.5; B31.2; D8.30
(4)(a), (b) A25.8
6(2) .... A27.1, A 27.3
8 .... A27A.1, A 27A.4
7 .... A25.8, A27.2
23 .... F5.24A
(4) F5.4
27 .... A25.18
28 .... A26.4B, A27.2
(2) ..... A25.7, A25.8, A 26.4
(3) A25.7, A25.8
(b)(ii) A26.4
37(1) A27.3A
(3) A25.7
Sch 2
Pt 1
para 5 .... A 27.3A
Mobile Telephones (Re-programming) Act 2002
s 2 .... A39.3

N

National Assistance Act 1948
s 47 .... F 5.50
National Assistance (Amendment) Act 1951
s 1 .... F 5.50
Nationality, Immigration and Asylum Act 2002
.... A81.3
Night Poaching Act 1828
.... A86.31
s 1 .... A86.9, A86.19
2 .... A86.9
9 .... A86.10
13 .... A86.17
Noise Act 1996 .... A84.33

O

Obscene Publications Act 1959
s 3 .... F5.4
Offences Against the Person Act 1861...... A11.11; C 16C.3
s 16 .... A59.1, A59.4, A59.5
18 .... A15.18A; B47.1
20 .... A 15.18A, A70.1, A70.2, A70.5, A70.20; B47.1
35 .... B 18.17
38 .... A7.1, A 7.4
44 .... A15.21
47 ... A8.1, A 8.31, A15.47
Offender Rehabilitation Act 2014
s 1 .... B 15.22A, B34.53
Official Secrets Act 1920

P

Poaching Prevention Act 1862
.... A 86.31
Police Act 1861
s 89 .... A 9.10
Police Act 1996
s 89 .... A9.4, A9A.4
(2) .. A 9.5, A47, A47.15
Police and Criminal Evidence Act 1954
s 8 .... F 5.17
Policing and Crime Act 2009
s 34(1) .... B 35.1
Policing and Crime Act 2009
s 34(1) .... B 35.1
(2), (3) .... B 35.2
(4) .... B 35.3
(5) .... B 35.2
35(3)–(5) .... B 35.3
(7) .... B 35.3
36(2) .... B 35.3
(3)–(5) .... B 35.4
(6), (7) .... B 35.5
37, 38 .... B 35.6
39(1) .... B 35.7
40(1)–(3) .... B 35.9
41(1), (2) .... B 35.9

Policing and Crime Act 2009 – *cont.*
s 41(4) .... B 35.9
42(1)–(6) .... B 35.10
43(2)–(5) .... B 35.11
(7)(a), (b) .... B 35.11
44(2)–(4) .... B 35.11
45(2) .... B 35.12
(4), (5) .... B 35.12
46 .... B 35.11
46A .... B 35.14
46B(1)–(3) .... B 35.13
47 .... B 35.2
49(1) .... B 35.11
Sch 5
para 2(1) .... B 35.11
Sch 5A
Pt 1 .... B 35.14
2 .... B 35.14
Police and Criminal Evidence Act 1984.... A57.2; D 4.9A; F5.24A, F5 46
s 2 .... A9.5
(3) A9.8
8 ...... F5.5, F5.10, F5.17A
(1) .... F 5.20A
(a) F5.7
(b) F5.7, F5.17A
(c) F5.7
(d) F5.16
(e) F5.7
(5) F5.8
15(6)(b) ..... F5.9, F 5.20A
17 .... A9.8
19, 20 .... F 5.20A
22(2)–(4) .... F 1.3
24(2) A20.18
(4) A20.18
(5)(e) A20.18
28(3) .... A 9.8
30A D8.55
30CB D8.55
38(6) .... E 3.8
47(1E) D8.56
58(1) C23.6A
63B . A23.3, A24.1, A24.2, A27.1; D8.30
78 .... C22.23A, C23.6A
82 .... C23.6A, C32A.6
Code B
para 3 .... F 5.17A
Police and Justice Act 2006 .... D8.22A
s 39 .... A 43.9
Police (Property) Act 1897 ... B12.31, B18.5, B18.16
s 1 .... F 1.1
(1) .... F 1.21
Police Reform Act 2002
s 46 .... A9.3, A47.10
Policing and Crime Act 2017 .... D8.56
Powers of Criminal Courts (Sentencing) Act 2000 .... B21.1
s 1ZA B16.4
1A B16
1B B16
(2)(c) B16.20
(3) B16.20
1C .... B16, B 16.21
1D B16
1E B16
1F B16
3 ... A17.3, A 80.5, B4.4, B 8.1, B 8.2, B 8.6, B8.10, B8.11, B8.14, B16.21, B21.33, B33.10, B34.46; D 4.5
(2) .... B 8.5, B 8.8, B 8.9
3A .... B8.14, D 4.5
(1), (2) B8.1
(5) B8.1
3(b) B19.11; E5.1
3B . B8.14; D 4.12; E3.18C, E3.18E, E3.18H
3C .... B8.14; E 3.18C, E3.18E, E4.2
4 .... B8.14
(2) B8.8
(4), (5) B8.8
(7) B8.9
4A B8.14
(4), (5) .... E 3.18H
5(1) B8.8
(2) B8.9
5A(2) .... E 3.18H
6 . B8.15, B22.7, B49.24; E 3.18H
(4)(e) B34.46
7 .... E 3.18H
(2) B8.15
8 .... B40.3; E5.1

Powers of Criminal Courts (Sentencing) Act 2000 – *cont.*
s 8(6) .... E 4.2
9(1) E5.1
10 .... B40.1
12 .... B22; E 4.2
(6) B5.20
(7) B22.8
13 .... E 4.2
(5) .... B 8.14, B22.7
14, 15 .... E 4.2
16 .... B39; E 4.2
17(1), (2) B39.7
26 .... C 5.6
31, 32 .... B11.2
60 .... B4; E4.2
61, 62 .... E4.2
69–72 .... B1, B1.1
73 .... B41; E 4.2
74, 75 .... E 4.2
78 ...... A37.1, A38.1; B34
83 .... B 15.8
89, 90 .... E4.2
91 .... E3.18, E4.2, E5.1
(1) ..... E3.18E, E 3.18H
(3) ..... E3.18C, E 3.18H
96 .... B21, B 21.0, B21.37
100 .... B19
101(3)–(6) B19.8
(8) B19.6A
(11), (12) B19.6A
103(1) B19.9
(2)–(3) B19.9
(4)(1) B19.9
(6), (7) B19.9
104(1)–(3D) B19.9
(4A) B19.9
104A, 104B B19.9
105 .... B19.9
(1)–(4) B19.10
(3)(a) B19.10
(4) B19.10
106(1) **B19.10**
110 ...... A25.3, A 26.5, A 27.3, A 27A.4, A 27B.4
111 .... A12.4, A12.20; B45.46
130 ...... A 72.8, A 72.8A; B10, B10.19; E 4.2
(1) B45.2
(2A) .... B 10.1
(3) B45.2

Powers of Criminal Courts (Sentencing) Act 2000 – *cont.*
s 130(4) .... B 10.6
131 .... B10, B10.19; E 4.2
(1A) B10.6
132 .... B10; E 4.2
133 .... B 10.6; E 4.2
134 .... B10; E 4.2
135 .... B28.93; E 4.2
137 .... B10
(4) B28.8
138 .... B10
139(2) B11.2
143 .... B18, B 18.5; F 1.21
(6), (7) .... B 18.17
144 .... B 18.17
(1)(b) .... **F 1.21**
146 ... B5.45; C5.5, C5.45, C6.2
147 .... C5.6, C6.2
147A, 147B C5.7
148 .... B42
150 ..... B5.20; E 4.2, E5.1
151(2) .... B 8.3
161 .... B 8.3
164(1) .... E 1.2
200 .... E 1.2
Sch 7
para 1 .... E 1.2
Sch 8 .... E 4.2
15B .... B 8.1
Prevention of Corruption Act 1906.................. A 89.4
Prevention of Corruption Act 1916.................. A 89.4
Prevention of Crime Act 1953 .. A 9.10, A11.1, A11.13, A11.8; B45.46
s 1 .... A11.1
(1) A11.15
1A E5.1
1(4) A11.5
Prison Act 1952
s 40CA A11.15
Proceeds of Crime Act 2002 .... B18.2; F 5.46
s 10 .... B11.1
13 .. A38.4, A40.12, A45.8, A54.6, A 57.37, A57.37A, A58.8, A 89.11
50(2) B11.1

Proceeds of Crime Act 2002 – *cont.*
s 242(2)(b) F5.47A
294 .... F5.47
298(1) F5.47
(2) F2.20; F5.47
299(2) F5.47A
329 .... A40.11
Prosecution of Offences Act 1985
s 16 .... B12.1
(1) .... A 84.31
(6), (6A) B12.16
(6C) ... B12.16, B12.16A
17 .... B12.1
(2) B12.4
(6) B12.6
18 .... B12.1
19 ... B12.1, B12.19; D6.12
(1) .... B 12.19
(3B)(b)(i) D6.4C
19A ..... B 12.19, B 12.20; D6.12
19B B12.20A; D6.12
21A(1), (2) B14.1
(4) B14.1
21B B14.1
(1) B14.2
21C, 21D B14.1
21E .. B14.1, B 14.4, B50.4
21F B14.1
22 .... D8.51
Protection from Harassment Act 1997 .... A41.10
s 1 .... A43.4
(1) .... A 41.8A
(2) .... A 41.8
(3) .... A 41.8, A41.8C
(a) .... A 41.10
(c) .... A 41.8
1A A41.7
2 .... A41.3, A41.6, A41.7, A41.12, A41.13
(1) A41.11
2A A41.3B, A41.6, A41.8A, A41.12
4 .... A41.1, A41.2, A41.7, A41.10, A41.11A, A41.13
(1) A41.7
(3) A41.8C
4A A41.3A, A41.8B, A41.11A
Protection from Harassment Act 1997 – *cont.*
s 4A(1)(b)(i) A41.8B
(4) A41.8C
5 .... A17A.4, A19A.4, A41.11A, A41.12, A59.5; B26.4
(1) A41.13
(4) A46.5
(5) .. A46.1, A46.3, A46.4
(5A) A46.4
(6) A46.3
5A(1) A41.13
7 .... A41.7
Protection of Children Act 1978
s 1 .... A43.1, A43.4, A43.12
(1)(b) A43.6
(4) A43.8
5 .... A43.11
7(4) A43.3
(4A) A43.3
Protection of Freedoms Act 2012 .... A 14.6, A 19.32
Psychoactive Substances Act 2016 A22.3, A87.1, A87.6; B 38A.1
s 4 .... A 87.2, A 87.9
5 .... A 87.9
(1), (2) .... A 87.2
6 .... A 87.5, A 87.9
7 .... A 87.2, A 87.9
8 .... A 87.9
(1), (2) .... A 87.2
(4) .... A 87.4
9 .... A 87.2
11 .... B 38A.2
12 .... A 87.9; B 38A.2
13(6) .... B 38A.3
14 .... B 38A.4
15 .... B 38A.3, B 38A.4
17(1) .... B 38A.5
18 .... B 38A.5
19(2) .... A 87.9
20(2) .... B 38A.6
21 .... B 38A.7
22(3)–(6) .... B 38A.8
23 .... B 38A.8, B 38A.9
24, 25 .... B 38A.8
26, 27 .... B 38A.9
28 ...... A 87.10; B 38A.10
29, 30 .... A 87.10
31 ...... A 87.10; B 38A.10

Psychoactive Substances Act 2016 – *cont.*
s 32(1)–(3) .... A 87.9
33 ...... B 38A.7, B 38A.10
54(3), (4) .... A 87.8
Sch 1, 2 .... A 87.4
Public Order Act 1986
s 2(1) A67.1
3 .... A2.1
(1) A2.5
4(1) .. A21.1, A21.5, A21.7
(a) B29.4
4A A21.2
(2) A21.9
5 . A 9.5, A20.1, A20.3B, A 20.5, A20.18; B29.4
(3) .... A 20.17
8 .... A20.3B
Pt III (ss 17–29) A21.9; B29.4
Public Bodies Corrupt Practices Act 1889............ A 89.4
Public Passenger Vehicles Act 1981
Pt II (ss 6–29) A56.2
s 181 .... A35.4

R

Refuse Disposal (Amenity) Act 1978
s 2(1)(a) A83.2
(b) A83.10
Regulation of the Railways Act 1889
s 5(1) A48.1, A48.9
(3) A48.9
(a) ...... A48.3, A 48.4
(b), (c) A48.3
Rehabilitation of Offenders Act 1974
s 7(5) B5.20
Restriction of Offensive Weapons Act 1959........ A11.4
Road Safety Act 1967
s 2–4 .... A 47.9
Road Safety Act 2006
...... C1.6, C25.5, C46.1, C49.1
s 3, 4 .... C8.8
35 .... C22.56
Road Traffic Act 1988
.... C5.49
s 1A .... C 16B.7
2 .. C16.1, C25.16, C46.16
2A(3) C16.8
2B .... C16A.1, C 16A.7, C 16A.10
3 . C16A.7, C25.1, C25.16, C25.20, C46.1, C46.16
3A ...... C 20.1, C 22.1, C 22A.1, C23.1, C23.2, C25.5
(2) (ba) .... C 22A.4
3ZA C25.5, C46.2
3ZB C16B.1, C16B.5A, C16B.6
3ZC C16B.1, C16D.1
3ZD(2) C16D.2
4 .. B 29.7, B31.2; C 20.19, C 22A.4
(1) ..... C20.1, C20.18, C 22.1, C 22A.1, C23.1,C 20.1
(2) . C20.18, C21.1, C21.5
(3) C22A.5
5 ...... B29.7, B31.2; C9.7, C23.2
(1)(a) ...... C20.1, C22.1, C22.31, C22.32, C 22A.1, C23.1
(b) C22.31, C22.62, C22.65
(2) ..... C20.1, C 22.1, C 22A.1, C22A.5, C23.1
5A **C22A.2**, C22A.7
(3)–(6) C22A.5
6 .... C22.10, C23.3
6A, 6B C24.2
6C C22A.4, C24.2
6D C22A.4
6(4) C24.1
7 .... B18.17
(1A) C22A.4
(6) .... C 20.1, C 22.1, C 22A.1, C23.1, C23.3, C23.6, C23.8; D6.23
7A .. B18.17; C23.1, C23.5
(6) .... C20.1, C 22.1, C 22A.1, C23.1
11 .... D8.9
14 .... C48.1
15 .... C22A.4, C48.1

Road Traffic Act 1988 – *cont.*
s 15(2) C22A.6, C48.9
(3A) C22A.6
16(4) C35.1
20(8) C49.4
24 .... C22.31, C22A.4
25 .... C32A.2
26 .... C32A.2
(1) B8.15
27 .... C32A.2
34 .... C10.1
(4) C5.6
35(1) C5.24
35A C5.7
36 .... C52.1
38(7) C3.1
40A C10.1
41A(b) C9.1, C50.1, C53.1
41B C38.1
41C C38A.1
42 .... C34.4, C36.1, C37.1
45, 45A C22A.4
47 .... C8.9
(1) C51.1
75(7)(c) C8.21
87 .... C18.1, C18.2
(1) C16B.1
103 .. C19.1, C19.8, C21.5
(1)(b) . C16B.1, C16D.1
Pt VI (ss 143–162) C9.7
s 143 . C8.9, C16B.1, C33.1, C 33.6, C33.23
144A C8.9
145(3)(a) ... C32A.9, C33.9
148(2)(e) C32A.9
164, 165 .... C17.3
168 .... C46.5
170(2), (3) .... B 18.17
(4) C31.1, C31.17, C32.1
(7) C31.16
172 .. C8.9, C8.21, C32A.1
(2) C32A.9
(a) .. C8.22, C32A.1, C32A.3, C32A.6
(b) C32A.1
(3) C32A.1,C32A.6, C32A.7, C32A.9
(4) C32A.6, C32A.9
(7)(b) . C32A.4, C32A.7

Road Traffic Act 1988 – *cont.*
s 178 .... C 5.6
185 .... C 9.7
192(1) C32A.2
Sch 2 .... C 22A.4
Pt 1 .... C10.1
Road Traffic Act 1991 .... C16.1, C49.4
s 24 .... C20.18
Road Traffic (Driver Licensing and Information Systems) Act 1989............ C18.31
Road Traffic Offenders Act 1988 .... C5.32
s 2 .... C49.3
12 .... C32A.23
15(2) C22.23
20 .... C49.4; D 6.17B
24 .... C16A.8, C20.18, C25.17, C46.17
26(1) B8.15
34 .... C 5.7, C22.56; D 6.44A
(1), (2) .... C 5.6
(3) .... C 5.6
(4) .... C 5.6
(4A), (4B) .... C 5.6
34A .... C 5.7
(3) C22.57
35 . C 5.7, C5.20, C5.37; D 6.44A
35A, 35B .... C 5.7
36 .... C5.38
(4) C16A.10, C16B.6
Sch 2 .... C52.1
3 .... C 5.6
Road Traffic Regulation Act 1984.................. C6.2
s 5 .... C9.4
14 .... C49.2, C49.35A
16 .... C49.2, C49.22, C49.35A
17 .. C49.1, C49.2, C49.19
25(5) C39.1, C40.1
64 .... C52.1
81 .... C49.1, C49.10
84 .. C49.1, C49.2, C49.22
85(1), (2) C49.15
(4) C49.15
86 .. C49.1, C49.2, C49.25
88 .... C49.2, C49.31
89 .... C49.1, C49.4

Road Traffic Regulation Act 1984 – *cont.*
s 89(1) C49.36

S

Safeguarding Vulnerable Groups Act 2006............. B44.2
Safety of Sports Grounds Act 1975.................. A34.7
s 10 .... A34.17
Senior Courts Act 1981 .... D6.48
s 29 .... D6.48
31 .... D6.48
Serious Crime Act 2007
s 19 .... B45.2A
Serious Crime Act 2015
s 69 .... A 43.2
76 .... A17A.1, A17A.4
(2), (3) A17A.1
(4)–(6) A17A.2
(8)–(10) A17A.3
Serious Organised Crime and Police Act 2005....... A41.5
s 73, 74 ... A3.5, A5.3, A5.5, A 10.3, A11.15, A14.6, A16.7, A17A.4, A18.32, A19A.4, A19.32, A23.3, A24.2, A25.16, A 26.5, A 27.3, A27A.4, A 27B.4, A28.9, A29.4, A30.3, A34.15, A36.10, A38.4, A40.12, A41.11A, A41.12, A43.9, A44.4, A45.8, A46.4, A47.15, A48.9, A49.4, A50.4, A51.3, A52.12, A53.10A, A54.6, A56.7, A 57.37, A57.37A, A58.8, A59.5, A61.15, A63.6, A65.18;A68.6, A 72.8, A 72.8A, A 80.20, A 89.11; B44.8; B45.2A; C19.8, C20.19, C21.5, C22.32, C22.65, C23.8, C23.9, C25.20, C31.17, C33.23, C49.36
Serious Organised Crime and Police Act 2005 – *cont.*
s 76(3) A4.18
110 .... A20.18
126 .... A41.5
Sex Offenders Act 1997 .... B22.9
Sexual Offences Act 1956
s 33–36 .... A 44.1
Sexual Offences Act 2003 ... A 14.6, A44.4, A51.3, A52.13, B21.10
s 3 . A 52.4, A53.1; B 31.2; E 3.18C
4 .... A53.2
7 ..... A52.1, A52.5, A52.7
8 .... A 52.1
(1), (2) .... A 52.5
9 .... A52.1, A52.2, A52.5, A52.7, A52.12, A53.7
10 ... A 52.1, A52.2, A53.7
11 ... A 52.1, A52.2, A53.7
(1)(c) A52.6
12 ... A 52.1, A52.2, A53.7
13 .... A53.7
14, 15 .... A 52.3, A53.7
15A .... A 52.3
16–19 ...... A 52.3; B 44.3
25, 26 ..... B 44.3; E 3.18C
45 .... A43.5
48 .... A14.1, A14.3, A14.6
49 .... A14.1, A14.3, A14.6
50 .... A14.1, A14.3
51 .... A82.2
(1) A14.3
(2) A14.4, A44.3
(3) A14.5
51A .... A29.1, A 82.1
52 . A29.1, A29.2A; B 31.2
53 . A29.2, A29.2A, A29.4; B 31.2
53A ..... A29.2, A29.2A, A 82.1
54 .... A29.2A
66 ... A30.1, A30.3; B 31.2
67 .... B 31.2
(1), (2) A68.1
(3), (4) A68.1
67A(1)–(3) A68.1
68 .... A68.4
71 .... A51.1, A51.2
73 .... A52.7

Sexual Offences Act 2003 – *cont.*
s 74 .... A68.4
77 .... A52.3
78 .... A 52.4
79 .... A 52.4, A68.4
Pt II (ss 80–136)
.... A52.14
s 80 .... A14.6, A68.5
83(1) A50.1
84(1) A50.1
(4)(b) A50.1
85(1) A50.1
86(1) A50.1
87(4) A50.1
89(2)(b) A50.1
(4) A52.14
91 .... A50.4, A52.14
(1) A50.1
91A–91F A52.15
92 .... A52.14
95(1) A50.1
103A(1), (2) B44.2
(4) B44.4
103B(1) B44.2, B44.6
103B (2)–(7) B44.6
103C(2), (3) B44.5
103D(1)–(7) B44.5
103E–103H .... B 44.7
107(2) B44.3
108(2) B44.2
(5) B44.3
Pt IIA (ss 136A–136R)
.... A26.12
s 136B(7)(b) . B 7.1, B 7.2, B 7.4
136C(3) .... B 7.3
(a) .... B 7.1
(d) .... B 7.2
(4) .... B 7.3
136D .... B 7.1
136F(2) .... B 7.3
(4) .... B 7.3
136H–136J .... B 7.4
136K .... B 7.5
136M .... B 7.6
Sch 3 .... A14.6, A52.14, A53.9, A68.5; B 44.2, B 44.3
para 60 .... B 44.6
Sch 5 .... B 44.2, B 44.6
Sexual Offences (Amendment) Act 1992........ D 1B.7
Social Security Administration Act 1992
s 111A .... A 31.3, A54.1, A54.3, A54.6
(1A) A54.5
112 .. A54.3, A54.1, A54.3, A54.4, A54.6
(1) A54.1
116(2) A54.4
Sporting Events (Control of Alcohol etc) Act 1985
.... A35.7
s 1 .... B29.7
(2)–(4) A35.1, A35.2
1A A35.4
(3), (4) .... A 35.2
2 .... B29.4
(1), (2) ... A34.15, A35.1, A35.2
2A A35.9
(1) .... A 35.2
Statutory Declarations Act 1835
.... F 5.57
Street Offences Act 1959
s 1(4) .... A 82.2; B 39.8

T

Tax Credits Act 1992
s 35 .... A55.4
Tax Credits Act 2002
s 35 .... A54.3, A55.1
Taxes Management Act 1970
s 106A A36.10
Theft Act 1968 .... A37.3, A57.7, A57.17; B10.3, B10.19
s 1 . A57.37, A57.37A, B31.2
(1) A57.1
3 .... A21.6
6(1) A57.32
9 ... A12.20, A13.19; B31.2
(1)(a) A12.1, A13.1
(b) A12.1, A13.1
(3)(a) A12.14
(4) A12.14
12 ..... A65.18; C1.6, C5.6
(1) A65.1, A66.8A
(5) A65.2
12A C1.6
(1) A66.1

Theft Act 1968 – *cont.*
s 12A(2)(a), (b) A66.1, A66.8A, A66.17
(c), (d) A66.1, A66.8A, A66.16
(3) A66.10
13 .... A1.1; B31.2
15, 15A A22.1
17 .. A31.1, A36.10, A54.6
22 .... A40.1, A40.11, A 40.12; B31.2
(1) A40.6
24 .... A 36.7
25 ... A38.3, A58.1, A58.8; B31.2; C5.6
(1) A58.6
(3) A58.5
(5) A58.3
26 .... F5.4, F5.21
34(2)(a) .... **A 31.3**
Theft Act 1978 . A37.3, A37.4
s 3 .... A45.1, A45.8, A57.22
Town Police Clauses Act 1847
s 45 .... A56.2
Trade Descriptions Act 1968
.... A75.3
s 1 .... A75.1
Trade Marks Act 1994
s 10–12 .... A60.3
92(1) B31.2
(a) A60.1, A60.3
(b) A60.1, A60.3
(c) A60.1, A60.3
(2) B31.2
(a)–(c) A60.1
(3)(a), (b) A60.1
(4), (5) A60.3
Transport Act 1968
s 96 .... D 1B.12
Transport Act 1985
s 10 .... A56.2

U

UK Borders Act 2007
s 32 .... B17.8
(5) B17.9
33 .... B17.9

V

Vagrancy Act 1824
.... A79.9
s 4 .... A79.1
Value Added Tax Act 1983
s 22 .... A62
Value Added Tax Act 1994
s 13(5) A62.2
35, 36 .... A62.2
39, 40 .... A62.2
72(1) A62
Vehicle Excise and Registration Act 1994.... B11.1, B28.38, B50.2
s 29(3) C47.2
(3A) C47.1, C47.2
31A C47.2
31B C47.25
33 .... C8.9
42, 43 .... C8.9
44 .... A 64.1, A 64.3, A64.3A
Sch 2 .... C47.17
Violent Crime Reduction Act 2006...... A 11.10; B 25.1, B29.33, B29.37
s 6–8 .... B27.1
23 .... A 3.3
28 .... E 3.18C
29 .... E 3.18C
(3) ..... E 3.18, E 3.18D

W

Wireless Telegraphy Act 1949
.... A61.1
s 8 .... A61.1
35 .... A61.1

Y

Youth Justice and Criminal Evidence Act 1999...... B 13.4; D8.22A
s 16, 17 ..... D6.4A, D6.13A
27, 28 .... D4.12; E 5.1
35 .... D6.13A
36 .... D6.4A

Youth Justice and Criminal Evidence Act 1999 – *cont.*
s 38 .... D6.4A
45(4)–(8) .... D 1B.7
45A .... D 1B.7
46 .... D 1B.7
49 .... E2.5

Youth Justice and Criminal Evidence Act 1999 – *cont.*
s 53 .... A 52.8
55 .... A52.6
Sch 1A D6.13A
2A .... D 1B.7

Table of Statutory Instruments

Paragraph references printed in **bold** type indicate where the Statutory Instrument is set out in part or in full.

A

Anti-social Behaviour, Crime and Policing Act 2014 (Commencement No 7, Saving and Transitional Provisions) Order 2014, SI 2014/2590
art 3(a) B25.1

Anti-social Behaviour, Crime and Policing Act 2014 (Commencement No 8, Saving and Transitional Provisions) Order 2015, SI 2015/373
art 4(a) B2.2, B13.1

C

Children (Secure Accommodation) Regulations 1991, SI 1991/1505
reg 16 .... E3.8

Civil Legal Aid (Merits Criteria) Regulations 2013, SI 2013/104 .... D7.1

Civil Legal Aid (Procedure) Regulations 2012, SI 2012/3098 .... D7.1

Civil Procedure Rules 1998, SI 1998/3132
Pt 6 .... D1B.7A
54 .... D6.48

Community Charges (Administration and Enforcement) (Amendment) Regulations 1989, SI 1989/712
reg 41 .... F4.16

Consumer Protection from Unfair Trading Regulations 2008, SI 2008/1277
reg 8(1) A75.1
(2) A75.4
9–12 ...... A75.1, A75.5
14, 15 .... A75.3
16–18 .... A75.5

Costs in Criminal Cases (General) Regulations 1986, SI 1986/1335
reg 14(4) B12.16

Council Tax (Administration and Enforcement) Regulations 1992, SI 1992/613
.... F4.1
reg 34(7)(b) F4.9A
36A F4.6
47(2), (3) F4.12
52 .... F4.11

Crime and Courts Act 2013 (Commencement No 18) Order 2018, SI 2018/1423
.... B9.23

Criminal Justice Act 1988 (Offensive Weapons) (Amendment) Order 1988, SI 1988/2019 .... A 11.3
Criminal Justice Act 2003 (Surcharge) Order 2012, SI 2012/1696 ... B 10.1, B50.1, B50.2
art 7 .... B50.2
Criminal Justice Act 2003 (Surcharge) (Amendment) Order 2014 SI 2014/2120 .... B50.2
Criminal Justice Act 2003 (Surcharge) (No 2) Order 2007, SI 2007/1079 .... B50.2
Criminal Justice (European Investigation Order) Regulations 2017, SI 2017/730 .... F5.47B
Criminal Justice (European Protection Order) (England and Wales) Regulations 2014, SI 2014/3300 .... B 26.1
reg 4 .... B26.2
Schedule B26.3
Criminal Legal Aid (Contribution Orders) Regulations 2013, SI 2013/483
Pt 2 (regs 5–39) D7.11
3 (regs 40–44) D7.11
4 (regs 45, 46) D7.11
Criminal Legal Aid (Determinations by a Court and Choice of Representative) Regulations 2013, SI 2013/614
Pt 3 .... D7.10
Criminal Legal Aid (Financial Resources) Regulations 2013, SI 2013/471 .... D7.4, D7.7
Criminal Legal Aid (General) Regulations 2013, SI 2013/9 .... D7.3
Pt 2 (regs 7, 8) D7.4
reg 9 .... D7.4
Criminal Legal Aid (General) Regulations 2013, SI 2013/9 – *cont.*
reg 12 .... D7.4
Pt 6 (regs 31–39) D7.6
Criminal Procedure Rules 2005, SI 2005/384 .... D6.23
Pt 1 .... D6.6
r 1.2(1)(a)–(c) C22.23A
(e) C22.23A
Pt 3
r 3.2(2)(a) C22.23A
3.3(1), (2) C22.23A
3.11 .... C22.23A
Pt 34 .... D6.16
35 .... D6.14, D6.15
Criminal Procedure Rules 2010, SI 2010/60 .... D6.21
Pt 31 .... A41.13
42
r 28.3 .... A52.14
Pt 50 .... A41.13
Criminal Procedure Rules 2012, SI 2012/1726
Pt 29
Section 5 .... D1B.7
Pt 44 .... B9.25
Criminal Procedure Rules 2013, SI 2013/1554 .... B12.19, D6.24
Pt 3
r 3.2 .... D6.3
Pt 14
r 14.2 .... B 8.9
Pt 19
r 19.11 .... D8.63, D8.80
Pt 42
r 42.2 .... B38.2
Pt 44 .... E4.2
50
r 50.2 .... B29.18
Pt 76
r 76.2(6), (7) B12.16A
Criminal Procedure Rules 2014, SI 2014/1610 .... D6.23
Pt 5 .... F5.24A
37 .... D1B.1

Criminal Procedure Rules 2014, SI 2014/1610 – *cont.*
Pt 42
r 42.2 .... A52.14
Pt 62
Section 3 .... D3.8
Pt 63 .... D3.16
Criminal Procedure Rules 2015, SI 2015/1490 .. D6.5, D6.17
Pt 1
r 1.1(2)(e) D6.3
Pt 3
r 3.2 .... D6.3
3.3(2) D6.3
3.5 .... D9.18
(3) D6.3
3.9(2)(b) D6.3
3.27 .... **D6.4A**
3.28(8) D6.4C, D6.37
Pt 4
r 4.4(2)(a) .. C32A.4, C32A.8
Pt 5C D6.19A
6
r 6.6 .... D1B.8
6.9 .... D1B.8, D1B.10
Pt 8 .... D6.3
r 8.2 .... **D6.11**
8.3 .... D6.3, D6.11
Pt 9
r 9.1 .... D6.3
9.7(5)(a)(i), (ii)
.... D6.3
Pt 14
r 14.6 .... D8.56
14.20–14.21 .... D8.56
Pt 15 .... D6.12
17 .... D6.4A
18 .... D6.4A
r 18.8–18.22 .... D1B.7
Pt 20 .... D6.4A,D6.16
21 .... D6.4A, D6.14
23 .... D6.4A
24 .... D6.4AA
r 24.9 .... D6.14A
24.11(9)(a) D6.3
24.17 .... D5.64
Pt 25
r 25.16(7)(a) D6.3
Criminal Procedure Rules 2015, SI 2015/1490 – *cont.*
Pt 28
r 28.3 .... A53.9
28.4 .... B28.4
Pt 31 .... A87.9
r 31.2 .... B13.3
31.3 .... **B13.3**
(5) B44.5
31.6–31.8 .... B13.4
31.10 .... B26.3
Pt 35 .... D6.15
45 .... B12.2
47 .... F5.1, F5.17A
48
Section 2 (reg 48.3–48.8)
.... D1B.10
r 48.5, 48.6 .... **D3.7**
48.9–48.17 .... D3.8
Pt 50 .... B44.1

D

Dangerous Dogs Compensation and Exemption Schemes Order 1991, SI 1991/1744
.... A72.8A
art 3 .... A72.20
Drug Driving (Specified Limits) (England and Wales) Regulations 2014, SI 2014/2868 .... C22A.3

E

Education (Parenting Contracts and Parenting Orders) (England) Regulations 2007, SI 2007/1869 .... B37.3
Education (Parenting Contracts and Parenting Orders) (Wales) Regulations 2010, SI 2010/2954 .... B37.3
Employer's Contributions Reimbursement Amendment Regulations 1999, SI 1999/286
reg 74 .... C22.45

F

Fines Collection Regulations 2006, SI 2006/501
reg 3 .... B28.63
4 .... B28.38
Firearms (Dangerous Air Weapons) Rules 1969, SI 1969/1490 .... A76.7
Football Spectators (Prescription) Order 2004, SI 2004/2409
reg 3, 4 .... **B29.2**
Framework Decision, Criminal Justice and Data Protection (Protocol No 26) Regulations 2014, SI 2014/3141 .... D8.76

G

Gambling Act 2005 (Commencement No 6 and Transitional Provisions) Order 2006, SI 2006/3272 .... F3.1

H

Housing Benefit (General) Regulations 1987, SI 19871971 .... A78.9
Immigration (European Economic Area) Regulations 2006, SI 2006/1003 .... B17.9

J

Justices' Clerks Rules 1999, SI 1999/2784 ..... D9.6, D9.18
Justices of the Peace (Training and Development Committee) Rules 2007, SI 2007/1609 .... E2.1

L

Legal Aid, Sentencing and Punishment of Offenders Act 2012 (Commencement No – *cont.*
11) Order 2015, SI 2015/504 .. C1.1, C8.9, C9.1, C10.1, C16.1, C16A, C16B.1, C16C.1, C19.1, C20.1, C22.1, C23.1, C25.1, C31.1, C32.1, C33.1, C38.1, C46.1
art 2 .... B28.3
Legal Aid, Sentencing and Punishment of Offenders Act 2012 (Fines on Summary Conviction) Regulations 2015, SI 2015/664 .... C1.1
Licensing Act 2003 (Persistent Selling of Alcohol to Children) (Prescribed Form of Closure Notice) Regulations 2012, SI 2012/963 .... F2.27
Licensing Act 2003 (Premises licences and club premises certificates) (Amendment) Regulations 2005, SI 2005/42 .... F2.2
Licensing Act 2003 (Premises licences and club premises certificates) (Amendment) Regulations 2012, SI 2012/955 .... F2.2
Litigants in Person (Costs and Expenses) (Magistrates' Courts) Order 2001, SI 2001/3438 .... B12.1

M

Magistrates' Courts (Children and Young Persons) Rules 1992, SI 1992/2071 .... E3.8
Magistrates' Courts (Detention and Forfeiture of Cash) Rules 2002, SI 2002/2998 .... F5.47

Magistrates' Courts (Detention and Forfeiture of Cash) (Amendment) Rules 2012, SI 2012/1275 .... F5.47
Magistrates' Courts (Injunctions: Anti-Social Behaviour) Rules 2015, SI 2015/423
r 4 .... B48.7
6 .... B48.8
7 .... B48.5
8(3) B48.9
9 .... B48.9
10 .... B48.5
11 .... B48.10
15, 16 .... B48.1
Magistrates' Courts (Injunctions: Gang-related Violence) Rules 2015, SI 2015/421
r 2, 3 .... B35.6
4 .... B35.7
5 .... B35.5
6 .... B35.10
7, 8 .... B35.11
10–13 .... B35.14
14 .... B35.10
15 .... B35.4
16 .... B35.8
Magistrates' Courts (Parenting Orders) Rules 2004, SI 2004/247 .... B37.3; A8
Magistrates Courts Rules 1981, SI 1981/552
r 14 .... F2.17
34 .... F2.18
Motor Cycles (Protective Helmets) Regulations 1980, SI 1980/1279
reg 4 .... C35.1
Motor Vehicles (Driving Licences) Regulations 1987, SI 1987/1378 .... C18.2
Motor Vehicles (Wearing of Seat Belts by Children in Front Seats) Regulations 1993, SI 1993/31 .... C48.10
Motor Vehicles (Wearing of Seat Belts) Regulations 1993, SI 1993/176 ..... C48.1, C48.3
Offender Rehabilitation Act 2014 (Commencement No 2) Order 2015, SI 2015/40
art 2 .... B15.22A, B34.53

P

Pelican Pedestrian Crossings Regulations and General Directions 1987, SI 1987/16
reg 17 .... C39.1
Policing and Crime Act 2009 (Commencement No. 4) Order 2010, SI 2010/507 .... A82.2
Proceeds of Crime Act 2002 (Recovery of Cash in Summary Proceedings: Minimum Amount) Order 2006, SI 2006/1699 .... F5.47
Prosecution of Offences Act 1985 (Criminal Courts Charge) Regulations 2015, SI 2015/796 .... B14.3
reg 2 .... B14.2
Prosecution of Offences Act 1985 (Criminal Courts Charge) Regulations 2015, SI 2015/1970
reg 3 .... B14.3

R

Road Safety Act 2006 (Commencement No 2) Order 2007, SI 2007/2472 .... C8.21, C10.1
Road Safety Act 2006 (Commencement No. 4) Order 2008, SI 2008/1918 .... C16A.1, C16B.1
Road Vehicles (Construction and Use) Regulations 1986, SI 1986/1078 ..... C5.32, C6.2
reg 18 .... C9.1
27 .... C53.1
29 .... C50.1
66 .... C38.1

Road Vehicles (Construction and Use) Regulations 1986, SI 1986/1078 – *cont.*
reg 75–79 .... C38.2
80 .... C38.1
103 .... C36.1
105 .... C37.1
Sch 8 .... C38.2
Road Vehicles Lighting Regulations 1989, SI 1989/1796
reg 23(1) C34.4
24(1) C34.4
25(1) C34.4
27 .... C34.4

S

Serious Organised Crime and Police Act 2005 (Commencement) (No. 7) Order 2006, SI 2006/1871
art 2 .... B37.1
Sexual Offences Act 2003 (Notification Requirements) (England and Wales) Regulations 2012, SI 2012/1876 .... A52.14
art 8 .... A52.14
Sexual Offences Act 2003 (Travel Notification Requirements) Regulations 2004, SI 2004/1220 .... A52.14
Sports Grounds and Sporting Events (Designation) Order 2005, SI 2005/3204 .... A35.5

T

Ticket Touting (Designation of Football Matches) Order 2007, SI 2007/790 .... A34.6A
Traffic Signs Regulations and General Directions 2002, SI 2002/3113 .... C49.10
reg 10 .... C52.1
Sch 17
Item 10 .... C49.15
Traffic Signs Regulations and General Directions 2002, SI 2016/362
reg 14 . C39.1, C40.1, C52.1
(2) C49.10
Sch 10 .... C49.10

Y

Youth Courts (Constitution of Committees and Right to Preside) Rules 2007, SI 2007/1611 .... E2.1

Z

"Zebra" Pedestrian Crossings Regulations 1971, SI 1971/1524
reg 8 .... C39.1
9 .... C40.1
12 .... C40.7
Zebra, Pelican and Puffin Pedestrian Crossings Regulations and General Directions 1997, SI 1997/2400 ..... C39.1,C6.2
reg 18 .... C40.1
24(1)(b) C39.10

Table of Cases

A

A v Director of Public Prosecutions [2017] EWHC 821 (Admin), [2017] All ER (D) 78 (Apr) .... A 15.11
A County Council v C [2013] EWHC 1757 (Admin), 177 JP 567, [2013] All ER (D) 241 (Apr) .... A 49.3
A Metropolitan Borough Council v DB. See B (a minor) (treatment and secure accommodation), Re
ADT v United Kingdom [2000] 2 FLR 697, [2000] Fam Law 797, [2000] Crim LR 1009, 9 BHRC 112, ECtHR .... A 15.11
Abdul v DPP [2011] EWHC 247 (Admin), 175 JP 190, [2011] Crim LR 553, 175 CL&J 127, [2011] All ER (D) 181 (Feb) .. A 20.5
Akhurst v Enfield Magistrates' Court [2009] EWHC 806 (Admin), 173 JP 499, (2009) Times, 13 April, [2009] All ER (D) 126 (Mar) .... A 79.4
Aldis v DPP [2002] EWHC 403 (Admin), (2002) Times, 6 March, [2002] All ER (D) 128 (Feb) .... E 1.2
Ali v DPP [2009] EWHC 3353 (Admin), 174 JP 149, [2009] All ER (D) 256 (Nov) .... A 9.5, 9.7
Anderson v Miller [1976] Crim LR 743, 120 Sol Jo 735, DC . A 33.3
Angus v United Kingdom Border Agency [2011] EWHC 461 (Admin), [2011] All ER (D) 138 (Mar) .... F 5.47A
Arrowsmith v Jenkins [1963] 2 QB 561, [1963] 2 All ER 210, [1963] 2 WLR 856, 61 LGR 312, 127 JP 289, 107 Sol Jo 215 .... C 36.2
Atkin v DPP (1989) 89 Cr App Rep 199, 153 JP 383, [1989] Crim LR 581, DC .... A 21.5
Atkins v DPP [2000] 2 All ER 425, [2000] 1 WLR 1427, [2000] 2 Cr App Rep 248, [2000] IP & T 639, [2000] All ER (D) 301, DC .... A 43.3
Atkinson v DPP [2004] EWHC 1457 (Admin), [2004] 3 All ER 971, [2005] 1 WLR 96, 168 JP 472, [2004] All ER (D) 247 (Jun) .... A 5.2
Atkinson v DPP [2011] EWHC 3363 (Admin), [2012] RTR 171, 176 CL&J 274, [2012] All ER (D) 33 (Jan) .... C 34A.9
A-G v Leveller Magazine Ltd [1979] AC 440, [1979] 1 All ER 745, [1979] 2 WLR 247, 68 Cr App Rep 342, 143 JP 260, 123 Sol Jo 129, HL .... D 1B.4
A-G's Reference (No 1 of 1980) [1981] 1 All ER 366, [1981] 1 WLR 34, 72 Cr App Rep 60, 145 JP 165, [1981] Crim LR 41, 124 Sol Jo 881, CA A31.3A
A-G's Reference (No 1 of 1981) [1982] QB 848, [1982] 2 All ER 417, [1982] 2 WLR 875, 75 Cr App Rep 45, [1982] Crim LR 512, 126 Sol Jo 210, CA .... A 4.6
A-G's Reference (No 1 of 1999) [2000] 1 QB 365, [1999] 3 WLR 769, [1999] 2 Cr App Rep 418, 163 JP 769, CA .... A 69.6

A-G's Reference (No 1 of 2000) [2001] 1 WLR 331, [2001] 1 Cr App Rep 218, [2001] Crim LR 127, (2000) Times, November 28, (2000) Independent, November 30, [2000] All ER (D) 1882, CA .... A 78.6
A-G's Reference (No 4 of 2000) [2001] EWCA Crim 780 [2001] RTR 415, [2001] 2 Cr App Rep 417, [2001] Crim LR 578 .... C 16.5
A-G's Reference (No 1 of 2001) [2002] EWCA Crim 1768, [2002] 3 All ER 840, [2003] 1 WLR 395, [2003] 1 Cr App Rep 131, [2002] Crim LR 844, [2002] 37 LS Gaz R 36, (2002) Times, 7 August, 146 Sol Jo LB 192, [2002] All ER (D) 165 (Jul) .... A 78.8
A-G's Reference (No 64 of 2003) [2003] EWCA Crim 3514, [2004] 2 Cr App Rep (S) 106, [2004] Crim LR 241, (2003) Times, 1 December, [2003] All ER (D) 288 (Nov) .... A 1.4
A-G's Reference (No 1 of 2004), R v Edwards [2004] EWCA Crim 1025, [2005] 4 All ER 457, [2004] 1 WLR 2111, [2004] 2 Cr App Rep 424, [2004] Crim LR 832, [2004] 20 LS Gaz R 34, (2004) Times, 30 April, 148 Sol Jo LB 568, [2004] BPIR 1073, [2004] All ER (D) 318 (Apr) .... A 69.7
A-G's Reference (No 2 of 2004) [2005] EWCA Crim 1415, [2006] 1 All ER 988, [2005] 1 WLR 3642, [2005] 2 Cr App Rep 527, [2006] Crim LR 148, (2005) Times, 22 June, 149 Sol Jo LB 712, [2005] All ER (D) 447 (May) .... A 25.8 A
A-G's Reference (No 4 of 2004), R v D [2005] EWCA Crim 889, [2005] 1 WLR 2810, (2005) Times, 17 May, [2005] All ER (D) 332 (Apr) .... A 20.6
Austen v Crown Prosecution Service [2016] EWHC 2247 (Admin), 181 JP 181 .... A 15.31
Axn v Worboys [2012] EWHC 1730 (QB), [2012] All ER (D) 212 (Jun) .... C 33.9

B

B (a minor) (treatment and secure accommodation), Re [1997] 1 FCR 618, sub nom A Metropolitan Borough Council v DB [1997] 1 FLR 767, [1997] Fam Law 400 .... E 3.7
B v Chief Constable of Avon and Somerset Constabulary [2001] 1 All ER 562, [2001] 1 WLR 340 .... A 52.15
Baker v Crown Prosecution Service [2009] EWHC 299 (Admin), 173 JP 215, [2009] All ER (D) 237 (Jan) .... A 9.8
Baker v Quantum Clothing Group [2011] UKSC 17, [2011] 4 All ER 223, [2011] 1 WLR 1003, [2011] ICR 523, [2011] 17 LS Gaz R 13, (2011) Times, 14 April, 155 Sol Jo (no 15) 38, [2011] All ER (D) 137 (Apr) .... A 80.19
Balshaw v Crown Prosecution Service [2009] EWCA Crim 470, [2009] 2 Cr App Rep 95, [2009] 2 Cr App Rep (S) 712, 173 JP 242, [2009] Crim LR 532, [2009] All ER (D) 184 (Mar) ...... B 12.8
Bannister v Clarke [1920] 3 KB 598, 85 JP 12, 90 LJKB 256, 26 Cox CC 641, 124 LT 28, 36 TLR 778, DC .... B 38.5

Barker v Royal Society for the Prevention of Cruelty to Animals [2018] EWHC 880 (Admin), [2018] 2 Cr App Rep (S) 92, [2018] PTSR 1582, 168 NLJ 7791, (2018) Times, 10 May, [2018] All ER (D) 168 (Jan) .... A 5.4
Barnfather v Islington Education Authority [2003] EWHC 418 (Admin), [2003] 1 WLR 2318, [2003] ELR 263, (2003) Times, 20 March, [2003] All ER (D) 89 (Mar) .... A 49.3
Bastable v Little [1907] 1 KB 59, 5 LGR 279, 71 JP 52, 76 LJKB 77, 21 Cox CC 354, 51 Sol Jo 49, 96 LT 115, 23 TLR 38, [1904–7] All ER Rep Ext 1147, DC .... A 47.9
Bauer v DPP (Liberty intervening) [2013] EWHC 634 (Admin), [2013] 1 WLR 3617, 177 JP 297, [2013] All ER (D) 13 (Apr) .... A 21.5A
Baxter, Re [2002] EWHC 300 (Admin), [2002] All ER (D) 218 (Jan) A31.3A
Bayliss v DPP 167 JPN 103, [2003] All ER (D) 71 (Feb) ... A 11.7, A 11.12
Beattie v Crown Prosecution Service [2018] EWHC 787 (Admin) .... C 22.23
Beckford v R [1988] AC 130, [1987] 3 All ER 425, [1987] 3 WLR 611, 85 Cr App Rep 378, [1988] Crim LR 116, 131 Sol Jo 1122, [1987] LS Gaz R 2192, [1987] NLJ Rep 591, PC ..... A 8.18, A 8.19
Begum v West Midlands Police [2012] EWHC 2304 (Admin), [2013] 1 All ER 1261, [2013] 1 WLR 3595, 176 CL&J 690, [2012] All ER (D) 101 (Nov) .... F 5.47A
Bennett v Brown (1980) 71 Cr App Rep 109 .... A 76.17
Bennett v Horseferry Road Magistrates' Court. See R v Horseferry Road Magistrates' Court, ex p Bennett
Bennett v Secretary of State for Work and Pensions [2012] EWHC 371 (Admin), 176 JP 181, [2012] All ER (D) 160 (Jan) .... A 54.4
Best v United Kingdom (2005) Times, 10 March .... B 28.50
Betts v Stevens [1910] 1 KB 1, 7 LGR 1052, 73 JP 486, 79 LJKB 17, 22 Cox CC 187, 101 LT 564, 26 TLR 5, [1908–10] All ER Rep Ext 1245 .... A 47.9
Bingham v Bruce [1962] 1 All ER 136, [1962] 1 WLR 70, 60 LGR 79, 126 JP 81, 105 Sol Jo 1086, DC .... C 32A.3
Birmingham City Council v Dixon [2009] EWHC 761 (Admin), 173 JP 233, (2009) Times, 13 April .... B 13.6
Birmingham City Council v Oakley [2001] 1 AC 617, [2001] 1 All ER 385, [2000] 3 WLR 1936, [2001] LGR 110, [2000] 48 LS Gaz R 38, [2000] NLJR 1824, (2000) Times, 30 November, 144 Sol Jo LB 290, [2000] All ER (D) 2037, HL .... A 84.3
Birmingham City Council v S. See A (a child) (disclosure of child's existence to paternal grandparents), Re
Birmingham City Council v Sharif [2019] EWHC 1268 (QB), [2019] LLR 494, [2019] All ER (D) 08 (Jun) .... B 8A.6
Blackburn v Bowering [1994] 3 All ER 380, [1994] 1 WLR 1324, [1995] Crim LR 38, CA .... A 9.7
Blake v DPP [2002] EWHC 2014 (Admin), [2002] All ER (D) 125 (Sep) .... C 25.9

Boggeln v Williams [1978] 2 All ER 1061, [1978] 1 WLR 873, 67 Cr App Rep 50, 142 JP 503, [1978] Crim LR 242, 122 Sol Jo 94, DC .... A 1.3
Bond v Chief Constable of Kent [1983] 1 All ER 456, [1983] 1 WLR 40, 76 Cr App Rep 56, 4 Cr App Rep (S) 324, 147 JP 107, [1983] Crim LR 166, 126 Sol Jo 707, [1983] LS Gaz R 29 .... B 10.2
Bonner v DPP [2004] EWHC 2415 (Admin), [2004] All ER (D) 74 (Oct) .... A 9.8
Booth v Crown Prosecution Service [2006] EWHC 192 (Admin), (2006) 170 JP 305, 170 JPN 513, [2006] All ER (D) 225 (Jan) .... A 18.31
Bourne v Scarborough Magistrates' Court [2017] EWHC 2828 (Admin), [2018] 4 WLR 29, 182 JP 49, [2018] Crim LR 258, [2017] All ER (D) 93 (Nov) .... D 9.18
Bradford Metropolitan District Council v Booth (2002), unreported .... F 2.20
Brants v DPP [2011] EWHC 754 (Admin), 175 JP 246, [2011] All ER (D) 92 (Mar) .... D 1B.12
Breckon v DPP [2007] EWHC 2013 (Admin), [2007] All ER (D) 135 (Aug) .... C 22.16
Bremme v Dubery [1964] 1 All ER 193, [1964] 1 WLR 119, 128 JP 148, 107 Sol Jo 911, DC .... A 48.4
Briffet and Bradshaw v DPP [2001] EWHC Admin 841 (2001) 166 JP 66, sub nom Briffett v Crown Prosecution Service [2002] EMLR 203 .... A 52.11; D 1B.7
Briscoe v Shattock [1999] 1 WLR 432, 163 JP 201, [1999] Crim LR 396 .... A 72.24
BBC Litigation Department, Re [2002] All ER (D) 69 (Apr), CA .... A 52.11; D 1B.7
Bromley London Borough Council v C [2006] EWHC 1110 (Admin), [2006] ELR 358, (2006) Times, 12 April, [2006] All ER (D) 80 (Mar) .... A 49.3
Brooker v DPP [2005] EWHC 1132 (Admin), 169 JP 368, (2005) Times, 5 May, [2005] All ER (D) 139 (Apr), DC .... A 11.9
Brooks v Blackpool Borough Council [2013] EWHC 3735 (Admin), [2014] RTR 173, 178 JP 79, [2013] All ER (D) 41 (Dec) .... C 39.10
Broome v DPP [1974] AC 587, [1974] 1 All ER 314, [1974] 2 WLR 58, [1974] IRLR 26, [1974] ICR 84, [1974] Crim LR 311, 118 Sol Jo 50, HL .... A 85.3
Brown v Stott [2001] 2 All ER 97, [2001] 2 WLR 817, [2001] RTR 121, 145 Sol Jo LB 100, PC .... C 8.22
Browne v Chief Constable of Greater Manchester [2004] EWHC 490 (Admin), 168 JP 448, [2004] NLJR 468, (2004) Times, 30 March, [2004] All ER (D) 269 (Mar) .... C 32A.3
Browning v Floyd [1946] KB 597, [1946] 2 All ER 367, 44 LGR 247, 110 JP 308, [1947] LJR 245, 90 Sol Jo 332, 175 LT 135, 62 TLR 405, DC .... A 48.4
Brutus v Cozens [1973] AC 854, [1972] 2 All ER 1297, [1972] 3 WLR 521, 56 Cr App Rep 799, 136 JP 636, 116 Sol Jo 647, HL .... A 20.5

Bryan v Mott (1975) 62 Cr App Rep 71, [1976] Crim LR 64, 119 Sol Jo 743, DC .... A 13
Burns v Currell [1963] 2 QB 433, [1963] 2 All ER 297, [1963] 2 WLR 1106, 61 LGR 356, 127 JP 397, 107 Sol Jo 272, DC ..... C 9.7
Buchanan v Crown Prosecution Service [2018] EWHC 1773 (Admin), [2018] LLR 668 .... A 85.3A

C

C v Crown Prosecution Service [2008] EWHC 854 (Admin), 172 JP 273, (2008) Times, 20 February, [2008] All ER (D) 112 (Feb) .... D 1B.7
C-T Aviation Solutions Ltd v R (Health and Safety Executive) [2015] EWCA Crim 1620, [2016] RTR 55, [2015] All ER (D) 86 (Oct) .... A 80.9
Cambridge City Council v Alex Nestling Ltd [2006] EWHC 1374 (Admin), 170 JP 539, 170 JPN 975, (2006) Times, 11 July, [2006] All ER (D) 252 (May) .... F 2.20
Cambridgeshire County Council v Associated Lead Mills Ltd [2005] EWHC 1627 (Admin), [2006] RTR 82, 169 JP 489, [2005] All ER (D) 318 (Jul) .... C 9.4
Campbell v Bromley Magistrates' Court [2017] EWCA Civ 1161, [2017] Crim LR 987, [2017] All ER (D) 104 (Aug) .... F 5.47
Carroll v DPP [2009] EWHC 554 (Admin), 173 JP 285, [2009] All ER (D) 35 (Mar) .... A 28.5
Castle v DPP (1998) Times, 3 April .... A 33.9, A 77.9
Castle v Wakefield and Pontefract Magistrates' Court [2014] EWHC 587 (Admin), [2014] RTR 268, 178 JP 285, 178 CL&J 182, 178 CL&J 62, [2014] All ER (D) 169 (Jan) .... C 49.35A
Caurti v DPP [2001] EWHC Admin 867, [2002] Crim LR 131, [2001] All ER (D) 287 (Oct) .... A 41.7
Cawthorn v DPP [2000] RTR 45, sub nom Cawthorn v Newcastle upon Tyne Crown Court 164 JP 527 .... C 18.9
Chahal v DPP [2010] EWHC 439 (Admin), [2010] 2 Cr App Rep 33, [2010] All ER (D) 37 (Apr) .... A 11.12, A 11.13
Chalupa v Crown Prosecution Service [2009] EWHC 3082 (Admin), 174 JP 111, [2009] All ER (D) 09 (Nov), DC ...... C 23.6A
Chambers v DPP [2012] EWHC 2157 (Admin), [2013] 1 All ER 149, [2013] 1 WLR 1833, [2013] 1 Cr App Rep 1, 176 JP 737, 176 CL&J 482, [2012] All ER (D) 346 (Jul) .... A 16.2
Chambers and Edwards v DPP [1995] Crim LR 896 .... A 20.8
Cherpion v DPP [2013] EWHC 615 (Admin), 177 CL&J 225, [2013] All ER (D) 44 (Feb) .... D 6.17C
Chief Constable of Avon and Somerset v Fleming [1987] 1 All ER 318, [1987] RTR 378, 84 Cr App Rep 345, [1987] Crim LR 277 .... A 63.5, A 65.6; C 9.7
Chief Constable of Cheshire Constabulary v Hunt (1983) 147 JP 567 .... A 25.7
Chief Constable of Cleveland Police v Vaughan [2009] EWHC 2831 (Admin) .... F 5.47

Chief Constable of Cumbria Constabulary v Wright [2006] EWHC 3574 (Admin), [2007] 1 WLR 1407, [2006] All ER (D) 265 (Nov) .... A 26.12
Chief Constable of Merseyside Police v Doyle [2019] EWHC 2180 (Admin), [2019] All ER (D) 82 (Aug) .... A 72.15
Chief Constable of Merseyside Police v Harrison (Secretary of State for the Home Department intervening) [2006] EWHC 1106 (Admin), [2006] 3 WLR 171, 170 JP 523, (2006) Times, 14 April, 150 Sol Jo LB 469, [2006] All ER (D) 115 (Apr) ... A 26.12
Chief Constable of Merseyside Police v Owens [2012] EWHC 1515 (Admin), 176 JP 688, 176 CL&J 353, [2012] All ER (D) 03 (Jun) .... B 18.5; F 1.3, F 1.7, F 1.21
Chief Constable of North Yorkshire Police v Saddington [2000] EWHC 409 (Admin), [2001] RTR 227, (2001) 165 JP 122, [2001] Crim LR 41, (2000) Times, 1 November, (2000) Independent, 3 November, [2000] Lexis Citation 3984, [2000] All ER (D) 1530, DC .... C 9.7
Childs v Coghlan (1968) 112 Sol Jo 175, DC .... C 9.7
Clark (a protected party suing by his Mother and litigation friend Nicola Woods) v Farleyand [2018] EWHC 1007 (QB), [2019] RTR 239, [2018] PIQR P306, 168 NLJ 7793, [2018] All ER (D) 23 (May) .... C 16.6
Clark (Procurator Fiscal, Kirkcaldy) v Kelly [2003] UKPC D1, [2004] 1 AC 681, [2003] 1 All ER 1106, [2003] 2 WLR 1586, (2003) Times, 12 February, 2003 SLT 308, 2003 SCCR 194, 147 Sol Jo LB 234, 14 BHRC 369, [2003] All ER (D) 139 (Feb) .. D 9.17
Clarke v Kato [1998] 4 All ER 417, [1998] 1 WLR 1647, [1998] 43 LS Gaz R 31, [1998] NLJR 1640, 142 Sol Jo LB 278, sub nom Clarke v General Accident Fire and Life Assurance Corpn plc [1999] RTR 153, 163 JP 502, HL ..... C 18.16
Clay v Clerk to the South Cambridgeshire Justices [2014] EWHC 321 (Admin), [2015] RTR 1, [2014] All ER (D) 171 (Jan) ... D 1B.12
Clear v Smith [1981] 1 WLR 399, [1980] Crim LR 246, 125 Sol Jo 256 .... A 54.4
Cleveland Police v Haggas [2009] EWHC 3231 (Admin), [2010] 3 All ER 506, [2011] 1 WLR 2512, [2010] All ER (D) 119 (Jan) .... B 44.4
Clifford v Bloom [1977] RTR 351, [1977] Crim LR 485, 121 Sol Jo 559, DC .... A 64.3
Coates v Crown Prosecution Service [2011] EWHC 2032 (Admin), 175 JP 401, [2011] All ER (D) 34 (Aug) .... C 9.7
Coffin v Smith (1980) 71 Cr App Rep 221, DC .... A 9.5
Collins v Wilcock [1984] 3 All ER 374, [1984] 1 WLR 1172, 79 Cr App Rep 229, 148 JP 692, [1984] Crim LR 481, 128 Sol Jo 660, [1984] LS Gaz R 2140 .... A 15.10
Condron v United Kingdom (Application 35718/97) (2000) 21 EHRR 1, [2000] Crim LR 679, 8 BHRC 290, ECtHR .... D 1A.3, D 6.22
Connell v DPP [2011] EWHC 158 (Admin), 175 JP 151, [2011] All ER (D) 155 (Jan) .... C 49.4

Coombes v DPP [2006] EWHC 3263 (Admin), [2007] RTR 383, 171 JP 271, (2006) Times, 29 December, [2006] All ER (D) 296 (Dec) .... C 49.15
Cooper v Metropolitan Police Comr (1985) 82 Cr App Rep 238, DC .... A 85.3
Corbyn v Saunders [1978] 2 All ER 697, [1978] 1 WLR 400, 67 Cr App Rep 7, 142 JP 458, [1978] Crim LR 169, 122 Sol Jo 15, DC .... A 48.4
Covington v Wright [1963] 2 QB 469, [1963] 2 All ER 212, [1963] 2 WLR 1232, 61 LGR 342, 107 Sol Jo 477, DC .... A 48.4
Cowan v DPP [2013] EWHC 192 (Admin), 177 JP 474, [2013] All ER (D) 116 (Jan) .... C 20.8
Cox v Riley (1986) 83 Cr App Rep 54, [1986] Crim LR 460 .... A 18.22
Cracknell v Willis [1988] AC 450, [1987] 3 All ER 801, [1987] 3 WLR 1082, [1988] RTR 1, 86 Cr App Rep 196, 154 JP 728, 131 Sol Jo 1514, 154 Sol Jo 728, [1987] LS Gaz R 3502, HL, [1987] NLJ Rep 1061, HL .... C 22.23
Crader v Chief Constable of Hampshire Constabulary [2015] EWHC 3553 (Admin), 180 JP 199 .... C 49.4
Crawley Borough Council v Attenborough [2006] EWHC 1278 (Admin), 170 JP 593, 171 JPN 69, [2006] All ER (D) 104 (May) .... F 2.20
Cresswell v DPP. See Currie v DPP
Criminal Practice Directions [2013] EWCA Crim 1631 .... A 80.5
Criminal Practice Directions 2015 Amendment No. 8 [2019] EWCA Crim 495, [2019] All ER (D) 149 (Mar) .... D 6.5
Croitoru v Crown Prosecution Service [2016] EWHC 1645 (Admin), [2017] 1 WLR 1130, [2017] RTR 216, 180 JP 451 ... C 9.7
Crown Prosecution Service v C [2017] Crim L R 62 .... 22.23A
Crown Prosecution Service v Humphries. See DPP v Humphries
Crown Prosecution Service v T. See DPP v T
Cumberbatch v Crown Prosecution Service [2009] EWHC 3353 (Admin), 174 JP 149, [2009] All ER (D) 256 (Nov) ..... A 9.5, 47.11
Currie v DPP [2006] EWHC 3379 (Admin), [2006] All ER (D) 429 (Nov), sub nom Cresswell v DPP; Currie v DPP 171 JP 233, 151 Sol Jo LB 500 .... A 18.19
Customs and Excise Comrs v Brunt (1998) 163 JP 161 .... A 4.19
Customs and Excise Comrs v Duffy [2002] EWHC 425 (Admin), (2002) Times, 4 April, [2002] All ER (D) 01 (Mar), DC .... F 5.47
Customs and Excise Comrs v Newbury [2003] EWHC 702 (Admin), [2003] 2 All ER 964, [2003] 1 WLR 2131, [2003] 23 LS Gaz R 39 .... B 18.19
Cutter v Eagle Star Insurance Co Ltd [1998] 4 All ER 417, [1998] 1 WLR 1647, [1999] RTR 153, 163 JP 502, [1998] 43 LS Gaz R 31, [1998] NLJR 1640, 142 Sol Jo LB 278, HL .... C 9.10

D

D v DPP [2005] EWHC 967 (Admin), [2005] Crim LR 962, [2005] All ER (D) 260 (May) A8.7, A15.4, A70.5

D Ltd v A [2017] EWCA Crim 1172, [2018] Crim LR 993, [2018] All ER (D) 163 (Jul) .... D 1B.12
D and R v DPP (1995) 160 LG Rev 481, 160 JP 275, sub nom D (a minor) v DPP 16 Cr App Rep (S) 1040, [1995] 3 FCR 725, [1995] 2 FLR 502, [1995] Fam Law 595, [1995] Crim LR 748, [1995] NLJR 560 .... B 28.10
DLA Piper UK LLP v BDO LLP [2013] EWHC 3970 (Admin), [2014] 1 WLR 4425, [2013] All ER (D) 175 (Dec) .... B 12.20
Daley v Hargreaves [1961] 1 All ER 552, [1961] 1 WLR 487, 59 LGR 136, 125 JP 193, 105 Sol Jo 111, DC .... C 9.7
Dannenberg v Secretary of State for the Home Department. See R v Secretary of State for the House Department ex p Dannenberg
Darroch v DPP (1990) 90 Cr App Rep 378, 154 JP 844, [1990] Crim LR 814 .... A 82.2
Darroux v The Crown [2018] EWCA Crim 1009, [2018] 2 Cr App Rep 311, [2018] All ER (D) 71 (May) .... A 57.9
Davies v Health and Safety Executive. See R v Davies
Davies v Leighton (1978) 68 Cr App Rep 4, [1978] Crim LR 575, 122 Sol Jo 641, DC .... A 57.22
Dehal v DPP [2005] EWHC 2154 (Admin), [2005] All ER (D) 152 (Sep), sub nom Dehal v Crown Prosecution Service 169 JP 581 .... A 21.5A
Delaney v Secretary of State for Transport [2015] EWCA Civ 172, [2015] 3 All ER 329, [2015] 2 CMLR 914, [2015] RTR 169, [2015] Lloyd's Rep IR 441, [2015] PIQR P 266, [2015] All ER (D) 97 (Mar) .... C 33.21
Demetriou (Leon) v DPP (2012) 156 Sol Jo (no 18) 31, [2012] All ER (D) 165 (Apr) .... A 9.8
Devon County Council v Gateway Foodmarkets Ltd (1990) 154 JP 557, [1990] COD 324, DC .... A 85.3
Dewar v DPP [2010] All ER (D) 83 (Jan), DC .... A 8.18
Dibble v Ingleton [1972] 1 QB 480, [1972] 2 WLR 163, [1972] RTR 161, 116 Sol Jo 97, sub nom Ingleton v Dibble [1972] 1 All ER 275, 136 JP 155 .... A 47.9
Dica, Re (5 May 2004, unreported), CA .... A 70.5
DPP v A [2000] All ER (D) 1247 .... A 70.5
DPP v Alderton [2003] EWHC 2917 (Admin), [2004] RTR 367, 147 Sol Jo LB 1398, [2003] All ER (D) 360 (Nov) .... C 18.8
DPP v Barber (1998) 163 JP 457 .... C 22.23
DPP v Barker (2004) 168 JP 617, [2004] All ER (D) 246 (Oct), DC .... C 5.38
DPP v Baker (2004) 169 JP 140, [2004] All ER (D) 28 (Nov), DC .... A 41.7; C 19.7
DPP v Beaumont [2008] EWHC 523 (Admin), [2008] 1 WLR 2186, [2008] 2 Cr App Rep (S) 549, 172 JP 283, [2008] Crim LR 572, [2008] All ER (D) 36 (Mar) .... B 29.7
DPP v Bennett [1993] RTR 175, 157 JP 493, [1993] Crim LR 71 .... C 31.2
DPP v Berry [2019] EWCA Civ 825, [2019] Crim LR 789 .. D 6.4AA
DPP v Bird [2015] EWHC 4077 (Admin), [2016] 4 WLR 82, [2016] 2 Cr App Rep 149, 180 JP 217 .... A 18.3
DPP v Bristow [1998] RTR 100, 161 JP 35 .... C 22.25

DPP v Broomfield [2002] EWHC 1962 (Admin), [2003] RTR 108, 166 JP 736 .... C 8.21, C 32A.6
DPP v Bulmer [2015] EWHC 2323 (Admin), 165 NLJ 7666, [2015] WLR (D) 355, [2015] All ER (D) 342 (Jul) .... B 13.5
DPP v Butterworth [1995] 1 AC 381, [1994] 3 All ER 289, [1994] 3 WLR 538, [1994] RTR 330, 159 JP 33, [1995] Crim LR 71, [1994] NLJR 1043, HL .... D 6.23
Director of Public Prosecutions v Camp [2017] EWHC 3119 (Admin), [2018] Crim LR 406, [2018] All ER (D) 45 (Jan) .... C 23.5
DPP v Chajed [2013] EWHC 188 (Admin), [2013] 2 Cr App Rep 60, 177 JP 350, [2013] Crim LR 603, 177 CL&J 63, [2013] All ER (D) 119 (Jan) .... B 38.5
DPP v Cheshire Justices [2002] EWHC 466 (Admin), [2002] All ER (D) 93 (Mar) .... D 6.17B
DPP v Chippendale [2004] EWHC 464 (Admin), [2004] Crim LR 755, [2004] All ER (D) 308 (Jan) .... A 21.7
DPP v Christof [2015] EWHC 4096 (Admin), [2016] 2 Cr App Rep 56 .... A 11.5
DPP v Clarke (1991) 94 Cr App Rep 359, 156 JP 267, 135 Sol Jo LB 135, DC .... A 20.17
DPP v Collins [2006] UKHL 40, [2006] 4 All ER 602, [2006] 1 WLR 2223, [2007] 1 Cr App Rep 49, 170 JP 712, [2006] IP & T 875, [2006] NLJR 1212, 171 JPN 162, (2006) Times, 21 July, 150 Sol Jo LB 987, [2006] All ER (D) 249 (Jul) .... A 16.2
DPP v Cove [2008] EWHC 441 (Admin), [2008] All ER (D) 199 (Feb) .... C 22.25
DPP v Darwin [2007] EWHC (Admin) 337 .... C 23.3
DPP v Denning [1991] 2 QB 532, [1991] 3 All ER 439, [1991] 3 WLR 235, 94 Cr App Rep 272, 155 JP 1003, [1991] Crim LR 699, (1991) Times, 9 April, DC .... B 12.19
DPP v Distill [2017] EWHC 2244 (Admin), [2017] All ER (D) 31 (Sep) .... A 20.3B, A 21.9
DPP v Drury [1989] RTR 165, 153 JP 417, DC .... C 32.6
DPP v Dunn (2008) 165 JP 130 .... A 41.7
DPP v Everest [2005] EWHC 1124 (Admin), 169 JP 345, [2005] All ER (D) 363 (May) .... D 6.23
DPP v Fearon [2010] EWHC 340 (Admin), [2010] 2 Cr App Rep 169, 174 JP 145, [2010] Crim LR 646, [2010] All ER (D) 32 (Mar) .... A 82.2
DPP v Gane (1991) 155 JP 846, [1991] Crim LR 711, DC .... B 36.1
Director of Public Prosecutions v Giles [2019] EWHC 2015 (Admin), [2019] All ER (D) 175 (Jul) .... D 6.25
DPP v Glendinning [2005] EWHC 2333 (Admin), 169 JP 649, [2005] All ER (D) 130 (Oct) .... A 47.9
DPP v Gowing [2013] EWHC 4614 (Admin), 178 JP 181 .. D 1B.12
DPP v Gregson (1992) 96 Cr App Rep 240, 157 JP 201, [1992] 34 LS Gaz R 34, 136 Sol Jo LB 245 .... A 11.12, A 11.13
DPP v H [1997] 1 WLR 1406, [1998] RTR 200, [1997] 18 LS Gaz R 31, sub nom DPP v Harper 161 JP 697 .... C 20.3
DPP v Halahan [2014] EWCA Crim 2079, [2014] All ER (D) 284 (Oct) .... D 1B.12

DPP v Hall [2005] EWHC 2612 (Admin), [2006] 3 All ER 170, [2006] 1 WLR 1000, 170 JP 11, [2005] All ER (D) 37 (Oct) .. A 46.5
DPP v Hammerton [2009] EWHC 921 (Admin), [2009] All ER (D) 258 (Oct), [2010] QB 79, [2009] 3 WLR 1085, [2009] 2 Cr App Rep 322, 174 JP 17 .... D 6.23
DPP v Hardy [2008] EWHC 2874 (Admin), 173 JP 10, [2008] All ER (D) 315 (Oct) .... A 41.7
DPP v Harper. See DPP v H
DPP v Hastings [1993] RTR 205, 158 JP 118 .... C 18.9
DPP v Hay [2005] EWHC 1395 (Admin), [2006] RTR 32, (2005) 169 JP 429, (2005) Times, 13 July, [2005] All ER (D) 90 (Jun) .... C 18.17, C 32.6, C 32.18
DPP v Heritage [2002] EWHC 2139 (Admin), (2002) 166 JP 772 .... C 33.23A
DPP v Heywood [1998] RTR 1, DC .... C 23.3
DPP v Holden [2006] All ER (D) 363 (Feb) .... C 8.21
DPP v Humphries [2000] RTR 52, sub nom Crown Prosecution Service v Humphries [2000] 2 Cr App Rep (S) 1, 164 JP 502 ...... C 22.25
DPP v Janman [2004] EWHC 101 (Admin), [2004] Crim LR 478, [2004] All ER (D) 171 (Jan) .... C 21.4, C 22.64
DPP v K (a minor) [1990] 1 All ER 331, [1990] 1 WLR 1067, 91 Cr App Rep 23, 154 JP 192, [1990] Crim LR 321, 134 Sol Jo 636, [1989] NLJR 1455 .... A 8.8
DPP v Karamouzis [2006] EWHC 2634 (Admin), [2006] All ER (D) 109 (Oct) .... C 23.3
DPP v Kemsley [2004] EWHC 278 (Admin), [2004] All ER (D) 53 (Feb), sub nom Kemsley v DPP 169 JP 148 .... C 25.10
DPP v King [2008] EWHC 447 (Admin), 172 JP 401, [2008] All ER (D) 170 (Feb) .... A 66.5, C 9.7
DPP v M [1998] QB 913, [1997] 2 All ER 749, [1998] 2 WLR 604, [1997] 2 Cr App Rep 70, [1997] 2 FLR 804, [1998] Fam Law 11, 161 JP 491 .... A 52.8
DPP v M [2004] EWHC 1453 (Admin), [2004] 1 WLR 2758, 148 Sol Jo LB 660, [2004] All ER (D) 358 (May) .... A 18.17
DPP v McCarthy [1999] RTR 323, 163 JP 585 .... C 31.8
DPP v McKeown and Jones [1997] 1 All ER 737, [1997] 1 WLR 295, [1997] 2 Cr App Rep 155, 161 JP 356, [1997] Crim LR 522, [1997] NLJR 289, (1997) Times, 21 February, HL ...... C 22.23
Director of Public Prosecutions v Melvyne John Woods [2017] EWHC 1070 (Admin), 181 JP 395 .... D 6.13
DPP v Memery [2002] EWHC 1720 (Admin), [2003] RTR 249, 167 JP 238, (2002) Times, 9 July, [2002] All ER (D) 64 (Jul) ...... C 22.23
DPP v Mills [1997] QB 300, [1996] 3 WLR 1093, [1997] 2 Cr App Rep 6, 160 JP 377, [1996] Crim LR 746 .... A 69.4
DPP v Milton [2006] EWHC 242 (Admin), (2006) 170 JP 319, 170 JPN 533, 150 Sol Jo LB 166, [2006] All ER (D) 04 (Feb) ..... C 49.7
DPP v Noe [2000] RTR 351, [2000] 20 LS Gaz R 43 .... C 23.4
DPP v Oram [2005] EWHC 964 (Admin), [2005] All ER (D) 57 (May) .... C 22.24

DPP v P [2007] EWHC 946 (Admin), 171 JP 349, 171 JPN 659, [2007] All ER (D) 244 (Apr) .... E 3.2, E 3.25
DPP v Pal [2000] Crim LR 756 .... A 20.6
DPP v Parmenter [1992] 1 AC 699, sub nom R v Parmenter [1991] 2 All ER 225, [1991] 2 WLR 408, 92 Cr App Rep 68, 164, 154 JP 941, [1991] Crim LR 41, 134 Sol Jo 1368, [1990] NLJR 1231, CA; revsd sub nom DPP v Parmenter [1992] 1 AC 699, [1991] 3 WLR 914, 94 Cr App Rep 193, 155 JP 935, sub nom R v Parmenter [1991] 4 All ER 698, HL .... A 8.7
DPP v Patterson [2004] All ER (D) 239 (Oct), DC .... A 11.13
DPP v Petrie [2015] EWHC 48 (Admin), 179 JP 251, [2015] Crim LR 385, [2015] All ER (D) 140 (Jan) .... D 1B.12, D 6.17B
DPP v Picton [2006] EWHC 1108 (Admin), 170 JP 567, 170 JPN 954, [2006] All ER (D) 83 (May) .... D 6.17A
DPP v Revitt [2006] EWHC 2266 (Admin), [2006] 1 WLR 3172, [2007] 1 Cr App Rep 266, 170 JP 729, [2007] Crim LR 238, [2006] NLJR 1476, 171 JPN 251, (2006) Times, 14 September, [2006] All ER (D) 34 (Sep) .... D 6.26
DPP v Richards [1988] QB 701, [1988] 3 All ER 406, [1988] 3 WLR 153, 88 Cr App Rep 97, 152 JP 333, 132 Sol Jo 623, DC .... A 10.2; D 8.85
DPP v Robertson [2002] 15 LS Gaz R 33 .... C 22.10
DPP v S [2007] All ER (D) 148 (Dec), DC .... D 6.21
DPP v Santra-Bermudez [2003] EWHC 2908 (Admin), (2003) 168 JP 373, [2004] Crim LR 471, [2003] All ER (D) 168 (Nov) .... A 8.8
DPP v Selvanayagam (1999) Times, 23 June, DC .... A 41.10
DPP v Shuttleworth [2002] EWHC 621 (Admin), 166 JP 417, [2002] All ER (D) 101 (Mar) .... D 6.17A
DPP v Smith [1961] AC 290, sub nom R v Smith [1960] 2 All ER 450, [1960] 3 WLR 92, 104 Sol Jo 510, CCA; revsd sub nom DPP v Smith [1961] AC 290, [1960] 3 All ER 161, [1960] 3 WLR 546, 44 Cr App Rep 261, 124 JP 473, 104 Sol Jo 683, HL .... A 70.6; C 16C.3
DPP v Smith (Michael Ross) [2006] EWHC 94 (Admin), [2006] 2 All ER 16, [2006] 1 WLR 1571, (2006) Times, 19 January, 150 Sol Jo LB 130, [2006] All ER (D) 69 (Jan) .... A 8.9
DPP v Smith [2017] EWHC 359 (Admin), 181 JP 258, [2017] All ER (D) 198 (Feb) .... A 16.2
DPP v Spriggs [1994] RTR 1, 157 JP 1143, [1993] Crim LR 622 .... A 65.4
DPP v Spurrier [2000] RTR 60, sub nom R v Crown Prosecution Service, ex p Spurrier 164 JP 369 .... C 22.23
DPP v Stoke on Trent Magistrates' Court [2003] EWHC 1593 (Admin), [2003] 3 All ER 1086, [2004] 1 Cr App Rep 55, 167 JP 436, [2003] Crim LR 804, [2003] NLJR 1063 .... A 34.11
Director of Public Prosecutions v Sugden [2018] EWHC 544 (Admin), [2018] RTR 247, [2018] 2 Cr App Rep 101, [2018] Crim LR 752, [2018] All ER (D) 139 (Mar) .... C 22.23A
DPP v T [2006] EWHC 728 (Admin), [2006] 3 All ER 471, [2006] 3 FCR 184, [2006] All ER (D) 41 (Apr), sub nom Crown Prosecution Service v T 170 JP 470, (2006) Times, 13 April .... B 2.4

DPP v Taylor [1992] QB 645, [1992] 1 All ER 299, [1992] 2 WLR 460, 95 Cr App Rep 28, [1992] Fam Law 377, 155 JP 713, [1991] Crim LR 904 .... A 15.5
DPP v Teixeira (2001) 166 JP 1 .... C 22.23
DPP v Thornley [2006] EWHC 312 (Admin), [2006] 09 LS Gaz R 32, 170 JPN 656, [2006] All ER (D) 41 (Feb) .... C 49.4
Director of Public Prosecutions v Vicky Patterson [2017] EWHC 2820 (Admin), [2018] 1 Cr App Rep 412 .... A 36.7
DPP v Vince [2016] EWHC 3014 (Admin), [2017] 4 WLR 3, [2017] RTR 97, [2017] Crim LR 307 .... C 22.23
DPP v Warren [1993] AC 319, [1992] 4 All ER 865, [1992] 3 WLR 884, [1993] RTR 58, 96 Cr App Rep 312, 157 JP 297, [1992] 45 LS Gaz R 26, [1992] NLJR 1684, HL .... C 23.6
DPP v Watkins [1989] QB 821, [1989] 1 All ER 1126, [1989] 2 WLR 966, [1989] RTR 324, 89 Cr App Rep 112, 154 JP 370, 133 Sol Jo 514, [1989] 19 LS Gaz R 45, [1989] NLJR 365 ... C 21.3
DPP v Whittaker [2015] EWHC 1850 (Admin), 179 JP 321, [2015] All ER (D) 47 (Jul) .... C 33.6
DPP v Wood [2006] EWHC 32 (Admin), (2006) 170 JP 177, [2006] NLJR 146, 170 JPN 414, (2006) Times, 8 February, [2006] All ER (D) 101 (Jan) .... C 22.16, C 22.23; D 6.12
DPP v Woods [2002] EWHC 85 (Admin) [2002] All ER (D) 154 (Jan) .... A 8.16, A 15.7, A 18.18
DPP v Ziegler and others [2019] EWHC 71 (Admin), [2019] 2 WLR 1451, [2019] 1 Cr App Re[32, [2019] Crim LR 728 .. A 85.3A
Director of the Assets Recovery Agency v Green [2005] EWHC 3168 (Admin), (2006) Times, 27 February, [2005] All ER (D) 261 (Dec) .... F 5.47A
Dixon v Atfield [1975] 3 All ER 265, [1975] 1 WLR 1171, 73 LGR 357, 139 JP 799, 119 Sol Jo 542, DC .... A 85.3
Dixon v Crown Prosecution Service [2018] EWHC 3154 (Admin), [2018] 4 WLR 160, [2019] 1 Cr App Rep 255, [2019] Crim LR 619, [2018] All ER (D) 129 (Nov) .... A 9.5
Donnelly v Jackman [1970] 1 All ER 987, [1970] 1 WLR 562, 54 Cr App Rep 229, 134 JP 352, 114 Sol Jo 130 .... A 9.5
Donovan v Gavin [1965] 2 QB 648, [1965] 2 All ER 611, [1965] 3 WLR 352, 129 JP 404, 109 Sol Jo 373, DC .... A 44.3
Dougall v Crown Prosecution Service [2018] EWHC 1367 (Admin), [2018] Crim LR 763 .... D 6.23
Dowler v Merseyrail [2009] EWHC 558 (Admin), 173 JP 332, [2009] All ER (D) 97 (May) .... B 12.16
Dragjoshi v Croydon Magistrates' Court [2017] EWHC 2840 (Admin), [2017] All ER (D) 115 (Nov) .... A 2.4
Dulgheriu v London Borough of Ealing [2018] EWHC 1667 (Admin), [2018] 4 All ER 881, 168 NLJ 7801, [2018] All ER (D) 07 (Jul); affd sub nom Dulgheriu v Ealing London Borough Council [2019] EWCA Civ 1490, [2019] All ER (D) 89 (Aug) .... B 8A 8
Dumble v Metropolitan Police Comr [2009] All ER (D) 66 (Feb) .... A 26.12
Durose v Wilson (1907) 71 JP 263, 21 Cox CC 421, 96 LT 645, DC .... A 44.3

E

Earl v Roy [1969] 2 ALL ER 684, 133 JP 520 .... C 22.22
East Lindsey District Council v Hanif (Zaraf Restaurant & Takeaway) (2016) [2016] EWHC 1265 (Admin) .... F 2.19
Elliott v DPP (1989) Times, 19 January, DC .... A 44.3
Ellis v Burton [1975] 1 All ER 395, [1975] 1 WLR 386, 139 JP 199, [1975] Crim LR 32, 119 Sol Jo 114 .... A 15.31
Evans v Barker [1971] RTR 453 .... C 36.4
Evans v Serious Fraud Office [2015] EWHC 263 (QB), [2015] 1 WLR 3595, [2015] All ER (D) 148 (Feb) .... B 12.19
Ewing v Highbury Corner Magistrates Court [2015] EWHC 3788 (Admin), [2016] RVR 174, [2016] All ER (D) 26 (Jan) .... F 4.9A

F

F and R (Section 8 order: grandparents' application), Re. See R (minors), Re,
Fawcett v Gasparics [1986] RTR 375, [1987] Crim LR 53 ... C 22.23
Felix v DPP [1998] Crim LR 657 .... A 83.21
Filmer v DPP [2006] EWHC 3450 (Admin), [2007] RTR 330, [2006] All ER (D) 08 (Nov) .... C 20.8
Flack v Baldry [1988] 1 All ER 673, [1988] 1 WLR 393, 87 Cr App Rep 130, 152 JP 418, [1988] Crim LR 610, 132 Sol Jo 334, [1988] 12 LS Gaz R 39, [1988] NLJR 63, (1988) Times, 26 February, HL .... A 76A.4
Flintshire County Council v Reynolds [2006] EWHC 195 (Admin), 170 JP 73, [2006] All ER (D) 130 (Jan) .... A 54.4
Foulkes v Chief Constable of Merseyside Police [1998] 3 All ER 705, [1999] 1 FCR 98, [1998] 2 FLR 798, [1998] Fam Law 661, [1998] All ER (D) 254, CA .... A 9.8
Francis v DPP [2004] EWHC 591 (Admin), (2004) 168 JP 492, [2004] All ER (D) 443 (Mar) .... C 8.21, C 34A.6

G

G v DPP [2004] EWHC 183 (Admin), (2004) 168 JP 313, 148 Sol Jo LB 149, [2004] All ER (D) 278 (Jan) .... A 15.7, A 20.6
Gearing v DPP [2008] EWHC 1695 (Admin), [2009] RTR 72 .... C 23.6A
Gillingham v Walker (1881) 45 JP 470, 29 WR 896, [1881–5] All ER Rep 710, 44 LT 715, DC .... A 48.4
Glenn & Co (Essex) Ltd v Revenue and Customs Comrs and East Berkshire Magistrates' Court [2011] EWHC 2998 (Admin), [2012] 1 Cr App Rep 291, 176 JP 65, [2012] Crim LR 464, [2011] All ER (D) 149 (Nov) .... F 5.7
Godwin v DPP (1992) 96 Cr App Rep 244, 157 JP 197 ...... A 11.9
Gordon v Thorpe [1986] RTR 358, [1986] Crim LR 61, DC . C 22.23

Gorman v Standen [1964] 1 QB 294, [1963] 3 All ER 627, [1963] 3 WLR 917, 48 Cr App Rep 30, 128 JP 28, 107 Sol Jo 811, DC .... A 44.3
Gough v Chief Constable of the Derbyshire Constabulary [2001] EWHC 554 (Admin), [2002] QB 459, [2001] 4 All ER 289, [2001] 3 WLR 1392, [2001] 3 CMLR 613, [2001] 31 LS Gaz R 30, (2001) Times, 19 July, 145 Sol Jo LB 186, [2001] All ER (D) 169 (Jul); affd [2002] EWCA Civ 351, [2002] QB 1213, [2002] 2 All ER 985, [2002] 3 WLR 289, (2002) Times, 10 April, [2002] All ER (D) 308 (Mar) .... B 29.22, B 29.33
Gough v Chief Constable of West Midland Police [2004] EWCA Civ 206, (2004) Times, 4 March, 148 Sol Jo LB 298, [2004] All ER (D) 45 (Mar) .... F 1.17
Gough v Director Of Public Prosecutions [2013] EWHC 3267 (Admin), 177 JP 669 .... A 20.5A
Government of the United Arab Emirates v Allen [2012] EWHC 1712 (Admin), [2012] 1 WLR 3419, [2012] All ER (D) 14 (Jul) .... A 36.7
Grace v DPP (1988) 153 JP 491, [1989] Crim LR 365, DC .... A 77.9
Grant v Crown Court at Kingston [2015] EWHC 767 (Admin), [2015] 2 Cr App Rep (S) 110, [2015] All ER (D) 337 (Feb) .... B 44.5
Green v DPP (1991) 155 JP 816, [1991] Crim LR 782, DC .... A 47.9
Green v Dunn [1953] 1 All ER 550, DC .... C 32.6
Griffiths v DPP [2002] EWHC 792 (Admin), (2002) 166 JP 629, [2002] All ER (D) 132 (Apr) .... C 22.30
Griffiths v DPP [2007] EWHC 619 (Admi'n), [2007] All ER (D) 356 (Mar) .... C 49.4
Guardian News and Media Ltd v Incedal [2014] EWCA Crim 1861, [2015] 1 Cr App Rep 36, (2014) Times, 29 October .... D 1B.2
Gunnell v DPP [1993] Crim LR 619 .... C 18.8

H

H v Crown Prosecution Service [2010] EWHC 1374 (Admin), 174 CL&J 271, [2010] All ER (D) 56 (Apr) .... A 15.11
H v DPP [2005] EWHC 2459 (Admin), (2005) 170 JP 4, [2005] All ER (D) 177 (Nov) .... A 28.4
H v Liverpool City Court [2001] Crim LR 897 .... A 66.11
HB v Switzerland (Application No 26899/95) (2001) 37 EHRR 1000, [2001] ECHR 26899/95, ECtHR .... D 8.2
Haggard v Mason [1976] 1 All ER 337, [1976] 1 WLR 187, 140 JP 198, 120 Sol Jo 7, DC .... A 26.4B
Haggis v DPP [2003] EWHC 2481 (Admin), [2004] 2 All ER 382, [2004] Crim LR 583, [2003] All ER (D) 113 (Oct) .... C 22.23
Hallett v DPP [2011] EWHC 488 (Admin), [2011] All ER (D) 91 (Mar) .... C 20.8
Hallinan v DPP [1998] Crim LR 754 .... C 31.3
Hambleton v Callinan [1968] 2 QB 427, [1968] 2 All ER 943, [1968] 3 WLR 235, 132 JP 461, 112 Sol Jo 503, DC .... A 25.7
Hammond v DPP [2004] EWHC 69 (Admin), [2004] All ER (D) 50 (Jan) .... A 21.5

Hampshire Police Authority v Smith [2009] EWHC 174 (Admin), 173 JP 207, [2009] All ER (D) 117 (Feb) .... A 26.16

Haralambous v St Albans Crown Court [2016] EWHC 916 (Admin), [2016] 1 WLR 3073, [2016] 2 Cr App Rep 224, 180 JP 428, [2016] Crim LR 664, [2016] All ER (D) 161 (Apr) ..... F 5.24A

Harding v Price [1948] 1 KB 695, [1948] 1 All ER 283, 46 LGR 142, 112 JP 189, [1948] LJR 1624, 92 Sol Jo 112, 64 TLR 111, DC .... C 32.6

Haringey London Borough Council v Jowett [1999] LGR 667, 78 P & CR D24, 32 HLR 308, [1999] NPC 52, [1999] EGCS 64, [1999] All ER (D) 420, DC .... A 84.3

Harrington, Re [1984] AC 473, [1984] 3 WLR 142, 79 Cr App Rep 305, 149 JP 211, [1984] Crim LR 622, 128 Sol Jo 434, [1984] LS Gaz R 2142, sub nom Harrington v Roots [1984] 2 All ER 474, HL .... D 6.17D

Harriott v DPP [2005] EWHC 965 (Admin), (2005) 170 JP 494, [2005] All ER (D) 28 (May) .... A 11.8

Harris v DPP [1993] 1 All ER 562, [1993] 1 WLR 82, 96 Cr App Rep 235, 157 JP 205, [1992] 32 LS Gaz R 35, 136 Sol Jo LB 228 .... A 11.9

Harrogate Borough Council v Barker (1995) 159 LG Rev 889, 159 JP 809, [1995] RVR 193 .... F 4.11

Harvey v DPP [2011] EWHC 3992 (Admin), 176 JP 265, [2012] Crim LR 553, [2011] 47 LS Gaz R 20, [2011] All ER (D) 143 (Nov) .... A 20.8

Hashman and Harrup v United Kingdom (2000) 30 EHRR 241, [2000] Crim LR 185, 8 BHRC 104, ECtHR .... B 5.6, B 5.20

Haw v City of Westminster Magistrates' Court [2007] EWHC 2960 (Admin), [2008] QB 888, [2008] 2 All ER 326, [2008] 3 WLR 465, 172 JPN 309, 172 JP 122, [2007] All ER (D) 164 (Dec) .... D 3.16

Hayes v Chief Constable of Merseyside Police [2011] EWCA Civ 911, [2012] 1 WLR 517, [2011] 2 Cr App Rep 434, [2012] Crim LR 35, (2011) Times, 19 August, [2011] All ER (D) 286 (Jul) A20.18

Hayes v DPP [2004] EWHC 277 (Admin), [2004] All ER (D) 55 (Feb) .... C 8.22

Hayes v Willoughby [2013] UKSC 17, [2013] 2 All ER 405, [2013] 1 WLR 935, [2013] 2 Cr App Rep 115, [2013] NLJR 25, (2013) Times, 28 May, [2013] All ER (D) 190 (Mar) .... A 41.10

Haystead v Chief Constable of Derbyshire [2000] 3 All ER 890, [2000] 2 Cr App Rep 339, [2000] Crim LR 758, sub nom Haystead v DPP 164 JP 396 .... A 15.6

Henderson v Commissioner of Police for the Metropolis [2018] EWHC 666 (Admin), [2018] 1 WLR 5029, [2018] All ER (D) 56 (Apr) .... A 72.10

Henderson v Crown Prosecution Service [2016] EWHC 464 (Admin), [2016] 1 WLR 1990, [2016] 2 Cr App Rep 62, [2016] Crim LR 422, [2016] All ER (D) 86 (Mar) .... B 36.1

HM Solicitor General v Cox [2016] EWHC 1241 (QB), [2016] 2 Cr App Rep 193, 166 NLJ 7702, [2016] All ER (D) 03 (Jun) . D 1B.9

Hertfordshire County Council v Bolden (1986) 151 JP 252, [1987] BTLC 272 .... A 85.3
Hills v Chief Constable of Essex Police [2006] EWHC 2633 (Admin), 171 JP 14, [2006] All ER (D) 35 (Oct) .... B 13.6
Hills v Ellis [1983] QB 680, [1983] 1 All ER 667, [1983] 2 WLR 234, 76 Cr App Rep 217, 148 JP 379, [1983] Crim LR 182, 126 Sol Jo 768, [1983] LS Gaz R 153, 133 NLJ 280, DC .... A 47.9
Hinchcliffe v Sheldon [1955] 3 All ER 406, [1955] 1 WLR 1207, 120 JP 13, 99 Sol Jo 797, DC .... A 47.9
Hinchley v Rankin [1961] 1 All ER 692, [1961] 1 WLR 421, 59 LGR 190, 125 JP 293, 105 Sol Jo 158, DC .... A 49.3
Hirst and Agu v Chief Constable of West Yorkshire (1986) 85 Cr App Rep 143, 151 JP 304, [1987] Crim LR 330 .... A 85.3
Hogan v DPP [2007] EWHC 978 (Admin), (2007) Times, 28 February, [2007] All ER (D) 253 (Feb) .... A 40.11
Hollis v Dudley Metropolitan Borough Council [1998] 1 All ER 759, [1999] 1 WLR 642, 30 HLR 902, [1998] 18 EG 133 ... A 84.31
Hooper v United Kingdom (App No 42317/98) (2004) Times, 19 November, [2004] All ER (D) 254 (Nov), ECtHR .... B 5.6
Hounslow London Borough Council v Thames Water Utilities Ltd [2004] All ER (D) 94 (Feb) .... A 84.9
Hudson v Crown Prosecution Service [2017] EWHC 841 (Admin), [2017] 4 WLR 108, [2017] 2 Cr App Rep (S) 177, 181 JP 346, (2017) Times, 13 June, [2017] 2 P & CR D27, [2017] All ER (D) 15 (May) .... A 12.14
Hughes v DPP [2012] EWHC 606 (Admin), [2012] All ER (D) 180 (Jan) .... A 21.7
Hussain v United Kingdom (Application 8866/04) (2006) 43 EHRR 437, (2006) Times, 5 April, [2006] ECHR 8866/04, [2006] All ER (D) 83 (Mar), ECtHR .... B 12.16

I

I v DPP, M v DPP, H v DPP [2001] UKHL 10, [2002] 1 AC 285, [2001] 2 All ER 583, [2001] 2 WLR 765, [2001] 2 Cr App Rep 216, 165 JP 437, [2001] Crim LR 491, [2001] 20 LS Gaz R 40, 151 NLJ 385, (2001) Times, 9 March, 145 Sol Jo LB 101, [2001] All ER (D) 83 (Mar) .... A 2.5, A 2.6
Idrees v DPP [2011] All ER (D) 156 (Feb) .... A 36.6
Ingleton v Dibble. See Dibble v Ingleton
Isle of Wight Council v Platt [2017] UKSC 28, [2017] 3 All ER 623, (2017) 181 JP 237 .... A 49.3
Islington London Borough Council v TD [2011] EWHC 990 (Admin), [2011] All ER (D) 265 (Mar) .... A 49.3
Ivey v Genting Casinos (UK) Ltd (trading as Crockfords) [2017] UKSC 67, [2018] AC 391, [2018] 2 All ER 406, [2017] 3 WLR 1212, [2018] 1 Cr App Rep 180, [2018] Crim LR 395, (2017) Times, 13 November, [2017] All ER (D) 134 (Oct), SC .... A 36.7

J

JB v DPP [2012] EWHC 72 (Admin), [2012] 1 WLR 2357, [2012] 2 Cr App Rep 9, 176 JP 97, [2012] All ER (D) 120 (Jan) .... B 2.4
Jaggard v Dickinson [1981] QB 527, [1980] 3 All ER 716, [1981] 2 WLR 118, 72 Cr App Rep 33, [1980] Crim LR 717, 124 Sol Jo 847 .... A 18.19
James v Birmingham City Council [2010] EWHC 282 (Admin), 174 JP 250, [2010] All ER (D) 218 (Feb) .... B 2.2
James v DPP [2012] EWHC 1317 (Admin), 176 JP 346, 176 CL&J 291, [2012] All ER (D) 150 (Apr) .... F 5.4
James and Chorley v DPP (1997) 163 JP 89, [1997] Crim LR 831 .... A 47.12
Jenkins v Howells [1949] 2 KB 218, [1949] 1 All ER 942, 47 LGR 394, 113 JP 292, [1949] LJR 1468, 93 Sol Jo 302, 65 TLR 305, DC .... A 49.3
Jones v Brimingham City Council [2018] EWCA Civ 1189, [2018] 3 WLR 1695, [2018] 2 Cr App Rep 353, 168 NLJ 7795, [2018] All ER (D) 129 (May) .... B 35.2, B 48.1
Jones v Chief Constable of West Mercia Police Authority (2000) 165 JP 6 .... C 5.20
Jones v DPP (1992) 96 Cr App Rep 130, 156 JP 866, (1992) Times, 4 June, DC .... A 44.3
Jones v DPP [2010] EWHC 523 (Admin), [2010] 3 All ER 1057, [2011] 1 WLR 833, 174 JP 278, 174 CL&J 172, [2010] All ER (D) 230 (Feb) .... A 20.6
Jones v DPP [2004] EWHC 236 (Admin), [2004] RTR 331, 168 JP 393, [2004] Crim LR 667, [2004] All ER (D) 319 (Jan) .... C 8.21, C 32A.6
Jones v DPP [2011] EWHC 50 (Admin), 175 JP 129 .... C 49.15
Jones v South East Surrey Local Justice Area [2010] EWHC 916 (Admin), 174 JP 342 .... D 6.13A
Joseph v DPP [2003] EWHC 3078 (Admin), [2004] RTR 341, 168 JP 575, [2004] 02 LS Gaz R 29, [2003] All ER (D) 326 (Nov) .... C 23.6

K

Kang v DPP [2016] EWHC 3014 (Admin), [2017] 4 WLR 3, [2017] RTR 97, [2017] Crim LR 307 .... C 22.23
Karsten v Wood Green Crown Court [2014] EWHC 2900 (Admin), [2014] All ER (D) 286 (Oct) .... A 16.2
Katsonis v Crown Prosecution Service [2011] EWHC 1860 (Admin), 175 JP 396, [2011] All ER (D) 16 (Jul) . A8.7, A15.4, A70.5
Keating v Knowsley Metropolitan Borough Council. See R (on the application of K) v Knowsley Metropolitan Borough Council
Kelly v DPP [2002] All ER (D) 177 (Jun) .... A 41.7
Kelly v Purvis [1983] QB 663, [1983] 1 All ER 525, [1983] 2 WLR 299, 76 Cr App Rep 165, 147 JP 135, [1983] Crim LR 185, 127 Sol Jo 52, DC .... A 44.3
Kemsley v DPP. See DPP v Kemsley

Kennedy v DPP [2002] EWHC 2297 (Admin), [2004] RTR 77, 167 JP 267, [2003] Crim LR 120, [2002] All ER (D) 77 (Nov), DC .... C 23.6A
Kennet District Council v Young [1999] RTR 235, 163 JP 622, 163 JP 854 .... C 8.21
Khan v DPP. See R (on the application of Khan) v DPP
Kingsnorth v DPP [2003] All ER (D) 235 (Mar) .... C 19.6
Kirkup v DPP [2003] EWHC 2354 (Admin), (2003) 168 JP 255, [2004] Crim LR 230, [2003] All ER (D) 53 (Oct) .... C 23.4
Knight v DPP [2012] EWHC 605 (Admin), 176 JP 177 .... A 21.7
Krishevsky v DPP [2014] EWHC 1755 (Admin), 178 JP 369, [2014] All ER (D) 22 (Jun), DC .... C 34A 4

L

L, Re (1990) 155 JP 273, [1991] Crim LR 633, (1990) Times, 11 December, DC .... D 1B.2
L v Crown Prosecution Service [2007] EWHC 1843 (Admin), [2007] All ER (D) 224 (Jul) .... A 79.5
L v Crown Prosecution Service [2010] EWHC 341 (Admin), 174 JP 209, [2010] All ER (D) 128 (Feb) .... A 72.2
LCC v DPP [2001] EWHC Admin 453, 165 JP 806, [2001] All ER (D) 303 (May) .... B 19.8
Langdon v Howells (1879) 4 QBD 337, 43 JP 717, 48 LJMC 133, 27 WR 657, 40 LT 880, DC .... A 48.4
Lambert (A) Flat Management Ltd v Lomas [1981] 2 All ER 280, [1981] 1 WLR 898, 125 Sol Jo 218 .... A 84.17
Lamont-Perkins v Royal Society for the Prevention of Cruelty to Animals [2012] EWHC 1002 (Admin), 176 JP 369, [2012] All ER (D) 149 (Apr) .... A 5.2
Lau v DPP [2000] 1 FLR 799, [2000] Fam Law 610, [2000] Crim LR 580 .... A 41.7
Leary v Chief Constable of West Midlands Police [2012] EWHC 639 (Admin), 176 CL&J 143, [2012] All ER (D) 137 (Feb) .. A 26.12
Leeds City Council v G [2007] EWHC 1612 (Admin), (2007) Times, 11 September, [2007] All ER (D) 114 (Jul) .... B 2.2
Leeson v DPP [2010] EWHC 994 (Admin), 174 JP 367, [2010] 17 LS Gaz R 16, 174 CL&J 284, [2010] All ER (D) 84 (Apr) .... A 2.6
Lester v Torrens (1877) 2 QBD 403, 41 JP 821, 46 LJMC 280, 25 WR 691, DC .... A 28.7
Letherbarrow v Warwickshire County Council [2014] EWHC 4820 (Admin), 179 JP 307, [2015] All ER (D) 34 (Jun) .... A 5.2
Levine v DPP (6 May 2010, unreported), QBD .... A 21.9
Lewington v The Motor Insurance Bureau [2017] EWHC 2848 (Comm), [2018] RTR 259 ....C 9.7
Lewis v Cox [1985] QB 509, [1984] 3 All ER 672, [1984] 3 WLR 875, 80 Cr App Rep 1, 148 JP 601, [1984] Crim LR 756, 128 Sol Jo 596, [1984] LS Gaz R 2538, DC .... A 47.8
Lewis v DPP [2004] EWHC 3081 (Admin), [2005] All ER (D) 66 (Jan) .... C 20.7

Lewisham London Borough Council v Hall [2002] EWHC 960 (Admin), [2002] All ER (D) 83 (May) .... A 84.4
Liverpool City Council v Pleroma Distribution Ltd [2002] EWHC 2467 (Admin), [2003] RA 34, [2003] 04 LS Gaz R 33, (2002) Times, 2 December, [2002] All ER (D) 302 (Nov) .... B 38.6
Liverpool v DPP [2008] EWHC 2540 (Admin), [2008] All ER (D) 50 (Oct) .... A 21.6
Loade v DPP [1990] 1 QB 1052, [1990] 1 All ER 36, [1989] 3 WLR 1281, 90 Cr App Rep 162, 153 JP 674, [1989] Crim LR 808, [1989] NLJR 1231, DC .... A 21.5
Loake v Crown Prosecution Service [2017] EWHC 2855 (Admin), [2018] 2 WLR 1159, [2018] 1 Cr App Rep 238, [2018] Crim LR 336, [2017] All ER (D) 128 (Nov) .... A 41.11
London, Midland and Scottish Rly Co v Greaver [1937] 1 KB 367, [1936] 3 All ER 333, 34 LGR 579, 100 JP 511, 106 LJKB 180, 30 Cox CC 487, 80 Sol Jo 878, 155 LT 535, 53 TLR 75, DC .... A 48.4
Longstaff v DPP [2008] EWHC 303 (Admin), [2008] RTR 212, [2008] All ER (D) 276 (Jan) .... C 23.6
Lord Howard of Lympne v Director of Public Prosecutions [2018] EWHC 100 (Admin), [2018] Crim LR 489, [2018] All ER (D) 179 (Feb) .... C 34A.6
Lunt v DPP [1993] Crim LR 534, [1993] COD 430, DC ...... A 47.9
Lynes v Director of Public Prosecutions [2012] EWHC 1300 (Admin), [2013] RTR 13, [2013] Crim L R 333 .... C 32A.3

M

M (a minor), Re [1995] Fam 108, [1995] 3 All ER 407, [1995] 2 WLR 302, [1995] 2 FCR 373, [1995] 1 FLR 418, 138 Sol Jo LB 241, CA .... E 3.7, E 3.8
MF (Nigeria) v Secretary of State for the Home Department [2013] EWCA Civ 1192, [2014] 2 All ER 543, [2014] 1 WLR 544, (2013) Times, 17 December, [2013] All ER (D) 78 (Oct) .... B 17.8
McCann v Crown Prosecution Service [2015] EWHC 2461 (Admin), [2016] 1 Cr App Rep 82, 179 JP 470, [2016] Crim LR 59, [2015] All ER (D) 106 (Aug) .... A 9.5
McCaskill v DPP [2005] EWHC 3208 (Admin), 170 JP 301, 170 JPN 554, [2005] All ER (D) 292 (Dec) .... A 46.3
McConnell v Chief Constable of the Greater Manchester Police [1990] 1 All ER 423, [1990] 1 WLR 364, 91 Cr App Rep 88, 154 JP 325, 134 Sol Jo 457, CA .... A 9.8
McCrone v J and L Rigby (Wigan) Ltd (1951) 50 LGR 115, [1951] WN 626, 95 Sol Jo 712, [1951] 2 TLR 911, DC .... C 9.7
Macdonald v Carmichael 1941 JC 27, 106 JP Jo 53 .... C 9.7
McKeon v DPP [2007] EWHC 3216 (Admin), [2008] RTR 165, [2007] All ER (D) 314 (Dec) .... C 23.4
McKerry v Teesdale and Wear Valley Justices (2000) 164 JP 355, [2000] Crim LR 594, [2000] COD 199, [2001] EMLR 127, sub nom McKerry v DPP [2000] 11 LS Gaz R 36, 144 Sol Jo LB 126, CA .... D 1A.2

McKoen v Ellis [1987] RTR 26, 151 JP 60, [1987] Crim LR 54 .... C 18.9
McMillan v Crown Prosecution Service [2008] EWHC 1457 (Admin), 172 JP 485, 172 JPN 646, 172 JPN 694, [2008] All ER (D) 142 (May) .... A 28.3
McNeil v DPP [2008] EWHC 1254 (Admin), [2008] All ER (D) 375 (Apr) .... C 23.6
Magee v Crown Prosecution Service [2014] EWHC 4089 (Admin), 179 JP 261, [2014] All ER (D) 370 (Oct) ... A 18.19; C 31.8, C 32.6
Maharaj v Solomon [1987] RTR 295, DC .... C 22.23
Malvern Justices, Ex Parte Evans [1988] QB 540, [1988] 2 WLR 218, (1987) Times, 1 August .... D 1B.2
Marsden v Crown Prosecution Service [2014] EWHC 3359 (Admin), [2014] 178 JP 497, [2014] All ER (D) 199 (Oct) .... A 9.5
Marsh v Director of Prosecutions [2015] EWHC 1022 (Admin), [2015] Crim LR 713, [2015] All ER (D) 347 (Mar) .... A 8.18
Marshall v Crown Prosecution Service (appeals Unit) [2015] EWHC 2333 (Admin), 180 JP 33 .... C 34A.9
Martin v DPP [2000] RTR 188, [2000] 2 Cr App Rep (S) 18, 164 JP 405, [2000] Crim LR 320 .... C 5.19
Martiner v DPP [2004] EWHC 2484 (Admin), [2004] All ER (D) 122 (Oct) .... C 23.3
Mawdesley v Chief Constable of Cheshire Constabulary [2003] EWHC 1586 (Admin), [2004] 1 All ER 58, [2004] 1 WLR 1035, [2004] RTR 209, 168 JP 23, [2004] Crim LR 232, [2003] NLJR 1384, (2003) Times, 11 September, [2003] All ER (D) 21 (Aug) .... C 32A.6
May v DPP [2005] EWHC 1280 (Admin), [2005] All ER (D) 182 (Apr) .... C 16A.5, C 20.7, C 25.4
Mayon v DPP [1988] RTR 281, DC .... C 22.23
Mepstead v DPP (1995) 160 JP 475, [1996] Crim LR 111, [1996] COD 13 .... A 9.8
Metropolitan Police Comr v B [2014] EWHC 546 (Admin), 178 JP 158, [2014] All ER (D) 25 (Mar) .... F 5.24A
Metropolitan Police Comr v Hooper [2005] EWHC 340 (Admin), [2005] 4 All ER 1095, [2005] 1 WLR 1995, 169 JP 409, (2005) Times, 3 March, [2005] All ER (D) 245 (Feb) .... A 26.12
Metropolitan Police Comr v Thorpe [2015] EWHC 3339 (Admin), [2016] 4 WLR 7, [2016] 1 Cr App Rep (S) 291, 180 JP 16, [2015] All ER (D) 166 (Nov) .... B 29.1
Miller v DPP [2004] EWHC 595 (Admin), [2004] 17 LS Gaz R 30, [2004] All ER (D) 477 (Mar) .... C 5.24
Mills v DPP [2008] EWHC 3304 (Admin), [2009] RTR 143, 173 JP 157, [2008] All ER (D) 39 (Dec) .... C 19.6
Milton v DPP [2007] EWHC 532 (Admin), [2007] All ER (D) 285 (Mar) .... C 16.8
Mohammed v Chief Constable of South Yorkshire Police [2002] EWHC 406 (Admin), [2002] All ER (D) 374 (Feb) .... A 11.12
Mohindra v DPP [2004] EWHC 490 (Admin), (2004) 168 JP 448, [2004] NLJR 468, [2004] All ER (D) 269 (Mar) . C 8.22, C 32A.1, C 32A.3, C 32A.5
Monks v Pilgrim [1979] Crim LR 595 .... A 61.4

Moore v Gooderham [1960] 3 All ER 575, [1960] 1 WLR 1308, 124 JP 513, 104 Sol Jo 1036, DC .... A 33.8, A 76.6
Moore v Green [1983] 1 All ER 663 .... A 47.8
Moran v DPP [2002] EWHC 89 (Admin), (2002) 166 JP 467, (2002) Times, 8 February, [2002] All ER (D) 268 (Jan) .... D 6.21
Moss v McLachlan [1985] IRLR 76, 149 JP 167 .... A 9.5
Muir v Smith [1978] Crim LR 293 .... A 25.7A

N

N v DPP [2011] EWHC 1807 (Admin), 175 JP 337, [2011] All ER (D) 04 (Jul), DC .... A 11.13
Najib and Sons Ltd v Crown Prosecution Service [2018] EWCA Crim 1554, [2018] 4 WLR 144 .... B 12.19
Nagy v Weston [1965] 1 All ER 78, [1965] 1 WLR 280, 129 JP 104, 109 Sol Jo 215, DC .... A 85.3
National Probation Service v Blackfriars Crown Court and others [2019] EWHC 529 (Admin), [2019] 2 Cr App Rep (S) 177, [2019] All ER (D) 51 (Mar) .... B 9.10
Nedic v South Staffordshire Council [2005] EWHC 1481 (Admin), [2005] All ER (D) 182 (Jun) .... B 12.2
Newcombe v Crown Prosecution Service [2013] EWHC 2160 (Admin), [2013] 6 Costs LO 905 .... B 12.16
Ng v DPP [2007] EWHC 36 (Admin), [2007] RTR 431, (2007) Times, 7 February, [2007] All ER (D) 214 (Jan) .... C 22.30
Nicolson v Grant Thornton UK LLP [2016] EWHC 710 (Admin), [2016] 2 Costs L.R. 211 .... F 4.9A
Noble v Killick (1891) 60 LJMC 61, DC .... A 48.4
Norbert Dentressangle Continental Ltd v Wing (1998), unreported .... C 38.20
Norwood v DPP [2003] EWHC 1564 (Admin), [2003] Crim LR 888, (2003) Times, 30 July, [2003] All ER (D) 59 (Jul) .... A 20.17

O

Oddy v Bug Bugs Ltd [2003] All ER (D) 156 (Nov) .... B 12.19
O'Halloran v United Kingdom (Application Nos 15809/02 and 25624/02) (2007) Times, 13 July, [2007] All ER (D) 07 (Jul), ECtHR .... C 8.22
Ohlson v Hylton [1975] 2 All ER 490, [1975] 1 WLR 724, 139 JP 531, 119 Sol Jo 255, DC .... A 11.5
Oldham Borough Council v Mohammed Sajjad [2016] EWHC 3597 (Admin), [2018] RTR 45 .... C 33.9
O'Leary International Ltd v Chief Constable of North Wales Police [2012] EWHC 1516 (Admin), 176 JP 514, 176 CL&J 370, [2012] All ER (D) 27 (Jun) .... B 18.5; F 1.21
Oraki v Crown Prosecution Service [2018] EWHC 115 (Admin), [2018] 2 WLR 1725, [2018] 1 Cr App Rep 402, [2018] Crim LR 655 .... A 47.12, A 47.15
Osman v DPP (1999) 163 JP 725 .... A 9.5

Ostler v Elliott [1980] Crim LR 584, DC .... A 47.8
O'Toole v Knowsley Metropolitan Borough Council [1999] LS Gaz R 36 .... A 84.3
Oxford v Baxendale [1987] RTR 247, DC .... C 22.23
Oxford County Council v L (3 March 2010, unreported), DC .... A 49.3
Oxfordshire County Council v L (3 March 2010, unreported) .... A 49.3

P

Pamplin v Gorman [1980] RTR 54, [1980] Crim LR 52, DC ...... C 34A.5
Parker v Smith [1974] RTR 500, [1974] Crim LR 426, DC ... C 23.4
Parry v DPP [2004] EWHC 3112 (Admin), [2004] All ER (D) 335 (Dec) .... A 18.17
Patel and a defendant's costs order, Re [2012] EWCA Crim 1508, [2012] All ER (D) 115 (Jul) .... B 12.17
Pattison v DPP [2005] EWHC 2938 (Admin), [2006] 2 All ER 317, [2005] All ER (D) 237 (Dec) .... C 19.6
Peake v DPP [2010] EWHC 286 (Admin), 174 JP 457, [2010] All ER (D) 223 (Feb) .... C 49.15
Peek v Towle [1945] KB 458, [1945] 2 All ER 611, 43 LGR 286, 109 JP 160, 114 LJKB 540, 173 LT 360, 61 TLR 399, DC .... C 32.6
Percy v DPP [2001] EWHC Admin 1125, 166 JP 93, [2002] Crim LR 835, (2002) Times, 21 January, [2001] All ER (D) 387 (Dec) .... A 20.17, A 21.5
Percy v Smith [1986] RTR 252 .... C 9.7
Phiri v Director of Public Prosecutions [2017] EWHC 2546 (Admin), [2017] All ER (D) 118 (Nov) .... C 34A.7
Pipe v DPP [2012] EWHC 1821 (Admin), [2012] All ER (D) 238 (May) .... C 49.7
Pitcher v Lockett [1966] Crim LR 283 .... A 85.3
Planton v DPP [2001] EWHC Admin 450 (2001) 166 JP 324, [2001] 27 LS Gaz R 40 .... A 36.3; C 18.8
Plunkett v DPP [2004] EWHC 1937 (Admin), [2004] All ER (D) 82 (Jul) .... C 22.5
Polychronakis v Richards and Jerrom Ltd [1998] JPL 588, [1998] Env LR 347 .... A 84.17
Power-Hynes v Norwich Magistrates' Court [2009] EWHC 1512 (Admin), 173 JP 573, [2009] All ER (D) 277 (Jun) .... F 5.9
Practice Direction (Criminal: Consolidated) [2002] 3 All ER 90 .... A 10.2; B 5.55
Practice Direction (magistrates' courts: anti-social behaviour orders: composition of benches) (24 February 2006, unreported) .... B 8.4
Practice Direction (Cost in Criminal Proceedings) (CLW/10/32/26) (30 July 2010, unreported) .... B 20.2A
Practice Direction (Costs in Criminal Proceedings) [2013] EWCA Crim 1632, [2013] 1 WLR 3255, 177 CL&J 674, [2013] All ER (D) 53 (Oct) .... B 12.16

Practice Direction (Costs in Criminal Proceedings) (No 2) [2014] EWCA Crim 1570, [2014] 1 WLR 3037, [2014] All ER (D) 215 (Jul) .... B 12.16
Practice Direction (Committal for Contempt of Court - Open Court) [2015] 2 All ER 541, [2015] All ER (D) 03 (Apr) .... D 3.7
Pratt v DPP [2001] EWHC Admin 483, (2001) 165 JP 800 ... A 41.7
Price v Cheshire East Borough Council [2012] EWHC 2927 (Admin), [2013] 1 WLR 1232 .... A 75.2
Prosecution Appeal (No 32 of 2007) [2008] EWCA Crim 1223, [2008] 1 WLR 2684, [2009] 1 Cr App Rep 56, (2008) Times, 25 August, [2008] All ER (D) 112 (Jun) .... D 6.21
Prosecution Appeal [2011] EWCA Crim 1508, [2011] 4 All ER 761, 175 CL&J 404, 175 CL&J 517, [2011] All ER (D) 135 (Jun); revsd sub nom R v Hughes [2013] UKSC 56, [2013] 1 WLR 2461, (2013) Times, 20 August, [2013] All ER (D) 388 (Jul) .... C 16B.5A
Pulton v Leader [1949] 2 All ER 747, 48 LGR 146, 113 JP 537, 94 Sol Jo 33, 65 TLR 687, DC .... C 32A.1
Pumbien v Vines [1996] RTR 37, [1996] Crim LR 124 . C 9.4, C 33.8, C 51.5
Pye v Leeds Youth Court [2006] EWHC 2527 (Admin), [2006] All ER (D) 16 (Oct) .... B 15.6, B 19.6

R

R v AH [2002] EWCA Crim 2938, (2003) 167 JP 30 .... E 3.18C
R v Abdulaziz [2016] EWCA Crim 887, [2016] 1 WLR 4366, [2016] 2 Cr App Rep 367, [2016] Crim LR 939, [2016] All ER (D) 145 (Jul) .... D 1B.7
R v Abdullahi [2006] EWCA Crim 2060, [2007] 1 WLR 225, [2007] 1 Cr App Rep 206, [2007] Crim LR 184, (2006) Times, 24 August, [2006] All ER (D) 334 (Jul) .... A 52.6
R v Aberdare Justices, ex p DPP (1990) 155 JP 324, DC ... D 6.17A
R (on the application of Robinson) v Abergavenny Magistrates' Court [2007] EWHC 2005 (Admin), 171 JP 683, 172 JPN 188, [2007] All ER (D) 210 (Jul) ..... D 6.4, D 6.7, D 6.17B
R (on the application of Denny) v Acton Youth Court (2004) Independent, 24 May .... E 3.24
R v Akhtar [2015] EWCA Crim 176, [2015] 1 WLR 3046, [2015] 2 Cr App Rep 81, [2015] All ER (D) 299 (Feb) ...... A 11.5; B 36.1
R (on the application of Harper) v Aldershot Magistrates' Court [2010] EWHC 1319 (Admin), 174 JP 410, 174 CL&J 383, [2010] All ER (D) 11 (Jun) .... D 1B.7
R (on the application of O'Connor and Jerrard) v Aldershot Magistrates' Court [2016] EWHC 2792, [2017] 181 JP 117 .. D 1B.2
R v Ali [2015] EWCA Crim 43, [2015] 1 Cr App Rep 494, [2015] All ER (D) 48 (Feb) .... A 81.5

R v Allen [1985] 1 All ER 148, [1985] 1 WLR 50, 79 Cr App Rep 265, [1984] Crim LR 498, 128 Sol Jo 660, [1984] LS Gaz R 1994, CA; affd [1985] AC 1029, [1985] 2 All ER 641, [1985] 3 WLR 107, 81 Cr App Rep 200, 149 JP 587, [1985] Crim LR 739, 129 Sol Jo 447, [1985] LS Gaz R 2740, [1985] NLJ Rep 603, HL .... A 45.6A, A 45.7
R v Amey [1983] 1 All ER 865, [1983] 1 WLR 345, [1983] RTR 192, 76 Cr App Rep 206, 4 Cr App Rep (S) 410, 147 JP 124, [1983] Crim LR 268, 127 Sol Jo 85, CA .... B 10.6, B 10.9
R v Andrew Smith (2000) 164 JP 681, CA .... B 19.4
R v Antoine [2014] EWCA Crim 1971, [2015] 1 Cr App Rep 81, 178 CL&J 647, [2014] All ER (D) 172 (Oct) .... D 1B.12
R v Antoniou [1989] Crim LR 436, CA .... A 38.3
R v Applied Language Solutions Ltd [2013] EWCA Crim 326, [2013] 1 WLR 3820, [2013] 2 Cr App Rep 169, [2013] 3 Costs LR 430, [2013] All ER (D) 239 (Mar) .... B 12.20A
R v Arbery and Mobley [2008] EWCA Crim 702, 172 JP 291 .... B 29.7
R v Argent [1997] 2 Cr App Rep 27, 161 JP 190, [1997] Crim LR 346, CA .... D 6.22
R v Asfaw [2008] UKHL 31, [2008] 1 AC 1061, [2008] 3 All ER 775, [2008] 2 WLR 1178, [2008] NLJR 788, (2008) Times, 26 May, 152 Sol Jo (no 22) 30, 25 BHRC 87, [2008] All ER (D) 274 (May) .... A 81.8A
R v Ashley [2003] EWCA Crim 2571, [2004] 1 WLR 2057, [2004] 1 Cr App Rep 299, 167 JP 548, [2004] Crim LR 297, [2003] All ER (D) 106 (Aug) .... D 8.92
R v Ashton [2006] EWCA Crim 794, [2007] 1 WLR 181, [2006] 2 Cr App Rep 231, (2006) Times, 18 April, [2006] All ER (D) 62 (Apr) .... B 8.12
R v Ashton-Rickardt [1978] 1 All ER 173, [1978] 1 WLR 37, 65 Cr App Rep 67, 142 JP 90, [1977] Crim LR 424, 121 Sol Jo 774, CA .... A 25.7
R v Augunas [2013] EWCA Crim 2046, [2014] 1 Cr App Rep 240 .... A 36.7
R v Auguste [2003] EWCA Crim 3929, [2004] 4 All ER 373, [2004] 1 WLR 917, [2004] 2 Cr App Rep 173, [2004] 05 LS Gaz R 28, (2003) Times, 15 December, [2003] All ER (D) 159 (Dec) .... A 27A.2
R v Ayhan [2011] EWCA Crim 3184, [2012] 1 WLR 1775, [2012] 1 Cr App Rep 391, [2012] 2 Cr App Rep (S) 207, 176 JP 121, [2012] Crim LR 299, 176 CL&J 13, (2012) Times, 18 January, [2011] All ER (D) 147 (Dec) .... B 8.10
R (on the application of Gray) v Aylesbury Crown Court [2013] EWHC 500 (Admin), [2013] 3 All ER 346, 177 JP 329, [2013] All ER (D) 157 (Mar) .... A 5.2
R (on the application of Y) v Aylesbury Crown Court, Crown Prosecution Service and Newsquest Media Group Ltd [2012] EWHC 1140 (Admin), [2012] All ER (D) 89 (May) . A 52.11; D 1B.7
R v Aziz [2012] EWCA Crim 1063, [2012] Crim LR 801 ... A 27.3A
R v Aziz [2016] EWCA Crim 1945, [2017] 1 Cr App Rep (S) 199, [2017] Crim LR 414 .... C 16C.4

R v B [2000] Crim LR 870 .... B 19.7
R v B [2012] EWCA Crim 770, [2012] 3 All ER 1093, [2013] 1 WLR 499, [2012] 2 Cr App Rep 164, 176 JP 312, [2013] Crim LR 90, 176 CL&J 273, (2012) Times, 30 July, [2012] All ER (D) 146 (Apr) .... A 68.3
R v B (D) [2016] EWCA Crim 474, [2016] 1 WLR 4157, [2016] 2 Cr App Rep 333 .... A 43.4A
R v BM [2018] EWCA Crim 560, [2018] 2 Cr App Rep 1, [2018] All ER (D) 13 (Apr) .... A 15.15
R (on the application of R) v Balham Youth Justices [2002] EWHC 2426 (Admin), [2002] All ER (D) 73 (Sep) .... E 3.18C
R v Ball [2002] EWCA Crim 2777, [2003] 2 Cr App Rep (S) 92, [2003] Crim LR 122 .... B 18.9
R v Bannister [2009] EWCA Crim 1571, (2009) Times, 24 August, 153 Sol Jo (no 30) 30, [2009] All ER (D) 289 (Jul) .... C 16.8
R v Barker [2010] EWCA Crim 4, [2011] Crim LR 233, (2010) Times, 5 February, [2010] All ER (D) 126 (Jan) .... A 52.8
R (on the application of Ethos Recycling Ltd) v Barking and Dagenham Magistrates' Court [2009] EWHC 2885 (Admin), [2010] PTSR 787, 174 JP 25, 173 CL&J 766, (2010) Times, 2 February, [2009] All ER (D) 162 (Nov) .... A 84.8
R (on the application of Cabot Global Ltd) v Barkingside Magistrates Court [2015] EWHC 1458 (Admin), [2015] 2 Cr App Rep 355, [2015] Crim LR 821, [2015] All ER (D) 182 (May) .... F 5.20A
R (on the application of P) v Barking Youth Court [2002] EWHC 734 (Admin), [2002] 2 Cr App Rep 294, 166 JP 641, [2002] All ER (D) 93 (Apr) .... E 3.25
R v Barnes [2004] EWCA Crim 3246, [2005] 2 All ER 113, [2005] 1 WLR 910, [2005] 1 Cr App Rep 507, [2005] Crim LR 381, (2005) Times, 10 January, [2004] All ER (D) 338 (Dec) ...... A 15.18
R v Barrett [2009] EWCA Crim 2213, [2010] 1 Cr App Rep (S) 572, [2010] Crim LR 159, (2009) Times, 5 October, [2009] All ER (D) 40 (Sep) .... B 34.39A
R v Barrick (1985) 81 Cr App Rep 78, 7 Cr App Rep (S) 142, 149 JP 705, [1985] Crim LR 602, 129 Sol Jo 416, [1985] LS Gaz R 3173, [1985] NLJ Rep 509, CA .... A 57.38
R (on the application of Spiteri (Elliott)) v Basildon Crown Court [2009] EWHC 665 (Admin), 173 JP 327, [2009] 5 Costs LR 772, [2009] All ER (D) 197 (Mar) .... B 12.16
R (on the application of Ricketts) v Basildon Magistrates' Court [2010] EWHC 2358 (Admin), [2011] 1 Cr App Rep 202, [2011] PTSR 180, [2011] Crim LR 505, [2010] All ER (D) 129 (Jul) .... A 57.22
R v Bassett [2008] EWCA Crim 1174, [2009] 1 WLR 1032, [2009] 1 Cr App Rep 90, 172 JP 491, 172 JPN 708, (2008) Times, 18 June, [2008] All ER (D) 48 (Jun) .... A 68.3
R v Bateman [2012] EWCA Crim 2158, [2013] 1 WLR 1710, [2013] 2 Cr App Rep (S) 174, 177 JP 137, [2013] Crim LR 352, [2012] All ER (D) 307 (Nov) .... B 8.15, B 34.46
R v Bayliss and Oliver [1978] Crim LR 361 .... A 25.7

R v Bebbington [2005] EWCA Crim 2395, [2006] 1 Cr App Rep (S) 690, 169 JP 621, [2006] Crim LR 160, (2005) Times, 24 October, [2005] All ER (D) 153 (Oct) .... B 13.6
R v Beckford [2018] EWCA Crim 2997, [2019] 1 Cr App Rep (S) 449, [2019] Crim LR 552 .... B 10.1
R v Beckles [2004] EWCA Crim 2766, [2005] 1 All ER 705, [2005] 1 WLR 2829, [2005] 1 Cr App Rep 377, [2005] Crim LR 560, (2004) Times, 17 November, 148 Sol Jo LB 1432, [2004] All ER (D) 226 (Nov) .... D 6.22
R v Becouarn [2005] UKHL 55, [2005] 4 All ER 673, [2005] 1 WLR 2589, [2006] 1 Cr App Rep 19, [2006] Crim LR 373, [2005] NLJR 1416, (2005) Times, 1 August, [2005] All ER (D) 412 (Jul) .... D 6.22
R v Beech [2016] EWCA Crim 1746, [2016] 4 WLR 182, [2017] RTR 111, [2017] Crim LR 238 .... C 5.38
R v Belmarsh Magistrates' Court, ex p Watts [1999] 2 Cr App Rep 188, [1999] All ER (D) 114, DC .... D 4.11
R v Bennet (Billy) [2013] EWCA Crim 323, [2013] 2 Cr App Rep (S) 460, [2013] Crim LR 533, 177 CL&J 251, [2013] All ER (D) 313 (Mar) .... B 45.55
R v Bentham [2005] UKHL 18, [2005] 2 All ER 65, [2005] 1 WLR 1057, 169 JP 181, [2005] Crim LR 648, [2005] NLJR 545, (2005) Times, 11 March, 149 Sol Jo LB 358, [2005] All ER (D) 161 (Mar) .... A 33.9A, A 77.9A, A 76.6
R v Berry [1989] 10 LS Gaz R 41, CA .... A 25.7
R v Bewley [2012] EWCA Crim 1457, [2013] 1 All ER 1, [2013] 1 WLR 137, [2012] 2 Cr App Rep 329, [2013] Crim LR 57, 176 CL&J 433, (2012) Times, 13 September, [2012] All ER (D) 82 (Jul) .... A 33.9, A 76.6, A 77.8
R v Bezzina [1994] 3 All ER 964, [1994] 1 WLR 1057, 158 JP 671, 138 Sol Jo LB 11, CA .... A 72.3, A 72.5
R v Billinghurst [1978] Crim LR 553, Crown Ct .... A 15.18
R v Bina [2014] EWCA Crim 1444, [2014] 2 Cr App Rep 496, [2015] Crim LR 287 .... A 81.5
R v Bingham [2015] EWCA Crim 1342, [2016] 1 Cr App Rep (S) 10, [2016] Crim LR 70 .... B 44.2
R v Bingley [2017] EWCA Crim 1464, [2018] 1 WLR 2969, [2018] 1 Cr App Rep (S) 107, [2017] Crim LR 91 .... B 44.5
R v Birchall (Leevon) (2018) [2018] EWCA Crim 1267, [2018] 2 Cr App Rep (S) 343 .... B 34.31
R v Bird [1985] 2 All ER 513, [1985] 1 WLR 816, 81 Cr App Rep 110, [1985] Crim LR 388, 129 Sol Jo 362, [1985] LS Gaz R 1709, CA .... A 8.18
R v Birmingham Justices, ex p F (1999) 164 JP 523, [2000] Crim LR 588 .... E 2.2
R v Birmingham Justices, ex p Lamb [1983] 3 All ER 23, [1983] 1 WLR 339, 147 JP 75, [1983] Crim LR 329, 127 Sol Jo 119, DC .... D 6.17 D
R (on the application of Blackwood) v Birmingham Magistrates Court [2006] EWHC 1800 (Admin), 170 JP 613, 171 JPN 19, [2006] All ER (D) 324 (Jun) .... F 2.19

R (on the application of Harrison) v Birmingham Magistrate's Court [2011] EWCA Civ 332, [2011] 14 LS Gaz R 21, [2011] All ER (D) 294 (Mar) .... F 5.47A
R (on the application of Director Of Public Prosecutions) v Birmingham Magistrates Court [2017] EWHC 3444 (Admin) .... D 6.17C
R (on the application of Mills) v Birmingham Magistrates' Court [2005] EWHC 2732 (Admin), (2005) 170 JP 237, 170 JPN 473, 170 JPN 457, [2005] All ER (D) 94 (Oct) .... B 13.6
R (on application of Johnson (Craig Matthew)) v Birmingham Magistrates' Court and Crown Prosecution Services [2012] EWHC 596 (Admin), 176 JP 298 .... B 11.1, B 28.76
R v Bishop [2004] EWCA Crim 2956, [2004] All ER (D) 116 (Dec) .... B 9.25
R (on the application of the DPP) v Blackfriars Crown Court [2001] EWHC Admin 56, [2001] All ER (D) 205 (Jan) .... D 8.52
R (on the application of the F, J and K) v Blackfriars Crown Court [2014] EWHC 1541 (Admin) .... F 5.20A
R (on the application of Crown Prosecution Service) v Blaydon Youth Court [2004] EWHC 2296 (Admin), (2004) 168 JP 638, [2005] Crim LR 495, [2004] All ER (D) 45 (Oct) .. A 15.3, A 41.9, B 36.1
R v Bloxham [1983] 1 AC 109, [1982] 1 All ER 582, [1982] 2 WLR 392, [1982] RTR 129, 74 Cr App Rep 279, 146 JP 201, [1982] Crim LR 436, 126 Sol Jo 154, HL .... A 40.6
R v Boggild [2011] EWCA Crim 1928, 175 CL&J 502, (2011) Times, 05 September, [2011] All ER (D) 167 (Jul) .... B 29.18
R v Bollom [2003] EWCA Crim 2846, [2004] 2 Cr App Rep 50, (2003) Times, 15 December, [2003] All ER (D) 143 (Dec) .. A 70.6, C 16C.3
R v Bolton (Simon David) [2010] EWCA Crim 1177 .... B 44.3
R v Boness [2005] EWCA Crim 2395, [2006] 1 Cr App Rep (S) 690, 169 JP 621, [2006] Crim LR 160, (2005) Times, 24 October, [2005] All ER (D) 153 (Oct) .... B 13.6
R v Bostan (Amar) (2018) [2018] EWCA Crim 494, [2018] 2 Cr App Rep (S) 112 .... B 34.46
R v Bouchereau: 30/77 [1978] QB 732, [1981] 2 All ER 924n, [1978] 2 WLR 250, [1977] ECR 1999, [1977] 2 CMLR 800, 66 Cr App Rep 202, 122 Sol Jo 79, ECJ .... B 17.9
R v Bow [1977] RTR 6, 64 Cr App Rep 54, [1977] Crim LR 176, CA .... A 65.4
R v Bown [2003] EWCA Crim 1989, 167 JP 429, [2003] 33 LS Gaz R 27, (2003) Times, 14 July, [2003] All ER (D) 299 (Jun) .... A 11.12
R v Boyesen [1982] AC 768, [1982] 2 All ER 161, [1982] 2 WLR 882, 75 Cr App Rep 51, 146 JP 217, [1982] Crim LR 596, 126 Sol Jo 308, HL .... A 25.7
R v Bradfield [2006] EWCA Crim 2917, [2006] All ER (D) 394 (Nov) .... A 46.5
R v Bradish [1990] 1 QB 981, [1990] 1 All ER 460, [1990] 2 WLR 223, 90 Cr App Rep 271, 154 JP 21, [1990] Crim LR 723, 133 Sol Jo 1605, (1989) Times, 30 August .... A 76A.4

R v Bradish [2004] EWCA Crim 1340, (2004) 148 Sol Jo LB 474, [2004] All ER (D) 40 (Apr) .... A 77.6
R v Braxton [2004] EWCA Crim 1374, [2005] 1 Cr App Rep (S) 167 .... B 8.13
R v Brazil [2004] EWCA Crim 1975, [2004] All ER (D) 348 (Jun) .... B 10.5
R (on the application of Visvaratnam) v Brent Magistrates' Court [2009] EWHC 3017 (Admin), 174 JP 61, [2009] All ER (D) 293 (Oct) .... D 6.17B
R (on the application of B) v Brent Youth Court [2010] All ER (D) 76 (Jul) .... D 8.77
R (on the application of W) v Brent Youth Court and the Crown Prosecution Service (Interested Party) [2006] EWHC Admin 95, (2006) 170 JP 198 .... E 3.18C
R v Brightling [1991] Crim LR 364 .... A 7.3
R v Bristol [2007] EWCA Crim 3214, 172 JP 161, 172 JPN 421, [2007] All ER (D) 47 (Dec) .... A 9.8
R v Bristol City Council, ex p Everett [1999] 2 All ER 193, [1999] 1 WLR 1170, [1999] LGR 513, 31 HLR 1102, [1999] 13 LS Gaz R 31, [1999] NLJR 370, [1999] EGCS 33, 143 Sol Jo LB 104, CA .... A 84.3
R v Britton [1973] RTR 502, [1973] Crim LR 375, CA .... A 47.9
R v Brock (1991) 165 JP 331, CA .... A 27A.2
R (on the application of Harrington) v Bromley Magistrates Court [2007] EWHC 2896 (Admin), [2007] All ER (D) 199 (Nov) .... B 8.7
R v Brooks and Brooks (1982) 76 Cr App Rep 66, [1983] Crim LR 188, 126 Sol Jo 855, CA .... A 45.6A
R v Brown [1970] 1 QB 105, [1969] 3 All ER 198, [1969] 3 WLR 370, 53 Cr App Rep 527, 133 JP 592, 113 Sol Jo 639, CA .... A 40.6
R v Brown [1985] Crim LR 212, CA .... A 12.7, A 13.6
R v Brown (1989) 11 Cr App Rep (S) 263, [1989] Crim LR 750, CA .... E 1.2
R v Brown [1992] QB 491, [1992] 2 All ER 552, [1992] 2 WLR 441, 94 Cr App Rep 302, 156 JP 475, [1992] 15 LS Gaz R 31, [1992] NLJR 275, 136 Sol Jo LB 90, CA; affd [1994] 1 AC 212, [1993] 2 All ER 75, [1993] 2 WLR 556, 97 Cr App Rep 44, 157 JP 337, [1993] Crim LR 583, [1993] NLJR 399, HL .... A 15.11
R v Brown (Benjamin Adam) [2011] EWCA Crim 1223 .... B 44.3
R v Brown (Dean Patrick) [2012] EWCA Crim 1152 .... A 41.14
R v Browne-Morgan [2016] EWCA Crim 1903, [2017] 4 WLR 118, [2017] 1 Cr App Rep (S) 279 .... B 13.5
R v Buckley (1994) 15 Cr App Rep (S) 695, [1994] Crim LR 387, CA .... C 5.9
R v Burnham Justices, ex p Ansorge [1959] 3 All ER 505, [1959] 1 WLR 1041, 123 JP 539, 103 Sol Jo 920, DC .... B 36.1
R (on the application of M) v Burnley, Pendle & Rossendale Magistrates' Court [2009] EWHC 2874 (Admin), 174 JP 102, [2009] All ER (D) 315 (Nov) .... D 6.19
R v Burroughes [2000] All ER (D) 2032, CA .... A 40.6
R (on the application of DPP) v Bury Magistrates' Court [2007] All ER (D) 208 (Dec) .... B 12.19

R v Buxton [2010] EWCA Crim 2923, [2011] 1 WLR 857, [2011] Bus LR 448, [2011] 2 Cr App Rep (S) 121, [2011] Crim LR 332, (2011) Times, 21 February, [2010] All ER (D) 215 (Dec) A41.13
R v C [2016] EWCA Crim 1617, 181 JP 143, [2016] All ER (D) 28 (Nov); affd [2017] UKSC 58, [2017] 1 WLR 3006, 167 NLJ 7758, [2017] All ER (D) 20 (Aug) .... C 60.3
R v Cakmak [2002] EWCA Crim 500, [2002] 2 Cr App Rep 158, (2002) Times, 28 March, [2002] All ER (D) 119 (Feb) .... A 18A.2
R (on the application of Dragoman) v Camberwell Green Magistrates' Court [2012] EWHC 4105 (Admin), 177 JP 372 .... B 9.15
R (on the application of Stone) v Camberwell Green Magistrates' Court [2010] EWHC 2333 (Admin), [2010] All ER (D) 242 (Jun) .... F 5.47
R v Camberwell Green Magistrates' Court, ex p Ibrahim (1983) 148 JP 400 .... B 38.5
R v Camberwell Green Youth Court, ex p G [2005] UKHL 4, [2005] 1 All ER 999, [2005] 1 WLR 393, [2005] 2 Cr App Rep 1, [2005] 1 FCR 365, 169 JP 105, [2005] Crim LR 497, (2005) Times, 1 February, 149 Sol Jo LB 146, [2005] All ER (D) 259 (Jan) .... E 3.22
R (on the application of the DPP) v Camberwell Youth Court [2004] EWHC 1805 (Admin), [2004] 4 All ER 699, [2005] 1 Cr App Rep 89, 168 JP 481, [2005] Crim LR 165, (2004) Times, 12 August, [2004] All ER (D) 413 (Jul) .... E 3.18C
R (on the application of H) v Camberwell Youth Court [2004] EWHC 1805 (Admin), [2004] 4 All ER 699, [2005] 1 Cr App Rep 89, 168 JP 481, [2005] Crim LR 165, (2004) Times, 12 August, [2004] All ER (D) 413 (Jul) .... E 3.18C
R (on the application of Middleton) v Cambridge Magistrates' Court [2012] EWHC 2122 (Admin), 176 JP 569, [2012] All ER (D) 35 (Jul) .... B 12.8
R v Campbell [2006] EWCA Crim 726, [2006] 2 Cr App Rep (S) 626, [2006] All ER (D) 137 (Mar) .... B 21.0
R v Campbell [2009] EWCA Crim 2459, [2010] 2 Cr App Rep (S) 175, 174 JP 73, [2010] Crim LR 241, [2009] All ER (D) 295 (Nov) .... C 16A.10
R v Capital Translation and Interpreting Ltd [2014] EWCA Crim 3460, (2015) JP 36 .... B 12.20A
R v Carmona [2006] EWCA Crim 508, [2006] 1 WLR 2264, [2006] 2 Cr App Rep (S) 662, (2006) Times, 13 April, [2006] All ER (D) 186 (Mar) .... B 17.11
R v Carr-Briant [1943] KB 607, [1943] 2 All ER 156, 41 LGR 183, 29 Cr App Rep 76, 107 JP 167, 112 LJKB 581, 169 LT 175, 59 TLR 300, CCA .... A 10.2, A 19A.3, A 41.11, A 66.10
R v Carrington [2014] EWCA Crim 325, [2014] 2 Cr App Rep (S) 337 .... B 10.6
R v Cartwright [2010] EWCA Crim 2803, [2011] 2 Cr App Rep (S) 54, 175 JP 33 .... B 29.7
R v Cash [1985] QB 801, [1985] 2 All ER 128, [1985] 2 WLR 735, 80 Cr App Rep 314, [1985] Crim LR 311, 129 Sol Jo 268, [1985] LS Gaz R 1330, CA .... A 40.5

R v Cawthorn [2001] Crim LR 51, (2000) Times, 27 October, CA .... B 19.4
R (on the application of A) v Central Criminal Court [2017] EWHC 70 (Admin), [2017] 1 WLR 3567, [2017] All ER (D) 138 (Jan) .... F 5.16
R (on the application of JC) v Central Criminal Court [2014] EWHC (Admin), (2014) 178 JP 188 .... D 1B.7
R (on the application of Rawlinson and Hunter Trustees) v Central Criminal Court [2012] EWHC 2254 (Admin), [2013] 1 WLR 1634, [2012] All ER (D) 06 (Aug) .... F 5.1
R v Central Criminal Court, ex p Bennett (1999) Times, 25 January .... D 8.53
R v Central Criminal Court, ex p Bright [2001] 2 All ER 244, [2001] 1 WLR 662, [2001] EMLR 79, [2000] All ER (D) 1042, DC .... F 5.7
R v Central Criminal Court, ex p Johnson [1999] 2 Cr App Rep 51 .... D 8.53
R v Chan-Fook [1994] 2 All ER 552, [1994] 1 WLR 689, 99 Cr App Rep 147, [1994] Crim LR 432, [1994] JPIL 332, CA .... A 8.9
R v Chapman [2017] EWCA Crim 1743, [2018] 1 WLR 726, [2018] 1 Cr App Rep 122, 182 JP 115 .... A 87.4
R v Chargot Ltd (t/a Contract Services) [2007] EWCA Crim 3032, [2008] 2 All ER 1077, [2008] ICR 517, [2007] All ER (D) 198 (Dec); affd [2008] UKHL 73, [2009] 2 All ER 645, [2009] 1 WLR 1, (2008) Times, 16 December, 153 Sol Jo (no 1) 32, [2008] All ER (D) 106 (Dec) .... A 80.19
R v Charles [2004] EWCA Crim 1977, [2005] 1 Cr App Rep (S) 253 .... A 76.19
R v Charles [2009] EWCA Crim 1570, [2010] 4 All ER 553, [2010] 1 Cr App Rep 38, 173 JP 481, [2010] Crim LR 303, (2009) Times, 25 August, [2009] All ER (D) 290 (Jul) .... B 2.4
R v Charlton (2000) 164 JP 685, CA .... B 19.4
R v Chatwood [1980] 1 All ER 467, [1980] 1 WLR 874, 70 Cr App Rep 39, [1980] Crim LR 46, 124 Sol Jo 396, CA .... A 25.7A
R v Cheeseman [2019] EWCA Crim 149, [2019] 1 WLR 3621, [2019] 1 Cr App Rep 488, [2019] Crim LR 714 .... A 8.20
R (on the application of Nicholas) v Chester Magistrates' Court [2009] EWHC 1504 (Admin), 173 JP 542, [2009] All ER (D) 267 (Oct) .... B 8.7; D 6.33
R v Chichester Justices, ex p Crouch (1981) 146 JP 26 .... C 5.49
R (on the application of Laporte) v Chief Constable of Gloucestershire Constabulary [2004] EWCA Civ 1639, [2005] QB 678, [2005] 1 All ER 473, [2005] 2 WLR 789, [2005] Crim LR 467, (2004) Times, 13 December, [2004] All ER (D) 118 (Dec); revsd in part sub nom R (on the application of Laporte) v Chief Constable of Gloucestershire Constabulary (Chief Constable of Thames Valley Police, interested parties) [2006] UKHL 55, [2007] 2 AC 105, [2007] 2 All ER 529, [2007] 2 WLR 46, (2006) Times, 14 December, 22 BHRC 38, [2007] 4 LRC 468, [2006] All ER (D) 172 (Dec) .... D 1.7

R (on the application of Laporte) v Chief Constable of Gloucestershire Constabulary (Chief Constable of Thames Valley Police) [2006] UKHL 55, [2007] 2 AC 105, [2007] 2 All ER 529, [2007] 2 WLR 46, (2006) Times, 14 December, 22 BHRC 38, [2007] 4 LRC 468, [2006] All ER (D) 172 (Dec) .... A 9.5
R (on the application of Shufflebottom) v Chief Constable of Greater Manchester [2003] EWHC 246 (Admin), (2003) 167 JP 153 .... A 72.21
R (on the application of Ali) v Chief Constable of Merseyside [2014] EWHC 4772 (Admin), 179 JP 333, [2015] Crim LR 645 .... A 72.20
R (on the application of Bates) v Chief Constable of the Avon and Somerset Police [2009] EWHC 942 (Admin), 173 JP 313, [2009] All ER (D) 59 (May) .... F 5.16
R (on the application of S,F and L) v Chief Constable of the British Transport Police [2013] EWHC 2189 (Admin), [2014] 1 All ER 268, [2014] 1 WLR 1647, 178 JP 221, [2013] All ER (D) 335 (Jul) .... F 5.1
R v Chippenham Magistrates' Court, ex p Thompson (1995) 160 JP 207 .... B 32.1
R v Chopra [2006] EWCA Crim 2133, [2007] 1 Cr App Rep 225, [2006] All ER (D) 44 (Dec) .... D 6.14
R (on the application of Crown Prosecution Service) v Chorley Justices [2002] EWHC 2162 (Admin), (2002) 166 JP 764, sub nom R (on the application of DPP) v Chorley Justices [2002] 43 LS Gaz R 34 .... D 8.63
R v Christie (1977) 65 Cr App Rep 253, CA .... A 27A.2
R (on the application of Decani) v City Of London Magistrates Court [2017] EWHC 3422 (Admin) .... D 6.17C
R (on the application of Sharer) v City of London Magistrates Court [2016] EWHC 1412 (Admin), 181 JP 48 ... F 5.16
R (on the application of the Chief Constable of Greater Manchester Police) v City of Salford Magistrates' Court [2008] EWHC 1651 (Admin), [2009] 1 WLR 1023, 172 JP 497, 172 JPN 708, [2008] All ER (D) 272 (Jul) .... F 5.47A
R (on the application of Haigh) v City of Westminster Magistrates' Court [2017] EWHC 232 (Admin), 181 JP 325, [2017] 1 Costs LR 175, [2017] All ER (D) 140 (Feb) .... B 12.9
R (on the application of Hope and Glory Public House Ltd) v City of Westminster Magistrates' Court (Lord Mayor and Citizens of the City of Westminster, interested party) [2011] EWCA Civ 31, [2011] 3 All ER 579, [2011] PTSR 868, 175 JP 77, [2011] 18 EG 110, [2011] 2 EGLR 53, [2011] All ER (D) 206 (Jan) .... F 2.19
R (on the application of Williamson) v City of Westminster Magistrates' Court [2012] EWHC 1444 (Admin), [2012] 2 Cr App Rep 299, [2012] Crim LR 975, [2012] All ER (D) 242 (May) .... B 38.5
R v Clancy [2012] EWCA Crim 8, [2012] 1 WLR 2536, [2012] 2 Cr App Rep 71, 176 JP 111, [2012] Crim LR 548, [2012] All ER (D) 97 (Jan) .... A 11.12, 11.13

R v Clark [1998] 2 Cr App Rep 137, [1998] 2 Cr App Rep (S) 95, [1998] Crim LR 227, [1998] 02 LS Gaz R 22, (1997) Times, 4 December, 142 Sol Jo LB 27, CA .... A 57.38
R v Clarke [1986] 1 All ER 846, [1986] 1 WLR 209, 82 Cr App Rep 308, [1986] Crim LR 334, 130 Sol Jo 110, [1986] LS Gaz R 287 .... A 76A.4
R v Clarke [1997] 1 Cr App Rep (S) 323, CA .... A 76.20
R v Clarke [2000] 1 Cr App Rep (S) 224, CA .... D 8.91
R v Cliff [2004] EWCA Crim 3139, [2005] RTR 147, [2005] 2 Cr App Rep (S) 118, [2005] Crim LR 250, (2004) Times, 1 December, [2004] All ER (D) 400 (Nov) .... C 5.45
R v Cohen [1951] 1 KB 505, [1951] 1 All ER 203, 49 LGR 216, 34 Cr App Rep 239, 115 JP 91, 95 Sol Jo 124, [1951] 1 TLR 251, CCA .... A 4.4
R v Coid [1998] Crim LR 199, CA .... A 27A.2
R v Coker (Isaac) [2019] EWCA Crim 420, [2019] 4 WLR 41, [2019] 2 Cr App Rep 81, [2019] Crim LR 542 .... A 26.4A
R v Colchester Magistrates' Court, ex p Abbott (2001)165 JP 386, [2001] Crim LR 564, DC .... D 4.9
R v Cole [2007] EWCA Crim 1924, [2007] 1 WLR 2716, [2008] 1 Cr App Rep 81, (2007) Times, 2 October, [2007] All ER (D) 472 (Jul) .... D 6.16
R v Coleman (1985) 150 JP 175, [1986] Crim LR 56, CA .... A 40.6
R v Collier [2004] EWCA Crim 1411, [2005] 1 WLR 843, [2005] 1 Cr App Rep 129, [2004] 27 LS Gaz R 29, (2004) Times, 13 July, [2004] All ER (D) 82 (Jun) .... A 43.8
R v Collins [1973] QB 100, [1972] 2 All ER 1105, [1972] 3 WLR 243, 56 Cr App Rep 554, 136 JP 605, 116 Sol Jo 432, CA . A 12.17, A 13.17
R v Colohan [2001] EWCA Crim 1251, [2001] 3 FCR 409, [2001] 2 FLR 757, [2001] Fam Law 732, 165 JP 594, [2001] Crim LR 845, [2001] All ER (D) 230 (May) .... A 41.8
R v Colyer [1974] Crim LR 243, Crown Ct .... A 25.7
R (on the application of Moos) v Comr of Police for the Metropolis [2012] EWCA Civ 12, 176 CL&J 94, [2012] All ER (D) 83 (Jan) .... A 9.5
R (on the application of Taylor) v Comr of the Metropolitan Police [2009] EWHC 264 (Admin), 173 JP 121, [2009] All ER (D) 156 (Jun) .... A 26.17
R v Connor [2019] EWCA Crim 234, [2019] 4 WLR 76, [2019] 2 Cr App Rep (S) 139, [2019] All ER (D) 24 (Mar) .... B 44.3
R v Condron and Condron [1997] 1 WLR 827, [1997] 1 Cr App Rep 185, 161 JP 1, [1997] Crim LR 215, CA .... D 6.22
R v Corboz [1984] Crim LR 629, CA .... A 38.3
R v Cornish [2016] EWHC 779 (QB), [2016] Crim LR 560, [2016] All ER (D) 167 (Apr) .... B 12.9
R v Court [1989] AC 28, [1988] 2 All ER 221, [1988] 2 WLR 1071, 87 Cr App Rep 144, 152 JP 422, [1988] Crim LR 537, 132 Sol Jo 658, [1988] NLJR 128, HL .... A 53.4
R v Cousins [1982] QB 526, [1982] 2 All ER 115, [1982] 2 WLR 621, 74 Cr App Rep 363, 146 JP 264, [1982] Crim LR 444, 126 Sol Jo 154, CA .... A 59.3

R (on the application of McAuley (Clarke)) v Coventry Crown Court and Crown Prosecution Service [2012] EWHC 680 (Admin), [2012] 3 All ER 519, [2012] 1 WLR 2766, 176 JP 418, [2012] Crim LR 697, 176 CL&J 206, [2012] All ER (D) 144 (Mar) .... D 8.52
R (on the application of Khan) v Coventry Magistrates' Court [2011] EWCA Civ 751, [2011] All ER (D) 226 (Jun) .... F 2.18
R v Cowan [1996] QB 373, [1995] 4 All ER 939, [1995] 3 WLR 818, [1996] 1 Cr App Rep 1, 160 JP 165, [1996] Crim LR 409, [1995] 38 LS Gaz R 26, [1995] NLJR 1611, 139 Sol Jo LB 215, CA .... D 6.22
R v Cox (Jacqueline) (2004) Times, 20 February, CA .... A 72.9
R v Cox (Rodney) [2019] EWCA Crim 71, [2019] 4 WLR 88, [2019] 2 Cr App Rep (S) 39 .... B 38.2
R (on the application of White) v Crown Court at Blackfriars [2008] EWHC 510 (Admin), [2008] 2 Cr App Rep (S) 542, 172 JP 321, [2008] Crim LR 575 .... B 29.18
R (on the application of Golding) v Crown Court at Maidstone [2019] EWHC 2029 (Admin), [2019] All ER (D) 64 (Aug) ... A 72.20
R v Crown Court at Isleworth, ex p Buda [2000] 1 Cr App Rep (S) 538, [2000] Crim LR 111, [1999] All ER (D) 1127, DC ...... B 8.11
R v Crown Court at Knightsbridge, ex p Dunne [1993] 4 All ER 491, [1994] 1 WLR 296, 158 JP 213, [1993] Crim LR 853, [1993] NLJR 1479n .... A 72.20
R (on the application of Holland) v Crown Court at Leeds [2002] EWHC 1862 (Admin), [2003] Crim LR 272, [2002] All ER (D) 430 (Jul) .... D 8.52
R v Crown Court at Leeds, ex p Bagoutie (1999) Times, 31 May .... D 8.53
R v Crown Court at Lincoln, ex p Jude [1997] 3 All ER 737, [1998] 1 WLR 24, [1998] 1 Cr App Rep 130, 161 JP 589, 141 Sol Jo LB 138 .... B 5.6
R (on the application of McCann) v Crown Court at Manchester [2001] 1 WLR 358, sub nom R v Crown Court at Manchester, ex p McCann 165 JP 225, [2001] 02 LS Gaz R 40, 144 Sol Jo LB 287; affd [2001] EWCA Civ 281 [2001] 4 All ER 264, [2001] 1 WLR 1084, 165 JP 545 .... B 8.4
R (on the application of Haralambous) v Crown Court at St Albans [2018] UKSC 1, [2018] 2 All ER 303, [2018] 2 WLR 357, [2018] 1 Cr App Rep 372, [2018] Crim LR 672, (2018) Times, 29 January, [2018] All ER (D) 95 (Jan), SC .... F 5.24
R v Crown Court at St Albans, ex p O'Donovan [2000] 1 Cr App Rep (S) 344 .... C 22.24
R (on the applications of Golfrate Property Management Ltd) v Crown Court at Southwark [2014] EWHC 840 (Admin), [2014] 2 Cr App Rep 145, [2014] Crim LR 830, [2014] All ER (D) 267 (Mar) .... F 5.1
R (on the application of Smith) v Crown Court at Woolwich [2002] EWHC 995 (Admin) [2002] All ER (D) 05 (May) ..... D 8.53
R (on the application of Pepushi) v Crown Prosecution Service [2004] EWHC 798 (Admin), (2004) Times, 21 May, [2004] All ER (D) 129 (May) .... A 81.8A

R v Crown Prosecution Service, ex p Spurrier. See DPP v Spurrier
R (on the application of Bhatti) v Croydon Magistrates' Court [2010] EWHC 522 (Admin), [2010] 3 All ER 671, [2011] 1 WLR 948, 174 JP 213, 174 CL&J 125, [2010] All ER (D) 28 (Feb) .... F 5.10
R (on the application of Trinity Mirror plc) v Croydon Crown Court. See Trinity Mirror plc, Re
R (on the application of Desouza) v Croydon Magistrates' Court [2012] EWHC 1362 (Admin), 176 JP 624 .... A 84.31
R (on the application of DPP) v Croydon Youth Court (2000) 165 JP 181, 165 JPN 34 .... E 3.25
R v Croydon Youth Court, ex p DPP [1997] 2 Cr App Rep 411, DC .... B 38.5
R v Cugullere [1961] 2 All ER 343, [1961] 1 WLR 858, 45 Cr App Rep 108, 125 JP 414, 105 Sol Jo 386, CCA .... A 11.7
R v Cunningham [1957] 2 QB 396, [1957] 2 All ER 412, [1957] 3 WLR 76, 41 Cr App Rep 155, 121 JP 451, 101 Sol Jo 503, CCA .... A 15.4, A 70.5
R v Currie [2007] EWCA Crim 926, [2007] RTR 450, [2007] 2 Cr App Rep 246, 151 Sol Jo LB 609, [2007] All ER (D) 233 (Apr) .... C 49.3
R v Curtis (Lewis Cash) [2009] EWCA Crim 1225, [2010] 1 Cr App Rep (S) 193 .... B 29.18
R v Curtis [2010] EWCA Crim 123, [2010] 3 All ER 849, [2010] 1 WLR 2770, [2010] 1 Cr App Rep 457, [2010] Crim LR 638, 174 CL&J 156, [2010] All ER (D) 94 (Feb) .... A 14.7, A 41.7
R v D [2000] Crim LR 867, CA .... B 19.4
R v D (contempt of court: illegal photography) (2004) Times, 13 May .... D 3.4, D 3.15
R v D (sexual offences: prevention order) [2005] EWCA Crim 3660, [2006] 2 All ER 726, [2006] 1 WLR 1088, [2006] 2 Cr App Rep (S) 204, [2006] 1 FLR 1085, [2006] Fam Law 273, [2006] Crim LR 364, (2006) Times, 3 January, [2005] All ER (D) 254 (Dec) .... B 44.2
R v D [2019] EWCA Crim 45, [2019] 1 Cr App Rep 482, [2019] Crim LR 436, [2019] All ER (D) 165 (Jan) .... A 11.9
R v D [2019] EWCA Crim 209, [2019] RVR 198 .... A 36.8
R v Dang [2014] EWCA Crim 348, [2014] 1 WLR 3797, [2014] 2 Cr App Rep 23, [2014] 2 Cr App Rep (S) 391, [2014] Crim LR 675, [2014] All ER (D) 66 (Mar) .... A 27.3
R v Danga [1992] QB 476, [1992] 1 All ER 624, [1992] 2 WLR 277, 94 Cr App Rep 252, 13 Cr App Rep (S) 408, 156 JP 382, 135 Sol Jo LB 190, CA .... E 1.2
R (on the application of Aldous) v Dartford Magistrates' Court [2011] EWHC 1919 (Admin), [2012] RA 11, 175 JP 445, [2011] All ER (D) 237 (Jul) .... F 4.12
R v Daubney (2000) 164 JP 519, CA .... A 11.9
R v Davies [2002] EWCA Crim 2949, [2002] All ER (D) 275 (Dec), [2003] ICR 486, [2003] 09 LS Gaz R 27, [2003] JPN 42, sub nom Davies v Health and Safety Executive [2003] IRLR 170, 147 Sol Jo LB 29 .... A 80.19

R v Davies [2010] EWCA Crim 1923, 174 CL&J 574, [2010] All ER (D) 25 (Aug) .... A 72.15
R v Davis [1998] Crim LR 564, [1998] Lexis Citation 4349, CA .... A 11.9
R v Deakin [1972] 3 All ER 803, [1972] 1 WLR 1618, 56 Cr App Rep 841, 137 JP 19, 116 Sol Jo 944, CA .... A 40.6
R v Dealy [1995] 1 WLR 658, [1995] 2 Cr App Rep 398, [1995] STC 217, [1994] 46 LS Gaz R 30, CA .... A 62.3
R v Debnath [2005] EWCA Crim 3472, [2006] 2 Cr App Rep (S) 169, [2005] All ER (D) 49 (Dec) .... A 41.13
R v De Jesus [2015] EWCA Crim 1118, [2015] 2 Cr App Rep (S) 343 .... B 18.10
R v Delgado [1984] 1 All ER 449, [1984] 1 WLR 89, 78 Cr App Rep 175, [1984] IRLR 169, 148 JP 431, 128 Sol Jo 32, [1984] LS Gaz R 38, CA .... A 26.4A
R v Dempsey and Dempsey (1985) 82 Cr App Rep 291, 150 JP 213, [1986] Crim LR 171, CA .... A 26.4A
R v Densu [1998] 1 Cr App Rep 400, [1998] Crim LR 345, [1998] 02 LS Gaz R 22, 141 Sol Jo LB 250, CA .... A 11.13
R (on the application of Hussain) v Derby Magistrates' Court [2001] EWHC Admin 507 [2001] 1 WLR 2454, [2002] 1 Cr App Rep 37, 145 Sol Jo LB 168 .... D 8.92
R (on the application of P) v Derby Youth Court [2015] EWHC 573 (Admin), (2015) 179 JP 139 .... E 3.18C
R v Derwentside Magistrates' Court, ex p Swift [1997] RTR 89, 160 JP 468 .... C 19.6
R v Devizes Youth Court, ex p A (2000) 164 JP 330 .... E 3.18C
R v Deyemi [2007] EWCA Crim 2060, [2008] 1 Cr App Rep 345, 172 JP 137, [2008] Crim LR 327, [2007] All ER (D) 369 (Oct) .... A 76A.4
R v Dillon (Reyon Menelek) (2018) [2017] EWCA Crim 2642, [2019] 1 Cr App Rep (S) 155, [2019] Crim LR 247 .... B 40.3
R v DPP [2001] EWHC Admin 17, 165 JP 349, [2001] All ER (D) 120 (Jan) .... A 41.7
R v DPP [2006] EWHC 1375 (Admin), 171 JPN 140, [2006] All ER (D) 250 (May) .... A 20.3A
R (on the application of Cooke) v DPP [2008] EWHC 2703 (Admin), 172 JP 596, [2008] All ER (D) 202 (Oct) .... B 13.6
R (on the application of Khan) v DPP [2004] EWHC 2505 (Admin), sub nom Khan v DPP [2004] All ER (D) 134 (Oct) . C 22.25
R (on the application of Reda) v DPP [2011] EWHC 1550 (Admin), 175 JP 329, [2011] All ER (D) 167 (Jun) A9.5, A20.8
R (on the application of Traves) v DPP [2005] EWHC 1482 (Admin), 169 JP 421, sub nom Traves v DPP [2005] All ER (D) 381 (Jun) .... C 18.8, C 18.9
R (on the application of W) v DPP [2005] EWCA Civ 1333, (2005) 169 JP 435, sub nom W v DPP (2005) Times, 20 June, [2005] All ER (D) 29 (Jun) .... B 2.4
R v Dolan [1976] Crim LR 145 .... A 40.5
R v Doncaster Justices, ex p Hannan (1998) 163 JP 182, [1998] 32 LS Gaz R 30, [1998] RVR 254, 142 Sol Jo LB 218 ...... B 28.52

R (on the application of Blick) v Doncaster Magistrates' Court [2008] EWHC 2698 (Admin), 172 JP 651, [2008] All ER (D) 51 (Oct) .... B 38.5
R (on the application of Culley) v Dorchester Crown Court [2007] EWHC 109 (Admin), 171 JP 373, 171 JPN 706, [2007] All ER (D) 295 (Jan) .... D 8.92
R v Dosanjh [1998] 3 All ER 618, [1999] 1 Cr App Rep 371, [1999] 1 Cr App Rep (S) 107, [1998] Crim LR 593, [1998] 22 LS Gaz R 28, 142 Sol Jo LB 163, CA .... A 4.17
R v Doukas [1978] 1 All ER 1061, [1978] 1 WLR 372, 66 Cr App Rep 228, [1978] Crim LR 177, 122 Sol Jo 30, CA .... A 36.9, A 38.3
R v Dover Magistrates' Court, ex p Pamment (1994) 15 Cr App Rep (S) 778, 158 JP 665, [1994] Crim LR 471, DC .... B 8.6
R v Doyle [2012] EWCA Crim 995, 176 JP 337, 176 CL&J 322, [2012] All ER (D) 130 (May) .... B 29.1, B 29.7
R v Doyle [2012] EWCA Crim 2158, [2013] 1 WLR 1710, [2013] 2 Cr App Rep (S) 174, 177 JP 137, [2013] Crim LR 352, [2012] All ER (D) 307 (Nov) .... B 8.15, B 34.46
R v Draz [2006] EWCA Crim 794, [2007] 1 WLR 181, [2006] 2 Cr App Rep 231, (2006) Times, 18 April, [2006] All ER (D) 62 (Apr) .... B 8.12
R v Dudley Magistrates' Court, ex p DPP (1992) 157 JP 177, DC .... D 6.17E
R v Dunbar [1958] 1 QB 1, [1957] 2 All ER 737, [1957] 3 WLR 330, 41 Cr App Rep 182, 121 JP 506, 101 Sol Jo 594, CCA . A 41.11
R (on the application of the DPP) v Dykes (2008) 173 JP 88, [2009] Crim LR 449 .... A 20.6
R v EGS Ltd [2009] EWCA Crim 1942 .... A 80.19
R (on the application of Louis) v Ealing Magistrates' Court [2009] EWHC 521 (Admin), 173 JP 248, [2009] All ER (D) 215 (Feb) .... B 28.70
R v Ealing Magistrates' Court [2001] 165 JP 82 .... D 6.19A
R v Ealing Magistrates' Court, ex p Fanneran (1995) 160 JP 409, 8 Admin LR 351 .... A 72.10
R v Ealing Magistrates' Court, ex p Sahota (1997) 162 JP 73, [1997] 45 LS Gaz R 29, 141 Sol Jo LB 251 .... B 38.5
R (on the application of Bahbahani) v Ealing Magistrates' Court [2019] EWHC 1385 (Admin) .... D 4.3
R (on the application of Singh) v Ealling Magistrates Court [2014] EWHC 1443 (Admin), 178 JP 253, [2014] All ER (D) 174 (May) .... B 12.19
R (on the application of Developing Retail Ltd) v East Hampshire Magistrates' Court [2011] EWHC 618 (Admin), [2011] All ER (D) 29 (Apr) .... F 2.19
R v Ebbs [2019] EWCA Crim 175, [2019] All ER (D) 142 (Feb) .... B 15.17
R v Edmunds [2000] 2 Cr App Rep (S) 62, CA .... C 5.48
R v Edwards [2011] EWCA Crim 3028, [2012] Crim LR 563, [2011] All ER (D) 108 (Nov) .... D 6.13A
R v Ellames [1974] 3 All ER 130, [1974] 1 WLR 1391, 60 Cr App Rep 7, 138 JP 682, 118 Sol Jo 578, CA .... A 38.3, A 58.6

R v Ellis and Street (1986) 84 Cr App Rep 235, [1987] Crim LR 44, 130 Sol Jo 649, [1986] LS Gaz R 2996, CA .... A 4.5
R (on the application of S) v Enfield Youth Court and the Crown Prosecution Service (Interested Party) [2006] EWHC Admin 95, (2006) 170 JP 198 .... E 3.18C
R v Engen [2004] EWCA Crim 1536, [2004] All ER (D) 117 (Jun) .... B 28.22
R v Evans [2004] EWCA Crim 3102, [2005] 1 WLR 1435, [2005] 1 Cr App Rep 546, 169 JP 129, [2005] Crim LR 654, (2004) Times, 10 December, [2004] All ER (D) 80 (Dec) .... A 46.3
R v Evans [2011] EWCA Crim 2842, [2012] 1 WLR 1192, [2012] 2 Cr App Rep 279, 176 JP 139, (2012) Times, 16 January . A 10.2; D 8.85
R v Evans [2013] EWCA Crim 125, [2013] 1 Cr App Rep 457, (2013) Times, 21 February, [2013] All ER (D) 21 (Jun) ...... A 81.8A
R v Evesham Justices, ex p McDonagh [1988] QB 553, [1988] 1 All ER 371, [1988] 2 WLR 227, 87 Cr App Rep 28, 152 JP 65, [1988] Crim LR 181, 131 Sol Jo 1698, [1988] 2 LS Gaz R 36, [1987] NLJ Rep 757, DC .... D 1B.6
R v Eyck [2000] 3 All ER 569, [2000] 1 WLR 1389, [2000] 2 Cr App Rep 50, [2000] Crim LR 299, [2000] 05 LS Gaz R 34, 144 Sol Jo LB 59, CA .... A 81.5, A 81.8
R v F [2006] EWCA Crim 686, [2006] 3 All ER 562, 170 JPN 716, [2006] All ER (D) 410 (Mar) .... B 13.6
R v F [2011] EWCA Crim 726, [2011] 2 Cr App Rep 145, 175 CL&J 213, [2011] All ER (D) 275 (Mar) .... D 1B.12
R v Falmouth and Truro Port Health Authority, ex p South West Water Services [2001] QB 445, [2000] 3 All ER 306, [2000] All ER (D) 429, [2000] 3 WLR 1464, [2000] NPC 36, [2000] EGCS 50, [2000] EHLR 306, [2000] Env LR 658, CA .... A 84.8
R (on the application of Gosport Borough Council) v Fareham Magistrates' Court [2006] EWHC 3047 (Admin), [2007] 1 WLR 634, 171 JP 102, 171 JPN 363, (2006) Times, 18 December, [2006] All ER (D) 267 (Nov) .... B 8.5
R v Farhad Hakimzadeh [2009] EWCA Crim 959, [2010] 1 Cr App Rep (S) 49, [2009] Crim LR 676, [2009] All ER (D) 210 (Jun) .... B 17.8
R v Farr [1982] Crim LR 745, [1982] LS Gaz R 1257, CA .. A 27.3A
R v Farrell (1988) 10 Cr App R (S) 74 .... B 18.2
R v Faversham and Sittingbourne Magistrates' Court, ex p Ursell [1992] RA 99, 156 JP 765 .... F 4.14
R v Felixstowe, Ipswich and Woodbridge Magistrates' Court and Ipswich Borough Council, ex p Herridge [1993] RA 83, 158 JP 307, DC .... F 4.13
R v Finn [2012] EWCA Crim 881, [2012] 2 Cr App Rep (S) 569 .... B 34.50
R v Fitzgerald [2012] 3 Costs LR 437 .... B 12.19
R v Flack [2008] EWCA Crim 204, [2008] 2 Cr App Rep (S) 395 .... A 72.15, A 72.20
R v Flax Bourton Magistrates' Court, ex p Customs and Excise Comrs (1996) 160 JP 481, [1996] Crim LR 907, DC .... B 8.6

R (on the application of Beach) v Folkestone Magistrates Court [2018] EWHC 2843 (Admin) .... B 11.1, B 11.2
R (on the application of Gonzales) v Folkestone Magistrates' Court [2010] EWHC 3428 (Admin), 175 JP 453, [2010] All ER (D) 172 (Dec) A41.13
R v Formosa [1991] 2 QB 1, [1991] 1 All ER 131, [1990] 3 WLR 1179, 92 Cr App Rep 11, 155 JP 97, [1990] Crim LR 868, 134 Sol Jo 1191, [1990] 41 LS Gaz R 35, (1990) Times, 23 July . A 76A.4
R v Francis [2006] EWCA Crim 3323, [2007] 1 WLR 1021, [2007] All ER (D) 179 (May) .... A 21.9
R v Freeman [1970] 2 All ER 413, [1970] 1 WLR 788, 54 Cr App Rep 251, 134 JP 462, 114 Sol Jo 336, CA .... A 33.9, A 77.8
R v Friskies Petcare Ltd [2000] 2 Cr App Rep (S) 401, [2000] Lexis Citation 06, CA .... A 80.22
R v G (Autrefois Acquit) [2001] EWCA Crim 1215 [2001] 1 WLR 1727, [2001] 2 Cr App Rep 615, 165 JP 513, 145 Sol Jo LB 126 .... A 15.31
R v G [2003] UKHL 50, [2004] 1 AC 1034, [2003] 4 All ER 765, [2003] 3 WLR 1060, [2004] 1 Cr App Rep 237, 167 JP 621, [2004] Crim LR 369, [2003] 43 LS Gaz R 31, [2004] 2 LRC 546, [2003] All ER (D) 257 (Oct) .... A 18.31
R v Galbraith [1981] 2 All ER 1060, [1981] 1 WLR 1039, 73 Cr App Rep 124, 144 JP 406, [1981] Crim LR 648, 125 Sol Jo 442, CA .... D 6.21
R v Ganyo (Molly and Prize) [2011] EWCA Crim 2491, [2012] 1 Cr App Rep (S) 650, 176 JP 396 .... B 10.6
R v Garcia (1987) 87 Cr App Rep 175, [1988] Crim LR 115, CA .... A 78.9
R v Gass [2015] EWCA Crim 579, [2015] 2 Cr App Rep (S) 196, [2015] Crim LR 732 .... B 44.3
R v Gedminintaite [2008] EWCA Crim 814, 172 JP 413 ... A 72.3, A 72.5
R v Gent [2002] EWCA Crim 943 [2002] All ER (D) 46 (Apr) .... A 76.18
R v George [2015] EWCA Crim 1096, [2015] 2 Cr App Rep (S) 409, [2015] Crim LR 916 .... B 9.25
R v George (Steven George) (2018) [2018] EWCA Crim 417, [2018] 2 Cr App Rep (S) 76 .... A 43.12
R v Ghafoor [2002] EWCA Crim 1857, [2003] 1 Cr App Rep (S) 428, 166 JP 601, [2002] Crim LR 739, [2002] All ER (D) 295 (Jul) .... E 1.2, E 5.1
R v Gheorghiu (Christian) [2013] EWCA Crim 281, [2013] 2 Cr App Rep (S) 497 .... B 17.9
R v Ghosh [1982] QB 1053, [1982] 2 All ER 689, [1982] 3 WLR 110, 75 Cr App Rep 154, 146 JP 376, [1982] Crim LR 608, 126 Sol Jo 429, CA .... A 36.7
R v Gilbert [2012] EWCA Crim 2392, [2012] All ER (D) 251 (Nov) .... A 36.6
R v Gillette (1999) Times, 3 December, CA .... B 21.18, B 34.16
R v Gilmartin [1983] QB 953, [1983] 1 All ER 829, [1983] 2 WLR 547, 76 Cr App Rep 238, 147 JP 183, [1983] Crim LR 330, 127 Sol Jo 119, CA .... A 36.7

R v Gimbert [2018] EWCA Crim 2190, [2019] 2 WLR 72, [2019] 1 Cr App Rep 189, [2019] Crim LR 258, [2018] All ER (D) 80 (Oct) .... A 57.18
R v Gingell [2000] 1 Cr App Rep 88, 163 JP 648, [1999] 19 LS Gaz R 27, CA .... A 40.6
R v Glidewell (1999) 163 JP 557, CA .... A 11.13
R (on the application of the Crown Prosecution Service) v Gloucester Justices [2008] EWHC 1488 (Admin), 172 JP 506, 172 JPN 723, [2008] All ER (D) 197 (Jun) .... D 6.13A
R v Gloucester Magistrates' Court, ex p Chung (1988) 153 JP 75 .... C 16.19
R v Golechha [1989] 3 All ER 908, [1989] 1 WLR 1050, 90 Cr App Rep 241, [1990] Crim LR 865, CA .... A 31.3
R v Golding [2014] EWCA Crim 889, [2014] Crim LR 686, [2014] All ER (D) 73 (May) .... A 70.6
R v Goldsborough [2015] EWCA Crim 1278, [2015] 1 WLR 4921, [2015] 2 Cr App Rep 407, [2015] Crim LR 887, [2015] All ER (D) 223 (Jul) .... A 76.7, A 76A.4
R v Goldie Steadman [2013] EWCA Crim 2031 .... B 34.24
R v Goodard [1992] Crim LR 588, CA .... A 26.4B
R v Gough (2001) 165 JPN 895 .... D 6.22
R (on the application of A) v Governor of Huntercombe Young Offender Institution [2006] EWHC 2544 (Admin), 171 JP 65, 171 JPN 345, [2006] All ER (D) 226 (Oct) .... B 19.7
R v Graham-Kerr [1988] 1 WLR 1098, 88 Cr App Rep 302, 153 JP 171, 132 Sol Jo 1299, [1988] 45 LS Gaz R 41, CA .... A 43.4
R v Grant [1996] 1 Cr App Rep 73, CA .... A 26.4A
R v Gravesend Justices, ex p Dexter [1977] Crim LR 298 .... B 38.3
R (on the application of AS) v Great Yarmouth Youth Court [2011] EWHC 2059 (Admin), [2012] Crim LR 478 .... D 6.13A
R v Green (Victoria) [2016] EWCA Crim 1888, [2017] 1 Cr App Rep (S) 161 .... A 36.10
R (on the application of Pearson) v Greenwich Magistrates' Court [2008] EWHC 300 (Admin), sub nom Pearson v Greenwich Borough Council [2008] RVR 234, [2008] All ER (D) 256 (Jan) .... A 54.4
R (on the application of Thomas) v Greenwich Magistrates' Court [2009] EWHC 1180 (Admin), 173 JP 345, [2009] Crim LR 800, [2009] All ER (D) 85 (May) .... D 8.92
R v Griffin (Daniel) [2019] EWCA Crim 563, [2019] 2 Cr App Rep (S) 237 .... C 5.45
R v Grout [2011] EWCA Crim 299, [2011] 1 Cr App Rep 472, 175 JP 209, [2011] Crim LR 584, [2011] All ER (D) 21 (Mar) .... A 52.5
R v Grundy [1977] Crim LR 543, CA .... C 16C.3
R (on the application of RSPCA) v Guildford Crown Court [2012] EWHC 3392 (Admin), 177 JP 154, [2012] All ER (D) 24 (Nov) .... A 5.4
R (on the application of Stokes) v Gwent Magistrates' Court [2001] EWHC 569 (Admin), [2001] All ER (D) 125 (Jul), 165 JP 766 .... B 28.50

R v Gwent Magistrates' Court, ex p Carey (1996) 160 JP 613, DC .... B 38.5
R v Gwynn [2002] EWCA Crim 2951, [2003] 2 Cr App Rep (S) 267, [2003] Crim LR 421, [2003] All ER (D) 318 (Dec) .... A 18.3
R v H [2005] EWCA Crim 732, [2005] 2 All ER 859, [2005] 1 WLR 2005, [2005] Crim LR 735, (2005) Times, 8 February, [2005] All ER (D) 16 (Feb) .... A 52.4, A 52.5, A 53.4
R v H [2010] EWCA Crim 1931, 174 CL&J 573, 154 Sol Jo (no 31) 28, [2010] All ER (D) 14 (Aug) .... A 8.10, A 20.6
R v H [2011] EWCA Crim 1508, [2011] 4 All ER 761, 175 CL&J 404, 175 CL&J 517, [2011] All ER (D) 135 (Jun); revsd sub nom R v Hughes [2013] UKSC 56, [2013] 1 WLR 2461, (2013) Times, 20 August, [2013] All ER (D) 388 (Jul) .... C 16B.5A
R v Hackett [2011] EWCA Crim 380, [2011] 2 Cr App Rep 35, 175 JP 503, [2011] Crim LR 879, [2011] All ER (D) 28 (Mar) .... D 6.22
R v Hahn [2003] EWCA Crim 825, [2003] 2 Cr App Rep (S) 636, [2003] All ER (D) 230 (Jun) .... E 1.2
R v Hall (1985) 81 Cr App Rep 260, [1985] Crim LR 377, 129 Sol Jo 283, [1985] LS Gaz R 1485, [1985] NLJ Rep 604, CA ... A 40.10
R v Hall (Ronnie) [2013] EWCA Crim 323, [2013] 2 Cr App Rep (S) 460, [2013] Crim LR 533, 177 CL&J 251, [2013] All ER (D) 313 (Mar) .... B 45.55
R v Hall-Chung [2002] EWCA Crim 3088, [2003] All ER (D) 113 (Feb) .... A 76.3
R v Hamidi [2010] EWCA Crim 66, [2010] Crim LR 578, [2010] All ER (D) 33 (Feb) .... D 6.22
R (on the application of Cuns) v Hammersmith Magistrates' Court [2016] EWHC 748 (Admin), [2016] Crim LR 580 .... C 23.4
R v Hanson [2005] EWCA Crim 824, [2005] 1 WLR 3169, [2005] 2 Cr App Rep 299, 169 JP 250, (2005) Times, 24 March, [2005] All ER (D) 380 (Mar) .... D 6.14
R v Haque [2011] EWCA Crim 1871, [2012] 1 Cr App Rep 48, [2011] Crim LR 962, (2011) Times, 20 September, [2011] All ER (D) 238 (Jul) .... A 41.7
R v Hargreaves [1985] Crim LR 243, CA .... A 58.6
R v Harris [1969] 2 All ER 599n, [1969] 1 WLR 745, 53 Cr App Rep 376, 133 JP 422, 113 Sol Jo 363 .... B 36.1
R v Harris [1996] 1 Cr App Rep 369, [1996] Crim LR 36, CA .... A 27.3A
R v Harrison [2003] EWCA Crim 3514, [2004] 2 Cr App Rep (S) 106, [2004] Crim LR 241, (2003) Times, 1 December, [2003] All ER (D) 288 (Nov) .... A 1.4
R v Harrison [2007] EWCA Crim 2976, [2008] 1 Cr App Rep 387, [2007] All ER (D) 72 (Dec) .... A 43.3
R (on the application of Holloway) v Harrow Crown Court [2019] EWHC 1731 (Admin), [2019] All ER (D) 155 (Jul) .... B 12.9
R v Havant Justices, ex p Palmer (1985) 149 JP 609, [1985] Crim LR 658, DC .... D 3.5
R (Health and Safety Executive) v Havering Borough Council [2017] EWCA Crim 242, [2017] 2 Cr App Rep (S) 54, [2017] All ER (D) 86 (Mar) .... A 80.20

R (on the application of the DPP) v Havering Magistrates' Court [2001] 3 All ER 997, [2001] 1 WLR 805, [2001] 2 Cr App Rep 12, (2001) Times, 7 February, (2001) Independent, 12 February, [2000] All ER (D) 2307, DC .... D 8.2
R v Haynes [2004] EWCA Crim 390, (2004) Times, 27 February, [2004] All ER (D) 235 (Mar) .... A 72.17
R v Heard [2007] EWCA Crim 125, [2007] 3 All ER 306, [2007] 3 WLR 475, [2007] Crim LR 654, (2007) Times, 6 March, [2007] All ER (D) 158 (Feb) .... A 52.4, A 53.5
R v Heathcote-Smith (Benjamin) and Melton (Christopher Timothy) [2011] EWCA Crim 2846, [2012] 2 Cr App Rep (S) 133, [2012] Crim LR 304 .... B 45.2
R v Hehl (1976) 65 Cr App Rep 45, [1977] Crim LR 285, CA .... A 40.5
R v Hemsley [2010] EWCA Crim 225, [2010] 3 All ER 965, 174 CL&J 172, [2010] All ER (D) 203 (Feb) .... B 44.4
R v Henderson [2016] EWCA Crim 965, [2016] 4 WLR 172, [2017] 1 Cr App Rep 29, 181 JP 229, [2017] Crim LR 233 ... A 11.6
R v Hennigan [1971] 3 All ER 133, [1971] RTR 305, 55 Cr App Rep 262, 135 JP 504, 115 Sol Jo 268, CA .... C 16A.6
R v Hereford Magistrates' Court, ex p Rowlands [1998] QB 110, [1997] 2 WLR 854, 161 JP 258, DC .... D 6.17A
R v Herrington [2017] EWCA Crim 889, [2018] 4 WLR 35, [2017] 2 Cr App Rep (S) 327 .... A 41.14
R v Hester-Wox [2016] EWCA Crim 1397, [2016] 2 Cr App Rep (S) 463, 181 JP 132, [2017] Crim LR 154 .... B 34.46
R v Hewitt [2018] EWCA Crim 2309, [2019] 1 Cr App Rep (S) 227 .... B 44.3
R v Hichens [2011] EWCA Crim 1626, [2011] 2 Cr App Rep 370, [2011] Crim LR 873, (2011) Times, 20 July, [2011] All ER (D) 81 (Jun) .... A 8.20
R (on the application of Cleary) v Highbury Corner Magistrates' Court [2006] EWHC 1869 (Admin), (2006) Times, 12 September, 150 Sol Jo LB 1052, [2006] All ER (D) 376 (Jul) .... A 26.12
R (on the application of Raphael (t/a Orleans)) v Highbury Corner Magistrates Court [2011] EWCA Civ 462, [2012] PTSR 427, [2011] All ER (D) 224 (Apr) .... F 2.19
R (on the application of Turner) v Highbury Corner Magistrates Court [2005] EWHC 2568 (Admin), [2006] 1 WLR 220, 170 JP 93, (2005) Times, 26 October, [2005] All ER (D) 105 (Oct) .... A 26.12, B 7.1
R (on the application of Walden) v Highbury Corner Magistrates Court [2003] EWHC 708 (Admin), [2003] All ER (D) 285 (Mar) .... D 6.17C
R v Highbury Corner Magistrates' Court, ex p Uchendu (1994) 158 LGR 481, [1994] RA 51, 158 JP 409 .... F 4.12
R v Hinks [2001] 2 AC 241, [2000] 4 All ER 833, [2000] 3 WLR 1590, [2001] 1 Cr App Rep 252, 165 JP 21, [2000] 43 LS Gaz R 37, 144 Sol Jo LB 265, HL .... A 57.8
R v Holland [2002] EWCA Crim 1585, [2003] 1 Cr App Rep (S) 288, [2002] All ER (D) 113 (Jun) .... A 72.17

R v Holmes (John) [2019] EWCA Crim 612, [2019] 2 Cr App Rep (S) 207 .... B 9.4
R v Horseferry Road Magistrates' Court, ex p Bennett [1994] 1 AC 42, [1993] 3 WLR 90, 98 Cr App Rep 114, 137 Sol Jo LB 159, sub nom Bennett v Horseferry Road Magistrates' Court [1993] 3 All ER 138, [1993] 3 LRC 94, HL .... D 1B.11
R v Horseferry Road Metropolitan Stipendiary Magistrate, ex p Siadatan [1991] 1 QB 260, [1991] 1 All ER 324, [1990] 3 WLR 1006, 92 Cr App Rep 257, [1990] Crim LR 598, [1990] NLJR 704 .... A 21.6
R v Horsham Justices, ex p Farquharson [1982] QB 762, [1982] 2 All ER 269, [1982] 2 WLR 430, 126 Sol Jo 49, DC; affd [1982] QB 762, [1982] 2 All ER 269, [1982] 2 WLR 430, 76 Cr App Rep 87, 126 Sol Jo 98, CA .... D 1B.7
R v Horsham Justices, ex p Richards [1985] 2 All ER 1114, [1985] 1 WLR 986, 82 Cr App Rep 254, 7 Cr App Rep (S) 158, 149 JP 567, 129 Sol Jo 467, [1985] LS Gaz R 2499 .... B 10.5
R v Howard [2012] EWCA Crim 671, [2012] All ER (D) 43 (Apr) .... A 55.3
R v Howells [1977] QB 614, [1977] 3 All ER 417, [1977] 2 WLR 716, 65 Cr App Rep 86, 141 JP 641, 121 Sol Jo 154, CA ... A 76.8A
R v Howells [1999] 1 All ER 50, [1999] 1 WLR 307, [1999] 1 Cr App Rep 98, [1999] 1 Cr App Rep (S) 335, 162 JP 731, [1998] Crim LR 836, CA .... B 45.34
R v Howlett [1999] All ER (D) 777, CA .... A 4.17
R v Huddart [1999] Crim LR 568, CA .... A 72.2
R (on the application of AB) v Huddersfield Magistrates' Court [2014] EWHC 1089 (Admin), [2014] 4 All ER 500, [2014] 2 Cr App Rep 409, 178 JP 265, 178 CL&J 270, [2014] All ER (D) 167 (Apr) .... F 5.1, F 5.20A
R v Hughes. See Prosecution Appeal
R v Hughes. See R v H [2011] EWCA Crim 1508
R v Hussain [1981] 2 All ER 287, [1981] 1 WLR 416, 72 Cr App Rep 143, 146 JP 23, 125 Sol Jo 166, CA .... A 76.8A
R v Hussain [2010] EWCA Crim 970, [2011] QB 1, [2010] 3 WLR 808, [2010] 2 Cr App Rep 78, (2010) Times, 17 March, [2010] All ER (D) 183 (Jan) .... A 26.4A
R v Hussain (Tayyab) [2018] EWCA Crim 780, [2018] 2 Cr App Rep (S) 89, [2018] Crim LR 770 .... B 45.46, B 45.46A
R v Iles [2012] EWCA Crim 1610, 176 JP 601, [2012] All ER (D) 212 (Jul) .... E 3.18G
R v Ingram (2004) Telegraph, 27 May, CA .... B 33.16
R (on the application of Brown) v Inner London Crown Court [2003] EWHC 3194 (Admin), [2003] All ER (D) 256 (Dec) . A 34.17; B 29.5
R v Inner London Youth Court, ex p DPP (1996) 161 JP 178, [1996] Crim LR 834, DC .... E 3.18C
R (on the application of DPP) v Ipswich Magistrates Court [2013] EWHC 1388 (Admin), 177 CL&J 397, [2013] All ER (D) 01 (Jun) .... D 6.17C
R v Iqbal (Naseen) [2011] EWCA Crim 1294, [2011] 2 Cr App Rep 250, (2011) Times, 21 April .... D 7.10

R v Ireland [1998] AC 147, [1997] 4 All ER 225, [1997] 3 WLR 534, [1998] 1 Cr App Rep 177, [1998] 1 FLR 105, [1998] Fam Law 137, [1997] Crim LR 810, [1997] NLJR 1273, HL .... A 8.9
R v Isaac [2004] EWCA Crim 1082, 168 JP 417, [2004] All ER (D) 209 (Apr) .... A 60.3
R (on the application of Sandhu) v Isleworth Crown Court [2012] EWHC 1658 (Admin), 176 JP 537, 176 CL&J 339, [2012] All ER (D) 183 (May) .... A 72.15
R (on the application of Mohuddin Khan) v Isleworth Crown Court and Hillingdon London Borough of Council (Interested Party) [2011] EWHC 3164 (Admin), 176 JP 6 ..... A 84.8
R v Jack McGeechan [2019] EWCA Crim 235, [2019] 2 Cr App Rep (S) 91, [2019] Crim LR 554 .... B 19.10
R v Jackson [2012] EWCA Crim 2602, 177 JP 147 .... B 44.3
R v Janes [2016] EWCA Crim 676, [2016] 2 Cr App Rep (S) 256, [2016] Crim LR 785 .... B 13.5
R v Jayson [2002] EWCA Crim 683, [2003] 1 Cr App Rep 212 .... A 43.3
Rv Jenkins [2012] EWCA Crim 2909, [2013] RTR 21 ...... C 16A.6
R v Johnson [1995] RTR 15, 158 JP 788, [1995] Crim LR 250, [1994] 13 LS Gaz R 35, CA .... A 64.3A
R v Johnstone [2003] UKHL 28, [2003] 3 All ER 884, [2003] 1 WLR 1736, [2003] 2 Cr App Rep 493, [2003] FSR 748, 167 JP 281, [2004] Crim LR 244, [2003] IP & T 901, [2003] 26 LS Gaz R 36, (2003) Times, 29 May, 147 Sol Jo LB 625, [2003] All ER (D) 323 (May) .... A 60.3; D 1.8
R v Jolie [2003] EWCA Crim 1543, [2004] 1 Cr App Rep 44, 167 JP 313, [2003] Crim LR 730, (2003) Times, 30 May, [2003] All ER (D) 356 (May) .... A 11.12
R v Jones [1995] QB 235, [1995] 3 All ER 139, [1995] 2 WLR 64, [1995] 1 Cr App Rep 262, 159 JP 94, [1995] Crim LR 416, [1994] 39 LS Gaz R 38, 138 Sol Jo LB 194, CA .... A 33.4
R v Jones [2003] 1 AC 1, [2002] 2 All ER 113, [2002] 2 WLR 524, [2002] 2 Cr App Rep 128, 166 JP 333, [2002] 13 LS Gaz R 26, (2002) Times, 21 February, 146 Sol Jo LB 61, [2002] 5 LRC 50, [2002] UKHL 5, [2002] All ER (D) 275 (Feb), HL .. D 6.17A, D 6.19
R v Jones [2006] UKHL 16, [2006] 2 All ER 741, [2006] 2 WLR 772, [2006] 15 LS Gaz R 20, [2006] NLJR 600, (2006) Times, 30 March, 150 Sol Jo LB 433, [2006] All ER (D) 419 (Mar) .... A 8.20A, A 18.19
R v Jones [2007] EWCA Crim 1118, [2008] QB 460, [2007] 4 All ER 112, [2007] 3 WLR 907, [2007] 2 Cr App Rep 267, [2007] Crim LR 979, (2007) Times, 8 June, [2007] All ER (D) 235 (May) .... A 52.5
R v Jones [2014] EWCA Crim 1859, [2015] 1 Cr App Rep (S) 68 .... B 44.2
R v Jones (Rowan) [2017] EWCA Crim 2192, [2018] 1 Cr App Rep (S) 248 .... B 18.1
R v Jordan [1998] Crim LR 353, CA .... A 17.3
R v Josephs (1977) 65 Cr App Rep 253, CA .... A 27A.2
R v Junab [2012] EWCA Crim 2660, [2013] 2 Cr App Rep (S) 159, [2013] Crim LR 348 .... B 17.10

R v K [2011] EWCA Crim 1843, 175 JP 378, [2011] All ER (D) 230 (Jul) A41.13
R v Kanwar [1982] 2 All ER 528, [1982] 1 WLR 845, 75 Cr App Rep 87, 146 JP 283, [1982] Crim LR 532, 126 Sol Jo 276, CA .... A 40.6
R v Kefford [2002] EWCA Crim 519 [2002] Crim LR 432 .... B 34.6
R v Kelly [2001] EWCA Crim 1751, [2002] 1 Cr App Rep (S) 360, [2001] Crim LR 836, [2001] All ER (D) 195 (Jul) .... B 45.2B
R v Kelly [2001] RTR 45, CA .... A 18.3, A 66.2; D 4.9
R v Kelt [1977] 3 All ER 1099, [1977] 1 WLR 1365, 65 Cr App Rep 74, 142 JP 60, 121 Sol Jo 423, CA .... A 33.3, A 77.6
R v Ketteridge [2014] EWCA Crim 1962, [2015] RTR 40, [2015] 1 Cr App Rep (S) 89 .... C 5.40
R v Khan [2015] EWCA Crim 835, [2015] 2 Cr App Rep (S) 313 .... B9.23A
R v Khellaf (Bilal) (2016) [2016] EWCA Crim 1297, [2017] 1 Cr App Rep (S) 1 .... A 41.14
R v Kimpriktzis [2013] EWCA Crim 734, [2014] 1 Cr App Rep (S) 23 .... B 44.3
R v Kimsey [1996] Crim LR 35, CA .... C 16A.6
R v King [1993] RTR 245, 13 Cr App Rep (S) 668, CA .... C 5.9
R v King's Lynn Magistrates' Court, ex p Hyman (CO/1320/91) (Unreported) .... B 34.24
R (on the application of M) v Kingston Crown Court [2014] EWHC 2702 (Admin), [2015] 1 Cr App Rep 27, 178 JP 438, [2015] Crim LR 436, 164 NLJ 7627, [2014] All ER (D) 02 (Oct) .... B 33.21
R v Kingston-upon-Hull Stipendiary Magistrate, ex p Hartung [1981] RTR 262, 72 Cr App Rep 26, [1981] Crim LR 42 .... B 18.8
R v Kluxen [2010] EWCA Crim 1081, [2011] 1 Cr App Rep (S) 249, [2010] Crim LR 657, 174 CL&J 380, (2010) Times, 23 June, [2010] All ER (D) 124 (May) .... B 17.9
R (on the application of K) v Knowsley Metropolitan Borough Council [2004] EWHC 1933 (Admin), 168 JP 461, sub nom Keating v Knowsley Metropolitan Borough Council [2004] All ER (D) 383 (Jul) .... B 8.7
R v Koffi (Sharon) [2019] EWCA Crim 300, [2019] 2 Cr App Rep (S) 127 .... B 40.3
R v Konzani [2005] EWCA Crim 706, [2005] All ER (D) 292 (Mar) .... A 70.5
R v L [2012] EWCA Crim 1336, [2013] 1 Cr App Rep (S) 317 .... B 19.4
R v LM [2002] EWCA Crim 3047, [2003] 2 Cr App Rep (S) 124, [2003] Crim LR 205, [2002] All ER (D) 35 (Dec) .... B 19.4
R v Lambert [2001] 1 All ER 1014, [2001] 2 WLR 211, [2001] 1 Cr App Rep 205, [2000] 35 LS Gaz R 36, 144 Sol Jo LB 226, CA; affd sub nom [2001] UKHL 37, [2002] 2 AC 545, [2001] 3 All ER 577, [2001] 3 WLR 206, [2001] 2 Cr App Rep 511, [2001] 31 LS Gaz R 29, (2001) Times, 6 July, (2001) Independent, 19 July, 145 Sol Jo LB 174, [2002] 1 LRC 584, [2001] All ER (D) 69 (Jul) .... A 25.7, A 25.10, A 26.4D

R (on the application of Vella) v Lambeth London Borough Council [2005] TLR 533, QBD .... A 84.3
R v Lancaster [2010] EWCA Crim 370, [2010] 1 WLR 2558, [2010] 2 Cr App Rep 45, [2010] HLR 647, (2010) Times, 2 June, [2010] 3 All ER 402 .... A 31.3
R v Land [1999] QB 65, [1998] 1 All ER 403, [1998] 3 WLR 322, [1998] 1 Cr App Rep 301, [1998] 1 FLR 438, [1998] Fam Law 133, [1998] Crim LR 70, [1997] 42 LS Gaz R 32, CA .... A 43.5
R v Lang [2005] EWCA Crim 2864, [2006] 2 All ER 410, [2006] 1 WLR 2509, [2006] Crim LR 174, (2005) Times, 10 November, 149 Sol Jo LB 1450, [2005] All ER (D) 54 (Nov) .... E 5.1
R v Lavery [2008] EWCA Crim 2499, [2009] 3 All ER 295, 172 JP 561, 172 JPN 806, (2008) Times, 20 October, [2008] All ER (D) 227 (Oct) .... B 45.9
R v Law [2015] EWCA Crim 5, [2016] 1 WLR 189, [2016] 1 Cr App Rep 188 .... A 76.7, A 76A.4
R v Lawson [2006] EWCA Crim 2674, [2007] All ER (D) 61 (Mar) .... B 2.4
R v Lee (2001) 165 JP 634 .... A 7.3
R (on the application of Lee) v Leeds Crown Court [2006] EWHC 2550 (Admin), [2006] All ER (D) 18 (Oct) .... A 46.5
R (on the application of W) v Leeds Crown Court [2011] EWHC 2326 (Admin), [2012] 1 Cr App Rep 162, 175 JP 467, [2012] Crim LR 160, [2011] All ER (D) 52 (Oct) .... B 40.5
R v Leeds Crown Court [2016] EWHC 1230 (Admin), 180 JP 282 .... B 19.8
R v Leeds Crown Court, ex p Wardle [2001] UKHL 12, [2002] 1 AC 754, [2001] 2 All ER 1, [2001] 2 WLR 865, [2001] 2 Cr App Rep 301, 165 JP 465, [2001] 21 LS Gaz R 39, [2001] NLJR 386, (2001) Times, March 13, 145 Sol Jo LB 117, [2001] All ER (D) 85 (Mar) .... D 8.54
R v Leeds Justices, ex p Kennett [1996] RVR 53 .... F 4.12
R (on the application of Grimshaw) v Leeds Magistrates' Court [2001] EWHC Admin 880 [2001] All ER (D) 350 (Oct) ...... D 8.23
R (on the application of Kenny) v Leeds Magistrates' Court [2003] EWHC 2963 (Admin), [2004] 1 All ER 1333, 168 JP 125, [2003] All ER (D) 104 (Dec); affd sub nom R (on the application of M) v Secretary of State for Constitutional Affairs and Lord Chancellor [2004] EWCA Civ 312, [2004] 2 All ER 531, [2004] 1 WLR 2298, [2004] LGR 417, 168 JP 529, 148 Sol Jo LB 385, [2004] All ER (D) 345 (Mar) .... B 8.7
R v Leonard [2012] EWCA Crim 277, [2012] 2 Cr App Rep 138, 176 CL&J 466, [2012] All ER (D) 235 (Jul) .... A 43.3
R v Levesconte [2011] EWCA Crim 2754, [2012] 2 Cr App Rep (S) 80, 176 JP 204, [2012] Crim LR 236, [2011] 47 LS Gaz R 21, [2011] All ER (D) 183 (Nov) .... B 34.47
R (on the application of Lonergan) v Lewes Crown Court (Secretary of State for the Home Department, interested party) [2005] EWHC 457 (Admin), [2005] 2 All ER 362, [2005] 1 WLR 2570, 169 JP 324, (2005) Times, 25 April, [2005] All ER (D) 382 (Mar) .... B 8.5

R v Lewis [2016] EWCA Crim 1020, [2017] 1 Cr App Rep (S) 5, [2017] Crim LR 147 .... 44.2
R (on the application of A) v Lewisham Youth Court [2011] EWHC 1193 (Admin), [2012] 1 WLR 34, 175 JP 321, [2011] All ER (D) 99 (May) .... E 3.4
R v Lincolnshire (Kesteven) Justices, ex p O'Connor [1983] 1 All ER 901, [1983] 1 WLR 335, 147 JP 97, [1983] Crim LR 621, 127 Sol Jo 121 .... B 32.1
R v Little (14 April 1976, unreported), CA 28.23
R (on the application of P) v Liverpool City Magistrates' Court [2006] EWHC 887 (Admin), 170 JP 453, [2006] All ER (D) 211 (Mar) .... A 49.3A
R v Longman (Mark) [2010] EWCA Crim 2046 .... B 44.3
R v Longworth [2004] EWCA Crim 2145, [2005] 1 Cr App Rep (S) 419, (2004) Times, 17 August, [2004] All ER (D) 439 (Jul); revsd [2006] UKHL 1, [2006] 1 All ER 887, [2006] 1 WLR 313, [2006] 2 Cr App Rep (S) 401, (2006) Times, 1 February, 150 Sol Jo LB 132, [2006] All ER (D) 182 (Jan) .... A 43.12, A 52.14
R (on the application of A) v Lowestoft Magistrates' Court [2013] EWHC 659 (Admin), [2014] 1 WLR 1489, 177 JP 377, [2013] Crim LR 763, [2013] All ER (D) 278 (Mar) .... D 1B.7
R v Lucas [1995] Crim LR 400, CA .... A 26.4A; D 6.22
R v M [2008] EWCA Crim 3329 .... E 5.1
R v M [2011] EWCA Crim 2752, [2012] Crim LR 789 .... A 43.4
R v MV [2010] EWCA Crim 2400, [2011] 1 Cr App Rep 432, [2010] All ER (D) 181 (Oct) A32.2A
R v Mabee (Craig) [2007] EWCA Crim 3230, [2008] 2 Cr App Rep (S) 143 .... B 29.7
R v McAuley [2009] EWCA Crim 2130, [2010] 1 Cr App Rep 148, 173 JP 585, [2010] Crim LR 336 .... A 11.12
R v McCalla (1988) 87 Cr App Rep 372, 152 JP 481, CA .... A 11.12
R v McCreadie and Tume (1993] 157 JP 541 .... A 1.3
R v McGarrick (Shaun) [2019] EWCA Crim 530, [2019] 2 Cr App Rep (S) 231 .... A 9A.6
R v McGillivray [2005] EWCA Crim 604, [2005] 2 Cr App Rep (S) 366, [2005] Crim LR 484, [2005] All ER (D) 208 (Jan) .... B 45.2B
R v McGrath [2003] EWCA Crim 2062, (2003) 167 JP 554, [2004] Crim LR 142, [2003] All ER (D) 397 (Jun) .... A 12.5, A 13.4
R v McGrath [2005] EWCA Crim 353, [2005] 2 Cr App Rep (S) 525, [2005] NLJ 826, [2005] All ER (D) 81 (May) .... B 8.5
R v McLellan [2017] EWCA Crim 1464, [2018] 1 WLR 2969, [2018] 1 Cr App Rep (S) 107, [2017] Crim LR 91 .... B 44.5
R v McNamara (1988) 87 Cr App Rep 246, 152 JP 390, [1988] Crim LR 440, 132 Sol Jo 300, [1988] 11 LS Gaz R 42, CA .... A 25.7
R v Macrae (1993) 159 JP 359, [1994] Crim LR 363, CA .... A 64.3
R v Maginnis [1987] AC 303, [1987] 1 All ER 907, [1987] 2 WLR 765, 85 Cr App Rep 127, 151 JP 537, [1987] Crim LR 564, 131 Sol Jo 357, [1987] LS Gaz R 1141, [1987] NLJ Rep 244, HL .... A 26.4A
R v Mahmood [2007] EWCA Crim 13, [2007] All ER (D) 28 (May) .... A 69.4

R v Mahmood (Abdullah) [2019] EWCA Crim 788, sub nom *New Case [2019] 2 Cr App Rep (S) 169 .... B 44.3
R v Major [2010] EWCA Crim 3016, [2011] 1 Cr App Rep 322, [2011] 2 Cr App Rep (S) 139, [2011] Crim LR 328, (2010) Times, 14 December A41.13
R v Mallett [1978] 3 All ER 10, [1978] 1 WLR 820, 67 Cr App Rep 239, 142 JP 528, 122 Sol Jo 295, CA A31.3A
R v Malvern Justices, ex p Evans [1988] QB 553, [1988] 1 All ER 371, [1988] 2 WLR 227, 87 Cr App Rep 28, 152 JP 65, [1988] Crim LR 181, 131 Sol Jo 1698, [1988] 2 LS Gaz R 36, [1987] NLJ Rep 757, DC .... D 1B.5
R (DPP) v Manchester and Salford Magistrates' Court [2017] EWHC 1708 (Admin) .... C 22.23
R (on the application of Coxon) v Manchester City Magistrates Court [2010] EWHC 712 (Admin), 174 CL&J 221, [2010] All ER (D) 123 (Mar) .... C 22.16
R (on the application of D) v Manchester City Youth Court [2001] EWHC 860 (Admin), [2002] 1 Cr App Rep (S) 573, 166 JP 15, [2002] Crim LR 149, 165 JPN 874, [2001] All ER (D) 406 (Oct) .... E 3.18C
R (on the application of Manchester City Council) v Manchester Magistrates' Court (2005) Times, 8 March, [2005] All ER (D) 103 (Feb) .... B 8.7
R v Mann (2000) 144 Sol Jo LB 150, CA .... A 41.13, A 46.3
R v Manning [1999] QB 980, [1998] 4 All ER 876, [1999] 1 WLR 430, [1998] 2 Cr App Rep 461, [1999] Crim LR 151, CA A31.3A
R v Marchese [2008] EWCA Crim 389, [2009] 1 WLR 992, [2008] 2 Cr App Rep 147, [2008] Crim LR 797, (2008) Times, 6 March, [2008] All ER (D) 150 (Feb) .... A 58.6
R v Marsh [1997] 1 Cr App Rep 67, [1997] Crim LR 205, 140 Sol Jo LB 157, CA .... A 66.8A
R v Marsham, ex p Pethick Lawrence [1912] 2 KB 362, 76 JP 284, 81 LJKB 957, 23 Cox CC 77, [1911–13] All ER Rep 639, 107 LT 89, 28 TLR 391, DC .... B 38.5
R v Martin [1998] 2 Cr App Rep 385, CA .... A 4.7
R v Martin and Brimecome [2014] EWCA Crim 1940, [2015] 1 WLR 588, [2015] 1 Cr App Rep 132, [2015] Crim LR 83 ... A 26.4A
R v Martindale [1986] 3 All ER 25, [1986] 1 WLR 1042, 84 Cr App Rep 31, 150 JP 548, [1986] Crim LR 736, 130 Sol Jo 613, [1986] LS Gaz R 2412, CA .... A 25.8
R v Mateta [2013] EWCA Crim 1372, [2013] All ER (D) 19 (Aug) .... A 81.8A
R v Matthews [2003] EWCA Crim 813, [2004] QB 690, [2003] 3 WLR 693, [2003] 2 Cr App Rep 302, 147 Sol Jo LB 383 .... A 11.13
R v Maunder [2015] EWCA Crim 778, [2015] 2 Cr App Rep (S) 247 .... B 34.46
R v Maxwell [2017] EWCA Crim 1233, [2018] 1 Cr App Rep 76, [2017] Crim LR 60, [2017] All ER (D) 100 (Aug) ..... D 4.9A, D 5.1
R v Metharam [1961] 3 All ER 200, 45 Cr App Rep 304, 125 JP 578, 105 Sol Jo 632, CCA .... A 70.6
R v Melin [2019] EWCA Crim 557, [2019] 3 WLR 150, [2019] 2 Cr App Rep 63 .... A 15.11

R v Miller [1954] 2 QB 282, [1954] 2 All ER 529, [1954] 2 WLR 138, 38 Cr App Rep 1, 118 JP 340, 98 Sol Jo 62 .... A 8.9
R v Miller (1993) 15 Cr App Rep (S) 505, [1994] Crim LR 231, CA .... C 5.38
R v Miller [2010] EWCA Crim 809, [2011] 1 Cr App Rep (S) 7, [2010] Crim LR 648 .... A12.4
R v Mills [2002] EWCA Crim 26, [2002] 2 Cr App Rep (S) 51, [2002] Crim LR 331, 146 Sol Jo LB 29 .... B 34.6
R v Mintchev [2011] EWCA Crim 499, [2011] 2 Cr App Rep (S) 465, [2011] Crim LR 483 .... B 17.8
R v Mobeen Ul Haq [2013] EWCA Crim 1478, [2014] 1 Cr App Rep (S) 307 .... B 17.10
R v Monaghan (Rudie Aaron) [2009] EWCA Crim 2699, [2010] 2 Cr App Rep (S) 343, [2010] Crim LR 322, [2010] 2 LS Gaz R 17, [2009] All ER (D) 225 (Dec) .... B 34.39A
R v More [1987] 3 All ER 825, [1987] 1 WLR 1578, 86 Cr App Rep 234, [1988] Crim LR 176, 11 LDAB 46, 131 Sol Jo 1550, [1987] LS Gaz R 3577, HL .... A 78.6
R v Morgan [2017] EWCA Crim 2163, [2018] 1 WLR 2409, [2018] 1 Cr App Rep (S) 307 .... B 44.3
R v Morris [1995] 2 Cr App Rep 69, 159 JP 1, CA .... A 26.4A
R v Morris [2013] EWCA Crim 436, [2014] 1 WLR 16, [2013] RTR 22, [2013] 2 Cr App Rep 89, [2013] All ER (D) 134 (Apr) .... A 45.6A
R v Morris and King (1984) 79 Cr App Rep 104, 149 JP 60, [1984] Crim LR 442, [1984] LS Gaz R 1518, CA . A 33.9A, A 77.9A
R v Mowatt [1968] 1 QB 421, [1967] 3 All ER 47, [1967] 3 WLR 1192, 51 Cr App Rep 402, 131 JP 463, 111 Sol Jo 716, CA .. A 70.5
R v Muir (1986) 83 Cr App Rep 375, CA .... A 15.17
R v Myers [2007] EWCA Crim 599, [2007] RTR 425, [2007] 2 Cr App Rep 258, [2007] All ER (D) 241 (Feb) .... C 49.3
R v N Ltd [2008] EWCA Crim 1223, [2008] 1 WLR 2684, [2009] 1 Cr App Rep 56, (2008) Times, 25 August, [2008] All ER (D) 112 (Jun) .... D 6.21
R v NC (2016) [2016] EWCA Crim 1448, [2017] 1 Cr App Rep (S) 87, [2017] Crim LR 334 .... B 44.2
R v NPS London Ltd [2019] EWCA Crim 228, [2019] 2 Cr App Rep (S) 132, 169 NLJ 7831, [2019] All ER (D) 148 (Feb) ... A 80.20
R v NW [2010] EWCA Crim 404, [2010] 2 Cr App Rep 54, [2010] Crim LR 723, (2010) Times, 29 April, [2010] All ER (D) 34 (Mar) .... A 67.4
R v Nafel (2004), unreported .... B 33.8
R (on the application of Singh (also known as Virdee) v National Crime Agency [2018] EWHC 1119 (Admin), [2018] 1 WLR 5073, [2019] 1 Cr App Rep 139 .... F 5.5
R v Nazari [1980] 3 All ER 880, [1980] 1 WLR 1366, 71 Cr App Rep 87, 2 Cr App Rep (S) 84, 145 JP 102, [1980] Crim LR 447, 124 Sol Jo 359, CA .... B 17.9
R v Neville (1987) 9 Cr App Rep (S) 222, [1987] Crim LR 585, CA .... B 18.2

R v Newcastle under Lyme Justices, ex p Massey [1995] 1 All ER 120, 158 JP 1037, [1994] NLJR 1444, sub nom R v Stoke-on-Trent Justices, ex p Knight [1994] 1 WLR 1684, DC .... F 4.17
R v Newcastle upon Tyne Justices, ex p Devine [1998] RA 97, 162 JP 602, [1998] 20 LS Gaz R 33, 142 Sol Jo LB 155 .... F 4.16
R (on the application of Craik, Chief Constable of Northumbria Police) v Newcastle Upon Tyne Magistrates' Court (Price, interested party's) [2010] EWHC 935 (Admin), 174 CL&J 334, [2010] 5 Archbold Review 2, [2010] All ER (D) 223 (Apr) .... D 4.11
R v Nicholson [2006] EWCA Crim 1518, (2006) 170 JP 573, (2006) Times, 13 June, [2006] All ER (D) 218 (May) .... B 8.13
R v Nolan [2012] EWCA Crim 671, [2012] All ER (D) 43 (Apr) .... A 55.3
R v Norfolk Justices, ex p DPP [1950] 2 KB 558, 48 LGR 483, 34 Cr App Rep 120, 94 Sol Jo 436, sub nom R v South Greenhoe Justices, ex p DPP [1950] 2 All ER 42, 114 JP 312, 66 (pt 2) TLR 452, DC .... B 38.5
R v Norman [2007] EWCA Crim 624, [2007] All ER (D) 523 (Mar) .... B 18.17
R v Norris (2000) 164 JP 689, [2000] Lexis Citation 4381 .... B 19.8
R (on the application of Wood) v North Avon Magistrates' Court [2009] EWHC 3614 (Admin), 174 JP 157, [2009] All ER (D) 133 (Nov) .... F 5.6
R (on the application of Durham County Council) v North Durham Justices [2004] EWHC 1073 (Admin), (2004) 168 JP 269, [2004] All ER (D) 260 (Apr) .... D 6.48
R (on the application of Costello) v North East Essex Magistrates' Court [2006] EWHC 3145 (Admin), 171 JP 153, 171 JPN 393, [2006] All ER (D) 294 (Nov) .... D 6.17B
R (on the application of Lloyd) v North Essex Justices (2000) 165 JP 117, (2000) Times, 14 November, 144 Sol Jo LB 274, [2000] All ER (D) 1814, DC .... B 8.5, B 8.7
R v North Sefton Magistrates' Court, ex p Marsh (1994) 16 Cr App Rep (S) 401, 159 JP 9, [1994] Crim LR 865, CA .... B 8.6
R v Northallerton Magistrates' Court, ex p Dove [2000] 1 Cr App Rep (S) 136, 163 JP 657, [1999] Crim LR 760 .... B 12.8
R (on the application of Trigger) v Northampton Magistrates' Court (Northamptonshire Probation Trust and Northamptonshire Crown Prosecution Service, Interested Parties) [2011] EWHC 149 (Admin), (2011) 175 JP 101, [2011] All ER (D) 35 (Feb) .... B 7.2
R (on the application of the Crown Prosecution Service) v Norwich Magistrates' Court [2011] EWHC 82 (Admin), [2011] All ER (D) 249 (Apr) .... D 6.21
R v Norwood [2002] Crim LR 888 .... A 20.11
R (on the application of SR) v Nottingham Magistrates' Court [2001] EWHC Admin 802 (2001) 166 JP 132 .... E 3.17
R v Nottingham Magistrates' Court, ex p Fohmann (1986) 84 Cr App Rep 316, 151 JP 49 .... B 12.2
R v O [2010] EWCA Crim 2233, [2011] 2 All ER 656, 174 JP 529, [2011] Crim LR 403, [2010] All ER (D) 71 (Dec) A31.3A

R v O'Callaghan [2005] EWCA Crim 317, [2005] 2 Cr App Rep (S) 514, [2005] Crim LR 486, [2005] All ER (D) 114 (Feb) .. B 45.2B
R v Odam [2008] EWCA Crim 1087, [2009] 1 Cr App Rep (S) 120 .... A 68.5
R v O'Hare [2006] EWCA Crim 471, [2006] Crim LR 950, [2006] All ER (D) 155 (Mar) .... D 6.19
R v Okoro (No 3) [2018] EWCA Crim 1929, [2019] 1 WLR 1638, [2019] 1 Cr App Rep 15, [2019] Crim LR 447, [2018] All ER (D) 23 (Sep) .... A 43.3
R v Olaniregun (Joseph) [2019] EWCA Crim 1294 .... B 12.8
R v Oldham Justices, ex p Cawley [1997] QB 1, [1996] 1 All ER 464, [1996] 2 WLR 681, 160 JP 133 .... B 28.50, B 28.86
R v Oliver (Gary Lee) (2016) [2016] EWCA Crim 2017 .... C 5.7
R v Olliver and Olliver (1989) 11 Cr App Rep (S) 10, 153 JP 369, [1989] Crim LR 387, CA .... B 10.6
R v O'Neill [2016] EWCA Crim 92, [2016] 2 Cr App Rep 112, 180 JP 252, [2016] All ER (D) 216 (Mar) .... A 41.7
R v O'Reilly [2006] EWCA Crim 794, [2007] 1 WLR 181, [2006] 2 Cr App Rep 231, (2006) Times, 18 April, [2006] All ER (D) 62 (Apr) .... B 8.12
R v Osman (Twana Tofiq) (2017) [2017] EWCA Crim 2178, [2018] 1 Cr App Rep 337 .... A 10.2; D 4.2, D 5.1
R v Owen [1988] 1 WLR 134, 86 Cr App Rep 291, [1988] Crim LR 120, 131 Sol Jo 1696, [1988] 1 LS Gaz R 34, CA .... A 43.4
R v P [2006] All ER (D) 238 (Oct), CA .... A 43.6
R v P (2007) Times, 17 March, CA .... A 19.8
R v P (10 May 2012, unreported) .... B 44.3
R v P W [2016] EWCA Crim 745, [2017] 4 WLR 79, [2016] RTR 844, [2016] 2 Cr App Rep 351 .... A 43.7
R v Page [2004] EWCA Crim 3358, (2004) Times, 23 December, 149 Sol Jo LB 26, [2004] All ER (D) 108 (Dec) .... A 57.38
R v Pakes [2010] EWCA Crim 2803, [2011] 2 Cr App Rep (S) 54, 175 JP 33 .... B 29.7
R v Panayi (No 2) [1989] 1 WLR 187, 88 Cr App Rep 267, [1989] Crim LR 210, 132 Sol Jo 1697, CA .... A 4.5
R v Panton [2001] 19 LS Gaz R 36, CA .... A 26.4
R v Park (1987) 87 Cr App Rep 164, [1988] Crim LR 238, [1988] 14 LS Gaz R 45, CA .... A 40.6
R v Parmenter. See DPP v Parmenter
R v Parsons [2017] EWCA Crim 2163, [2018] 1 WLR 2409, [2018] 1 Cr App Rep (S) 307 .... B 44.3
R v Passmore [2007] EWCA Crim 2053, [2008] 1 Cr App Rep 165, 171 JP 519, 171 JPN 888, (2007) Times, 28 June, [2007] All ER (D) 178 (Jun) .... A 54.3
R v Patel (1994) 16 Cr App Rep (S) 756, [1995] Crim LR 440, CA .... C 5.5
R v Patrascu [2004] EWCA Crim 2417, [2004] 4 All ER 1066, [2005] 1 WLR 3344, [2005] 1 Cr App Rep 577, 168 JP 589, [2005] Crim LR 593, [2004] All ER (D) 167 (Oct) .... A 69.4
R v Pawlicki [1992] 3 All ER 902, [1992] 1 WLR 827, 95 Cr App Rep 246, [1992] Crim LR 584, [1992] 21 LS Gaz R 27, [1992] 30 LS Gaz R 32, 136 Sol Jo LB 104, CA .... A 33.3, A 76.3

R v Pearce [1973] Crim LR 321, CA .... A 65.4
R v Peart [1970] 2 QB 672, [1970] 2 All ER 823, [1970] 3 WLR 63, 54 Cr App Rep 374, 114 Sol Jo 418, CA .... A 65.9
R v Peaston (1978) 69 Cr App Rep 203, [1979] Crim LR 183, [1978] LS Gaz R 1201, CA .... A 25.7
R v Peevey (1973) 57 Cr App Rep 554, CA .... A 25.7
R v Penfold (1995) 16 Cr App Rep (S) 1016, [1995] Crim LR 666, CA .... B 22.7
R v Pereira-Lee (Cheyenn) (2016) [2016] EWCA Crim 1705, [2017] 1 Cr App Rep (S) 122, [2017] Crim LR 243 .... B 9.4
R v Perkins (Robert) [2013] EWCA Crim 323, [2013] 2 Cr App Rep (S) 460, [2013] Crim LR 533, 177 CL&J 251, [2013] All ER (D) 313 (Mar) .... B 45.55
R v Peterborough Magistrates' Court, ex p Allgood (1994) 159 JP 627 .... E 3.18B
R v Phillips (1988) 10 Cr App Rep (S) 419, [1989] Crim LR 160, CA .... B 10.6
R v Pitham (1976) 65 Cr App Rep 45, [1977] Crim LR 285, CA .... A 40.5
R v Plavecz (2002), unreported .... A 2.6
R (on the application of Sainsbury's Supermarkets Ltd) v Plymouth Magistrates Court [2006] EWHC 1749 (Admin), 171 JPN 219, [2006] All ER (D) 137 (Jun) .... D 6.23
R (on the application of Williams) v Pontefract Magistrates' Court [2002] All ER (D) 465 (May) .... F 4.8
R v Porter [2006] EWCA Crim 560, [2007] 2 All ER 625, [2006] 1 WLR 2633, [2006] 2 Cr App Rep 359, (2006) Times, 21 June, 150 Sol Jo LB 396, [2006] All ER (D) 236 (Mar) .... A 43.3
R v Porter [2008] EWCA Crim 1271, [2008] ICR 1259, (2008) Times, 9 July, [2008] All ER (D) 249 (May) .... A 80.19
R v Potter (Marcus) [2019] EWCA Crim 461, [2019] 2 Cr App Rep (S) 36 .... B 13.6
R (on the application of the DPP) v Prestatyn Magistrates' Court [2002] EWHC 1177 (Admin), [2002] Crim LR 924, (2002) Times, 17 October, [2002] All ER (D) 421 (May), DC . A 18.6; D 4.9
R (on the application of Langley) v Preston Crown Court [2008] EWHC 2623 (Admin), [2009] 3 All ER 1026, [2009] 1 WLR 1612, 172 JP 605, 172 JPN 845, [2008] All ER (D) 300 (Oct) .... B 8.12
R v Price [2013] EWCA Crim 1283, [2014] 1 Cr App Rep (S) 216 .... A 17.5; B 9.12
R v Prior [2004] EWCA Crim 1147, [2004] Crim LR 849, [2004] All ER (D) 115 (May) .... A 26.4B
R v Qosja (Robert) (2016) [2016] EWCA Crim 1543, [2017] 1 WLR 311 .... A 41.8B
R v Quayle [2005] EWCA Crim 1415, [2006] 1 All ER 988, [2005] 1 WLR 3642, [2005] 2 Cr App Rep 527, [2006] Crim LR 148, (2005) Times, 22 June, 149 Sol Jo LB 712, [2005] All ER (D) 447 (May) .... A 25.8A
R v Rafferty [1999] 1 Cr App Rep 235, [1998] 2 Cr App Rep (S) 449, 162 JP 353, [1998] Crim LR 433, CA .... B 8.13

R v Rampley [2006] EWCA Crim 2203, [2007] 1 Cr App Rep (S) 542 .... B 44.2
R v Ramsgate Justices, ex p Kazmarek (1984) 80 Cr App Rep 366, 149 JP 16, DC .... B 32.1
R v Rana [2007] EWCA Crim 2261, [2007] All ER (D) 183 (Nov) .... D 6.22
R v Raphael [2008] EWCA Crim 1014, [2008] All ER (D) 159 (May) .... A 57.32
R v Rashid [1977] 2 All ER 237, [1977] 1 WLR 298, 64 Cr App Rep 201, 141 JP 305, [1977] Crim LR 237, 120 Sol Jo 856, CA .... A 38.3
R v Ray [2017] EWCA Crim 1391, [2018] 2 WLR 1148, [2018] 1 Cr App Rep 64, 181 JP 493, [2018] Crim LR 342, [2017] All ER (D) 111 (Sep) .... A 8.20
R (on the application of the Crown Prosecution Service) v Redbridge Youth Court [2005] EWHC 1390 (Admin), 169 JP 393, (2005) Times, 13 July, [2005] All ER (D) 21 (Jun) ...... E 3.18C
R v Rhodes [2015] EWCA Crim 155, [2015] 2 Cr App Rep 235, [2015] Crim LR 445 .... A 76A.4
R v Richards [2006] EWCA Crim 2519, [2007] 1 WLR 847, [2007] 1 Cr App Rep (S) 734, [2007] Crim LR 173, (2006) Times, 13 November, [2006] All ER (D) 338 (Oct) .... B 44.2
R v Rivano (1993) 14 Cr App Rep (S) 578, 158 JP 288, CA .... C 5.9
R v Roberts [2003] EWCA Crim 2753, [2004] 1 WLR 181, 167 JP 675, [2004] Crim LR 141, [2003] 44 LS Gaz R 30, 147 Sol Jo LB 1238, [2003] All ER (D) 325 (Oct) .... A 11.8
R v Robinson-Pierre [2013] EWCA Crim 2396, [2014] 1 WLR 2638, [2014] 1 Cr App Rep 305, 178 JP 45, [2013] All ER (D) 223 (Dec) .... A 72.3
R v Rochester [2018] EWCA Crim 1936, [2019] 1 WLR 1257, [2019] 1 Cr App Rep 208, [2018] Crim LR 1002 .... A 87.4
R v Rogers [2007] UKHL 8, [2007] 2 AC 62, [2007] 2 All ER 433, [2007] 2 WLR 280, [2007] 2 Cr App Rep 99, (2007) Times, 1 March, [2007] All ER (D) 359 (Feb) .... A 18.17, A 20.6
R v Rowe [2008] EWCA Crim 2712, 172 JP 585, 172 JPN 845, [2008] All ER (D) 17 (Nov) .... A 43.3, A 43.7
R v Russell (1991) 94 Cr App Rep 351, CA .... A 27.3A
R v S [2000] 1 Cr App R (S)18 .... E 5.1
R v S (crime: delay in prosecution) [2006] EWCA Crim 756, [2006] 2 Cr App Rep 341, 170 JP 434, [2007] Crim LR 296, 170 JPN 760, (2006) Times, 29 March, [2006] All ER (D) 73 (Mar) .... D 1B.12
R v Saeed Ali [2011] EWCA Crim 2747, 176 JP 1 .... B 16.17
R v Sainthouse [1980] Crim LR 506, CA .... A 40.5
R v Sakalauskas [2013] EWCA Crim 2278, [2014] 1 All ER 1231, [2014] 1 WLR 1204, [2014] 2 Cr App Rep 141, 178 JP 30, [2013] All ER (D) 189 (Nov) .... A 38.3
R v Salisbury and Tisbury and Mere Combined Juvenile Court, ex p Ball [1986] 1 FLR 1, [1985] Fam Law 313, 149 JP 346 ..... F 1.20
R v Salisbury Magistrates' Court, ex p Gray [2000] 1 Cr App Rep (S) 267, 163 JP 732, DC .... D 6.35

R v Sallis [2003] EWCA Crim 233, [2003] 2 Cr App Rep (S) 394, 167 JP 103, [2003] Crim LR 291, (2003) Times, 7 February, [2003] All ER (D) 275 (Jan) .... B 8.9
R v Sanchez (1996) 160 JP 321, [1996] Crim LR 572, CA ...... A 2.6
R v Sanders (1982) 75 Cr App Rep 84, [1982] Crim LR 695, CA .... A 40.6
R v Sarker [2018] EWCA Crim 1341, [2018] 4 All ER 694, [2018] 1 WLR 6023, [2019] 1 Cr App Rep 27, [2018] Crim LR 843, [2018] All ER (D) 61 (Jun) .... D 1B.7
R v Saunders [1985] Crim LR 230, [1985] LS Gaz R 1005, CA .... A 70.6
R v Savage [1992] 1 AC 699, [1991] 2 All ER 220, [1991] 2 WLR 418n, 91 Cr App Rep 317, 154 JP 757, [1990] Crim LR 709, CA; affd [1992] 1 AC 699, [1991] 4 All ER 698, [1991] 3 WLR 914, 94 Cr App Rep 193, 155 JP 935, HL .... A 8.7
R v Scott [2007] EWCA Crim 2757, 172 JP 149, 172 JPN 325, [2007] All ER (D) 191 (Oct) .... D 8.85
R (on the application of Collins) v Secretary of State for Justice [2016] EWHC 33 (Admin), [2016] 3 All ER 490, [2016] 2 WLR 1303, [2016] 1 Cr App Rep 363, [2016] Crim LR 438, (2016) Times, 23 February, [2016] All ER (D) 83 (Jan) .... A 8.20
R (on the application of Gibson) v Secretary of State for Justice [2015] EWCA Civ 1148, [2016] 4 All ER 244, [2017] 1 WLR 1115, 165 NLJ 7678, [2015] All ER (D) 107 (Nov); revsd [2018] UKSC 2, [2018] 2 All ER 478, [2018] 1 WLR 629, [2018] 1 Cr App Rep (S) 389, (2018) Times, 30 January, [2018] All ER (D) 99 (Jan), SC .... B 11.2
R (on the application of OP) v Secretary of State for Justice, Cheltenham Magistrates' Court, CPS (Interested Parties) and Just for Kids (Intervener) [2014] EWHC 1944 (Admin), [2015] 1 Cr App Rep 70, 178 JP 377, [2015] Crim LR 79, [2014] All ER (D) 134 (Jun) .... D 6.13A
R (on the application of Hussain) v Secretary of State for the Home Department [2001] EWHC 555 (Admin) .... A 81.8A
R (on the application of Prothero) v Secretary of State for the Home Department [2013] EWHC 2830 (Admin), [2014] 1 WLR 1195, 155 Sol Jo (no 37) 37, [2013] All ER (D) 156 (Sep) ... A 52.14
R (on the application of the Koppers) v Secretary of State for the Home Department [2015] EWHC 1071 (Admin), [2015] All ER (D) 145 (Apr) .... A 9.5
R (on the application of M) v Secretary of State for Constitutional Affairs and Lord Chancellor. See R (on the application of Kenny) v Leeds Magistrates' Court
R (on the application of Adebowale) v Secretary of State for the Department of Transport [2004] EWHC 1741 (Admin), [2004] All ER (D) 335 (Jun) .... C 5.48
R v Shahabi-Shack [2014] EWCA Crim 2842, [2015] 1 WLR 2602, [2015] 1 Cr App Rep 391, [2015] All ER (D) 117 (Jan) .... A 76A.4
R v Shahadat [2017] EWCA Crim 822, [2017] 2 Cr App Rep (S) 282, [2017] All ER (D) 153 (Jun) .... A 26.5

R v Shanahan [2010] EWCA Crim 98, 174 JP 172, [2010] All ER (D) 157 (Feb) .... A 54.3
R v Sheffield City Justices, ex p Foster (1999) Times, 2 November .... B 38.2
R (on the application of Director of Public Prosecutions) v Sheffield Crown Court [2014] EWHC 2014 (Admin), 178 CL&J 397, [2014] All ER (D) 167 (Jun) .... B 12.19
R v Sheffield Crown Court and Sheffield Stipendiary Magistrate, ex p DPP 15 Cr App Rep (S) 768, (1994) 158 JP 334, [1994] Crim LR 470, DC .... B 8.6
R (on the application of Broadhurst) v Sheffield Justices (2000) 164 JP 870 .... F 4.11
R (on the application C and D) v Sheffield Youth Court [2003] EWHC 35 (Admin), 167 JP 159, [2003] 12 LS Gaz R 29, (2003) Times, 3 February, [2003] All ER (D) 189 (Jan) .... E 3.18C
R (on the application of D) v Sheffield Youth Court [2008] EWHC 601 (Admin), 172 JP 576, [2008] All ER (D) 70 (Mar) ..... B 38.3, B 38.4, B 38.5
R (on the application of D) v Sheffield Youth Court [2008] EWHC 601 (Admin), [2008] All ER (D) 70 (Mar), DC .... B 7.3, B 7.4
R v Sherif [2008] EWCA Crim 2653, [2009] 2 Cr App Rep (S) 235, [2008] All ER (D) 203 (Nov) .... B 34.39A
R v Singh [1989] Crim LR 724, CA .... A 33.8, A 76.6
R v Singh [2000] 1 Cr App Rep 31, [1999] Crim LR 681, CA .... A 69.9
R v Skelton [1995] Crim LR 635, CA .... C 16A.6
R v Skitt [2004] EWCA Crim 3141, [2005] 2 Cr App Rep (S) 122, [2004] All ER (D) 401 (Nov) .... C 5.40
R v Sloggett [1972] 1 QB 430, [1971] 3 All ER 264, [1971] 3 WLR 628, 55 Cr App Rep 532, 135 JP 539, 115 Sol Jo 655, CA .... A 40.6
R v Smethurst [2001] EWCA Crim 772, [2002] 1 Cr App Rep 50, 165 JP 377, [2001] Crim LR 657, (2001) Times, April 13, [2001] All ER (D) 231 (Mar) .... A 43.4
R v Smith [1960] 2 All ER 450. See DPP v Smith [1961] AC 290
R v Smith (Andrew Benjamin) (2000) 164 JP 681, [2000] Crim LR 613, CA .... B 19.4
R v Smith [2002] EWCA Crim 683, [2003] 1 Cr App Rep 212 .... A 43.3; B 29.5
R v Smith [2011] EWCA Crim 66, [2011] 1 Cr App Rep 379, [2011] Crim LR 719, (2011) Times, 28 March, [2011] All ER (D) 105 (Jan) .... A 57.17
R v Smith [2011] EWCA Crim 1772, [2012] 1 All ER 451, [2012] 1 WLR 1316, [2012] 1 Cr App Rep (S) 468, [2011] Crim LR 967, [2011] All ER (D) 189 (Jul) .... B 44.3
R v Smith [2012] EWCA Crim 2566, [2013] 2 All ER 804, [2013] 1 WLR 1399, [2013] 2 Cr App Rep (S) 191, 177 JP 183, [2013] Crim LR 250, [2012] All ER (D) 359 (Nov) .... A 41.13
R (on the application of Purnell) v Snaresbrook Crown Court [2011] EWHC 934 (Admin), [2011] RTR 452, 175 JP 233, [2011] All ER (D) 334 (Mar) .... C 32A 5, C34A.8

R (on the application of Smith) v Snaresbrook Crown Court [2008] EWHC 1282 (Admin), 172 JP 473, 172 JPN 675, [2008] All ER (D) 98 (Jun) .... A 26.12
R v Sofroniou [2003] EWCA Crim 3681, [2004] QB 1218, [2004] 3 WLR 161, [2004] 1 Cr App Rep 460, [2004] Crim LR 381, [2004] 06 LS Gaz R 31, (2004) Times, 5 January, [2003] All ER (D) 362 (Dec) .... A 37.3
R v Sokolowski [2017] EWCA Crim 1903, [2018] 1 Cr App Rep (S) 216, [2018] Crim LR 412 .... B 44.2, B 44.3
R (on the application of Lees) v Solihull Magistrates' Court [2013] EWHC 3779 (Admin), [2014] Lloyd's Rep FC 233, [2013] All ER (D) 60 (Dec) ....F 5.20A
R (on the application of Drinkwater) v Solihull Magistrates Court and Crown Prosecution Service [2012] EWHC 765 (Admin), 176 JP 401, [2012] All ER (D) 206 (Mar) ... D 6.3, D 6.4AA, D 6.17A, D 6.19
R (on the application of Howe) v South Durham Justices [2004] EWHC 362 (Admin), 168 JP 424, [2004] All ER (D) 226 (Feb) .... C 19.6
R v South Tameside Magistrates' Court, ex p Rowland [1983] 3 All ER 689, 148 JP 202 .... D 6.26
R v South Tyneside Justices, ex p Martin (1995) Independent, 20 September .... F 4.10
R (on the application of DPP) v South Tyneside Youth Court [2015] EWHC 1455 (Admin), [2015] 2 Cr App Rep (S) 411, [2015] Crim LR 746, [2015] All ER (D) 186 (May) .... E 3.18C, E 3.18H, E 5.1
R (on the application of Eastenders Barking Ltd) v South Western Magistrates' Court (March 22 2011, unreported), QBD .... F 5.7
R (on the application of Rhodes-Presley) v South Worcestershire Magistrates' Court [2008] EWHC 2700 (Admin), [2008] All ER (D) 92 (Nov) .... B 38.2
R (on the application of Flegg) v Southampton and New Forest Justices [2006] EWHC 396 (Admin), 170 JP 373, (2006) 170 JPN 615, [2006] All ER (D) 271 (Feb) .... C 8.20, C 32A.6
R (on the application of Rathor) v Southampton Magistrates Court [2018] EWHC 3278 (Admin), [2019] Crim LR 431 . B 38.5, D 6.19A
37, [2005] Crim LR 395, [2004] All ER (D) 38 (Dec) .... E 5.1
R (on the application of W) v Southampton Youth Court [2002] EWHC 1640 (Admin), [2003] 1 Cr App Rep (S) 455, 166 JP 569, [2002] Crim LR 750, [2002] All ER (D) 331 (Jul) ...... E 3.18C
R (on the application of Mathialagan) v Southwark London Borough Council [2004] EWCA Civ 1689, [2005] RA 43, (2004) Times, 21 December, [2004] All ER (D) 179 (Dec) .. B 38.4, B 38.6; F 4.6
R v Spence [1999] RTR 353, 163 JP 754, [1999] Crim LR 975, CA .... C 20.8
R v Spencer [2013] EWCA Crim 2286, [2014] 2 Cr App Rep (S) 127, [2013] All ER (D) 50 (Dec) .... B 44.3
R v Stapylton (Ben) [2012] EWCA Crim 728, [2012] All ER (D) 84 (Apr) .... B 10.5

R v Steane [1947] KB 997, [1947] 1 All ER 813, 45 LGR 484, 32 Cr App Rep 61, 111 JP 337, [1947] LJR 969, 91 Sol Jo 279, 177 LT 122, 63 TLR 403, CCA .... A 48.4
R v Steed (1990) 12 Cr App Rep (S) 230, [1990] Crim LR 816, CA .... E 1.2
R v Steele [1993] Crim LR 298, CA .... A 76.8A
R v Stockport Justices, ex p Conlon [1997] 2 All ER 204, 161 JP 81 .... B 28.86
R v Stoke-on-Trent Justices, ex p Knight. See R v Newcastle under Lyme Justices, ex p Massey
R v Stokes [1983] RTR 59, [1982] Crim LR 695, CA .... A 65.4
R (on the application of Newham London Borough Council) v Stratford Magistrates' Court [2008] EWHC 125 (Admin), [2008] RA 108, 173 JP 30, [2008] All ER (D) 17 (Jan) .... B 38.6
R (on the application of Singh) v Stratford Magistrates' Court [2007] EWHC 1582 (Admin), (2007) Times, 13 August, [2007] All ER (D) 30 (Jul) .... B 33.2
R (on the application of the Director of Public Prosecutions) v Stratford Magistrates' Court [2017] EWHC 1794 (Admin), [2017] All ER (D) 112 (Jul) .... A 8.20A
R v Stratford Youth Court, ex p S [1998] 1 WLR 1758, 162 JP 552, [1999] Crim LR 146, [1998] NLJR 870, [1998] All ER (D) 224 .... D 8.51
R v Strong [1989] 10 LS Gaz R 41, CA .... A 25.7
R (on the application of Parashar) v Sunderland Magistrates' Court [2019] EWHC 514 (Admin), [2019] 2 Cr App Rep 18, [2019] LLR 360, [2019] Crim LR 627, [2019] All ER (D) 103 (Mar) .... D 6.17A
R v Sundhers [1998] Crim LR 497, CA A31.3A
R v Swindell [1992] 1 WLR 827, 95 Cr App Rep 246, [1992] Crim LR 584, [1992] 21 LS Gaz R 27, 136 Sol Jo LB 104, CA .. A 33.3, A 76.3
R v T [2008] EWCA Crim 815, [2008] 3 WLR 923, [2008] 2 Cr App Rep 235, 172 JP 335, (2008) Times, 5 May, [2008] All ER (D) 215 (Apr); affd sub nom R v JTB [2009] UKHL 20, [2009] 3 All ER 1, [2009] 2 WLR 1088, [2009] 2 Cr App Rep 189, 173 JP 289, [2009] Crim LR 581, [2009] NLJR 672, 153 Sol Jo (no 18) 27, [2009] All ER (D) 211 (Apr) .... E 3.2
R v Taaffe [1984] AC 539, [1984] 1 All ER 747, [1984] 2 WLR 326, 78 Cr App Rep 301, 148 JP 510, [1984] Crim LR 356, 128 Sol Jo 203, [1984] LS Gaz R 1051, HL .... A 4.5
R v Tait [1990] 1 QB 290, [1989] 3 All ER 682, [1989] 3 WLR 891, 90 Cr App Rep 44, [1989] Crim LR 834, CA .... A 59.4
R v Taj [2018] EWCA Crim 1743, [2018] All ER (D) 153 (Jul) .... A 8.20
R v Tangerine Confectionery Ltd [2011] EWCA Crim 2015, 176 JP 349 .... A 80.19
R v Tao [1977] QB 141, [1976] 3 All ER 65, [1976] 3 WLR 25, 63 Cr App Rep 163, 140 JP 596, [1976] Crim LR 516, 120 Sol Jo 420, CA .... A 27A.2
R v Tata Steel UK Ltd [2017] EWCA Crim 704, [2017] 2 Cr App Rep (S) 233, 167 NLJ 7750, [2017] All ER (D) 32 (Jun) ..... A 80.20

R v Taylor [2016] UKSC 5, [2016] 1 WLR 500, [2016] 1 Cr App Rep 423, 180 JP 165, [2016] Crim LR 366, (2016) Times, 15 February, [2016] All ER (D) 38 (Feb) .... A 66.8A
R v Taylor [2017] EWCA Crim 2209, [2018] 1 Cr App Rep (S) 273 .... A 14.13
R (on the application of Richards) v Teesside Magistrates Court [2015] EWCA Civ 7, [2015] 1 WLR 1695, [2015] 1 Cr App Rep (S) 412, 179 JP 119, [2015] Crim LR 461, (2015) Times, 24 February, [2015] All ER (D) 86 (Jan) .... B 44.2
R v Terry [1984] AC 374, [1984] 1 All ER 65, [1984] 2 WLR 23, [1984] RTR 129, 78 Cr App Rep 101, 128 Sol Jo 34, [1984] LS Gaz R 510, HL .... A 64.4
R v Thelwall [2016] EWCA Crim 1755, [2017] Crim LR 240, [2016] All ER (D) 193 (Oct) .... B 45.1
R v Thorpe [1987] 2 All ER 108, [1987] 1 WLR 383, 85 Cr App Rep 107, [1987] Crim LR 493, 131 Sol Jo 325, [1987] LS Gaz R 819, CA .... A 33.8, A 76.6
R v Tilley [2009] EWCA Crim 1426, 173 JP 393, (2009) Times, 5 August, [2009] All ER (D) 200 (Jul) .... A 54.5
R v Tobierre [1986] 1 All ER 346, [1986] 1 WLR 125, 82 Cr App Rep 212, [1986] Crim LR 243, 130 Sol Jo 35, [1986] LS Gaz R 116, CA .... A 78.8
R (on the application of Reverend Nicolson) v Tottenham Magistrates [2015] EWHC 1252 (Admin), [2015] LGR 867, [2015] RA 543, [2015] PTSR 1045, 179 JP 421, [2015] PLSCS 148, 165 NLJ 7653, [2015] All ER (D) 54 (May) .... F 4.9A
R v Tottenham Youth Court, ex p Fawzy [1998] 1 All ER 365, [1999] 1 WLR 1350, 162 JP 241, sub nom R v Haringey Justices, ex p Fawzy [1998] 1 Cr App Rep 411, DC .... E 1.3
R v Townsend [2018] EWCA Crim 875, [2018] 2 Cr App Rep (S) 278, [2018] Crim LR 870 .... B 8.16
R (on the application of Morsby) v Tower Bridge Magistrates' Court [2007] EWHC 2766 (Admin), 172 JP 155, 172 JPN 372, [2007] All ER (D) 464 (Oct) .... D 6.19
R v Trafford Magistrates' Court, ex p Riley (1995) 160 JP 418 .... A 72.2
R v Trott [2011] EWCA Crim 2395, 175 JP 458 .... A 41.13
R v Tsap [2008] EWCA Crim 2580, 173 JP 4, [2008] All ER (D) 194 (Oct) .... A 11.13
R v Tucker [2016] EWCA Crim 13, 180 JP 225, [2016] All ER (D) 122 (Feb) .... A 11.5
R v Turner [2010] EWCA Crim 2897, [2011] 2 Cr App Rep (S) 102 .... B 17.8
R v Ukoh [2004] EWCA Crim 3270, [2005] Crim LR 314, (2004) Times, 28 December, [2005] All ER (D) 58 (Jan) .... B 17.2
R v Unah [2011] EWCA Crim 1837, 175 JP 391, [2011] 30 LS Gaz R 24, 175 CL&J 503, (2011) Times, 02 August, [2011] All ER (D) 97 (Jul) A32.2A
R (on the application of Akpinar) v Upper Tribunal (Immigration and Asylum Chamber) [2014] EWCA Civ 937, [2015] 2 All ER 870, [2015] 1 WLR 466, (2014) Times, 17 July, [2014] All ER (D) 233 (Jul) .... B 17.8

R v Uxbridge Justices, ex p Metropolitan Police Comr [1981] 1 All ER 940, [1981] 1 WLR 112, 144 JP 432, 124 Sol Jo 828; affd [1981] QB 829, [1981] 3 All ER 129, [1981] 3 WLR 410, 146 JP 42, 125 Sol Jo 445, CA .... F 1.20
R (on the application of Thornhill) v Uxbridge Magistrates' Court [2008] EWHC 508 (Admin), 172 JP 297, 172 JPN 580, [2008] All ER (D) 08 (Mar) .... D 6.23
R v Uxbridge Magistrates' Court, ex p Adimi [2001] QB 667, [1999] 4 All ER 520, [2000] 3 WLR 434, [1999] Imm AR 560, [1999] INLR 490, DC .... A 81.8A
R v Uxbridge Youth Court, ex p Howard (1998) 162 JP 327 . B 49.23
R v Vann and Davis [1996] Crim LR 52, CA .... A 76.8A
R v Vasili [2011] EWCA Crim 615, [2011] 2 Cr App Rep 56, 175 JP 185, [2011] All ER (D) 246 (Feb) A11.5
R v Venna [1976] QB 421, [1975] 3 All ER 788, [1975] 3 WLR 737, 61 Cr App Rep 310, 140 JP 31, 119 Sol Jo 679, CA ... A 8.7, A 15.4
R v Veolia ES (UK) Ltd [2011] EWCA Crim 2015, 176 JP 349 .... A 80.19
R v Vinall [2011] EWCA Crim 2652, [2012] 1 Cr App Rep 400, 175 JP 517, [2012] Crim LR 386, [2011] All ER (D) 107 (Nov) .... A 57.32
R v Vittles [2004] EWCA Crim 1089, [2005] 1 Cr App Rep (S) 31, [2004] All ER (D) 334 (May) .... B 8.3
R v W [2006] EWCA Crim 686, [2006] 3 All ER 562, 170 JPN 716, [2006] All ER (D) 410 (Mar) .... B 13.6
R v Waka [2018] EWCA Crim 125, [2018] 1 Cr App Rep (S) 419, [2018] Crim LR 675 .... A 87.6
R v Wallace [2007] EWCA Crim 1760, [2008] 1 WLR 572, 171 JP 543, [2007] Crim LR 976, [2007] All ER (D) 219 (Jul) .... D 6.14
R v Waller [1991] Crim LR 381, CA .... A 76.8A
R (on the application of Khan) v Waltham Forest Magistrates' Court [2007] EWHC 1801 (Admin), [2007] All ER (D) 29 (Jul) .... D 6.4B, D 6.5
R v Wang [2003] EWCA Crim 3228, (2003) 168 JP 224, [2003] All ER (D) 299 (Dec) .... A 11.12
R v Warley Magistrates' Court, ex p DPP [1999] 1 All ER 251, [1999] 1 WLR 216, [1998] 2 Cr App Rep 307, [1999] 1 Cr App Rep (S) 156, 162 JP 559, [1998] Crim LR 684, [1998] 24 LS Gaz R 33, [1998] NLJR 835, 142 Sol Jo LB 165, DC .... B 8.5
R v Warneford and Gibbs [1994] Crim LR 753, CA .... A 78.6
R v Warwick Quarter Sessions, ex p Patterson (1971) 115 Sol Jo 484 .... B 38.5
R (on the application of Dyer) v Watford Magistrates Court [2013] EWHC 547 (Admin), 177 JP 265, [2013] All ER (D) 88 (Jan) .... B 36.1
R v Watton (1978) 68 Cr App Rep 293, [1979] Crim LR 246, CA .... D 8.93
R v Webbe [2001] EWCA Crim 1217, [2002] 1 Cr App Rep (S) 22 .... A 40.11
R v Webster [2003] EWCA Crim 3597, [2004] 2 Cr App Rep (S) 126, [2004] Crim LR 238, [2003] All ER (D) 313 (Nov) ...... A 12.4

R v Webster [2006] EWCA Crim 415, (2006) Times, 15 March, [2006] All ER (D) 41 (Mar) .... C 16.6
R v West [1964] 1 QB 15, [1962] 2 All ER 624, [1962] 3 WLR 218, 46 Cr App Rep 296, 126 JP 352, 106 Sol Jo 514, CCA .. B 38.5
R (on the application of Knight) v West Dorset Magistrates' Court [2002] EWHC 2152 (Admin), 166 JP 705 .... E 3.25
R (on the application of Hassani) v West London Magistrates' Court [2017] EWHC 1270 (Admin), 181 JP 253, [2017] Crim LR 720, [2017] 3 Costs LR 477 ..... C 22.23, C 22.23A
R (on the application of Vickers) v West London Magistrates' Court [2003] EWHC 1809 (Admin), (2003) 167 JP 473, [2003] All ER (D) 211 (Jul) .... D 8.92
R (on the application of TP) v West London Youth Court [2005] EWHC 2583 (Admin), [2006] 1 All ER 477, [2006] 1 WLR 1219, [2006] 1 Cr App Rep 402, 170 JP 82, 170 JPN 333, [2005] All ER (D) 260 (Nov) .... E 3.25
R v Whibley [1938] 3 All ER 777, 36 LGR 438, 26 Cr App Rep 184, 102 JP 326, 31 Cox CC 58, 82 Sol Jo 478, 158 LT 527, CCA .... A 19.20
R v White (1871) LR 1 CCR 331, 36 JP 134, 40 LJMC 134, 12 Cox CC 83, 19 WR 783, 24 LT 637 .... A 19.19
R v White [2001] EWCA Crim 216 [2001] 1 WLR 1352, [2001] Crim LR 576 .... A 20.6
R v White (2002) Times, 9 December .... D 8.91
R v Whitely (1991) 93 Cr App Rep 25, 155 JP 917, [1991] Crim LR 436, 135 Sol Jo 249, CA .... A 18.22
R v Whiteside [1989] Crim LR 436, CA .... A 38.3
R v Whitton [2006] EWCA Crim 3229, [2007] 2 Cr App Rep (S) 67 .... B 44.2
R v Wickins (1958) 42 Cr App Rep 236, 122 JP 518, CCA ..... C 5.2
R v Widdows [2011] EWCA Crim 1500, [2011] 2 FLR 869, [2011] Fam Law 937, 175 JP 345, [2011] Crim LR 959, [2011] 27 LS Gaz R 22, 175 CL&J 404, [2011] All ER (D) 136 (Jun) .... A 41.7
R (on the application of McDonough) v Wigan Magistrates' Court [2004] EWHC 3272 (Admin), [2005] All ER (D) 304 (Feb) .. B 28.70
R v Wiggins [2001] RTR 37, CA .... C 5.38
R v Wilkinson (James) (2018) [2018] EWCA Crim 2154, [2019] RTR 233 .... A 45.6
R (on the application of Imbeah) v Willesden Magistrates' Court [2016] EWHC 1760 (Admin), [2017] 1 Cr App Rep 24, [2016] All ER (D) 44 (Aug) .... D 6.17B
R v Williams [2010] EWCA Crim 2552, [2011] 3 All ER 969, [2011] 1 WLR 588, [2011] RTR 463, 174 JP 606, [2011] Crim LR 471, 174 CL&J 751, [2010] All ER (D) 19 (Nov) ...... C 16B.5A
R v Wills (Alan Paul) [2011] EWCA Crim 1938, [2012] 1 Cr App Rep 16, [2012] Crim LR 565 .... D 6.13A
R v Wilson [1997] QB 47, [1996] 3 WLR 125, [1996] 2 Cr App Rep 241, [1996] Crim LR 573, 140 Sol Jo LB 93, CA .... A 15.16
R v Wilson [2018] EWCA Crim 1184, [2019] 1 WLR 3916, [2019] RTR 267 .... C 16B.5A

R (on the application of Shea) v Winchester Crown Court [2013] EWHC 1050 (DC) .... D 8.66
R v Windsor [2011] EWCA Crim 143, [2011] 2 Cr App Rep 71, 175 CL&J 110, (2011) Times, 03 March, [2011] All ER (D) 91 (Feb) .... F 5.7
R v Winston [1999] 1 Cr App Rep 337, 162 JP 775, [1999] Crim LR 81, [1998] 34 LS Gaz R 32, 142 Sol Jo LB 246, CA .... A 78.9
R (on the application of Daniel Thwaites plc) v Wirral Borough Magistrates' Court [2008] EWHC 838 (Admin), [2009] 1 All ER 239, 172 JP 301, [2008] NLJR 707, [2008] All ER (D) 61 (May) .... F 2.19
R (on the application of Jermyn) v Wirral Magistrates' Court [2001] Crim LR 45, [2000] All ER (D) 1478, DC .... B 8.2
R v Wise (Darren) [2012] EWCA Crim 995, 176 JP 337, 176 CL&J 322, [2012] All ER (D) 130 (May) .... B 29.7
R v Wise (Ryan) [2012] EWCA Crim 995, 176 JP 337, 176 CL&J 322, [2012] All ER (D) 130 (May) .... B 29.7
R v Wolstenholme [2016] EWCA Crim 638, [2016] 2 Cr App Rep (S) 168 .... B 34.50
R v Wolverhampton Stipendiary Magistrate, ex p Mould (1992) Times, 16 November .... F 4.15
R v Woods [2005] EWCA Crim 2065, [2006] 1 Cr App Rep (S) 477, [2005] Crim LR 982 .... A 1.4
R v Woodward [2017] EWHC 1008 (Admin), 181 JP 405, [2017] Crim LR 884, [2017] All ER (D) 41 (May) .... A 5.2
R v Wright (1975) 62 Cr App Rep 169, 119 Sol Jo 825, CA .. A 25.7
R v Wright [2011] EWCA Crim 1180, [2011] 2 Cr App Rep 168 .... A26.4
R v Yehou [1997] 2 Cr App Rep (S) 48, CA .... B 10.6
R v ZN [2013] EWCA Crim 989, [2013] 4 All ER 331, [2013] 1 WLR 3900, [2013] 2 Cr App Rep 275, 177 JP 639, (2013) Times, 07 August, [2013] All ER (D) 159 (Jun) .... A 69.4
R v Zinga [2012] EWCA Crim 2357, [2013] Crim LR 226, [2012] All ER (D) 92 (Nov) .... F 5.1
R (on the application of Virgin Media Ltd) v Zinga [2014] EWCA Crim 1823, [2015] 1 Cr App Rep 14, [2015] 1 Cr App Rep (S) 74, 178 JP 449, [2014] 5 Costs LR 879, [2014] All ER (D) 90 (Sep) .... B 12.6
R & S Pilling trading as Phoenix Engineering v UK Insurance Ltd [2019] UKSC 16, [2019] 3 All ER 917, [2019] 2 WLR 1015, [2019] RTR 358, 169 NLJ 7835, [2019] All ER (D) 132 (Mar), SC .... C 33.9
Radford v Kent County Council (1998) 162 JP 697 .... D 6.22
Rafiq v DPP (1997) 161 JP 412, DC .... A 72.5
Read v Donovan [1947] KB 326, [1947] 1 All ER 37, 45 LGR 28, 111 JP 46, [1947] LJR 849, 91 Sol Jo 101, 176 LT 124, 63 TLR 89, DC .... A 33.8, A 76.6
Reader v Bunyard [1987] RTR 406, 85 Cr App Rep 185, [1987] Crim LR 274, DC .... C 9.7
Reading Borough Council v Ali [2019] EWHC 200 (Admin), [2019] 1 WLR 2635, [2019] RTR 405, [2019] LLR 389, [2019] All ER (D) 64 (Feb) A56.2

Redhead Freight Ltd v Shulman [1989] RTR 1, [1988] Crim LR 696 .... C 9.5
Redknapp v Comr of the City of London Police Department [2008] EWHC 1177 (Admin), 172 JP 388, [2008] NLJR 861, 172 JPN 548, (2008) Times, 16 June, [2008] All ER (D) 319 (May) .... F 5.20A
Redmond-Bate v DPP (1999) 163 JP 789, [1999] Crim LR 998, 7 BHRC 375, DC .... A 9.5, A 47.13
Regentford Ltd v Thanet District Council [2004] EWHC 246 (Admin), [2004] RA 113, [2004] 11 LS Gaz R 35, [2004] TLR 143, (2004) Times, 4 March, [2004] All ER (D) 285 (Feb) ...... F 4.2
Regina v B [2018] EWCA Crim 1439, [2019] 1 WLR 3177, [2019] 1 Cr App Rep 498, CA .... A 52.6
Regina v Jackson (David Gareth) [2018] EWCA Crim 1840, [2019] 4 WLR 43, [2019] 2 Cr App Rep 56, CA .... A 52.4
Reynolds v Beasley [1919] 1 KB 215, 17 LGR 29, 83 JP 35, 88 LJKB 466, 120 LT 271, 35 TLR 115, DC .... A 48.6
Rice v Connolly [1966] 2 QB 414, [1966] 2 All ER 649, [1966] 3 WLR 17, 130 JP 322, 110 Sol Jo 371, DC .... A 47.9
Richards v National Probation Service [2007] EWHC 3108 (Admin), 172 JP 100, 172 JPN 293, 172 JPN 357, [2007] All ER (D) 454 (Nov) .... A 17.2
Richardson v Director of Public Prosecutions [2019] EWHC 428 (Admin), [2019] 4 WLR 46, [2019] Crim LR 733, [2019] All ER (D) 39 (Mar) .... C 20.7
Ricketts v Cox (1981) 74 Cr App Rep 298, [1982] Crim LR 184, DC .... A 47.9
Ridehalgh v Horsefield [1994] Ch 205, [1994] 3 All ER 848, [1994] 3 WLR 462, [1994] 2 FLR 194, [1994] Fam Law 560, [1994] BCC 390, (1994) Times, 28 January .... B 12.19
Riley v Crown Prosecution Service [2016] EWHC 2531 (Admin), 181 JP 96, [2017] Crim LR 222, [2016] All ER (D) 146 (Oct) .... A 5.2, D 6.13
Robinson v DPP [2003] EWHC 2718 (Admin), (2003) 168 JP 522, [2004] Crim LR 670, [2003] All ER (D) 05 (Nov) .... C 22.25
Roper v Taylor's Central Garages (Exeter) Ltd. See Taylor's Central Garages (Exeter) Ltd v Roper
Ross v Moss [1965] 2 QB 396, [1965] 3 All ER 145, [1965] 3 WLR 416, 63 LGR 321, 129 JP 537, 109 Sol Jo 475 .... A 62.3
Royal Society for the Prevention of Cruelty to Animals v Johnson [2009] EWHC 2702 (Admin), [2009] All ER (D) 177 (Oct) .... A 5.2
Royal Society for the Prevention of Cruelty to Animals v Mccormick [2016] EWHC 928 (Admin), [2016] 1 WLR 2641, 180 JP 288, 166 NLJ 7698, [2016] All ER (D) 05 (May) ...... A 5.2
Rudd v Secretary of State for Trade and Industry [1987] 2 All ER 553, [1987] 1 WLR 786, 85 Cr App Rep 358, 151 JP 610, 131 Sol Jo 805, [1987] LS Gaz R 2192, HL .... A 61.3
Ruiz Torija v Spain (1994) 19 EHRR 542, ECtHR .... D 1A.3
Rushmoor Borough Council v Richards (1996) 160 LG Rev 460 .... F 2.14
Rweikiza v DPP [2008] EWHC 386 (Admin), [2008] All ER (D) 259 (Jan) .... C 23.3

Rymer v DPP [2010] EWHC 1848 (Admin), [2011] RTR 65, 174 JP 473, 174 CL&J 526, [2010] All ER (D) 219 (Jul) .... D 6.26

S

S v DPP [2006] EWHC 1207 (Admin), 170 JP 707, 171 JPN 161, [2006] All ER (D) 280 (Apr) .... D 6.17B
S v DPP (8 February 2008, unreported) .... A 10.3A
S (an infant) v Manchester City Recorder [1971] AC 481, [1969] 3 All ER 1230, [1970] 2 WLR 21, 134 JP 3, 113 Sol Jo 872, HL .... B 38.5; D 6.26
S v Poole Borough Council [2002] EWHC 244 (Admin) [2002] All ER (D) 143 (Feb) .... B 8.4
Sagnata Investments Ltd v Norwich Corpn [1971] 2 QB 614, [1971] 2 All ER 1441, [1971] 3 WLR 133, 69 LGR 471, 115 Sol Jo 406, CA .... F 2.19
Sahin v Havard [2016] EWCA Civ 1202, [2017] 4 All ER 157, [2017] 1 WLR 1853, [2017] 2 All ER (Comm) 851, [2017] RTR 118, [2017] Lloyd's Rep IR 110, [2016] All ER (D) 21 (Dec) . C 33.9
Sayce v Coupe [1953] 1 QB 1, [1952] 2 All ER 715, 116 JP 552, 96 Sol Jo 748, [1952] 2 TLR 664, DC .... A 4.4
Schneider v Dawson [1960] 2 QB 106, [1959] 3 All ER 583, [1959] 3 WLR 960, 124 JP 7, 103 Sol Jo 962, DC .... A 4.4
Secretary of State for the Environment, Transport and the Regions v Holt [2000] RTR 309 .... C 47.7
Secretary of State for the Home Department v AV (Democratic Republic of the Congo) [2014] EWCA Civ 937, [2015] 2 All ER 870, [2015] 1 WLR 466, (2014) Times, 17 July, [2014] All ER (D) 233 (Jul) .... B 17.8
Secretary of State for the Home Department v Tuncel [2012] EWHC 402 (Admin), [2012] 1 WLR 3355, (2012) Times, 10 May, [2012] All ER (D) 191 (Feb) .... F 5.47
Sekfali v DPP [2006] EWHC 894 (Admin), 170 JPN 736, [2006] All ER (D) 381 (Feb) .... A 47.9
Selby v Chief Constable of Avon and Somerset [1988] RTR 216 .... C 31.8
Sharma v Director Of Public Prosecutions [2018] EWHC 3330 (Admin), [2019] 2 Cr App Rep 111 .... A 11.9
Shaw v DPP [2007] EWHC 207 (Admin), 171 JP 254, 171 JPN 460, [2007] All ER (D) 197 (Jan) .... D 6.23
Sheldrake v DPP [2003] EWHC 273 (Admin), [2004] QB 487, [2003] 2 All ER 497, [2003] 2 WLR 1629, [2003] 2 Cr App Rep 206, 167 JP 333, [2004] RTR 13, [2003] 13 LS Gaz R 30; revsd [2004] UKHL 43, [2004] 3 WLR 976 .... C 21.4A, C 22.64
Sills v DPP [2006] EWHC 3383 (Admin), 171 JP 201, 171 JPN 514, [2006] All ER (D) 165 (Oct) .... A 11.5
Singh v DPP [1999] RTR 424, 164 JP 82, [1999] Crim LR 914 .... C 19.6
Singleton v Ellison [1895] 1 QB 607, 59 JP 119, 64 LJMC 123, 18 Cox CC 79, 15 R 201, 43 WR 426, 72 LT 236, [1895–9] All ER Rep Ext 2181, DC .... A 44.3

Skinner v DPP [2004] EWHC 2914 (Admin), [2005] RTR 202, [2004] All ER (D) 441 (Nov) .... C 22.23
Smith v DPP and Morris [2000] RTR 36, 164 JP 96, [1999] 32 LS Gaz R 34, [1999] 34 LS Gaz R 34 .... C 25.11
Smith v Royal Society For The Prevention Of Cruelty To Animals [2017] EWHC 3536 (Admin) .... D 6.17C
Sobczak v DPP [2012] EWHC 1319 (Admin), 176 JP 575, 176 CL&J 371, [2012] All ER (D) 29 (May) .... A 9.5, A 9.8
Soni (appeal against a wasted costs order), Re [2019] EWCA Crim 1304, [2019] 4 WLR 103, [2019] All ER (D) 33 (Aug) .... B 12.20
Southard v DPP [2006] EWHC 3449 (Admin), [2006] All ER (D) 101 (Nov) .... A 20.3A
Stannard v Crown Prosecution Service [2019] EWHC 84 (Admin), [2019] All ER (D) 107 (Jan) .... B 8A.5
Steel v United Kingdom (1999) 28 EHRR 603, [1998] Crim LR 893, 5 BHRC 339, ECtHR .... B 5.20
Stepney Borough Council v Joffe [1949] 1 KB 599, [1949] 1 All ER 256, 47 LGR 189, 113 JP 124, [1949] LJR 561, 93 Sol Jo 119, 65 TLR 176, DC .... F 2.19
Stevens and Stevens v Christy (1987) 85 Cr App Rep 249, 151 JP 366, [1987] Crim LR 503, DC .... A 44.3
Stewart v Doncaster Youth Offending Team [2003] EWHC 1128 (Admin), 167 JP 381, [2003] All ER (D) 269 (May) .... B 19.9
Stinton v Stinton [1995] RTR 167, [1995] 01 LS Gaz R 37, sub nom Stinton v Motor Insurers Bureau 159 JP 656, [1999] Lloyd's Rep IR 305, CA .... C 9.4
Strath v Foxon [1956] 1 QB 67, [1955] 3 All ER 398, [1955] 3 WLR 659, 39 Cr App Rep 162, 119 JP 581, 99 Sol Jo 799, DC .... A 44.3
Street v DPP [2004] EWHC 86 (Admin), (2004) Times, 23 January, [2004] All ER (D) 70 (Jan) .... A 71.3
Sunworld Ltd v Hammersmith and Fulham London Borough Council [2000] 2 All ER 837, [2000] 1 WLR 2102, [2018] LLR 646, [1999] All ER (D) 1306 .... D 6.48
Swanston v DPP (1996) 161 JP 203, DC .... A 21.7
Sweet v Parsley [1970] AC 132, [1969] 1 All ER 347, [1969] 2 WLR 470, 53 Cr App Rep 221, 133 JP 188, 113 Sol Jo 86, 209 Estates Gazette 703, HL .... A 66.8A
Syed v DPP [2010] EWHC 81 (Admin), [2010] 1 Cr App Rep 480, 174 JP 97, [2010] 04 LS Gaz R 14, (2010) Times, 26 January, [2010] All ER (D) 48 (Jan) .... A 9.8

T

T (a minor), Re. See KDT (a minor)
T v DPP [2003] EWHC 266 (Admin), [2003] Crim LR 622 .... A 8.9
T v DPP [2004] EWHC 183 (Admin), (2004) 168 JP 313, 148 Sol Jo LB 149, [2004] All ER (D) 278 (Jan) .... A 8.9, A 15.7, A 20.6
Talbot v DPP [2000] 1 WLR 1102, 164 JP 169, [2000] Crim LR 326, [2000] 05 LS Gaz R 33, sub nom Talbot v Oxford City Magistrates' Court [2000] 2 Cr App Rep 60 .... A 79.3

Taylor v DPP [2006] EWHC 1202 (Admin), 170 JP 485, 170 JPN 856, (2006) Times, 14 June, [2006] All ER (D) 271 (Apr) .. A 20.6, A 20.8
Taylor's Central Garages (Exeter) Ltd v Roper [1951] WN 383, 115 JP 445, sub nom Roper v Taylor's Central Garages (Exeter) Ltd [1951] 2 TLR 284 .... C 9.6
Telegraph Group plc, ex p [2001] EWCA Crim 1075, [2001] 1 WLR 1983, (2001) Times, 12 June, CA .... D 1B.7
Tester v DPP [2015] EWHC 1353 (Admin), [2015] Crim LR 812 .... A 9.5
Thomas v News Group Newspapers Ltd [2001] EWCA Civ 1233, [2001] 34 LS Gaz R 43, (2001) Times, 25 July, 145 Sol Jo LB 207, [2002] EMLR 78, [2001] All ER (D) 246 (Jul) .... A 41.7
Thomson (Procurator Fiscal) v Jackson [2010] HCJAC 96, [2011] RTR 210, 2010 SCCR 915, HC of Justiciary (Sc) .... C 8.21
Thornton v CPS [2010] 2 Cr App Rep (S) 434, [2010] Crim LR 514, 174 CL&J 109, [2010] All ER (D) 48 (Feb), DC .... B 8.7
Thornton v Crown Prosecution Service [2010] EWHC 346 (Admin), 174 JP 121 .... D 6.33
Times Newspapers Ltd, Re [2016] EWCA Crim 887, [2016] 1 WLR 4366, [2016] 2 Cr App Rep 367, [2016] Crim LR 939, [2016] All ER (D) 145 (Jul) .... D 1B.7
Tora Tolinos v Spain (No 23816/94) (17 May 1995, unreported), ECtHR .... C 8.22
Torbay Borough Council v Cross (1995) 159 JP 682 .... A 85.3
Torbay Council v Singh [1999] 2 Cr App Rep 451, [2000] FSR 158, 163 JP 744, [1999] IP & T 54, [1999] NLJR 1002, [1999] All ER (D) 625 .... A 60.3
Trans Berckx BVBA v North Avon Magistrates' Court [2011] EWHC 2605 (Admin) .... B 18.9
Travel-Gas (Midlands) Ltd v Reynolds [1989] RTR 75 ...... C 38.16
Traves v DPP. See R (on the application of Traves) v DPP
Trinity Mirror plc (A and B (Minors, acting by the Official Solicitor to the Supreme Court) Intervening), Re [2008] EWCA Crim 50, [2008] 2 All ER 1159, [2008] 3 WLR 51, [2008] 2 Cr App Rep 1, (2008) Times, 13 February, [2008] All ER (D) 12 (Feb), sub nom R (on the application of Trinity Mirror plc) v Croydon Crown Court [2008] QB 770, [2008] Crim LR 554, [2009] EMLR 61 .... D 1B.7
Troughton v Metropolitan Police [1987] Crim LR 138, DC . A 45.6A

U

UK Insurance Ltd v Holden [2016] EWHC 264 (QB), [2016] 3 All ER 727, [2016] 4 WLR 38, [2016] 2 CMLR 1104, [2016] RTR 233, [2016] Lloyd's Rep IR 349, [2016] All ER (D) 228 (Feb); revsd sub nom UK Insurance Ltd v R&S Pilling trading as Phoenix Engineering [2017] EWCA Civ 259, [2017] 4 All ER 199, [2017] 3 WLR 450, [2017] RTR 385, [2017] Lloyd's Rep IR 463, (2017) Times, 30 May, [2017] All ER (D) 122 (Apr) . C 33.9

V

Vehicle and Operator Services Agency v F & S Gibbs Transport Services Ltd [2006] EWHC 1109 (Admin), (2006) 170 JP 586, [2006] All ER (D) 84 (May) .... C 38.18A
Vehicle Inspectorate v Nuttall (t/a Redline Coaches) [1999] 3 All ER 833, [1999] 1 WLR 629, [1999] RTR 264, [1999] IRLR 656, [1999] Crim LR 674, [1999] 16 LS Gaz R 36, 143 Sol Jo LB 111, HL .... C 9.6
Verderers of the New Forest v Young [2004] EWHC 2954 (Admin), [2004] All ER (D) 14 (Dec) .... F 4.6
Vigon v DPP (1997) 162 JP 115, [1998] Crim LR 289 .... A 20.9

W

W v DPP. See R (on the application of W) v DPP
W v Hertfordshire County Council. See Hertfordshire County Council v W
Waite v Smith [1986] Crim LR 405, [1985] Lexis Citation 2144, DC .... C 22.23
Waite v Taylor (1985) 149 JP 551, [1985] LS Gaz R 1092 .... A 85.3
Walker v Comr of the Police of the Metropolis [2014] EWCA Civ 897, [2015] 1 WLR 312, [2015] 1 Cr App Rep 283, (2014) Times, 16 July, [2014] All ER (D) 22 (Jul) .... A 9.8
Walkling v DPP (2004) Independent, 26 January .... B 8.13
Waltham Forest London Borough Council v Mills (1979) 78 LGR 248, [1980] RTR 201, [1980] Crim LR 243, DC .... A 85.3
Ward (Anthony) v Royal Society for the Prevention of Cruelty to Animals [2010] EWHC 347 (Admin) .... A 5.4
Wastell v Woodward [2017] Lloyd's Rep IR 474 .... C 33.9
Webb v Chief Constable of Avon and Somerset Constabulary (Secretary of State for Food Environment and Rural Affairs intervening) [2017] EWHC 3311 (Admin), (2018) Times, 31 January, [2018] All ER (D) 68 (Jan) .... A 72.10
Weightman v DPP [2007] EWHC 634 (Admin), [2007] RTR 565, [2007] All ER (D) 77 (Mar), DC .... C 34A.9
Weise v UK Border Agency (Christopher Hendrik) (29 June 2012, unreported), CA .... F 5.47A
Welham v DPP [1961] AC 103, [1960] 1 All ER 805, [1960] 2 WLR 669, 44 Cr App Rep 124, 124 JP 280, 104 Sol Jo 308, HL .... A 64.4
Wellingborough District Council v Gordon (1990) 155 JP 494, [1991] JPL 874 .... A 84.17
Welton v Taneborne (1908) 6 LGR 891, 72 JP 419, 21 Cox CC 702, 99 LT 668, 24 TLR 873, DC .... B 36.1
West Midlands Probation Board v Sutton Coldfield Magistrates' Court [2008] EWHC 15 (Admin), [2008] 3 All ER 1193, 172 JP 169, [2008] NLJR 102, [2008] All ER (D) 03 (Jan), sub nom West Midlands Probation Board v Sadler [2008] 1 WLR 918 .... A 17.2

West Yorkshire Probation Board v Boulter [2005] EWHC 2342 (Admin), [2006] 1 WLR 232, 169 JP 601, [2005] 42 LS Gaz R 24, (2005) Times, 11 October, [2005] All ER (D) 54 (Oct) .... A 17.2
West Yorkshire Probation Board v Cruickshanks [2010] EWHC 615 (Admin), 174 JP 305, [2010] All ER (D) 239 (Mar) ...... B 34.46
West Yorkshire Probation Board v Robinson and Tinker [2009] EWHC 2468 (Admin), 174 JP 13, [2009] All ER (D) 197 (Jul) .... B 9.24
West Yorkshire Trading Standards Service v Lex Vehicle Leasing Ltd [1996] RTR 70 .... C 9.4
Westminster City Council v Haw [2002] All ER (D) 59 (Oct) . C 36.4
Westminster City Council v Owadally [2017] EWHC 1092 (Admin), [2017] 2 Cr App Rep 223, [2017] Crim LR 806, (2017) Times, 22 June, [2017] All ER (D) 114 (May) .... D 4.3
Whiley v DPP [1995] Crim LR 39 .... A 61.3
Whiteside v DPP [2011] EWHC 3471 (Admin), 176 JP 103, [2011] All ER (D) 191 (Dec) .... C 34A.7
Whittaker v Campbell [1984] QB 318, [1983] 3 All ER 582, [1983] 3 WLR 676, [1984] RTR 220, 77 Cr App Rep 267, [1983] Crim LR 812, 127 Sol Jo 714 .... A 65.8
Wildman v DPP [2001] EWHC Admin 14, 165 JP 453, (2001) Times, 8 February, [2001] All ER (D) 137 (Jan) .... D 8.52
Williams v DPP [1992] Crim LR 503 .... A 28.6
Williams v DPP [2009] EWHC 2354 (Admin), [2009] All ER (D) 292 (Jul) .... D 6.23
Williams v East Northamptonshire District Council [2016] EWHC 470 (Admin), [2016] RA 191, [2016] All ER (D) 95 (Mar) .... F 4.9A
Williams v Richards (1997) Times, 29 July .... C 51.10
Winn v DPP (1992) 156 JP 881, [1992] NLJR 527, DC .... A 21.5
Winter v Woolfe [1931] 1 KB 549, 29 LGR 89, 95 JP 20, 100 LJKB 92, 29 Cox CC 214, [1930] All ER Rep 623, 144 LT 311, 47 TLR 145, CCA .... A 44.3
Wisdom v McDonald [1983] RTR 186, [1982] Crim LR 758, DC .... C 36.2
Wolverton UDC v Willis (t/a S G Willis & Sons) [1962] 1 All ER 243, [1962] 1 WLR 205, 60 LGR 135, 126 JP 84, 106 Sol Jo 153, DC .... A 85.3
Wood v DPP [2008] EWHC 1056 (Admin), (2008) Times, 23 May, [2008] All ER (D) 162 (May) .... A 9.8
Woolls v North Somerset Council [2016] EWHC 1410 (Admin), [2016] Crim LR 765 .... D 1B.11
Wragg v DPP [2005] EWHC 1389 (Admin), [2005] All ER (D) 131 (Jun) .... A 9.5, A 9.8
Wright v Taplin [1986] RTR 388n, DC .... C 22.23

Y

Yagci and Sargin v Turkey (Applications 16419/90, 16426/90) (1995) 20 EHRR 505, ECtHR .... D 1A.4

Z

Zafar v DPP [2004] EWHC 2468 (Admin), [2005] RTR 220, 169 JP 208, (2005) Times, 7 January, 148 Sol Jo LB 1315, [2004] All ER (D) 06 (Nov) .... C 23.3
Zofar v DPP (2004) Times, 1 November .... C 22.10
Zykin v Crown Prosecution Service [2009] EWHC 1469 (Admin), 173 JP 361, [2009] All ER (D) 303 (Oct) .... B 38.5

Section A

Criminal offences dealt with in magistrates' courts

Index to criminal offences and table of maximum penalties

Set out below are a number of maximum penalties for some common offences. If an offence is dealt with more fully in this book the relevant paragraph is stated.

† or + Penalty on summary conviction of an offence triable either way.

* Indicates that the police may issue a fixed penalty ticket

For index and penalties for road traffic offences, see **C[1]**

Absconding level 5 and 3 months **A[10]**

Abstracting/using electricity level 5 and/or 6 months † **A[1]**

Abusive words or behaviour level 5 and 6 months **A[21]**

Actual bodily harm level 5 and 6 months † **A[8]**

Affray level 5 and 6 months † **A[2]**

Aggravated vehicle-taking level 5 and 6 months **A[66]**

Air gun in public place (FA 1968, s 22(5)) level 3 forfeiture **A[71]**

Airports (Aviation Security Act 1982)
false statements relating to baggage, cargo, etc (s 21A) level 5
false statements in connection with identity documents (s 21B) level 5
unauthorised presence in restricted zone (s 21C) level 5
unauthorised presence on board aircraft (s 21D) level 5
intentionally obstructing an authorised person (s 21E(1)(a)) level 5
impersonating an authorised person (s 21E(1)(b)) level 5

Alcohol sale offences level 3 **A[3]**

Alcohol/tobacco, fraudulently evade duty (See Customs duty) **A[4]**

Ammunition (FA 1968, s 1) (*See* Firearms) level 5 and 6 months, forfeiture **A[36]**

Animal cruelty £20,000 and/or 6 months (ss 4, 8 and 9) level 5 and 6 months **A[5]**

Animals straying on highway level 3

Anti-social behaviour order – breach level 5 and 6 months † **A[6]**, **B[2]** and **B[8.15]**

Arson (see Criminal damage)

Article with blade or point in public place (CJA 1988, s 139) level 5 and 6 months † **A[11]**

Assault (*See* Actual bodily harm, Common assault, Indecent assault, Grievous bodily harm, Wounding)

Assault on police constable or person assisting police constable level 5 and 6 months **A[9]**

Assault with intent to resist arrest level 5 and 6 months † **A[7]**

Assaulting an emergency worker (Assaults on Emergency Workers (Offences) Act 2018, s 3) 6 months **A[9A]**

Avoiding customs duty (*See* Customs duty) **A[4]**

Bail, failure to surrender (Bail Act 1976, s 6) 12 months **A[10]**

Bankrupt (undischarged, obtaining credit) level 5 and 6 months †

Begging level 3

Bladed article/offensive weapon, possession of (PCA 1953, s 1(1), CJA 1988, ss 139(1), 139A(1), (2) and PA 1952, 40CA) 4 years **A[11]**

Breach of disqualification from keeping an animal (Animal Welfare Act 2006, s 32) 6 months' **A[5.5]**

Breach of the peace (*See* Insulting words, and *see* **B[5] for Binding over) A[21]**

Breach of a non-molestation order (Family Law Act 1996, s 42A) level 5 and 6 months † **A[46]**

Bribery (Bribery Act 2010)
Bribing another person (s 1) level 5 and/or 6 months † **A[89]**
Being bribed (s 2) level 5 and/or 6 months † **A[89]**
Bribery of foreign public officials (s 6) level 5 and/or 6 months † **A[89]**
Failure of commercial organisations to prevent bribery (s 7) indictable only **A[89]**

Breach of a protective order (restraining and non- molestation orders) (Protection from Harassment Act 1997, s 5, Family Law Act 1996, s 42A) 5 years' **A[46]**

Brothel level 3 and 3 months; level 4 and 6 months (second or subsequent offence in relation to a brothel) **For keeping a brothel used for prostitution** see **A[44]**

Builder's skip
depositing on highway level 3
not complying with a condition level 3
unlit on roadway level 3

Burglary in a dwelling (domestic burglary) level 5 and 6 months † **A[12]**

Burglary in a building other than a dwelling (non-domestic burglary) level 5 and/or 6 months † **A[13]**

Car dumping (*See* Litter) **A[83]**

Child prostitution and pornography (includes possession of extreme photographic images) level 5 and 6 months † **A[14]**

Children (cruelty to) level 5 and 6 months † **A[19]**

Chimes level 5 **A[34]**

Common assault level 5 and 6 months **A[15]**

Communications network offences Communications Act 2003, s 127 (1) and (2)) level 5 and/or 6 months **A[16]**

Community order, breach of (CJA, 2003, Sch 8, for powers of the court see) **A[17]**

Computers (Computer Misuse Act 1990)
unauthorised access to computer material (s 1) level 5 and 6 months
unauthorised access with intent to commit or facilitate further offences (s 2) level 5 and 6 months
unauthorised modification of computer material (s 3) level 5 and 6 months †

Contempt of court level 4 and 1 month **D[3]**

Controlling or coercive behaviour in an intimate or family relationshi (SCA 2015, s 76) 5 years' **A[17A]**

Controlled drugs Penalty varies with classification of drug **A[22]**

Copying false instrument level 5 and 6 months † **A[78]**

Court security officer
assault level 5 and 6 months **A[9]**
obstruction level 3 **A[47]**

Criminal damage Penalties vary with value of property **A[18]–A[18B]**

Crossbow (draw weight 1.4kg or more) (Crossbows Act 1987)
sell or lease to person under 17 level 5 and 6 months, forfeiture
buying or hiring by person under 17 level 3, forfeiture
possession of by person under 17 level 3, forfeiture

Cruelty to animals £20,000 fine and/or 6 months (ss 4 and 8) level 5 and 6 months (s 9) **A[5]**

Cruelty to a child level 5 and 6 months † **A[19]**

Customs duty (avoiding) 3 times value of goods or £5,000 and 6 months (**12months)† **A[4]**

Damaging property Penalty varies with value of damage **A[18]–A[18B]**

Dangerous dog A[72]

Dangerous drugs (*See* Controlled drugs) **A[22]**

Dangerous machinery level 5†

Disclosing private sexual images (CJCA 2015, s 33) 2 years' **A[19A]**

Dishonestly handling level 5 and 6 months † **A[49]**

Disorderly behaviour (Public Order Act 1986, s 5) level 3 **A[20]**

Displaying indecent matter level 5

Disposal of property in police possession A[66]

Dogs
Dangerous Dogs Act 1991
- breeding or parting with, etc, fighting dogs (s 1(2)) level 5 and 6 months
- fighting dog in public place without muzzle and lead (s 1(2)) level 5 and 6 months
- dog dangerously out of control (whether or not in a public place) and injury to a person or death/injury of an assistance dog level 5 and 6 months + (if aggravated offence) **A[72]**

control order (Dogs Act 1871) **A[72]**
dog worrying livestock level 3 **A[73]**

Domestic Violence (see breach of a non-molestation order)

Drugs (controlled) Penalty varies with classification of drug **A[22]–A[27B]**

Drunk in a highway, public place or licensed premises level 2 **A[28]**

Drunk and disorderly level 3 **A[28]**

Drunk at, or on the way to, a football match level 2 **A[76]**

Earnings of prostitution (living on) level 5 and 6 months †

Electricity, abstract/use without authority level 5 and/or 6 months † **A[1]**

Enclosed premises (found on) level 3 or 3 months (**level 3 only) **A[79]**

Excessive noise (nuisance order) level 5 **A[74]**

Exclusion order (licensed premises), breach of level 4 and 1 month **B[27]**

Exploitation of Prostitution – causing or inciting prostitution for gain; controlling prostitution for gain (Sexual Offences Act 2003, ss 52, 53) level 5 and 6 months † **A[29]**

Exposure (Sexual Offences Act 2003, s 66) level 5 and/or 6 months † A[30]

Failure to maintain oneself or a dependant
level 3 or (and, depending on the facts) 3 months (National Assistance Act 1948, s 51)
level 4 and 3 months (**level 4 only) (Social Security Administration Act 1992, s 105)

False accounting (Theft Act 1968, s 17) level 5 and 6 months † **A[31]**

False identity documents (Identity Documents Act 2010, s 6(1)) level 5 and 6 months † **A[32]**

False instrument, using level 5 and 6 months † **A[78]**

False statement to obtain social security level 5 and 3 months (Social Security Administration Act 1992, s 112) **A[54]**

False representation to obtain benefit level 5 and 6 months † (Social Security Administration Act 1992, s 111A) **A[54]**

Firearm (forfeiture for each of the following) (Firearms Act 1968)
air weapon in public place level 5 and 6 months (s 19) **A[71]**
air weapon (preventing minor from having with him) level 3 (s 24ZA) **A[71A]**
firearm (other than air weapon) in public place level 5 and 6 months † (s 19) **A[33]**
firearms: prohibition of certain weapons and control of arms traffic **A[76A]**
purchasing, possession, etc, without certificate level 5 and 6 months † (s 1) **A[76]**
trespassing in a building level 5 and 6 months **A[77]**
trespassing on land level 4 and 3 months **A[77]**

Food (selling food not of quality demanded) (Food Safety Act 1990, s 14) £20,000 and 6 months †

Football-related offences (may attract a football banning order)
Possession of alcohol whilst entering or trying to enter ground level 3 **A[34]**
Being drunk in, or whilst trying to enter, ground level 2 **A[35]**
throwing missile, indecent or racist chanting; going into prohibited areas level 3 **A[34]**
unauthorised sale or attempted sale of tickets level 5 **A[34]**

Forgery level 5 and 6 months † **A[78]**

Found on enclosed premises level 3 or 3 months (**level 3 only) **A[79]**

Fraud level 5 and/or 6 months † **A[36]–A[39]**
fraud by false representation (s 1 (2) (a)) **A[36]**
fraud by failing to disclose information (s 1 (2) (b)) **A[36]**
fraud by abuse of position (s 1 (2) (c)) **A[36]**
banking and insurance fraud, and obtaining credit through fraud, benefit fraud, and revenue fraud **A[36]**
confidence **A[36]**
obtaining services dishonestly (s 11) **A[37]**
possession of articles for fraud (s 6) **A[38]**
possessing, making or supplying articles for use in fraud (ss 6, 7 and 1) **A[38]**
making, adapting, supplying or offering to supply articles for fraud (s 7) **A[39]**

Fraudulently receiving programmes (see Television licence below)

Game (trespassing on land in day time in search of game) level 3; level 5 if 5 or more trespassers (Game Act 1831, s 30) **A[86]**

Glue sniffing, supplying level 5 and 6 months

Going equipped for theft level 5 and 6 months † A[58]

Grievous bodily harm level 5 and 6 months † A[70]

Gross indecency level 5 and 6 months †

Handling stolen goods level 5 and 6 months † A[40]

Harassing residential occupier (Protection from Eviction Act 1977, s 1) level 5 and 6 months †

Harassment (Protection from Harassment Act 1997, s 4) 6 months' A[41]

Harassment (putting people in fear of violence) (Protection from Harassment Act 1997, s 4) 10 years' A[41]

Harassment, alarm or distress/disorderly behaviour (Public Order Act 1986, s 5) level 3* A[20]

Health and Safety at Work Act 1974
failure to discharge a duty imposed by ss 2–6 fine not exceeding £20,000 and/or 6 months A[80]
contravention of s 7 fine not exceeding £20,000 and 6 months †
contravention of s 8 fine not exceeding £20,000 and 6 months †
contravention of s 9 fine not exceeding £20,000 †
an offence under s 33(1)(c) fine not exceeding £20,000 and 6 months †
an offence under s 33(1)(d) level 5 fine
an offence under s 33(1)(e), (f) or (g) fine not exceeding £20,000 and 6 months †
an offence under s 33(1)(h) level 5 and/or 6 months
an offence under s 33(1)(i) level 5 †
an offence under s 33(1)(j) fine not exceeding £20,000 and 6 months †
an offence under s 33(1)(k), (l) or (m) fine not exceeding £20,000 and 6 months †
an offence under s 33(1)(n) level 5 fine
an offence under s 33(1)(o) fine not exceeding £20,000 and 6 months †
an offence under the existing statutory provisions for which no other penalty is specified fine not exceeding £20,000 and 6 months † A[80]

Health Act 2006 (*See* Smoking)

Highway
builder's skip (depositing or leaving unlit) level 3
straying animals on level 3
wilful obstruction level 3 A[85]

Housebreaking implements (*See* Going equipped to steal) A[58]

Immigration offences (Immigration Act 1971, ss 24 – 26) A[81]

Income tax evasion (Finance Act 2000, s 144) level 5 and 6 months † A[42]

Indecent photographs of children level 5 and 6 months † A[43]

Indecent display level 5

Insulting magistrate, etc level 4 and 1 month D[3]

Insulting words or behaviour level 5 and 6 months A[21]

Interference with vehicle level 4 and 3 months A[63]

Intoxicating liquor
possessing at, or on the way to, a designated sporting event level 3 and 3 months A[76]
selling outside permitted hours level 3
selling to persons under 18 level 3 and forfeiture of licence (on second or subsequent conviction within 5 years)
selling without a licence level 4 and 6 months; forfeiture of liquor and containers. For

a subsequent offence defendant can be disqualified from holding a licence
persistently sell alcohol to persons aged less than 18 years, fine not exceeding £10,000, the holder of a premises licence may have the licence suspended by the court up to three months

Intoxicating substance, supplying level 5 and 6 months

Keeping a brothel used for prostitution (Sexual Offences Act 2003, s 55) level 5 and/or 6 months † **A[44]**

Kerb crawling level 3 **A[82]**

Kill, threatening to (Offences Against the Person Act 1861, s 16) level 5 and/or 6 months † **A[59]**

Landlord and tenant (unlawful eviction or harassment) level 5 and 6 months †

Litter (including car dumping)
(i) Environmental Protection Act 1990 **A[83.18]**
(ii) Refuse Disposal (Amenity) Act 1978 level 4 and 3 months **A[83]**

Living on earnings of prostitution level 5 and 6 months †

Loudspeakers level 5 **A[74]**

Making off without payment level 5 and 6 months † **A[45]**

Malicious communications level 5 and 6 months

Measuring equipment (false or unjust) level 5 (and 6 months if fraud), and forfeiture (Weights and Measures Act 1985, s 17)

Messages, offensive or threatening level 5 and 6 months (Malicious Communications Act 1988, s(1))

Misbehaviour in court level 4 and 1 month **D[3]**

Misuse of drugs (*See* Controlled drugs) **A[22]–A[27B]**

Mobile phones level 3 or level 4 for HGVs and PSVs*

National insurance, failing to pay contributions level 3 plus arrears of contributions for two years

Noise (excessive) A[74]

Noise or nuisance on NHS premises A[74]

Nuisance A[84]

Obscenely exposing person level 3 or 3 months (Vagrancy Act 1824, s 4); level 3 or 14 days (**not imprisonable for offences from a date to be appointed) (Town Police Clauses Act 1847, s 28)

Obstructing highway level 3 **A[85]**

Obstructing or resisting a police officer (or a person assisting a police officer) level 3 and 1 month **A[47]**

Offensive weapon and threatening with offensive weapon level 5 and 6 months, forfeiture † **A[11]**

Payment, making off without level 5 and 6 months † **A[45]**

Pedlar
trading without certificate (Pedlars Act 1871, s 4) level 1

Poaching (For hunting wild mammals with dogs and hare coursing see the Hunting Act 2004, ss 1–5)
day time offence level 3; level 5 if 5 or more trespassers (Game Act 1831, s 30) **A[86]**
night time offences level 3; level 4 and 6 months where violence is used or offered

(Night Poaching Act 1828, ss 1 and 2) or 3 or more being armed (s 9) A[86.9]

Point, article with, in public place (CJA 1988, s 139) level 5 or 6 months + A[11]

Possessing certain false documents level 5 and 6 months † (Immigration Act 1971, ss 26, 26A) A[81.3]

Property (damaging or destroying) Penalty varies with value A[18] to A[18B]

Property (obtaining property by deception) level 5 and 6 months † A[22]

Prostitutes (see also exploitation of prostitution)
living on earnings of level 5 and 6 months †
soliciting by prostitutes level 2/level 3 or Support and Engagement Order A[82.2]

Psychoactive substances 6 months and/or an unlimited fine A[87]

Public telephone (see **Telephone**) (Telecommunications Act 1984 – Communications Act 2003
fraudulent use of (s 42) level 5 and 6 months †
indecent or false telephone calls (s 43) level 5 and 6 months

Racially or religiously aggravated offences
wounding level 5 and 6 months † A[48]
actual bodily harm level 5 and 6 months † A[8.2]
common assault level 5 and 6 months A[8.2]
criminal damage level 5 and 6 months † A[18]
disorderly behaviour level 3 A[20]
harassment 6 months' A[41]
harassment (putting people in fear of violence) 14 years' A[41]
stalking 2 years' A[41]
stalking (involving fear of violence or serious alarm or distress) 14 years' A[41]
threatening behaviour/intentional harassment alarm or distress level 5 and 6 months + A[21]

Railway fare evasion
avoid fare level 3 or 3 months A[48]
giving false name or address level 3 or 3 months A[48.2]

Resisting a constable or a person assisting a constable level 3 and 1 month A[47]

Scales (unjust) level 5 (and 6 months if fraud), and forfeiture (Weights and Measures Act 1985, s 17)

School attendance, parent not ensuring (Education Act 1996, s 444) level 3 Aggravated offence level 4 and 3 months A[49]

Selling food not of quality demanded (Food Safety Act 1990, s 14) £20,000 and 6 months †

Sexual activity with child level 5 and 6 months † A[52]

Sexual activity in a public lavatory level 5 and 6 months † A[51]

Sexual assault level 5 and 6 months † A[53]

Sex Offenders register – fail to comply with notification requirements (Sexual Offences Act 2003, s 91) 5 years' A[50]

Shotgun
purchasing or possessing, etc, without certificate level 5 and 6 months †, forfeiture A[88]
loaded shotgun in a public place level 5 and 6 months +, forfeiture A[33]

Skip

depositing on highway level 3
not complying with condition level 3
unlit level 3

Smuggling 3 times value of goods or £5,000 and 6 months † **A[19]**

Social security
Dishonest statement/representation for obtaining benefit etc level 5 and/or six months

† (Social Security Administration Act 1992, s 111A) **A[54]**
false statement/representation to obtain level 5 and 3 months (Social Security Administration Act 1992, s 112) **A[54]**
persistently refusing or neglecting to maintain oneself or a dependant level 4 and 3 months (**no longer imprisonable for offences from a date to be appointed) (Social Security Administration Act 1992, s 105)

Soliciting by prostitutes level 2/level 3 or Support and Engagement Order **A[82.2]**

Soliciting women for prostitution level 3 **A[82]**

Solvent, supplying for intoxication level 5 and 6 months

Smoking (Health Act 2006)
Smoking in a smoke free place (£200 – a fixed penalty of £50 reduced to £30 if paid before the end of 15 days)
Failing to display the required no-smoking signs (£1,000 – a fixed penalty of £200 reduced to £150 if paid before the end of 15 days) – this offence is committed by anyone who manages or occupies smoke-free premises or a vehicle
Failing to prevent smoking in a smoke-free place (£2,500 – no fixed penalty) – this offence is committed by anyone who manages or controls smoke-free premises or a vehicle

Sporting event (may attract a football banning order)
football banning order **B[27]**
intoxicating liquor, possessing at/on the way to level 3 and 3 months **A[35]**
drunk at/on the way to level 2 **A[35]**

Squatting in a residential building level 5 and 6 months

Stalking (Protection from harassment Act 1997, s 4A) 6 month' **A[41]**

Stalking (involving fear of violence or serious alarm or distress)
(Protection from harassment Act 1997, s 4A) 10 years' **A[41]**

Statutory nuisance (noise) A[61]

Stealing level 5 and 6 months † **A[57]**

Taking motor vehicle or conveyance level 5 and 6 months, disqualification **A[65]**

Tattooing a minor level 3

Tax credit fraud level 5 and 6 months † (Tax Credits Act 2005, s 35) **A[55]**

Taxi-touting/soliciting for hire level 4 (Criminal Justice and Public Order Act 1994, s 167) **A[56]**

Telephone (Telecommunications Act 1984 – Communications Act 2003)

NB: Ss 42, 42A and 43 below were replaced by ss 125–127 of the Communications Act 2003 effective from 25/7/03 by virtue of SI 2003/1900 as amended. **A[16]**
fraudulent use of public telephone (s 42) level 5 and 6 months †
indecent or false calls (s 43) level 5 and 6 months *

Television licence payment evasion (Communications Act 2003, s 363) level 3 **A[61]**

[Fraudulently receiving programmes] (Copyright, Designs and Patents Act 1988, s 297) level 5 **F[3]**

Terrorism offences (Terrorism Act 2000, ss 15–18) level 5 or 6 months†
(Breach of notification provisions under the Counter-Terrorism Act 2008) level 5 or 6 months† *See also* **B[30]**

Theft (covers breach of trust; in a dwelling; from the person and from a shop) level 5 and 6 months† **A[57]**

Threatening to damage or destroy property level 5 and 6 months † **A[18A]**

Threatening letters level 4

Threats to kill (Offences Against the Person Act 1861, s 16) 10 years' **A[59]**

Threatening words or behaviour (Public Order Act 1986, s 4) level 5 and 6 months **A[21]**

Ticket Touting (unauthorised sale or disposal of tickets for designated football matches (CJPOA 1994, s 166 as amended) level 5 **A[34]**

Trade mark, unauthorised use of etc (Trade Marks Act 1994, s 92) level 5 and/or 6 months † **A[60]**

Trespassing on land during day time in search of game, etc level 3/level 5 (if 5 or more trespassers) (Game Act 1831, s 30) **A[65]**

Trespassing with firearm in a building level 5 and 6 months + (if not an air weapon) forfeiture **A[38]**

Trespassing with firearm on land level 4 and 3 months, forfeiture **A[38]**

Unauthorised taking of motor vehicle level 5 and 6 months, disqualification **A[77]**

Unfair or prohibited commercial practices level 5† **A[75]**

Using false (or copy of false) instrument level 5 and 6 months + (Forgery etc Act 1981) **A[78]**

VAT evasion (VATA 1994, s 72) level 5 and/or 6 months † **A[62]**

Vehicle interference level 4 and 3 months **A[63]**

Vehicle taking, without consent level 5 and 6 months, disqualification **A[65]**

Vehicle-taking (aggravated) level 5 and 6 months **A[66]**

Violent disorder level 5 and/or 6 months † **A[67]**

Voyeurism (Sexual Offences Act 2003, s 67) level 5 and/or 6 months † **A[68]**

Weighing equipment (unjust) level 5 (and 6 months if fraud), and forfeiture

Wilful obstruction of highway level 3 **A[63]**

Wilful obstruction of police constable (or person assisting police constable) level 3 and 1 month **A[47]**

Witness intimidation level 5 and/or 6 months † **A[69]**

Wounding level 5 and 6 months † **A[70]**

A[1]

Electricity – Abstracting/Use without authority

Charge (Electricity abstracting/use without authority)

A[1.1] **Dishonestly uses without due authority, or dishonestly causes to be wasted or diverted, any electricity**

Theft Act 1968, s 13

Maximum penalty – 6 months' imprisonment and/or fine level 5 (for offences committed on or after 12 March 2015 an unlimited fine). Triable either way.

Crown Court – 5 years' imprisonment and unlimited fine.

Mode of trial

A[1.2] Consider the SGC Guideline at A[1.4] below.

Legal notes and definitions

A[1.3] **Dishonestly.** See the notes at A[57.5] onwards.

Where a defendant's electricity supply was cut off for non-payment and he then reconnected the supply knowing that he did not have the electricity board's consent to do so, that knowledge did not of itself make his conduct dishonest. Whether he acted dishonestly was a question of fact to be answered subjectively having regard to the defendant's state of mind when he reconnected the supply: *Boggeln v Williams* [1978] 2 All ER 1061, [1978] 1 WLR 873, DC.

It is sufficient for the prosecution to establish electricity was used without the authority of the relevant provider (company) and with no intention to pay (*R v McCreadie and Tume* (1993) 157 JP 541).

Sentencing
SC Guideline – Electricity, abstract/use without authority

A[1.4]

OFFENCE SERIOUSNESS (CULPABILITY AND HARM) A. IDENTIFY THE APPROPRIATE STARTING POINT Starting points based on first time offender pleading not guilty		
Example of nature of activity	**Starting point**	**Range**
Where the offence results in substantial commercial gain, a custodial sentence may be appropriate		
Offence involving evidence of planning and indication that the offending was intended to be continuing, such as using a device to interfere with the electricity meter or re-wiring or to by-pass the meter.	Medium level community order	Band A fine to high level community order

OFFENCE SERIOUSNESS (CULPABILITY AND HARM)
B. CONSIDER THE EFFECT OF AGGRAVATING AND MITIGATING FACTORS (OTHER THAN THOSE WITHIN EXAMPLES ABOVE) Common aggravating and mitigating factors are identified at **B[45.2A]**. The following may be particularly relevant but **these lists are not exhaustive**
Factor indicating greater degree of harm 1. Risk of danger caused to property and/or life
FORM A PRELIMINARY VIEW OF THE APPROPRIATE SENTENCE, THEN CONSIDER OFFENDER MITIGATION Common factors are identified at B[45.2A] – see also note (c) below
CONSIDER A REDUCTION FOR A GUILTY PLEA
CONSIDER ANCILLARY ORDERS, INCLUDING COMPENSATION **Refer to Part B for available ancillary orders and in particular B[10] for guidance on compensation.** This may be ordered in respect of any injury loss or damage resulting from the offence. Maximum is £5,000 per offence. It may be ordered in addition to another sentence, or as a substantive penalty by itself. If a monetary penalty is appropriate and the defendant's means are limited, preference must be given to ordering compensation instead of a fine.
DECIDE SENTENCE **GIVE REASONS**

Electricity, abstract/use without authority – factors to be taken into consideration

Key factors

(a) The starting points and sentencing ranges in this guideline are based on the assumption that the offender was motivated by greed or a desire to live beyond his or her means. To avoid double counting, such a motivation should not be treated as a factor that increases culpability.

(b) When assessing the harm caused by this offence, the starting point should be the loss suffered by the victim. In general, the greater the loss, the more serious the offence. However, the monetary value of the loss may not reflect the full extent of the harm caused by the offence. The court should also take into account the impact of the offence on the victim, any harm to persons other than the direct victim, and any harm in the form of public alarm or erosion of public confidence.

(c) The following matters of offender mitigation may be relevant to this offence:

(i) *Offender motivated by desperation or need.* The fact that an offence has been committed in desperation or need arising from particular hardship may count as offender mitigation in exceptional circumstances.

(ii) *Voluntary restitution.* Whether and the degree to which payment for stolen electricity constitutes a matter of offender mitigation will depend on an assessment of the circumstances and, in particular, the voluntariness and timeliness of the payment.

(iii) Impact on sentence of offender's dependency. Many offenders convicted of acquisitive crimes are motivated by an addiction, often to drugs, alcohol or gambling. This does not mitigate the seriousness of the offence, but an offender's dependency may properly influence the type of sentence imposed. In particular, it may sometimes be appropriate to impose a drug rehabilitation requirement or an alcohol treatment requirement as part of a community order or a suspended sentence order in an attempt to break the cycle of addiction and offending, even if an immediate custodial sentence would otherwise be warranted (see B[15.17]).

The Court of Appeal gave guidance on the approach to making drug treatment and testing orders, which also applies to imposing a drug rehabilitation requirement in *Attorney General's Reference No 64 of 2003 (R v Boujettif and Harrison) v Sanchez* [2003] EWCA Crim 3514 and *R v Woods and Collins* [2005] EWCA Crim 2065 summarised in the Sentencing Guidelines Council Guideline Judgments Case Compendium (Section (A) Generic Sentencing Principles) available at: sent encingcouncil.judiciary.gov.uk.

New guidelines apply to offences sentenced on or after 1 February 2016. These are reproduced at A[57.37].

A[2]
Affray

Charge (Affray)

A[2.1] **Using or threatening unlawful violence towards another such that the conduct would cause a person of reasonable firmness present at the scene to fear for his personal safety**

Public Order Act 1986, s 3

Maximum penalty – 6 months' imprisonment and/or fine level 5 (for offences committed on or after 12 March 2015 an unlimited fine). Triable either way. Specified violent offence under Sch 15, Part 1, CJA 2003

Crown Court – 3 years' imprisonment and unlimited fine.

Mode of trial

A[2.2] Consider the **SGC Guideline** at A[2.15] below.

Legal notes and definitions

A[2.3] **The charge.** Only one offence is created.

A[2.4] **Using or threatening.** Where two or more persons use or threaten the violence, it is the conduct of them taken together that must be considered for the purpose of the offence.

To be guilty of affray there need not be an attribution of individual roles to the participants; thus, where the court found that there had been a group of people fighting in a street and that the defendant had been part of that group, all of whom had been fighting, the court was entitled to convict even though it could not be sure of the defendant's involvement in a specific incident of assault: *Dragjoshi v Croydon Magistrates' Court* [2017] EWHC 2840 (Admin), [2017] All ER (D) 115 (Nov).

A[2.5] **Threats.** Cannot be made by way of words alone, there must be at least a physical gesture towards someone. For the purposes of s 3(1), the carrying of dangerous weapons by a group of persons can in some circumstances constitute a threat of violence without those weapons being waved or brandished, but the mere possession of a weapon, without threatening circumstances, is insufficient to constitute such a threat. Nor can carrying a concealed weapon itself be such a threat. However, the visible carrying in public of primed petrol bombs by a large number of what is obvious a gang out for no good is clearly capable of constituting a threat of unlawful violence: *I v DPP, M v DPP, H v DPP* [2001] UKHL 10, [2002] AC 285, [2001] 2 All ER 583, [2001] 2 WLR 765.

A[2.6] **Person of reasonable firmness** need not actually be or be likely to be present at the scene, it is the hypothetical reasonable bystander who has to be put in fear for his personal safety, not just the victim himself (*R v Sanchez* (1996) 160 JP 321, [1996] Crim LR 572, CA). In *R v Plavecz* (2002) it is made clear that an assault does not turn into an affray because it is in a public place. There must be evidence that anyone watching would have been put in fear themselves.

The purpose of the legislation was to address public order. The authorities made it plain that the facts in particular circumstances required careful study before the legal principle was applied. It was difficult to see how, when viewed contextually, the evidence in the instant case, supported the appellant's conviction for affray. The incident had consisted of brief exchanges which were essentially private in nature. Further, there was no realistic possibility of a notional third party entering the premises and fearing for his own safety: *R (on the application of Leeson) v DPP* [2010] EWHC 994 (Admin), 174 JP 367, [2010] 17 LS Gaz R 16. It does not necessarily follow that because a person is present at a location where a gang are carrying petrol bombs there is a threat of violence towards that person; whether the latter is the case will depend on the facts of the actual case: *I v DPP, M v DPP, H v DPP* (above).

A[2.7]–[2.8] Violence. Violence does not include violence justified in law (self-defence or prevention of crime). The violence must be directed towards another, ie not property – such as kicking a door. However, the violence is not restricted to violence causing or intended to cause injury and includes violent conduct such as throwing a missile of a kind capable of causing injury even though it misses or falls short.

A[2.9] Intent. The accused must intend to use or threaten violence or be aware that his conduct may be violent or threaten violence.

A[2.10]–[2.14] Intoxication. See under the offence of violent disorder at A[67]. Affray can be committed in a public or private place.

Sentencing
SC Guideline – Affray

A[2.15]

OFFENCE SERIOUSNESS (CULPABILITY AND HARM)
A. IDENTIFY THE APPROPRIATE STARTING POINT
Starting points based on first time offender pleading not guilty

Examples of nature of activity	Starting point	Range
Brief offence involving low-level violence, no substantial fear created	Low level community order	Band C fine to medium level community order
Degree of fighting or violence that causes substantial fear	High level community order	Medium level community order to 12 weeks custody
Fight involving a weapon/throwing objects, or conduct causing risk of injury	18 weeks custody	12 weeks custody to Crown Court

OFFENCE SERIOUSNESS (CULPABILITY AND HARM)
B. CONSIDER THE EFFECT OF AGGRAVATING AND MITIGATING FACTORS (OTHER THAN THOSE WITHIN EXAMPLES ABOVE)
Common aggravating and mitigating factors are identified at **B[45.2A]**. The following may be particularly relevant but these lists are not exhaustive:

Factors indicating higher culpability	*Factors indicating lower culpability*
1. Group action 2. Threats 3. Lengthy incident	1. Did not start the trouble 2. Provocation 3. Stopped as soon as police arrived
Factors indicating greater degree of harm 1. Vulnerable person(s) present 2. Injuries caused 3. Damage to property	

FORM A PRELIMINARY VIEW OF THE APPROPRIATE SENTENCE, THEN CONSIDER OFFENDER MITIGATION

Common factors are identified at B[45.2A].
CONSIDER A REDUCTION FOR A GUILTY PLEA
CONSIDER ANCILLARY ORDERS, INCLUDING COMPENSATION AND FOOTBALL BANNING ORDER (where appropriate) Refer to Part B for guidance on ancillary orders and in particular B[10] for guidance on compensation.
DECIDE SENTENCE GIVE REASONS

A[2.16] Domestic violence. For domestic violence offences see SC Definitive Guideline 'Overarching Principles: Domestic Abuse'.

A[3]
Alcohol sale offences

Charge (Alcohol sale offences)

A[3.1] Sale of alcohol to a person who is drunk

Licensing Act 2003, s 141

NB: For the sale of alcohol to a drunk person under s 141 LA 2003, a fixed penalty of £80 is available

A[3.2] Sale of alcohol to children

Licensing Act 2003, s 146

NB: For the sale of alcohol to a person under 18 a fixed penalty of £80 is available for staff under s 146 Licensing Act 2003. Licensees should be the subject of a summons

A[3.3] Allowing the sale of alcohol to children

Licensing Act 2003, s 147

Maximum penalty – level 3 fine for a s 141 offence; level 5 fine (for offences committed on or after 12 March 2015 an unlimited fine) for ss 146 and 147 offences

Section 23 of the Violent Crime Reduction Act 2006 created a new offence of persistently selling alcohol to children, which came into force on April 6, 2007. This is committed if, on three or more different occasions within a period of three consecutive months, alcohol is unlawfully sold on the same premises to a person under 18. The offence is summary only and the maximum penalty is an unlimited fine. **Consult your legal adviser for guidance on the approach to sentencing and the court's powers in relation to liquor licences.**

Legal notes and definitions

A[3.4] The provisions apply to any person who works at the premises in a capacity, whether paid or unpaid, which gives him authority to sell the alcohol concerned (see s,141 (2) for further definitions).

The provisions apply equally to the sale or supply of alcohol in club premises.

Sentencing
SC Guideline – Alcohol sale offences

Alcohol sale offences (Revised 2017)

A[3.5]

Licensing Act 2003, s 41 (sale of alcohol to drunk person); s 46 (sale of alcohol to children); s 47 (allowing sale of alcohol to children)

Effective from: 24 April 2017

Triable only summarily:

Maximum: Level 3 fine (s 141); Unlimited fine (ss 46 and 147)

Offence range: Conditional Discharge–Band C fine

Note

This guideline may also be relevant when sentencing offences under s 147A of the Licensing Act 2003, persistently selling alcohol to children, which is committed if, on three or more different occasions within a period of three consecutive months, alcohol is unlawfully sold on the same premises to a person under 18. The offence is summary only and the maximum penalty is an unlimited fine. The court should refer to the sentencing approach in this guideline, adjusting the starting points and ranges bearing in mind the increased seriousness of this offence.

STEP 1
Determining the offence category

The Court should determine the offence category using the table below.

Category 1	Higher culpability **and** greater harm
Category 2	Higher culpability **and** lesser harm **or** lower culpability **and** greater harm
Category 3	Lower culpability **and** lesser harm

The court should determine the offender's culpability and the harm caused with reference **only** to the factors below. Where an offence does not fall squarely into a category, individual factors may require a degree of weighting before making an overall assessment and determining the appropriate offence category.

CULPABILITY demonstrated by one or more of the following:

Factors indicating higher culpability

- No attempt made to establish age
- Sale for consumption by group of intoxicated persons
- Sale intended for consumption by a child or young person
- Offender in management position (or equivalent)
- Evidence of failure to police the sale of alcohol

Factors indicating lower culpability

- Offender deceived by false identification
- Evidence of substantial effort to police the sale of alcohol
- Offender acting under direction

HARM demonstrated by one or more of the following:

Factors indicating greater harm

- Supply to younger child/children
- Supply causes or contributes to antisocial behaviour
- Large quantity of alcohol supplied

Factors indicating lesser harm

- All other cases

STEP 2
Starting point and category range

Having determined the category at step one, the court should use the starting point to reach a sentence within the appropriate category range in the table below. The starting point applies to all offenders irrespective of plea or previous convictions.

Offence Category	Starting Point	Range
Category 1	Band C fine	Band B fine–Band C fine
Category 2	Band B fine	Band A fine–Band C fine
Category 3	Band A fine	Conditional discharge–Band B fine

Note: refer to fines for offence committed for 'commercial' purposes

The court should then consider adjustment for any aggravating or mitigating factors. The following is a **non-exhaustive** list of additional factual elements providing the context of the offence and factors relating to the offender. Identify whether any combination of these, or other relevant factors, should result in an upward or downward adjustment from the sentence arrived at so far.

Factors increasing seriousness

Statutory aggravating factors:

- Previous convictions, having regard to a) the **nature** of the offence to which the conviction relates and its **relevance** to the current offence; and b) the **time** that has elapsed since the conviction
- Offence committed whilst on bail
- Offence motivated by, or demonstrating hostility based on any of the following characteristics or presumed characteristics of the victim: religion, race, disability, sexual orientation or transgender identity

Other aggravating factors:

- Failure to comply with current court orders
- Offence committed on licence or post sentence supervision

Factors reducing seriousness or reflecting personal mitigation

- No previous convictions **or** no relevant/recent convictions
- Offence committed as the result of substantial intimidation

STEP 3
Consider any factors which indicate a reduction, such as assistance to the prosecution

The court should take into account sections 73 and 74 of the Serious Organised Crime and Police Act 2005 (assistance by defendants: reduction or review of sentence) and any other rule of law by virtue of which an offender may receive a discounted sentence in consequence of assistance given (or offered) to the prosecutor or investigator.

STEP 4
Reduction for guilty pleas

The court should take account of any potential reduction for a guilty plea in accordance with section 144 of the Criminal Justice Act 2003 and the *Guilty Plea* guideline.

STEP 5
Totality principle

If sentencing an offender for more than one offence, or where the offender is already serving a sentence, consider whether the total sentence is just and proportionate to the overall offending behaviour in accordance with the *Offences Taken into Consideration and Totality* guideline.

STEP 6
Compensation and ancillary orders

In all cases, the court should consider whether to make compensation and/or other ancillary orders including deprivation and/or forfeiture or suspension of personal liquor licence.

STEP 7
Reasons

Section 174 of the Criminal Justice Act 2003 imposes a duty to give reasons for, and explain the effect of, the sentence.

A[4]
Alcohol/tobacco, fraudulently evade duty

Charge (Alcohol/tobacco, fraudulently evade duty)

A[4.1] **(1) Knowingly acquiring possession of any of the following goods:**

- **goods which have been unlawfully removed from a warehouse or Queen's warehouse;**
- **goods which are chargeable with a duty which has not been paid;**
- **goods with respect to the importation or exportation of which any prohibition or restriction is for the time being in force under or by virtue of any enactment; or**

knowingly concerned in carrying, removing, depositing, harbouring, keeping or concealing or in any manner dealing with any such goods,

with intent to defraud Her Majesty of any duty payable on the goods or to evade any such prohibition or restriction with respect to the goods he shall be guilty of an offence under this section and may be arrested.

Customs and Excise Management Act 1979, s 170(1)

OR

(2) In relation to any goods, in any way knowingly concerned in any fraudulent evasion or attempt at evasion:

- **of any duty chargeable on the goods;**
- **of any prohibition or restriction for the time being in force with respect to the goods under or by virtue of any enactment; or**
- **of any provision of the Customs and Excise Acts 1979 applicable to the goods.**

Customs and Excise Management Act 1979, s 170(2)

Maximum penalty – Three times the value of the goods or £20,000 (for offences committed on or after 12 March 2015 - for prior offences £5,000) fine whichever is the greater and 6 months. Triable either way.

Crown Court – 7 years' imprisonment and unlimited fine.

A[4.2] **Drugs** – Different penalties will apply in both the magistrates' court and the Crown Court if drugs are involved and in the Crown Court where there is the import or export of counterfeit money. For drugs see A[27B].

Mode of trial

A[4.3] See general notes at D[4].

Legal notes and definitions

A[4.4] **Offence (1): knowingly and intent to defraud.** The possession by a defendant of dutiable goods raises a presumption that they were knowingly in his possession; the intent to defraud may be inferred from the surrounding circumstances: *R v Cohen* [1951] 1 KB 505, [1951] 1 All ER 203, 115 JP 91; *Sayce v Coupe* [1953] 1 QB 1, [1952] 2 All ER 715, 116 JP 552; *Schneider v Dawson* [1960] 2 QB 106,[1959] 3 All ER 584, 124 JP 7.

A[4.5] **Offence (2): knowingly concerned.** What is required is a specific intent to be knowingly concerned in any fraudulent evasion of a prohibition. Where the case concerns the importation of drugs, to found a conviction the prosecution must establish that, at the time of the offence, the accused intended dishonestly to evade the prohibition and import the drugs by entering UK territorial waters, and knew that they had in fact entered those waters. Merely running the risk of entering UK waters did not suffice: *R v Panayi (No 2)* [1989] 1 WLR 187, 88 Cr App Rep 267, CA. 'Knowingly concerned' involves not merely knowledge of the smuggling operation, but also that the substance is one the importation of which is prohibited. Where the defendant smuggled cannabis into the UK believing it was currency, he could not be convicted of the offence even though he wrongly thought that smuggling currency was prohibited: *R v Taafe* [1984] AC 539, [1984] 1 All ER 747, 148 JP 510, HL. Where, however, a defendant smuggled drugs believing they were pornographic goods, believing correctly that the importation of such goods was prohibited, he was liable to conviction: *R v Ellis* (1987) 84 Cr App Rep 235, [1987] Crim LR 44.

A[4.6] **Offence (2): fraudulent evasion or attempt.** The prosecution must prove fraudulent conduct in the sense of dishonest conduct deliberately intended to evade the prohibition or restriction with respect to, or the duty chargeable on, goods as the case may be. There is no necessity for the prosecution to prove acts of deceit practised on a customs officer in his presence: *Re A-G's Reference (No 1 of 1981)* [1982] QB 848, [1982] 2 All ER 417.

A[4.7] **Duplicity.** Offence (2) is an 'activity' offence. Sometimes it will arise in relation to only one transaction and in other cases there will be many giving rise to continuity of activity which may be charged as one offence. Nevertheless s 170(2) does not permit two different activities to be charged as one offence, see *R v Martin* [1998] 2 Cr App Rep 385, CA.

A[4.8] **The prosecution.** Must be authorised by HM Revenue and Customs. Neither the police nor a private citizen can instigate proceedings on their own authority.

A[4.9] **Death of informant.** If the informant (or person authorised by HM Revenue and Customs) dies, is dismissed or is absent then the Revenue and Customs can nominate another person to proceed with the case.

A[4.10] **Presumptions against the defendant.** The Act is so worded that it gives to the prosecution a number of advantages in presuming certain points to be in the prosecution's favour.

For example, if a defendant claims that the goods were lawfully imported or lawfully unloaded from a ship or aircraft the burden of proving these points rests on the defendant. However, the burden of proof is not to establish his defence beyond all reasonable doubt but to satisfy the magistrates that on the balance of probabilities his defence is true.

A[4.11]–[4.15] **Mistake.** If the customs officer makes a mistake and undercharges the duty, no offence is committed by a person who pays the duty realising the mistake, provided that he has not given false information or induced the error.

Sentencing

SC Guideline – Alcohol/tobacco, fraudulently evade duty

A[4.16] Refer to the Revenue Fraud guideline at A[36].

A[4.17] **Value of goods.** The value of the goods, for the purpose of determining the penalty, shall be the price they might reasonably be expected to have fetched on the open market, after duty has been paid, at or about the time of the commission of the offence. See *R v Dosanjh* [1998] 3 All ER 618, [1999] 1 Cr App Rep 371, CA for aggravating features and the use of imprisonment and *R v Howlett* [1999] All ER (D) 777, CA which suggest that cases involving a loss of duty under £10,000 may be dealt with by sentences of under six months' imprisonment.

A[4.18] Financial reporting order. A conviction for an offence under s 170 of the Customs and Excise Management Act 1979 (including attempting, conspiring, inciting, aiding, abetting, counselling or procuring the commission of the offence) is one that is mentioned in s 76(3) of the Serious Organised Crime and Police Act 2005. The court when sentencing or otherwise dealing with an offender convicted on or after 4 May 4 2007 may also make a financial reporting order.

A[4.19] Appeal. Note that HM Revenue and Customs may appeal any decision of the court including sentence (*Customs and Excise Comrs v Brunt* (1998) 163 JP 161).

A[5]

Animal cruelty

Charges (Animal cruelty)

A[5.1] **1. A person commits an offence if –**

(a) **an act of his, or a failure of his to act, causes an animal to suffer;**
(b) **he knew, or ought reasonably to have known, that the act, or failure to act, would have that effect or be likely to do so,**
(c) **the animal is a protected animal, and**
(d) **the suffering is unnecessary.**

Animal Welfare Act 2006, s 4(1).

2. A person commits an offence if –

(a) **he is responsible for an animal,**
(b) **an act, or failure to act, of another person causes the animal to suffer,**
(c) **he permitted that to happen or failed to take such steps (whether by supervising the other person or otherwise) as were reasonable in all the circumstances to prevent that happening, and**
(d) **the suffering is unnecessary.**

Animal Welfare Act 2006, s 4(2).

3. Fighting etc

A person commits an offence if he –

(a) **causes an animal fight to take place, or attempts to do so;**
(b) **knowingly receives money for an animal fight;**
(c) **knowingly publicises an animal fight; . . .**

Animal Welfare Act 2006, s 8(1).

NB: Offences under (d)–(i) omitted and subsections (2) and (3). Different types of offences are caught by this section including being present at an animal fight. For ease of space not all offences under section 8 have been included in this section.

4. A person commits an offence if –

he does not take such steps as are reasonable in all the circumstances to ensure that the needs of an animal for which he is responsible are met to the extent required by good practice.

Animal Welfare Act 2006, s 9

Maximum penalty

(1) 6 months' imprisonment or an unlimited fine or both – triable only summarily.
(2) 6 months' imprisonment or an unlimited fine or both – triable only summarily.
(3) 6 months' imprisonment or an unlimited fine or both – triable only summarily.
(4) 6 months' imprisonment or level 5 fine (for offences committed on or after 12 March 2015 an unlimited fine) or both – triable only summarily.

Legal notes and definitions

A[5.2] Each of the types of cruelty alleged above are separate offences. The legislation appears designed to catch not only owners or persons in charge of an animal but in specified circumstances any other person 'responsible' for an animal (see below). If a defendant causes suffering etc to a number of different animals on the same occasion there does not appear to be any objection to a single charge being preferred eg under s 4 (1). The mutilation of animals is a separate offence covered by s 5 while the docking of animal tails is provided for by s 6 of the AWA 2006.

Animal. Is defined in s 1 and means a vertebrate other than man.

Protected animal. The legislation covers mostly domesticated animals as defined in s 2.

Responsibility for animals. In the AWA 2006:

(1) References to a person responsible for an animal are to a person responsible for an animal whether on a permanent or temporary basis.
(2) References to being responsible for an animal include being in charge of it.
(3) A person who 'owns' an animal should always be regarded as being a person who is responsible for it.
(4) A person should be 'treated' as responsible for any animal for which a person under the age of 16 years of whom he has actual care and control is responsible.

Whether suffering unnecessary. In the AWA 2006, the considerations to which it is relevant to have regard when determining for the purposes of this section whether suffering is unnecessary include:

(1) Whether the suffering could reasonably have been avoided or reduced.
(2) Whether the conduct which caused the suffering was in compliance with any relevant enactment or any relevant provisions of a licence or code of practice issued under any enactment.
(3) Whether the conduct which caused the suffering was proportionate to the purpose of the conduct concerned.
(4) Whether the conduct concerned was in all the circumstances that of a reasonably competent and humane person.
(5) Nothing in (1)–(4) above applies to the destruction of an animal in an appropriate and humane manner.

Does not take steps as are reasonable in all the circumstances. It is the circumstances which determine what steps are reasonable to take to prevent an animal from suffering unreasonably, and knowledge of those circumstances is thus an essential element of charge. Accordingly, the offence under s 4(2) is not one of strict liability; it requires at least an element of culpability: *Riley v Crown Prosecution Service* [2016] EEWHC 2531 (Admin), [2017] 1 WLR 505, (2017) 181 JP 96, [2017] Crim L R 222.

Knew or ought reasonably to have known. The prosecution had to establish that the defendant knew or ought reasonably to have known both that his or her act or failure would cause an animal to suffer and that the suffering was unnecessary: *R (on the application of Gray and Gray) v Aylesbury Crown Court, RSPCA (interested party)* [2013] EWHC 500 (Admin), (2013) 177 JP 329.

Difference between 'cruelty' offence (s 4) and the 'welfare' offence (s 9). The difference is whether the animal has suffered unnecessarily and not as to the mental state of the person concerned; s 9(1) sets a purely objective standard: *R (on the application of Gray and Gray) v Aylesbury Crown Court, RSPCA (interested party)* [2013] EWHC 500 (Admin), (2013) 177 JP 32.

A conviction for a s 9 offence will not be bad for duplicity if it is based on the same findings of fact as a conviction for a s 4 offence. There can be no objection to a person being convicted of both offences if the conduct proved in relation to the s 9 offence is wider than the conduct which can be proved to have caused actual suffering to the animal: *R (on the application of Gray and Gray) v Aylesbury Crown Court, RSPCA (interested party)*, above.

Section 8 – meaning of 'animal fight'.

This is defined by AWA 2006, s 8(7) as 'an occasion on which a protected animal is placed with an animal, or with a human, for the purpose of fighting, wrestling or baiting . . . '. In *Royal Society for the Prevention of Cruelty to Animals v McCormick and others* [2016] EWHC 928 (Admin), [2016] 1 WLR 2641, 180 JP 288 a group would go into the countryside at night with one or more 'protected animals', namely dogs, to seek out wild animals with the purpose of setting the dogs to attack and kill them. When caught, each animal would fight to protect itself. The RSPCA contended that this constituted an 'animal fight'. However, the Administrative Court upheld the acquittal (on a submission of no case to answer). 'Placed with' could not be equated with the release of a protected animal into the actual or potential unrestricted vicinity of another animal. It required a contrived or artificial creation specifically for the purpose of a fight during which the other animal had no natural means of escape. There could be no hunt to chase to find the other animal, and there had to be control in the sense that the other animal, whose instinct would be to escape, could not do so. Whether or not restraint was required depended on the facts. On the facts of the present case it was, but in a case where two dogs were bred for fighting there was no such requirement because the other dog would fight and not attempt to escape. The involvement of money was not, however, a necessary ingredient. (The activities may well, however, have amounted to offences under the Hunting Act 2004.)

Time limits for prosecution.

The usual six month limit in s 127 of the Magistrates' Courts Act 1980 may be extended if the information is laid before the end of the period of three years beginning with the date of the commission of the offence, and before the end of the period of six months beginning with the date on which evidence which the prosecutor thinks is sufficient to justify the proceedings comes to his knowledge: Animal Welfare Act 2006, s 31(1). For these purposes a certificate signed by or on behalf of the prosecutor and stating the date on which such evidence came to his knowledge shall be conclusive evidence of that fact, and a certificate stating that matter and purporting to be so signed shall be treated as so signed unless the contrary is proved: Animal Welfare Act 2006, s 31(2).

'The prosecutor' for the purposes of s 31 is not limited to a person or organisation who/which prosecutes pursuant to a power conferred by statute, but applies to anyone who initiates a prosecution under the 2006 Act: *Lamont-Perkins v Royal Society for the Prevention of Cruelty to Animals* [2012] EWHC 1002 (Admin), (2012) 176 JP 369. Where reliance is placed on a certificate, if it conforms to the criteria specified in s 31(2) it can only be challenged on the basis: (i) it constitutes a fraud; or (ii) the certificate is plainly wrong. Where the latter is claimed the challenge should be mounted in relation to the jurisdiction of the court and not as an abuse of process: *Atkinson v DPP* [2004] EWHC 1457 (Admin), [2004] 3 ALL ER 971, [2005] 1 WLR 96; *Lamont-Perkins v Royal Society for the Prevention of Cruelty to Animals* (supra).

In *Letherbarrow v Warwickshire County Council* [2014] EWHC 4820 (Admin), (2015) 179 JP, [2015] All ER (D) 34 (Jun) the prosecutor began an investigation on 19 March 2013. On 3 April an animal health officer issued a caution to the defendant. Further visits took place that month and the officer concerned, after various exchanges of correspondence with the defendant, prepared an internal report. She passed it to a team manager who recommended prosecution and passed that recommendation to his superior, the Group Manager (Trading Standards). She decided that the appellant should be prosecuted on all charges. Summonses were issued, all dated 25 November 2013. The defendant raised the time bar point at the first hearing before the justices on 20th January 2014. The prosecution had not issued a certificate by that stage, but at the next hearing, on 11 February, a certificate was produced to the effect that the date on which sufficient evidence came to the prosecutor's knowledge to justify the proceedings was 5 August 2013 (the date on which the Group Manager made her decision).

The questions which arose were: who is the prosecutor for the purposes of s 31? When does that person have the required knowledge? Can a certificate be issued after a challenge has been made? Is a certificate essential where reliance is placed on s 31?

In *RSPCA v Johnson* [2009] EWHC 2702 (Admin), [2009] All ER (D) 177 (Oct) the Administrative Court had taken the view that the prosecutor for the purposes of s 31 was the RSPCA's case manager given responsibility for making the important decision of whether to prosecute. Time did not begin to run just because some other employee of the RSPCA may have had prior knowledge of the relevant evidence. The court in the present case agreed with that approach. There is no principle that knowledge in a prosecutor begins immediately any employee of the prosecutor has the relevant knowledge. A careful decision is required as to whether the evidence is sufficient to justify a prosecution. This will involve a consideration of what is in the interests of justice and usually involve the opportunity for the defendant to make a statement either at interview or in writing by way of mitigation. This involves the exercise of a judgment by the individual who is given responsibility for making the important decision whether to prosecute. It is the individual with responsibility for deciding whether a prosecution should go forward whose thoughts and beliefs are relevant. While a prosecutor is not entitled to 'shuffle papers' or sit on information to extend a time limit, time runs from when that person makes the decision to prosecute.

In *Riley v Crown Prosecution Service*, supra, the prosecution arose from an incident at a slaughterhouse. DEFRA had responsibility for animals in slaughterhouses and had contracted out responsibility for their welfare to Food Standards Agency veterinary staff. However, the FSA had no prosecution powers; therefore, the prosecutor was the CPS, which issued its certificate in time. It was regrettable that the CPS had not received the evidence sooner, but the delay had not cast any doubt on the fairness of the proceedings, there was nothing to undermine the certificate, consequently the proceedings had been commenced in time.

A certificate under s 31(2) can be issued after a challenge has been raised in court proceedings, but a certificate is not essential because the prosecution may, alternatively, adduce evidence of fact showing who made the decision that a prosecution was justified and when.

A number of issues arose in *R v Woodward* [2017] EWHC 1008 (Admin), 181 JP 405, [2017] Crim LR 884, arising principally from a crucial omission in the first certificate. It was held as follows. There is no reason why, a certificate having been found to be deficient, the prosecutor cannot issue a new certificate. Whilst conceptually, the repeated issue of certificates might amount to an abuse of process, in practice, it is unlikely to do so, absent fraud. Where, after a first certificate valid on its face, a second certificate is issued with a different date of knowledge, that may well require some form of explanation from the prosecutor. Where there is no certificate to be relied upon – because either none was issued, or any certificate issued was defective – then the court must still go on to consider and determine whether the prosecution was brought within the time required by section 31(1)(b) by considering all the available evidence, including documents such as reports even if not supported by a statement, although the weight to be given to that evidence, without being the subject of any supporting statement or cross-examination, is a matter for the court.

Sentencing

SC Guideline – Animal cruelty

Animal cruelty (Revised 2017)

A[5.3]

Animal Welfare Act 2006, s 4 (unnecessary suffering), s 8 (fighting etc), s 9 (breach of duty of person responsible for animal to ensure welfare)

Effective from: 24 April 2017

Triable only summarily:

Maximum: Unlimited fine and/or 6 months

Offence range: Band A fine–26 weeks' custody

STEP 1
Determining the offence category

The court should determine culpability and harm caused with reference only to the factors below. Where an offence does not fall squarely into a category, individual factors may require a degree of weighting before making an overall assessment and determining the appropriate offence category.

CULPABILITY demonstrated by one or more of the following:

Factors indicating high culpability

- Deliberate or gratuitous attempt to cause suffering
- Prolonged or deliberate ill treatment or neglect
- Ill treatment in a commercial context
- A leading role in illegal activity

Factors indicating medium culpability

- All cases not falling into high or low culpability

Factors indicating low culpability

- Well intentioned but incompetent care
- Mental disorder or learning disability, where linked to the commission of the offence

HARM demonstrated by one or more of the following:

Factors indicating greater harm

- Death or serious injury/harm to animal
- High level of suffering caused

Factors indicating lesser harm

- All other cases

STEP 2
Starting point and category range

Having determined the category at step one, the court should use the corresponding starting point to reach a sentence within the category range below. The starting point applies to all offenders irrespective of plea or previous convictions.

A case of particular gravity, reflected by multiple features of culpability in step one, could merit upward adjustment from the starting point before further adjustment for aggravating or mitigating features, set out below.

	High culpability	Medium culpability	Low culpability
Greater harm	**Starting point** 18 weeks' custody	**Starting point** Medium level community order	**Starting point** Band C fine
	Category range 12–26 weeks' custody	**Category range** Low level community order–High level community order	**Category range** Band B fine–Low level community order
Lesser harm	**Starting point** High level community order	**Starting point** Low level community order	**Starting point** Band B fine
	Category range Low level community order–12 weeks' custody	**Category range** Band C fine–Medium level community order	**Category range** Band A fine–Band C fine

The court should then consider further adjustment for any aggravating or mitigating factors. The following is a **non-exhaustive** list of additional factual elements providing the context of the offence and factors relating to the offender. Identify whether any combination of these, or other relevant factors, should result in an upward or downward adjustment from the sentence arrived at so far.

Factors increasing seriousness

Statutory aggravating factors:

- Previous convictions, having regard to a) the **nature** of the offence to which the conviction relates and its **relevance** to the current offence; and b) the **time** that has elapsed since the conviction
- Offence committed whilst on bail
- Offence motivated by, or demonstrating hostility based on any of the following characteristics or presumed characteristics of the owner/keeper of the animal: religion, race, disability, sexual orientation or transgender identity

Other aggravating factors:

- Distress caused to owner where not responsible for the offence
- Failure to comply with current court orders
- Offence committed on licence or post sentence supervision
- Use of weapon
- Allowing person of insufficient experience or training to have care of animal(s)
- Use of technology to publicise or promote cruelty
- Ignores warning/professional advice/declines to obtain professional advice
- Use of another animal to inflict death or injury
- Offender in position of responsibility
- Animal requires significant intervention to recover
- Animal being used in public service or as an assistance dog

Factors reducing seriousness or reflecting personal mitigation

- No previous convictions or no relevant/recent convictions
- Remorse
- Good character and/or exemplary conduct
- Serious medical condition requiring urgent, intensive or long-term treatment
- Age and/or lack of maturity where it affects the responsibility of the offender
- Mental disorder or learning disability, where not linked to the commission of the offence
- Sole or primary carer for dependent relatives
- Offender has been given an inappropriate level of trust or responsibility
- Voluntary surrender of animals to authorities
- Cooperation with the investigation
- Isolated incident

STEP 3
Consider any factors which indicate a reduction, such as assistance to the prosecution

The court should take into account sections 73 and 74 of the Serious Organised Crime and Police Act 2005 (assistance by defendants: reduction or review of sentence) and any other rule of law by virtue of which an offender may receive a discounted sentence in consequence of assistance given (or offered) to the prosecutor or investigator.

STEP 4
Reduction for guilty pleas

The court should take account of any potential reduction for a guilty plea in accordance with section 144 of the Criminal Justice Act 2003 and the *Guilty Plea* guideline.

STEP 5
Totality principle

If sentencing an offender for more than one offence, or where the offender is already serving a sentence, consider whether the total sentence is just and proportionate to the overall offending behaviour in accordance with the *Offences Taken into Consideration and Totality* guideline.

STEP 6
Compensation and ancillary orders

In all cases, the court should consider whether to make compensation and/or other ancillary orders including deprivation of ownership and disqualification of ownership of animals.

STEP 7
Reasons

Section 174 of the Criminal Justice Act 2003 imposes a duty to give reasons for, and explain the effect of, the sentence.

STEP 8
Consideration for time spent on bail

The court must consider whether to give credit for time spent on bail in accordance with section 240A of the Criminal Justice Act 2003.

A[5.4] Deprivation of ownership. If the person convicted of an offence under eg ss 4 or 9 above, is the owner of an animal in relation to which the offence was committed, the court may, instead of or in addition, make an order depriving him of ownership of the animal and for its disposal (Animal Welfare Act 2006, s 33).

Destruction of animal. After conviction the court, if satisfied on the evidence of a veterinary surgeon that it is in the interests of the animal, it may order the animal to be destroyed. The defendant or another person (such as the owner) can be ordered to pay the costs involved. There is a right of appeal to the Crown court except where the court considers that it is in the interests of the animal not to delay the destruction order (Animal Welfare Act 2006, s 37).

Disqualification. The court may disqualify the defendant:

(a) from owning animals;
(b) from keeping animals;
(c) from participating in the keeping of animals; and,
(d) from being party to an arrangement under which he is entitled to control or influence the way in which animals are kept (Animal Welfare Act 2006, s 34).

Such a disqualification must include all the activities specified above: *R (on the application of the RSPCA) v Guildford Crown Court* [2012] EWHC 3392 (Admin), (2013) 177 JP, 154. However, '[10] Under s 3 of the Human Rights Act, legislation must be read, where possible, so as to comply with Convention rights. It may be that in an exceptional case it would be possible to read down the section so as to allow the court a discretion to choose not to apply the disqualification to all the specified acts if that were necessary to protect a Convention right (and, in practice, the right which would be likely to apply would be art 8).' (per Elias LJ)

Alternatively, or additionally, a court may:

(a) disqualify a person from dealing in animals; and/or
(b) disqualify a person from transporting animals and from arranging for the transport of animals.

A disqualification may be imposed in relation to animals generally or in relation to animals of one or more kinds.

The following observations were made by Kerr J in *Barker v RSPCA* [2018] EWHC 8880 (Admin), [2018] 1 Cr App R (S) 13 as to the disqualification provisions:

> '48 First there can be an "all animals" order, that is to say a prohibition against owning, keeping etc any animals at all. An example in an extreme case would be a case where there was no insight whatever into the need to protect the welfare of the animals in question and a culture of uncaring indifference towards them. Contrary to any suggestion from (counsel), I do not accept that an "all animals" prohibition is wrong in principle. A person's treatment of a dog may, in principle, shed light on his or her likely treatment of a cat or a parrot.
>
> 49 Secondly, there can be an order covering some kind of animals but not others. An example would be a prohibition against owning, keeping etc, particular kinds of animals by reference to their inclusion within terms of the order. A simple example would be a prohibition against owning or keeping rabbits because of a repeated failure to protect outdoor rabbit hutches against foxes forcing entry and eating the rabbits. Another example is that proffered in the course of argument by [counsel]: a prohibition against keeping etc horses where a person without any malice or cruelty keeps horses in unacceptable conditions because he or she lacks the resources to maintain proper stables.
>
> 50 Thirdly, there can be what I could call an exclusory order, that is to say an order prohibiting the ownership etc of all animals except those of certain kinds. An example would be where there is a particular reason for finding that defendants are unfit to keep animals generally, but subject to an exception because on the evidence harm to a particular kind of animal in their keeping is considered unlikely.
>
> 51 I note that under s 34(5) it is not permissible to prohibit the ownership etc of individual animals; thus, you cannot make an order prohibiting defendants from owning animals except for one particular terrapin. The prohibition must be framed by reference either to all animals or to kinds of animals, by reference to their genus of species. Here the order made was in the third category. It covered all animals except terrapins. Therefore, it does not preclude the appellant from owning as many terrapins as they wish. They could lawfully keep an army, or perhaps I should say a navy of terrapins.'

If the court decides not to order disqualification it must state its reasons in open court.

The court may specify a period during which no application may be made to terminate the disqualification. If no such period is specified, such an application may be made after the expiry of one year.

The disqualification may be for such period as the court deems fit. If the disqualification order is breached the maximum penalty is a level 5 fine or 51 weeks. The offence is triable summarily only.

Pursuant to s 143 (2) CJA 2003, the court is entitled to have regard to the previous convictions of the offender (as an aggravating factor) for causing unnecessary suffering to an animal. Ten years' disqualification from keeping equine animals upheld on appeal where a farmer had two previous convictions for similar offences: *Anthony Ward v Royal Society for the Prevention of Cruelty to Animals* [2010]) EWHC 347 (Admin).

After the disqualification order has been in force for 12 months the defendant can apply for its removal unless the court specified a different minimum period when imposing the order or a previous application has been refused less than 12 months ago (Animal Welfare Act 2006, s 43).

Sentencing

SC Guideline – Breach of disqualification from keeping an animal

Breach of disqualification from keeping an animal

A[5.5]

Animal Welfare Act 2006, s 32

Effective from: 1 October 2018

Triable: either way

Maximum: 6 months' custody

Offence range: Dishcarge–26 weeks' custody

STEP 1
Determining the offence category

The court should determine the offence category with reference only to the factors listed in the tables below. In order to determine the category the court should assess culpability and harm.

Culpability

A	Serious and/or persistent breach
B	All other cases

Harm

The level of harm is determined by weighing up all the factors of the case to determine the harm that has been caused or was at risk of being caused.

In assessing any risk of harm posed by the breach, consideration should be given to the original offence(s) for which the order was imposed and the circumstances in which the breach arose.

Category 1	• Breach causes or risks death or very serious harm or suffering to animal(s) • Breach results in risk of or actual serious harm to individual(s)
Category 2	• Cases falling between categories 1 and 3
Category 3	• Breach causes or risks little or no harm or suffering to animal(s) • Breach results in very low risk of or little or no harm to individual(s)

STEP 2
Starting point and category range

Having determined the category at step one, the court should use the corresponding starting point to reach a sentence within the category range from the appropriate sentence table below. The starting point applies to all offenders irrespective of plea or previous convictions. The court should then consider further adjustment within the category range for aggravating or mitigating features.

	Culpability	
Harm	**A**	**B**
Category 1	**Starting point** 16 weeks' custody **Category range** 6 weeks' – 26 weeks' custody	**Starting point** 8 weeks' custody **Category range** Medium level community order – 16 weeks' custody
Category 2	**Starting point** 8 weeks' custody **Category range** Medium level community order – 16 weeks' custody	**Starting point** Medium level community order **Category range** Band C Fine – High level community order
Category 3	**Starting point** Medium level community order **Category range** Band C Fine – High level community order	**Starting point** Band A Fine **Category range** Discharge – Band B Fine

The table below contains a **non-exhaustive** list of additional factual elements providing the context of the offence and factors relating to the offender. Identify whether any combination of these, or other relevant factors, should result in an upward or downward adjustment from the starting point. In some cases, having considered these factors, it may be appropriate to move outside the identified category range.

Factors increasing seriousness

Statutory aggravating factors:
Previous convictions, having regard to a) the **nature** of the offence to which the conviction relates and its **relevance** to the current offence; and b) the **time** that has elapsed since the conviction
Offence committed whilst on bail
Other aggravating factors:
Breach committed immediately or shortly after order made
History of disobedience to court orders
Breach conducted in commercial context
Breach involves deceit regarding ownership of/responsibility for animal
Harm risked or caused to multiple animals (where not taken into account at step one)
Offence committed on licence or while subject to post sentence supervision

Factors reducing seriousness or reflecting personal mitigation

Breach committed after long period of compliance
Genuine misunderstanding of terms of order
Prompt voluntary surrender/admission of breach or failure
Age and/or lack of maturity where it affects the responsibility of the offender
Mental disorder or learning disability where linked to the commission of the offence
Sole or primary carer for dependent relatives

STEP 3
Consider any factors which indicate a reduction for assistance to the prosecution

The court should take into account sections 73 and 74 of the Serious Organised Crime and Police Act 2005 (assistance by defendants: reduction or review of

sentence) and any other rule of law by virtue of which an offender may receive a discounted sentence in consequence of assistance given (or offered) to the prosecutor or investigator.

STEP 4
Reduction for guilty pleas

The court should take account of any reduction for a guilty plea in accordance with section 144 of the Criminal Justice Act 2003 and the Guilty Plea guideline.

STEP 5
Totality principle

If sentencing an offender for more than one offence, or where the offender is already serving a sentence, consider whether the total sentence is just and proportionate to the overall offending behaviour in accordance with the *Offences Taken into Consideration and Totality* guideline.

STEP 6
Ancillary orders

In all cases the court should consider whether to make compensation and/or ancillary orders.

STEP
Reasons

Section 174 of the Criminal Justice Act 2003 imposes a duty to give reasons for, and explain the effect of, the sentence.

STEP 8
Consideration for time spent on bail

The court must consider whether to give credit for time spent on bail in accordance with section 240A of the Criminal Justice Act 2003.

A[6]

Anti-social behaviour order, breach of

A[6.1] See B[2] and B[2.5].

A[7]

Assault with intent to resist arrest

Charge (Assault with intent to resist arrest)

A[7.1] **Whosoever shall assault any person with intent to resist or prevent the lawful apprehension or detainer of himself or any other person for any offence, shall be guilty of [an offence]**

Offences Against the Person Act 1861, s 38

Maximum penalty – 6 months' imprisonment and/or fine level 5 (for offences committed on or after 12 March 2015 an unlimited fine). Triable either way. Violent specified offence under Sch 15, Part 1, CJA 2003.

Crown Court – 2 years' imprisonment and unlimited fine.

Mode of trial

A[7.2] Consider the SC Guideline at **A**[7.4] below.

Legal notes and definitions

A[7.3] The prosecution must establish:

(1) That the arrest was lawful.
(2) An intention by the defendant to resist arrest.
(3) Knowledge that the person assaulted, who might or might not be a police officer, was a person who was seeking to arrest him.

An honest belief by the defendant that the arrest was unlawful is irrelevant (*R v Lee* (2001) 165 JP 344, CA).

Where the person carrying out the arrest was a police officer, it is not necessary for the prosecution to establish that the defendant knew he/she was a police officer (*R v Brightling* [1991] Crim LR 364).

Sentencing
SC Guideline – Assault with intent to resist arrest

A[7.4] Offences Against the Person Act 1861, section 38

This is a specified offence for the purposes of section 224 of the Criminal Justice Act 2003

Triable either way

Maximum when tried summarily: 6 months' imprisonment and/or fine level 5 (for offences committed on or after 12 March 2015 an unlimited fine)

Maximum when tried on indictment: 2 years' custody

Offence range: Fine – 51 weeks' custody

This guideline applies to all offenders aged 18 and older, who are sentenced on or after 13 June 2011. The definitions of 'starting point' and 'first time offender' do not apply for this guideline. Starting point and category ranges apply to all offenders in all cases, irrespective of plea or previous convictions.

STEP ONE
Determining the offence category

The court should determine the offence category using the table below.

Category 1	Greater harm and higher culpability
Category 2	Greater harm and lower culpability; or lesser harm and higher culpability
Category 3	Lesser harm and lower culpability

The court should determine the offender's culpability and the harm caused, or intended, by reference **only** to the factors identified in the table below (as demonstrated by the presence of one or more). These factors comprise the principal factual elements of the offence and should determine the category.

Factors indicating greater harm
Sustained or repeated assault on the same victim
Factors indicating lesser harm
Injury which is less serious in the context of the offence
Factors indicating higher culpability
Statutory aggravating factors:
Offence racially or religiously aggravated
Offence motivated by, or demonstrating, hostility to the victim based on his or her sexual orientation (or presumed sexual orientation)
Offence motivated by, or demonstrating, hostility to the victim based on the victim's disability (or presumed disability)
Other aggravating factors:
A significant degree of premeditation
Use of weapon or weapon equivalent (for example, shod foot, headbutting, use of acid, use of animal)
Intention to commit more serious harm than actually resulted from the offence
Deliberately causes more harm than is necessary for commission of offence
Leading role in group or gang
Offence motivated by, or demonstrating, hostility based on the victim's age, sex, gender identity (or presumed gender identity)
Factors indicating lower culpability
Subordinate role in group or gang Lack of premeditation
Mental disorder or learning disability, where linked to commission of the offence

STEP TWO
Starting point and category range

Having determined the category, the court should use the corresponding starting points to reach a sentence within the category range below. The starting point applies to all offenders irrespective of plea or previous convictions. A case of particular gravity, reflected by multiple features of culpability in step one, could merit upward adjustment from the starting point before further adjustment for aggravating or mitigating features, set out below.

Offence Category	Starting Point *(Applicable to all offenders)*	Category Range *(Applicable to all offenders)*
Category 1	26 weeks – custody	12 weeks – custody – Crown Court (51 weeks – custody)
Category 2	Medium level community order	Low level community order – High level community order
Category 3	Band B fine	Band A fine – Band C fine

The table below contains a **non-exhaustive** list of additional factual elements providing the context of the offence and factors relating to the offender. Identify whether any combination of these, or other relevant factors, should result in an upward or downward adjustment from the starting point. In some cases, having considered these factors, it may be appropriate to move outside the identified category range.

When sentencing **category 1** offences, the court should consider whether the sentence can be suspended.

Factors increasing seriousness

Statutory aggravating factors:

Previous convictions, having regard to a) the nature of the offence to which the conviction relates and its relevance to the current offence; and b) the time that has elapsed since the conviction

Offence committed whilst on bail

Other aggravating factors include:

Location of the offence

Timing of the offence

Ongoing effect upon the victim

Gratuitous degradation of victim

Failure to comply with current court orders

Offence committed whilst on licence

An attempt to conceal or dispose of evidence

Failure to respond to warnings or concerns expressed by others about the offender's behaviour

Commission of offence whilst under the influence of alcohol or drugs

Established evidence of community impact

Any steps taken to prevent the victim reporting an incident, obtaining assistance and/or from assisting or supporting the prosecution

Offences taken into consideration (TICs)

Factors reducing seriousness or reflecting personal mitigation

No previous convictions or no relevant/recent convictions

Single blow

Remorse

Good character and/or exemplary conduct

Determination and/or demonstration of steps taken to address addiction or offending behaviour

Serious medical conditions requiring urgent, intensive or long-term treatment

Isolated incident

Age and/or lack of maturity where it affects the responsibility of the defendant

Mental disorder or learning disability, where not linked to the commission of the offence

Sole or primary carer for dependent relatives

STEP THREE
Consider any other factors which indicate a reduction, such as assistance to the prosecution

The court should take into account any rule of law by virtue of which an offender may receive a discounted sentence in consequence of assistance given (or offered) to the prosecutor or investigator.

STEP FOUR
Reduction for guilty pleas

The court should take account of any potential reduction for a guilty plea in accordance with section 144 of the Criminal Justice Act 2003 and the *Guilty Plea* guideline.

STEP FIVE
Dangerousness

Assault with intent to resist arrest is a specified offence within the meaning of Chapter 5 of the Criminal Justice Act 2003 and at this stage the court should consider whether having regard to the criteria contained in that Chapter it would be appropriate to award an extended sentence.

STEP SIX
Totality principle

If sentencing an offender for more than one offence or where the offender is already serving a sentence, consider whether the total sentence is just and proportionate to the offending behaviour.

STEP SEVEN
Compensation and ancillary orders

In all cases, the court should consider whether to make compensation and/or other ancillary orders.

STEP EIGHT
Reasons

Section 174 of the Criminal Justice Act 2003 imposes a duty to give reasons for, and explain the effect of, the sentence.

STEP NINE
Consideration for remand time

(Now obligatory.)

A[7.5] Licensed premises. If the offence takes place on licensed premises an exclusion order may be made. See B[27].

A[8]

Assault occasioning actual bodily harm and racially/religiously aggravated assault occasioning ABH

Charge (Assault occasioning actual bodily harm)

A[8.1] **Assault occasioning actual bodily harm**

Offences Against The Person Act 1861, s 47

Maximum penalty – 6 months' imprisonment and/or fine level 5 (for offences committed on or after 12 March 2015 an unlimited fine). Triable either way. Violent specified offence under Sch 15, Part 1, CJA 2003.

Crown Court – 5 years' imprisonment and unlimited fine.

A[8.2] **Racially or religiously aggravated assault occasioning actual bodily harm**

Crime and Disorder Act 1998, s 29

Maximum penalty – 6 months' imprisonment and/or fine level 5 (for offences committed on or after 12 March 2015 an unlimited fine). Triable either way. Specified violent offence under Sch 15, Part 1, CJA 2003

Crown Court – 7 years' imprisonment and unlimited fine.

Mode of trial

A[8.3]–[8.4] Consider the SC Guideline at A[8.31] below. For cases of domestic violence. See SC Definitive Guideline: "Overarching Principles: Domestic Violence".

Owing to the nature of charges of assault it is particularly important that magistrates hear an outline of the facts before making their decision.

Legal notes and definitions

A[8.5]–[8.6] **Assault.** See under 'Common assault' at A[15].

A[8.7] **Intent.** The defendant must intend to cause his victim to apprehend immediate and unlawful violence, or be reckless whether such apprehension be caused (*R v Venna* [1976] QB 421, [1975] 3 All ER 788, CA). The offence of assault occasioning actual bodily harm is made out upon proof of an assault together with proof of the fact that actual bodily harm was occasioned by the assault. The prosecution are not obliged to prove that the defendant intended to cause some actual bodily harm or was reckless as to whether such harm would be caused (*R v Savage* [1992] 1 AC 699, [1991] 4 All ER 698, *R v Parmenter* [1991] 4 All ER 698, HL).

In principle it was open to justices to convict on the basis of recklessness even where the prosecution simply alleged a deliberate assault: *D v DPP* [2005] EWHC 967 (Admin) considered. However, the justices had failed to identify what was the unlawful act of K leading to the assault. Recklessness had only been a possible conclusion if the justices had found that K had thrown a punch, albeit without intending it to land, or was flailing his arms about in an agitated and aggressive manner. The conviction could not stand in the light of the findings of fact made by the justices: *Katsonis v Crown Prosecution Service* [2011] EWHC 1860 (Admin), 175 JP 396.

A[8.8] In *DPP v K (a minor)* [1990] 1 All ER 331, [1990] 1 WLR 1067, a schoolboy who put acid in a hot air dryer recklessly but in a mindless panic rather than with any intention to cause harm was nonetheless guilty of assault. In *DPP v Santra-Bermudez* [2003] EWHC 2908, [2003] All ER (D) 168 (Nov) the offence was made out when a police officer pricked her finger on a needle while carrying out a lawful search of a man who had told her that he had no needles in his pocket.

A[8.9] Actual bodily harm. This is less serious than grievous bodily harm. There need not be permanent injury. Any hurt or injury calculated to interfere with health or comfort can be actual bodily harm, so can an assault causing unconsciousness or an hysterical or nervous condition (*R v Miller* [1954] 2 QB 282, [1954] 2 All ER 529), ie some psychiatric damage and not just distress or panic (*R v Chan-Fook* [1994] 2 All ER 552, [1994] 1 WLR 689, CA). Significant psychological symptoms caused by a series of telephone calls, followed by silence can constitute an assault causing actual bodily harm (*R v Ireland* [1998] AC 147, [1997] 4 All ER 225, HL). Where a victim suffered great pain immediately and for some time thereafter suffered tenderness and soreness, that was sufficient for the court to infer that there was actual bodily harm notwithstanding that no physically discernible injury had been occasioned. This would include the victim's unconsciousness without the appearance of physical injury (*T v DPP* [2004] EWHC 183 (Admin), [2004] All ER (D) 278 (Jan)). Where there is evidence that a blow was struck, the justices are entitled if they see fit to infer that some bodily harm, however slight, has resulted.

Cutting off a substantial part of the victim's hair was capable in law of amounting to an assault which occasioned actual bodily harm (*DPP v Smith (MR)* [2006] EWHC 94 (Admin), [2006] 2 All ER 16).

A[8.10]–[8.15] Racial, religious, disability, sexual orientation or transgender identity aggravation. This means that at the time of committing the offence, or immediately before or after doing so, the offender demonstrates towards the victim of the offence either hostility based on the victim's membership (or presumed membership) of a racial or religious group or their disability or presumed sexual orientation; or, the offence is motivated (wholly or partly) by hostility towards members of a racial or religious group based on their membership of that group, or persons of a particular sexual orientation, transgender identity or disability. See *R v H* [2010] EWCA Crim 1931, 174 CL&J 573, 154 Sol Jo (no 31) 28 which reviews the authorities.

A[8.16] When considering whether an offence was racially motivated for the purposes of the CDA 1998, s 28 (1)(a) in the light of words uttered immediately prior to the offence, the following matters were irrelevant: (i) victim's perception of the words used; (ii) any additional reason unrelated to race, for uttering the words (CDA 1998, s 28(3)(b)); and (iii) the fact that in the defendant's frame of mind at the time he uttered the words, he would have abused anyone by reference to an obvious physical characteristic (*DPP v Woods* [2002] EWHC 85 (Admin), [2002] All ER (D) 154 (Jan)). However, see **A[20.6]** for more recent case law.

It is immaterial whether or not the offender's hostility is based, to any extent on any other factor not mentioned above. See **A[15.33]** for sentencing.

A[8.17] Provocation is not a defence but can be taken into consideration when deciding sentence.

A[8.18]–[8.19] Reasonable force for purposes of self-defence etc. A person may use reasonable force to defend himself, his property or another. Where self-defence is put forward to justify the use of violence, the onus is on the prosecution to disprove the defence beyond reasonable doubt. A person must not use force in attacking or retaliating, or revenging himself. It is permissible to use force not merely to counter an actual attack but to ward off an attack honestly believed to be imminent. The reasonableness or otherwise of the belief is only relevant in ascertaining whether he actually held the belief or not (*Beckford v R* [1988] AC 130, [1987] 3 All ER 425, PC).

The fact that the use of force was instinctive rather than based on a conscious decision can be important when judging honest belief, but it does not negate this and can, indeed, be potent evidence pointing the other way; nor does it negate self defence that the defendant regretted what he had done seconds later, or that he apologised immediately afterwards, especially where the apology included the explanation that the use of force had been in the defence of another: *Dewar v DPP* [2010] EWHC 1050 (Admin), [2010] ALL ER (D) 83 (Jan).

Proof that the accused tried to retreat or call off the fight might be a cast-iron method of rebutting the suggestion that he was an attacker or retaliator or trying to revenge himself. It is to be stressed, however, that this is not the only method of doing so, and it depends on the circumstances of the particular case (*R v Bird* [1985] 2 All ER 513, [1985] 1 WLR 816, CA). The common law defence of self defence and the defence under s 3 of the Criminal Law Act 1967, extended to the use of violence against an innocent third party: *R v Hichens* [2011] EWCA Crim 1626, [2011] 2 Cr App Rep 370, [2011] Crim LR 873.

In *Marsh v DPP* [2015] EWHC 1022 (Admin), [2015] Crim LR 713, [2015] All ER (D) 347 (Mar) M was charged with assault by beating. His defence at trial was that he was not the aggressor and that the victim had approached him in a manner which had led him to believe that he needed to defend himself. He did this by head butting the victim because he suffered from osteoporosis and could not, therefore, use his arms. The justices were not sure who the original aggressor was, but they were sure that M had used more force than was necessary to defend himself and they accordingly convicted him. M appealed by way of case stated, but was unsuccessful. The proper approach was to focus on the violent act and to determine whether it was done in self defence. There was no need to show who the initial aggressor was. In the present case the justices had been entitled to conclude that M had gone over the top and had used force out of all proportion to the anticipated attack.

A[8.20] A man who is attacked can defend himself but can only do what is objectively reasonable in the circumstances as the defendant believes them to be. In relation to self defence, prevention of crime or effecting or assisting in the lawful arrest of another, s 76 of the Criminal Justice and Immigration Act 2008 codified the common law. It has subsequently been amended by both the Legal Aid, Sentencing and Punishment of Offenders Act 2012 (which inserted subs(6A)) and the Crime and Courts Act 2013 (which inserted subs(5A), (8A)–(8F). It provides as follows:

(1) This section applies where in proceedings for an offence—
  (a) an issue arises as to whether a person charged with the offence ("D") is entitled to rely on a defence within subsection (2), and
  (b) the question arises whether the degree of force used by D against a person ("V") was reasonable in the circumstances.

(2) The defences are—
  (a) the common law defence of self-defence;
  (aa) the common law defence of defence of property; and
  (b) the defences provided by section 3(1) of the Criminal Law Act 1967 (c 58) or section 3(1) of the Criminal Law Act (Northern Ireland) 1967 (c 18 (NI)) (use of force in prevention of crime or making arrest).

(3) The question whether the degree of force used by D was reasonable in the circumstances is to be decided by reference to the circumstances as D believed them to be, and subsections (4) to (8) also apply in connection with deciding that question.

(4) If D claims to have held a particular belief as regards the existence of any circumstances—
  (a) the reasonableness or otherwise of that belief is relevant to the question whether D genuinely held it; but
  (b) if it is determined that D did genuinely hold it, D is entitled to rely on it for the purposes of subsection (3), whether or not–
    (i) it was mistaken, or

(ii) (if it was mistaken) the mistake was a reasonable one to have made.

(5) But subsection (4) (b) does not enable D to rely on any mistaken belief attributable to intoxication that was voluntarily induced.

(5A) In a householder case, the degree of force used by D is not to be regarded as having been reasonable in the circumstances as D believed them to be if it was grossly disproportionate in those circumstances.

(6) In a case other than a householder case, the degree of force used by D is not to regarded as having been reasonable in the circumstances as D believed them to be if it was disproportionate in those circumstances.

(6A) In deciding the question mentioned in subsection (3), a possibility that D could have retreated is to be considered (so far as relevant) as a factor to be taken into account, rather than as giving rise to a duty to retreat.

(7) In deciding the question mentioned in subsection (3) the following considerations are to be taken into account (so far as relevant in the circumstances of the case)—

(a) that a person acting for a legitimate purpose may not be able to weigh to a nicety the exact measure of any necessary action; and

(b) that evidence of a person having only done what the person honestly and instinctively thought was necessary for a legitimate purpose constitutes strong evidence that only reasonable action was taken by that person for that purpose.

(8) Subsections (6A) and (7) are not to be read as preventing other matters from being taken into account where they are relevant in deciding the question mentioned in subsection (3).

(8A) For the purposes of this section "a householder case" is a case where—

(a) the defence concerned is the common law defence of self-defence,

(b) the force concerned is force used by D while in or partly in a building, or part of a building, that is a dwelling or is forces accommodation (or is both),

(c) D is not a trespasser at the time the force is used, and

(d) at that time D believed V to be in, or entering, the building or part as a trespasser.

(8B) Where—

(a) a part of a building is a dwelling where D dwells,

(b) another part of the building is a place of work for D or another person who dwells in the first part,

(c) that other part is internally accessible from the first part,

that other part, and any internal means of access between the two parts, are each treated for the purposes of subsection (8A) as a part of a building that is a dwelling.

(8C) Where—

(a) a part of a building is forces accommodation that is living or sleeping accommodation for D,

(b) another part of the building is a place of work for D or another person for whom the first part is living or sleeping accommodation, and

(c) that other part is internally accessible from the first part, that other part, and any internal means of access between the two parts, are each treated for the purposes of subsection (8A) as a part of a building that is forces accommodation.

(8D) Subsections (4) and (5) apply for the purposes of subsection (8A)(d) as they apply for the purposes of subsection (3).

(8E) The fact that a person derives title from a trespasser, or has the permission of a trespasser, does not prevent the person from being a trespasser for the purposes of subsection (8A).

(8F) In subsections (8A) to (8C)—

"building" includes a vehicle or vessel, and

"forces accommodation" means service living accommodation for the purposes of Part 3 of the Armed Forces Act 2006 by virtue of section 96(1)(a) or (b) of that Act.

(9) This section, except so far as making different provision for householder cases, is intended to clarify the operation of the existing defences mentioned in subsection (2).

(10) In this section—

(a) "legitimate purpose" means—

(i) the purpose of self-defence under the common law,

(ia) the purpose of defence of property under the common law, or

(ii) the prevention of crime or effecting or assisting in the lawful arrest of persons mentioned in the provisions referred to in subsection (2)(b);

(b) references to self-defence include acting in defence of another person; and

(c) references to the degree of force used are to the type and amount of force used.

Section 76(5) provides that the defendant may not rely on any mistaken belief attributable to intoxication that was voluntarily induced. It was held in *R v Taj* [2018] EWCA crim 1743, [2018] ALL ER (D) 153 (Jul) that the words 'attributable to intoxication' were broad enough to encompass both: (i) a mistaken state of mind as a result of being drunk or intoxicated at the time; and (ii) a mistaken state of mind immediately and proximately consequent on earlier drink or drug-taking, so that even though the person concerned was not drunk or intoxicated at the time, the short-term effects could be shown to have triggered subsequent episodes of, for example, paranoia. That conclusion did not extend to long-term mental illness precipitated (perhaps over a considerable period) by alcohol or drug misuse. Accordingly, the judge had been right that the phrase 'attributable to intoxication' was not confined to cases in which alcohol or drugs were still present in a defendant's system.

The so-called householder's defence was considered in *R (Collins) v Secretary of State for Justice* [2016] EWHC 333 (Admin), [2016] 2 WLR 1303, [2016] 1 Cr App R 25. The combined effect of s 76(3) and s 76(5A) was that the nature and degree of force had to be reasonable in the circumstances as the defendant believed them to be. Section 76(5A) automatically excluded a degree of force which was grossly disproportionate from being reasonable; it did not direct that a lesser degree of force was reasonable. The latter was an issue that would depend on the particular facts and circumstances of the case. This did not breach the UK's positive obligation under art 2.1 of the ECHR to secure the right to life by putting in place an appropriate and legal and administrative framework to deter the commission of offences against the person. The approach to be adopted was: did the defendant genuinely believe it was necessary for the defendant to use force to defend him/herself? If so, was the degree of force which the defendant used grossly disproportionate in the circumstances as he/she believed them to be? If not, was the degree of force which the defendant used reasonable in the circumstances as he/she believed them to be? The answers to these questions had to be 'yes', 'no' and 'yes' for the defence to succeed.

The decision in *R (Collins) v Secretary of State for Justice* on the householder's defence under s 76 of the 2008 Act was affirmed by the Court of Appeal in *R v Ray* [2017] EWCA Crim 1391, [2018] 1 Cr App R 4, 181 JP 493, a decision of particular authority since the court comprised of five judges presided over by the Lord Chief Justice. The judgment is particularly valuable for the practical guidance it gives in householder cases. An unreasonable degree of force used when confronting an aggressive individual in a club might not be so when used by a householder confronting an intruder in his own home. The householder is entitled to some latitude as to the degree of force used and, if it is not 'completely over the top', the court must examine all the circumstances in determining whether the prosecution have proved that the degree of force used was unreasonable. It is this context that differentiates the householder case. The circumstances to consider might, for example, include the shock of coming upon an intruder, the time of day, the presence of other help, the desire to protect the home and its occupants, the vulnerability of the occupants, particularly children, or the picking up of an object (such as a knife or stick that would lawfully be to hand in the home), and the conduct of the intruder at the time (or on any relevant previous occasion if known to the defendant). Each of these might lead to the view that what was done, such as using a knife, which otherwise in a different context might be unreasonable, in the circumstances of a householder coming on an intruder might, in all the circumstances of such a case, be reasonable. Another useful illustration may be the question of retreat. Section 76(6A) makes clear that there is no duty to retreat; the possibility of retreat is but a factor in determining whether the degree of force used was reasonable. If there is a threat of confrontation in the street, then the option to retreat may be important in determining whether the use of any force was reasonable. In the case of an intruder in the home, however, the option of retreat is unlikely to arise in many cases and therefore the degree of force used, although otherwise appearing to be disproportionate, might nonetheless be assessed as reasonable.

The householder defence is available where a person entered premises lawfully but thereafter became a trespasser: *R v Cheeseman* [2019] EWCA Crim 149, [2019] 1 WLR 3505, [2019] 1 Cr App R 34.

A[8.20A] **Use of force to prevent crime or effect an arrest: Criminal Law Act 1967, s 3(1).** The defence under s 3(1) of the CLA 1967 has been considered exhaustively by the House of Lords in *R v Jones* [2006] UKHL 16, [2007] 1 AC 136, [2006] 2 WLR 772, [2006] 2 Cr App Rep 136 and subsequently by the Administrative Court in *R (DPP) v Stratford Magistrates' Court* [2017] EWHC 1794. This was in part in response to attempts to invoke the defence in cases of protest and direct action against activities alleged to be unlawful under domestic or international law.

There are two questions to ask. First, did the defendant honestly (even if mistakenly), believe that he or she was acting to prevent a crime? Second, if so, was the force that was used reasonable, in the circumstances that the defendant believed them to be?

General principles applying to the defence are these. Firstly, ordinary citizens who apprehend a breach of the law are normally expected to call the police and not take the law into their own hands. Secondly, the use of force to prevent crime may be legitimate and give rise to the defence in a moment of emergency, when individual action is necessary to prevent some imminent crime. Thirdly, the right of a citizen to use force is even more circumscribed when not in defence of his own person or property, but deployed to enforce the law in the interest of the community at large. Fourthly, while the law recognises conscientious protests and civil disobedience, the honestly held beliefs of protestors as to the legality of certain activities cannot be allowed to subvert the forensic process. Fifthly, in the light of these points, a Court should be prepared to conclude that the defence under s 3(1) is not available to a defendant.

The defence under s 3(1) of the CLA 1967 operates as a justification for the use of force rather than an excuse to use force, and is linked to the concept of necessity.

Firstly, there must be an apprehension of a need to use force (or, in an appropriate case something less than force – see infra) to prevent an imminent or immediate crime, or an actual and inevitable danger. There must be a clear nexus between the use of force and the prevention of crime, and there is a clear difference between a protest against what is regarded as objectionable and even illegal conduct on the one hand, and the use of force to prevent an imminent and immediate crime on the other. Secondly, the court should not countenance the demand for disclosure or the calling of evidence (expert or otherwise) which relates to what cannot properly be characterised as an imminent or immediate crime. If the commission of such crimes are not within the direct knowledge of a defendant, they are unlikely to fall into that category. Thirdly, on an application to consider the ambit of a defence under s 3(1) of the CLA 1967, a court should consider whether, on the most favourable view of the facts, such a defence is available. If there is no proper evidential basis on which the defence can be said to be available, it should be withdrawn from consideration. Fourthly, in the magistrates' court it is particularly important to consider carefully: (1) the proper ambit of the defence, and (2) when making findings, the questions which need to be posed and how they should be answered. The sincerity of the defendant's beliefs relation to a matter about which he or she is protesting, for example, is irrelevant to the second question which the court must address.

The defence applies to the direct application of force, although the force will not necessarily have to be applied directly against a person. It will apply, for example, to defendants who attach themselves to a lorry which is believed to be carrying chemical weapons, or a case where the defendants tie themselves to tractors rather than attacking the tractor drivers. In contrast, the defence will not be available to those who lie down in the road in front of lorries making their way to a place where crimes are believed to be taking place or who block access by chaining themselves to gates.

Notwithstanding the apparent anomaly that force may be relied on as a statutory defence but that something less than force does not come within this defence, something short of the application of force may give rise to a defence to a criminal offence, but that, as in the case of the statutory defence, there must be a nexus between the conduct and the criminality.

A[8.21] Misadventure. See A[15.8].

A[8.22] **Consent and reasonable chastisement.** See A[15.10]–A[15.17].

A[8.23]–[8.30] **Lawful sport.** See A[15.18].

Reduction of charge/alternative verdict. The court cannot reduce this charge to common assault or consider an alternative verdict but, if a separate charge of common assault is preferred, a conviction for that may be possible.

Sentencing

SC Guideline – Assault occasioning actual bodily harm and Racially/religiously aggravated ABH

Assault occasioning actual bodily harm

Offences Against the Person Act 1861 (section 47)

Racially/religiously aggravated ABH

Crime and Disorder Act 1998 (section 29)

A[8.31]–[8.32] These are specified offences for the purposes of section 224 of the Criminal Justice Act 2003

Triable either way

Section 47

Maximum when tried summarily: Level 5 fine and/or 26 weeks' custody

Maximum when tried on indictment: 5 years' custody

Section 29

Maximum when tried summarily: Level 5 fine and/or 26 weeks' custody

Maximum when tried on indictment: 7 years' custody

Offence range: Fine – 3 years' custody

This guideline applies to all offenders aged 18 and older, who are sentenced on or after 13 June 2011. The definitions of 'starting point' and 'first time offender' do not apply for this guideline. Starting point and category ranges apply to all offenders in all cases, irrespective of plea or previous convictions.

STEP ONE
Determining the offence category

The court should determine the offence category using the table below.

Category 1	Greater harm and higher culpability
Category 2	Greater harm and lower culpability; or lesser harm and higher culpability
Category 3	Lesser harm and lower culpability

The court should determine the offender's culpability and the harm caused, or intended, by reference only to the factors identified in the table below (as demonstrated by the presence of one or more). These factors comprise the principal factual elements of the offence and should determine the category.

Factors indicating greater harm

Injury (which includes disease transmission and/or psychological harm) which is serious in the context of the offence (must normally be present)

Victim is particularly vulnerable because of personal circumstances

Sustained or repeated assault on the same victim

Factors indicating lesser harm

Injury which is less serious in the context of the offence

Factors indicating higher culpability

Statutory aggravating factors:

Offence motivated by, or demonstrating, hostility to the victim based on his or her sexual orientation (or presumed sexual orientation)

Offence motivated by, or demonstrating, hostility to the victim based on the victim's disability (or presumed disability)

Other aggravating factors:

A significant degree of premeditation

Use of weapon or weapon equivalent (for example, shod foot, headbutting, use of acid, use of animal)

Intention to commit more serious harm than actually resulted from the offence

Deliberately causes more harm than is necessary for commission of offence

Deliberate targeting of vulnerable victim

Leading role in group or gang

Offence motivated by, or demonstrating, hostility based on the victim's age, sex, gender identity (or presumed gender identity)

Factors indicating lower culpability
Subordinate role in group or gang
A greater degree of provocation than normally expected
Lack of premeditation
Mental disorder or learning disability, where linked to commission of the offence
Excessive self defence

STEP TWO

Starting point and category range

Having determined the category, the court should use the corresponding starting points to reach a sentence within the category range below. The starting point applies to all offenders irrespective of plea or previous convictions. A case of particular gravity, reflected by multiple features of culpability in step one, could merit upward adjustment from the starting point before further adjustment for aggravating or mitigating features, set out below.

Offence Category	Starting Point *(Applicable to all offenders)*	Category Range *(Applicable to all offenders)*
Category 1	Crown Court	Crown Court
Category 2	26 weeks' custody	Low level community order – Crown Court (51 weeks' custody)
Category 3	Medium level community order	Band A fine – High level community order

The table below contains a **non-exhaustive** list of additional factual elements providing the context of the offence and factors relating to the offender. Identify whether any combination of these, or other relevant factors, should result in an upward or downward adjustment from the starting point. In some cases, having considered these factors, it may be appropriate to move outside the identified category range.

When sentencing **category 2** offences, the court should also consider the custody threshold as follows:

- has the custody threshold been passed?
- if so, is it unavoidable that a custodial sentence be imposed?
- if so, can that sentence be suspended?

When sentencing **category 3** offences, the court should also consider the community order threshold as follows:

- has the community order threshold been passed?

Factors increasing seriousness
Statutory aggravating factors:
Previous convictions, having regard to a) the nature of the offence to which the conviction relates and its relevance to the current offence; and b) the time that has elapsed since the conviction
Offence committed whilst on bail
Other aggravating factors include:
Location of the offence
Timing of the offence
Ongoing effect upon the victim

Offence committed against those working in the public sector or providing a service to the public
Presence of others including relatives, especially children or partner of the victim
Gratuitous degradation of victim
In domestic violence cases, victim forced to leave their home
Failure to comply with current court orders
Offence committed whilst on licence
An attempt to conceal or dispose of evidence
Failure to respond to warnings or concerns expressed by others about the offender's behaviour
Commission of offence whilst under the influence of alcohol or drugs
Abuse of power and/or position of trust
Exploiting contact arrangements with a child to commit an offence
Established evidence of community impact
Any steps taken to prevent the victim reporting an incident, obtaining assistance and/or from assisting or supporting the prosecution
Offences taken into consideration (TICs)
Factors reducing seriousness or reflecting personal mitigation
No previous convictions **or** no relevant/recent convictions
Single blow
Remorse
Good character and/or exemplary conduct
Determination and/or demonstration of steps taken to address addiction or offending behaviour
Serious medical conditions requiring urgent, intensive or long-term treatment
Isolated incident
Age and/or lack of maturity where it affects the responsibility of the offender
Lapse of time since the offence where this is not the fault of the offender
Mental disorder or learning disability, where **not** linked to the commission of the offence
Sole or primary carer for dependent relatives

Section 29 offences only: The court should determine the appropriate sentence for the offence without taking account of the element of aggravation and then make an addition to the sentence, considering the level of aggravation involved. It may be appropriate to move outside the identified category range, taking into account the increased statutory maximum.

STEP THREE
Consider any other factors which indicate a reduction, such as assistance to the prosecution

The court should take into account any rule of law by virtue of which an offender may receive a discounted sentence in consequence of assistance given (or offered) to the prosecutor or investigator.

STEP FOUR
Reduction for guilty pleas

The court should take account of any potential reduction for a guilty plea in accordance with section 144 of the Criminal Justice Act 2003 and the *Guilty Plea* guideline.

STEP FIVE
Dangerousness

Assault occasioning actual bodily harm and racially/religiously aggravated ABH are specified offences within the meaning of Chapter 5 of the Criminal Justice Act 2003 and at this stage the court should consider whether having regard to the criteria contained in that Chapter it would be appropriate to award an extended sentence.

STEP SIX
Totality principle

If sentencing an offender for more than one offence, or where the offender is already serving a sentence, consider whether the total sentence is just and proportionate to the offending behaviour.

STEP SEVEN
Compensation and ancillary orders

In all cases, the court should consider whether to make compensation and/or other ancillary orders.

STEP EIGHT
Reasons

Section 174 of the Criminal Justice Act 2003 imposes a duty to give reasons for, and explain the effect of, the sentence.

STEP NINE
Consideration for remand time

(Now obligatory.)

A[8.33] Licensed premises. An assault committed on licensed premises will enable the court to make an exclusion order. See B[27].

A[8.34] Domestic violence. For domestic violence offences see SC Definitive Guideline 'Overarching Principles: Domestic Abuse'.

A[9]

Assaulting a police constable (or a person assisting the police) Assaulting a court security officer

Charge (Assaulting a police constable)

A[9.1] Assaulting a constable in the execution of his duty

or

Assaulting a person assisting a constable in the execution of his duty

Police Act 1996, s 89

and

Assaulting a court security officer in the execution of his duty

Criminal Justice Act 1991, s 78 [from 1 April 2005 contrary to Courts Act 2003, s 57]

Maximum penalty – 6 months' imprisonment and/or fine level 5 (for offences committed on or after 12 March 2015 an unlimited fine). Triable only summarily.

Legal notes and definitions

A[9.2] Assault. See under Common assault at A[8].

A[9.3] Constable. Includes a special constable and any member of the police irrespective of actual rank. Offences against designated and accredited persons acting in the execution of their duty ie community support officer, investigating officer, detention officer or escort officer are catered for under the Police Reform Act 2002, s 46. Assaults carry a maximum penalty of a level 5 fine and/or six months imprisonment.

A[9.4] Court security officer. A person appointed by the Lord Chancellor or provided under a contract and designated by the Lord Chancellor as a court security officer (s 51 Courts Act 2003).

A[9.5] In the execution of his duty. The constable must be carrying out his duty at the time of the assault. If he goes beyond his duty, for example by catching hold of a person whom he is not arresting, then this offence is not committed by a person resisting him with reasonable force. The line between duty and what lies beyond is not easily discernible. This needs reference to many decided cases in the higher courts – see, for example, *Donnelly v Jackman* [1970] 1 All ER 987, [1970] 1 WLR 562 and *Osman v DPP* (1999) 163 JP 725. Police acting on a reasonable expectation of a breach of the peace are acting within their duty (*Wragg v DPP* [2005] EWHC 1389 (Admin), [2005] All ER (D) 131 (Jun)).

It was held in *Metcalf v CPS* [2015] EWHC 1071 (Admin), (2015) 179 JP 288, [2015] 2 Cr App R 25, [2015] Crim L R 722 that an officer was entitled to use reasonable force (by pushing away) against a person who had made it clear by his words and actions that he intended to continue to obstruct that and another officer as they were attempting to take away two men who had been arrested following a public disturbance. Lord Justice Burnton added that, in any event, the push had no bearing on the question whether the appellant's conduct before that time amounted to wilful obstruction. An unlawful push cannot retrospectively render conduct lawful, which was otherwise criminal.

In *R (on the application of Reda) v DPP* [2011] EWHC 1550 (Admin), 175 JP 329, the appellant was walking with other youths past an empty police van when he raised his voice and uttered the words 'fuck the police'. At the material time there were no members of the public present other than the youths and two police officers who were emerging from a nearby block of flats. The first officer heard the specific words used and decided to arrest the appellant for causing harassment, alarm or distress contrary to s 5 of the Public Order Act 1986. Following his arrest the appellant kicked the police officer on the leg.

The Queen's Bench Division concluded that there were reasonable grounds to suspect that an offence had been or was about to be committed. The offending words were said in a public place and, whilst it could not be established that the police officer had himself seen other people present at the material time, nevertheless he could reasonably proceed on the footing that there were or may have been. Furthermore, the arresting officer's colleague was in hearing distance of what was said and the other youths were present. He could not necessarily have taken it that the other boys would not themselves have been insulted or alarmed by what this appellant was shouting or saying. Accordingly, the officer was acting lawfully in the execution of his duty.

In *McCann v Crown Prosecution Service* [2015] EWHC 2461 (Admin), (2015) 179 JP 470, [2016] 1 Cr App R 6, [2016] Crim L R 59 in the course of an anti 'fracking' protest the defendant and other were seated in the middle of the road, locked together and thereby preventing lorries heading for the drilling site from passing. The local police inspector instructed the defendant and those locked with her to move. They refused on the ground, subsequently accepted to be correct, that the passageway was a private road with a public footpath. The inspector believed the road to be a public highway and the defendant was arrested for obstructing the highway. Shortly afterwards, the appellant was further arrested for obstructing a police officer, contrary to s 89(2) of the Police Act 1996 and this was the charge which proceeded to trial.

It was submitted by the defence that even if the officer had been acting in good faith or that the error was reasonable, it did not make the request to move lawful and, consequently, the inspector was not acting in the execution of his duty. The District Judge rejected this argument, holding that it mattered not that the officer had the wrong offence in mind because her belief, albeit mistaken, was reasonable, she acted in response to the same activity and the same mischief and the facts could have lent themselves to another offence (aggravated trespass).

The appeal proceeded on two grounds only: whether the mistake of fact regarding the classification of the road was unreasonable so as to place the inspector outside the execution of her duty; and whether in the circumstances the inspector could not be acting within the execution of her duty on the basis that another offence, namely aggravated trespass, may have been committed. The Administrative Court upheld the conviction. It was not necessary for the officer to have had the correct offence in mind at the time the direction to move was given. It was sufficient for the officer to have taken steps which reasonably appeared to her to be necessary for preventing crime. The fact that the officer in fact had an offence of which the appellant was not guilty in mind did not prevent her from taking steps which in the circumstances, as she believed them to be, reasonably appeared to her to be necessary for preventing crime. In the light of the findings that the officer reasonably believed at the material time that the road was a public highway and that she had reasonable grounds to suspect that an offence was being committed and she was, accordingly, acting within the execution of her duty.

If a constable apprehends on reasonable grounds that a breach of the peace may be committed, he is not only entitled, but is under a duty, to take reasonable steps to prevent that breach occurring. Provided the constable honestly and reasonably forms the opinion that there is a real risk of a breach of the peace in the sense that it is in close proximity both in place and time, then the conditions exist for reasonable preventive action. Accordingly, where police officers stopped a convoy of striking miners whom they believed were intending to demonstrate and form a mass picket at one or more of four collieries in the area, it was held that the police officers acted reasonably and in the execution of their duty by preventing the striking miners from passing through the police cordon and, when they did attempt to force their way through the cordon, were justified in arresting them on the ground that if they proceeded it was feared a breach of the peace would occur at one of the collieries (*Moss v McLachlan* (1984) 149 JP 167, [1985] IRLR 76).

Officers who helped a youth leader eject persons from a youth club and were subsequently assaulted, were in the execution of their duty (*Coffin v Smith* (1980) 71 Cr App Rep 221).

In *R (on the application of Laporte) v Chief Constable of Gloucestershire Constabulary* [2006] UKHL 55, [2007] 2 AC 105, [2007] 2 All ER 529, [2007] 2 WLR 46, persons travelling by coach to a demonstration were stopped, the coaches were prevented from proceeding and were forcibly returned and the protesters were detained on the coaches throughout the return journey. The question arose as to whether this police action, which was short of arrest, was legitimate. The House of Lords held that the common law entitled and bound all police officers and citizens alike to seek to prevent, by arrest or action short of arrest, any breach of the peace occurring in their presence, or which they reasonably believed was about to occur, but where no breach of the peace had yet occurred a reasonable apprehension of an imminent breach was required before any form of preventive action was permissible. The police could not, therefore, take whatever action short of arrest they reasonably judged to be reasonable to prevent a breach of the peace which was not sufficiently imminent to justify arrest. Since there had been no indication of any imminent breach of the peace when the coaches were intercepted and searched, and since the defendant had not considered that such a breach was then likely to occur, the action taken in preventing the claimant from continuing to the demonstration had been an interference with her right to demonstrate at a lawful assembly which was not prescribed by domestic law.

The test of the reasonableness of a constable's action is objective in the sense that it is for the court to decide not whether the view taken by the constable fell within the broad band of rational decisions but whether in the light of what he knew and perceived at the time the court is satisfied that it was reasonable to fear an imminent breach of the peace. Accordingly, although reasonableness of belief is a question for the court, it is to be evaluated without the qualifications of hindsight. The court must restrict itself to considering the reasonableness, in the context of the events, of the constable's assessment of the imminence of a breach of the peace; it is not for the court to form its own assessment of that imminence (*R (on the application of Moos and another) v Commissioner of Police for the Metropolis* [2012] EWCA Civ 12, [2012] All ER (D) 83 (Jan)). The next and critical question for the constable, and in turn for the court, is where the threat is coming from, because it is there that the preventative action must be directed. If there is no real threat, no question of intervention for breach of the peace arises. If the defendant is being so provocative that someone in the crowd, without behaving wholly unreasonably, might be moved to violence, the constable is entitled to ask him to stop and arrest him if he will not. If the threat of disorder or violence is coming from passers-by who are taking that opportunity to react so as to cause trouble, then it is they and not the defendant who should be asked to desist and arrested if they will not (*Redmond-Bate v DPP* (1999) 163 JP 789, [1999] Crim LR 998– constable held not to be acting in the execution of his duty when he required three women preachers to stop preaching from the steps of a cathedral because some of those in the crowd that had gathered were showing hostility towards the preachers and he feared a breach of the peace).

Where a constable is given permission to enter premises, it is necessary to approach with common sense the terms of the licence given by the occupier. Thus, where a constable was asked to enter premises to remove that party's partner, the common sense terms of the constable's licence permitted him to speak to the partner to get his side of the story, and when the partner said to the constable 'Fuck off this is nothing to do with you' this could, but did not necessarily, amount to a request to leave the premises since other constructions, for example, the mere use of abuse, were capable of being made: *Marsden v CPS* [2014] EWHC 3359 (Admin), [2014] 178 JP 497.

If a person is unlawfully arrested (due to lack of reasonable grounds for suspicion) that person cannot be guilty of resisting not only the arresting officer, but also any officer who comes to assist them to complete the arrest (unless they have used unreasonable force against the first officer); similarly, while a police officer is entitled to use reasonable force to prevent a breach of the peace, if the actual or threatened breach of the peace is indissolubly linked with the unlawful arrest of another and is not directed at anyone else, any officer seeking to prevent that interference or protest is not acting in the course of their duty any more than the arresting officer, though the position would be different if the breach of the peace were independent and free-standing: *Cumberbatch v Crown Prosecution Service; Ali v DPP* [2009] EWHC 3353 (Admin), 174 JP 149 (though see infra). There is a distinction, however, between an unlawful act and an act which is not unlawful but is intended to lead to an unlawful act. Thus, where a community support officer put out her hand to stop a person she intended (unlawfully) to detain to be searched for drugs by a police constable but did not make physical contact with that person, and that person pushed past the officer causing her to stumble, the officer was acting in the execution of her duty. It was irrelevant that within a short while she would not have been so acting: *D v DPP* [2010] EWHC 3400 (Admin), [2011] 1 WLR 882, applied in *Tester v DPP* [2015] EWHC 1353 (Admin), [2015] Crim LR 812. Where an officer's search of a person was unlawful (owing to non-compliance with the requirements of s 2 of PACE 1984), a sufficient gap in time (a matter for the judgment of the court) may make a subsequent incident separate and distinct so that the officer is then acting in the execution of their duty: *Sobczak v DPP* [2012] EWHC 1319 (Admin), 176 JP 575, [2013] Crim LR 515, 176 CL & J 371.

Cumberbatch was distinguished in *Dixon v Crown Prosecution Service* [2018] EWHC 3353 (Admin), [2018] 4 WLR 160. A was cycling in the early hours, when he was spotted by three police constables who were on patrol in an unmarked vehicle. A fitted the description of persons who, according to an earlier intelligence briefing, might be carrying drugs or weapons. One officer, H, got out of the vehicle and asked A to stop. When he failed to do so, H took hold of his arm. He was not arresting the appellant nor exercising powers of stop and search. A fight ensued and H was joined by another officer, B, who struggled to restrain A. They were then joined by a third officer, D. D went to restrain A's arm because he believed that A might be reaching for a weapon, or something to use as a weapon, in his waistband. D understood that H and B were trying to detain A. A bit D on the arm. He knew when doing so that he was biting a police officer. A was charged with assaulting all three officers acting in the execution of their duty. The justices acquitted A of the charges relating to H and B, but convicted him of the charge relating to D. The Crown Court dismissed the appeal against conviction and A appealed by way of case stated.

The appeal was dismissed. There was an independent reason for D to use reasonable force to prevent A from unlawfully attacking the other officers with a weapon. There was nothing artificial or untoward in holding that a constable who acts reasonably to protect a fellow officer from unjustified assault is acting lawfully and in the execution of his duty, even if this involves assisting an officer who is acting unlawfully. While A could not be expected to distinguish between the first two officers and D, the relevance of that was to whether the defendant was acting lawfully in resisting restraint, and not to whether each of the individual officers was acting lawfully in trying to restrain him. Whether a police officer is acting lawfully and in the execution of their duty depends on the reasonable beliefs and intentions of the officer. It does not depend on the knowledge or beliefs of the defendant, save that in principle self-defence is available as a defence if the force used was justified in the circumstances as the defendant honestly believed them to be.

A[9.6] A court security officer shall not be regarded as acting in the execution of his duty unless he is readily identifiable by a badge or uniform (powers of court security officers are found in the Courts Act 2003, s 51(3)).

A[9.7] The burden of proof that the constable was acting in the execution of his duty rests on the prosecution but the prosecution does not have to prove that the defendant knew that the constable was a constable, nor that the defendant knew that the constable was acting in the execution of his duty. The offence may be established even if the court accepts that the defendant (who must take his victim as he finds him) did not know that his victim was a police officer. Where the accused is unaware that his victim is a police officer and believes there are circumstances which would justify the use of reasonable force, eg self-defence, he should have a defence (*Blackburn v*

Bowering [1994] 3 All ER 380, [1994] 1 WLR 1324, CA. See also *Ali v DPP* [2009] EWHC 3353 (Admin), 174 JP 149. See A[8.8] for defences).

A[9.8] If a police officer touches a person to draw his attention that contact must be acceptable by ordinary standards and for no longer than necessary to remain within the execution of the officer's duty (*Mepstead v DPP* (1995) 160 JP 475, [1996] Crim LR 111). When a police officer, who was not exercising his common law power, restrained a person, but had no intended or purported to arrest a person at that time, he committed an assault, even if the arrest had been justified. To be lawful arrest: (1) There must be reasonable grounds to suspect that a person had committed an arrestable offence (2) That person had to be informed that he was under arrest, either at the time of the arrest or within a reasonable time thereafter (*Wood v DPP* [2008] EWHC 1056 (Admin)).

The issue in *Walker v Commissioner of Police for the Metropolis* [2014] EWCA Civ 897, [2015] 1 WLR 312, [2015] 1 Cr App R 22 was the adequacy of the reasons given by the police officer for the claimant's arrest. The police attended at the home of the claimant's girlfriend to investigate an alleged assault. While the police were at the property an officer blocked the claimant in a doorway, detaining him for a few seconds without touching him. That initial detention was for the purpose of pursuing inquiries, rather than for arrest. Shortly thereafter the officer arrested the claimant, giving 'public order' as the reason for the arrest. The claimant, contending that the initial detention had been unlawful and that he had not been given a proper reason for the subsequent arrest, as required by s 28(3) of the Police and Criminal Evidence Act 1984, brought an action against the police claiming damages for, inter alia, false imprisonment.

It was held that in the circumstances of the case the utterance by the police officer of the words 'public order' were legally and factually sufficient to meet the requirements of s 28(3). 'Although in some situations legal labels may matter more than in others, I do not think that the particular legal label of a particular offence matters so much if the arrested person knows that he is being arrested for the conduct he has immediately carried out, a fortiori in the face of the arresting officer, and after warnings that such conduct may lead to his arrest' (per Sir Brian Rix at para 44).

Plain clothes officers carrying out a drugs search are not acting in the execution of their duty if they fail to comply with the requirements of s 2(3), PACE 1984 (*Bonner v DPP* [2004] EWHC 2415 (Admin), [2004] All ER (D) 74 (Oct); *R v Bristol* [2007] EWCA Crim 3214, (2007) 172 JP 161).

A police officer exercising a power of entry to premises, pursuant to s 17 of the Police and Criminal Evidence Act 1984, 'in order to save life or limb or serious damage to property', was acting lawfully where he sought to search the occupant based on a reasonable belief that she was in possession of a knife (*Baker v Crown Prosecution Service* [2009] EWHC 299 (Admin), 173 JP 215).

Concern for the welfare of somebody within the premises is not enough. It was clear that Parliament intended that the right of entry by force without warrant should be confined to cases where there is an apprehension that something serious was likely to occur or had occurred within premises (*Syed v DPP* [2010] EWHC 81 (Admin),[2010] 1 Cr App Rep 480, 174 JP 97).

In current times, distinguishing between violence in the home and in the street was long gone. Cases that attempted to do so could not be relied on and were out of date, *Foulkes v Chief Constable of Merseyside* [1998] 3 All ER 705, [1999] 1 FCR 98, CA and *McConnell v Chief Constable of Greater Manchester Police* [1990] 1 All ER 423, [1990] 1 WLR 364, CA are no longer good law. The correct approach was to draw a contrast between the ability of those on the street to go their own way, and in a domestic setting where that might not be possible, *Wragg v DPP* [2005] EWHC 1389 (Admin), [2005] All ER (D) 131 (Jun) applied: *Leon Demetriou v DPP*(2012) 156 Sol Jo (no 18) 31.

Although a pat-down search was authorised by the Criminal Law Act 1967, s 3, a police officer was required by s 2 of the Police and Criminal Evidence Act 1984 to take reasonable steps to bring certain matters to the attention of the person being searched. They included his name and police station, the object of the search and his grounds for proposing to make it. It meant that the officer's search of a defendant on this occasion was unlawful. However, there was a sufficient gap in time between the search of the defendant and an assault by the defendant on H to make the events separate and distinct. What the officer was doing was no more than to prevent harm to a woman in accordance with his common law duty and to prevent her from further contributing to violence. It followed that the justices had been entitled to find that the officer had been acting lawfully in the execution of his duty: *Sobczak v DPP* [2012] EWHC 1319 (Admin), 176 JP 575, 176 CL&J 371.

A[9.9] Reduction of charge/alternative verdict. The court cannot reduce this charge to common assault, but if a separate charge for common assault is preferred, a conviction for that offence may be possible.

Sentencing
SC Guideline – Assault on a police constable in the execution of his duty

A[9.10] Assault on a police constable in execution of his duty

Police Act 1996 (section 89)

Triable only summarily

Maximum: Level 5 and/or 26 weeks' custody

Offence range: Fine – 26 weeks' custody

This guideline applies to all offenders aged 18 years and older, who are sentenced on or after 13 June 2011. The definitions of 'starting point' and 'first time offender' do not apply for this guideline. Starting point and category ranges apply to all offenders in all cases, irrespective of plea or previous convictions.

STEP ONE
Determining the offence category

The court should determine the offence category using the table below.

Category 1	Greater harm and higher culpability
Category 2	Greater harm and lower culpability; or lesser harm and higher culpability
Category 3	Lesser harm and lower culpability

The court should determine the offender's culpability and the harm caused, or intended, by reference only to the factors below (as demonstrated by the presence of one or more). These factors comprise the principal factual elements of the offence and should determine the category.

Factors indicating greater harm
Sustained or repeated assault on the same victim
Factors indicating lesser harm
Injury which is less serious in the context of the offence
Factors indicating higher culpability
Statutory aggravating factors:
Offence racially or religiously aggravated

Offence motivated by, or demonstrating, hostility to the victim based on his or her sexual orientation (or presumed sexual orientation)
Offence motivated by, or demonstrating, hostility to the victim based on the victim's disability (or presumed disability)
Other aggravating factors:
A significant degree of premeditation
Use of weapon or weapon equivalent (for example, shod foot, headbutting, use of acid, use of animal)
Intention to commit more serious harm than actually resulted from the offence
Deliberately causes more harm than is necessary for commission of offence
Leading role in group or gang
Offence motivated by, or demonstrating, hostility based on the victim's age, sex, gender identity (or presumed gender identity)
Factors indicating lower culpability
Subordinate role in group or gang Lack of premeditation
Mental disorder or learning disability, where linked to commission of the offence

STEP TWO
Starting point and category range

Having determined the category, the court should use the corresponding starting points to reach a sentence within the category range below. The starting point applies to all offenders irrespective of plea or previous convictions. A case of particular gravity, reflected by multiple features of culpability in step one, could merit upward adjustment from the starting point before further adjustment for aggravating or mitigating features, set out below.

Offence Category	Starting Point *(Applicable to all offenders)*	Category Range *(Applicable to all offenders)*
Category 1	12 weeks' custody	Low level community order – 26 weeks' custody
Category 2	Medium level community order	Low level community order – High level community order
Category 3	Band B fine	Band A fine – Band C fine

The table below contains a **non-exhaustive** list of additional factual elements providing the context of the offence and factors relating to the offender. Identify whether any combination of these, or other relevant factors, should result in an upward or downward adjustment from the starting point. In some cases, having considered these factors, it may be appropriate to move outside the identified category range.

When sentencing **category 1** offences, the court should also consider the custody threshold as follows:

- has the custody threshold been passed?
- if so, is it unavoidable that a custodial sentence be imposed?
- if so, can that sentence be suspended?

Factors increasing seriousness
Statutory aggravating factors:
Previous convictions, having regard to a) the nature of the offence to which the conviction relates and its relevance to the current offence; and b) the time that has elapsed since the conviction

Offence committed whilst on bail
Other aggravating factors include:
Location of the offence
Timing of the offence
Ongoing effect upon the victim
Gratuitous degradation of victim
Failure to comply with current court orders
Offence committed whilst on licence
An attempt to conceal or dispose of evidence
Failure to respond to warnings or concerns expressed by others about the offender's behaviour
Commission of offence whilst under the influence of alcohol or drugs
Established evidence of community impact
Any steps taken to prevent the victim reporting an incident, obtaining assistance and/or from assisting or supporting the prosecution
Offences taken into consideration (TICs)
Factors reducing seriousness or reflecting personal mitigation
No previous convictions or no relevant/recent convictions
Single blow
Remorse
Good character and/or exemplary conduct
Determination and/or demonstration of steps taken to address addiction or offending behaviour
Serious medical conditions requiring urgent, intensive or long-term treatment
Isolated incident
Age and/or lack of maturity where it affects the responsibility of the offender
Lapse of time since the offence where this is not the fault of the offender
Mental disorder or learning disability, where **not** linked to the commission of the offence
Sole or primary carer for dependent relatives

STEP THREE
Consider any other factors which indicate a reduction, such as assistance to the prosecution

The court should take into account any rule of law by virtue of which an offender may receive a discounted sentence in consequence of assistance given (or offered) to the prosecutor or investigator.

STEP FOUR
Reduction for guilty pleas

The court should take account of any potential reduction for a guilty plea in accordance with section 144 of the Criminal Justice Act 2003 and the *Guilty Plea* guideline.

STEP FIVE
Totality principle

If sentencing an offender for more than one offence, or where the offender is already serving a sentence, consider whether the total sentence is just and proportionate to the offending behaviour.

STEP SIX
Compensation and ancillary orders

In all cases, courts should consider whether to make compensation and/or other ancillary orders.

STEP SEVEN
Reasons

Section 174 of the Criminal Justice Act 2003 imposes a duty to give reasons for, and explain the effect of, the sentence.

STEP EIGHT
Consideration for remand time

Sentencers should take into consideration any remand time served in relation to the final sentence. The court should consider whether to give credit for time spent on remand in custody or on bail in accordance with ss 240 and 240A of the Criminal Justice Act 2003.

A[9.11] Licensed premises. If the offence takes place on licensed premises an exclusion order may be made. See B[27].

A[9A]

Assaulting an emergency worker

Charge (Assaulting an emergency worker)

A[9A.1] **Assaulting an emergency worker acting in the exercise of functions as such a worker**

Assaults on Emergency Workers (Offences) Act 2018, s 1(2).

Maximum penalty – 6 months' imprisonment and/or fine.

Crown Court – 12 months' imprisonment and/or a fine.

Legal notes and definitions

A[9A.2] The offence applies to offences of common assault and battery committed against an emergency worker who is exercising functions as such a worker, whether or not the offence takes place during his/her work time: Assaults on Emergency Workers (Offences) Act 2018, s 1(2), (3).

A[9A.3] 'Emergency worker' is defined to include a:

- constable or person with the powers of a constable or otherwise employed for police purposes or engaged to provide services for police purposes;
- National Crime Agency officer;
- prison officer or other person employed or engaged to carry out corresponding functions in a custodial institution;
- prison custody officer carrying out escort functions;
- person employed or engaged to provide fire services or fire and rescue services, or search services or rescue services (or both); or
- person employed or engaged to provide NHS health or NHS health support services whose general activities in doing so involve face-to-face interaction with patients or other members of the public.

Assaults on Emergency Workers (Offences) Act 2018, s 3(1).

The employment/engagement may be paid or unpaid: Assaults on Emergency Workers (Offences) Act 2018, s 3(2)

A[9A.4] In relation to police constables, this offence is generally preferred to the offence of assaulting a police officer in the execution of his duty, contrary to s 89 of the Police Act 1996. In addition to the higher penalty it provides, the phrase 'acting in the exercise of functions as such a worker' is arguable broader than 'in the execution of his duty', and the constable need not be on duty at the relevant time.

Aggravating the seriousness of other offences

A[9A.5] Where the court is dealing with one of the offences listed in s 2 of the Act, and the offence was committed against an emergency worker acting in the exercise of functions as such a worker, again whether on duty or not, the court must in sentencing treat that fact as an aggravating factor and state so in open court: Assaults on Emergency Workers (Offences) Act 2018, s 2.

Sentencing

A[9A.6] There is currently no SC guideline for this offence.

The Court of Appeal has held that there are no existing sentencing guidelines to which resort can usefully be had by analogy. Sentencing should be by reference to the overarching requirements that any sentence must be just and proportionate and no more than commensurate with the seriousness of the offending. Courts must also bear in mind the clear legislative intent that assaults on public servants doing their work as part of the emergency services should be sentenced more severely than hitherto: *R v Shaun James McGarrick* [2019] EWCA Crim 530, [2019] 2 Cr App R (S) 31.

A[10]

Bail, failure to surrender

Charge (Bail, failure to surrender)

A[10.1] Having been released on bail in criminal proceedings fails without reasonable cause to surrender to custody

Bail Act 1976, s 6(1)

or

Having been released on bail in criminal proceedings, and having reasonable cause therefore, has failed to surrender to custody, fails to surrender to custody at the appointed place as soon as after the appointed time as is reasonably practicable

Bail Act 1976, s 6(2).

Maximum penalty – 3 months' imprisonment and/or fine level 5 (for offences committed on or after 12 March 2015 an unlimited fine) (if not committed for sentence).

Crown Court – 12 months' imprisonment or an unlimited fine

Legal notes and definitions

A[10.2] 'Fails without reasonable cause'. The fact that a defendant mistakenly formed the opinion he was required to surrender on a later date does not amount to a 'reasonable cause': *Laidlaw v Atkinson* (1986) The Times, 2 August.

'Surrender to custody'. It has been held: ' . . . if a court provides a procedure which, by some form of direction, by notice or orally, instructs a person surrendering to bail to report to a particular office or to a particular official, when he complies with that direction he surrenders to his bail. Thereafter, albeit he may not be physically restrained, albeit he may be allowed to sit in the court concourse and visit the court canteen, he is in the custody of the court. I have already suggested that he is under an implied, if not an express obligation, not to leave the building without consent until the case is called on. The argument that section 7(2) would have no meaning if that were not the correct construction is one which seems to me to be correct. I emphasise that if a person simply goes to the courthouse and does not report to anybody he has not surrendered to his bail. That is not enough. He has to report to somebody and do whatever he is directed to do, but when he does comply with the procedure which he is directed to follow by the court, then I emphasise that he has surrendered' (per Glidewell LJ in *DPP v Richards* [1988] QB 701). As to the position in the Crown Court, see *R v Evans* [2011] EWCA Crim 2842, [2012] 1 WLR 1192, [2012] 2 Cr App Rep 279, 176 JP 139. In the absence of special arrangements either particular to the court or to the individual case, surrender is accomplished when the defendant presents himself to the custody officers by entering the dock or where a hearing commences at which he is formally identified as present.

Burden of proof on accused. An accused who raises this defence is required to establish it on a balance of probabilities: *R v Carr-Briant* (1943) 107 JP 167.

Prosecution. See the detailed notes at **D[8.82]** onwards.

Committal to the Crown Court. In certain circumstances, a magistrates' court may commit to the Crown Court for sentence. See s 6(6) of the Bail Act 1976 and consult your legal adviser for guidance. An offence of failing to answer bail cannot in any circumstances be committed to the Crown Court for trial: *R v Osman* [2017] EWCA Crim 2178, [2018] 1 Cr App R (S) 23.

Sentencing
SC Guideline – Bail, failure to surrender

A[10.3] This guideline is taken from the SGC's definitive guideline *Fail to Surrender to Bail.*

Faliure to surrender to bail

Bail Act 1976, s 6

Effective from: 1 October 2018

Triable either way

Maximum: 12 months' custody

Offence range: Discharge – 26 weeks' custody

Where offence committed in a domestic context, also refer to the *Overarching principles: Domestic abuse guideline*

STEP 1
DETERMINING THE OFFENCE CATEGORY

The court should determine the offence category with reference only to the factors listed in the tables below. In order to determine the category the court should assess **culpability and harm.**

Culpability	
A	Failure to surrender represents deliberate attempt to evade or delay justice
B	Cases falling between categories A and C
C	Reason for failure to surrender just short of reasonable cause

Harm

The level of **harm** is determined by weighing up all the factors of the case to determine the harm that has been caused or was intended to be caused.

In assessing any risk of harm posed by the breach, consideration should be given to the original offence(s) for which the order was imposed and the circumstances in which the breach arose.

Category 1	Failure to attend Crown Court hearing results in substantial delay and/or interference with the administration of justice
Category 2	Failure to attend magistrates' court hearing results in substantial delay and/or interference with the administration of justice*
Category 3	Cases in either the magistrates' court or Crown Court not in categories 1 and 2

* In particularly serious cases where the failure to attend is in the magistrates' court and the consequences of the delay have a severe impact on victim(s) and /or witness(es) warranting a sentence outside of the powers of the magistrates' court, the case should be committed to the Crown Court pursuant to section 6(6)(a) of the Bail Act 1976 and the Crown Court should sentence the case according to the range in Category A1.

STEP 2
STARTING POINT AND CATEGORY RANGE

Having determined the category at step one, the court should use the corresponding starting point to reach a sentence within the category range in the table below. The starting point applies to all offenders irrespective of plea or previous convictions.

Where a custodial sentence is available within the category range and the substantive offence attracts a custodial sentence, a consecutive custodial sentence should normally be imposed for the failure to surrender offence.

	Culpability		
Harm	A	B	C
Category 1	**Starting point** 6 weeks' custody **Category range** 28 days' – 26 weeks' custody[1]	**Starting point** 21 days' custody **Category range** High level community order* – 13 weeks' custody	**Starting point** Medium level community order* **Category range** Low level community order* – 6 weeks' custody
Category 2	**Starting point** 21 days' custody **Category range** High level community order* – 13 weeks' custody	**Starting point** Medium level community order* **Category range** Band B fine – 6 weeks' custody	**Starting point** Band B fine **Category range** Band A fine – Low level community order
Category 3	**Starting point** 14 days' custody **Category range** Low level community order* – 6 weeks' custody	**Starting point** Band C fine **Category range** Band A fine – Medium level community order*	**Starting point** Band A fine **Category range** Discharge – Band B fine

* To include a curfew and/or unpaid work requirement only

1 In A1 cases which are particularly serious and where the consequences of the delay have a severe impact on victim(s) and /or witness(es), a sentence in excess of the specified range may be appropriate.

Maximum sentence in magistrates' court – 3 months' imprisonment

Maximum sentence in Crown Court – 12 months' imprisonment

The table below contains a **non-exhaustive** list of additional factual elements providing the context of the offence and factors relating to the offender. Identify whether any combination of these, or other relevant factors, should result in an upward or downward adjustment from the starting point. In some cases, having considered these factors, it may be appropriate to move outside the identified category range.

FACTORS INCREASING SERIOUSNESS

Statutory aggravating factors:
Previous convictions, having regard to a) the **nature** of the offence to which the conviction relates and its **relevance** to the current offence; and b) the **time** that has elapsed since the conviction
Other aggravating factors:
History of breach of court orders or police bail
Distress to victim(s) and /or witness(es)

Offence committed on licence or while subject to post sentence supervision

FACTORS REDUCING SERIOUSNESS OR REFLECTING PERSONAL MITIGATION

Genuine misunderstanding of bail or requirements
Prompt voluntary surrender
Sole or primary carer for dependent relatives

STEP 3
CONSIDER ANY FACTORS WHICH INDICATE A REDUCTION, SUCH AS ASSISTANCE TO THE PROSECUTION

The court should take into account sections 73 and 74 of the Serious Organised Crime and Police Act 2005 (assistance by defendants: reduction or review of sentence) and any other rule of law by virtue of which an offender may receive a discounted sentence in consequence of assistance given (or offered) to the prosecutor or investigator.

STEP 4
REDUCTION FOR GUILTY PLEAS

The court should take account of any potential reduction for a guilty plea in accordance with section 144 of the Criminal Justice Act 2003 and the *Guilty Plea* guideline.

STEP 5
TOTALITY PRINCIPLE

If sentencing an offender for more than one offence, or where the offender is already serving a sentence, consider whether the total sentence is just and proportionate to the overall offending behaviour in accordance with the *Offences Taken into Consideration and Totality* guideline.

STEP 6
ANCILLARY ORDERS

In all cases, the court must consider whether to make a compensation order and/or other ancillary orders.

STEP 7
REASONS

Section 174 of the Criminal Justice Act 2003 imposes a duty to give reasons for, and explain the effect of, the sentence.

STEP 8
CONSIDERATION FOR TIME SPENT ON BAIL

The court must consider whether to give credit for time spent on bail in accordance with section 240A of the Criminal Justice Act 2003.

A[11]

Bladed articles/offensive weapons, possession of

Charge (Bladed article/offensive weapon)

A[11.1] **Having an article which has a blade (or is sharply pointed) namely a [. . . . .] in a public place or on school premises [or]**

[Has an article with a blade or point or offensive weapon on school premises, unlawfully and intentionally threatens another person with the weapon, and does so in such a way that there is an immediate risk of serious physical harm to that other person]

Criminal Justice Act 1988, s 139 and s 139A [and 139AA]*

Having, without lawful authority or reasonable excuse, an offensive weapon in any public place [or]

[Has an offensive weapon with him in a public place, unlawfully and intentionally threatens another person with the weapon, and does so in such a way that there is an immediate risk of serious physical harm to that other person.]

Prevention of Crime Act 1953, s 1 [and 1A]

Maximum penalty:

(a) In relation to the 'possession' offences, whether in a public place or on school premises, triable either way: maximum penalty on summary conviction six months' imprisonment and/or fine level 5 (for offences committed on or after 12 March 2015 an unlimited fine); on indictment four years' imprisonment. *Note: The Prevention of Crime Act 1953 and the Criminal Justice Act 1988 were amended by s 28 of, and Sch 5 to, the Criminal Justice and Courts Act 2015 to require courts to impose 'an appropriate custodial sentence' for repeat offences involving offences weapons and pointed/bladed articles, unless the court is of the opinion that there are particular circumstances which (a) relate to the offence, to the previous offence or to the offender, and (b) would make it unjust to do so in all the circumstances.*
'An appropriate custodial sentence' is a minimum of 6 months' imprisonment for offenders aged at least 18 on the date of conviction, and four months' detention and training for those aged 16 or 17 on the date of conviction. Credit for pleading guilty changes the duty in relation to offenders aged at least 18 to a duty to impose a sentence of not less than 80% of the minimum term; in relation to offenders aged 16 or 17 the duty is further reduced and the court is not prevented from passing any sentence it considers appropriate after taking the plea and the circumstances in which it was indicated into account. The commencement date is 17 July 2015 and the new provisions apply only where the second/subsequent offence was committed after commencement.

(b) In relation to the threatening offences, triable either way with the same maximum on indictment, but on summary conviction, fine level 5 (for offences committed on or after 12 March 2015 an unlimited fine) or 12 months' imprisonment *and* the court (magistrates or Crown) must pass 'an appropriate custodial sentence' if the offender is aged 16 or over unless there are particular circumstances which relate to the offence or the offender which would make it unjust to do so. The minimum sentences are: offenders aged 16 and 17 – four months' DTO; older offenders six months' imprisonment (or 80% of these minimum terms where the offender pleads guilty).

Crown Court – 4 years' imprisonment (for offences committed on or after 12/2/2007) and unlimited fine

A[11.2] Mode of trial. Consider the SGC Guidelines at A[11.15] below.

Legal notes and definitions

A[11.3] General. The possession of offensive weapons is also controlled by several other statutes. The Crossbows Act 1987 regulates the sale or hire of crossbows to persons under 17 years, and the purchase or possession of crossbows by such persons. The Firearms Act 1968 controls the possession and use of airguns, shotguns and firearms and the possession of articles with blades or sharp points is governed by the Criminal Justice Act 1988 (see **A[5]**).

'Samurai swords' are on the list of prohibited articles. Accordingly, with a number of small exemptions the manufacture, sale, hire and importation of samurai swords is an offence. A later amendment order covered swords with a curved blade of 50 centimetres or more: Criminal Justice Act (Offensive Weapons) (Amendment) Order 2008, SI 2008/973.

A[11.4] Controls are also imposed on the manufacturers of and dealers in or persons who lend or give 'flick-knives' by the Restriction of Offensive Weapons Act 1959 and the Criminal Justice Act 1988 extends such controls to offensive weapons specified by the Home Office such as weapons used in martial arts, stun guns and so-called stealth knives. Selling a knife to a person under the age of 18 is an offence by virtue of amendments brought into force in January 1997. The maximum penalty for contravention of such regulations is a fine on level 5 and 6 months' imprisonment.

A[11.5] Offensive weapon. A police constable may arrest without warrant anyone carrying or suspected of carrying an offensive weapon in a public place. In order to convict the prosecution must first prove that the defendant was in possession of an offensive weapon. An offensive weapon means any article either:

(a) made or adapted for use for causing injury to the person; or
(b) intended by the person having it with him for such use by him or by some other person (s 1(4) Prevention of Crime Act 1953).

Articles in category (a), such as knuckle dusters and flick-knives and disguised knives, are always offensive weapons. An article in category (b), such as for example a milk bottle, only becomes an offensive weapon when the person carrying it has the intention of using it to cause injury to the person. The prosecution must prove this intention.

An object which bears all the characteristics of a flick-knife does not cease to be or lose its characteristic as a flick-knife because it has the secondary character of being a lighter. It is just as much an offensive weapon and potentially dangerous as if the lighter function were not there: *R v Vasili* [2011] EWCA Crim 615, [2011] 2 Cr App Rep 56, 175 JP 185.

In relation to category (a), in *Sills v DPP* [2006] EWHC 3383 (Admin), [2006] All ER (D) 165 (Oct), justices had been entitled to conclude that half of a pool cue, which had been unscrewed from its counterpart, and which the defendant maintained he had taken with him to scare off any attacker, was an article adapted for use for causing injury to the person within the meaning of s 1(4) above.

A petrol bomb is offensive 'per se': *R v Akhtar* [2015] EWCA Crim 176, [2015] 1 WLR 3046, [2015] 2 Cr App R 7. Similarly, where a leather belt had a detachable buckle in the form of a knuckle duster, the buckle was made or designed to cause injury and, thus, was offensive per se, even though it also served the purpose of being a belt buckle: *Director of Public Prosecutions v Christof* [2015] EWHC 4096 (Admin), [2016] 2 Cr App R 6. (However, the buckle also had two holes, one for the belt to fit to it and the other for the purpose of tightening the belt; therefore, the item might have been made so as to make the belt with the buckle a fashion item rather than for the purpose of causing injury, even though the buckle might have been put to that use when removed from the belt. Therefore the case was remitted for further consideration.)

In relation to (b), the necessary intent must be formed before an occasion to use actual violence arises. Thus, where a carpenter on his way home with the tools of his trade got into a dispute with another man and immediately took a hammer from his briefcase and struck the other man with it, the carpenter was not guilty of possessing an offensive weapon: *Ohlson v Hylton* [1975] 2 All ER 490, [1975] 1 WLR 724. Where, however, a person emerged from premises with a cricket bat and charged at a group involved in an affray, the court had been entitled to conclude that the bat had been introduced with intent to injure prior to it being used offensively and that the offence had, accordingly, been committed: *R v Tucker* [2016] EWCA Crim 13, (2016) 180 JP, 225, [2016] All ER (D) 122 (Feb).

A[11.6] **Have with him.** The prosecution must prove that the defendant knowingly was 'carrying' the offensive weapon with him. 'Carrying' would not include the situation where the accused seized a clasp knife, which he had not been carrying, for instant use on his victim.

In *R v Henderson* [2016] EWCA Crim 965, [2016] 4 WLR 172, [2017] 1 Cr App R 4, [2017] Crim L R 233 the defendant was with his family in a second floor flat when the police found his car keys while searching the premises. The car was in a communal car park at the rear of the flats. The police found a lock knife in the car boot. It was agreed that the car park was a public place, but the defendant submitted there was no case to answer as he did not have the lock knife 'with him' for the purposes of s 139(1). The judge rejected this submission, but the Court of Appeal allowed the appeal against conviction: (1) The defendant was not near his car; (2) there was no evidence that the defendant had shortly left or was shortly to return to the car; (3) there was no evidence that the knife in the car was linked in any way to his presence in the flat on that day or at all; and (4) there was no evidence linking the knife to any ongoing or indeed any criminal enterprise. In short, there was no close geographical, temporal or purposive link between the knife which was in a public place and the defendant who was in a private flat.

A[11.7] **Knowledge of possession.** The accused must have acquired the weapon knowingly (eg it was not slipped into his pocket unawares) (*R v Cugullere* [1961] 2 All ER 343, [1961] 1 WLR 858, 45, CCA). He still has it if he subsequently forgets it is there (*R v McCalla* (1988) 87 Cr App Rep 372, 152 JP 481, CA; *Bayliss v DPP* [2003] All ER (D) 71 (Feb)) until he or another does something to rid him of it. See below as to forgetfulness and 'good reason'.

A[11.8] **In a public place.** This includes any highway and any other premises or place to which at the material time the public have or are permitted to have access, whether on payment or otherwise. (*R v Roberts* [2003] EWCA Crim 2753, [2003] All ER (D) 325 (Oct)). In *Harriot v DPP* [2005] EWHC 965 (Admin), (2005) 170 JP 494, the Divisional Court held that a "public place" is not a term of legal art and that the statutory definition under the Prevention of Crime Act 1953 was illustrative not exhaustive. Accordingly, the open area between a bail hostel building and a road, was, on the face of it, private premises.

A[11.9] **Bladed article** – the prosecution merely has to prove that the accused had an article to which this offence applies and it is then up to the accused to justify its possession. The prosecution has a lesser burden of proof, than in the offence described at A[64]. The defendant does not discharge this burden merely by providing an explanation uncontradicted by prosecution evidence if the justices disbelieve his explanation (*Godwin v DPP* (1992) 96 Cr App Rep 244, 157 JP 197). However the prosecution must prove the defendant had knowledge of his possession of the blade (*R v Daubney* (2000) 164 JP 519, CA).

It is suggested that having regard to the legitimate aims of the legislation the legal burden of proof which rests with the accused is ECHR compliant.

Exceptions. This offence does not apply to a folding pocket knife except if the cutting edge of its blade exceeds 3 inches. Folding knife does not include a knife where the blade is secured in the open position by a locking device (*Harris v DPP* [1993] 1 All ER 562, [1993] 1 WLR 82).

To be a folding pocket knife a knife has to be immediately foldable at all times, simply by the folding process and without any further process such as the pressing of a button or catch: *Sharma v DPP* [2018] EWHC 3330 (Admin), [2019] 2 Cr App R 13.

'A pocketknife' is not an apt description of a cut-throat razor. The items have distinct characteristics, as reflected both in their descriptive names and in their functions. A razor is an article of sufficient sharpness to be used to shave. That would not be normally done by a pocketknife (per Simon LJ in *R v D* [2019] EWCA Crim 45, at para 22).

The section applies to articles which have a blade or are sharply pointed, falling into the same broad category as a knife or sharply pointed instrument; it does not apply to a screwdriver just because it has a blade: *R v Davis* [1998] Crim LR 564.

It is unnecessary for the blade to be sharp; the words of the statute, namely 'any article that has a blade' are unqualified and will, thus, include a blunt butter knife: *Brooker v DPP* [2005] EWHC (Admin) 1132, 169 JP 368.

A[11.10] **School premises** includes any land used for the purposes of a school but excludes a dwelling occupied by a person employed at the school.

From **31 May 2007** (England only) by virtue of the Violent Crime Reduction Act 2006, school staff with reasonable grounds for suspecting that a pupil may have possession of a blade or offensive weapon, may search the pupil or his possessions for such articles. The persons authorised to search are a Head teacher or someone authorised by the Head teacher. Similar authority is a available to carry out searches of students in **higher education.**

A[11.11] **'Threatening' offences.** The use of the weapon must be unlawful. Therefore, the defences of self-defence, defence of others' or own property, etc, are available. 'Serious physical harm' is defined as 'grievous bodily harm' for the purposes of the Offences Against the Person Act 1861. If a person is found not guilty of the aggravated offence, but it is proved that he committed the relevant possession offence, a conviction can be returned on the latter.

See also A[11.13] below.

A[11.12] **Good reason or lawful authority.** Good reason or lawful authority includes cases where the accused had the article with him:

(a) for use at work;
(b) for religious reasons (eg a Sikh) but not where the reason was connected with a martial art ancillary to a religious practice (*R v Wang* [2003] EWCA Crim 3228, [2003] All ER (D) 299 (Dec)); or
(c) as part of any national costume (eg a Scotsman's dirk).The defendant cannot rely on forgetfulness as constituting a good reason for having a weapon with him even where at an earlier period he was in lawful possession of the article (*DPP v Gregson* (1992) 96 Cr App Rep 240, 157 JP 201); or, in the case of the school offence:
(d) for educational purposes.

The words 'good reason' are both very general words and ordinary words which Parliament must have intended would normally be applied and interpreted by a jury or other fact-finding tribunal such as justices: *R v McAuley* [2009] EWCA Crim 2130, [2010] 1 Cr App Rep 148, 173 JP 585, [2010] Crim LR 336. A fear of attack can constitute a good reason and it therefore follows that the defendant's state of mind is not wholly irrelevant; if the court considers that defendant's view of the facts was wholly unreasonable, for example, because he was drunk or had taken drugs or was suffering from mental illness, it may be unlikely to conclude that the defence has been made out, but it is a matter ultimately for the court to determine: *R v Clancy* [2012] EWCA Crim 8, [2012] 1 WLR 2536, [2012] 2 Cr App Rep 71. Forgetfulness is not sufficient to prevent the state of possession from continuing (see above), but there may be circumstances in which forgetfulness can be relevant to the 'good reason' defence: for instance, if the reason that the defendant forgot that a bladed instrument, usually used for his work, was in his possession was a relevant illness or was occasioned by medication for such an illness: *Bayliss v DPP* (2003) 167 JPN 103. See also: *R v McCalla* (1988) 87 Cr App Rep 372; *DPP v Gregson* (1992) 157 JP 201. In *R v Jolie* [2003] EWCA Crim 1543, [2004] 1 Cr App Rep 44, (2003) 167

JP 313, [2003] Crim LR 730 it was affirmed that forgetfulness does not bring possession to an end; that forgetfulness cannot be a good reason, though it can be part of a good reason; and that the words 'good reason' do not require a judicial gloss. As to when forgetfulness might assist a defendant the court gave the example (in para 16) of a parent who, having bought a kitchen knife and put in the glove compartment of a car out of reach of a child then forgot to retrieve it when he got home; it seemed to the court contrary to Parliament's intention that such a person would be committing an offence the next time he drove the vehicle on a public road. See also *Chahal v DPP* [2010] EWHC 439 (Admin), [2010] 2 Cr App R 5. The defendant was found in possession of a knife. He claimed he had used it at work, put it in his coat, forgotten about it and then, at the time of the offence, when he realised it was in his jacket he decided to return home. The justices accepted that the defendant used the knife at work, but found that the work was of a casual nature, that the defendant did not regularly need the knife for work and, therefore, he did not have a 'good reason' for its possession at the relevant time. The appeal by way of case stated succeeded. The justices had been misled into thinking that the nature of the defendant's work deprived him of the statutory defence. The real question was whether the defendant had genuinely forgotten about the knife and at the time when his recollection was restored whether he continued to have 'good reason for possession of the knife.

A reason may be capable of being a good reason, but fail to amount to a good reason on the facts of the case (see *Mohammed v Chief Constable of South Yorkshire Police* [2002] EWHC 406 (Admin), [2002] All ER (D) 374 (Feb), where the defendant took a meat cleaver to sharpen it but had it in his possession for that purpose for longer than he needed to). It cannot be a good reason to possess a knife that you may wish to commit self harm with it at some time the following day: *R v Bown* [2003] EWCA Crim 1989, [2003] 33 LS Gaz R 27, (2003) 167 JP 429, [2004] Crim LR 67.

A[11.13] Without lawful authority or reasonable excuse. If the prosecution has established that an offensive weapon was carried in a public place then the onus shifts to the defendant to prove that lawful authority or reasonable excuse existed. The degree of proof is not to establish this beyond all reasonable doubt but that on the balance of probabilities it is true. The common excuse put forward is that the article was carried for use in self-defence. As the authority or excuse relates to the reason for carrying the offensive weapon, not to a use for which it is subsequently employed, one has to look at the situation when the defendant was carrying it. Accordingly, fear of being attacked, arising from the experience of friends and general violence in the neighbourhood, has been held not to be a reasonable excuse for carrying a metal ball and chain for self-protection. Self-protection from an actual or imminent attack might provide a 'reasonable excuse'. There would be no excuse or authority for a bouncer at a dance carrying an offensive weapon.

A claim by the accused that he did not know that the article in question was an offensive weapon cannot amount to a defence of reasonable excuse (*R v Densu* [1998] 1 Cr App Rep 400, [1998] Crim LR 345, CA). However, forgetfulness that one has unintended possession of an offensive weapon, may be relevant as part of a wider set of circumstances relied on as providing reasonable excuse: *R v Glidewell* (1999) 163 JP 557, CA; *R v Tsap* [2008] EWCA Crim 2580, 173 JP 4; *Chahal v DPP* [2010] EWHC 439 (Admin), [2010] 2 Cr App Rep 33.

The burden on the defendant to show a reasonable excuse was a heavy one where the weapon (a butterfly knife) was offensive per se, but the court still has a wide discretion on the facts (*DPP v Patterson* [2004] All ER (D) 239 (Oct), DC; but see *R v Tsap* immediately above and *Garry v Crown Prosecution Service* immediately below.

The case of *Garry v Crown Prosecution Service* [2019] EWHC 636 (Admin), [2019] 1 WLR 3630, [2019] 2 Cr App R 4 concerned a butterfly knife, which is a weapon offensive per se. The defendant claimed he used the knife for his work as a plumber, electrician and gas electrician, and that this innocent purpose afforded him with a 'reasonable excuse' for its possession in a public place. However, this argument failed in the magistrates' court and in the Crown Court on appeal, and the defendant's subsequent appeal by way of case stated was similarly unsuccessful. The key passages in the judgement, given by Rafferty LJ, are these:

'16. A tribunal of fact has a wide discretion in determining whether reasonable excuse is made out. An innocent purpose for having an offensive weapon in a public place does not equate to a reasonable excuse, rather the court is entitled to consider necessity or immediate temporal connection between possession and the purpose for which it is carried. In this case the evidence did not lead to a finding of fact that for the quotidian tasks of opening access panels and stripping aluminium sheathing no other implement would suffice. The evidence also included the attention of police being attracted since they suspected him of smoking cannabis.

17. Conclusive proof of a habit of using the weapon for work might prompt review of whether that use was reasonable: the wedding planner supplies a sword for cake-cutting, the chef tenderises meat using knuckle dusters.

18. The starting point is *Bryan v Mott* [1975] 62 Cr App R 71 where the Lord Chief Justice said: "In deciding whether a reasonable excuse is made out for the carrying of an offensive weapon in a public place the court should ask whether a reasonable man would accept that in the particular circumstances it was a proper occasion for carrying such a weapon."

19. It is thus clear that the Appellant's proof of his habitual carrying of the butterfly knife for work is simply evidence of what he suggests is the reasonableness of its possession. That falls short of proof of habitual carrying for work being dispositive of the issue.

20. The tribunal of fact would then review the balance of evidence capable of affecting its ultimate conclusion, which would include the type of weapon, and where it was found. In this case the weapon was a butterfly knife, specifically mentioned in *Patterson* as setting a high hurdle for discharge of a defendant's burden of proof, found not in a tool bag or box or overalls pocket but in the glovebox of his personal vehicle.

21. Additionally, context plays a part. Temporal connection could be important. Here, discovery was on a Saturday afternoon. The applicant, employed by the local council, did not lead worksheets or customer confirmation or any other evidence that he worked on Saturdays, let alone on Saturday afternoons.

22. The court, should it reject temporal proximity, will then consider whether he might have forgotten to move it out of the public place: *DPP v Gregson* (1992) 96 Cr App R 240.

23. Those consequential questions underline that proof that the weapon was for use at work is not dispositive of reasonable excuse. If it were, neither would be posed.

24. Under the 1953 Act, the questions, applied to these facts, are whether the Appellant proved it is more probable than not that a reasonable man would think he had a reasonable excuse for carrying the butterfly knife in the circumstances of that Saturday afternoon, and whether his assertion that the butterfly knife was used for work were credible.'

It might be a reasonable excuse that a person carrying a weapon was at risk of immediate attack and so carried the weapon for his own defence, but the 1953 Act never intended to sanction the continued carrying of an offensive weapon. A person under that kind of threat had to seek protection via other means such as contacting the police. Each case had to be determined on its own facts and no assistance was to be derived from comparing the facts of other cases. It remained for a jury to determine how soon and how likely the anticipated attack had to be to constitute reasonable excuse for carrying an offensive weapon. Further, there was no authority to support the proposition that reasonable excuse should be determined subjectively. Nor was there any basis for importing the self-defence test. Accordingly, when a defendant claimed he had reasonable excuse it was for him to prove both belief and the reasonableness of the belief on a balance of probabilities. Otherwise any defendant could claim that he had been at risk of immediate attack: see *N v DPP* [2011] EWHC 1807 (Admin), 175 JP 337. The defendant's state of mind might be relevant to the question as to whether she had a 'good reason' for possession of a bladed article: *R v Clancy* [2012] EWCA Crim 8, [2012] 1 WLR 2536, [2012] 2 Cr App Rep 71. This last decision went too far on the facts. The defendant was no longer at risk of an immediate attack and the excuse put forward lacked merit or foundation.

ECHR: In the light of *R v Matthews* [2003] EWCA Crim 813, [2004] QB 690, it is submitted that the imposition of a reverse legal burden on the accused is proportionate in accordance with art 6(2) of the ECHR.

Sentencing

SC Guideline – Bladed articles and offensive weapons – possession

A[11.15] This guideline is taken from the Sentencing Council's definitive guideline, published on 1 March 2018, effective from 1 June 2018.

Bladed articles and offensive weapons – possession

Possession of an offensive weapon in a public place

Prevention of Crime Act 1953 (section 1(1))

Possession of an article with blade/point in a public place

Criminal Justice Act 1988 (section 139(1))

Possession of an offensive weapon on school premises

Criminal Justice Act 1988 (section 139A(2))

Possession of an article with blade/point on school premises

Criminal Justice Act 1988 (section 139A(1))

Unauthorised possession in prison of a knife or offensive weapon

Prison Act 1952 (section 40CA)

This guideline applies only to offenders aged 18 and older

Triable either way

Maximum: 4 years' custody

Offence range: Fine – 2 years 6 months' custody

This guideline applies only to offenders aged 18 and older

This offence is subject to statutory minimum sentencing provisions.

See STEP THREE for further details.

STEP ONE
DETERMING THE OFFENCE CATEGORY

The court should determine the offence category with reference only to the factors listed in the tables below. In order to determine the category, the court should assess culpability and harm.

The court should weigh all the factors set out below in determining the offender's culpability.

Where there are characteristics present which fall under different levels of culpability, the court should balance these characteristics to reach a fair assessment of the offender's culpability.

Culpability demonstrated by one or more of the following:

A	• Possession of a bladed article • Possession of a highly dangerous weapon* • Offence motivated by, or demonstrating hostility based on any of the following characteristics or presumed characteristics of the victim: religion, race, disability, sexual orientation or transgender identity
B	• Possession of weapon (other than a bladed article or a highly dangerous weapon) – used to threaten or cause fear
C	• Possession of weapon (other than a bladed article or a highly dangerous weapon) – not used to threaten or cause fear
D	• Possession of weapon falls just short of reasonable excuse

* NB an offensive weapon is defined in legislation as 'any article made or adapted for use for causing injury, or is intended by the person having it with him for such use'. A highly dangerous weapon is, therefore, a weapon, including a corrosive substance (such as acid), whose dangerous nature must be substantially above and beyond this. The court must determine whether the weapon is highly dangerous on the facts and circumstances of the case.

Harm

The court should consider the factors set out below to determine the level of harm that has been caused or was risked

Category 1	• Offence committed at a school or other place where vulnerable people are likely to be present • Offence committed in prison • Offence committed in circumstances where there is a risk of serious disorder • Serious alarm/distress
Category 2	• All other cases

STEP TWO
STARTING POINT AND CATEGORY RANGE

Having determined the category at step one, the court should use the corresponding starting point to reach a sentence within the category range below. The starting point applies to all offenders irrespective of plea or previous convictions. A case of particular gravity, reflected by multiple features of culpability or harm in step one, could merit upward adjustment from the starting point before further adjustment for aggravating or mitigating features, set out on the next page.

	Culpability			
Harm	A	B	C	D
Category 1	**Starting point** 1 year 6 months' custody **Category range** 1 – 2 years' 6 months' custody	**Starting point** 9 months' custody **Category range** 6 months' – 1 year 6 months' custody	**Starting point** 3 months' custody **Category range** High level community order – 6 months' custody	**Starting point** High level community order **Category range** Medium level community order – 3 months' custody

Harm	Culpability A	B	C	D
Category 2	**Starting point** 6 months' custody	**Starting point** High level community order	**Starting point** Medium level community order	**Starting point** Low level community order
	Category range 3 months' – 1 year's custody	**Category range** Medium level community order – months' custody	**Category rangeLow** level community order – High level community order	**Category range** Band C fine – Medium level community order

The table below contains a **non-exhaustive** list of additional factual elements providing the context of the offence and factors relating to the offender. Identify whether any combination of these, or other relevant factors, should result in an upward or downward adjustment from the sentence arrived at so far. In particular, relevant recent convictions are likely to result in an upward adjustment. In some cases, having considered these factors, it may be appropriate to move outside the identified category range.

FACTORS INCREASING SERIOUSNESS

Statutory aggravating factors:
Previous convictions, having regard to a) the **nature** of the offence to which the conviction relates and its **relevance** to the current offence; and b) the **time** that has elapsed since the conviction (unless the convictions will be relevant for the purposes of the statutory minimum sentencing provisions – see step three)
Offence committed whilst on bail
Other aggravating factors:
Offence was committed as part of a group or gang
Attempts to conceal identity
Commission of offence whilst under the influence of alcohol or drugs
Attempts to conceal/dispose of evidence
Failure to comply with current court orders
Offence committed on licence or post sentence supervision
Offences taken into consideration
Failure to respond to warnings about behaviour

FACTORS REDUCING SERIOUSNESS OR REFLECTING PERSONAL MITIGATION

No previous convictions or no relevant/recent convictions
Good character and/or exemplary conduct
Serious medical condition requiring urgent, intensive or long-term treatment
Age and/or lack of maturity where it affects the responsibility of the offender
Mental disorder or learning disability
Sole or primary carer for dependent relatives
Co-operation with the police

STEP THREE
MINIMUM TERMS – SECOND OR FURTHER RELEVANT OFFENCE

When sentencing the offences of:

- possession of an offensive weapon in a public place;
- possession of an article with a blade/point in a public place;
- possession of an offensive weapon on school premises; and
- possession of an article with blade/point on school premises

a court must impose a sentence of at least 6 months' imprisonment where this is a second or further relevant offence **unless the court is of the opinion that there are particular circumstances relating to the offence, the previous offence or the offender which make it unjust to do so in all the circumstances.**

A 'relevant offence' includes those offences listed above and the following offences:

- threatening with an offensive weapon in a public place;
- threatening with an article with a blade/point in a public place;
- threatening with an article with a blade/point on school premises; and
- threatening with an offensive weapon on school premises.

Unjust in all of the circumstances

In considering whether a statutory minimum sentence would be 'unjust in all of the circumstances' the court must have regard to the particular circumstances of the offence and the offender. If the circumstances of the offence, the previous offence or the offender make it unjust to impose the statutory minimum sentence then the court **must impose either a shorter custodial sentence than the statutory minimum provides or an alternative sentence.**

The offence:

Having reached this stage of the guideline the court should have made a provisional assessment of the seriousness of the current offence. In addition, the court must consider the seriousness of the previous offence(s) and the period of time that has elapsed between offences. Where the seriousness of the combined offences is such that it falls far below the custody threshold, or where there has been a significant period of time between the offences, the court may consider it unjust to impose the statutory minimum sentence.

The offender:

The court should consider the following factors to determine whether it would be unjust to impose the statutory minimum sentence;

- any strong personal mitigation;
- whether there is a realistic prospect of rehabilitation;
- whether custody will result in significant impact on others.

STEP FOUR
CONSIDER ANY FACTORS WHICH INDICATE A REDUCTION FOR ASSISTANCE TO THE PROSECUTION

The court should take into account sections 73 and 74 of the Serious Organised Crime and Police Act 2005 (assistance by defendants: reduction or review of sentence) and any other rule of law by virtue of which an offender may receive a discounted sentence in consequence of assistance given (or offered) to the prosecutor or investigator.

STEP FIVE
REDUCTION FOR GUILTY PLEAS

The court should take account of any potential reduction for a guilty plea in accordance with section 144 of the Criminal Justice Act 2003 and the *Guilty Plea* guideline.

Where a statutory minimum sentence has been imposed, the court must ensure that any reduction for a guilty plea does not reduce the sentence to less than 80 per cent of the statutory minimum.

STEP SIX
TOTALITY PRINCIPLE

If sentencing an offender for more than one offence, or where the offender is already serving a sentence, consider whether the total sentence is just and proportionate to the overall offending behaviour in accordance with the *Offences Taken into Consideration and Totality* guideline.

STEP SEVEN
ANCILLARY ORDERS

In all cases the court should consider whether to make ancillary orders.

STEP EIGHT
REASONS

Section 174 of the Criminal Justice Act 2003 imposes a duty to give reasons for, and explain the effect of, the sentence.

STEP NINE
CONSIDERATION FOR TIME SPENT ON BAIL

The court must consider whether to give credit for time spent on bail in accordance with section 240A of the Criminal Justice Act 2003.

A[12]

Domestic burglary

Charge (Domestic burglary)

A[12.1] Entering a dwelling-house (or part of a dwelling-house) as a trespasser with intent to steal therein (or with intent to do unlawful damage)

or

Having entered a dwelling-house (or part of a dwelling-house) as a trespasser stole (or attempted to steal)

Theft Act 1968, s 9(1)(a) and s 9(1)(b) respectively

Maximum penalty – 6 months' imprisonment and/or fine level 5 (for offences committed on or after 12 March 2015 an unlimited fine). Triable either way. Specified violent offence under Sch 15, Part 1, CJA 2003 if the offence is committed with intent to (i) inflict GBH on a person; or (ii) do unlawful damage to a dwelling or anything in it.

Crown Court – 14 years' imprisonment or life following a third separate conviction (for burglaries involving a dwelling) and unlimited fine.

Mode of trial or allocation

A[12.2] Aggravated burglary is the commission of a burglary whilst armed with a firearm or other weapon of offence at the time of entry and is triable only at the Crown Court. Crime and Disorder Act 1998, s 51 applies.

A[12.3] Burglary comprising the commission of, or an intention to commit, an offence of rape or grievous bodily harm may only be heard at the Crown Court. Crime and Disorder Act 1998, s 51 applies.

A[12.4] Consult the legal adviser. Where the charge is burglary of a dwelling and the accused has two separate convictions for dwelling house burglaries, the charge may only be heard at the Crown Court (PCC(S) A 2000, s 111). See *R v Webster* [2003] EWCA Crim 3597, [2003] All ER (D) 313 (Nov) for an example of a third offence becoming indictable only. Crime and Disorder Act 1998, s 51 applies.

NB: In *R v Miller* [2010] EWCA Crim 809, [2011] 1 Cr App Rep (S) 7, [2010] Crim LR 648, it was stated that where a burglary has not been charged as burglary of a dwelling, it could not be treated as such for sentencing purposes pursuant to PCC(S)A 2000, s 111.

A[12.5] Otherwise a magistrates' court can try the case unless it is alleged that the defendant used, or threatened, violence to someone in the dwelling-house in which case the Crime and Disorder Act 1998, s 51 applies (*R v McGrath* [2003] EWCA Crim 2062, 167 JP 554, [2004] Crim LR 142, [2003] All ER (D) 397 (Jun)).

A[12.6] Where the offence is triable either way consider the SC Guidelines at A[12.18] below.

Legal notes and definitions

A[12.7]–[12.9] **Entering.** Whether the defendant can properly be described as entering or having entered the building is a question of fact for the magistrates. They will have to decide whether the accused had made an effective entry into the building (*R v Brown* [1985] Crim LR 212, CA). An effective entry can be made by the burglar putting his hand through a broken shop window and stealing therefrom. It can be sufficient for only a part of the burglar's body to enter the premises.

A[12.10]–[12.13] **Building.** The offence is committed by one who is lawfully in part of a building but trespasses into another part.

A[12.14] **Dwelling.** See *Hudson v Crown Prosecution Service* [2017] EWHC 841 (Admin), (2017) 181 JP 346, [2017] 2 Cr App R (S) 23, [2017] Crim L R 703, Times, 13 June 2017. The property in question was fully furnished in all rooms and fully habitable, but between tenancies. It was affirmed that whether or not a building was a 'dwelling' was a question of fact. Unlike vehicles or vessels (see s 9(4) of the Theft Act 1968) the word 'inhabited' is not used in s 9(3)(a). If the premises had been unoccupied for an extended period and had not been fit for habitation, different questions would have arisen, but, on the facts of the present case – the building had been occupied until two days before the burglary – on a natural meaning of the word, the building on the date of the burglary was a 'dwelling'. The more habitable a building is the more, all things being equal, it is likely to be a 'dwelling'. This avoids fine distinctions and niceties and leaves the risk on the burglar. Further, no unfairness is involved. The fact that premises are temporarily vacant can be reflected in arguments as to mitigation.

However, while each case is fact specific, burglary of a communal area in a block of facts, without entering any individual flat, should be sentenced on the basis the burglary was non-domestic within the guidelines: *R v Ogungbile* [2017] EWCA Crim 1826, [2018] 1 Cr App R (S) 31.

A[12.15] An inhabited vehicle (eg a caravan) or vessel is within the section notwithstanding that the occupant is absent at the time of the offence.

A[12.16] **Stealing** is dishonestly appropriating another person's property with the intention of permanently depriving the other person of it. See **A[79]**.

A[12.17] **Trespass.** Accidental trespass would not be an offence. The defendant must know, or be reckless as to whether, he is trespassing (*R v Collins* [1973] QB 100, [1972] 2 All ER 1105, CA). If there is doubt whether the defendant was trespassing, consult the legal adviser.

A[12.18]–[12.19] **Third conviction.** Where magistrates have before them a defendant who appears to be facing a third time domestic burglary, the case must be committed for trial at Crown Court (see **A[12.4]**). In all cases of burglary dwelling the court should announce in open court for the record that the defendant has been convicted of a qualifying offence.

Sentencing

SC Guideline – Domestic burglary

Domestic burglary (came into force on 16 January 2012)

A[12.20] This is a serious specified offence for the purposes of s 224 of the Criminal Justice Act 2003 if it was committed with intent to: (a) inflict grievous bodily harm on a person, or (b) do unlawful damage to a building or anything in it.

Triable either way

Maximum when tried summarily: Level 5 fine and/or 26 weeks' custody.

Maximum when tried on indictment: 14 years' custody.

Offence range: Community order – 6 years' custody.

Where sentencing an offender for a qualifying third domestic burglary, the Court must apply s 111 of the Powers of the Criminal Courts (Sentencing) Act 2000 and impose a custodial term of at least three years, unless it is satisfied that there are particular circumstances which relate to any of the offences or to the offender which would make it unjust to do so.

This guideline applies to all offenders aged 18 and older, who are sentenced on or after 16 January 2012. The definitions of 'starting point' and 'first time offender' do not apply for this guideline. Starting point and category ranges apply to all offenders in all cases, irrespective of plea or previous convictions.

STEP ONE
Determining the offence category

The court should determine the offence category using the table below.

Category 1	Greater harm and higher culpability
Category 2	Greater harm and lower culpability; or lesser harm and higher culpability
Category 3	Lesser harm and lower culpability

The court should determine the offender's culpability and the harm caused, or intended, by reference only to the factors below which comprise the principal factual elements of the offence. Where an offence does not fall squarely into a category, individual factors may require a degree of weighting before making an overall assessment and determining the appropriate category range.

Factors indicating greater harm
Theft of/damage to property causing a significant degree of loss to the victim (whether economic, sentimental or personal value)
Soiling, ransacking or vandalism of property
Occupier at home (or returns home) while offender present
Trauma to the victim, beyond the normal inevitable consequence of intrusion and theft
Violence used or threatened against victim
Context of general public disorder
Factors indicating lesser harm
Nothing stolen or only property of very low value to the victim (whether economic, sentimental or personal)
Limited damage or disturbance to property
Factors indicating higher culpability
Victim or premises deliberately targeted (for example, due to vulnerability or hostility based on disability, race, sexual orientation)
A significant degree of planning or premeditation
Knife or other weapon carried (where not charged separately)
Equipped for burglary (for example, implements carried and/or use of vehicle)
Member of a group or gang
Factors indicating lower culpability
Offence committed on impulse, with limited intrusion into property
Offender exploited by others
Mental disorder or disability, where linked to the commission of the offence

STEP TWO
Starting point and category range

Having determined the category, the court should use the corresponding starting points to reach a sentence within the category range below. The starting point applies to all offenders irrespective of plea or previous convictions.

Where the defendant is dependant on or a propensity to misuse drugs and there is sufficient prospect of success, a community order with a drug rehabilitation requirement under s 229 of the Criminal Justice Act 2003 may be a proper alternative to a short or moderate custodial sentence.

A case of particular gravity, reflected by multiple features of culpability in step one, could merit adjustment from the starting point before further adjustment for aggravating or mitigating features, set out below.

Offence Category	Starting Point *(Applicable to all offenders)*	Category Range *(Applicable to all offenders)*
Category 1	Crown Court	Crown Court
Category 2	1 year's custody	High level community order Crown Court (2 years' custody)
Category 3	High level community order	Low level community order – 26 weeks' custody

The table below contains a **non-exhaustive** list of additional factual elements providing the context of the offence and factors relating to the offender. Identify whether any combination of these, or other relevant factors, should result in an upward or downward adjustment from the starting point. In some cases, having considered these factors, it may be appropriate to move outside of the identified category range.

When sentencing **category** 3 offences, the court should consider the custody threshold as follows:

- Has the custody threshold been passed?
- If so is it unavoidable that a custodial sentence be imposed?
- If so, can the sentence be suspended?

Factors increasing seriousness
Statutory aggravating factors:
Previous convictions, having regard to a) the nature of the offence to which the conviction relates and its relevance to the current offence; and b) the time that has elapsed since the conviction*
Offence committed whilst on bail
Other aggravating factors include:
Child at home (or returns home) when offence committed
Offence committed at night
Gratuitous degradation of victim
Any steps taken to prevent the victim reporting an incident, obtaining assistance and/or from assisting or supporting the prosecution
Victims compelled to leave their home (in particular victims of domestic violence) Established evidence of community impact
Established evidence of community impact
Commission of offence whilst under the influence of alcohol or drugs
Failure to comply with current court orders
Offence committed whilst on licence

Offences taken into consideration (TICs)
Factors reducing seriousness or reflecting personal mitigation
Offender has made voluntary reparation to the victim
Subordinate role in a group or gang
No previous convictions or no relevant recent convictions
Remorse
Good character and/or exemplary conduct
Determination and/or demonstration of steps taken to address addiction or offending behaviour
Isolated incident
Serious medical conditions requiring urgent, intensive or long-term treatment
Age and/or lack of maturity where it affects the responsibility of the defendant
Lapse of time since the offence where this is not the fault of the offender
Mental disorder or learning disability, where not linked to the commission of the offence
Sole or primary carer for dependent relatives

* Where sentencing an offender for a qualifying third domestic burglary, the Court must apply section 111 of the Powers of the Criminal Courts (Sentencing) Act 2000 and impose a custodial term of at least three years, unless it is satisfied that there are particular circumstances which relate to any of the offences or to the offender which would make it unjust to do so.

STEP THREE
Consider any other factors which indicate a reduction, such as assistance to the prosecution

The court should take into account any rule of law by virtue of which an offender may receive a discounted sentence in consequence of assistance given (or offered) to the prosecutor or investigator.

STEP FOUR
Reduction for guilty pleas

The court should take account of any potential reduction for a guilty plea in accordance with section 144 of the Criminal Justice Act 2003 and the *Guilty Plea* guideline.

Where a minimum mandatory sentence is imposed under section 111 Powers of Criminal Courts (Sentencing) Act, the discount for an early guilty plea must not exceed 20 per cent.

STEP FIVE
Dangerousness

A burglary offence under section 9 of the Theft Act 1968 is a serious specified offence within the meaning of chapter 5 of the Criminal Justice Act 2003 if it was committed with the intent to (a) inflict grievous bodily harm on a person, or (b) do unlawful damage to a building or anything in it. The court should consider whether having regard to the criteria contained in that chapter it would be appropriate to award imprisonment for public protection or an extended sentence. Where offenders meet the dangerousness criteria, the notional determinate sentence should be used as the basis for the setting of a minimum term.

STEP SIX
Totality principle

If sentencing an offender for more than one offence or where the offender is already serving a sentence, consider whether the total sentence is just and proportionate to the offending behaviour.

STEP SEVEN
Compensation and ancillary orders

In all cases, the court should consider whether to make compensation and/or other ancillary orders.

STEP EIGHT
Reasons

Section 174 of the Criminal Justice Act 2003 imposes a duty to give reasons for, and explain the effect of, the sentence.

STEP NINE
Consideration for remand time

(Now obligatory.)

A[13]
Non-domestic burglary

Charge (Non-domestic burglary)

A[13.1] Entering a building (or part of a building) as a trespasser with intent to steal therein (or with intent to do unlawful damage)

or

Having entered a building (or part of a building) as a trespasser stole (or attempted to steal)

Theft Act 1968, s 9(1)(a) and s 9(1)(b) respectively

Maximum penalty – 6 months' imprisonment and/or fine level 5 (for offences committed on or after 12 March 2015 an unlimited fine). Triable either way. Specified violent offence under Sch 15, Part 1, CJA 2003 if the offence is committed with intent to (i) inflict GBH on a person; or (ii) do unlawful damage to a building or anything in it.

Crown Court – 10 years and unlimited fine.

Mode of trial

A[13.2] Aggravated burglary is the commission of a burglary whilst armed with a firearm or other weapon of offence at the time of entry and is triable only at the Crown Court. Crime and Disorder Act 1998, s 51 applies.

A[13.3] Burglary comprising the commission of, or an intention to commit, an offence of rape or grievous bodily harm may only be heard at the Crown Court. Crime and Disorder Act 1998, s 51 applies.

A[13.4] If the building is a non-dwelling a magistrates' court can try the case unless it is alleged that the defendant used, or threatened, violence to someone in the non-dwelling in which case the Crime and Disorder Act 1998, s 51 applies (*R v McGrath* [2003] EWCA Crim 2062, 167 JP 554, [2004] Crim LR 142, [2003] All ER (D) 397 (Jun)).

A[13.5] Where the offence is triable either way consider the **SGC Guideline** at A[13.19] below and the general notes at D[4].

Legal notes and definitions

A[13.6] **Entering.** Whether the defendant can properly be described as entering or having entered the building is a question of fact for the magistrates. They will have to decide whether the accused had made an effective entry into the building (*R v Brown* [1985] Crim LR 212, CA). An effective entry can be made by the burglar putting his hand through a broken shop window and stealing therefrom. It can be sufficient for only a part of the burglar's body to enter the premises.

A[13.7]–[13.15] **Building.** The offence is committed by one who is lawfully in part of a building but trespasses into another part. An inhabited vehicle (eg a caravan) or vessel is within the section notwithstanding that the occupant is absent at the time of the offence.

A[13.16] Stealing is dishonestly appropriating another person's property with the intention of permanently depriving the other person of it. See A[79].

A[13.17]–[13.18] **Trespass.** Accidental trespass would not be an offence. The defendant must know, or be reckless as to whether, he is trespassing (*R v Collins* [1973] QB 100, [1972] 2 All ER 1105, CA). If there is doubt whether the defendant was trespassing, consult the legal adviser.

Sentencing
SC Guideline – Non-domestic burglary

Non-domestic burglary (came into force on 16 January 2012)

A[13.19] This is a serious specified offence for the purposes of section 224 Criminal Justice Act 2003 if it was committed with intent to: (a) inflict grievous bodily harm on a person, or (b) do unlawful damage to a building or anything in it.

Triable either way

Maximum when tried summarily: Level 5 fine and/or 26 weeks' custody.

Maximum when tried on indictment: 10 years' custody.

Offence range: Fine – 5 years' custody.

This guideline applies to all offenders aged 18 and older, who are sentenced on or after 16 January 2012. The definitions of 'starting point' and 'first time offender' do not apply for this guideline. Starting point and category ranges apply to all offenders in all cases, irrespective of plea or previous convictions.

STEP ONE
Determining the offence category

The court should determine the offence category using the table below.

Category 1	Greater harm **and** higher culpability
Category 2	Greater harm **and** lower culpability; **or** lesser harm **and** higher culpability
Category 3	Lesser harm **and** lower culpability

The court should determine the offender's culpability and the harm caused, or intended, by reference **only** to the factors below which comprise the principal factual elements of the offence. Where an offence does not fall squarely into a category, individual factors may require a degree of weighting before making an overall assessment and determining the appropriate category range.

Factors indicating greater harm

Theft of/damage to property causing a significant degree of loss to the victim (whether economic, sentimental or personal value)

Soiling, ransacking or vandalism of property

Victim on the premises (or returns) while offender present

Trauma to the victim, beyond the normal inevitable consequence of intrusion and theft

Violence used or threatened against victim

Context of general public disorder

Factors indicating lesser harm

Nothing stolen or only property of very low value to the victim (whether economic, sentimental or personal)

Limited damage or disturbance to property

Factors indicating higher culpability

Premises or victim deliberately targeted (to include pharmacy or doctor's surgery and targeting due to vulnerability of victim or hostility based on disability, race, sexual orientation and so forth)

A significant degree of planning or premeditation
Knife or other weapon carried (where not charged separately)
Equipped for burglary (for example, implements carried and/or use of vehicle)
Member of a group or gang
Factors indicating lower culpability
Offence committed on impulse, with limited intrusion into property
Offender exploited by others
Mental disorder or disability, where linked to the commission of the offence

STEP TWO
Starting point and category range

Having determined the category, the court should use the corresponding starting points to reach a sentence within the category range below. The starting point applies to all offenders irrespective of plea or previous convictions.

Where the defendant is dependant on or a propensity to misuse drugs and there is sufficient prospect of success, a community order with a drug rehabilitation requirement under s 229 of the Criminal Justice Act 2003 may be a proper alternative to a short or moderate custodial sentence.

A case of particular gravity, reflected by multiple features of culpability in step one, could merit adjustment from the starting point before further adjustment for aggravating or mitigating features, set out below.

Category 1	Crown Court	Crown Court
Category 2	18 weeks' custody	Low level community order – 51 weeks' custody)
Category 3	Medium level community order	Band B fine – low level – 18 weeks' custody

The table below contains a **non-exhaustive** list of additional factual elements providing the context of the offence and factors relating to the offender. Identify whether any combination of these, or other relevant factors, should result in an upward or downward adjustment from the starting point. In some cases, having considered these factors, it may be appropriate to move outside of the identified category range.

When sentencing **category 2 or 3 offences**, the court should consider the custody threshold as follows:

- Has the custody threshold been passed?
- If so is it unavoidable that a custodial sentence be imposed?
- If so, can the sentence be suspended?

Factors increasing seriousness
Statutory aggravating factors:
Previous convictions, having regard to a) the nature of the offence to which the conviction relates and its relevance to the current offence; and b) the time that has elapsed since the conviction
Offence committed whilst on bail
Other aggravating factors include:
Offence committed at night, particularly where staff present or likely to be present
Abuse of a position of trust

Gratuitous degradation of victim
Any steps taken to prevent the victim reporting an incident, obtaining assistance and/or from assisting or supporting the prosecution
Established evidence of community impact
Commission of offence whilst under the influence of alcohol or drugs
Failure to comply with current court orders
Offence committed whilst on licence
Offences taken into consideration (TICs)
Factors reducing seriousness or reflecting personal mitigation
Offender has made voluntary reparation to the victim
Subordinate role in a group or gang
No previous convictions or no relevant recent convictions
Remorse
Good character and/or exemplary conduct
Determination and/or demonstration of steps taken to address addiction or offending behaviour
Isolated incident
Serious medical conditions requiring urgent, intensive or long-term treatment
Age and/or lack of maturity where it affects the responsibility of the defendant
Lapse of time since the offence where this is not the fault of the offender
Mental disorder or learning disability, where not linked to the commission of the offence
Sole or primary carer for dependent relatives

STEP THREE
Consider any other factors which indicate a reduction, such as assistance to the prosecution

The court should take into account any rule of law by virtue of which an offender may receive a discounted sentence in consequence of assistance given (or offered) to the prosecutor or investigator.

STEP FOUR
Reduction for guilty pleas

The court should take account of any potential reduction for a guilty plea in accordance with section 144 of the Criminal Justice Act 2003 and the *Guilty Plea* guideline.

STEP FIVE
Dangerousness

A burglary offence under section 9 of the Theft Act 1968 is a serious specified offence within the meaning of chapter 5 of the Criminal Justice Act 2003 if it was committed with the intent to (a) inflict grievous bodily harm on a person, or (b) do unlawful damage to a building or anything in it. The court should consider whether having regard to the criteria contained in that chapter it would be appropriate to award imprisonment for public protection or an extended sentence. Where offenders meet the dangerousness criteria, the notional determinate sentence should be used as the basis for the setting of a minimum term.

STEP SIX
Totality principle

If sentencing an offender for more than one offence or where the offender is already serving a sentence, consider whether the total sentence is just and proportionate to the offending behaviour.

STEP SEVEN
Compensation and ancillary orders

In all cases, the court should consider whether to make compensation and/or other ancillary orders.

STEP EIGHT
Reasons

Section 174 of the Criminal Justice Act 2003 imposes a duty to give reasons for, and explain the effect of, the sentence.

STEP NINE
Consideration for remand time

(Now obligatory.)

A[14]

Child prostitution and pornography

Charge (Child prostitution and pornography)

A[14.1] **Intentionally causes or incites another person (B) to become a prostitute or to be involved in pornography in any part of the world, and either—**

(i) **B is under 18, and a does not reasonably believe that B is 18 or over, or**
(ii) **B is under 13.**

Sexual Offences Act 2003, s 48

Intentionally controls any of the activities of another person (B) relating to B's prostitution or involvement in pornography in any part of the world, and either–

(i) **B is under 18, and A does not reasonably believe that B is over 18, or**
(ii) **B is under 13.**

Sexual Offences Act 2003, s 49.

Intentionally arranges or facilitates the prostitution or involvement in pornography in any part of the world of another person (B), and either—

(i) **B is under 18, and A does not reasonably believe that B is over 18 or over, or**
(ii) **B is under 13.**

Sexual Offences Act, 2003, s 50.

Maximum penalty – 6 months' imprisonment and/or fine level 5 (for offences committed on or after 12 March 2015 an unlimited fine). Triable either way. Specified sexual offence under Sch 15, Part 2, CJA 2003

Crown Court – 14 years' imprisonment and unlimited fine.

A[14.1A] **NB:** From 26/1/09, section 63 of the Criminal Justice and Immigration Act 2008 created a new offence of possession of extreme pornographic images.

An image is 'pornographic' if it is of such a nature that it must reasonably be assumed to have been produced solely or principally for the purpose of sexual arousal.

An 'extreme image is one which portrays, in an explicit and realistic way, any of the following –

- an act which threatens a person's life
- an act which results, or is likely to result, in serious injury to a person's anus, breasts or genitals
- an act which involves interference with a human corpse, or
- a person performing an act of intercourse or oral sex with an animal (whether dead or alive),
- and a reasonable person looking at the image would think that any such person or animal was real; *and*
- the image is grossly offensive, disgusting or otherwise of an obscene character.

Section 63 was amended by s 37 of the Criminal Justice and Courts Act 2015 to add to the list of 'extreme images' images which portray, in an explicit and realistic way, either of the following:

(a) an act which involves the non-consensual penetration of a person's vagina, anus or mouth by another with the other person's penis, or
(b) an act which involves the non-consensual sexual penetration of a person's vagina or anus by another with a part of the other person's body or anything else, and a reasonable person looking at the image would think that the persons were real.

The amendments took effect on 13 April 2015. The amendments made by s 37 of the Act do not apply to possession of an image which occurs before 13 April 2015.

An 'image' means a moving or still image (produced by any means); or, data (stored by any means) which is capable of conversion into an image.

Classified films are exempted under s 64. See ss 65 and 66 for defences.

Defences Section 65 provides a general defence to an offence under s 63, which the defendant bears the burden of proving on a balance of probabilities:

(a) that the person had a legitimate reason for being in possession of the image concerned; or
(b) that the person had not seen the image concerned and did not know, nor had any cause to suspect, it to be an extreme pornographic image; or
(c) that the person:
  (i) was sent the image concerned without any prior request having been made by or on behalf of the person; and
  (ii) did not keep it for an unreasonable time.

Section 66 adds a defence of participation in consensual acts, but this does not apply to images which portray a person performing an act of intercourse or oral sex with an animal (whether dead or alive). Again, the burden of proof is on the defendant and the standard is a balance of probabilities.

The defence is:

(a) that D directly participated in the act or any of the acts portrayed; and
(b) that the act or acts did not involve the infliction of any non-consensual harm on any person; and
(c) if the image portrays an act which involves interference with a human corpse, that what is portrayed as a human corpse was not in fact a corpse; and
(d) if the image portrays an act of non-consensual penetration (the new category added by the Criminal Justice and Courts Act 2015) what is portrayed as non-consensual was in fact consensual.

For this purpose harm inflicted on a person is 'non-consensual' harm if:

(a) the harm is of such a nature that the person cannot, in law, consent to it being inflicted on himself or herself; or
(b) where the person can, in law, consent to it being so inflicted, the person does not in fact consent to it being so inflicted

Maximum penalty – For images that portray any 'relevant act', 6 months' imprisonment and/or fine level 5 (for offences committed on or after 12 March 2015 an unlimited fine). Triable either way.

Crown Court – 3 years' imprisonment and unlimited fine.

For images that do not portray any 'relevant act' the same penalty applies on summary conviction but the maximum term of imprisonment in the Crown Court is reduced to 2 years' imprisonment.

'Relevant act' means:

(a) an act which threatens a person's life; or
(b) an act which results, or is likely to result, in serious injury to a person's anus, breasts or genitals; or
(c) an act which involves the non-consensual penetration of a person's vagina, anus or mouth by another with the other person's penis; or
(d) an act which involves the non-consensual sexual penetration of a person's vagina or anus by another with a part of the other person's body or anything else.

NB: (1) Proceedings for an offence may not be instituted in England and Wales except by or with the consent of the Director of Public Prosecutions.

(2) There is currently no SC Guideline.

Mode of trial

A[14.2] Consider the SC Guideline at A[14.5] below.

Legal notes and definitions

A[14.3] **Pornography.** For the purposes of ss 48 to 50, a person is involved in pornography if an indecent image of that person is recorded; and similar expressions, and 'pornography', are to be interpreted accordingly (Sexual Offences Act 2003, s 51(1)).

A[14.4] **Prostitute.** Means a person (A) who, on at least one occasion and whether or not compelled to do so, offers or provides sexual services to another person in return for **payment** or a promise of payment to A or to a third person; and "prostitution" is to be interpreted accordingly (Sexual Offences Act 2003, s 51(2)).

A[14.5] **Payment.** As in A[14.4] "payment" means any financial advantage, including the discharge of an obligation to pay or the provision of goods or services (including sexual services) gratuitously or at a discount (Sexual Offences Act 2003, s 51(3)).

Sentencing

SC Guideline – Child prostitution and pornography

A[14.6] This guideline is taken from the Sentencing Council's definitive guideline *Sexual Offences*, effective from 1 April 2014.

Causing or inciting child prostitution or pornography

Sexual Offences Act 2003 (section 48)

Controlling a child prostitute or child involved in pornography

Sexual Offences Act 2003 (section 49)

Arranging or facilitating child prostitution or pornography

Sexual Offences Act 2003 (section 50)

Triable either way

Maximum: 14 years' custody

Offence range:	Victim aged under 13	1 – 13 years' custody
	Victim aged 13–15	26 weeks' – 11 years' custody
	Victim aged 16–17	Community order – 7 years' custody

For offences committed on or after 3 December 2012, these are offences listed in Part 1 of Schedule 15B for the purposes of sections 224A (life sentence for second listed offence) of the Criminal Justice Act 2003.

For convictions on or after 3 December 2012 (irrespective of the date of commission of the offence), these are specified offences for the purposes of section 226A (extended sentence for certain violent or sexual offences) of the Criminal Justice Act 2003.

The terms 'child prostitute', 'child prostitution' and 'child involved in pornography' are used in this guideline in accordance with the statutory language contained in the Sexual Offences Act 2003.

STEP ONE
Determining the offence category

The court should determine which categories of harm and culpability the offence falls into by reference only to the tables below.

For offences that involve wide scale commercial and/or international activity sentences above the category range may be appropriate.

Harm	Culpability
Category 1	A
• Victims involved in penetrative sexual activity	Directing or organising child prostitution or pornography on significant commercial basis
• Abduction/detention	Expectation of significant financial or other gain
• Violence or threats of violence	Abuse of trust Exploitation of victim(s) known to be trafficked
• Sustained and systematic psychological abuse	Significant involvement in limiting the freedom of the victim(s)
• Victim(s) participated in unsafe/degrading sexual activity beyond that which is inherent in the offence	Grooming of a victim to enter prostitution or pornography including through cultivation of a dependency on drugs or alcohol
• Victim(s) passed around by the offender to other "customers" and/or moved to other brothels	B
Category 2	Close involvement with inciting, controlling, arranging or facilitating child prostitution or pornography (where offender's involvement is not as a result of coercion)
Factor(s) in category 1 not present	C
	Performs limited function under direction
	Close involvement but engaged by coercion/intimidation/exploitation

STEP TWO
Starting point and category range

Having determined the category, the court should use the corresponding starting points to reach a sentence within the category range below. The starting point applies to all offenders irrespective of plea or previous convictions. Having determined the starting point, step two allows further adjustment for aggravating or mitigating features, set out on the next page.

A case of particular gravity, reflected by multiple features of culpability or harm in step one, could merit upward adjustment from the starting point before further adjustment for aggravating or mitigating features, set out on the next page.

Where there is a sufficient prospect of rehabilitation, a community order with a sex offender treatment programme requirement under section 202 of the Criminal Justice Act 2003 can be a proper alternative to a short or moderate length custodial sentence.

		A	B	C
Category 1	U 13	**Starting point** 10 years' custody	**Starting point** 8 years' custody	**Starting point** 5 years' custody
		Category range 8 – 13 years' custody	**Category range** 6 – 11 years' custody	**Category range** 2 – 6 years' custody
	13–15	**Starting point** 8 years' custody	**Starting point** 5 years' custody	**Starting point** 2 years 6 months' custody
		Category range 6 – 11 years' custody	**Category range** 4 – 8 years' custody	**Category range** 1 – 4 years' custody
	16–17	**Starting point** 4 years' custody	**Starting point** 2 years' custody	**Starting point** 1 years' custody
		Category range 3 – 7 years' custody	**Category range** 1 – 4 years' custody	**Category range** 26 weeks' – 2 years' custody
Category 2	U 13	**Starting point** 8 years' custody	**Starting point** 6 years' custody	**Starting point** 2 years' custody
		Category range 6 – 11 years' custody	**Category range** 4 – 9 years' custody	**Category range** 1 – 4 years' custody
	13–15	**Starting point** 6 years' custody	**Starting point** 3 years' custody	**Starting point** 1 years' custody
		Category range 4 – 9 years' custody	**Category range** 2 – 5 years' custody	**Category range** 26 weeks' – 2 years' custody
	16–17	**Starting point** 3 years' custody	**Starting point** 1 year's custody	**Starting point** 26 weeks' custody
		Category range 2 – 5 years' custody	**Category range** 26 weeks' – 2 years' custody	**Category range** High level community order – 1 year's custody

The table below contains a **non-exhaustive** list of additional factual elements providing the context of the offence and factors relating to the offender. Identify whether any combination of these, or other relevant factors, should result in an upward or downward adjustment from the starting point. **In particular, relevant recent convictions are likely to result in an upward adjustment.** In some cases, having considered these factors, it may be appropriate to move outside the identified category range.

When sentencing appropriate category 2 offences, the court should also consider the custody threshold as follows:

- has the custody threshold been passed?
- if so, is it unavoidable that a custodial sentence be imposed?

- if so, can that sentence be suspended?

Aggravating factors	Mitigating factors
Statutory aggravating factors	No previous convictions or no relevant/recent convictions
Previous convictions, having regard to a) the nature of the offence to which the conviction relates and its relevance to the current offence; and b) the time that has elapsed since the conviction	Remorse
Offence committed whilst on bail	Previous good character and/or exemplary conduct*
Other aggravating factors	Age and/or lack of maturity where it affects the responsibility of the offender
Failure to comply with current court orders	Mental disorder or learning disability, particularly where linked to the commission of the offence
Offence committed whilst on licence	* Previous good character/exemplary conduct is different from having no previous convictions. The more serious the offence, the less the weight which should normally be attributed to this factor. Where previous good character/exemplary conduct has been used to facilitate the offence, this mitigation should not normally be allowed and such conduct may constitute an aggravating factor. In the context of this offence, previous good character/exemplary conduct should not normally be given any significant weight and will not normally justify a reduction in what would otherwise be the appropriate sentence.
Deliberate isolation of victim(s)	
Vulnerability of victim(s)	
Threats made to expose victim(s) to the authorities (for example, immigration or police), family/friends or others	
Harm threatened against the family/friends of victim(s)	
Passport/identity documents removed	
Victim(s) prevented from seeking medical treatment	
Victim(s) prevented from attending school	
Food withheld	
Earnings withheld/kept by offender or evidence of excessive wage reduction or debt bondage, inflated travel or living expenses or unreasonable interest rates	
Any steps taken to prevent the victim reporting an incident, obtaining assistance and/or from assisting or supporting the prosecution	
Attempts to dispose of or conceal evidence	
Timescale over which the operation has been run	

STEP THREE

Consider any factors which indicate a reduction, such as assistance to the prosecution

The court should take into account sections 73 and 74 of the Serious Organised Crime and Police Act 2005 (assistance by defendants: reduction or review of sentence) and any other rule of law by virtue of which an offender may receive a discounted sentence in consequence of assistance given (or offered) to the prosecutor or investigator.

STEP FOUR
Reduction for guilty pleas

The court should take account of any potential reduction for a guilty plea in accordance with section 144 of the Criminal Justice Act 2003 and the *Guilty Plea* guideline.

STEP FIVE
Dangerousness

The court should consider whether having regard to the criteria contained in Chapter 5 of Part 12 of the Criminal Justice Act 2003 it would be appropriate to award a life sentence (section 224A) or an extended sentence (section 226A). When sentencing offenders to a life sentence under these provisions, the notional determinate sentence should be used as the basis for the setting of a minimum term.

STEP SIX
Totality principle

If sentencing an offender for more than one offence, or where the offender is already serving a sentence, consider whether the total sentence is just and proportionate to the offending behaviour.

STEP SEVEN
Ancillary orders

The court must consider whether to make any ancillary orders. The court must also consider what other requirements or provisions may automatically apply. Further information is included at Annex A on page 153.

STEP EIGHT
Reasons

Section 174 of the Criminal Justice Act 2003 imposes a duty to give reasons for, and explain the effect of, the sentence.

STEP NINE
Consideration for time spent on bail

The court must consider whether to give credit for time spent on bail in accordance with section 240A of the Criminal Justice Act 2003.

Key factors

A[14.7] Notification requirements. See A[52.15].

A[15]

Common assault and racially/religiously aggravated assault

Charge (Common & racially/religiously aggravated assault)

A[15.1] **Did assault [. . . . .] [by beating]**

Contrary to the Criminal Justice Act 1988, s 39.

Maximum penalty – 6 months' imprisonment and/or fine level 5 (for offences committed on or after 12 March 2015 an unlimited fine). Triable only by magistrates.

(By virtue of s 10 of the Domestic Violence, Crime and Victims Act 2004, from July 1, 2007 common assault is to become an arrestable offence.)

A[15.2] **Racially/religiously aggravated assault**

Contrary to the Crime and Disorder Act 1998, s 29.

Maximum penalty – 6 months' imprisonment and/or fine level 5 (for offences committed on or after 12 March 2015 an unlimited fine). Triable either way. Specified violent offence under Sch 15, Part 1, CJA 2003.

Crown Court – 2 years' imprisonment and unlimited fine.

Legal notes and definitions

A[15.3] The basic offence is triable only by magistrates but may be alleged as an alternative charge at a trial at the Crown Court if the prosecution chooses with a maximum penalty of £5,000 and 6 months (51 weeks). Racially or religiously aggravated assault is triable either way. The two offences may be tried together in the alternative (*R (CPS) v Blaydon Youth Court* [2004] EWHC 2296 (Admin), 168 JP 638).

A[15.4] **Intent.** The defendant must intend to cause his victim to apprehend immediate and unlawful violence, or be reckless whether such apprehension be caused (*R v Venna* [1976] QB 421, [1975] 3 All ER 788, CA). 'Reckless' means that the accused foresaw the risk and went on to take it (*R v Cunningham* [1957] 2 QB 396, [1957] 2 All ER 412, CA).

In principle it was open to justices to convict on the basis of recklessness even where the prosecution simply alleged a deliberate assault: *D v DPP* [2005] EWHC 967 (Admin) considered. However, the justices had failed to identify what was the unlawful act of K leading to the assault. Recklessness had only been a possible conclusion if the justices had found that K had thrown a punch albeit, without intending it to land, or was flailing his arms about in an agitated and aggressive manner. The conviction could not stand in the light of the findings of fact made by the justices: *Katsonis v Crown Prosecution Service* [2011] EWHC 1860 (Admin), 175 JP 396.

A[15.5] **Assault.** Does not require any contact between the two parties, a threatening gesture is enough. Words, however insulting, are probably not an assault but any attempt to commit a battery, even if the blow does not connect, can be an assault. It is not necessary that the other party should receive an actual injury, but there must have been a hostile intent. In modern usage the term assault will now include a battery, ie the actual application of force as opposed to its threatened use, and this is how it is used in most statutes. But if a charge alleges 'did assault and batter' then 'assault' will be taken to mean assault in its pure form and the charge will be as bad as being duplicitous. If anything other than 'did assault' is to be alleged it should be 'did assault by beating' (*DPP v Taylor and Little* (1991)). A reckless act which causes injury will suffice, for example a man who having fallen to the ground when struggling with the police lashed out wildly with his legs, striking the officer and fracturing a bone in his hand, was held to have been properly convicted. Just placing a hand on someone's shoulder to call his attention to something is not an assault. Throwing something at a person, even if it misses, may be an assault.

A[15.6] If a man strikes at another but at such a distance that it would be quite impossible for it to connect then it is not an assault (although it might be an attempt). If the other person is actually touched then it is a battery which includes an assault. Equally a punch to a mother causing her to drop her baby is an assault on the baby (*Haystead v Chief Constable of Derbyshire* [2000] 3 All ER 890, [2000] 2 Cr App Rep 339).

A[15.7] Racially or religiously aggravated. This means that at the time of committing the offence, or immediately before or after doing so, the offender demonstrates towards the victim of the assault, hostility based on the victim's membership (or presumed membership) of a racial/religious group, or the offence is motivated (wholly or partly) by hostility towards members of a racial/ religious group based on their membership of that group. It is immaterial whether or not the offender's hostility is also based on other factor not mentioned above. The prosecution can proceed on one or both limbs and will not need to specify which (*G v DPP; T v DPP* [2004] EWHC 183 (Admin), [2004] All ER (D) 278 (Jan)) (*DPP v Woods* [2002] EWHC 85 (Admin), [2002] All ER (D) 154 (Jan)) The victim's perception of the words used is irrelevant, as is the defendant's frame of mind at the time he uttered the words. This offence may also be aggravated by a motivation towards the victim's disability, sexual orientation or transgender identity but not as a separate offence.

A[15.8] Misadventure. If a horse out of control strikes a person that is not an assault. In an old decision a soldier drilling in the ranks fired his gun as a man was passing unexpectedly and this was held not to be an assault.

A[15.9] Accidental jostling. In a crowd there is not an assault as there is an implied consent to the physical contacts of ordinary life.

A[15.10] Hostile intent. See *Collins v Wilcock* [1984] 1 WLR 1172.

A[15.11]–[15.15] Consent. Consent of the victim is a defence but there are limits to this. The test is whether it is in the public interest to allow the activity complained of. In 1981 the Lord Chief Justice decided consent was irrelevant where two youths settled an argument in a public street by agreeing to have a fight. It was not in the public interest for people to cause each other actual bodily harm for no good reason. A similar principle has been applied by the House of Lords to assault which took place in the course of sado-masochistic activities (*R v Brown* [1992] QB 491, [1992] 2 All ER 552, CA; affd [1994] 1 AC 212, [1993] 2 All ER 75, HL). But see *ADT v United Kingdom* [2000] 2 FLR 697, [2000] Fam Law 797, ECtHR for protection from prosecution for such genuinely 'private' activities.

Where a registered tattooist and body piercer also did body modifications, and had no medical qualifications, and was charged with three counts of causing grievous bodily harm with intent in consequence of carrying out operations without anaesthetic: to remove an ear; to remove a nipple; and to split a person's tongue to resemble a reptile's tongue, the consent of the clients concerned did not provide a defence. There was no easy articulated principle by which novel situations could be judged, but most of the exceptions to consent as a defence had a basis in some discernible social benefit, such as sport, or dangerous exhibitions as social entertainment or religious ritual: *R v BM; R v M* [2018] EWCA Crim 560, [2018] 2 Cr App Rep 1. As to sport, see further **A[15.18]**.

In *R v Melin* [2019] EWCA Crim 557, [2019] 3 WLR 150, [2019] 2 Cr App Rep 63 the defendant administered what purported to be Botox injections for cosmetic purposes to the two complainants, who were unaware that he was not medically qualified. Both complainants suffered very serious harm as a result of severe reactions to their injections. The Crown's case was that each complainant's apparent consent to her treatment had been vitiated by the defendant's deception as to his medical qualifications. The defendant contended that deception as to a qualification was insufficient to vitiate consent. The defendant was convicted and appealed.

It was held that deception as to a person's status as a doctor could as a matter of law amount to deception as to his identity, capable of vitiating consent to an act that would otherwise be an assault, where that status was inextricably bound up with his or her identity for the purposes of the specific activity he or she was performing. If, as a matter of fact, a complainant would not have consented to the administration of an injection if it had been given by someone who was not a medically qualified practitioner, then that person's status as a medical practitioner was part of his or her identity for the purposes of whether the complainant's consent to the injection had been vitiated. In relation to one of the complainants the appeal was allowed since there was insufficient evidence that her consent had been dependent on the defendant's identity as a doctor; however, in the case of the other complaint there was sufficient evidence of this, so her consent had been vitiated.

It is not a defence to assault that the complainant is a teacher at a special needs school and, by taking that job, consents to the risk of being assaulted. Knowledge of the risk does not imply consent to assault: *H v Crown Prosecution Service* [2010] EWHC 1374 (Admin), 174 CL&J 271, followed in *A v DPP* [2017] EWHC 821 (Admin).

A[15.16] Consensual activity between husband and wife in the privacy of the matrimonial home was held not to be a proper matter for criminal investigation in *R v Wilson* [1997] QB 47, [1996] 3 WLR 125, CA. Lawful sport would be unimpeachable as being in the public interest and the exercise of a legal right.

A[15.17] Defendants who maintained that they had been engaged in rough and undisciplined horseplay, had not intended any harm, and had thought that the victims were consenting to what had occurred, were entitled to have their defence considered by the court (*R v Muir* (1986) 83 Cr App Rep 375, CA).

A[15.18] An injury inflicted on an opponent by deliberately flouting the rules of the game may form the basis of a criminal prosecution: *R v Billinghurst* [1978] Crim LR 553. Most organised sports have their own disciplinary procedures to uphold their rules and standards of play; criminal prosecutions should, therefore, be brought only in cases that are so grave as to be properly categorised as criminal. If what occurs goes beyond what a player can reasonably be regarded as having accepted by taking part in the sport, this indicates that the conduct will not be covered by the defence of consent; on the other hand, the fact that the play is within the rules and practice of the game and does not go beyond them, will be a firm indication that what has happened is not criminal: *R v Barnes* [2004] EWCA Crim 3246, [2005] 2 All ER 113, [2005] 1 Cr App Rep 507, [2005] Crim LR 381 in which the following guidance was given. It must be borne in mind that in highly competitive sports conduct outside the rules could be expected to occur in the heat of the moment and even if conduct justified not only being penalised but also a warning or even a sending off it still might not reach the threshold level required for it to be criminal. The type of sport, the level at which it was played, the nature of the act, the degree of force used, the extent of the risk of injury and the state of mind of the defendant were all likely to be relevant in determining whether the defendant's actions went beyond the threshold and warranted criminal proceedings.

A[15.18A] **Reasonable chastisement** is a defence available to a parent accused of assaulting their child; however the chastisement must be reasonable and moderate. This is assessed by:

(i) the nature and context of the defendant's behaviour
(ii) the duration
(iii) physical/ mental consequences to the child (injury will make it unlawful)
(iv) age and characteristics of the child

While reasonable chastisement can (depending on the circumstances) justify an assault by beating (but not an offence under ss 18, 20, or 47 of the Offences Against the Person Act 1861, or s 1 of the Children and Young Persons Act 1933), battery of a child causing actual bodily harm cannot be justified in any civil proceedings on the ground that it constituted reasonable punishment (Children Act 2004, s 58).

A[15.19] **Self-defence.** See A[8.18]–A[8.20].

Self-defence – onus of proof. Once the defendant raises the issue of self-defence the onus is on the prosecution to disprove the defence beyond reasonable doubt.

A[15.20] **Execution of legal process.** An officer of justice acting on a court order can, if he is resisted, use whatever force is necessary to carry out the order of the court.

A[15.21]–[15.30] **Justification or triviality.** In a case of common assault where the information was preferred by or on behalf of the party aggrieved, if the court finds that an assault has been committed but that either it was justified or that it was so trifling as not to merit any punishment, they may dismiss the charge and issue a certificate of dismissal (see OATPA 1861, s 44).

A[15.31] **Certificate of dismissal.** If the justices upon hearing any case of assault or battery upon the merits, where the information was preferred by or on behalf of the person aggrieved, find the offence not proved or find the assault or battery to have been justified, or so trifling as not to merit any punishment, and accordingly dismiss the information, they must make out a certificate stating the fact of such dismissal and must deliver the certificate to the party against whom the complaint was preferred: OATPA 1861, s 44.

Note, the dismissal must be on the merits; this means the evidence must be thoroughly gone into: *Ellis v Burton* [1975] 1 ALL ER 395, 139 JP 199. Note also, s 44 is confined to private prosecutions; when the CPS undertakes a prosecution it does not do so on behalf of the person aggrieved, it is acting in the public interest: *Austen v CPS* [2016] EWHC 2247 (Admin), (2017) 181 JP 181. It is also worth noting that where a person pleads not guilty to a charge of assault occasioning actual bodily harm and no evidence is offered, he/she cannot then be tried for common assault on the same facts: *R v G (autrefois acquit)* [2001] EWCA Crim 1215, [2001] 1 WLR 1727.

A[15.32] **Provocation.** This is not a defence but may be put forward to mitigate the penalty.

Sentencing

SC Guideline – Common assault and racially/religiously aggravated common assault

A[15.33] **Common Assault**

Criminal Justice Act 1988 (section 39)

Racially/religiously aggravated common assault

Crime and Disorder Act 1998 (section 29)

Racially/religiously aggravated assault is a specified offence for the purposes of section 224 of the Criminal Justice Act 2003

Section 39

Triable only summarily

Maximum: Level 5 and/or 26 weeks' custody

Section 29

Triable either way

Maximum when tried summarily: Level 5 fine and/or 26 weeks' custody

Maximum when tried on indictment: 2 years' custody

Offence range: Discharge – 26 weeks' custody

This guideline applies to all offenders aged 18 and older, who are sentenced on or after 13 June 2011. The definitions of 'starting point' and 'first time offender' do not apply for this guideline. Starting point and category ranges apply to all offenders in all cases, irrespective of plea or previous convictions.

STEP ONE
Determining the offence category

The court should determine the offence category using the table below.

Category 1	Greater harm **and** higher culpability
Category 2	Greater harm **and** lower culpability; **or** lesser harm **and** higher culpability
Category 3	Lesser harm **and** lower culpability

The court should determine the offender's culpability and the harm caused, or intended, by reference **only** to the factors below (as demonstrated by the presence of one or more). These factors comprise the principal factual elements of the offence and should determine the category.

Factors indicating greater harm
Injury (which includes disease transmission and/or psychological harm) which is serious in the context of the offence (must normally be present)
Victim is particularly vulnerable because of personal circumstances
Sustained or repeated assault on the same victim
Factors indicating lesser harm
Injury which is less serious in the context of the offence
Factors indicating higher culpability
Statutory aggravating factors:
Offence motivated by, or demonstrating, hostility to the victim based on his or her sexual orientation (or presumed sexual orientation)
Offence motivated by, or demonstrating, hostility to the victim based on the victim's disability (or presumed disability)
Other aggravating factors:
A significant degree of premeditation
Threatened or actual use of weapon or weapon equivalent (for example, shod foot, headbutting, use of acid, use of animal)
Intention to commit more serious harm than actually resulted from the offence
Deliberately causes more harm than is necessary for commission of offence
Deliberate targeting of vulnerable victim
Leading role in group or gang
Offence motivated by, or demonstrating, hostility based on the victim's age, sex, gender identity (or presumed gender identity)
Factors indicating lower culpability
Subordinate role in group or gang

A greater degree of provocation than normally expected
Lack of premeditation
Mental disorder or learning disability, where linked to commission of the offence
Excessive self defence

STEP TWO
Starting point and category range

Having determined the category, the court should use the corresponding starting points to reach a sentence within the category range below. The starting point applies to all offenders irrespective of plea or previous convictions. A case of particular gravity, reflected by multiple features of culpability in step one, could merit upward adjustment from the starting point before further adjustment for aggravating or mitigating features, set out below.

Offence Category	Starting Point *(Applicable to all offenders)*	Category Range *(Applicable to all offenders)*
Category 1	High level community order	Low level community order – 26 weeks' custody
Category 2	Medium level community order	Band A fine – High level community order
Category 3	Band A fine	Discharge – Band C fine

The table below contains a **non-exhaustive** list of additional factual elements providing the context of the offence and factors relating to the offender. Identify whether any combination of these, or other relevant factors, should result in an upward or downward adjustment from the starting point. In some cases, having considered these factors, it may be appropriate to move outside the identified category range.

When sentencing **category 1** offences, the court should also consider the custody threshold as follows:

- has the custody threshold been passed?
- if so, is it unavoidable that a custodial sentence be imposed?
- if so, can that sentence be suspended?

When sentencing **category 2** offences, the court should also consider the community order threshold as follows:

- has the community order threshold been passed?

Factors increasing seriousness
Statutory aggravating factors:
Previous convictions, having regard to a) the nature of the offence to which the conviction relates and its relevance to the current offence; and b) the time that has elapsed since the conviction
Offence committed whilst on bail
Other aggravating factors include:
Location of the offence
Timing of the offence
Ongoing effect upon the victim
Offence committed against those working in the public sector or providing a service to the public
Presence of others including relatives, especially children or partner of the victim

Gratuitous degradation of victim
In domestic violence cases, victim forced to leave their home
Failure to comply with current court orders
Offence committed whilst on licence
An attempt to conceal or dispose of evidence
Failure to respond to warnings or concerns expressed by others about the offender's behaviour
Commission of offence whilst under the influence of alcohol or drugs
Abuse of power and/or position of trust
Exploiting contact arrangements with a child to commit an offence
Established evidence of community impact
Any steps taken to prevent the victim reporting an incident, obtaining assistance and/or from assisting or supporting the prosecution
Offences taken into consideration (TICs)
Factors reducing seriousness or reflecting personal mitigation
No previous convictions **or** no relevant/recent convictions
Single blow
Remorse
Good character and/or exemplary conduct
Determination and/or demonstration of steps taken to address addiction or offending behaviour
Serious medical conditions requiring urgent, intensive or long-term treatment
Isolated incident
Age and/or lack of maturity where it affects the responsibility of the offender
Lapse of time since the offence where this is not the fault of the offender
Mental disorder or learning disability, where **not** linked to the commission of the offence
Sole or primary carer for dependent relatives

Section 29 offences only: The court should determine the appropriate sentence for the offence without taking account of the element of aggravation and then make an addition to the sentence, considering the level of aggravation involved. It may be appropriate to move outside the identified category range, taking into account the increased statutory maximum.

STEP THREE
Consider any other factors which indicate a reduction, such as assistance to the prosecution

The court should take into account any rule of law by virtue of which an offender may receive a discounted sentence in consequence of assistance given (or offered) to the prosecutor or investigator.

STEP FOUR
Reduction for guilty pleas

The court should take account of any potential reduction for a guilty plea in accordance with section 144 of the Criminal Justice Act 2003 and the *Guilty Plea* guideline.

STEP FIVE
Dangerousness

Inflicting grievous bodily harm/unlawful wounding and racially/religiously aggravated GBH/unlawful wounding are specified offences within the meaning of Chapter

5 of the Criminal Justice Act 2003 and at this stage the court should consider whether having regard to the criteria contained in that Chapter it would be appropriate to award an extended sentence

STEP SIX
Totality principle

If sentencing an offender for more than one offence, or where the offender is already serving a sentence, consider whether the total sentence is just and proportionate to the offending behaviour.

STEP SEVEN
Compensation and ancillary orders

In all cases, the court should consider whether to make compensation and/or other ancillary orders.

STEP EIGHT
Reasons

Section 174 of the Criminal Justice Act 2003 imposes a duty to give reasons for, and explain the effect of, the sentence.

STEP NINE
Consideration for remand time

(Now obligatory.)

A[15.34] Domestic violence. For domestic violence offences see SC Definitive Guideline 'Overarching Principles: Domestic Abuse'.

A[16]
Communications network offences

Charge (Communications network offences)

A[16.1] **A person is guilty of an offence if he—**

(a) **sends by means of a public electronic communications network a message or other matter that is grossly offensive or of an indecent, obscene or menacing character; or**
(b) **causes any such matter to be so sent**

Communications Act 2003, s 127(1)

A person is guilty of an offence if he—

(a) **sends by means of a public electronic communications network, a message that he knows to be false,**
(b) **causes such a message to be sent; or**
(c) **persistently makes use of a public electronic communications network**

Communications Act 2003, s 127(2)

Maximum penalty – 6 months' imprisonment and/or fine level 5 (for offences committed on or after 12 March 2015 an unlimited fine). Triable summarily only.

Legal notes and definitions

A[16.2]–[16.6] **Elements of the offence.** In *DPP v Collins* [2006] UK 40, [2006] 4 All ER 602, [2006] 1 WLR 2223, (2006) 170 JP 712, [2007] 1 Cr App R 5, [2007] Crim LR 98 the House of Lords held that the purpose and elements of the offence under s 127(1)(a) were as follows. The object was to prohibit the use of a service provided and funded by the public for the benefit of the public, for the transmission of communications that contravened the basic standards of society. The proscribed act was the sending of the message of the proscribed character by the defined means, and the offence was complete when the message was sent. It was for the court, applying the standards of an open and just multiracial society and taking account of the context and all relevant circumstances, to determine as a question of fact whether a message was grossly offensive. It was necessary to show that the defendant intended his words to be grossly offensive to those to whom the message related, or that he was aware that they might be taken to be so. Although s 127(1)(a) interfered with the right to freedom of expression under art 10 of the Convention, it went no further than was necessary in a democratic society for achieving the legitimate objective of preventing the use of the public electronic communications network for attacking the reputations and rights of others.

In *Chambers v DPP* [2012] EWHC 2157 (Admin), [2013] 1 All ER 149, [2013] 1 Cr App Rep 1 the defendant was a registered user of Twitter and 'tweeted' in his own name. When he learned of the closure of an airport owing to adverse weather conditions he tweeted '... You've got a week and a bit to get your shit together otherwise I am blowing the airport sky high!!' This was posted onto the public time line, which meant it was available to be read by about 600 Twitter followers of the defendant. The conviction was quashed by the Divisional Court. At the time the tweet was posted it was a 'message' within s 127, but on an objective assessment there was no proper basis for concluding that the tweet constituted or included a message of a menacing character. There was no evidence that any Twitter follower of the defendant, or anyone else who may have seen the tweet, had found it to be menacing or even slightly alarming. 'The message must be credible as an immediate threat to the mind of an ordinary person of normal stability and courage . . . it is difficult to imagine a serious threat in which warning of it is given to a large number of tweet "followers" in ample time for the threat to be reported and extinguished' (per Lord Judge CJ at paras 30 and 31). His Lordship added this regarding the mental element of the offence. No different test applied to 'menacing' messages than those which were 'grossly offensive'. The mental element is satisfied 'if the offender is proved to have been aware or to have recognised the risk at the time of sending the message that it may create fear or apprehension in any reasonable member of the public who reads or sees it. We would merely emphasise that, even expressed in these terms, the mental element of the offence is directed exclusively to the state of the mind of the offender, and that if he may have intended the message as a joke, even if a joke in bad taste, it is unlikely that the mens rea required before conviction for the offence of sending a message of a menacing character will be established' (at para 37).

See also *Karsten v Wood Green Crown Court* [2014] EWHC 2900 (Admin), [2014] All ER (D) 286 (Oct). The conviction was quashed; the defendant had used nasty, anti-Semitic words, but they could not be regarded as menacing in the sense demanded by authority.

The above authorities were considered in *Director of Public Prosecutions v Smith (Kingsley Anthony)* [2017] EWHC 359 (Admin), (2017) 181 JP 258. The respondent used his Google+ account to post four messages for public view. Each was attached to a YouTube video which the respondent had downloaded to his account. One of the charges concerned a Vice News video entitled 'The Islamic State', which depicted images of execution by crucifixion and beheading. To this the respondent attached the message 'Allahu Akbar, kill the Kuffir'. The four films attracted a very large number of hits and thousands of comments. Despite deprecating the comments and noting that they were not jokes but typical expressions of anger and bigotry, the District Judge 'could not find that these messages created menace. They did not create fear or apprehension in those to whom they were communicated ... they represented empty bombast or ridiculous banter'. The judge was influenced in coming to these conclusions by the seeming lack of concern by the police for the impact of the messages on those seeing them, and the lack of expedition with which the police took action following the discovery of the texts, also there was no evidence of people complaining or being upset or being encouraged to act. The language used was 'inconsistent with the writer intending them to taken as serious warnings of actions he genuinely intended'.

The prosecutor's appeal by way of case stated was upheld. This case was very different from *Chambers*. The messages were not a joke. The lack of evidence from anyone seeing them was unsurprising. It was perfectly reasonable for the police to prioritise other cases, and there was evidence that it was very difficult to take down things posted online. The District Judge had, therefore, inappropriately taken these matters into account or, at least, given them too much weight. The District Judge had to ask himself whether, as a question of fact, taking account of the context and all relevant circumstances, and applying the standards of a reasonable person in an open and just multi-racial and multi-faith society, it was proved that the message was grossly offensive to those to whom it related or was of a menacing character in that it would have created a sense of apprehension or feat in a person of reasonable firmness who received and read it. However, the judge had not asked himself that question at all, nor had he recorded any reasoned conclusion as to whether the messages were grossly offensive, when there was a clear case that they were. Those errors fatally undermined all the findings of fact the judge had made as to the actus reus of the offence.

Sentencing

SC Guideline – Communications network offences

Communication network offences (Revised 2017)

A[16.7]

Communications Act 2003, ss 127(1) and 127(2)

Effective from: 24 April 2017

Triable only summarily:

Maximum: Unlimited fine and/or 6 months

Offence range: Band A fine–15 weeks' custody

STEP 1
Determining the offence category

The Court should determine the offence category using the table below.

Category 1	Higher culpability and greater harm
Category 2	Higher culpability and lesser harm or lower culpability and greater harm
Category 3	Lower culpability and lesser harm

The court should determine the offender's culpability and the harm caused with reference only to the factors below. Where an offence does not fall squarely into a category, individual factors may require a degree of weighting before making an overall assessment and determining the appropriate offence category.

CULPABILITY demonstrated by one or more of the following:

Factors indicating higher culpability

- Targeting of a vulnerable victim
- Targeting offending (in terms of timing or location) to maximise effect
- Use of threats (including blackmail)
- Threat to disclose intimate material or sexually explicit images
- Campaign demonstrated by multiple calls and/or wide distribution
- False calls to emergency services
- Offence motivated by, or demonstrating, hostility based on any of the following characteristics or presumed characteristics of the victim(s): religion, race, disability, sexual orientation or transgender identity

Factors indicating lower culpability

- All other cases

HARM demonstrated by one or more of the following:

Factors indicating greater harm

- Substantial distress or fear to victim(s) or moderate impact on several victims
- Major disruption

Factors indicating lesser harm

- All other cases

STEP 2
Starting point and category range

Having determined the category at step one, the court should use the corresponding starting point to reach a sentence within the category range in the table below. The starting point applies to all offenders irrespective of plea or previous convictions.

Offence Category	Starting Point	Range
Category 1	9 weeks' custody	High level community order–15 weeks' custody
Category 2	Medium level community order	Low level community order–High level community order

Offence Category	Starting Point	Range
Category 3	Band B fine	Band A fine–Band C fine

The court should then consider adjustment for any aggravating or mitigating factors. The following is a **non-exhaustive** list of additional factual elements providing the context of the offence and factors relating to the offender. Identify whether any combination of these, or other relevant factors, should result in an upward or downward adjustment from the sentence arrived at so far.

Factors increasing seriousness

Statutory aggravating factors:

- Previous convictions, having regard to a) the **nature** of the offence to which the conviction relates and its **relevance** to the current offence; and b) the **time** that has elapsed since the conviction
- Offence committed whilst on bail

Other aggravating factors:

- Failure to comply with current court orders including restraining order
- Offence committed on licence or post sentence supervision
- Offence committed whilst subject to sex offender notification requirements
- Offence linked to domestic abuse
- Abuse of trust
- Targeting emergency services (where not taken into account at step one)

Factors reducing seriousness or reflecting personal mitigation

- No previous convictions **or** no relevant/recent convictions
- Remorse
- Good character and/or exemplary conduct
- Isolated incident
- Age and/or lack of maturity where it affects the responsibility of the offender
- Mental disorder or learning disability
- Sole or primary carer for dependent relatives
- Limited awareness or understanding of the offence

STEP 3

Consider any factors which indicate a reduction, such as assistance to the prosecution

The court should take into account sections 73 and 74 of the Serious Organised Crime and Police Act 2005 (assistance by defendants: reduction or review of sentence) and any other rule of law by virtue of which an offender may receive a discounted sentence in consequence of assistance given (or offered) to the prosecutor or investigator.

STEP 4

Reduction for guilty pleas

The court should take account of any potential reduction for a guilty plea in accordance with section 144 of the Criminal Justice Act 2003 and the *Guilty Plea* guideline.

STEP 5

Totality principle

If sentencing an offender for more than one offence, or where the offender is already serving a sentence, consider whether the total sentence is just and proportionate to the overall offending behaviour in accordance with the *Offences Taken into Consideration and Totality* guideline.

STEP 6
Compensation and ancillary orders

In all cases, the court should consider whether to make compensation and/or other ancillary orders including restraining orders.

STEP 7
Reasons

Section 174 of the Criminal Justice Act 2003 imposes a duty to give reasons for, and explain the effect of, the sentence.

STEP 8
Consideration for time spent on bail

The court must consider whether to give credit for time spent on bail in accordance with section 240A of the Criminal Justice Act 2003.

A[17]

Community order, breach of

Charge (Community order, breach of)

A[17.1] That the offender has failed without reasonable excuse to comply with any of the requirements of a community order made on x date by x court. Contrary to Criminal Justice Act 2003, Sch 8.

Legal notes and definitions

A[17.2] **Burden and standard of proof.** The burden is on the prosecutor; the standard of proof is beyond a reasonable doubt (*West Yorkshire Probation Board v Boulter* [2005 [EWHC 2342 (Admin), (2005) 169 JP 601).

Reasonable excuse. A community order takes effect when it is imposed and it remains in full force and effect until and unless it is quashed on appeal or revoked or amended by order of the court. Although the concept of "reasonable excuse" is broad there is no statutory provision which automatically suspends the operation of a community order pending an appeal against it (or the conviction on which it is based). It is not therefore a reasonable excuse for a defendant to fail to carry out the community order despite the lodging of a notice of appeal (*West Midlands Probation Board v Sutton Coldfield Magistrates' Courts* [2005] EWHC 15 (Admin)).

Failed. An offender who "fails to keep in touch" with his responsible officer in accordance with such instructions as he may from time to time be given by that officer, in the absence of documentary or supporting evidence to explain the failure, provided within a specified period of time eg 7 days, breaches the terms of the community order (*Richards v National Probation Service* [2007] EWHC 3108 (Admin)).

Sentencing
SC Guideline – Breach offences definitive guideline

A[17.3] This guideline includes a section on breach of a community order. This is reproduced at **B**[9.27], post.

Options in breach proceedings:

When dealing with breaches of community orders for offences committed after 4 April 2005, the court must either:

- **amend the terms of the original order so as to impose more onerous requirements.** The court may extend the duration of particular requirements within the order, but it cannot extend the overall length of the original order (NB: s 38 of the Criminal Justice and Immigration Act 2008 reduces from 40 hours to 20 hours the minimum period of unpaid work that can be imposed on breach, provided that the order did not previously contain an unpaid work requirement); or
- **fine,** by ordering the offender to pay a fine of an amount not exceeding £2,500; or
- **revoke the original order and proceed to sentence for the original offence.** Where an offender has wilfully and persistently failed to comply with an order made in respect of an offence that is not punishable by imprisonment, the court can impose of to six months custody (CJA, Sch 8, para 9(1)(c)).

NB: revocation and re-sentence: in the case of an offence triable either way this does not include committal to the Crown Court for sentence pursuant to s 3 PCC (S) Act 2000 (*R v Jordan* [1998] Crim LR 353).

Approach to breach proceedings:

- having decided that a community order is commensurate with the seriousness of the offence, the primary objective when sentencing for breach of requirements is to ensure that those requirements are completed;
- a court sentencing for breach must take account of the extent to which the offender has complied with the requirements of the original order, the reasons for the breach, and the point at which the breach has occurred;
- if increasing the onerousness of requirements, sentencers should take account of the offender's ability to comply and should avoid precipitating further breach by overloading the offender with too many or conflicting requirements;
- there may be cases where the court will need to consider re-sentencing to a differently constructed community order in order to secure compliance with the purposes of the original sentence, perhaps where there has already been partial compliance or where events since the sentence was imposed have shown that a different course of action is likely to be effective;
- where available, custody should be the last resort, reserved for those cases of deliberate and repeated breach where all reasonable efforts to ensure that the offender complies have failed.

Where the original order was made by the Crown court, breach proceedings must be commenced in that court, unless the order provided that any failure to comply with its requirements may be dealt with a magistrates' court. **Consult your legal adviser for further guidance when dealing with breach of a community order made in the Crown Court.**

A[17A]

Controlling or coercive behaviour in an intimate or family relationship

Charge

A[17A.1] **Repeatedly or continuously engaged in controlling or coercive behaviour towards another person (B), at a time when the parties were personally connected, and the behaviour had a serious effect on B, which the defendant knew or ought to have known.**

Serious Crime Act 2015, s 76

Maximum penalty – 6 months' imprisonment and/or an unlimited fine.

Crown Court – 5 years imprisonment and/or unlimited fine.

Legal notes and definitions

A[17A.2] 'Personally connected' means: in an intimate personal relationship; living together and being members of the same family; or previously being in an intimate personal relationship with each other: SCA 2015, s 76(2). No offence is committed, however, if at the time of the behaviour the perpetrator (A) had parental responsibility for the other party (B) and B was under 16: SCA 2015, s 76(3).

A and B are members of the 'same family' if: they are or have been married to each other or are or have been civil partners of each other; they are relatives within the meaning given by s 63(1) of the Family Law Act 1996; they are or have been engaged to marry each other or are or have been in a civil partnership agreement within the meaning of s 73 of the Civil Partnership Act 2004; they are both parents of the same child (under 18); or they have, or have had, parental responsibility within the meaning provided by the Children Act 1989 for the same child (under 18): SCA s 76(6).

Behaviour has a 'serious effect' on B if: it causes B to fear, on at least two occasions, that violence will be used against him/her; or it causes B serious alarm or distress which has a substantial adverse effect on B's usual day-to-day activities: CSA 2015, s 76(4).

A 'ought to know' that which a reasonable person in possession of the same information would know: SCA 2015, s 76(5).

Defences

A[17A.3] Subject to the below, it is a defence for A to show that in engaging in the relevant behaviour A believed that he/she was acting in B's best interests, and the behaviour was in all the circumstances reasonable: SCA 2015, s 76(8). A is taken to have shown these facts if he/she has adduced sufficient evidence to raise an issue with respect to them and the contrary is not proved beyond reasonable doubt: SCA 2015, s 76(9).

The defence is not available in relation to behaviour which causes B to fear he/she will suffer violence: SCA 2015, s 76(10).

Sentencing

SC Guideline – Controlling or coercive behaviour in an intimate or family relationship

A[17A.4] This guideline is taken from the Sentencing Council's Intimidatory offences: Definitive guideline, published on 5 July 2018, coming into effect on 1 October 2018.

Controlling or coercive behaviour in an intimate or family relationship

Serious Crime Act 2015, s 76

Effective from: 1 October 2018

Triable either way

Maximum: 5 years' custody

Offence range: Community order – 4 years' custody

Also refer to the *Overarching principles: Domestic abuse* guideline

STEP 1
Determining the offence category

The court should determine the offence category with reference only to the factors in the tables below. In order to determine the category the court should assess culpability and harm.

The level of **culpability** is determined by weighing up all the factors of the case. **Where there are characteristics present which fall under different levels of culpability, the court should balance these characteristics to reach a fair assessment of the offender's culpability.**

Culpability demonstrated by one or more of the following:

A – Higher culpability	• Conduct intended to maximise fear or distress • Persistent action over a prolonged period • Use of multiple methods of controlling or coercive behaviour • Sophisticated offence • Conduct intended to humiliate and degrade the victim
B – Medium culpability	• Conduct intended to cause some fear or distress • Scope and duration of offence that falls between categories A and C • All other cases that fall between categories A and C
C – Lesser culpability	• Offender's responsibility substantially reduced by mental disorder or learning disability • Offence was limited in scope and duration

Harm

The level of harm is assessed by weighing up all the factors of the case.

Category 1	• Fear of violence on many occasions • Very serious alarm or distress which has a substantial adverse effect on the victim • Significant psychological harm
Category 2	• Fear of violence on at least two occasions • Serious alarm or distress which has a substantial adverse effect on the victim

STEP 2
Starting point and category range

Having determined the category at step one, the court should use the corresponding starting point to reach a sentence within the category range in the table below. The starting point applies to all offenders irrespective of plea or previous convictions.

	Culpability		
Harm	A	B	C
Category 1	**Starting point** 2 years 6 months' custody **Category range** 1–4 years' custody	**Starting point** 1 years' custody **Category range** 26 weeks' – 2 years 6 months' custody	**Starting point** 26 weeks' custody **Category range** High level community order – 1 year's custody
Category 2	**Starting point** 1 years' custody **Category range** 26 weeks – 2 years 6 months' custody	**Starting point** 26 weeks' custody **Category range** High level community order – 1 year's custody	**Starting point** Medium level community order **Category range** Low level community order – 26 weeks' custody

The court should then consider any adjustment for any aggravating or mitigating factors. Below is a **non-exhaustive** list of additional factual elements providing the context of the offence and factors relating to the offender.

Identify whether any combination of these, or other relevant factors, should result in an upward or downward adjustment from the starting point.

Factors increasing seriousness

Statutory aggravating factors:
Previous convictions, having regard to a) the **nature** of the offence to which the conviction relates and its **relevance** to the current offence; and b) the **time** that has elapsed since the conviction
Offence committed whilst on bail
Offence motivated by, or demonstrating hostility based on any of the following characteristics or presumed characteristics of the victim: religion, race, disability, sexual orientation, or transgender identity
Other aggravating factors:
Steps taken to prevent the victim reporting an incident
Steps taken to prevent the victim obtaining assistance
A proven history of violence or threats by the offender in a domestic context
Impact of offence on others particularly children
Exploiting contact arrangements with a child to commit the offence
Victim is particularly vulnerable (not all vulnerabilities are immediately apparent)
Victim left in debt, destitute or homeless
Failure to comply with current court orders
Offence committed on licence or post sentence supervision
Offences taken into consideration

Factors reducing seriousness or reflecting personal mitigation

No previous convictions or no relevant/recent convictions
Remorse
Good character and/or exemplary conduct
Serious medical condition requiring urgent, intensive or long-term treatment
Age and/or lack of maturity

Mental disorder or learning disability (where not taken into account at step one)
Sole or primary carer for dependent relatives
Determination and/or demonstration of steps having been taken to address offending behaviour

STEP 3
Consider any factors which indicate a reduction, such as assistance to the prosecution

The court should take into account sections 73 and 74 of the Serious Organised Crime and Police Act 2005 (assistance by defendants: reduction or review of sentence) and any other rule of law by virtue of which an offender may receive a discounted sentence in consequence of assistance given (or offered) to the prosecutor or investigator.

STEP 4
Reduction for guilty pleas

The court should take account of any potential reduction for a guilty plea in accordance with section 144 of the Criminal Justice Act 2003 and the *Guilty Plea* guideline.

STEP 5
Totality principle

If sentencing an offender for more than one offence, or where the offender is already serving a sentence, consider whether the total sentence is just and proportionate to the overall offending behaviour in accordance with the *Offences Taken into Consideration and Totality* guideline.

STEP 6
Compensation and ancillary orders

In all cases, the court must consider whether to make a compensation order and/or other ancillary orders.

Compensation order

The court should consider compensation orders in all cases where personal injury, loss or damage has resulted from the offence. The court must give reasons if it decides not to award compensation in such cases.

Other ancillary orders available include:
Restraining order

Where an offender is convicted of any offence, the court may make a restraining order (section 5 of the Protection from Harassment Act 1997).

The order may prohibit the offender from doing anything for the purpose of protecting the victim of the offence, or any other person mentioned in the order, from further conduct which amounts to harassment or will cause a fear of violence.

The order may have effect for a specified period or until further order.

STEP 7
Reasons

Section 174 of the Criminal Justice Act 2003 imposes a duty to give reasons for, and explain the effect of, the sentence.

STEP 8
Consideration for time spent on bail

The court must consider whether to give credit for time spent on bail in accordance with section 240A of the Criminal Justice Act 2003.

A[18]
Damage to property

Criminal damage (including by fire (arson)) and racially/ religiously aggravated criminal damage

Charge (Damage to property)

A[18.1] **Without lawful excuse destroyed (or damaged) property namely [. . . . .] belonging to [. . . . .] intending to destroy (or damage) it or being reckless as to whether such property would be destroyed or damaged**

Criminal Damage Act 1971, s 1

NB: Where the damage is under £500 and not normally over £300 a fixed penalty of £90 is available

A[18.2] **Maximum penalty and venue for trial** – Where the damage or destruction is caused by fire (arson) the offence is triable either way without regard to the value of the damage caused and the maximum penalty is 6 months' imprisonment and/or fine level 5 (for offences committed on or after 12 March 2015 an unlimited fine). If it is alleged in the charge that the accused intended to endanger life, or was reckless as to whether life would be endangered, the offence is triable only on indictment and is punishable in the Crown Court with life imprisonment. Where the offence involves racial aggravation it will always be an either way offence (see below).

Offences of arson (s 1(3)) or where life is endangered (s 1(2)) are specified violent offences under Sch 15, Part 1, CJA 2003.

A[18.3] The plea before venue procedure only applies to criminal damage allegations in excess of £5,000 (*R v Kelly* [2001] RTR 45, CA). If the value is ascertained as £5,000 or under the court must proceed to summary trial and the sentence will be restricted to a maximum of a level 4 fine and/or 3 months' imprisonment – or 6 months for two offences (*R v Gwynn* [2002] EWCA Crim 2951, [2003] All ER (D) 318 (Dec)).

Note: while small value criminal damage can be tried only summarily it is nevertheless an either way offence for other purposes, eg time limits for commencing prosecutions: see *DPP v Bird* [2015] EWHC 4077 (Admin), [2016] 4 WLR 82, (2016) 180 JO 217.

A[18.4] Where the defendant does not indicate a guilty plea and it is unclear to the court whether the value of the damage is more than £5,000 or not the court must decide whether the value is more or less than that sum (it is not necessary to decide what the value is, simply whether it is above £5,000). If the court decides that the value of the damage exceeds £5,000 (and it may hear representations from the prosecution and defence to assist in arriving at a decision) then the offence is triable either way as in the preceding paragraph. Likewise if the court reaches a decision that the value of the damage does not exceed £5,000 the offence is triable summarily, as above. In those cases where the court is unable to decide whether the value is more or less than £5,000 the accused must be told that if he wishes he may consent to be tried summarily, and if he does he will be so tried and will be liable to a maximum penalty on level 4 and 3 months (level 5 and 6 months in a case of aggravated vehicle taking). If the accused then consents, the trial will proceed summarily.

A[18.5] If he does not consent, the court proceeds as for an ordinary either way offence, with the plea before venue and mode of trial procedure as is appropriate.

A[18.6] **Assessing the value of the damage.** Unless the damage was caused by fire, or racial aggravation was involved, where property has been destroyed the mode of trial depends upon its value. This means what it would probably have cost to buy in the open market at the material time. See (*R (on application of DPP) v Prestatyn Magistrates' Courts* [2002] All ER (D) 421 (May)) for further guidance.

A[18.7] If the allegation is one of damage (excluding damage caused by fire) the mode of trial depends upon the value of the damage. If, immediately after the damage was caused, the property was capable of repair (eg a car windscreen) then the value of the damage is the lesser of: (a) what would probably have been the market price for the repair of the damage immediately after the damage was caused (this would, for example, not include the cost of repairing further deterioration since the offence); or (b) what the property would probably have cost to buy in the open market at the material time, whichever is the less. Thus, if it would cost more to repair the property than its probable market value, then the value of the damage for the purposes of deciding the venue of trial would be the probable market price. If, immediately after the damage was caused, the property was beyond repair (eg a shattered crystal decanter) then the value for trial purposes is its probable cost in the open market at the time of the offence.

A[18.8] The use of the word 'probable' in the Act indicates that the court must make up its mind in the light of the available information.

A[18.9] **Multiple offences.** Where an accused is charged with a series of offences of damage or destruction the offences are only triable either way if their aggregate value is in excess of £5,000.

A[18.10]–[18.15] **Mode of trial considerations.** See the SC Guidelines below.

Charge (Damage to property) [cont.]

A[18.16] **Racially/religiously aggravated criminal damage**

Crime and Disorder Act 1998, s 30

Maximum penalty – level 5 and 6 months' imprisonment. Triable either way. Crown Court – 14 years' imprisonment and unlimited fine.

A[18.17] **Racially/religiously aggravated.** This means that at the time of committing the offence, of immediately before or after doing so, the offender demonstrates towards the victim's property hostility based on the victim's membership (or presumed membership) of a racial or religious group (see *Parry v DPP* [2004] EWHC 3112 (Admin), [2004] All ER (D) 335 (Dec) for guidance on immediacy); or the offence is motivated (wholly or partly) by hostility towards members of a racial or religious group based on their membership of that group. In *DPP v M* [2004] EWHC 1453 (Admin), [2004] All ER (D) 358 (May) the term 'bloody foreigners' was held to be a group defined by nationality and was hostile. In *R v Rogers* [2007] UKHL 8, it was decided that the term "foreigners" could constitute a racial group within the meaning of s 28(4) of the Crime and Disorder Act 1998. Whether the evidence in any particular case, taken as a whole, proved that the offender's conduct demonstrated hostility to such a group, or was motivated by such hostility, was a question of fact for the court.

A[18.18] The victim's perceptions of the words used is irrelevant here, as is the fact that the defendant would have used those words to anyone with the victim's characteristics (*DPP v Woods* [2002] EWHC 85 (Admin), [2002] All ER (D) 154 (Jan)).

It is immaterial whether the offender's hostility is also based to any extent on any other factor not mentioned above.

Legal notes and definitions

A[18.19] **Without lawful excuse.** It is a defence if the defendant proves he had a lawful excuse for destroying or damaging the property. He only has to establish that this defence is probably true, he does not have to establish it beyond reasonable doubt. Section 5(2) provides that, inter alia, the following can be lawful excuses:

(a) that at the time he destroyed or damaged the property he believed that a person or persons entitled to consent to the destruction or damage had given consent; or that person or persons would have consented if he or they had known of the destruction or damage and the circumstances; or
(b) that at the time he destroyed or damaged the property he believed that property belonging to himself or another was in immediate need of protection and that the adopted or proposed means of protection were reasonable in all the circumstances.

It has been held that, provided that the defendant honestly held such a belief, it is immaterial whether the belief was justified or not (even if the defendant was drunk) (*Jaggard v Dickinson* [1981] QB 527, [1980] 3 All ER 716, [1981] 2 WLR 118, 72 Cr App Rep 33, [1980] Crim LR 717, 124 Sol Jo 847). It has been stated, however, that the continuing validity of *Jaggard* was questionable, and in a case of failing to stop after an accident where D was intoxicated and was found to have genuinely believed that there had been no accident the conviction was upheld – there was no reason why D should be allowed to pray in aid her own state of drunkenness as the reason for the mistake: *Magee v CPS* [2014] EWHC 4089 (Admin), 179 JP 261.

Individuals facing charges for criminal damage and aggravated trespass arising out of their actions in protesting against the war in Iraq could not argue that they were using **reasonable force** to prevent the commission of a crime under s 3 of the Criminal Law Act 1967, nor that the activities of the activities of the Crown at military bases were unlawful (*R v Jones* [2006] UKHL 16).

The destruction of badger traps were not justified under s 5(2)(b) because the defendants did not cause the damage in order to protect property belonging to themselves or another person (*Currie v DPP* [2006] EWHC AER (D) 429 (Nov)).

A[18.20] **Destroy or damage.** Where a defendant was initially unaware that he had done an act that in fact set in train events which, by the time he became aware of them, would make it obvious to anyone who troubled to give his mind to them that they presented a risk that property belonging to another would be damaged, he would be guilty if he did not try to prevent or reduce the damage because he gave no thought to the possibility of such a risk or having done so he decided not to prevent or reduce the risk. An example would be the man who, unawares, drops a lighted cigarette down a chair and later, on discovering the chair is smouldering, leaves the room not caring whether the chair catches light or not.

A[18.21] **Property** is defined at length in s 10(1). It means property of a tangible nature and includes money. It also includes wild creatures which have been tamed or are ordinarily kept in captivity. It does not include mushrooms, fungus, flowers, fruit or foliage of a plant, shrub or tree which are growing wild on any land.

A[18.22] **Damage.** Defendants who had painted graffiti on a pavement with a water-soluble whitewash in the expectation that the graffiti would be washed away by rainwater, were guilty especially since expense and inconvenience had been caused to the local authority which removed the marks before it rained. 'Damage' may be used in the sense of mischief to property. The 'temporary functional derangement' of a police officer's cap by the defendant's stamping on it constituted damage although it could be pushed back into shape. Accordingly the erasure of a computer program on a plastic circuit card was damage and although it could be restored, this necessitated time, labour and expense (*Cox v Riley* (1986) 83 Cr App Rep 54, [1986] Crim LR 460). A computer 'hacker' who obtains unauthorised entry to a computer system and makes alterations impairing its proper use can be convicted of criminal damage, although the damage to the magnetic particles in the disk are not perceptible without using the computer. Tangible property has been damaged even though the damage itself is not tangible. Impairment of usefulness does not require breaking, cutting or removal of a part: *R v Whiteley* [1991] Crim LR 436.

A[18.23] **Belonging to another person** (s 10(2)). In addition to an ordinary owner this includes a person who had the custody or control of the property, or a proprietary right or interest in the property (except for an equitable interest arising only from an agreement to transfer or grant an interest), or who had a charge on the property.

A[18.24] As far as trust property is concerned, it can be treated for the purposes of this offence as belonging to any person having the right to enforce the trust (s 10(3)).

A[18.25]–[18.30] **Intending.** The court must decide whether the defendant intended the damage by considering all the evidence and drawing from it such inferences as appear proper in the circumstances.

A[18.31] **Reckless.** A person is reckless with respect to:

(a) a circumstance when he is aware of a risk, that it exists or will exist;
(b) a result, when he is aware of a risk that it will occur; and
(c) it is, in the circumstances known to him, unreasonable to take the risk (*R v G* [2003] UKHL 50, [2004] 1 AC 1034, [2003] 4 All ER 765, HL).

For a more recent example of the application of the test of recklessness see *Booth v Crown Prosecution Service* [2006] EWHC 192 (Admin), (2006) 170 JP 305, QBD.

Sentencing
SC Guideline – Arson (criminal damage by fire)

A[18.32] This is the text of the Sentencing Council's Definitive guideline, taking effect from 1 October 2019.

Arson (criminal damage by fire)

Criminal Damage Act 1971, s 1

Effective from: 1 October 2019

This is a serious specified offence for the purposes of section 224 of the Criminal Justice Act 2003.

Triable either way

Maximum when tried summarily: Level 5 fine and/or 6 months' custody

Maximum when tried on indictment: Life

Offence range: Discharge – 8 years' custody

Where offence committed in a domestic context, refer to the *Overarching principles: domestic abuse guideline*

Courts should consider requesting a report from: liaison and diversion services, a medical practitioner, or where it is necessary, ordering a psychiatric report, to ascertain both whether the offence is linked to a mental disorder or learning disability (to assist in the assessment of culpability) and whether any mental health disposal should be considered.

STEP 1
DETERMINING THE OFFENCE CATEGORY

The court should determine the offence category with reference only to the factors in the tables below. In order to determine the category the court should assess **culpability** and **harm.**

The level of **culpability** is determined by weighing up all the factors of the case. **Where there are characteristics present which fall under different levels of culpability, the court should balance these characteristics to reach a fair assessment of the offender's culpability.**

Culpability demonstrated by one or more of the following:

A – Higher culpability	• High degree of planning or premeditation • Revenge attack • Use of accelerant • Intention to cause very serious damage to property • Intention to create a high risk of injury to persons
B – Medium culpability	• Some planning • Recklessness as to whether very serious damage caused to property • Recklessness as to whether serious injury caused to persons • Other cases that fall between categories A and C because: – Factors are present in A and C which balance each other out and/or – The offender's culpability falls between the factors described in A and C
C – Lesser culpability	• Little or no planning; offence committed on impulse • Recklessness as to whether some damage to property caused • Offender's responsibility substantially reduced by mental disorder or learning disability • Involved through coercion, intimidation or exploitation

Harm

The level of harm is assessed by weighing up all the factors of the case.

Category 1	• Serious physical and/or psychological harm caused • Serious consequential economic or social impact of offence • High value of damage caused
Category 2	• Harm that falls between categories 1 and 3
Category 3	• No or minimal physical and/or psychological harm caused • Low value of damage caused

STEP 2
STARTING POINT AND CATEGORY RANGE

Having determined the category at step one, the court should use the corresponding starting point to reach a sentence within the category range below. The starting point applies to all offenders irrespective of plea or previous convictions.

Where the offender is dependent on or has a propensity to misuse drugs or alcohol, **which is linked to the offending**, a community order with a drug rehabilitation requirement under section 209, or an alcohol treatment requirement under section 212 of the Criminal Justice Act 2003 may be a proper alternative to a short or moderate custodial sentence.

Where the offender suffers from a medical condition that is susceptible to treatment but does not warrant detention under a hospital order, a community order with a mental health treatment requirement under section 207 of the Criminal Justice Act 2003 may be a proper alternative to a short or moderate custodial sentence.

In exceptional cases within category 1A, sentences of above 8 years may be appropriate.

Harm	Culpability A	B	C
Category 1	**Starting point** 4 years' custody **Category range** 2 – 8 years' custody	**Starting point** 1 year 6 months' custody **Category range** 9 months – 3 years' custody	**Starting point** 9 months' custody **Category range** 6 months – 1 year 6 months' custody
Category 2	**Starting point** 2 years' custody **Category range** 1 – 4 years' custody	**Starting point** 9 months' custody **Category range** 6 months – 1 year 6 months' custody	**Starting point** High level community order **Category range** Medium level community order – 9 months' custody
Category 3	**Starting point** 1 year's custody **Category range** 6 months – 2 years' custody	**Starting point** High level community order **Category range** Medium level Community order – 9 months' custody	**Starting point** Low level community order **Category range** Discharge – High level community order

The court should then consider any adjustment for any aggravating or mitigating factors. Below is a **non-exhaustive** list of additional factual elements providing the context of the offence and factors relating to the offender.

Identify whether any combination of these, or other relevant factors, should result in an upward or downward adjustment from the starting point.

FACTORS INCREASING SERIOUSNESS

Statutory aggravating factors:
Previous convictions, having regard to a) the **nature** of the offence to which the conviction relates and its **relevance** to the current offence; and b) the **time** that has elapsed since the conviction
Offence committed whilst on bail
Offence motivated by, or demonstrating hostility based on any of the following characteristics or presumed characteristics of the victim: religion, race, disability, sexual orientation, or transgender identity
Other aggravating factors:
Commission of offence whilst under the influence of alcohol or drugs
Offence committed for financial gain
Offence committed to conceal other offences
Victim is particularly vulnerable
Offence committed within a domestic context
Fire set in or near a public amenity
Damage caused to heritage and/or cultural assets
Significant impact on emergency services or resources
Established evidence of community/wider impact
Failure to comply with current court orders
Offence committed on licence or post sentence supervision
Offences taken into consideration

FACTORS REDUCING SERIOUSNESS OR REFLECTING PERSONAL MITIGATION

No previous convictions or no relevant/recent convictions
Steps taken to minimise the effect of the fire or summon assistance
Remorse
Good character and/or exemplary conduct
Serious medical condition requiring urgent, intensive or long-term treatment
Age and/or lack of maturity
Mental disorder or learning disability (where not taken into account at step one)
Sole or primary carer for dependent relatives
Determination and/or demonstration of steps having been taken to address offending behaviour

STEP 3
CONSIDER ANY FACTORS WHICH INDICATE A REDUCTION, SUCH AS ASSISTANCE TO THE PROSECUTION

The court should take into account sections 73 and 74 of the Serious Organised Crime and Police Act 2005 (assistance by defendants: reduction or review of sentence) and any other rule of law by virtue of which an offender may receive a discounted sentence in consequence of assistance given (or offered) to the prosecutor or investigator.

STEP 4
REDUCTION FOR GUILTY PLEAS

The court should take account of any potential reduction for a guilty plea in accordance with section 144 of the Criminal Justice Act 2003 and the guideline for Reduction in Sentence for a Guilty Plea (where first hearing is on or after 1 June 2017, or first hearing before 1 June 2017).

STEP 5
DANGEROUSNESS

The court should consider whether having regard to the criteria contained in Chapter 15 of Part 12 of the Criminal Justice Act 2003 it would be appropriate to impose a life sentence (section 225) or an extended sentence (section 226A). When sentencing offenders to a life sentence under these provisions the notional determinate sentence should be used as the basis for the setting of a minimum term.

STEP 6
TOTALITY PRINCIPLE

If sentencing an offender for more than one offence, or where the offender is already serving a sentence, consider whether the total sentence is just and proportionate to the overall offending behaviour in accordance with the *Totality* guideline.

STEP 7
COMPENSATION AND ANCILLARY ORDERS

In all cases, the court must consider whether to make a compensation order and/or other ancillary orders.

Compensation order

The court should consider compensation orders in all cases where personal injury, loss or damage has resulted from the offence. The court must give reasons if it decides not to award compensation in such cases.

STEP 8
REASONS

Section 174 of the Criminal Justice Act 2003 imposes a duty to give reasons for, and explain the effect of, the sentence.

STEP 9
CONSIDERATION FOR TIME SPENT ON BAIL (TAGGED CURFEW)

The court must consider whether to give credit for time spent on bail in accordance with section 240A of the Criminal Justice Act 2003.

Sentencing
SC Guideline – Criminal damage – other than by fire – value exceeding £5,000
SC Guideline – Racially or religiously aggravated criminal damage

A[18.33] This is the text of the Sentencing Council's Definitive guideline, taking effect from 1 October 2019.

Criminal damage – other than by fire – value exceeding £5,000
Racially or religiously aggravated criminal damage

Crime and Disorder Act 1998, s 30, Criminal Damage Act 1971, s 1(1)

Effective from: 1 October 2019

Criminal damage (other than by fire) value exceeding £5,000, Criminal Damage Act 1971, s 1(1)

Triable either way

Maximum: 10 years' custody

Offence range: Discharge – 4 years' custody

Note: Where an offence of criminal damage is added to the indictment at the Crown Court the statutory maximum sentence is 10 years' custody regardless of the value of the damage. In such cases where the value does not exceed £5,000 regard should also be had to the not exceeding £5,000 guideline.

Racially or religiously aggravated criminal damage, Crime and Disorder Act 1998, s 30

Triable either way

Maximum: 14 years' custody

Where offence committed in a domestic context, refer to the *Overarching principles: domestic abuse guideline*

STEP 1
DETERMINING THE OFFENCE CATEGORY

The court should determine the offence category with reference only to the factors in the tables below. In order to determine the category the court should assess **culpability** and **harm.**

The level of **culpability** is determined by weighing up all the factors of the case. **Where there are characteristics present which fall under different levels of culpability, the court should balance these characteristics to reach a fair assessment of the offender's culpability.**

Culpability demonstrated by one or more of the following:

A – Higher culpability	• High degree of planning or premeditation • Revenge attack • Intention to cause very serious damage to property • Intention to create a high risk of injury to persons
B – Medium culpability	• Some planning • Recklessness as to whether very serious damage caused to property • Recklessness as to whether serious injury caused to persons • Other cases that fall between categories A and C because: – Factors are present in A and C which balance each other out **and/or** – The offender's culpability falls between the factors described in A and C
C – Lesser culpability	• Little or no planning; offence committed on impulse • Recklessness as to whether some damage to property caused • Offender's responsibility substantially reduced by mental disorder or learning disability • Involved through coercion, intimidation or exploitation

Harm

The level of harm is assessed by weighing up all the factors of the case.

Category 1	• Serious distress caused • Serious consequential economic or social impact of offence • High value of damage
Category 2	• Harm that falls between categories 1 and 3
Category 3	• No or minimal distress caused • Low value damage

STEP 2
STARTING POINT AND CATEGORY RANGE

Having determined the category at step one, the court should use the corresponding starting point to reach a sentence within the category range below. The starting point applies to all offenders irrespective of plea or previous convictions.

Where the offender is dependent on or has a propensity to misuse drugs or alcohol, which **is linked to the offending**, a community order with a drug rehabilitation requirement under section 209, or an alcohol treatment requirement under section 212 of the Criminal Justice Act 2003 may be a proper alternative to a short or moderate custodial sentence.

Where the offender suffers from a medical condition that is susceptible to treatment but does not warrant detention under a hospital order, a community order with a mental health treatment requirement under section 207 of the Criminal Justice Act 2003 may be a proper alternative to a short or moderate custodial sentence.

Maximum: 10 years' custody (basic offence)

Harm	Culpability A	Culpability B	Culpability C
Category 1	**Starting point** 1 year 6 months' custody **Category range** 6 months – 4 years' custody	**Starting point** 6 months' custody **Category range** High level community order – 1 year 6 months' custody	**Starting point** High level community order **Category range** Medium level community order – 9 months' custody
Category 2	**Starting point** 6 months' custody **Category range** High level community order – 1 year 6 months' custody	**Starting point** High level community order **Category range** Medium level community order – 9 months' custody	**Starting point** Low level community order **Category range** Band C fine – High level community order
Category 3	**Starting point** High level community order **Category range** Medium level community order – 9 months' custody	**Starting point** Low level community order **Category range** Band C fine – High level community order	**Starting point** Band B fine **Category range** Discharge – Low level community order

The court should then consider any adjustment for any aggravating or mitigating factors. Below is a **non-exhaustive** list of additional factual elements providing the context of the offence and factors relating to the offender.

Identify whether any combination of these, or other relevant factors, should result in an upward or downward adjustment from the starting point.

FACTORS INCREASING SERIOUSNESS

Statutory aggravating factors:
Previous convictions, having regard to a) the **nature** of the offence to which the conviction relates and its **relevance** to the current offence; and b) the **time** that has elapsed since the conviction
Offence committed whilst on bail
Offence motivated by, or demonstrating hostility based on any of the following characteristics or presumed characteristics of the victim: religion, race, disability, sexual orientation, or transgender identity
Other aggravating factors:
Damaged items of great value to the victim (whether economic, commercial, sentimental or personal value)
Commission of offence whilst under the influence of alcohol or drugs
Victim is particularly vulnerable
Offence committed within a domestic context
Damage caused to heritage and/or cultural assets
Significant impact on emergency services or resources

Established evidence of community/wider impact
Failure to comply with current court orders
Offence committed on licence or post sentence supervision
Offences taken into consideration

FACTORS REDUCING SERIOUSNESS OR REFLECTING PERSONAL MITIGATION

No previous convictions or no relevant/recent convictions
Remorse
Good character and/or exemplary conduct
Serious medical condition requiring urgent, intensive or long-term treatment
Age and/or lack of maturity
Mental disorder or learning disability (where not taken into account at step one)
Sole or primary carer for dependent relatives
Determination and/or demonstration of steps having been taken to address offending behaviour

RACIALLY OR RELIGIOUSLY AGGRAVATED CRIMINAL DAMAGE OFFENCES ONLY

Having determined the category of the basic offence to identify the sentence of a non-aggravated offence, the court should now consider the level of racial or religious aggravation involved and apply an appropriate uplift to the sentence in accordance with the guidance below. The following is a list of factors which the court should consider to determine the level of aggravation. Where there are characteristics present which fall under different levels of aggravation, the court should balance these to reach a fair assessment of the level of aggravation present in the offence.

Maximum sentence for the aggravated offence on indictment is 14 years' custody (maximum for the basic offence is 10 years' custody)

Care should be taken to avoid double counting factors already taken into account in assessing the level of harm at step one

High level of racial or religious aggravation	**Sentence uplift**
Racial or religious aggravation was the predominant motivation for the offence. Offender was a member of, or was associated with, a group promoting hostility based on race or religion. Aggravated nature of the offence caused severe distress to the victim or the victim's family (**over and above the distress already considered at step one**). Aggravated nature of the offence caused serious fear and distress throughout local community or more widely.	Increase the length of custodial sentence if already considered for the basic offence or consider a custodial sentence, if not already considered for the basic offence.

Medium level of racial or religious aggravation	Sentence uplift
Racial or religious aggravation formed a significant proportion of the offence as a whole. Aggravated nature of the offence caused some distress to the victim or the victim's family (**over and above the distress already considered at step one**). Aggravated nature of the offence caused some fear and distress throughout local community or more widely.	Consider a significantly more onerous penalty of the same type **or consider** a more severe type of sentence than for the basic offence.
Low level of racial or religious aggravation	**Sentence uplift**
Aggravated element formed a minimal part of the offence as a whole. Aggravated nature of the offence caused minimal or no distress to the victim or the victim's family (**over and above the distress already considered at step one**).	Consider a more onerous penalty of the same type identified for the basic offence.

Magistrates may find that, although the appropriate sentence for the basic offence would be within their powers, the appropriate increase for the aggravated offence would result in a sentence in excess of their powers. If so, they must commit for sentence to the Crown Court.

The sentencer should state in open court that the offence was aggravated by reason of race or religion, and should also state what the sentence would have been without that element of aggravation.

STEP 3
CONSIDER ANY FACTORS WHICH INDICATE A REDUCTION, SUCH AS ASSISTANCE TO THE PROSECUTION

The court should take into account sections 73 and 74 of the Serious Organised Crime and Police Act 2005 (assistance by defendants: reduction or review of sentence) and any other rule of law by virtue of which an offender may receive a discounted sentence in consequence of assistance given (or offered) to the prosecutor or investigator.

STEP 4
REDUCTION FOR GUILTY PLEAS

The court should take account of any potential reduction for a guilty plea in accordance with section 144 of the Criminal Justice Act 2003 and the guideline for Reduction in Sentence for a Guilty Plea (where first hearing is on or after 1 June 2017, or first hearing before 1 June 2017).

STEP 5
TOTALITY PRINCIPLE

If sentencing an offender for more than one offence, or where the offender is already serving a sentence, consider whether the total sentence is just and proportionate to the overall offending behaviour in accordance with the *Totality* guideline.

STEP 6
COMPENSATION AND ANCILLARY ORDERS

In all cases, the court must consider whether to make a compensation order and/or other ancillary orders.

Compensation order

The court should consider compensation orders in all cases where personal injury, loss or damage has resulted from the offence. The court must give reasons if it decides not to award compensation in such cases.

STEP 7
REASONS

Section 174 of the Criminal Justice Act 2003 imposes a duty to give reasons for, and explain the effect of, the sentence.

STEP 8
CONSIDERATION FOR TIME SPENT ON BAIL (TAGGED CURFEW)

The court must consider whether to give credit for time spent on bail in accordance with section 240A of the Criminal Justice Act 2003.

Sentencing
SC Guideline – Criminal damage – other than by fire – value not exceeding £5,000
SC Guideline – Racially or religiously aggravated criminal damage

A[18.34] This is the text of the Sentencing Council's Definitive guideline, taking effect from 1 October 2019.

Criminal damage – other than by fire – value exceeding £5,000

Racially or religiously aggravated criminal damage

Crime and Disorder Act 1998, s 30, Criminal Damage Act 1971, s 1(1)

Effective from: 1 October 2019

Criminal damage (other than by fire) value not exceeding £5,000, Criminal Damage Act 1971, s 1(1)

Triable only summarily

Maximum: Level 4 fine and/or 3 months' custody

Offence range: Discharge – 3 months' custody

Note: Where an offence of criminal damage is added to the indictment at the Crown Court the statutory maximum sentence is 10 years' custody regardless of the value of the damage. In such cases where the value does not exceed £5,000, the exceeding £5,000 guideline should be used but regard should also be had to this guideline.

Racially or religiously aggravated criminal damage, Crime and Disorder Act 1998, s 30

Triable either way

Maximum: 14 years' custody

Where offence committed in a domestic context, refer to the *Overarching principles: domestic abuse guideline*

STEP 1
DETERMINING THE OFFENCE CATEGORY

The court should determine the offence category with reference only to the factors in the tables below. In order to determine the category the court should assess **culpability and harm.**

The level of **culpability** is determined by weighing up all the factors of the case. **Where there are characteristics present which fall under different levels of culpability, the court should balance these characteristics to reach a fair assessment of the offender's culpability.**

Culpability demonstrated by one or more of the following:

A – Higher culpability	• High degree of planning or premeditation • Revenge attack • Intention to cause very serious damage to property • Intention to create a high risk of injury to persons
B – Medium culpability	• Some planning • Recklessness as to whether very serious damage caused to property • Recklessness as to whether serious injury caused to persons • Other cases that fall between categories A and C because: – Factors are present in A and C which balance each other out and/or – The offender's culpability falls between the factors described in A and C
C – Lesser culpability	• Little or no planning; offence committed on impulse • Recklessness as to whether some damage to property caused • Offender's responsibility substantially reduced by mental disorder or learning disability • Involved through coercion, intimidation or exploitation

Harm

The level of harm is assessed by weighing up all the factors of the case.

Category 1	• Serious distress caused • Serious consequential economic or social impact of offence • High value of damage
Category 2	• All other cases

STEP 2
STARTING POINT AND CATEGORY RANGE

Having determined the category at step one, the court should use the corresponding starting point to reach a sentence within the category range below. The starting point applies to all offenders irrespective of plea or previous convictions.

Where the offender is dependent on or has a propensity to misuse drugs or alcohol, which is **linked to the offending**, a community order with a drug rehabilitation requirement under section 209, or an alcohol treatment requirement under section 212 of the Criminal Justice Act 2003 may be a proper alternative to a short or moderate custodial sentence.

Where the offender suffers from a medical condition that is susceptible to treatment but does not warrant detention under a hospital order, a community order with a mental health treatment requirement under section 207 of the Criminal Justice Act 2003 may be a proper alternative to a short or moderate custodial sentence.

Maximum Level 4 fine and/or 3 months custody (basic offence)

	Culpability		
Harm	**A**	**B**	**C**
Category 1	**Starting point** High level community order **Category range** Medium level community order – 3 months' custody	**Starting point** Low level community order **Category range** Band C fine – High level community order	**Starting point** Band B fine **Category range** Discharge – Low level community order
Category 2	**Starting point** Low level community order **Category range** Band C fine – High level community order	**Starting point** Band B fine **Category range** Discharge – Low level community order	**Starting point** Band A fine **Category range** Discharge – Band B fine

The court should then consider any adjustment for any aggravating or mitigating factors. Below is a **non-exhaustive** list of additional factual elements providing the context of the offence and factors relating to the offender.

Identify whether any combination of these, or other relevant factors, should result in an upward or downward adjustment from the starting point.

FACTORS INCREASING SERIOUSNESS

Statutory aggravating factors:
Previous convictions, having regard to a) the **nature** of the offence to which the conviction relates and its **relevance** to the current offence; and b) the **time** that has elapsed since the conviction
Offence committed whilst on bail
Offence motivated by, or demonstrating hostility based on any of the following characteristics or presumed characteristics of the victim: religion, race, disability, sexual orientation, or transgender identity
Other aggravating factors:
Damaged items of great value to the victim (whether economic, commercial, sentimental or personal value)
Commission of offence whilst under the influence of alcohol or drugs
Victim is particularly vulnerable
Offence committed within a domestic context
Damage caused to heritage and/or cultural assets
Significant impact on emergency services or resources
Established evidence of community/wider impact

Failure to comply with current court orders
Offence committed on licence or post sentence supervision
Offences taken into consideration

FACTORS REDUCING SERIOUSNESS OR REFLECTING PERSONAL MITIGATION

No previous convictions or no relevant/recent convictions
Remorse
Good character and/or exemplary conduct
Serious medical condition requiring urgent, intensive or long-term treatment
Age and/or lack of maturity
Mental disorder or learning disability (where not taken into account at step one)
Sole or primary carer for dependent relatives
Determination and/or demonstration of steps having been taken to address offending behaviour

RACIALLY OR RELIGIOUSLY AGGRAVATED CRIMINAL DAMAGE OFFENCES ONLY

Having determined the category of the basic offence to identify the sentence of a non-aggravated offence, the court should now consider the level of racial or religious aggravation involved and apply an appropriate uplift to the sentence in accordance with the guidance below. The following is a list of factors which the court should consider to determine the level of aggravation. Where there are characteristics present which fall under different levels of aggravation, the court should balance these to reach a fair assessment of the level of aggravation present in the offence.

Maximum sentence for the aggravated offence on indictment is 14 years' custody (maximum for the basic offence is 10 years' custody)

Care should be taken to avoid double counting factors already taken into account in assessing the level of harm at step one

High level of racial or religious aggravation	**Sentence uplift**
Racial or religious aggravation was the predominant motivation for the offence. Offender was a member of, or was associated with, a group promoting hostility based on race or religion. Aggravated nature of the offence caused severe distress to the victim or the victim's family (**over and above the distress already considered at step one**). Aggravated nature of the offence caused serious fear and distress throughout local community or more widely.	Increase the length of custodial sentence if already considered for the basic offence or consider a custodial sentence, if not already considered for the basic offence.
Medium level of racial or religious aggravation	**Sentence uplift**

Racial or religious aggravation formed a significant proportion of the offence as a whole. Aggravated nature of the offence caused some distress to the victim or the victim's family (**over and above the distress already considered at step one**). Aggravated nature of the offence caused some fear and distress throughout local community or more widely.	Consider a significantly more onerous penalty of the same type **or consider** a more severe type of sentence than for the basic offence.
Low level of racial or religious aggravation	**Sentence uplift**
Aggravated element formed a minimal part of the offence as a whole. Aggravated nature of the offence caused minimal or no distress to the victim or the victim's family (**over and above the distress already considered at step one**).	Consider a more onerous penalty of the same type identified for the basic offence.

Magistrates may find that, although the appropriate sentence for the basic offence would be within their powers, the appropriate increase for the aggravated offence would result in a sentence in excess of their powers. If so, they must commit for sentence to the Crown Court.

The sentencer should state in open court that the offence was aggravated by reason of race or religion, and should also state what the sentence would have been without that element of aggravation.

STEP 3
CONSIDER ANY FACTORS WHICH INDICATE A REDUCTION, SUCH AS ASSISTANCE TO THE PROSECUTION

The court should take into account sections 73 and 74 of the Serious Organised Crime and Police Act 2005 (assistance by defendants: reduction or review of sentence) and any other rule of law by virtue of which an offender may receive a discounted sentence in consequence of assistance given (or offered) to the prosecutor or investigator.

STEP 4
REDUCTION FOR GUILTY PLEAS

The court should take account of any potential reduction for a guilty plea in accordance with section 144 of the Criminal Justice Act 2003 and the guideline for Reduction in Sentence for a Guilty Plea (where first hearing is on or after 1 June 2017, or first hearing before 1 June 2017).

STEP 5
TOTALITY PRINCIPLE

If sentencing an offender for more than one offence, or where the offender is already serving a sentence, consider whether the total sentence is just and proportionate to the overall offending behaviour in accordance with the *Totality* guideline.

STEP 6
COMPENSATION AND ANCILLARY ORDERS

In all cases, the court must consider whether to make a compensation order and/or other ancillary orders.

Compensation order

The court should consider compensation orders in all cases where personal injury, loss or damage has resulted from the offence. The court must give reasons if it decides not to award compensation in such cases.

STEP 7
REASONS

Section 174 of the Criminal Justice Act 2003 imposes a duty to give reasons for, and explain the effect of, the sentence.

STEP 8
CONSIDERATION FOR TIME SPENT ON BAIL (TAGGED CURFEW)

The court must consider whether to give credit for time spent on bail in accordance with section 240A of the Criminal Justice Act 2003.

A[18A]

Threatening to destroy or damage property

(Criminal Damage Act 1971, s 2(a))

Charge (Threatening to destroy or damage property)

A[18A.1] Without lawful excuse made to [. . . . .] a threat to destroy (or damage) property belonging to that other person (or belonging to a third person), intending that the other person would fear it would be carried out

Maximum penalty – Fine level 5 and 6 months. Triable either way.

The legal notes and definitions relating to the previous offence at A[18] also apply here, except for the reference to compensation and mode of trial. The threats can be spoken or in writing.

Crown Court – 10 years' imprisonment and unlimited fine.

A[18A.2] The gist of the offence under both parts of s 2 is the threat; the nature of the threat has to be considered objectively so that it does not matter what the person threatened thought was embraced within the threat or whether he feared the threat would be carried out, though the prosecution must prove that the defendant intended that the person threatened would fear that the threat would be carried out: *R v Cakmak* [2002] EWCA Crim 500, [2002] 2 Cr App Rep 158, [2002] Crim LR 581.

A[18B]

Possessing anything with intent to destroy or damage property

(Criminal Damage Act 1971, s 3(a))

Charge (Intent to destroy or damage property)

A[18B.1] **Had in his custody (or under his control) a [...............] intending without lawful excuse to use it to destroy (or damage) property belonging to another person**

Maximum penalty – 6 months' imprisonment and/or fine level 5 (for offences committed on or after 12 March 2015 an unlimited fine). Triable either way.

The legal notes and definitions relating to offence no 1 at **A[18]** also apply here except for mode of trial.

Crown Court – 10 years' imprisonment and unlimited fine.

A[19]

Cruelty to a child

Charge (Cruelty to a child)

A[19.1] **Having responsibility for a child or young person under the age of 16 and wilfully assaulting, ill-treating, neglecting, abandoning, or exposing him in a manner likely to cause him unnecessary suffering or injury to health**

Children and Young Persons Act 1933, s 1, as amended

Maximum penalty – 6 months' imprisonment and/or fine level 5 (for offences committed on or after 12 March 2015 an unlimited fine). Triable either way. Specified violent offence under Sch 15, Part 1, CJA 2003.

Crown Court – 10 years' imprisonment and unlimited fine.

Mode of trial

A[19.2] Consider the SC Guideline at A[19.32] below.

A[19.3] All or any of the types of cruelty listed in the charge above can be included in a single information but on conviction one penalty must cover the lot.

A[19.4] The offence of cruelty can only be committed by a person over the age of 16.

A[19.5] **Reasonable punishment.** In relation to this offence, battery cannot be justified on the ground that it constituted reasonable punishment: Children Act 2004, s 58.

A[19.6] **A child.** Means someone under 14 years of age. As a result of amendments made to s 1 by the Serious Crime Act 2015, s 66, the ill treatment may be physical or otherwise; thus the harm may be psychological.

A[19.7] **A young person.** Means for this offence someone aged 14 or 15 years.

A[19.8] **Wilfully.** Offences under s 1(1) are not offences of strict liability, thus the prosecution need to prove a deliberate or reckless act or failure: a genuine lack of appreciation through stupidity, ignorance or personal inadequacy will be a good defence. The offence is not to be judged by the objective test of what a reasonable parent would have done: *R v Sheppard* [1981] AC 394, [1980] 3 All ER 899, 72 Cr App Rep 82. That the parents acted in the deluded belief that the children were possessed by spirits is not mitigation and does not reduce the culpability of the offences: *R v P* (2007) Times 17 March, CA.

A[19.9]–[19.15] **Assaulting.** See under the charge of 'Common assault', at A[15].

A[19.16] **Ill-treating.** Actual assault or battery need not be proved. Bullying or frightening or any course of conduct calculated to cause unnecessary suffering or injury to health will suffice.

A[19.17] **Neglecting.** Means omitting to take such steps as a reasonable parent would take and can include failing to apply for state benefits. Failure to obtain medical care can amount to neglect. It is a question of fact which the magistrates have to determine in each case.

A[19.18] **Abandoning.** Means leaving the child to his fate. In one case a child was carefully packed in a hamper and sent by train to the father's address and although the child came to no harm it was held that the child had been abandoned: *R v Boulden* (1957) 41 Cr App Rep 105.

A[19.19] In another case a child had been left on his doorstep and the father knew he was there and permitted the child to remain there during an October night for six hours. It was held that he had abandoned the child: *R v White* (1871) LR 1 CCR 311, 36 JP 134.

A[19.20] Leaving children at a youth court has been held not to be an offence under this section: *R v Whibley* [1938] 3 All ER 777, 102 JP 326.

A[19.21] **Exposing.** It is not necessary to prove that the defendant intended to cause suffering or injury to health. The requisite is that the defendant exposed the child or young person in a manner which was likely to cause unnecessary suffering or injury to health.

A[19.22] **In a manner likely to cause him unnecessary suffering or injury to health.** This part of the offence must be proved in addition to wilfully assaulting, ill-treating, neglecting, abandoning or exposing as set out in the charge. As a result of amendments made to s 1 by the Serious Crime Act 2015, s 66, the suffering or injury may be of a physical or psychological nature.

A[19.23] **Presumption of guilt.** A parent or other person legally liable to maintain a child or young person, or the legal guardian of a child or young person will be presumed to have neglected the child or young person in a manner likely to cause injury to health if he has failed to provide adequate food, clothing, medical aid or lodging. If the parent has been unable to provide any of these things he will still be presumed to have neglected him if he fails to apply for them under state benefits. (However the prosecution must still establish that this neglect was 'wilful'.)

Where it is proved that the death of an infant under three years of age was caused by suffocation (not being suffocation caused by disease or the presence of any foreign body in the throat or air passages of the infant) while the infant was in bed with some other person who has attained the age of 16 years, that other person shall, if he was, when he went to bed (or at any later time before the suffocation], under the influence of drink [or a prohibited drug), be deemed to have neglected the infant in a manner likely to cause injury to its health. Being 'in bed' with another includes a reference to the infant lying next to the adult in or on any kind of furniture or surface being used by the adult for the purpose of sleeping.

A[19.24]–[19.30] **Dealing with the children.** As the defendant is almost always over the age of 18, this offence is usually tried in the adult court.

A[19.31] The court may direct that nothing may be published or broadcast which would identify any child concerned.

Sentencing

SC Guideline – Cruelty to children

A[19.32] This guideline is taken from the Sentencing Council's definitive guideline *Child Cruelty* published on 6 September 2018, effective from 1 January 2019.

***The court *must* inform the defendant that the Independent Safeguarding Authority (now the Disclosure and Barring Service constituted under the Protection of Freedoms Act 2012) will automatically ban him/her from working with children and/or vulnerable adults. As the court has no role in the decision if the defendant needs any further advice he/she should consult a solicitor.**

Cruelty to a child – assault and ill treatment, abandonment, neglect, and failure to protect

Children and Young Persons Act 1933 (section 1(1))

Triable either way

Maximum: 10 years' custody

Offence range: Community order – 8 years' custody

This is a specified offence for the purposes of section 226A (extended sentence for certain violent or sexual offences) of the Criminal Justice Act 2003.

STEP ONE
DETERMINING THE OFFENCE CATEGORY

The court should determine the offence category with reference **only** to the factors listed in the tables below. In order to determine the category, the court should assess **culpability** and **harm.**

The court should weigh all the factors set out below in determining the offender's culpability.

Where there are characteristics present which fall under different levels of culpability, the court should balance these characteristics to reach a fair assessment of the offender's culpability.

Culpability demonstrated by one or more of the following:

A	**High culpability:** • Prolonged and/or multiple incidents of serious cruelty, including serious neglect • Gratuitous degradation of victim and/or sadistic behaviour • Use of very significant force • Use of a weapon • Deliberate disregard for the welfare of the victim • Failure to take any steps to protect the victim from offences in which the above factors are present • Offender with professional responsibility for the victim (where linked to the commission of the offence)
B	**Medium culpability:** • Use of significant force • Prolonged and/or multiple incidents of cruelty, including neglect • Limited steps taken to protect victim in cases with category A factors present • Other cases falling between A and C because: – Factors in both high and lesser categories are present which balance each other out; and/or – The offender's culpability falls between the factors as described in high and lesser culpability
C	**Lesser culpability:** • Offender's responsibility substantially reduced by mental disorder or learning disability or lack of maturity • Offender is victim of domestic abuse, including coercion and/or intimidation (where linked to the commission of the offence) • Steps taken to protect victim but fell just short of what could reasonably be expected • Momentary or brief lapse in judgement including in cases of neglect • Use of some force or failure to protect the victim from an incident involving some force • Low level of neglect

Harm

The court should consider the factors set out below to determine the level of harm that has been caused or was intended to be caused to the victim.

Psychological, developmental or emotional harm

A finding that the psychological, developmental or emotional harm is **serious** may be based on a clinical diagnosis but the court may make such a finding based on other evidence from or on behalf of the victim that serious psychological, developmental or emotional harm exists. It is important to be clear that the absence of such a finding does **not** imply that the psychological, developmental or emotional harm suffered by the victim is minor or trivial.

Category 1	• Serious psychological, developmental, and/or emotional harm • Serious physical harm (including illnesses contracted due to neglect)
Category 2	• Cases falling between categories 1 and 3 • A high likelihood of category 1 harm being caused
Category 3	• Little or no psychological, developmental, and/or emotional harm • Little or no physical harm

STEP TWO
STARTING POINT AND CATEGORY RANGE

Having determined the category at step one, the court should use the corresponding starting point to reach a sentence within the category range below. The starting point applies to all offenders irrespective of plea or previous convictions.

Where a case does not fall squarely within a category, adjustment from the starting point may be required before adjustment for aggravating or mitigating features.

	Culpability		
Harm	A	B	C
Category 1	**Starting point** 6 years' custody **Category range** 4–8 years' custody	**Starting point** 3 years' custody **Category range** 2–6 years' custody	**Starting point** 1 year's custody **Category range** High level community order – 2 years 6 months' custody
Category 2	**Starting point** 3 years' custody **Category range** 2–6 years' custody	**Starting point** 1 year's custody **Category range** High level community order – 2 years 6 months' custody	**Starting point** High level community order **Category range** Medium level community order – 1 year's custody
Category 3	**Starting point** 1 year's custody **Category range** High level community order – 2 years 6 months' custody	**Starting point** High level community order **Category range** Medium level community order – 1 year's custody	**Starting point** Medium level community order **Category range** Low level community order – 6 months' custody

The table below contains a **non-exhaustive** list of additional factual elements providing the context of the offence and factors relating to the offender. Identify whether any combination of these, or other relevant factors, should result in an upward or downward adjustment from the sentence arrived at so far. In particular, relevant recent convictions are likely to result in an upward adjustment. In some cases, having considered these factors, it may be appropriate to move outside the identified category range.

FACTORS INCREASING SERIOUSNESS

Statutory aggravating factors:
Previous convictions, having regard to a) the **nature** of the offence to which the conviction relates and its **relevance** to the current offence; and b) the **time** that has elapsed since the conviction
Offence committed whilst on bail
Other aggravating factors:
Failure to seek medical help (where not taken into account at step one)
Commission of offence whilst under the influence of alcohol or drugs
Deliberate concealment and/or covering up of the offence
Blame wrongly placed on others
Failure to respond to interventions or warnings about behaviour
Threats to prevent reporting of the offence
Failure to comply with current court orders
Offence committed on licence or post sentence supervision
Offences taken into consideration
Offence committed in the presence of another child

FACTORS REDUCING SERIOUSNESS OR REFLECTING PERSONAL MITIGATION

No previous convictions or no relevant/recent convictions
Remorse
Determination and demonstration of steps having been taken to address addiction or offending behaviour, including co-operation with agencies working for the welfare of the victim
Sole or primary carer for dependent relatives (**see step five for further guidance on parental responsibilities**)
Good character and/or exemplary conduct (where previous good character/exemplary conduct has been used to facilitate or conceal the offence, this should not normally constitute mitigation and such conduct may constitute aggravation)
Serious medical condition requiring urgent, intensive or long-term treatment
Mental disorder, learning disability or lack of maturity (where not taken into account at step one)
Co-operation with the investigation

STEP THREE
CONSIDER ANY FACTORS WHICH INDICATE A REDUCTION FOR ASSISTANCE TO THE PROSECUTION

The court should take into account sections 73 and 74 of the Serious Organised Crime and Police Act 2005 (assistance by defendants: reduction or review of sentence) and any other rule of law by virtue of which an offender may receive a discounted sentence in consequence of assistance given (or offered) to the prosecutor or investigator.

STEP FOUR
REDUCTION FOR GUILTY PLEAS

The court should take account of any potential reduction for a guilty plea in accordance with section 144 of the Criminal Justice Act 2003 and the Guilty Plea guideline.

STEP FIVE
PARENTAL RESPONSIBILITIES OF SOLE OR PRIMARY CARERS

In the majority of child cruelty cases the offender will have parental responsibility for the victim.

When considering whether to impose custody the court should step back and review whether this sentence will be in the best interests of the victim (as well as other children in the offender's care). This must be balanced with the seriousness of the offence and all sentencing options remain open to the court but careful consideration should be given to the effect that a custodial sentence could have on the family life of the victim and whether this is proportionate to the seriousness of the offence. This may be of particular relevance in lower culpability cases or where the offender has otherwise been a loving and capable parent/carer.

Where custody is unavoidable consideration of the impact on the offender's children may be relevant to the length of the sentence imposed. For more serious offences where a substantial period of custody is appropriate, this consideration will carry less weight.

STEP SIX
DANGEROUSNESS

The court should consider whether having regard to the criteria contained in Chapter 5 of Part 12 of the Criminal Justice Act 2003 it would be appropriate to impose an extended sentence (section 226A).

STEP SEVEN
TOTALITY PRINCIPLE

If sentencing an offender for more than one offence, or where the offender is already serving a sentence, consider whether the total sentence is just and proportionate to the overall offending behaviour in accordance with the *Offences Taken into Consideration and Totality* guideline.

STEP EIGHT
ANCILLARY ORDERS

In all cases the court should consider whether to make ancillary orders.

STEP NINE
REASONS

Section 174 of the Criminal Justice Act 2003 imposes a duty to give reasons for, and explain the effect of, the sentence.

STEP TEN
CONSIDERATION FOR TIME SPENT ON BAIL (TAGGED CURFEW)

The court must consider whether to give credit for time spent on bail in accordance with section 240A of the Criminal Justice Act 2003.

A[19.33] Available sentences. See Table A at B[43.1A].

If two or more children are concerned in the same occasion then all of them can be included in one charge and if this is done then only one penalty can be imposed for the one collective charge and not a penalty for each child (s 14). If the prosecution has brought a separate charge for each child, then a separate penalty can be ordered for each charge.

A[19.34] As mentioned above, if in the case of an individual child one information is laid alleging assault, ill-treatment, neglect, etc, only one penalty may be imposed.

A[19A]

Disclosing private sexual photographs and films with intent to cause distress

Charge

A[19A.1] Disclosing a private sexual photograph or film without the consent of the individual who appears in the photograph or film and with the intent of causing that individual distress.

Criminal Justice and Courts Act 2015, s 33.

Maximum penalty – 6 months' imprisonment and/or an unlimited fine

Crown Court – 2 years' imprisonment and/or an unlimited fine

Legal notes and definitions

A[19A.2] The disclosure must be to a party other than the individual shown in the photograph or film: CJCA 2015, s 33(2). A person is not to be taken to have disclosed a photograph or film with the intention of causing distress merely because that was a natural and probable consequence of the disclosure: CJCA 2015, s 33(8).

A person 'discloses' something to a person if, by any means, he or she gives or shows or makes it available to that person: CJCA 2015, s 34(2). The disclosure need not be for reward and need not be the first disclosure of the photograph or film to that person: CJCA 2015, s 34(3).

'Consent' to a disclosure may be of a general kind covering the disclosure or to the particular disclosure: CJCA 2015, s 33(7)(a).

'Photograph or film' means a still or moving image in any form which appears to and in fact consists of one or more photographed or filmed images: CJCA 2015, s 34(4). This includes altered images: CJCA 2015, s 34(5) (though see below).

'Photograph or film' includes negatives, and data stored by any means which is capable of conversion into an image: CJCA 2015, s 34(8).

'Photographed or filmed image' means a, or a part of a, still or moving image which was originally captured by photography or filming: CJCA 2015, s 34(6).

'Filming' means making a recording on any medium from which a moving image may be produced by any means: CJCA 2015, s 34(7).

'Private' means something that is not of a kind ordinarily seen in public: CJCA 2015, s 35(2).

A photograph or film is 'sexual' if it shows all/part of a person's exposed genitalia/pubic area, or shows something which a reasonable person would consider to be sexual because of its nature, or its content taken as a whole is such that a reasonable person would consider it to be sexual: CJCA 2015, s 35(3).

A photograph or film is not 'private and sexual' if it was not or did not include originally a photographed or filmed image which was itself private and sexual and it was only by virtue of being altered or being combined with one or more photographed or filmed images or with something else that it became a photograph or film which was private and sexual: CJCA 2015, s 35(5).

Defences

A[19A.3] (a) It is a defence for the defendant to prove that he/she reasonably believed that the disclosure was necessary for the purposes of preventing, detecting or investigating crime: CJCA 2015, s 33(3).

(b) It is a defence for the defendant to show that the disclosure was made in the course of, or with a view to, the publication of journalistic material and he/she reasonably believed that, in the particular circumstances, publication of the journalistic material was, or would be, in the public interest: CJCA 2015, s 33(4). 'Publication' means to the public at large or to a section of it: CJCA 2015, s 33(7)(b).

(c) It is a defence for the defendant to show that he/she reasonably believed that the photograph or film had previously been disclosed for reward, whether by the person shown in the photograph or film or by somebody else, and he/she had no reason to believe that the previous disclosure for reward was made without the consent of the person shown in the photograph or film: CJCA 2015, s 33(5).

In relation to defence (a), the standard of proof is on the balance of probabilities: *R v Carr-Briant* [1943] KB 607, [1943] 2 All ER 156. In relation to defences (b) and (c), a defendant is taken to have shown the matters mentioned if he/she adduces sufficient evidence to raise an issue with respect to it and the contrary is not proved beyond reasonable doubt: CJCA 2015, s 33(6).

Sentencing

SC Guideline – Disclosing private sexual images

A[19A.4] This text is taken from the Sentencing Council's Intimidatory offences: Definitive guideline, published on 5 July 2018, taking effect from 1 October 2018.

Disclosing private sexual images

Criminal Justice and Courts Act 2015, s 33

Effective from: 1 October 2018

Triable either way

Maximum: 2 years' custody

Offence range: Discharge – 1 year 6 months' custody

Where offence committed in a domestic context, also refer to the *Overarching principles: Domestic abuse guideline*

STEP 1
DETERMINING THE OFFENCE CATEGORY

The court should determine the offence category with reference only to the factors in the tables below. In order to determine the category the court should assess **culpability** and **harm.**

The level of **culpability** is determined by weighing up all the factors of the case. **Where there are characteristics present which fall under different levels of culpability, the court should balance these characteristics to reach a fair assessment of the offender's culpability.**

Culpability demonstrated by one or more of the following:

A – Higher culpability	• Conduct intended to maximise distress and/or humiliation • Images circulated widely/publically • Significant planning and/or sophisticated offence • Repeated efforts to keep images available for viewing
B – Medium culpability	• Some planning • Scope and duration of offence that falls between categories A and C • All other cases that fall between categories A and C

C – Lesser culpability	• Offender's responsibility substantially reduced by mental disorder or learning disability • Little or no planning • Conduct intended to cause limited distress and/or humiliation • Offence was limited in scope and duration

Harm

The level of harm is assessed by weighing up all the factors of the case.

Category 1	• Very serious distress caused to the victim • Significant psychological harm caused to the victim • Offence has a considerable practical impact on the victim
Category 2	• Harm that falls between categories 1 and 3, and in particular: • Some distress caused to the victim • Some psychological harm caused to the victim • Offence has some practical impact on the victim
Category 3	• Limited distress or harm caused to the victim

STEP 2
STARTING POINT AND CATEGORY RANGE

Having determined the category at step one, the court should use the corresponding starting point to reach a sentence within the category range in the table below. The starting point applies to all offenders irrespective of plea or previous convictions.

	Culpability		
Harm	**A**	**B**	**C**
Category 1	**Starting point** 1 year's custody **Category range** 26 weeks' custody – 1 year 6 months' custody	**Starting point** 26 weeks' custody **Category range** 12 weeks' – 1 year's custody	**Starting point** 12 weeks' custody **Category range** High level community order – 26 weeks' custody
Category 2	**Starting point** 26 weeks' custody **Category range** 12 weeks – 1 year's custody	**Starting point** 12 weeks' custody **Category range** High level community order – 26 weeks' custody	**Starting point** High level community order **Category range** Low level community order – 12 weeks' custody
Category 3	**Starting point** 12 weeks' custody **Category range** High level community order – 26 weeks' custody	**Starting point** High level community order **Category range** Low level community order – 12 weeks' custody	**Starting point** Low level community order **Category range** Discharge – High level community order

The court should then consider any adjustment for any aggravating or mitigating factors. Below is a **non-exhaustive** list of additional factual elements providing the context of the offence and factors relating to the offender.

Identify whether any combination of these, or other relevant factors, should result in an upward or downward adjustment from the starting point.

FACTORS INCREASING SERIOUSNESS

Statutory aggravating factors:
Previous convictions, having regard to a) the **nature** of the offence to which the conviction relates and its **relevance** to the current offence; and b) the **time** that has elapsed since the conviction
Offence committed whilst on bail
Offence motivated by, or demonstrating hostility based on any of the following characteristics or presumed characteristics of the victim: religion, race, disability, sexual orientation, or transgender identity
Other aggravating factors:
Impact of offence on others, particularly children
Victim is particularly vulnerable (not all vulnerabilities are immediately apparent)
Failure to comply with current court orders
Offence committed on licence or post sentence supervision
Offences taken into consideration

FACTORS REDUCING SERIOUSNESS OR REFLECTING PERSONAL MITIGATION

No previous convictions or no relevant/recent convictions
Offender took steps to limit circulation of images
Remorse
Good character and/or exemplary conduct
Serious medical condition requiring urgent, intensive or long-term treatment
Age and/or lack of maturity
Mental disorder or learning disability (where not taken into account at step one)
Sole or primary carer for dependent relatives
Determination and/or demonstration of steps having been taken to address offending behaviour

STEP 3
CONSIDER ANY FACTORS WHICH INDICATE A REDUCTION, SUCH AS ASSISTANCE TO THE PROSECUTION

The court should take into account sections 73 and 74 of the Serious Organised Crime and Police Act 2005 (assistance by defendants: reduction or review of sentence) and any other rule of law by virtue of which an offender may receive a discounted sentence in consequence of assistance given (or offered) to the prosecutor or investigator.

STEP 4
REDUCTION FOR GUILTY PLEAS

The court should take account of any potential reduction for a guilty plea in accordance with section 144 of the Criminal Justice Act 2003 and the *Guilty Plea* guideline.

STEP 5
TOTALITY PRINCIPLE

If sentencing an offender for more than one offence, or where the offender is already serving a sentence, consider whether the total sentence is just and proportionate to the overall offending behaviour in accordance with the *Offences Taken into Consideration and Totality* guideline.

STEP 6
COMPENSATION AND ANCILLARY ORDERS

In all cases, the court must consider whether to make a compensation order and/or other ancillary orders.

Compensation order

The court should consider compensation orders in all cases where personal injury, loss or damage has resulted from the offence. The court must give reasons if it decides not to award compensation in such cases.

Other ancillary orders available include:
Restraining order

Where an offender is convicted of any offence, the court may make a restraining order (section 5 of the Protection from Harassment Act 1997).

The order may prohibit the offender from doing anything for the purpose of protecting the victim of the offence, or any other person mentioned in the order, from further conduct which amounts to harassment or will cause a fear of violence.

The order may have effect for a specified period or until further order.

STEP 7
REASONS

Section 174 of the Criminal Justice Act 2003 imposes a duty to give reasons for, and explain the effect of, the sentence.

STEP 8
CONSIDERATION FOR TIME SPENT ON BAIL

The court must consider whether to give credit for time spent on bail in accordance with section 240A of the Criminal Justice Act 2003.

A[20]

Disorderly behaviour (harassment, alarm or distress) Racially/religiously aggravated disorderly behaviour (harassment, alarm or distress)

Charges (Disorderly behaviour)

A[20.1] **Using threatening or abusive words or behaviour or disorderly behaviour (or displaying any writing, sign or other visible representation which is threatening or abusive) within the hearing or sight of a person likely to be caused harassment, alarm or distress thereby**

Public Order Act 1986, s 5

Maximum penalty – Fine level 3. Triable only by magistrates.

NB: A fixed penalty of £80 is available for a s 5 offence of disorderly behaviour

A[20.2] Racially or religiously aggravated threats, threatening or abusive or disorderly behaviour.

Crime and Disorder Act 1998, s 31

Maximum penalty – Fine level 4. Triable only by magistrates.

Legal notes and definitions

A[20.3] This offence is designed to deal with such cases as groups of youths persistently shouting abuse and obscenities, rowdy behaviour in the street late at night, hooligans causing disturbances in the common parts of flats, banging on doors, knocking over dustbins and throwing items downstairs.

A[20.3A] **Harassment; alarm; distress.** Distress by its very nature involved an element of emotional disturbance or upset. The same could not be said of harassment. A person could be seriously harassed without any emotional disturbance or upset (*Southard v DPP* [2006] All ER (D) 101 (Nov), distinguishing on the facts *R v DPP* [2006] All ER (D) 250 (May)).

Taking a photograph of the complainant; transferring the photograph onto a computer followed by a posting of the same on the internet with the words 'C'mon I'd love to eat you! We're the Covance Cannibals' held to amount to *intentional harassment* etc where the complainant was shown a hard copy some five months later (*S v DPP* judgment delivered February 8, 2008).

A[20.3B] **Dwelling.** The offence can be committed in public or in private place, but no offence is committed where the words, etc, are used by a person inside a dwelling and the other person is inside that or another dwelling. 'Dwelling' is defined by s 8. This refers to 'structure' and 'occupation as a person's home or other living accommodation'. It was accordingly held in *DPP v Distill* [2017] EWHC 2244 (Admin), [2017] ALL ER (D) 31 (Sep) that an offence under s 5 can be committed where, at the relevant time, both parties were within their adjoining private gardens. A different conclusion might be appropriate, in respect of gardens which formed an integral part of a structure, but this will not be the case with typical gardens of typical homes.

A[20.4] **The charge.** Only one offence is created. However, the racially/religiously aggravated offence can be heard at the same time as alternative offences (*R (CPS) v Blaydon Youth Court* (2004)).

A[20.5] Threatening; abusive; ECHR. See A[21] and A[21.5].

In *Abdul v DPP* [2011] EWHC 247, (2011) 175 JP 190, [2011] Crim L R 553 the relevant principles between s 5 of the Public Order Act 1986 and art 10 of the ECHR came under consideration. It was held:

(i) 'The starting point is the importance of the right to freedom of expression.

(ii) Illegitimate protest can be offensive at least to some – and on occasions must be, if it is to have impact. Moreover, the right to freedom of expression would be unacceptably devalued if it did no more than protect those holding popular, mainstream views; it must plainly extend beyond that so that minority views can be freely expressed, even if distasteful.

(iii) Interference with the right to freedom of expression must be convincingly established. Art 10 does not confer an unqualified right to freedom of expression, but the restrictions contained in Art 10.2 are to be narrowly construed.

(iv) There is not and cannot be any universal test for resolving when speech goes beyond legitimate protest, so attracting the sanction of the criminal law. The justification for invoking the criminal law is the threat to public order. Inevitably, the context of the particular occasion will be of the first importance.

(v) The relevance of the threat to public order should not be taken as meaning that the risk of violence by those reacting to the protest is, without more, determinative; sometimes it may be that protesters are to be protected. That said in striking the right balance when determining whether speech is 'threatening, abusive or insulting', the focus on minority rights should not result in overlooking the rights of the majority.

(vi) Plainly, if there is no prima facie case that speech was 'threatening, abusive or insulting' or that the other elements of the s 5 offence can be made good, then no question of prosecution will arise. However, even if there is otherwise a prima facie case for contending that an offence has been committed under s 5, it is still for the Crown to establish that prosecution is a proportionate response, necessary for the preservation of public order.

(vii) If the line between legitimate freedom of expression and a threat to public order has indeed been crossed, freedom of speech will not have been impaired by 'ruling out' threatening, abusive or insulting speech: per Lord Reid, in *Brutus v Cozens* [1973] AC 854, [1972] 2 All ER 1297, [1972] 3 WLR 521,HL, at p 862.

(viii) [The High Court] should not interfere [with decisions of the magistrates] unless, on well-known grounds, the appellants can establish that the decision to which the district judge has come is one she could not properly have reached.'

(at para [49] per Gross LJ)

It is for the CPS to decide whether or not prosecution is a proportionate approach and it is not for a magistrates' court to review such a decision under the guise, for example, of abuse of process: *James v DPP* [2015] EWHC 3296 (Admin), (2016) 180 JP 1.

See further, A[20.17], below.

A[20.5A] Disorderly. A court is entitled to conclude that walking naked through a town centre violates public order and is thus 'disorderly': *Gough v DPP* [2013] EWHC 3267 (Admin), (2013) 177 JP 669.

A[20.6]–[20.7] Racially/religiously aggravated. Section 28(1) provides: 'An offence is racially or religiously aggravated . . . if

(a) at the time of committing the offence, or immediately before or after doing so, the offender demonstrates towards the victim of the offence hostility based on the victim's membership (or presumed membership) of a racial or religious group; or

(b) the offence is motivated (wholly or partly) by hostility towards members of a racial or religious group based on their membership of that group.'

It is immaterial for the purposes of (a) or (b) whether or not the offender's hostility is also based, to any extent, on any other factor: CDA 1998, s 28(3).

Section 28(1)(a) involves no examination of motivation or subjective intent; it merely requires the demonstration of racial hostility: *Jones v DPP* [2010] EWHC 523 (Admin), [2010] 3 All ER 1057, (2010) 174 JP 278. See also *R v H(S)* [2010] EWCA Crim 1931, [2011] 1 Cr App R 14.

Cases may arise where it is legitimate to require the prosecution to make clear whether it is proceeding under subpara (a), or (b), or both: *G v DPP and T v DPP* [2004] EWHC 183 (Admin), (2004) 168 JP 313.

The key difference between (a) and (b) is the latter's concern with the defendant's motivation; the use of racially offensive language may provide evidence of the offence, but if it was not the motivation for the offence there can be no conviction pursuant to (b): *R (on the application of the DPP) v Dykes* [2008] EWHC 2775 (Admin), 173 JP 88. See also *Jones v Director of Public Prosecutions* [2010] EWHC 523 (Admin), 174 JP 278. See further *Taylor v Director of Public Prosecutions* [2006] EWHC 1202 (Admin), 170 JP 485 where the defendant used racially abusive language, but there was no evidence that any of those who heard or were in a position to hear the language were persons to whom the defendant demonstrated racial hostility or were from the racial group referred to by the defendant's words. Section 28(1)(a) could not, therefore, apply. However, 'the use of phrases such as "fucking nigger" and "fucking coon bitch", patently not used in a jesting fashion, must, in the circumstances of this case, have led any judge to find that the s 5 offence was motivated, at least in part, by racial hostility as described in s 28(1)(b)' (per Keene LJ at para 20).

The statute intends a broad, non-technical approach rather than a construction which invites nice distinctions. So that it does not matter, for example, whether the use of the word 'Paki' demonstrated hostility to all who came from the Indian Sub-continent or simply those who came from Pakistan. It is also the same whether the group is defined exclusively by reference to what its members are not, eg some description implying they are not British such as 'bloody foreigners' or inclusively by reference to what they are eg 'bloody Spaniards'. However, to demonstrate hostility no particular words need be used. The necessary hostility can be demonstrated in ways such as the wearing of a swastika or the singing of certain songs, although it will normally be proved by some well known terms of abuse. Accordingly, those who were not of a British origin do constitute a 'racial group' as do 'foreigners'. Whether the evidence proves that the offender's conduct demonstrated hostility to such a group, or was motivated by such hostility is a question of fact for the court: *R v Rogers* [2007] UKHL 8, [2007] 2 AC 62, [2007] 2 All ER 433, 2007] 2 WLR 280, [2007] 2 Cr App R). In an earlier authority, the word 'immigrant doctor' itself was held to be specific enough to denote membership of a 'racial group' within the meaning in sub-s (4) of the 1998 Act where the court was satisfied that in the factual context the defendant's hostility was based on his perception of the victim's non-Britishness derived from his race and/or his colour and/or his nationality and/or his ethnic or national origins: *A-G's Reference (No 4 of 2004)* [2005] EWCA Crim 889, [2005] 1 WLR 2810.

The hostility must be towards the victim as a member of a racial group. Where the hostility is towards the victim's conduct such as associating with members of another racial group, then, depending on the facts, the conduct may not amount to being 'racially aggravated': see *DPP v Pal* [2000] Crim LR 756, DC. Whilst it may be unusual, and may be more difficult to establish that the hostility is of racial, ethnic or national origin, a person may show hostility to his own kind, whether racial, ethnic or national: *R v White* [2001] EWCA Crim 216, [2001] 1 WLR 1352, [2001] Crim LR 576.

A[20.8] **Another person.** The defendant's behaviour must be within the hearing or sight of a person likely to be caused harassment etc. The prosecution must identify the person who was likely to have been alarmed etc though he need not be called as a witness. In *Chambers and Edwards v DPP* [1995] Crim LR 896 demonstrators made it difficult for a surveyor to carry out his work. Although the surveyor was in no fear for his safety, his annoyance and inconvenience were sufficient to meet the requirements of the section. For further developments see *R (on the application of Reda) v DPP* [2011] EWHC 1550 (Admin) at **A[9.5]**. In *Harvey v DPP* [2011] EWHC 3992 (Admin), 176 JP 265, [2012] Crim LR 553, commonplace swear words used by the appellant were capable of causing police officers to experience harassment, alarm or distress. Much would depend on the facts, but where a witness was silent on the point, it would be wrong to draw inferences. Accordingly, there was no evidence whereby the justices could have concluded that either police officer had been caused or was likely to have been caused harassment, alarm or distress. As for a group of young people who gathered during the exchanges, the words uttered were commonplace swear words in contrast to the far more offensive terms used in the case of *Taylor v DPP* [2006] EWHC 1202 (Admin), 170 JP 485, 170 JPN 856. It was wrong to infer, in the absence of evidence of evidence from any of them, that one or more persons would have experienced harassment, alarm or distress. As for neighbours and people in the adjoining flats, there was no evidence that anybody other than the group of young people was within earshot. If there had been evidence, for example, of apparently frightened neighbours leaning out of windows or of similar passers-by within earshot, that might have formed the basis of a finding that such persons were caused alarm or distress.

A[20.9] *Vigon v DPP* (1997) 162 JP 115, [1998] Crim LR 289 – A concealed camera in a changing cubicle is capable of being disorderly [and insulting] behaviour.

A[20.10] **Intent.** The accused must intend his words or behaviour etc to be, or be aware that his words etc may be threatening, abusive, or intend his behaviour to be or is aware that it may be disorderly.

A[20.11]–[20.15] **Visible Representation.** *Norwood v DPP* [2003] EWHC 1564 (Admin), [2003] Crim LR 888 set out the four elements that need to be proved in such a case, namely: (1) a fact – display by a defendant of a visible representation; (2) a value judgment that the representation is threatening, abusive or insulting; (3) a fact – that the defendant either intended, or was aware that it might be, threatening, abusive or insulting; and (4) a mixed fact and value judgment – that the display was within sight of a person likely to be caused, harassment, alarm or distress by it.

A[20.16] **Intoxication.** See under the offence of violent disorder, at A[67]. Disorderly conduct may be committed in a public or private place. For offences committed in dwelling-houses see under the offence of threatening behaviour below, at **A[21]**.

A[20.17] **Defences.** Where the accused proves

(a) that he had no reason to believe that there was any person within hearing or sight who was likely to be caused harassment, alarm or distress, or
(b) that he was inside a dwelling and had no reason to believe that the words or behaviour used, or the writing, sign or other visible representation displayed, would be heard or seen by a person outside that or any other dwelling, or
(c) that his conduct was reasonable,

he must be acquitted. He does not have to establish his defence beyond a reasonable doubt, but only on the balance of probabilities.

It was stated in *Norwood v DPP*, above, that '[20 . . . in this statutory context, whatever the nature of the burden cast on the defence, it is, in any event, hard to find much of a role for any of the s 5(3) defences, directed, as they are, to an objective assessment by the court of the reasonableness of the accused's conduct. That is because the essentials of the basic s 5 offence require the court to be satisfied as to the accused's subjective state of mind, namely that he intended that the representation should be, or was aware that it might be, threatening, abusive or insulting. See eg *DPP v Clarke* (1991) 94 Cr App Rep 359, per Nolan LJ. If the s 5(3) burden on the defence is to be "read down" to an evidential burden so as to make it Convention compliant, with the result of casting upon the prosecution the burden of disproving it, it would be harder to find any sensible role for s 5(3) . . . '.

The defence of reasonable conduct is to be viewed objectively: *DPP v Clarke* (1991) 156 JP 267. In a case involving the defacement of the American flag (the defendant's own property) near the gate of an RAF base, in the course of a protest against the use of weapons of mass destruction and American military policy including the national missile defence system, it was held that the court had to presume that the defendant's conduct was protected by art 10 unless and until it was established that a restriction on her freedom was strictly necessary. While the district judge had been entitled to find that there was a pressing social need in a multicultural society to prevent the denigration of objects of veneration and symbolic importance for one social group, the next stage was to assess whether or not interference, by means of prosecution, with the defendant's right to free expression by using her own property to convey a lawful message, was a proportionate response to that aim, and the fact that the defendant could have demonstrated in other ways was only one factor to be taken into account when determining the overall reasonableness of the defendant's behaviour and the state's response to it: *Percy v DPP* [2001] EWHC Admin 1125, (2001) 166 JP 93, [2002] Crim LR 835.

A[20.18] **Power of arrest.** Police powers of arrest under what was s 5 of the Public Order Act 1986 are now governed by s 24 of the Police and Criminal Evidence Act 1984 as substituted by Part 3, s 110 of the Serious Organised Crime and Police Act 2005.

For the police to justify an arrest a constable has to show two things: first, under the Police and Criminal Evidence Act 1984, s 24(2), that he had reasonable grounds for suspecting that an offence had been committed and that H was guilty of it; second, that he had reasonable grounds for believing that it was necessary to arrest H to allow the prompt and effective investigation of the offence, as per s 24(4) and s 24(5)(e): see *Hayes v Chief Constable of Merseyside* [2011] EWCA Civ 911, [2012] 1 WLR 517, [2011] 2 Cr App Rep 434.

Sentencing

A[20.19] **Domestic violence.** See SC Definitive Guideline: "Overarching Principles: Domestic Violence".

Available sentences. See Table C at B[43.3].

These offences are is not imprisonable and therefore sentences such as detention in a young offender institution are *not* available.

SC Guideline – (1) Disorderly behaviour (harassment, alarm or distress)
(2) Racially or religiously aggravated disorderly behaviour

OFFENCE SERIOUSNESS (CULPABILITY AND HARM) A. IDENTIFY THE APPROPRIATE STARTING POINT Starting points based on first time offender pleading not guilty		
Examples of nature of activity	**Starting point**	**Range**
Shouting, causing disturbance for some minutes	Band A fine	Conditional discharge to band B fine
Substantial disturbance caused	Band B fine	Band A fine to band C fine

OFFENCE SERIOUSNESS (CULPABILITY AND HARM) B. CONSIDER THE EFFECT OF AGGRAVATING AND MITIGATING FACTORS (OTHER THAN THOSE WITHIN THE EXAMPLES ABOVE) Common aggravating and mitigating factors are identified at B[45.2A]. The following may be particularly relevant but **these lists are not exhaustive**	
Factors indicating higher culpability	*Factors indicating lower culpability*

1. Group action 2. Lengthy incident	1. Stopping as soon as police arrvied 2. Brief/minor incident 3. Provocation
Factors indicating greater degree of harm 1. Vulnerable person(s) present 2. Offence committed at school, hospital or other place where vulnerable persons may be present 3. Victim providing public service	
FORM A PRELIMINARY VIEW OF THE APPROPRIATE SENTENCE IF OFFENDER CHARGED AND CONVICTED OF THE RACIALLY OR RELIGIOUSLY AGGRAVATED OFFENCE, INCREASE THE SENTENCE TO REFLECT THIS ELEMENT Refer to B[45.2B] for guidance	
CONSIDER OFFENDER MITIGATION Common factors are identified at B[45.2A]	
CONSIDER A REDUCTION FOR A GUILTY PLEA	
CONSIDER ANCILLARY ORDERS, INCLUDING COMPENSATION AND FOOTBALL BANNING ORDER (where appropriate) Consult your legal adviser on guidance for available ANCILLARY ORDERS	
DECIDE SENTENCE GIVE REASONS	

A[20.20] **Bind over.** See the amended Consolidated Criminal Practice Direction and associated notes at B[10] onwards.

A[21]

(1) Threatening behaviour
(2) Racially or religiously aggravated threatening behaviour
(3) Disorderly behaviour with intent to cause harassment, alarm or distress
(4) Racially or religiously aggravated disorderly behaviour with intent to cause harassment, alarm or distress

Charge 1 (Threatening behaviour etc)

A[21.1] Using towards another threatening, abusive or insulting words or behaviour (or distributing or displaying to another person any writing, sign or other visible representation being threatening, abusive or insulting) intending to cause that other person to believe that immediate unlawful violence would be used against him or another by any person, or to provoke the immediate use of unlawful violence by that person or another or whereby that other person was likely to believe that such violence would be used or it was likely that such violence would be provoked

Public Order Act 1986, s 4(1)

Maximum penalty – 6 months' imprisonment and/or fine level 5 (for offences committed on or after 12 March 2015 an unlimited fine). Triable only by magistrates.

Charge 2 (Threatening behaviour etc)

A[21.2] A person is guilty of an offence if with intent to cause a person harassment, alarm and distress, he

(a) uses threatening, abusive or insulting words or behaviour, or
(b) displays any writing, sign or visible representation which is threatening, abusive or insulting,

thereby causing that or another person harassment, alarm or distress

Public Order Act 1986, s 4A

Maximum penalty – Fine level 4 and 6 months. Triable only by magistrates.

Charge 3 (Threatening behaviour etc)

A[21.3] Using towards another threatening, abusive or insulting words or behaviour etc which was racially or religiously aggravated.

Crime and Disorder Act 1998, s 31

Maximum penalty – see Charge 4 below.

Charge 4 (Threatening behaviour etc)

A[21.4] Intentional harassment alarm or distress etc which is racially or religiously aggravated.

Crime and Disorder Act 1998, s 31

Maximum penalty – 6 months' imprisonment and/or fine level 5 (for offences committed on or after 12 March 2015 an unlimited fine). Triable either way. Specified violent offence under Sch 15, Part 1, CJA 2003.

Crown Court – 2 years' imprisonment and unlimited fine.

Legal notes and definitions

A[21.5] Although s 4(1) creates only one offence, that offence may be committed in four different ways. Common to all four is the requirement that the accused must intend or be aware that his words or behaviour are or may be threatening, abusive or insulting, and must be directed to another person: see *Winn v DPP* (1992) 156 JP 881. The words 'uses towards another person' mean that threatening words must be addressed directly to another person who is present and either in earshot or aimed at as being putatively in earshot: *Atkin v DPP* (1989) 153 JP 383, [1989] Crim LR 581, DC. It is inappropriate to use the words 'another person' in an information charging an offence under s 4 because the person in whom the belief that unlawful violence would be used has to be the same person as the person threatened, abused or insulted: see *Loade v DPP* (1990) 90 Cr App Rep 162.

Threatening; abusive; insulting. (The following comments are based on repealed legislation but still seem applicable.) The High Court has described these as being 'all very strong words'. If the evidence shows that the words or behaviour used fell short of being abusive, insulting or threatening but merely annoying then the case should be dismissed. The words 'f . . . off' shouted at a police officer who was trying to prevent a breach of the peace have been held to be 'insulting'. Shouting encouragement to a gang throwing stones at another gang is sufficient for a conviction under this section. See *Hammond v DPP* [2004] EWHC 69 (Admin), [2004] All ER (D) 50 (Jan) and *Percy v DPP* [2001] EWHC 1125 (Admin), 166 JP 93, [2002] Crim LR 835, [2001] All ER (D) 387 (Dec). Insulting words or an insulting sign should cause harassment, alarm or distress to another not just strong disagreement.

A[21.5A] ECHR. In *Dehal v DPP* [2005] EWHC 2154 (Admin), (2005) 169 JP 581, the defendant had entered a Sikh Temple and affixed a notice to a notice board which, inter alia, described the president of the Temple as a hypocrite. The Administrative Court held that in order to justify the interference with a right to freedom of expression as set out in art 10 of the ECHR, the prosecution had to demonstrate that the prosecution was being brought in pursuance of a legitimate aim and that the prosecution was the minimum necessary response to that aim. Accordingly, the prosecution of the defendant had not been a proportionate response to his conduct. However, there were indications in *Bauer v DPP* [2013] EWHC 634 (Admin), [2013] WLR 3616, (2013) 177 JP 177 by the same judge (Moses LJ) at para 40 that the imposition of such a burden on the prosecution might be open to question, and it is submitted that it is difficult to reconcile with the well established line of authority that it is not for courts to question how prosecutorial discretion is exercised.

A[21.6] Violence does not include violence justified by law (eg self-defence or prevention of crime). The violence apprehended must be immediate which does not mean 'instantaneous' but connotes proximity in time and causation (*R v Horseferry Road Metropolitan Stipendiary Magistrate, ex p Siadatan* [1991] 1 QB 260, [1991] 1 All ER 324). Where the defendant threatened to shoot the complainant coupled with a shooting gesture with his hand, the combination of the hand gesture together with his loud and threatening language satisfied the test of 'immediacy' (*Liverpool v DPP* [2008] EWHC 2540 (Admin), [2008] All ER (D) 50 (Oct)). For what is included under the offence of violent disorder see A[67].

A[21.7] **Intent.** The accused must *intend* his words or behaviour etc to be, or be aware that his words etc may be, threatening, abusive or insulting and intend the apprehension of unlawful violence etc. It does not have to be shown what the other person in fact believed; it has to be shown that the defendant had the intention to cause that person to believe. This can be proved by any admissible evidence and it is not necessary for the person to whom the threats or insulting behaviour were directed to give evidence: *Swanston v DPP* (1996) 161 JP 203.

In order to ensure that an arrest is lawful the defendant must be warned first about his conduct. This warning is not however part of the offence and so a case can still be determined where the arrest was not lawful (*DPP v Chippendale* [2004] EWHC 464 (Admin), [2004] All ER (D) 308 (Jan)).

Where an appellant had struggled whilst restrained by nightclub doormen, a magistrates' court was entitled to convict him under s 4(1) of the Public Order Act 1986 on the basis that he had intended to cause the doormen to believe that he would use unlawful violence against them if they released him: *Knight v DPP* [2012] EWHC 605 (Admin), 176 JP 177.

By contrast, a court erred in concluding that the appellant had intended to cause his victim to believe that unlawful violence would be used against him, where the appellant had approached the victim in such a way that the victim had not realised that he was about to be attacked: *Hughes v DPP* [2012] EWHC 606 (Admin), [2012] All ER (D) 180 (Jan). The appellant should have been charged with assault by beating.

A[21.8] **Intoxication.** See under the offence of violent disorder at A[67].

A[21.9] Threatening etc behaviour may be committed in a public or private place. If the threatening etc words or behaviour are used inside a dwelling-house, the offence can only be committed if the other person is not inside that or another dwelling-house, but parts of a dwelling not occupied as a person's house or living accommodation do not count as a dwelling for this purpose, eg the shop underneath the owner's flat; a laundry used by the residents of a block of flats: *Ian Norman Levine v DPP* [2010] May 6, 2010, QBD. A tent, caravan, vehicle, vessel or other temporary or movable structure may be a dwelling for this purpose where it is occupied as a person's house or as other living accommodation. A police cell could not be classified as a dwelling or living accommodation for the purposes of s 4A (2) of the Public Order Act 1986 (*R v Francis* [2007] EWCA Crim 3323).

In *DPP v Distill* [2017] EWHC 2244 (Admin), [2017] 4 WLR 177, (2018) 182 JP 1, [2018] Crim L R 170 racial abuse was hurled by one neighbour to another when both parties were in their adjoining back gardens. The case was dismissed in the magistrates' court on the basis that both parties were inside 'dwellings'. The decision was reversed on appeal by way of case stated. The 'dwelling' must in the first place be something which can truly be described as a 'structure' or 'part of a structure'. If, on the particular facts, a garden cannot properly be so it will fall outside the definition of a 'dwelling' in s 8. The word 'structure' carries its ordinary English meaning. There can be many kinds of garden and in every case the facts will be different. A roof garden or winter garden or some other form of garden contained within a residential building will be, as a matter of fact, 'part of a structure', whereas a normal garden to the front or rear of a suburban detached, semi-detached or terraced house would not normally fit that description There may be 'structures' within gardens, eg a gazebo or a greenhouse, but that does not make the garden itself a 'structure'. Neither does the means of enclosure, such as the wall or fence around the garden, even though that wall or fence may itself be a 'structure'.

A[21.10]–[21.15] **Racial/religious aggravation.** See A[20.6]–A[20.7], ante.

Sentencing
SC Guideline – (1) Threatening behaviour (2) Racially or religiously aggravated threatening behaviour

A[21.16] (Section 4A disorderly behaviour and the racially/religiously aggravated – SC Guideline is at A[21.17] below)

Domestic violence. See SC Definitive Guideline: "Overarching Principles: Domestic Violence"

OFFENCE SERIOUSNESS (CULPABILITY AND HARM) A. IDENTIFY THE APPROPRIATE STARTING POINT Starting points based on first time offender pleading not guilty		
Examples of nature of activity	**Starting point**	**Range**
Fear or threat of low level immediate unlawful violence such as push, shove or spit	Low level community penalty	Band B fine to medium level community order
Fear or threat or medium level immediate unlawful violence such as punch	High level community order	Low level community order to 12 weeks custody
Fear or threat of high level immediate unlawful violence such as use of weapon; missile thrown; gang involvement	12 weeks custody	6 to 26 weeks custody

OFFENCE SERIOUSNESS (CULPABILITY AND HARM) B. CONSIDER THE EFFECT OF AGGRAVATING AND MITIGATING FACTORS (OTHER THAN THOSE WITHIN EXAMPLES ABOVE) Common aggravating and mitigating factors are identified at B[45.2A]. The following may be particularly relevant but **these lists are not exhaustive**	
Factors indicating higher culpability 1. Planning 2. Offender deliberately isolates victim 3. Group action 4. Threat directed at victim because of job 5. History of antagonism towards victim	*Factors indicating lower culpability* 1. Impulsive action 2. Short duration 3. Provocation
Factors indicating greater degree of harm 1. Offence committed at school, hospital or other place where vulnerable victims may be present 2. Offence committed on enclosed premises such as public transport 3. Vulnerable victim(s) 4. Victim needs medical help/counselling	

FORM A PRELIMINARY VIEW OF THE APPROPRIATE SENTENCE IF OFFENDER CHARGED AND CONVICTED OF THE RACIALLY OR RELIGIOUSLY AGGRAVATED OFFENCE, INCREASE THE SENTENCE TO REFLECT THE ELEMENT Common factors are identified at B[45.2B]
CONSIDER OFFENDER MITIGATION Common factors are identified at B[45.2A]
CONSIDER A REDUCTION FOR A GUILTY PLEA
CONSIDER ANCILLARY ORDERS, INCLUDING COMPENSATION AND FOOTBALL BANNING ORDER (where appropriate) Refer to B[10] for guidance on compensation.
DECIDE SENTENCE

GIVE REASONS

SC Guideline – (3) Disorderly behaviour with intent etc (4) Racially or religiously aggravated threatening behaviour with intent etc

A[21.17] (Section 4 threatening behaviour and the racially/religiously aggravated SC Guideline is at A[21.16] above)

Domestic violence. See SC Definitive Guideline: "Overarching Principles: Domestic Violence"

OFFENCE SERIOUSNESS (CULPABILITY AND HARM) A. IDENTIFY THE APPROPRIATE STARTING POINT Starting points based on first time offender pleading not guilty		
Examples of nature of activity	**Starting point**	**Range**
Threats, abuse or insults made more than once but on same occasion against the same person eg while following down the street	Band C fine	Band B fine to low level community order
Group action or deliberately planned action against targeted victim	Medium level community order	Low level community order to 12 weeks custody
Weapon brandished or used or threats against vulnerable victim – course of conduct over longer period	12 weeks custody	High level community order to 26 weeks custody

OFFENCE SERIOUSNESS (CULPABILITY AND HARM) B. CONSIDER THE EFFECT OF AGGRAVATING AND MITIGATING FACTORS (OTHER THAN THOSE WITHIN EXAMPLES ABOVE) Common aggravating and mitigating factors are identified at B[45.2A]. The following may be particularly relevant but **these lists are not exhaustive**	
Factors indicating higher culpability 1. High degree of planning 2. Offender deliberately isolates victim	*Factors indicating lower culpability* 1. Very short period 2. Provocation
Factors indicating greater degree of harm 1. Offence committed in vicinity of victim's home 2. Large number of people in vicinity 3. Actual or potential escalation into violence 4. Particularly serious impact on victim	
FORM A PRELIMINARY VIEW OF THE APPROPRIATE SENTENCE	
IF OFFENDER CHARGED AND CONVICTED OF THE RACIALLY OR RELIGIOUSLY AGGRAVATED OFFENCE, INCREASE THE SENTENCE TO REFLECT THE ELEMENT Common factors are identified at B[45.2B]	
CONSIDER OFFENDER MITIGATION	

Common factors are identified at B[45.2A]
CONSIDER A REDUCTION FOR A GUILTY PLEA
CONSIDER ANCILLARY ORDERS, INCLUDING COMPENSATION AND FOOTBALL BANNING ORDER (where appropriate) **Refer to B[10] for guidance on compensation.**
DECIDE SENTENCE **GIVE REASONS**

A[21.18] **Bind over.** See the amended Consolidated Criminal Practice Direction and associated notes at B[5] onwards.

A[22]
Drugs

A[22.1] The misuse of drugs is made unlawful by the Misuse of Drugs Act 1971, which introduced the term 'controlled drugs' (ie drugs, the use of which is controlled by the Act). The second schedule of the Act allocates controlled drugs to Classes A, B or C and maximum penalties vary according to the class to which a controlled drug belongs.

A[22.2] The text below concerns two drug offences which seem likely to be among the most frequently committed offences created by the Act. These are the offences created by the Misuse of Drugs Act 1971, ss 5(2) and 5(3).

Psychoactive substances

A[22.3] The Psychoactive Substances Act 2016 bans the production, distribution, sale and supply and importation of psychoactive substances (or 'legal highs') in the United Kingdom. Exceptions are made in respect of such scheduled products as food, alcohol, tobacco, caffeine, medicinal products and controlled drugs, and certain health and scientific research activities are also exempted. In addition to creating offences, the Act makes provision for prohibition notices, premises notices, prohibition orders and premises orders as well as powers to stop and search persons, vehicles and vessels, to enter and search premises (under warrant) and to forfeit seized psychoactive substances and other items.

These provisions came into effect on 26 May 2016. The offences are dealt with at A[87]. The provisions on prohibition and premises orders are dealt with in Section B.

A[23]

Drugs – class A – failure to attend initial/remain for initial assessment

(Drugs Act 2005, s 12)

Charge (Drugs – class A – assessment)

A[23.1] A person who, by virtue of s 9 (2) of the Drugs Act 2005, without good cause—

(a) **fails to attend an initial drugs assessment at the specified time and place, or**
(b) **attends the assessment at the specified time and place but fails to remain for its duration**

shall be guilty of an offence.

Drugs Act 2005, s 12

Maximum penalty. A person guilty of an offence under s 12 is liable on summary conviction to a punishment not exceeding 3 months or to a level 4 fine or both.

Legal notes and definitions

A[23.2] If a person fails to attend an initial assessment at the specified time and place, any requirement imposed on him by virtue of s 10(2) ie a "follow-up assessment" ceases to have effect.

Sentencing
SC Guideline – Drugs – class A – fail to attend/remain for initial assessment

Drugs – class A – fail to attend/remain for initial assessment (Revised 2017)

A[23.3]

Drugs Act 2005, s 12

Effective from: 24 April 2017

Triable only summarily:

Maximum: Level 4 fine and/or 3 months

Offence range: Band A fine–High level community order

STEP 1
Determining the offence category

The Court should determine the offence category using the table below.

Category 1	Higher culpability and greater harm
Category 2	Higher culpability and lesser harm or lower culpability and greater harm
Category 3	Lower culpability and lesser harm

The court should determine the offender's culpability and the harm caused with reference **only** to the factors below. Where an offence does not fall squarely into a category, individual factors may require a degree of weighting before making an overall assessment and determining the appropriate offence category.

CULPABILITY demonstrated by one or more of the following:

Factor indicating higher culpability

- Deliberate failure to attend/remain

Factor indicating lower culpability

- All other cases

HARM demonstrated by one or more of the following:

Factor indicating greater harm

- Aggressive, abusive or disruptive behaviour

Factor indicating lesser harm

- All other cases

STEP 2
Starting point and category range

Having determined the category at step one, the court should use the corresponding starting point to reach a sentence within the category range in the table below. The starting point applies to all offenders irrespective of plea or previous convictions.

Offence Category	Starting Point	Range
Category 1	Medium level community order	Low level community order–High level community order
Category 2	Band C fine	Band B fine–Low level community order
Category 3	Band B fine	Band A fine–Band C fine

The court should then consider further adjustment for any aggravating or mitigating factors. The following is a **non-exhaustive** list of additional factual elements providing the context of the offence and factors relating to the offender. Identify whether any combination of these, or other relevant factors, should result in an upward or downward adjustment from the sentence arrived at so far.

Factors increasing seriousness

Statutory aggravating factors:

- Previous convictions, having regard to a) the **nature** of the offence to which the conviction relates and its **relevance** to the current offence; and b) the **time** that has elapsed since the conviction
- Offence committed whilst on bail
- Offence motivated by, or demonstrating hostility based on any of the following characteristics or presumed characteristics of the victim: religion, race, disability, sexual orientation or transgender identity

Other aggravating factors:

- Failure to comply with current court orders
- Offence committed on licence or post sentence supervision
- Offender's actions result in a waste of resources

Factors reducing seriousness or reflecting personal mitigation

- No previous convictions or no relevant/recent convictions

- Remorse
- Good character and/or exemplary conduct
- Serious medical condition requiring urgent, intensive or long-term treatment
- Age and/or lack of maturity where it affects the responsibility of the offender
- Mental disorder or learning disability
- Sole or primary carer for dependent relatives
- Determination and/or demonstration of steps having been taken to address addiction or offending behaviour
- Attempts made to re-arrange appointments

STEP 3
Consider any factors which indicate a reduction, such as assistance to the prosecution

The court should take into account sections 73 and 74 of the Serious Organised Crime and Police Act 2005 (assistance by defendants: reduction or review of sentence) and any other rule of law by virtue of which an offender may receive a discounted sentence in consequence of assistance given (or offered) to the prosecutor or investigator.

STEP 4
Reduction for guilty pleas

The court should take account of any potential reduction for a guilty plea in accordance with section 144 of the Criminal Justice Act 2003 and the *Guilty Plea* guideline.

STEP 5
Totality principle

If sentencing an offender for more than one offence, or where the offender is already serving a sentence, consider whether the total sentence is just and proportionate to the overall offending behaviour in accordance with the *Offences Taken into Consideration and Totality* guideline.

STEP 6
Consider ancillary orders

In all cases, the court should consider whether to make compensation and/or other ancillary orders.

STEP 7
Reasons

Section 174 of the Criminal Justice Act 2003 imposes a duty to give reasons for, and explain the effect of, the sentence.

A[24]

Drugs – class A – fail/refuse to provide a sample

(Police and Criminal Evidence Act 1984, s 63B)

Charge (Drugs – class A – fail/refuse to provide a sample)

A[24.1] A person who by virtue of this section, fails without good cause to give any sample which may be taken from him shall be guilty of an offence.

Police and Criminal Evidence Act 1984, s 63B

Maximum penalty. A person guilty of an offence under s 63B is liable on summary conviction to a punishment not exceeding 3 months or to a level 4 fine or both.

Sentencing
SGC Guideline – Drugs – class A – fail/refuse to provide a sample

Drugs – class A – fail/refuse to provide a sample (Revised 2017)

A[24.2]

Police and Criminal Evidence Act 1984, s 63B

Effective from: 24 April 2017

Triable only summarily:

Maximum: Level 4 fine and/or 3 months

Offence range: Band A fine–High level community order

STEP 1
Determining the offence category

The Court should determine the offence category using the table below.

Category 1	Higher culpability and greater harm
Category 2	Higher culpability and lesser harm or lower culpability and greater harm
Category 3	Lower culpability and lesser harm

The court should determine the offender's culpability and the harm caused with reference **only** to the factors below. Where an offence does not fall squarely into a category, individual factors may require a degree of weighting before making an overall assessment and determining the appropriate offence category.

CULPABILITY demonstrated by one or more of the following:

Factors indicating higher culpability

- Deliberate refusal

Factors indicating lower culpability

- All other cases

HARM demonstrated by one or more of the following:

Factors indicating greater harm

- Aggressive, abusive or disruptive behaviour

Factors indicating lesser harm

- All other cases

STEP 2

Starting point and category range

Having determined the category at step one, the court should use the starting point to reach a sentence within the appropriate category range in the table below. The starting point applies to all offenders irrespective of plea or previous convictions.

Offence Category	Starting Point	Range
Category 1	Medium level community order	Low level community order–High level community order
Category 2	Band C fine	Band B fine–Low level community order
Category 3	Band B fine	Band A fine–Band C fine

The court should then consider adjustment for any aggravating or mitigating factors. The following is a **non-exhaustive** list of additional factual elements providing the context of the offence and factors relating to the offender. Identify whether any combination of these, or other relevant factors, should result in an upward or downward adjustment from the sentence arrived at so far.

Factors increasing seriousness

Statutory aggravating factors:

- Previous convictions, having regard to a) the **nature** of the offence to which the conviction relates and its **relevance** to the current offence; and b) the **time** that has elapsed since the conviction
- Offence committed whilst on bail
- Offence motivated by, or demonstrating hostility based on any of the following characteristics or presumed characteristics of the victim: religion, race, disability, sexual orientation or transgender identity

Other aggravating factors:

- Failure to comply with current court orders
- Offence committed on licence or post sentence supervision
- Offender's actions result in a waste of resources

Factors reducing seriousness or reflecting personal mitigation

- No previous convictions **or** no relevant/recent convictions
- Remorse
- Good character and/or exemplary conduct
- Serious medical condition requiring urgent, intensive or long-term treatment
- Age and/or lack of maturity where it affects the responsibility of the offender
- Mental disorder or learning disability
- Sole or primary carer for dependent relatives
- Determination and/or demonstration of steps having been taken to address addiction or offending behaviour

STEP 3

Consider any factors which indicate a reduction, such as assistance to the prosecution

The court should take into account sections 73 and 74 of the Serious Organised Crime and Police Act 2005 (assistance by defendants: reduction or review of

sentence) and any other rule of law by virtue of which an offender may receive a discounted sentence in consequence of assistance given (or offered) to the prosecutor or investigator.

STEP 4
Reduction for guilty pleas

The court should take account of any potential reduction for a guilty plea in accordance with section 144 of the Criminal Justice Act 2003 and the *Guilty Plea* guideline.

STEP 5
Totality principle

If sentencing an offender for more than one offence, or where the offender is already serving a sentence, consider whether the total sentence is just and proportionate to the overall offending behaviour in accordance with the *Offences Taken into Consideration and Totality* guideline.

STEP 6
Consider ancillary orders

In all cases, the court should consider whether to make compensation and/or other ancillary orders.

STEP 7
Reasons

Section 174 of the Criminal Justice Act 2003 imposes a duty to give reasons for, and explain the effect of, the sentence.

A[25]

Possession of a controlled drug

(Misuse of Drugs Act 1971, s 5(2))

Charge (Possession of a controlled drug)

A[25.1] Having a quantity of a controlled drug, namely [. . . . .], in his possession

Maximum penalty

Class A	level 5 and 6 months
Class B	£2,500 and 3 months
Class C	£1,000 and 3 months

Court can order forfeiture but see 'Forfeiture' below.

Crown Court -

Class A	7 years and fine
Class B	5 years and fine
Class C	2 years and fine

Triable either way in respect of any class of drug although see A[25.3] below.

Mode of trial

A[25.2] See the SC Guidelines below.

A[25.3] Possession of Class A drugs – see SC Guideline at A[25.16] below.

It should be noted that the Powers of Criminal Courts (Sentencing) Act 2000, s 110 makes provision for the imposition of a minimum seven-year custodial sentence on 18-year-olds and above who have been convicted of a third Class A drug trafficking offence.

A[25.4] Possession of class B or C drugs – see SC Guideline at A[25.16] below.

Legal notes and definitions

A[25.5] **Quantity.** The charge should state the quantity involved. If it is a diminutive quantity consult the legal adviser. Scrapings from a pocket can be enough. A few droplets in a tube only discernible microscopically are not enough; the court must be satisfied that there is sufficient there to amount to something. If the quantity is very small it may be relevant to the question of the accused's knowledge that it was in his possession.

A[25.6] **Expert examination.** The court should be satisfied that an expert has confirmed that the substance is the controlled drug alleged. In a contested case this would have to be proved by the prosecution or admitted by the defendant.

A[25.7] **Possession.** The Act does not contain a definition of 'possession' but the nature of possession has received extensive consideration in case law, in particular by the House of Lords in *R v Lambert* [2001] UKHL 37, [2002] 2 AC 545, [2001] 3 All ER 577, [2001] 3 WLR 206 (see below).

Possession embraces both a factual and a mental element.

The factual element is control. Section 37(3) provides that for the purposes of the Act the things which a person has in his possession shall be taken to include anything subject to his control which is in the custody of another. In *R v Wright* (1975) 119 Sol Jo 825 a distinction was made between mere physical custody of an object, and its possession for the commission of an offence. The defendant was given a container and told to throw it away, which he did instantly: he could not be convicted although he suspected it might contain drugs. A person having given directions to a supplier, following which he receives a parcel containing a drug through his letter-box, becomes the possessor of the drug once the parcel is put through the letter-box: *R v Peaston* [1979] Crim LR 183. If a person smokes cannabis resin he must have cannabis resin in his possession at the time of smoking: *Chief Constable of Cheshire Constabulary v Hunt* (1983) 147 JP 567. Once a controlled drug has been consumed and has changed in character, the consumer could not then be said to be 'in possession' of it, though it might be evidence of possession immediately before he consumed it: *Hambleton v Callinan* [1968] 2 QB 427, [1968] 2 All ER 943, 132 JP 461.

The mental element. The mental element in offences contrary to s 5 was exhaustively considered by the House of Lords in *R v Lambert*, above from which the following propositions are derived.

The prosecution must prove:

(a) the defendant was in possession of something;
(b) the defendant knew he was in possession of that something; and
(c) the thing which the defendant possessed was a controlled drug.

Lack of knowledge. The prosecution is not required to prove that the defendant knew that the thing which he possessed was a controlled drug but if the prosecution have adduced sufficient evidence to prove (a)–(c), s 28(2), (3) post, stipulates the way in which lack of knowledge etc can be a defence in proceedings. To bring himself within the provisions of s 28 (2), (3) the defendant must satisfy an evidential burden of adducing evidence which is sufficient to raise the issue of knowledge. If sufficient evidence is adduced to raise the issue, it will be for the prosecution to show beyond reasonable doubt that the defence is not made out by the evidence.

Quantity is of importance in two respects when determining whether or not an accused person has a controlled drug in his possession. First, is the quantity sufficient to enable a court to find as a matter of fact that it amounts to something? If it is visible, tangible and measurable, it is certainly something. The question is one of fact for the commonsense of the tribunal. Secondly, quantity may be relevant to the issue of knowledge. If the quantity in custody or control is minute, the question arises – was it so minute that it cannot be proved that the accused knew he had it? If knowledge cannot be proved, possession is not established: *R v Boyeson* [1982] AC 768, [1982] 2 All ER 161, 146 JP 217, HL. See also *R v Colyer* [1974] Crim LR 243 (minute quantity) and *R v Ashton Rickardt* [1977] Crim LR 424. As to aggregating several amounts of a drug, see *R v Bayliss and Oliver* [1978] Crim LR 361. As to conviction for possessing a lesser amount than charged, see *R v Peevey* (1973) 57 Cr App Rep 554, CA.

Mere presence in the same vehicle as cannabis, even if someone had said there was cannabis in the car, is not sufficient to prove possession: *R v Strong* and *R v Berry* [1989] 10 LS Gaz R 41, CA.

Once the prosecution proves that the defendant had control of a box which he was delivering on his motor cycle and knew it contained something, which was in fact the drug alleged, he has the onus of bringing himself within the provisions of s 28(3): see *R v McNamara* (1988) 87 Cr App Rep 246, 152 JP 390 approved in *R v Lambert*, above.

A[25.7A] **Controlled drug.** Where an experienced drug user admits possession of a substance which he himself identifies as a controlled drug, that admission and identification are sufficient to provide prima facie evidence of the nature of the substance and of unlawful possession of a controlled drug: see *R v Chatwood* [1980]

1 All ER 467, [1980] 1 WLR 874. It is important that the prosecution should prove possession of the drug as charged: see *Muir v Smith* [1978] Crim LR 293 where the prosecution failed as it could not be ascertained whether the substance was cannabis or herbal cannabis.

A[25.8] **Defences.** Each of the following defences is expressly provided by the Act, but a defendant is also entitled to rely on other common law defences (see **A[25.8A]** below).

(a) Authorised by regulation (s 7). After consulting the Advisory Council on the Misuse of Drugs, the Home Secretary is empowered to introduce regulations exempting certain persons (eg doctors, dentists, veterinary surgeons, pharmacists) and controlled drugs (in certain circumstances) from the scope of this offence.

or

(b) Knowing or suspecting it was a controlled drug, the defendant took possession of it to prevent another person from committing or continuing to commit an offence with it; and further that as soon as possible after taking possession of it he took all reasonable steps to destroy it or to deliver it to a person lawfully entitled to take it (s 5(4)(a)).

or

(c) Knowing or suspecting it was a controlled drug, the defendant took possession of it to deliver it to a person lawfully entitled to it and as soon as possible he took all reasonable steps to deliver it to that person (s 5(4)(b)).

or

(d) The defendant neither knew nor suspected, nor had reason to suspect, the existence of any fact (except whether the article was a controlled drug, see (e) below) which the prosecution must prove if the defendant is to be convicted (s 28(2)); eg he did not know he possessed anything (this is where quantity might be relevant). Possession is not dependent on the accused's *recollection* that he has it. Where a man had knowingly placed some cannabis in his wallet and had later forgotten it was there, he was still in possession of it. Of course it would be otherwise if a third party had slipped it in his pocket unawares so that he never knew it was there (*R v Martindale* [1986] 3 All ER 25, [1986] 1 WLR 1042, CA). [Where the defendant knew he possessed something but denies he knew it was a controlled drug the next defence ((e) below) is appropriate.]

or

(e) In cases where the prosecution must prove that the substance or product was the controlled drug alleged in the charge and has done so, the defendant shall not be acquitted by reason only of proving that he neither knew or suspected that the substance was the particular drug alleged but shall be acquitted if he proves either:
   (i) that he neither believed nor suspected nor had reason to suspect that the substance or product was *any kind* of controlled drug, ie not just that it was not the controlled drug referred to in the charge; or
   (ii) that he believed it to be a controlled drug and that he also believed the circumstances were such that he would not be committing any offence (s 28(3)).

A[25.8A] **Common law defence of necessity.** In *R v Quayle and other appeals; Attorney General's Reference (No 2 of 2004)* [2005] EWCA Crim 1415, [2006] 1 All ER 988, the Court of Appeal held that the common law defence of necessity was not available for individuals who contended that they genuinely and reasonably believed that the cultivation, production, importation and possession of cannabis had been necessary to avoid them suffering serious pain or injury by reason of their medical condition.

A[25.9] **Burden of proof upon the defendant.** A defendant relying upon one of the above defences does not have to establish it beyond reasonable doubt. He need only establish it was more probable than not (see **ECHR** (A[25.10]) below)

A[25.10] ECHR. In the light of *R v Lambert* [2001] UKHL 37, [2002] 2 AC 545, it appears that the imposition of a legal burden of proof on the accused may be disproportionate to a fair trial as required by art 6(2) ECHR. Accordingly, the MDA 1971 should be read as imposing an evidential burden on the accused ie the accused only bears the burden of raising the defence. Once raised it is for the prosecution to negative the defence beyond a reasonable doubt.

A[25.11]–[25.15] Cannabis. Means the whole or any part of the plant except cannabis resin or the separated mature stalk, fibre produced from the mature stalk or the seed.

Sentencing
SC Sentencing Guideline – Possession of a controlled drug

Misuse of Drugs Act 1971 (section 5(2))

A[25.16] This guideline applies to all offenders aged 18 years and older, who are sentenced on or after 27 February 2012. The definitions of 'starting point' and 'first time offender' do not apply for this guideline. Starting point and category ranges apply to all offenders in all cases, irrespective of plea or previous convictions. Triable either way.

Class A

Maximum: 7 years' custody

Offence range: Fine – 51 weeks' custody

Class B

Maximum: 5 years' custody

Offence range: Discharge – 26 weeks' custody

Class C

Maximum: 2 years' custody

Offence range: Discharge – Community order

STEP ONE
Determining the offence category

The court should identify the offence category based on the class of drug involved.

Category 1	Class A drug
Category 2	Class B drug
Category 3	Class C drug

STEP TWO
Starting point and category range

The court should use the table below to identify the corresponding starting point. The starting point applies to all offenders irrespective of plea or previous convictions. The court should then consider further adjustment within the category range for aggravating or mitigating features, set out on the opposite page.

Where the defendant is dependent on or has a propensity to misuse drugs and there is sufficient prospect of success, a community order with a drug rehabilitation requirement under section 209 of the Criminal Justice Act 2003 can be a proper alternative to a short or moderate length custodial sentence.

Offence category	Starting point (applicable to all offenders)	Category range (applicable to all offenders)
Category 1 (class A)	Band C fine	Band A fine – 51 weeks' custody
Category 2 (class B)	Band B fine	Discharge – 26 weeks' custody
Category 3 (class C)	Band A fine	Discharge – medium level community order

The table below contains a **non-exhaustive** list of additional factual elements providing the context of the offence and factors relating to the offender. Identify whether any combination of these, or other relevant factors, should result in an upward or downward adjustment from the starting point. **In particular, possession of drugs in prison is likely to result in an upward adjustment.** In some cases, having considered these factors, it may be appropriate to move outside the identified category range.

Where appropriate, consider the custody threshold as follows:

- has the custody threshold been passed?
- if so, is it unavoidable that a custodial sentence be imposed?
- if so, can that sentence be suspended?

Where appropriate, the court should also consider the community threshold as follows:

- has the community threshold been passed?

Factors increasing seriousness
Statutory aggravating factors:
Previous convictions, having regard to a) nature of the offence to which conviction relates and relevance to current offence; and b) time elapsed since conviction
Offence committed on bail
Other aggravating factors include:
Possession of drug in prison
Presence of others, especially children and/or non-users
Possession of drug in a school or licensed premises
Failure to comply with current court orders
Offence committed on licence
Attempts to conceal or dispose of evidence, where not charged separately
Charged as importation of a very small amount
Established evidence of community impact
Factors reducing seriousness or reflecting personal mitigation
No previous convictions or no relevant or recent convictions
Remorse
Good character and/or exemplary conduct
Offender is using cannabis to help with a diagnosed medical condition
Determination and/or demonstration of steps having been taken to address addiction or offending behaviour

Serious medical conditions requiring urgent, intensive or long-term treatment
Isolated incident
Age and/or lack of maturity where it affects the responsibility of the offender
Mental disorder or learning disability
Sole or primary carer for dependent relatives

STEP THREE
Consider any factors which indicate a reduction, such as assistance to the prosecution

The court should take into account sections 73 and 74 of the Serious Organised Crime and Police Act 2005 (assistance by defendants: reduction or review of sentence) and any other rule of law by virtue of which an offender may receive a discounted sentence in consequence of assistance given (or offered) to the prosecutor or investigator.

STEP FOUR
Reduction for guilty pleas

The court should take account of any potential reduction for a guilty plea in accordance with section 144 of the Criminal Justice Act 2003 and the *Guilty Plea* guideline.

STEP FIVE
Totality principle

If sentencing an offender for more than one offence, or where the offender is already serving a sentence, consider whether the total sentence is just and proportionate to the offending behaviour.

STEP SIX
Ancillary orders

In all cases, the court should consider whether to make ancillary orders.

STEP SEVEN
Reasons

Section 174 of the Criminal Justice Act 2003 imposes a duty to give reasons for, and explain the effect of, the sentence.

STEP EIGHT
Consideration for remand time

(Now obligatory.)

A[25.17] Available sentences (Class A, B and C drugs). See Table A at B[43.1A].

A[25.18] Forfeiture (s 27). The court can order the controlled drugs, or anything proved to relate to the offence, to be forfeited and either destroyed or otherwise dealt with as the court may order. However, if a person claims to be owner of the drug or item to be forfeited, or to be otherwise interested in it, he must first be given an opportunity to show cause why a forfeiture order should not be made.

A[26]

Supplying or offering to supply a controlled drug Possessing a controlled drug with intent to supply it to another

(Misuse of Drugs Act 1971, ss 4(3) and 5(3))

Charge (Possessing a controlled drug with intent to supply)

A[26.1] **1. (a) To supply or offer to supply a controlled drug to another; or (b) to be concerned in the supplying of a controlled drug to another; or (c) to be concerned in the making to another of an offer to supply a controlled drug.**
2. Having in his possession a quantity of [. . . . . . .] a controlled drug of Class [. . . . . . .] with intent to supply it to another person

Maximum penalty –

Class A	£5,000 and 6 months
Class B	£5,000 and 6 months
Class C	£2,500 and 3 months

Court can order forfeiture, but see 'Forfeiture' above.

Crown Court –

Class A	Life imprisonment and fine
Class B	14 years and fine
Class C	14 years and fine

Triable either way in respect of any class of drug but see A[25.3]

Mode of trial

A[26.2] See SC Guideline at A[26.5] below.

Legal notes and definitions

A[26.3] The notes in respect of the previous offence at A[25] also apply here except that the defences numbered (b) and (c) in A[25.8] are not applicable.

A[26.4] **Intent to supply to another person.** In deciding whether or not the defendant had this intention, the court must consider all the evidence drawing such inferences from it as appear proper in the circumstances. An involuntary keeper of drugs can be guilty of supply (*R v Panton* [2001] 19 LS Gaz R 36, CA).

In *R v Wright* [2011] EWCA Crim 1180, [2011] 2 Cr App Rep 168, there was no suggestion that W had intended to supply the immature cannabis plants which he had produced and was in possession of at the material time. The core offence was the production of cannabis under s 4 and the seriousness of that offence depended, inter alia, on whether the cannabis was being grown for W's own use or for supply to others. That question could be resolved within the sentencing process for the offence of production, if necessary by a Newton hearing. It had been unnecessary therefore to add a count of possession with intent to supply in order to determine the purpose for which the cannabis was being produced.

The prosecution only has to establish that the accused was in possession of the controlled drug as charged with the necessary intent; the accused will not be able to avail himself of the defences in s 28(2) or 28(3)(b)(ii) where he believed the substance to be a different drug from that alleged by the prosecution as it is not necessary for the prosecution to prove which controlled drug it was to obtain a conviction. The only purpose of specifying the class of drug in the particulars of the offence is that that factor affects the sentence which can be passed on conviction: *R v Leeson* [2000] 1 Cr App Rep 233, 164 JP 224, [2000] Crim LR 195.

A[26.4A] **Supply and being concerned in supplying.** 'Supply' covers a wide range of transactions, of which a feature common to all of those transactions is a transfer of physical control of a drug from one person to another: *R v Delgado* [1984] 1 All ER 449, [1984] 1 WLR 89, 148 JP 431, CA; but the transfer must be for the purposes of the transferee: *R v Maginnis* [1987] AC 303,[1987] 1 All ER 907. Where a defendant intends to supply drugs to a courier, even a commercial courier, for eventual supply to a person outside the jurisdiction, there is no contravention of s 4(1) (ante) since there is no intention to supply for the purposes of the transferee (the courier) and the offence does not have extraterritorial effect: *R v Hussain (Shabbir)* [2010] EWCA Crim 970, [2011] QB 1, [2010] 2 WLR 808, [2010] 2 Cr App R 11.

A person in unlawful possession of a controlled drug which has been deposited with him for safe keeping has the intent to supply that drug to another if his intention is to return the drug to the person who deposited it with him: *R v Maginnis*, above. However, 'supply' in s 4(2)(a) implies an act designed to benefit the recipient and does not cover the deposit of a controlled drug with someone for safe keeping: *R v Dempsey* (1985) 82 Cr App Rep 291, 150 JP 213.

Evidence of large amounts of money in the possession of the defendant or an extravagant life style prima facie explicable only if derived from drug dealing is admissible in cases of possession of drugs with intent to supply if it is of probative significance to an issue in the case: *R v Morris* [1995] 2 Cr App Rep 69, 159 JP 1 and see *R v Lucas* [1995] Crim LR 400, CA. Moreover, the finding of money, whether in the home of the defendant or perhaps, more cogently, in the possession of the defendant when away from his home, and in conjunction with a substantial quantity of drugs, is capable of being relevant to the issue of whether there is proved an intent to supply: *R v Grant* [1996] 1 Cr App Rep 73.

The offence of being concerned in supplying a controlled drug is designed to provide a means of proceeding against the 'trafficker', and individuals who have connived rather than contrived, and so have escaped prosecution for aiding and abetting the commission of an offence; for example, someone assisting in the injection of a drug into someone else. It is also sufficient to involve people who may be at some distance from the actual making of the offer: *R v Blake* (1979) 68 Cr App Rep 1. To prove an offence under s 4(3)(b) or (c), the prosecution has to prove (1) the supply of a drug to another or, as the case may be, the making of an offer to supply a drug to another in contravention of s 4(1); (2) participation by the defendant in an enterprise involving such supply, or as the case may be, such offer to supply; and (3) knowledge by the defendant of the nature of the enterprise, ie that it involved supply of a drug or, as the case may be, offering to supply a drug (*R v Hughes* (1985) 81 Cr App Rep 344). The offence under s 4(3)(b) does not require an actual supply to another; it includes a transaction which is the process of supply where there would in due course be delivery to another person: *R v Martin and Brimecome* [2014] EWCA Crim 1940, [2015] 1 WLR 588, [2015] 1 Cr App Rep 132. The above authorities were followed in *R v Coker* [2019] EWCA Crim 420, [2019] 4 WLR 41, [2019] 2 Cr App R 10, [2019] Crim LR 542. Section 4(3) creates three distinct offences, and where there is doubt as to whether a case falls within s 4(3)(b) or (3)(c), both offences should be charged, albeit to be treated as alternatives for the purposes of conviction.

A[26.4B] **Offer to supply.** It is an offence to offer to supply a controlled drug even though the substance in the defendant's possession is not such a drug (but not if the offence charged is supplying): *Haggard v Mason* [1976] 1 All ER 337, 140 JP 198. The offence is complete when the offer to supply a controlled drug is made, regardless of whether the offeror intends to carry the offer into effect by actually supplying the drug: *R v Goddard* [1992] Crim LR 588. Whether the words spoken and the circumstances in which they were uttered amounted to an offer is a question of fact having regard to the effect of the words and any relevant circumstances apparent to the offeree. An offer once made cannot be withdrawn, any attempt to withdraw may only be relevant to the issue whether there was an offer in the first place. There is no need for the offer to meet the specificity as to date and time of delivery of the civil law and it does not matter whether the offeror or the offeree took the initiative: *R v Prior* [2004] EWCA Crim 1147, [2004] Crim LR 849.

A[26.4C] Aggravation of offence of supply of controlled drug. A new s 4A was added to the Misuse of Drugs Act 1971 by the Drugs Act 2005, s 1. This section applies if –

(a) a court is considering the seriousness of an offence under s 4(3) of the 1971 Act, and
(b) at the time the offence was committed the offender had attained the age of 18 years.

If either of the following conditions is met the court must treat the fact that the condition is met as an aggravating factor ie a factor that increases the seriousness of the offence and when giving its reasons in open court must state that the offence is so aggravated. The conditions are:
(a) the offence was committed on or in the vicinity of school premises at the relevant time;
(b) in connection with the commission of the offence the offender used a courier who, at the time the offence was committed, was under the age of 18 years.

A[26.4D] Defences and ECHR. See A[25.9] onwards and (*R v Lambert* [2001] 1 All ER 1014, [2001] 2 WLR 211, CA; affd sub nom R v Lambert [2001] UKHL 37, [2002] 2 AC 545, [2001] 3 All ER 577) and Misuse of Drugs Act 1971, s 28.

Sentencing
SC Sentencing Guideline – Supplying or offering to supply a controlled drug

Misuse of Drugs Act 1971 (section 4(3))

Possession of a controlled drug with intent to supply it to another

Misuse of Drugs Act 1971 (section 5(3))

A[26.5] Triable either way unless the defendant could receive the minimum sentence of seven years for a third drug trafficking offence under section 110 Powers of Criminal Courts (Sentencing) Act 2000 in which case the offence is triable only on indictment.

Class A

Maximum: Life imprisonment

Offence range: Community order – 16 years' custody

A class A offence is a drug trafficking offence for the purpose of imposing a minimum sentence under section 110 Powers of Criminal Courts (Sentencing) Act 2000

Class B

Maximum: 14 years' custody and/or unlimited fine

Offence range: Fine – 10 years' custody

Class C

Maximum: 14 years' custody and/or unlimited fine

Offence range: Fine – 8 years' custody

STEP ONE
Determining the offence category

The court should determine the offender's culpability (role) and the harm caused (quantity/type of offender) with reference to the tables below.

In assessing culpability, the sentencer should weigh up all the factors of the case to determine role. Where there are characteristics present which fall under different role categories, the court should balance these characteristics to reach a fair assessment of the offender's culpability.

In assessing harm, quantity is determined by the weight of the product. Purity is not taken into account at step 1 but is dealt with at step 2. Where the offence is **street dealing*** or **supply of drugs in prison by a prison employee,** the quantity of the product is less indicative of the harm caused and therefore the **starting point is not based on quantity.**

Where the operation is on the most serious and commercial scale, involving a quantity of drugs significantly higher than category 1, sentences of 20 years and above may be appropriate, depending on the role of the offender.

* 'Street dealing' is a term of art. The supply does not have to take place on a 'street'; the essence of street dealing is that it involves selling directly to users: *R v Shahadat* [2017] EWCA Crim 822, [2017] All ER (D) 153 (Jun).

Culpability demonstrated by offender's role

One or more of these characteristics may demonstrate the offender's role. These lists are not exhaustive.

LEADING role:

- directing or organising buying and selling on a commercial scale;
- substantial links to, and influence on, others in a chain;
- close links to original source;
- expectation of substantial financial gain;
- uses business as cover;
- abuses a position of trust or responsibility, for example prison employee, medical professional.

SIGNIFICANT role:

- operational or management function within a chain;
- involves others in the operation whether by pressure, influence, intimidation or reward;
- motivated by financial or other advantage, whether or not operating alone;
- some awareness and understanding of scale of operation;
- supply, other than by a person in a position of responsibility, to a prisoner for gain without coercion.

LESSER role:

- performs a limited function under direction;
- engaged by pressure, coercion, intimidation;
- involvement through naivety/exploitation;
- no influence on those above in a chain;
- very little, if any, awareness or understanding of the scale of operation;
- if own operation, absence of any financial gain, for example joint purchase for no profit, or sharing minimal quantity between peers on non-commercial basis.

Category of harm

Indicative quantity of drug concerned (upon which the starting point is based):

Category 1

- heroin, cocaine – 5kg;
- ecstasy – 10,000 tablets;
- LSD – 250,000 squares;
- amphetamine – 20kg;
- cannabis – 200kg;
- ketamine – 5kg.

Category 2

- heroin, cocaine – 1kg;
- ecstasy – 2,000 tablets;
- LSD – 25,000 squares;
- amphetamine – 4kg;
- cannabis – 40kg;
- ketamine – 1kg.

Category 3

Where the offence is selling directly to users* ('street dealing'), the starting point is not based on a quantity,

OR

where the offence is supply of drugs in prison by a prison employee, the starting point is not based on a quantity – see shaded box on page 232,

OR

- heroin, cocaine – 150g;
- ecstasy – 300 tablets;
- LSD – 2,500 squares;
- amphetamine – 750g;
- cannabis – 6kg;
- ketamine – 150g.

* Including test purchase officers

Category 4

- heroin, cocaine – 5g;
- ecstasy – 20 tablets;
- LSD – 170 squares;
- amphetamine – 20g;
- cannabis – 100g;
- ketamine – 5g;

OR

where the offence is selling directly to users* ('street dealing') the starting point is not based on quantity – go to category 3.

* Including test purchase officers

STEP TWO
Starting point and category range

Having determined the category, the court should use the corresponding starting point to reach a sentence within the category range below. The starting point applies to all offenders irrespective of plea or previous convictions. The court should then consider further adjustment within the category range for aggravating or mitigating features, set out on page 236. In cases where the offender is regarded as being at the very top of the 'leading' role it may be justifiable for the court to depart from the guideline.

Where the defendant is dependent on or has a propensity to misuse drugs and there is sufficient prospect of success, a community order with a drug rehabilitation requirement under section 209 of the Criminal Justice Act 2003 can be a proper alternative to a short or moderate length custodial sentence.

For **class A** cases, section 110 of the Powers of Criminal Courts (Sentencing) Act 2000 provides that a court should impose a minimum sentence of at least seven years' imprisonment for a third class A trafficking offence except where the court is of the opinion that there are particular circumstances which (a) relate to any of the offences or to the offender; and (b) would make it unjust to do so in all the circumstances.

CLASS A	Leading role	Significant role	Lesser role
Category 1	**Starting point** 14 years' custody **Category range** 12 – 16 years' custody	**Starting point** 10 years' custody **Category range** 9 – 12 years' custody	**Starting point** 7 years' custody **Category range** 6 – 9 years' custody
Category 2	**Starting point** 11 years' custody **Category range** 9 – 13 years' custody	**Starting point** 8 years' custody **Category range** 6 years 6 months' – 10 years' custody	**Starting point** 5 years' custody **Category range** 3 years 6 months' – 7 years' custody
Category 3	**Starting point** 8 years 6 months' custody **Category range** 6 years 6 months' – 10 years' custody	**Starting point** 4 years 6 months' custody **Category range** 3 years 6 months' – 7 years' custody	**Starting point** 3 years' custody **Category range** 2 – 4 years 6 months' custody
Category 4	**Starting point** 5 years 6 months' custody **Category range** 4 years 6 months' – 7 years 6 months' custody	**Starting point** 3 years 6 months' custody **Category range** 2 – 5 years' custody	**Starting point** 18 months' custody **Category range** High level community order – 3 years' custody

CLASS B	Leading role	Significant role	Lesser role
Category 1	**Starting point** 8 years' custody **Category range** 7 – 10 years' custody	**Starting point** 5 years 6 months' custody **Category range** 5 – 7 years' custody	**Starting point** 3 years' custody **Category range** 2 years 6 months' – 5 years' custody
Category 2	**Starting point** 6 years' custody **Category range** 4 years 6 months' – 8 years' custody	**Starting point** 4 years' custody **Category range** 2 years 6 months' – 5 years' custody	**Starting point** 1 year's custody **Category range** 26 weeks' – 3 years' custody

CLASS B	Leading role	Significant role	Lesser role
Category 3	**Starting point**	**Starting point**	**Starting point**
	4 years' custody	1 year's custody	High level community order
	Category range	**Category range**	**Category range**
	2 years 6 months' – 5 years' custody	26 weeks' – 3 years' custody	Low level community order – 26 weeks' custody
Category 4	**Starting point**	**Starting point**	**Starting point**
	18 months' custody	High level community order	Low level community order
	Category range	**Category range**	**Category range**
	26 weeks' – 3 years' custody	Medium level community order – 26 weeks' custody	Band B fine – medium level community order

CLASS C	Leading role	Significant role	Lesser role
Category 1	**Starting point**	**Starting point**	**Starting point**
	5 years' custody	3 years' custody	18 months' custody
	Category range	**Category range**	**Category range**
	4 – 8 years' custody	2 – 5 years' custody	1 – 3 years' custody
Category 2	**Starting point**	**Starting point**	**Starting point**
	3 years 6 months' custody	18 months' custody	26 weeks' custody
	Category range	**Category range**	**Category range**
	2 – 5 years' custody	1 – 3 years' custody	12 weeks' – 18 months' custody
Category 3	**Starting point**	**Starting point**	**Starting point**
	18 months' custody	26 weeks' custody	High level community order
	Category range	**Category range**	**Category range**
	1 – 3 years' custody	12 weeks' – 18 months' custody	Low level community order – 12 weeks' custody
Category 4	**Starting point**	**Starting point**	**Starting point**
	26 weeks' custody	High level community order	Low level community order
	Category range	**Category range**	**Category range**
	High level community order – 18 months' custody	Low level community order – 12 weeks' custody	Band A fine – medium level community order

The table below contains a **non-exhaustive** list of additional factual elements providing the context of the offence and factors relating to the offender. Identify whether any combination of these, or other relevant factors, should result in an upward or downward adjustment from the starting point. In some cases, having considered these factors, it may be appropriate to move outside the identified category range.

For appropriate **class B** and **C** ranges, consider the custody threshold as follows:

- has the custody threshold been passed?
- if so, is it unavoidable that a custodial sentence be imposed?
- if so, can that sentence be suspended?

For appropriate class B and C ranges, the court should also consider the community threshold as follows:

- has the community threshold been passed?

Factors increasing seriousness
Statutory aggravating factors:
Previous convictions, having regard to a) nature of the offence to which conviction relates and relevance to current offence; and b) time elapsed since conviction (see shaded box at page 234 if third drug trafficking conviction)
Offender used or permitted a person under 18 to deliver a controlled drug to a third person
Offender 18 or over supplies or offers to supply a drug on, or in the vicinity of, school premises either when school in use as such or at a time between one hour before and one hour after they are to be used
Offence committed on bail
Other aggravating factors include:
Targeting of any premises intended to locate vulnerable individuals or supply to such individuals and/or supply to those under 18
Exposure of others to more than usual danger, for example drugs cut with harmful substances
Attempts to conceal or dispose of evidence, where not charged separately
Presence of others, especially children and/or non-users
Presence of weapon, where not charged separately
Charged as importation of a very small amount
High purity
Failure to comply with current court orders
Offence committed on licence
Established evidence of community impact
Factors reducing seriousness or reflecting personal mitigation
Involvement due to pressure, intimidation or coercion falling short of duress, except where already taken into account at step 1
Supply only of drug to which offender addicted
Mistaken belief of the offender regarding the type of drug, taking into account the reasonableness of such belief in all the circumstances
Isolated incident
Low purity
No previous convictions or no relevant or recent convictions
Offender's vulnerability was exploited
Remorse
Good character and/or exemplary conduct
Determination and/or demonstration of steps having been taken to address addiction or offending behaviour
Serious medical conditions requiring urgent, intensive or long-term treatment
Age and/or lack of maturity where it affects the responsibility of the offender
Mental disorder or learning disability
Sole or primary carer for dependent relatives

STEP THREE
Consider any factors which indicate a reduction, such as assistance to the prosecution

The court should take into account sections 73 and 74 of the Serious Organised Crime and Police Act 2005 (assistance by defendants: reduction or review of sentence) and any other rule of law by virtue of which an offender may receive a discounted sentence in consequence of assistance given (or offered) to the prosecutor or investigator.

STEP FOUR
Reduction for guilty pleas

The court should take account of any potential reduction for a guilty plea in accordance with section 144 of the Criminal Justice Act 2003 and the *Guilty Plea* guideline.

For class A offences, where a minimum mandatory sentence is imposed under section 110 Powers of Criminal Courts (Sentencing) Act, the discount for an early guilty plea must not exceed 20 per cent.

STEP FIVE
Totality principle

If sentencing an offender for more than one offence, or where the offender is already serving a sentence, consider whether the total sentence is just and proportionate to the offending behaviour.

STEP SIX
Confiscation and ancillary orders

In all cases, the court is required to consider confiscation where the Crown invokes the process or where the court considers it appropriate. It should also consider whether to make ancillary orders.

STEP SEVEN
Reasons

Section 174 of the Criminal Justice Act 2003 imposes a duty to give reasons for, and explain the effect of, the sentence.

STEP EIGHT
Consideration for remand time

(Now obligatory.)

A[26.6]–[26.9] Available sentences (Class A, B and C drugs). See Table A at B[43.1A].

A[26.10]–[26.11] Custodial sentence. See B[15].

A[26.12]–[26.15] "Crack Houses" – Closure orders – S 2 Anti-Social Behaviour Act 2003

Closure orders. Section 1 of the Anti-social Behaviour Act 2003 made provision for the closure of premises associated with the unlawful use of drugs. This and other powers of closure have been replaced and consolidated into a new power to close premises associated with nuisance or disorder. The provisions governing the exercise of this power will be found in ss 76–91 of the Anti-social Behaviour, Crime and Policing Act 2014.

For the closure of premises associated with persistent disorder or nuisance see Part 1A of the Anti-Social Behaviour Act 2003.

(For closure orders for premises used for activities related to certain **sexual offences** see ss 22 and 22 and schedule 2 of the Policing and Crime Act 2009 which added a new Part 2A to the Sexual Offences Act 2003. These provisions came into force on **1 April 2010.**)

Within 48 hours of the serving of a closure notice an application must be made to a magistrates' court. If satisfied that:

(a) the premises have been used for the production or supply of a class 'A' drug;
(b) that use is associated with disorder or serious public nuisance; and
(c) the order is necessary to prevent reoccurrence,

the court can order closure of the premises for a period no longer than 3 months.

An application can be to extend the closure order for up to a further three months pursuant to s 5(4) of the 2003 Act; but a closure order may not exceed a total of six months: s 5(5). The court should simply ask whether it had been proved that an extension was necessary and proportionate to prevent the occurrence of further disorder or nuisance; and if so how long the extension should be (*R (on the application of Smith)v Snaresbrook Crown Court* [2008] EWHC 1282 (Admin)).

Closure order applications are civil proceedings. Although closure order applications should be dealt with as a matter of urgency in *R (on the application of Turner v Highbury Corner Magistrates' Court and Commissioner of the Metropolis (Interested Party)* [2005] EWHC 2568 (Admin), [2006] 1 WLR 220, it was decided that the general power of a magistrates' court to grant an adjournment co-existed with the limited and specific power granted under s 2(6) of the Anti-Social Behaviour Act 2003. Accordingly, an adjournment of more than 14 days could be granted where the court was satisfied that there was a need for such an adjournment consonant with the interests of justice (*Metropolitan Police Comr v Hooper* [2005] EWHC 340 (Admin) explained).

The standard of proof applicable to making an order under s 2(3)(a) and (b) of the 2003 Act was the civil standard of proof, namely on a balance of probabilities (*Chief Constable of Merseyside v Harrison* [2006] EWHC 1106 (Admin), [2006] 3 WLR 171).

For general guidance on disclosure of evidence in s 2 applications and observations on the admissibility of and weight to be accorded to hearsay evidence see *R (on the application of Cleary) v Highbury Corner Magistrates' Court and the Comr of Police of the Metropolis and the Secretary of State for the Home Department* [2006] EWHC 1869 (Admin), (2006) Times, 12 September; and more recently *R (on the application of Errington) v Metropolitan Police Authority* (2007) 171 JP 89.

When applying for a closure order it was not necessary for the police and local authority to demonstrate they had first considered and/or tried other less draconian methods first, so as to comply with the ECHR, article 8. Further, it was not possible to adjust the terms of a closure order to exclude visitors from the premises but to allow an occupier to remain there: *Leary v Chief Constable of the West Midlands Police* [2012] EWHC 639 (Admin), 176 CL&J 143.

On a true construction of the Act, the requirement of s 2(3)(b) of disorder or serious nuisance had to derive from the drug use required by s 2(3)(a). The purpose of the legislation was to grant powers to deal with 'crack houses' and it followed that the disturbance(s) required by s 2(3)(b) had to be linked to the drug use referred to in s 2(3)(a). The Act was intended to deal with a present and continuing situation. An order might be obtained if there was a short hiatus in the disorder, although not if the disorder had permanently ceased. Historical evidence was therefore admissible if relevant to a continuing situation (*Chief Constable of Cumbria Constabulary v Wright* [2006] EWHC 3574 (Admin)). In *Dumble v Metropolitan Police Commissioner* [2009] All ER (D) 66 (Feb) for the purposes of s 2(3)(b) the justices were entitled to consider the ongoing nature of disorder and violence at the appellant's premises including the 'few' incidents which had taken place immediately prior to the making of the application. On the facts, the legitimate aim of preventing crime and disorder was a trump card overriding the appellant's Art 8 ECHR rights.

An offence in contravention of the order is punishable summarily by 6 months' imprisonment or a level 5 fine (ss 2 and 4 of the Anti-Social Behaviour Act 2003).

For the closure of **'noisy premises'** see s 40 of the ABA 2003 at A[84.7] onwards.

A[26.16] **Appeal.** Section 6 of the Anti-Social Behaviour Act 2003 states that an appeal against a decision or order must be brought before the end of the period of 21 days beginning with the day on which the order or decision is made. Section 6(1) has been interpreted to mean that an appellant has 21 days from the date of the order or decision to issue the notice of appeal. Further, there was no power to extend the time for appeal under s 6(2): *Hampshire Police Authority v Smith* [2009] EWHC 174 (Admin), 173 JP 207.

A[26.17] **Costs.** A magistrates' court has jurisdiction to make an award of costs between the parties under s 64 of the Magistrates' Courts Act 1980: *R (on the application of Taylor) v Comr of the Metropolitan Police* [2009] EWHC 264 (Admin), 173 JP 121.

A[26.18] **Community sentence.** See B[9].

A[26.19] **Forfeiture.** See A[25.18].

A[26.20] **Drug trafficking.** For the power of the Crown Court to make a confiscation order in respect of the proceeds of drug trafficking offences, see **B[11]**.

A[27]

Drugs – Cultivation of Cannabis Plant
Drugs – Production of a controlled drug

(Misuse of Drugs Act 1971, s 6(2))
(Misuse of Drugs Act 1971, s 4(2)(a) or (b))

Charge (Cultivation of Cannabis)

A[27.1] On X date at . . . . the accused unlawfully cultivated cannabis

On X date at . . . . unlawfully produced a controlled drug (namely . . . .); or was concerned in the production of a controlled drug (namely . . . .)

Maximum penalty –

6 months' imprisonment and/or fine level 5 (for offences committed on or after 12 March 2015 an unlimited fine). Triable either way.

Crown Court

- Class A: Life imprisonment and unlimited fine
- Class B: 14 years' imprisonment and unlimited fine
- Class C: 14 years' imprisonment and unlimited fine

A[27.2] This offence is subject to s 7 (authorisation of activities otherwise unlawful) and s 28 (proof of lack of knowledge etc to be a defence in proceedings for certain offences.

Mode of trial

A[27.3] See SC Guideline at A[27.4] below. However, a person can be concerned in the production of a controlled drug as a principal offender whether or not he is the actual producer: *R v Dang* [2014] EWCA Crim 348, [2014] 2 Cr App Rep 23.

Legal notes and definitions

A[27.3A] Produce and be concerned in production. 'Produce', where the reference is to producing a controlled drug, means producing it by manufacture, cultivation or any other method, and 'production' has a corresponding meaning: s 37(1) of the Misuse of Drugs Act 1971.

Conversion from one form of a drug to another can amount to production: *R v Russell* (1991) 94 Cr App Rep 351, CA. The preparation of plants so as to discard the parts which are not usable for the drug and to put together those which are amounts to 'production' of cannabis: *R v Harris* [1996] 1 Cr App Rep 369, [1996] Crim LR 36, CA. Making an infusion out of B-Caapi and Chacruna amounts to 'producing' a controlled drug (DMT) by making a 'preparation': *R v Aziz* [2012] EWCA Crim 1063, [2012] Crim LR 801. See further para 5 of Pt 1 (Class A) to Sch 2, post, which provides ' . . . any preparation or other product containing a substance or product for the time being specified in any of the paragraphs 1 to 4 above [is a Class A controlled drug]'.

There must be established some identifiable participation in the process of producing a controlled drug before a person can be convicted: *R v Farr* [1982] Crim LR 745, CA.

Sentencing

SC Sentencing Guideline – Production of a controlled drug

Misuse of Drugs Act 1971 (section 4(2)(a) or (b))

A[27.4] Triable either way unless the defendant could receive the minimum sentence of seven years for a third drug trafficking offence under section 110 Powers of Criminal Courts (Sentencing) Act 2000 in which case the offence is triable only on indictment.

Class A

Maximum: Life imprisonment

Offence range: Community order – 16 years' custody

A class A offence is a drug trafficking offence for the purpose of imposing a minimum sentence under section 110 Powers of Criminal Courts (Sentencing) Act 2000

Class B

Maximum: 14 years' custody

Offence range: Discharge – 10 years' custody

Class C

Maximum: 14 years' custody

Offence range: Discharge – 8 years' custody

Cultivation of cannabis plant

Misuse of Drugs Act 1971 (section 6(2))

Maximum: 14 years' custody

Offence range: Discharge – 10 years' custody

STEP ONE
Determining the offence category

The court should determine the offender's culpability (role) and the harm caused (output or potential output) with reference to the tables below.

In assessing culpability, the sentencer should weigh up all of the factors of the case to determine role. Where there are characteristics present which fall under different role categories, the court should balance these characteristics to reach a fair assessment of the offender's culpability.

In assessing harm, output or potential output is determined by the weight of the product or number of plants/scale of operation. For production offences, purity is not taken into account at step 1 but is dealt with at step 2.

Where the operation is on the most serious and commercial scale, involving a quantity of drugs significantly higher than category 1, sentences of 20 years and above may be appropriate, depending on the role of the offender.

Culpability demonstrated by offender's role

One or more of these characteristics may demonstrate the offender's role. These lists are not exhaustive.

LEADING role:

- directing or organising production on a commercial scale;
- substantial links to, and influence on, others in a chain;
- expectation of substantial financial gain;
- uses business as cover;
- abuses a position of trust or responsibility.

SIGNIFICANT role:

- operational or management function within a chain;
- involves others in the operation whether by pressure, influence, intimidation or reward;
- motivated by financial or other advantage, whether or not operating alone;
- some awareness and understanding of scale of operation.

LESSER role:

- performs a limited function under direction;
- engaged by pressure, coercion, intimidation;
- involvement through naivety/exploitation;
- no influence on those above in a chain;
- very little, if any, awareness or understanding of the scale of operation;
- if own operation, solely for own use (considering reasonableness of account in all the circumstances).

Category of harm

Indicative output or potential output (upon which the starting point is based):

Category 1

- heroin, cocaine – 5kg;
- ecstasy – 10,000 tablets;
- LSD – 250,000 tablets;
- amphetamine – 20kg;
- cannabis – operation capable of producing industrial quantities for commercial use;
- ketamine – 5kg.

Category 2

- heroin, cocaine – 1kg;
- ecstasy – 2,000 tablets;
- LSD – 25,000 squares;
- amphetamine – 4kg;
- cannabis – operation capable of producing significant quantities for commercial use;
- ketamine – 1kg.

Category 3

- heroin, cocaine – 150g;
- ecstasy – 300 tablets;
- LSD – 2,500 squares;
- amphetamine – 750g;
- cannabis – 28 plants;*
- ketamine – 150g.

Category 4

- heroin, cocaine – 5g;
- ecstasy – 20 tablets;
- LSD – 170 squares;
- amphetamine – 20g;
- cannabis – 9 plants (domestic operation);*
- ketamine – 5g.

* With assumed yield of 40g per plant

STEP TWO
Starting point and category range

Having determined the category, the court should use the corresponding starting point to reach a sentence within the category range below. The starting point applies to all offenders irrespective of plea or previous convictions. The court should then consider further adjustment within the category range for aggravating or mitigating features, set out on page 243. In cases where the offender is regarded as being at the very top of the 'leading' role it may be justifiable for the court to depart from the guideline.

Where the defendant is dependent on or has a propensity to misuse drugs and there is sufficient prospect of success, a community order with a drug rehabilitation requirement under section 209 of the Criminal Justice Act 2003 can be a proper alternative to a short or moderate length custodial sentence.

For **class A** cases, section 110 of the Powers of Criminal Courts (Sentencing) Act 2000 provides that a court should impose a minimum sentence of at least seven years' imprisonment for a third class A trafficking offence except where the court is of the opinion that there are particular circumstances which (a) relate to any of the offences or to the offender; and (b) would make it unjust to do so in all the circumstances.

CLASS A	Leading role	Significant role	Lesser role
	Starting point	**Starting point**	**Starting point**
	14 years' custody	10 years' custody	7 years' custody
	Category range	**Category range**	**Category range**
	12 – 16 years' custody	9 – 12 years' custody	6 – 9 years' custody
Category 2	**Starting point**	**Starting point**	**Starting point**
	11 years' custody	8 years' custody	5 years' custody
	Category range	**Category range**	**Category range**
	9 – 13 years' custody	6 years 6 months' – 10 years' custody	3 years 6 months' – 7 years' custody
Category 3	**Starting point**	**Starting point**	**Starting point**
	8 years 6 months' custody	5 years' custody	3 years 6 months' custody
	Category range	**Category range**	**Category range**
	6 years 6 months' – 10 years' custody	3 years 6 months' – 7 years' custody	2 – 5 years' custody
Category 4	**Starting point**	**Starting point**	**Starting point**
	5 years 6 months' custody	3 years 6 months' custody	18 months' custody
	Category range	**Category range**	**Category range**
	4 years 6 months' – 7 years 6 months' custody	2 – 5 years' custody	High level community order – 3 years' custody

CLASS B	Leading role	Significant role	Lesser role
Category 1	**Starting point**	**Starting point**	**Starting point**
	8 years' custody	5 years 6 months' custody	3 years' custody
	Category range	**Category range**	**Category range**
	7 – 10 years' custody	5 – 7 years' custody	2 years 6 months' – 5 years' custody
Category 2	**Starting point**	**Starting point**	**Starting point**
	6 years' custody	4 years' custody	1 year's custody
	Category range	**Category range**	**Category range**
	4 years 6 months' – 8 years' custody	2 years 6 months' – 5 years' custody	26 weeks' – 3 years' custody
Category 3	**Starting point**	**Starting point**	**Starting point**
	4 years' custody	1 year's custody	High level community order
	Category range	**Category range**	**Category range**
	2 years 6 months' – 5 years' custody	26 weeks' – 3 years' custody	Low level community order – 26 weeks' custody
Category 4	**Starting point**	**Starting point**	**Starting point**
	1 year's custody	High level community order	Band C fine
	Category range	**Category range**	**Category range**
	High level community order – 3 years' custody	Medium level community order – 26 weeks' custody	Discharge – medium level community order

CLASS C	Leading role	Significant role	Lesser role
Category 1	**Starting point**	**Starting point**	**Starting point**
	5 years' custody	3 years' custody	18 months' custody
	Category range	**Category range**	**Category range**
	4 – 8 years' custody	2 – 5 years' custody	1 – 3 years' custody
Category 2	**Starting point**	**Starting point**	**Starting point**
	3 years 6 months' custody	18 months' custody	26 weeks' custody
	Category range	**Category range**	**Category range**
	2 – 5 years' custody	1 – 3 years' custody	High level community order – 18 months' custody
Category 3	**Starting point**	**Starting point**	**Starting point**
	18 months' custody	26 weeks' custody	High level community order
	Category range	**Category range**	**Category range**
	1 – 3 years' custody	High level community order – 18 months' custody	Low level community order – 12 weeks' custody
Category 4	**Starting point**	**Starting point**	**Starting point**
	26 weeks' custody	High level community order	Band C fine
	Category range	**Category range**	**Category range**

CLASS C	Leading role	Significant role	Lesser role
	High level community order – 18 months' custody	Low level community order – 12 weeks' custody	Discharge – medium level community order

The table below contains a **non-exhaustive** list of additional factual elements providing the context of the offence and factors relating to the offender. Identify whether any combination of these, or other relevant factors, should result in an upward or downward adjustment from the starting point. In some cases, having considered these factors, it may be appropriate to move outside the identified category range.

Where appropriate, consider the custody threshold as follows:

- has the custody threshold been passed?
- if so, is it unavoidable that a custodial sentence be imposed?
- if so, can that sentence be suspended?

Where appropriate, the court should also consider the community threshold as follows:

- has the community threshold been passed?

Factors increasing seriousness
Statutory aggravating factors:
Previous convictions, having regard to a) nature of the offence to which conviction relates and relevance to current offence; and b) time elapsed since conviction (see shaded box at page 241 if third drug trafficking conviction)
Offence committed on bail
Other aggravating factors include:
Nature of any likely supply
Level of any profit element
Use of premises accompanied by unlawful access to electricity/other utility supply of others
Ongoing/large scale operation as evidenced by presence and nature of specialist equipment
Exposure of others to more than usual danger, for example drugs cut with harmful substances
Attempts to conceal or dispose of evidence, where not charged separately
Presence of others, especially children and/or non-users
Presence of weapon, where not charged separately
High purity or high potential yield
Failure to comply with current court orders
Offence committed on licence
Established evidence of community impact
Factors reducing seriousness or reflecting personal mitigation
Involvement due to pressure, intimidation or coercion falling short of duress, except where already taken into account at step 1
Isolated incident
Low purity
No previous convictions **or** no relevant or recent convictions
Offender's vulnerability was exploited
Remorse
Good character and/or exemplary conduct

Determination and/or demonstration of steps having been taken to address addiction or offending behaviour
Serious medical conditions requiring urgent, intensive or long-term treatment
Age and/or lack of maturity where it affects the responsibility of the offender
Mental disorder or learning disability
Sole or primary carer for dependent relatives

STEP THREE
Consider any factors which indicate a reduction, such as assistance to the prosecution

The court should take into account sections 73 and 74 of the Serious Organised Crime and Police Act 2005 (assistance by defendants: reduction or review of sentence) and any other rule of law by virtue of which an offender may receive a discounted sentence in consequence of assistance given (or offered) to the prosecutor or investigator.

STEP FOUR
Reduction for guilty pleas

The court should take account of any potential reduction for a guilty plea in accordance with section 144 of the Criminal Justice Act 2003 and the *Guilty Plea* guideline.

For class A offences, where a minimum mandatory sentence is imposed under section 110 Powers of Criminal Courts (Sentencing) Act, the discount for an early guilty plea must not exceed 20 per cent.

STEP FIVE
Totality principle

If sentencing an offender for more than one offence, or where the offender is already serving a sentence, consider whether the total sentence is just and proportionate to the offending behaviour.

STEP SIX
Confiscation and ancillary orders

In all cases, the court is required to consider confiscation where the Crown invokes the process or where the court considers it appropriate. It should also consider whether to make ancillary orders.

STEP SEVEN
Reasons

Section 174 of the Criminal Justice Act 2003 imposes a duty to give reasons for, and explain the effect of, the sentence.

STEP EIGHT
Consideration for remand time

(Now obligatory.)

A[27A]

Drugs – Permitting premises to be used

(Misuse of Drugs Act 1971, s 8)

Charge (Drugs – Permitting premises to be used)

A[27A.1] **Being the occupier or concerned in the management of premises at . . . . on X date knowingly permits or suffers the following activity:**

(a) **producing or attempting to produce a controlled drug in contravention of section 4(1);**
(b) **supplying or attempting to supply a controlled drug to another in contravention of section 4(1), or offering to supply a controlled drug in contravention of section 4(1);**
(c) **preparing opium for smoking;**
(d) **smoking cannabis, cannabis resin or prepared opium.**

Maximum penalty – 6 months' imprisonment and/or fine level 5 (for offences committed on or after 12 March 2015 an unlimited fine). Triable either way.

Crown Court

– Class A: 14 years' imprisonment and unlimited fine
– Class B: 14 years' imprisonment and unlimited fine
– Class C: 14 years' imprisonment and unlimited fine

Legal notes and definitions

A[27A.2] Occupier, concerned in the management of premises and knowingly permits. 'Occupier' includes anyone in occupation of premises whose degree of occupation was such that he could exclude anyone likely to commit an offence under the Act: *R v Tao* [1977] QB 141, [1976] 3 All ER 65, 140 JP 596. The fact that one person can be identified as an occupier, even if enjoying a legal title or tenancy, does not preclude the application of that description to another person: *R v Coid* [1998] Crim LR 199.

If a person is exercising control over premises, running them or managing them, the fact that he is not lawfully in possession of them is irrelevant: *R v Josephs* and *R v Christie* (1977) 65 Cr App Rep 253.

To establish the offence of permitting the prosecution must prove: (i) knowledge, actual or by closing ones eyes to the obvious, that dealing in controlled drugs is taking place; and (ii) unwillingness to prevent it, which can be inferred from failure to take steps readily available to prevent it. A defendant's belief that he has taken reasonable steps is irrelevant; it is not for the defendant to judge his own conduct: *R v Brock* (1991) 165 JP 331, CA. The commission of the offence requires the actual smoking of cannabis; mere tentative permission to smoke cannabis is insufficient: *R v Auguste* [2003] EWCA Crim 3929, [2004] 4 All ER 373, [2004] 1 WLR 917, [2004] Cr App Rep 173.

Mode of trial

A[27A.3] See SC Guideline at A[27A.4] below.

Sentencing
SC Sentencing Guideline – Permitting premises to be used

Misuse of Drugs Act 1971 (section 8)

A[27A.4] Triable either way unless the defendant could receive the minimum sentence of seven years for a third drug trafficking offence under section 110 Powers of Criminal Courts (Sentencing) Act 2000 in which case the offence is triable only on indictment.

Class A

Maximum: 14 years' custody

Offence range: Community order – 4 years' custody

A class A offence is a drug trafficking offence for the purpose of imposing a minimum sentence under section 110 Powers of Criminal Courts (Sentencing) Act 2000

Class B

Maximum: 14 years' custody

Offence range: Fine – 18 months' custody

Class C

Maximum: 14 years' custody

Offence range: Discharge – 26 weeks' custody

STEP ONE
Determining the offence category

The court should determine the offender's culpability and the harm caused (extent of the activity and/or the quantity of drugs) with reference to the table below.

In assessing harm, quantity is determined by the weight of the product. Purity is not taken into account at step 1 but is dealt with at step 2.

Category 1	Higher culpability and greater harm
Category 2	Lower culpability and greater harm; or higher culpability and lesser harm
Category 3	Lower culpability and lesser harm

Factors indicating culpability (non-exhaustive)

Higher culpability:

Permits premises to be used primarily for drug activity, for example crack house

Permits use in expectation of substantial financial gain

Uses legitimate business premises to aid and/or conceal illegal activity, for example public house or club

Lower culpability:

Permits use for limited or no financial gain

No active role in any supply taking place

Involvement through naivety

Factors indicating harm (non-exhaustive)

Greater harm:

Regular drug-related activity

Higher quantity of drugs, for example:

- heroin, cocaine – more than 5g;
- cannabis – more than 50g.

Lesser harm:

Infrequent drug-related activity

Lower quantity of drugs, for example:

- heroin, cocaine – up to 5g;
- cannabis – up to 50g.

STEP TWO
Starting point and category range

Having determined the category, the court should use the table below to identify the corresponding starting point to reach a sentence within the category range. The starting point applies to all offenders irrespective of plea or previous convictions. The court should then consider further adjustment within the category range for aggravating or mitigating features, set out over the page.

Where the defendant is dependent on or has a propensity to misuse drugs and there is sufficient prospect of success, a community order with a drug rehabilitation requirement under section 209 of the Criminal Justice Act 2003 can be a proper alternative to a short or moderate length custodial sentence.

For class A cases, section 110 of the Powers of Criminal Courts (Sentencing) Act 2000 provides that a court should impose a minimum sentence of at least seven years' imprisonment for a third class A trafficking offence except where the court is of the opinion that there are particular circumstances which (a) relate to any of the offences or to the offender; and (b) would make it unjust to do so in all the circumstances.

CLASS A

Offence category	Starting point (applicable to all offenders)	Category range (applicable to all offenders)
Category 1	2 years 6 months' custody	18 months' – 4 years' custody
Category 2	36 weeks' custody	High level community order – 18 months' custody
Category 3	Medium level community order	Low level community order – high level community order

CLASS B

Offence category	Starting point (applicable to all offenders)	Category range (applicable to all offenders)
Category 1	1 year's custody	26 weeks' – 18 months' custody
Category 2	High level community order	Low level community order – 26 weeks' custody
Category 3	Band C fine	Band A fine – low level community order

CLASS C

Offence category	Starting point (applicable to all offenders)	Category range (applicable to all offenders)
Category 1	12 weeks' custody	High level community order – 26 weeks' custody*
Category 2	Low level community order	Band C fine – high level community order
Category 3	Band A fine	Discharge – band C fine

*When tried summarily, the maximum penalty is 12 weeks' custody.

The table below contains a **non-exhaustive** list of additional factual elements providing the context of the offence and factors relating to the offender. Identify whether any combination of these, or other relevant factors, should result in an upward or downward adjustment from the starting point. In some cases, having considered these factors, it may be appropriate to move outside the identified category range.

Where appropriate, consider the custody threshold as follows:

- has the custody threshold been passed?
- if so, is it unavoidable that a custodial sentence be imposed?
- if so, can that sentence be suspended?

Where appropriate, the court should also consider the community threshold as follows:

- has the community threshold been passed?

Factors increasing seriousness
Statutory aggravating factors:
Previous convictions, having regard to a) nature of the offence to which conviction relates and relevance to current offence; and b) time elapsed since conviction (see shaded box at page 247 if third drug trafficking conviction)
Offence committed on bail
Other aggravating factors include:
Length of time over which premises used for drug activity
Volume of drug activity permitted
Premises adapted to facilitate drug activity
Location of premises, for example proximity to school
Attempts to conceal or dispose of evidence, where not charged separately
Presence of others, especially children and/or non-users
High purity
Presence of weapons, where not charged separately
Failure to comply with current court orders
Offence committed on licence
Established evidence of community impact
Factors reducing seriousness or reflecting personal mitigation
Involvement due to pressure, intimidation or coercion falling short of duress
Isolated incident
Low purity
No previous convictions or no relevant or recent convictions
Offender's vulnerability was exploited

Remorse
Good character and/or exemplary conduct
Determination and/or demonstration of steps having been taken to address addiction or offending behaviour
Serious medical conditions requiring urgent, intensive or long-term treatment
Age and/or lack of maturity where it affects the responsibility of the offender
Mental disorder or learning disability
Sole or primary carer for dependent relatives

STEP THREE
Consider any factors which indicate a reduction, such as assistance to the prosecution

The court should take into account sections 73 and 74 of the Serious Organised Crime and Police Act 2005 (assistance by defendants: reduction or review of sentence) and any other rule of law by virtue of which an offender may receive a discounted sentence in consequence of assistance given (or offered) to the prosecutor or investigator.

STEP FOUR
Reduction for guilty pleas

The court should take account of any potential reduction for a guilty plea in accordance with section 144 of the Criminal Justice Act 2003 and the *Guilty Plea* guideline.

For class A offences, where a minimum mandatory sentence is imposed under section 110 Powers of Criminal Courts (Sentencing) Act, the discount for an early guilty plea must not exceed 20 per cent.

STEP FIVE
Totality principle

If sentencing an offender for more than one offence or where the offender is already serving a sentence, consider whether the total sentence is just and proportionate to the offending behaviour.

STEP SIX
Confiscation and ancillary orders

In all cases, the court is required to consider confiscation where the Crown invokes the process or where the court considers it appropriate. It should also consider whether to make ancillary orders.

STEP SEVEN
Reasons

Section 174 of the Criminal Justice Act 2003 imposes a duty to give reasons for, and explain the effect of, the sentence.

STEP EIGHT
Consideration for remand time

(Now obligatory.)

A[27B]

Fraudulent evasion of a prohibition by bringing into or taking out of the UK a controlled drug

(Misuse of Drugs Act 1971, section 3)
(Customs and Excise Management Act 1979, section 170)

Charge (Controlled drug: fraudulent evasion of prohibition)

A[27B.1] **A on the . . . . day of . . . . was knowingly concealed in concealing goods, that is to say a quantity of a controlled drug, namely . . . with intent to evade the prohibition on importation of the said goods then in force pursuant to section 3 of the Misuse of Drugs Act 1971**

Maximum penalty – Three times the value of the goods or £20,000 (for offences committed on or after 12 March 2015 - for prior offences £5,000) fine whichever is the greater and 6 months. Triable either way.

Crown Court – 7 years' imprisonment and unlimited fine.

A[27B.2] **Knowingly concerned.** See para A[4.5], above, for detailed consideration of the meaning of 'knowingly concerned'.

Mode of trial

A[27B.3] See SC Guideline at **A[27B.4]** below.

Sentencing
SC Sentencing Guideline – Fraudulent evasion of a prohibition by bringing into or taking out of the UK a controlled drug

Misuse of Drugs Act 1971 (section 3)
Customs and Excise Management Act 1979
(section 170(2))

A[27B.4] **Triable either way unless the defendant could receive the minimum sentence of seven years for a third drug trafficking offence under section 110 Powers of Criminal Courts (Sentencing) Act 2000 in which case the offence is triable only on indictment.**

Class A

Maximum: Life imprisonment

Offence range: 3 years 6 months' – 16 years' custody

A class A offence is a drug trafficking offence for the purpose of imposing a minimum sentence under section 110 Powers of Criminal Courts (Sentencing) Act 2000

Class B

Maximum: 14 years' custody and/or unlimited fine

Offence range: 12 weeks' – 10 years' custody

Class C

Maximum: 14 years' custody and/or unlimited fine

Offence range: Community order – 8 years' custody

STEP ONE
Determining the offence category

The court should determine the offender's culpability (role) and the harm caused (quantity) with reference to the tables below.

In assessing culpability, the sentencer should weigh up all the factors of the case to determine role. Where there are characteristics present which fall under different role categories, the court should balance these characteristics to reach a fair assessment of the offender's culpability.

In assessing harm, quantity is determined by the weight of the product. Purity is not taken into account at step 1 but is dealt with at step 2.

Where the operation is on the most serious and commercial scale, involving a quantity of drugs significantly higher than category 1, sentences of 20 years and above may be appropriate, depending on the role of the offender.

Culpability demonstrated by offender's role

One or more of these characteristics may demonstrate the offender's role. These lists are not exhaustive.

LEADING role:

- directing or organising buying and selling on a commercial scale;
- substantial links to, and influence on, others in a chain;
- close links to original source;
- expectation of substantial financial gain;
- uses business as cover;
- abuses a position of trust or responsibility.

SIGNIFICANT role:

- operational or management function within a chain;
- involves others in the operation whether by pressure, influence, intimidation or reward;
- motivated by financial or other advantage, whether or not operating alone;
- some awareness and understanding of scale of operation.

LESSER role:

- performs a limited function under direction;
- engaged by pressure, coercion, intimidation;
- involvement through naivety/exploitation;
- no influence on those above in a chain;
- very little, if any, awareness or understanding of the scale of operation;
- if own operation, solely for own use (considering reasonableness of account in all the circumstances).

Category of harm

Indicative quantity of drug concerned (upon which the starting point is based):

Category 1

- heroin, cocaine – 5kg;
- ecstasy – 10,000 tablets;

- LSD – 250,000 squares;
- amphetamine – 20kg;
- cannabis – 200kg;
- ketamine – 5kg.

Category 2

- heroin, cocaine – 1kg;
- ecstasy – 2,000 tablets;
- LSD – 25,000 squares;
- amphetamine – 4kg;
- cannabis – 40kg;
- ketamine – 1kg.

Category 3

- heroin, cocaine – 150g;
- ecstasy – 300 tablets;
- LSD – 2,500 squares;
- amphetamine – 750g;
- cannabis – 6kg;
- ketamine – 150g.

Category 4

- heroin, cocaine – 5g;
- ecstasy – 20 tablets;
- LSD – 170 squares;
- amphetamine – 20g;
- cannabis – 100g;
- ketamine – 5g.

STEP TWO
Starting point and category range

Having determined the category, the court should use the corresponding starting point to reach a sentence within the category range below. The starting point applies to all offenders irrespective of plea or previous convictions. The court should then consider further adjustment within the category range for aggravating or mitigating features, set out over the page. In cases where the offender is regarded as being at the very top of the 'leading' role it may be justifiable for the court to depart from the guideline.

Where the defendant is dependent on or has a propensity to misuse drugs and there is sufficient prospect of success, a community order with a drug rehabilitation requirement under section 209 of the Criminal Justice Act 2003 can be a proper alternative to a short or moderate length custodial sentence.

For class A cases, section 110 of the Powers of Criminal Courts (Sentencing) Act 2000 provides that a court should impose a minimum sentence of at least seven years' imprisonment for a third class A trafficking offence except where the court is of the opinion that there are particular circumstances which (a) relate to any of the offences or to the offender; and (b) would make it unjust to do so in all the circumstances.

CLASS A	Leading role	Significant role	Lesser role
Category 1	Starting point	Starting point	Starting point
	14 years' custody	10 years' custody	8 years' custody
	Category range	Category range	Category range
	12 – 16 years' custody	9 – 12 years' custody	6 – 9 years' custody
Category 2	Starting point	Starting point	Starting point
	11 years' custody	8 years' custody	6 years' custody

CLASS A	Leading role	Significant role	Lesser role
	Category range	Category range	Category range
	9 – 13 years' custody	6 years 6 months' – 10 years' custody	5 – 7 years' custody
Category 3	Starting point	Starting point	Starting point
	8 years 6 months' custody	6 years 6 months' – 10 years' custody	4 years 6 months' custody
	Category range	Category range	Category range
	6 years' custody	5 – 7 years' custody	3 years 6 months' – 5 years' custody
Category 4	Where the quantity falls below the indicative amount set out for category 4 on the previous page, first identify the role for the importation offence, then refer to the starting point and ranges for possession or supply offences, depending on intent. Where the quantity is significantly larger than the indicative amounts for category 4 but below category 3 amounts, refer to the category 3 ranges above.		

CLASS B	Leading role	Significant role	Lesser role
Category 1	Starting point	Starting point	Starting point
	8 years' custody	5 years 6 months' custody	4 years' custody
	Category range	Category range	Category range
	7 – 10 years' custody	5 – 7 years' custody	2 years 6 months' – 5 years' custody
Category 2	Starting point	Starting point	Starting point
	6 years' custody	4 years' custody	2 years' custody
	Category range	Category range	Category range
	4 years 6 months' – 8 years' custody	2 years 6 months' – 5 years' custody	18 months' – 3 years' custody
Category 3	Starting point	Starting point	Starting point
	4 years' custody	2 years' custody	1 year's custody
	Category range	Category range	Category range
	2 years 6 months' – 5 years' custody	18 months' – 3 years' custody	12 weeks' – 18 months' custody
Category 4	Where the quantity falls below the indicative amount set out for category 4 on the previous page, first identify the role for the importation offence, then refer to the starting point and ranges for possession or supply offences, depending on intent. Where the quantity is significantly larger than the indicative amounts for category 4 but below category 3 amounts, refer to the category 3 ranges above.		

CLASS C	Leading role	Significant role	Lesser role
Category 1	Starting point	Starting point	Starting point
	5 years' custody	3 years' custody	18 months' custody
	Category range	Category range	Category range
	4 – 8 years' custody	2 – 5 years' custody	1 – 3 years' custody
Category 2	Starting point	Starting point	Starting point
	3 years 6 months' custody	18 months' custody	26 weeks' custody

CLASS C	Leading role	Significant role	Lesser role
	Category range	Category range	Category range
	2 – 5 years' custody	1 – 3 years' custody	12 weeks' – 18 months' custody
Category 3	Starting point	Starting point	Starting point
	18 months' custody	26 weeks' custody	High level community order
	Category range	Category range	Category range
	1 – 3 years' custody	12 weeks' – 18 months' custody	Medium level community order – 12 weeks' custody
Category 4	Where the quantity falls below the indicative amount set out for category 4 on the previous page, first identify the role for the importation offence, then referto the starting point and ranges for possession or supply offences, depending on intent. Where the quantity is significantly larger than the indicative amounts for category 4 but below category 3 amounts, refer to the category 3 ranges above.		

The table below contains a **non-exhaustive** list of additional factual elements providing the context of the offence and factors relating to the offender. Identify whether any combination of these, or other relevant factors, should result in an upward or downward adjustment from the starting point. In some cases, having considered these factors, it may be appropriate to move outside the identified category range.

For appropriate **class C** ranges, consider the custody threshold as follows:

- has the custody threshold been passed?
- if so, is it unavoidable that a custodial sentence be imposed?
- if so, can that sentence be suspended?

Factors increasing seriousness
Statutory aggravating factors:
Previous convictions, having regard to a) nature of the offence to which conviction relates and relevance to current offence; and b) time elapsed since conviction
Offender used or permitted a person under 18 to deliver a controlled drug to a third person
Offence committed on bail
Other aggravating factors include:
Sophisticated nature of concealment and/or attempts to avoid detection
Attempts to conceal or dispose of evidence, where not charged separately
Exposure of others to more than usual danger, for example drugs cut with harmful substances
Presence of weapon, where not charged separately
High purity
Failure to comply with current court orders
Offence committed on licence
Factors reducing seriousness or reflecting personal mitigation
Lack of sophistication as to nature of concealment
Involvement due to pressure, intimidation or coercion falling short of duress, except where already taken into account at step 1

Mistaken belief of the offender regarding the type of drug, taking into account the reasonableness of such belief in all the circumstances
Isolated incident
Low purity
No previous convictions or no relevant or recent convictions
Offender's vulnerability was exploited
Remorse
Good character and/or exemplary conduct
Determination and/or demonstration of steps having been taken to address addiction or offending behaviour
Serious medical conditions requiring urgent, intensive or long-term treatment
Age and/or lack of maturity where it affects the responsibility of the offender
Mental disorder or learning disability
Sole or primary carer for dependent relatives

STEP THREE
Consider any factors which indicate a reduction, such as assistance to the prosecution

The court should take into account sections 73 and 74 of the Serious Organised Crime and Police Act 2005 (assistance by defendants: reduction or review of sentence) and any other rule of law by virtue of which an offender may receive a discounted sentence in consequence of assistance given (or offered) to the prosecutor or investigator.

STEP FOUR
Reduction for guilty pleas

The court should take account of any potential reduction for a guilty plea in accordance with section 144 of the Criminal Justice Act 2003 and the *Guilty Plea* guideline.

For class A offences, where a minimum mandatory sentence is imposed under section 110 Powers of Criminal Courts (Sentencing) Act, the discount for an early guilty plea must not exceed 20 per cent.

STEP FIVE
Totality principle

If sentencing an offender for more than one offence, or where the offender is already serving a sentence, consider whether the total sentence is just and proportionate to the offending behaviour.

STEP SIX
Confiscation and ancillary orders

In all cases, the court is required to consider confiscation where the Crown invokes the process or where the court considers it appropriate. It should also consider whether to make ancillary orders.

STEP SEVEN
Reasons

Section 174 of the Criminal Justice Act 2003 imposes a duty to give reasons for, and explain the effect of, the sentence.

STEP EIGHT
Consideration for remand time

(Now obligatory.)

A[28] Drunkenness

Charges (Drunkenness)

A[28.1] **1 Being found drunk in any highway, public place, or on licensed premises**

Licensing Act 1872, s 12

Maximum penalty – Fine level 2.

A[28.2] **2 In a public place namely [. . . . .] was guilty while drunk of disorderly behaviour**

Criminal Justice Act 1967, s 91

Maximum penalty – Fine level 3.

NB: A fixed penalty of £80 is available

Legal notes and definitions

A[28.3] **Found.** Means 'ascertained to be', not 'discovered'.

Lawfulness of arrest.

Police were called to a disturbance in a private garden at 4am. A police officer led the defendant by the arm out of the garden onto a public path. The defendant continued to disturb the peace and was arrested. Placing the events in context and taking a common sense approach, the officer, in acting as he had done, had acted in conformity with the general accepted standards of conduct. A conviction for drunk and disorderly was upheld (*McMillan v Crown Prosecution Service* [2008] EWHC 1457 (Admin), [2008] All ER (D) 142 (May)).

A[28.4] **Drunk.** Typical evidence of drunkenness is strong smell of drink, falling over, swaying, stumbling, showing evidence of a lack of co-ordination, slurred thick speech, rapid pulse, redness in the face, glazed expression, drowsiness or semi-coma and no evidence of any other cause for these symptoms. A person exhibiting these symptoms as a result of 'glue sniffing' is not drunk for the purposes of this offence or the offence of being drunk and disorderly.

The offence is constituted by the state of drunkenness. The inability of the defendant to take care of himself may permit a constable to arrest the defendant. On a charge of being drunk and disorderly it is the disorderly behaviour that normally provides the trigger for an arrest without warrant (*H v DPP* [2005] EWHC 2459 (Admin), 170 JP 4).

A[28.5] **Disorderly.** The term 'drunk and disorderly' should be given its natural and ordinary meaning. It was a question of fact and degree whether or not the accused had exhibited 'disorderly behaviour' (*Carroll v DPP* [2009] All ER (D) 35 (Mar), 173 JP 285).

A[28.6] **Public place.** Includes buildings and any place to which the public has access whether on payment or otherwise, as well as buses or taxis. The entrance hall of a block of flats where admission was controlled by an intercom and a security lock was not a public place (*Williams v DPP* [1992] Crim LR 503).

A[28.7] **'Licensed premises'.** Means premises in respect of which a premises licence has effect: Licensing Act 2003, s 193. A licensee cannot be convicted of being found drunk on his own licensed premises after the house has closed because the premises are then his private place: *Lester v Torrens* (1877) 2 QBD 403, 41 JP 821.

Sentencing

SC Guideline – Drunk and disorderly in a public place

A[28.8] NB: There is no published guideline for being drunk in a highway. Consider whether a fine or discharge is appropriate?

Drunk and disorderly in a public place (Revised 2017)

A[28.9]

Criminal Justice Act 1967, s 91

Effective from: 24 April 2017

Triable only summarily:
Maximum: Level 3 fine

Offence range: Conditional discharge–Band C fine

STEPS 1 and 2
Determining the offence seriousness
The starting point applies to all offenders irrespective of plea or previous convictions.

Starting Point	Range
Band A fine	Conditional discharge–Band C fine

The court should then consider adjustment for any aggravating or mitigating factors. The following is a **non-exhaustive** list of additional factual elements providing the context of the offence and factors relating to the offender. Identify whether any combination of these, or other relevant factors, should result in an upward or downward adjustment from the sentence arrived at so far.

Factors increasing seriousness

Statutory aggravating factors:

- Previous convictions, having regard to a) the **nature** of the offence to which the conviction relates and its **relevance** to the current offence; and b) the **time** that has elapsed since the conviction
- Offence committed whilst on bail
- Offence motivated by, or demonstrating hostility based on any of the following characteristics or presumed characteristics of the victim: religion, race, disability, sexual orientation or transgender identity

Other aggravating factors:

- Substantial disturbance caused
- Offence ties up disproportionate police resource
- Disregard of earlier warning regarding conduct
- Failure to comply with current court orders
- Offence committed on licence or post sentence supervision
- Location of the offence
- Timing of the offence
- Offence committed against those working in the public sector or providing a service to the public
- Presence of others including, especially children or vulnerable people

Factors reducing seriousness or reflecting personal mitigation

- Minimal disturbance caused
- No previous convictions or no relevant/recent convictions
- Remorse
- Good character and/or exemplary conduct
- Age and/or lack of maturity where it affects the responsibility of the offender
- Mental disorder or learning disability

STEP 3
Consider any factors which indicate a reduction, such as assistance to the prosecution

The court should take into account sections 73 and 74 of the Serious Organised Crime and Police Act 2005 (assistance by defendants: reduction or review of sentence) and any other rule of law by virtue of which an offender may receive a discounted sentence in consequence of assistance given (or offered) to the prosecutor or investigator.

STEP 4
Reduction for guilty pleas

The court should take account of any potential reduction for a guilty plea in accordance with section 144 of the Criminal Justice Act 2003 and the *Guilty Plea* guideline.

STEP 5
Totality principle

If sentencing an offender for more than one offence, or where the offender is already serving a sentence, consider whether the total sentence is just and proportionate to the overall offending behaviour in accordance with the *Offences Taken into Consideration and Totality* guideline.

STEP 6
Compensation and ancillary orders

In all cases, the court should consider whether to make compensation and/or other ancillary orders, including a football banning order (where appropriate).

STEP 7
Reasons

Section 174 of the Criminal Justice Act 2003 imposes a duty to give reasons for, and explain the effect of, the sentence.

A[29]

Exploitation of prostitution

Charges (Exploitation of prostitution)

A[29.1] **1. Intentionally causes or incites another person to become a prostitute in any part of the world, and does so for or in the expectation of gain for himself or a third person.**

Sexual Offences Act 2003, s 52.

Maximum penalty – 6 months' imprisonment and/or fine level 5 (for offences committed on or after 12 March 2015 an unlimited fine). Triable either way.

Specified sexual offence under Sch 15, Part 2, CJA 2003.

Crown Court – 7 years' imprisonment or an unlimited fine.

NB: A new s 51A of the 2003 Act has been added by the Policing and Crime Act 2009. From **1 April 2010** this makes it an offence for a person in a street or public place to solicit another (B) for the purposes of obtaining B's sexual services as a prostitute. References to a person is a street or public place include a person in a vehicle in a street or public place. The offence is a summary only offence carrying a maximum level 3 fine.

A[29.2] **2. Intentionally controls any of the activities of another person relating to that person's prostitution in any part of the world, and does so for or in the expectation of gain for himself or a third person.**

Sexual Offences Act 2003, s 53.

Maximum penalty – 6 months' imprisonment and/or fine level 5 (for offences committed on or after 12 March 2015 an unlimited fine). Triable either way.

Specified sexual offence under Sch 15, Part 2, CJA 2003.

Crown Court – 7 years' imprisonment or an unlimited fine.

NB: A new s 53A of the 2003 Act has been added by the Policing and Crime Act 2009. From **1 April 2010** this makes it an offence to pay for the services of a prostitute subjected to force etc. The offence is a summary only offence carrying a maximum level 3 fine.

A[29.2A] For the purposes of the offences under ss 52, 53 and 53A,

'gain' means:

(a) any financial advantage, including the discharge of an obligation to pay or the provision of goods or services (including sexual services) gratuitously or at a discount; or

(b) the goodwill of any person which is or appears likely, in time, to bring financial advantage;

'prostitute' means a person (A) who, on at least one occasion and whether or not compelled to do so, offers or provides sexual services to another person in return for payment or a promise of payment to A or a third person; and

'payment' means any financial advantage, including the discharge of an obligation to pay or the provision of goods or services (including sexual services) gratuitously or at a discount (Sexual Offences Act 2003, s 54).

Mode of trial

A[29.3] See SC Guideline at A[29.4] below.

Note

Where an offender has profited from his or her involvement in the prostitution of others, the court should consider making a confiscation order approximately equivalent to the profits enjoyed. Such an order may be made only in the Crown Court.

Sentencing

Magistrates' Court Sentencing Guidelines – Exploitation of prostitution

A[29.4] This guideline is taken from the Magistrates' Court Sentencing Guidelines, effective from 1 April 2014.

Causing or inciting prostitution for gain

Sexual Offences Act 2003 (section 52)

Controlling prostitution for gain

Sexual Offences Act 2003 (section 53)

Triable either way

Maximum: 7 years' custody

Offence range: Community order – 6 years' custody

For convictions on or after 3 December 2012 (irrespective of the date of commission of the offence), these are specified offences for the purposes of section 226A (extended sentence for certain violent or sexual offences) of the Criminal Justice Act 2003.

The terms 'prostitute' and 'prostitution' are used in this guideline in accordance with the statutory language contained in the Sexual Offences Act 2003.

STEP ONE
Determining the offence category

The court should determine which categories of harm and culpability the offence falls into by reference only to the tables below.

Harm	Culpability
Category 1	A
• Abduction/detention	Causing, inciting or controlling prostitution on significant commercial basis
• Violence or threats of violence	Expectation of significant financial or other gain
• Sustained and systematic psychological abuse	Abuse of trust
• Individual(s) forced or coerced to participate in unsafe/degrading sexual activity	Exploitation of those known to be trafficked

Harm	Culpability
• Individual(s) forced or coerced into seeing many 'customers'	Significant involvement in limiting the freedom of prostitute(s)
• Individual(s) forced/coerced/deceived into prostitution	Grooming of individual(s) to enter prostitution including through cultivation of a dependency on drugs or alcohol
Category 2	B
Factor(s) in category 1 not present	Close involvement with prostitute(s), for example control of finances, choice of clients, working conditions, etc (where offender's involvement is not as a result of coercion)
	C
	Performs limited function under direction
	Close involvement but engaged by coercion/intimidation/exploitation

STEP TWO
Starting point and category range

Having determined the category, the court should use the corresponding starting points to reach a sentence within the category range on the next page. The starting point applies to all offenders irrespective of plea or previous convictions. Having determined the starting point, step two allows further adjustment for aggravating or mitigating features, set out on the next page.

A case of particular gravity, reflected by multiple features of culpability or harm in step one, could merit upward adjustment from the starting point before further adjustment for aggravating or mitigating features, set out on the next page.

Where there is a sufficient prospect of rehabilitation, a community order with a sex offender treatment programme requirement under section 202 of the Criminal Justice Act 2003 can be a proper alternative to a short or moderate length custodial sentence.

	A	B	C
Category 1	Starting point 4 years' custody	Starting point 2 years 6 months' custody	Starting point 1 years' custody
	Category range 3– 6 years' custody	Category range 2 – 4 years' custody	Category range 26 weeks' – 2 years' custody
Category 2	Starting point 2 years 6 months' custody	Starting point 1 year's custody	Starting point Medium level community order
	Category range 2 – 5 years' custody custody	Category range High level community order – 2 year's custody	Category range Low level community order – High level community order

The table below contains a **non-exhaustive** list of additional factual elements providing the context of the offence and factors relating to the offender. Identify whether any combination of these, or other relevant factors, should result in an upward or downward adjustment from the starting point. **In particular, relevant recent convictions are likely to result in an upward adjustment.** In some cases, having considered these factors, it may be appropriate to move outside the identified category range.

When sentencing appropriate **category 2 offences**, the court should also consider the custody threshold as follows:

- has the custody threshold been passed?
- if so, is it unavoidable that a custodial sentence be imposed?
- if so, can that sentence be suspended?

Aggravating factors	Mitigating factors
Statutory aggravating factors	No previous convictions or no relevant/recent convictions
Previous convictions, having regard to a) the nature of the offence to which the conviction relates and its relevance to the current offence; and b) the time that has elapsed since the conviction	Remorse
Offence committed whilst on bail	Previous good character and/or exemplary conduct*
Other aggravating factors	Age and/or lack of maturity where it affects the responsibility of the offender
Failure to comply with current court orders	Mental disorder or learning disability, particularly where linked to the commission of the offence
Offence committed whilst on licence	Demonstration of steps taken to address offending behaviour
Deliberate isolation of prostitute(s)	* Previous good character/exemplary conduct is different from having no previous convictions. The more serious the offence, the less the weight which should normally be attributed to this factor. Where previous good character/exemplary conduct has been used to facilitate the offence, this mitigation should not normally be allowed and such conduct may constitute an aggravating factor.
Threats made to expose prostitute(s) to the authorities (for example, immigration or police), family/friends or others	
Harm threatened against the family/friends of prostitute(s)	
Passport/identity documents removed	
Prostitute(s) prevented from seeking medical treatment	
Food withheld	
Victim(s) prevented from attending school	
Food withheld	
Earnings withheld/kept by offender or evidence of excessive wage reduction or debt bondage, inflated travel or living expenses or unreasonable interest rates	
Any steps taken to prevent the reporting of an incident, obtaining assistance and/or from assisting or supporting the prosecution	
Attempts to dispose of or conceal evidence	
Prostitute(s) forced or coerced into pornography	
Timescale over which operation has been run	

STEP THREE
Consider any factors which indicate a reduction, such as assistance to the prosecution

The court should take into account sections 73 and 74 of the Serious Organised Crime and Police Act 2005 (assistance by defendants: reduction or review of sentence) and any other rule of law by virtue of which an offender may receive a discounted sentence in consequence of assistance given (or offered) to the prosecutor or investigator.

STEP FOUR
Reduction for guilty pleas

The court should take account of any potential reduction for a guilty plea in accordance with section 144 of the Criminal Justice Act 2003 and the *Guilty Plea* guideline.

STEP FIVE
Dangerousness

The court should consider whether having regard to the criteria contained in Chapter 5 of Part 12 of the Criminal Justice Act 2003 it would be appropriate to award an extended sentence (section 226A).

STEP SIX
Totality principle

If sentencing an offender for more than one offence, or where the offender is already serving a sentence, consider whether the total sentence is just and proportionate to the offending behaviour.

STEP SEVEN
Ancillary orders

The court must consider whether to make any ancillary orders. The court must also consider what other requirements or provisions may automatically apply. Further information is included on page 303.

STEP EIGHT
Reasons

Section 174 of the Criminal Justice Act 2003 imposes a duty to give reasons for, and explain the effect of, the sentence.

STEP NINE
Consideration for time spent on bail

The court must consider whether to give credit for time spent on bail in accordance with section 240A of the Criminal Justice Act 2003.

A[29.5] Closure orders: see **B**[7].

A[30]

Exposure

Charge (Exposure)

A[30.1] **Intentionally exposes his genitals, and he intends that someone will see them and be caused alarm or distress.**

Sexual Offences Act 2003, s 66.

Maximum penalty – 6 months' imprisonment and/or fine level 5 (for offences committed on or after 12 March 2015 an unlimited fine). Triable either way.

Specified sexual offence under Sch 15, Part 2, CJA 2003.

Crown Court – 2 years' imprisonment and unlimited fine.

Mode of trial

A[30.2] See SGC Guideline and Notes at A[30.3] below.

Sentencing
Magistrates' Court Sentencing Guidelines – Exposure

A[30.3] This guideline is taken from the Magistrates' Court Sentencing Guidelines, effective from 1 April 2014.

Exposure

Sexual Offences Act 2003 (section 66)

Triable either way

Maximum: 2 years' custody

Offence range: Fine – 1 year's custody

For convictions on or after 3 December 2012 (irrespective of the date of commission of the offence), this is a specified offence for the purposes of section 226A (extended sentence for certain violent or sexual offences) of the Criminal Justice Act 2003.

STEP ONE
Determining the offence category

The court should determine the offence category using the table below.

Category 1	Raised harm **and** raised culpability
Category 2	Raised harm **or** raised culpability
Category 3	Exposure **without** raised harm or culpability factors present

The court should determine culpability and harm caused or intended, by reference only to the factors below, which comprise the principal factual elements of the offence. Where an offence does not fall squarely into a category, individual factors may require a degree of weighting before making an overall assessment and determining the appropriate offence category.

Factors indicating raised harm	Factors indicating raised culpability
Victim followed/pursued	Specific or previous targeting of a particularly vulnerable victim
Offender masturbated	Abuse of trust
	Use of threats (including blackmail)
	Offence racially or religiously aggravated
	Offence motivated by, or demonstrating, hostility to the victim based on his or her sexual orientation (or presumed sexual orientation) or transgender identity (or presumed transgender identity)
	Offence motivated by, or demonstrating, hostility to the victim based on his or her disability (or presumed disability)

STEP TWO
Starting point and category range

Having determined the category, the court should use the corresponding starting points to reach a sentence within the category range on the next page. The starting point applies to all offenders irrespective of plea or previous convictions. Having determined the starting point, step two allows further adjustment for aggravating or mitigating features, set out on the next page.

A case of particular gravity, reflected by multiple features of culpability or harm in step one, could merit upward adjustment from the starting point before further adjustment for aggravating or mitigating features, set out on the next page.

Where there is a sufficient prospect of rehabilitation, a community order with a sex offender treatment programme requirement under section 202 of the Criminal Justice Act 2003 can be a proper alternative to a short or moderate length custodial sentence.

Category 1	**Starting point** 26 weeks' custody
	Category range 12 weeks' – 1 year's custody
Category 2	**Starting point** High level community order
	Category range Medium level community order – 26 weeks' custody
Category 3	**Starting point** Medium level community order
	Category range Band A fine – High level community order

The table below contains a **non-exhaustive** list of additional factual elements providing the context of the offence and factors relating to the offender. Identify whether any combination of these, or other relevant factors, should result in an upward or downward adjustment from the starting point. **In particular, relevant recent convictions are likely to result in an upward adjustment.** In some cases, having considered these factors, it may be appropriate to move outside the identified category range.

When sentencing **category 2 offences**, the court should also consider the custody threshold as follows:

- has the custody threshold been passed?
- f so, is it unavoidable that a custodial sentence be imposed?
- if so, can that sentence be suspended?

When sentencing **category 3 offences**, the court should also consider the community order threshold as follows:

Aggravating factors	Mitigating factors
Statutory aggravating factors	No previous convictions or no relevant/recent convictions
Previous convictions, having regard to a) the nature of the offence to which the conviction relates and its relevance to the current offence; and b) the time that has elapsed since the conviction	Remorse
Offence committed whilst on bail	Previous good character and/or exemplary conduct*
Other aggravating factors	Age and/or lack of maturity where it affects the responsibility of the offender
Location of offence	Mental disorder or learning disability, particularly where linked to the commission of the offence
Timing of offence Any steps taken to prevent the victim reporting an incident, obtaining assistance and/or from assisting or supporting the prosecution	Demonstration of steps taken to address offending behaviour
Failure to comply with current court orders	* Previous good character/exemplary conduct is different from having no previous convictions. The more serious the offence, the less the weight which should normally be attributed to this factor. Where previous good character/exemplary conduct has been used to facilitate the offence, this mitigation should not normally be allowed and such conduct may constitute an aggravating factor.
Offence committed whilst on licence	
Commission of offence whilst under the influence of alcohol or drugs Presence of others, especially children	

STEP THREE
Consider any factors which indicate a reduction, such as assistance to the prosecution

The court should take into account sections 73 and 74 of the Serious Organised Crime and Police Act 2005 (assistance by defendants: reduction or review of sentence) and any other rule of law by virtue of which an offender may receive a discounted sentence in consequence of assistance given (or offered) to the prosecutor or investigator.

STEP FOUR
Reduction for guilty pleas

The court should take account of any potential reduction for a guilty plea in accordance with section 144 of the Criminal Justice Act 2003 and the *Guilty Plea* guideline.

STEP FIVE
Dangerousness

The court should consider whether having regard to the criteria contained in Chapter 5 of Part 12 of the Criminal Justice Act 2003 it would be appropriate to award an extended sentence (section 226A).

STEP SIX
Totality principle

If sentencing an offender for more than one offence, or where the offender is already serving a sentence, consider whether the total sentence is just and proportionate to the offending behaviour.

STEP SEVEN
Ancillary orders

The court must consider whether to make any ancillary orders. The court must also consider what other requirements or provisions may *automatically* apply. Further information is included on page 303.

STEP EIGHT
Reasons

Section 174 of the Criminal Justice Act 2003 imposes a duty to give reasons for, and explain the effect of, the sentence.

STEP NINE
Consideration for time spent on bail

The court must consider whether to give credit for time spent on bail in accordance with section 240A of the Criminal Justice Act 2003.

A[31]

False accounting

Charge (False accounting)

A[31.1] **Dishonestly and with a view to gain for himself or another or with intent to cause loss to another—**

(a) destroys, defaces, conceals or falsifies any account or any record or document made or required for any accounting purpose; or

(b) in furnishing information for any purpose produces or makes use of any account, or any such record or document as aforesaid, which to his knowledge is or may be misleading, false or deceptive in any material particular.

Theft Act 1968, s 17

Maximum penalty – 6 months' imprisonment and/or fine level 5 (for offences committed on or after 12 March 2015 an unlimited fine).

Crown Court – 7 years' imprisonment and unlimited fine.

Mode of trial

A[31.2] See general notes at D[4] and SC Guidelines below.

Legal notes and definitions

A[31.3] 'Gain' and 'loss'. These terms are defined in s 34(2)(a) of the Theft Act as:

> '"gain" and "loss" are to be construed as extending only to gain or loss in money or other property, but as extending to any such gain or loss whether temporary or permanent; and–
>
> (i) "gain" includes a gain by keeping what one has, as well as a gain by getting what one has not; and
>
> (ii) "loss" includes a loss by not getting what one might get, as well as a loss by parting with what one has;'

The use of falsified bills of exchange with a view to securing a bank's forbearance from enforcing repayment of existing debts does not constitute falsification with a view to 'gain' within the meaning of this section, *R v Golechha* [1989] 3 All ER 908, [1989] 1 WLR 1050, CA.

This section applies generally to the falsification of accounting documents for the purpose of obtaining financial gain or causing financial loss. It does not require that such gain or loss should in fact result. It is to be contrasted to the statutory scheme under s 111A of the Social Security Administration Act 1992 where the mischief aimed at is not falsification of documents but dishonest failure by a recipient of public benefits to notify the relevant authority of a change of circumstances which would make a difference to the computation of his benefit: *R v Lancaster* [2010] EWCA Crim 370, [2010] 3 All ER 402, [2010] 2 Cr App R 7, [2010] Crim LR 776.

A[31.3A] 'Accounting purpose' and 'material particular'. In *Re A-G's Reference (No 1 of 1980)* [1981] 1 All ER 366, [1981] 1 WLR 34 it was held, on the facts of that reference, that a personal loan proposal form was a document 'required for any accounting purpose'. A claim form submitted in respect of a home insurance policy may be a document made or required for an accounting purpose in that the insurance company may use the form as a basis for keeping its accounting records, but the court must receive some evidence that it is in fact used for this purpose and the court cannot draw its own conclusion from the nature and form of the claim form: *R v Sundhers* [1998] Crim LR 497, CA. A court is entitled, however, without any further direct evidence of the accounting practices of the lender, to conclude that an application for a mortgage or a loan made to a commercial institution is a document required for an accounting purpose: *R v O and B* [2010] EWCA Crim 2233, [2011] 2 All ER 656, [2011] 1 WLR 2936, [2011] 2 Cr App R 33(in this regard not following *Sundhers*). See also *R v Manning* [1999] QB 980, [1998] 4 All ER 876, [1998] 2 Cr App Rep 461, CA (court entitled to conclude that insurance cover note an accounting document as it set out on the document what was owed by the client), and *Re Baxter* [2002] All ER (D) 218 (Jan), (2002) JPN 99 (a certificate, included in an application pack for an investment scheme, by which an insurance company purportedly stood behind the investment programme concerned could be regarded as a document made or required for an accounting purpose, but another document that was a general solicitation, any response to which would have resulted in the issue of accounting documents, could not be so regarded).

Although the document itself must be made or required for an accounting purpose, the material particular in question does not have to be one which is directly connected with the accounting purpose of the document: *R v Mallett* [1978] 3 All ER 10.

A[31.4]–[31.7] The offence information and guidelines on fraud – banking and insurance fraud, and obtaining credit through fraud, benefit fraud, revenue fraud and confidence – can now be found at A[36.10].

A[32]

False identity documents

Charge (False identity documents)

A[32.1] Have in his possession or under his control, without reasonable excuse—

(a) an identify document that is false,
(b) an identity document that was improperly obtained,
(c) an identity document that relates to someone else,
(d) any apparatus, article or material which, to his knowledge, is or has been specially designed or adapted for he making of false identify documents or to be used in the making of such documents, or
(e) any article or material which, to his knowledge, is or has been specially designed or adapted to be used in the making of such documents.

Identity Documents Act 2010, s 6(1)*

Maximum penalty – 6 months' imprisonment and/or fine level 5 (for offences committed on or after 12 March 2015 an unlimited fine).

Crown Court – 2 years' imprisonment and unlimited fine.

*NB: From 21 January 2011 this legislation repealed the Identity Cards Act 2006.

Mode of trial

A[32.2] See the SC Guideline below.

Defences

A[32.2A] Section 31(1) of the Immigration and Asylum Act 1999 provides a defence to certain offences, including those under ss 4 and 6 of the Identity Documents Act 2010, based on Art 31(1) of the United Nations Convention relating to the Status of Refugees. It states:

> (1) It is a defence for a refugee charged with an offence to which this section applies to show that, having come to the United Kingdom directly from a country where his life or freedom was threatened (within the meaning of the Refugee Convention), he–
> (a) presented himself to the authorities in the United Kingdom without delay;
> (b) showed good cause for his illegal entry or presence; and
> (c) made a claim for asylum as soon as was reasonably practicable after his arrival in the United Kingdom.

The term 'refugee' bears its Convention meaning, namely:

> 'a refugee is a person who has left his own country owing to a well-founded fear of being persecuted for reasons of race, religion, nationality, membership of a particular social group or political opinion.'

Provided that the defendant can adduce sufficient evidence in support of his claim to refugee status to raise the issue, the prosecution bears the burden of proving to the usual standard that he is not in fact a refugee. Different considerations apply, however, in relation to the other matters which have to be established under s 31(1). The burden, here, is legal rather than merely evidential.

The defence is qualified, however, by s 32(2). This provides:

'If, in coming from the country where his life or freedom was threatened, the refugee stopped in another country outside the United Kingdom, subsection (1) applies only if he shows that he could not reasonably have expected to be given protection under the Refugee Convention in that other country.'

See further, **A[81.8A]**, below.

In *R v MV* [2010] EWCA Crim 2400, [2011] 1 Cr App Rep 432, the appellant had come into the UK on a flight from Italy. Given his inability to say whether his flight had stopped during his journey from Somalia and to account for where he had spent one and a half days, a jury could have inferred that he had in all probability remained in Italy. Even if no legal advice had been given regarding the availability of a defence under s 31 of the Immigration and Asylum Act 1999, there was no reasonable prospect of that defence succeeding.

The absence of words in what was subsection (5) of s 25 of the Identity Cards Act 2006, such as are found in subsection (1) of s 25, indicates that a defendant who does not know or believe that a document is false cannot of itself, per se, amount to a reasonable excuse (even for an offence under what is now s 6(1)). However, lack of knowledge or belief might be relevant to a defence of reasonable excuse. The defence is found in various statutory contexts and it is par excellence a matter for the jury whether or not a reasonable excuse has been established. A judge ought to withdraw that issue from the jury only if no reasonable jury could conclude on the facts alleged that the explanation was capable of constituting a reasonable excuse. Nothing in s 25 suggested that honest belief in the genuineness of the document is a factor which the jury is obliged to ignore. Accordingly, the defendant was entitled to rely upon her genuine belief that the document was valid while contending that she had a reasonable excuse for having the false passport in her possession: see *R v Unah* [2011] EWCA Crim 1837, 175 JP 391, [2011] 30 LS Gaz R 24.

Sentencing
SC Guideline – False identity documents

A[32.3] Note: possession of a false identity document with an improper intention of using it is an indictable only offence (Identity Documents Act 2010, s 4(1)). The maximum penalty is 10 years' imprisonment and an unlimited fine.

OFFENCE SERIOUSNESS (CULPABILITY AND HARM) A. IDENTIFY THE APPROPRIATE STARTING POINT Starting points based on first time offender pleading not guilty		
Examples of nature of activity	**Starting point**	**Range**
Single document possessed	Medium community order	Band C fine to high level community order
Small number of documents, no evidence of dealing	12 weeks custody	6 weeks custody to Crown Court
Considerable number of documents possessed, evidence of involvement in larger operation	Crown Court	Crown Court

OFFENCE SERIOUSNESS (CULPABILITY AND HARM) B. CONSIDER THE EFFECT OF AGGRAVATING AND MITIGATING FACTORS (OTHER THAN THOSE WITHIN EXAMPLES ABOVE) Common aggravating and mitigating factors are identified at **B[45.2A]**. The following may be particularly relevant but **these lists are not exhaustive**	
Factors indicating higher culpability	*Factor indicating lower culpability*

1. Clear knowledge that documents false 2. Number of documents possessed (where not in offence descriptions above)	1. Genuine mistake or ignorance
Factors indicating greater degree of harm 1. Group activity 2. Potential impact of use (where not in offence descriptions above)	
FORM A PRELIMINARY VIEW OF THE APPROPRIATE SENTENCE, THEN CONSIDER OFFENDER MITIGATION Common factors are identified at B[45.2A]	
CONSIDER A REDUCTION FOR A GUILTY PLEA	
DECIDE SENTENCE **GIVE REASONS**	

A[33]
Firearm, carrying in a public place

Charge (Firearm, carrying in a public place)

A[33.1] Without lawful authority or reasonable excuse having in a public place (a loaded shotgun), (a firearm loaded or not and ammunition suitable for use in the said firearm) (an air weapon loaded or not) or (an imitation firearm)

Firearms Act 1968, s 19

Maximum penalty -

Firearm: 6 months' imprisonment and/or fine level 5 (for offences committed on or after 12 March 2015 an unlimited fine). Triable either way.

Air weapon: 6 months' imprisonment and/or fine level 5 (for offences committed on or after 12 March 2015 an unlimited fine) and forfeiture. Triable only by magistrates.

Crown Court – 7 years' imprisonment and unlimited fine (12 months for imitation firearm).

Where the offence is committed in respect of certain, specified firearms or ammunition the court must pass an 'appropriate custodial sentence' of at least the 'required minimum term' (three years for offenders aged under 18, five years for older offenders) unless the court is of the opinion that there are 'exceptional circumstances relate to the offence or to the offender which justify its not doing so': Firearms Act 1968, s 51A.

Mode of trial

A[33.2] See the SC Guideline below.

Legal notes and definitions

A[33.3] 'Public place' and 'has with him'. Public place 'includes any highway, premises or place to which the public at the material time has access whether on payment or otherwise': Firearms Act 1968, s 57(4). In *Anderson v Miller* [1976] Crim LR 743, the space behind a counter in a shop was held to be a public place.

To prove that the accused had with him a firearm the prosecution must establish more than mere possession, namely that the accused had a close physical link and immediate control over the firearm; but it is not necessary to establish that he had been carrying it: *R v Kelt* [1977] 3 All ER 1099, 142 JP 60 and see *R v Pawlicki* and *R v Swindell* [1992] 1 WLR 827, [1992] Crim LR 584, CA.

A[33.4] Without lawful authority or reasonable excuse. The Firearms Act 1968 expressly places on the defendant the burden of proving that he had lawful authority or reasonable excuse. He only has to prove that on the balance of probabilities he had lawful authority or reasonable excuse. He does not have to prove this beyond all reasonable doubt.

(a) A certificate for a firearm was not in itself lawful authority under the Firearms Act 1968, s 19, for the holder of the certificate to have the firearm and ammunition for it in a public place.
(b) The mistaken belief by the holder of an invalid firearm certificate that it was valid and that it was lawful authority under the Firearms Act 1968, s 19 was not capable of being a reasonable excuse and therefore a defence under that section

(*R v Jones* [1995] QB 235, [1995] 3 All ER 139, CA).

A[33.5] **ECHR.** Having regard to the legitimate aims of the legislation, it is suggested that the shifting of the legal burden of proof to the accused is necessary and proportionate in ECHR terms.

A[33.6] **Shotgun.** Although the firearm need not be loaded a shotgun must be loaded to establish this offence. A shotgun is a smooth bore gun whose barrel is 24 inches or longer with a bore not exceeding two inches and which is not a revolver nor has an illegal magazine, not being an air gun.

A[33.7] **Air weapon.** An air weapon may be loaded or not to establish this offence. An air weapon is an air gun, air rifle or an air pistol of a type which has not been declared by the Home Office to be specially dangerous (see **A[76.7]**).

A[33.8] **Firearm.** This is defined by s 57(1) of the Firearms Act 1968 as:

(1) In this Act, the expression 'firearm' means a lethal barrelled weapon of any description from which any shot, bullet or other missile can be discharged and includes–
- (a) any prohibited weapon, whether it is such a lethal weapon as aforesaid or not; and
- (b) any component part of such a lethal or prohibited weapon; and
- (c) any accessory to any such weapon designed or adapted to diminish the noise or flash caused by firing the weapon.

'Lethal weapon' includes a weapon not designed to kill or inflict injury but capable of doing so if misused: *Read v Donovan* [1947] KB 326, [1947] 1 All ER 37, 111 JP 46 (signal pistol); *Moore v Gooderham* [1960] 3 All ER 575, 124 JP 513 (air gun); *R v Thorpe* [1987] 2 All ER 108, [1987] 1 WLR 383 (revolver powered by compressed carbon dioxide); *R v Singh* [1989] Crim LR 724 (flare launcher).

A[33.9] An imitation firearm which is so constructed or adapted as to be readily convertible into a firearm is to be treated as a firearm even though it has not been so converted: *Castle v DPP* (1998) The Times, April 3. A starting pistol which could be adapted for firing bullets if the barrel was drilled was held to be a firearm in *R v Freeman* [1970] 2 All ER 413, [1970] 1 WLR 788, CA.

In *R v Bewley* [2012] EWCA Crim 1457, [2013] 1 All ER 1, [2013] 1 WLR 137 the weapon in question was a starting pistol, which was originally designed to fire blank cartridges. A 2cm hole had been drilled into the solid barrel and the top of the hammer had been broken off. A senior forensic scientist was able to fire it by placing it in a vice, inserting a specially selected lead pellet and using a mallet and punch to strike the firing pin. The judge ruled that the pistol was a lethal-barrelled weapon from which a missile '(could) be discharged', but the Court of Appeal quashed the conviction. Although the Firearms Act 1982 had not amended the Firearms Act 1968, the two had to be construed as creating a single code. It was the clear legislative intention of the 1982 Act to exclude from the 1968 Act imitation firearms which could only be readily convertible into firearms by equipment or tools not in common use.

A[33.9A] **Imitation firearm.** An imitation firearm means anything which has the appearance of being a firearm (other than any weapon designed or adapted for the discharge of any noxious liquid, gas or other thing) whether or not it is capable of discharging any shot, bullet or other missile: Firearms Act 1968, s 57(4). The test is whether the thing looked like a firearm at the time when the accused had it for that purpose: *R v Morris and King* (1984) 149 JP 60, 79 Cr App Rep 104, CA. Two fingers inside the defendant's pocket cannot constitute possession of an imitation firearm under s 17(2) of the Act: *R v Bentham* [2005] UKHL 18, [2005] 2 All ER 65, HL.

A[33.10] An offence is committed whether the firearm is loaded or not but the defendant must have with him ammunition suitable for use in that firearm.

Sentencing
SC Guideline – Firearm, carrying in a public place

A[33.11]

<table>
<tr><td colspan="3">OFFENCE SERIOUSNESS (CULPABILITY AND HARM)
A. IDENTIFY THE APPROPRIATE STARTING POINT
Starting points based on first time offender pleading not guilty</td></tr>
<tr><td>Examples of nature of activity</td><td>Starting point</td><td>Range</td></tr>
<tr><td>Carrying an unloaded air weapon</td><td>Low level community order</td><td>Band B fine to medium level community order</td></tr>
<tr><td>Carrying loaded air weapon/imitation firearm/unloaded shotgun without ammunition</td><td>High level community order</td><td>Medium level community order to 26 weeks custody (air weapon) Medium level community order to Crown Court (imitation firearm, unloaded shotgun)</td></tr>
<tr><td>Carrying loaded shotgun/carrying shotgun or any other firearm together with ammunition with it</td><td>Crown Court</td><td>Crown Court</td></tr>
<tr><td colspan="3">OFFENCE SERIOUSNESS (CULPABILITY AND HARM)
B. CONSIDER THE EFFECT OF AGGRAVATING AND MITIGATING FACTORS (OTHER THAN THOSE WITHIN EXAMPLES ABOVE)
Common aggravating and mitigating factors are identified at B[45.2A]. The following may be particularly relevant but these lists are not exhaustive</td></tr>
<tr><td colspan="2">Factors indicating higher culpability
1. Brandishing the firearm
2. Carrying firearm in a busy place
3. Planned illegal use</td><td>Factors indicating lower culpability
1. Firearm not in sight
2. No intention to use forearm
3. Firearm to be used for lawful purpose (not amounting to a defence)</td></tr>
<tr><td colspan="2">Factors indicating greater degree of harm
1. Person or people put in fear
2. Offender participating in violent incident</td><td></td></tr>
<tr><td colspan="3">FORM A PRELIMINARY VIEW OF THE APPROPRIATE SENTENCE, THEN CONSIDER OFFENDER MITIGATION
Common factors are identified at B[45.2A]</td></tr>
<tr><td colspan="3">CONSIDER A REDUCTION FOR A GUILTY PLEA</td></tr>
<tr><td colspan="3">CONSIDER ANCILLARY ORDERS, INCLUDING COMPENSATION, FORFEITURE OR SUSPENSION OF PERSONAL LIQUOR LICENCE AND FOOTBALL BANNING ORDER (where appropriate)
Refer to B[10] for guidance on compensation and Part B for guidance on available ancillary orders</td></tr>
<tr><td colspan="3">DECIDE SENTENCE
GIVE REASONS</td></tr>
</table>

A[33.12] **Available sentences.** See Table A at **B**[43.1A] (firearms) and Table B at **B**[43.2] (air weapons).

A[33.13] Forfeiture. The court can order the firearm (imitation, or shotgun or air weapon) to be forfeited to the police or to be disposed of as the court thinks fit. The court can also cancel any firearm or shotgun certificate held by the defendant.

A[34]

Football-related offences

(For other related drunkenness offences see A[35] below)

Charges (Football-related offences)

A[34.1] **1 Being a person at a regulated football match and throwing anything at or towards (the playing area, or any area adjacent to the playing area to which spectators are not generally admitted) (any area in which spectators or other persons are or may be present) without lawful authority or lawful excuse**

Football (Offences) Act 1991, s 2

A[34.2] **2 Taking part at a regulated football match in chanting of an indecent or racialist nature**

Football (Offences) Act 1991, s 3

A[34.3] **3 At a regulated football match going onto the playing area, or any area adjacent to the playing area to which spectators are not generally admitted, without lawful authority or lawful excuse**

Football (Offences) Act 1991, s 4

Maximum penalty (for each offence) – Fine level 3.

A[34.4] **4 Being an unauthorised person, did sell, or offer or expose for sale, a ticket for a designated football match in any public place or place to which the public has access or, in the course of a trade or business, in any other place.**

Criminal Justice and Public Order Act 1994, s 166.

Maximum penalty – Fine level 5 (for offences committed on or after 12 March 2015 an unlimited fine).

Legal notes and definitions

A[34.5] The creation of these offences follows the recommendations of the Taylor report into the Hillsborough Disaster. They can be committed only in respect of matches in England and Wales.

A[34.6] **Designated football matches for the purposes of the Football (Offences) Act 1991.** The Football (Offences) (Designation of Football Matches) Order 2004, SI 2004/2410, as amended, designates football matches for the purpose of this Act. A designated football match is an association football match in which one or both of the participating teams represents a club which is for the time being a member (whether a full or associate member) of the Football League, the Football Association Premier League, the Football Conference, the Scottish Football League or the Welsh Premier League, or whose home ground is for the time being situated outside England and Wales, or represents a country or territory. A designated match is also an association football match in competition for the Football Association Cup (other than in a preliminary or qualifying round).

A[34.6A] Designated football match (ticket touting). The Ticket Touting (Designation of Football Matches) Order 2007, SI 2007/790 designates the following matches:

(1) an association football match played in England and Wales in which one or both of the participating teams represents:

(a) a club which is for the time being a member (whether a full or associate member) of the Football League, the Football Association Premier League, the Football Conference or the League of Wales;
(b) a club whose home ground is for the time being situated outside England and Wales; or
(c) a country or territory.

(2) an association football match played outside England and Wales involving:
(a) a national team appointed by the Football Association to represent England or appointed by the Football Association of Wales to represent Wales;
(b) a team representing a club which is for the time being a member (whether a full or associate member) of the Football League, the Football Association Premier League, the Football Conference or the League of Wales;
(c) a team representing any country or territory whose football association is for the time being a member of FIFA, where:
(i) the match is part of a competition or tournament organised by, or under the authority of, FIFA or UEFA, and
(ii) the competition or tournament is one in which a team referred to in sub-paragraph (a) is eligible to participate or has participated; or
(d) a team representing a club which is for the time being a member (whether a full or associate member) of, or affiliated to, a national football association which is a member of FIFA, where:
(i) the match is part of a competition or tournament organised by, or under the authority of, FIFA or UEFA, and
(ii) the competition or tournament is one in which a club referred to in sub-paragraph (b) is eligible to participate or has participated.

A[34.7] In addition, the match must take place on a ground occupied by a Football (or Premier) League Club or which is designated under the Safety of Sports Grounds Act 1975.

A[34.8] Being or taking part at. The offence may be committed in a period beginning two hours before the start of the match or, if earlier, two hours before the time it is advertised to start and ending one hour after the end of the match. Where a match is postponed or cancelled, the period includes the two hours before and one hour after the advertised starting time.

A[34.9] Without lawful authority or lawful excuse. The defendant must establish this but he only has to establish that his defence is probably true, he does not have to establish it beyond reasonable doubt.

A[34.10] Charge 1: Throwing an object. The prosecution only has to prove that the object was thrown, not that a particular person was aimed at or caused alarm or distress thereby.

A[34.11]–[34.14] Charge 2: Indecent or racialist chanting. 'Chanting' means the repeated uttering of any words or sounds alone or with one or more others. 'Racialist nature' means consisting of or including matter which is threatening, abusive or insulting to a person by reason of his colour, race, nationality (including citizenship) or ethnic or national origins, whether alone or in concert with one or more others. In *DPP v Stoke on Trent Magistrates' Court* [2003] EWHC 1593 (Admin), [2003] 3 All ER 1086, for example, 'Paki' was racially offensive.

Sentencing

SC Guideline – Football related offences

Football related offences (Revised 2017)

A[34.15]

Criminal Justice and Public Order Act 1994: s 166 (unauthorised sale or attempted sale of tickets); Football Offences Act 1991: s 2 (throwing missile); s 3 (indecent or racist chanting); s 4 (going onto prohibited areas)., Sporting Events (Control of Alcohol etc.) Act 1985: s 2(1) (possession of alcohol whilst entering or trying to enter ground); s 2(2) (being drunk in, or whilst trying to enter, ground).

Effective from: 24 April 2017

Triable only summarily:

Maximum:

Level 2 fine (being drunk in ground)

Level 3 fine (throwing missile; indecent or racist chanting; going onto prohibited areas)

Unlimited fine (unauthorised sale of tickets)

Level 3 fine and/or 3 months (possession of alcohol)

Offence range:

Conditional discharge–High level community order (possession of alcohol) Conditional discharge–Band C fine (all other offences)

STEP 1
Determining the offence category

The Court should determine the offence category using the table below.

Category 1	Higher culpability and greater harm
Category 2	Higher culpability and lesser harm or lower culpability and greater harm
Category 3	Lower culpability and lesser harm

The court should determine the offender's culpability and the harm caused with reference only to the factors below. Where an offence does not fall squarely into a category, individual factors may require a degree of weighting before making an overall assessment and determining the appropriate offence category.

CULPABILITY demonstrated by one or more of the following:

Factors indicating higher culpability

- Deliberate or flagrant action
- Disregard of warnings
- Commercial operation
- Inciting others
- (Possession of) Large quantity of alcohol
- Targeted abuse

Factors indicating lower culpability

- All other cases

HARM demonstrated by one or more of the following:

Factor indicating greater harm

- Distress or alarm caused
- Actual injury or risk of injury
- Significant financial loss to others

Factors indicating lesser harm

- All other cases

STEP 2
Starting point and category range

Having determined the category at step one, the court should use the starting point to reach a sentence within the appropriate category range in the table below. The starting point applies to all offenders irrespective of plea or previous convictions.

Offence Category	Starting Point	Range
Category 1	Band C fine	Band C fine
Category 2	Band B fine	Band A fine–and C fine
Category 3	Band A fine	Conditional discharge–Band B fine

Possession of alcohol only

Offence Category	Starting Point	Range
Category 1	Band C fine	Band C fine–High level community order
Category 2	Band B fine	Band A fine–Band C fine
Category 3	Band A fine	Conditional discharge–Band B fine

The court should then consider adjustment for any aggravating or mitigating factors. The following is a **non-exhaustive** list of additional factual elements providing the context of the offence and factors relating to the offender. Identify whether any combination of these, or other relevant factors, should result in an upward or downward adjustment from the sentence arrived at so far.

Factors increasing seriousness

Statutory aggravating factors:

- Previous convictions, having regard to a) the **nature** of the offence to which the conviction relates and its **relevance** to the current offence; and b) the **time** that has elapsed since the conviction
- Offence committed whilst on bail
- Offence motivated by, or demonstrating hostility based on any of the following characteristics or presumed characteristics of the owner/keeper of the animal: religion, race, disability, sexual orientation or transgender identity

Other aggravating factors:

- Presence of children
- Offence committed on licence or post sentence supervision

Factors reducing seriousness or reflecting personal mitigation

- Remorse
- Admissions to police in interview
- Ready co-operation with authorities
- Minimal disturbance caused
- No previous convictions **or** no relevant/recent convictions
- Good character and/or exemplary conduct
- Age and/or lack of maturity where it affects the responsibility of the offender
- Mental disorder or learning disability

STEP 3
Consider any factors which indicate a reduction, such as assistance to the prosecution

The court should take into account sections 73 and 74 of the Serious Organised Crime and Police Act 2005 (assistance by defendants: reduction or review of sentence) and any other rule of law by virtue of which an offender may receive a discounted sentence in consequence of assistance given (or offered) to the prosecutor or investigator.

STEP 4
Reduction for guilty pleas

The court should take account of any potential reduction for a guilty plea in accordance with section 144 of the Criminal Justice Act 2003 and the *Guilty Plea* guideline.

STEP 5
Totality principle

If sentencing an offender for more than one offence, or where the offender is already serving a sentence, consider whether the total sentence is just and proportionate to the overall offending behaviour in accordance with the *Offences Taken into Consideration and Totality* guideline.

STEP 6
Compensation and ancillary orders

In all cases, the court should consider whether to make compensation and/or other ancillary orders, including a football banning order.

STEP 7
Reasons

Section 174 of the Criminal Justice Act 2003 imposes a duty to give reasons for, and explain the effect of, the sentence.

A[34.16] Available sentences. See Table C at B[43.3].

A[34.17] In addition to any sentence it may impose, the court will normally make a football banning order (at B[29]). These orders prevent the defendant from attending football matches in England and Wales or outside England and Wales under s 10 of the Act, if the court is satisfied, on conviction of a relevant offence, that there are reasonable grounds for believing that such an order will help prevent disorder at football matches (*R (on the application of Brown) v Inner London Crown Court* [2003] EWHC 3194 (Admin), [2003] All ER (D) 256 (Dec)). If the court is not so satisfied, it must state that fact in open court and give its reasons. Those reasons will be recorded in the court register.

A[35]

Football-related offences: Sporting events (control of alcohol etc)

Charges (Football-related offences (control of alcohol etc))

A[35.1] 1(a) **Being the operator (or hirer) (or his servant or agent) knowingly causing or permitting intoxicating liquor to be carried on a public service vehicle which was being used for the principal purpose of carrying passengers for the whole or part of a journey to or from a designated sporting event**

OR

(b) **Possessing intoxicating liquor whilst on such a vehicle**

OR

(c) **Being drunk on such a vehicle**

Sporting Events (Control of Alcohol etc) Act 1985, 1(2), 1(3) and 1(4) (See para A[35.4] for like offences in respect of drivers and keepers of, and passengers on, minibuses.)

A[35.2] 2 (a) **Possessing intoxicating liquor (or an article specified by the Act namely [. . . . .]) at a time during the period of a designated sporting event when in an area of a designated sports ground from which the event might have been directly viewed (or while entering or trying to enter such an event)**

OR

(b) **Being drunk in a designated sports ground at a time during the period of a designated sporting event (or, being drunk while entering or trying to enter such an event)**

Sporting Events (Control of Alcohol etc) Act 1985, 2(1) and 2(2)

OR

(c) **Possessing an article to which s 2A of the Sporting Events (Control of Alcohol etc) Act 1985 applies:**

(i) **at any time during the period of a designated sporting event when he is in any area of a designated sports ground from which the event may be directly viewed, or**

(ii) **while entering or trying to enter a designated sports ground at any time during the period of a designated sporting event at the ground.**

Sporting Events (Control of Alcohol etc) Act 1985, s 2A

Maximum penalties –

Offences under	s 1(2) (or 1A(2)) – Fine level 4
	ss 1(3), 1A(3), 2(1), 2A(1) – Fine level 3 and 3 months
	ss 1(4), 1A(4), and 2(2) – Fine level 2.

Legal notes and definitions

A[35.3] These offences were created in an attempt to deal with rowdy behaviour at football matches primarily where teams belonging to the Football (or Premier)

League are involved (including their reserve and youth teams) but generally not at games exclusively concerning 'non-league' or amateur clubs. In addition, the Act provides for a total ban on the sale of alcohol at such matches although there is the opportunity for the club to apply to the relevant local authority for an order modifying this prohibition (see Section F).

A[35.4] **Public service vehicle** means a motor vehicle adapted to carry more than eight passengers for hire or reward. (For this and the definition of 'operator' see the Public Passenger Vehicles Act 1981, s 181.) This offence also applies to a person who knowingly causes or permits intoxicating liquor to be carried in these circumstances on a railway passenger vehicle which he has hired. The Sporting Events (Control of Alcohol etc) Act 1985, s 1A makes provision for offences similar to those under s 1(a), (b) and (c) for drivers and keepers of a minibus, ie not a public service vehicle, but one which is adapted to carry more than eight passengers, and is being used for the principal purpose of carrying two or more passengers for the whole or part of a journey to or from a designated sporting event.

A[35.5] **Designated sports grounds and sporting events.** The Sports Grounds and Sporting Events (Designation) Order 2005, SI 2005/3204, as amended, designates the following:

(1) Grounds
Any sports ground in England or Wales.

(2) Classes of Sporting Events
- (a) Association football matches in which one or both of the participating teams represents a club which is a member (whether a full or associate member) of the Football League, the Football Association Premier League, the Football Conference National Division, the Scottish Professional Football League or Welsh Premier League, or whose home ground is situated outside England and Wales, or represents a country or territory.
- (b) Association football matches in competition for the Football Association Cup (other than in a preliminary or qualifying round).
- (c) Association football matches at a sports ground outside England and Wales in which one or both of the participating teams represents a club which is for the time being a member (whether a full or associate member) of the Football League, the Football Association Premier League, the Football Conference National division, the Scottish Professional Football League or Welsh Premier League, or represents the Football Association or the Football Association of Wales.

A[35.6] **Period of the event.** The prohibitions apply to a period beginning two hours before the start of the event or, if earlier, two hours before the time it is advertised to start and ends one hour after the end of the event. Where a match is postponed or cancelled, the period includes the two hours before and one hour after the advertised start of the event. A shorter restricted period starting 15 minutes before and ending 15 minutes after the event applies to private boxes overlooking the ground.

A[35.7] **Exceptions.** Apart from those clubs or matches not covered by the designation, eg games exclusively concerning 'non-league' clubs, the Sporting Events (Control of Alcohol etc) Act 1985 does not apply to matches where all competitors take part without reward *and* all spectators are admitted free of charge.

A[35.8] **Prohibited articles.** As well as intoxicating liquor this includes any article capable of causing injury to a person struck by it being a bottle, can or other portable container (including such a container when crushed or broken) which is for holding *any* drink and which when empty is of a kind normally discarded or returned to the supplier, or part of such a container eg a beer glass. Thus a vacuum flask containing tea would be exempt. Also exempted are containers for holding medicinal products.

A[35.9] Prohibited articles also include under s 2A any article or substance whose main purpose is the emission of a flare for purposes of illuminating or signalling (as opposed to igniting or heating) or the emission of smoke or visible gas, eg distress flares, fog signals, pellets for fumigating, but not matches, lighters, or heaters; fireworks are also prohibited. It is a defence if the accused proves that he was in possession of an article under s 2A with lawful authority.

A[35.10]–[35.15] Designated sports ground. These are the home grounds of all Football Association clubs (ie not necessarily just those clubs in the Football (or Premier) League) including any ground used occasionally or temporarily by such a club, Wembley Stadium and any ground used for any international association match. However, it should be noted that all the restrictions apply only to a designated sporting event and so where, for example, a boxing match is held on a Football League ground the provisions of the Act do not apply.

Sentencing

A[35.16] SC Guideline. Football related offences – see A[34.15] above.

A[35.17] For the power to make banning orders on persons convicted of certain offences in relation to football matches see B[29].

A[36]
Fraud
(a) Fraud by false representation (s 1(2)(a))
(b) Fraud by failing to disclose information (s 1(2)(b))
(c) Fraud by abuse of position (s 1(2)(c))

Charges (Fraud)

A[36.1] (1)

(a) **Dishonestly makes a false representation, and intends, by making the representation—**
  (i) **to make a gain for himself or another, or**
  (ii) **to cause loss to another or to expose another to a risk of loss.**

Fraud Act 2006, s 1(2)(a)

A[36.2] (1)

(b) **Dishonestly fails to disclosed to another person information which he is under a legal duty to disclose, and intends, by failing to disclose that information—**
  (i) **to make a gain for himself or another, or**
  (ii) **to cause loss to another or to expose another to a risk of loss.**

Fraud Act 2006, s 1(2)(b)

A[36.3] (1)

(c) **Occupies a position in which he is expected to safeguard, or not to act against, the financial interests of another person, dishonestly abuses that position, and intends, by means of the abuse of that position—**
  (i) **to make a gain for himself or another, or**
  (ii) **to cause loss to another or to expose another to a risk of loss.**

Fraud Act 2006, s 1(2)(c)

A[36.4] Maximum penalty – 6 months' imprisonment and/or fine level 5 (for offences committed on or after 12 March 2015 an unlimited fine). Triable either way.

Crown Court – 10 years and unlimited fine.

Mode of trial

A[36.5] Consider first the notes at D[4]. In general, offences of fraud should be tried summarily except for the presence of one or more of the following factors (not an exhaustive list):

(a) breach of trust by a person in a person of substantial authority or in whom a high degree of trust has been placed;
(b) there has been sophisticated hiding or disguising of the offence;
(c) the offence has been committed by an organised gang;
(d) the victim was particularly vulnerable;
(e) there is unrecovered property of high value.

Legal notes and definitions

A[36.6] Fraud by false representation: s 1(2)(a). This offence is further defined in s 2 of the Act. The effect is to create a very broad offence which consists of lying for economic purposes. This is a "conduct crime". There is no requirement that a gain or anything else should have been obtained, or that a loss should have been caused, or that any risk of loss should have been created. Note, however, the words 'intends by'. It is a matter of fact in each case whether the required causative link between the intention and the false representation has been established: *R v Gilbert* [2012] EWCA Crim 2392, [2012] All ER (D) 251, where G was party to providing false information to open a bank account, but it was not suggested that she was party to a subsequent scheme to obtain computer equipment by means of post-dated cheques drawn on that account which were subsequently stopped, causing a loss of £130,000 to the supplier. The need to be sure of the above causative link had not been properly addressed and the conviction was, therefore, quashed.

A magistrates' court was correct to find a case to answer against the appellant who was alleged to have committed fraud by false representation. There was overwhelming evidence that the appellant had had another person impersonate him for the purposes of sitting a theory driving test: *Idrees v DPP* [2011] All ER (D) 156 (Feb), QBD.

A[36.7] **Dishonesty.** The test for dishonesty, which had stood unquestioned since *R v Ghosh* [1982] QB 1053, [2982] 2 All ER 689 (CA), mixed subjective and objective elements. The questions to be asked were, (1) was what was done dishonest according to the ordinary standards and reasonable and honest people? and (2) must the defendant have realised that what he/she was doing was dishonest according to those standards?

The meaning of 'dishonesty' was reviewed by the Supreme Court in *Ivey v Genting Casinos (UK) Ltd (trading as Crockfords)* [2017] UKSC 67, [2017] 3 WLR 1212. This was in the context of whether the offence of cheating under s 42 of the Gaming Act 2005 required proof of dishonesty and, if so, whether it was a defence – following the decision in *R v Ghosh* [1982] QB 1053, [1982] 2 All ER 689, 75 Cr App R 154 – that the defendant did not consider that what he had done was dishonest according to the ordinary standards of reasonable and honest people, even though it plainly was. The Court concluded that the mixture of subjective and objective elements contained in the *Ghosh* formulation was wrong, and that there was no justification for 'dishonesty' to bear a different meaning according to whether it arose in a civil or criminal context. The proper test was that which had been clearly established for some time in civil law, namely, 'Although a dishonest state of mind is a subjective mental state, the standard by which the law determines whether it is dishonest is objective. If by ordinary standards a defendant's mental state would be characterised as dishonest, it is irrelevant that the defendant judges by different standards. The Court of Appeal held this to be a correct state of the law and their Lordships agree.'

This part of the decision in *Ivey* was obiter since the Court concluded that dishonesty was not, in law, an element of the offence of cheating. Accordingly, as a matter of strict precedent, it remains open to the Court of Appeal to follow the decision in *Ghosh*, but it was stated by Sir Brian Leveson P in *Patterson v DPP* [2017] EWHC 2820 (Admin) that it would be 'difficult to imagine the Court of Appeal preferring *Ghosh* to *Ivey* in the future'.

Representation. A representation is 'false' if it is untrue or misleading and the person making it knows that it is, or might be, untrue or misleading. The term "representation" is widely defined as any representation as to fact or law, including a representation as to the state of the mind of –

(a) the person making the representation, or
(b) any other person.

In *Government of the United Arab Emirates v Allen* [2012] EWHC 1712 (Admin), [2012] 1 WLR 3419, the defendant, a British national, obtained a mortgage from a bank in the United Arab Emirates. The loan was for a period of 20 years, repayable by monthly instalments to be debited from the defendant's credit card account held with the bank. As security, the defendant provided the bank with an undated cheque in a sum approximately equal to the loan amount. Some 19 months later, the defendant defaulted on her loan payments and the bank presented the cheque for payment, but it 'bounced'. The defendant returned to the UK and thereafter was convicted in her absence in the UAE of an offence of issuing an uncovered cheque. The UAE sought her extradition, but this was refused on the basis that the 'dual criminality' requirement was not satisfied since the default on a loan agreement supported by the security of an undated cheque could not of itself amount to an offence in the United Kingdom of fraud by false representation contrary to s 2 of the Fraud Act 2006 (the UK offence relied on by the UAE). This decision was upheld on appeal. A 'representation' for the purposes of s 2 had to be capable of being expressed as a statement of the past or present, and did not include a simple promise of future action. While the issue of a post-dated cheque can convey an implied representation of existing fact – see *R v Gilmartin* [1983] QB 953 – it was necessary to consider the commercial context and what a reasonable person would have understood from the defendant's conduct in so doing. The defendant's contractual promises to the bank were not representations for the purposes of s 2. By agreeing to provide an undated cheque as security against a default on her loan, the defendant had not thereby impliedly represented that her current financial circumstances were such as to be able to say with confidence that in the event of that contingency occurring, at any time during the term of the loan, the cheque would in the ordinary course be met. Furthermore, there was no basis for concluding that the defendant had made any implied representation as to her financial circumstances which continued at the time when the cheque was presented. The only representation which could be inferred from the defendant's conduct was that she intended, at the time the loan agreement had been entered into, to honour its terms, but it was not alleged that such representation had been false.

A representation may be express or implied and is wide enough to include deceiving a mechanical device such as a machine (s 2(5)).

Knowing a representation is, or might be, misleading. The test is subjective, ie it is what the accused knows is or may be misleading and not what a reasonable person in his position would have known or suspected. '. . . the safest course for a judge to adopt is to pose to the jury the question for them in words as close as possible to those of the statute. Elaboration will rarely assist. It may be that some direction as to the consequences of an accused wilfully shutting his eyes to the obvious may be required, but rarely will more be needed': *R v Augunas* [2013] EWCA Crim 2046, [2014] 1 Cr App Rep 240 (per McCombe LJ at para 19).

Gain and loss. See s 5 of the Act. The terms are defined in the same terms as s 24 of the Theft Act 1968 and are to be construed as extending only to gain or loss in money or other property, but as extending to any such gain or loss whether temporary or permanent; and –

(i) "gain" includes a gain by keeping what one has, as well as gain by getting what one has not; and
(ii) "loss" includes a loss by not getting what one might get, as well as loss by parting with what one has.

A[36.8] Fraud by failing to disclose information: s 1(2)(b). This offence is further defined in s 3 of the Act. The section is narrower than s 1(2)(a) above, but there is some overlap between the two types of offence.

Dishonesty. There is no statutory definition. See A[36.7] above.

Gain and loss. Defined in A[36.7] above.

Legal duty. There is no statutory definition. The Law Commission report on Fraud (Law Com No 276, Cm 5560, 2002) explained the concept of legal duty as:

> '7.28 . . . Such a duty may derive from statute (such as the provisions governing company prospectuses), from the fact that the transaction in question is one of the utmost good faith (such as a contract of insurance), from the express or implied terms of a contract, from the custom of a particular trade or market, or from a fiduciary relationship between the parties (such as that of agent and principal).

> 7.29 For this purpose there is a legal duty to disclose information not only if the defendant's failure to disclose it gives the victim a cause of action for damages, but also if the law gives the victim a right to set aside any change in his or her legal position to which he or she may consent as a result of the non-disclosure. For example, a person in a fiduciary position has a duty to disclose material information when entering into a contract with his or her beneficiary, in the sense that a failure to make such disclosure will entitle the beneficiary to rescind the contract and to reclaim any property transferred under it.'

Liability to pay council tax is not to be equated with a liability to disclose residence, and under the statutory council tax scheme no such liability can be implied; accordingly, such a failure to disclose information cannot give rise to an offence under s 3: *R v D* [2019] EWCA Crim 209, [2019] 2 Cr App R 15, [2019] Crim L R 789.

It is no defence to claim a lack of knowledge as to the duty to disclose; nevertheless, the accused may claim a lack of **dishonesty.**

A[36.9] **Fraud by abuse of position: s 1(2)(c).** This offence is further defined in s 4 of the Act. It is the most controversial of the three forms of fraud and was criticised in Parliament as a "catch all provision that will be a nightmare of judicial interpretation". The section is intended to criminalise the secret profiteer such as the wine waiter selling his own bottles passing them off as a belonging to the restaurant (a form of cheat): see *R v Doukas* [1978] 1 All ER 1071. There is no legal requirement for the conduct to be "secret" and the government also emphasised that the potential for s 4 to combat legacy fraud with an expectation that charities will benefit to the tune of £2–3 million per annum.

Abuse. There is no statutory definition.

Dishonesty. There is no statutory definition. See A[36.7] above.

Position. The Law Commission report on Fraud (Law Com No 276, Cm 5560, 2002) explained the meaning of 'position' as:

> '7.38 The necessary relationship will be present between trustee and beneficiary, director and company, professional person and client, agent and principal, employee and employer, or between partners. It may arise otherwise, for example within a family, or in the context of voluntary work, or in any context where the parties are not at arm's length. In nearly all cases where it arises, it will be recognised by the civil law as imposing fiduciary duties, and any relationship that is so recognised will suffice. We see no reason, however, why the existence of such duties should be essential. This does not of course mean that it would be entirely a matter for the fact-finders whether the necessary relationship exists. The question whether the particular facts alleged can properly be described as giving rise to that relationship will be an issue capable of being ruled upon by a judge and, if the case goes to the jury, of being the subject of directions.'

The breadth of the offence gives rise to the potential for all sorts of civil law disputes within the family or employment to become issues of criminal law. As elsewhere the element of **dishonesty** may prove crucial.

A[36.10] Update 12 of the Magistrates' Court sentencing guidelines took in the new definitive guideline of the Sentencing Council on fraud, bribery and money laundering. The same kind of fraud may be charged in a number of ways and the guidelines reflect this. The categories are: fraud by false representation, failing to disclose information and by abuse of position; possessing, making or supplying articles for use in fraud; revenue fraud; benefit fraud; money laundering; bribery; and corporate offences fraud, bribery and money laundering.

The guidelines on fraud by false representation, failing to disclose information and by abuse of position; and revenue fraud are reproduced below. (There are separate guidelines for corporate offenders which are not reproduced since cases are rarely heard in the magistrates' court.)

Fraud

Fraud by false representation, fraud by failing to disclose information, fraud by abuse of position

Fraud Act 2006 (section 1)

Triable either way

Conspiracy to defraud

Common law

Triable on indictment only

Maximum: 10 years' custody

Offence range: Discharge – 8 years' custody

False accounting

Theft Act 1968 (section 17)

Triable either way

Maximum: 7 years' custody

Offence range: Discharge – 6 years and 6 months' custody

STEP ONE
Determining the offence category

The court should determine the offence category with reference to the tables below. In order to determine the category the court should assess **culpability** and **harm.**

Culpability demonstrated by one or more of the following:

A – High culpability
A leading role where offending is part of a group activity Involvement of others through pressure, influence
Abuse of position of power or trust or responsibility
Sophisticated nature of offence/significant planning
Fraudulent activity conducted over sustained period of time
Large number of victims
Deliberately targeting victim on basis of vulnerability
B – Medium culpability
Other cases where characteristics for categories A or C are not present
A significant role where offending is part of a group activity
C – Lesser culpability
Involved through coercion, intimidation or exploitation
Not motivated by personal gain
Peripheral role in organised fraud
Opportunistic 'one-off' offence; very little or no planning
Limited awareness or understanding of the extent of fraudulent activity

Where there are characteristics present which fall under different levels of culpability, the court should balance these characteristics to reach a fair assessment of the offender's culpability.

Harm is initially assessed by the actual*, intended or risked loss as may arise from the offence.

The values in the table below are to be used for **actual** or **intended** loss only.

Intended loss relates to offences where circumstances prevent the actual loss that is intended to be caused by the fraudulent activity.

* Where consequential loss is alleged it must be proved to the criminal standard that it was caused as a direct result of the offending: *RR v Green* [2016] EWCA Crim 1888, [2017] 1 Cr App R (S) 22.

Risk of loss (for instance in mortgage frauds) involves consideration of both the likelihood of harm occurring and the extent of it if it does. Risk of loss is less serious than actual or intended loss. Where the offence has caused risk of loss but no (or much less) actual loss the normal approach is to move down to the corresponding point in the next category. This may not be appropriate if either the likelihood or extent of risked loss is particularly high.

Harm A – Loss caused or intended		
Category 1	£500,000 or more	Starting point based on £1 million
Category 2	£100,000 – £500,000 or Risk or category 1 harm	Starting point based on £300,000
Category 3	£20,000 – £100,000 or Risk of category 2 harm	Starting point based on £50,000
Category 4	£5,000 – £20,000 or Risk of category 3 harm	Starting point based on £12,500
Category 5	Less than £5,000 or Risk of category 4 harm	Starting point based on £2,500
Risk of category 5 harm, move down the range within the category		

Harm B – Victim impact demonstrated by one or more of the following:
The court should then take into account the level of harm caused to the victim(s) or others to determine whether it warrants the sentence being moved up to the corresponding point in the next category or further up the range of the initial category.
High impact – move up a category; if in category 1 move up the range
Serious detrimental effect on the victim whether financial or otherwise, for example substantial damage to credit rating
Victim particularly vulnerable (due to factors including but not limited to their age, financial circumstances, mental capacity)
Medium impact – move upwards within the category range
Considerable detrimental effect on the victim whether financial or otherwise
Lesser impact – no adjustment
Some detrimental impact on victim, whether financial or otherwise

STEP TWO
Starting point and category range

Having determined the category at step one, the court should use the appropriate starting point (as adjusted in accordance with step one above) to reach a sentence within the category range in the table below. The starting point applies to all offenders irrespective of plea or previous convictions.

Where the value is larger or smaller than the amount on which the starting point is based, this should lead to upward or downward adjustment as appropriate.

Where the value greatly exceeds the amount of the starting point in category 1, it may be appropriate to move outside the identified range.

TABLE 1

Section 1 Fraud Act 2006

Conspiracy to defraud

Maximum: 10 years' custody

	A	B	C
Category 1 £500,000 or more	**Starting point** 7 years' custody	**Starting point** 5 years' custody	**Starting point** 3 years' custody
Starting point based on £1 million	**Category range** 5 – 8 years' custody	**Category range** 3 – 6 years' custody	**Category range** 18 months' – 4 years' custody
Category 2 £100,000–£500,000	**Starting point** 5 years' custody	**Starting point** 3 years' custody	**Starting point** 18 months' custody
Starting point based on £300,000	**Category range** 3 – 6 years' custody	**Category range** 18 months' – 4 years' custody	**Category range** 26 weeks' – 3 years' custody
Category 3 £20,000 - £100,000	**Starting point** 3 years' custody	**Starting point** 18 months' custody	**Starting point** 26 weeks' custody
Starting point based on £50,000	**Category range** 18 months' – 4 years' custody	**Category range** 26 weeks' – 3 years' custody	**Category range** Medium level community order – 1 year's custody
Category 4 £5,000- £20,000	**Starting point** 18 months' custody	**Starting point** 26 weeks' custody	**Starting point** Medium level community order
Starting point based on £12,500	**Category range** 26 weeks' – 3 years' custody	**Category range** Medium level community order – 1 year's custody	**Category range** Band B fine – High level community order
Category 5 Less than £5,000	**Starting point** 36 weeks' custody	**Starting point** Medium level community order	**Starting point** Band B fine
Starting point based on £2,500	**Category range** High level community order – 1 year's custody	**Category range** Band B fine – 26 weeks' custody	**Category range** Discharge – Medium level community order

TABLE 2

Section 17 Theft Act 1968: false accounting

Maximum: 7 years' custody

	A	B	C
Category 1 £500,000 or more	**Starting point** 5 years 6 months' custody	**Starting point** 4 years' custody	**Starting point** 2 years 6 months' custody
Starting point based on £1 million	**Category range** 4 years' – 6 years 6 months' custody	**Category range** 2 years 6 months' – 5 years' custody	**Category range** 15 months' – 3 years 6 months' custody
Category 2 £100,000–£500,000	**Starting point** 4 years' custody	**Starting point** 2 years 6 months' custody	**Starting point** 15 months' custody
Starting point based on £300,000	**Category range** 2 years 6 months' – 5 years' custody	**Category range** 15 months' – 3 years 6 months' custody	**Category range** 26 weeks' – 2 years 6 months' custody
Category 3 £20,000 - £100,000	**Starting point** 2 years 6 months' custody	**Starting point** 15 months' custody	**Starting point** High level community order
Starting point based on £50,000	**Category range** 15 months' – 3 years 6 months' custody	**Category range** High level community order – 2 years 6 months' custody	**Category range** Low level community order – 36 weeks' custody
Category 4 £5,000- £20,000	**Starting point** 15 months' custody	**Starting point** High level community order	**Starting point** Low level community order
Starting point based on £12,500	**Category range** High level community order – 2 years 6 months' custody	**Category range** Low level community order – 36 weeks' custody	**Category range** Band B fine – Medium level community order
Category 5 Less than £5,000	**Starting point** 26 weeks' custody	**Starting point** Low level community order	**Starting point** Band B fine
Starting point based on £2,500	**Category range** Medium level community order – 36 weeks' custody	**Category range** Band B fine – Medium level community order	**Category range** Discharge – Low level community order

The table below contains a non-exhaustive list of additional factual elements providing the context of the offence and factors relating to the offender.

Identify whether any combination of these or other relevant factors should result in an upward or downward adjustment from the sentence arrived at so far.

Consecutive sentences for multiple offences may be appropriate where large sums are involved.

Factors increasing seriousness	**Factors reducing seriousness or reflecting personal mitigation**
Statutory aggravating factors	No previous convictions or no relevant/recent convictions
Previous convictions, having regard to a) the nature of the offence to which the conviction relates and its relevance to the current offence; and b) the time that has elapsed since the conviction	Remorse

Factors increasing seriousness	Factors reducing seriousness or reflecting personal mitigation
Offence committed whilst on bail	Good character and/or exemplary conduct
Other aggravating factors	Little or no prospect of success
Steps taken to prevent the victim reporting or obtaining assistance and/or from assisting or supporting the prosecution	Serious medical conditions requiring urgent, intensive or long-term treatment
Attempts to conceal/dispose of evidence	Age and/or lack of maturity where it affects the responsibility of the offender
Established evidence of community/wider impact	Lapse of time since apprehension where this does not arise from the conduct of the offender
Failure to comply with current court orders	Mental disorder or learning disability
Offence committed on licence	Sole or primary carer for dependent relatives
Offences taken into consideration	Offender co-operated with investigation, made early admissions and/or voluntarily reported offending
Failure to respond to warnings about behaviour	Determination and/or demonstration of steps having been taken to address addiction or offending behaviour
Offences committed across borders	Activity originally legitimate
Blame wrongly placed on others	

STEP THREE
Consider any factors which indicate a reduction, such as assistance to the prosecution

The court should take into account sections 73 and 74 of the Serious Organised Crime and Police Act 2005 (assistance by defendants: reduction or review of sentence) and any other rule of law by virtue of which an offender may receive a discounted sentence in consequence of assistance given (or offered) to the prosecutor or investigator.

STEP FOUR
Reduction for guilty pleas

The court should take account of any potential reduction for a guilty plea in accordance with section 144 of the Criminal Justice Act 2003 and the *Guilty Plea* guideline.

STEP FIVE
Totality principle

If sentencing an offender for more than one offence, or where the offender is already serving a sentence, consider whether the total sentence is just and proportionate to the overall offending behaviour.

STEP SIX
Confiscation, compensation and ancillary orders

The court must proceed with a view to making a confiscation order if it is asked to do so by the prosecutor or if the court believes it is appropriate for it to do so.

Where the offence has resulted in loss or damage the court must consider whether to make a compensation order.

If the court makes both a confiscation order and an order for compensation and the court believes the offender will not have sufficient means to satisfy both orders in full, the court must direct that the compensation be paid out of sums recovered under the confiscation order (section 13 of the Proceeds of Crime Act 2002).

The court may also consider whether to make ancillary orders. These may include a deprivation order, a financial reporting order, a serious crime prevention order and disqualification from acting as a company director.

STEP SEVEN
Reasons

Section 174 of the Criminal Justice Act 2003 imposes a duty to give reasons for, and explain the effect of, the sentence.

STEP EIGHT
Consideration for time spent on bail

The court must consider whether to give credit for time spent on bail in accordance with section 240A of the Criminal Justice Act 2003.

Revenue fraud

Fraud – Conspiracy to defraud (common law)

Triable on indictment only

Fraud Act 2006 (section 1)

Triable either way

Maximum: 10 years' custody

Offence range: Low level community order – 8 years' custody

False accounting

Theft Act 1968 (section 17)

Fraudulent evasion of VAT; False statement for VAT purposes; Conduct amounting to an offence

Value Added Tax Act 1994 (section 72)

Fraudulent evasion of income tax

Taxes Management Act 1970 (section 106A)

Fraudulent evasion of excise duty; Improper importation of goods

Customs and Excise Management Act 1979 (sections 50, 170 and 170B)

Triable either way

Maximum: 7 years' custody

Offence range: Band C fine – 6 years and 6 months' custody

Fraud – Cheat the public revenue (common law)

Triable on indictment only

Maximum: Life imprisonment

Offence range: 3 – 17 years' custody

STEP ONE
Determining the offence category

The court should determine the offence category with reference to the tables below. In order to determine the category the court should assess **culpability** and **harm.**

The level of culpability is determined by weighing up all the factors of the case to determine the offender's role and the extent to which the offending was planned and the sophistication with which it was carried out.

A – High culpability
A leading role where offending is part of a group activity Involvement of others through pressure, influence
Abuse of position of power or trust or responsibility
Sophisticated nature of offence/significant planning
Fraudulent activity conducted over sustained period of time
Large number of victims
B – Medium culpability
Other cases where characteristics for categories A or C are not present
A significant role where offending is part of a group activity
C – Lesser culpability
Involved through coercion, intimidation or exploitation
Not motivated by personal gain
Peripheral role in organised fraud
Opportunistic 'one-off' offence; very little or no planning
Limited awareness or understanding of the extent of fraudulent activity

Where there are characteristics present which fall under different levels of culpability, the court should balance these characteristics to reach a fair assessment of the offender's culpability.

Category 1
£50 million or more Starting point based on £80 million
Category 2
£10 million–£50 million Starting point based on £30 million
Category 3
£2 million–£10 million Starting point based on £5 million
Category 4
£500,000–£2 million Starting point based on £1 million
Category 5
£100,000–£500,000 Starting point based on £300,000
Category 6
£20,000–£100,000 Starting point based on £50,000

Category 7
Less than £20,000 Starting point based on £12,500

STEP TWO
Starting point and category range

Having determined the category at step one, the court should use the appropriate starting point to reach a sentence within the category range in the table below. The starting point applies to all offenders irrespective of plea or previous convictions.

Where the value is larger or smaller than the amount on which the starting point is based, this should lead to upward or downward adjustment as appropriate.

Where the value greatly exceeds the amount of the starting point in category 1, it may be appropriate to move outside the identified range.

TABLE 1

Section 1 Fraud Act 2006

Conspiracy to defraud (common law)

Maximum: 10 years' custody

	A	**B**	**C**
Category 4 **£500,000 or more**	**Starting point** 7 years' custody	**Starting point** 5 years' custody	**Starting point** 3 years' custody
Starting point based on £1 million	**Category range** 5 – 8 years' custody	**Category range** 3 – 6 years' custody	**Category range** 18 months' – 4 years' custody
Category 5 **£100,000–£500,000**	**Starting point** 5 years' custody	**Starting point** 3 years' custody	**Starting point** 18 months' custody
Starting point based on £300,000	**Category range** 3 – 6 years' custody	**Category range** 18 months' – 4 years' custody	**Category range** 26 weeks' – 3 years' custody
Category 6 **£20,000 - £100,000**	**Starting point** 3 years' custody	**Starting point** 18 months' custody	**Starting point** 26 weeks' custody
Starting point based on £50,000	**Category range** 18 months' – 4 years' custody	**Category range** 26 weeks' – 3 years' custody	**Category range** Medium level community order – 1 year's custody
Category 7 Less than £20,000	**Starting point** 18 months' custody	**Starting point** 36 weeks' custody	**Starting point** Medium level community order
Starting point based on £12,500	**Category range** 36 weeks' – 3 years' custody	**Category range** Medium level community order – 1 year's custody	**Category range** Low level community order – High level community order

TABLE 2

Section 17 Theft Act 1968: False Accounting

Section 72(1) Value Added Tax Act 1994: Fraudulent evasion of VAT

Section 72(3) Valued Added Tax Act 1994: False statement for VAT purposes

Section 72(8) Value Added Tax Act 1994: Conduct amounting to an offence

Section 106(a) Taxes Management Act 1970: Fraudulent evasion of income tax

Section 170(1)(a)(i), (ii), (b), 170(2)(a), 170B

Customs and Excise Management Act 1979: Fraudulent evasion of excise duty

Section 50(1)(a), (2)

Customs and Excise Management Act 1979: Improper importation of goods

Maximum: 7 years' custody

Harm	A	B	C
Category 4 £500,000 or more	**Starting point** 5 years 6 months' custody	**Starting point** 4 years' custody	**Starting point** 2 years 6 months' custody
Starting point based on £1 million	**Category range** 4 years' – 6 years 6 months' custody	**Category range** 2 years 6 months' – 5 years' custody	**Category range** 15 months' – 3 years 6 months' custody
Category 5 £100,000–£500,000	**Starting point** 4 years' custody	**Starting point** 2 years 6 months' custody	**Starting point** 15 months' custody
Starting point based on £300,000	**Category range** 2 years 6 months' – 5 years' custody	**Category range** 15 months' – 3 years 6 months' custody	**Category range** 26 weeks' – 2 years 6 months' custody
Category 6 £20,000 –£100,000	**Starting point** 2 years 6 months' custody	**Starting point** 15 months' custody	**Starting point** High level community order
Starting point based on £50,000	**Category range** 15 months' – 3 years 6 months' custody	**Category range** High level community order – 2 years 6 months' custody	**Category range** Low level community order – 36 weeks' custody
Category 7 Less than £20,000	**Starting point** 15 months' custody	**Starting point** 26 weeks' custody	**Starting point** Low level community order
Starting point based on £12,500	**Category range** High level community order – 2 years 6 months' custody	**Category range** Medium level community order – 15 months' custody	**Category range** Band C fine – High level community order

TABLE 3

Cheat the Revenue (common law)

Maximum: Life imprisonment

Where the offending is on the most serious scale, involving sums significantly higher than the starting point in category 1, sentences of 15 years and above may be appropriate depending on the role of the offender. In cases involving sums below £2 million the court should refer to Table 1.

Harm	A	B	C
Category 1 £50 million or more	Starting point 12 years' custody	Starting point 8 years' custody	Starting point 6 years' custody
Starting point based on £80 million	Category range 10 – 17 years' custody	Category range 7 – 12 years' custody	Category range 4 – 8 years' custody
Category 2 £10 million–£50 million	Starting point 10 years' custody	Starting point 7 years' custody	Starting point 5 years' custody
Starting point based on £30 million	Category range 8 – 13 years' custody	Category range 5 – 9 years' custody	Category range 3 – 6 years' custody
Category 3 £2 million–£10 million	Starting point 8 years' custody	Starting point 6 years' custody	Starting point 4 years' custody
Starting point based on £5 million	Category range 6 – 10 years' custody	Category range 4 – 7 years' custody	Category range 3 – 5 years' custody

The table below contains a non-exhaustive list of additional factual elements providing the context of the offence and factors relating to the offender.

Identify whether any combination of these or other relevant factors should result in any further upward or downward adjustment from the starting point.

Consecutive sentences for multiple offences may be appropriate where large sums are involved.

Factors increasing seriousness	Factors reducing seriousness or reflecting personal mitigation
Statutory aggravating factors	No previous convictions or no relevant/recent convictions
Previous convictions, having regard to a) the nature of the offence to which the conviction relates and its relevance to the current offence; and b) the time that has elapsed since the conviction	Remorse
Offence committed whilst on bail	Good character and/or exemplary conduct
Other aggravating factors	Little or no prospect of success
Involves multiple frauds	Serious medical conditions requiring urgent, intensive or long-term treatment
Number of false declarations	Age and/or lack of maturity where it affects the responsibility of the offender
Attempts to conceal/dispose of evidence	Lapse of time since apprehension where this does not arise from the conduct of the offender
Failure to comply with current court orders	Mental disorder or learning disability
Offence committed on licence	Sole or primary carer for dependent relatives

Factors increasing seriousness	Factors reducing seriousness or reflecting personal mitigation
Offences taken into consideration	Offender co-operated with investigation, made early admissions and/or voluntarily reported offending
Failure to respond to warnings about behaviour	Determination and/or demonstration of steps having been taken to address addiction or offending behaviour
Blame wrongly placed on others	Activity originally legitimate
Damage to third party (for example as a result of identity theft)	
Dealing with goods with an additional health risk	
Disposing of goods to under age purchasers	

STEP THREE
Consider any factors which indicate a reduction, such as assistance to the prosecution

The court should take into account sections 73 and 74 of the Serious Organised Crime and Police Act 2005 (assistance by defendants: reduction or review of sentence) and any other rule of law by virtue of which an offender may receive a discounted sentence in consequence of assistance given (or offered) to the prosecutor or investigator.

STEP FOUR
Reduction for guilty pleas

The court should take account of any potential reduction for a guilty plea in accordance with section 144 of the Criminal Justice Act 2003 and the *Guilty Plea* guideline.

STEP FIVE
Totality principle

If sentencing an offender for more than one offence, or where the offender is already serving a sentence, consider whether the total sentence is just and proportionate to the overall offending behaviour.

STEP SIX
Confiscation, compensation and ancillary orders

The court must proceed with a view to making a confiscation order if it is asked to do so by the prosecutor or if the court believes it is appropriate for it to do so.

Where the offence has resulted in loss or damage the court must consider whether to make a compensation order.

If the court makes both a confiscation order and an order for compensation and the court believes the offender will not have sufficient means to satisfy both orders in full, the court must direct that the compensation be paid out of sums recovered under the confiscation order (section 13 of the Proceeds of Crime Act 2002).

The court may also consider whether to make ancillary orders. These may include a deprivation order, a financial reporting order, a serious crime prevention order and disqualification from acting as a company director.

STEP SEVEN
Reasons

Section 174 of the Criminal Justice Act 2003 imposes a duty to give reasons for, and explain the effect of, the sentence.

STEP EIGHT
Consideration for time spent on bail

The court must consider whether to give credit for time spent on bail in accordance with section 240A of the Criminal Justice Act 2003.

A[37]
Fraud: obtaining services dishonestly

Charge (Fraud: obtaining services dishonestly)

A[37.1] **(1) Obtains services for himself or another—**

(a) by a dishonest act, and
(b) in breach of subsection (2)

(2)

(a) the services are made available on the basis that payment has been, is being or will be made for or in respect of them,
(b) obtains them without any payment having been made for or in respect of them or without payment having been made in full, and
(c) when he obtains them, he knows—
  (i) that they are being made available on the basis as described in paragraph (a), or
  (ii) that they might be

but intends that payment will not be made, or will not be made in full.

Fraud Act 2006, s 11.

Maximum penalty – 6 months' imprisonment and/or fine level 5 (for offences committed on or after 12 March 2015 an unlimited fine). Triable either way

(**NB:** Until repealed by the CJA 2003, the general limit on a magistrates' court is to impose imprisonment up to a maximum of six months for one offence: s 78 PCC (S) Act 2000.)

Crown Court – five years and an unlimited fine.

Mode of trial

A[37.2] Consider first the notes at D[4]. In general, offences of obtaining services dishonestly should be tried summarily except for the presence of one or more of the following factors (not an exhaustive list):

(a) breach of trust by a person in position of substantial authority or in whom a high degree of trust has been placed;
(b) there has been a sophisticated hiding or disguising of the offence;
(c) the offence has been committed by an organised gang;
(d) the victim was particularly vulnerable;
(e) there is unrecovered property of high value.

Legal notes and definitions

A[37.3] **Services.** As with the 1978 Act it applies only to services for which payment is required. There must be an act and an obtaining of the service.

Intention. The new offence is wider than the old offence in that it can cover obtaining services through a wholly automated process; however, it is narrower than the old offence because the defendant must intend to avoid payment which presents problems if D knows that the bank will pay.

Act. The new offence extends well beyond the machine 'deception' offences, to encompass eg cases where the defendant climbs a wall to watch a football match without paying the entrance fee (even though not deceiving the provider of the service directly); this is because the defendant is obtaining a service which is provided on the basis that people will pay for it.

As under the Theft Acts 1968 and 1978, an application for a bank account or credit card will only be caught if the service is to be paid for (see *R v Sofroniou* [2003] EWCA Crim 3681).

Dishonesty. There is no statutory definition. See **A[36.7]** above.

Sentencing
Fraud – Obtaining Services Dishonestly (Fraud Act 2006, s 11)

A[37.4] Triable either way:

Maximum when tried summarily: Level 5 fine and/or 6 months

Maximum when tried on indictment: 5 years

The offence of **obtaining services dishonestly** may be committed in circumstances that otherwise could be charged as an offence contrary to s 1 of the Fraud Act 2006 or may be more akin to *making off without payment*, contrary to s 3 of the Theft Act 1978.

For this reason, it has not been included specifically within any of the guidelines for fraud, and one of the following approaches should be used:

- where it involves conduct which can be characterised as a fraud offence (such as obtaining credit through fraud or payment card fraud), the court should apply the guideline for the relevant type of fraud (see **A[31]** and **A[36]**); or
- where the conduct could be characterised as *making off without payment* (where an offender, knowing that payment on the spot for any goods supplied or service done is required or expected, dishonestly makes off without having paid and with intent to avoid payment), the guideline for that offence should be used: **A[21.16]**.

A[38]
Possession of articles for fraud

Charge (Possession of articles for fraud)

A[38.1] The defendant [person] had in his possession or under this control any article for use in the course of or in connection with any fraud

Fraud Act 2006, s 6.

Maximum penalty – 6 months' imprisonment and/or fine level 5 (for offences committed on or after 12 March 2015 an unlimited fine). Triable either way.

(**NB:** until repealed by the CJA 2003, the general limit on a magistrates' courts sentencing powers is six months imprisonment for a single offence: s 78 PCC(S)A 2000).

Crown Court – 5 years' imprisonment and unlimited fine.

An on-line introduction to the legislation can be found on **Crimeline** (see issue 203, crimeline.info).

Mode of trial

A[38.2] Consider first the general notes at D[4]. In general, offences of possessing articles for fraud should be tried summarily except for the presence of one or more of the following factors (not an exhaustive list):

(a) offence committed by a person in a position of substantial authority or in whom a high degree of trust has been placed;
(b) sophisticated offence or disguising of the offence;
(c) the offence has been committed by an organised gang;
(d) targeting of a vulnerable victim;
(e) property acquired of high value (or would have been).

Legal notes and definitions

A[38.3] This is another very wide offence. It was created in order to meet concerns that the s 25 of the Theft Act 1968 offence of going equipped, was outdated in relation to its application to modern fraud cases eg given that many frauds are now perpetrated from home computers. Unlike s 25, there is no requirement to prove that the relevant articles were carried or used outside the defendant's "place of abode".

When the words 'or cheat' (repealed by this Act) appeared in the offence of going equipped for theft in s 25 of the Theft Act 1968, they were interpreted as follows. In *R v Rashid* [1977] 2 All ER 237, 141 JP 305, because of a misdirection to the jury, the defendant was held to have been wrongly convicted of possession of bread and tomatoes with which he intended to make sandwiches for sale to passengers on a train on which he was a steward. In that case the Court of Appeal, in an obiter dicta, expressed the view that on the facts of the case there was probably no obtaining by deception and that it was not appropriate to exalt a breach of contractual duty owed to the defendant's employers into a criminal offence. But *R v Rashid*, was distinguished in *R v Doukas* [1978] 1 All ER 1061, where a wine waiter in an hotel was held to have been properly convicted of having with him his own wine which he dishonestly intended to sell to customers as property of his employers. In the latter case it was held that it had to be assumed that the hypothetical customer against whom the intended deception was to be practised was reasonably honest and intelligent, and that it was unlikely that any customer to whom the true situation was made clear would willingly make himself a party to what was a fraud by the waiter on his employer. See also *R v Corboz* [1984] Crim LR 629 and *R v Whiteside* and *R v Antoniou* [1989] Crim LR 436, CA.

Article. Includes "any program or data held in electronic form" – Fraud Act 2006, s 8. The offence is designed to combat the growing menace of computer programs used to generate credit card numbers and blank utility bills.

Intention. It is not necessary to prove intended use in a particular fraud. The Crown must prove that the defendant had a general intention that the article be used by someone for a fraudulent purpose (as with the interpretation of intent in going equipped: see *R v Ellames* [1974] 3 AER 130. The article must, however, be with the defendant for the purpose or intention that it will be used for fraud then or in the future. It is insufficient that the article may have been used for fraud in the past: *R v Sakalauskas* [2013] EWCA Crim 2278, (2014) 178 JP 30(applying *Ellames*).

Possession or control. It is submitted that the said terms will be construed analogous to offences under eg the Misuse of Drugs Act 1971 (see **A[25.7]**).

Sentencing
Fraud – Possessing, making or supplying articles for use in fraud

A[38.4]–[38.6] Possession of articles for use in frauds

Fraud Act 2006 (section 6)

Triable either way

Maximum: 5 years' custody

Offence range: Band A fine – 3 years' custody

Making or supplying articles for use in frauds

Fraud Act 2006 (section 7)

Triable either way

Maximum: 10 years' custody

Offence range: Band C fine – 7 years' custody

STEP ONE
Determining the offence category

The court should determine the offence category with reference to the tables below. In order to determine the category the court should assess **culpability** and **harm.**

The level of **culpability** is determined by weighing up all the factors of the case to determine the offender's role and the extent to which the offending was planned and the sophistication with which it was carried out.

Culpability demonstrated by one or more of the following:

A – High culpability
A leading role where offending is part of a group activity Involvement of others through pressure, influence
Involvement of others through pressure, influence
Abuse of position of power or trust or responsibility
Sophisticated nature of offence/significant planning
Fraudulent activity conducted over sustained period of time

Articles deliberately designed to target victims on basis of vulnerability
B – Medium culpability
Other cases where characteristics for categories A or C are not present
A significant role where offending is part of a group activity
C – Lesser culpability
Performed limited function under direction
Involved through coercion, intimidation or exploitation
Not motivated by personal gain
Opportunistic 'one-off' offence; very little or no planning
Limited awareness or understanding of the extent of fraudulent activity

Where there are characteristics present which fall under different levels of culpability, the court should balance these characteristics to reach a fair assessment of the offender's culpability.

HARM

This guideline refers to preparatory offences where no substantive fraud has been committed. The level of **harm** is determined by weighing up all the factors of the case to determine the harm that would be caused if the article(s) were used to commit a substantive offence.

Greater harm
Large number of articles created/supplied/in possession
Article(s) have potential to facilitate fraudulent acts affecting large number of victims
Article(s) have potential to facilitate fraudulent acts involving significant sums Use of third party identities
Offender making considerable gain as result of the offence
Lesser harm
All other offences

STEP TWO
Starting point and category range

Having determined the category at step one, the court should use the appropriate starting point to reach a sentence within the category range in the table below. The starting point applies to all offenders irrespective of plea or previous convictions.

Section 6 Fraud Act 2006: Possessing articles for use in fraud

Maximum: 5 years' custody

	Culpability		
	A	**B**	**C**
Greater	**Starting point** 18 months' custody	**Starting point** 36 weeks' custody	**Starting point** High level community order
	Category range 36 weeks' custody – 3 years' custody	**Category range** High level community order – 2 years' custody	**Category range** Medium level community order – 26 weeks' custody
Lesser	**Starting point** 26 weeks' custody	**Starting point** Medium level community order	**Starting point** Band B fine

	Culpability		
	A	B	C
	Category range High level community order – 18 months' custody	Category range Low level community order – 26 weeks' custody	Category range Band A fine – Medium level community order

Section 7 Fraud Act 2006: Making or adapting or supplying articles for use in fraud

Maximum: 10 years' custody

	Culpability		
	A	B	C
Greater	Starting point 4 years 6 months' custody	Starting point 2 years 6 months' custody	Starting point 1 year's custody
	Category range 3 – 7 years' custody	Category range 18 months' – 5 years' custody	Category range High level community order – 3 years' custody
Lesser	Starting point 2 years' custody	Starting point 36 weeks' custody	Starting point Medium level community order
	Category range 26 weeks' – 4 years' custody	Category range Low level community order – 2 years' custody	Category range Band C fine – 26 weeks' custody

The table below contains a non-exhaustive list of additional factual elements providing the context of the offence and factors relating to the offender.

Identify whether any combination of these or other relevant factors should result in an upward or downward adjustment from the sentence arrived at so far.

Consecutive sentences for multiple offences may be appropriate where large sums are involved.

Factors increasing seriousness	Factors reducing seriousness or reflecting personal mitigation
Statutory aggravating factors	No previous convictions or no relevant/recent convictions
Previous convictions, having regard to a) the nature of the offence to which the conviction relates and its relevance to the current offence; and b) the time that has elapsed since the conviction	Remorse
Offence committed whilst on bail	Good character and/or exemplary conduct
Other aggravating factors	Little or no prospect of success
Steps taken to prevent the victim reporting or obtaining assistance and/or from assisting or supporting the prosecution	Serious medical conditions requiring urgent, intensive or long-term treatment
Attempts to conceal/dispose of evidence	Age and/or lack of maturity where it affects the responsibility of the offender

Factors increasing seriousness	Factors reducing seriousness or reflecting personal mitigation
Established evidence of community/wider impact	Lapse of time since apprehension where this does not arise from the conduct of the offender
Failure to comply with current court orders	Mental disorder or learning disability
Offence committed on licence	Sole or primary carer for dependent relatives
Offences taken into consideration	Offender co-operated with investigation, made early admissions and/or voluntarily reported offending
Failure to respond to warnings about behaviour	Determination and/or demonstration of steps having been taken to address addiction or offending behaviour
Offences committed across borders	Activity originally legitimate
Blame wrongly placed on others	

STEP THREE
Consider any factors which indicate a reduction, such as assistance to the prosecution

The court should take into account sections 73 and 74 of the Serious Organised Crime and Police Act 2005 (assistance by defendants: reduction or review of sentence) and any other rule of law by virtue of which an offender may receive a discounted sentence in consequence of assistance given (or offered) to the prosecutor or investigator.

STEP FOUR
Reduction for guilty pleas

The court should take account of any potential reduction for a guilty plea in accordance with section 144 of the Criminal Justice Act 2003 and the *Guilty Plea* guideline.

STEP FIVE
Totality principle

If sentencing an offender for more than one offence, or where the offender is already serving a sentence, consider whether the total sentence is just and proportionate to the overall offending behaviour.

STEP SIX
Confiscation, compensation and ancillary orders

The court must proceed with a view to making a confiscation order if it is asked to do so by the prosecutor or if the court believes it is appropriate for it to do so.

Where the offence has resulted in loss or damage the court must consider whether to make a compensation order.

If the court makes both a confiscation order and an order for compensation and the court believes the offender will not have sufficient means to satisfy both orders in full, the court must direct that the compensation be paid out of sums recovered under the confiscation order (section 13 of the Proceeds of Crime Act 2002).

The court may also consider whether to make ancillary orders.

STEP SEVEN
Reasons

Section 174 of the Criminal Justice Act 2003 imposes a duty to give reasons for, and explain the effect of, the sentence.

STEP EIGHT
Consideration for time spent on bail

The court must consider whether to give credit for time spent on bail in accordance with section 240A of the Criminal Justice Act 2003.

A[39]

Making, adapting, supplying or offering to supply articles for fraud

Charge (Making, adapting, supplying etc articles for fraud)

A[39.1] **The defendant [person] makes, adapts, supplies or offers to supply any article –**

(a) **knowing that it is designed or adapted for use in the course of or in connection with fraud, or**
(b) **intending it to be used to commit, or assist in the commission of, fraud**

Fraud Act 2006, s 7.

Maximum penalty – 6 months' imprisonment and/or fine level 5 (for offences committed on or after 12 March 2015 an unlimited fine). Triable either way.

Crown Court – 10 years' imprisonment and an unlimited fine.

Mode of trial

A[39.2] Consider first the general notes at D[4]. In general, offences of making/adapting articles etc for fraud should be tried summarily except for the presence of one or more of the following factors (not an exhaustive list):

(a) offence committed by a person in a position of substantial authority or in whom a high degree of trust has been placed;
(b) sophisticated offence or disguising of the offence;
(c) the offence has been committed by an organised gang;
(d) targeting of a vulnerable victim;
(e) property acquired or high value (or would have been).

Legal notes and definition

A[39.3] This offence is aimed at, amongst others, the manufacturers of the 'black boxes' (which caused electricity meters to under-record consumption) in the well-known case of *R v Hollinshead* [1985] AC 975. The defendants in that case were convicted of conspiracy to defraud at common law (still preserved under the Fraud Act 2006). It would no longer be necessary to rely on the common law in such a case.

Parliament has created numerous specific offences to tackle similar behaviour see eg Communications Act 2003, s 126; Mobile Telephones (Re-programming) Act 2002, s 2; but this is a valuable general offence wide enough to catch eg software manufacturers producing programmes designed for criminal purposes.

It is not clear what the difference is, if any, between 'in the course of' (s 7(1)(a)) and 'in the commission of' (s 7(1)(b)).

A[39.4] **Article.** Includes any "program or data held in electronic form" – Fraud Act 2006, s 8.

Makes. It is submitted that the term would be accorded its ordinary dictionary meaning.

Adapts. It is submitted that the term would be accorded its ordinary dictionary meaning.

Supplies. It is submitted that the term will be given its ordinary everyday meaning similar to eg under the Misuse of Drugs Act 1971. The offence does not appear to require proof of payment or reward. 'Supply' connotes more than a mere transfer of physical control of some chattel or object from one person to another. There is an additional concept namely that of enabling the recipient to apply the thing transferred for his own nefarious desires or purposes (see *R v Maginnis* [1987] AC 303, HL).

Offers to supply. It is inappropriate to introduce civil notions of offer and acceptance. The offence lies in the making of the offer to supply any article, It is submitted, therefore, that an offer to supply can be made by words or conduct.

Knowledge. Means actual knowledge. Mere suspicion would not appear to be sufficient for the purposes of s 7.

Intention. The accused must intend the article to be used to commit, or assist in the commission of the fraud.

Sentencing

Fraud – Making, adapting, supplying or offering to supply articles for fraud (Fraud Act 2006, s 7)

A[39.5] Triable either way:

Maximum when tried summarily: Level 5 fine and/or 6 months.

Maximum when tried on indictment: 10 years.

See the relevant guideline at A[38.4] onwards.

A[40]
Handling stolen goods

Charge (Handling stolen goods)

A[40.1] **Handled stolen goods, namely [. . . . .], knowing or believing them to have been stolen**

Theft Act 1968, s 22

Maximum penalty – 6 months' imprisonment and/or fine level 5 (for offences committed on or after 12 March 2015 an unlimited fine). Triable either way.

Crown Court – 14 years' imprisonment and unlimited fine.

Mode of trial

A[40.2] Consider the SC Guidelines below.

Legal notes and definitions

A[40.3] The prosecution must prove that the goods were:

(a) stolen; or
(b) obtained by deception; or
(c) obtained by blackmail.

Also that the defendant knew or believed the goods had been obtained by one of those methods (see below).

A[40.4] **Handling.** A person handles stolen goods if, otherwise than in the course of the stealing, knowing or believing them to be stolen goods he:

(a) dishonestly receives the goods; or
(b) dishonestly undertakes in the retention, removal, disposal or realisation of the goods by or for the benefit of another; or
(c) dishonestly assists in the retention, removal, disposal or realisation of the goods by or for the benefit of another; or
(d) arranges to do (a) or (b) or (c).

Thus a defendant who has not himself personally handled goods can be convicted for this offence.

A[40.5] **Otherwise than in the course of the stealing.** If a person handles goods he has stolen subsequent to the theft he may be guilty of both theft and handling, though normally theft and handling will be alternative charges: see *R v Dolan* [1976] Crim LR 145 and *R v Sainthouse* [1980] Crim LR 506. See also *R v Pitham and Hehl* [1977] Crim LR 285, where the defendants were convicted of handling, having been taken to a house and sold furniture by the thief who thereby appropriated furniture left in his care: their buying was nevertheless not 'in the course of the stealing'.

In the ordinary case where there is no evidence that the defendant was the thief, the prosecution is not required to prove affirmatively that the defendant was not the thief, because handling the goods 'otherwise than in the course of the stealing' is not an essential ingredient of the offence. However, where the defendant is in possession of stolen goods so recently after they are stolen that the inevitable inference is that he is the thief then, if he is charged only with handling, the words 'otherwise than in the course of the stealing' are relevant since the prosecution can only prove the offence of handling if it proves affirmatively that the defendant was not the thief: *R v Cash* [1985] QB 801, [1985] 2 All ER 128, CA.

A[40.6] **Forms of handling.** 'Assists' means helping or encouraging amongst other things; there must be either affirmative or circumstantial evidence of help or encouragement: *R v Coleman* (1985) 150 JP 175, [1986] Crim LR 56. Something must be done by the defendant; a mere failure to act, where no duty to act existed in law, does not amount to an offence: *R v Burroughes* [2000] All ER (D) 2032, CA.

The words 'by or for the benefit of another person', 'govern retention', 'removal', 'disposal' and 'realisation', and should be included in the charge where retention, removal, disposal or realisation is alleged: *R v Sloggett* [1972] 1 QB 430, [1971] 3 All ER 264, 135 JP 539. If the accused knows that the stolen goods are hidden on his property, mere failure to reveal their presence does not in itself amount to assisting in their retention but would afford strong evidence of providing accommodation for the goods which may amount to assisting in their retention: *R v Brown* [1970] 1 QB 105, [1969] 3 All ER 198, 133 JP 592. Merely using stolen goods in the possession of another does not constitute the offence of assisting in their retention, because something must be done by the offender, and done intentionally and dishonestly, for the purpose of enabling the goods to be retained: *R v Kanwar* [1982] 2 All ER 528, 146 JP 283; *R v Sanders* [1982] Crim LR 695.

'Realisation' merely involves the exchange of the goods for money; and he who pays is just as much involved in the realisation as he who receives the payment: *R v Deakin* [1972] 3 All ER 803, 137 JP 19. A person who has bona fide acquired goods for value does not commit an offence of dishonestly undertaking the disposal or realisation of stolen property for the benefit of another if when he sells the goods he knows or believes them to be stolen, because it is the purchase, not the sale, which is for the purchaser's benefit: *R v Bloxham* [1983] 1 AC 109, [1982] 1 All ER 582, 146 JP 201.

The word 'another' in s 22(1) cannot be construed to embrace a co-accused on the same charge: *R v Gingell* (1999) 163 JP 648, [2000] 1 Cr App Rep 88, CA.

'Arranges' does not cover the situation where the goods are not yet stolen: *R v Park* [1988] Crim LR 238.

A[40.7] **Goods.** Includes money and every kind of property except land. The term also includes things severed from land by stealing.

A[40.8] **Knowledge or belief.** Mere suspicion which does not amount to knowledge or belief is not sufficient to justify conviction. The state of the defendant's mind must be judged subjectively, ie what did *this* defendant know, or believe, not what did he suspect.

A[40.9] The term 'belief' connotes its ordinary meaning of holding something to be true.

A[40.10] In *R v Hall* (1985) 81 Cr App R 260, the Lord Chief Justice presided in a court which gave some examples of what might amount to knowledge and what might amount to belief. A man might be said to *know* that goods were stolen when he was told by someone with first-hand knowledge, such as the thief, that such was the case. *Belief* was something short of knowledge. It might be said to be the state of mind of a person who said to himself: 'I cannot say I know for certain that those goods are stolen, but there can be no other reasonable conclusion in the light of all the circumstances of all I have heard and seen.' It was enough for belief even if the person said to himself: 'Despite all that I have seen and heard, I refuse to believe what my brain tells me is obvious.'

A[40.11] What was insufficient was a mere suspicion: 'I suspect that these goods may be stolen but on the other hand they may not be stolen.' That state of mind does not fall within the words 'knowing or believing'. [Contrast the intention under s 22 with an offence under say, s 329 of the Proceeds of Crime Act 2002 (acquisition, use and possession of criminal property). In *Hogan v DPP* [2007] EWHC 978 (Admin), [2007] All ER (D) 253 (Feb) once a defendant raise the issue that consideration had been paid in respect of criminal property in his possession it was for the prosecution to prove to the criminal standard that the consideration paid was not adequate.]

Sentencing
SC Guideline – Handling stolen goods

A[40.12] Theft Act 1968 (section 22)

Triable either way

Maximum: 14 years' custody

Offence range: Discharge – 8 years' custody

STEP ONE
Determining the offence category

The court should determine the offence category with reference **only** to the factors identified in the following tables. In order to determine the category the court should assess **culpability** and **harm.**

The level of culpability is determined by weighing up all the factors of the case to determine the offender's role and the extent to which the offending was **planned** and the **sophistication** with which it was carried out.

CULPABILITY demonstrated by one or more of the following:

A – High culpability
A leading role where offending is part of a group activity
Involvement of others through coercion, intimidation or exploitation
Abuse of position of power or trust or responsibility
Professional and sophisticated offence
Advance knowledge of the primary offence
Possession of very recently stolen goods from a domestic burglary or robbery
B – Medium culpability
A significant role where offending is part of a group activity
Offender acquires goods for resale
All other cases where characteristics for categories A or C are not present
C – Lesser culpability
Performed limited function under direction Involved through coercion, intimidation or exploitation
Little or no planning
Limited awareness or understanding of offence
Goods acquired for offender's personal use

Where there are characteristics present which fall under different levels of culpability, the court should balance these characteristics to reach a fair assessment of the offender's culpability.

HARM

Harm is assessed by reference to the **financial value** (to the loser) of the handled goods **and any significant additional harm** associated with the underlying offence on the victim or others – examples of additional harm may include **but are not limited to:**

Property stolen from a domestic burglary or a robbery (unless this has already been taken into account in assessing culpability)

Items stolen were of substantial value to the loser, regardless of monetary worth
Metal theft causing disruption to infrastructure
Damage to heritage assets

Category 1	High value goods stolen (above £100,000) **or** High value with significant additional harm to the victim or others
Category 2	High value goods stolen (£10,000 to £100,000) **and** no significant additional harm **or** Medium value with significant additional harm to the victim or others
Category 3	Medium value goods stolen (£1,000 to £10,000) **and** no significant additional harm **or** Low value with significant additional harm to the victim or others
Category 4	Low value goods stolen (up to £1,000) **and** Little or no significant additional harm to the victim or others

STEP TWO
Starting point and category range

Having determined the category at step one, the court should use the starting point to reach a sentence within the appropriate category range in the table below.

The starting point applies to all offenders irrespective of plea or previous convictions.

	Culpability		
Harm	A	B	C
Category 1 Where the value greatly exceeds £100,000, it may be appropriate to move outside the identified range. Adjustment should be made for any significant additional harm where very high value stolen goods are handled	**Starting point** 5 years' custody	**Starting point** 3 years' custody	**Starting point** 1 year's custody
	Category range 3 – 8 years' custody	**Category range** 1 year 6 months' – 4 years' custody	**Category range** 26 weeks' – 1 year 6 months' custody
Category 2	**Starting point** 3 years' custody	**Starting point** 1 year's custody	**Starting point** High level community order
	Category range 1 year 6 months' – 4 years' custody	**Category range** 26 weeks' – 1 year 6 months' custody	**Category range** Low level community order – 26 weeks' custody
Category 3	**Starting point** 1 year's custody	**Starting point** High level community order	**Starting point** Band C fine
	Category range 26 weeks' – 2 years' custody	**Category range** Low level community order – 26 weeks' custody	**Category range** Band B fine – Low level community order

	Culpability		
Harm	A	B	C
Category 4	**Starting point** High level community order	**Starting point** Low level community order	**Starting point** Band B fine
	Category range Medium level community order – 26 weeks' custody	**Category range** Band C fine – High level community order	**Category range** Discharge – Band C fine

Consecutive sentences for multiple offences may be appropriate – please refer to the *Offences Taken Into Consideration and Totality* guideline.

The court should then consider further adjustment for any aggravating or mitigating factors. The following is a **non-exhaustive** list of additional factual elements providing the context of the offence and factors relating to the offender. Identify whether any combination of these, or other relevant factors, should result in an upward or downward adjustment from the sentence arrived at so far.

Factors increasing seriousness	Factors reducing seriousness or reflecting personal mitigation
Statutory aggravating factors	No previous convictions or no relevant/recent convictions
Previous convictions, having regard to a) the **nature** of the offence to which the conviction relates and its **relevance** to the current offence; and b) the **time** that has elapsed since the conviction	Good character and/or exemplary conduct
Offence committed whilst on bail	Serious medical condition requiring urgent, intensive or long-term treatment
Other aggravating factors	Age and/or lack of maturity where it affects the responsibility of the offender
Seriousness of the underlying offence, for example, armed robbery	Mental disorder or learning disability
Deliberate destruction, disposal or defacing of stolen property	Sole or primary carer for dependent relatives
Damage to a third party	Determination and/or demonstration of steps having been taken to address addiction or offending behaviour
Failure to comply with current court orders	
Offence committed on licence	
Offences taken into consideration	
Established evidence of community/wider impact	

STEP THREE

Consider any factors which indicate a reduction, such as assistance to the prosecution

The court should take into account sections 73 and 74 of the Serious Organised Crime and Police Act 2005 (assistance by defendants: reduction or review of sentence) and any other rule of law by virtue of which an offender may receive a discounted sentence in consequence of assistance given (or offered) to the prosecutor or investigator.

STEP FOUR
Reduction for guilty pleas

The court should take account of any potential reduction for a guilty plea in accordance with section 144 of the Criminal Justice Act 2003 and the *Guilty Plea* guideline.

STEP FIVE
Totality principle

If sentencing an offender for more than one offence, or where the offender is already serving a sentence, consider whether the total sentence is just and proportionate to the overall offending behaviour in accordance with the *Offences Taken into Consideration and Totality* guideline.

STEP SIX
Confiscation, compensation and ancillary orders

The court must proceed with a view to making a confiscation order if it is asked to do so by the prosecutor or if the court believes it is appropriate for it to do so.

Where the offence has resulted in loss or damage the court must consider whether to make a compensation order.

If the court makes both a confiscation order and an order for compensation and the court believes the offender will not have sufficient means to satisfy both orders in full, the court must direct that the compensation be paid out of sums recovered under the confiscation order (section 13 of the Proceeds of Crime Act 2002).

The court may also consider whether to make ancillary orders. These may include a deprivation order, or a restitution order.

STEP SEVEN
Reasons

Section 174 of the Criminal Justice Act 2003 imposes a duty to give reasons for, and explain the effect of, the sentence.

STEP EIGHT
Consideration for time spent on bail

The court must consider whether to give credit for time spent on bail in accordance with section 240A of the Criminal Justice Act 2003.

A[41]

Harassment

Harassment – putting people in fear of violence
Stalking – involving fear of violence or serious alarm or distress
Racially or religiously aggravated harassment – putting people in fear of violence
Racially or religiously aggravated stalking – involving fear of violence or serious alarm or distress
Harassment
Stalking
Racially or religiously aggravated harassment
Racially or religiously aggravated stalking

Charges (Harassment)

A[41.1] **1 Did pursue a course of conduct on two or more occasions, causing another to fear that violence would be used against him, which he knew or ought to have known would cause that other person to fear violence would be used against him**

Protection from Harassment Act 1997, s 4

Maximum penalty – 6 months' imprisonment and/or fine level 5 (for offences committed on or after 12 March 2015 an unlimited fine). Triable either way. Specified violent offence under Sch 15, Part 1, CJA 2003.

Crown Court – 5 years' imprisonment and unlimited fine.

A[41.2] **2 Racially/religiously aggravated course of conduct on two or more occasions causing fear of violence etc**

Crime and Disorder Act 1998, s 32

Maximum penalty – 6 months' imprisonment and/or fine level 5 (for offences committed on or after 12 March 2015 an unlimited fine). Triable either way. Sch 15, Part 1, CJA 2003 does not identify this offence as a "specified violent offence". This would appear to be a drafting error given the classification of the basic offence under s 4 PHA 1997 above. The SGC Guideline (below) recognises this offence as a specified violent offence.

Crown Court – 7 years' imprisonment and unlimited fine.

A[41.3] **3 Did pursue a course of conduct amounting to harassment of another which he knew or ought to have known amounted to harassment**

Protection from Harassment Act 1997, s 2

Maximum penalty – 6 months' imprisonment and/or fine level 5 (for offences committed on or after 12 March 2015 an unlimited fine) summary only.

A[41.3A] **3A Did pursue a course of conduct which amounted to stalking and either:**

(a) caused another (B) to fear, on at least two occasions, that violence would be used against B, or

(b) caused B serious alarm or distress which had a substantial adverse effect on B's usual day-to-day activities,

knowing that the course of conduct would cause B so to fear on each of those occasions or would cause B such alarm or distress.

Protection from Harassment Act 1997, s 4A

Maximum penalty – 6 months' imprisonment and/or fine level 5 (for offences committed on or after 12 March 2015 an unlimited fine). Triable either way. Specified violent offence under CJA 2003, Sch 15, Pt 1.

Crown Court – 5 years' imprisonment and unlimited fine.

A[41.3B] **3B Did pursue a course of conduct amounting to harassment of another and the acts or omissions involved in that court of conduct were ones associated with stalking, which he knew or ought to have known amounted to harassment of that person.**

Protection from Harassment Act 1997, s 2A

Maximum penalty – 6 months' imprisonment and/or fine level 5 (for offences committed on or after 12 March 2015 an unlimited fine) summary only.

A[41.4] **4 Racially/religiously aggravated conduct amounting to harassment of another etc**

Crime and Disorder Act 1998, s 32

Maximum penalty – 6 months' imprisonment and/or fine level 5 (for offences committed on or after 12 March 2015 an unlimited fine). Triable either way.

Crown Court – 2 years' imprisonment and unlimited fine.

A[41.5] **Harassment of a person in his home.** In response to animal rights protests and the like the Serious Organised Crime and Police Act 2005 amended the Protection from Harassment Act 1997 to make it an offence to harass two or more persons with the intention of persuading them not to do something they are required or entitled to do, or to do something they are not required to do. A course of conduct may involve conduct on just one occasion for each victim if there is more than one.

Section 126 of the Act adds s 42A to the Criminal Justice and Police Act 2001 and creates an offence of harassment of a person in his home. Punishable with fine level 4 and 6 months (**the maximum term of imprisonment may be subject to alteration under s 280(2) CJA 2003). Triable only by magistrates.

Mode of trial

A[41.6] Consider the SC Guidelines below.

Note that the Crown Court can bring in an alternative verdict under the Protection from Harassment Act 1997, s 2 or s 2A, but magistrates cannot.

Legal notes and definitions

A[41.7] It has been held that the 'course of conduct' under s 4 must be a course of conduct amounting to harassment under s 1: *R v Curtis* [2010] EWCA Crim 123, [2010] 3 All ER 849, [2010] WLR 2770, [2010] Crim LR 638; followed in *R v Widdows* [2011] EWCA Crim 1500, (2011) 175 JP 345. These decisions were followed, with reluctance, in *R v Haque* [2011] EWCA Crim 1871, [2012] 1 Cr App R 5, [2011] Crim LR 962. The result of this is that a prosecution under s 4 requires, in addition to the elements expressly set out: (a) proof of harassment; (b) that the conduct was targeted at an individual; and (c) that it was calculated to produce the consequence of alarm or distress. See further *Thomas v News Group Newspapers Ltd* [2001] EWCA Civ 1233, [2002] EMLT 68, in which it was noted that the 1997 Act does not purport to provide a comprehensive definition of harassment, and it does not attempt to define the type of conduct that is capable of constituting harassment. "Harassment" is, however, a word which has a meaning which is generally understood. It describes conduct targeted at an individual which is calculated to produce the consequences described in section 7 and which is oppressive and unreasonable. The practice of stalking is a prime example of such conduct.' (per Lord Phillips MR at para 30.) See also *R v N* [2016] EWCA Crim 92, (2016) 180 JP 242, [2016] 2 Cr App R 10: 'The requirement of oppression – always and of course to be considered in context – serves as a yardstick, helping the law to draw a sensible line between the give and take of daily life and conduct which justifies the sanction of the criminal law' (per Gross LJ at para 32).

Course of conduct denotes actions taking place on at least two occasions. In the case of a s 4 offence the victim must have been put in fear that violence would have been used against him on at least two of those occasions (*Caurti v DPP* [2002] EWHC 867 (Admin), [2002] Crim LR 131). The fewer the incidents and the wider apart they are spread, the less likely it is that a finding of harassment can reasonably be made (*Lau v DPP* [2000] 1 FLR 799, [2000] Fam Law 610). In *Pratt v DPP* [2001] EWHC 483 (Admin), (2001) 165 JP 800 incidents three months apart were said to be borderline, while in *Kelly v DPP* [2002] All ER (D) 177 (Jun) nine telephone calls all within five minutes amounted to a course of conduct even though the victim listened to them as recorded messages at the same time. A threat to harm a person's dog may be inferred to be a threat directed at them (*R v DPP* [2001] EWHC 17 (Admin), (2001) 165 JP 349).

Events between May 2005 and November 2005 constituted a "course of conduct" and could not be regarded as one continuous episode of intimidation (*Buckley v CPS* [2008] All ER (D) 06 (Jan)). At least one of the incidents relied on by the prosecution must have occurred within the 6 month limitation period for summary proceedings (*DPP v Baker* (2004) 169 JP 140, [2004] All ER (D) 28 (Nov), DC).

Conduct which may begin with what is or may be a legitimate inquiry (in this case by telephone) may become harassment within the meaning of section 1, by reason of the manner of its being pursued and its persistence: see *DPP v Hardy* [2008] EWHC 2874 (Admin), 173 JP 10. A series of six incidents, over the course of nine months during a volatile relationship with aggression on both sides, could not on the facts be described as a course of conduct and giving rise to an offence under s 4(1): *R v Curtis* [2010] EWCA Crim 123, [2010] 3 All ER 849, [2010] 1 Cr App Rep 457. See also *R v Widdows* [2011] EWCA Crim 1500, [2011] 2 FLR 869, [2011] Fam Law 937.

Two or more complainants. See A[41.5] above. **Two or more complainants** may be named in one charge under s 2 and such a charge is not necessarily bad for duplicity: see *DPP v Dunn* (2008) 165 JP 130. For a s 4 offence, the interpretation is slightly narrower in that the course of conduct complained of must cause at least one of the complainants to fear, on at least two occasions, that violence will be used against him, as opposed to another: see *Caurti v DPP* [2002] EWHC 867 (Admin), [2002] Crim LR 131.

A[41.8] Knows or ought to have known. In the case of the defendant this means that he will be presumed to have that knowledge if a reasonable person in possession of the same information would think the course of conduct would amount to harassment or cause the other person to fear violence would be used against him. The defendant's mental disorder (paranoid schizophrenia) was not to be considered as a relevant condition of the hypothetical reasonable man under s 1(2) or to be taken into account when assessing whether the defendant's conduct was reasonable under s 1(3)(c); both s 1(2) and s 1(3) involved objective test: *R v Colohan* [2001] EWCA Crim 1251, [2001] Crim LR 845.

As to the availability of the defence of insanity, see **A[41.11]** post.

A[41.8A] The basic offence of stalking, contrary to s 2A, consists of:

(a) pursuing a course of conduct in breach of s 1(1); and
(b) the course of conduct amounts to stalking.

A person's course of conduct amounts to stalking of another person if:

(a) it amounts to harassment of that person;
(b) the acts or omissions involved are ones associated with stalking; and
(c) the person whose course of conduct it is knows or ought to know that the course of conduct amounts to harassment of the other person.

Subsection (3) provides the following examples of acts or omissions which, in particular circumstances, are ones associated with stalking:

(a) following a person;
(b) contacting, or attempting to contact, a person by any means;
(c) publishing any statement or other material:
  (i) relating or purporting to relate to a person; or
  (ii) purporting to originate from a person,
(d) monitoring the use by a person of the internet, email or any other form of electronic communication;
(e) loitering in any place (whether public or private);
(f) interfering with any property in the possession of a person;
(g) watching or spying on a person.

A[41.8B] The aggravated offence of stalking, contrary to s 4A, consists of a course of conduct which:

(a) amounts to stalking by 'A'; and
(b) either:
  (i) causes another ('B') to fear, on at least two occasions, that violence will be used against B; or
  (ii) causes B serious alarm or distress which has a substantial adverse effect on B's usual day-to-day activities,

and A knows or ought to know that A's course of conduct will cause B so to fear on each of those occasions or (as the case may be) will cause such alarm or distress.

For the purposes of s 4A:

(a) A ought to know that A's course of conduct will cause B to fear that violence will be used against B on any occasion if a reasonable person in possession of the same information would think the course of conduct would cause B so to fear on that occasion; or
(b) A ought to know that A's course of conduct will cause B serious alarm or distress which has a substantial adverse effect on B's usual day-to-day activities if a reasonable person in possession of the same information would think the course of conduct would cause B such alarm or distress.

In *R v Qosja* [2016] EWCA Crim 1543, [2017] 1 WLR 311 the issue centred on whether the jury could be sure that on at least two occasions the appellant had caused the complainant to fear that he, the appellant, would use violence against the complainant and that on at least two occasions he knew, or ought as a reasonable person to have known, that his course of conduct would cause her to fear that violence would be used against her. Whilst the first incident was accepted as being within the legislation, as to the second, the complainant had testified that she was scared that he had come back to her house on the second incident and that he could still break in again. If her housemates weren't in she would be alone and that would make her feel 'dangerous' (sic) (her first language was not English).

The appellant contended that the fear of violence on any second occasion was too speculative, but the Court did not agree. The statute does not specify the need for a fear of immediate violence such as is required for common assault and battery in s 39 of the Criminal Justice Act 1988. The limiting factor lies in the requirement that the reasonable man would have to think that the fear would be caused. A plain and natural reading of the wording of s 4A(1)(b)(i) of the Protection from Harassment

Act 1997 reveals that the section is wide enough to look to incidents of violence in the future and not only to incidents giving rise to a fear of violence arising directly out of the incident in question. Nor is there any requirement for the fear to be of violence on a particular date or time in the future, or at a particular place or in a particular manner, or for there to be a specific threat of violence. There can be a fear of violence sufficient for the statute where that fear of violence is of violence on a separate and later occasion. The position can be tested simply by reference to the example of somebody saying 'I'll come back and get you'. There was therefore sufficient evidence for the case to be left to the jury.

A[41.8C] **Defences.** Section 4A(4) provides the same three defences as s 1(3)and s 4(3), which are considered at **A**[4.10], below.

A[41.9] **Racial aggravation.** See A[8.10] and A[15.7].

May be heard together with a harassment charge as an alternative (*R (CPS) v Blaydon Youth Court* [2004] EWHC Admin 2296, (2004) 168 JP 638).

A[41.10] **Defences.** The Protection from Harassment Act 1997, s 1 gives three possible defences if the defendant can show:

(a) his course of conduct was pursued for the purposes of preventing or detecting crime;
(b) that it was pursued under an enactment or rule of law;
(c) that in the particular circumstances the course of conduct was reasonable and in the case of a s 4 offence that it was reasonable for the protection of himself or another or his or another's property.

'Purpose' is not a wholly subjective test. The purpose does not have to be 'reasonable' but it must be 'rational'.

> 'Before an alleged harasser can be said to have had the purpose of preventing or detecting crime, he must have sufficiently applied his mind to the matter. He must have thought rationally about the material suggesting the possibility of criminality and formed the view that the conduct said to constitute harassment was appropriate for the purpose of preventing or detecting it. If he has done these things, then he has the relevant purpose. The court will not test his conclusions by reference to the view which a hypothetical reasonable man in his position would have formed. If, on the other hand, he has not engaged in these minimum mental processes necessary to acquire the relevant state of mind, but proceeds anyway on the footing that he is acting to prevent or detect crime, then he acts irrationally. In that case, two consequences will follow. The first is that the law will not regard him as having had the relevant purpose at all. He has simply not taken the necessary steps to form one. The second is that the causal connection which section 1(3)(a) posits between the purpose of the alleged harasser and the conduct constituting the harassment, will not exist. The effect of applying a test of rationality to the question of purpose is to enable the court to apply to private persons a test which would in any event apply to public authorities engaged in the prevention or detection of crime as a matter of public law. It is not a demanding test, and it is hard to imagine that Parliament can have intended anything less.' (per Lord Sumption SCJ in *Hayes v Willoughby* [2013] UKSC 17, [2013] 1 WLR 935, at para 15)

It is not reasonable to pursue a course of conduct which is in breach of a court injunction designed to prevent it: *DPP v Selvanayagam* (1999) Times, 23 June, DC. As to the relevance of mental illness to 'reasonable', see **A**[41.8], above.

In our view, the standard of proof is on a preponderance of probabilities: *R v Carr-Briant* [1943] KB 607, [1943] 2 All ER 156, 107 JP 167, *R v Dunbar* [1958] 1 QB 1, [1957] 2 All ER 737, [1957] 3 WLR 330. It is arguable, however, that it will be held that the ECHR requires s 1(3) to be 'read down' to impose only an evidential burden on the defendant.

A[41.11] In *Loake v Crown Prosecution Service* [2017] EWHC 2855 (Admin), [2017] All ER (D) 128 (Nov), the issue was whether insanity could be a defence to a charge under s 2(1) of the Protection from Harassment Act 1997. It has held, not following *Director of Public Prosecutions v Harper* [1997] 1 WLR 1406, that the defence was available to offences of strict liability, and to offences in which the mental element is objective. Insanity is wider than simply a means of claiming lack of mens rea (which in practice adds nothing to criminal proceedings in magistrates' courts) and is available where the defendant did have the requisite mens rea but claims he/she did not know that what he/she was doing was wrong.

Sentencing
SC Guideline – Harassment (putting people in fear of violence)
SC Guideline – Stalking (involving fear of violence or serious alarm or distress)
SC Guideline – Racially or religiously aggravated harassment (putting people in fear of violence)
SC Guideline – Racially or religiously aggravated stalking (involving fear of violence or serious alarm or distress)

A[41.11A] This text is taken from the Sentencing Council's Intimidatory offences: Definitive guideline, published on 5 July 2018, taking effect from 1 October 2018.

Harassment (putting people in fear of violence)

Protection from Harassment Act 1997 (section 4)

Stalking (involving fear of violence or serious alarm or distress)

Protection from Harassment Act 1997 (section 4A)

Triable either way

Maximum: 10 years' custody

Offence range: Fine–8 years' custody

Racially or religiously aggravated harassment (putting people in fear of violence)

Crime and Disorder Act 1998 (section 32(1)(b))

Racially or religiously aggravated stalking (involving fear of violence or serious alarm or distress)

Crime and Disorder Act 1998 (section 32(1)(b))

Triable either way

Maximum: 14 years' custody

The racially or religiously aggravated offence is a specified offence for the purposes of section 226A (extended sentence for certain violent or sexual offences) of the Criminal Justice Act 2003

Where offence committed in a domestic context, also refer to the *Overarching principles: Domestic abuse guideline*

STEP 1
DETERMINING THE OFFENCE CATEGORY

The court should determine the offence category with reference only to the factors in the tables below. In order to determine the category the court should assess culpability and harm.

The level of culpability is determined by weighing up all the factors of the case. Where there are characteristics present which fall under different levels of culpability, the court should balance these characteristics to reach a fair assessment of the offender's culpability.

Culpability demonstrated by one or more of the following:

A	**Very high culpability** – the extreme nature of one or more culpability B factors or the extreme culpability indicated by a combination of culpability B factors may elevate to category A.
B	**High culpability:** • Conduct intended to maximise fear or distress • High degree of planning and/or sophisticated offence • Persistent action over a prolonged period • Offence motivated by, or demonstrating, hostility based on any of the following characteristics or presumed characteristics of the victim: age, sex, disability, sexual orientation or transgender identity
C	**Medium culpability:** • Cases that fall between categories B and D, and in particular: • Some planning • Scope and duration of offence that falls between categories B and D
D	**Lesser culpability:** • Offender's responsibility substantially reduced by mental disorder or learning disability • Conduct unlikely to cause significant fear or distress • Little or no planning • Offence was limited in scope and duration

Harm

The level of harm is assessed by weighing up all the factors of the case.

Category 1	• Very serious distress caused to the victim • Significant psychological harm caused to the victim • Victim caused to make considerable changes to lifestyle to avoid contact
Category 2	• Harm that falls between categories 1 and 3, and in particular: • Some distress caused to the victim • Some psychological harm caused to the victim • Victim caused to make some changes to lifestyle to avoid contact
Category 3	• Limited distress or harm caused to the victim

STEP 2
STARTING POINT AND CATEGORY RANGE

Having determined the category at step one, the court should use the corresponding starting point to reach a sentence within the category range in the table below. The starting point applies to all offenders irrespective of plea or previous convictions.

Sentencers should consider whether to ask for psychiatric reports in order to assist in the appropriate sentencing (hospital orders, or mental health treatment requirements) of certain offenders to whom this consideration may be relevant.

Maximum: 10 years' custody (basic offence)

Harm	Culpability A	B	C	D
Category 1	**Starting point** 5 year's custody **Category range** 3 years 6 months' – 8 years' custody	**Starting point** 2 years 6 months' custody **Category range** 1 – 4 year's custody	**Starting point** 36 weeks' custody **Category range** 12 weeks – 1 year 6 months' custody	**Starting point** 12 weeks' custody **Category range** High level community order – 36 weeks' custody
Category 2	**Starting point** 2 years 6 months' custody **Category range** 1 – 4 years' custody	**Starting point** 36 weeks' custody **Category range** 12 weeks' – 1 year 6 months' custody	**Starting point** 12 weeks' custody **Category range** High level community order – 36 weeks' custody	**Starting point** High level community order **Category range** Low level community order – 12 weeks' custody
Category 3	**Starting point** 36 weeks' custody **Category range** 12 weeks' – 1 year 6 months' custody	**Starting point** 12 weeks' custody **Category range** High level community order – 36 weeks' custody	**Starting point** High level community order **Category range** Low level community order – 12 weeks' custody	**Starting point** Band C fine – High level community order

The court should then consider any adjustment for any aggravating or mitigating factors. Below is a **non-exhaustive** list of additional factual elements providing the context of the offence and factors relating to the offender.

Identify whether any combination of these, or other relevant factors, should result in an upward or downward adjustment from the starting point.

FACTORS INCREASING SERIOUSNESS

Statutory aggravating factors:
Previous convictions, having regard to a) the **nature** of the offence to which the conviction relates and its **relevance** to the current offence; and b) the **time** that has elapsed since the conviction
Offence committed whilst on bail
Other aggravating factors:
Using a position of trust to facilitate the offence
Victim is particularly vulnerable (not all vulnerabilities are immediately apparent)
Grossly violent or offensive material sent
Impact of offence on others, particularly children
Exploiting contact arrangements with a child to commit the offence
Offence committed against those working in the public sector or providing a service to the public
Failure to comply with current court orders
Offence committed on licence or post sentence supervision
Offences taken into consideration

FACTORS REDUCING SERIOUSNESS OR REFLECTING PERSONAL MITIGATION

No previous convictions or no relevant/recent convictions
Remorse
Good character and/or exemplary conduct
Serious medical condition requiring urgent, intensive or long-term treatment
Age and/or lack of maturity
Mental disorder or learning disability (where not taken into account at step one)
Sole or primary carer for dependent relatives
Determination and/or demonstration of steps having been taken to address offending behaviour

RACIALLY OR RELIGIOUSLY AGGRAVATED HARASSMENT/STALKING OFFENCES ONLY

Having determined the category of the basic offence to identify the sentence of a non-aggravated offence, the court should now consider the level of racial or religious aggravation involved and apply an appropriate uplift to the sentence in accordance with the guidance below. The following is a list of factors which the court should consider to determine the level of aggravation. Where there are characteristics present which fall under different levels of aggravation, the court should balance these to reach a fair assessment of the level of aggravation present in the offence.

Maximum sentence for the aggravated offence on indictment is 14 years' custody (maximum for the basic offence is 10 years' custody)

HIGH LEVEL OF RACIAL OR RELIGIOUS AGGRAVATION	SENTENCE UPLIFT
• Racial or religious aggravation was the predominant motivation for the offence. • Offender was a member of, or was associated with, a group promoting hostility based on race or religion (where linked to the commission of the offence). • Aggravated nature of the offence caused severe distress to the victim or the victim's family (over and above the distress already considered at step one). • Aggravated nature of the offence caused serious fear and distress throughout local community or more widely.	Increase the length of custodial sentence if already considered for the basic offence or consider a custodial sentence, if not already considered for the basic offence.

MEDIUM LEVEL OF RACIAL OR RELIGIOUS AGGRAVATION	SENTENCE UPLIFT
• Racial or religious aggravation formed a significant proportion of the offence as a whole. • Aggravated nature of the offence caused some distress to the victim or the victim's family (over and above the distress already considered at step one). • Aggravated nature of the offence caused some fear and distress throughout local community or more widely.	Consider a significantly more onerous penalty of the same type or consider a more severe type of sentence than for the basic offence.
LOW LEVEL OF RACIAL OR RELIGIOUS AGGRAVATION	**SENTENCE UPLIFT**
• Aggravated element formed a minimal part of the offence as a whole. • Aggravated nature of the offence caused minimal or no distress to the victim or the victim's family (over and above the distress already considered at step one).	Consider a more onerous penalty of the same type identified for the basic offence.

Magistrates may find that, although the appropriate sentence for the basic offence would be within their powers, the appropriate increase for the aggravated offence would result in a sentence in excess of their powers. If so, they must commit for sentence to the Crown Court.

The sentencer should state in open court that the offence was aggravated by reason of race or religion, and should also state what the sentence would have been without that element of aggravation.

STEP 3
CONSIDER ANY FACTORS WHICH INDICATE A REDUCTION, SUCH AS ASSISTANCE TO THE PROSECUTION

The court should take into account sections 73 and 74 of the Serious Organised Crime and Police Act 2005 (assistance by defendants: reduction or review of sentence) and any other rule of law by virtue of which an offender may receive a discounted sentence in consequence of assistance given (or offered) to the prosecutor or investigator.

STEP 4
REDUCTION FOR GUILTY PLEAS

The court should take account of any potential reduction for a guilty plea in accordance with section 144 of the Criminal Justice Act 2003 and the *Guilty Plea* guideline.

STEP 5
DANGEROUSNESS

The court should consider whether having regard to the criteria contained in Chapter 5 of Part 12 of the Criminal Justice Act 2003 it would be appropriate to impose an extended sentence (section 226A).

STEP 6
TOTALITY PRINCIPLE

If sentencing an offender for more than one offence, or where the offender is already serving a sentence, consider whether the total sentence is just and proportionate to the overall offending behaviour in accordance with the *Offences Taken into Consideration and Totality* guideline.

STEP 7
COMPENSATION AND ANCILLARY ORDERS

In all cases, the court must consider whether to make a compensation order and/or other ancillary orders.

Compensation order

The court should consider compensation orders in all cases where personal injury, loss or damage has resulted from the offence. The court must give reasons if it decides not to award compensation in such cases.

Other ancillary orders available include:
Restraining order

Where an offender is convicted of any offence, the court may make a restraining order (section 5 of the Protection from Harassment Act 1997).

The order may prohibit the offender from doing anything for the purpose of protecting the victim of the offence, or any other person mentioned in the order, from further conduct which amounts to harassment or will cause a fear of violence.

The order may have effect for a specified period or until further order.

STEP 8
REASONS

Section 174 of the Criminal Justice Act 2003 imposes a duty to give reasons for, and explain the effect of, the sentence.

STEP 9
CONSIDERATION FOR TIME SPENT ON BAIL (TAGGED CURFEW)

The court must consider whether to give credit for time spent on bail in accordance with section 240A of the Criminal Justice Act 2003.

Sentencing
SC Guideline – Harassment
SC Guideline – Stalking
SC Guideline – Racially or religiously aggravated harassment
SC Guideline – Racially or religiously aggravated stalking

A[41.12] This text is taken from the Sentencing Council's Intimidatory offences: Definitive guideline, published on 5 July 2018, taking effect from 1 October 2018.

Harassment

Protection from Harassment Act 1997 (section 2)

Stalking

Protection from Harassment Act 1997 (section 2A)

Triable either way

Maximum: 6 months' custody

Offence range: Discharge – 26 weeks' custody

Racially or religiously aggravated harassment

Crime and Disorder Act 1998 (section 32(1)(a))

Racially or religiously aggravated stalking

Crime and Disorder Act 1998 (section 32(1)(a))

Triable either way

Maximum: 2 years' custody

Where offence committed in a domestic context, also refer to the *Overarching principles: Domestic abuse guideline*

STEP 1
DETERMINING THE OFFENCE CATEGORY

The court should determine the offence category with reference only to the factors in the tables below. In order to determine the category the court should assess **culpability and harm.**

The level of culpability is determined by weighing up all the factors of the case. **Where there are characteristics present which fall under different levels of culpability, the court should balance these characteristics to reach a fair assessment of the offender's culpability.**

Culpability demonstrated by one or more of the following:

A	High culpability: • Conduct intended to maximise fear or distress • High degree of planning and/or sophisticated offence • Persistent action over a prolonged period • Threat of serious violence • Offence motivated by, or demonstrating, hostility based on any of the following characteristics or presumed characteristics of the victim: age, sex, disability, sexual orientation or transgender identity
B	Medium Culpability: • Cases that fall between categories A and C, in particular: • Conduct intended to cause some fear or distress • Some planning • Threat of some violence Scope and duration of offence that falls between categories A and C
C	Lesser culpability: • Offender's responsibility substantially reduced by mental disorder or learning disability • Little or no planning • Offence was limited in scope and duration

Harm

The level of harm is assessed by weighing up all the factors of the case.

Category 1	• Very serious distress caused to the victim • Significant psychological harm caused to the victim • Victim caused to make considerable changes to lifestyle to avoid contact
Category 2	• Harm that falls between categories 1 and 3, and in particular: • Some distress caused to the victim • Some psychological harm caused to the victim • Victim caused to make some changes to lifestyle to avoid contact
Category 3	• Limited distress or harm caused to the victim

STEP 2
STARTING POINT AND CATEGORY RANGE

Having determined the category at step one, the court should use the corresponding starting point to reach a sentence within the category range below. The starting point applies to all offenders irrespective of plea or previous convictions.

Maximum: months' custody (basic offence)

	Culpability		
Harm	A	B	C
Category 1	**Starting point** 12 weeks' custody **Category range** High level community order – 26 weeks' custody	**Starting point** High level community order **Category range** Medium level community order – 16 weeks' custody	**Starting point** Medium level community order **Category range** Low level community order – 12 weeks' custody
Category 2	**Starting point** High level community order **Category range** Medium level community order – 16 weeks' custody	**Starting point** Medium level community order **Category range** Low level community order – 12 weeks' custody	**Starting point** Low level community order **Category range** Band B fine – Medium level community order
Category 3	**Starting point** Medium level community order **Category range** Medium level community order 12 weeks' custody	**Starting point** Low level community order **Category range** Band B fine – Medium level community order	**Starting point** Band B fine **Category range** Discharge – Low level community order

The court should then consider any adjustment for any aggravating or mitigating factors. Below is a **non-exhaustive** list of additional factual elements providing the context of the offence and factors relating to the offender.

Identify whether any combination of these, or other relevant factors, should result in an upward or downward adjustment from the starting point.

FACTORS INCREASING SERIOUSNESS

Statutory aggravating factors:
Previous convictions, having regard to a) the **nature** of the offence to which the conviction relates and its **relevance** to the current offence; and b) the **time** that has elapsed since the conviction
Offence committed whilst on bail
Other aggravating factors:
Using a position of trust to facilitate the offence
Victim is particularly vulnerable (not all vulnerabilities are immediately apparent)
Grossly violent or offensive material sent
Impact of offence on others, particularly children
Exploiting contact arrangements with a child to commit the offence
Offence committed against those working in the public sector or providing a service to the public
Failure to comply with current court orders
Offence committed on licence or post sentence supervision
Offences taken into consideration

FACTORS REDUCING SERIOUSNESS OR REFLECTING PERSONAL MITIGATION

No previous convictions or no relevant/recent convictions
Remorse
Good character and/or exemplary conduct
Serious medical condition requiring urgent, intensive or long-term treatment
Age and/or lack of maturity
Mental disorder or learning disability (where not taken into account at step one)
Sole or primary carer for dependent relatives
Determination and/or demonstration of steps having been taken to address offending behaviour

RACIALLY OR RELIGIOUSLY AGGRAVATED HARASSMENT/STALKING OFFENCES ONLY

Having determined the category of the basic offence to identify the sentence of a non-aggravated offence, the court should now consider the level of racial or religious aggravation involved and apply an appropriate uplift to the sentence in accordance with the guidance below. The following is a list of factors which the court should consider to determine the level of aggravation. Where there are characteristics present which fall under different levels of aggravation, the court should balance these to reach a fair assessment of the level of aggravation present in the offence.

Maximum sentence for the aggravated offence on indictment is 2 years' custody (maximum for the basic offence is 6 months' custody)

HIGH LEVEL OF RACIAL OR RELIGIOUS AGGRAVATION	SENTENCE UPLIFT
• Racial or religious aggravation was the predominant motivation for the offence. • Offender was a member of, or was associated with, a group promoting hostility based on race or religion (where linked to the commission of the offence). • Aggravated nature of the offence caused severe distress to the victim or the victim's family (over and above the distress already considered at step one). • Aggravated nature of the offence caused serious fear and distress throughout local community or more widely.	Increase the length of custodial sentence if already considered for the basic offence or consider a custodial sentence, if not already considered for the basic offence.
MEDIUM LEVEL OF RACIAL OR RELIGIOUS AGGRAVATION	**SENTENCE UPLIFT**
• Racial or religious aggravation formed a significant proportion of the offence as a whole. • Aggravated nature of the offence caused some distress to the victim or the victim's family (over and above the distress already considered at step one). • Aggravated nature of the offence caused some fear and distress throughout local community or more widely.	Consider a significantly more onerous penalty of the same type or consider a more severe type of sentence than for the basic offence.
LOW LEVEL OF RACIAL OR RELIGIOUS AGGRAVATION	**SENTENCE UPLIFT**
• Aggravated element formed a minimal part of the offence as a whole. • Aggravated nature of the offence caused minimal or no distress to the victim or the victim's family (over and above the distress already considered at step one).	Consider a more onerous penalty of the same type identified for the basic offence.

Magistrates may find that, although the appropriate sentence for the basic offence would be within their powers, the appropriate increase for the aggravated offence would result in a sentence in excess of their powers. If so, they must commit for sentence to the Crown Court.

The sentencer should state in open court that the offence was aggravated by reason of race or religion, and should also state what the sentence would have been without that element of aggravation.

STEP 3
CONSIDER ANY FACTORS WHICH INDICATE A REDUCTION, SUCH AS ASSISTANCE TO THE PROSECUTION

The court should take into account sections 73 and 74 of the Serious Organised Crime and Police Act 2005 (assistance by defendants: reduction or review of sentence) and any other rule of law by virtue of which an offender may receive a discounted sentence in consequence of assistance given (or offered) to the prosecutor or investigator.

STEP 4
REDUCTION FOR GUILTY PLEAS

The court should take account of any potential reduction for a guilty plea in accordance with section 144 of the Criminal Justice Act 2003 and the *Guilty Plea* guideline.

STEP 5
TOTALITY PRINCIPLE

If sentencing an offender for more than one offence, or where the offender is already serving a sentence, consider whether the total sentence is just and proportionate to the overall offending behaviour in accordance with the *Offences Taken into Consideration and Totality* guideline.

STEP 6
COMPENSATION AND ANCILLARY ORDERS

In all cases, the court must consider whether to make a compensation order and/or other ancillary orders.

Compensation order

The court should consider compensation orders in all cases where personal injury, loss or damage has resulted from the offence. The court must give reasons if it decides not to award compensation in such cases.

Other ancillary orders available include:
Restraining order

Where an offender is convicted of any offence, the court may make a restraining order (section 5 of the Protection from Harassment Act 1997).

The order may prohibit the offender from doing anything for the purpose of protecting the victim of the offence, or any other person mentioned in the order, from further conduct which amounts to harassment or will cause a fear of violence.

The order may have effect for a specified period or until further order.

STEP 7
REASONS

Section 174 of the Criminal Justice Act 2003 imposes a duty to give reasons for, and explain the effect of, the sentence.

STEP 8
CONSIDERATION FOR TIME SPENT ON BAIL (TAGGED CURFEW)

The court must consider whether to give credit for time spent on bail in accordance with section 240A of the Criminal Justice Act 2003.

A[41.13] Restraining orders. On *conviction* pursuant to s 5(1) of the Protection from Harassment Act 1997 as amended, from **30 September** 2009, restraining orders can be issued for *any* offence rather than just offences covered by ss 2 or 4 of the 1997 Act. The order can be made for a determinate or indeterminate period of time.

On *acquittal* by virtue of s 5A of the Protection from Harassment Act 1997 (as inserted by s 12 of the Domestic Violence, Crime and Victims Act 2004). Again restraining orders can be issued for any offence on acquittal, not just for offences covered by the PHA 1997. The order can be made for a determinate or indeterminate period of time. This legislation came into force on **30 September 2009**. The legislation states that the court 'may', if it considers it necessary to do so to protect a person from harassment by the defendant . . . make an order. Despite a declaration that that legislation complies with the European Convention of Human Rights difficulties arise eg what is the evidential basis and standard for making an order?

In *R v Major* [2010] EWCA Crim 3016, [2011] 1 Cr App Rep 322, [2011] 2 Cr App Rep (S) 139, it was held that s 5A(1) of the Act was inserted to deal with those cases where there is clear evidence that the victim needs protection but there is insufficient evidence to convict of the particular charges before the court. The victim need not have been blameless and the court's added powers avoided the need for alternative proceedings to protect the victim, added costs and delay. The fact that a criminal court was unsure that the alleged conduct amounted to harassment did not mean that there was no risk of future harassment. Even though the required criminal standard of proof might not have been met, a retraining order was a civil order and the civil standard of proof applied. (2) A restraining order made on acquittal is not a sentence. However, the requirements of s 174(1) of the Criminal Justice Act 2003 and the Consolidated Criminal Practice Direction at III.31.4 should be applied (see now Part 31 of the CrimPR 2015). Accordingly, a court imposing a restraining order should state in open court, its reasons for doing so. In the instant case, while there may have been good reason for making the order, it was not apparent from the Judge's remarks as to whether or not the order was justified. *R v Major* was followed just two weeks later in *R (on the application of Gonzales) v Folkestone Magistrates' Court* [2010] EWHC 3428 (Admin), 175 JP 453.

In *R v Smith (Mark John)* [2012] EWCA Crim 2566; [2013] 1 WLR 1399; [2013] 2 Cr App R (S) 28 the court considered s 5A(1) and concluded:

> '29. There are other fundamental problems with the order. Since the purpose of such an order is to protect a person from harassment by an acquitted defendant, the court must first be satisfied that the defendant is likely to pursue a course of conduct which amounts to harassment within the meaning of s 1. Pursuit of a course of conduct requires intention.
>
> 30. Further, the power to make an order under s5A is circumscribed by the important words "necessary . . . to protect a person from harassment by the defendant". The word "necessary" is not to be diluted. To make an order prohibiting a person who has not committed any criminal offence from doing an act which is otherwise lawful, on pain of imprisonment, is an interference with that person's freedom of action which could be justified only when it is truly necessary for the protection of some other person.'

See further *R v Taylor* [2017] EWCA Crim 2209, [2018] 1 Cr App R (S) 39, where an order was quashed because the necessity test had not been made out.

In the case of a prison sentence a copy of the order should be sent to the prison. Any order should be specific and name parties protected by it (*R v Mann* (2000) 144 Sol Jo LB 150, CA).

Section 5 and Sch 1 of the Interpretation Act 1978 provide that when the word appears in a statute, unless a contrary intention appears "person" includes a body of persons corporate or unincorporated. If there is evidence to indicate that there is a real fear of actual harassment or violence in the future, a restraining order can therefore be imposed in appropriate circumstances either to protect a limited company or its employees. However, in this particular case, the practical sense of the imposition of the order had to be balanced against the failure of the Crown, which had not originally intended applying for restraining orders, to adduce any evidence that there was actual harassment or anything close to it or any perceived danger from anything said or done by any particular defendant to put anybody in fear of violence (*R v Buxton* [2010] EWCA Crim 2923, [2011] 1 WLR 857, [2011] Bus LR 448).

In *R v Debnath* [2005] EWCA Crim 3472, the Court of Appeal stated that when considering whether or not to make a restraining order the following principles applied: (i) the purpose of a restraining order was to prohibit particular conduct with a view to protecting the complainant from further offences; (ii) the order had to be clear and in precise terms so that there could be no doubt as to what the defendant was prohibited from doing; (iii) the order had to be practical in its terms; (iv) when considering the terms, or the extent of an order, the court had to have regard to the issue of proportionality; and (v) the power to vary or discharge an order was an important safeguard and the Court of Appeal would be unlikely to interfere with the order where an application could be made to the court that made the order for its variation or discharge.

Under s 12 above gives any person mentioned in a restraining order the right to make representations in court if an application is made to vary or discharge an order.

In *R v K* [2011] EWCA Crim 1843, 175 JP 378, a restraining order was quashed because at the hearing no consideration appeared to have been given to the provisions of either s 5A of the 1997 Act or the Criminal Procedure Rules 2010. The serious nature of a restraining order was underpinned by the provisions of Part 50 of the Criminal Procedure Rules 2010 which identified the steps which had to be taken in order to ensure that any person to whom any such order was directed was given a proper opportunity to understand what was being proposed and why and to make representations at a hearing. In the instant case, no procedural steps were taken either before or after the Crown offered no evidence, and the limited evidence before the court could not provide a sound evidential basis upon which to make the restraining order. See also *R v Trott* [2011] EWCA Crim 2395, 175 JP 458.

A[41.14] The views of the complainant. When deciding whether to impose a restraining order the authorities set out the following propositions:

> '(1) a court should take into account the views of the person to be protected by such an order as to whether an order should be made. We do not say that there will never be a case where it would be inappropriate to make a restraining order, even though the subject of the order does not seek one, but the views of the victim will clearly be relevant. Nor do we say that a court must have direct evidence of the views of the victim. That may prove impossible. The court may be able to draw a proper inference as to those views, or may conclude that a restraining order should be made whatever the views of the victim, although clearly if a victim does not want an order to be made because she wants to have contact, that may make such an order impractical. But we accept that in normal circumstances the views of the victim should be obtained. It is the responsibility of the prosecution to ensure that the necessary enquiries are made;
>
> (2) an order should not be made unless the judge concludes that it is necessary to make an order in order to protect the victim;
>
> (3) the terms of the order should be proportionate to the harm that it is sought to prevent; and
>
> (4) particular care should be taken when children are involved to ensure that the order does not make it impossible for contact to take place between a parent and a child if that is otherwise inappropriate (sic).'

(per Saunders J giving the judgment of the court): *R v Khellaf* [2016] EWCA Crim 1297, [2017] 1 Cr App R (S) 1.

However, the jurisdiction to make a restraining order cannot be used in a case where the victim does not want an order and wishes to continue living with the defendant, even though the victim is at risk of suffering further violence. The court must respect a decision by an adult which is unambiguous and freely made, whether or not the court considers the decision to be wise having regard to the risk of further violence that person may be exposing herself to. If there is concern about the safety of a child of the family, the proper forum for determining what action needs to be taken is the family proceedings court, to which an application can be made by social services; this is not a task with which the criminal court is equipped to deal: *R v Herrington (Wayne)* [2017] EWCA Crim 889, [2017] 2 Cr App R (S) 38.

A[42] Income tax evasion

Charge (Income tax evasion)

A[42.1] Being knowingly concerned in the fraudulent evasion of income tax by him or another person.

Finance Act 2000, s 144

Maximum penalty – Fine level 5 and 6 months' imprisonment †

Crown Court – 7 years' imprisonment and unlimited fine.

Mode of trial

A[42.2] See general notes at **D**[4] and SC Guideline below.

Sentencing

A[42.3] Refer to guidelines *Fraud – banking and insurance fraud and obtaining credit through fraud, benefit fraud and revenue fraud* at **A**[36.10].

A[43]
Indecent photographs of children

Charges (Indecent photographs of children)

A[43.1] **Did take or make an indecent photograph of a child or**

Distribute or show such photographs or

Possess such photographs with a view to distribution or

Publish an advertisement conveying that the advertiser distributes or shows such photographs.

Protection of Children Act 1978, s 1

Possession of indecent photograph of child

Criminal Justice Act 1988, s 160

Possession of a prohibited image of a child

Coroners and Justice Act 2009, s 62**

Maximum penalty – 6 months' imprisonment and/or fine level 5 (for offences committed on or after 12 March 2015 an unlimited fine). Triable either way. Specified sexual offence under Sch 15, Part 2, CJA 2003.

Crown Court – 10 years' imprisonment (3 years if committed before 11/01/2001) and unlimited fine. **(3 years' imprisonment and unlimited fine for an offence under s 62 above.)

Note; Section 69 of the Serious Crime Act 2015 creates an offence of possession of paedophile material, defined as any item that contains advice or guidance about abusing children sexually. This came into force on 3 May 2015.

Mode of trial

A[43.2] Consider the SC Guideline at A[43.8] below. Possession of indecent photographs of children may be tried in the magistrates' court but the court must have regard to an ascending level of seriousness as set out at **A[43.8]** below.

Legal Notes and definitions

A[43.3] **Indecent photographs or pseudo-photographs.** The section makes it an offence to make an indecent photograph, pseudo photograph, copy, negative or data stored on a computer disc. A person who downloads indecent images of children from an internet site and prints or saves them is also making an indecent photograph (*R v Smith, R v Jayson* [2002] EWCA Crim 683, [2003] 1 Cr App Rep 212, CA).

The offence of possession under s 160(1) is not committed unless the defendant knows that he has the photographs in his possession: *Atkins v DPP* [2000] 2 All ER 425, [2000] 1 WLR 1427, [2000] 2 Cr App Rep 248, DC.

'Possession' means physically in one's custody or under one's physical control. A defendant is not in 'possession' of indecent images which he has deleted from his computer, if he cannot retrieve or gain access to them as he no longer has custody or control of them. Whether he is able to retrieve items deleted from the recycle bin will depend on a finding of fact about his computer skills and ownership of the requisite software. There may also be practical reasons why an accused is not charged with possession at the time when he viewed the images until he deleted them: *R v Porter* [2006] EWCA Crim 560, [2007] 2 All ER 625, [2006] 1 WLR 2633, [2006] 2 Cr App R 25. See also *R v Rowe* [2008] EWCA Crim 2712, 172 JP 585, considered at A[43.7]. Problems can be resolved if the indictment addresses the deletion issue by alleging possession of the indecent image over a period covering either the date of the deletion (if it can be established) or between the dates when the defendant assumed control of the computer and the date when the images were found. If that were done, it would not be the end of the case as it would be open to the defendant to advance any of the statutory defences provided in s 160(2), and, if convicted, if the defendant had truly tried to rid himself of the material, that would be likely to provide substantial mitigation: *R v Leonard* [2012] EWCA Crim 277, [2012] 2 Cr App Rep 138, 176 CL&J 466.

The authorities on possession were considered by Irwin LJ in *R v Okoro (Cyprian)* [2018] EWCA Crim 1929, [2019] 1 WLR 1638, [2019] 1 Cr App R 2 in the context of images which, the defendant claimed, had been sent to him uninvited via WhatsApp. It was held:

> '43 It cannot be the law that a defendant must be shown to be aware of all the relevant content of a digital file on his device. If that were necessary, then the statutory defences in s.160(2) CJA 1988 would be redundant. The question is whether it is enough that the accused should know that digital files had been sent to him, say, as an attachment to an email, or perhaps more likely as an encrypted file by one of the many apps by which digital content may be transmitted. Can possession be established by demonstrating that material is contained in an attachment to an unopened email in an inbox? Or, as claimed here, where the information was transmitted through WhatsApp without any invitation from the accused, and without him viewing any or all of the material.
>
> 44 There is such a volume of information in the memory of modern devices that proof of knowledge of all transmitted content would be impossible. For commercial reasons, many of the great internet business corporations collect and store information on phone and computer memories, individual to the user, but quite unknown and indeed inaccessible to the user.
>
> 45 We are clear that the statute requires proof by the Crown of possession of the pornography or images of child abuse, as a preliminary step before the burden of proof shifts to the accused, to establish the statutory defences. An accused cannot be convicted in relation to material of which he was genuinely totally unaware. Nor could a defendant be said to be in possession of a digital file if it was in practical terms impossible for him to access that file. However, for these statutory purposes we are clear that possession is established if the accused can be shown to have been aware of a relevant digital file or package of files which he has the capacity to access, even if he cannot be shown to have opened or scrutinised the material. That represents the closest possible parallel to the test laid down in the authorities set out above, and appears to us to be consistent with the criminal law of possession in other fields, such as unlawful possession of drugs.
>
> 46 It follows that in this case, two elements had to be made out in order for an individual to have possession: (1) the images must have been within the appellant's custody or control, i.e. so that he was capable of accessing them; and (2) he must have known that he possessed an image or a group of images. It is clear that knowledge of the content of those images is not required to make out the basic ingredients of the offence; instead that issue is dealt with by the statutory defences. Where unsolicited images are sent on WhatsApp, and automatically downloaded to the phone's memory, it is highly likely that the first element will be fulfilled. The second element will depend on whether the defendant knew that he received an image or images.'

'Pop-ups' that occur when a computer user visits particular websites are made by the user and not the website designer; and in 'pop-up' cases the offence of possession is committed where: (a) the images stored there are of persons under age and are of an indecent nature; and (b) the defendant was the person responsible for accessing the images, and he knew that such material would then be automatically stored to the hard drive and that his browsing would or could access illegal images, or be likely to do so: *R v Harrison* [2007] EWCA Crim 2976, [2008] 1 Cr App R 29.

From 8 July 2008, the meaning of 'photograph' in s 7(4) of the Protection of Children Act 1978 was extended by the Criminal Justice and Immigration Act 2008 to include:

> (4A)(a) a tracing or other image, whether made by electronic or other means (of whatever nature) –
>
> (i) which is not itself a photograph or pseudo-photograph, but
>
> (ii) which is derived from the whole or part of a photograph or pseudo-photograph (or a combination of either or both); and
>
> (b) data stored on a computer disc or by other electronic means which is capable of conversion into an image within paragraph (a);
>
> and subsection (8) applies in relation to such an image as it applies in relation to a pseudo-photograph.

A[43.4] Indecent photographs or pseudo-photographs: marriage etc. From April 6, 2010, ss 62–69 of the Coroners and Justice Act 2009 came into force. Section 69 amends s 1A of the Protection of Children Act 1978 and s 160A of the Criminal Justice Act 1988 to insert a reference to 'pseudo-photograph'.

The age of the child is a material consideration for the court in determining whether the photograph of the child was in fact indecent: *R v Owen* [1988] 1 WLR 134, 86 Cr App Rep 291, CA. To convict a person of taking an indecent photograph, it must be proved that the defendant took the photograph deliberately and intentionally. If so satisfied, the court must then decide whether the photograph was indecent by applying the recognised standards of propriety, but for this purpose the circumstances in which the photograph was taken and the motivation of the taker are irrelevant: *R v Graham-Kerr* [1988] 1 WLR 1098, 153 JP 171, CA. Articles 8 and 10 of the European Convention on Human Rights do not require a reconsideration of the interpretation of s 1 of the 1978 Act as the exceptions in art 8(2) and 10(2) apply as the Act is there for the prevention of crime, for the protection of morals, and in particular for the protection of children from being exploited, which is a matter necessary in a democratic society: *R v Smethurst* [2001] EWCA 772, 165 JP 377, [2001] Crim LR 657, [2002] 1 Cr App Rep 50.

A[43.4A] Prohibited images. Section 162 of the Coroners and Justice Act 2009 created an offence of possession of prohibited images of children. Section 162(2) defines a prohibited image as one which is pornographic (subsections (6) and (7) elaborate on this) and subsection (3) provides 'an image is "pornographic" if it is of such a nature that it must reasonably be assumed to have been produced solely or principally for the purpose of sexual arousal'.

In *R v Baddiel* [2016] EWCA Crim 474, [2016] 1 WLR 4157, [2016] 2 Cr App R 25 the Court of Appeal rejected a submission that the relevant purpose had to be that of the person who sent the image to the defendant rather than that of the photographer(s) who took the original images: '15 To our minds these are very simple provisions. Subsection (3) asks what is reasonably to be assumed that the purpose of the production of the image was: was it solely or principally for the purpose of sexual arousal? In other words, in our judgment, it means simply was it produced (and by whom is utterly immaterial) for the purpose of sexual arousal of anyone who comes to have it, be that the producer himself, a distributor or ultimate recipient (per McCombe LJ).'

A[43.5] Evidence. It is for the court to decide on the evidence as a whole whether a child in a photograph was under age at the material time (*R v Land* [1999] QB 65, [1998] 1 All ER 403, CA).

Child includes 16 and 17 year olds: Sexual Offences Act 2003, s 45.

A[43.6] **Distribution.** A person distributes an indecent photograph if he parts with possession of it, or exposes or offers it to another person.

Section 1(1)(b) ("to distribute or show") created an offence of strict liability, in which it was not necessary for the prosecution to prove the defendant's knowledge that a CD which he had given to another person, had contained indecent images at the time of his parting with possession. That section was subject only to the statutory defences, in which knowledge was in issue (*R v P* [2006] All ER (D) 238 (Oct).

A[43.7] **Knowledge.** Deletion of files may be directly relevant to the accused's lack of knowledge of possession of the material particularly where specialist software would be needed to recover the deleted files (*R v Rowe* [2008] EWCA Crim 2712, 172 JP 585).

There are different approaches to the mens rea of the s 1(1)(a) offence between what is meant by 'makes' in the context of images made by being downloaded to a computer or phone from the internet or via email and the making of an image by the act of photographing or filming. Given particular considerations relating to a phone or computer user's awareness as to what he is downloading, a different approach has been adopted for that situation; the mens rea includes a requirement of knowledge that the image made was likely to be an indecent one of a child. But where the making of an indecent image takes place through the more direct action of photographing or filming, the offence is made out by the deliberate act of photographing or filming without more: *R v W* [2016] EWCA Crim 745, [2016] 2 Cr App R 27.

A[43.8] **Defences.** Section 1(4) of the Protection of Children Act 1978 provides that it is a defence for a person to prove that he had a legitimate reason for possessing, distributing or showing the photographs, or that he had not himself seen the photographs and did not know or have cause to suspect them to be indecent.

The above defences are limited to persons who distribute or are in possession of such material for a legitimate reason (eg the police) or an individual who was ignorant of and had no reason to believe that he was in possession of or distributing indecent material or in the case of simple possession, who received it unsolicited and gets rid of it with reasonable promptness. No statutory defence is available for the person who creates the material or advertises its availability. It is also not a defence that a person did not know nor had any cause to suspect that the photograph depicted persons who were 16 years or older: *R v Land* [1998]) 1 All ER 403, [1998] 3 WLR 322, [1998] 1 Cr App Rep 301.

In respect of 16 and 17 year olds specific defences are provided that the defendant can show:

(a) the child was 16 or over or they were married or in an enduring family relationship;
(b) there was consent or a reasonable belief the child consented;
(c) the photograph is not of the child and another person other than the defendant.

Whilst the 1978 Act does not impede an accused from engaging in sexual intercourse with a person who is aged 17, he is not permitted to make such a person the subject of pornography. The defence does not apply to a 'one night stand' as a defence which includes a 'brief sexual relationship' would diminish the protection provided and would risk the re-introduction of issues as to the circumstances in which the photograph was taken and the motivation for taking or making it. The legislation strikes the balance between keeping interference by the State in the private lives of individuals to the minimum and maintaining under the law maximum protection for children from sexual abuse and exploitation: *R v M* [2011] EWCA Crim 2752, [2012] Crim LR 789.

There is also a defence for those involved in law enforcement activities.

In relation to the offence under s 160(1) of the Criminal Justice Act 1988, it shall be a defence for the accused to prove:

(a) that they had a legitimate reason for having the photograph or pseudo-photograph in his possession; or
(b) that they had not themselves seen the photograph or pseudo-photograph and did not know, nor had any cause to suspect, it to be indecent; or
(c) that the photograph or pseudo-photograph was sent to them without any prior request made by them or on their behalf and that they did not keep it for an unreasonable time.

Criminal Justice Act 1988, s 160(2).

The 'it' referred to in (b) above refers to an indecent image of a child and not an indecent image alone; thus, the defence is available where the defendant had reasonable cause to suspect the image was indecent but not that it was an indecent image of a child: *R v Collier* [2004] EWCA Crim 1411, [2005] 1 WLR 843, [2005] 1 Cr App R 9, [2005] Crim LR 1039.

Sentencing
SC Guideline – Indecent photographs of children

A[43.9] This guideline is taken from the SC's definitive guideline *Sexual Offences Act 2003* effective from 1 April 2014.

Triable either way

Maximum: 10 years' custody

Offence range: Community order – 9 years' custody

For section 1 offences committed on or after 3 December 2012, this is an offence listed in Part 1 of Schedule 15B for the purposes of section 224A (life sentence for second listed offence) of the Criminal Justice Act 2003.

For convictions on or after 3 December 2012 (irrespective of the date of commission of the offence), these are specified offences for the purposes of section 226A (extended sentence for certain violent or sexual offences) of the Criminal Justice Act 2003.

STEP ONE
Determining the offence category

The court should determine the offence category using the table below.

	Possession	Distribution*	Production**
Category A	Possession of images involving penetrative sexual activity	Sharing images involving penetrative sexual activity	Creating images involving penetrative sexual activity
	Possession of images involving sexual activity with an animal or sadism	Sharing images involving sexual activity with an animal or sadism	Creating images involving sexual activity with an animal or sadism
Category B	Possession of images involving non-penetrative sexual activity	Sharing of images involving non-penetrative sexual activity	Creating images involving non-penetrative sexual activity
Category C	Possession of other indecent images not falling within categories A or B	Sharing of other indecent images not falling within categories A or B	Creating other indecent images not falling within categories A or B

* Distribution includes possession with a view to distributing or sharing images.

** Production includes the taking or making of any image at source, for instance the original image. Making an image by simple downloading should be treated as possession for the purposes of sentencing.

In most cases the intrinsic character of the most serious of the offending images will initially determine the appropriate category. If, however, the most serious images are unrepresentative of the offender's conduct a lower category may be appropriate. A lower category will not, however, be appropriate if the offender has produced or taken (for example photographed) images of a higher category.

STEP TWO

Starting point and category range

Having determined the category, the court should use the corresponding starting points to reach a sentence within the category range below. The starting point applies to all offenders irrespective of plea or previous convictions. Having determined the starting point, step two allows further adjustment for aggravating or mitigating features, set out on the next page.

Where there is a sufficient prospect of rehabilitation, a community order with a sex offender treatment programme requirement under section 202 of the Criminal Justice Act 2003 can be a proper alternative to a short or moderate length custodial sentence.

	Possession	Distribution	Production
Category A	**Starting point** 1 year's custody	**Starting point** 3 years' custody	**Starting point** 6 years' custody
	Category range 26 weeks' – 3 years' custody	**Category range** 2 – 5 years' custody	**Category range** 4 – 9 years' custody
Category B	**Starting point** 26 weeks' custody	**Starting point** 1 year's custody	**Starting point** 2 years' custody
	Category range High level community order – 18 months' custody	**Category range** 26 weeks' – 2 years' custody	**Category range** 1 – 4 years' custody
Category C	**Starting point** High level community order	**Starting point** 13 weeks' custody	**Starting point** 18 months' custody
	Category range Medium level community order – 26 weeks' custody	**Category range** High level community order – 26 weeks' custody	**Category range** 1 – 3 years' custody

The table below contains a **non-exhaustive** list of additional factual elements providing the context of the offence and factors relating to the offender. Identify whether any combination of these, or other relevant factors, should result in an upward or downward adjustment from the starting point. **In particular, relevant recent convictions are likely to result in an upward adjustment. In some cases, having considered these factors, it may be appropriate to move outside the identified category range.**

When sentencing appropriate **category B or C offences**, the court should also consider the custody threshold as follows:

- has the custody threshold been passed?
- if so, is it unavoidable that a custodial sentence be imposed?

- if so, can that sentence be suspended?

Aggravating factors	Child depicted known to the offender
Statutory aggravating factors	Active involvement in a network or process that facilitates or commissions the creation or sharing of indecent images of children
Previous convictions, having regard to a) the nature of the offence to which the conviction relates and its relevance to the current offence; and b) the time that has elapsed since the conviction	Commercial exploitation and/or motivation
Offence committed whilst on bail	Deliberate or systematic searching for images portraying young children, category A images or the portrayal of familial sexual abuse
Other aggravating factors	Large number of different victims
Failure to comply with current court orders	Child depicted intoxicated or drugged
Offence committed whilst on licence	**Mitigating factors**
Age and/or vulnerability of the child depicted+	No previous convictions or no relevant/recent convictions
Discernable pain or distress suffered by child depicted	Remorse
Period over which images were possessed, distributed or produced	Previous good character and/or exemplary conduct*
High volume of images possessed, distributed or produced	Age and/or lack of maturity where it affects the responsibility of the offender
Placing images where there is the potential for a high volume of viewers	Mental disorder or learning disability, particularly where linked to the commission of the offence
Collection includes moving images	Demonstration of steps taken to address offending behaviour
Attempts to dispose of or conceal evidence	
Abuse of trust	

+ Age and/or vulnerability of the child should be given significant weight. In cases where the actual age of the victim is difficult to determine sentencers should consider the development of the child (infant, pre-pubescent, post-pubescent)

* Previous good character/exemplary conduct is different from having no previous convictions. The more serious the offence, the less the weight which should normally be attributed to this factor. Where previous good character/exemplary conduct has been used to facilitate the offence, this mitigation should not normally be allowed and such conduct may constitute an aggravating factor.

STEP THREE

Consider any factors which indicate a reduction, such as assistance to the prosecution

The court should take into account sections 73 and 74 of the Serious Organised Crime and Police Act 2005 (assistance by defendants: reduction or review of sentence) and any other rule of law by virtue of which an offender may receive a discounted sentence in consequence of assistance given (or offered) to the prosecutor or investigator.

STEP FOUR
Reduction for guilty pleas

The court should take account of any potential reduction for a guilty plea in accordance with section 144 of the Criminal Justice Act 2003 and the *Guilty Plea* guideline.

STEP FIVE
Dangerousness

The court should consider whether having regard to the criteria contained in Chapter 5 of Part 12 of the Criminal Justice Act 2003 it would be appropriate to award a life sentence (section 224A) or an extended sentence (section 226A). When sentencing offenders to a life sentence under these provisions, the notional determinate sentence should be used as the basis for the setting of a minimum term.

STEP SIX
Totality principle

If sentencing an offender for more than one offence, or where the offender is already serving a sentence, consider whether the total sentence is just and proportionate to the overall offending behaviour.

STEP SEVEN
Ancillary orders

The court must consider whether to make any ancillary orders. The court must also consider what other requirements or provisions may automatically apply. Further information is included on page 303.

STEP EIGHT
Reasons

Section 174 of the Criminal Justice Act 2003 imposes a duty to give reasons for, and explain the effect of, the sentence.

STEP NINE
Consideration for time spent on bail

The court must consider whether to give credit for time spent on bail in accordance with section 240A of the Criminal Justice Act 2003.

A[43.10] Available sentences. See Table A at B[43.1A].

A[43.11] Forfeiture.

Section 5 of the 1978 Act has been amended by s 39 of the Police and Justice Act 2006 to specifically provide for the forfeiture of indecent photographs and pseudo-photographs.

A[43.12] Notification requirements. See A[52.15]. Requirements apply even on the making of a conditional discharge (*R v Longworth* [2004] EWCA Crim 2145, [2005] 1 Cr App Rep (S) 419, (2004) Times, 17 August).

Offences under s 1 of the Protection of Children Act 1978 can relate to children aged 16 or 17; therefore, it needs to be clear that the child shown in the photograph was under 16 or a notification requirement will not arise: *R v George* [2018] EWCA Crim 417, [2018] 2 Cr App R (s) 10.

A[44]
Keeping a brothel used for prostitution

Charge (Keeping a brothel used for prostitution)

A[44.1] **Did keep, or to manage, or act or assist in the management of, a brothel to which people resort for practices involving prostitution (whether or not also for other practices)**

Sexual Offences Act 1956, s 33A

Maximum penalty – 6 months' imprisonment and/or fine level 5 (for offences committed on or after 12 March 2015 an unlimited fine). Triable either way. Specified sexual offence under Sch 15, Part 2, CJA 2003

Crown Court – 7 years' imprisonment and unlimited fine.

Section 33A was inserted by s 55 of the Sexual Offences Act 2003. The Sexual Offences Act 1956 also provides offences of: keeping a brothel (s 33); letting premises for use as brothel (s 34); tenant permitting premises to be used as a brothel (s 35); and tenant permitting premises to be sued for prostitution (s 36). These offences are summary only. The maximum penalty is a fine level 3 and three months, or, for second or subsequent conviction, a fine level 4 and six months.

Mode of trial

A[44.2] Consider the SC Guideline at A[44.4] below. Note, where an offender has profited from his or her involvement in the prostitution of others, the courts should always consider making a confiscation order approximately equivalent to the profits enjoyed. Such an order can only be made in the Crown Court.

Legal notes and definitions

A[44.3] **Brothel.** A brothel is a place where people of opposite sexes are allowed to resort for illicit intercourse, whether the women are common prostitutes or not: *Winter v Woolfe* [1931] 1 KB 549, 95 JP 20. A house occupied by one woman and used by her for prostitution but not allowed by her to be used by other women for a like purpose, is not a brothel: *Singleton v Ellison* [1895] 1 QB 607, 59 JP 119. However, the facts justified a finding that premises were used as a brothel where two women, one being the tenant and occupier both used the premises for prostitution: *Gorman v Standen, Palace-Clark v Standen* [1964] 1 QB 294, [1963] 3 All ER 627, 128 JP 28. On other facts it has been held that two flats in one building, separately let to prostitutes, did not justify a finding that the building was used as a brothel: *Strath v Foxon* [1956] 1 QB 67, [1955] 3 All ER 398, 119 JP 581; but a block of flats, inhabited by different women and used by them for prostitution was held, on the facts, to be a brothel: *Durose v Wilson* (1907) 71 JP 263; and where there was use by three prostitutes in separate rooms, separately let to them, in such proximity as to constitute a 'nest' of prostitutes, it was held that the premises were a brothel: *Donovan v Gavin* [1965] 2 QB 648, [1965] 2 All ER 611, 129 JP 404. Similarly where premises were used by a team of different prostitutes, but no more than one used the premises each day, the premises were held to constitute a brothel: *Stevens v Christy* (1987) 151 JP 366, [1987] Crim LR 503.

Assisting in the management. Evidence of normal sexual intercourse provided on the premises is not essential to prove a charge of assisting in the management of a brothel; it is sufficient to prove that more than one woman offered herself as a participant in physical acts of indecency for the sexual gratification of men: *Kelly v Purvis* [1983] QB 663, [1983] 1 All ER 525, 76 Cr App Rep 165. Women in a massage parlour, who not only performed lewd acts, but also discussed the nature of the acts to be performed and negotiated the terms of payment for their services, were held to be assisting in the management of a brothel: *Elliott v DPP* (1989) Times, 19 January, DC. To establish the offence of assisting in the management it is not necessary to show that the defendant exercised some sort of control over the management, nor is it necessary to show there was a specific act of management for that would be acting in the management: *Jones and Wood v DPP* (1992) 156 JP 866.

Prostitution. Has the same meaning as give by s 51(2) of the Sexual Offences Act 2003.

Sentencing
SC Guideline – Keeping a brothel used for prostitution

A[44.4] This guideline is taken from the SC's definitive guideline *Sexual Offences Act 2003* effective from 1 April 2014.

Triable either way

Maximum: 7 years' custody

Offence range: Community order – 6 years' custody

The terms 'prostitute' and 'prostitution' are used in this guideline in accordance with the statutory language contained in the Sexual Offences Act 2003.

STEP ONE
Determining the offence category

The court should determine which categories of harm and culpability the offence falls into by reference **only** to the tables below.

Harm		Culpability
Category 1	• Under 18 year olds working in brothel	A
	• Abduction/detention	Keeping brothel on significant commercial basis Involvement in keeping a number of brothels
	• Violence or threats of violence	Expectation of significant financial or other gain
	• Sustained and systematic psychological abuse	Abuse of trust
	• Those working in brothel forced or coerced to participate in unsafe/degrading sexual activity	Exploitation of those known to be trafficked
	• Those working in brothel forced or coerced into seeing many 'customers'	Significant involvement in limiting freedom of those working in brothel
	• Those working in brothel forced/coerced/deceived into prostitution	Grooming of a person to work in the brothel including through cultivation of a dependency on drugs or alcohol
	• Established evidence of community impact	B
Category 2	Factor(s) in category 1 not present	Keeping/managing premises

Harm		Culpability
		Close involvement with those working in brothel, for example control of finances, choice of clients, working conditions, etc (where offender's involvement is not as a result of coercion)
		C
		Performs limited function under direction
		Close involvement but engaged by coercion/intimidation/ exploitation

STEP TWO
Starting point and category range

Having determined the category, the court should use the corresponding starting points to reach a sentence within the category range on the next page. The starting point applies to all offenders irrespective of plea or previous convictions. Having determined the starting point, step two allows further adjustment for aggravating or mitigating features, set out on the next page.

A case of particular gravity, reflected by multiple features of culpability or harm in step one, could merit upward adjustment from the starting point before further adjustment for aggravating or mitigating features, set out on the next page.

Where there is a sufficient prospect of rehabilitation, a community order with a sex offender treatment programme requirement under section 202 of the Criminal Justice Act 2003 can be a proper alternative to a short or moderate length custodial sentence.

	A	B	C
Category 1	**Starting point** 3 – 6 years' custody	**Starting point** 2 – 5 years' custody	**Starting point** High level community order – 18 months' custody
	Category range 5 – 8 years' custody	**Category range** 3 – 6 years' custody	**Category range** 18 months' – 4 years' custody
Category 2	**Starting point** 3 years' custody	**Starting point** 12 months' custody	**Starting point** Medium level community order
	Category range 2 – 5 years' custody	**Category range** 26 weeks' – 2 years' custody	**Category range** Low level community order – High level community order

The table below contains a **non-exhaustive** list of additional factual elements providing the context of the offence and factors relating to the offender. Identify whether any combination of these, or other relevant factors, should result in an upward or downward adjustment from the starting point. **In particular, relevant recent convictions are likely to result in an upward adjustment. In some cases, having considered these factors, it may be appropriate to move outside the identified category range.**

When sentencing appropriate **category 1 offences**, the court should also consider the custody threshold as follows:

- has the custody threshold been passed?
- if so, is it unavoidable that a custodial sentence be imposed?
- if so, can that sentence be suspended?

Aggravating factors	Any steps taken to prevent those working in brothel reporting an incident, obtaining assistance and/or from assisting or supporting the prosecution
Statutory aggravating factors	Attempts to dispose of or conceal evidence
Previous convictions, having regard to a) the nature of the offence to which the conviction relates and its relevance to the current offence; and b) the time that has elapsed since the conviction	Those working in brothel forced or coerced into pornography
Offence committed whilst on bail	Timescale over which operation has been run
Other aggravating factors	**Mitigating factors**
Failure to comply with current court orders	No previous convictions or no relevant/recent convictions
Offence committed whilst on licence	Remorse
Deliberate isolation of those working in brothel	Previous good character and/or exemplary conduct*
Threats made to expose those working in brothel to the authorities (for example, immigration or police), family/friends or others	Age and/or lack of maturity where it affects the responsibility of the offender
Harm threatened against the family/friends of those working in brothel	Mental disorder or learning disability, particularly where linked to the commission of the offence
Passport/identity documents removed	Demonstration of steps taken to address offending behaviour
Those working in brothel prevented from seeking medical treatment	
Food withheld	
Those working in brothel passed around by offender and moved to other brothels	
Earnings of those working in brothel withheld/kept by offender or evidence of excessive wage reduction or debt bondage, inflated travel or living expenses or unreasonable interest rates	

* Previous good character/exemplary conduct is different from having no previous convictions. The more serious the offence, the less the weight which should normally be attributed to this factor. Where previous good character/exemplary conduct has been used to facilitate the offence, this mitigation should not normally be allowed and such conduct may constitute an aggravating factor.

STEP THREE

Consider any factors which indicate a reduction, such as assistance to the prosecution

The court should take into account sections 73 and 74 of the Serious Organised Crime and Police Act 2005 (assistance by defendants: reduction or review of

sentence) and any other rule of law by virtue of which an offender may receive a discounted sentence in consequence of assistance given (or offered) to the prosecutor or investigator.

STEP FOUR
Reduction for guilty pleas

The court should take account of any potential reduction for a guilty plea in accordance with section 144 of the Criminal Justice Act 2003 and the *Guilty Plea* guideline.

STEP FIVE
Totality principle

If sentencing an offender for more than one offence, or where the offender is already serving a sentence, consider whether the total sentence is just and proportionate to the overall offending behaviour.

STEP SIX
Ancillary orders

The court must consider whether to make any ancillary orders. The court must also consider what other requirements or provisions may automatically apply. Further information is included on page 303.

STEP SEVEN
Reasons

Section 174 of the Criminal Justice Act 2003 imposes a duty to give reasons for, and explain the effect of, the sentence.

STEP EIGHT
Consideration for time spent on bail

The court must consider whether to give credit for time spent on bail in accordance with section 240A of the Criminal Justice Act 2003.

A[45]
Making off without payment

Charge (Making off without payment)

A[45.1] **Knowing that payment on the spot for certain goods supplied [or service done] was required or expected dishonestly made off without having paid as required or expected and with intent to avoid payment of the amount due**

Theft Act 1978, s 3

A[45.2] **Maximum penalty** – 6 months' imprisonment and/or fine level 5 (for offences committed on or after 12 March 2015 an unlimited fine). Triable either way.

Crown Court – 2 years and unlimited fine.

Mode of trial

A[45.3] Consider the SC Guideline at A[45.8] below.

Legal notes and definitions

A[45.4] The basis of this offence is dishonesty. Dishonesty can be inferred from the surrounding circumstances. It is an offence whether the advantage is obtained for the defendant or for someone else.

A[45.5] **Dishonesty.** See A[36.7], ante.

A[45.6] **Payment on the spot** includes payment at the time of collecting goods on which work has been done, or in respect of which a service has been provided, eg collecting one's car from a garage after repair.

In the case of a journey by taxi, the service is not performed until the cab reaches the agreed destination, and if the journey is cut short as a result of any argument between the driver and their fare, the latter will not be guilty of making off without payment: *R v Wilkinson* [2018] EWCA Crim 2154, [2019] RTR 20 (see further A[45.7]).

A[45.6A] **Making off.** 'Making off' involves a departure from the spot where payment is required: *R v Brooks* (1983) 76 Cr App Rep 66. In the case of a taxi, payment might be made while sitting in the taxi or standing by the window. Payment might be requested whilst the fares are still in the cab and at this stage the fares might be disputed. The fact that the taxi driver then drives off to a police station, or somewhere else, locking the door, does not mean that when the defendant runs off he could not be making off without having paid, dishonestly intending to avoid payment. It is the time at which he makes off which is critical at which he had to have formed the intention to avoid payment. But to apply the words too literally would be to misunderstand the legislation. Thus, if a passenger were to explain (honestly) to the taxi driver that he had to enter his house in order to obtain the fare, the moment for payment would be deferred for him to do so. A decision not to return to the taxi would mean that, from that moment, the passenger is making off without payment. See *R v Morris* [2013] EWCA Crim 436, [2013] 2 Cr App R 9, [2013] RTR 22.

A breach of contract by the party claiming payment may mean that the defendant may not have been in a situation in which he was bound to pay or even tender the money and, thus, cannot be charged with making off: *Troughton v Metropolitan Police* [1987] Crim LR 138.

A[45.7] **With intent to avoid payment of the amount due.** This means with intent *never* to pay the sum due. An intent merely to defer or delay payment is not enough for a 'making off' offence (*R v Allen* [1985] 1 All ER 148, [1985] 1 WLR 50, CA; affd [1985] AC 1029, [1985] 2 All ER 641, HL).

Sentencing
SC Guideline – Making off without payment

A[45.8] Theft Act 1978 (section 3)

Triable either way

Maximum: 2 years' custody

Offence range: Discharge – 36 weeks' custody

STEP ONE
Determining the offence category

The court should determine the offence category with reference **only** to the factors identified in the following tables. In order to determine the category the court should assess **culpability** and **harm.**

The level of culpability is determined by weighing up all the factors of the case to determine the offender's role and the extent to which the offending was **planned** and the **sophistication** with which it was carried out.

CULPABILITY demonstrated by one or more of the following:

A – High culpability
A leading role where offending is part of a group activity
Involvement of others through coercion, intimidation or exploitation
Sophisticated nature of offence/significant planning
Offence involving intimidation or the use or threat of force
Deliberately targeting victim on basis of vulnerability
B – Medium culpability
A significant role where offending is part of a group activity
Some degree of planning involved
All other cases where characteristics for categories A or C are not present
C – Lesser culpability
Performed limited function under direction
Involved through coercion, intimidation or exploitation
Little or no planning
Limited awareness or understanding of offence

Where there are characteristics present which fall under different levels of culpability, the court should balance these characteristics to reach a fair assessment of the offender's culpability.

HARM

Harm is assessed by reference to the **actual loss** that results from the offence **and any significant additional harm** suffered by the victim – examples of additional harm may include **but are not limited to:**

Greater harm

A high level of inconvenience caused to the victim
Emotional distress
Fear/loss of confidence caused by the crime
A greater impact on the victim due to the size or type of their business
All other cases

Category 1	Goods or services obtained above £200 or Goods/services up to £200 with significant additional harm to the victim
Category 2	Goods or services obtained up to £200 and Little or no significant additional harm to the victim

STEP TWO

Starting point and category range

Having determined the category at step one, the court should use the starting point to reach a sentence within the appropriate category range in the table below

The starting point applies to all offenders irrespective of plea or previous convictions.

	Culpability		
Harm	A	B	C
Category 1 Where the value greatly exceeds £200, it may be appropriate to move outside the identified range. Adjustment should be made for any significant additional harm for offences above £200.	**Starting point** 12 weeks' custody	**Starting point** Low level community order	**Starting point** Band B fine
	Category range High level community order – 36 weeks' custody	**Category range** Band C fine – High level community order	**Category range** Band A fine – Low level community order
Category 2	**Starting point** Low level community order – 12 weeks' custody	**Starting point** Band C fine	**Starting point** Band A fine
	Category range Medium level community order – 12 weeks' custody	**Category range** Band B fine – Low level community order	**Category range** Discharge – Band B fine

Consecutive sentences for multiple offences may be appropriate – please refer to the *Offences Taken Into Consideration and Totality* guideline.

The court should then consider further adjustment for any aggravating or mitigating factors. The following is a **non-exhaustive** list of additional factual elements providing the context of the offence and factors relating to the offender.

Identify whether any combination of these, or other relevant factors, should result in an upward or downward adjustment from the starting point.

Factors increasing seriousness	Factors reducing seriousness or reflecting personal mitigation
Statutory aggravating factors	No previous convictions or no relevant/recent convictions
Previous convictions, having regard to a) the **nature** of the offence to which the conviction relates and its **relevance** to the current offence; and b) the **time** that has elapsed since the conviction	Remorse, particularly where evidenced by voluntary reparation to the victim
Offence committed whilst on bail	Good character and/or exemplary conduct
Offence motivated by, or demonstrating hostility based on any of the following characteristics or presumed characteristics of the victim: religion, race, disability, sexual orientation or transgender identity	Serious medical condition requiring urgent, intensive or long-term treatment
Other aggravating factors	Age and/or lack of maturity where it affects the responsibility of the offender
Steps taken to prevent the victim reporting or obtaining assistance and/or from assisting or supporting the prosecution	Mental disorder or learning disability
Attempts to conceal/dispose of evidence	Sole or primary carer for dependent relatives
Failure to comply with current court orders	Determination and/or demonstration of steps having been taken to address addiction or offending behaviour
Offence committed on licence	
Offences taken into consideration	
Established evidence of community/wider impact	

STEP THREE
Consider any factors which indicate a reduction, such as assistance to the prosecution

The court should take into account sections 73 and 74 of the Serious Organised Crime and Police Act 2005 (assistance by defendants: reduction or review of sentence) and any other rule of law by virtue of which an offender may receive a discounted sentence in consequence of assistance given (or offered) to the prosecutor or investigator.

STEP FOUR
Reduction for guilty pleas

The court should take account of any potential reduction for a guilty plea in accordance with section 144 of the Criminal Justice Act 2003 and the *Guilty Plea* guideline.

STEP FIVE
Totality principle

If sentencing an offender for more than one offence, or where the offender is already serving a sentence, consider whether the total sentence is just and proportionate to the overall offending behaviour in accordance with the *Offences Taken into Consideration and Totality* guideline.

STEP SIX
Confiscation, compensation and ancillary orders

The court must proceed with a view to making a confiscation order if it is asked to do so by the prosecutor or if the court believes it is appropriate for it to do so.

Where the offence has resulted in loss or damage the court must consider whether to make a compensation order.

If the court makes both a confiscation order and an order for compensation and the court believes the offender will not have sufficient means to satisfy both orders in full, the court must direct that the compensation be paid out of sums recovered under the confiscation order (section 13 of the Proceeds of Crime Act 2002).

The court may also consider whether to make ancillary orders. These may include a deprivation order, or a restitution order

STEP SEVEN
Reasons

Section 174 of the Criminal Justice Act 2003 imposes a duty to give reasons for, and explain the effect of, the sentence.

STEP EIGHT
Consideration for time spent on bail

The court must consider whether to give credit for time spent on bail in accordance with section 240A of the Criminal Justice Act 2003.

A[46]

Protective order, breach of

Charges (Protective order, breach of)

A[46.1] **1 Without reasonable excuse the defendant breached the terms of his restraining order in that he [specify] thereby making him guilty of an offence.**

Protection from Harassment Act 1997, s 5(5).

2. Without reasonable excuse the defendant breached the terms of his non-molestation order in that he [specify] thereby making him guilty of an offence.

Family Law Act 1996, s 42A(1).

Maximum penalty – (in either case) 6 months' imprisonment and/or fine level 5 (for offences committed on or after 12 March 2015 an unlimited fine). Triable either way. Specified violent offence under Sch 15, Part 1, CJA 2003.

Crown Court – 5 years' imprisonment and unlimited fine.

Mode of trial

A[46.2] Consider the SC Guideline at A[46.4] below.

Legal notes and definitions

A[46.3] **Non-molestation – duplicity.** An information couched in the form of a s 1 offence (ie it referred to a 'course of conduct') and alleging this to be in breach of the terms of a restraining order, contrary to s 5(5) and (6), was held not to be bad for duplicity in *McCaskill v DPP* [2005] EWHC 3208 (Admin), (2006) 170 JP 301.

Harassment – terms of order. An order under s.5 must identify by name those who are protected by it (*R v Mann* [2000] The Times, April 11, CA).

Interpretation. The interpretation of ordinary words in a court order is a question of fact; the criminal context is not a reason for giving a narrow or strained meaning to words which bear their ordinary meaning, and the application of that meaning to the facts is a matter for the fact-finding tribunal: *R v Evans* [2004] EWCA Crim 3102, (2005) 169 JP 129, [2005] 1 Cr App Rep 546, [2005] Crim LR 654 (parking a car so that it blocked in the van of somebody visiting the complainants' property was held to breach a restraining order that prohibited the defendant from 'abusive action' towards the complainants).

Sentencing

Sentencing Council – Protective order (restraining and non-molestation orders), breach of

A[46.4] This guideline is taken from the Sentencing Council's Breach offences: Definitive guideline, published on 7 June 2018, taking effect from 1 October 2018.

For cases of domestic violence. See SC Definitive Guideline: "Overarching Principles: Domestic Violence".

Breach of a protective order (restraining and non-molestation orders)

Restraining orders:
Protection from Harassment Act 1997 (section 5(5) and (5A))

Non-molestation orders:

Family Law Act 1996, s 42A

Effective from: 1 October 2018

Triable either way

Maximum: 5 years' custody

Offence range: Fine–4 years' custody

STEP 1
DETERMINING THE OFFENCE CATEGORY

The court should determine the offence category with reference only to the factors listed in the tables below. In order to determine the category the court should assess **culpability** and **harm.**

Culpability

In assessing culpability, the court should consider the **intention** and **motivation** of the offender in committing any breach.

A	• Very serious or persistent breach
B	• Deliberate breach falling between A and C
C	• Minor breach • Breach just short of reasonable excuse

Harm

The level of **harm** is determined by weighing up all the factors of the case to determine the harm that has been caused or was at risk of being caused.

In assessing any risk of harm posed by the breach, consideration should be given to the original offence(s) or activity for which the order was imposed and the circumstances in which the breach arose.

Category 1	Breach causes very serious harm or distress
Category 2	Cases falling between categories 1 and 3
Category 3	Breach causes little or no harm or distress*

* where a breach is committed in the context of a background of domestic abuse, the sentencer should take care not to underestimate the harm which may be present in a breach

STEP 2
STARTING POINT AND CATEGORY RANGE

Having determined the category at step one, the court should use the corresponding starting point to reach a sentence within the category range in the table below. The starting point applies to all offenders irrespective of plea or previous convictions.

	Culpability		
Harm	**A**	**B**	**C**
Category 1	**Starting point** 2 years' custody **Category range** 1–4 years' custody	**Starting point** 1 years' custody **Category range** High level community order – 2 years' custody	**Starting point** 12 weeks' custody **Category range** Medium level community order – 1 year's custody

	Culpability		
Harm	A	B	C
Category 2	**Starting point** 1 years' custody **Category range** High level community order – 2 years' custody	**Starting point** 12 weeks' custody **Category range** Medium level community order – 1 year's custody	**Starting point** High level community order **Category range** Low level community order – 26 weeks' custody
Category 3	**Starting point** 12 weeks' custody **Category range** Medium level community order – 1 year's custody	**Starting point** High level community order **Category range** Low level community order – 26 weeks' custody	**Starting point** Low level community order **Category range** Band B fine – High level community order

The table above refers to single offences. Where there are multiple offences consecutive sentences may be appropriate – please refer to the *Offences Taken Into Consideration and Totality* guideline.

The table below contains a **non-exhaustive** list of additional factual elements providing the context of the offence and factors relating to the offender. Identify whether any combination of these, or other relevant factors, should result in an upward or downward adjustment from the starting point. In some cases, having considered these factors, it may be appropriate to move outside the identified category range.

FACTORS INCREASING SERIOUSNESS

Statutory aggravating factors:
Previous convictions, having regard to a) the **nature** of the offence to which the conviction relates and its **relevance** to the current offence; and b) the **time** that has elapsed since the conviction
Offence committed whilst on bail
Other aggravating factors:
Breach committed shortly after order made
History of disobedience to court orders (where not already taken into account as a previous conviction)
Breach involves a further offence (where not separately prosecuted)
Using contact arrangements with a child/children to instigate offence and/or proven history of violence or threats by offender
Breach results in victim or protected person being forced to leave their home
Impact upon children or family members
Victim or protected subject of order breached is particularly vulnerable
Offender takes steps to prevent victim or subject harmed by breach from reporting an incident or seeking assistance
Offence committed on licence or while subject to post sentence supervision

FACTORS REDUCING SERIOUSNESS OR REFLECTING PERSONAL MITIGATION

Breach committed after long period of compliance

Prompt voluntary surrender/admission of breach or failure
Age and/or lack of maturity where it affects the responsibility of the offender
Mental disorder or learning disability where linked to the commission of the offence
Sole or primary carer for dependent relatives
Contact not initiated by offender – a careful examination of all the circumstances is required before weight is given to this factor

STEP 3
CONSIDER ANY FACTORS WHICH INDICATE A REDUCTION, SUCH AS ASSISTANCE TO THE PROSECUTION

The court should take into account sections 73 and 74 of the Serious Organised Crime and Police Act 2005 (assistance by defendants: reduction or review of sentence) and any other rule of law by virtue of which an offender may receive a discounted sentence in consequence of assistance given (or offered) to the prosecutor or investigator.

STEP 4
REDUCTION FOR GUILTY PLEAS

The court should take account of any reduction for a guilty plea in accordance with section 144 of the Criminal Justice Act 2003 and the guideline for Reduction in Sentence for a Guilty Plea (where first hearing is on or after 1 June 2017, or first hearing before 1 June 2017).

STEP 5
TOTALITY PRINCIPLE

If sentencing an offender for more than one offence, or where the offender is already serving a sentence, consider whether the total sentence is just and proportionate to the overall offending behaviour in accordance with the *Offences Taken into Consideration and Totality* guideline.

STEP 6
ANCILLARY ORDERS

In all cases, the court should consider whether to make compensation and/or ancillary orders.

STEP 7
REASONS

Section 174 of the Criminal Justice Act 2003 imposes a duty to give reasons for, and explain the effect of, the sentence.

STEP 8
CONSIDERATION FOR TIME SPENT ON BAIL

The court must consider whether to give credit for time spent on bail in accordance with section 240A of the Criminal Justice Act 2003.

Variation

A[46.5] Variation of restraining order. Where a restraining order has been made for a specified period of time, on a true construction of s 5(4), a court had power to vary a restraining order by extending the expiry date of the order (*DPP v Kevin Hall* [2005] EWHC 2612 (Admin), [2006] 3 All ER 170). The refusal by a magistrates' court to vary or discharge a restraining order on an application under s 5(4) was not subject to a right of appeal to the Crown Court as such an order was not a sentence (or "order") for the purposes of s 108 MCA 1980 (*R (on the application of Lee) v Leeds Crown Court* [2006] All ER (D) 18 (Oct). The same argument was canvassed in *R v Bradfield* [2006] All ER (D) 394 (Nov) in relation to s 9 of the Criminal Appeal Act 1968 but the Court of Appeal did not find it necessary to decide the point. The case of *Lee*, therefore, remains good law).

A[47]

Obstructing or resisting a constable in the execution of his duty Obstructing a court security officer in the execution of his duty

Charges (Obstructing etc constable in execution of duty)

A[47.1] **1 Resisting a constable in the execution of his duty**

A[47.2] **2 Resisting a person assisting a constable in the execution of his duty**

A[47.3] **3 Wilfully obstructing a constable in the execution of his duty**

A[47.4] **4 Wilfully obstructing a person assisting a constable in the execution of his duty**

Police Act 1996, s 89(2)

Maximum penalty – Fine level 3 and one month.

A[47.5] **5 Wilfully obstructing a court security officer in the execution of his duty**

Courts Act 2003, s 57

Maximum penalty – Fine level 3.

Legal notes and definitions

A[47.6] The offences of resisting and wilfully obstructing will usually involve some other activity than an assault on the police or a court security officer (which would constitute a different charge). A person exercising their right to silence does not commit the offence of obstructing a police officer.

A[47.7] **Resisting.** Means striving against, opposing or trying to impede. For the intention which the defendant must have to commit the offence see **A[9]** (police assault).

A[47.8] **Wilfully.** A person wilfully obstructs a police constable in the execution of his duty if he deliberately does an act which, though not necessarily 'aimed at' or 'hostile to' the police, in fact prevents a constable from carrying out his duty or makes it more difficult for him to do so, and if he knows and intends (whether or not that is his predominant intention) that his conduct will have that effect; the motive with which the act is committed is irrelevant unless it constitutes a lawful excuse for the obstruction: *Lewis v Cox* [1985] QB 509, [1984] 3 All ER 672, 148 JP 601. It is immaterial that the defendant does not appreciate that his action amounted to obstruction: *Moore v Green* [1983] 1 All ER 663. A person cannot obstruct a police officer in the execution of his duty when he reasonably believes that he is not a police officer: *Ostler v Elliott* [1980] Crim LR 584.

A[47.9] **Obstructing.** A person who simply gave drivers of motor cars notice of a 'police trap' was held not guilty of obstruction under an enactment replaced by this sub-section: *Bastable v Little* [1907] 1 KB 59, 71 JP 52. But, where cars when warned of a police trap are being driven at an illegal speed, the person so warning may be convicted of obstruction: *Betts v Stevens* [1910] 1 KB 1, 73 JP 486. In *R (on the application of DPP) v Glendinning* [2005] EWHC Admin 2333, (2005) 169 JP 649 it was re-affirmed that a conviction for obstruction required evidence that there were vehicles that were speeding or were likely to speed at the location of the speed trap.

A person's mere refusal to answer a constable's questions which, in the circumstances, he was not legally obliged to answer, is not caught by the section: *Rice v Connolly* [1966] 2 QB 414, [1966] 2 All ER 649, 130 JP 322, but in *Ricketts v Cox* (1981) 74 Cr App Rep 298, [1982] Crim LR 184, it was held that a defendant who was abusive, uncooperative and positively hostile to police officers, using obscene language calculated to provoke and antagonise the officers, was guilty of obstruction.

Running off to avoid apprehension amounts to an act that is capable of constituting the wilful obstruction of a police officer: *Sekfall, Banamira and Ouham v DPP* [2006] EWHC 894 (Admin), (2006) 170 JP 393. While it is lawful for a third party to advise a suspect of his right not to answer questions put to him by a police officer, if the third party by his abusive, persistent and unruly behaviour, acts in a way that goes well beyond the exercise of his legal rights and prevents communication between the officer and the suspect, or makes it more difficult, he will be guilty of obstructing the police: see *Green v DPP* (1991) 155 JP 816, DC. In *Ingleton v Dibble* [1972] 1 QB 480, [1972] 1 All ER 275, 136 JP 155, it was held that there was a distinction between a refusal to act (as in *Rice v Connolly*, above) and the doing of some positive act, and that it was not necessary to show, where the obstruction consists of a positive act, that it must be unlawful independently. It was held that the driver of a motor car who drank whisky after being asked to take a breath test with the object and effect of frustrating the procedure under ss 2 and 3 of the Road Safety Act 1967 was guilty of obstructing the police, and in *R v Britton* [1973] Crim LR 375 a similar action with a bottle of beer led to a conviction for the common law misdemeanour of attempting to defeat the due course of justice.

A private citizen can never have a lawful excuse for interfering with an arrest by a police officer which is lawful: *Hills v Ellis* [1983] QB 680, [1983] 1 All ER 667.

A person who shouted, outside a public house, outside 'permitted hours', that the police were waiting to enter, was rightly convicted: *Hinchliffe v Sheldon* [1955] 3 All ER 406, 120 JP 13.

Failure to accord entry to police officers acting under s 4 of the Road Traffic Act 1988 may be a wilful obstruction: *Lunt v DPP* [1993] Crim LR 534.

A[47.10] **Constable.** A constable includes a special constable and member of the police force of any rank however high. Offences against designated and accredited persons acting in the execution of their duty ie community support officer, investigating officer, detention officer and escort officer are catered for by the Police Reform Act 2002, s 46. Wilful obstruction carries on conviction imprisonment of one month or a level 3 fine.

A[47.11] **In the execution of his duty.** See A[9.5], where this topic is considered in detail in relation to the offence of assaulting a constable acting in the execution.

A[47.12] This type of defence sometimes raises difficult questions of law as to whether, for example, a constable had a right to be on private premises when not in possession of a search warrant, or whether a constable had a right to detain a person without there being in force a warrant for arrest. See *James and Chorley v DPP* (1997) 161 JP 89, [1997] Crim LR 831 where a defendant had ceased driving thus ending a constable's right to arrest for driving whilst disqualified. His friend did not obstruct the constable by preventing an arrest as the arrest was not lawful.

Self-defence is available as a defence to obstructing a police officer in the execution of their duty: *Oraki v Crown Prosecution Service* [2018] EWHC 115 (Admin), [2018] 1 Cr App R 27.

A[47.13] The burden of proof that the constable was acting in the execution of his duty rests on the prosecution (*Redmond-Bate v DPP* (1999) 163 JP 789, [1999] Crim LR 998).

A[47.14] **Police officer and court security officer.** See A[9.4] for definitions.

Sentencing
SC Guideline – Obstruct/resist a constable in the execution of duty

Obstruct/resist a police constable in execution of duty (Revised 2017)

A[47.15]

Police Act 1996, s 89(2)

Effective from: 24 April 2017

Triable only summarily:

Maximum: Level 3 fine and/or one month

Offence range: Conditional Discharge–Medium level community order

Defences. Self-defence is available as a defence to obstructing a police officer in the execution of his duty: *Oraki v Crown Prosecution Service* [2018] EWHC 115 (Admin), [2018 1 Cr App R 27.

STEP 1
Determining the offence category

The Court should determine the offence category using the table below.

Category 1	Higher culpability and greater harm
Category 2	Higher culpability and lesser harm or lower culpability and greater harm
Category 3	Lower culpability and lesser harm

The court should determine the offender's culpability and the harm caused with reference only to the factors below. Where an offence does not fall squarely into a category, individual factors may require a degree of weighting before making an overall assessment and determining the appropriate offence category.

CULPABILITY demonstrated by one or more of the following:

Factors indicating higher culpability

- Deliberate obstruction or interference
- Use of force, aggression or intimidation
- Group action

Factors indicating lower culpability

- All other cases

HARM demonstrated by one or more of the following:

Factors indicating greater harm

- Offender's actions significantly increase risk to officer or other(s)
- Offender's actions result in a suspect avoiding arrest
- Offender's actions result in a significant waste of resources

Factors indicating lesser harm

- All other cases

STEP 2
Starting point and category range

Having determined the category at step one, the court should use the corresponding starting point to reach a sentence within the category range below. The starting point applies to all offenders irrespective of plea or previous convictions.

Offence Category	Starting Point	Range
Category 1	Low level community order	Band C fine–Medium level community order
Category 2	Band B fine	Band A fine–Band C fine
Category 3	Band A fine	Conditional discharge–Band B fine

The court should then consider adjustment for any aggravating or mitigating factors. The following is a **non-exhaustive** list of additional factual elements providing the context of the offence and factors relating to the offender. Identify whether any combination of these, or other relevant factors, should result in an upward or downward adjustment from the sentence arrived at so far.

Factors increasing seriousness

Statutory aggravating factors:

- Previous convictions, having regard to a) the **nature** of the offence to which the conviction relates and its **relevance** to the current offence; and b) the **time** that has elapsed since the conviction
- Offence committed whilst on bail
- Offence motivated by, or demonstrating hostility based on any of the following characteristics or presumed characteristics of the victim: religion, race, disability, sexual orientation or transgender identity

Other aggravating factors:

- Failure to comply with current court orders
- Offence committed on licence or post sentence supervision
- Blame wrongly placed on others
- Injury caused to an officer/another
- Giving false details

Factors reducing seriousness or reflecting personal mitigation

- No previous convictions **or** no relevant/recent convictions
- Remorse
- Brief incident
- Acting under direction or coercion of another
- Genuinely held belief if coming to the aid of another, that the other was suffering severe medical difficulty
- Good character and/or exemplary conduct
- Serious medical condition requiring urgent, intensive or long-term treatment
- Age and/or lack of maturity where it affects the responsibility of the offender
- Mental disorder or learning disability
- Sole or primary carer for dependent relatives

STEP 3
Consider any factors which indicate a reduction, such as assistance to the prosecution

The court should take into account sections 73 and 74 of the Serious Organised Crime and Police Act 2005 (assistance by defendants: reduction or review of sentence) and any other rule of law by virtue of which an offender may receive a discounted sentence in consequence of assistance given (or offered) to the prosecutor or investigator.

STEP 4
Reduction for guilty pleas

The court should take account of any potential reduction for a guilty plea in accordance with section 144 of the Criminal Justice Act 2003 and the *Guilty Plea* guideline.

STEP 5
Totality principle

If sentencing an offender for more than one offence, or where the offender is already serving a sentence, consider whether the total sentence is just and proportionate to the overall offending behaviour in accordance with the *Offences Taken into Consideration and Totality* guideline.

STEP 6
Compensation and ancillary orders

In all cases, the court should consider whether to make compensation and/or other ancillary orders.

STEP 7
Reasons

Section 174 of the Criminal Justice Act 2003 imposes a duty to give reasons for, and explain the effect of, the sentence.

A[48]
Railway fare evasion

Charge 1 (Railway fare evasion)

A[48.1] Failure to give name and address following a failure to produce a valid ticket

Regulation of Railways Act 1889, s 5(1)

Maximum penalty – Fine level 2 (Railway Company or London Transport)

Charge 2 (Railway fare evasion)

A[48.2] Travelling on a railway without having previously paid the fare with the intention of avoiding payment

OR

Having paid a fare knowingly and wilfully travelling beyond the distance paid for without previously paying for an additional distance with the intention of avoiding additional fare

OR

Giving a false name and address following a failure to pay

Regulation of the Railways Act 1889, s 5(3)(a), (b), and (c) respectively

Maximum penalty – Fine level 3 or 3 months (Railway Company or London Transport).

Byelaws. All railway operators and Railtrack have adopted the Framework Railway Byelaws. Penalty for a breach of a byelaw is a level 3 fine.

Legal notes and definitions

A[48.3] A fare must be paid to the railway authority or one of its employees.

The request for a traveller's name and address must be made by an officer of the railway operator.

A[48.4]–[48.6] Intention. A person travelling with a return ticket of another person may be rightly convicted for travelling without having paid his fare, and with intent to avoid payment: *Langdon v Howells* (1879) 4 QBD 337, 43 JP 717; *London, Midland and Scottish Rly Co v Greaver* [1937] 1 KB 367, [1936] 3 All ER 333, 100 JP 511.

Payment of fare means payment to the railway company, or to their servant or agent. The intent to avoid payment thereof is proved by travelling on a non-transferable ticket issued to someone else. It is not necessary to show that the offender knew the ticket was non-transferable. The transferor is guilty of aiding and abetting him in the commission of the offence: *Reynolds v Beasley* [1919] 1 KB 215, 83 JP 35.

Proof of intent to defraud is not required; there need only be proof of intent to avoid payment: *Browning v Floyd* [1946] KB 597, [1946] 2 All ER 367, 110 JP 308. A dishonest intention is not necessarily imported and an offence is committed if a passenger travels or attempts to travel intending not to pay what, in fact, turns out to be the proper fare: see *Covington v Wright* [1963] 2 QB 469, [1963] 2 All ER 212.

But there must be proof of intent to avoid payment and the burden of proof remains throughout on the prosecution: *R v Steane* [1947] KB 997, [1947] 1 All ER 813, 111 JP 387.

'His fare' means the fare by the train and for the class of carriage in which the passenger travels; so a person travelling in a first-class carriage with a second-class ticket, and fraudulently intending to avoid payment of first-class fare, may be convicted for travelling 'without having previously paid his fare': *Gillingham v Walker* (1881) 45 JP 470. In such circumstances, the passenger may be convicted on proof that he declined to pay the excess fare demanded: *Noble v Killick* (1891) 60 LJMC 61.

The intent to avoid payment refers in point of time to the period of travel and this continues at least until the traveller reaches the ticket barrier: *Bremme v Dubery* [1964] 1 All ER 193, 128 JP 148; *Murphy v Verati* [1967] 1 All ER 861. There is no reason for importing the adverb 'permanently' into s 5(3)(a); an intention not to pay the proper fare unless and until he was tracked down and payment requested is sufficient to constitute an intent to avoid payment: *Corbyn v Saunders* [1978] 2 All ER 697, 142 JP 458.

A[48.7] **Travelling.** This includes the time between leaving the railway carriage and proceeding to the exit barrier. Thus an offence is committed if a passenger decides to avoid the fare at that stage of the journey.

A[48.8] **Wilfully.** This means deliberately.

Sentencing

SC Guideline – Railway fare evasion

Railway fare evasion (Revised 2017)

A[48.9]

Regulation of Railways Act 1889, s 5(3) (travelling on railway without paying fare, with intent to avoid payment); s 5(1) (failing to produce ticket)

Effective from: 24 April 2017

Triable only summarily:

Maximum:

Level 2 fine (s 5(1) failing to produce ticket)

Level 3 fine and/or 3 months (s 5(3) travelling on railway with intent to avoid payment)

Offence range:

Conditional Discharge–Band C fine (s 5(1))

Conditional Discharge–Low level community order (s 5(3))

STEP 1
Determining the offence category

The Court should determine the offence category using the table below.

Category 1	Higher culpability and greater harm
Category 2	Higher culpability and lesser harm or lower culpability and greater harm

Category 3 Lower culpability and lesser harm

The court should determine the offender's culpability and the harm caused with reference **only** to the factors below. Where an offence does not fall squarely into a category, individual factors may require a degree of weighting before making an overall assessment and determining the appropriate offence category.

CULPABILITY demonstrated by one or more of the following:

Factors indicating higher culpability

- Aggressive, abusive or disruptive behaviour

Factors indicating lower culpability

- All other cases

HARM demonstrated by one or more of the following:

Factors indicating greater harm

- High revenue loss

Factors indicating lesser harm

- All other cases

STEP 2
Starting point and category range

Having determined the category at step one, the court should use the corresponding starting point to reach a sentence within the category range below. The starting point applies to all offenders irrespective of plea or previous convictions.

Travelling on railway without paying fare, with intent

Offence Category	Starting Point	Range
Category 1	Band C fine	Band B fine–Low level community order
Category 2	Band B fine	Band A fine–Band C fine
Category 3	Band A fine	Conditional discharge–Band B fine

Failing to Produce a ticket

Offence Category	Starting Point	Range
Category 1	Band B fine	Band B fine–Band C fine
Category 2	Band A fine	Band A fine–Band B fine
Category 3	Band A fine	Conditional discharge–Band B fine

The court should then consider adjustment for any aggravating or mitigating factors. The following is a **non-exhaustive** list of additional factual elements providing the context of the offence and factors relating to the offender. Identify whether any combination of these, or other relevant factors, should result in an upward or downward adjustment from the sentence arrived at so far.

Factors increasing seriousness

Statutory aggravating factors:

- Previous convictions, having regard to a) the **nature** of the offence to which the conviction relates and its **relevance** to the current offence; and b) the **time** that has elapsed since the conviction

- Offence committed whilst on bail
- Offence motivated by, or demonstrating hostility based on any of the following characteristics or presumed characteristics of the victim: religion, race, disability, sexual orientation or transgender identity

Other aggravating factors:

- Offender has avoided paying any of the fare
- Offender produces incorrect ticket or document to pass as legitimate fare payer
- Failure to comply with current court orders
- Abuse to staff
- Offence committed on licence or post sentence supervision

Factors reducing seriousness or reflecting personal mitigation

- No previous convictions or no relevant/recent convictions
- Remorse
- Good character and/or exemplary conduct
- Serious medical condition requiring urgent, intensive or long-term treatment
- Age and/or lack of maturity where it affects the responsibility of the offender
- Mental disorder or learning disability
- Sole or primary carer for dependent relatives

STEP 3
Consider any factors which indicate a reduction, such as assistance to the prosecution

The court should take into account sections 73 and 74 of the Serious Organised Crime and Police Act 2005 (assistance by defendants: reduction or review of sentence) and any other rule of law by virtue of which an offender may receive a discounted sentence in consequence of assistance given (or offered) to the prosecutor or investigator.

STEP 4
Reduction for guilty pleas

The court should take account of any potential reduction for a guilty plea in accordance with section 144 of the Criminal Justice Act 2003 and the *Guilty Plea* guideline.

STEP 5
Totality principle

If sentencing an offender for more than one offence, or where the offender is already serving a sentence, consider whether the total sentence is just and proportionate to the overall offending behaviour in accordance with the *Offences Taken into Consideration and Totality* guideline.

STEP 6
Compensation and ancillary orders

In all cases, the court should consider whether to make compensation and/or other ancillary orders.

STEP 7
Reasons

Section 174 of the Criminal Justice Act 2003 imposes a duty to give reasons for, and explain the effect of, the sentence.

A[48.10] See Table B at B[43.2] for available sentences.

A[49]
School non-attendance

Charge 1 (School non-attendance)

A[49.1] **Being the parent of a child [identify] of compulsory school age and who is a registered pupil at a school [specify], [identify child] failed to attend regularly at the school.**

Education Act 1996, s 444(1).

Maximum penalty – Level 3 fine.

Charge 2 (School non-attendance)

A[49.2] **Being the parent of a child [identify] of compulsory school age and who is a registered pupil at a school namely [specify], knowing that the child [identify] is failing to attend regularly at that school, fails without justification to cause the child to do so.**

Education Act 1996, s 444 (1A).

Maximum penalty – Level 4 fine and/or 3 months.

Legal notes and definitions

A[49.3] 'Compulsory school age' and 'school' is defined by Education Act 1996, s 8.

'Registered pupil' in relation to a school, means a person registered as a pupil at the school in the register kept under the Education Act 1996, s 434.

'Parent' is defined by Education Act 1996, s 576.

'Regularly' is not defined. The issue which arose in *Isle of Wight Council v Platt* [2017] UKSC 28, [2017] 3 All ER 623, (2017) 181 JP 237 was, effectively, whether parents could remove their children from school during term time for the purpose of taking a holiday.

Baroness Hale, in giving the judgment of the Supreme Court identified at least three possible meanings of 'regularly' in this provision: (a) evenly spaced, as in 'he attends Church regularly every Sunday'; (b) sufficiently often, as in 'he attends Church regularly, almost every week'; or (c) in accordance with the rules, as in 'he attends Church when he is required to do so'. The Divisional Court in *London Borough of Bromley v C* [2006] EWHC 1110 (Admin), [2006] ELR 358 and in this case, made the assumption that 'regularly' means 'sufficiently frequently'. In the present case the Supreme Court undertook a thorough and informative historical review of the legislation and its predecessors. Whilst accepting that definition (b) above, sufficiently frequently, might well be the meaning assumed by many people at first reading there were many reasons to think that this was not what Parliament intended, either in the 1944 or 1996 Education Acts:

> 'Finally, given the strictness of the previous law, Parliament is unlikely to have found it acceptable that parents could take their children out of school in blatant disregard of the school rules, either without having asked for permission at all or, having asked for it, been refused. This is not an approach to rule-keeping which any educational system can be expected to find acceptable. It is a slap in the face to those obedient parents who do keep the rules, whatever the cost or inconvenience to themselves.'

Her Ladyship also dealt with what worried the Divisional Court, namely that the consequence that a single missed attendance without leave or unavoidable cause could lead to criminal liability, and referred to sensible prosecution policy and recourse to fixed penalties as a means of avoiding criminal proceedings. If such cases are prosecuted, the court can deal with them by an absolute or conditional discharge if appropriate. But it must be borne in mind that the aim is to bring home to parents how important it was that they ensured that their children went to school.

Subject to the defences set out in s 444(1), the offence is one of strict liability; which does not contravene article 6(2) of the ECHR (*Barnfather v Islington Education Authority* [2003] 1 WLR 2318). Where the parent asserted that the child was receiving a suitable education outside of school, the burden lay on the parent to prove that defence albeit on a balance of probabilities: *Oxford County Council v L* (unreported) 3/3/10, DC.

It is a defence to a charge under s 444(1A) for the defendant to prove that he had a reasonable justification for his failure to cause the child to attend regularly at the school: s 444(1B). A child shall not, however, be taken to have failed to attend regularly at the school at any time if the parent proves that at that time the child was prevented from attending by reason of sickness or any unavoidable cause (discussed below): s 444(2A).Therefore, if 'unavoidable cause' is raised it should be considered first because if it is made out there can be no conviction of under s 444(1) or s 444(1A): *A County Council v C* [2013] EWHC 1757, (2013) 177 JP 567.

In *Islington London Borough Council v TD* [2011] EWHC 990 (Admin), it was held that the Education Act created two distinct offences and two distinct defences for non-school attendance. It was a defence that the child was prevented from attending regularly by reason of sickness, or any unavoidable cause. 'Unavoidable cause' had to be in relation to the child and had to be something in the nature of an emergency. On the facts there was no question of something in the nature of an emergency that stopped the child from going to school and the fact that P was unable to persuade the child to go to school was not a defence. The magistrates had applied the wrong test. The fact that P had done all she reasonably could do to ensure the child's attendance went to mitigation only. See also *West Sussex County Council v C*, above (the mother's chaotic lifestyle could not constitute an 'unavoidable cause'). See further *Jenkins v Howells* [1949] 2 KB 218, (1949) 113 JP 292.

A[49.3A] If, on the trial of an offence under subsection (1A), the court finds the defendant not guilty of that offence but is satisfied that he is guilty of an offence under subsection (1), the court may find him guilty of that offence: Education Act 1996, s 444(8B). It is not obligatory to convict of an offence under subsection (1) although as a general proposition, if the offence under subsection (1A) is not made out, magistrates ought to convict of an offence under subsection (1) because it is an absolute offence; none the less the interests of justice may dictate to the contrary: *R (P) v Liverpool City Magistrates' Court* [2006] EWHC 887 (Admin), 170 JP 453. See also *West Sussex County Council v C*, above. Though the child concerned had attained 16 and the mother was on benefits, remitting the case with a direction to convict of the lesser offence was 'far from being pointless'. The mother had another child whose education was being seriously disrupted.

Sentencing

SC Guideline – School non-attendance

School non-attendance (Revised 2017)

A[49.4]

Education Act 1996, s 444(1) (parent fails to secure regular attendance at school of registered pupil); s 444(1A) (Parent knowingly fails to secure regular attendance at school of registered pupil)

Effective from: 24 April 2017

Triable only summarily

Maximum:

Level 3 fine (s 444(1) parent fails to secure regular attendance at school);

Level 4 fine and/or 3 months (s.444(1A) parent knowingly fails to secure regular attendance at school)

Offence range:

Conditional discharge–Band C fine (s 444(1))

Band A fine–High level community order (s 444(1A))

STEP 1
Determining the offence seriousness

The Court should determine the offence category using the table below.

Category 1	Higher culpability and greater harm
Category 2	Higher culpability and lesser harm or lower culpability and greater harm
Category 3	Lower culpability and lesser harm

The court should determine the offender's culpability and the harm caused with reference only to the factors below. Where an offence does not fall squarely into a category, individual factors may require a degree of weighting before making an overall assessment and determining the appropriate offence category.

CULPABILITY demonstrated by one or more of the following:

Factors indicating higher culpability

- Refusal/failure to engage with guidance and support offered
- Threats to teachers and/or officials
- Parent encouraging non attendance

Factors indicating lower culpability

- Genuine efforts to ensure attendance
- Parent concerned by child's allegations of bullying
- Parent put in fear of violence and/or threats from the child

HARM demonstrated by one or more of the following:

Factors indicating greater harm

- Significant and lengthy period of education missed
- Adverse influence on other children of the family

Factors indicating lesser harm

- All other cases

STEP 2
Starting point and category range

Having determined the category at step one, the court should use the corresponding starting point to reach a sentence within the category range below. The starting point applies to all offenders irrespective of plea or previous convictions.

s 444(1A) (Parent knowingly fails to secure regular attendance at school of registered pupil)

Offence Category	Starting Point	Range
Category 1	Medium level community order	Low level community order–High level community order
Category 2	Band C fine	Band B fine–Low level community order
Category 3	Band B fine	Band A fine–Band C fine

s 444(1) (parent fails to secure regular attendance at school of registered pupil)

Offence Category	Starting Point	Range
Category 1	Band C fine	Band B fine–Band C fine
Category 2	Band B fine	Band A fine–Band B fine
Category 3	Band A fine	Conditional Discharge–Band B fine

The court should then consider adjustment for any aggravating or mitigating factors. The following is a **non-exhaustive** list of additional factual elements providing the context of the offence and factors relating to the offender. Identify whether any combination of these, or other relevant factors, should result in an upward or downward adjustment from the sentence arrived at so far.

Factors increasing seriousness

Statutory aggravating factors:

- Previous convictions, having regard to a) the **nature** of the offence to which the conviction relates and its **relevance** to the current offence; and b) the **time** that has elapsed since the conviction
- Offence committed whilst on bail

Other aggravating factors:

- Failure to comply with current court orders
- Offence committed on licence or post sentence supervision

Factors reducing seriousness or reflecting personal mitigation

- No previous convictions **or** no relevant/recent convictions
- Remorse
- Good character and/or exemplary conduct
- Serious medical condition requiring urgent, intensive or long-term treatment
- Age and/or lack of maturity where it affects the responsibility of the offender
- Mental disorder or learning disability (of offender)
- Parent unaware of child's whereabouts
- Previously good attendance

STEP 3
Consider any factors which indicate a reduction, such as assistance to the prosecution

The court should take into account sections 73 and 74 of the Serious Organised Crime and Police Act 2005 (assistance by defendants: reduction or review of sentence) and any other rule of law by virtue of which an offender may receive a discounted sentence in consequence of assistance given (or offered) to the prosecutor or investigator.

STEP 4
Reduction for guilty pleas

The court should take account of any potential reduction for a guilty plea in accordance with section 144 of the Criminal Justice Act 2003 and the *Guilty Plea* guideline.

STEP 5
Totality principle

If sentencing an offender for more than one offence, or where the offender is already serving a sentence, consider whether the total sentence is just and proportionate to the overall offending behaviour in accordance with the *Offences Taken into Consideration and Totality* guideline.

STEP 6
Compensation and ancillary orders

In all cases, the court should consider whether to make compensation and/or other ancillary orders including parenting orders.

STEP 7
Reasons

Section 174 of the Criminal Justice Act 2003 imposes a duty to give reasons for, and explain the effect of, the sentence.

A[50]

Sex offenders register – fail to comply with notification requirements

Charge (Sex offenders register)

A[50.1] A person commits an offence if he—

(a) fails, without reasonable excuse, to comply with section 83 (1), 84 (1), 84 (4) (b), 85 (1), 87 (4) or 89 (2) (b) or any requirement imposed by regulations made under section 86 (1); or

(b) notifies to the police, in purported compliance with section 83 (1), 84 (1) or 95 (1) or any requirement imposed by regulations made under section 86 (1), any information which he knows to be false.

Sexual Offences Act 2003, s 91 (1).

Maximum penalty – 6 months' imprisonment and/or fine level 5 (for offences committed on or after 12 March 2015 an unlimited fine). Triable either way.

Crown Court – 5 years' imprisonment and unlimited fine

Mode of trial

A[50.2] See SC Guideline at **A**[50.4] below.

Legal notes and definitions

A[50.3] As to the obligation to register see **A**[52.15].

Sentencing
SC Guideline – Fail to comply with notification requirements

A[50.4] The text of this guideline is taken from the Sentencing Council's Breach offences: Definitive guideline, published on 4 July 2018, taking effect from 1 October 2018.

Fail to comply with notification requirements

Sexual Offences Act 2003, s 91

Effective from: 1 October 2018

Triable either way

Maximum: 5 years' custody

Offence range: Fine – 4 years' custody

Where offence committed in a domestic context, also refer to the *Overarching principles: Domestic abuse guideline*

STEP 1
DETERMINING THE OFFENCE CATEGORY

The court should determine the offence category with reference only to the factors in the tables below. In order to determine the category the court should assess **culpability** and **harm**.

Culpability

In assessing culpability, the court should consider the intention and motivation of the offender in committing any breach.

A	• Determined attempts to avoid detection Long period of non compliance
B	• Deliberate failure to comply with requirement
C	• Minor breach • Breach just short of reasonable excuse

Harm

The level of harm is assessed by weighing up all the factors of the case.

In assessing any risk of harm posed by the breach, consideration should be given to the original offence(s) for which the order was imposed and the circumstances in which the breach arose.

Category 1	Breach causes or risks very serious harm or distress
Category 2	Cases falling between categories 1 and 3
Category 3	Breach causes or risks little or no harm or distress

STEP 2
STARTING POINT AND CATEGORY RANGE

Having determined the category at step one, the court should use the corresponding starting point to reach a sentence within the category range in the table below. The starting point applies to all offenders irrespective of plea or previous convictions.

	Culpability		
Harm	A	B	C
Category 1	**Starting point** 2 year's custody **Category range** 1 year's – 4 years' custody	**Starting point** 1 year's custody **Category range** 26 weeks' – 2 year's custody	**Starting point** 36 weeks' custody **Category range** 26 weeks' – 1 year 6 months' custody
Category 2	**Starting point** 1 years' custody **Category range** 26 weeks – 2 years' custody	**Starting point** 36 weeks' custody **Category range** 26 weeks' – 1 year 6 months' custody	**Starting point** High level community order **Category range** Medium level community order – 36 weeks' custody
Category 3	**Starting point** 36 weeks' custody **Category range** 26 weeks' – 1 year 6 months' custody	**Starting point** High level community order **Category range** Medium level community order – 36 weeks' custody	**Starting point** Low level community order **Category range** Band B fine – Medium level community order

The table below contains a **non-exhaustive** list of additional factual elements providing the context of the offence and factors relating to the offender. Identify whether any combination of these, or other relevant factors, should result in an upward or downward adjustment from the starting point. In some cases, having considered these factors, it may be appropriate to move outside the identified category range.

FACTORS INCREASING SERIOUSNESS

Statutory aggravating factors:
Previous convictions, having regard to a) the **nature** of the offence to which the conviction relates and its **relevance** to the current offence; and b) the **time** that has elapsed since the conviction
Offence committed whilst on bail
Other aggravating factors:
Breach committed shortly after order made
History of disobedience of court orders (where not already taken into account as a previous conviction)
Breach constitutes a further offence (where not separately prosecuted)
Offence committed on licence or while subject to post sentence supervision

FACTORS REDUCING SERIOUSNESS OR REFLECTING PERSONAL MITIGATION

Breach committed after long period of compliance
Prompt voluntary surrender/admission of breach or failure
Good character and/or exemplary conduct
Mental disorder or learning disability where linked to the commission of the offence
Sole or primary carer for dependent relatives

STEP 3
CONSIDER ANY FACTORS WHICH INDICATE A REDUCTION, SUCH AS ASSISTANCE TO THE PROSECUTION

The court should take into account sections 73 and 74 of the Serious Organised Crime and Police Act 2005 (assistance by defendants: reduction or review of sentence) and any other rule of law by virtue of which an offender may receive a discounted sentence in consequence of assistance given (or offered) to the prosecutor or investigator.

STEP 4
REDUCTION FOR GUILTY PLEAS

The court should take account of any potential reduction for a guilty plea in accordance with section 144 of the Criminal Justice Act 2003 and the *Guilty Plea* guideline.

STEP 5
TOTALITY PRINCIPLE

If sentencing an offender for more than one offence, or where the offender is already serving a sentence, consider whether the total sentence is just and proportionate to the overall offending behaviour in accordance with the *Offences Taken into Consideration and Totality* guideline.

STEP 6
COMPENSATION AND ANCILLARY ORDERS

In all cases, the court must consider whether to make a compensation order and/or other ancillary orders.

The order may have effect for a specified period or until further order.

STEP 7
REASONS

Section 174 of the Criminal Justice Act 2003 imposes a duty to give reasons for, and explain the effect of, the sentence.

STEP 8
CONSIDERATION FOR TIME SPENT ON BAIL

The court must consider whether to give credit for time spent on bail in accordance with section 240A of the Criminal Justice Act 2003.

A[51]

Sexual activity in a public lavatory

Charge (Sexual activity in a public lavatory)

A[51.1] **The accused was in a lavatory to which the public or a section of the public has or were permitted to have access, whether on payment or otherwise; that he intentionally engaged in an activity and, the activity was sexual.**

Sexual Offences Act 2003, s 71.

Maximum penalty – 6 months' imprisonment and/or fine level 5 (for offences committed on or after 12 March 2015 an unlimited fine).

Legal Notes and definitions

A[51.2] For the purposes of s 71, an activity is sexual if a reasonable person would, in all the circumstances but regardless of any person's purpose, consider it to be sexual.

Sentencing
SC Guideline – Sexual activity in a lavatory

Sexual activity in a public lavatory
(Revised 2017)

A[51.3]

Sexual Offences Act 2003, s 71

Effective from: 24 April 2017

Triable only summarily:

Maximum: Unlimited fine and/or 6 months

Offence range: Band A fine–High level community order

STEP 1
Determining the offence category

The Court should determine the offence category using the table below.

Category 1	Higher culpability **and** greater harm
Category 2	Higher culpability **and** lesser harm **or** lower culpability **and** greater harm
Category 3	Lower culpability **and** lesser harm

The court should determine the offender's culpability and the harm caused with reference **only** to the factors below. Where an offence does not fall squarely into a category, individual factors may require a degree of weighting before making an overall assessment and determining the appropriate offence category.

CULPABILITY demonstrated by one or more of the following:

Factors indicating higher culpability

- Intimidating behaviour/threats of violence to member(s) of the public
- Blatant behaviour

Factors indicating lower culpability

- All other cases

HARM demonstrated by one or more of the following:

Factors indicating greater harm

- Distress suffered by members of the public
- Children or young persons present

Factors indicating lesser harm

- All other cases

STEP 2
Starting point and category range

Having determined the category at step one, the court should use the starting point to reach a sentence within the appropriate category range in the table below. The starting point applies to all offenders irrespective of plea or previous convictions.

Offence Category	Starting Point	Range
Category 1	Low level community order	Band C fine–High level community order
Category 2	Band C fine	Band B fine–Low level community order
Category 3	Band B fine	Band A fine–Band C fine

Persistent offending of this nature may justify an upward adjustment outside the category range and may cross the community threshold even though the offence otherwise warrants a lesser sentence.

The court should then consider adjustment for any aggravating or mitigating factors. The following is a **non-exhaustive** list of additional factual elements providing the context of the offence and factors relating to the offender. Identify whether any combination of these, or other relevant factors, should result in an upward or downward adjustment from the sentence arrived at so far.

Factors increasing seriousness

Statutory aggravating factors:

- Previous convictions, having regard to a) the **nature** of the offence to which the conviction relates and its **relevance** to the current offence; and b) the **time** that has elapsed since the conviction
- Offence committed whilst on bail

Other aggravating factors:

- Failure to comply with current court orders
- Offence committed on licence or post sentence supervision
- Offences taken into consideration
- Location
- Presence of children
- Established evidence of community/wider impact

Factors reducing seriousness or reflecting personal mitigation

- No previous convictions **or** no relevant/recent convictions
- Remorse
- Good character and/or exemplary conduct
- Serious medical condition requiring urgent, intensive or long-term treatment

- Age and/or lack of maturity where it affects the responsibility of the offender
- Mental disorder or learning disability

STEP 3
Consider any factors which indicate a reduction, such as assistance to the prosecution

The court should take into account sections 73 and 74 of the Serious Organised Crime and Police Act 2005 (assistance by defendants: reduction or review of sentence) and any other rule of law by virtue of which an offender may receive a discounted sentence in consequence of assistance given (or offered) to the prosecutor or investigator.

STEP 4
Reduction for guilty pleas

The court should take account of any potential reduction for a guilty plea in accordance with section 144 of the Criminal Justice Act 2003 and the *Guilty Plea* guideline.

STEP 5
Totality principle

If sentencing an offender for more than one offence, or where the offender is already serving a sentence, consider whether the total sentence is just and proportionate to the overall offending behaviour in accordance with the *Offences Taken into Consideration and Totality* guideline.

STEP 6
Compensation and ancillary orders

In all cases, the court should consider whether to make compensation and/or other ancillary orders.

STEP 7
Reasons

Section 174 of the Criminal Justice Act 2003 imposes a duty to give reasons for, and explain the effect of, the sentence.

A[52]

Sexual offences against children

A. Children aged under 13

Charge

A[52.1] **(1) Intentionally touching a child under 13 in a sexual manner**

Sexual Offences Act 2003, s 7

Maximum penalty – Fine level 5 and 6 months. Triable either way. Specified sexual offence under Sch 15, Part 2, CJA 2003.

Crown Court – 14 years' imprisonment and unlimited fine.

(2) Intentionally causing or inciting a child under 13 to engage in sexual activity

Sexual Offences Act 2003, s 8

Maximum penalty – Fine level 5 and 6 months. Triable either way. Specified sexual offence under Sch 15, Part 2, CJA 2003. Triable only on indictment if the activity involved penetration.

B. Children aged under 16 – defendants aged 18 or over**

Charge

A[52.2] **(3) Intentionally touching a child (B) in a sexual manner and:**

(i) **B is under 16 and the defendant did not reasonably believe that B was 16 or over; or**
(ii) **B is under 13.**

Sexual Offences Act 2003, s 9

Maximum penalty – Fine level 5 and 6 months. Triable either way. Specified sexual offence under Sch 15, Part 2, CJA 2003. Triable only on indictment if the activity involved penetration.

(4) Intentionally causing or inciting a child (B) to engage in sexual activity and:

(i) **B is under 16 and the defendant did not reasonably believe that B was 16 or over; or**
(ii) **B is under 13.**

Sexual Offences Act 2003, s 10

Maximum penalty – Fine level 5 and 6 months. Triable either way. Specified sexual offence under Sch 15, Part 2, CJA 2003. Triable only on indictment if the activity involved penetration

(5) Intentionally engaging in sexual activity for the purpose of obtaining sexual gratification when another person (B) is present or is in a place to observe and knowing or believing that B is aware, or intending that B should be aware, that the defendant is engaging in it, and:

(i) **B is under 16 and the defendant does not reasonably believe that B is 16 or over; or**
(ii) **B is under 13.**

Sexual Offences Act 2003, s 11

(6) For the purpose of obtaining sexual gratification, intentionally cause a child (B) to watch a third person or an image of that person engaging in a sexual activity and:

(i) **B is under 16 and the defendant did not reasonably believe that B was 16 or over, or**
(ii) **B is under 13.**

Sexual Offences Act 2003, s 12

Maximum penalty – Fine level 5 and 6 months. Triable either way. Specified sexual offence under Sch 15, Part 2, CJA 2003.

*** The offences under ss 9–12 can also be committed by offenders aged under 18, but the maximum penalty on indictment is then reduced to five years.*

A[52.3] Further offences against children (excluding familial offences). The Sexual Offences Act 2003 additionally creates offences of: arranging or facilitating commission of a child sex offence (s 14); meeting a child following sexual grooming (s 15) (this offence was amended by the Criminal Justice and Courts Act 2015 to reduce to one the number of prior meetings/communications required to be made in the grooming – where only one instance is relied on it must have occurred after this amendment came into force, namely 13 April 2015); and abuse of a position sexual activity (s 16), causing or inciting sexual activity (s 17), sexual activity in the presence of a child (s 18) and causing a child to watch a sexual act (s 19).
Section 67 of the Serious Crime Act 2015 inserted s 15A into the Sexual Offences Act 2003 to create an offence of sexual communication with a child.

A[52.4] Sexual activity. An activity is sexual if a reasonable person would conclude:

(a) whatever the circumstances or purpose, it is because of its nature sexual; or
(b) because of its nature it may be sexual and because of the circumstances and or purpose it is sexual (s 78).

In relation to (b), two distinct questions should be identified for the court/jury (both of which must be answered in the affirmative to find the defendant guilty), namely: (i) whether they, as reasonable people, consider that the touching, in the particular circumstances before them, because of its nature, may be sexual; and (ii) whether they, as 12 reasonable people, consider that the touching, in view of its circumstances, or the purpose of any person in relation to it, or both, was in fact sexual. In relation to the first question, evidence as to the circumstances before and after the touching, and evidence of the purpose of any person in relation to that touching is irrelevant. However, in most cases, the answer will be same whether the two-stage approach is adopted or whether the matter is looked at as a whole: *R v H* [2005] EWCA Crim 732, [2005] 2 All ER 859, [2005] 2 Cr App R 9, [2005] Crim LR 735.

Purpose is only relevant where the circumstances are ambiguous and the intent or purpose of the offender may help establish whether right-minded people would consider the assault sexual: *R v DJ* [2018] EWCA Crim 1840, [2019] 4 WLR 43, [2019] 2 Cr App R 7.

Touching. This includes touching with any part of the body, with anything else, through anything and in particular touching amounting to penetration (s 79). If, whether intoxicated or otherwise, the touching is unintentional the offence is not committed. Thus, to flail about resulting in unintended touching, objectively sexual, does not make out the offence. However, the offence under s 3 is not an offence of 'specific intent', since purpose is not an element that falls under consideration. Therefore, voluntary intoxication preventing the defendant from intending to touch is not available as a defence: *R v Heard* [2007] EWCA Crim 125, [2008] QB 43, [2007] 3 All ER 306, [2007] 3 WLR 475, [2007] 1 Cr App R 37.

Legal notes and definitions

A[52.5] Causing or inciting. The following propositions are derived from the case of *R v Grout* [2011] EWCA Crim 299, (2011) 175 JP 209, [2011] 1 Cr App R 38, [2011] Crim LR 584.

(a) Section 8(1) creates two basic offences. The first is intentionally causing a child to engage in sexual activity. The second is intentionally inciting a child to engage in sexual activity. Intentional incitement means the intentional seeking by encouragement or persuasion to bring something about, namely the child engaging in sexual activity, though it is unnecessary to prove that the defendant intended that sexual activity should take place.
(b) The offences are not concerned with whether the defendant engages in sexual activity.
(c) There is no definition of 'activity'. (For the purposes of the appeal it was accepted that it could embrace conversation or text or other messages.)
(d) The questions to be considered when deciding whether or not a particular 'activity' is 'sexual' were set out in *R v H* (see A[52.4], above).
(e) Because s 8 creates two, if not four (by reason of the higher penalties prescribed for cases within s 8(2)), offences a charge must be drawn with particular care to avoid duplicity.

The offence under s 8 can be committed by a person who, with the requisite intention, makes a statement which in specific terms directly incites a child or children under the age of 13 to engage in sexual activity; it does not matter that it is not possible to identify any specific or identifiable person to whom the statement was addressed because the criminality is directed at the incitement: *R v Jones* [2007] EWCA Crim 1118, [2008] QB 460, [2007] 4 All ER 112, [2007] 3 WLR 907, [2007] 2 Cr App Rep 267 (where the defendant left explicit messages on trains, etc, seeking girls aged between 8 and 13 for sex, offering payment and including a contact text number).

A[52.6] **Sexual gratification.** The sexual gratification need not be taken immediately. It can extend to a longer term plan to obtain further or greater sexual gratification in the form of the eventual working out of a particular sexual fantasy or activity involving the child. The purpose may involve both short-term and long-term sexual gratification; immediate or deferred, or immediate and deferred gratification: *R v Abdullahi* [2006] EWCA Crim 2060, [2007] 1 WLR 225, [2007] 1 Cr App R 14, [2007] Crim LR 184 at para 117.

The prosecution must prove a link between 'for the purposes of obtaining sexual gratification' within s 11(1)(c) of the SOA 2003 and the presence or observation of a child; the offence is not made out unless the child's presence or observation is for the purpose of obtaining sexual gratification: *R v B and L* [2018] EWCA Crim 1439, [2019] 1 WLR 3177, [2019] 1 Cr App R 35.

Defences

A[52.7] Consent is not a defence to any of the charges. Where the victim is aged 13-16, it must additionally be proved that the defendant did not reasonably believe that the victim was 16 or over. A mistake as to age is otherwise relevant only to sentence.

Section 73 of the Sexual Offences Act 2003 provides exceptions to aiding, abetting and counselling the offences under (inter alia) ss 7 and 9 where the person acts for one of the four stated purposes, eg to protect the child from sexually transmitted infection, and not for the purpose of obtaining sexual gratification.

Evidence

A[52.8] **Competence.** A court may not refuse to admit the evidence of a child complainant by reason of age only. The court should assess whether the child is capable of giving intelligible testimony either by watching a video of the child or by questioning the complainant themselves: *DPP v M* [1998] QB 913, [1997] 2 All ER 749. See *R v Barker* [2011] Crim LR 233, (2010) Times, 5 February in which comprehensive guidance was given in relation to the statutory test of competence prescribed by s 53 of the Youth Justice and Criminal Evidence Act 1999. Where the issue is raised, it is for the party calling a witness to establish competence to the civil standard.

A[52.9] Special measures. See section D[6.13A].

Privacy and anonymity

A[52.10] **Privacy: clearing the court.** The magistrates can order the court to be cleared (except for those directly concerned with the case and the press) whilst the child or young person is testifying: Children and Young Persons Act 1933, s 37 as amended.

A[52.11] **Anonymity of victim.** The general prohibition on revealing the identity of the victim of a sexual offence applies n the case of persons under 18 the existing power under s 39 of the Children and Young Persons Act 1933 (as amended) is preserved. The court may direct that any press, radio or television report of the case must not reveal the name, address, school or identity of any child or young person concerned in the proceedings including the defendant. However, such an order must be clear as to precisely what is prohibited: *Briffet v DPP* [2001] EWHC 841 (Admin), (2001) 166 JP 66, sub nom *Briffett and Bradshaw v Crown Prosecution Service* [2002] EMLR 203 and should be in writing: *Re BBC Litigation Department* [2002] All ER (D) 69 (Apr), CA. This topic is considered in detail at D[1B.7].

It has been doubted whether an order under s 39 can embrace reporting in digitised or other form not in existence when s 39 was enacted: *MXB v East Sussex Hospitals NHS Trust* [2012] EWHC 32769, (2012) 177 JP 177.

A decision to vary reporting restrictions in relation to a young offender pursuant to the Children and Young Persons Act 1933, s 39 was quashed as the proper test had not been applied and inadequate reasons had been given to justify the variation. In deciding whether to impose reporting restrictions under s 39, a court had to balance the welfare of the child, the public interest and the requirements of the ECHR, art 10, and to restrict publication if the factors were evenly balanced. Prior to conviction, the former is likely to prevail. After conviction, the defendant's age and the gravity of the crime are likely to be particularly relevant: *R (on the application of Y) v Aylesbury Crown Court, Crown Prosecution Service and Newsquest Media Group Ltd* [2012] EWHC 1140 (Admin), [2012] Crim LR 893.

Sentencing
SC Guideline – Sexual assault and Sexual assault of a child under 13

A[52.12] These guidelines are taken from the SC's definitive guideline *Sexual Offences Act 2003* effective from 1 April 2014.

Triable either way

Maximum: 14 years' custody

Offence range: Community order – 9 years' custody

For offences committed on or after 3 December 2012, this is an offence listed in Part 1 of Schedule 15B for the purposes of section 224A (life sentence for second listed offence) of the Criminal Justice Act 2003.

For convictions on or after 3 December 2012 (irrespective of the date of commission of the offence), this is a specified offence for the purposes of section 226A (extended sentence for certain violent or sexual offences) of the Criminal Justice Act 2003.

STEP ONE
Determining the offence category

The court should determine which categories of harm and culpability the offence falls into by reference **only** to the tables below.

Harm		Culpability
Category 1	• Severe psychological or physical harm	A
	• Abduction	Significant degree of planning
	• Violence or threats of violence	Offender acts together with others to commit the offence
	• Forced/uninvited entry into victim's home	Use of alcohol/drugs on victim to facilitate the offence
Category 2	• Touching of naked genitalia or naked breast area	Grooming behaviour used against victim
	• Prolonged detention/sustained incident	Previous violence against victim
	• Additional degradation/humiliation	Abuse of trust
	• Child is particularly vulnerable due to extreme youth and/or personal circumstances	Offence committed in course of burglary
Category 3	Factor(s) in categories 1 and 2 not present	Sexual images of victim recorded, retained, solicited or shared
		Deliberate isolation of victim
		Commercial exploitation and/or motivation
		Offence racially or religiously aggravated
		Offence motivated by, or demonstrating, hostility to the victim based on his or her sexual orientation (or presumed sexual orientation) or transgender identity (or presumed transgender identity)
		Offence motivated by, or demonstrating, hostility to the victim based on his or her disability (or presumed disability)
		B
		Factor(s) in category A not present

STEP TWO
Starting point and category range

Having determined the category, the court should use the corresponding starting points to reach a sentence within the category range on the next page. The starting point applies to all offenders irrespective of plea or previous convictions. Having determined the starting point, step two allows further adjustment for aggravating or mitigating features, set out on the next page.

A case of particular gravity, reflected by multiple features of culpability or harm in step one, could merit upward adjustment from the starting point before further adjustment for aggravating or mitigating features, set out on the next page.

Where there is a sufficient prospect of rehabilitation, a community order with a sex offender treatment programme requirement under section 202 of the Criminal Justice Act 2003 can be a proper alternative to a short or moderate length custodial sentence.

	A	B
Category 1	**Starting point** 6 years' custody	**Starting point** 4 years' custody
	Category range 4 – 9 years' custody	**Category range** 3 – 7 years' custody
Category 2	**Starting point** 4 years' custody	**Starting point** 2 years' custody
	Category range 3 – 7 years' custody	**Category range** 1 – 4 years' custody
Category 3	**Starting point** 1 year's custody	**Starting point** 26 weeks' custody
	Category range 26 weeks' – 2 years' custody	**Category range** High level community order – 1 year's custody

The table below contains a **non-exhaustive** list of additional factual elements providing the context of the offence and factors relating to the offender. Identify whether any combination of these, or other relevant factors, should result in an upward or downward adjustment from the starting point. **In particular, relevant recent convictions are likely to result in an upward adjustment.** In some cases, having considered these factors, it may be appropriate to move outside the identified category range.

Aggravating factors	Any steps taken to prevent the victim reporting an incident, obtaining assistance and/or from assisting or supporting the prosecution
Statutory aggravating factors	Attempts to dispose of or conceal evidence
Previous convictions, having regard to a) the nature of the offence to which the conviction relates and its relevance to the current offence; and b) the time that has elapsed since the conviction	Commission of offence whilst under the influence of alcohol or drugs
Offence committed whilst on bail	Victim encouraged to recruit others
Other aggravating factors	**Mitigating factors**
Specific targeting of a particularly vulnerable child	No previous convictions **or** no relevant/recent convictions
Blackmail or other threats made (where not taken into account at step one)	Remorse
Location of offence	Previous good character and/or exemplary conduct*
Timing of offence	Age and/or lack of maturity where it affects the responsibility of the offender

Use of weapon or other item to frighten or injure	Mental disorder or learning disability, particularly where linked to the commission of the offence**
Victim compelled to leave their home, school, etc	
Failure to comply with current court orders	
Offence committed whilst on licence	
Exploiting contact arrangements with a child to commit an offence	
Presence of others, especially children	

* Previous good character/exemplary conduct is different from having no previous convictions. The more serious the offence, the less the weight which should normally be attributed to this factor. Where previous good character/exemplary conduct has been used to facilitate the offence, this mitigation should not normally be allowed and such conduct may constitute an aggravating factor.

** In the context of this offence, previous good character/exemplary conduct should not normally be given any significant weight and will not normally justify a reduction in what would otherwise be the appropriate sentence.

STEP THREE
Consider any factors which indicate a reduction, such as assistance to the prosecution

The court should take into account sections 73 and 74 of the Serious Organised Crime and Police Act 2005 (assistance by defendants: reduction or review of sentence) and any other rule of law by virtue of which an offender may receive a discounted sentence in consequence of assistance given (or offered) to the prosecutor or investigator.

STEP FOUR
Reduction for guilty pleas

The court should take account of any potential reduction for a guilty plea in accordance with section 144 of the Criminal Justice Act 2003 and the *Guilty Plea* guideline.

STEP FIVE
Dangerousness

The court should consider whether having regard to the criteria contained in Chapter 5 of Part 12 of the Criminal Justice Act 2003 it would be appropriate to award a life sentence (section 224A) or an extended sentence (section 226A). When sentencing offenders to a life sentence under these provisions, the notional determinate sentence should be used as the basis for the setting of a minimum term.

STEP SIX
Totality principle

If sentencing an offender for more than one offence, or where the offender is already serving a sentence, consider whether the total sentence is just and proportionate to the overall offending behaviour.

STEP SEVEN
Ancillary orders

The court must consider whether to make any ancillary orders. The court must also consider what other requirements or provisions may automatically apply. Further information is included on page 303.

STEP EIGHT
Reasons

Section 174 of the Criminal Justice Act 2003 imposes a duty to give reasons for, and explain the effect of, the sentence.

STEP NINE
Consideration for time spent on bail

The court must consider whether to give credit for time spent on bail in accordance with section 240A of the Criminal Justice Act 2003.

A[52.13] For other sexual offences involving children, see Part 3A of the definitive guidance of the Sentencing Guidelines Council on offences under the Sexual Offences Act 2003, issued in April 2007. Custody for at least six months is appropriate for forms of contact more serious than contact not involving touching the genitalia of either the defendant or the victim.

A[52.14] **Sexual Offences Act 2003 (Part 2).** Under r 28.3 of the CrimPR 2015, on conviction the court must explain the notification requirements to the defendant.

Persons who have committed certain sexual offences (subject in some cases, to the age of the victim and/or the nature of the disposal) are required to notify their names and addresses and other details to the police for a specified period: Part 2 of the Sexual Offences Act 2003.

The Sexual Offences Act (Travel Notification Requirements) Regulations 2004, SI 2004/1220, as amended, and the Sexual Offences Act (Notification Requirements) (England and Wales) Regulations 2012, SI 2012/1876 give further effect to the notification regime. The former regulations oblige relevant offenders intending to travel out of the UK to notify this intention and provide certain information more than seven days before the intended date of departure. If the relevant offender does not state the date of his return and the point of his arrival back in the UK, this information must be given within three days of his return. The latter regulations include requirements to give information about bank accounts and credit cards. The obligation of a person on the sex offenders' register to provide bank account details does not contravene art 8. The Sexual Offences Act 2003 (Notification Requirements) (England and Wales) Regulations 2012 have a legitimate policy objective, namely the ability to trace an offender quickly, to guard against the risk of an offender using another identity or to have a means of obtaining quick access to a credit card account, and the means employed are practical and proportionate to provide further protection to prevent other persons from becoming potential victims of those on the register: *R (on the application of Prothero) v Secretary of State for the Home Department* [2013] EWHC 2830 (Admin), [2014] 1 WLR 1195, 155 Sol Jo (no 37) 37.

Where the defendant is under the age of 18 years, the court may make a parental direction whereby the obligations which would otherwise be imposed on the defendant are to be treated instead as obligations on the parent until the defendant attains the age of 18 or for such shorter period as the court may direct: SOA 2003, s 89. An application for a parental direction may be made by a chief officer of police by way of complaint: s 89(4).

The court by or before which a person is convicted or is found to have committed such an offence may state in open court and certify that the offence is one to which the notification requirements of the Sexual Offences Act 2003 apply and, if it does so, the certificate shall be evidence of that fact: SOA 2003, s 92. Failure, without reasonable excuse, to comply with the notification requirements is an offence triable either way: SOA 2003, s 91.

A notification requirement does not arise, or survive, if sentence is passed on a later occasion than the date of conviction and the offender is sentenced to an absolute discharge: *R v Longworth* [2006] UKHL 1, [2006] 1 All ER 887, [2006] 1 WLR 313.

A[52.15] Provision has been made for the review of indefinite notification requirements by the insertion of ss 91A–91F of the Sexual Offences Act 2003, inserted by SI 2012/1883.

A[53] Sexual assault

Charge (Sexual assault)

A[53.1] Intentionally touching another person (B) in a sexual manner without B's consent and without reasonable belief that B consents

Sexual Offences Act 2003, s 3

Maximum penalty – 6 months' imprisonment and/or fine level 5 (for offences committed on or after 12 March 2015 an unlimited fine). Triable either way. Specified sexual offence under Sch 15, Part 2, CJA 2003.

Crown Court – 10 years' imprisonment and unlimited fine.

Mode of trial

A[53.2] Consider first the general notes at **D**[4] and the SC definitive guidance set out at A[52.14] above.

Legal notes and definitions

A[53.3] Touching and sexual manner. See A[52.4] above.

A[53.4] An accused's explanation for the assault, whether or not it reveals a sexual motive, is admissible to support or negative that the touching was sexual and was so intended by the accused: *R v Court* [1989] AC 28, [1988] 2 All ER 221, HL. See also *R v H* [2005] EWCA Crim 732, [2005] 2 All ER 859 (grabbing a girl's tracksuit bottoms coupled with the request 'Do you fancy a shag?').

A[53.5] Defences. Consent of the alleged victim is a defence except if obtained by force or fraud. A reasonable belief that the person consents is a defence, as would be non-intentional touching. The defence that voluntary intoxication had rendered a defendant unable to form the intent to touch is not open to him: *R v Heard* [2007] EWCA Crim 125. See further para **A**[52.3] above.

Consent is not a defence if the victim is aged under 16: see **A**[52.7] above.

A[53.6] Special measures. See section **D**[6.13A].

A[53.7] Privacy and anonymity. See **A**[52.11] above.

A[53.8] Sentencing. See A[52.12] above.

A[53.9] Sexual Offences Act 2003 (Sch 3) Under r 28.3 of the CrimPR 2015, on conviction the court must explain the notification requirements to the defendant.

As to notification requirements, see **A**[52.14], ante.

A[53.10] Sexual harm prevention order The Anti-social Behaviour, Crime and Policing Act 2014 introduced sexual harm prevention orders (and sexual risk orders), which replace, in England and Wales: sexual offences prevention orders; risk of sexual harm orders; and foreign travel orders. Narrative on the new order will be found in Section B Sentencing at **B**[44].

Sentencing

SC Guideline – Sexual assault

A[53.10A] This guideline is taken from the SC's definitive guideline *Sexual Offences Act 2003* effective from 1 April 2014.

Triable either way

Maximum: 10 years' custody

Offence range: Community order – 7 years' custody

For convictions on or after 3 December 2012 (irrespective of the date of commission of the offence), this is a specified offence for the purposes of section 226A (extended sentence for certain violent or sexual offences) of the Criminal Justice Act 2003.

STEP ONE
Determining the offence category

The court should determine which categories of harm and culpability the offence falls into by reference **only** to the tables below.

Harm		Culpability
Category 1	• Severe psychological or physical harm	A
	• Abduction	Significant degree of planning
	• Violence or threats of violence	Offender acts together with others to commit the offence
	• Forced/uninvited entry into victim's home	Use of alcohol/drugs on victim to facilitate the offence
Category 2	• Touching of naked genitalia or naked breasts	Abuse of trust
	• Prolonged detention/sustained incident	Previous violence against victim
	• Additional degradation/humiliation	Offence committed in course of burglary
	• Victim is particularly vulnerable due to personal circumstances*	Recording of offence
Category 3	Factor(s) in categories 1 and 2 not present	Commercial exploitation and/or motivation
		Offence racially or religiously aggravated
		Offence motivated by, or demonstrating, hostility to the victim based on his or her sexual orientation (or presumed sexual orientation) or transgender identity (or presumed transgender identity)
		Offence motivated by, or demonstrating, hostility to the victim based on his or her disability (or presumed disability)
		B
		Factor(s) in category A not present

STEP TWO
Starting point and category range

Having determined the category, the court should use the corresponding starting points to reach a sentence within the category range on the next page. The starting point applies to all offenders irrespective of plea or previous convictions. Having determined the starting point, step two allows further adjustment for aggravating or mitigating features, set out on the next page.

A case of particular gravity, reflected by multiple features of culpability or harm in step one, could merit upward adjustment from the starting point before further adjustment for aggravating or mitigating features, set out on the next page.

Where there is a sufficient prospect of rehabilitation, a community order with a sex offender treatment programme requirement under section 202 of the Criminal Justice Act 2003 can be a proper alternative to a short or moderate length custodial sentence.

	A	B
Category 1	**Starting point** 4 years' custody	**Starting point** 2 years 6 months' custody
	Category range 3 – 7 years' custody	**Category range** 2 – 4 years' custody
Category 2	**Starting point** 2 years' custody	**Starting point** 1 year's custody
	Category range 1 – 4 years' custody	**Category range** High level community order – 2 years' custody
Category 3	**Starting point** 26 weeks' custody	**Starting point** High level community order
	Category range High level community order – 1 year's custody	**Category range** Medium level community order – 26 weeks' custody

The table below contains a **non-exhaustive** list of additional factual elements providing the context of the offence and factors relating to the offender. Identify whether any combination of these, or other relevant factors, should result in an upward or downward adjustment from the starting point. **In particular, relevant recent convictions are likely to result in an upward adjustment.** In some cases, having considered these factors, it may be appropriate to move outside the identified category range.

When sentencing appropriate **category 2 or 3 offences**, the court should also consider the custody threshold as follows:

- has the custody threshold been passed?
- if so, is it unavoidable that a custodial sentence be imposed?
- if so, can that sentence be suspended?

Aggravating factors	Any steps taken to prevent those working in brothel reporting an incident, obtaining assistance and/or from assisting or supporting the prosecution
Statutory aggravating factors	Attempts to dispose of or conceal evidence

Previous convictions, having regard to a) the nature of the offence to which the conviction relates and its relevance to the current offence; and b) the time that has elapsed since the conviction	Commission of offence whilst under the influence of alcohol or drugs
Offence committed whilst on bail	**Mitigating factors**
Other aggravating factors	No previous convictions or no relevant/recent convictions
Specific targeting of a particularly vulnerable victim	Remorse
Blackmail or other threats made (where not taken into account at step one)	Previous good character and/or exemplary conduct*
Location of offence	Mental disorder or learning disability, particularly where linked to the commission of the offence
Timing of offence	Demonstration of steps taken to address offending behaviour
Use of weapon or other item to frighten or injure	
Victim compelled to leave their home (including victims of domestic violence)	
Failure to comply with current court orders	
Offence committed whilst on licence	
Exploiting contact arrangements with a child to commit an offence	
Presence of others, especially children	

* Previous good character/exemplary conduct is different from having no previous convictions. The more serious the offence, the less the weight which should normally be attributed to this factor. Where previous good character/exemplary conduct has been used to facilitate the offence, this mitigation should not normally be allowed and such conduct may constitute an aggravating factor.

STEP THREE
Consider any factors which indicate a reduction, such as assistance to the prosecution

The court should take into account sections 73 and 74 of the Serious Organised Crime and Police Act 2005 (assistance by defendants: reduction or review of sentence) and any other rule of law by virtue of which an offender may receive a discounted sentence in consequence of assistance given (or offered) to the prosecutor or investigator.

STEP FOUR
Reduction for guilty pleas

The court should take account of any potential reduction for a guilty plea in accordance with section 144 of the Criminal Justice Act 2003 and the *Guilty Plea* guideline.

STEP FIVE
Dangerousness

The court should consider whether having regard to the criteria contained in Chapter 5 of Part 12 of the Criminal Justice Act 2003 it would be appropriate to award an extended sentence (section 226A).

STEP SIX
Totality principle

If sentencing an offender for more than one offence, or where the offender is already serving a sentence, consider whether the total sentence is just and proportionate to the overall offending behaviour.

STEP SEVEN
Ancillary orders

The court must consider whether to make any ancillary orders. The court must also consider what other requirements or provisions may *automatically* apply. Further information is included on page 303.

STEP EIGHT
Reasons

Section 174 of the Criminal Justice Act 2003 imposes a duty to give reasons for, and explain the effect of, the sentence.

STEP NINE
Consideration for time spent on bail

The court must consider whether to give credit for time spent on bail in accordance with section 240A of the Criminal Justice Act 2003.

A[54] Social security benefit, false statement/representation to obtain

Charges (Social security benefit)

A[54.1] **1. The accused, for the purpose of obtaining any benefit or other payment under the relevant social security legislation whether or himself or some other person, or for any other purpose connected with that legislation –**

(a) **makes a statement or representation which he knows to be false; or**
(b) **produces or furnishes, or knowingly causes or knowingly allows to be produced or furnished, any document or information which he knows to be false in a material particular.**

Social Security Administration Act 1992, s 112(1).

Maximum penalty – 3 months' imprisonment and/or fine level 5 (for offences committed on or after 12 March 2015 an unlimited fine).

2. The accused dishonestly –

(a) **makes a statement or representation or;**
(b) **produces or furnishes, or causes or allows to be produced or furnished, any document or information which is false in a material particular;**

With a view to obtaining any benefit or other payment or advantage under the relevant social security legislation (whether for himself or for some other person).

Social Security Administration Act 1992, s 111A.

Maximum penalty – 6 months' imprisonment and/or fine level 5 (for offences committed on or after 12 March 2015, an unlimited fine). Triable either way.

Crown Court – 7 years' imprisonment and unlimited fine.

As to further offences under ss 111A and 112, see A[54.3] below.

Mode of trial

A[54.2] For charge 2 consider the SC definitive guidance set out at A[54.5] below.

More serious charges may well be charged under the Fraud Act 2006.

Legal notes and definitions

A[54.3] Charge 2 requires proof of dishonesty unlike charge 1. For the definition of dishonesty see A[60.5].

The provisions of ss 111A or 112 do not apply in any case where the benefit or other payment or advantage is or relates to, or the failure to notify relates to, tax credit (see Tax Credits Act 2002, s 35 and A[55]).

Sections 111A and 112 create a number of further offences concerning failure to notify a change in circumstances affecting entitlement to benefit. The same maximum penalties apply. The essential difference, again, is the added element of dishonesty in the s 111A offences.

The change of circumstances must have made a difference to the amount of benefit which the recipient was entitled to claim: *R v Passmore* [2007] EWCA Crim 2053,

[2008] 1 Cr App Rep 165, 171 JP 519. Where a defendant has more than one new source of income arising from her gaining employment, eg working tax credits and child tax credits, all those sources are disclosable if at the time each would have made a difference to the computation of the defendant's entitlement to benefit. But if there had been disclosure of one source which extinguished liability, there would be no requirement to notify further sources: *London Borough of Croydon v Shanahan* [2010] EWCA Crim 98, 174 JP 172.

A[54.4] Under s 112 the offence is committed where there is a false representation made which the person making the claim knows to be false; the proof of intent to defraud is not necessary (*Clear v Smith* [1981] 1 WLR 399, HL). The offence under s 112 does not require proof of dishonesty. However, "constructive knowledge" ie that the defendant neglected to make such inquiries as a reasonable and prudent person would make (as distinct from deliberately closing one's eyes to an obvious means of knowledge) is insufficient to found liability (*Flintshire County Council v Reynolds* [2006] EWHC 195 (Admin), 170 JP 73).

In *Pearson v Greenwich Borough Council* [2008] All ER [D] 256 (Jan), the accused owned two properties. A council tax form required the accused to provide details of the name and address of the property for which he sought to receive a council tax reduction. The subsequent allegation was that he had made representations that he only owned one property for the purposes of obtaining benefit. The charge failed because the accused's omission did not necessarily mean he had made representations to the effect that he only owned one house.

By virtue of s 116(2) of the 1992 Act, a prosecution could be started at any time from 3 months or 12 months, whichever period last expired. The time limits for an offence under s 112 had been satisfied where it had been brought within 12 months even thought there had been some evidence available for a prosecution within three months, as the offence was a continuing offence and the investigations were ongoing: *Bennett v Secretary of State for Work and Pensions* [2012] EWHC 371 (Admin), 176 JP 181.

A[54.5] Causes or Allows. The word 'causes' suggests that the defendant did something that 'caused' the recipient of the benefit not to report a change of circumstances (alternatively, the defendant could be guilty of aiding and abetting an offence under s 111A(1A)). The word 'allows' normally means there has to be some act that the defendant could have taken which could have resulted in the recipient of benefit discharging his/her liability to report. The one exception might be where the defendant is aware of circumstances that he knew affected the recipient's entitlement to benefit (*R v Tilley* [2009] EWCA Crim 1426, 173 JP 393).

Sentencing

SC Guideline – Benefit fraud

A[54.6] Update 12 of the Magistrates' Court sentencing guidelines took in the new definitive guideline of the Sentencing Council on fraud, bribery and money laundering. The same kind of fraud may be charged in a number of ways and the guidelines reflect this. The categories are: fraud by false representation, failing to disclose information and by abuse of position; possessing, making or supplying articles for use in fraud; revenue fraud; benefit fraud; money laundering; bribery; and corporate offences fraud, bribery and money laundering. The guidelines on benefit fraud are reproduced below.

Dishonest representations for obtaining benefit etc

Social Security Administration Act 1992 (section 111A)

Tax Credit fraud

Tax Credits Act 2002 (section 35)

False accounting

Theft Act 1968 (section 17)

Triable either way

Maximum: 7 years' custody

Offence range: Discharge – 6 years 6 months' custody

False representations for obtaining benefit etc

Social Security Administration Act 1992 (section 112)

Triable summarily only

Maximum: Level 5 fine and/or 3 months' custody

Offence range: Discharge – 12 weeks' custody

Fraud by false representation, fraud by failing to disclose information, fraud by abuse of position

Fraud Act 2006 (section 1)

Triable either way

Conspiracy to defraud

Common law

Triable on indictment only

Maximum: 10 years' custody Offence range:

Discharge – 8 years' custody

STEP ONE
Determining the offence category

The court should determine the offence category with reference to the tables below. In order to determine the category the court should assess **culpability** and **harm.**

The level of **culpability** is determined by weighing up all the factors of the case to determine the offender's role and the extent to which the offending was planned and the sophistication with which it was carried out.

Culpability demonstrated by one or more of the following:

A – High culpability
A leading role where offending is part of a group activity Involvement of others through pressure, influence
Involvement of others through pressure, influence
Abuse of position of power or trust or responsibility
Sophisticated nature of offence/significant planning
B – Medium culpability
Other cases where characteristics for categories A or C are not present
Claim not fraudulent from the outset
A significant role where offending is part of a group activity

C – Lesser culpability
Involved through coercion, intimidation or exploitation
Performed limited function under direction

Where there are characteristics present which fall under different levels of culpability, the court should balance these characteristics to reach a fair assessment of the offender's culpability.

Harm – Amount obtained or intended to be obtained
Category 1 £500,000–£2 million Starting point based on £1 million
Category 2 £100,000–£500,000 Starting point based on £300,000
Category 3 £50,000–£100,000 Starting point based on £75,000
Category 4 £10,000–£50,000 Starting point based on £30,000
Category 5 £2,500–£10,000 Starting point based on £5,000
Category 6 Less than £2,500 Starting point based on £1,000

STEP TWO
Starting point and category range

Having determined the category at step one, the court should use the appropriate starting point to reach a sentence within the category range in the table below. The starting point applies to all offenders irrespective of plea or previous convictions.

Where the value is larger or smaller than the amount on which the starting point is based, this should lead to upward or downward adjustment as appropriate.

Where the value greatly exceeds the amount of the starting point in category 1, it may be appropriate to move outside the identified range.

TABLE 1

Section 111A Social Security Administration Act 1992: Dishonest representations to obtain benefit etc

Section 35 Tax Credits Act 2002: Tax Credit fraud

Section 17 Theft Act 1968: False accounting

Maximum: 7 years' custody

	Culpability		
Harm	A	B	C
Category 1 £500,000 or more	Starting point 5 years 6 months' custody	Starting point 4 years' custody	Starting point 2 years 6 months' custody

	Culpability		
Harm	A	B	C
Starting point based on £1 million	Category range 4 years' – 6 years 6 months' custody	Category range 2 years 6 months' – 5 years' custody	Category range 15 months' – 3 years 6 months' custody
Category 2 £100,000–£500,000	Starting point 4 years' custody	Starting point 2 years 6 months' custody	Starting point 1 year's custody
Starting point based on £300,000	Category range 2 years 6 months' – 5 years' custody	Category range 15 months' – 3 years 6 months' custody	Category range 26 weeks' – 2 years 6 months' custody
Category 3 £50,000–£100,000	Starting point 2 years 6 months' custody	Starting point 1 year's custody	Starting point 26 weeks' custody
Starting point based on £75,000	Category range 2 years' – 3 years 6 months' custody	Category range 26 weeks' – 2 years 6 months' custody	Category range High level community order – 36 weeks' custody
Category 4 £10,000–£50,000	Starting point 18 months' custody	Starting point 36 weeks' custody	Starting point Medium level community order
Starting point based on £30,000	Category range 36 weeks' – 2 years 6 months' custody	Category range Medium level community order – 21 months' custody	Category range Low level community order – 26 weeks' custody
Category 5 £2,500–£10,000	Starting point 36 weeks' custody	Starting point Medium level community order	Starting point Low level community order
Starting point based on £5,000	Category range Medium level community order – 18 months' custody	Category range Low level community order – 26 weeks' custody	Category range Band B fine – Medium level community order
Category 6 Less than £2,500	Starting point Medium level community order	Starting point Low level community order	Starting point Band A fine
Starting point based on £1,000	Category range Low level community order – 26 weeks' custody	Category range Band A fine – Medium level community order	Category range Discharge – Band B fine

TABLE 2

Section 112 Social Security Administration Act 1992: False representations for obtaining benefit etc

Maximum: Level 5 fine and/or 3 months' custody

	Culpability		
	A	B	C
Category 5 Above £2,500	Starting point High level community order	Starting point Medium level community order	Starting point Low level community order

	Culpability		
	A	**B**	**C**
Starting point based on £5,000	**Category range** Medium level community order – 12 weeks' custody	**Category range** Band B fine – High level community order	**Category range** Band A fine – Medium level community order
Category 6 Less than £2,500	**Starting point** Medium level community order	**Starting point** Band B fine	**Starting point** Band A fine
Starting point based on £1,000	**Category range** Low level community order – High level community order	**Category range** Band A fine – Band C fine	**Category range** Discharge – Band B fine

TABLE 3

Section 1 Fraud Act 2006

Conspiracy to defraud (common law)

Maximum: 10 years' custody

	Culpability		
Harm	**A**	**B**	**C**
Category 1 £500,000 or more	**Starting point** 7 years' custody	**Starting point** 5 years' custody	**Starting point** 3 years' custody
Starting point based on £1 million	**Category range** 5 – 8 years' custody	**Category range** 3 – 6 years' custody	**Category range** 18 months' – 4 years' custody
Category 2 £100,000–£500,000	**Starting point** 5 years' custody	**Starting point** 3 years' custody	**Starting point** 15 months' custody
Starting point based on £300,000	**Category range** 3 – 6 years' custody	**Category range** 18 months' – 4 years' custody	**Category range** 26 weeks' – 3 years' custody
Category 3 £50,000–£100,000	**Starting point** 3 years' custody	**Starting point** 15 months' custody	**Starting point** 36 weeks' custody
Starting point based on £75,000	**Category range** 2 years 6 months' – 4 years' custody	**Category range** 36 weeks' – 3 years' custody	**Category range** 26 weeks' – 1 year's custody
Category 4 £10,000–£50,000	**Starting point** 21 months' custody	**Starting point** 1 year's custody	**Starting point** High level community order
Starting point based on £30,000	**Category range** 1 year's – 3 years' custody	**Category range** High level community order – 2 years' custody	**Category range** Low level community order – 26 weeks' custody
Category 5 £2,500–£10,000	**Starting point** 1 year's custody	**Starting point** High level community order	**Starting point** Medium level community order
Starting point based on £5,000	**Category range** High level community order – 2 years' custody	**Category range** Low level community order – 26 weeks' custody	**Category range** Band C fine – High level community order

Harm	Culpability A	B	C
Category 6 Less than £2,500	**Starting point** High level community order	**Starting point** Low level community order	**Starting point** Band B fine
Starting point based on £1,000	**Category range** Low level community order – 26 weeks' custody	**Category range** Band B fine – Medium level community order	**Category range** Discharge – Band C fine

The table below contains a non-exhaustive list of additional factual elements providing the context of the offence and factors relating to the offender.

Identify whether any combination of these or other relevant factors should result in an upward or downward adjustment from the sentence arrived at so far.

Consecutive sentences for multiple offences may be appropriate where large sums are involved.

Factors increasing seriousness	**Factors reducing seriousness or reflecting personal mitigation**
Statutory aggravating factors	No previous convictions or no relevant/recent convictions
Previous convictions, having regard to a) the nature of the offence to which the conviction relates and its relevance to the current offence; and b) the time that has elapsed since the conviction	Remorse
Offence committed whilst on bail	Good character and/or exemplary conduct
Other aggravating factors	Serious medical condition requiring urgent, intensive or long term treatment
Claim fraudulent from the outset	Legitimate entitlement to benefits not claimed
Proceeds of fraud funded lavish lifestyle	Little or no prospect of success
Length of time over which the offending was committed	Age and/or lack of maturity where it affects the responsibility of the offender
Number of false declarations	Lapse of time since apprehension where this does not arise from the conduct of the offender
Attempts to conceal/dispose of evidence	Mental disorder or learning disability
Failure to comply with current court orders	Sole or primary carer for dependent relatives
Offence committed on licence	Offender co-operated with investigation, made early admissions and/or voluntarily reported offending
Offences taken into consideration	Determination and/or demonstration of steps having been taken to address addiction or offending behaviour

Factors increasing seriousness	Factors reducing seriousness or reflecting personal mitigation
Failure to respond to warnings about behaviour	Offender experiencing significant financial hardship or pressure at time fraud was committed due to exceptional circumstances
Blame wrongly placed on others	
Damage to third party (for example as a result of identity theft)	

STEP THREE
Consider any factors which indicate a reduction, such as assistance to the prosecution

The court should take into account sections 73 and 74 of the Serious Organised Crime and Police Act 2005 (assistance by defendants: reduction or review of sentence) and any other rule of law by virtue of which an offender may receive a discounted sentence in consequence of assistance given (or offered) to the prosecutor or investigator.

STEP FOUR
Reduction for guilty pleas

The court should take account of any potential reduction for a guilty plea in accordance with section 144 of the Criminal Justice Act 2003 and the *Guilty Plea* guideline.

STEP FIVE
Totality principle

If sentencing an offender for more than one offence, or where the offender is already serving a sentence, consider whether the total sentence is just and proportionate to the overall offending behaviour.

STEP SIX
Confiscation, compensation and ancillary orders

The court must proceed with a view to making a confiscation order if it is asked to do so by the prosecutor or if the court believes it is appropriate for it to do so.

Where the offence has resulted in loss or damage the court must consider whether to make a compensation order.

If the court makes both a confiscation order and an order for compensation and the court believes the offender will not have sufficient means to satisfy both orders in full, the court must direct that the compensation be paid out of sums recovered under the confiscation order (section 13 of the Proceeds of Crime Act 2002).

The court may also consider whether to make ancillary orders.

STEP SEVEN
Reasons

Section 174 of the Criminal Justice Act 2003 imposes a duty to give reasons for, and explain the effect of, the sentence.

STEP EIGHT
Consideration for time spent on bail

The court must consider whether to give credit for time spent on bail in accordance with section 240A of the Criminal Justice Act 2003.

A[55]
Tax credit fraud

Charge (Tax credit fraud)

A[55.1] **The accused was knowingly concerned in any fraudulent activity undertaken with a view to obtaining payments of a tax credit by him or any other person.**

Tax Credits Act 2002, s 35.

Maximum penalty – 6 months' imprisonment and/or fine level 5 (for offences committed on or after 12 March 2015 an unlimited fine). Triable either way.

Crown Court – 7 years' imprisonment and unlimited fine.

Mode of trial

A[55.2] Consider first the general notes at D[4] and the SC definitive guidance set out at A[54.6] above.

More serious charges may well be charged under the Fraud Act 2006.

Legal notes and definitions

A[55.3] Administrative penalties may be levied under ss 31–34 in respect of incorrect statements, failure to comply with requirements and failure by employer to make correct payments.

In order to prove 'fraudulent activity' for the purposes of s 35, an offender had to behave in a manner calculated to achieve false benefits payments. A passive receipt of funds and a deliberate failure to notify the benefits agency of an overpayment, while dishonest, fell short of fraudulent activity: *R v Nolan; R v Howard* [2012] EWCA Crim 671, [2012] All ER (D) 43 (Apr).

Sentencing

A[55.4] Offences under s 35 of the Tax Credit Act 1992 are included within the SC Guideline on benefit fraud, which is reproduced at A[54.6], above.

A[56]

Taxi-touting/soliciting for hire

Charge (Taxi-touting/soliciting for hire)

A[56.1] The accused, in a public place, solicited persons to hire vehicles to carry them as passengers.

Criminal Justice and Public Order Act 1994, s 167.

Maximum penalty – Fine level 4

Legal notes and definitions

A[56.2] No offence is committed where soliciting persons to hire licensed taxis is permitted by a scheme under the Transport Act 1985, s 10.

It is a defence for the accused to show (on a balance of probabilities) that he was soliciting for passengers to be carried at separate fares by public service vehicles for public service vehicles on behalf of the holder of a PSV operator's licence for those vehicles whose authority he had at the time of the alleged offence.

"Public place" includes any highway and any other premises or place to which at the material time the public have or are permitted to have access (whether on payment or otherwise); "Public service vehicle" and "PSV operator's licence" have the same meaning as in Part II of the Public Passengers Act 1981 (Criminal Justice and Public Order Act 1994, s 167(5))

Bookings via mobile phone apps – Uber. In relation to the offence of plying for hire without a hackney carriage licence, contrary to s 45 of the Town Police Clauses Act 1847, in *Reading Borough Council v Ali* [2019] EWHC 200 (Admin), [2019] 1 WLR 2635, [2019] All ER (D) 64 (Feb) it was held that the system used by Uber to enable private hire vehicles to be booked did not contravene s 45. A person wishing to use the service had to download the app. When booking via the app the user would be told that there were vehicles in the vicinity, but no vehicle or driver would be specifically identified and the user would be unable to select a particular vehicle. The exhibition of a vehicle's location was not equivalent to it displaying a 'for hire' sign. This merely showed a potentially available vehicle. This was not an express or implied solicitation of custom so as to amount to plying for hire. A private hire vehicle would only proceed to the pick-up point after the hirer had confirmed the booking and the driver had accepted it. Whatever the precise contractual relationship between Uber and its drivers, the transaction remained a private hire booking through the operator, with the app merely replacing telephone booking, a system which operators had been using for many years.

Sentencing
SC Guideline – Taxi-touting/soliciting for hire

A[56.3] **Note:** refer to B[28.24] for approach to fines for offences committed for commercial purposes.

Taxi touting/soliciting for hire (Revised 2017)

Criminal Justice and Public Order Act 1994, s 167

Effective from: 24 April 2017

Triable only summarily: Maximum: Level 4 fine

Offence range: Conditional Discharge–Band C fine

STEP 1
Determining the offence category

The Court should determine the offence category using the table below.

Category 1	Higher culpability and greater harm
Category 2	Higher culpability and lesser harm or lower culpability and greater harm
Category 3	Lower culpability and lesser harm

The court should determine the offender's culpability and the harm caused with reference **only** to the factors below. Where an offence does not fall squarely into a category, individual factors may require a degree of weighting before making an overall assessment and determining the appropriate offence category.

CULPABILITY demonstrated by one or more of the following:

Factors indicating higher culpability

- Targeting of vulnerable/unsuspecting victim(s) (including tourists)
- Commercial business/large scale operation
- Offender not licensed to drive
- Positive step(s) taken to deceive

Factors indicating lower culpability

- All other cases

HARM demonstrated by one or more of the following:

Factors indicating greater harm

- Passenger safety compromised by vehicle condition
- Passenger(s) overcharged

Factors indicating lesser harm

- All other cases

STEP 2
Starting point and category range

Having determined the category at step one, the court should use the starting point to reach a sentence within the appropriate category range in the table below. The starting point applies to all offenders irrespective of plea or previous convictions.

Offence Category	Starting Point	Range
Category 1	Band C fine	Band B fine–Band C fine and disqualification 6–12 months
Category 2	Band B fine	Band A fine–Band B fine and consider disqualification 3–6 months
Category 3	Band A fine	Conditional discharge–Band A fine and consider disqualification 1–3 months

Note: refer to fines for offence committed for 'commercial' purposes

The court should then consider adjustment for any aggravating or mitigating factors. The following is a **non-exhaustive** list of additional factual elements providing the context of the offence and factors relating to the offender. Identify whether any combination of these, or other relevant factors, should result in an upward or downward adjustment from the sentence arrived at so far.

Factors increasing seriousness

Statutory aggravating factors:

- Previous convictions, having regard to a) the **nature** of the offence to which the conviction relates and its **relevance** to the current offence; and b) the **time** that has elapsed since the conviction
- Offence committed whilst on bail

Other aggravating factors:

- Failure to comply with current court orders
- Offence committed on licence or post sentence supervision
- PHV licence refused/ ineligible

Factors reducing seriousness or reflecting personal mitigation

- No previous convictions or no relevant/recent convictions
- Remorse
- Good character and/or exemplary conduct
- Mental disorder or learning disability
- Sole or primary carer for dependent relatives

STEP 3
Consider any factors which indicate a reduction, such as assistance to the prosecution

The court should take into account sections 73 and 74 of the Serious Organised Crime and Police Act 2005 (assistance by defendants: reduction or review of sentence) and any other rule of law by virtue of which an offender may receive a discounted sentence in consequence of assistance given (or offered) to the prosecutor or investigator.

STEP 4
Reduction for guilty pleas

The court should take account of any potential reduction for a guilty plea in accordance with section 144 of the Criminal Justice Act 2003 and the *Guilty Plea* guideline.

STEP 5
Totality principle

If sentencing an offender for more than one offence, or where the offender is already serving a sentence, consider whether the total sentence is just and proportionate to the overall offending behaviour in accordance with the *Offences Taken into Consideration and Totality* guideline.

STEP 6
Compensation and ancillary orders

In all cases, the court should consider whether to make compensation and/or other ancillary orders, including disqualification from driving and the deprivation of a vehicle.

STEP 7
Reasons

Section 174 of the Criminal Justice Act 2003 imposes a duty to give reasons for, and explain the effect of, the sentence.

A[57]

Theft

(Covers (1) Theft – breach of trust (2) Theft – person (3) Theft – shop (4) Theft – dwelling

Charge (Theft)

A[57.1] **Stealing**

Theft Act 1968, s 1(1)

Maximum penalty – 6 months' imprisonment and/or fine level 5 (for offences committed on or after 12 March 2015 an unlimited fine). Triable either way, except for low value shoplifting (see below).

Crown Court – 7 years' imprisonment and unlimited fine.

Motor vehicles. See A[77].

Theft, going equipped for. See A[58].

NB: A fixed penalty of £90 is available for theft from a shop but only where the goods are under £200, and not normally where the goods are over £100

Mode of trial

A[57.2] Consider first the general notes at D[4] and the SC Guidelines at A[57.37] onwards below.

Section 176 of the Anti-social Behaviour, Crime and Policing Act 2014 inserted new s 22A of the Magistrates' Court Act 1980 to make 'low value shoplifting' triable only summarily, but where the accused is an adult and appears before the court before the summary trial of the offence begins, the court must give him the opportunity to elect Crown Court trial and, if he so elects, he must be sent to the Crown Court for trial. The preservation of the right to elect may lead one to question the administrative benefits of this reform; only in very rare circumstances would magistrates decline jurisdiction. The answer, however, appears to be this. The right to elect applies only where the accused appears before the summary trial begins. Otherwise, the offence is summary for all purposes (save those mentioned below). Thus, the written plea of guilty procedure under the Magistrates' Courts Act 1980, s 12, can be invoked; or the court can proceed to try the defendant in his absence without a prior mode of trial procedure (and thereby avoiding the need to issue an arrest warrant before conviction).

'Low-value shoplifting' is defined as theft of goods where the value does not exceed £200, the goods were being offered for sale in shop or any other premises, stall, vehicle or place from which there is carried on a trade or business, and at the time the accused was or was purporting to be a customer or potential customer of the person offering the goods for sale.

The value of the goods is defined as the price at which they were being offered for sale at the time. In our view this requires a clear verbal or written representation as to the price. Where a person is charged on the same occasion with two or more offences of low-value shoplifting the reference to the value is a reference to the aggregate of the values involved.

A person convicted of low-value shoplifting may not appeal against conviction to the Crown Court on the ground that the convicting court was mistaken as to whether the offence was one of low-value shoplifting.

These provisions apply to secondary parties as well as principal offenders.

Amendments to the Criminal Attempts Act 1981 and the Police and Criminal Evidence Act 1984 preserve, respectively, the ability to charge an offence of attempt and the inclusion of low-value shoplifting in any reference to an 'indictable offence'.

Legal notes and definitions

A[57.3] Theft or stealing means dishonestly appropriating property belonging to another person with the intention of permanently depriving the other person of it. It does not matter whether the purpose of the theft was gain or not. Nor does it matter if the theft was for the benefit of the defendant or another person.

A[57.4] The prosecution does not have to prove that the property was appropriated without the owner's consent. However, if the defendant believed he had the owner's consent that could be relevant in deciding whether the defendant acted dishonestly.

1 Dishonestly

A[57.5] The appropriation can be dishonest even though the defendant was willing to pay for the property.

A[57.6] As to the general test for dishonesty, see A[36.7], ante.

A[57.7] The Theft Act 1968 provides that appropriation in the following circumstances is not 'dishonest':

(a) if the defendant believed he had the legal right to deprive the other of the property, either for himself or a third party; or
(b) if the defendant believed the other person would have consented had the other person known of the appropriation and the circumstances of the appropriation; or
(c) if the defendant believed the person to whom the property belonged could not be discovered by taking reasonable steps (but this defence is not available if the property came to the defendant as a trustee or a personal representative).

2 Appropriates

A[57.8] Any assumption of the rights of an owner amounts to appropriation. If the defendant came by the property (innocently or otherwise) without stealing it and later assumed a right to it by keeping it or dealing with it as an owner, he has appropriated it. An appropriation may occur even though the owner has consented to the property being taken (*R v Hinks* [2001] 2 AC 241, [2000] 4 All ER 833, HL).

A[57.9] The following are examples of dishonest appropriation:

(a) a parent whose child has brought home someone else's property and who retains the property; or
(b) a person who has found property (but see (1)(c) above); or
(c) a person who has acquired property through another person's mistake and has taken advantage of the error; or
(d) a person who switches price labels in a supermarket in order to obtain the goods at a price lower than the original marked price.

In *R v Darroux* [2018] EWCA Crim 1009, [2018] 2 Cr App R 21 the defendant ran a residential care home operated by a housing association. She had responsibility for the payroll of all the staff, including herself. She was entitled to claim certain additional payments, such as overtime. Relevant claims were sent on a monthly basis to a company which provided payroll services. This company was permitted to operate the housing association's bank account and the sums in question were paid from that account by BACS. The defendant had no control over this account. An audit established that the defendant had submitted a number of false claims for overtime, etc. She was charged with nine counts of theft, all alleging that she had stolen 'monies' belonging to the housing association. The convictions were quashed on appeal. A chose in action, here a credit balance in a bank account, could be stolen, but in submitting false claims the defendant had not assumed any of the rights of an owner with regard to the account. The forms she submitted did not, themselves, confer any rights regarding the account, she had no contact with the bank and no control over the account. Conduct which was ultimately causally operative in reducing a bank account did not necessarily become an assumption of the rights of the owner with regard to the bank balance simply and solely through the causation process. There was no evidence that the payroll company automatically had to give effect, at the behest of the defendant, to the forms she submitted.

A[57.10]–[57.15] **Repentance.** It is important in some cases to appreciate the moment when the offence is complete. Sometimes, for example, the shoplifter decides either to put the goods back or to pay for them. Once the offence is completed such action is evidence of repentance only and may affect the sentence, but it does not establish innocence.

A[57.16] **Acquiring in good faith.** If the defendant in good faith gave value for the property and later found that the vendor (or other person from whom he acquired the property) had no right to the goods, then the defendant is not guilty of theft in the event of his keeping or disposing of the property.

3 Property

A[57.17] Includes money, stocks and shares, bills of exchange, insurance policies and all kinds of goods and property.

Nothing in the 1968 Act suggested that what would otherwise constitute or be regarded as 'property' for the purposes of the Act ceased to be so because its possession or control was, for whatever reason, unlawful or illegal or prohibited. The criminal law was concerned with keeping the Queen's peace, not vindicating individual property rights: *R v Smith* [2011] EWCA Crim 66, [2011] 1 Cr App Rep 379, [2011] Crim LR 719.

A[57.18] **Land.** Land or anything forming part of land cannot be stolen except in the following circumstances:

(a) dishonest appropriation by trustees, personal representatives, liquidators of companies, persons holding a power of attorney and certain similar persons; or
(b) dishonest appropriation of something forming part of land by a person not in possession of the land (eg removing soil); or
(c) dishonest appropriation by tenants of fixtures let to be used with land.

The power of attorney exception cannot apply where the power of attorney was null and void by reason of the person's lack of capacity and lack of registration: *R v Gimbert* [2018] EWCA Crim 2190, [2019] 2 WLR 72, [2019] Crim LR 258.

A[57.19] **Attempting the impossible.** A person may be guilty of an attempt to steal even though the facts are such that the commission of the offence of theft is impossible, for example by placing one's hand into an empty pocket.

A[57.20] **Things growing wild.** If mushrooms, flowers, fruit or foliage from a plant which is growing wild are picked, that only amounts to theft if it is done for reward, or for sale or any other commercial purpose.

A[57.21] **Wild creatures.** Appropriating a wild creature can only amount to theft if it has been reduced into the possession of someone else who has not lost or abandoned such possession of the creature; or if someone else is in the course of reducing it into his possession.

4 Belonging to another

A[57.22] The property must be treated as belonging to anyone having possession or control of it or having any proprietary right or interest in it. Petrol ceases to belong to another when it is put in a vehicle's petrol tank at a self-service filling station (this accounts for the offence under s 3 of the Theft Act 1978 – see A[45]). When goods in a supermarket are for convenience or hygiene bagged, weighed and priced by an assistant they remain the property of the supermarket until paid for, and may therefore be the subject of the theft:*Davies v Leighton* [1978] Crim LR 575.

Where items were left by unknown donors outside a charity shop and were then dishonestly appropriated, while it could not be said that the charity had acquired possession or assumed control simply by reason of the items being left in close proximity, it was open to the court to infer that the items had not been abandoned; the donors had attempted to effect delivery but it would not be complete until the charity took up possession and, until then, the donors had not given up ownership; if, alternatively, the items had been placed in bins provided by the charity near their shop premises, the court could conclude that the bins were controlled by the charity with the result that anything put in them belonged to the charity in addition to the donors: *R (Ricketts) v Basildon Magistrates' Court* [2010] EWHC 2358, [2011] 1 Cr App R 15.

A[57.23] **Trust property.** Must be treated as belonging to anyone having a right to enforce the trust. An intention to defeat the trust shall be treated as an intention to deprive the person entitled to enforce the trust of the property.

A[57.24] **Being entrusted with property.** If a defendant (eg the treasurer of a holiday fund or Christmas club) has received property and is under an obligation to retain it or deal with it in a particular way, the property shall be treated as belonging to the beneficiary and not to the defendant.

A[57.25]–[57.30] **Getting property by mistake.** If the defendant obtained property by a mistake on the part of another person, and is under a legal (as opposed to a moral or social) obligation to restore it, then the property must be treated as belonging to the other person.

A[57.31] If the court considers the defendant formed an intention not to restore the property, he must be deemed to have intended to deprive the other person of the property.

5 With the intention of permanently depriving

A[57.32] The court must be satisfied that the defendant had this intention; or alternatively that he intended treating the property as his own to dispose of regardless of the owner's rights. The court must decide the defendant's intention by considering all the evidence and drawing from it such inferences as appear proper in the circumstances.

An offer, not to return a person's car to him in exactly the same condition that it had been when it was removed from his possession and control, but to sell his property back to him, and to make its return subject to a condition or conditions inconsistent with his right to possession of his own property fell within the definition of s 6(1): See *R v Raphael* [2008] EWCA Crim 1014.

In *R v Vinall* [2011] EWCA Crim 6252, [2012] 1 Cr App Rep 400, 175 JP 517 on a charge of robbery the judge should have invited the jury to consider whether the subsequent abandonment of D's bicycle was evidence from which it could be inferred that when the appellants appropriated the bicycle they intended to treat the bicycle as their own to dispose of regardless of D's rights. If such a direction had been given, an explicit direction would also have been required explaining that an intention formed only upon abandonment of the bicycle at the bus shelter was inconsistent with and fatal to the robbery count. In the absence of a proper direction the verdicts were unsafe. The jury was discharged from reaching a verdict on count 2. This was not a case in which the court should substitute a conviction for theft or taking a pedal cycle as those alternatives were not left to the jury.

A[57.33] **Borrowing or lending.** Can be used to establish that the defendant had the intention of permanently depriving the owner if, and only if, the borrowing or lending were for a period and the circumstances of the case make it equivalent to an outright taking or disposal. Ordinary borrowing or lending would not have this effect.

A[57.34] **Reduction of the charge (motor vehicles).** If the property is a motor vehicle a magistrates' court cannot reduce the charge of theft to one of 'taking a conveyance', see A[65].

A[57.35] **Proof of stealing one article enough.** If the charge alleges the theft of several articles, the court can convict of theft if it decides that only one of the articles was stolen. The announcement of decision and court register should make the decision clear.

A[57.36] **Partnership property.** A partner can be convicted of stealing property which he and another or other partners own.

Sentencing

SC Guideline – Theft Offences

A[57.37] This guideline is taken from the SC's definitive guideline *Theft Offences* effective from 1 February 2016.

Applicability of guideline

In accordance with section 120 of the Coroners and Justice Act 2009, the Sentencing Council issues this definitive guideline. It applies to all offenders aged 18 and older, who are sentenced on or after 1 February 2016, regardless of the date of the offence.

Section 125(1) of the Coroners and Justice Act 2009 provides that when sentencing offences committed after 6 April 2010:

'Every court –

(a) must, in sentencing an offender, follow any sentencing guidelines which are relevant to the offender's case, and

(b) must, in exercising any other function relating to the sentencing of offenders, follow any sentencing guidelines which are relevant to the exercise of the function,

unless the court is satisfied that it would be contrary to the interests of justice to do so.'

This guideline applies only to offenders aged 18 and older. General principles to be considered in the sentencing of youths are in the Sentencing Guidelines Council's definitive guideline, *Overarching Principles – Sentencing Youths.*

Structure, ranges and starting points

For the purposes of section 125(3)–(4) of the Coroners and Justice Act 2009, the guideline specifies *offence ranges* – the range of sentences appropriate for each type of offence. Within each offence, the Council has specified a number of categories which reflect varying degrees of seriousness. The offence range is split into *category ranges* – sentences appropriate for each level of seriousness. The Council has also identified a starting point within each category.

Starting points define the position within a category range from which to start calculating the provisional sentence. The court should consider further features of the offence or the offender that warrant adjustment of the sentence within the range, including the aggravating and mitigating factors set out at step two. Starting points and ranges apply to all offenders, whether they have pleaded guilty or been convicted after trial. Credit for a guilty plea is taken into consideration only at step four in the decision making process, after the appropriate sentence has been identified.

Information on community orders and fine bands is set out in the annex at page 35.

General Theft

Theft Act 1968 (section 1)

Including:

Theft from the person

Theft in a dwelling

Theft in breach of trust

Theft from a motor vehicle

Theft of a motor vehicle

Theft of a pedal bicycle and all other section 1

Theft Act 1968 offences, excluding theft from a shop or stall

Triable either way

Maximum: 7 years' custody

Offence range: Discharge – 6 years' custody

STEP ONE
Determining the offence category

Culpability demonstrated by one or more of the following:

A – High culpability
A leading role where offending is part of a group activity
Involvement of others through coercion, intimidation or exploitation
Breach of a high degree of trust or responsibility
Sophisticated nature of offence/significant planning
Theft involving intimidation or the use or threat of force
Deliberately targeting victim on basis of vulnerability
B – Medium culpability
A significant role where offending is part of a group activity
Some degree of planning involved
Breach of some degree of trust or responsibility
All other cases where characteristics for categories A or C are not present
C – Lesser culpability
Performed limited function under direction
Involved through coercion, intimidation or exploitation
Little or no planning
Limited awareness or understanding of offence

Where there are characteristics present which fall under different levels of culpability, the court should balance these characteristics to reach a fair assessment of the offender's culpability.

HARM

Harm is assessed by reference to the **financial loss** that results from the theft **and any significant additional harm** suffered by the victim or others – examples of significant additional harm may include **but are not limited to:**

Items stolen were of substantial value to the loser – regardless of monetary worth
High level of inconvenience caused to the victim or others
Consequential financial harm to victim or others
Emotional distress
Fear/loss of confidence caused by the crime
Risk of or actual injury to persons or damage to property
Impact of theft on a business
Damage to heritage assets
Disruption caused to infrastructure

Intended loss should be used where actual loss has been prevented.

Category 1	Very high value goods stolen (above £100,000) or High value with significant additional harm to the victim or others
Category 2	High value goods stolen (£10,000 to £100,000) and no significant additional harm or Medium value with significant additional harm to the victim or others
Category 3	Medium value goods stolen (£500 to £10,000) and no significant additional harm or Low value with significant additional harm to the victim or others
Category 4	Low value goods stolen (up to £500) and Little or no significant additional harm to the victim or others

STEP TWO
Starting point and category range

Having determined the category at step one, the court should use the starting point to reach a sentence within the appropriate category range in the table below.

The starting point applies to all offenders irrespective of plea or previous convictions.

	Culpability		
Harm	**A**	**B**	**C**
Category 1 Adjustment should be made for any significant additional harm factors where very high value goods are stolen.	**Starting point** 3 years 6 months' custody	**Starting point** 2 years' custody	**Starting point** 1 year's custody
	Category range 2 years 6 months' – 6 years' custody	**Category range** 1 – 3 years 6 months' custody	**Category range** 26 weeks' – 2 years' custody

	Culpability		
Harm	**A**	**B**	**C**
Category 2	**Starting point** 2 years' custody	**Starting point** 1 year's custody	**Starting point** High level community order
	Category range 1 – 3 years 6 months' custody	**Category range** 26 weeks' – 2 years' custody	**Category range** Low level community order – 36 weeks' custody
Category 3	**Starting point** 1 year's custody	**Starting point** High level community order	**Starting point** Band C fine
	Category range 26 weeks' – 2 years' custody	**Category range** Low level community order – 36 weeks' custody	**Category range** Band B fine – Low level community order
Category 4	**Starting point** High level community order	**Starting point** Low level community order	**Starting point** Band B fine
	Category range Medium level community order – 36 weeks' custody	**Category range** Band C fine – Medium level community order	**Category range** Discharge – Band C fine

The table above refers to single offences. Where there are multiple offences, consecutive sentences may be appropriate: please refer to the *Offences Taken Into Consideration and Totality* guideline. Where multiple offences are committed in circumstances which justify consecutive sentences, and the total amount stolen is in excess of £1 million, then an aggregate sentence in excess of 7 years may be appropriate.

> Where the offender is dependent on or has a propensity to misuse drugs or alcohol and there is sufficient prospect of success, a community order with a drug rehabilitation requirement under section 209, or an alcohol treatment requirement under section 212 of the Criminal Justice Act 2003 may be a proper alternative to a short or moderate custodial sentence.
>
> Where the offender suffers from a medical condition that is susceptible to treatment but does not warrant detention under a hospital order, a community order with a mental health treatment requirement under section 207 of the Criminal Justice Act 2003 may be a proper alternative to a short or moderate custodial sentence.

The court should then consider further adjustment for any aggravating or mitigating factors. The following is a **non-exhaustive** list of additional factual elements providing the context of the offence and factors relating to the offender. Identify whether any combination of these, or other relevant factors, should result in an upward or downward adjustment from the sentence arrived at so far

Factors increasing seriousness	**Factors reducing seriousness or reflecting personal mitigation**
Statutory aggravating factors	No previous convictions or no relevant/recent convictions
Previous convictions, having regard to a) the **nature** of the offence to which the conviction relates and its **relevance** to the current offence; and b) the **time** that has elapsed since the conviction	Remorse, particularly where evidenced by voluntary reparation to the victim

Factors increasing seriousness	Factors reducing seriousness or reflecting personal mitigation
Offence committed whilst on bail	Good character and/or exemplary conduct
Offence motivated by, or demonstrating hostility based on any of the following characteristics or presumed characteristics of the victim: religion, race, disability, sexual orientation or transgender identity	Serious medical condition requiring urgent, intensive or long-term treatment
Other aggravating factors	Age and/or lack of maturity where it affects the responsibility of the offender
Stealing goods to order	Mental disorder or learning disability
Steps taken to prevent the victim reporting or obtaining assistance and/or from assisting or supporting the prosecution	Sole or primary carer for dependent relatives
Offender motivated by intention to cause harm or out of revenge	Determination and/or demonstration of steps having been taken to address addiction or offending behaviour
Offence committed over sustained period of time	Inappropriate degree of trust or responsibility
Attempts to conceal/dispose of evidence	
Failure to comply with current court orders	
Offence committed on licence	
Offences taken into consideration	
Blame wrongly placed on others	
Established evidence of community/wider impact (for issues other than prevalence)	
Prevalence – see below	

Prevalence

There may be exceptional local circumstances that arise which may lead a court to decide that prevalence should influence sentencing levels. The pivotal issue in such cases will be the harm caused to the community.

It is essential that the court before taking account of prevalence:

- has supporting evidence from an external source, for example, Community Impact Statements, to justify claims that a particular crime is prevalent in their area, and is causing particular harm in that community, **and**
- is satisfied that there is a compelling need to treat the offence more seriously than elsewhere.

STEP THREE
Consider any factors which indicate a reduction, such as assistance to the prosecution

The court should take into account sections 73 and 74 of the Serious Organised Crime and Police Act 2005 (assistance by defendants: reduction or review of sentence) and any other rule of law by virtue of which an offender may receive a discounted sentence in consequence of assistance given (or offered) to the prosecutor or investigator.

STEP FOUR
Reduction for guilty pleas

The court should take account of any potential reduction for a guilty plea in accordance with section 144 of the Criminal Justice Act 2003 and the *Guilty Plea* guideline.

STEP FIVE
Totality principle

If sentencing an offender for more than one offence, or where the offender is already serving a sentence, consider whether the total sentence is just and proportionate to the overall offending behaviour in accordance with the *Offences Taken into Consideration and Totality* guideline.

STEP SIX
Confiscation, compensation and ancillary orders

The court must proceed with a view to making a confiscation order if it is asked to do so by the prosecutor or if the court believes it is appropriate for it to do so.

Where the offence has resulted in loss or damage the court must consider whether to make a compensation order.

If the court makes both a confiscation order and an order for compensation and the court believes the offender will not have sufficient means to satisfy both orders in full, the court must direct that the compensation be paid out of sums recovered under the confiscation order (section 13 of the Proceeds of Crime Act 2002).

The court may also consider whether to make ancillary orders. These may include a deprivation order, or a restitution order.

STEP SEVEN
Reasons

Section 174 of the Criminal Justice Act 2003 imposes a duty to give reasons for, and explain the effect of, the sentence.

STEP EIGHT
Consideration for time spent on bail

The court must consider whether to give credit for time spent on bail in accordance with section 240A of the Criminal Justice Act 2003.

SC Guideline – Theft from a shop or stall

A[57.37A] Theft Act 1968 (section 1)

Triable either way

Maximum: 7 years' custody

(except for an offence of low-value shoplifting which is treated as a summary only offence in accordance with section 22A of the Magistrates' Courts Act 1980 where the maximum is 6 months' custody)

Offence range: Discharge – 3 years' custody

STEP ONE
Determining the offence category

The court should determine the offence category with reference **only** to the factors identified in the following tables. In order to determine the category the court should assess **culpability** and **harm.**

The level of culpability is determined by weighing up all the factors of the case to determine the offender's role and the extent to which the offending was **planned** and the **sophistication** with which it was carried out.

CULPABILITY demonstrated by one or more of the following:

A – High culpability
A leading role where offending is part of a group activity
Involvement of others through coercion, intimidation or exploitation
Sophisticated nature of offence/significant planning
Significant use or threat of force
Offender subject to a banning order from the relevant store
Child accompanying offender is actively used to facilitate the offence (not merely present when offence is committed)
B – Medium culpability
A significant role where offending is part of a group activity
Some degree of planning involved
Limited use or threat of force
All other cases where characteristics for categories A or C are not present
C – Lesser culpability
Performed limited function under direction
Involved through coercion, intimidation or exploitation
Little or no planning
Mental disorder/learning disability where linked to commission of the offence

Where there are characteristics present which fall under different levels of culpability, the court should balance these characteristics to reach a fair assessment of the offender's culpability.

HARM

Harm is assessed by reference to the **financial loss** that results from the theft **and any significant additional harm** suffered by the victim or others – examples of significant additional harm may include **but are not limited to:**

Emotional distress
Damage to property
Effect on business
A greater impact on the victim due to the size or type of their business
A particularly vulnerable victim

Intended loss should be used where actual loss has been prevented.

Category 1	High value goods stolen (above £1,000) **or** Medium value with significant additional harm to the victim
Category 2	Medium value goods stolen (£200 to £1,000) **and** no significant additional harm **or** Low value with significant additional harm to the victim
Category 3	Low value goods stolen (up to £200) **and** Little or no significant additional harm to the victim

STEP TWO
Starting point and category range

Having determined the category at step one, the court should use the starting point to reach a sentence within the appropriate category range in the table below.

The starting point applies to all offenders irrespective of plea or previous convictions.

	Culpability		
Harm	**A**	**B**	**C**
Category 1 Where the value greatly exceeds £1,000 it may be appropriate to move outside the identified range. Adjustment should be made for any significant additional harm where high value goods are stolen.	**Starting point** 26 weeks' custody	**Starting point** Medium level community order	**Starting point** Band C fine
	Category range 12 weeks' – 3 years' custody	**Category range** Low level community order – 26 weeks' custody	**Category range** Band B fine – Low level community order
Category 2	**Starting point** 12 weeks' custody	**Starting point** Low level community order	**Starting point** Band B fine
	Category range High level community order – 26 weeks' custody	**Category range** Band C fine – Medium level community order	**Category range** Band A fine – Band C fine
Category 3	**Starting point** High level community order	**Starting point** Band C fine	**Starting point** Band A fine
	Category range Low level community order – 12 weeks' custody	**Category range** Band B fine – Low level community order	**Category range** Discharge – Band B fine

Consecutive sentences for multiple offences may be appropriate – please refer to the *Offences Taken Into Consideration and Totality* guideline.

Previous diversionary work with an offender does not preclude the court from considering this type of sentencing option again if appropriate.

Where the offender is dependent on or has a propensity to misuse drugs or alcohol and there is sufficient prospect of success, a community order with a drug rehabilitation requirement under section 209, or an alcohol treatment requirement under section 212 of the Criminal Justice Act 2003 may be a proper alternative to a short or moderate custodial sentence.

Where the offender suffers from a medical condition that is susceptible to treatment but does not warrant detention under a hospital order, a community order with a mental health treatment requirement under section 207 of the Criminal Justice Act 2003 may be a proper alternative to a short or moderate custodial sentence.

The court should then consider further adjustment for any aggravating or mitigating factors. The following is a **non-exhaustive** list of additional factual elements providing the context of the offence and factors relating to the offender. Identify whether any combination of these, or other relevant factors, should result in an upward or downward adjustment from the sentence arrived at so far.

Factors increasing seriousness	Factors reducing seriousness or reflecting personal mitigation
Statutory aggravating factors	No previous convictions or no relevant/recent convictions
Previous convictions, having regard to a) the nature of the offence to which the conviction relates and its relevance to the current offence; and b) the time that has elapsed since the conviction Relevant recent convictions may justify an upward adjustment, including outside the category range. In cases involving significant persistent offending, the community and custodial thresholds may be crossed even though the offence otherwise warrants a lesser sentence. Any custodial sentence must be kept to the necessary minimum	Remorse, particularly where evidenced by voluntary reparation to the victim
Offence committed whilst on bail	Good character and/or exemplary conduct
Offence motivated by, or demonstrating hostility based on any of the following characteristics or presumed characteristics of the victim: religion, race, disability, sexual orientation or transgender identity	Serious medical condition requiring urgent, intensive or long-term treatment
Other aggravating factors	Age and/or lack of maturity where it affects the responsibility of the offender
Stealing goods to order	Mental disorder or learning disability (where not linked to the commission of the offence)
Steps taken to prevent the victim reporting or obtaining assistance and/or from assisting or supporting the prosecution	Sole or primary carer for dependent relatives
Attempts to conceal/dispose of evidence	Determination and/or demonstration of steps having been taken to address addiction or offending behaviour
Offender motivated by intention to cause harm or out of revenge	Offender experiencing exceptional financial hardship
Failure to comply with current court orders	
Offence committed on licence	
Offences taken into consideration	
Established evidence of community/wider impact (for issues other than prevalence)	
Prevalence – see below	

Prevalence

There may be exceptional local circumstances that arise which may lead a court to decide that prevalence should influence sentencing levels. The pivotal issue in such cases will be the harm caused to the community.

It is essential that the court before taking account of prevalence:

- has supporting evidence from an external source, for example, Community Impact Statements, to justify claims that a particular crime is prevalent in their area, and is causing particular harm in that community, and
- is satisfied that there is a compelling need to treat the offence more seriously than elsewhere.

STEP THREE
Consider any factors which indicate a reduction, such as assistance to the prosecution

The court should take into account sections 73 and 74 of the Serious Organised Crime and Police Act 2005 (assistance by defendants: reduction or review of sentence) and any other rule of law by virtue of which an offender may receive a discounted sentence in consequence of assistance given (or offered) to the prosecutor or investigator.

STEP FOUR
Reduction for guilty pleas

The court should take account of any potential reduction for a guilty plea in accordance with section 144 of the Criminal Justice Act 2003 and the *Guilty Plea* guideline.

STEP FIVE
Totality principle

If sentencing an offender for more than one offence, or where the offender is already serving a sentence, consider whether the total sentence is just and proportionate to the overall offending behaviour in accordance with the *Offences Taken into Consideration and Totality* guideline.

STEP SIX
Confiscation, compensation and ancillary orders

The court must proceed with a view to making a confiscation order if it is asked to do so by the prosecutor or if the court believes it is appropriate for it to do so.

Where the offence has resulted in loss or damage the court must consider whether to make a compensation order.

If the court makes both a confiscation order and an order for compensation and the court believes the offender will not have sufficient means to satisfy both orders in full, the court must direct that the compensation be paid out of sums recovered under the confiscation order (section 13 of the Proceeds of Crime Act 2002).

The court may also consider whether to make ancillary orders. These may include a deprivation order, or a restitution order.

STEP SEVEN
Reasons

Section 174 of the Criminal Justice Act 2003 imposes a duty to give reasons for, and explain the effect of, the sentence.

STEP EIGHT
Consideration for time spent on bail

The court must consider whether to give credit for time spent on bail in accordance with section 240A of the Criminal Justice Act 2003.

A[57.38] Structure of the sentencing decision. See B[9.6].

A[57.39] Compensation. This may be ordered up to £5,000 either as part of a wider sentence or by itself as a substantive penalty. The court may deprive the defendant of any property in his possession when arrested if it was used, or intended for use, in the commission of a crime.

A[57.40] Motor vehicles. If the property was a motor vehicle (defined as a mechanically propelled vehicle intended or adapted for use on a road) the court may disqualify but there is no endorsement or penalty points.

A[58]

Theft, burglary – going equipped for

Charge (Theft, burglary – going equipped for)

A[58.1] **Having, when not at his place of abode, an article, namely a [. . . . .], for use in the course of burglary or theft**

Theft Act 1968, s 25

Maximum penalty – 6 months' imprisonment and/or fine level 5 (for offences committed on or after 12 March 2015 an unlimited fine). Triable either way.

Crown Court – 3 years' imprisonment and unlimited fine.

Motor vehicles. If the defendant intended to steal or take a motor vehicle the offence is not endorsable nor are penalty points applicable but disqualification may be ordered.

Mode of trial

A[58.2] See the SC Guideline at **A**[58.8] below.

Legal notes and definitions

A[58.3] **Theft** includes taking a conveyance without the owner's consent: Theft Act 1968, s 25(5).

A[58.4] The words 'or cheat' were removed from this offence by the Fraud Act 2006. For the offence of possession of articles for fraud, see **A**[38], above.

A[58.5] If the article was made or adapted for use in committing a burglary or theft, the court can treat that as evidence that the defendant had the article with him for such use: Theft Act 1968, s 25(3).

A[58.6] The offence can be committed by day or night. The offence cannot take place at the defendant's place of abode: s 25(1). It must be proved that he had the articles with him for the purpose of using them in connection with burglary or theft, though it is not necessary for the prosecution to prove that the defendant intended to use them himself: *R v Ellames* [1974] 3 All ER 130, 138 JP 682. An intention to use the item if the opportunity arose would be sufficient to convict the accused, but it would not be sufficient where he had not actually decided whether to use the item if the opportunity presented itself: *R v Hargreaves* [1985] Crim LR 243, CA.

A[58.7] More than one article may be specified in the charge without offending the rule against duplicity.

Sentencing
SC Guideline – Going equipped for theft or burglary

A[58.8] Theft Act 1968 (section 25)

Triable either way

Maximum: 3 years' custody

Offence range: Discharge – 18 months' custody

STEP ONE
Determining the offence category

The court should determine the offence category with reference **only** to the factors identified in the following tables. In order to determine the category the court should assess **culpability** and **harm.**

The level of culpability is determined by weighing up all the factors of the case to determine the offender's role and the extent to which the offending was **planned** and the **sophistication** with which it was carried out.

CULPABILITY demonstrated by one or more of the following:

A – High culpability
A leading role where offending is part of a group activity
Involvement of others through coercion, intimidation or exploitation
Significant steps taken to conceal identity and/or avoid detection
Sophisticated nature of offence/significant planning
Offender equipped for robbery or domestic burglary
B – Medium culpability
A significant role where offending is part of a group activity
All other cases where characteristics for categories A or C are not present
C – Lesser culpability
Involved through coercion, intimidation or exploitation
Limited awareness or understanding of offence
Little or no planning

HARM

This guideline refers to preparatory offences where no theft has been committed. The level of harm is determined by weighing up all the factors of the case to determine the harm that would be caused if the item(s) were used to commit a substantive offence.

Greater harm
Possession of item(s) which have the potential to facilitate an offence affecting a large number of victims
Possession of item(s) which have the potential to facilitate an offence involving high value items
Lesser harm
All other cases

STEP TWO
Starting point and category range

Having determined the category at step one, the court should use the starting point to reach a sentence within the appropriate category range in the table below

The starting point applies to all offenders irrespective of plea or previous convictions.

Harm	Culpability A	Culpability B	Culpability C
Greater	**Starting point** 1 year's custody	**Starting point** 18 weeks' custody	**Starting point** Medium level community order
	Category range 26 weeks' – 1 year 6 months' custody	**Category range** High level community order – 36 weeks' custody	**Category range** Low level community order – High level community order
Lesser	**Starting point** 26 weeks' custody	**Starting point** High level community order	**Starting point** Band C fine
	Category range 12 weeks' – 36 weeks' custody	**Category range** Medium level community order – 12 weeks' custody	**Category range** Discharge – Medium level community order

Consecutive sentences for multiple offences may be appropriate – please refer to the *Offences Taken Into Consideration and Totality* guideline.

The court should then consider further adjustment for any aggravating or mitigating factors. The following is a **non-exhaustive** list of additional factual elements providing the context of the offence and factors relating to the offender. Identify whether any combination of these, or other relevant factors, should result in an upward or downward adjustment from the sentence arrived at so far.

Factors increasing seriousness	Factors reducing seriousness or reflecting personal mitigation
Statutory aggravating factors	No previous convictions or no relevant/recent convictions
Previous convictions, having regard to a) the **nature** of the offence to which the conviction relates and its **relevance** to the current offence; and b) the **time** that has elapsed since the conviction	Good character and/or exemplary conduct
Offence committed whilst on bail	Serious medical condition requiring urgent, intensive or long-term treatment
Other aggravating factors	Age and/or lack of maturity where it affects the responsibility of the offender
Attempts to conceal/dispose of evidence	Mental disorder or learning disability
Established evidence of community/wider impact	Sole or primary carer for dependent relatives
Failure to comply with current court orders	Determination and/or demonstration of steps having been taken to address addiction or offending behaviour
Offence committed on licence	
Offences taken into consideration	

STEP THREE
Consider any factors which indicate a reduction, such as assistance to the prosecution

The court should take into account sections 73 and 74 of the Serious Organised Crime and Police Act 2005 (assistance by defendants: reduction or review of

sentence) and any other rule of law by virtue of which an offender may receive a discounted sentence in consequence of assistance given (or offered) to the prosecutor or investigator.

STEP FOUR
Reduction for guilty pleas

The court should take account of any potential reduction for a guilty plea in accordance with section 144 of the Criminal Justice Act 2003 and the *Guilty Plea* guideline.

STEP FIVE
Totality principle

If sentencing an offender for more than one offence, or where the offender is already serving a sentence, consider whether the total sentence is just and proportionate to the overall offending behaviour in accordance with the *Offences Taken into Consideration and Totality* guideline.

STEP SIX
Confiscation, compensation and ancillary orders

The court must proceed with a view to making a confiscation order if it is asked to do so by the prosecutor or if the court believes it is appropriate for it to do so.

Where the offence has resulted in loss or damage the court must consider whether to make a compensation order.

If the court makes both a confiscation order and an order for compensation and the court believes the offender will not have sufficient means to satisfy both orders in full, the court must direct that the compensation be paid out of sums recovered under the confiscation order (section 13 of the Proceeds of Crime Act 2002).

The court may also consider whether to make ancillary orders. These may include a deprivation order.

STEP SEVEN
Reasons

Section 174 of the Criminal Justice Act 2003 imposes a duty to give reasons for, and explain the effect of, the sentence.

STEP EIGHT
Consideration for time spent on bail

The court must consider whether to give credit for time spent on bail in accordance with section 240A of the Criminal Justice Act 2003.

A[59]

Threats to kill

Charge (Threats to kill)

A[59.1] **Without lawful excuse makes to another a threat intending that that other would fear it would be carried out, to kill that other or a third person**

Offences Against the Person Act 1861, s 16

Maximum penalty – 6 months' imprisonment and/or fine level 5 (for offences committed on or after 12 March 2015 an unlimited fine). Triable either way. Specified violent offence under Sch 15, Part 1, CJA 2003.

Crown Court – 10 years' imprisonment and unlimited fine.

An allegation must particularise only one threat; there is no offence of making multiple threats to kill: *R v Marchese* [2008] EWCA Crim 389, [2009] 1 WLR 992, [2008] 2 Cr App R 12, [2008] Crim LR 797.

Mode of trial

A[59.2] See the SC Guideline at A[59.5] below.

Legal notes and definitions

A[59.3] **Lawful excuse.** Making a threat where it is for the prevention of crime or self-defence can amount to a defence if it is reasonable in the circumstances to make such a threat. Once the issue is raised by the defence the onus is on the prosecution to prove that there was no lawful excuse, beyond a reasonable doubt (*R v Cousins* [1982] 2 All ER 115, CA).

A[59.4] **Person.** A foetus in utero is not a person distinct from its mother; therefore a threat to cause the mother to have a miscarriage is not an offence under s 16. However, a threat to kill a child after its birth when it is still in foetus does amount to an offence under s 16 (*R v Tait* [1989] 3 All ER 682, CA).

Sentencing
SC Guideline – Threats to kill

A[59.5] The text of this guideline is taken from the Sentencing Council's Intimidatory offences: Definitive guideline, published on 5 July 2018, taking effect from the 1 October 2018.

Threats to kill

Offences against the Person Act 1861, s 16

Effective from: 1 October 2018

Triable either way

Maximum: 10 years' custody

Offence range: Community order – 7 years' custody

This is a specified offence for the purposes of section 226A (extended sentence for certain violent or sexual offences) of the Criminal Justice Act 2003

Where offence committed in a domestic context, also refer to the *Overarching principles: Domestic abuse guideline*

STEP 1
DETERMINING THE OFFENCE CATEGORY

The court should determine the offence category with reference only to the factors in the tables below. In order to determine the category the court should assess **culpability and harm.**

The level of **culpability** is determined by weighing up all the factors of the case. **Where there are characteristics present which fall under different levels of culpability, the court should balance these characteristics to reach a fair assessment of the offender's culpability.**

Culpability demonstrated by one or more of the following:

A – Higher culpability	• Significant planning and/or sophisticated offence • Visible weapon • Threat(s) made in the presence of children • History of and/or campaign of violence towards the victim • Threat(s) with significant violence
B – Medium culpability	Cases that fall between categories A and C because: • Factors are present in A and C which balance each other out and/or • The offender's culpability falls between the factors described in A and C
C – Lesser culpability	• Offender's responsibility substantially reduced by mental disorder or learning disability • Offence was limited in scope and duration

Harm

The level of harm is assessed by weighing up all the factors of the case.

Category 1	• Very serious distress caused to the victim • Significant psychological harm caused to the victim • Offence has a considerable practical impact on the victim
Category 2	Harm that falls between categories 1 and 3, and in particular: • Some distress caused to the victim • Some psychological harm caused to the victim • Offence has some practical impact on the victim
Category 3	• Little or no distress or harm caused to the victim

STEP 2
STARTING POINT AND CATEGORY RANGE

Having determined the category at step one, the court should use the corresponding starting point to reach a sentence within the category range in the table below. The starting point applies to all offenders irrespective of plea or previous convictions.

	Culpability		
Harm	A	B	C
Category 1	**Starting point** 4 years' custody **Category range** 2–7 years' custody	**Starting point** 2 years' custody **Category range** 1–4 years' custody	**Starting point** 1 years' custody **Category range** 26 weeks'–2 years 6 months' custody
Category 2	**Starting point** 2 years' custody **Category range** 1–4 years' custody	**Starting point** 1 years' custody **Category range** 26 weeks'–2 years 6 months' custody	**Starting point** 26 weeks' **Category range** High level community order–1 years' custody
Category 3	**Starting point** 1 years' custody **Category range** 26 weeks'–2 years 6 months' custody	**Starting point** 26 weeks' custody **Category range** High level community order–1 years' custody	**Starting point** Medium level community order **Category range** Low level community order–High level community order

The court should then consider any adjustment for any aggravating or mitigating factors. Below is a **non-exhaustive** list of additional factual elements providing the context of the offence and factors relating to the offender.

Identify whether any combination of these, or other relevant factors, should result in an upward or downward adjustment from the starting point.

FACTORS INCREASING SERIOUSNESS

Statutory aggravating factors:
Previous convictions, having regard to a) the **nature** of the offence to which the conviction relates and its **relevance** to the current offence; and b) the **time** that has elapsed since the conviction
Offence committed whilst on bail
Offence motivated by, or demonstrating hostility based on any of the following characteristics or presumed characteristics of the victim: religion, race, disability, sexual orientation, or transgender identity
Other aggravating factors:
Offence committed against those working in the public sector or providing a service to the public
Impact of offence on others, particularly children
Victim is particularly vulnerable (not all vulnerabilities are immediately apparent)
Failure to comply with current court orders
Offence committed on licence or post sentence supervision
Offences taken into consideration

FACTORS REDUCING SERIOUSNESS OR REFLECTING PERSONAL MITIGATION

No previous convictions or no relevant/recent convictions

Remorse
Good character and/or exemplary conduct
Serious medical condition requiring urgent, intensive or long-term treatment
Age and/or lack of maturity
Mental disorder or learning disability (where not taken into account at step one)
Sole or primary carer for dependent relatives
Determination and/or demonstration of steps having been taken to address offending behaviour

STEP 3
CONSIDER ANY FACTORS WHICH INDICATE A REDUCTION, SUCH AS ASSISTANCE TO THE PROSECUTION

The court should take into account sections 73 and 74 of the Serious Organised Crime and Police Act 2005 (assistance by defendants: reduction or review of sentence) and any other rule of law by virtue of which an offender may receive a discounted sentence in consequence of assistance given (or offered) to the prosecutor or investigator.

STEP 4
REDUCTION FOR GUILTY PLEAS

The court should take account of any potential reduction for a guilty plea in accordance with section 144 of the Criminal Justice Act 2003 and the *Guilty Plea* guideline.

STEP 5
DANGEROUSNESS

The court should consider whether having regard to the criteria contained in Chapter 5 of Part 12 of the Criminal Justice Act 2003 it would be appropriate to impose an extended sentence (section 226A).

STEP 6
TOTALITY PRINCIPLE

If sentencing an offender for more than one offence, or where the offender is already serving a sentence, consider whether the total sentence is just and proportionate to the overall offending behaviour in accordance with the *Offences Taken into Consideration and Totality* guideline.

STEP 7
COMPENSATION AND ANCILLARY ORDERS

In all cases, the court must consider whether to make a compensation order and/or other ancillary orders.

Compensation order

The court should consider compensation orders in all cases where personal injury, loss or damage has resulted from the offence. The court must give reasons if it decides not to award compensation in such cases.

Other ancillary orders available include:

Restraining order

Where an offender is convicted of any offence, the court may make a restraining order (section 5 of the Protection from Harassment Act 1997).

The order may prohibit the offender from doing anything for the purpose of protecting the victim of the offence, or any other person mentioned in the order, from further conduct which amounts to harassment or will cause a fear of violence.

The order may have effect for a specified period or until further order.

STEP 8
REASONS

Section 174 of the Criminal Justice Act 2003 imposes a duty to give reasons for, and explain the effect of, the sentence.

STEP 9
CONSIDERATION FOR TIME SPENT ON BAIL (TAGGED CURFEW)

The court must consider whether to give credit for time spent on bail in accordance with section 240A of the Criminal Justice Act 2003.

A[60]
Trade mark, unauthorised use of etc

Charge (Trade mark, unauthorised use of etc)

A[60.1] **(1) With a view to gain for himself or another, or with intent to cause loss to another, and without the consent of the proprietor—**

(a) **applies to goods or their packaging a sign identical to, or likely to be mistaken for, a registered trade mark, or**
(b) **sells or lets for hire, offers or exposes for sale or hire or distributes goods which bear, or the packaging of which bears, such a sign, or**
(c) **has in his possession, custody or control in the course of a business any such goods with a view to the doing of anything, by himself or another, which would be an offence under paragraph (b).**

Trade Marks Act 1994, s 92(1)

(2) With a view to gain for himself or another, or with intent to cause loss to another, and without the consent of the proprietor—

(a) **applies a sign identical to, or likely to be mistaken for, a registered trade mark to material intended to be used—**
  (i) **for labelling or packaging goods,**
  (ii) **as a business paper in relation to goods, or**
  (iii) **as advertising goods, or**
(b) **uses in the course of a business material bearing such a sign for labelling or packaging goods, as a business paper in relation to goods, or for advertising goods, or**
(c) **has in his possession, custody or control in the course of a business any such material with a view to the doing of anything, by himself or another, which would be an offence under** paragraph (b).

Trade Marks Act, 1994, s 92(2)

(3) With a view to gain for himself or another, or with intent to cause loss to another, and without the consent of the proprietor—

(a) **makes an article specifically designed for or adapted for making copies of a sign identical to, or likely to be mistaken for, a registered trade mark, or**
(b) **has such an article in his possession, custody or control in the course of a business,**

Knowing or having reason to believe that it has been, or is to be, used to produce goods, or material for labelling or packaging goods, as a business paper in relation to goods, or for advertising goods.

Trade Marks Act 1994, s 92(3)

Maximum penalty – 6 months' imprisonment and/or fine level 5 (for offences committed on or after 12 March 2015 an unlimited fine).

Crown Court – 10 years' imprisonment and unlimited fine.

Mode of trial

A[60.2] See the SC Guideline at A[60.5] below.

Legal notes and definitions

A[60.3] The offences set out in s 92(1)(a), (b) and (c) are not cumulative, but separate, and its provisions are not a disproportionate breach of a defendant's rights under article 1 of Protocol 1 to the European Convention for the Protection of Human Rights and Fundamental Freedoms. Where persons have no proprietary right in the trade marks, they have a right in the goods which they have bought. The 1994 Act does not stop them selling them, except if they wish to do so whilst still with the misleading and infringing trade mark attached. The 1994 Act does not, therefore, deprive the defendants of any property which they have. The most it does is to regulate their use or the manner of their disposal of the goods: *R v M* [2017] UKSC 58, [2017] 1 WLR 3006.

Grey goods. The offence under s 92(1)(b) applies to 'grey goods' as well as to counterfeit goods. 'Grey goods' are goods which are manufactured with the authority and bear the mark of the trade mark proprietor, but that proprietor has not consented to the sale, distribution or possession of the goods because, for example, they are faulty or they constitute surplus production: *R v C and others* [2016] EWCA Crim 1617, [2017] 1 Cr App R 20, (2017) 181 JP 143. See further *R v M*, supra. Examples of unauthorised sales include, but are not limited to: an excess number of garments deliberately manufactured so that the balance can be sold for the defendant's benefit; or, even without that original ulterior intention, as precautionary spare capacity planned and approved by the trade mark owner but then put on the market without his consent; or made under a permission which was cancelled by the trade mark owner, eg where the trade mark owner was dissatisfied with the quality

Defences. A criminal offence under s 92 cannot be committed unless there is a civil infringement of a trade mark (see ss 10–12); the civil defences will not apply in every case. Once a defence has been raised it is for the prosecution to disprove it (*R v Johnstone* [2003] UKHL 28; *R v Isaac* [2004] EWCA Crim 1082, 168 JP 417).

Section 92(4) provides that a person does not commit an offence unless –

(a) the goods are goods in respect of which the trade mark is registered, or
(b) the trade mark has a reputation in the UK and the use of the sign takes or would take unfair advantage of, or is or would be detrimental to, the distinctive character or repute of the trade mark.

The validity of the registration of a trade mark cannot be tried in criminal proceedings. If there is a challenge to the validity, the court must adjourn to allow that challenge to be determined against the trademark owner; albeit, not where the challenge is made late or is frivolous (*R v Johnstone* [2003] 3 All ER 884).

Section 92(5) provides that it a defence to show that the accused believed on reasonable grounds that the use of the sign in the manner in which it was used, or was to be used, was not an infringement of the registered trade mark.

The burden of proof rests with the accused to establish the defence on a balance of probabilities (*R v Johnstone* [2003] 3 All ER 884).

It was held in *Torbay Council v Singh* [1999] 2 Cr App Rep 451, [1999] 163 JP 744 that to establish criminal liability for offences under this section it was not necessary for the prosecution to prove knowledge or intent to infringe a registered trademark; the statutory defence related to a reasonable belief that the manner of use of a sign did not infringe the registered trademark and it presupposed an awareness of the registration. This view was doubted, however, in *R v Johnstone*, above (which concerned 'bootleg' CDs that bore the names of the performers and those performers had previously registered their names as trademarks).

> 'Section 92(5) is concerned to provide a defence where the person charged has a reasonable belief in the lawfulness of what he did. Those who act honestly and reasonably are not to be visited with criminal sanctions. It makes no sense to confine this defence to cases where the defendant is aware of the existence of the registered trade mark and exclude altogether those cases where the defendant is not. Section 92(5) provides a defence where the defendant believes on reasonable grounds his use of the sign does not infringe a registered trade mark of whose existence he is aware. It would be extraordinary if the subsection does not equally furnish a defence in the stronger case where the reason why the defendant believes

his use of the sign does not infringe a registered trade mark is that he reasonably believes no relevant trade mark is registered. Section 92(5) is to be interpreted as including the latter case as well as the former' (per Lord Nicholls at para 43).

A[60.4] **Companies.** For offences committed by partnerships and bodies corporate see s 101.

Sentencing
SC Guideline – Trade mark, unauthorised use of

A[60.5] *This may be an offence for which it is appropriate to combine a fine with a community order. Consult your legal adviser for further guidance.

<table>
<tr><td colspan="4" align="center">OFFENCE SERIOUSNESS (CULPABILITY AND HARM)
A. IDENTIFY THE APPROPRIATE STARTING POINT
Starting points based on first time offender pleading not guilty</td></tr>
<tr><td>Examples of nature of activity</td><td colspan="2">Starting point</td><td>Range</td></tr>
<tr><td>Small number of counterfeit items</td><td colspan="2">Band C fine</td><td>Band B fine to low level community order</td></tr>
<tr><td>Larger number of counterfeit items but no involvement in wider operation</td><td colspan="2">Medium level community order, plus fine*</td><td>Low level community order to 12 weeks custody, plus fine*</td></tr>
<tr><td>High number of counterfeit items or involvement in wider operation eg. Manufacture or distribution</td><td colspan="2">12 weeks custody</td><td>6 weeks to Crown Court</td></tr>
<tr><td>Central role in large-scale operation</td><td colspan="2">Crown Court</td><td>Crown Court</td></tr>
<tr><td colspan="4" align="center">OFFENCE SERIOUSNESS (CULPABILITY AND HARM)
B. CONSIDER THE EFFECT OF AGGRAVATING AND MITIGATING FACTORS (OTHER THAN THOSE WITHIN EXAMPLES ABOVE)
Common aggravating and mitigating factors are identified at B[45.2A]. The following may be particularly relevant but these lists are not exhaustive</td></tr>
<tr><td colspan="2">Factors indicating higher culpability
1. High degree of professionalism
2. High level of profit</td><td colspan="2">Factor indicating lower culpability
1. Mistake or ignorance about provenance of goods</td></tr>
<tr><td colspan="2">Factor indicating greater degree of harm
1. Purchasers at risk of harm eg from counterfeit drugs</td><td colspan="2"></td></tr>
<tr><td colspan="4" align="center">FORM A PRELIMINARY VIEW OF THE APPROPRIATE SENTENCE, THEN CONSIDER OFFENDER MITIGATION
Common factors are identified at B[45.2A]</td></tr>
<tr><td colspan="4" align="center">CONSIDER A REDUCTION FOR A GUILTY PLEA</td></tr>
<tr><td colspan="4" align="center">CONSIDER ANCILLARY ORDERS
Refer to B[10] for guidance on compensation and Part B for available ancillary orders
Consider ordering forfeiture and destruction of the goods</td></tr>
<tr><td colspan="4" align="center">DECIDE SENTENCE
GIVE REASONS</td></tr>
</table>

A[61]

TV licence payment evasion

Charge (TV licence payment evasion)

A[61.1] Installation or use of a television receiver without a licence.

Communications Act 2003, s 363(2)

Has a television receiver in his possession or under his control who –

(a) **intends to install or use it in contravention of subsection (1), or**
(b) **knows, or has reasonable grounds for believing, that another person intends to install or use it in contravention of that subsection.**

Communications Act 2003, s 363(3)

NB: The Wireless Telegraphy Act 1949, was repealed by the Wireless Telegraphy Act 2006. See ss 8 and 35 for further provision concerning the use of television and wireless apparatus.

Maximum penalty – Fine level 3.

Legal notes and definitions

A[61.2] The charge should allege either that the apparatus was used or was installed.

A[61.3] Using should be given its natural and ordinary meaning. This might create problems for enforcing authorities. They would if necessary have to persuade the court to draw the inference that the apparatus in question had been used by the defendant during the relevant period. If, for example, a television set in working order was found in the sitting-room of a house occupied by the defendant, it would not be difficult for a court to draw the necessary inference in the absence of some credible explanation by the defendant to the effect that it was not being used (*Rudd v Secretary of State for Trade and Industry* [1987] 2 All ER 553, [1987] 1 WLR 786, HL) and (*Whiley v DPP* [1995] Crim LR 39) in respect of a radio scanner.

A[61.4] A user does not have to be an owner or hirer. Therefore where a set belonged to a husband but the wife switched it on, she was convicted of using it (*Monks v Pilgrim* [1979] Crim LR 595).

A[61.5] **Licence.** Applies to the person named on the licence, his family and domestic staff living with him on the premises. The prosecution does not have to prove that the defendant did not have a valid licence (see s 101 MCA 1980).

A[61.6] Applies to the premises named on the licence. Also covers members of family living away as full-time students at educational establishments using a portable television set (black and white or colour as described in the licence) in any other place provided:

(a) they normally reside at the licence holder's address; and
(b) the equipment is powered by internal batteries; and
(c) is not permanently installed.

There are concessions for touring caravans.

A[61.7] **Duration.** Normally one year. If the licence is paid for by a subsequently dishonoured cheque, it continues in force until it is properly revoked. It may be short-dated if it is not renewed immediately on the expiry of the previous licence.

A[61.8] A licence is required where a television set is used to receive BBC, ITV, satellite or cable television programmes, whether or not it is used for other purposes such as a home computer.

A[61.9]–[61.14] Concessions and exemptions are made under regulations for particular categories of persons. The number of sets that may be used on the same or different premises is also regulated by secondary legislation.

Sentencing
SC Guideline – TV licence payment evasion

TV licence payment evasion (Revised 2017)

A[61.15]

Communications act 2003, s 363

Effective from: 24 April 2017

Triable only summarily:

Maximum: Level 3 fine

Offence range: Band A fine–Band B fine

STEP 1
Determining the offence category

The Court should determine the offence category using the table below.

Category 1	Higher culpability and greater harm
Category 2	Higher culpability and lesser harm or lower culpability and greater harm
Category 3	Lower culpability and lesser harm

The court should determine the offender's culpability and the harm caused with reference only to the factors below. Where an offence does not fall squarely into a category, individual factors may require a degree of weighting before making an overall assessment and determining the appropriate offence category.

CULPABILITY demonstrated by one or more of the following:

Factors indicating higher culpability

- No attempt to obtain TV Licence
- Had additional subscription television service
- Attempts made to evade detection

Factors indicating lower culpability

- Accidental oversight or belief licence held (eg failure of financial arrangement)
- Confusion of responsibility
- Licence immediately obtained
- Significant efforts made to be licensed

HARM demonstrated by one or more of the following:

Factor indicating greater harm

- Prolonged period without TV licence (over 6 months unlicensed use)

Factors indicating lesser harm

- Short period without television licence (under 6 months unlicensed use)

STEP 2
Starting point and category range

Having determined the category at step one, the court should use the starting point to reach a sentence within the appropriate category range in the table below. The starting point applies to all offenders irrespective of plea or previous convictions.

Offence Category	Starting Point	Range
Category 1	Band B fine	Band B fine
Category 2	Band B fine	Band A fine–Band B fine
Category 3	Band A fine	Conditional discharge–Band A fine

The court should then consider adjustment for any aggravating or mitigating factors. The following is a **non-exhaustive** list of additional factual elements providing the context of the offence and factors relating to the offender. Identify whether any combination of these, or other relevant factors, should result in an upward or downward adjustment from the sentence arrived at so far.

Factors increasing seriousness

Statutory aggravating factors:

- Previous convictions, having regard to a) the **nature** of the offence to which the conviction relates and its **relevance** to the current offence; and b) the **time** that has elapsed since the conviction
- Offence committed whilst on bail

Other aggravating factors:

- Failure to comply with current court orders
- Offence committed on licence or post sentence supervision

Factors reducing seriousness or reflecting personal mitigation

- No previous convictions **or** no relevant/recent convictions
- Remorse, especially if evidenced by immediate purchase of television licence
- Good character and/or exemplary conduct
- Age and/or lack of maturity where it affects the responsibility of the offender
- Mental disorder or learning disability
- Offender experiencing significant financial hardship at time of offence due to **exceptional** circumstances

STEP 3
Consider any factors which indicate a reduction, such as assistance to the prosecution

The court should take into account sections 73 and 74 of the Serious Organised Crime and Police Act 2005 (assistance by defendants: reduction or review of sentence) and any other rule of law by virtue of which an offender may receive a discounted sentence in consequence of assistance given (or offered) to the prosecutor or investigator.

STEP 4
Reduction for guilty pleas

The court should take account of any potential reduction for a guilty plea in accordance with section 144 of the Criminal Justice Act 2003 and the *Guilty Plea* guideline.

STEP 5
Totality principle

If sentencing an offender for more than one offence, or where the offender is already serving a sentence, consider whether the total sentence is just and proportionate to the overall offending behaviour in accordance with the *Offences Taken into Consideration and Totality* guideline.

STEP 6
Compensation and ancillary orders

In all cases, the court should consider whether to make compensation and/or other ancillary orders.

STEP 7
Reasons

Section 174 of the Criminal Justice Act 2003 imposes a duty to give reasons for, and explain the effect of, the sentence.

A[62]

VAT evasion

Charge (VAT evasion)

A[62.1] **Being knowingly concerned in, or in the taking of steps with a view to, the fraudulent evasion of VAT by him or any other person.**

Value Added Tax Act, s 72(1)

Maximum penalty – 6 months' imprisonment and/or fine statutory maximum of three times the amount of the VTA, whichever is the greater (for offences committed on or after 12 March 2015, £20,000 or three times the amount of the VAT, whichever is the greater).

Crown Court – 7 years' imprisonment and unlimited fine.

Mode of trial

A[62.1A] See general notes at **D[4]** and SC Guideline at **A[36.10]** below.

Legal notes and definitions

A[62.2] **Evasion of VAT.** Includes a reference to the obtaining of –

(a) the payment of a VAT credit; or
(b) a refund under ss 35, 36 or 40 of this Act or s 22 of the 1983 Act; or
(c) a refund under any regulations made by virtue of s 13 (5); or
(d) a repayment under s 39;

and any reference in those subsections to the amount of VAT shall be construed –

(i) in relation to VAT itself or a Vat credit, as a reference to the aggregate of the amount (if any) falsely claimed by way of credit for input tax and the amount (if any) by which output tax was falsely understated, and
(ii) in relation to a refund or repayment falling within paragraph (b), (c) or (d) above, as a reference to the amount falsely claimed by way of refund or repayment.

A[62.3] **Knowingly.** Can include "deliberately looking the other way" (*Ross v Moss* [1965] 2 QB 396, (1965) 129 JP 537).

Evasion. Means a deliberate non-payment when payment is due. There is no need therefore for the Crown to prove an intention permanently to deprive (*R v Dealy* [1995] 1 WLR 658).

Sentencing
VAT evasion

A[62.4] See the SC definitive guidance on revenue fraud, reproduced at **A[36.10]** above.

A[63] Vehicle interference

Charge (Vehicle interference)

A[63.1] **Interfered with a motor vehicle or anything carried in or on the same with the intention that an offence of theft of the said motor vehicle or part of it or of anything carried in or on the said motor vehicle or an offence of taking and driving it away without consent should be committed**

Criminal Attempts Act 1981, s 9(1)

Maximum penalty – Fine level 4 and/or 3 months.

Legal notes and definitions

A[63.2] This offence applies to trailers. A trailer means a vehicle drawn by a motor vehicle.

A[63.3] **Interfere.** It will be for the court to decide whether a particular activity amounts to interference; simply keeping a vehicle under observation in the hope that an opportunity will arise to commit an offence would not be interference. In many cases the alleged activity would support a charge of attempting to steal which, unlike this offence is triable either way but this offence may be easier to prove because of the provision regarding 'intent'.

A[63.4] **Intent.** There must be evidence of an intention to commit theft of the vehicle, trailer, any parts of them or anything carried in or on them, or to commit the offence of unauthorised taking of the vehicle or trailer. The prosecution does not have to prove precisely which of these offences the accused intended. In some cases, for example, the prosecution would be unable to prove whether the intention was to take the vehicle, steal it, or steal goods from inside it.

A[63.5] **Motor vehicle.** Means a mechanically propelled vehicle intended or adapted for use on the road.

The test of whether a vehicle is 'intended or adapted for use on roads' is whether a reasonable person, looking at the vehicle, and forming a view as to its general user, would say the vehicle might well be used on the road: *Chief Constable of Avon and Somerset v Fleming* [1987] 1 All ER 318, [1987] RTR 378.

Sentencing

SC Guideline – Vehicle interference

Vehicle interference (Revised 2017)

A[63.6]

Criminal Attempts Act 1981, s 9

Effective from: 24 April 2017

Triable only summarily:

Maximum: Level 4 fine and/or 3 months

Offence range: Band A fine–12 weeks' custody

STEP 1
Determining the offence category

The Court should determine the offence category using the table below.

Category 1	Higher culpability and greater harm
Category 2	Higher culpability and lesser harm or lower culpability and greater harm
Category 3	Lower culpability and lesser harm

The court should determine the offender's culpability and the harm caused with reference only to the factors below. Where an offence does not fall squarely into a category, individual factors may require a degree of weighting before making an overall assessment and determining the appropriate offence category.

CULPABILITY demonstrated by one or more of the following:

Factors indicating higher culpability

- Leading role where offending is part of a group activity
- Targeting of particular vehicles and/or contents
- Planning

Factors indicating lower culpability

- All other cases

HARM demonstrated by one or more of the following:

Factors indicating greater harm

- Damage caused significant financial loss, inconvenience or distress to victim
- Vehicle left in a dangerous condition

Factors indicating lesser harm

- All other cases

STEP 2
Starting point and category range

Having determined the category at step one, the court should use the corresponding starting point to reach a sentence within the category range in the table below. The starting point applies to all offenders irrespective of plea or previous convictions.

Offence Category	Starting Point	Range
Category 1	High level community order	Medium level community order–12 weeks' custody
Category 2	Medium level community order	Band C fine–High level community order
Category 3	Band C fine	Band A fine–Low level community order

The court should then consider adjustment for any aggravating or mitigating factors. The following is a **non-exhaustive** list of additional factual elements providing the context of the offence and factors relating to the offender. Identify whether any combination of these, or other relevant factors, should result in an upward or downward adjustment from the sentence arrived at so far.

Factors increasing seriousness

Statutory aggravating factors:

- Previous convictions, having regard to a) the nature of the offence to which the conviction relates and its relevance to the current offence; and b) the time that has elapsed since the conviction
- Offence committed whilst on bail

Other aggravating factors:

- Failure to comply with current court orders
- Offence committed on licence or post sentence supervision
- Part of a spree
- Offence against emergency services vehicle

Factors reducing seriousness or reflecting personal mitigation

- No previous convictions or no relevant/recent convictions
- Good character and/or exemplary conduct
- Age and/or lack of maturity where it affects the responsibility of the offender
- Mental disorder or learning disability
- Sole or primary carer for dependent relatives

STEP 3
Consider any factors which indicate a reduction, such as assistance to the prosecution

The court should take into account sections 73 and 74 of the Serious Organised Crime and Police Act 2005 (assistance by defendants: reduction or review of sentence) and any other rule of law by virtue of which an offender may receive a discounted sentence in consequence of assistance given (or offered) to the prosecutor or investigator.

STEP 4
Reduction for guilty pleas

The court should take account of any potential reduction for a guilty plea in accordance with section 144 of the Criminal Justice Act 2003 and the *Guilty Plea* guideline.

STEP 5
Totality principle

If sentencing an offender for more than one offence, or where the offender is already serving a sentence, consider whether the total sentence is just and proportionate to the overall offending behaviour in accordance with the *Offences Taken into Consideration and Totality* guideline.

STEP 6
Compensation and ancillary orders

In all cases, the court should consider whether to make compensation and/or other ancillary orders, including disqualification from driving.

STEP 7
Reasons

Section 174 of the Criminal Justice Act 2003 imposes a duty to give reasons for, and explain the effect of, the sentence.

STEP 8
Consideration for time spent on bail

The court must consider whether to give credit for time spent on bail in accordance with section 240A of the Criminal Justice Act 2003.

A[63.7] See Table B at B[43.2] for available sentences.

A[64]
Vehicle registration/trade plate fraud

Charge (Vehicle registration/trade plate fraud)

A[64.1] Forging, or fraudulently altering, or fraudulently using, or fraudulently lending, or fraudulently allowing to be used by another person and of the following: a registration mark; a registration document; or a trade plate (including a replacement plate)

Vehicle Excise and Registration Act 1994, s 44.

Maximum penalty – Fine level 5 (for fines see **B[28]**).

Crown Court – Unlimited fine and 2 years' imprisonment. Triable either way.

Mode of trial

A[64.2] See the SC Guideline at A[64.4] below.

Note: Custody only available in Crown Court.

Legal notes and definitions

A[64.3] **Forgery.** The definition of forgery in the Forgery and Counterfeiting Act 1981, s 1, should be applied. Accordingly a person charged under s 44 with forgery of a licence will be guilty of an offence if (i) he made a false licence; (ii) with the intent that he or another should use it to include another to accept it as genuine; and (iii) by reason of so accepting it to do or not to do some act, to his own or another's prejudice as a result of such acceptance of the false licence as genuine in connection with the performance of any duty: *R v Macrae* (1993) 159 JP 359, [1994] Crim LR 363. In *Clifford v Bloom* [1977] RTR 351, where the terminal letter on registration plates was altered, 'forges' was defined as the making of a false registration mark upon a number plate with the intention that it should be regarded as genuine.

A[64.3A] **Fraudulently using.** The offence of fraudulently using a vehicle licence is only committed where there is evidence that the vehicle was being or had been used on a public road while displaying the offending licence. Accordingly, exhibiting an altered licence on private land, with an intention to use the vehicle with the licence in future, is insufficient to constitute an offence: *R v Johnson (Tony)* (1994) 158 JP 788, [1995] RTR 15, [1995] Crim LR 250, CA.

(Note, as part of the paperless initiative, tax discs no longer exist and they, together with trade licences and nil licences, were accordingly removed from s 44 of the VEA by the Finance Act 2014.)

A[64.4] **Fraudulently.** In *R v Terry* [1984] AC 374, [1984] 1 All ER 65, 78 Cr App Rep 101 'fraudulently' was given a wide meaning, following *Welham v DPP* [1961] AC 103, [1960] 1 All ER 805, 124 JP 280, not confined to economic loss but including the purpose of deceiving a police officer into thinking a motor car was properly licensed.

Sentencing
SC Guideline – Vehicle licence/registration fraud

A[64.5]

OFFENCE SERIOUSNESS (CULPABILITY AND HARM)
A. IDENTIFY THE APPROPRIATE STARTING POINT
Starting points based on first time offender pleading not guilty

Examples of nature of activity	Starting point	Range
Use of unaltered licence from another vehicle	Band B fine	Band B fine
Forged licence bought for own use, or forged/altered for own use	Band C fine	Band C fine
Use of number plates from another vehicle; or licence/number plates forged or altered for sale to another	High level community order	Medium level community order to Crown Court Note: custody only available in Crown Court

OFFENCE SERIOUSNESS (CULPABILITY AND HARM)
B. CONSIDER THE EFFECT OF AGGRAVATING AND MITIGATING FACTORS (OTHER THAN THOSE WITHIN EXAMPLES ABOVE)
Common aggravating and mitigating factors are identified at **B[45.2A]**. The following may be particularly relevant but **these lists are not exhaustive**

Factors indicating higher culpability	*Factors indicating lower culpability*
1. LGV/PSV/LGV/taxi etc	1. Licence/registration mark from another vehicle owned by defendant
2. Long-term fraudulent use	2. Short-term use
Factors indicating greater degree of harm	
1. High financial gain 2. Innocent victim deceived 3. Legitimate owner inconvenienced	

FORM A PRELIMINARY VIEW OF THE APPROPRIATE SENTENCE, THEN CONSIDER OFFENDER MITIGATION
Common factors are identified at **B[45.2A]**

CONSIDER A REDUCTION FOR A GUILTY PLEA

CONSIDER ANCILLARY ORDERS
Refer to **B[10]** for guidance on compensation and **Part B** for available ancillary orders

CONSIDER DISQUALIFICATION FROM DRIVING AND DEPRIVATION OF PROPERTY (including vehicle)

DECIDE SENTENCE
GIVE REASONS

A[65]

Vehicle taking, without consent

Charge (Vehicle taking, without consent)

A[65.1] **Without the consent of the owner or other lawful authority taking a conveyance, namely a [. . . . .] for his own use (or for another person's use)**

Theft Act 1968, s 12(1)

Note – It is also an offence to drive a conveyance, or allow oneself to be carried in or on it, if one knows the conveyance has been taken without such authority; the penalty for such offences is the same as for the offence of unauthorised taking.

Maximum penalty – 6 months' imprisonment and/or fine level 5 (for offences committed on or after 12 March 2015 an unlimited fine). Triable only by magistrates.

Motor vehicles. The defendant may be disqualified but no endorsement or penalty points are applicable.

Legal notes and definitions

A[65.2] Pedal cycles. The Theft Act 1968, s 12(5) applies a special provision if the conveyance is a pedal cycle. The maximum penalty is a fine up to level 3.

A[65.3] If the circumstances amounted to theft and theft is alleged, the notes at A[57.3] will apply.

A[65.4] Taking. An offence is committed if the conveyance is taken. 'Driving away' does not have to be proved but there must be evidence of some movement and that the vehicle was used as a conveyance. Accordingly, the moving of a motor car round the corner as a practical joke to lead the owner to believe it had been stolen was not an offence as it was not established that anyone rode inside it (*R v Stokes* [1983] RTR 59, [1982] Crim LR 695, CA). But where a defendant allowed a vehicle to roll down a hill by climbing in it and releasing the handbrake, he was guilty of the offence (*R v Bow* [1977] RTR 6, 64 Cr App Rep 54, CA). It would be otherwise if he did not get inside the vehicle. It is not a defence that the conveyance was stolen, as opposed to being taken. Nor is it a defence that the vehicle had been previously taken (*DPP v Spriggs* [1994] RTR 1, 157 JP 1143, [1993] Crim LR 622).

The offence does not require the propelling of the conveyance 'in its own element'; thus a conviction was upheld where a defendant had loaded an inflatable rubber dinghy on a trailer which he then drove away: *R v Pearce* [1973] Crim LR 321.

A[65.5] Conveyance. Means a conveyance constructed or adapted for carrying one or more persons by land, water or air. It does not include a conveyance which can only be controlled by a person not carried in or on it.

A[65.6] Motor vehicle. A motor vehicle is a mechanically propelled vehicle intended or adapted for use on a road.

The test of whether a vehicle is 'intended or adapted for use on roads' is whether a reasonable person, looking at the vehicle, and forming a view as to its general user, would say the vehicle might well be used on the road: *Chief Constable of Avon and Somerset v Fleming* [1987] 1 All ER 318, [1987] RTR 378.

A[65.7] Owner. Includes a person in possession of the conveyance under a hiring or hire-purchase agreement.

A[65.8] **Owner's consent.** Where the owner is induced by fraud to part with possession of his vehicle, no offence under this section has been committed (*Whittaker v Campbell* [1984] QB 318, [1983] 3 All ER 582). The owner has in fact consented even though in the civil law he may have a remedy against the fraudster.

A[65.9] No offence was committed where consent was obtained by a false pretence as to the destination and purpose of the journey (*R v Peart* [1970] 2 QB 672, [1970] 2 All ER 823, CA). Nor where consent of an owner to allow a vehicle to be hired was obtained by the fraudulent misrepresentation of the hirer as to his identity and the holding of a full driving licence.

A[65.10] **Reduction of charge from theft of conveyance.** If a defendant is tried in a magistrates' court for stealing a conveyance, the court cannot reduce the charge to this offence of taking the conveyance.

A[65.11]–[65.15] **Time Limits.** Like many summary road traffic offences, proceedings may be commenced within six months of the day the prosecution had knowledge of the offence subject to an overall time limit of three years from the commission of the offence.

A[65.16] **Successful defence.** If the court is satisfied the defendant acted in the belief that he had lawful authority, or that the owner would have consented if the owner knew the circumstances, then he must be acquitted. The defendant only has to raise the defence. The absence of lawful authority or the owner's consent is an essential ingredient of the offence and it remains the prosecutor's duty to prove the allegation beyond a reasonable doubt.

A[65.17] **Aggravated vehicle-taking.** See A[66].

Sentencing
SC Guideline – Vehicle taking, without consent

Vehicle taking, without consent (Revised 2017)

A[65.18]

Theft Act 1968, s 12

Effective from: 24 April 2017

Triable only summarily:

Maximum: Unlimited fine and/or 6 months

Offence range: Band B fine–26 weeks' custody

STEP 1
Determining the offence category

The Court should determine the offence category using the table below.

Category 1	Higher culpability and greater harm
Category 2	Higher culpability and lesser harm or lower culpability and greater harm
Category 3	Lower culpability and lesser harm

The court should determine the offender's culpability and the harm caused with reference only to the factors below. Where an offence does not fall squarely into a category, individual factors may require a degree of weighting before making an overall assessment and determining the appropriate offence category.

CULPABILITY demonstrated by one or more of the following:

Factors indicating higher culpability

- A leading role where offending is part of a group activity
- Involvement of others through coercion, intimidation or exploitation
- Sophisticated nature of offence/significant planning
- Abuse of position of power or trust or responsibility
- Commission of offence in association with or to further other criminal activity

Factors indicating lower culpability

- Performed limited function under direction
- Involved through coercion, intimidation or exploitation
- Limited awareness or understanding of offence
- Exceeding authorised use of e.g. employer's or relative's vehicle
- Retention of hire car for short period beyond return date

HARM demonstrated by one or more of the following:

Factors indicating greater harm

- Vehicle later burnt
- Vehicle belonging to elderly/disabled person
- Emergency services vehicle
- Medium to large goods vehicle
- Passengers carried
- Damage to lock/ignition
- Vehicle taken from private premises

Factors indicating lesser harm

- All other cases

STEP 2
Starting point and category range

Having determined the category at step one, the court should use the appropriate starting point to reach a sentence within the category range in the table below. The starting point applies to all offenders irrespective of plea or previous convictions.

Level of seriousness	Starting Point	Range	Disqualification
Category 1	High level community order	Medium level community order–26 weeks' custody	Consider disqualification 9 to 12 months (Extend if imposing immediate custody)
Category 2	Medium level community order	Low level community order–High level community order	Consider disqualification 5 to 8 months
Category 3	Low level community order	Band B fine–Medium level community order	Consider disqualification

- **Extend any disqualification if imposing immediate custody**

The court should then consider further adjustment for any aggravating or mitigating factors. The following is a **non-exhaustive** list of additional factual elements providing the context of the offence and factors relating to the offender. Identify whether any combination of these, or other relevant factors, should result in an upward or downward adjustment from the sentence arrived at so far.

Factors increasing seriousness

Statutory aggravating factors:

- Previous convictions, having regard to a) the nature of the offence to which the conviction relates and its relevance to the current offence; and b) the time that has elapsed since the conviction
- Offence committed whilst on bail

Other aggravating factors:

- Failure to comply with current court orders
- Offence committed on licence or post sentence supervision

Factors reducing seriousness or reflecting personal mitigation

- No previous convictions or no relevant/recent convictions
- Remorse
- Good character and/or exemplary conduct
- Age and/ or lack of maturity where it affects the responsibility of the offender
- Mental disorder or learning disability
- Sole or primary carer for dependent relatives
- Co-operation with the investigation

STEP 3
Consider any factors which indicate a reduction, such as assistance to the prosecution

The court should take into account sections 73 and 74 of the Serious Organised Crime and Police Act 2005 (assistance by defendants: reduction or review of sentence) and any other rule of law by virtue of which an offender may receive a discounted sentence in consequence of assistance given (or offered) to the prosecutor or investigator.

STEP 4
Reduction for guilty pleas

The court should take account of any potential reduction for a guilty plea in accordance with section 144 of the Criminal Justice Act 2003 and the *Guilty Plea* guideline.

STEP 5
Totality principle

If sentencing an offender for more than one offence, or where the offender is already serving a sentence, consider whether the total sentence is just and proportionate to the overall offending behaviour in accordance with the *Offences Taken into Consideration and Totality* guideline.

STEP 6
Compensation and ancillary orders

In all cases, the court should consider whether to make compensation and/or other ancillary orders, including disqualification from driving.

STEP 7
Reasons

Section 174 of the Criminal Justice Act 2003 imposes a duty to give reasons for, and explain the effect of, the sentence.

STEP 8
Consideration for time spent on bail

The court must consider whether to give credit for time spent on bail in accordance with section 240A of the Criminal Justice Act 2003.

A[65.19] Available sentences. See Table B at B[4.2].

A[65.20] Disqualification may be ordered in the case of a motor vehicle (no points available).

A[66]

(1) Vehicle-taking (aggravated) – damage caused to property other than the vehicle in accident or damage caused to the vehicle (ss 12A(2)(c) and (d)) (2) Vehicle-taking (aggravated) – dangerous driving or accident causing injury (ss 12A(2)(a) and (b))

Charges (Aggravated vehicle taking)

A[66.1] **Taking a mechanically propelled vehicle without the owner's consent or other lawful authority (or driving, or allowing oneself to be carried in or on it, knowing it to have been taken without the owner's consent etc) and at any time after it had been unlawfully taken (whether by him or another) and before it was recovered:**

(a) **the vehicle was driven dangerously on a road or other public place;**
(b) **owing to the driving of the vehicle, an accident occurred by which injury was caused to any person;**
(c) **owing to the driving of the vehicle an accident occurred by which damage was caused to any property, other than the vehicle;**
(d) **damage was caused to the vehicle.**

Theft Act 1968, s 12A(1)

Maximum penalty – 6 months' imprisonment and/or fine level 5 (for offences committed on or after 12 March 2015 an unlimited fine). Specified violent offence under Sch 15, Part 1, CJA 2003 if the offence involves an accident causing the death of any person.

Mandatory disqualification for one year and endorsement. Penalty points 3–11.

Crown Court – 2 years' imprisonment (14 years where death has been caused) and unlimited fine.

Mode of trial

A[66.2] See the SC Guideline at A[66.16] and A[66.17] below.

Where no allegation is made other than damage to property or the vehicle concerned, the offence is triable only before magistrates where the total value of the damage concerned does not exceed £5,000 (*R v Kelly* [2001] RTR 45, CA). The value of the damage to property other than the vehicle involved in the offence is what it would probably have cost to buy the property in the open market at the time of the offence. The value of the damage to the vehicle taken is assessed in a similar manner to that where property has been damaged. Otherwise the offence is triable either way.

A[66.3]–[66.4] For the procedure where it is not clear whether the damage is above or below £5,000, see A[18.4].

Legal notes and definitions

A[66.5] Mechanically propelled vehicle ie a vehicle intended or adapted for use on a road. This includes, inter alia, a Mantis City electric scooter (*DPP v King* [2008] EWHC 447 (Admin), 172 JP 401).

A[66.6] Vehicle recovered ie when it is restored to its owner or to other lawful possession or custody.

A[66.7] Owner includes a person in possession under a hiring or hire-purchase agreement.

A[66.8] **Dangerous driving**

A vehicle is driven dangerously if it is driven in any way which falls far below what would be expected of a competent and careful driver and it would be obvious to a competent and careful driver that driving the vehicle in that way would be dangerous.

A[66.8A] **'Owing to the driving of the vehicle'**

It was held in *R v Marsh* [1997] 1 Cr App R 67, CA that it was not a defence that the accident occurred through no fault of the vehicle taker, but this decision was overruled in *R v Taylor* [2016] UKSC 5, [2016] 1 WLR 500, [2016] 1 Cr App Rep 423.

> '28 The one respect in which section 12A imposes strict liability is that the offence may be committed not only by the driver but by anyone else who was party to the basic offence under section 12(1) and is in or in the immediate vicinity of the vehicle at the time of the dangerous driving, injury or damage. That emerges unequivocally from the statutory language. But it is important to note that it is also a rational response to the mischief of the enactment, which has close analogies to the principle underlying cases of strict liability identified by Lord Diplock in *Sweet v Parsley* [1970] AC 132. The Act treats someone who has been party to the taking of a vehicle without authority as having control over it thereafter. He is in a position to take positive steps to ensure that it is driven safely and not in a manner which causes personal injury or damage to property. That is the rationale of the proviso that he must have been in or in the immediate vicinity of the vehicle at the time when the dangerous driving, injury or damage occurred. His responsibility continues to be engaged while he is present. 29 However, it is one thing for the legislature to make a person who has taken a car without authority responsible for the fault of another person who drives it in his presence. It is another thing altogether to make him responsible for personal injury or damage which could not have been prevented, because it occurred without fault or was entirely the fault of the victim. That would be a sufficiently remarkable extension of the scope of the strict liability to require clear language, such as the draftsman has actually employed to impose liability on a taker who is not the driver. There is no such language in section 12A. Of the four aggravating circumstances identified in subsection (2), (a) expressly imports a requirement of fault (the car must have been driven dangerously), while (b), (c) and (d) contain nothing which expressly excludes such a requirement. As Lord Reid explained in *Sweet v Parsley* [1970] AC 132, 149 d–e , this difference cannot itself be enough to make (b), (c) and (d) operate independent of fault. On the contrary, in the case of (b) and (c), it is implicit in the requirement that the accident must have occurred "owing to the driving of the vehicle", that there will have been something wrong with the driving. As this court pointed out in *R v Hughes* [2013] 1 WLR 2461, the driving cannot be said to have caused the accident if it merely explained how the vehicle came to be in the place where the accident occurred (per Lord Sumption JSC).'

A[66.9] **Road or public place.** See C[22.5], C[22.6].

A[66.10] **Defence.** The defendant is not guilty of this offence if he proves that, as regards any such proven driving, injury or damage as the offence refers to, either:

(a) that the driving accident or damage occurred before he committed the basic offence ; or

(b) that he was neither in, nor on, nor in the immediate vicinity of the vehicle when that driving etc occurred: Theft Act 1968, s 12A(3).

The standard of proof is on a balance of probabilities: *R v Carr-Briant* (1943) 107 JP 167.

A[66.11]–[66.15] Reduction of charge/alternative verdict. The court may find the defendant guilty of the basic offence if it decides to dismiss the aggravated version. (*H v Liverpool City Youth Court* [2001] Crim LR 897)

Sentencing

SC Guideline – Vehicle taking (aggravated) – Damage caused to property etc – ss 12A(2)(c) and (d)

A[66.16] Must endorse and disqualify for at least 12 months

Must disqualify for at least two years if offender has had two or more disqualifications for periods of 56 days or more in preceding 3 years – consult your legal adviser for further guidance

If there is a delay in sentencing after conviction, consider interim disqualification

OFFENCE SERIOUSNESS (CULPABILITY AND HARM) A. IDENTIFY THE APPROPRIATE STARTING POINT Starting points based on first time offender pleading not guilty		
Examples of nature of activity	Starting point	Range
Relative's vehicle; exceeding authorised use of eg. employer's vehicle; retention of hire car beyond return date; minor damage to taken vehicle	Medium level community order	Low level community order to high level community order
Greater damage to taken vehicle and/or moderate damage to another vehicle and/or property	High level community order	Medium level community order to 12 weeks custody
Vehicle taken as part of burglary or from private premises; severe damage	18 weeks custody	12 to 26 weeks custody (Crown Court if damage over £5,000)

OFFENCE SERIOUSNESS (CULPABILITY AND HARM) B. CONSIDER THE EFFECT OF AGGRAVATING AND MITIGATING FACTORS (OTHER THAN THOSE WITHIN EXAMPLES ABOVE) Common aggravating and mitigating factors are identified at B[45.2A]. The following may be particularly relevant but these lists are not exhaustive	
Factors indicating greater degree of harm 1. Vehicle deliberately damaged/destroyed 2. Offender under influence of alcohol/drugs	*Factors indicating lower culpability* 1. Misunderstanding with owner 2. Damage resulting from actions of another (where this does not provide a defence)
Factors indicating greater degree of harm 1. Passengers carried 2. Vehicle belonging to elderly or disabled person	

3. Emergency services vehicle 4. Medium to large goods vehicle 5. Damage caused in moving traffic accident	

FORM A PRELIMINARY VIEW OF THE APPROPRIATE SENTENCE, THEN CONSIDER OFFENDER MITIGATION Common factors are identified at **B**[45.2A]
CONSIDER A REDUCTION FOR A GUILTY PLEA
CONSIDER ANCILLARY ORDERS, INCLUDING COMPENSATION Refer to **B**[10] for guidance on compensation and **Part B** for available ancillary orders
DECIDE SENTENCE **GIVE REASONS**

SC Guideline – Vehicle taking (aggravated) – Dangerous driving or accident causing injury – ss 12A(2)(a) and (b)

A[66.17] Must endorse and disqualify for at least 12 months

Must disqualify for at least two years if offender has had two or more disqualifications for periods of 56 days or more in preceding 3 years – consult your legal adviser for further guidance

If there is a delay in sentencing after conviction, consider interim disqualification

OFFENCE SERIOUSNESS (CULPABILITY AND HARM) **A. IDENTIFY THE APPROPRIATE STARTING POINT** Starting points based on first time offender pleading not guilty		
Examples of nature of activity	**Starting point**	**Range**
Taken vehicle involved in single incident of bad driving where little or no damage or risk of personal injury	High level community order	Medium level community order to 12 weeks custody
Taken vehicle involved in incident(s) involving excessive speed or showing off, especially on busy roads or in built-up area	18 weeks custody	12 to 26 weeks custody
Taken vehicle involved in prolonged bad driving involving deliberate disregard for safety of others	Crown Court	Crown Court

OFFENCE SERIOUSNESS (CULPABILITY AND HARM) **B. CONSIDER THE EFFECT OF AGGRAVATING AND MITIGATING FACTORS (OTHER THAN THOSE WITHIN EXAMPLES ABOVE)** Common aggravating and mitigating factors are identified at **B**[45.2A]. The following may be particularly relevant but **these lists are not exhaustive**	
Factors indicating greater degree of harm 1. Disregarding warnings of others 2. Evidence of alcohol or drugs	

3. Carrying out other tasks while driving 4. Carrying passengers or heavy load 5. Tiredness 6. Trying to avoid arrest 7. Aggressive driving, such as driving much too close to vehicle in front, inappropriate attempts to overtake, or cutting in after overtaking	
Factors indicating greater degree of harm 1. Injury to others 2. Damage to other vehicles or property	
FORM A PRELIMINARY VIEW OF THE APPROPRIATE SENTENCE, THEN CONSIDER OFFENDER MITIGATION Common factors are identified at **B[45.2A]**	
CONSIDER A REDUCTION FOR A GUILTY PLEA	
CONSIDER ORDERING DISQUALIFICATION UNTIL APPROPRIATE DRIVING TEST PASSED **CONSIDER ANCILLARY ORDERS, INCLUDING COMPENSATION** Refer to **B[10]** for guidance on compensation and **Part B** for available ancillary orders	
DECIDE SENTENCE **GIVE REASONS**	

A[67]

Violent disorder

Charge (Violent disorder)

A[67.1] Being one of three or more persons present together and using or threatening unlawful violence so that the conduct taken together is such as would cause a person of reasonable firmness present at the scene to fear for his personal safety

Public Order Act 1986, s 2(1)

Maximum penalty – 6 months' imprisonment and/or fine level 5 (for offences committed on or after 12 March 2015 an unlimited fine). Triable either way. Specified violent offence under Sch 15, Part 1, CJA 2003.

Crown Court – 5 years' imprisonment and unlimited fine.

Mode of trial

A[67.2] Cases of violent disorder should generally be considered for trial on indictment. See SC Guideline at **A[67.10]** below.

Legal notes and definitions

A[67.3] **The charge.** Only one offence is created.

A[67.4] **Three or more persons.** The defendants need not be using or threatening violence simultaneously. The term 'present together' meant no more than being present in the same place at the same time; the prosecution are not required to prove a common purpose among those using or threatening violence: *R v NW* [2010] EWCA Crim 404, [2010] 2 Cr App Rep 54, [2010] Crim LR 723.

A[67.5] **Violence** does not include violence justified by law (eg self-defence or prevention of crime) but apart from that includes violent conduct towards property or persons and is not restricted to conduct causing or intended to cause injury or damage but includes any other violent conduct (for example, throwing at or towards a person a missile of a kind capable of causing injury which does not hit or falls short).

A[67.6] **Person of reasonable firmness** need not actually be or be likely to be, present at the scene. See **A[2.6]**.

A[67.7] **Intent.** A person may be guilty only if he intends to use or threaten violence, or is aware that his conduct may be violent or threaten violence.

A[67.8] **Intoxication.** A person whose awareness is impaired by intoxication shall be taken to be aware of that of which he would be aware if not intoxicated, unless he shows that his intoxication was not self-induced, or that it was caused solely by the taking of a substance in the course of medical treatment. 'Intoxication' may be caused by drink, drugs or other means.

A[67.9] **Violent disorder** may be committed in a public or private place.

Sentencing
SC Guideline – Violent disorder

A[67.10]

OFFENCE SERIOUSNESS (CULPABILITY AND HARM)
A. IDENTIFY THE APPROPRIATE STARTING POINT Starting points based on first time offender pleading not guilty
These offences should normally be dealt with in the Crown Court. However, there may be rare cases involving missile violence or threats of violence leading to no or minor injury, with few people involved and no weapon or missiles, in which a custodial sentence within the jurisdiction of a magistrates' court may be appropriate.

A[67.11] **Available sentences.** See Table A at B[43.1A].

A[68]
Voyeurism

Charge (Voyeurism)

A[68.1] **For the purpose of obtaining sexual gratification, observed another person doing a private act, and he knows that the other person does not consent to being observed for sexual gratification.**

Sexual Offences Act 2003, s 67(1)

Operates equipment with the intention of enabling another to observe, for sexual gratification, a third person (B) doing a private act and know that B does not consent to his operating equipment with that intention.

Sexual Offences Act 2003, s 67(2)

Records another person (B) doing a private act with the intention that he (A) or a third person will, for the purpose of obtaining sexual gratification, look at an image of B doing the act, and A knows that B does not consent to his recording the act with that intention.

Sexual Offences Act 2003, s 67(3)

Installs equipment, or constructs or adapts a structure or part of a structure, with the intention of enabling himself or another person to commit an offence under subsection (1).

Sexual Offences Act 2003, s 67(4)

Operates equipment beneath the clothing of another person (B), and does so with the intention of enabling him (A) or another person (C), for a purpose mentioned in subsection (3)*, to observe B's genitals or buttocks (whether exposed or covered with underwear), or the underwear covering B's genitals or buttocks, in circumstances where the genitals, buttocks or underwear would not otherwise be visible, and A does so without B's consent, and without reasonably believing that B consents.**

Sexual Offences Act 2003, s 67A(1)

Records an image beneath the clothing of another person (B), and the image is of B's genitals or buttocks (whether exposed or covered with underwear), or the underwear covering B's genitals or buttocks, in circumstances where the genitals, buttocks or underwear would not otherwise be visible, and does so with the intention that he (A) or another person (C) will look at the image for a purpose mentioned in subsection (3)*, and A does so without B's consent, and without reasonably believing that B consents.**

Sexual Offences Act 2003, s 67A(2)

*The purposes referred to in s 67A(3) are: (a) obtaining sexual gratification (whether for A or C); (b) humiliating, alarming or distressing B.

** These offences were inserted by the Voyeurism (Offences) Act 2019 and criminalise the conduct commonly known as 'up-skirting', which previously had to be charged as outraging public decency.

Maximum penalty – 6 months' imprisonment and/or fine level 5 (for offences committed on or after 12 March 2015 an unlimited fine). Triable either way. Specified sexual offence under Sch 15, Part 2, CJA 2003.

Crown Court – 2 years' imprisonment and unlimited fine.

Mode of trial

A[68.2] See the SC Guideline at A[68.5] below.

Legal notes and definitions

A[68.3] The purpose of obtaining sexual gratification forms part of the relevant act; thus, where a defendant was unfit to plead and the jury had to determine whether or not he had committed the relevant act, it was necessary for the jury to find both deliberate observation and the purpose of sexual gratification: *R v B* [2012] EWCA Crim 770, [2012] 3 All ER 1093, [2013] 1 WLR 499.

For the purpose of this offence 'private act' means an act carried out in a place which, in the circumstances, would reasonably be expected to provide privacy, and the person's genitals, buttocks or breasts are exposed or covered only in underwear; or the person is using a lavatory; or the person is doing a sexual act that is of a kind not ordinarily done in public (the offence does not extend solely to 'ogling male breasts'): *R v Bassett* [2008] EWCA Crim 1174.

A[68.4] Definitions. See the notes at the end of the SC Guideline at A[68.5] below. "Private Act" and "structure" are defined by s 68.

There must be a private act in order for offences of voyeurism to be committed. Section 68 is then concerned to bring within the meaning of the private act those parts of the body for which people conventionally expect or normally expect privacy. The clear intention of Parliament therefore was to mean the female "breast" or breasts" and not the male breast (see the notes to A[68.5] below)

"Observes" and "image" are further defined by s 79.

For "consent" see s 74.

Sentencing

A[68.5] In accordance with s 80 of and Sch 3 to the Sexual Offences Act 2003, automatic notification requirements apply upon conviction to an offender aged 18 or over where:

(1) a victim was under 18; or
(2) a term of imprisonment or a community sentence of at least 12 months is imposed.

For notification requirements generally, see A[52.15].

NB: A community order with a requirement to carry out 120 hours unpaid work was not a community sentence of at least 12 months for the purposes of Sch 3 and therefore the offender was not subject to the notification requirements of the legislation (*R v Odam* [2008] EWCA Crim 1087).

Sentencing
SC Guideline – Voyeurism

A[68.6] This guideline is taken from the SC's definitive guideline *Sexual Offences Act 2003* effective from 1 April 2014.

Triable either way

Maximum: 2 years' custody

Offence range: Fine – 18 months' custody

For convictions on or after such date (irrespective of the date of commission of the offence), these are specified offences for the purposes of section 226A (extended sentence for certain violent or sexual offences) of the Criminal Justice Act 2003.

STEP ONE
Determining the offence category

The court should determine the offence category using the table below.

Category 1	Raised harm **and** raised culpability
Category 2	Raised harm **or** raised culpability
Category 3	Voyeurism **without** raised harm or culpability factors present

The court should determine culpability and harm caused or intended, by reference **only** to the factors below, which comprise the principal factual elements of the offence. Where an offence does not fall squarely into a category, individual factors may require a degree of weighting before making an overall assessment and determining the appropriate offence category.

Factors indicating raised harm	**Factors indicating raised culpability**
Image(s) available to be viewed by others	Significant degree of planning
Victim observed or recorded in their own home or residence	Image(s) recorded
	Abuse of trust
	Specific or previous targeting of a particularly vulnerable victim
	Commercial exploitation and/or motivation
	Offence racially or religiously aggravated
	Offence motivated by, or demonstrating, hostility to the victim based on his or her sexual orientation (or presumed sexual orientation) or transgender identity (or presumed transgender identity)
	Offence motivated by, or demonstrating, hostility to the victim based on his or her disability (or presumed disability)

STEP TWO
Starting point and category range

Having determined the category, the court should use the corresponding starting points to reach a sentence within the category range on the next page. The starting point applies to all offenders irrespective of plea or previous convictions. Having determined the starting point, step two allows further adjustment for aggravating or mitigating features, set out on the next page.

A case of particular gravity, reflected by multiple features of culpability or harm in step one, could merit upward adjustment from the starting point before further adjustment for aggravating or mitigating features, set out on the next page.

Where there is a sufficient prospect of rehabilitation, a community order with a sex offender treatment programme requirement under section 202 of the Criminal Justice Act 2003 can be a proper alternative to a short or moderate length custodial sentence.

Category 1	**Starting point** 26 weeks' custody
	Category range 12 weeks' – 18 months' custody
Category 2	**Starting point** High level community order
	Category range Medium level community order – 26 weeks' custody
Category 3	**Starting point** Medium level community order
	Band A fine – High level community order

The table below contains a **non-exhaustive** list of additional factual elements providing the context of the offence and factors relating to the offender. Identify whether any combination of these, or other relevant factors, should result in an upward or downward adjustment from the starting point. **In particular, relevant recent convictions are likely to result in an upward adjustment.** In some cases, having considered these factors, it may be appropriate to move outside the identified category range.

When sentencing **category 2 offences**, the court should also consider the custody threshold as follows:

- has the custody threshold been passed?
- if so, is it unavoidable that a custodial sentence be imposed?
- if so, can that sentence be suspended?

When sentencing **category 3 offences**, the court should also consider the community order threshold as follows:

- has the community order threshold been passed?

Aggravating factors	Any steps taken to prevent victim reporting an incident, obtaining assistance and/or from assisting or supporting the prosecution
Statutory aggravating factors	Attempts to dispose of or conceal evidence
Previous convictions, having regard to a) the nature of the offence to which the conviction relates and its relevance to the current offence; and b) the time that has elapsed since the conviction	**Mitigating factors**
Offence committed whilst on bail	No previous convictions or no relevant/recent convictions
Other aggravating factors	Remorse
Location of offence	Previous good character and/or exemplary conduct*
Timing of offence	Age and/or lack of maturity where it affects the responsibility of the offender
Failure to comply with current court orders	Mental disorder or learning disability, particularly where linked to the commission of the offence

Offence committed whilst on licence	Demonstration of steps taken to address offending behaviour
Distribution of images, whether or not for gain	
Placing images where there is the potential for a high volume of viewers	
Period over which victim observed	
Period over which images were made or distributed	

* Previous good character/exemplary conduct is different from having no previous convictions. The more serious the offence, the less the weight which should normally be attributed to this factor. Where previous good character/exemplary conduct has been used to facilitate the offence, this mitigation should not normally be allowed and such conduct may constitute an aggravating factor.

STEP THREE
Consider any factors which indicate a reduction, such as assistance to the prosecution

The court should take into account sections 73 and 74 of the Serious Organised Crime and Police Act 2005 (assistance by defendants: reduction or review of sentence) and any other rule of law by virtue of which an offender may receive a discounted sentence in consequence of assistance given (or offered) to the prosecutor or investigator.

STEP FOUR
Reduction for guilty pleas

The court should take account of any potential reduction for a guilty plea in accordance with section 144 of the Criminal Justice Act 2003 and the *Guilty Plea* guideline.

STEP FIVE
Dangerousness

The court should consider whether having regard to the criteria contained in Chapter 5 of Part 12 of the Criminal Justice Act 2003 it would be appropriate to award an extended sentence (section 226A).

STEP SIX
Totality principle

If sentencing an offender for more than one offence, or where the offender is already serving a sentence, consider whether the total sentence is just and proportionate to the overall offending behaviour.

STEP SEVEN
Ancillary orders

The court must consider whether to make any ancillary orders. The court must also consider what other requirements or provisions may automatically apply. Further information is included on page 303.

STEP EIGHT
Reasons

Section 174 of the Criminal Justice Act 2003 imposes a duty to give reasons for, and explain the effect of, the sentence.

STEP NINE
Consideration for time spent on bail

The court must consider whether to give credit for time spent on bail in accordance with section 240A of the Criminal Justice Act 2003.

A[69]

Witness intimidation

Charge 1 (Witness intimidation)

A[69.1] Did intimidate [. . . . .] **knowing or believing [. . . . .] is assisting an investigation/is a witness or potential witness in proceedings with the intention that the investigation/course of justice would be interfered/perverted/obstructed**

Criminal Justice and Public Order Act 1994, s 51(1)

See Charge 2 for penalty.

Charge 2 (Witness intimidation)

A[69.2] Did harm or threaten with harm [. . . . .] intending to harm him knowing or believing that [. . . . .] has assisted in an investigation or has given evidence in proceedings for an offence because he believes/ knows that assistance or evidence was given

Criminal Justice and Public Order Act 1994, s 51(2)

Maximum penalty – 6 months' imprisonment and/or fine level 5 (for offences committed on or after 12 March 2015 an unlimited fine). Triable either way.

Crown Court – maximum 5 years' imprisonment.

Note that similar offences carrying the same maximum penalty may now be charged under the Criminal Justice and Police Act 2001, ss 39 and 40. These offences are specifically aimed at incidents not covered by CJPOA 1994, s 51 and cover both civil and criminal proceedings.

Mode of trial

A[69.3] See the SC Guideline at **A[69.11]** below.

Legal notes and definitions

A[69.4] A person does an act to another person with the intention of intimidating/harming not only when it is done directly but also when it is done to a third party with the same intention. The threat may be at a distance, eg over the telephone: *DPP v Mills* [1997] QB 300, [1996] 3 WLR 1093.

In *R v Patrascu* [2004] EWCA Crim 2417, [2014] 4 All ER 1066, [2005] 1 WLR 3344, [2005] 1 Cr App R 35 it was held that 'to intimidate' normally means 'to put someone in fear', another meaning is 'to force to or deter from some action by threats of violence'. However, the person intended to be intimidated must in fact be intimidated: *R v ZN* [2013] EWCA Crim 989, [2013] 4 All ER 331, [2013] 1 WLR 3900, [2013] 2 Cr App R 25 (not following *Patrascu* in this respect). (If the victim is sufficiently steadfast not to be intimidated a charge of attempt remains possible.)

It was not enough to describe the defendant's behaviour as objectively intimidating, but rather, there had to have been an act that had intimidated and had been intended to intimidate the victim: *R v Mahmood* [2007] EWCA Crim 13. The requirement of actual intimidation is inconsistent, however, with *Patrascu*, and it is submitted that the former authority is to be preferred on this point.

A[69.5] Harm may be financial/physical to a person or property.

A[69.6] **Intention.** The intention or motive required for the two charges need not be the only or predominant motive or intention with which the act is done or threatened. A threat to harm a witness relayed via a third party constitutes an offence under this section. If a threat to harm a witness takes place within one year after the trial the prosecution do not have to prove a connection between the threat and the trial: *A-G's Reference (No 1 of 1999)*. If the prosecution can prove the act/threat and the defendant's knowledge/belief in the circumstances then the resultant motive/intention shall be presumed unless the contrary is proven.

A[69.7] **Knowingly and ECHR.** Section 51(7) of the CJPOA 1994 provides that if the defendant knowingly commits an act of intimidation it will be presumed that the defendant intended to interfere with the course of justice unless otherwise proven. The fact that the legislation imposes a reverse burden of proof on the defence is both justiciable and proportionate in ECHR terms having regard to the stated aims of the legislation and *Attorney General's Reference (No 1 of 2004)* [2004] EWCA Crim 1025, [2004] 1 WLR 2111.

A[69.8] **Witness** includes jurors or potential jurors in the Crown Court.

A[69.9] **Investigation into an offence** means an investigation by police or such other person charged with the duty of investigating offences or charging offenders. The prosecution must prove that there was an investigation under way, not merely that the defendant believed there to be one: *R v Singh* [2000] 1 Cr App Rep 31, [1999] Crim LR 681, CA.

A[69.10] **Offence** includes an alleged or suspected offence.

Sentencing
SC Guideline – Witness intimidation

A[69.11] Where offence committed in a domestic context, see SC Definitive Guideline: "Overarching Principles: Domestic Violence".

OFFENCE SERIOUSNESS (CULPABILITY AND HARM) A. IDENTIFY THE APPROPRIATE STARTING POINT Starting points based on first time offender pleading not guilty		
Examples of nature of activity	**Starting point**	**Range**
Sudden outburst in chance encounter	6 weeks custody	Medium level community order to 18 weeks custody
Conduct amounting to a threat; staring at, approaching or following witnesses; talking about the case; trying to alter or stop evidence	18 weeks custody	12 weeks custody to Crown Court
Threats of violence to witnesses and/or their families; deliberately seeking out witnesses	Crown Court	Crown Court

OFFENCE SERIOUSNESS (CULPABILITY AND HARM) B. CONSIDER THE EFFECT OF AGGRAVATING AND MITIGATING FACTORS (OTHER THAN THOSE WITHIN EXAMPLES ABOVE) Common aggravating and mitigating factors are identified at B[45.2A]. The following may be particularly relevant but these lists are not exhaustive	
Factors indicating higher culpability 1. Breach of bail conditions	

2. Offender involves others	
Factors indicating greater degree of harm 1. Detrimental impact on administration of justice 2. Contact made at or in vicinity of victim's home	
FORM A PRELIMINARY VIEW OF THE APPROPRIATE SENTENCE, THEN CONSIDER OFFENDER MITIGATION Common factors are identified at B[45.2A]	
CONSIDER A REDUCTION FOR A GUILTY PLEA	
CONSIDER ANCILLARY ORDERS, INCLUDING COMPENSATION Refer to **B[10]** for guidance on compensation and **Part B** for available ancillary orders	
DECIDE SENTENCE **GIVE REASONS**	

A[70]

Wounding/causing grievous bodily harm, and racially/religiously aggravated grievous bodily harm and malicious wounding

(Offences Against the Person Act 1861, s 20; Crime and Disorder Act 1998, s 29)

Charges (Grievous bodily harm)

A[70.1] **Unlawfully and maliciously inflicting grievous bodily harm**

A[70.2] **Unlawfully and maliciously wounding**

Offences Against the Person Act 1861, s 20

Maximum penalty – 6 months' imprisonment and/or fine level 5 (for offences committed on or after 12 March 2015 an unlimited fine). Triable either way. Specified violent offence under Sch 15, Part 1, CJA 2003.

Crown Court – 5 years and unlimited fine.

Racially/religiously aggravated offences.

Maximum penalty – Fine level 5 and 6 months. Triable either way. Specified violent offence under Sch 15, Part 1, CJA 2003.

Crown Court – 7 years and unlimited fine.

Mode of trial

A[70.3] For cases of domestic violence. See SC Definitive Guideline: "Overarching Principles: Domestic Violence".

A[70.4] See the SC Guideline at A[70.20] below

Legal notes and definitions

A[70.5] **Intent.** 'Maliciously' means intentionally or recklessly (*R v Mowatt* [1968] 1 QB 421, [1967] 3 All ER 47, CA) and 'recklessly' means that the accused foresaw the particular risk and yet went on to take it (*R v Cunningham* [1957] 2 QB 396, [1957] 2 All ER 412, CCA). In offences under the Offences Against The Person Act 1861, s 20 what must be intended or foreseen is that some physical harm might occur, not necessarily amounting to grievous bodily harm or wounding. An intention to frighten is not enough. (*DPP v A* [2000] All ER (D) 1247). In *Re Dica* (5 May 2004, unreported), CA it was held that where a person, knowing he suffers from a serious sexual disease, infects another through consensual sex (but not deliberately intending to pass on the disease) he will be guilty of the offence, so long as the victim did not consent to the risk of infection. An honest belief in an informed consent will amount to a defence (*R v Konzani* [2005] EWCA Crim 706, [2005] All ER (D) 292 (Mar)).

In principle it was open to justices to convict on the basis of recklessness even where the prosecution simply alleged a deliberate assault: *D v DPP* [2005] EWHC 967 (Admin) considered. However, the justices had failed to identify what was the unlawful act of K leading to the assault. Recklessness had only been a possible conclusion if the justices had found that K had thrown a punch albeit, without intending it to land, or was flailing his arms about in an agitated and aggressive manner. The conviction could not stand in the light of the findings of fact made by the justices: *Katsonis v Crown Prosecution Service* [2011] EWHC 1860 (Admin), 175 JP 396.

A[70.6] **Grievous bodily harm.** To constitute grievous bodily harm, really serious bodily harm must be caused; *R v Metharam* [1961] 3 All ER 200, 45 Cr App Rep 304, CCA; *DPP v Smith* [1961] AC 290, [1960] 3 All ER 161, HL). 'Grievous' means no more and no less than 'really serious', and there is no distinction between the phrases 'serious bodily harm' and 'really serious bodily harm'; see *R v Saunders* [1985] Crim LR 230, [1985] LS Gaz R 1005, CA. In *R v Bollom* [2003] EWCA Crim 2846, [2004] 2 Cr App Rep 50, (2003) Times, 15 December the question arose as to whether the degree of a harm had to be considered with or without reference to the health or other particular factors relating to the person harmed (in this case a 17-month-old baby who had suffered extensive bruising and some abrasions). It was held that it was necessary to consider the injuries in their real context and there was no pre-condition to a finding that the injuries amounted to grievous bodily harm that the victim should require treatment or that the harm would have lasting consequences; however, where it is alleged that the injuries collectively, though not individually, amount to grievous bodily harm the court must be satisfied that they were inflicted in a single assault and not in a series of assaults. In *R v Golding* [2014] EWCA Crim 889, [2014] Crim LR 686 it was confirmed that the herpes virus might be added to the list of communicable diseases that are considered sufficiently serious to constitute really serious harm. (See the commentary in the Criminal Law Review for a discussion on this topic.)

A[70.7] **Provocation** is no defence, but can be taken into account when sentencing.

A[70.8] **Racial/religious aggravation** (See **A[20.6]–A[20.7]**.)

A[70.9] **Misadventure** (See **A[8.8]**.)

A[70.10] **Consent** (See **A[8.10]–A[8.17]**.)

A[70.11]–[70.15] **Self-defence etc** (See **A[8.18]–A[8.20]**.)

A[70.16] **Lawful sport** (See **A[15.18]**.)

A[70.17]–[70.18] **Trespasser on property** (See **A[15.21]–A[15.30]**.)

A[70.19] **Reduction of charge/alternative verdict.** The court cannot reduce this charge to a less serious one (eg actual bodily harm or common assault); but if a separate charge for a lesser offence has been preferred there could be a conviction for that. Consult a legal adviser and **A[15.31]** on the effect of a dismissal for common assault.

Sentencing

SC Guideline – Wounding/causing grievous bodily harm and Racially/religiously aggravated GBH/Unlawful wounding

Grievous bodily harm

Inflicting grievous bodily harm/Unlawful wounding

Offences Against the Person Act 1861 (section 20)

Racially/religiously aggravated GBH/Unlawful wounding

Crime and Disorder Act 1998 (section 29)

A[70.20] These are specified offences for the purposes of section 224 of the Criminal Justice Act 2003

Triable either way

Section 20

Maximum when tried summarily: Level 5 fine and/or 26 weeks' custody

Maximum when tried on indictment: 5 years' custody

Section 29

Maximum when tried summarily: Level 5 fine and/or 26 weeks' custody

Maximum when tried on indictment: 7 years' custody

Offence range: Community order – 4 years' custody

This guideline applies to all offenders aged 18 and older, who are sentenced on or after 13 June 2011. The definitions of 'starting point' and 'first time offender' do not apply for this guideline. Starting point and category ranges apply to all offenders in all cases, irrespective of plea or previous convictions.

STEP ONE
Determining the offence category

The court should determine the offence category using the table below.

Category 1	Greater harm and higher culpability
Category 2	Greater harm and lower culpability; or lesser harm and higher culpability
Category 3	Lesser harm and lower culpability

The court should determine the offender's culpability and the harm caused, or intended, by reference only to the factors below (as demonstrated by the presence of one or more). These factors comprise the principal factual elements of the offence and should determine the category.

Factors indicating greater harm
Injury (which includes disease transmission and/or psychological harm) which is serious in the context of the offence (must normally be present)
Victim is particularly vulnerable because of personal circumstances
Sustained or repeated assault on the same victim
Factors indicating lesser harm
Injury which is less serious in the context of the offence
Factors indicating higher culpability
Statutory aggravating factors:
Offence motivated by, or demonstrating, hostility to the victim based on his or her sexual orientation (or presumed sexual orientation)
Offence motivated by, or demonstrating, hostility to the victim based on the victim's disability (or presumed disability)
Other aggravating factors:
A significant degree of premeditation
Use of weapon or weapon equivalent (for example, shod foot, headbutting, use of acid, use of animal)
Intention to commit more serious harm than actually resulted from the offence

Deliberately causes more harm than is necessary for commission of offence
Deliberate targeting of vulnerable victim
Leading role in group or gang
Offence motivated by, or demonstrating, hostility based on the victim's age, sex, gender identity (or presumed gender identity)
Factors indicating lower culpability
Subordinate role in a group or gang
A greater degree of provocation than normally expected
Lack of premeditation
Mental disorder or learning disability, where linked to commission of the offence
Excessive self defence

STEP TWO
Starting point and category range

Having determined the category, the court should use the corresponding starting points to reach a sentence within the category range below. The starting point applies to all offenders irrespective of plea or previous convictions. A case of particular gravity, reflected by multiple features of culpability in step one, could merit upward adjustment from the starting point before further adjustment for aggravating or mitigating features, set out below.

Offence Category	**Starting Point** *(Applicable to all offenders)*	**Category Range** *(Applicable to all offenders)*
Category 1	Crown Court	Crown Court
Category 2	Crown Court	Crown Court
Category 3	High level community order	Low level community order – Crown Court (51 weeks' custody)

The table below contains a **non-exhaustive** list of additional factual elements providing the context of the offence and factors relating to the offender. Identify whether any combination of these, or other relevant factors, should result in an upward or downward adjustment from the starting point. In some cases, having considered these factors, it may be appropriate to move outside the identified category range.

When sentencing **category 3** offences, the court should also consider the custody threshold as follows:

- has the custody threshold been passed?
- if so, is it unavoidable that a custodial sentence be imposed?
- if so, can that sentence be suspended?

Factors increasing seriousness
Statutory aggravating factors:
Previous convictions, having regard to a) the nature of the offence to which the conviction relates and its relevance to the current offence; and b) the time that has elapsed since the conviction
Offence committed whilst on bail
Other aggravating factors include:
Location of the offence
Timing of the offence
Ongoing effect upon the victim

Offence committed against those working in the public sector or providing a service to the public
Presence of others including relatives, especially children or partner of the victim
Gratuitous degradation of victim
In domestic violence cases, victim forced to leave their home
Failure to comply with current court orders
Offence committed whilst on licence
An attempt to conceal or dispose of evidence
Failure to respond to warnings or concerns expressed by others about the offender's behaviour
Commission of offence whilst under the influence of alcohol or drugs
Abuse of power and/or position of trust
Exploiting contact arrangements with a child to commit an offence
Established evidence of community impact
Any steps taken to prevent the victim reporting an incident, obtaining assistance and/or from assisting or supporting the prosecution
Offences taken into consideration (TICs)
Factors reducing seriousness or reflecting personal mitigation
No previous convictions **or** no relevant/recent convictions
Single blow
Remorse
Good character and/or exemplary conduct
Determination and/or demonstration of steps taken to address addiction or offending behaviour
Serious medical conditions requiring urgent, intensive or long-term treatment
Isolated incident
Age and/or lack of maturity where it affects the responsibility of the offender
Lapse of time since the offence where this is not the fault of the offender
Mental disorder or learning disability, where **not** linked to the commission of the offence
Sole or primary carer for dependent relatives

Section 29 offences only: The court should determine the appropriate sentence for the offence without taking account of the element of aggravation and then make an addition to the sentence, considering the level of aggravation involved. It may be appropriate to move outside the identified category range, taking into account the increased statutory maximum.

STEP THREE
Consider any other factors which indicate a reduction, such as assistance to the prosecution

The court should take into account any rule of law by virtue of which an offender may receive a discounted sentence in consequence of assistance given (or offered) to the prosecutor or investigator.

STEP FOUR
Reduction for guilty pleas

The court should take account of any potential reduction for a guilty plea in accordance with section 144 of the Criminal Justice Act 2003 and the *Guilty Plea* guideline.

STEP FIVE
Dangerousness

Inflicting grievous bodily harm/unlawful wounding and racially/religiously aggravated GBH/unlawful wounding are specified offences within the meaning of Chapter 5 of the Criminal Justice Act 2003 and at this stage the court should consider whether having regard to the criteria contained in that Chapter it would be appropriate to award an extended sentence.

STEP SIX
Totality principle

If sentencing an offender for more than one offence, or where the offender is already serving a sentence, consider whether the total sentence is just and proportionate to the offending behaviour.

STEP SEVEN
Compensation and ancillary orders

In all cases, the court should consider whether to make compensation and/or other ancillary orders.

STEP EIGHT
Reasons

Section 174 of the Criminal Justice Act 2003 imposes a duty to give reasons for, and explain the effect of, the sentence.

STEP NINE
Consideration for remand time

(Now obligatory.)

A[71]

Air guns – possession by person under 18

Charge (Air guns)

A[71.1] **Being a person under 18 having with him an air weapon or ammunition**

Firearms Act 1968, s 22(4)

Maximum penalty – Fine level 3 or any other adjudication to which a young person is liable, bearing in mind the offence is not punishable with imprisonment.

Forfeiture of the air weapon or ammunition can be ordered.

Legal notes and definitions

A[71.2] **Possession,** a close physical link and immediate control over the firearm but not necessarily that he had been carrying it. It is not an offence where he is under the supervision of someone of or over 21 years.

A[71.3] **Air weapon** means an air rifle, air gun or air pistol of a type which has not been declared to be specially dangerous in rules made by the Home Office. See *Street v DPP* [2004] EWHC 86 (Admin), (2004) Times, 23 January, [2004] All ER (D) 70 (Jan) where a low powered ball bearing gun was included in the definition.

A[71.4] **Public place** includes any highway or premises or place to which at the material time the public had access whether for payment or otherwise.

A[71.5] It is not an offence for a person of 14 or over to have with him an air weapon on private premises with the consent of the occupier.

Section 23(1) provides that it is not an offence under s 22(4) for a person to have with him an air weapon or ammunition while he is under the supervision of a person of or over the age of 21; but where a person has with him an air weapon on any premises in circumstances where he would be prohibited from having it with him but for this subsection, it is an offence for the person under whose supervision he is to allow him to use it for firing any missile beyond those premises. In proceedings against a person this offence it shall be a defence for him to show that the only premises into or across which the missile was fired were premises the occupier of which had consented to the firing of the missile (whether specifically or by way of a general consent): Firearms Act 1968, s 23(1A).

A[71.6] He does not commit an offence if he is engaged in target practice as a member of a club approved by the Home Office or if the weapon and ammunition are being used at a shooting gallery where only air weapons or miniature rifles of 0.23 calibre or less are used (Firearms Act 1968, s 23(2)).

Sentencing

A[71.7] **No SC Guideline.** For available sentences see Table C at B[43.3].

A[71.8] **Fines.** See B[28].

A[71A]

Air guns – failing to prevent possession by person under 18

Charge (Air guns) [cont.]

A[71A.1] (1) It is an offence for a person in possession of an air weapon to fail to take reasonable precautions to prevent any person under the age of eighteen from having the weapon with him.

(2) Subsection (1) does not apply where by virtue of section 23 of this Act (see A[71.5], above) the person under the age of eighteen is not prohibited from having the weapon with him.

Firearms Act 1968, s 24ZA

Maximum penalty – Fine level 3 or any other adjudication to which a young person is liable, bearing in mind the offence is not punishable with imprisonment.

Forfeiture of the air weapon or ammunition can be ordered.

Legal notes and definitions

A[71A.2] In proceedings for an offence under subsection (1) it is a defence to show that the person charged with the offence—

(a) believed the other person to be aged eighteen or over; and
(b) had reasonable ground for that belief.

A person shall be taken to have shown the matters specified in subsection (3) if—

(a) sufficient evidence of those matters is adduced to raise an issue with respect to them; and
(b) the contrary is not proved beyond a reasonable doubt.

Sentencing

A[71A.3] No SC Guideline. For available sentences see Table C at B[43.3].

A[72]
Dangerous dogs

Offences under the Dangerous Dogs Act 1991

A[72.1] **Being the owner (person for the time being in charge) of a dog which on [. . . . .] was dangerously out of control in a place (whether or not a public place) namely [. . . . .] (and which injured a person or assistance dog)**

Dangerous Dogs Act 1991, s 3

Maximum penalty Non-aggravated offences: 6 months' imprisonment and/or fine level 5 (for offences committed on or after 12 March 2015 an unlimited fine). Triable only summarily.

Aggravated offences: 14 years if a person dies as a result of being injured; 5 years in other cases where a person is injured; 3 years where an assistance dog is killed. Triable either way.

Significant amendments to the 1991 Act were made by the Anti-social Behaviour, Crime and Policing Act 2014, ss 106 and 107. In particular, the offence was extended to private places (subject to a householder defence), and maximum penalties were increased for aggravated offences.

Legal notes and definitions

A[72.2] **Owner.** Includes, where the dog is owned by a person who is less than 16 years old, the head of the household of which that person is a member. In *L v CPS* [2010] EWHC 341 (Admin), (2010) 174 JP 209 the appellant, who had charge of a dog but was not the owner, handed the lead to another person while he tied his shoe lace and that other person deliberately released the dog, which proceeded to bite somebody. It was held that the appellant remained in charge of the dog. The short and temporary transfer did not prevent this. The appellant had the right and power to take the dog back any time and was able to control it since the dog responded to his commands.

In proceedings for an offence under s 3(1) it is a defence for the accused to prove that the dog was at the material time in charge of a person whom he reasonably believed to be a fit and proper person to be in charge of it: s 3(2). A contention, however, that different members of a family looked after a dog at different times fell well outside the ambit of the s 3(2) defence, which was intended to cover situations such as a dog being left with a neighbour for a period of time: *R v Huddart* [1999] Crim LR 568.

Natural justice requires that the known owner of the dog be notified of any prosecution where a conviction will result in the destruction of the dog: *R v Trafford Magistrates' Court, ex p Riley* (1995) 160 JP 418, DC.

A[72.3] **Standard of liability.** Section 3(1) creates an offence of strict liability. Nevertheless, liability is not absolute. As has been seen, s 3(2) makes available a defence in certain circumstances to an owner of a dog placed in the charge of another. Also, there must be some causal connection between having charge of the dog and the prohibited state of affairs that has arisen. Section 3(1) requires proof by the prosecution of an act or omission of the defendant (with or without fault) that to some (more than minimal) degree caused or permitted the prohibited state of affairs to come about: *R v Robinson-Pierre* [2013] EWCA Crim 2396, 178 JP 45 (explaining *R v Bezzina* [1994] 1 WLR 1057, 158 JP 671) (In Robinson-Pierre the dog was in a public place only as a result of escaping from the house when police broke down the door executing a search warrant. The offence under s 3(1) can now be committed in private, as well as public, places. It is submitted, however, that this has no bearing on the principles established by the case).

The behaviour of the dog in that it bit a person and the fact that it was not controlled by its handler when on a lead was ample evidence of the dog being dangerously out of control in a public place (*R v Gedminintaite and Collier* [2008] EWCA Crim 814).

A[72.4] **Householder cases.** The extension of the law to private places was accompanied by a 'householder' defence mirroring the provisions of s 76(8B) to 8(F) of the Criminal Justice and Immigration Act 2008 (use of force at place of residence).

A person is not guilty of the offence under s 3(1) in a case which is a householder case, defined as a case where:

(a) the dog is dangerously out of control while in or partly in a building, or part of a building, that is a dwelling (or forces accommodation, or both); and
(b) at that time the person to whom the dog is dangerously out of control is in, or entering, the building or part as a trespasser and the defendant (if present at that time) believed that person to be in, or entering, the building or part as a trespasser. The reasonableness of the defendant's belief is relevant to the question as to whether he genuinely held it, but if it is determined the belief was genuine D may rely on it whether or not it was mistaken or, if mistaken, the mistake was a reasonable one. The defendant cannot, however, rely on a mistaken belief attributable to voluntary intoxication: s 3(1B).

A[72.5] **Dangerously out of control.** This term is partly defined by s 10(3), which provides: 'For the purposes of this Act a dog shall be regarded as dangerously out of control on any occasion on which there are grounds for reasonable apprehension that it will injure any person or assistance dog, whether or not it actually does so, but references to a dog injuring a person or assistance dog or there being grounds for reasonable apprehension that it will do so do not include references to any case in which the dog is being used for a lawful purpose by a constable or a person in the service of the Crown'.

Section 10(3) sets an objective standard of reasonable apprehension, not related to the state of mind of the dog owner; it is no defence that the owner had no realisation that his dog might behave in such a way: see *R v Bezzina* [1994] 1 WLR 1057, 158 JP 671. Where injury in fact results there must have been, immediately before, reasonable apprehension that injury would occur: *Rafiq v DPP* (1997) 161 JP 412. Note, however, that s 10(3) does not provide an exhaustive definition and the court is entitled to go back to the straightforward words of s 3: *R v Gedminitaite and Collier* [2008] EWCA Crim 814, 172 JP 413.

'Assistance dog' has the meaning given to it by the Equality Act 2010, s 173(1) (dog trained to assist the blind, deaf or persons with certain disabilities).

A[72.6]–[72.7] **Sentencing.** The following guidelines are effective from 1 July 2016 and take in the significant changes made by the Anti-social behaviour, Crime and Policing Act 2014.

The 2014 Act also amended the criteria for determining whether or not a dog would constitute a danger to public safety. The changes are noted at A[72.10]–[72.14].

Sentencing

SC Sentencing Guideline – Owner or person in charge of a dog dangerously out of control in any place in England or Wales (whether or not a public place) where a person is injured

A[72.8] Dangerous Dogs Act 1991 (section 3(1))

Triable either way

Maximum: 5 years' custody

Offence range: Discharge – 4 years' custody

STEP ONE
Determining the offence category

In order to determine the category the court should assess **culpability** and **harm**. The court should determine the offence category with reference only to the factors in the tables below.

The level of culpability is determined by weighing up all the factors of the case. **Where there are characteristics present which fall under different levels of culpability, the court should balance these characteristics to reach a fair assessment of the offender's culpability.**

*CULPABILITY **demonstrated by one or more of the following:***

A – High culpability

Dog used as a weapon or to intimidate people

Dog known to be prohibited

Dog trained to be aggressive

Failure to respond to official warnings or to comply with orders concerning the dog

Offender disqualified from owning a dog, or failed to respond to official warnings, or to comply with orders concerning the dog

B – Medium culpability

All other cases where characteristics for categories A or C are not present, and in particular:

Failure to respond to warnings or concerns expressed by others about the dog's behaviour

Failure to act on prior knowledge of the dog's aggressive behaviour

Lack of safety or control measures taken in situations where an incident could reasonably have been foreseen

Failure to intervene in the incident (where it would have been reasonable to do so)

Ill treatment or failure to ensure welfare needs of the dog (where connected to the offence and where not charged separately)

C – Lesser culpability

Attempts made to regain control of the dog and/or intervene

Provocation of the dog without fault of the offender

Evidence of safety or control measures having been taken

Incident could not have reasonably been foreseen by the offender

Momentary lapse of control/attention

HARM

The level of **harm** is assessed by weighing up all the factors of the case.

Category 1	Serious injury (which includes disease transmission) Serious psychological harm
Category 2	Harm that falls between categories 1 and 3
Category 3	Minor injury and no significant psychological harm

STEP TWO

Starting point and category range

Having determined the category at step one, the court should use the corresponding starting point to reach a sentence within the category range below. The starting point applies to all offenders irrespective of plea or previous convictions.

Culpability

Harm	A	B	C
Category 1	**Starting point**	**Starting point**	**Starting point**
	3 years' custody	1 year 6 months' custody	High level community order
	Category range	**Category range**	**Category range**
	2 years 6 months' – 4 years' custody	6 months' – 2 years 6 months' custody	Medium level community order – 6 months' custody
Category 2	**Starting point**	**Starting point**	**Starting**
	2 years' custody	6 months' custody	Band C fine
	Category range	**Category range**	**Category range**
	1 year – 3 years' custody	Medium level community order – 1 year's custody	Band B fine – High level community order
Category 3	**Starting point**	**Starting point**	**Starting point**
	6 months' custody	Low level community order	Band B fine
	Category range	**Category range**	**Category range**
	High level community order – 1 year 6 months' custody	Band C fine – 6 months' custody	Discharge – Band C fine

The table is for single offences. Concurrent sentences reflecting the overall criminality of offending will ordinarily be appropriate where offences arise out of the same incident or facts: please refer to the *Offences Taken into Consideration and Totality* guideline.

The court should then consider any adjustment for any aggravating or mitigating factors. On the next page is a **non-exhaustive** list of additional factual elements providing the context of the offence and factors relating to the offender.

Identify whether any combination of these, or other relevant factors, should result in an upward or downward adjustment from the starting point.

Factors increasing seriousness
Statutory aggravating factors:
Previous convictions, having regard to a) the**nature** of the offence to which the conviction relates and its **relevance** to the current offence; and b) the **time** that has elapsed since the conviction
Offence committed whilst on bail

Offence motivated by, or demonstrating hostility based on any of the following characteristics or presumed characteristics of the victim: religion, race, disability, sexual orientation or transgender identity.
Other aggravating factors include:
Victim is a child or otherwise vulnerable because of personal circumstances
Location of the offence
Sustained or repeated attack
Significant ongoing effect on witness(es) to the attack
Serious injury caused to others (where not charged separately)
Significant practical and financial effects of offence on relatives/carers
Allowing person insufficiently experienced or trained, to be in charge of the dog
Lack or loss of control of dog due to influence of alcohol or drugs
Offence committed against those working in the public sector or providing a service to the public
Injury to other animals
Established evidence of community/wider impact
Failure to comply with current court orders (except where taken into account in assessing culpability)
Offence committed on licence
Offences taken into consideration
Factors reducing seriousness or reflecting personal mitigation
No previous convictions or no relevant/recent convictions
Isolated incident
No previous complaints against, or incidents involving the dog
Evidence of responsible ownership
Remorse
Good character and/or exemplary conduct
Serious medical condition requiring urgent, intensive or long-term treatment
Age and/or lack of maturity where it affects the responsibility of the offender
Mental disorder or learning disability
Sole or primary carer for dependent relatives
Determination and/or demonstration of steps having been taken to address offending behaviour

STEP THREE

Consider any factors which indicate a reduction, such as assistance to the prosecution

The court should take into account sections 73 and 74 of the Serious Organised Crime and Police Act 2005 (assistance by defendants: reduction or review of sentence) and any other rule of law by virtue of which an offender may receive a discounted sentence in consequence of assistance given (or offered) to the prosecutor or investigator.

STEP FOUR

Reduction for guilty pleas

The court should take account of any potential reduction for a guilty plea in accordance with section 144 of the Criminal Justice Act 2003 and the *Guilty Plea* guideline.

STEP FIVE
Totality principle

If sentencing an offender for more than one offence, or where the offender is already serving a sentence, consider whether the total sentence is just and proportionate to the overall offending behaviour in accordance with the *Offences Taken into Consideration and Totality* guideline.

STEP SIX
Compensation and ancillary orders

In all cases, the court must consider whether to make a compensation order and/or other ancillary orders.

Compensation order

The court should consider compensation orders in all cases where personal injury, loss or damage has resulted from the offence. The court must give reasons if it decides not to award compensation in such cases.

Other ancillary orders available include:

Disqualification from having a dog

The court **may** disqualify the offender from having custody of a dog. The test the court should consider is whether the offender is a fit and proper person to have custody of a dog.

Destruction order/contingent destruction order

In any case where the offender is not the owner of the dog, the owner must be given an opportunity to be present and make representations to the court.

If the dog is a **prohibited dog** refer to the guideline for possession of a prohibited dog in relation to destruction/contingent destruction orders.

The court **shall** make a destruction order unless the court is satisfied that the dog would not constitute a danger to public safety.

In reaching a decision, the court should consider the relevant circumstances which **must** include:

- the temperament of the dog and its past behaviour;
- whether the owner of the dog, or the person for the time being in charge of it is a fit and proper person to be in charge of the dog;

and **may** include:

- other relevant circumstances.

If the court is satisfied that the dog would not constitute a danger to public safety and the dog is not prohibited, it **may** make a contingent destruction order requiring the dog be kept under proper control. A contingent destruction order may specify the measures to be taken by the owner for keeping the dog under proper control, which include:

- muzzling;
- keeping on a lead;
- neutering in appropriate cases; and
- excluding it from a specified place.

Where the court makes a destruction order, it **may** appoint a person to undertake destruction and order the offender to pay what it determines to be the reasonable expenses of destroying the dog and keeping it pending its destruction.

Fit and proper person

In determining whether a person is a fit and proper person to be in charge of a dog the following non-exhaustive factors may be relevant:

- any relevant previous convictions, cautions or penalty notices;
- the nature and suitability of the premises that the dog is to be kept at by the person;
- where the police have released the dog pending the court's decision whether the person has breached conditions imposed by the police; and
- any relevant previous breaches of court orders.

STEP SEVEN
Reasons

Section 174 of the Criminal Justice Act 2003 imposes a duty to give reasons for, and explain the effect of, the sentence.

STEP EIGHT
Consideration for time spent on bail

The court must consider whether to give credit for time spent on bail in accordance with section 240A of the Criminal Justice Act 2003.

Owner or person in charge of a dog dangerously out of control in any place in England or Wales (whether or not a public place) where an assistance dog is injured or killed

Dangerous Dogs Act 1991 (section 3(1))

Triable either way

Maximum: 3 years' custody

Offence range: Discharge – 2 years 6 months' custody

STEP ONE
Determining the offence category

In order to determine the category the court should assess **culpability** and **harm**. The court should determine the offence category with reference only to the factors in the tables below.

The level of culpability is determined by weighing up all the factors of the case. **Where there are characteristics present which fall under different levels of culpability, the court should balance these characteristics to reach a fair assessment of the offender's culpability.**

Culpability demonstrated by one or more of the following:

A – High culpability

Dog used as a weapon or to intimidate people or dogs

Dog known to be prohibited

Dog trained to be aggressive

Offender disqualified from owning a dog, or failed to respond to official warnings, or to comply with orders concerning the dog

Offence motivated by, or demonstrating hostility to the victim (assisted person) based on the victim's disability (or presumed disability)

B – Medium culpability

All other cases where characteristics for categories A or C are not present, and in particular:

Failure to respond to warnings or concerns expressed by others about the dog's behaviour

Failure to act on prior knowledge of the dog's aggressive behaviour

Lack of safety or control measures taken in situations where an incident could reasonably have been foreseen

Failure to intervene in the incident (where it would have been reasonable to do so)

Ill treatment or failure to ensure welfare needs of the dog (where connected to the offence and where not charged separately)

C – Lesser culpability

Attempts made to regain control of the dog and/or intervene

Provocation of the dog without fault of the offender

Evidence of safety or control measures having been taken

Incident could not have reasonably been foreseen by the offender

Momentary lapse of control/attention

HARM

The level of **harm** is assessed by weighing up all the factors of the case.

Category 1	Fatality or serious injury to an assistance dog and/or Serious impact on the assisted person (whether psychological or other harm caused by the offence)
Category 2	Harm that falls between categories 1 and 3
Category 3	Minor injury to assistance dog and impact of the offence on the assisted person is limited

STEP TWO

Starting point and category range

Having determined the category at step one, the court should use the corresponding starting point to reach a sentence within the category range below. The starting point applies to all offenders irrespective of plea or previous convictions.

Culpability

Harm	A	B	C
Category 1	**Starting point**	**Starting point**	**Starting point**
	2 years' custody	9 months' custody	Medium level community order
	Category range	**Category range**	**Category range**
	1 year – 2 years 6 months' custody	Medium level community order – 1 year's custody	Low level community order – High level community order

Harm	A	B	C
Category 2	Starting point	Starting point	Starting point
	1 years' custody	High level community order	Band B fine
	Category range	Category range	Category range
	6 months' – 1 year 6 months' custody	Low level community order – 6 months' custody	Band A fine – Low level community order
Category 3	Starting point	Starting point	Starting point
	High level community order	Band C fine	Band A fine
	Category range	Category range	Category range
	Medium level community order – 6 months' custody	Band B fine – High level community order	Discharge – Band B fine

The court should then consider any adjustment for any aggravating or mitigating factors. On the next page is a **non-exhaustive** list of additional factual elements providing the context of the offence and factors relating to the offender.

Identify whether any combination of these, or other relevant factors, should result in an upward or downward adjustment from the starting point.

Factors increasing seriousness

Statutory aggravating factors:

Previous convictions, having regard to a) the **nature** of the offence to which the conviction relates and its **relevance** to the current offence; and b) the **time** that has elapsed since the conviction

Offence committed whilst on bail

Offence motivated by, or demonstrating hostility based on any of the following characteristics or presumed characteristics of the victim: religion, race, sexual orientation or transgender identity

Other aggravating factors:

Location of the offence

Sustained or repeated attack

Significant ongoing effect on witness(es) to the attack

Allowing person insufficiently experienced or trained, to be in charge of the dog

Lack or loss of control of the dog due to influence of alcohol or drugs

Offence committed against those working in the public sector or providing a service to the public

Injury to other animals

Cost of retraining an assistance dog

Established evidence of community/wider impact

Failure to comply with current court orders (except where taken into account in assessing culpability)

Offence committed on licence

Offences taken into consideration

Factors reducing seriousness or reflecting personal mitigation

No previous convictions or no relevant/recent convictions

Isolated incident

No previous complaints against, or incidents involving the dog

Evidence of responsible ownership
Remorse
Good character and/or exemplary conduct
Serious medical condition requiring urgent, intensive or long-term treatment
Age and/or lack of maturity where it affects the responsibility of the offender
Mental disorder or learning disability
Sole or primary carer for dependent relatives
Determination and/or demonstration of steps having been taken to address offending behaviour

STEP THREE
Consider any factors which indicate a reduction, such as assistance to the prosecution

The court should take into account sections 73 and 74 of the Serious Organised Crime and Police Act 2005 (assistance by defendants: reduction or review of sentence) and any other rule of law by virtue of which an offender may receive a discounted sentence in consequence of assistance given (or offered) to the prosecutor or investigator.

STEP FOUR
Reduction for guilty pleas

The court should take account of any potential reduction for a guilty plea in accordance with section 144 of the Criminal Justice Act 2003 and the *Guilty Plea* guideline.

STEP FIVE
Totality principle

If sentencing an offender for more than one offence, or where the offender is already serving a sentence, consider whether the total sentence is just and proportionate to the overall offending behaviour in accordance with the *Offences Taken into Consideration and Totality* guideline.

STEP SIX
Compensation and ancillary orders

In all cases, the court must consider whether to make a compensation order and/or other ancillary orders.

Compensation order

The court should consider compensation orders in all cases where personal injury, loss or damage has resulted from the offence. The court must give reasons if it decides not to award compensation in such cases.

Other ancillary orders available include:

Disqualification from having custody of a dog

The court may disqualify the offender from having custody of a dog. The test the court should consider is whether the offender is a fit and proper person to have custody of a dog.

Destruction order/contingent destruction order

In any case where the offender is not the owner of the dog, the owner must be given an opportunity to be present and make representations to the court.

If the dog is a **prohibited dog** refer to the guideline for possession of a prohibited dog in relation to destruction/contingent destruction orders.

The court **shall** make a destruction order unless the court is satisfied that the dog would not constitute a danger to public safety.

In reaching a decision, the court should consider the relevant circumstances which **must** include:

- the temperament of the dog and its past behaviour;
- whether the owner of the dog, or the person for the time being in charge of it is a fit and proper person to be in charge of the dog;

and **may** include:

- other relevant circumstances.

If the court is satisfied that the dog would not constitute a danger to public safety and the dog is not prohibited, it **may** make a contingent destruction order requiring the dog be kept under proper control. A contingent destruction order may specify the measures to be taken by the owner for keeping the dog under proper control, which include:

- muzzling;
- keeping on a lead;
- neutering in appropriate cases; and
- excluding it from a specified place.

Where the court makes a destruction order, it **may** appoint a person to undertake destruction and order the offender to pay what it determines to be the reasonable expenses of destroying the dog and keeping it pending its destruction.

Fit and proper person

In determining whether a person is a fit and proper person to be in charge of a dog the following non-exhaustive factors may be relevant:

- any relevant previous convictions, cautions or penalty notices;
- the nature and suitability of the premises that the dog is to be kept at by the person;
- where the police have released the dog pending the court's decision whether the person has breached conditions imposed by the police; and
- any relevant previous breaches of court orders.

STEP SEVEN
Reasons

Section 174 of the Criminal Justice Act 2003 imposes a duty to give reasons for, and explain the effect of, the sentence.

STEP EIGHT
Consideration for time spent on bail

The court must consider whether to give credit for time spent on bail in accordance with section 240A of the Criminal Justice Act 2003.

Owner or person in charge of a dog dangerously out of control in any place in England or Wales (whether or not a public place)

A[72.8A] Dangerous Dogs Act 1991 (section 3(1))

Triable only summarily

Maximum: 6 months' custody

Offence range: Discharge – 6 months' custody

STEP ONE
Determining the offence category

In order to determine the category the court should assess **culpability** and **harm**. The court should determine the offence category with reference only to the factors in the tables below.

The level of culpability is determined by weighing up all the factors of the case. **Where there are characteristics present which fall under different levels of culpability, the court should balance these characteristics to reach a fair assessment of the offender's culpability.**

CULPABILITY demonstrated by one or more of the following:

A – Higher culpability

Dog used as a weapon or to intimidate people

Dog known to be prohibited

Dog trained to be aggressive

Offender disqualified from owning a dog, or failed to respond to official warnings, or to comply with orders concerning the dog

B – Lower culpability

Attempts made to regain control of the dog and/or intervene

Provocation of dog without fault of the offender

Evidence of safety or control measures having been taken

Incident could not have reasonably been foreseen by the offender

Momentary lapse of control/attention

HARM

The level of harm is assessed by weighing up all the factors of the case.

Greater harm	Presence of children or others who are vulnerable because of personal Greater harm circumstances Injury to other animals
Lesser harm	Low risk to the public

STEP TWO
Starting point and category range

Having determined the category at step one, the court should use the corresponding starting point to reach a sentence within the category range below. The starting point applies to all offenders irrespective of plea or previous convictions.

Culpability

Harm	A	B
Greater harm	Starting point	Starting point
	Medium level community order	Band B fine
	Category range	Category range
	Band C fine – 6 months' custody	Band A fine – Band C fine
Lesser harm	Starting point	Starting point
	Band C fine	Band A fine
	Category range	Category range
	Band B fine – Low level community order	Discharge – Band B fine

The court should then consider any adjustment for any aggravating or mitigating factors. On the next page is a **non-exhaustive** list of additional factual elements providing the context of the offence and factors relating to the offender.

Identify whether any combination of these, or other relevant factors, should result in an upward or downward adjustment from the starting point.

Factors increasing seriousness

Statutory aggravating factors:

Previous convictions, having regard to a) the **nature** of the offence to which the conviction relates and its **relevance** to the current offence; and b) the **time** that has elapsed since the conviction

Offence committed whilst on bail

Offence motivated by, or demonstrating hostility based on any of the following characteristics or presumed characteristics of the victim: religion, race, disability, sexual orientation or transgender identity

Other aggravating factors:

Location of the offence

Significant ongoing effect on the victim and/or others

Failing to take adequate precautions to prevent the dog from escaping

Allowing person insufficiently experienced or trained, to be in charge of the dog

Ill treatment or failure to ensure welfare needs of the dog (where connected to the offence and where not charged separately)

Lack or loss of control of the dog due to influence of alcohol or drugs

Offence committed against those working in the public sector or providing a service to the public

Established evidence of community/wider impact

Failure to comply with current court orders (unless this has already been taken into account in assessing culpability)

Offence committed on licence

Offences taken into consideration

Factors reducing seriousness or reflecting personal mitigation

No previous convictions or no relevant/recent convictions

Isolated incident

No previous complaints against, or incidents involving the dog

Evidence of responsible ownership

Remorse

Good character and/or exemplary conduct
Serious medical condition requiring urgent, intensive or long-term treatment
Age and/or lack of maturity where it affects the responsibility of the offender
Mental disorder or learning disability
Sole or primary carer for dependent relatives
Determination and/or demonstration of steps having been taken to address offending behaviour

STEP THREE
Consider any factors which indicate a reduction, such as assistance to the prosecution

The court should take into account sections 73 and 74 of the Serious Organised Crime and Police Act 2005 (assistance by defendants: reduction or review of sentence) and any other rule of law by virtue of which an offender may receive a discounted sentence in consequence of assistance given (or offered) to the prosecutor or investigator.

STEP FOUR
Reduction for guilty pleas

The court should take account of any potential reduction for a guilty plea in accordance with section 144 of the Criminal Justice Act 2003 and the *Guilty Plea* guideline.

STEP FIVE
Totality principle

If sentencing an offender for more than one offence, or where the offender is already serving a sentence, consider whether the total sentence is just and proportionate to the overall offending behaviour in accordance with the *Offences Taken into Consideration and Totality* guideline.

STEP SIX
Compensation and ancillary orders

In all cases, the court must consider whether to make a compensation order and/or other ancillary orders.

Compensation order

The court should consider compensation orders in all cases where personal injury, loss or damage has resulted from the offence. The court must give reasons if it decides not to award compensation in such cases.

Other ancillary orders available include:

Disqualification from having a dog

The court may disqualify the offender from having custody of a dog. The test the court should consider is whether the offender is a fit and proper person to have custody of a dog.

Destruction order/contingent destruction order

In any case where the offender is not the owner of the dog, the owner must be given an opportunity to be present and make representations to the court.

If the dog is a prohibited dog refer to the guideline for possession of a prohibited dog in relation to destruction/contingent destruction orders.

If the dog is not prohibited and the court is satisfied that the dog would constitute a danger to public safety the court **may** make a destruction order.

In reaching a decision, the court should consider the relevant circumstances which **must** include:

- temperament of the dog and its past behaviour;
- whether the owner of the dog, or the person for the time being in charge of it is a fit and proper person to be in charge of the dog;

and **may** include:

- other relevant circumstances.

If the court is satisfied that the dog would not constitute a danger to public safety and the dog is not prohibited, it **may** make a contingent destruction order requiring the dog be kept under proper control. A contingent destruction order may specify the measures to be taken by the owner for keeping the dog under proper control, which include:

- muzzling;
- keeping on a lead;
- neutering in appropriate cases; and
- excluding it from a specified place.

Where the court makes a destruction order, it **may** appoint a person to undertake destruction and order the offender to pay what it determines to be the reasonable expenses of destroying the dog and keeping it pending its destruction.

Fit and proper person

In determining whether a person is a fit and proper person to be in charge of a dog the following non-exhaustive factors may be relevant:

- any relevant previous convictions, cautions or penalty notices;
- the nature and suitability of the premises that the dog is to be kept at by the person;
- where the police have released the dog pending the court's decision whether the person has breached conditions imposed by the police; and
- any relevant previous breaches of court orders.

STEP SEVEN
Reasons

Section 174 of the Criminal Justice Act 2003 imposes a duty to give reasons for, and explain the effect of, the sentence.

STEP EIGHT
Consideration for time spent on bail

The court must consider whether to give credit for time spent on bail in accordance with section 240A of the Criminal Justice Act 2003.

Possession of a prohibited dog

Dangerous Dogs Act 1991 (section 1(7))

Breeding, selling, exchanging or advertising a prohibited dog

Dangerous Dogs Act 1991 (section 1(7))

Triable only summarily

Maximum: 6 months' custody

Offence range: Discharge – 6 months' custody

STEP ONE
Determining the offence category

In order to determine the category the court should assess **culpability** and **harm.** The court should determine the offence category with reference only to the factors in the tables below.

The level of culpability is determined by weighing up all the factors of the case. **Where there are characteristics present which fall under different levels of culpability, the court should balance these characteristics to reach a fair assessment of the offender's culpability.**

CULPABILITY demonstrated by one or more of the following:

A – Higher culpability:

Possessing a dog known to be prohibited

Breeding from a dog known to be prohibited

Selling, exchanging or advertising a dog known to be prohibited

Offence committed for gain

Dog used to threaten or intimidate

Permitting fighting

Training and/or possession of paraphernalia for dog fighting

B – Lower culpability:

All other cases

HARM

The level of harm is assessed by weighing up all the factors of the case.

Greater harm	High risk to the public and/or animals
Lesser harm	Low risk to the public and/or animals

STEP TWO
Starting point and category range

Having determined the category at step one, the court should use the corresponding starting point to reach a sentence within the category range below. The starting point applies to all offenders irrespective of plea or previous convictions.

Culpability

Harm	**A**	**B**
Greater harm	**Starting point**	**Starting point**
	Medium level community order	Band B fine
	Category range	**Category range**

	Band C fine – 6 months' custody	Band A fine – Low level community order
Lesser harm	**Starting point**	**Starting point**
	Band C fine	Band A fine
	Category range	**Category range**
	Band B fine – Medium level community order	Discharge – Band B fine

The court should then consider any adjustment for any aggravating or mitigating factors. Below is a **non-exhaustive** list of additional factual elements providing the context of the offence and factors relating to the offender.

Identify whether any combination of these, or other relevant factors, should result in an upward or downward adjustment from the starting point.

Factors increasing seriousness

Statutory aggravating factors:

Previous convictions, having regard to a) the **nature** of the offence to which the conviction relates and its **relevance** to the current offence; and b) the **time** that has elapsed since the conviction

Offence committed whilst on bail

Other aggravating factors:

Presence of children or others who are vulnerable because of personal circumstances

Ill treatment or failure to ensure welfare needs of the dog (where connected to the offence and where not charged separately)

Established evidence of community/wider impact

Failure to comply with current court orders

Offence committed on licence

Offences taken into consideration

Factors reducing seriousness or reflecting personal mitigation

No previous convictions or no relevant/recent convictions

Unaware that dog was prohibited type despite reasonable efforts to identify type

Evidence of safety or control measures having been taken by owner

Prosecution results from owner notification

Evidence of responsible ownership

Remorse

Good character and/or exemplary conduct

Serious medical condition requiring urgent, intensive or long-term treatment

Age and/or lack of maturity where it affects the responsibility of the offender

Mental disorder or learning disability

Sole or primary carer for dependent relatives

Determination and/or demonstration of steps having been taken to address offending behaviour

Lapse of time since the offence where this is not the fault of the offender

STEP THREE

Consider any factors which indicate a reduction, such as assistance to the prosecution

The court should take into account sections 73 and 74 of the Serious Organised Crime and Police Act 2005 (assistance by defendants: reduction or review of

sentence) and any other rule of law by virtue of which an offender may receive a discounted sentence in consequence of assistance given (or offered) to the prosecutor or investigator.

STEP FOUR
Reduction for guilty pleas

The court should take account of any potential reduction for a guilty plea in accordance with section 144 of the Criminal Justice Act 2003 and the *Guilty Plea* guideline.

STEP FIVE
Totality principle

If sentencing an offender for more than one offence, or where the offender is already serving a sentence, consider whether the total sentence is just and proportionate to the overall offending behaviour in accordance with the *Offences Taken into Consideration and Totality* guideline.

STEP SIX
Compensation and ancillary orders

In all cases, the court must consider whether to make a compensation order and/or other ancillary orders.

Compensation order

The court should consider compensation orders in all cases where personal injury, loss or damage has resulted from the offence. The court must give reasons if it decides not to award compensation in such cases.

Other ancillary orders available include:

Disqualification from having a dog

The court **may** disqualify the offender from having custody of a dog for such period as it thinks fit. The test the court should consider is whether the offender is a fit and proper person to have custody of a dog.

Destruction order/contingent destruction order

In any case where the offender is not the owner of the dog, the owner must be given an opportunity to be present and make representations to the court.

The court **shall** make a destruction order unless the court is satisfied that the dog would not constitute a danger to public safety.

In reaching a decision, the court should consider the relevant circumstances which **must** include:

- the temperament of the dog and its past behaviour;
- whether the owner of the dog, or the person for the time being in charge of it is a fit and proper person to be in charge of the dog;

and **may** include:

- other relevant circumstances.

If the court is satisfied that the dog would not constitute a danger to public safety, it **shall** make a contingent destruction order requiring that the dog be exempted from the prohibition on possession or custody within the requisite period.

Where the court makes a destruction order, it **may** appoint a person to undertake destruction and order the offender to pay what it determines to be the reasonable expenses of destroying the dog and keeping it pending its destruction.

Fit and proper person

In determining whether a person is a fit and proper person to be in charge of a dog the following non-exhaustive factors may be relevant:

- any relevant previous convictions, cautions or penalty notices;
- the nature and suitability of the premises that the dog is to be kept at by the person;
- where the police have released the dog pending the court's decision whether the person has breached conditions imposed by the police; and
- any relevant previous breaches of court orders.

Note: the court must be satisfied that the person who is assessed by the court as a fit and proper person can demonstrate that they are the owner or the person ordinarily in charge of that dog at the time the court is considering whether the dog is a danger to public safety. Someone who has previously not been in charge of the dog should not be considered for this assessment because it is an offence under the Dangerous Dogs Act 1991 to make a gift of a prohibited dog.

STEP SEVEN
Reasons

Section 174 of the Criminal Justice Act 2003 imposes a duty to give reasons for, and explain the effect of, the sentence.

STEP EIGHT
Consideration for time spent on bail

The court must consider whether to give credit for time spent on bail in accordance with section 240A of the Criminal Justice Act 2003.

A[72.9] Available sentences. See Table B at B[43.2]; for aggravated offences see Table A at B[43.1A]. In *R v Cox* (2004) Times, 20 February, CA a sentence of 3 months was upheld for an aggravated offence where a pack of dogs attacked a child resulting in hospitalisation.

A[72.10]–[72.14] Order for destruction. Before making a destruction order the court must consider ss 4(1A)(a), 4A(4) and 4A(5) – see A[72.15] below. Where a person is convicted of an offence under s 3(1) the court may order the destruction of the dog and must do so in the case of an aggravated offence, unless the court is satisfied the dog does not constitute a danger to public safety. In deciding whether or not a dog would constitute a danger to public safety, the court must consider the dog's temperament and past behaviour, and whether the owner or the person for the time being in charge of the dog, is a fit and proper person to be in charge of the dog; the court may also consider any other relevant circumstances: Dangerous Dogs Act 1991, s 4(1B).

It was held in *Webb v Chief Constable of Avon and Somerset* [2017] EWHC 3311 (Admin), The Times, 31 January, 2018, a case on the identical wording used in s 4B(2A) (destruction orders otherwise than on conviction following seizure of a dog) that the court is not permitted to find that someone who is not 'an owner' or 'a person for the time being in charge of the dog' is a fit and proper person to be in charge of it; the court can consider only someone from that limited class. Whether or not someone is 'for the time being in charge' of a dog is fact sensitive. The concept has to relate to having responsibility for the dog and it is at least possible that somebody who walks a dog on a regular basis and has responsibility for it during that time meets that description. 'For the time being' does not mean at the time of the seizure, but there are some temporal limits. The concept involves contact in the past or present, but cannot extend to the future. *Webb* was applied in *Henderson v Commissioner of Police of the Metropolis* [2018] EWHC 666 (Admin), [2018] 1 WLR 5029. A person who has never owned, possessed or been in charge of a dog has no standing to intervene in an application under s 4B(1) to contend that the dog is not one to which s 1 of the Act applies; the fitness of such a person cannot be a relevant circumstances for the purposes of s 4B(2A)(b); and such a person does not have standing to contend that the dog would not constitute a danger to public safety.

A court should not make an order for destruction without giving the dog's owner an opportunity to be heard (*R v Ealing Magistrates' Court, ex p Fanneran* (1995) 160 JP 409, 8 Admin LR 351). Any person having custody of the dog may be required to deliver it up to a person appointed by the court to undertake its destruction which will be suspended pending the determination of any appeal. Note that disobedience of a court order to deliver up for destruction is a criminal offence. The maximum penalty under these provisions is a level 5 fine.

A[72.15] **Order for contingent destruction.** Section 4(1A) of the Dangerous Dogs Act 1991 allows for a contingent destruction order even if a mandatory or discretionary order is appropriate. For example, the court may order that the dog will be destroyed unless the owner keeps it under proper control, and that it was to be muzzled and on a lead at all times in any public place. The legal principles were outlined in *R v Flack* [2008] EWCA Crim 204, [2008] 2 Cr App Rep (S) 395; *R v Grant David Robert Davies* [2010] EWCA Crim 1923, 174 CL&J 574.

The Crown Court had no power to impose conditions when it made contingent destruction orders under the Dangerous Dogs Act 1991, s 4A in relation to two pit bull terriers, the possession of which was prohibited under s 1 of the Act: *R (on the application of Sandhu) v Isleworth Crown Court* [2012] EWHC 1658 (Admin), 176 JP 537, 176 CL&J 339.

A contingent destruction order under the Dangerous Dogs Act 1991 can be varied or enforced under s 63 of the MCA 1980: *Chief Constable of Merseyside Police v Doyle* [2019] EWHC 2180 (Admin), [2019] All ER (D) 82 (Aug).

A[72.16] **Additional powers.** A person convicted under s 3(1) may be ordered to keep the dog under proper control or failing that the dog shall be destroyed. The court may also specify measures for keeping the dog under proper control such as muzzling, keeping on a lead or excluding the dog from entering specific places. The court may also order a male dog to be neutered.

A[72.17] **Disqualification.** Whether or not there is an order for destruction of the dog the court may disqualify the person convicted (ie not necessarily the owner) for having custody of a dog for a period specified in the order. A person disqualified for having custody of a dog may apply to the court after one year to terminate the disqualification having regard to his character, conduct and any other circumstances (*R v Holland* [2002] EWCA Crim 1585, [2002] All ER (D) 113 (Jun), CA). Where an application is refused, no further application can be considered for a further year. Costs may be awarded.

Note there is no power to make a disqualification order under s 4(1)(b) that would allow for a single dog to be kept, nor is there power to attach other conditions (*R v Haynes* [2004] EWCA Crim 390, (2004) Times, 27 February, [2004] All ER (D) 235 (Mar), CA).

A[72.18] Having custody of a dog in contravention of a disqualification is an offence, maximum penalty a fine on level 5.

A[72.19] **Right to appeal to the Crown Court.** A person convicted of an offence has an automatic right to appeal to the Crown Court against his conviction, sentence or any order made. In addition, where an order has been made for the destruction of a dog owned by a person other than the offender, then, unless the order was one which the court was required to make the owner may appeal to the Crown Court against the destruction order.

Other offences

A[72.20] The Dangerous Dogs Act 1991 creates a number of offences in connection with 'fighting dogs' which are defined as pit bull terriers, Japanese Tosas and other dogs specified by the Secretary of State. It is unlawful to breed, sell, exchange, advertise for sale or to make a gift of such a dog. Accordingly, these dogs will decline in numbers with the effluxion of time. Those persons who already possess such dogs must obtain a certificate of exemption and comply with the stringent conditions attached thereto. The Dangerous Dogs Exemptions Schemes (England and Wales) Order 2015, SI 2015/138 replaced the Dangerous Dogs Compensation and Exemptions Schemes Order 1991 and continued, with adjustments, the scheme for conditions and requirements for prohibited dogs that a court has decided can be exempt from the prohibition under the Dangerous Dogs Act 1991. Provisions are made for interim orders pending a court considering a case and restrictions on change of ownership on the death or serious illness of the registered person without approval of the court. It is an offence for an owner to have such a dog which is not registered, or to abandon it. The most common charge is for the owner or person for the time being in charge of such a dog to allow it to stray or to be in a public place without being muzzled and kept on a lead: maximum penalty 6 months' imprisonment and a level 5 fine – triable only by magistrates. It should be noted that a dog 'of the type known as a pit bull terrier' is not to be taken as being synonymous with the definition breed (*R v Crown Court at Knightsbridge, ex p Dunne* [1993] 4 All ER 491, [1994] 1 WLR 296). The provisions relating to destruction and disqualification apply as for 'aggravated offences' under s 3 of the 1991 Act. Except that where no destruction order is made in the case of a designated dog, the court must order that unless a certificate of exemption is obtained for the dog within two months of the date of the order the dog shall be destroyed. If a certificate is not obtained the court has a discretion to extend the two-month period.

If a dog is exempted within the period it may not be destroyed, even if it subsequently ceases to be exempt. There is nothing in the exemption scheme which spells out the consequences of loss of exemption, save that it follows from Art 3 of the Exemption Scheme and s 1(3) of the Act that the prohibition imposed by the latter is revived, which engages all the statutory consequences of that prohibition. There is no provision for 'automatic' destruction of a dog which ceases to be exempt – the normal statutory steps must be followed with an application under ss 4, 4A or 4B of the Act: *R(Ali) v Chief Constable of Merseyside* [2014] EWHC 4772 (Admin), (179) JP 333, [2015] Crim LR 646.

Fighting dogs – destruction orders otherwise than on conviction. Provision is made by s 4B of the Dangerous Dogs Act 1991 for the making of destruction orders in respect of fighting dogs otherwise than on conviction. If the dog is one to which s 1 of the Act applies, the court must order its destruction unless it is satisfied the dog would not constitute a danger to public safety. The matters to be considered in this regard are set out in s 4B(2A). It was argued in *R (on the application of Golding) v Crown Court at Maidstone* [2019] EWHC 2029 (Admin), [2019] All ER (D) 64 (Aug) that, in addition to the matters specified in subs (2A) the court should take into account the mandatory conditions of exemption, which require particular controls, but this was rejected. The only matters to be taken into account in determining the issue of danger to public safety in respect of a particular pit bull are those set out at section 4B(2A) of the 1991 Act. The approach in a civil case, therefore, differs from that which is taken in a criminal case under s 4 (see *R v Flack, in A* at [72.15]

Control or destruction order

(Dogs Act 1871, as amended)

A[72.21] As an alternative to prosecution under the Dangerous Dogs Act 1991 the pre-existing civil remedy under the Dogs Act 1871 is still available and is not confined to public places nor where the dog has injured a person, but is determined by where the dog resides (*R (on the application of Shufflebottom) v Chief Constable of Greater Manchester Police* [2003] EWHC 246 (Admin), 167 JP 153). The introduction of a national jurisdiction under the Courts Act 2003 means that the case could be heard at any venue within England and Wales. In practice, jurisdiction will usually be exercised by reference to residence or where the cause of action arose.

Legal notes and definitions

A[72.22] **Application for dangerous dog to be kept under control or destroyed.** Application may be made to a magistrates' court for an order that the dog be destroyed or kept under proper control by the owner. The magistrates may in their discretion make a destruction order without the option of a control order. A dog is not allowed his 'one bite' although in most cases a control order is sufficient for the first transgression. Costs can be awarded by the court to the successful party.

A[72.23] The proceedings must be in the form of a **complaint** and not as an **information** for an offence.

A[72.24] The court must be satisfied (a) that the dog *is* dangerous and (b) that it *is* not kept under proper control. The dog need not be dangerous to mankind. It is sufficient if it is proved that the dog injured cattle or chased sheep. It need not be proved that the owner knew his dog was dangerous. Moreover the dog need not be dangerous by temperament if he is shown to have been dangerous on one occasion. Evidence of the temperament of the animal, however, is admissible if it shows the likelihood of its being dangerous on a particular occasion. The correct approach is for the justices to ask themselves whether on the facts the behaviour of the dog showed that it had a dangerous disposition (*Briscoe v Shattock* [1999] 1 WLR 432, 163 JP 201, [1999] Crim LR 396).

A[72.25]–[72.30] **Change of ownership.** If the owner of the dog establishes in court that he is no longer the owner of the dog but has made a bona fide transfer of the dog to some other person no order can be made against him for the dog's destruction or its proper control; but the order can be made against the new owner provided that a complaint is made against the new owner within six months from the date of the cause of the complaint.

A[72.31] **Procedure at the hearing.** If the **complaint** is accompanied by an **information** alleging some additional offence (such as worrying livestock) then the **information** should be dealt with first and the **complaint** afterwards. The legal adviser should be consulted in such cases.

A[72.32] **Control order.** The court may specify the measures to be taken for keeping the dog under proper control, whether by muzzling, keeping on a lead, excluding it from specified places, or otherwise. Where the dog is male, the court may order it to be neutered if thereby it would be less dangerous.

A[72.33] **Destruction order.** Any person having custody of the dog may be required to deliver it up to a person appointed by the court to undertake its destruction which will be suspended pending the determination of any appeal.

A[72.34] **Disqualification.** A court which makes a destruction order may disqualify the owner for having custody of a dog for a period specified in the order. Disqualification may also be imposed on conviction of an offence of failure to comply with a court order (either to keep the dog under proper control or deliver it up for destruction), maximum penalty a fine on level 3.

A[72.35] A person disqualified for having custody of a dog may apply to the court after one year to terminate the disqualification having regard to his character, conduct and any other circumstances. Where an application is refused, no further application can be considered for a further year. Costs may be awarded.

A[72.36] Disobedience of a court order for control or to deliver up for destruction is a criminal offence, maximum penalty a fine on level 3.

A[72.37] Having custody of a dog in contravention of a disqualification is an offence, maximum penalty a fine on level 5.

A[72.38] **Right of appeal to the Crown Court.** If an order is made for control or destruction, the owner can appeal to the Crown Court. Appeal against conviction and sentence for the criminal offences lie to the Crown Court in the normal way.

A[73]

Dog worrying livestock

Charge (Dog worrying livestock)

A[73.1] **Being the owner of (or being in charge of) a dog worrying livestock namely [. . . . .] on agricultural land situated at [. . . . .]**

Dogs (Protection of Livestock) Act 1953, s 1, as amended

Maximum penalty – Fine level 3.

Legal notes and definitions

A[73.2] A dog's owner or the person in charge of a dog commits an offence if the dog worries livestock on agricultural land. A prosecution for livestock worrying can only be brought by or with the consent of the chief officer of the police, or by the occupier of the agricultural land or the owner of the livestock.

A[73.3] Worrying livestock means:

(a) attacking livestock; or
(b) chasing livestock in such a way as may reasonably be expected to cause injury or suffering to the livestock, or abortion or loss or diminution in their produce; or
(c) being at large in a field where there are sheep except a dog owned by or in the charge of the occupier or the owner of the sheep or a person authorised by them or a police dog, guide-dog, trained sheep dog, working gun dog or pack of hounds.

Livestock is extensively defined by s 3 of the Act and means cattle, sheep, goats, swine, horses or poultry.

A[73.4] Possible lines of defence

(a) That the livestock were trespassing and the dog in question was owned by or in the charge of the occupier of the land on which the livestock were trespassing or the dog was in the charge of a person authorised by the occupier of the land. This defence is not available if the dog was deliberately set on the livestock.
(b) The owner of the dog is not liable if at the time of the attack on the livestock the dog was in the custody of a person whom the owner considered to be a fit and proper person to have charge of the dog.
(c) That the worrying took place on land that was not agricultural land. A street or a private garden is not therefore agricultural land and some moors and heaths are excluded from the definitions of agricultural land.
(d) That the Ministry of Agriculture, Fisheries and Food has directed that this offence shall not apply to the land in question.

A[73.5] No SC Guideline. For structure of the sentencing decision see B[9.6].

A[73.6] Fines. See B[28.16].

A[73.7] **Compensation.** This may be ordered up to a maximum of £5,000 on each charge, eg for the loss of livestock, either as part of a wider sentence or by itself as a substantive penalty. If the offender's means are limited and a monetary penalty is appropriate, preference must be given to ordering compensation instead of a fine.

A[74]

Excessive noise

(Prosecution)

A[74.1] Problems caused by noise amounting to a nuisance, eg caused by noisy neighbours, are dealt with by proceedings for a nuisance order, see A[84].

Causing a noise or disturbance on National Health Service premises is now an offence contrary to s 119 of the Criminal Justice and Immigration Act 2008. By s 120 a constable or 'authorised person' may remove persons causing a noise or disturbance from NHS premises.

Maximum penalty – Fine level 3.

Night time charge

A[74.2] Operating a loudspeaker in a street between 9 pm and 8 am

Control of Pollution Act 1974, s 62

Maximum penalty – Fine level 5 (and a further fine not exceeding £50 for each day on which the offence continues after the conviction). The notes which follow only apply to proceedings brought under the Control of Pollution Act 1974, s 62 and magistrates should confirm with their legal adviser that the proceedings are in fact being brought under that Act.

Legal notes and definitions

A[74.3] In certain circumstances loudspeakers are exempt from prosecutions as follows:

(a) those used by the police, fire, ambulance, water authority or local authority;
(b) those used for communicating with a vessel to direct it or any other vessel;
(c) those forming part of the public telephone system;
(d) those fitted to vehicles solely for the entertainment of persons in the vehicle or for communicating with persons in the vehicle or for giving warning to other vehicles if the loudspeaker forms part of the vehicle's horns or warning system but all such loudspeakers fitted to vehicles must not operate so loudly that they give reasonable cause for annoyance to persons in the vicinity or the exemption is forfeited;
(e) transport undertakings may use loudspeakers off the highways to make announcements to passengers, prospective passengers and staff;
(f) a travelling showman may use a loudspeaker on his fairground;
(g) loudspeakers may be used in an emergency.

Except for the above exemptions there is a complete ban on the use of loudspeakers in a street between 9 pm and 8 am.

A[74.4] **Loudspeaker.** Includes a megaphone and any other device for amplifying sound.

A[74.5] **Street.** Means any highway, road, footway, square or court which is for the time being open to the public.

Day time charge

A[74.6] Operating a loudspeaker in a street between 8 am and 9 pm for the purpose of advertising an entertainment, a trade or a business

Control of Pollution Act 1974, s 62

Maximum penalty – Fine level 5 (and a further fine not exceeding £50 for each day on which the offence continues after the conviction).

Legal notes and definitions

A[74.7] See under this heading at A[74.3].

A[74.8] Defences. It is permissible to use a loudspeaker in a street between the hours of 8 am and 9 pm except as outlined above for advertising. However, there is an exception to this ban on advertising in the following circumstances. Where the loudspeaker is:

(a) fixed to a vehicle conveying a perishable commodity for human consumption; and

(b) is used solely to inform the public (otherwise than by words) that the commodity is on sale from the vehicle; and

(c) is so operated as not to give reasonable cause for annoyance to persons in the vicinity,

it may be operated between the hours of noon and 7 pm on the same day. This is the provision, for example, under which ice cream vans are allowed to use chimes to advertise their wares.

Sentencing (Excessive noise)

A[74.9] No SC Guideline.

Noise amounting to a statutory nuisance. If a noise is persistent and seriously affects persons in an area then the local authority may serve a noise abatement notice or the person affected can lay a complaint alleging that the noise or vibration amounts to a statutory nuisance. See A[84].

A[75]

Offences relating to unfair or prohibited commercial practices

Offences

A[75.1] (From 26/5/08 s 1 of the Trade Description Act 1968 offences were repealed and replaced by a series of new offences contrary to the Consumer Protection from Unfair Trading Regulations 2008.)

Offence 1: Commercial practice contrary to professional diligence

(1) A trader is guilty of an offence if –

(a) **he knowingly or recklessly engages in a commercial practice which contravenes the requirements of professional diligence under regulation 3 (3) (a); and**

(b) **the practice materially distorts or is likely to materially distort the commercial behaviour of the average consumer with regard to the product under regulation 3 (3) (b).**

Regulation 8 of the Consumer Protection from Unfair Trading Regulations 2008

Offence 2: Commercial practice which is misleading

A trader is guilty of an offence if he engages in a commercial practice which is a misleading action under regulation 5 otherwise than by reason of the commercial practice satisfying the condition in regulation 5 (3) (b).

Regulation 9 of the Consumer Protection from Unfair Trading Regulations 2008

Offence 3: Commercial practice – misleading omission

A trader is guilty of an offence if he engages in a commercial practice which is a misleading omission under regulation 6.

Regulation 10 of the Consumer Protection from Unfair Trading Regulations 2008

Offence 4: Commercial practice – aggressive practice

A trader is guilty of an offence if he engages in commercial practice which is aggressive under regulation 17.

Regulation 11 of the Consumer Protection from Unfair Trading Regulations 2008

Offence 5: Banned commercial practices – contravenes schedule 1 (except paragraphs 11 and 28)

A trader is guilty of an offence if he engages in a commercial practice set out in any of the paragraphs 1 to 10, 12 to 27 and 29 to 31 of Schedule 1.

Regulation 12 of the Consumer Protection from Unfair Trading Regulations 2008

Maximum penalty in each case – Fine statutory maximum (£5,000 per offence, or, for offences committed on or after 12 March 2015, an unlimited fine). Triable either way.

Crown Court – 2 years' imprisonment and unlimited fine.

Mode of trial

A[75.2] See general notes at D[4].

What the justices must consider when determining mode of trial is whether or not the custody threshold is crossed; the test is not whether a custodial sentence is 'highly likely' but whether, on the facts, it should be open to the sentencing court to impose a custodial sentence: *Price v Cheshire East Borough Council* [2012] EWHC 2927 (Admin), (2012) 176 JP 697.

Legal notes and definitions

A[75.3] **General.** This is a detailed piece of legislation. A detailed three-part commentary to the 2008 regulations can be found at (2008) 172 JPN 516, 536 and 560 respectively.

Time limits for prosecution. These are provided for by regulation 14 and are similar to the repealed Trade Descriptions Act 1968.

Offences committed by bodies of persons. See regulation 15

A[75.4] **Mens rea – regulation 8.** Creates the only one of the five offence provisions which includes an element of mens rea. Regulation 8(2) defines the term "recklessly". It is submitted that it will suffice if the prosecution can show that the defendant trader did not have regard to the truth or falsity of his statement even though it cannot be shown that he was deliberately closing his eyes to the truth, or that he had any kind of dishonest mind.

A[75.5] **Defences.** Offence due to the act or default of another person – regulation 16 (applies to prosecutions under regulations 9–12).

Due diligence offence – regulation 17 (applies to prosecutions under regulations 9–12).

Innocent publication of advertisement – regulation 18 (applies to prosecutions under regulations 9–12).

A[75.6]–[75.7] **Definitions.** Commercial practice: "Any act, omission, course of conduct, representation or commercial communication (including advertising and marketing), by a trader, which is directly connected with the promotion, sale or supply of a product to or from consumers, whether occurring before, during or after a commercial transaction (if any) in relation to a product".

Consumer: "Any individual who in relation to a commercial practice is acting for purposes which are outside his business".

Product: "Any goods or service and includes immovable property, rights and obligations".

Transactional decision: "Any decision taken by a consumer, whether it is to act or to refrain from acting, concerning (a) whether, how and on what terms to purchase, make payment in whole or in part for, retain or dispose of a product; or (b) whether, how and on what terms to exercise a contractual right in relation to a product".

Trader: "Any person who in relation to a commercial practice is acting for purposes relating to his business (including acting in the name of or on behalf of a trader)".

Sentencing (Unfair or prohibited commercial practices)

A[75.8] **Compensation.** This may be ordered up to £5,000 either as part of a wider sentence or by itself as a substantive penalty. If the offender's means are limited and a monetary penalty is appropriate, preference must be given to ordering compensation instead of a fine.

A[75.9] **Crown Court.** Prison is appropriate only where there has been a deliberate dishonesty. Prison has been upheld in cases involving dishonest dealers eg traders who deliberately "clock" motor vehicles.

A[75.10] Fines. See B[28].

A[76]

Firearm: possessing, purchasing or acquiring without certificate

Charge (Possessing etc a firearm without certificate)

A[76.1] **Possessing, purchasing or acquiring a firearm (or ammunition) without certificate**

Firearms Act 1968, s 1

For shotguns see A[71].

Maximum penalty – 6 months' imprisonment and/or fine level 5 (for offences committed on or after 12 March 2015 an unlimited fine) and forfeiture. Triable either way.

Crown Court – 5 years' imprisonment and unlimited fine.

Mode of trial

A[76.2] See general notes at D[4].

Legal notes and definitions

A[76.3] **Possess, purchase or acquire.** These are three separate offences and the charge should only include one of these allegations. Possession can include where a person has a firearm in his custody for another for the purpose of cleaning it, and is not restricted to physical possession but includes proprietary control (*R v Pawlicki and Swindells* [1992] 3 All ER 902, [1992] 1 WLR 827, CA). More than one person can control a firearm at the same time (*R v Hall-Chung* [2002] EWCA Crim 3088, [2003] All ER (D) 113 (Feb)). 'Acquire' means hire, accept as a gift or borrow: Firearms Act 1968, s 58(4).

A[76.4] **Excessive ammunition.** It is also an offence to have in one's possession more ammunition than the quantity authorised by a firearms certificate.

A[76.5] **Certificate.** This is granted by the police. It may specify conditions. Failure to observe such conditions is an offence. The certificate may bear a photograph of the holder and, unless revoked or cancelled, remains in force for the period specified which may be up to three years.

A[76.6] **Firearm.** This is defined by s 57(1) of the Firearms Act 1968 as:

(1) (1)In this Act, the expression 'firearm' means a lethal barrelled weapon of any description from which any shot, bullet or other missile can be discharged and includes–

(a) any prohibited weapon, whether it is such a lethal weapon as aforesaid or not; and

(b) any component part of such a lethal or prohibited weapon; and

(c) any accessory to any such weapon designed or adapted to diminish the noise or flash caused by firing the weapon'.

'Lethal weapon'. This includes a weapon not designed to kill or inflict injury but capable of doing so if misused: *Read v Donovan* [1947] KB 326, [1947] 1 All ER 37, 111 JP 46 (signal pistol); *Moore v Gooderham* [1960] 3 All ER 575, 124 JP 513 (air gun); *R v Thorpe* [1987] 2 All ER 108, [1987] 1 WLR 383 (revolver powered by compressed carbon dioxide); *R v Singh* [1989] Crim LR 724 (flare launcher).

An imitation firearm which is so constructed or adapted as to be readily convertible into a firearm is to be treated as a firearm even though it has not been so converted. However, in *R v Bewley* [2012] EWCA Crim 1457, [2013] 1 All ER 1, [2013] 1 WLR 137 the weapon in question was a starting pistol, which was originally designed to fire blank cartridges. A 2cm hole had been drilled into the solid barrel and the top of the hammer had been broken off. A senior forensic scientist was able to fire it by placing it in a vice, inserting a specially selected lead pellet and using a mallet and punch to strike the firing pin. The judge ruled that the pistol was a lethal-barrelled weapon from which a missile '(could) be discharged', but the Court of Appeal quashed the conviction. Although the Firearms Act 1982 had not amended the Firearms Act 1968, the two had to be construed as creating a single code. It was the clear legislative intention of the 1982 Act to exclude from the 1968 Act imitation firearms which could only be readily convertible into firearms by equipment or tools not in common use. The capacity to discharge a missile by conversion (the need for extraneous tools in the present case amounted to a conversion) was now restricted to only imitation weapons which could be converted without any special skill or equipment or tools not in common use. On the facts this weapon did not fall within s 57(1). Nor was it a component part of 'such a lethal or prohibited weapon' within s 57(1)(b). If a starting pistol did not fall within the definition of firearm in s 57(1) no part of it could do so.

A[76.7] Excepted firearms under s 1 apply to every firearm except:

(a) a shot gun within the meaning of the Act, that is to say a smooth-bore gun (not being an air gun) which–
  (i) has a barrel not less than 24 inches in length and does not have any barrel with a bore exceeding 2 inches in diameter;
  (ii) either has no magazine or has a non-detachable magazine incapable of holding more than two cartridges; and
  (iii) is not a revolver gun; and

(b) an air weapon (that is to say, an air rifle, air gun or air pistol which does not fall within s 5(1) and which is not of a type declared by rules made by the Secretary of State under s 53 of this Act to be specially dangerous).

A gun which has been adapted to have such a magazine as is mentioned in (a)(ii) above shall not be regarded as falling within that provision unless the magazine bears a mark approved by the Secretary of State for denoting that fact and that mark has been made, and the adaptation has been certified in writing as having been carried out in a manner approved by him, either by one of the two companies mentioned in s 58(1) of the Act or by such other person as may be approved by him for that purpose.

Shot guns and air weapons may be 'firearms', however, for the purpose of other offences under the Act: see A[77.8], below.

The Firearms (Dangerous Air Weapons) Rules 1969, SI 1969/1490, as amended, declare certain air weapons to be specifically dangerous. Section 48 of the Firearms (Amendment) Act 1997 provides that any reference to an air rifle, pistol or air gun in the 1968 Act or these rules shall include a reference to a rifle, pistol or gun powered by compressed carbon dioxide.

The definition of 'air weapon' in (b) above excludes two different kinds of air weapon: those specifically prohibited under s 5(1) (eg despite their not being specially dangerous, any air rifle, air gun or air pistol which uses, or is designed or adapted for use with, a self-contained gas cartridge system); and those specially dangerous: *R v Law* [2015] EWCA Crim 5, [2016] 1 WLR 189, [2016] 1 Cr App R 13. The prohibition by s 5(1)(af) of any air rifle, air gun or air pistol which uses, or is designed or adapted for use with, a self-contained gas cartridge system came into force on 30 April 2004 and is subject to the saving provision of s 39(4) of the Anti-social Behaviour Act 2003, which provides that where a person had in his possession an air rifle, air gun or air pistol on the commencement day s 5(1) of the 1968 Act does not prevent its continued possession, s 1 of the 1968 Act shall apply and the certificate shall not be revoked in whole or in part, or not renewed, on the ground that the person does not have a good reason for possessing the air rifle, gun or pistol. In *R v Goldsborough* [2015] EWCA Crim 1278, [2015] 1 WLR 4921, [2015] 2 Cr App R

29, [2015] Crim L R 887 it was held that where a person possessed an air weapon on commencement day but did not have a firearms certificate, he could not be guilty of an offence under s 5 but only of an offence under s 1.

A[76.8] **Ammunition.** Means ammunition for any firearm as defined above. It also means grenades, bombs and other similar missiles. It also includes ammunition containing or adapted to contain any noxious liquid, gas or other noxious thing.

Section 1(4), however, makes the following exceptions:

(a) cartridges containing five or more shot, none of which exceeds 36 inch in diameter;
(b) ammunition for an air gun, air rifle or air pistol; and
(c) blank cartridges not more than one inch in diameter measured immediately in front of the rim or cannelure of the base of the cartridge.

A[A76.8A] **Mental element.** Section 1 is to be construed strictly and proof of mens rea is unnecessary: *R v Howells* [1977] QB 614, [1977] 3 All ER 417, 141 JP 641. It is immaterial that the accused did not know the nature of the article in his possession: *R v Hussain* [1981] 2 All ER 287, [1981] 1 WLR 416; *R v Waller* [1991] Crim LR 381, CA approved in *R v Vann and Davis* [1996] Crim LR 52, CA, or that possession of a container was for a matter of minutes without opportunity to discover that it contained a firearm: *R v Steele* [1993] Crim LR 298, CA.

A[76.9] **Exemptions.** If a defence is raised that a weapon or ammunition is not covered by the Act the legal adviser should be consulted.

A[76.10]–[76.15] Certain persons and organisations are exempted from having to hold firearms certificates such as the following:

(a) A registered dealer and his staff, an auctioneer, carrier or warehouseman in the course of his business, a licensed slaughterer in respect of his slaughtering instruments, ships and aircraft (Firearms Act 1968, ss 8–10 and 13).
(b) A person may carry a firearm or ammunition for another person who does hold a firearms certificate if he is acting under that other person's instructions and if that other person is to use the firearm or ammunition for sporting purposes only. Sporting purposes does not include the shooting of rats (Firearms Act 1968, s 11(1)). **NB:** If the person carrying the firearm etc is under 18 years, the other person must be 18 years or over.
(c) Members of rifle clubs, miniature rifle clubs and cadet corps in possession of Home Office approval do not require certificates for club or corps activities such as drilling or target practice (Firearms Act 1968, s 11(3) and Firearms (Amendment) Act 1988, s 15).
(d) A certificate is not necessary for weapons at a miniature rifle range if the miniature rifles do not exceed 0.23 calibre or if the weapons are air guns, air rifles or air pistols which have not been declared as dangerous by the Home Office (Firearms Act 1968, s 11(4)).
(e) Persons participating in a theatrical performance or rehearsal or in producing a film may have a firearm without a certificate (Firearms Act 1968, s 12).
(f) Starters aged 18 years or over at athletic meetings may have a firearm without a certificate (different rules for persons aged under 18 years apply for blank-firing weapons): Firearms Act 1968, s 11(2).
(g) A person who has obtained a permit from the police may have a firearm and ammunition, as authorised by that permit without holding a firearms certificate. The permit will usually be for short periods such as one month to allow, for example, the next of kin of the holder of a firearms certificate time to sell the weapons and ammunition after the holder has died (Firearms Act 1968, s 7).
(h) A person may borrow a shotgun or, if under 18 years, a rifle from the occupier of private premises (which includes land) and use it on those premises in the occupier's presence (Firearms Act 1968, s 11(5) and Firearms (Amendment) Act 1988, s 16).
(i) A person visiting Great Britain may have in his possession a firearm or shotgun without a certificate where he has been granted a visitor's permit. Such permits are granted by the police and may continue in force for up to 12 months (Firearms (Amendment) Act 1988, s 17).

(j) A person temporarily in Great Britain purchasing weapons for export (Firearms (Amendment) Act 1988, s 18).
(k) Museums granted a licence by the Secretary of State (Schedule to the Firearms (Amendment) Act 1988, para.1).

A[76.16] Degree of proof. A defendant wishing to establish one of the above exemptions does not have to satisfy the court beyond reasonable doubt; he need only satisfy the court that on the balance of probabilities his defence is true. Having regard to the legitimate aims of the above legislation, the shifting of the legal burden to the accused is necessary and proportionate in ECHR terms.

A[76.17] Antique firearms. The legislation does not apply to an antique firearm sold, transferred, purchased, acquired or possessed as a curiosity or ornament (Firearms Act 1968, s 58(2)). See *Bennett v Brown* (1980) 71 Cr App Rep 109.

Sentencing (Possessing etc a firearm without certificate)

A[76.18] No SC Guideline.

Structure of the sentencing decision. See B[9.6].

Should the case be committed for sentence? (*R v Gent* [2002] EWCA Crim 943 [2002] All ER (D) 46 (Apr)) 2 years' imprisonment for possession of a sawn-off shotgun.

A[76.19] Available sentences. See Table A at B[43.1A].

R v Charles [2004] EWCA Crim 1977, [2005] 1 Cr App Rep (S) 253 – 5 years when coupled with a siege and threats to the police.

A[76.20] Custodial sentence. See B[15]. See *R v Clarke* [1997] 1 Cr App Rep (S) 323, CA on the use of imprisonment.

A[76.21] Community sentence. See B[9].

A[76.22] Fines. See B[28].

A[76.23] Forfeiture. The court can order the firearm and ammunition to be forfeited to the police or disposed of as it thinks fit.

A[76.24] The court can cancel any firearm or shotgun certificate held by the defendant.

A[76A]

Firearms: prohibition of certain weapons and control of arms traffic

Charge (Prohibition of certain weapons and control of arms)

A[76A.1] Possessing, purchasing or acquiring a weapon subject to general prohibition, without authority

Firearms Act 1968, s 5(1)

Maximum penalty

(1) Possession, etc, of any of the weapons specified in s 5(1)(a)–(af) or (c) below is triable only on indictment with a maximum penalty of 10 years or an unlimited fine or both. NOTE the minimum sentence provisions of s 51A of the Firearms Act 1968 apply to these weapons.

(2) Possession, etc, of the weapon specified in s 5(1)(b) is triable either way with a maximum penalty of 6 months and/or a fine level 5 (for offences committed on or after 12 March 2015 an unlimited fine). Triable either way. Crown Court – 10 years or an unlimited fine or both.

(3) Possession, etc, of any a firearm disguised as another object s 5(1A)(a) is triable only on indictment with a maximum penalty 10 years or an unlimited fine or both. NOTE the minimum sentence provisions of s 51A of the Firearms Act 1968 apply to this offence.

(4) Possession, etc, of any of the prohibited weapons in s 5(1A) is triable either way with a maximum penalty of 6 months and/or a fine level 5 (for offences committed on or after 12 March 2015 an unlimited fine). Triable either way. Crown Court – 10 years or an unlimited fine or both.

Mode of trial

A[76A.2] See general notes at D[4].

The prohibited weapons

A[76A.3] Section 5 of the Firearms Act provides as follows:

'Prohibition of certain weapons and control of arms traffic

5 Weapons subject to general prohibition

(1) A person commits an offence if, without authority, he has in his possession, or purchases or acquires-

(a) any firearm which is so designed or adapted that two or more missiles can be successively discharged without repeated pressure on the trigger;

(ab) any self-loading or pump-action rifled gun other than one which is chambered for.22 rim-fire cartridges;

(aba) any firearm which either has a barrel less than 30 centimetres in length or is less than 60 centimetres in length overall, other than an air weapon, a muzzle-loading gun or a firearm as signalling apparatus;

(ac) any self-loading or pump-action smooth-bore gun which is not an air weapon or chambered for.22 rim-fire cartridges and either has a barrel less than 24 inches in length or an air weapon or is less than 40 inches in length overall;

(ad) any smooth-bore revolver gun other than one which is chambered for 9 mm rim-fire cartridges or a muzzle-loading gun;

(ae) any rocket launcher, or any mortar, for projecting a stabilised missile, other than a launcher or mortar designed for line-throwing or pyrotechnic purposes or as signalling apparatus;

(af) any air rifle, air gun or air pistol which uses, or is designed or adapted for use with, a self-contained gas cartridge system;

(b) any weapon of whatever description designed or adapted for the discharge of any noxious liquid, gas or other thing; and

(c) any cartridge with a bullet designed to explode on or immediately before impact, any ammunition containing or designed or adapted to contain any such noxious thing as is mentioned in paragraph (b) above and, if capable of being used with a firearm of any description, any grenade, bomb (or other like missile), or rocket or shell designed to explode as aforesaid.

(1A) Subject to section 5A of this Act, a person commits an offence if, without authority, he has in his possession, or purchases or acquires-

(a) any firearm which is disguised as another object;

(b) any rocket or ammunition not falling within paragraph (c) of subsection (1) of this section which consists in or incorporates a missile designed to explode on or immediately before impact and is for military use;

(c) any launcher or other projecting apparatus not falling within paragraph (ae) of that subsection which is designed to be used with any rocket or ammunition falling within paragraph (b) above or with ammunition which would fall within that paragraph but for its being ammunition falling within paragraph (c) of that subsection;

(d) any ammunition for military use which consists in or incorporates a missile designed so that a substance contained in the missile will ignite on or immediately before impact;

(e) any ammunition for military use which consists in or incorporates a missile designed, on account of its having a jacket and hard-core, to penetrate armour plating, armour screening or body armour;

(f) any ammunition which incorporates a missile designed or adapted to expand on impact;

(g) anything which is designed to be projected as a missile from any weapon and is designed to be, or has been, incorporated in-

(i) any ammunition falling within any of the preceding paragraphs; or

(ii) any ammunition which would fall within any of those paragraphs but for its being specified in subsection (1) of this section.

(2) The weapons and ammunition specified in subsections (1) and (1A) of this section (including, in the case of ammunition, any missiles falling within subsection (1A)(g) of this section) are referred to in this Act as "prohibited weapons" and "prohibited ammunition" respectively.

. . .

(7) For the purposes of this section and section 5A of this Act-

(a) any rocket or ammunition which is designed to be capable of being used with a military weapon shall be taken to be for military use;

(b)) references to a missile designed so that a substance contained in the missile will ignite on or immediately before impact include references to any missile containing a substance that ignites on exposure to air; and

(c) references to a missile's expanding on impact include references to its deforming in any predictable manner on or immediately after impact.

(8) For the purposes of subsection (1) (aba) and (ac) above, any detachable, folding, retractable or other movable butt-stock shall be disregarded in measuring the length of any firearm.

(9) Any reference in this section to a muzzle-loading gun is a reference to a gun which is designed to be loaded at the muzzle end of the barrel or chamber with a loose charge and a separate ball (or other missile).'

Legal notes and definitions

A[76A.4] Section 5 creates an absolute offence, and it is not open to the defence to prove that the accused did not know and could not reasonably have been expected to know that he was in possession of a prohibited weapon: *R v Bradish* [1990] 1 QB 981, [1990] 1 All ER 460, 154 JP 21, CA; followed in *R v Deyemi and Edwards* [2007] EWCA Crim 2060, (2008) 172 JP 137, [2008] 1 Cr App R 25, where it was held that, in 'container' cases, it was not a defence that the accused did not know what was in the container).

Adaptations to an authorised firearm may cause it to be a prohibited weapon if it involves the breach of a condition of the related firearms certificate: *R v Shahabi-Shack* [2014] EWCA Crim 2842, [2015] 1 WLR 2602, [2015] 1 Cr App R 25.

A firearm which is designed or adapted for automatic fire still remains so designed, and is therefore a prohibited weapon, despite the fact that an essential component such as the trigger may be missing: *R v Clarke* [1986] 1 All ER 846, [1986] 1 WLR 209, CA).

Section 5 does not import either explicitly or implicitly any intention on the part of the designer or the adapter. The weapon does not have to be designed or adapted for the purpose of burst or repeated fire; it is sufficient if it is capable of such fire even if only in the hands of an expert: *R v Law* [1999] Crim LR 837, CA. Similarly, a weapon which had not been designed for the purpose of discharging noxious gasses but which has the design capability of discharging gas cartridges is not lawful: *R v Rhodes* [2015] EWCA Crim 155, [2015] 2 Cr App R 16, [2015] Crim LR 445.

An air pistol is an air weapon within the terms of S 5(1)(aba) (and therefore not a prohibited weapon) only if the exclusions in s 1(3)(b) do not bite: *R v Law* [2015] EWCA Crim 5, [2016] 1 WLR 189, [2016] 1 Cr App R 13. See A[76.7], ante.

Section 5(1)(af) came into force on 30 April 2004 and is subject to the saving provision of s 39(4) of the Anti-social Behaviour Act 2003, (in Part 1, Magistrates' Courts, Procedure, ante) which provides that where a person had in his possession an air rifle, air gun or air pistol on the commencement day s 5(1) of the Firearms Act 1968 does not prevent its continued possession, s 1 of the Firearms Act 1968 (firearm certificate) shall apply and the certificate shall not be revoked in whole or part, or not renewed, on the ground that the person does not have a good reason for possessing the air rifle, air gun or air pistol. See *R v Goldsborough (Paul)* [2015] EWCA Crim 1278, [2015] 1 WLR 4921, [2015] 2 Cr App R 29, [2015] Crim LR 887, where the defendant possessed an air weapon on commencement date but did not have a firearms certificate. It was held that he could not be guilty of an offence under s 5 but only of an offence under s 1.

An empty bottle of Fairy Liquid filled with hydrochloric acid was held not to be a weapon designed or adapted for the discharge of the acid within the meaning of Section 5(1)(b) this paragraph because there had been no alteration to the bottle so as to make it fit for such use: *R v Formosa* [1991] 2 QB 1, [1991] 1 All ER 131, 155 JP 97, CA.

The emission of electricity from a stun device amounts to a 'discharge' within the meaning of s 5(1)(b); accordingly, a Lightning Strike hand-held electric stun device was held to be a weapon designed for the discharge of a noxious thing: *Flack v Baldry* [1988] 1 All ER 673, [1988] 1 WLR 393, 152 JP 418, HL.

Sentencing (Prohibition of certain weapons and control of arms)

A[76A.5] No SC Guideline.

A[76A.6] Structure of the sentencing decision. See B[43.1A].

A[76A.7] Available sentences. See Table A at B[43.1A].

A[77]

Firearm (trespassing in a building and on land)

Charges (Firearm (trespassing in a building and on land))

A[77.1] **1 Whilst having a firearm or imitation firearm with him, entering or being in any building or part of a building, as a trespasser and without reasonable excuse**

Firearms Act 1968, s 20(1)

Maximum penalty –

Firearm: 6 months' imprisonment and/or fine level 5 (for offences committed on or after 12 March 2015 an unlimited fine) and forfeiture. Triable either way.

Air weapon or imitation firearm: Fine level 5 and 6 months and forfeiture. Triable only by magistrates.

Crown Court – 7 years' imprisonment and unlimited fine.

A[77.2] **2 Whilst having a firearm or imitation firearm with him entering or being on any land as a trespasser and without reasonable excuse**

Firearms Act 1968, s 20(2)

Maximum penalty – Fine level 4 and 3 months and forfeiture.

Mode of trial

A[77.3] See general notes at D[4].

Legal notes and definitions

A[77.4] **Trespasser.** The court must be satisfied that the defendant was a trespasser which means that the defendant was personally within the domain of another person without his consent.

A[77.5] **Land.** The Act provides that 'land' includes 'land covered by water'.

A[77.6] **With him.** The prosecution must establish more than mere possession, namely, a close physical link and immediate control over the firearm, but not necessarily that he had been carrying it (*R v Kelt* [1977] 3 All ER 1099, [1977] 1 WLR 1365, CA). In the context of an offence under s 18 of the Act a defendant was said not to have a firearm with him when it was 2 or 3 miles away (*R v Bradish* [2004] EWCA Crim 1340, 148 Sol Jo LB 474, [2004] All ER (D) 40 (Apr), CA).

A[77.7] **Reasonable excuse.** The onus of establishing reasonable excuse for his presence, when a trespasser, in a building and in possession of a firearm rests on the defendant. He does not have to prove reasonable excuse beyond all reasonable doubt. He has only to prove that on the balance of probabilities he had reasonable excuse. For ECHR, see A[33.5] above.

A[77.8] **Firearm.** Means any lethal barrelled weapon of any description from which any shot, bullet or other missile can be discharged. A lethal weapon includes one capable of inflicting injury although not designed to do so, eg a signal pistol. An imitation firearm which is so constructed or adapted as to be readily converted into a firearm is to be treated as a firearm even though it has not been so converted. The Court of Appeal has ruled that a starting pistol which could be adapted to fire bullets if the barrel was drilled was a firearm. In this case the barrel was partly drilled: *R v Freeman* [1970] 2 All ER 413, [1970] 1 WLR 788. However, in *R v Bewley* [2012] EWCA Crim 1457, [2013] 1 All ER 1, [2013] 1 WLR 137 the weapon in question was a starting pistol, which was originally designed to fire blank cartridges. A 2cm hole had been drilled into the solid barrel and the top of the hammer had been broken off. A senior forensic scientist was able to fire it by placing it in a vice, inserting a specially selected lead pellet and using a mallet and punch to strike the firing pin. The judge ruled that the pistol was a lethal-barrelled weapon from which a missile '(could) be discharged', but the Court of Appeal quashed the conviction. Although the Firearms Act 1982 had not amended the Firearms Act 1968, the two had to be construed as creating a single code. It was the clear legislative intention of the 1982 Act to exclude from the 1968 Act imitation firearms which could only be readily convertible into firearms by equipment or tools not in common use. The capacity to discharge a missile by conversion (the need for extraneous tools in the present case amounted to a conversion) was now restricted to only imitation weapons which could be converted without any special skill or equipment or tools not in common use. On the facts this weapon did not fall within s 57(1). Nor was it a component part of 'such a lethal or prohibited weapon' within s 57(1)(b). If a starting pistol did not fall within the definition of firearm in s 57(1) no part of it could do so.

A[77.9] **Shotguns and air weapons** count as firearms for the purpose of this offence. An air weapon is an air rifle, air gun or air pistol of a type which has not been declared by the Home Office to be specially dangerous. Nevertheless, an air gun as a species of weapon is not, as a matter of law, a lethal weapon; the prosecution must prove that fact, either by expert evidence or by evidence of someone who has seen the gun fired and can indicate not only that it did work but what its observed effect was when it was fired: *Grace v DPP* (1988) 153 JP 491, DC. However, air rifles which had been tested and classified as in normal working order and capable of killing small vermin or of being used in target practice were held to have been properly found to be lethal barrelled weapons: *Castle v DPP* (1998) Times 3 April.

A[77.9A] **Imitation firearm.** An imitation firearm means anything which has the appearance of being a firearm (other than any weapon designed or adapted for the discharge of any noxious liquid, gas or other thing) whether or not it is capable of discharging any shot, bullet or other missile: s 57(4) of the Firearms Act 1968. The test is whether the thing looked like a firearm at the time when the accused had it for that purpose: *R v Morris and King* (1984) 149 JP 60, 79 Cr App Rep 104, CA. Two fingers inside the defendant's pocket cannot constitute possession of an imitation firearm under s 17(2) of the Act: *R v Bentham* [2005] UKHL 18, [2005] 2 All ER 65, HL.

Sentencing (Firearm (trespassing in a building and on land))

A[77.10]–[77.15] No SC Guideline but see A[28].

Structure of the sentencing decision. See B[9.6].

A[77.16] **Available sentences.** See Table A at B[43.1A] (firearms) and Table B at B[43.2] (air weapons and trespass on land).

A[77.17] **Forfeiture.** The court can order the weapon and ammunition to be forfeited to the police or disposed of as the court thinks fit.

A[77.18] The court can also cancel any firearm or shotgun certificate held by the defendant.

A[78]
Forgery

Charge (Forgery)

A[78.1] **1 Unlawfully making a false instrument with the intention that he (or another) should use it to induce somebody to accept it as genuine, and, by reason of so accepting it to do, or not to do, some act to that person's or some other person's prejudice**

Forgery and Counterfeiting Act 1981, s 1

A[78.2] **2 Unlawfully using a false instrument, which is and which he knows or believes to be false, with the intention of inducing somebody to accept it as genuine, as above**

Forgery and Counterfeiting Act 1981, s 3

A[78.3] **3 Unlawfully using a copy of a false instrument, which is and which he knows or believes to be false, as above**

Forgery and Counterfeiting Act 1981, s 4

Maximum penalty – 6 months' imprisonment and/or fine level 5 (for offences committed on or after 12 March 2015 an unlimited fine). Triable either way.

Crown Court – 10 years' imprisonment and unlimited fine.

Mode of trial

A[78.4] Consider first the general guidelines at D[4]. In general, forgery offences should be tried summarily except for the presence of one or more of the following factors:

(a) breach of trust by a person in a position of substantial authority or in whom a high degree of trust has been placed;
(b) there has been a sophisticated hiding or disguising of the offence;
(c) the offence has been committed by an organised gang;
(d) the victim was particularly vulnerable;
(e) there is unrecovered property of high value.

Legal notes and definitions

A[78.5] **Instrument.** Means any document whether of a formal or informal character, any stamp issued or sold by the Post Office, any Inland Revenue stamp and any disk, tape, soundtrack or other device on or in which information is recorded, or is stored by mechanical, electronic or other means.

A[78.6] The term 'false' is extensively defined in s 9 of the Forgery and Counterfeiting Act 1981. The essence of forgery is that the document must tell a lie about itself and not merely tell a lie. It was held in *R v Warneford and Gibbs* [1994] Crim LR 753, CA that any 'lie in the document must relate to the actual circumstances of the making of the document (and) a lie about other facts, extraneous to the document, does not suffice'. However, the Court of Appeal in *A-G's Reference (No 1 of 2000)* [2001] 1 Cr App Rep 218, [2001] Crim LR 127, CA, while agreeing with the above remarks, regarded that case as coming to the wrong conclusion on the facts and held that a tachograph record sheet would be false for the purposes of s 9(1)(g) if it was a document which required, before it could be made or altered, that a set of circumstances should exist or should have existed and those circumstances did not or had not existed (the false circumstance was that the record was being made during a period when there wrongly purported to be a second driver who was driving).

Where a defendant had stolen a cheque, opened a building society account in a name similar to that of the payee, paid the cheque into it and subsequently withdrew money from the account by completing a withdrawal form in the name in which he had opened the account, it was held that as the withdrawal form purported to be signed by the person who had opened the account, and had in that respect been accurate, it had not told a lie about itself and the defendant had not been guilty of forgery by making a false instrument under s 9(1)(h): *R v More* [1987] 3 All ER 825, [1987] 1 WLR 1578.

A[78.7] **Make.** A person makes a false instrument if he alters it so as to make it false in any respect, whether or not it is false in some other respect apart from that alteration. There is no further element of dishonesty required.

A[78.8] **Intention.** In *R v Tobierre* [1986] 1 All ER 346, [1986] 1 WLR 125, CA for an offence under s 3, it was held that the prosecution must prove both that the accused intended to induce somebody to accept the forgery as genuine *and* intended that by so doing he should act, or not act, to that person's or some other person's prejudice. In some cases, the demonstrated existence of a claim of right at the time when the false document was used may negative an intent to cause another to act to his prejudice; but where, in relation to the submission of a false expenses invoice by beneficiaries of a trust fund to the trustee, the evidence showed both an intention to induce the trustees to accept the false invoice as genuine, and an intention to cause them by reason of so accepting it to authorise and execute a cheque, which in the circumstances it was not their duty to do, both elements of the mens rea were present: *A-G's Reference (No 1 of 2002)* [2002] EWCA Crim 1768, [2002] 3 All ER 840, [2003] 1 Cr App Rep 131, [2002] Crim LR 844.

A[78.9] **Prejudice.** An act or omission intended to be induced is to be regarded as being to a person's prejudice only if it is one which *will* result (and not merely which has the *potential* to result (*R v Garcia* (1987) 87 Cr App Rep 175, [1988] Crim LR 115, CA):

(a) in his temporary or permanent loss of property;
(b) in his being deprived of the opportunity to earn remuneration, or greater remuneration;
(c) in his being deprived of an opportunity to gain a financial advantage otherwise than by way of remuneration; or would result in someone being given an opportunity;
(d) to earn remuneration, or greater remuneration from him; or
(e) to gain a financial advantage from him otherwise than by way of remuneration; or
(f) would be the result of his having accepted a false instrument as genuine, or a copy of a false instrument as a copy of a genuine one, in connection with the performance of a duty.

An act which a person has an enforceable duty to do and an omission to do an act which a person is not entitled to do shall be disregarded for the purposes of the Forgery and Counterfeiting Act 1981, s 10(2). Where the defendant had submitted forged documents in support of an application for housing benefit, although the contents of the documents were true, the local authority did not have an enforceable duty to pay the benefit as he was required to provide the evidence required by the Housing Benefit (General) Regulations 1987: *R v Winston* [1998] 1 Cr App Rep 337, 162 JP 775, [1998] Crim LR 81, DC.

Sentencing (Forgery)

A[78.10] No SC Guideline.

A[78.11]–[78.15] **Structure of the sentencing decision.** See B[9.6].

A[78.16] **Available sentences.** See Table A at B[43.1A].

A[78.17] **Compensation.** This may be ordered up to £5,000 either as part of a wider sentence or by itself as a substantive penalty. If the offender's means are limited and a monetary penalty is appropriate, preference must be given to ordering compensation instead of a fine.

A[79]

Found on enclosed premises

Charge (Found on enclosed premises)

A[79.1] **Being found in or upon any dwelling-house, warehouse, outhouse, or in any enclosed yard, garden or area for an unlawful purpose**

Vagrancy Act 1824, s 4

Maximum penalty – For a first offence fine level 3 or 3 months. For a subsequent offence the accused may sometimes be committed to the Crown Court as an incorrigible rogue for sentence.

**For an offence committed from a date to be appointed, the power to impose imprisonment will be repealed by the CJA 2003, Sch 25. In addition the power to commit the offender as an incorrigible rogue to the Crown Court will be repealed by the CJA 2003, Sch 37, Part 9.

Legal notes and definitions

A[79.2] **Found.** For an offence to be made out an individual had to be found, which meant that he had to be **seen** or **discovered**, with an unlawful purpose in mind at the time he was so found: *L v CPS* [2007] EWHC1843 (Admin).

A[79.3] **Enclosed.** The yard may still rate as being enclosed even if there is access through spaces in surrounding buildings, an archway, open gate, etc but does not include a room within a building (*Talbot v DPP* [2000] 1 WLR 1102, 164 JP 169, sub nom Talbot v Oxford City Magistrates' Court [2000] 2 Cr App Rep 60).

A[79.4] **Yard.** Would not include a very large area, such as a shipyard or railway sidings, the essential feature of a yard is that it should be a relatively small area ancillary to a building.

Area. There was no evidence that a university campus amounted to an 'enclosed area' within the terms of the section in *Akhurst v Enfield Magistrates' Court* [2009] EWHC 806 (Admin), 173 JP 499.

A[79.5] **Unlawful purpose.** Means that the defendant was there for the purpose of committing a criminal offence. In deciding whether the defendant had such a purpose, the court must consider all the evidence drawing such inferences from it as appear proper in the circumstances. "Unlawful purpose" meant that an individual was about to commit a criminal offence. Hiding from the police in order to escape detection for a criminal offence which had already occurred could not constitute an unlawful purpose: *L v CPS* [2007] EWHC 1843 (Admin).

Sentencing (Found on enclosed premises)

A[79.6] **No SC Guideline.** For structure of the sentencing decision. See B[9.6].

A[79.7] **Available sentences.** See Table B at B[43.2].

A[79.8] **Committal for sentence.** For a subsequent offence, as long as the previous offence was **not** dealt with by absolute or conditional discharge the court may commit the defendant to the Crown Court for sentence on bail or in custody as an incorrigible rogue. The Crown Court can impose imprisonment for up to one year. **For offences committed on or after a date to be appointed the power to imprison or commit for sentence has been repealed.

A[79.9] Even if there is no previous conviction for a similar offence but there is evidence of previous convictions under the Vagrancy Act 1824, then this procedure may still be available to the magistrates. **See **A[79.1]** above.

A[80]

Health and safety at work

Charges (Health and safety at work)

A[80.1] **Did fail to comply with an improvement or prohibition notice (specified)**

Health and Safety at Work Act 1974, s 33(1)(g)

A[80.2] **Did fail to comply with an order of the court to remedy (specified)**

Health and Safety at Work Act 1974, s 33(1)(o)

Maximum penalty – Fine £20,000 and 6 months. Triable either way.

Crown Court – 2 years' imprisonment and unlimited fine.

A[80.3] **Did fail to comply with a duty specified in the Health and Safety at Work Act 1974, ss 2–6 (for example), under s 3(1) did fail to conduct an undertaking in such a way as to ensure, so far as is reasonably practicable, that persons not in your employment, who may be affected thereby, were not exposed to risks to their health and safety.**

Health and Safety at Work Act 1974, s 33(1A)

Maximum penalty – Fine £20,000 and 6 months. Triable either way.

Crown Court – Unlimited fine.

A[80.4] **Other breaches of the Act or Regulations**

See the new Sch 3A to the Health and Safety at Work Act 1974 as added by Sch 1 to the Health and Safety (Offences) Act 2008.

Mode of trial

A[80.5]–[80.6] Section 85 of the Legal Aid, Sentencing and Punishment of Offenders Act 2012 enables magistrates' courts to impose unlimited fines for most offences previously punishable with a maximum fine on summary conviction of £5,000, however expressed. In anticipation of this the following annex was added to the Criminal Practice Directions 2015 [2015] EWCA Crim 1567.

'CPD XIII Annex 3

CASES INVOLVING VERY LARGE FINES IN THE MAGISTRATES' COURT

(1) This Annex applies when s.85 Legal Aid, Sentencing and Punishment of Offenders Act 2012 comes into force and the magistrates' court has the power to impose a maximum fine of any amount.

(2) An authorised DJ (MC) must deal with any allocation decision, trial and sentencing hearing in the following types of cases which are triable either way:

  (a) Cases involving death or significant, life changing injury or a high risk of death or significant, life-changing injury;

  (b) Cases involving substantial environmental damage or polluting material of a dangerous nature;

  (c) Cases where major adverse effect on human health or quality of life, animal health or flora has resulted;

(d) Cases where major costs through clean up, site restoration or animal rehabilitation have been incurred;
(e) Cases where the defendant corporation has a turnover in excess of £10 million but does not exceed £250 million, and has acted in a deliberate, reckless or negligent manner;
(f) Cases where the defendant corporation has a turnover in excess of £250 million;
(g) Cases where the court will be expected to analyse complex company accounts;
(h) High profile cases or ones of an exceptionally sensitive nature.

(3) The prosecution agency must notify the justices' clerk where practicable of any case of the type mentioned in paragraph 2 of this Annex, no less than 7 days before the first hearing to ensure that an authorised DJ (MC) is available at the first hearing.

(4) The justices' clerk shall contact the Office of the Chief Magistrate to ensure that an authorised DJ (MC) can be assigned to deal with such a case if there is not such a person available in the courthouse. The justices' clerk shall also notify a Presiding Judge of the Circuit that such a case has been listed.

(5) Where an authorised DJ (MC) is not appointed at the first hearing the court shall adjourn the case. The court shall ask the accused for an indication of his plea, but shall not allocate the case nor, if the accused indicates a guilty plea, sentence him, commit him for sentence, ask for a pre sentence report or give any indication as to likely sentence that will be imposed. The justices' clerk shall ensure an authorised DJ (MC) is appointed for the following hearing and notify the Presiding Judge of the Circuit that the case has been listed.

(6) When dealing with sentence, section 3 of the Powers of Criminal Courts (Sentence) Act 2000 can be invoked where, despite the magistrates' court having maximum fine powers available to it, the offence or combination of offences make it so serious that the Crown Court should deal with it as though the person had been convicted on indictment.

(7) An authorised DJ (MC) should consider allocating the case to the Crown Court or committing the accused for sentence.'

Legal notes and definitions

A[80.7] The Health and Safety at Work Act 1974 imposes general duties on employers towards their employees, self-employed persons, persons connected with premises other than employees and articles and substances for use at work in ss 2–6. Most prosecutions are now brought under these sections.

A[80.8] Specific offences are detailed in the Health and Safety at Work Act 1974, s 33.

A[80.9] **Offences by bodies corporate.** Where an offence committed by a body corporate is proved to have been committed with the consent or connivance of or attributable to neglect by a director, manager, secretary or other officer of the company, he as well as the company shall be guilty of that offence and may be proceeded against.

A[80.10]–[80.15] **Prosecution by inspectors.** An inspector if authorised by the enforcement authority may prosecute before a magistrates' court.

A[80.16] **Power to order remedial action.** Where it appears to the court that the defendant can remedy matters they may in addition to or instead of a punishment order him within a given time to remedy the matters complained of (s 42).

A[80.17] Work means work as an employee, or self-employed person. Regulations may extend the meaning of work to include at work.

A[80.18] **Article for use at work,** means any plant designed for use or operation by persons at work and any article designed for use as a component in any such plant.

Defences

A[80.19] Typical prosecutions involve breaches of duty to safeguard health and safety so far as **is reasonably practicable as well as specific requirements under regulations.** It is therefore a common defence that an employer has safe systems of work and has done all that was reasonably practicable to avoid a breach of duty.

(1) Although s 2 is concerned with ensuring safety and s 3 with ensuring an absence of risk to safety, the language of the statute signified that these two concepts are one and the same thing. It was also implicit from the leading decision in *R v Chargot Ltd (t/a Contract Services)* [2007] EWCA Crim 3032, [2008] 2 All ER 1077, [2008] ICR 517; affd [2008] UKHL 73, [2009] 2 All ER 645, [2009] 1 WLR 1. In each section the obligation is qualified by the words 'so far as is reasonably practicable'. An offence under s 2 is committed if there is a relevant risk to the safety of an employee and the defendant has not taken such steps as are reasonably practicable to avoid it; whilst an offence under s 3 is committed if there is a relevant risk to the safety of a non-employee who may be affected by the conduct of the undertaking and the defendant has not taken such steps as are reasonably practicable to avoid that. In the case of each section, s 40 places on the defendant a reverse onus of proof (on the balance of probabilities) on the issue of reasonable practicability.

(2) The offence in s 2 or s 3 lies in the failure to ensure safety so far as reasonably practicable, ie in exposure to risk of injury, not in the doing of actual injury. Causation of the injury, therefore, is not an ingredient of either offence: *R v Chargot*; *R v EGS Ltd* [2009] EWCA Crim 1942 followed.

(3) The risks with which both sections are concerned are those relating to the activities of the defendant. Although it will sometimes be necessary to address the source of a risk, the introduction of a separate test of 'derivation' is more likely to confuse than to illuminate. The jury should be asked to concentrate on two central issues:
   (i) exposure to risk and
   (ii) (assuming the issue is raised) whether it was reasonably practicable to avoid it.

(4) Foreseeability of risk (strictly foreseeability of danger) is relevant to the question whether a risk to safety exists. That accords with the ordinary meaning of risk, as is demonstrated by the concept of a risk assessment, which is itself an exercise in foresight. Whether a material risk exists or not is a jury question and the foreseeability (or lack of it) of some danger or injury is a part of the enquiry: *Baker v Quantum Clothing Group Ltd* [2011] UKSC 17, [2011] 4 All ER 223, [2011] 1 WLR 1003 followed. Nonetheless, the Crown is not required to prove that the accident which occurred was foreseeable. The sections impose, in effect, a duty on employers to think deliberately about things which are not obvious. In most cases, absent the sort of time factor which obtained in *Baker v Quantum*, it is likely that consideration of foreseeability will add little to the question whether there was a risk. In most cases, the principal relevance of foreseeability will be whether the employer took all reasonably practicable precautions to avoid that material risk: *R v Tangerine Confectionary Ltd; R v Veolia ES (UK) Ltd* [2011] EWCA Crim 2015, 176 JP 349.

(5) The prosecution must prove a real as opposed to a hypothetical risk. There is no objective standard or test applicable to every case by which the line may be drawn. But in most, if not every, case there will be one way or the other important indicia which the court is obliged to take into account to determine whether the risk is real or fanciful. None of them is determinative; but many (depending on the facts of any particular case) will be of importance. For example, the absence of any previous accident in circumstances which occur day after day will be highly relevant. Unless it can be said that the person was exposed to a real risk by the conduct of the undertaking, no question of the reasonable practicability of measures designed to avoid that risk arises: *R v Porter* [2008] EWCA Crim 1271, (2008) Times, 9 July. The case of *Porter* was considered in *R (on the application of the Health and Safety Executive)*

v C-T Aviation Solutions Ltd [2015] EWCA Crim 1620, [2016] RTR 3. The appellant company specialised in traffic management systems for UK airports. A woman died after being hit by a lorry on an access road. The driver was acquitted of causing death by careless driving. He gave evidence for the prosecution to the effect that the victim had been in the lorry's 'blind spot'. The company was convicted and appealed. The issue was whether the judge should have upheld a submission of no case to answer based on the absence of 'material risk'. The appeal was dismissed. *Porter* did not purport to depart from, or put a gloss on, the statutory test. It was open to the defence to contend that the possibility of pedestrians crossing the road and colliding with vehicles was an incidence of everyday life tolerated by society, and that the crossing was no different from many others. However, the issue was whether that crossing, in that location and designed as it was, had exposed pedestrians to a material risk to their health and safety, and there was ample evidence of such material risk. The company had remodelled or redesigned the road, parking and pedestrian system and the material risk created was 'pedestrian and vehicular conflict'. The combination of an overly wide gap in the crossing guard rail and the absence of give way markings had led to a situation where pedestrians with suitcases could enter the crossing unseen by a lorry.

ECHR. This is a legal rather than an evidential burden on the defendant and the reverse burden of proof is compatible with the presumption of innocence under the ECHR (*R v Davies* [2002] EWCA Crim 2949, [2002] All ER (D) 275 (Dec), sub nom *Davies v Health and Safety Executive* [2003] IRLR 170, 147 Sol Jo LB 29;*R v Chargot Ltd (t/a Contract Services)* [2007] EWCA Crim 3032, [2008] 2 All ER 1077, [2008] ICR 517; affd [2008] UKHL 73, [2009] 2 All ER 645, [2009] 1 WLR 1).

Sentencing (Health and safety at work)

A[80.20] The Sentencing Council has published a definitive guideline 'Health and Safety Offences, Corporate Manslaughter and Food Safety and Hygiene Offences'. This applies to all organisations and offenders sentenced on or after 1 February 2016. We reproduce below the part of the guideline which deals with the offences under ss 2 and 3 of the Health and Safety at Work Act 1974.

Organisations
Breach of duty of employer towards employees and non-employees
Breach of duty of self-employed to others

Health and Safety at Work Act 1974 (section 33(1)(a) for breaches of sections 2 and 3)

Breach of Health and Safety regulations

Health and Safety at Work Act 1974 (section 33(1)(c))

Triable either way

Maximum: when tried on indictment: unlimited fine

when tried summarily: unlimited fine

Offence range: £50 fine – £10 million fine

STEP ONE
Determining the offence category

The court should determine the offence category using only the culpability and harm factors in the tables below.

Culpability

Where there are factors present in the case that fall in different categories of culpability, the court should balance these factors to reach a fair assessment of the offender's culpability.

Very high

Deliberate breach of or flagrant disregard for the law

High

Offender fell far short of the appropriate standard; for example, by:

- failing to put in place measures that are recognised standards in the industry
- ignoring concerns raised by employees or others
- failing to make appropriate changes following prior incident(s) exposing risks to health and safety
- allowing breaches to subsist over a long period of time

Serious and/or systemic failure within the organisation to address risks to health and safety

Medium

Offender fell short of the appropriate standard in a manner that falls between descriptions in 'high' and 'low' culpability categories

Systems were in place but these were not sufficiently adhered to or implemented

Low

Offender did not fall far short of the appropriate standard; for example, because:

- significant efforts were made to address the risk although they were inadequate on this occasion
- there was no warning/circumstance indicating a risk to health and safety

Failings were minor and occurred as an isolated incident

HARM

Health and safety offences are concerned with failures to manage risks to health and safety and do not require proof that the offence caused any actual harm. **The offence is in creating a risk of harm.**

(1) Use the table below to identify an initial harm category based on the **risk of harm created by the offence**. The assessment of harm requires a consideration of **both**:
   – the seriousness of the harm risked (A, B or C) by the offender's breach; and
   – the likelihood of that harm arising (high, medium or low).

Seriousness of harm risked

	Level A	Level B	Level C
	• Death	• Physical or mental impairment, not amounting to Level A, which has a substantial and long-term effect on the sufferer's ability to carry out normal day-to-day activities or on their ability to return to work	• All other cases not falling within Level A or Level B

	Level A	Level B	Level C
	• Physical or mental impairment resulting in lifelong dependency on third party care for basic needs • Significantly reduced life expectancy	• A progressive, permanent or irreversible condition	
High likelihood of harm	Harm category 1	Harm category 2	Harm category 3
Medium likelihood of harm	Harm category 2	Harm category 3	Harm category 4
Low likelihood of harm	Harm category 3	Harm category 4	Harm category 4 (start towards bottom of range)

(2) **Next, the court must consider if the following factors apply. These two factors should be considered in the round in assigning the final harm category.**

(i) **Whether the offence exposed a number of workers or members of the public to the risk of harm.** The greater the number of people, the greater the risk of harm.

(ii) **Whether the offence was a significant cause of actual harm.** Consider whether the offender's breach was a **significant cause*** of actual harm and the extent to which other factors contributed to the harm caused. Actions of victims are unlikely to be considered contributory events for sentencing purposes. Offenders are required to protect workers or others who may be neglectful of their own safety in a way which is reasonably foreseeable.

If one or both of these factors apply the court must consider either moving up a harm category or substantially moving up within the category range at step two overleaf. If already in harm category 1 and wishing to move higher, move up from the starting point at step two on the following pages. The court should not move up a harm category** if actual harm was caused but to a lesser degree than the harm that was risked, as identified on the scale of seriousness above.

* A significant cause is one which more than minimally, negligibly or trivially contributed to the outcome. It does not have to be the sole or principal cause.

** While this precludes in these circumstances moving up a category it does not preclude moving up within the range: *R v Havering BC* [2017] EWCA Crim 242, [2017] 2 Cr App R (S) 9.

STEP TWO
Starting point and category range

Having determined the offence category, the court should identify the relevant table for the offender on the following pages. There are tables for different sized organisations.

At step two, the court is required to focus on the organisation's annual turnover or equivalent to reach a starting point for a fine. The court should then consider further adjustment within the category range for aggravating and mitigating features.

At step three, the court may be required to refer to other financial factors listed below to ensure that the proposed fine is proportionate.

Obtaining financial information

The offender is expected to provide comprehensive accounts for the last three years, to enable the court to make an accurate assessment of its financial status. In the absence of such disclosure, or where the court is not satisfied that it has been given sufficient reliable information, the court will be entitled to draw reasonable inferences as to the offender's means from evidence it has heard and from all the circumstances of the case, **which may include the inference that the offender can pay any fine.**

Normally, only information relating to the organisation before the court will be relevant, unless exceptionally it is demonstrated to the court that the resources of a linked organisation are available and can properly be taken into account.

(1) *For companies*: annual accounts. Particular attention should be paid to turnover; profit before tax; directors' remuneration, loan accounts and pension provision; and assets as disclosed by the balance sheet. Most companies are required to file audited accounts at Companies House. **Failure to produce relevant recent accounts on request may properly lead to the conclusion that the company can pay any appropriate fine.**

(2) *For partnerships*: annual accounts. Particular attention should be paid to turnover; profit before tax; partners' drawings, loan accounts and pension provision; assets as above. Limited liability partnerships (LLPs) may be required to file audited accounts with Companies House. *If adequate accounts are not produced on request, see paragraph 1.*

(3) *For local authorities, fire authorities and similar public bodies*: the Annual Revenue Budget ('ARB') is the equivalent of turnover and the best indication of the size of the organisation. It is unlikely to be necessary to analyse specific expenditure or reserves (where relevant) unless inappropriate expenditure is suggested.

(4) *For health trusts*: the independent regulator of NHS Foundation Trusts is Monitor. It publishes quarterly reports and annual figures for the financial strength and stability of trusts from which the annual income can be seen, available via www.monitor-nhsft.gov.uk. Detailed analysis of expenditure or reserves is unlikely to be called for.

(5) *For charities*: it will be appropriate to inspect annual audited accounts. Detailed analysis of expenditure or reserves is unlikely to be called for unless there is a suggestion of unusual or unnecessary expenditure.

Very large organisation

Where an offending organisation's turnover or equivalent very greatly exceeds* the threshold for large organisations, it may be necessary to move outside the suggested range to achieve a proportionate sentence.

* As to the approach where a company has a very large turnover, but is sustaining losses and is being kept alive as an operational concern by its parent company, see *R v Tata Steel Ltd* [2017] EWCA Crim 704, [2017] 2 Cr App R (S) 29. As to the proper approach where the court is dealing with parent companies or joint venture companies, see *R v NPS London Ltd* [2019] EWCA Crim 228, [2019] 2 Cr App R (S) 18.

Large
Turnover or equivalent: £50 million and over

	Starting point	Category range
Very high culpability		
Harm category 1	£4,000,000	£2,600,000 – £10,000,000
Harm category 2	£2,000,000	£1,000,000 – £5,250,000
Harm category 3	£1,000,000	£500,000 – £2,700,000
Harm category 4	£500,000	£240,000 – £1,300,000
High culpability		
Harm category 1	£2,400,000	£1,500,000 – £6,000,000
Harm category 2	£1,100,000	£550,000 – £2,900,000

	Starting point	Category range
Harm category 3	£540,000	£250,000 – £1,450,000
Harm category 4	£240,000	£120,000 – £700,000
Medium culpability		
Harm category 1	£1,300,000	£800,000 – £3,250,000
Harm category 2	£600,000	£300,000 – £1,500,000
Harm category 3	£300,000	£130,000 – £750,000
Harm category 4	£130,000	£50,000 – £350,000
Low culpability		
Harm category 1	£300,000	£180,000 – £700,000
Harm category 2	£100,000	£35,000 – £250,000
Harm category 3	£35,000	£10,000 – £140,000
Harm category 4	£10,000	£3,000 – £60,000

Medium
Turnover or equivalent: between £10 million and £50 million

	Starting point	Category range
Very high culpability		
Harm category 1	£1,600,000	£1,000,000 – £4,000,000
Harm category 2	£800,000	£400,000 – £2,000,000
Harm category 3	£400,000	£180,000 – £1,000,000
Harm category 4	£190,000	£90,000 – £500,000
High culpability		
Harm category 1	£950,000	£600,000 – £2,500,000
Harm category 2	£450,000	£220,000 – £1,200,000
Harm category 3	£210,000	£100,000 – £550,000
Harm category 4	£100,000	£50,000 – £250,000
Medium culpability		
Harm category 1	£540,000	£300,000 – £1,300,000
Harm category 2	£240,000	£100,000 – £600,000
Harm category 3	£100,000	£50,000 – £300,000
Harm category 4	£50,000	£20,000 – £130,000
Low culpability		
Harm category 1	£130,000	£75,000 – £300,000
Harm category 2	£40,000	£14,000 – £100,000
Harm category 3	£14,000	£3,000 – £60,000
Harm category 4	£3,000	£1,000 – £10,000

Small
Turnover or equivalent: between £2 million and £10 million

	Starting point	Category range
Very high culpability		
Harm category 1	£450,000	£300,000 – £1,600,000
Harm category 2	£200,000	£100,000 – £800,000
Harm category 3	£100,000	£50,000 – £400,000
Harm category 4	£50,000	£20,000 – £190,000
High culpability		

	Starting point	Category range
Harm category 1	£250,000	£170,000 – £1,000,000
Harm category 2	£100,000	£50,000 – £450,000
Harm category 3	£54,000	£25,000 – £210,000
Harm category 4	£24,000	£12,000 – £100,000
Medium culpability		
Harm category 1	£160,000	£100,000 – £600,000
Harm category 2	£54,000	£25,000 – £230,000
Harm category 3	£24,000	£12,000 – £100,000
Harm category 4	£12,000	£4,000 – £50,000
Low culpability		
Harm category 1	£45,000	£25,000 – £130,000
Harm category 2	£9,000	£3,000 – £40,000
Harm category 3	£3,000	£700 – £14,000
Harm category 4	£700	£100 – £5,000

Micro
Turnover or equivalent: not more than £2 million

	Starting point	Category range
Very high culpability		
Harm category 1	£250,000	£150,000 – £450,000
Harm category 2	£100,000	£50,000 – £200,000
Harm category 3	£50,000	£25,000 – £100,000
Harm category 4	£24,000	£12,000 – £50,000
High culpability		
Harm category 1	£160,000	£100,000 – £250,000
Harm category 2	£54,000	£30,000 – £110,000
Harm category 3	£30,000	£12,000 – £54,000
Harm category 4	£12,000	£5,000 – £21,000
Medium culpability		
Harm category 1	£100,000	£60,000 – £160,000
Harm category 2	£30,000	£14,000 – £70,000
Harm category 3	£14,000	£6,000 – £25,000
Harm category 4	£6,000	£2,000 – £12,000
Low culpability		
Harm category 1	£30,000	£18,000 – £60,000
Harm category 2	£5,000	£1,000 – £20,000
Harm category 3	£1,200	£200 – £7,000
Harm category 4	£200	£50 – £2,000

The table below contains a **non-exhaustive** list of factual elements providing the context of the offence and factors relating to the offender. Identify whether any combination of these, or other relevant factors, should result in an upward or downward adjustment from the starting point. **In particular, relevant recent convictions are likely to result in a substantial upward adjustment.** In some cases, having considered these factors, it may be appropriate to move outside the identified category range.

Factors increasing seriousness

Statutory aggravating factors:
Previous convictions, having regard to a) the nature of the offence to which the conviction relates and its relevance to the current offence; and b) the time that has elapsed since the conviction
Other aggravating factors include:
Cost-cutting at the expense of safety
Deliberate concealment of illegal nature of activity
Breach of any court order
Obstruction of justice
Poor health and safety record
Falsification of documentation or licences
Deliberate failure to obtain or comply with relevant licences in order to avoid scrutiny by authorities
Targeting vulnerable victims
Factors reducing seriousness or reflecting personal mitigation
No previous convictions or no relevant/recent convictions
Evidence of steps taken voluntarily to remedy problem
High level of co-operation with the investigation, beyond that which will always be expected
Good health and safety record
Effective health and safety procedures in place
Self-reporting, co-operation and acceptance of responsibility

STEPS THREE AND FOUR

The court should 'step back', review and, if necessary, adjust the initial fine based on turnover to **ensure that it fulfils the objectives of sentencing** for these offences. The court may adjust the fine upwards or downwards, including outside the range.

STEP THREE

Check whether the proposed fine based on turnover is proportionate to the overall means of the offender

General principles to follow in setting a fine

The court should finalise the appropriate level of fine in accordance with section 164 of the Criminal Justice Act 2003, which requires that the fine must reflect the seriousness of the offence and that the court must take into account the financial circumstances of the offender.

The level of fine should reflect the extent to which the offender fell below the required standard. The fine should meet, in a fair and proportionate way, the objectives of punishment, deterrence and the removal of gain derived through the commission of the offence; it should not be cheaper to offend than to take the appropriate precautions.

The fine must be **sufficiently substantial to have a real economic impact which will bring home to both management and shareholders the need to comply with health and safety legislation.**

Review of the fine based on turnover

The court should 'step back', review and, if necessary, adjust the initial fine reached at step two to *ensure that it fulfils the general principles* set out above. The court may adjust the fine upwards or downwards including outside of the range.

The court should examine the financial circumstances of the offender in the round to assess the economic realities of the organisation and the most efficacious way of giving effect to the purposes of sentencing.

In finalising the sentence, the court should have regard to the following factors:

- The profitability of an organisation will be relevant. If an organisation has a small profit margin relative to its turnover, downward adjustment may be needed. If it has a large profit margin, upward adjustment may be needed.
- Any quantifiable economic benefit derived from the offence, including through avoided costs or operating savings, should normally be added to the fine arrived at in step two. Where this is not readily available, the court may draw on information available from enforcing authorities and others about the general costs of operating within the law.
- Whether the fine will have the effect of putting the offender out of business will be relevant; in some bad cases this may be an acceptable consequence.

In considering the ability of the offending organisation to pay any financial penalty, the court can take into account the **power to allow time for payment or to order that the amount be paid in instalments,** if necessary over a number of years.

STEP FOUR
Consider other factors that may warrant adjustment of the proposed fine

The court should consider any wider impacts of the fine within the organisation or on innocent third parties; such as (but not limited to):

- the fine impairs offender's ability to make restitution to victims;
- impact of the fine on offender's ability to improve conditions in the organisation to comply with the law;
- impact of the fine on employment of staff, service users, customers and local economy (but not shareholders or directors).

Where the fine will fall on public or charitable bodies, the fine should normally be substantially reduced if the offending organisation is able to demonstrate the proposed fine would have a significant impact on the provision of its services.

STEP FIVE
Consider any factors which indicate a reduction, such as assistance to the prosecution

The court should take into account sections 73 and 74 of the Serious Organised Crime and Police Act 2005 (assistance by defendants: reduction or review of sentence) and any other rule of law by virtue of which an offender may receive a discounted sentence in consequence of assistance given (or offered) to the prosecutor or investigator.

STEP SIX
Reduction for guilty pleas

The court should take account of any potential reduction for a guilty plea in accordance with section 144 of the Criminal Justice Act 2003 and the *Guilty Plea* guideline.

STEP SEVEN
Compensation and ancillary orders

In all cases, the court must consider whether to make ancillary orders. These may include:

Remediation

Under section 42(1) of the Health and Safety at Work Act 1974, the court may impose a remedial order in addition to or instead of imposing any punishment on the offender.

An offender ought by the time of sentencing to have remedied any specific failings involved in the offence and if it has not, will be deprived of significant mitigation.

The cost of compliance with such an order should not ordinarily be taken into account in fixing the fine; the order requires only what should already have been done.

Forfeiture

Where the offence involves the acquisition or possession of an explosive article or substance, section 42(4) enables the court to order forfeiture of the explosive.

Compensation

Where the offence has resulted in loss or damage, the court must consider whether to make a compensation order. The assessment of compensation in cases involving death or serious injury will usually be complex and will ordinarily be covered by insurance. In the great majority of cases the court should conclude that compensation should be dealt with in the civil court, and should say that no order is made for that reason.

If compensation is awarded, priority should be given to the payment of compensation over payment of any other financial penalty where the means of the offender are limited.

Where the offender does not have sufficient means to pay the total financial penalty considered appropriate by the court, compensation and fine take priority over prosecution costs.

STEP EIGHT
Totality principle

If sentencing an offender for more than one offence, consider whether the total sentence is just and proportionate to the offending behaviour in accordance with the *Offences Taken into Consideration and Totality* guideline.

STEP NINE
Reasons

Section 174 of the Criminal Justice Act 2003 imposes a duty to give reasons for, and explain the effect of, the sentence.

Costs (Health and safety at work)

A[80.21] The prosecution will normally claim the costs of investigation and presentation. These may be substantial and can incorporate time and activity expended on containing and making the area safe.

Fines – practice and procedure

A[80.22] The Sentencing Council has issued a definitive guideline for the above offences (see infra) The Court of Appeal has recommended that when the Health and Safety Executive commences criminal proceedings, it should list in writing for the assistance of the court not only the facts of the case, but also any aggravating features which it says exist in the particular case. This should be served on the court and the defendant. If the defendants plead guilty they should submit a similar document setting out any mitigating features they wish the court to take into account. If by the time the matter comes to court there is agreement between the parties as to which are the relevant aggravating and mitigating factors that the court should take into account, and the plea is upon an agreed basis, that agreed basis should be put into writing so there is no doubt what is the proper basis upon which the court should pass sentence: *R v Friskies Petcare (UK) Ltd* 2 Cr App R (S) 401, CA

A[80.23] As to guilty pleas on a basis, see *R (Health and Safety Executive) v ATE Truck and Trailer Sales Ltd* [2018] EWCA Crim 752, [2018] 2 Cr App R (S) 29. There is much to be said for sensible agreement between the parties in an area where a specialist prosecution agency is involved. Such sensible agreement is to be encouraged and can be expected to be weighed heavily by any court before departing from it. Ultimately, however, sentencing is the function of the court.

The case is also instructive as to the meaning of low likelihood of harm. An absence of accident does not persuasively tell in favour of a low likelihood; everything depends on the circumstances of the case.

A[80.24] *Fire safety offences* The Sentencing Council chose to omit these offences from the definitive guideline because it felt that their inclusion had the potential for distorting sentence levels. However, it was held in *Mehmood Butt v Regina* [2018] EWCA Crim 1617, that the structure of the guidelines in identifying the steps involved in determining the seriousness of the offending might usefully be followed.

> '27 In prosecutions for a breach of the Order the harm risked will be at the highest level, level A in the Guideline, because of the risk of death or serious injury. The level of culpability will vary depending upon the circumstances of the offending. The likelihood of harm occurring depends upon the chances of fire breaking out. In most cases there will be no evidence of special risk of a fire breaking out, although in some there may be evidence of an enhanced risk. The law imposes a high standard for precautions to guard against the risk of fire. That is not only because of the very serious consequences that can flow from fire but also because it is so unpredictable how and when it will start. The severe penalties evident in cases of the breach of the Order do not depend upon such enhanced risk. Its presence would be a seriously aggravating factor. The two factors referred to in paragraph 9 of the Guideline (risk to many and actual harm) are aggravating features when sentencing for fire safety offences.
>
> 28 In the *Patel* case, as we have seen, a suspended sentence was combined with a substantial fine. A combination of a fine and a suspended or community sentence is available when sentencing. The Definitive Guideline on Offences Taken into Consideration and Totality indicates:
>
> "A fine should not generally be imposed in combination with a custodial sentence because of the effect of imprisonment on the means of the defendant. However, exceptionally, it may be appropriate to impose a fine in addition to a custodial sentence where:
>
> - The sentence is suspended;
> - A confiscation order is not contemplated; and
> - There is no obvious victim to whom compensation can be awarded; and
> - The offender has, or will have, resources from which a fine can be paid."
>
> 29 It is particularly apt when the offending is related to a defendant's business or employment, when dealing with offenders with substantial means, or when the sentence allows an offender to continue in well-remunerated work. For many, a substantial fine coupled with a suspended sentence or community sentence will be an appropriate punishment. Indeed, there may be cases where a substantial fine would be viewed as a greater punishment by an offender than the other part of the sentence.
>
> 30 "Resources" include both income and capital. Many Guidelines, including the Health and Safety Guideline, identify fines by reference to bands which are calculated by taking a multiple of a defendant's disposable income. Courts will be astute to recognise that income, evidenced by tax returns, when looking at the means of those in business, and especially family businesses, may not tell the whole story. Moreover, the wealth of an offender may be reflected in substantial capital rather than high income.
>
> 31 We would also wish to reiterate the need for defendants in health and safety and similar cases to place detailed evidence of their financial circumstances before the sentencing court . . . ' (per Lord Burnett CJ).

A[81]
Immigration offences

Charges (Immigration offences)

A[81.1] **1 Illegal entry and similar offences by a person who is not a British citizen**

Immigration Act 1971, s 24

Maximum penalty – Triable summary only. 6 months' imprisonment and/or fine level 5 (for offences committed on or after 12 March 2015 an unlimited fine).

A[81.2] **2 Assisting unlawful entry to a member state, assisting an asylum seeker to enter the UK and entry to the UK in breach or attempted breach* of an exclusion or deportation order.**

Immigration Act 1971, ss 25, 25A, 25B

* Words 'or attempted breach' inserted by Immigration Act 2016, s 75 and Sch 14.

Maximum penalty – 6 months' imprisonment and/or fine level 5 (for offences committed on or after 12 March 2015 an unlimited fine). Triable either way.

Crown Court – Unlimited fine and/or 14 years' imprisonment.

A[81.3] **3 Possession of false passports, work permits, registration cards etc and other offences in connection with the administration of the Act.**

Immigration Act 1971, ss 26, 26A

Maximum penalty – Triable summary only. 6 months' imprisonment and/or fine level 5 (for offences committed on or after 12 March 2015 an unlimited fine).

NB: The Nationality, Immigration and Asylum Act 2002 created a large number of related offences under the Act with effect from 10 February 2003. If charged under s 26A they are punishable with a maximum of ten years' imprisonment and a fine unless they only involve possession without reasonable excuse when the maximum penalty is two years' imprisonment and a fine. Both offences are triable either way carrying on summary conviction a fine level 5 and 6 months imprisonment.

Mode of trial

A[81.4] See general notes at D[4] and sentencing below for further guidance, although many cases will be most appropriately dealt with at Crown Court (*R v Uluc* [2001] EWCA Crim 2991 [2001] All ER (D) 273 (Dec)).

Legal notes and definitions

A[81.5] A person commits an offence of knowingly remaining beyond the time limit of a limited leave to stay on the day when he first knows that the time limit of his leave has expired. He continues to commit the offence (Immigration Act 1971, s 24(1)(b)(i)) throughout any period he is in the United Kingdom thereafter.

Assisting unlawful immigration to member state The conduct of a person charged with a s 25(1) offence must inevitably precede or be contemporaneous with any entry by those he is assisting. The material times for the knowledge or belief required by s 25(1) are the times at which the defendant makes or carries out the arrangements. Therefore, an offence under s 25(1)(a) may relate to a person who sought or intended to become an illegal entrant as well as to someone who had become an illegal entrant by reason of passing or attempting to pass through immigration control by concealment or deception. Similarly, an offence under s 25(1)(b) may relate to an intending asylum claimant: *R v Eyck* [2000] 3 All ER 569, [2000] 1 WLR 1389, CA.

A conviction under s 25 was upheld where the offences consisted of helping a person to submit a bogus application for a Certificate of Approval ('COA') in respect of an intended sham marriage; a sham bride is essential for a sham marriage and the defendant had been instrumental in finding her. A condition precedent for a sham marriage was an application for a COA, which the prosecution had proved the defendant had been instrumental in creating and submitting. Once the jury had been satisfied that the defendant had committed the acts it was for them to decide whether they had facilitated a breach of immigration law: *R v Ali* [2015] EWCA Crim 43, [2015] 1 Cr App Rep 494.

There is nothing in s 25 to indicate that the individual non-national of the European Union, whose breach of immigration law has been facilitated, needs to be a person who is not an applicant for asylum; and the entirely domestic offence of facilitating a breach of immigration law includes a breach of an immigration law having effect in a member state, and a conspiracy to commit such an offence is properly charged under s 1, and not s 1A, of the Criminal Law Act 1977: *R v Bina* [2014] EWCA Crim 1444, [2014] 2 Cr App Rep 496, [2015] Crim LR 287.

A[81.6] **Extended time limits for prosecution.** The normal time limit for laying an information for a summary offence is 6 months. However in cases charged under s 28(1)(a) (knowingly entering the United Kingdom in breach of a deportation order), s 28(1)(c)(having lawfully entered the United Kingdom remains without leave beyond the time allowed), s 26(1)(c) (making a false representation to an immigration officer) or 26(1)(d) (altering any relevant certificate, work permit or passport) an information relating to the offence may in England and Wales be tried by a magistrates' court if it is laid within six months after the commission of the offence, or if it is laid within three years after the commission of the offence and not more than two months after the date certified by a police officer above the rank of chief superintendent to be the date on which evidence sufficient to justify proceedings came to the notice of the police.

A[81.7] **Search warrants.** In the case of offences of illegal entry (s 24(1)(a)), obtaining leave to enter or remain by deception (s 24(1)(aa)) and remaining beyond a time-limited leave or failing to observe conditions of leave (s 24(1)(b)) may all be the subject of an arrest without warrant by a constable or immigration officer with reasonable grounds to suspect an offence has been committed. A justice of the peace may grant a warrant of entry of search to premises if satisfied by written information on oath that a person suspected of one of the above offences is to be found on those premises.

Immigration and Asylum Act 1999, s 7

A[81.8] **An immigration officer** is a person appointed by the Secretary of State or may be employed as a revenue and customs officer.

Facilitating entry is not an offence if it is done otherwise than for gain or by a bona fide organisation whose purpose is assisting asylum claimants.

Illegal entrant is not confined to persons who have actually entered the country but includes those seeking to enter (*R v Eyck* [2000] 3 All ER 569, [2000] 1 WLR 1389, CA).

Defence based on art 31 of the United Nations Convention relating to the Status of Refugees

A[81.8A] It is a defence for a refugee charged with one of the offences listed below to show that, having come to the UK directly from a country to which his life or freedom was threatened, he:

(a) presented himself to the authorities in the UK without delay;

(b) showed good cause for his illegal entry or presence; and
(c) made a claim for asylum as soon as was reasonably practicable after his arrival in the UK.

A refugee is defined by the Convention, Article 1.A(2) as any person who 'owing to a well-founded fear of being persecuted for reasons of race, religion, nationality, membership of a particular social group or political opinion, is outside the country of his nationality and is unable or, owing to such fear, is unwilling to avail himself of the protection of that country; or, who, not having a nationality and being outside the country of his former habitual residence . . . is unable or, owing to such fear, is unwilling to return to it . . . '. The Convention meaning is adopted by the Immigration and Asylum Act 1999, s 31(6).

The meaning of 'particular social group' was considered in *R v Evans* [2013] EWCA Crim 125, [2013] 1 Cr App R 34. It was held that there was no basis in logic or the evidence for either of the following collection of individuals to come within the term: (a) migrants of Jamaican origin returning to Jamaica after residing in the US, Canada or UK; or (b) persons deported back to Jamaica from any of those countries.

If the refugee stopped in another country en route to the UK the above defence is only available if he shows that he could not reasonably have expected to be given protection under the Convention in that other country: Immigration and Asylum Act 1999, s 31(1) and (2).

The burden on the refugee to establish his refugee status is an evidential burden only; once he has adduced sufficient evidence to raise the issue the prosecution bears the burden of proving beyond reasonable doubt that he is not a refugee. The burden of proving the other matters that must be established under s 31(1) is, however, the legal burden.

The offences are any offence or attempt to commit an offence under:

(a) the Forgery and Counterfeiting Act 1981, Part I;
(b) the Identity Cards Act 2006, s 25(1);
(c) the Immigration Act 1971, s 24A; and
(d) the 1971 Act, s 26(1).

Section 31 supersedes the interpretation of art 31 in *R v Uxbridge Magistrates' Court, ex p Adimi* [2001] QB 667, [1999] 4 All ER 520, [2000] 3 WLR 434, DC. The focus is now on the terms of the section, and not on art 31 as interpreted in *ex p Adimi*: *R (Hussain) v Secretary of State for the Home Department* [2001] EWHC Admin 555. Accordingly, there can be no legitimate expectation that the CPS will have regard to art 31 as, in instituting a prosecution, the CPS is required to apply the domestic law: *R (Pepushi) v Crown Prosecution Service* [2004] EWHC 798 (Admin), [2004] TLR 279. The disparity between the scope of art 31(1) and the scope of s 31 of the 1999 Act cannot be made good by a free-standing defence under art 31(1); it is not permissible for the courts effectively to add to the list of the offences set out in s 31. However, where a defendant faced two factually indistinguishable charges, only one of which was within the scope of s 31, once the statutory defence had been made out it was an abuse of process to proceed further on the other charge: *R v Asfaw* [2008] UKHL 31, [2008] 1 AC 1061, [2008] 3 All ER 775, [2008] 2 WLR 1178. Section 31 is not be read as limited to offences attributable to a refugee's illegal entry into or presence in this country, but provides immunity, if the other conditions are fulfilled, from the imposition of criminal penalties for offences attributable to the attempt of a refugee to leave the country in the continuing course of a flight from persecution even after a short stopover in transit: *R v Asfaw* (above).

See further, *R v Mateta* [2013] EWCA Crim 1372, [2013] All ER (D) 19 (Aug) (several convictions quashed despite guilty pleas; the defendants had either not been advised as to the s 31 defence or advised that it was unavailable on the facts when in fact s 31 defences would probably have succeeded).'

Sentencing (Immigration offences)

A[81.9] **No SC Guideline.** For structure of the sentencing decision. See **B**[9.6].

A[81.10]–[81.15] Available sentences. See Table A at B[43.1A] (either way offences) and Table B at B[43.2] (summary offences).

A[81.16] Immigration offences generally attract sentences in excess of the powers of magistrates' courts. Numerous examples are contained in para 3.306 of *Stone's Justices' Manual* and readers are advised to consult this narrative for guidance on sentencing levels for the various offences that can arise in connection with illegal immigration, etc.

A[81.17] Bail See D[8].

It may be the case that some asylum seekers face charges before the criminal courts. In these circumstances, the courts have no powers under immigration and asylum legislation to bail or detain them. Where the criminal proceedings have to be adjourned for any reason, magistrates are advised that defendants who are also asylum seekers should have their applications for bail under the Bail Act 1976 considered by the courts in the same way as any other defendant. Where the case proceeds to sentence, the courts have no additional powers to exercise in relation to the offender's immigration status, save for making a recommendation for deportation underthe Immigration Act 1971, s 3(6), where this is appropriate.

A[82]

Soliciting for prostitution

Charges (Soliciting for prostitution)

A[82.1] In a street or public place did solicit another for the purpose of obtaining that other's sexual services as a prostitute

Sexual Offences Act 2003, s 51A

Maximum penalty – Fine level 3

A further offence, with the same maximum penalty, is provided by s 53A of the 2003 Act of paying for sexual services of a prostitute subjected to force, etc. It is irrelevant whether or not the defendant knew or ought to have been aware of the force/other exploitation.

Legal notes and definitions

A[82.2] 'Street' has the meaning given by s 1(4) of the Street Offences Act 1959. The accused must have given some indication, by act or word, that he required the other's sexual services as a prostitute: *Darroch v DPP* (1990) 90 Cr App Rep 378, 154 JP 844. 'Prostitute' means a person who, on at least one occasion and whether or not compelled to do so, offers or provides sexual services to another for payment or a promise of payment either to the prostitute or another; 'payment' means any financial advantage: Sexual Offences Act 2003, s 51.

A single act on foot of soliciting for prostitution within a recognised area cannot amount in law to the common law offence of public nuisance: *DPP v Fearon* [2010] EWHC 340 (Admin), [2010] 2 Cr App Rep 169, 174 JP 145.

Sentencing (Soliciting for prostitution)

A[82.3] There is no SC Guideline.

Ancillary orders

A[82.4] ASBOs are often made for this offence, Alternatively, offenders can be bound over where a future breach of the peace is apprehended.

A[83]

Litter

(including dumping articles and car dumping)

A[83.1] Under the general term of **litter** there are three different offences: car dumping, dumping objects other than vehicles, and depositing general litter.

Charge 1 (Litter)

A[83.2] Without lawful authority abandoning on land in the open air or on land forming part of a highway a motor vehicle

Refuse Disposal (Amenity) Act 1978, s 2(1)(a)

Maximum penalty – Fine level 4 and 3 months' imprisonment. May be dealt with by a fixed penalty notice.

A removal charge can also be imposed if the local authority applies.

Legal notes and definitions

A[83.3] It is also an offence to abandon on such land a part of a motor vehicle if the vehicle was brought to that land and there dismantled and some part of the vehicle abandoned there.

A[83.4] Motor vehicle. This is defined in the Act as a mechanically propelled vehicle intended or adapted for use on roads whether or not it is in a fit state for such use. It includes a trailer, a chassis or body with or without wheels appearing to have formed part of a motor vehicle or trailer and anything attached to a motor vehicle or trailer.

A[83.5] Burden of proof. If the vehicle (or part of a vehicle) was left on the land in such circumstances or for such a period that it may be reasonably assumed that the defendant had abandoned it then he shall be deemed to have abandoned the vehicle (or part of a vehicle) unless he can prove the contrary. The degree of proof required of the defendant is not such as is necessary to establish this point beyond all reasonable doubt but only such as establishes that on the balance of probabilities it is true. Give the stated aims of the legislation and the fact that the reason for leaving [abandoning] the vehicle may peculiarly be within the knowledge of the accused, it is suggested that the shifting of the legal burden of proof to the accused is both necessary and proportionate and therefore ECHR compliant.

A[83.6] Land. The land must be land in the open air or land which forms part of the highway.

Sentencing

A[83.7] No SC Guideline.

Prison will rarely be appropriate but a fine will in most cases need to be such as to reflect the seriousness of the offence.

A[83.8] On application by police or local authority, a removal charge can also be imposed.

A[83.9] Disqualification from driving. See C[5.45].

Charge 2 (Litter)

A[83.10] Without lawful authority abandoning on land in the open air (or on land forming part of the highway) property namely [. . . . .] which he brought to the land for the purpose of abandoning it there

Refuse Disposal (Amenity) Act 1978, s 2(1)(b)

Maximum penalty – Fine level 4 and 3 months' imprisonment.

Legal notes and definitions

A[83.11]–[83.14] Although this offence does not apply to motor vehicles it does apply to a part of a motor vehicle which was dismantled elsewhere and then brought and abandoned.

A[83.15] **Land.** Means land in the open air or land forming part of a highway.

Sentencing

A[83.16] No SC Guideline.

A[83.17] **Disqualification from driving.** See C[5.45].

Charge 3 (Litter)

A[83.18] **Throwing down (or dropping or depositing) [in a public open place] [in a place to which this section applies] and there leaving certain articles namely [. . . . .] in such circumstances as to tend to lead to defacement by litter**

Environmental Protection Act 1990, s 87

Maximum penalty – Fine level 4.

Legal notes and definitions

A[83.19] The charge should allege one or other of the following:

A[83.20] **Throwing down; dropping; depositing.** If two or more of these words are included in the charge then it may be defective.

A[83.21] **Public open place.** Means a place in the open air to which the public are entitled or permitted to have access without payment. Any covered place open to the air on at least one side and available for public use is to be treated as a public open place. An enclosed telephone kiosk is not an open space (*Felix v DPP* [1998] Crim LR 657).

A[83.22] **Place to which the section applies.** Includes publicly maintained highways and motorways, local authority open spaces, certain Crown lands and land belonging to certain designated statutory undertakers and educational establishments. Also included is land designated by a local authority as a 'litter control area', eg a shopping mall.

A[83.23] **Time limit.** Proceedings must be commenced within six months of the litter being thrown down or dropped or deposited. If litter is left for a considerable period then the time limit of six months still commences from the time the litter was deposited.

A[83.24] **Leaving.** No offence is committed if the litter is not left; thus prompt clearing up can be a defence.

A[83.25]–[83.30] **Consent of the owner.** If the owner, occupier or person having control of the place consented to the depositing of the litter then no offence is committed.

Sentencing

A[83.31] No SC Guideline.

Aggravating factors to which the court may have regard may include the defacement by litter, but also the nature of the litter and any resulting risk of injury to persons or animals or of damage to property.

A[83.32] Whatever the circumstances the fine will usually need to be such as to reflect the prevalence of the offence in an area.

A[83.33] Fines. See B[28].

A[83.34] Disqualification from driving. See C[5.45].

A[84]
Nuisance

Introduction to nuisance

A[84.1] In addition to the remedies which the law affords in respect of nuisances in civil proceedings before the county court and the High Court, local authorities and private persons may bring proceedings for the abatement or restriction of a statutory nuisance before the magistrates' court. Further see A6 and A[74].

Statutory nuisance

(Environmental Protection Act 1990, s 79)

A[84.2] The following matters constitute statutory nuisances where they are such as to be prejudicial to health or a nuisance:

(a) the state of any premises;

(b) the emission of smoke from premises;

(c) the emission of fumes or gases from private dwellings;

(d) any dust, steam, smell or other effluvia arising on industrial, trade or business premises;

(e) any accumulation or deposit;

(f) the manner or keeping in such a place of any animal;

(fa) any insects emanating from relevant industrial, trade or business premises and being prejudicial to health or a nuisance;

(fb) artificial light emitted from premises so as to be prejudicial to health or a nuisance;

(g) noise emitted from premises;

(ga) noise that is prejudicial to health or a nuisance and is emitted from or caused by a vehicle; and also

(h) any other matter declared by any enactment to be a statutory nuisance.

A[84.3] Prejudicial to health. The expressions 'prejudicial to health' and 'injurious or likely to cause injury to health' are aimed at the effect on people's health of filthy or unwholesome premises and the like: in particular, the risk of disease or illness. There is nothing in s 79 to suggest that the powers were intended to protect against the danger of accidental physical injury; accordingly, premises that are in such a state as to create the likelihood of accident causing personal injury are not as a matter of law capable of giving rise to a statutory nuisance within s 79 (1)(a): *R v Bristol City Council, ex p Everett* [1999] 2 All ER 193, [1999] 1 WLR 1170, CA. The powers in this section are directed to the presence of some feature which in itself is prejudicial to health in that it is the source of possible infection or disease or illness such as dampness, mould, dirt or evil-smelling accumulations or the presence of rats. They do not extend to the arrangement of rooms otherwise not in themselves insanitary so as to be prejudicial to health, such as where the nearest facility for washing hands after use of a lavatory required access through kitchen or use of the kitchen sink: *Birmingham City Council v Oakley* [2001] 1 All ER 385, [2000] 3 WLR 1936, HL.

Evidence given by experts about the condition of premises is sufficient by itself, in the absence of evidence relating to the health and medical condition of the tenant, to establish a prima facie case that premises were prejudicial to health and a statutory nuisance: *O'Toole v Knowsley Metropolitan Borough Council* [1999] LS Gaz R 36.

The powers in this provision do not extend to a lack of adequate sound insulation for which there is a separate statutory code under which local authorities have express powers and, in serious cases, duties to deal with sound insulation: *R (Vella) v Lambeth Borough Council* [2005] TLR 533, QBD.

Traffic noise from vehicles, machinery or equipment in the street which renders premises to be in such a state as to be prejudicial to health or a nuisance does not constitute a statutory nuisance within the meaning of s 79(1)(a) because s 79(1)(ga) subject to the limitations in s 79(6A), deals directly with vehicle noise: *Haringey London Borough Council v Jowett* (1999) 78 P & CR D24, [1999] EGCS 64.

A[84.4] **Noise.** This includes vibration: Environmental Protection Act 1990, s 79(7). It is wrong for justices to refuse to convict of an offence under s 80(4) and (5) merely on the basis that no reliable acoustic measurement evidence has been adduced; however, where the evidence of the environmental enforcement officer is that the nuisance was 'marginal' justices are perfectly entitled to say that they are not sure and to acquit: *Lewisham Borough Council v Hall* [2002] EWHC 960 (Admin), [2002] All ER (D) 83 (May), [2002] JPN 378.

A[84.5] **Exceptions** are made to the definitions of a statutory nuisance given above. These include activities of the armed forces, smoke emissions covered by the Clean Air Acts (excluding bonfires), dark smoke from trade or industrial premises, smoke and steam from steam locomotives and noise from aircraft.

A[84.6] **Premises.** Includes land and any vessel (except one powered by steam reciprocating engines).

Proceedings by the local authority

(Environmental Protection Act 1990, s 82)

A[84.7] The local authority must from time to time cause its area to be inspected to detect the existence of any statutory nuisance and, where a complaint has been made, take such steps as are reasonably practicable to investigate the complaint (s 79).

Chapter 3 of Part 4 of the Anti-social, Crime and Policing Act 2014 empowers a senior police officer or a local authority to issue a closure notice if satisfied on reasonable grounds that the use of particular premises has resulted, or is likely soon to result, in nuisance to members of the public, or there has been, or is likely to be, disorder near those premises associated with the use of those premises, and that the notice is necessary to prevent the nuisance or disorder from continuing, recurring or occurring.

Such a notice lasts for 24 or 48 hours (see s 77) and must be followed (unless the notice is cancelled) by an application to a magistrates' court for a closure order. A closure order is an order prohibiting access to the specified premises and it may last for up to three months. Section 86 prescribes offences of breaching closure notices and closure orders; the offences are summary only and carry either three or six months' imprisonment (depending upon the nature of the contravention) or an unlimited fine.

A[84.8] **Abatement notice.** Where the local authority are satisfied that a statutory nuisance exists or is likely to occur or reoccur, the local authority must serve a notice requiring abatement or prohibiting or restricting its occurrence and if the means of abatement are required by the local authority the description of any steps necessary for this purpose and any times within which the required action is to be taken (*R v Falmouth and Truro Port Health Authority, ex p South West Water Services* [2001] QB 445, [2000] 3 All ER 306, [2000] All ER (D) 429, CA). The consent of the Secretary of State or the Environment Agency is not required prior to the issue of an abatement notice by a local authority: *R (on the application of Ethos Recycling Ltd v Barking and Dagenham Magistrates' Court* [2009] EWHC 2885 (Admin).

In *R (on the application of Mohuddin Khan) v Isleworth Crown Court and the London Borough of Hillingdon* [2011] EWHC 3164 (Admin), 176 JP 6, there was no dispute as to the facts of the nuisance itself, nor was there any dispute that the claimant was not at the premises. It was also accepted that the dog (the cause of the nuisance) did not belong to him. The Crown Court considered that the claimant should have made sensible arrangements to collect his post while he was absent from the relevant premises. It concluded that he was therefore responsible for the nuisance and dismissed an appeal from the magistrates' court. It as held that the claimant was not 'the person responsible' for the nuisance. He was not the person 'to whose act, default or sufferance the nuisance was attributable'. That person was manifestly another person whose dog it was, and who was plainly in control of the dog at all material times. The abatement notice should in the ordinary way have been served on him and he should have been prosecuted for its breach. Despite the claimant's failure to make a better arrangement to collect his post from the said premises, that failure could not properly deprive him of an opportunity to raise a cast iron point had he appealed to the magistrates' court.

A[84.9] Appeal. The person served with the notice may appeal within 21 days to the magistrates' court. These are civil proceedings by way of complaint and the court is unable to impose a criminal penalty (*Hounslow London Borough Council v Thames Water Utilities Ltd* [2004] All ER (D) 94 (Feb)).

A[84.10]–[84.15] Offence. Contravention of or failure to comply with the terms of a notice without reasonable excuse is an offence triable only by magistrates. The maximum penalty is a fine not exceeding level 5 on the standard scale together with a further fine of an amount equal to one-tenth of that level or, for offences committed in or after 12 March 2015 one-tenth of the greater of £5,000 or level 4 on the standard scale, for each day on which the offence continues after the conviction. For an offence on industrial, trade or business premises the fine is £20,000.

A[84.16] Defence. It is a defence for the defendant to prove that the best practicable means were used to prevent, or to counteract the effects of, the nuisance. However, the defence is not available:

(a) in the case of a nuisance falling within paragraph (a), (d), (e), (f), (fa) or (g) of A[84.2] above except where the nuisance arises on industrial, trade or business premises;
(b) in the case of a nuisance falling within paragraph (fb) of section **A[84.2]** above except where:
  (i) the artificial light is emitted from industrial, trade or business premises; or
  (ii) the artificial light (not being light to which sub-paragraph (i) applies) is emitted by lights used for the purpose only of illuminating an outdoor relevant sports facility;
(c) in the case of a nuisance falling within paragraph (ga) of **A[84.2]** above except where the noise is emitted from or caused by a vehicle, machinery or equipment being used for industrial, trade or business purposes;
(d) in the case of a nuisance falling within paragraph (b) of **A[84.2]** above except where the smoke is emitted from a chimney; and
(e) in the case of a nuisance falling within paragraph (c) or (h) of **A[84.2]** above.

Certain other defences are available where it is alleged that the activity is in conformity with consents or notices under control of pollution legislation.

A[84.17] If the defendant raises the defence of reasonable excuse under s 80(4) and (6) then it is for the prosecution to satisfy the court beyond reasonable doubt that the excuse was not reasonable: *Polychronakis v Richards and Jerrom Ltd* [1998] JPL 588, [1998] Env LR 347. 'Reasonable excuse' does not include matters that should have been raised on an appeal challenging the validity of the notice, unless there has been some special reason for not entering an appeal: *A Lambert Flat Management Ltd v Lomas* [1981] 2 All ER 280, [1981] 1 WLR 898. Mitigating factors, such as loud reggae music playing to celebrate a birthday, do not amount to a reasonable excuse if other ingredients of a nuisance are established: *Wellingborough Borough Council v Gordon* (1990) 155 JP 494.

A[84.18] **Appeal.** A person convicted of an offence may appeal against conviction and sentence to the Crown Court in the usual way.

Complaint by person aggrieved by a statutory nuisance

(Environmental Protection Act 1990, s 82)

A[84.19] A private individual may complain to the local authority about an alleged statutory nuisance and it will be the duty of the authority to take such steps as are reasonably practicable to investigate the complaint and if they consider it appropriate to serve an abatement notice as described above (Environmental Protection Act 1990, s 79).

A[84.20] However, a person may also lay a complaint before the magistrates on the ground that he is aggrieved by the existence of a statutory nuisance. Proceedings are normally brought against the person responsible for the nuisance; where he cannot be found it will be the owner or occupier of the premises.

A[84.21] **Notice of intention to bring proceedings** and the matters complained of should be served not less than 3 days before, in respect of noise, and 21 days before, in respect of any other allegation.

A[84.22] **Magistrates' order.** If the court is satisfied that the alleged nuisance exists or that, although abated, it is likely to reoccur, the court must make either one or both of the following orders:

(a) to abate the nuisance, within a time specified in the order, and to execute any works necessary for that purpose;
(b) prohibiting a recurrence of the nuisance, and requiring the defendant, within a time specified in the order, to execute any works necessary to prevent the recurrence.

The court may also impose a fine not exceeding £5,000 (level 5) (for offences committed on or after 12 March 2015 an unlimited fine).

A[84.23] Where the nuisance renders premises unfit for human habitation, the order may prohibit their use for this purpose until the court is satisfied they are fit for such use.

A[84.24] **Offence.** See A[74.9] for private premises.

A[84.25]–[84.30] **Defence.** See A[84.16]–A[84.17]. The 'best practicable means' defence is not available for a nuisance which is such as to render the premises unfit for human habitation.

A[84.31] **Costs.** Where the alleged nuisance is proved to have existed at the making of the complaint then, whether or not at the date of the hearing it still exists or is likely to recur, the court shall order the defendant to pay the complainant's proper costs. Such costs should include costs incurred in establishing that a statutory nuisance existed (*Hollis v Dudley Metropolitan Borough Council* [1998] 1 All ER 759, [1999] 1 WLR 642).

Such proceedings are not civil in nature. Any award of costs therefore cannot be made under 64 of the Magistrates' Courts Act 1980: see s 50 of the Magistrates' Courts Act 1980 and s 82(2) of the Environmental Protection Act 1990. The combined effect of those two provisions was that s 82 must be read as if the word 'information' is substituted for 'complaint' in subsection (1). The power to award costs in favour of a successful defendant, other than by a wasted costs order when an information is dismissed, is to be found only in s 16(1) of the Prosecution of Offences Act 1985: *R (on the application of DeSouza) v Croydon Magistrates' Court* [2012] EWHC 1362 (Admin), 176 JP 624.

A[84.32] Local authority. Where a person has been convicted of failing to comply with an order the court, after allowing the local authority an opportunity to be heard, may direct the authority to do anything which the person convicted was required to do by the order. Similarly, where the defendant cannot be found the court may direct the local authority to do that which it would have ordered him to do.

Noise Act 1996

A[84.33] **See the amendments as a result of s 84 and schedule, 1 to the Clean Neighbourhoods and Environment Act 2005 which applies to licensed premises with a penalty (after service of the relevant notice under para 4A of a fine not exceeding level 5.

If a warning notice has been served under this Act, in respect of noise emitted from premises, any person who is responsible for such a breach is liable to a fine not exceeding level 3.

A[84.34] Defence. It is open to the defendant to show he has reasonable excuse.

A[84.35] Forfeiture. Magistrates may direct the forfeiture of any equipment related to a noise conviction.

A[84.36] Before doing so the court must have regard:

(a) to the value of the equipment; and
(b) to the likely financial and other effects on the offender of the making of the order.

A[85]
Obstructing the highway

Charge (Obstructing the highway)

A[85.1] **Without lawful authority or excuse wilfully obstructing the free passage along a highway**

Highways Act 1980, s 137

Maximum penalty – Fine level 3.

Legal notes and definitions

A[85.2] This offence can be committed in a number of different ways apart from leaving a motor vehicle. It should not be confused with the offence of causing an unnecessary obstruction on a road with a motor vehicle or with a breach of parking regulations. See C[36].

A[85.3] The correct approach for magistrates dealing with an offence of obstruction is as follows:

(a) Was there an obstruction? Unless within the *de minimis* rule, any stopping on the highway is prima facie an obstruction.
(b) Was it wilful, ie deliberate?
(c) Have the prosecution proved that the obstruction was without lawful authority or excuse? Lawful authority includes permits and licences granted under statutory provision; lawful excuse embraces activities otherwise lawful in themselves which may or may not be reasonable in all the circumstances, including the length of time the obstruction continues, the place where it occurs, the purpose for which it is done and whether it does in fact cause an actual obstruction as opposed to a potential obstruction (*Hirst and Agu v Chief Constable of West Yorkshire* (1986) 85 Cr App Rep 143, 151 JP 304).

It was stated in *Dixon v Atfield* [1975] 3 All ER 265, [1975] 1 WLR 1171 that the broad interpretation of 'reasonable excuse' applied in the case of a temporary obstruction did not apply to a permanent obstruction; ie the longer an obstruction exists the more likely it will be found unreasonable. (The defendant erected a bollard on the pavement outside his shop to protect his property and customers from vehicles mounting the footpath – since this was meant to be permanent the case was remitted to the justices with a direction to convict.)

The test of whether a particular use of a highway, eg, by a vehicle, amounts to an obstruction is whether such use is unreasonable having regard to all the circumstances including its duration, position and purpose, and whether it causes an actual, as opposed to a potential, obstruction: *Nagy v Weston* [1965] 1 All ER 78, 129 JP 104.

Although, as noted above, the de minimis principle applies to obstruction cases, the principle is reserved for cases of fractional obstructions: *Torbay Borough Council v Cross* (1995) 159 JP 682 (displays of goods on the pavement outside a shop projecting by no more than 5% of the total width of the pavement held to be an obstruction which did not satisfy the de minimis principle).

A defendant selling hot dogs from a van parked in a line of parked vehicles in a busy street was properly convicted; as soon as his van turned itself into a shop it ceased to make a reasonable use of the road: *Pitcher v Lockett* [1966] Crim LR 283); applied in *Waltham Forest London Borough Council v Mills* [1980] RTR 201, [1980] Crim LR 243, where it was held that the selling of refreshments from a mobile snack bar on the highway was an unreasonable user.

The placing of shopping trolleys in three parallel rows outside a supermarket was held to constitute an unreasonable user because of the performance of the obstruction, the substantial nature of it, and its denial to the public of free access over the whole of the highway: *Devon County Council v Gateway Foodmarkets Ltd* (1990) 154 JP 557, DC.

Where a club tout approached groups of pedestrians on four occasions and on each of those occasions the free passage of other people using the highway was obstructed to an extent that members of the public passing were forced to step into the roadway, it was held that it was such an unreasonable use of the highway as to amount to an obstruction: *Cooper v Metropolitan Police Comr* (1985) 82 Cr App Rep 238.

An unauthorised encroachment restricting access to any part of the highway is such an obstruction and the prosecution is not obliged to allege or prove that any particular person was incommoded: see *Wolverton UDC v Willis* [1962] 1 All ER 243, 126 JP 84. Similarly, the display for sale of garden produce on a grass verge adjacent to a footpath, which formed part of the highway, was held to be an unreasonable user and, therefore, an obstruction, notwithstanding that the display did not encroach on the footpath itself and there was no evidence of anyone being inconvenienced: *Hertfordshire County Council v Bolden* (1986) 151 JP 252.

If stopping on a highway is merely part and parcel of reasonably passing and re-passing, it is not obstruction; to stand juggling with lighted firesticks, however, is not part and parcel of one's right to pass and re-pass, nor is it a user ancillary to that right: *Waite v Taylor* 149 JP 551, [1985] LS Gaz R 1092.

As to the application of s 131 to peaceful picketing in accordance with s 134 of the Industrial Relations Act 1971 (now s 220 of the Trade Union and Labour Relations Act (Consolidation) Act 1992), see *Broome v DPP* [1974] 1 All ER 314, 138 JP 105.

A[85.3A] **Lawful excuse and freedom of expression.** In *DPP v Ziegler and others* [2019] EWHC 71 (Admin), [2019] 2 WLR 1451, [2019] 1 Cr App Rep 32, [2019] Crim LR 728 the court gave guidance on the relevance of Articles 10 and 11 of the European Convention on Human Rights to the potential defence of 'lawful excuse' in a prosecution for obstructing the highway under section 137 of the Highways Act 1980. These Convention rights were qualified rather than 'absolute' rights and were not 'trump cards' that entitled political protestors to circumvent laws that related to the planning and use of the highways. Nevertheless, where these Convention rights were engaged, they were more than a significant consideration as had been held in the case of *Buchanan v Crown Prosecution Service* [2018] EWHC 1773 (Admin). In deciding whether an act of protest gave rise to lawful excuse, it was necessary to undertake a careful analysis of the proportionality of any interference to a person's freedom of expression and assembly and to consider whether a fair balance had been struck between the different rights and interests at stake. If the prosecution could show that the interference was proportionate then the defendant would have been acting unreasonably in all of the circumstances and would not be able to rely on the defence of lawful excuse. Conversely, if the interference was not proportionate then the defendant would have been acting reasonably and lawfully and the statutory defence would be made out. In such cases, the court suggested that the following questions should be asked:

(1) Is what the defendant did in exercise of one of the rights in Articles 10 and 11?
(2) If so, is there an interference by a public authority with that right?
(3) If there is an interference, is it 'prescribed by law'?
(4) If so, is the interference in pursuit of a legitimate aim as set out in paragraph (2) of Articles 10 and 11, for example the protection of the rights of others?
(5) If so, is the interference 'necessary in a democratic society' to achieve the legitimate aim?

The last question required a careful analysis of the proportionality of the interference in which the court would need to ask the following:

(1) Is the aim sufficiently important to justify interference with a fundamental right?
(2) Is there a rational connection between the means chosen and the aim in view?
(3) Are there less restrictive alternative means available to achieve that aim?

(4) Is there a fair balance between the rights of the individual and the general interest of the community, including the rights of others?

Whilst the type or content of certain types of expression, such as political or economic views, may well require them to be given greater weight than others, such as pornography or 'vapid tittle-tattle', the particular viewpoint being expressed was not something on which it was permissible for the court to express its own view by way of approval or disapproval.

A[85.4] Highway. A highway means the whole or part of a highway. Only a part of a highway needs to be obstructed to commit this offence and the highway, available to the general public, may be a wide road or a narrow passageway, only suitable for pedestrians. Bridges and tunnels used by the public are also highways.

Sentencing (Obstructing the highway)

A[85.5] No SC Guideline. This offence carries a fine only. See B[28.10]–[28.15].

A[86]
Poaching

1 Day time offence

A[86.1] **Trespassing by entering or being in the day time upon any land in search or pursuit of game, or woodcocks, snipes or conies**

Game Act 1831, s 30, as amended

Maximum penalty – Fine level 3. Triable only by magistrates.

Note – Where it is alleged that there were five or more persons together trespassing in pursuit of game the maximum penalty is a fine set at level 4 for each defendant, or level 5 where they are armed and any of them uses violence, etc.

For hunting wild mammals with dogs and hare coursing see ss 1–5 of the Hunting Act 2004.

Legal notes and definitions

A[86.2]–[86.4] A prosecution must be commenced within three calendar months after the commission of the offence (Game Act 1831, s 41). The charge creates only one offence, that of trespass, and the summons may refer to pursuit of more than one species.

A[86.5] Day time commences at the beginning of the last hour before sunrise and concludes at the expiration of the first hour after sunset (s 34).

A[86.6]–[86.7] Game means hares, pheasants, partridges, grouse, heath or moor game, and black game (s 2).

A[86.8] **Hunting.** This offence does not apply to hunting or coursing in fresh pursuit of deer, hare, or fox (Game Act 1831, s 35). **NB:** By virtue of the Hunting Act 2004, Sch 3, the words, "to any person hunting or coursing upon any land with hounds or greyhounds, and being in pursuit of any deer, hare or fox already started upon any other land, nor" have been repealed.

A[86.8A] Disqualification from driving. See C[5.45].

2 Night time offences

A[86.9] (a) **Unlawfully taking or destroying any game or rabbits by night in any land, open or enclosed or by night unlawfully entering or being on any land, whether open or enclosed, with any gun, net, engine, or other instrument for the purpose of taking or destroying game**

Night Poaching Act 1828, s 1, as amended

Maximum penalty – Fine level 3 (offence under s 2 where violence is offered to gamekeepers etc with the weapons described in charge (b) the maximum is a fine on level 4 and 6 months). Triable only by magistrates.

A[86.10]–[86.15] (b) **Three or more persons together by night unlawfully entering or being on any land, whether open or enclosed, for the purpose of taking or destroying game or rabbits, any of such persons being armed with gun, cross bow, firearms, bludgeon or any other offensive weapon**

Night Poaching Act 1828, s 9, as amended

Maximum penalty – Fine level 4 and 6 months. Triable only by magistrates.

Legal notes and definitions

A[86.16] **Claim of right.** (See above.).

A[86.17] **Game** includes hares, pheasants, partridges, grouse, heath or moor game, black game and bustards (Night Poaching Act 1828, s 13).

A[86.18] **Land** includes public roads, highways, or paths, or the sides thereof or at the opening, outlets, or gates, from any such land into any such road, highway or path.

A[86.19] **Charge.** Section 1 creates two offences and any information must allege only one offence.

A[86.20] **Unlawfully entering or being.** (See above.) This offence does not relate to the taking or destroying of rabbits.

A[86.21] **Night time** commences at the expiration of the first hour after sunset and concludes at the beginning of the last hour before sunrise.

A[86.22] **Three or more together.** It is not necessary for all the persons actually to enter provided they are associated together on a common purpose, some entering while others remain near enough to assist.

A[86.22A]–[86.30] **Disqualification from driving.** See C[5.45].

Sentencing (Poaching)

A[86.31] No SC Guideline.

Where the police have arrested a person for an offence under the Night Poaching Act 1828 or Game Act 1831 they may search him and may seize and detain any game or rabbits, or any gun or cartridges or other ammunition, or any nets, traps, snares or other devices of a kind used for the killing or taking of game or rabbits, which are found in his possession: Poaching Prevention Act 1862, s 2.

A[86.32] If convicted the court may order any of these items to be forfeited (whether or not the offence of which he was convicted concerned that game, rabbit etc) (Game Laws Amendment Act 1960, s 4).

A[86.32A] **Disqualification from driving.** See C[5.45].

A[87]

Psychoactive substances

Introduction to psychoactive substances

A[87.1] The Psychoactive Substances Act 2016 creates offences in respect of the production, supply, offer to supply, possession with intent to supply, importing, exporting, or possession in a custodial institution of psychoactive substances. In addition, the Act makes provision for prohibition notices, premises notices, prohibition orders and premises orders as well as powers to stop and search persons, vehicles and vessels, to enter and search premises (under warrant) and to forfeit seized psychoactive substances and other items.

These provisions came into effect on 26 May 2016. The provisions on prohibition and premises orders are dealt with in Section B.

Charges (Psychoactive substances)

A[87.2] 1. Intentionally produced a psychoactive substance knowing or suspecting that it was such a suspect and intending to consume it for its psychoactive effect or knowing or being reckless as to whether it was likely to be consumed by some other person for its psychoactive effect

Psychoactive Substances Act 2016, s 4

2. Intentionally supplied a psychoactive substance when D knew or suspected, or ought to have known or suspected, that it was such a substance and knew or was reckless as to whether it was likely to be consumed by the person to whom it was supplied, or by some other person, for its psychoactive effects

Psychoactive Substances Act 2016, s 5(1)

3. (D) Offered to supply a psychoactive substance to another person (R), knowing or being reckless as to whether that person, or some other person, would, if D supplied the substance to R in accordance with the offer, be likely to consume the substance for its psychoactive effects

Psychoactive Substances Act 2016, s 5(2)

4. Possessed a psychoactive substance knowing or suspecting it was such a substance and intending to supply it to another person for its consumption, whether by any person to whom it was supplied or by some other person, for its psychoactive effects

Psychoactive Substances Act 2016, s 7

5. Intentionally importing a psychoactive substance when D knew, or suspected, or ought to have known or suspected, that it was such a substance, intending to consume it for its psychoactive effects, or knowing or being reckless as to whether it was likely to be consumed by some other person for its psychoactive effects

Psychoactive Substances Act 2016, s 8(1)

6. Intentionally exporting a psychoactive substance when D knew, or suspected, or ought to have known or suspected, that it was such a substance, intending to consume it for its psychoactive effects, or knowing or being reckless as to whether it was likely to be consumed by some other person for its psychoactive effects

Psychoactive Substances Act 2016, s 8(2)

7. Possessing a psychoactive substance in a custodial institution, knowing or suspecting it was such a substance and intending to consume it for its psychoactive effects

Psychoactive Substances Act 2016, s 9

Maximum penalty 6 months' imprisonment and/or an unlimited fine

Crown Court 7 years' imprisonment and/or an unlimited fine except for offence 7 where the maximum term is 2 years

Mode of trial

A[87.3] Consider the general guidelines at D[4].

Legal notes and definitions

A[87.4] All the offences are subject to the exemptions in Schedule 2, which are concerned with health care and scientific research.

A 'psychoactive substance' is any substance capable of producing a psychoactive effect in a person who consumes it. In the case of offence 3 (offer to supply), the reference to psychoactive effects includes a reference to the psychoactive effects the substance would have had if it had been the substance D had offered to supply. The psychoactive effect may be produced directly or indirectly; both are encompassed. Thus, alkyl nitrites ('poppers'), which are largely used as a sexual aid, are caught though the 'rush' or 'high' they cause is an indirect effect caused by the dilation of blood vessels: *R v Rochester* [2018] EWCA Crim 1936, [2018] Crim LR 1002.

Exempted substances are listed in Schedule 1. These are: controlled drugs; medicinal products; alcohol (ethyl alcohol) and alcohol products; nicotine and tobacco products; caffeine and caffeine; and food (including drink). In the cases of the 'products' (apart from medicinal), the product must not contain any psychoactive substance.

A substance can be a medicinal product for one purpose, and thus exempt, but not for another. Where canisters of nitrous oxide gas, which is capable of bringing health benefits, had been produced for a catering purpose (as a propellant found in aerosols for whipped cream), and were in the possession of the defendants to be supplied as a recreational drug because it produced a psychoactive effect, this took it outside the definition of a medicinal product and, consequently, this exemption: *R v Chapman, R v Tesfay, R v Chroussis & R v Bryce* [2017] EWCA Crim 1743, [2018] 1 WLR 726, (2018) 172 JP 115 (citing *In Criminal Proceedings against D* [2014] PTSR 1217, in which the Luxembourg court concluded that for the purpose of determining whether a product falls within the definition of a medicinal product, the courts must proceed on a case-by-case basis, taking into account its characteristics and properties and the manner in which it is used).

Where a person imports/exports a controlled drug suspecting it to be a psychoactive substance, he/she is to be treated as if he/she had imported/exported a psychoactive substance suspecting it to be such a substance: Psychoactive Substances Act 2016, s 8(4).

Aggravation of offences of supplying or offering to supply

A[87.5] When considering seriousness in the case of an offender aged at least 18 , if any of the three conditions below is met the court must treat that as an aggravating factor and state in open court that the offence is so aggravated: Psychoactive Substances Act 2016, s 6.

(1) The offence was committed in the vicinity of school premises during or within one hour of the start or finish of the use of the premises by persons under the age of 18.
(2) The offender used a courier, either to a deliver a substance or a drug-related consideration, who was under the age of 18.
(3) The offence was committed in a custodial institution.

Sentencing

A[87.6] The sentencing guidelines for drug offences do not cover offences under the Psychoactive Substances Act 2016. Therefore, the guideline is not 'relevant' within the meaning of s 125(1) of the Coroners and Justice Act 2009. Nevertheless, it is relevant in a broader sense when sentencing for a similar offence (in the present case the substance was a cannaboid and the offender was also charged with a separate offence of possession of cannabis with intent to supply committed four months later, and both cases fell within 'street dealing'). Therefore, the court should have regard to the guidelines and impose a sentence which reflects the drug and factual situation in the guidelines representing the closest approximation to the facts before the court. Here, the closest comparable offence was street dealing of cannabis: *R v Waka (Mohammed Hussain)* [2018] EWCA Crim 125, [2018] 1 Cr App R (S) 54 (the offender was 19 at the time of sentencing and of good character, the sentence of 16 months' detention for the 2016 Act offence was reduced to seven months on the basis of a starting point of 11 months and a full reduction for the guilty pleas, bringing the total sentence down to 15 months' detention).

Structure of the sentencing decision. See B[9.6].

A[87.7] **Available sentences.** See Table A at B[43.1A].

A[87.8] **Forfeiture.** The court must order forfeiture of any psychoactive substance in respect of which the offence was committed, and the court may also order forfeiture of any other item that was used in the commission of the offence: Psychoactive Substances Act 2016, s 54(3), 4).

A[87.9] **Prohibition orders on conviction.** Where an offender is convicted of an offence under ss 4–8, or an offence of attempt, conspiracy, etc, relating to an offence under ss 4–8, the court may make a prohibition order if it considers it necessary and proportionate for the purpose of preventing the offender from carrying on any prohibited activity: Psychoactive Substances Act 2016, s 19. 'Prohibited activity' means producing, etc, a psychoactive substance or assisting or encouraging such production, etc: Psychoactive Substances Act 2016, s 12. If the offender is aged under 18 the order must be for a fixed term of no longer than three years.

As to procedure for a behaviour order, see Part 31 of the CrimPR 2015.

An order must be additional to any sentence or order of discharge imposed for the offence: Psychoactive Substances Act 2016, s 19(2).

Post conviction proceedings are civil and the standard of proof is the balance of probabilities: Psychoactive Substances Act 2016, s 32(1),(2). The court is not restricted to considering evidence that would have been admissible in the criminal proceedings: Psychoactive Substances Act 2016, s 32(3).

A[87.10] **Variation and appeals.** See Psychoactive Substances Act 2016, ss 28–31. Where an offender against whom a prohibition order has previously been made is convicted of a relevant offence it may vary that order. Again, this must be additional to any sentence or order of discharge made for the offence: Psychoactive Substances Act 2016, s 29.

A[88]

Shotgun (purchasing etc without shotgun certificate)

Charge (Shotgun (purchasing etc without certificate))

A[88.1] Possessing, or purchasing or acquiring a shotgun without holding a shotgun certificate

Firearms Act 1968, s 2(1)

Maximum penalty – 6 months' imprisonment and/or fine level 5 (for offences committed on or after 12 March 2015 an unlimited fine). Triable either way.

Crown Court – 5 years' imprisonment and unlimited fine.

Mode of trial

A[88.2] See general notes at D[4].

Legal notes and definitions

A[88.3] Purchasing, possessing, acquiring. These are three separate offences and the charge should only allege one of these. See **A**[76], above.

A[88.4] Shotgun. Means a smooth bore gun with a barrel of 24 inches or longer with a bore not exceeding two inches and which is not a revolver nor has an illegal magazine, which is not an air gun.

A[88.5] Certificate. This is granted by the police and it may contain conditions. Failure to observe the conditions is an offence which is also triable either way punishable on summary conviction by a fine of level 5 and/or 6 months' imprisonment; the offence carries five years on indictment and an unlimited fine (Firearms Act 1968, s 2(2)). The police can revoke the certificate if they are satisfied that it entails danger to public safety or peace.

A[88.6] Exemptions. These include visitors to Great Britain who are holders of a visitor's shotgun permit; persons using shotguns on occasions and at places approved by the police; a person who borrows a shotgun and uses it on the lender's private premises, in the presence of the lender; persons holding a Northern Ireland firearm certificate which authorises holders to possess shotguns. See also **A[76.9]**.

A[88.7] ECHR. The degree of proof required from the defendant is to establish that on the balance of probabilities he was exempt. He does not have to establish this beyond reasonable doubt. Having regard to the legitimate aims of the legislation it is suggested that the imposition of a legal burden on the accused is necessary and proportionate so as to accord with art 6(2) of the ECHR.

Sentencing (Shotgun (purchasing etc without certificate))

A[88.8] No SC Guideline. For structure of the sentencing decision see **B**[9.6].

A[88.9] Available sentences. See Table A at **B**[43.1A].

A[88.10] Forfeiture. The court can order the shotgun to be forfeited to the police or disposed of as it thinks fit.

A[88.11] The court can also cancel any firearm or shotgun certificate held by the defendant.

A[89]

General bribery offences

Charges (General bribery offences)

A[89.1] The following charges are available:

1. Bribing another person, or purchasing
Bribery Act 2010, s 1
Maximum penalty – 6 months' imprisonment and/or fine level 5 (for offences committed on or after 12 March 2015 an unlimited fine). Triable either way.
Crown Court – 10 years' imprisonment and unlimited fine.*

2. Offences relating to being bribed
Bribery Act 2010, s 2
Maximum penalty – 6 months' imprisonment and/or fine level 5 (for offences committed on or after 12 March 2015 an unlimited fine). Triable either way.
Crown Court – 10 years' imprisonment and unlimited fine.*

3. Bribery of foreign officials
Bribery Act 2010, s 6
Maximum penalty – Fine level 5 and 6 months. Triable either way.
Crown Court – 10 years' imprisonment and unlimited fine.*

4. Failure of commercial organisation to prevent bribery
Bribery Act 2010, s 7
Maximum penalty – 6 months' imprisonment and/or fine level 5 (for offences committed on or after 12 March 2015 an unlimited fine). Triable either way.
Crown Court – Unlimited fine.

*The maximum penalties above relate to individuals only.

No proceedings for an offence under this Act may be instituted in England and Wales except by or with the consent of—

(a) the Director of Public Prosecutions,
(b) the Director of the Serious Fraud Office, or
(c) the Director of Revenue and Customs Prosecutions

A[89.2] **1. Offences of bribing another person**

(1) A person ("P") is guilty of an offence if either of the following cases applies.
(2) Case 1 is where—
 (a) P offers, promises or gives a financial or other advantage to another person, and
 (b) P intends the advantage
  (i) to induce a person to perform improperly a relevant function or activity, or
  (ii) to reward a person for the improper performance of such a function or activity.
(3) Case 2 is where—
 (a) P offers, promises or gives a financial or other advantage to another person, and
 (b) P knows or believes that the acceptance of the advantage would itself constitute the improper performance of a relevant function or activity.
(4) In case 1 it does not matter whether the person to whom the advantage is offered, promised or given is the same person as the person who is to perform, or has performed, the function or activity concerned.
(5) In cases 1 and 2 it does not matter whether the advantage is offered, promised or given by P directly or through a third party.

2. Offences relating to being bribed

(1) A person ("R") is guilty of an offence if any of the following cases applies.
(2) Case 3 is where R requests, agrees to receive or accepts a financial or other advantage intending that, in consequence, a relevant function or activity should be performed improperly (whether by R or another person).
(3) Case 4 is where—
(a) R requests, agrees to receive or accepts a financial or other advantage, and
(b) the request, agreement or acceptance itself constitutes the improper performance by R of a relevant function or activity.
(4) Case 5 is where R requests, agrees to receive or accepts a financial or other advantage as a reward for the improper performance (whether by R or another person) of a relevant function or activity.
(5) Case 6 is where, in anticipation of or in consequence of R requesting, agreeing to receive or accepting a financial or other advantage, a relevant function or activity is performed improperly—
(a) by R, or
(b) by another person at R's request or with R's assent or acquiescence.
(6) In cases 3 to 6 it does not matter—
(a) whether R requests, agrees to receive or accepts (or is to request, agree to receive or accept) the advantage directly or through a third party,
(b) whether the advantage is (or is to be) for the benefit of R or another person.
(7) In cases 4 to 6 it does not matter whether R knows or believes that the performance of the function or activity is improper.
(8) In case 6, where a person other than R is performing the function or activity, it also does not matter whether that person knows or believes that the performance of the function or activity is improper.

3. Bribery of foreign public officials

(1) A person ("P") who bribes a foreign public official ("F") is guilty of an offence if P's intention is to influence F in F's capacity as a foreign public official.
(2) P must also intend to obtain or retain—
(a) business, or
(b) an advantage in the conduct of business.
(3) P bribes F if, and only if—
(a) directly or through a third party, P offers, promises or gives any financial or other advantage—
(i) to F, or
(ii) to another person at F's request or with F's assent or acquiescence, and
(b) F is neither permitted nor required by the written law applicable to F to be influenced in F's capacity as a foreign public official by the offer, promise or gift.
(4) References in this section to influencing F in F's capacity as a foreign public official mean influencing F in the performance of F's functions as such an official, which includes—
(a) any omission to exercise those functions, and
(b) any use of F's position as such an official, even if not within F's authority.
(5) "Foreign public official" means an individual who—
(a) holds a legislative, administrative or judicial position of any kind, whether appointed or elected, of a country or territory outside the United Kingdom (or any subdivision of such a country or territory)
(b) exercises a public function—
(i) for or on behalf of a country or territory outside the United Kingdom (or any subdivision of such a country or territory), or
(ii) for any public agency or public enterprise of that country or territory (or subdivision), or
(c) is an official or agent of a public international organisation.
(6) "Public international organisation" means an organisation whose members are any of the following—
(a) countries or territories,
(b) governments of countries or territories

(c) other public international organisations,
(d) a mixture of any of the above.

(7) For the purposes of subsection (3)(b), the written law applicable to F is—
(a) where the performance of the functions of F which P intends to influence would be subject to the law of any part of the United Kingdom, the law of that part of the United Kingdom,
(b) where paragraph (a) does not apply and F is an official or agent of a public international organisation, the applicable written rules of that organisation,
(c) where paragraphs (a) and (b) do not apply, the law of the country or territory in relation to which F is a foreign public official so far as that law is contained in—
(i) any written constitution, or provision made by or under legislation, applicable to the country or territory concerned, or
(ii) any judicial decision which is so applicable and is evidenced in published written sources.

(8) For the purposes of this section, a trade or profession is a business.

Mode of trial

A[89.3] See general notes at D[4].

Legal notes and definitions

A[89.4] The Bribery Act 2010 received Royal Assent on 8 April 2010 and came into force on 1 July 2011. Amendments by virtue of the Bribery Act 2010 (Consequential Amendments) Order 2011 reflect the abolition of the following offences:

(1) The common law offences of bribery and embracery.
(2) The Public Bodies Corrupt Practices Act 1889.
(3) The Prevention of Corruption Act 1906.
(4) The Prevention of Corruption Act 1916.

Section 1: Offences of bribing another person

A[89.5] Makes it an offence for a person ('P') to offer, promise or give a financial or other advantage to another person in one of two cases:

- Case 1 applies where P intends the advantage to bring about the improper performance by another person of a relevant function or activity or to reward such improper performance.
- Case 2 applies where P knows or believes that the acceptance of the advantage offered, promised or given in itself constitutes the improper performance of a relevant function or activity.

'Improper performance' is defined at ss 4 and 5 of the Bribery Act 2010. In summary, this means performance which amounts to a breach of an expectation that a person will act in good faith, impartially, or in accordance with a position of trust. The offence applies to bribery relating to any function of a public nature, connected with a business, performed in the course of a person's employment or performed on behalf of a company or another body of persons. Therefore, bribery in both the public and private sectors is covered.

For the purposes of deciding whether a function or activity has been performed improperly the test of what is expected is a test of what a reasonable person in the UK would expect in relation to the performance of that function or activity. Where the performance of the function or activity is not subject to UK law (for example, it takes place in a country outside UK jurisdiction) then any local custom or practice must be disregarded – unless permitted or required by the written law applicable to that particular country. Written law means any written constitution, provision made by or under legislation applicable to the country concerned or any judicial decision evidenced in published written sources.

By way of illustration, in order to proceed with a case under Bribery Act 2010, s 1 based on an allegation that hospitality was intended as a bribe, the prosecution would need to show that the hospitality was intended to induce conduct that amounts to a breach of an expectation that a person will act in good faith, impartially, or in accordance with a position of trust. This would be judged by what a reasonable person in the UK thought. So, for example, an invitation to foreign clients to attend a Six Nations match at Twickenham as part of a public relations exercise designed to cement good relations or enhance knowledge in the organisation's field is extremely unlikely to engage s 1 as there is unlikely to be evidence of an intention to induce improper performance of a relevant function.

Section 2: Offences relating to being bribed

A[89.6] This section defines the offence of bribery as it applies to the recipient or potential recipient of the bribe, who is called R. It distinguishes four cases, namely Case 3 to Case 6.

In Cases 3, 4 and 5 there is a requirement that R "requests, agrees to receive or accepts" an advantage, whether or not R actually receives it. This requirement must then be linked with the "improper performance" of a relevant function or activity. As with section 1, the nature of this function or activity is addressed in section 3, and "improper performance" is defined in section 4. The link between the request, agreement to receive or acceptance of an advantage and improper performance may take three forms:

- R may intend improper performance to follow as a consequence of the request, agreement to receive or acceptance of the advantage (Case 3, in subsection (2));
- requesting, agreeing to receive or accepting the advantage may itself amount to improper performance of the relevant function or activity (Case 4, in subsection (3));
- alternatively, the advantage may be a reward for performing the function or activity improperly (Case 5, in subsection (4)).

In Cases 3 and 5, it does not matter whether the improper performance is by R or by another person. In Case 4, it must be R's requesting, agreeing to receive or acceptance of the advantage which amounts to improper performance, subject to subsection (6).

In Case 6 (subsection (5)) what is required is improper performance by R (or another person, where R requests it, assents to or acquiesces in it). This performance must be in anticipation or in consequence of a request, agreement to receive or acceptance of an advantage. Subsection (6) is concerned with the role of R in requesting, agreeing to receive or accepting advantages, or in benefiting from them, in Cases 3 to 6. First, this subsection makes it clear that in Cases 3 to 6 it does not matter whether it is R, or someone else through whom R acts, who requests, agrees to receive or accepts the advantage (subsection (6)(a)). Secondly, subsection (6) indicates that the advantage can be for the benefit of R, or of another person (subsection (6)(b)).

Subsection (7) makes it clear that in Cases 4 to 6, it is immaterial whether R knows or believes that the performance of the function is improper. Additionally, by subsection (8), in Case 6 where the function or activity is performed by another person, it is immaterial whether that person knew or believed that the performance of the function is improper.

Section 3: Function or activity to which bribe relates

A[89.7] This section defines the fields within which bribery can take place, in other words the types of function or activity that can be improperly performed for the purposes of sections 1 and 2. The term "relevant function or activity" is used for this purpose.

The purpose of the section is to ensure that the law of bribery applies equally to public and to selected private functions without discriminating between the two. Accordingly the functions or activities in question include all functions of a public nature and all activities connected with a business, trade or profession. The phrase "functions of a public nature" is the same phrase as is used in the definition of "public authority" in section 6(3)(b) of the Human Rights Act 1998 but it is not limited in the way it is in that Act. In addition, the functions or activities include all activities performed either in the course of employment or on behalf of any body of persons: these two categories straddle the public/private divide.

Not every defective performance of one of these functions for reward or in the hope of advantage engages the law of bribery. Subsections (3) to (5) make clear that there must be an expectation that the functions be carried out in good faith (condition A), or impartially (condition B), or the person performing it must be in a position of trust (condition C).

Subsection (6) provides that the functions or activities in question may be carried out either in the UK or abroad, and need have no connection with the UK. This preserves the effect of section 108(1) and (2) of the Anti-terrorism, Crime and Security Act 2001 (which is repealed by the Act).

Section 4: Improper performance to which bribe relates

A[89.8] Section 4 defines "improper performance" as performance which breaches a relevant expectation, as mentioned in condition A or B (subsections (3) and (4) of section 3 respectively) or any expectation as to the manner in which, or reasons for which, a function or activity satisfying condition C (subsection (5) of section 3) will be performed. Subsection (1)(b) states that an omission can in some circumstances amount to improper "performance".

Subsection (3) addresses the case where R is no longer engaged in a given function or activity but still carries out acts related to his or her former function or activity. These acts are treated as done in performance of the function or activity in question.

Section 5: Expectation test

A[89.9] Section 5 provides that when deciding what is expected of a person performing a function or activity for the purposes of sections 3 and 4, the test is what a reasonable person in the UK would expect of a person performing the relevant function or activity. Subsection (2) makes it clear that in deciding what a reasonable person in the UK would expect in relation to functions or activities the performance of which is not subject to UK laws, local practice and custom must not be taken into account unless such practice or custom is permitted or required by written law. Subsection (3) defines what is meant by "written law" for the purposes of this section.

Section 6: Bribery of a foreign public official

A[89.10] Section 6 creates a stand alone offence of bribery of a foreign public official. The offence is committed where a person offers, promises or gives a financial or other advantage to a foreign public official with the intention of influencing the official in the performance of his or her official functions. The person offering, promising or giving the advantage must also intend to obtain or retain business or an advantage in the conduct of business by doing so. However, the offence is not committed where the official is permitted or required by the applicable written law to be influenced by the advantage.

A 'foreign public official' includes officials, whether elected or appointed, who hold a legislative, administrative or judicial position of any kind of a country or territory outside the UK. It also includes any person who performs public functions in any branch of the national, local or municipal government of such a country or territory or who exercises a public function for any public agency or public enterprise of such a country or territory, such as professionals working for public health agencies and officers exercising public functions in state-owned enterprises. Foreign public officials can also be an official or agent of a public international organisation, such as the UN or the World Bank.

Sections 1 and 6 may capture the same conduct but will do so in different ways. The policy that founds the offence at section 6 is the need to prohibit the influencing of decision making in the context of publicly funded business opportunities by the inducement of personal enrichment of foreign public officials or to others at the official's request, assent or acquiescence. Such activity is very likely to involve conduct which amounts to 'improper performance' of a relevant function or activity to which section 1 applies, but, unlike section 1, section 6 does not require proof of it or an intention to induce it. This is because the exact nature of the functions of persons regarded as foreign public officials is often very difficult to ascertain with any accuracy, and the securing of evidence will often be reliant on the co-operation of the state any such officials serve. To require the prosecution to rely entirely on section 1 would amount to a very significant deficiency in the ability of the legislation to address this particular mischief. That said, it is not the Government's intention to criminalise behaviour where no such mischief occurs, but merely to formulate the offence to take account of the evidential difficulties referred to above. In view of its wide scope, and its role in the new form of corporate liability at section 7, the Government offers the following further explanation of issues arising from the formulation of section 6.

Local law. For the purposes of section 6 prosecutors will be required to show not only that an 'advantage' was offered, promised or given to the official or to another person at the official's request, assent or acquiescence, but that the advantage was one that the official was not permitted or required to be influenced by as determined by the written law applicable to the foreign official.

In seeking tenders for publicly funded contracts Governments often permit or require those tendering for the contract to offer, in addition to the principal tender, some kind of additional investment in the local economy or benefit to the local community. Such arrangements could in certain circumstances amount to a financial or other 'advantage' to a public official or to another person at the official's request, assent or acquiescence. Where, however, relevant 'written law' permits or requires the official to be influenced by such arrangements they will fall outside the scope of the offence. So, for example, where local planning law permits community investment or requires a foreign public official to minimise the cost of public procurement administration through cost sharing with contractors, a prospective contractor's offer of free training is very unlikely to engage section 6. In circumstances where the additional investment would amount to an advantage to a foreign public official and the local law is silent as to whether the official is permitted or required to be influenced by it, prosecutors will consider the public interest in prosecuting. This will provide an appropriate backstop in circumstances where the evidence suggests that the offer of additional investment is a legitimate part of a tender exercise.

Hospitality, promotional, and other business expenditure. Bona fide hospitality and promotional, or other business expenditure which seeks to improve the image of a commercial organisation, better to present products and services, or establish cordial relations, is recognised as an established and important part of doing business and it is not the intention of the Act to criminalise such behaviour. The Government does not intend for the Act to prohibit reasonable and proportionate hospitality and promotional or other similar business expenditure intended for these purposes. It is, however, clear that hospitality and promotional or other similar business expenditure can be employed as bribes.

In order to amount to a bribe under section 6 there must be an intention for a financial or other advantage to influence the official in his or her official role and thereby secure business or a business advantage. In this regard, it may be in some circumstances that hospitality or promotional expenditure in the form of travel and accommodation costs does not even amount to 'a financial or other advantage' to the relevant official because it is a cost that would otherwise be borne by the relevant foreign Government rather than the official him or herself.

Where the prosecution is able to establish a financial or other advantage has been offered, promised or given, it must then show that there is a sufficient connection between the advantage and the intention to influence and secure business or a business advantage. Where the prosecution cannot prove this to the requisite standard then no offence under section 6 will be committed. There may be direct evidence to support the existence of this connection and such evidence may indeed relate to relatively modest expenditure. In many cases, however, the question as to whether such a connection can be established will depend on the totality of the evidence which takes into account all of the surrounding circumstances. It would include matters such as the type and level of advantage offered, the manner and form in which the advantage is provided, and the level of influence the particular foreign public official has over awarding the business. In this circumstantial context, the more lavish the hospitality or the higher the expenditure in relation to travel, accommodation or other similar business expenditure provided to a foreign public official, then, generally, the greater the inference that it is intended to influence the official to grant business or a business advantage in return.

The standards or norms applying in a particular sector may also be relevant here. However, simply providing hospitality or promotional, or other similar business expenditure which is commensurate with such norms is not, of itself, evidence that no bribe was paid if there is other evidence to the contrary; particularly if the norms in question are extravagant. Levels of expenditure will not, therefore, be the only consideration in determining whether a section 6 offence has been committed. But in the absence of any further evidence demonstrating the required connection, it is unlikely, for example, that incidental provision of a routine business courtesy will raise the inference that it was intended to have a direct impact on decision making, particularly where such hospitality is commensurate with the reasonable and proportionate norms for the particular industry; e.g. the provision of airport to hotel transfer services to facilitate an on-site visit, or dining and tickets to an event.

Sentencing (General bribery offences)

A[89.11] There are separate guidelines for corporate defendants. These are not reproduced since such cases are rarely heard in the magistrates' court.

Bribery

Bribing another person

Bribery Act 2010 (section 1)

Being bribed

Bribery Act 2010 (section 2)

Bribery of foreign public officials

Bribery Act 2010 (section 6)

Triable either way

Maximum: 7 years' custody

Offence range: Discharge – 8 years' custody

STEP ONE
Determining the offence category

The court should determine the offence category with reference to the tables below. In order to determine the category the court should assess **culpability** and **harm.**

The level of culpability is determined by weighing up all the factors of the case to determine the offender's role and the extent to which the offending was planned and the sophistication with which it was carried out.

Culpability demonstrated by one or more of the following:

A – High culpability

A leading role where offending is part of a group activity
Involvement of others through pressure, influence
Abuse of position of significant power or trust or responsibility
Intended corruption (directly or indirectly) of a senior official performing a public function Intended corruption (directly or indirectly) of a law enforcement officer
Sophisticated nature of offence/significant planning
Offending conducted over sustained period of time
Motivated by expectation of substantial financial, commercial or political gain
B – Medium culpability
All other cases where characteristics for categories A or C are not present
A significant role where offending is part of a group activity
C – Lesser culpability
Involved through coercion, intimidation or exploitation
Not motivated by personal gain
Peripheral role in organised fraud
Opportunistic 'one-off' offence; very little or no planning
Limited awareness or understanding of the extent of fraudulent activity

Where there are characteristics present which fall under different levels of culpability, the court should balance these characteristics to reach a fair assessment of the offender's culpability.

Harm is assessed in relation to any impact caused by the offending (whether to identifiable victims or in a wider context) and the actual or intended gain to the offender.

Harm demonstrated by one or more of the following factors:

Category 1	• Serious detrimental effect on individuals (for example by provision of substandard goods or services resulting from the corrupt behaviour)
	• Serious environmental impact
	• Serious undermining of the proper function of local or national government, business or public services
	• Substantial actual or intended financial gain to offender or another or loss caused to others
Category 2	• Significant detrimental effect on individuals
	• Significant environmental impact
	• Significant undermining of the proper function of local or national government, business or public services
	• Significant actual or intended financial gain to offender or another or loss caused to others
	• Risk of category 1 harm
Category 3	• Limited detrimental impact on individuals, the environment, government, business or public services
	• Risk of category 2 harm
Category 4	• Risk of category 3 harm

Risk of harm involves consideration of both the likelihood of harm occurring and the extent of it if it does. Risk of harm is less serious than the same actual harm. Where the offence has caused risk of harm but no (or much less) actual harm, the normal approach is to move to the next category of harm down. This may not be appropriate if either the likelihood or extent of potential harm is particularly high.

STEP TWO
Starting point and category range

Having determined the category at step one, the court should use the appropriate starting point (as adjusted in accordance with step one above) to reach a sentence within the category range in the table below. The starting point applies to all offenders irrespective of plea or previous convictions.

Where the value is larger or smaller than the amount on which the starting point is based, this should lead to upward or downward adjustment as appropriate.

Section 1 Bribery Act 2010: Bribing another person

Section 2 Bribery Act 2010: Being bribed

Section 6 Bribery Act 2010: Bribery of foreign public officials

Maximum: 10 years' custody

	A	B	C
Category 1	Starting point 7 years' custody	Starting point 5 years' custody	Starting point 3 years' custody
	Category range 5 – 8 years' custody	Category range 3 – 6 years' custody	Category range 18 months' – 4 years' custody
Category 2	Starting point 5 years' custody	Starting point 3 years' custody	Starting point 18 months' custody
	Category range 3 – 6 years' custody	Category range 18 months' – 4 years' custody	Category range 26 weeks' – 3 years' custody
Category 3	Starting point 3 years' custody	Starting point 18 months' custody	Starting point 26 weeks' custody
	Category range 18 months' – 4 years' custody	Category range 26 weeks' – 3 years' custody	Category range Medium level community order – 1 year's custody
Category 4	Starting point 18 months' custody	Starting point 26 weeks' custody	Starting point Medium level community order
	Category range 26 weeks' – 3 years' custody	Category range Medium level community order – 1 year's custody	Category range Band B fine – High level community order

The table below contains a non-exhaustive list of additional factual elements providing the context of the offence and factors relating to the offender.

Identify whether any combination of these or other relevant factors should result in an upward or downward adjustment from the starting point.

Consecutive sentences for multiple offences may be appropriate where large sums are involved.

Factors increasing seriousness	Factors reducing seriousness or reflecting personal mitigation
Statutory aggravating factors	No previous convictions or no relevant/recent convictions
Previous convictions, having regard to a) the nature of the offence to which the conviction relates and its relevance to the current offence; and b) the time that has elapsed since the conviction	Remorse
Offence committed whilst on bail	Good character and/or exemplary conduct
Other aggravating factors	Little or no prospect of success
Steps taken to prevent the victim reporting or obtaining assistance and/or from assisting or supporting the prosecution	Serious medical conditions requiring urgent, intensive or long-term treatment
Attempts to conceal/dispose of evidence	Age and/or lack of maturity where it affects the responsibility of the offender
Established evidence of community/wider impact	Lapse of time since apprehension where this does not arise from the conduct of the offender
Failure to comply with current court orders	Mental disorder or learning disability
Offence committed on licence	Sole or primary carer for dependent relatives
Offences taken into consideration	Offender co-operated with investigation, made early admissions and/or voluntarily reported offending
Failure to respond to warnings about behaviour	
Offences committed across borders	
Blame wrongly placed on others	
Pressure exerted on another party	
Offence committed to facilitate other criminal activity	

STEP THREE
Consider any factors which indicate a reduction, such as assistance to the prosecution

The court should take into account sections 73 and 74 of the Serious Organised Crime and Police Act 2005 (assistance by defendants: reduction or review of sentence) and any other rule of law by virtue of which an offender may receive a discounted sentence in consequence of assistance given (or offered) to the prosecutor or investigator.

STEP FOUR
Reduction for guilty pleas

The court should take account of any potential reduction for a guilty plea in accordance with section 144 of the Criminal Justice Act 2003 and the *Guilty Plea* guideline.

STEP FIVE
Totality principle

If sentencing an offender for more than one offence, or where the offender is already serving a sentence, consider whether the total sentence is just and proportionate to the overall offending behaviour.

STEP SIX
Confiscation, compensation and ancillary orders

The court must proceed with a view to making a confiscation order if it is asked to do so by the prosecutor or if the court believes it is appropriate for it to do so.

Where the offence has resulted in loss or damage the court must consider whether to make a compensation order.

If the court makes both a confiscation order and an order for compensation and the court believes the offender will not have sufficient means to satisfy both orders in full, the court must direct that the compensation be paid out of sums recovered under the confiscation order (section 13 of the Proceeds of Crime Act 2002).

The court may also consider whether to make ancillary orders. These may include a deprivation order, a financial reporting order, a serious crime prevention order and disqualification from acting as a company director.

STEP SEVEN
Reasons

Section 174 of the Criminal Justice Act 2003 imposes a duty to give reasons for, and explain the effect of, the sentence.

STEP EIGHT
Consideration for time spent on bail

The court must consider whether to give credit for time spent on bail in accordance with section 240A of the Criminal Justice Act 2003.

Section B

Sentencing and Orders

Index to sentencing

Absolute discharge B[22]

Activity requirement B[9.10]
or, for offences committed on or after 1 February 2015, a rehabilitation activity requirement.

Action plan order B[1]

Alcohol Treatment requirement B[9.21]

Anti-social behaviour orders – breach B[2.4] and B[2.5]

Assessment of fines B[3]

Attendance centre order (aged 10 to 21) B[4]

Binding over B[5]

Closure of premises associated with nuisance or disorder, etc B[6]

Closure order (specified prostitution offences) B[7]

Community orders B[9]
Breach of a requirement B[9.24], B[9.27], B[9.28] and A[9]

Committal to Crown Court for sentence B[8]

Community protection B[8A]

Community sentence: orders and requirement B[9]

Compensation order B[10]

Conditional discharge B[22]

Confiscation order B[11]

Costs B[12]

Criminal behaviour orders B[13]

Criminal behaviour orders – breach B[2.5]

Criminal courts charge B[14]

Curfew requirement B[9.13]

Custodial sentence B[15]

Deferred sentence B[16]

Deportation B[17]

Deprivation of property B[18]

Detention and training order B[19]

Detention
in courthouse B[20]
in young offender institution B[21]

Domestic violence protection notice B[23]

Domestic violence protection order B[24]

Drug rehabilitation requirement B[9.18]

European protection order B[26]

Exclusion requirement B[10]

Fines B[28]

(Assessment of fines) B[3]

Fines unpaid

enforcement procedure B[28.62]
means inquiry B[28.62]
18 to 21 age group B[28.85]
10 to 17 age group B[28.93]

Football banning orders B[29]

Foreign Travel Prohibition requirement B[9.14]

Foreign Travel Restriction order B[30]

Forfeiture B[18]

Forfeiture or suspension of liquor licence B[31]

Guardianship order B[32]

Hospital order B[33]

Imprisonment B[34]
suspended sentence B[34.40]

Injunctions for gang-related violence B[35]

Mental Health Treatment requirement B[9.16]

Mental Health Treatment at place other than that specified in the order B[9.17]

Multiplicity of charges B[36]

Parenting order B[37]

Power to review decisions B[38]

Premises and prohibition orders – psychoactive substances B[38A]

Process of sentencing B[45]

Programme requirement B[9.11]

Prohibited activity requirement B[9.12]

Referral order B[39]

Remission to another court B[40]

Reparation order B[41]

Residence requirement B[9]

Restitution order B[42]

Restraining order A[41.13]

Review of decisions B[38]

Sentencing tables B[43]

Sexual harm prevention orders B[44]

Structure B[45.2]
aggravating and mitigating features B[45.2A]
aggravated related to race, religion, disability or sexual orientation B[45.2B]

Supervision requirement B[9.22]

Surcharge (see fines, costs and compensation at B[10], B[12] and B[28].

Suspended sentence (See Imprisonment) B[34.40]

Transfer of criminal proceedings B[46]

Unpaid work requirement B[9.9]

Violent Offender Order B[47]

The (victims') surcharge B[50]

Youth injunctions B[48]

Youth Rehabilitation Order B[49]

YRO requirements (Sch 1, Pt 1 CJ & IA 2008) B[49.4] onwards)
The details are to be found in Schedule 1 of the Act and the relevant paragraph to the Schedule is indicated below in each of the available requirements:

(1) Intensive supervision and surveillance requirement
(2) Activity requirement (paras 6–8)
(3) Supervision requirement (para 9)
(4) Unpaid work requirement for those aged 16–17 years when convicted (para 10)
(5) Programme requirement (para 11)
(6) Attendance centre requirement (para 12)
(7) Prohibited activity requirement (para 13)
(8) Curfew requirement (para 14)
(9) Exclusion requirement (para 15)
(10) Residence requirement (para 16)
(11) Local authority residence requirement (paras 17 and 19)
(12) Fostering requirement (paras 4, 18–19)
(13) Mental health treatment requirement (paras 20–21)
(14) Drug treatment/drug testing requirement (paras 22–23)
(15) Intoxicating substance treatment requirement (para 24)
(16) Education requirement (para 25)
(17) Electronic monitoring requirement (para 26)

Breach of a YRO requirement **B[49.23]**
Commission of further offence **B[49.24]**
Application to revoke **B[49.25]**
Amendment **B[49.26]**

B[1]

Action plan orders

(PCC(S) Act 2000, ss 69–72)

Reports

B[1.1] Sections 69–72 of the 2000 Act have been repealed by the Criminal Justice and Immigration Act 2008. Action plan orders were replaced by the Youth Rehabilitation Order. See **B[49]** onwards.

B[2]

Anti-social behaviour orders (ASBOs)

(Crime and Disorder Act 1998, ss 1–4)

B[2.1] Anti-social behaviour orders were repealed by the Anti-social Behaviour, Crime and Policing Act 2014. Orders in civil proceedings were replaced by injunctions, with jurisdiction transferred to the county court for adults and to the youth court for those aged under 18. Narrative on injunctions in respect of youths can be found at **B**[48]. Anti-social behaviour orders on conviction (CrASBOs) were replaced by criminal behaviour orders (CBOs). Narrative on CBOs can be found at B[13]. These repeals are subject to saving and transitional provisions, which are described below.

B[2.2] Variation or discharge of ABSOs – The repeal of ASBOs (and certain other orders, eg individual support orders) is subject to the saving and transitional provisions set out in s 21 of the Anti-social Behaviour, Crime and Policing Act 2014. All such orders will be converted (with necessary modifications) to injunctions under the 2014 Act at the end of five years beginning with the commencement day.

As from the commencement day, ie 23 March 2015 (see SI 2015/373, art 4(a)), there may be no variation of such an order that extends the period of the order or any of its provisions. This overturns the decision in *Leeds City Council v G* [2007] EWHC 1612 (Admin), (2007) Times, 11 September, in which the Administrative Court held that a magistrates' court did have jurisdiction under s 1(8) of the Crime and Disorder Act 1998 to vary a civil order by extending the duration of the original order beyond the minimum period, ie two years. Subject to this, orders may be varied or discharged, as before .

Variation of an ASBO under s 1(8) does not require proof of a fresh act of anti-social behaviour. The court was entitled, in the exercise of its discretion, to consider a variation even if the applicant had the option of applying for a fresh ASBO (now injunction). A complaint to vary must simply be made within six months from an event or circumstance which it is alleged renders the original order inappropriate for one reason or another. On a purposive construction of s 1(8) the question is whether it is necessary to vary the order to protect the public: *James v Birmingham City Council* [2010] EWHC 282 (Admin), 174 JP 250.

B[2.3] Variation or discharge of CrASBOs – The repeal of anti-social behaviour orders on conviction (and individual support orders and drink banning orders on conviction) is subject to the saving and transitional provisions set out in s 33 of the Anti-social Behaviour, Crime and Policing Act 2014. Again, as from the commencement day (see **B**[2.2] above) there may be no variation that extends the period of the order or of any of its provisions and, again, at the end of the period of five years beginning with the commencement day any such order still in force will be converted (with necessary modifications) to a CBO under the 2014 Act.

B[2.4] Breach of an ASBO or CrASBO will result in the commission of a criminal offence triable either way.

Breach of an order – commission of a criminal offence – CDA 1998, s 8(2) – Although there is nothing inherently wrong in passing a consecutive sentence for breach of an anti-social behaviour order, if the new offence is derived from the same course of conduct, broadly speaking concurrent sentences should be imposed (*R v Lawson* [2006] EWCA Crim 2674, [2006] All ER (D) 61 (Mar)).

Breach – collateral attack on validity of the order or its terms – In *R (on the application of W) v DPP* [2005] EWCA Civ 1333, (2005) 169 JP 435 it was decided that an ASBO was to be treated as a valid order unless and until it was varied or declared invalid. The Court of Appeal said it was open to a magistrates' court considering an allegation of a breach of an order to determine whether the original order was ultra vires and therefore not a valid order. In *DPP v T* [2006] EWHC 728 (Admin), [2006] 3 All ER 471, [2006] 3 FCR 184; sub nom *CPS v T* (2006) 170 JP 470, (2006) Times, 13 April the Divisional Court reached a slightly different conclusion. The Divisional Court made reference to the normal rule that an order of the court was to be obeyed unless and until it was set aside. The Court noted that the person against whom an ASBO was made had a full opportunity to challenge that order on appeal or to apply to vary it. The policy consideration that a magistrates' court had jurisdiction to determine issues of the validity of a byelaw or an administrative decision was wholly absent when the issue was the validity of an order of the court. It was open to a magistrates' court to consider whether the provision lacked sufficient clarity to warrant a finding that the defendant's conduct did not amount to a breach of the order; or that the lack of clarity provided him with a reasonable excuse; or whether, assuming a breach was established, it was appropriate in the circumstances not to impose any penalty for the breach.

Breach – reasonable excuse – Section 1(10) of the CDA 1998 makes it a criminal offence to breach an ASBO in the following terms: 'If without reasonable excuse a person does anything which he is prohibited from doing by an anti-social behaviour order, he is guilty of an offence'. The Act only imposes an evidential burden of the defendant, the legal burden rests with the prosecution to prove that the defendant acted without reasonable excuse (*R v Charles* [2009] EWCA Crim 1570, [2010] 4 All ER 553, [2010] 1 Cr App Rep 38). The words 'without reasonable excuse' also apply to breaches of CBOs and it is submitted that the same burden and principles apply.

In the context of an ASBO, ignorance, forgetfulness or misunderstanding, whether arising from an error as to the terms of the order or lack of knowledge of where the defendant was at the material time, might be capable of constituting a defence of reasonable excuse (*R v Nicholson* [2006] EWCA Crim 1518, [2006] 1 WLR 2857, [2006] 2 Cr App Rep 429).

Section 1(10) did not require the Crown to prove a specific mental element on the part of a defendant at the time he committed an act which constituted a breach of an ASBO. However, if the defence of reasonable excuse was raised, the state of mind of the accused would usually be relevant and could, if the circumstances warranted, be taken into account in determining whether the Crown had proved there was no reasonable excuse. The burden of so proving lay with the Crown: *R v Charles* [2009] EWCA Crim 1570, [2010] 4 All ER 553, [2010] 1 Cr App Rep 38. In this case the judge was entitled to conclude that there was no reasonable excuse as the risk was obvious and JB had actually foreseen it. The alarm and distress had not been an accident but was caused by JB's reckless conduct in breaching the ASBO: *JB v DPP* [2012] EWHC 72 (Admin), [2012] 1 WLR 2357, [2012] 2 Cr App Rep 9.

SGC Guideline – Criminal behaviour order, breach of (also applicable to breach of an anti-social behaviour order)

B[2.5] The text of this guideline is taken from the Sentencing council's Breach offences: Definitive guideline, published on 4 July 2018, taking effect from 1 October 2018.

Breach of a criminal behaviour order (also applicable to breach of an anti-social behaviour order)

Triable either way

Maximum: 5 years' custody

Offence range: Fine – 4 years' custody

STEP 1
DETERMINING THE OFFENCE CATEGORY

The court should determine the offence category with reference only to the factors listed in the tables below. In order to determine the category the court should assess culpability and harm.

Culpability

A	• Very serious or persistent breach
B	• Deliberate breach falling between A and C
C	• Minor breach • Breach just short of reasonable excuse

Harm

The level of harm is determined by weighing up all the factors of the case to determine the harm that has been caused or was at risk of being caused.

In assessing any risk of harm posed by the breach, consideration should be given to the original offence(s) or activity for which the order was imposed and the circumstances in which the breach arose.

Category 1	• Breach causes very serious harm or distress • Breach demonstrates a continuing risk of serious criminal and/or anti-social behaviour
Category 2	• Cases falling between categories 1 and 3
Category 3	• Breach causes little or no harm or distress • Breach demonstrates a continuing risk of minor criminal and/or anti-social behaviour

STEP 2
STARTING POINT AND CATEGORY RANGE

Having determined the category at step one, the court should use the corresponding starting point to reach a sentence within the category range in the table below. The starting point applies to all offenders irrespective of plea or previous convictions.

	Culpability		
Harm	A	Starting Point	Range
Category 1	Starting point 2 years' custody Category range 1–4 years' custody	Starting point 1 years' custody Category range High level community order – 2 years' custody	Starting point 12 weeks' custody Category range Medium level community order – 1 year's custody

Harm	Culpability A	Starting Point	Range
Category 2	**Starting point** 1 years' custody **Category range** High level community order – 2 years' custody	**Starting point** 12 weeks' custody **Category range** Medium level community order – 1 year's custody	**Starting point** High level community order **Category range** Low level community order – 26 weeks' custody
Category 3	**Starting point** 12 weeks' custody **Category range** Medium level community order – 1 year's custody	**Starting point** High level community order **Category range** Low level community order – 26 weeks' custody	**Starting point** Medium level community order **Category range** Band B fine – High level community order

NOTE: A Conditional Discharge **MAY NOT** be imposed for breach of a criminal behaviour order.

The table below contains a **non-exhaustive** list of additional factual elements providing the context of the offence and factors relating to the offender. Identify whether any combination of these, or other relevant factors, should result in an upward or downward adjustment from the starting point. In some cases, having considered these factors, it may be appropriate to move outside the identified category range.

FACTORS INCREASING SERIOUSNESS

Statutory aggravating factors:
Previous convictions, having regard to a) the **nature** of the offence to which the conviction relates and its **relevance** to the current offence; and b) the **time** that has elapsed since the conviction
Offence committed whilst on bail
Other aggravating factors:
Offence is a further breach, following earlier breach proceedings
Breach committed shortly after order made
History of disobedience of court orders or orders imposed by local authorities
Breach constitutes a further offence (where not separately prosecuted)
Targeting of a person the order was made to protect or a witness in the original proceedings
Victim or protected subject of order breached is particularly vulnerable due to age, disability, culture, religion, language, or other factors
Offence committed on licence or while subject to post sentence supervision

FACTORS REDUCING SERIOUSNESS OR REFLECTING PERSONAL MITIGATION

Genuine misunderstanding of terms of order
Breach committed after long period of compliance
Prompt voluntary surrender/admission of breach or failure
Age and/or lack of maturity where it affects the responsibility of the offender

Mental disorder or learning disability	
Sole or primary carer for dependent relatives	

STEP 3
CONSIDER ANY FACTORS WHICH INDICATE A REDUCTION, SUCH AS ASSISTANCE TO THE PROSECUTION

The court should take into account sections 73 and 74 of the Serious Organised Crime and Police Act 2005 (assistance by defendants: reduction or review of sentence) and any other rule of law by virtue of which an offender may receive a discounted sentence in consequence of assistance given (or offered) to the prosecutor or investigator.

STEP 4
REDUCTION FOR GUILTY PLEAS

The court should take account of any potential reduction for a guilty plea in accordance with section 144 of the Criminal Justice Act 2003 and the *Guilty Plea* guideline.

STEP 5
TOTALITY PRINCIPLE

If sentencing an offender for more than one offence, or where the offender is already serving a sentence, consider whether the total sentence is just and proportionate to the overall offending behaviour in accordance with the *Offences Taken into Consideration and Totality* guideline.

STEP 6
ANCILLARY ORDERS

In all cases, the court should consider whether to make compensation and/or ancillary orders.

STEP 7
REASONS

Section 174 of the Criminal Justice Act 2003 imposes a duty to give reasons for, and explain the effect of, the sentence.

STEP 8
CONSIDERATION FOR TIME SPENT ON BAIL

The court must consider whether to give credit for time spent on bail in accordance with section 240A of the Criminal Justice Act 2003.

B[2.6] **Previous convictions.** For the purposes of this guideline a 'first time offender' is one who does not have a previous conviction for breach of an ASBO.

Key factors

B[2.7] (a) An ASBO may be breached in a very wide range of circumstances and may involve one or more terms not being complied with. The examples given below are intended to illustrate how the scale of the conduct that led to the breach, taken as a whole, might come within the three levels of seriousness:

No harm caused or intended – in the absence of intimidation or the causing of fear or violence, breaches involving being very drunk or begging at this level, as may prohibited use of public transport or entry into a prohibited area, where there is no evidence that harassment, alarm or distress was caused or intended.

Lesser degree of harm caused or intended – examples may include lesser degree of threats or intimidation, the use of seriously abusive language, or causing more than minor damage to property.

Serious harm caused or intended – breach at this level of seriousness will involve the use of violence, significant threats or intimidation or the targeting of individuals or groups of people in a manner that leads to a fear of violence.

(b) The suggested starting points are based on the assumption that the offender has the level of culpability.

(c) In the most serious cases, involving repeat offending and a breach causing serious harassment together with the presence of several aggravating factors, such as the use of violence, a sentence beyond the highest range will be justified.

(d) When imposing a community order, the court must ensure that the requirements imposed are proportionate to the seriousness of the breach, compatible with each other, and also with the prohibitions of the ASBO if the latter is to remain in force. Even where the threshold for a custodial sentence is crossed, a custodial sentence is not inevitable.

(e) An offender may be sentenced for more than one offence of breach, which occurred on different days. While consecutive sentences may be imposed in such cases, the overall sentence should reflect the totality principle.

B[2.8] **Sentencing of Young Offenders.** The normal approach is that the penalty is scaled down to reflect both reduced culpability (for example, due to a lesser ability to foresee the consequences of actions) and the more onerous effects of punishments on their education and personal development. For the same reasons, the sentencing framework differs significantly depending on the age of the young offender. Space does not permit a full discussion of the SAP advice. See **paragraphs 52–69** of the advice.

B[2.9] The court may not impose a conditional discharge following a breach.

B[3]

Assessment of Fines: Sentencing Process

Sentencing guidelines

B[3.1] Assessment of fines

1. DECIDE THAT A FINE IS APPROPRIATE
2. OFFENCE SERIOUSNESS A. IDENTIFY THE APPROPRIATE STARTING POINT In the offence guidelines, the starting point is identified as band A, B or C Each fine band provides a **starting point** and a **range** related to the **seriousness** of the offence expressed as a proportion of the offender's **relevant weekly income** – see B[28.16].
2. OFFENCE SERIOUSNESS B. CONSIDER THE EFFECT OF AGGRAVATING AND MITIGATING FACTORS **Move up or down from the starting point** to reflect aggravating or mitigating factors that affect the **seriousness** of the offence – this will usually be within the indicated range for the fine band but the court is not precluded from going outside the range where the facts justify it.
3. CONSIDER OFFENDER MITIGATION The court may consider it appropriate to make a further adjustment to the starting point in the light of any matters of offender mitigation.
4. FORM A VIEW OF THE POSITION OF THE OFFENCE WITHIN THE RANGE FOR THE FINE BAND THEN TAKE INTO ACCOUNT THE OFFENDER'S FINANCIAL CIRCUMSTANCES Require the offender to provide a statement of **financial circumstances**. Obtain further information through questioning if necessary. Failure to provide the information when required is an offence. The provision of financial information does not affect the seriousness of the offence or, therefore, the position of the offence within the range for the applicable fine band.
The initial consideration for the assessment of the fine is the offender's **relevant weekly income** – see B[28.17]. However, the court must take account of the offender's financial circumstances more broadly. These may have the effect of increasing or reducing the amount of the fine – see **B[28.18]–B[28.23]**. Where the court has insufficient information to make a proper determination of the offender's financial circumstances, it may make such determination as it thinks fit – see **B[28.18]**.
5. CONSIDER A REDUCTION FOR A GUILTY PLEA Reduce the fine by the appropriate proportion – see **B[45.46]**.
6. CONSIDER ANCILLARY ORDERS, INCLUDING COMPENSATION Must consider compensation in every case where the offending has resulted in personal injury, loss or damage – give reasons if order not made – see **B[10]**.
7. CONSIDER A REDUCTION FOR A GUILTY PLEA GIVE REASONS **The resulting fine must reflect the seriousness of the offence and must take into account the offender's financial circumstances**

Consider the proposed total financial penalty, including compensation, victims surcharge and costs. Where there are insufficient resources to pay the total amount, the order of priority is compensation, surcharge, fine, costs.

Must give reasons for the sentence passed, including any ancillary orders.

Must state if the sentence has been reduced to reflect ca guilty plea; indicate what the sentence would otherwise have been.

Must make a collection order unless this would be impracticable or inappropriate – see **B[28.38]** onwards above.

B[4]

Attendance centre orders (adults only)

(Powers of Criminal Courts (Sentencing) Act 2000, s 60; Criminal Justice Act 2003, s 177)

B[4.1] **Jurisdiction** – Offence must be punishable with imprisonment (even though the individual offender may not be).

B[4.2] **Age limits** – 18 to under 25 years (25 years old also when used as a fine default power).

B[4.3] **Maximum period** – 12 hours unless the court thinks that would be inadequate in which event the maximum periods are:

Offender aged 18 to under 25: 36 hours

Note – A further order may be made during the currency of a previous one, in which case the period of the later order may be determined as above without regard to the unexpired part of the previous order.

B[4.4] **Minimum period** – 12 hours.

B[4.5] **Availability.** Court must have been notified of the availability of a centre for persons of the offender's age and sex.

B[4.6] Regard must be paid to the accessibility of the centre to the offender.

B[4.7] **Juveniles.** A magistrates' court may not make this order against a juvenile but must remit him to a youth court.

B[4.8] **Community sentences.** Note the restrictions on imposing a community sentence, see **B**[9].

Ancillary orders

B[4.9] Anti-social behaviour orders **B**[2]

Binding over orders

Compensation at **B**[10]

Costs at **B**[12]

Deprivation of property and forfeiture at **B**[18]

Disqualification from driving at C[5]

Endorsement of driving licence at C[5]

Legal aid contribution order at B[38]

Restitution orders B[42]

How to announce

B[4.10]–[4.15] **We shall order you to attend the attendance centre at [................] for a total of [................] hours starting on [................].** You will be given a copy of the order which will show the date and time of your first attendance. After that you will attend as directed by the officer in charge. You will make up the period of [................] hours by attending on Saturday afternoons (or as the case may be) for two (or three, as the case may be) hours at a time. If you arrive late the officer in charge may not count that day's attendance. If you fail to attend without a very good excuse, or if you fail to carry out the officer's instructions properly, he will bring you back here and we shall deal with you. Do you understand?

General considerations for attendance centre orders (adults only)

B[4.16] The aims of the attendance centre have been described by the Home Office as follows:

(a) to vindicate the law by imposing loss of leisure, a punishment that is generally understood by offenders;
(b) to bring the offender for a period under the influence of representatives of the authority of the state; and
(c) to teach the offender constructive use of leisure and to guide him, on leaving, towards organisations or activities where he may use what he has learned. Centres usually require attendance for three-hour periods on alternate Saturday afternoons. Only one period of attendance may be required in any one day. The court must take into account the availability of suitable transport and the journey time from home to the centre. A distance of 15 miles or a 90–minutes journey would be the limit.

B[4.17] The court must announce for how many hours the defendant must attend. The court should also tell the defendant the date, time and place of the first attendance.

B[5]
Binding over

B[5.1] There have been significant developments to the making of binding over orders following amendments to the *Criminal Practice Directions 2015* [2015] EWCA Crim 1567 which for the sake of completeness is set out below at B[5.20]–[5.21]. The following notes therefore must be read in the light of that Practice Direction.

B[5.2] Maximum period – None, but the Practice Direction suggests generally not longer than 12 months.

B[5.3] Minimum period – None, but consistent with community orders generally not less than six months.

Ancillary orders

B[5.4] Costs at B[12]. It would appear that there is no power to award costs where a defendant is bound over under the court's inherent powers where the substantive charge is withdrawn or dismissed.

How to announce

B[5.5] **We are going to order you to enter a recognisance – that is a binding promise – that you will refrain from the following conduct or activity for the next** [*period*]. [Court to specify the specific conduct or activity from which the individual must refrain.]

The amount of that recognisance will be [*amount*] **and that means that if you repeat the kind of conduct or activity we have heard about today, during the next** [*period*] **we will order** you to pay that amount. Do you understand? Do you agree to making that promise and to guaranteeing to pay the [*amount*] if you break that promise?

Age limits – None. However, a refusal to enter a recognisance (see below) will result in imprisonment and as those under 21 [**18] may not be imprisoned the court would be powerless to enforce an order to enter into a recognisance.

General considerations for binding over

B[5.6] One or more sureties may also be required if the court thinks fit. This order is commonly and conveniently referred to as a binding over order but this tends to disguise its real form. The court orders the defendant to enter a recognisance in terms chosen by the court as to the duration and amount. The defendant or his legal representative must be given an opportunity to address the court in order not to breach Article 6 rights (*Hooper v UK* (2004) Times, 19 November, [2004] All ER (D) 254 (Nov), ECtHR). If the defendant so agrees, he is said to be bound over to keep the peace. If he refuses to enter the recognisance the only course left to the court is to send him to prison from which he will be released after a term fixed by the court of up to six months or when he enters the recognisance, whichever is the sooner. Great care should therefore be exercised before making such an order especially if there is any possibility of refusal to comply with it. An order to be of good behaviour should be avoided as it is imprecise and may breach the ECHR (*Hashman and Harrup v United Kingdom* (2000) 30 EHRR 241, [2000] Crim LR 185, ECtHR).

NB: The defendant's consent is not required if the binding over order is made as an ancillary penalty to a criminal sentence (*R v Crown Court at Lincoln, ex p Jude* [1997] 3 All ER 737, [1998] 1 WLR 24). This case must be read against the Consolidated Practice Direction set out below.

B[5.7] Before a court has any power to order a person to enter a recognisance to keep the peace, it must have grounds for believing that there is a possibility of a future breach of the peace.

B[5.8] Sometimes the court is asked to make this order by an applicant who has taken out a summons for that purpose. In addition to this, the court may on its own initiative consider the need to make the order when dealing with an offender. Moreover, a witness or complainant may also be ordered to enter a recognisance. Whenever the court takes the initiative it should explain to the person concerned what it has in mind to do and offer an opportunity to address the court before it is decided whether to make the order or not.

B[5.9]–[5.15] The procedure for binding over a complainant or witness must be followed punctiliously, and if this is in contemplation, the advice of the legal adviser should be followed.

B[5.16] There is no power generally to impose any conditions, and an order must be specific as to the conduct or activity which the individual must refrain from repeating. Also it appears that there may be a condition not to possess, carry or use firearms or as part of a community order (Firearms Act 1968, s 21(3)).

B[5.17] Breach of the order will be dealt with by forfeiting the recognisance, or any part of it. The defendant may be given time to pay and in default, after a means inquiry, he may be committed to prison, as if he owed a fine.

Binding over a parent

B[5.18] Either a magistrates' court or a youth court may require the parent of a young person (or an 18-year-old who was 17 when the proceedings commenced) who has been found guilty of an offence to enter a recognisance to take proper care of him and to exercise proper control over him. The court must exercise these powers where the juvenile has not attained 16 years if it is satisfied, having regard to the circumstances of the case, that it would be desirable in the interests of preventing the juvenile from committing further offences. If the court does not exercise the powers it must say so and give its reasons in open court. The court's duty to bind over the parent is replaced by a power where the juvenile has attained 16 years. In such a case the maximum amount of the recognisance is £1,000 and the maximum period is three years or until a young person attains 18, whichever is the shorter.

B[5.19] The parent must consent to the order. An unreasonable refusal is punishable by a fine of up to £1,000. A parent may appeal to the Crown Court against the bind over.

Criminal Practice Directions 2015

B[5.20]–[5.21] Section J of the CPD provides:

'J: BINDING OVER ORDERS AND CONDITIONAL DISCHARGES

J.1 This direction takes into account the judgments of the European Court of Human Rights in *Steel v United Kingdom* (1999) 28 EHRR 603, [1998] Crim. L.R.893 and in *Hashman and Harrup v United Kingdom* (2000) 30 EHRR 241, [2000]Crim. L.R. 185. Its purpose is to give practical guidance, in the light of those two judgments, on the practice of imposing binding over orders. The direction applies to orders made under the court's common law powers, under the Justices of the Peace Act 1361, under section 1(7) of the Justices of the Peace Act 1968 and under section 115 of the Magistrates' Courts Act 1980. This direction also gives guidance concerning the court's power to bind over parents or guardians under section 150 of the Powers of Criminal Courts (Sentencing) Act 2000 and the Crown Court's power to bind over to come up for judgment. The court's power to impose a conditional discharge under section 12 of the Powers of Criminal Courts (Sentencing) Act 2000 is also covered by this direction.

Binding over to keep the peace

J.2 Before imposing a binding over order, the court must be satisfied so that it is sure that a breach of the peace involving violence, or an imminent threat of violence, has occurred or that there is a real risk of violence in the future. Such violence may be perpetrated by the individual who will be subject to the order or by a third party as a natural consequence of the individual's conduct.

J.3 In light of the judgment in *Hashman*, courts should no longer bind an individual over "to be of good behaviour". Rather than binding an individual over to "keep the peace" in general terms, the court should identify the specific conduct or activity from which the individual must refrain.

Written order

J.4 When making an order binding an individual over to refrain from specified types of conduct or activities, the details of that conduct or those activities should be specified by the court in a written order, served on all relevant parties. The court should state its reasons for the making of the order, its length and the amount of the recognisance. The length of the order should be proportionate to the harm sought to be avoided and should not generally exceed 12 months.

Evidence

J.5 Sections 51 to 57 of the Magistrates' Courts Act 1980 set out the jurisdiction of the magistrates' court to hear an application made on complaint and the procedure which is to be followed. This includes a requirement under section 53 to hear evidence and the parties, before making any order. This practice should be applied to all cases in the magistrates' court and the Crown Court where the court is considering imposing a binding over order. The court should give the individual who would be subject to the order and the prosecutor the opportunity to make representations, both as to the making of the order and as to its terms. The court should also hear any admissible evidence the parties wish to call and which has not already been heard in the proceedings. Particularly careful consideration may be required where the individual who would be subject to the order is a witness in the proceedings.

J.6 Where there is an admission which is sufficient to found the making of a binding over order and / or the individual consents to the making of the order, the court should nevertheless hear sufficient representations and, if appropriate, evidence, to satisfy itself that an order is appropriate in all the circumstances and to be clear about the terms of the order.

J.7 Where there is an allegation of breach of a binding over order and this is contested, the court should hear representations and evidence, including oral evidence, from the parties before making a finding. If unrepresented and no opportunity has been given previously the court should give a reasonable period for the person said to have breached the binding over order to find representation.

Burden and standard of proof

J.8 The court should be satisfied so that it is sure of the matters complained of before a binding over order may be imposed. Where the procedure has been commenced on complaint, the burden of proof rests on the complainant. In all other circumstances, the burden of proof rests upon the prosecution.

J.9 Where there is an allegation of breach of a binding over order, the court should be satisfied on the balance of probabilities that the defendant is in breach before making any order for forfeiture of a recognisance. The burden of proof shall rest on the prosecution.

Recognisance

J.10 The court must be satisfied on the merits of the case that an order for binding over is appropriate and should announce that decision before considering the amount of the recognisance. If unrepresented, the individual who is made subject to the binding over order should be told he has a right of appeal from the decision.

J.11 When fixing the amount of recognisance, courts should have regard to the individual's financial resources and should hear representations from the individual or his legal representatives regarding finances.

J.12 A recognisance is made in the form of a bond giving rise to a civil debt on breach of the order.

Refusal to enter into a recognisance

J.13 If there is any possibility that an individual will refuse to enter a recognisance, the court should consider whether there are any appropriate alternatives to a binding over order (for example, continuing with a prosecution). Where there are no appropriate alternatives and the individual continues to refuse to enter into the recognisance, the court may commit the individual to custody. In the magistrates' court, the power to do so will derive from section 1(7) of the Justices of the Peace Act 1968 or, more rarely, from section 115(3) of the Magistrates' Courts Act 1980, and the court should state which power it is acting under; in the Crown Court, this is a common law power.

J.14 Before the court exercises a power to commit the individual to custody, the individual should be given the opportunity to see a duty solicitor or another legal representative and be represented in proceedings if the individual so wishes. Public funding should generally be granted to cover representation. In the Crown Court this rests with the Judge who may grant a Representation Order.

J.15 In the event that the individual does not take the opportunity to seek legal advice, the court shall give the individual a final opportunity to comply with the request and shall explain the consequences of a failure to do so.

Antecedents

J.16 Courts are reminded of the provisions of section 7(5) of the Rehabilitation of Offenders Act 1974 which excludes from a person's antecedents any order of the court "with respect to any person otherwise than on a conviction".

Binding over to come up for judgment

J.17 If the Crown Court is considering binding over an individual to come up for judgment, the court should specify any conditions with which the individual is to comply in the meantime and not specify that the individual is to be of good behaviour.

J.18 The Crown Court should, if the individual is unrepresented, explain the consequences of a breach of the binding over order in these circumstances.

Binding over of parent or guardian

J.19 Where a court is considering binding over a parent or guardian under section 150 of the Powers of Criminal Courts (Sentencing) Act 2000 to enter into a recognisance to take proper care of and exercise proper control over a child or young person, the court should specify the actions which the parent or guardian is to take.

Security for good behaviour

J.20 Where a court is imposing a conditional discharge under section 12 of the Powers of Criminal Courts (Sentencing) Act 2000, it has the power, under section 12(6) to make an order that a person who consents to do so give security for the good behaviour of the offender. When making such an order, the court should specify the type of conduct from which the offender is to refrain.

B[6]

Closure of premises associated with nuisance or disorder, etc – Anti-social Behaviour, Crime and Policing Act 2014, Pt 4, Ch 3

B[6.1] These provisions consolidated various previous powers.

See para **A[84.7]**, above, for the grounds for the issue of a closure notice. Such a notice may be issued by a police officer of at least the rank of inspector, or by a local authority. If issued by a police officer of at least the rank of superintendent, or, in the case of a notice issued by a local authority, if signed by the chief executive or a person designated by him for this purpose, the notice may last for a maximum of 48 hours; in all other cases the maximum period is 24 hours: ABCPA 2014, s 77.

A closure notice is a notice prohibiting access by all persons except those specified, or by all persons except those of a specified description; at all times, or at all times except those specified; and in all circumstances, or in all circumstances except those specified: a notice may not, however, prohibit access by people who habitually live on the premises or by the owner: ABCPA 2014, s 76.

Unless the notice is cancelled, an application must be made to a magistrates' court for a closure order and the application must be heard no later than 48 hours from service of the closure notice: ABCPA 2014, s 80(1).

B[6.2] The court may make a closure order if it is satisfied that a person has engaged, or is likely to engage, in disorderly, offensive or criminal behaviour on the premises; or that the use of the premises has resulted, or is likely to result, in serious nuisance to members of the public; or that there has been, or is likely to be, disorder near those premises associated with the use of those premises: ABCPA 2014, s 80(4).

'Offensive behaviour' means behaviour by a person which causes or is likely to cause harassment, alarm or distress to one or more other persons not of the same household as that person: ABCPA 2014, s 92(1).

The order may last for up to three months and may contain the same prohibitions as a closure notice: ABCPA 2014, s 80(6), (7).

Provision is made for the issue of temporary orders of up to 48 hours, and the extension of closure notices for up to 14 days if the court proceedings are adjourned: ABCPA 2014, s 81. Provision is also made for the extension of closure notices for up to three months subject to an overall maximum of six months, for the discharge of closure notices, and for appeals: ABCPA 2014, ss 82–84. Provision is also made for reimbursement of costs incurred in relation to the premises by the applicant, and for compensation to persons suffering financial loss in consequence of a closure notice order: ABCPA 2014, ss 88, 90.

B[6.3] *Enforcement* A person who without reasonable excuse: remains on or enters premises in contravention of a closure notice; remains on or enters premises in contravention of a closure order; or obstructs any person acting under s 79 (service of notices) or s 85(1) (securing premises) commits an offence. All these offences carry an unlimited fine, alternatively the court may imprison for up to three months (the first and third offences) or six months (the second offence).

B[7]

Closure Order (specified prostitution offences)

B[7.1] Part 2A of the Sexual Offences Act 2003 was inserted by the Policing and Crime Act 2009.

The provisions outlined below came into force on 1 April 2010. Section 136B of the SOA 2003 permits a police officer, not below the rank of superintendent, to authorise a closure order in relation to premises which are being used for certain activities; those activities are associated with "specified prostitution or pornography offences" as defined by the Act. The police must have consulted the local authority first.

Section 115 of, and Sch 6 to, the Anti-social, Behaviour, Crime and Policing Act 2014 amended Part 2A of the Sexual Offences Act 2003 by extending the closure powers. Section 116 of the 2014 Act gave power to require hotel owners, operators or managers to give information about guests where there is reasonable belief that the premises have been or will be used for child sexual exploitation or conduct preparatory thereto. A person issued with a notice under s 116 may appeal to a magistrates' court. The appeal must be brought within and the court may quash the notice, modify it or dismiss the appeal: Anti-social, Crime and Policing Act 2014, s 117.

If a closure order has been issued, a constable must apply under SOA 2003, s 136D to a magistrates' court for a closure order.

A closure order is an order that the premises (or part of the premises) in respect of which the order is made are closed to all persons for such period not exceeding 3 months as is specified in the order.

The application must be heard by the magistrates' court not later than 48 hours after the notice was served by the police in pursuance of SOA 2003, s 136C(3)(a).

The magistrates' court may adjourn the hearing for a closure order for a period of not more than 14 days to enable any of the following to show why a closure order should not be made: (a) an occupier of the premises; (b) a person who has control of or responsibility for the premises; (c) any other person who has an interest in the proceedings (see SOA 2003, s136B(7)(b)).

If the application is adjourned the magistrates' court may order that the closure order continues in effect until the end of the period of the adjournment.

Closure order applications are civil proceedings. Although closure order applications should be dealt with as a matter of urgency, a magistrates' court has a general power to grant a further adjournment under the MCA 1980, s 54: see *R (on the application of Turner) v Highbury Corner Magistrates Court* [2005] EWHC 2568 (Admin), [2006] 1 WLR 220, 170 JP 93.

B[7.2] A magistrates' court may make a closure order if satisfied three criteria have been made out:

(1) That the premises have been used, during the period 3 months ending on the day the closure order was issued by the police, for specified prostitution offences (except if only one person obtained all of the sexual services in question, whether or not on a single occasion) or for specified pornography offences.

(2) That the closure order is necessary to prevent the premises being used for one or other of the above activities.

(3) Reasonable steps have been taken to consult the relevant local authority and to establish the identity of any person (see SOA 2003, s 136B(7)(b) above); and, there has been compliance by the police with SOA 2003, s 136C(3)(d) ie a copy of the notice was given to the persons mentioned in s 136B(7)(b) of the SOA 2003.

B[7.3] **Enforcement and offences.** Enforcement is to be found in SOA 2003, s 136F. A person who obstructs a constable or an authorised person acting under s 136C(3) or (4) or s 136F(2) or (4) of the SOA 2003 commits an offence. The offence is summary only carrying a maximum penalty of 6 months' imprisonment (51 weeks if the CJA 2003 is brought into force) and/or a maximum fine of £5,000 (level 5).

B[7.4] **Extension, variation and discharge.** This is catered for by SOA 2003, ss 136H–J. On application a closure order may be extended for a further period of 3 months but a closure order cannot exceed 6 months in total. This would not prevent the police from making a fresh application for a closure order. There is provision for any of the person mentioned in SOA 2003, s 136B(7)(b) to apply for the order to be discharged.

B[7.5] **Appeal.** Any of the above mentioned may appeal to the Crown Court. The appeal must be lodged before the end of 21 days beginning with the day on which the order or decision was made: SOA 2003, s 136K.

B[7.6] There are miscellaneous provisions covering costs or compensation associated with the making of such orders eg see SOA 2003, s 136M. Magistrates would be well advised to consult their legal adviser.

B[8]
Committal for sentence of dangerous adult offenders

B[8.1] Where an adult offender is convicted of a specified offence within the meaning of s 224 of the Criminal Justice Act 2003 and it appears to the court that the criteria for the imposition of an extended sentence under s 226A of the Criminal Justice Act 2003 would be met, the court must commit the offender in custody or on bail to the Crown Court for sentence: Powers of Criminal Courts (Sentencing) Act 2000, s 3A(1) and (2). The criteria referred to above are:

(a) at the time the offence was committed, the offender had been convicted of an offence listed in Schedule 15B to the 2003 Act; or
(b) if the court were to impose an extended sentence of imprisonment, the term it would specify as the appropriate custodial term would be at least four years.

This does not, however, prevent the court from committing for sentence under s 3 of the 2000 Act (see below) where the provisions of that section are satisfied: Powers of Criminal Courts (Sentencing) Act 2000, s 3A(5).

The Crown Court may then deal with the offender in any way in which it could deal with him if he had just been convicted on indictment.

In reaching the above decision the court is not bound by any indication of sentence given during mode of trial; nor may its decision be challenged on the ground that it is inconsistent with such an indication.

Provision is made for the committal for sentence of other offences where a specified offence is committed under this power (see B[8.13] below).

Committal to the Crown Court for sentence (other than as a 'dangerous offender')

B[8.2] On conviction of an offence triable either way, the offender may be committed in custody or on bail to the Crown Court for sentence under s 3 of the Powers of Criminal Courts (Sentencing) Act 2000. It is unnecessary for justices to state their reasons for committing for sentence since the person so committed will have an opportunity to make full representations to the sentencing court: *R (on the application of Jermyn) v Wirral Magistrates Court* [2001] Crim LR 45, [2000] All ER (D) 1478, DC.

B[8.3] The court must be of opinion that the offence or the combination of the offence and one or more offences associated with it was so serious that the Crown Court should, in the court's opinion, have the power to deal with the offender in any way it could deal with him if he had been convicted on indictment or, in the case of a violent or sexual offence, that a sentence of imprisonment for term longer than the court has power to impose is necessary to protect the public from serious harm. The terms 'associated with it', 'violent offence', 'sexual offence' and 'serious harm' are all defined in s 161 of the Powers of Criminal Courts (Sentencing) Act 2000.

In considering the seriousness of any offence for this purpose, the court may take into account any previous convictions of the offender or any failure of his to respond to previous sentences. If such an offence was committed while the offender was on bail, the court must treat the fact that it was committed in those circumstances as an aggravating factor: Powers of Criminal Courts (Sentencing) Act 2000, s 151(2).

B[8.4] Where the court is minded to commit the offender for sentence it should first invite representations from the defence and, if it proceeds to commit, it should make clear its opinion when doing so, although this is not binding on the Crown Court.

Guidance on committal for sentence

B[8.5] Where an offender, or his representative, indicates, in accordance with s 17A(6) of the Magistrates' Courts Act 1980, that he would plead guilty if the offence were to proceed to trial the offender may be committed to the Crown Court for sentence if the court is of such opinion as is referred to above (see **B[8.3]**): Powers of Criminal Courts (Sentencing) Act 2000, s 3(2). Guidance on committal for sentence following an indicated guilty plea was given in *R v Warley Magistrates' Court, ex p DPP* [1999] 1 All ER 251, [1999] 1 WLR 216, DC. The National Mode of Trial Guidelines and the Magistrates' Courts Sentencing Guidelines are likely to be of the greatest assistance. Magistrates must also have regard to the discount to be granted on a plea of guilty. If the court is of the opinion that the gravity of the offence requires committal for sentence whatever the mitigation may be, it should be prepared to commit for sentence without seeking a pre-sentence report or hearing full mitigation, though a brief submission in opposition to committal may be allowed. If the facts are disputed and, on the defendant's version, the powers of the magistrates' court would be adequate, the court should proceed to hold a '*Newton*' hearing.

If the court considers that a restriction order under the Mental Health Act 1983 is appropriate, it will commit the offender for trial or sentence to the Crown Court as it does not itself possess this power. Similarly, justices may commit a defendant to the Crown Court for sentence if they are of the opinion that, while imprisonment would not be appropriate, the offence was so serious that a larger fine is merited that they have power to impose: *R (on the application of Lloyd) v North Essex Justices* (2000) 165 JP 117, (2000) Times, 14 November, DC.

There may be no committal for sentence, however, under s 3 of the Powers of Criminal Courts (Sentencing) Act 2000 for offences of criminal damage if the value involved is small: Magistrates' Courts Act 1980, s 33(1).

Committal for sentence following acceptance of summary trial

B[8.6] The opinion that the offence or offences are so serious as to require committal to the Crown Court may be formed after jurisdiction has been accepted and, it would seem, that opinion is not dependent on information showing the offence or offences to be more serious than they were originally thought to be received after the decision to try the case summarily was made: see *R v Sheffield Crown Court and Sheffield Stipendiary Magistrate, ex p DPP* 15 Cr App Rep (S) 768, (1994) 158 JP 334; *R v Dover Magistrates' Court, ex p Pamment* 15 Cr App Rep (S) 778, (1994) 158 JP 665; *R v North Sefton Magistrates' Court, ex p Marsh* (1994) 16 Cr App Rep (S) 401, 159 JP 9. Nevertheless, justices must still apply their minds to the matters which they are required by s 19(3) of the Magistrates' Courts Act 1980 to consider before deciding to accept summary jurisdiction: *R v Flax Bourton Magistrates, ex p Customs and Excise Comrs* (1996) 160 JP 481, [1996] Crim LR 907.

Previous convictions are now taken into account in mode of trial, but this does not prevent the court from exercising its power to commit for sentence under s 3 of the Powers of Criminal Courts (Sentencing) Act 2000 following a conviction.

B[8.7] A defendant may not be committed for sentence where he has been given a legitimate expectation that the case will be dealt with summarily: *R (on the application of Lloyd) v North Essex Justices* (2000) 165 JP 117, (2000) Times, 14 November, DC. Such an indication may be given expressly, or it may be given impliedly by, for example, adjourning for a pre sentence report or other inquiries without openly preserving the option of committal for sentence. A sentencing indication (however given) will not bind a subsequent bench, however, if it was so unreasonable to be perverse: see *R (on the application of Nicholas) v Chester Magistrates' Court* [2009] EWHC 1504 (Admin), 173 JP 542; and *R (on the application of Harrington) v Bromley Magistrates Court* [2007] EWHC 2896 (Admin), [2007] All ER (D) 199 (Nov). See also *Thornton v CPS* [2010] 2 Cr App Rep (S) 434, [2010] Crim LR 514 (indication not binding where the court failed to have regard to the sentencing guidelines, contrary to the duty imposed by s 172 of the Criminal Justice Act 2003).

Committal for sentence of either offences following an indication of guilty pleas where they are related to offences sent for trial

B[8.8] If the court does not form the opinion that its powers are insufficient but sends the offender to the Crown Court for trial for one or more 'related' offences (see below), it may also commit him to the Crown Court to be dealt with in accordance with the provisions of s 5(1) of the Powers of Criminal Courts (Sentencing) Act 2000: Powers of Criminal Courts (Sentencing) Act 2000, s 4(2). Section 5 provides that the Crown Court may deal with the offender in any way in which it could have dealt with him if he had just been convicted of the offence on indictment before the court. This is subject, however, to the exception stated below.

Where the court does commit the offender to the Crown Court to be dealt with, but it does not state that, in its opinion, it does have power so to commit him under s 3(2) of the Powers of Criminal Courts (Sentencing) Act 2000, the provisions of s 5 of the 2000 Act will not apply unless he is convicted before the Crown Court of one or more of the related offences: Powers of Criminal Courts (Sentencing) Act 2000, s 4(4).Where the provisions of s 5 do not apply, the Crown Court's powers to deal with the offender are limited to those of the magistrates' court: Powers of Criminal Courts (Sentencing) Act 2000, s 4(5).

Meaning of 'related'

B[8.9] For the purposes of a committal for sentence on the indication of a guilty plea under s 4 of the 2000 Act, one offence is related to another if, were they both to be prosecuted on indictment, the charges for them could be joined in the same indictment: Powers of Criminal Courts (Sentencing) Act 2000, s 4(7). Charges for any offences may be joined in the same indictment if those charges are founded on the same facts, or form or are a part of a series of offences of the same or a similar character: Criminal Procedure Rules 2013, r 14.2. Where the magistrates' court makes a mistake and instead of committing under s 3(2) commits under s 4 in circumstances where there are no related offences and does not state that it had power to commit under s 3(2) of the 2000 Act, the powers of the Crown Court are limited to those of the magistrates' court: Powers of Criminal Courts (Sentencing) Act 2000, s 5(2) and see *R v Sallis* [2003] EWCA Crim 233, [2003] 2 Cr App Rep (S) 394, 167 JP 103.

Effect of mistake in recording the basis of committal

B[8.10] Where issues concerning jurisdiction to commit for sentence arise, what matters is the power that was actually used rather than the power that was recorded as being used.

> 'In our judgment, provided the power of the magistrates' court to commit for sentence was properly exercised in respect of one or more either way offences in accordance with section 3 of the 2000 Act, a mistake in recording the statutory basis for a committal of summary only offences does not invalidate the committal. The principle is that thereafter the Crown Court must abide by the sentencing powers available to the magistrates' court in relation to the summary only offences. If that principle is not followed, then the sentences must be reduced to sentences which fall within the jurisdiction of the magistrates.' (Per Lord Judge CJ in *R v Ayhan* [2011] EWCA Crim 3184, [2012] 1 WLR 1775, [2012] 1 Cr App Rep 391, at para 22.)

Committal on a mistaken view of the facts

B[8.11] Where following plea before venue an offender is committed to the Crown Court for sentence, but before he is sentenced it is discovered that the decision to commit for sentence was taken on the wrong view of the facts, the proper approach will be to allow the offender to make an application to change his plea. If such an application is allowed, the Crown Court may then remit the case to the magistrates' court so that the matter may be considered on a proper view of the facts for the purposes of s 3 of the Powers of Criminal Courts (Sentencing) Act 2000: *R v Crown Court at Isleworth, ex p Buda* [2000] 1 Cr App Rep (S) 538, [2000] Crim LR 111.

Other error in committal

B[8.12] Where a case was erroneously committed to the Crown Court for sentence (the prior consent of the DPP, which was a prerequisite to the prosecution, had not been obtained by that stage, though it was given subsequently), it was unnecessary for the judge to use s 66 of the Courts Act 2003 to exercise the powers of district judge and re-commit the offender; the judge should instead have considered whether it was Parliament's intention that such a failure rendered the proceedings a nullity (however, the judge had been entitled to use his powers under s 66): *R v Ashton; R v Draz; R v O'Reilly* [2006] EWCA Crim 794, [2007] 1 WLR 181, [2006] Cr App Rep 231.

Bail or custody

B[8.13] When a person who has been on bail pleads at the plea before venue, the practice should normally be to continue bail, even if it is anticipated that a custodial sentence will be imposed by the Crown Court, unless there are good reasons for remanding the defendant in custody. If the defendant is in custody, then after entering a plea of guilty at the plea before venue, it will be unusual, if the reasons for remanding in custody remain unchanged, to alter the position: *R v Rafferty* [1999] 1 Cr App Rep 235, [1998] 2 Cr App Rep (S) 449.

Other powers of committal to the Crown Court for sentence

B[8.14] These arise where the offender is committed for sentence for another offence in accordance with any of the following:

- Powers of Criminal Courts (Sentencing) Act 2000, ss 3–4A (committal for sentence for offences triable either way);
- Powers of Criminal Courts (Sentencing) Act 2000, ss 13(5) (conditionally discharged person convicted of further offence);
- Criminal Justice Act 2003, Sch 12, para 11 (offender convicted during operational period of suspended sentence)

Powers of Criminal Courts (Sentencing) Act 2000, s 6

B[8.15] The powers of the Crown Court for offences committed under this provision are limited to those of the magistrates' court: see s 7 of the 2000 Act; see also *R v Bateman; R v Doyle* [2012] EWCA Crim 2518, [2013] 1 WLR 1710, [2013] 2 Cr App Rep (S) 174 – the exception made by s 7(2), namely committal of a person to be dealt with by the Crown Court in respect of a suspended sentence, refers to a suspended sentence imposed by the magistrates' court. Therefore, where offences were committed to the Crown Court for sentence because they were committed during the currency of a Crown Court suspended sentence, the Crown Court's powers were limited to those of the magistrates' court for those further offences.

In relation to these powers as well as the major power to commit for sentence, if the magistrates' court commits to the Crown Court for sentence, then if the offence on which it commits is an indictable offence, it may also commit the offender to be dealt with in respect of any other offence whatsoever in respect of which it has itself power to deal with him. If the offence is on the other hand a summary offence, it may also commit him for sentence if that offence is imprisonable or disqualifiable, or it may commit him in respect of any suspended sentence of imprisonment which it would itself have power to deal with. The committing court must not itself exercise any sentencing powers or duties but must leave them to the Crown Court; it may however impose an interim driving disqualification if that is appropriate: Road Traffic Offenders Act 1988, s 26(1).

A further power of committal to the Crown Court for sentence arises where a court convicts a person who, having been released on bail in criminal proceedings fails without reasonable cause to surrender to custody, and the court thinks that the circumstances of the offence are such that greater punishment should be inflicted for that offence than the court has power to inflict: Bail Act 1976, s 6(6).

Ordering pre-sentence reports on committal for sentence

B[8.16] See the Criminal Practice Directions 2015, 3A.8, 38.9. The magistrates' court should request a PSR for the use of the Crown Court if it considers: there is a realistic alternative to a custodial sentence; the defendant may satisfy the criteria for classification as a dangerous offender; or there is some other appropriate reason for doing so.

The Senior Presiding Judge has issued guidance, which goes on to say:

> 'When in doubt as to whether the case requires a pre-sentence report, the justices should decline to order the report. They should direct the defence practitioner to make an application to the Crown Court setting out the reason why they consider one to be necessary. The application will be considered administratively by a Crown Court Judge who will direct the preparation of a pre-sentence report if he/she thinks it appropriate to do so.'

Further guidance indicates that:

> 'It will usually be appropriate to order a report and in some of these cases a recent report may well be sufficient where:
>
> - the defendant is 17 and under;
> - the defendant is under 21 and is a first time offender/has not served a prison sentence;
> - the defendant falls to be assessed for "dangerousness";
> - there is a realistic alternative to a custodial sentence (check the Sentencing Guidelines).'

The guidance then lists a number of offences where it will not usually be appropriate to order a report. The list includes the supply of Class A drugs.

It is the role of the litigator, not the Probation Service, to put together the mitigation by gathering all the background information about the offender, and a report should not be requested where the sentencing guidelines indicate a prison sentence which cannot be suspended: *R v Townsend* [2018] EWCA Crim 875, [2018] 2 Cr App R (S) 30.

B[8A]
Community protection

B[8A.1] Part 4 of the Anti-social Behaviour, Crime and Policing Act 2014 provides for the making of Community Protection Notices and Public Spaces Protection Orders. We summarise these below. All the statutory references are to the ABCPA 2014.

Community protection notices

B[8A.2] An authorised person – a constable, or a relevant local authority or a person designated by it – may issue a CPN to a person aged 16 or over, or a body, if satisfied on reasonable grounds that the conduct of that individual or body is having a detrimental effect, of a persistent or continuing nature, on the quality of life of those in the vicinity, and the conduct is unreasonable: s 43(1). Prior written warning must be given that the CPN will be issued unless the above conduct ceases and the applicant must be satisfied that, despite having had enough time to deal with the matter, the recipient's conduct is still having that detrimental effect: s 43(5).

B[8A.3] A CPN is a notice that imposes requirements to: stop doing specified things; do specified things; or take reasonable steps to achieve specified results: s 43(3). The only requirements that may be imposed are ones that are reasonable to impose to prevent, or to reduce or to reduce the risk of, the detrimental effect from continuing or recurring: s 43(4). A CPN must identify the conduct referred to in B[8A.2], and explain the effect of ss 46–51 which deal with: appeals; remedial action by local authority; the offence of non-compliance; remedial orders; forfeiture of items used in the commission an offence of non-compliance; and seizure of such items. A CPN may specific periods within which, or times by which, requirements are to be complied with: s 43(8).

B[8A.4] Where the CPN arises from the state of land, the relevant local authority may undertake remedial work to remedy the failure if the land is open to air or, if it is not, it may specify the work it intends to carry out together with its estimated cost and invite the defaulter, and the owner of the premises if different, to consent to the work being carried out. The consent of the owner is not necessary where the authority has made reasonable efforts contact the owner but without success. Where work is carried out the defaulter is liable to meet the cost, but may challenge the amount by way of appeal to the magistrates' court within 21 days: s 47.

B[8A.5] Non-compliance with a CPN is an offence punishable with a fine level 4, but a person does not commit an offence if they took all reasonable steps to comply with the CPN or there is some other reasonable excuse for the non-compliance: s 48. It is not open to a person charged with breach of a CPN to argue by way of defence that the notice was invalid; such an argument must be raised by way of an appeal against the notice under s 46: *Stannard v Crown Prosecution Service* [2019] EWHC 84 (Admin), [2019] All ER (D) 107 (Jan). On conviction, the court may make whatever order it thinks appropriate to ensure that what the notice requires to be done is done: s 49.

Public spaces protection orders

B[8A.6] A local authority may make a public spaces protection order if it is satisfied on reasonable grounds that:

(a) activities carried on in a public space within the authority's area have had a detrimental effect (see below) on the quality of life or those in the locality; or
(b) it is likely that activities will be carried on in a public place within that area and that they will have such an effect; and
(c) the effect, or likely effect, of the activities is, or is likely to be, of a persistent or continuing nature, and is, or is likely to be, such as to make the activities unreasonable, and justifies the restrictions imposed by the notice: s 59(1)–(3).

Before deciding whether or not to make a PSPO, or the requirements it should include, or whether or for how long to extend the period of a PSPO, or whether or not to vary a PSPO or how, or whether or not to discharge a PSPO, a local authority must have particular regard to the rights of freedom of expression and freedom of assembly conferred by arts 10 and 11 of the ECHR: s 72.

The ability to apply for a PSPO does not prevent a local authority from alternatively seeking an injunction, which carries more severe sanctions in the event of breach, or prevent the court from granting such a remedy if it considers it justified and proportionate to do so: *Birmingham City Council v Sharif* [2019] EWHC 1268 (QB), [2019] All ER (D) 09 (Jun).

B[8A.7] A PSPO is an order which identifies the public place in question (the restricted area) and prohibits specified things from being done in that area, or requires specified things to be done by persons carrying on specified activities in that area, or both: s 59(4). It must identify the activities referred to in (a) above, explain (if relevant) the effect of consumption of alcohol in breach of the order, and the offence of failing to comply with the order: s 59(7).

The prohibitions or requirements must be reasonable to prevent the detrimental effect from continuing, occurring or recurring, or to reduce the detrimental effect or the risk of its continuance, occurrence or recurrence: s 59(5). A prohibition or requirement may be framed:

(a) to apply to all persons, or specified categories of persons, or to all persons except those in specified categories;
(b) to apply at all times, or only at specified times, or at all times except those specified;
(c) to apply in all circumstances, or only in specified circumstances' or in all circumstances except those specified: s 59(6).

Special considerations apply to orders restricting the public right of way over a highway: s 64.

B[8A.8] *Detrimental effect*. This term is not defined, and the courts should not fill this vacuum with a definition of their own. Local authorities have a wide discretion to decide what behaviours are troublesome and need to be addressed. Any attempt to lay down any general threshold with concepts such as 'intimidation', 'harassment', 'alarm', or 'distress' would almost certainly prove to be unhelpful and inappropriate, and no free-standing test of 'objectivity' referring to detrimental effect on the quality of life of a reasonable person was to be superimposed. The reference to 'quality of life of those in the locality' is not limited as referring to those who live or work in the relevant place or those who visit it regularly; if Parliament had intended such a limitation it could have so provided. A narrow approach would also potentially tie the local authority's hands when attempting to prohibit detrimental activities in public areas mainly populated by visitors: *Dulgheriu and another v Ealing London Borough Council* [2018] EWHC 1667 (Admin), [2018] 4 All ER 881 (dismissing an application under s 66 to challenge a public spaces protection order providing for a 'safe zone' around an abortion clinic, to protect staff and service users).

B[8A.9] Provision is made for the duration, variation and discharge of orders: ss 61, 62.

B[8A.10] Where alcohol is consumed in breach of a PSPO, the constable may require that person not to consume anything which is, or which the constable reasonably believes to be, alcohol, and to surrender anything which the constable reasonably believes to be or to contain alcohol, and it is an offence punishable with a fine not exceeding level 2 to fail to comply without reasonable excuse to such a requirement: s 63.

B[8A.11] An interested party may apply to the High Court to question the validity of a PSPO or a variation of a PSPO: s 66.

B[8A.12] It is an offence for a person without reasonable excuse to contravene prohibition, or to fail to comply with a requirement, of a PSPO, otherwise than by consumption of alcohol, unless the non-compliance relates to a prohibition or requirement which the local authority did not have power to include in the PSPO; the penalty is a fine not exceeding level 3 on the standard scale: s 67

B[9]

Community sentences: order and requirement

Introduction to community sentences: order and requirement

B[9.1] The Criminal Justice Act 2003 introduced the concept of a 'community order', ie a sentence which consists of or includes one or more requirements. This generic community order only applies to defendants over 18 years.

B[9.2] A court may not impose a community sentence unless:

(a) the offence is punishable with imprisonment (CJA 2003, s 150A);
(b) it is of the opinion that the offence was serious enough to warrant such a sentence taking into account all such information about the circumstances of the offence (including any associated offences or any aggravating or mitigating factors) as is available to it;
(c) the particular order or orders comprising or forming part of the sentence are such as in the opinion of the court is, or taken together are, the most suitable for the offender taking into account any information about the offender which is before it (such as a pre-sentence report, see below);
(d) the restrictions on liberty imposed by the order or orders are such as in the opinion of the court are commensurate with the seriousness of the offence, or the combination of the offence and other offences associated with it, taking into account information about the circumstances etc as in (a) above.

Note that there will still be cases where the community threshold has been passed but a fine or discharge is still an appropriate penalty (see CJA 2003, s 148(5)).

B[9.3] When considering seriousness of the current offence or offences previous convictions and previous failures to respond to court orders may be taken into account.

B[9.4] A community order may be made even where the offender has been subject to remand on a qualifying curfew for a period equivalent to a lengthy sentence of imprisonment. There is a distinction between custodial and community sentences; in the case of the former, credit is automatic, but in the case of the latter it is discretionary. In the present case, there was a specific need, in the public interest and in the offender's own interest, for him to undertake a programme requirement: *R v Pereira-Lee* [2016] EWCA Crim 705, [2017] 1 Cr App R (S) 17, [2017] Crim LR 243.

Similarly, in a case where the offender had extensive antecedents for similar offences, the court was entitled to make a community order with restrictions following a long period of remand in custody; this did not amount to being sentenced twice over: *R v Holmes* [2019] EWCA Crim 612, [2019] 2 Cr App R (S) 26.

Pre-sentence report

B[9.5] Where the court reaches the provisional view that a community order may be appropriate it should seek a pre-sentence report – written or verbal – unless the court is of the opinion that a report is unnecessary in all the circumstances of the case.

B[9.6] The Sentencing Council's definitive guideline 'Imposition of Community and Custodial Sentences' states:

> 'It may be helpful to indicate to the National Probation Service the court's preliminary opinion as to which of the three sentencing ranges is relevant (see **B[9.9]**, infra) and the purpose(s) of sentencing that the package of requirements is expected to fulfil. Ideally a pre-sentence report should be completed on the same

day to avoid adjourning the case. If an adjournment cannot be avoided, the information should be provided to the National Probations Service in written form and a copy retained on the court file for the benefit of the sentencing court. *However, the court must make clear to the offender that all sentencing options remain open including, in appropriate cases, committal for sentence to the Crown Court.*'

The sentencing decision

B[9.7]

SENTENCING FORM FOR PSR

A: PRE-SENTENCE ASSESSMENT STAGE

DATE: ☐ 1a) **DEFENDANT:** ☐

b) **D.O.B:** ☐ c) **ADDRESS:** ☐

2. **CUSTODY:** ☐ **BAIL:** ☐

3. **CHARGES:** ☐

4. **GUIDELINE SENTENCE:** Fine/discharge ☐ Community ☐ Custody ☐ Commit for Sentence ☐

5. **OFFENCE FACTORS INFLUENCING ASSESSMENT**

a) Aggravating factors: ☐

b) Mitigating factors: ☐

c) Culpability

intentional	☐	reckless	☐
knew likely outcome	☐	negligent	☐

d) Harm caused/risked: ☐

6. **OFFENDER FACTORS INFLUENCING ASSESSMENT**

☐

7. **SERIOUSNESS** (sentencing range justified by offence and offending factors)

			L	M	H
Fine/discharge (no **PSR**)	☐	Community (serious enough)	☐	☐	☐
Custody (so serious)	☐	Commit to Crown Court (too serious)	☐		

8. **MAIN (1) AND SECONDARY (2) PURPOSE(S) OF SENTENCE**

Punishment	☐	Rehabilitation	☐	Reduction in crime/ deterrence	☐
Protection of public	☐	Reparation	☐		

9. **REPORT TYPE:** Fast ☐ Standard ☐ Due: ☐

B: SENTENCING STAGES

10. FACTORS ARISING FROM REPORT
Including, if appropriate, a) why you have reached a different conclusion from the indications of seriousness and purpose already given, or b) why you are departing from the proposals in the report.

11. SENTENCE TO BE IMPOSED (referring to reasons)

12. CREDIT FOR GUILTY PLEA
Record a) the extent of credit given and reasons for it, or b) what the sentence would have been if a timely guilty plea had been entered. (NB: Do not double count credit)

13. ANCILLARY ORDERS
Details of compensation (or reasons for not awarding it), plus other ancillary orders.

14. REASONS FOR DEPARTING FROM SENTENCING COUNCIL GUIDELINES

15. EXPLAIN SENTENCE USING APPROPRIATE PRONOUNCEMENTS

Power to impose community sentence

B[9.8] The power to impose a community sentence is restricted to imprisonable offences.

Sections 147–150 of the Criminal Justice Act 2003 define community orders and the restrictions that apply to them. Any requirements imposed must be the most suitable for the offender and must be commensurate and proportionate with the seriousness of the offending. The court may take account of time spent on remand before sentence.

The court must set the end date for completion of all requirements (not later that three years from sentence), but may set different dates for different requirements. If a supervision requirement is included it must be for the full length of the order. The court must impose an electronic monitoring requirement with a curfew or exclusion requirement and may do so for various requirements.

B[9.9] The Sentencing Council's definitive guideline provides that the seriousness of the offence should be the initial factor in determining which requirements to include in a community order. Offence-specific guidelines refer to three ranges within the community order band: low, medium and high.

At least one requirement must be imposed for the purpose of punishment and/or a fine imposed in addition to the community order unless there are exceptional circumstances which relate to the offence or the offender that would make it unjust in all the circumstances to do so: CJA 2003, s 177(2A) and (2B). If the order does not contain a punitive requirement, the suggested fine levels are: Low Band A; Medium Band B; and High Band C.

LOW	MEDIUM	HIGH
Offences only just cross community order threshold, where a discharge or fine is inappropriate	Offences that obviously fall within the community order band	Offences only just fall below the custody threshold or the custody threshold is crossed but a community order is more appropriate in the circumstances
In general, only one requirement will be appropriate and the length may be curtailed if additional requirements are necessary		More intensive sentences which combine two or more requirements may be appropriate
Suitable requirements might include:	Suitable requirements might include:	Suitable requirements might include:
40–80 hours unpaid work	80–150 hours unpaid work	150–300 hours unpaid work
Curfew requirement eg up to 12 hours per day for a few weeks (see electronic monitoring below)	Curfew requirement eg up to 12 hours per day for 2–3 months (see electronic monitoring below)	Activity requirement up to the maximum of 60 days
Exclusion requirement, without electronic monitoring for a few months (see electronic monitoring below)	Exclusion requirement lasting in the region of 6 months (see electronic monitoring below)	Curfew requirement up to 12 hours per day for 4–6 months (see electronic monitoring below)
Prohibited activity requirement	Prohibited activity requirement	Exclusion order lasting in the region of 12 months (see electronic monitoring below)
Attendance centre requirement (where available)		

Note: *Electronic monitoring (if available in the area concerned)*. The court must impose an electronic monitoring requirement where it makes a community order with a curfew or exclusion requirement unless in the particular circumstances of the case it considers it inappropriate to do so (CJA 2003, s 177(3)), and may do so to secure compliance with other requirements (CJA 2003, s 215(1)(a)) except an alcohol abstinence and monitoring requirement (CJA 2003, s 215(5)), though see infra), but the court may not do so where there is a person (other than the offender) without whose co-operation it would not be practicable to secure the monitoring without that person's consent (CJA 2003, 215(2)).

If an order contains an alcohol abstinence and monitoring requirement, the court is not prevented from making an electronic monitoring requirement to secure compliance with other requirements (CJA 2003, s 215(6)).

As to an electronic monitoring of the offender's whereabouts otherwise than for the purpose of securing compliance with other requirements, see **B[9.23]**, post.

Where a relevant order imposes an electronic monitoring requirement, the offender must (in particular):

(a) submit, as required from time to time by the responsible officer or the person responsible for the monitoring, to:
  (i) being fitted with, or installation of, any necessary apparatus; and
  (ii) inspection or repair of any apparatus fitted or installed for the purposes of the monitoring,

(b) not interfere with, or with the working of, any apparatus fitted or installed for the purposes of the monitoring; and

(c) take any steps required by the responsible officer, or the person responsible for the monitoring, for the purpose of keeping in working order any apparatus fitted or installed for the purposes of the monitoring (CJA 2003, s 215(4A)).

Permissible requirements

(1) Unpaid work requirement

B[9.10] This is a requirement that the offender must perform unpaid work in accordance for the number of hours specified in the order such work at such times as he may be instructed by the responsible officer. Unless revoked, a community order imposing an unpaid work requirement remains in force until the offender has worked under it for the number of hours specified in it. The work required to be performed under an unpaid work requirement of a community order or a suspended sentence order must be performed during a period of twelve months. However, a community order with an unpaid work requirement can be extended as to the time for completion of the work after the end date specified in the order: *National Probation Service v Blackfriars Crown Court* [2019] EWHC 529 (Admin), [2019] All ER (D) 51 (Mar).

The number of hours which a person may be required to work under an unpaid work requirement must be specified in the relevant order and must be in the aggregate–

(a) not less than 40, and
(b) not more than 300.

The court may not impose an unpaid work requirement in respect of an offender unless after hearing (if the court thinks necessary) an appropriate officer, the court is satisfied that the offender is a suitable person to perform work under such a requirement.

Where the court makes orders in respect of two or more offences of which the offender has been convicted on the same occasion and includes unpaid work requirements in each of them, the court may direct that the hours of work specified in any of those requirements is to be concurrent or consecutive. However the total number of hours must not exceed the maximum of 300 hours.

(2) Activity requirement (for offences committed on or after 1 February 2015, a rehabilitation activity requirement – see below)

B[9.11] An activity requirement means a requirement that the offender must do either or both of the following-

(a) present himself to a person or persons specified in the relevant order at a place or places so specified on such number of days as may be so specified and comply with instructions given by, or under the authority of, the person in charge of that place.
(b) participate in activities specified in the order on such number of days as may be so specified.

The specified activities may consist of or include reparation, for example contact between the offender and victims affected by their offences.

A court may not include an activity requirement in a relevant order unless it has consulted either an officer of a local probation board or a member of a youth offending team, and it is satisfied that it is feasible to secure compliance with the requirement.

A court may not include an activity requirement in a relevant order if compliance with that requirement would involve the co-operation of a person other than the offender and the offender's responsible officer, unless that other person consents to its inclusion.

The aggregate of the number of days specified must not exceed 60.

A place specified in a requirement for the offender's attendance must be either,

(a) a community rehabilitation centre, or
(b) a place that has been approved by the local probation board for the area in which the premises are situated as providing facilities suitable for persons subject to activity requirements.

A requirement to participate in activities operates to require the offender,

(a) to participate in activities on the number of days specified in the order in accordance with instructions given by his responsible officer, and
(b) while participating, to comply with instructions given by, or under the authority of, the person in charge of the activities.

Rehabilitation activity requirement

B[9.11A] A rehabilitation activity requirement means a requirement that, during the period for which the community order remains in force, the offender must comply with any instructions given by the responsible officer to attend appointments or participate in activities or both.

A rehabilitation activity requirement must specify the maximum number of days for which the offender may be instructed to participate in activities.

Any instructions given by the responsible officer must be given with a view to promoting the offender's rehabilitation; but this does not prevent the responsible officer giving instructions with a view to other purposes.

The responsible officer may instruct the offender to attend appointments with the responsible officer or with someone else.

The responsible officer, when instructing the offender to participate in activities, may require the offender to:

(a) a) participate in specified activities and, while doing so, comply with instructions given by the person in charge of the activities; or
(b) go to a specified place and, while there, comply with any instructions given by the person in charge of the place.

The activities that responsible officers may instruct offenders to participate in include:

(a) activities forming an accredited programme (see section 202(2));

(b) activities whose purpose is reparative, such as restorative justice activities.

An activity is a restorative justice activity if:

(a) the participants consist of, or include, the offender and one or more of the victims;
(b) the aim of the activity is to maximise the offender's awareness of the impact of the offending concerned on the victims; and
(c) the activity gives a victim or victims an opportunity to talk about, or by other means express experience of, the offending and its impact.

Where compliance with an instruction would require the co-operation of a person other than the offender, the responsible officer may give the instruction only if that person agrees.

(3) Programme requirement

B[9.12] This requirement involves the offender in participation in an accredited programme in accordance with this section on the number of days specified in the order.

Accreditation is by the Secretary of State, and a programme means a systematic set of requirements.

A requirement to attend a programme requirement operates to require the offender,

(a) in accordance with instructions given by the responsible officer, to participate in the accredited programme that is from time to time specified by the responsible officer at the place that is so specified at the place specified in the order on the number of days specified in the order, and
(b) while at that place, to comply with instructions given by, or under the authority of, the person in charge of the programme.

The court cannot leave it to the probation officer to decide whether or not the defendant should attend a programme. The amendments to s 202 made by the Legal Aid, Sentencing and Punishment of Offenders Act 2012 give the responsible officer a wide discretion as to the appropriate programme to follow and the place where it must be undertaken, but they do not relieve the court of the duty to specify that an accredited programme needs to be undertaken and to specify the number of days: *R v Price* [2013] EWCA Crim 1283, [2014] 1 Cr App R (S) 36.

(4) Prohibited activity requirement

B[9.13] This means a requirement that the offender must refrain from participating in activities specified in the order—

(a) on a day or days so specified, or
(b) during a period so specified.

A court may not include a prohibited activity requirement in a relevant order unless it has consulted, either an officer of a local probation board or a member of a youth offending team.

The statute provides that the requirements that may be included in a relevant order include a requirement that the offender does not possess, use or carry a firearm within the meaning of the Firearms Act 1968.

(5) Curfew requirement

B[9.14] A curfew requirement[1] is a requirement that the offender must remain, for periods specified in the relevant order, at a place so specified. It may specify different places or different periods for different days, but may not specify periods which amount to less than two hours or more than sixteen hours in any one day.

The order may not exceed a period of twelve months beginning with the day on which it is made. For youths and curfew orders see B[48.12].

Before making a relevant order imposing a curfew requirement, the court must obtain and consider information about the place proposed to be specified in the order (including information as to the attitude of persons likely to be affected by the enforced presence there of the offender). An electronic monitoring requirement must be made unless it requires the co-operation of a third party which is not forthcoming.

---

1 Note: supervision requirements have been repealed and absorbed into the new rehabilitation activity requirement, but remain available for offences committed before 1 February 2015.

---

(6) *Exclusion requirement*

B[9.15] An exclusion requirement, is a provision prohibiting the offender from entering a place named in the order for a specified period of not more than two years.

An exclusion requirement,

(a) may provide for the prohibition to operate only during the periods specified in the order, and
(b) may specify different places or areas for different periods or days.

Subject to limited exceptions, the court must impose an electronic monitoring requirement where

it makes a community order with an exclusion requirement.

It is not the objective of an exclusion requirement to punish an offender, nor is it possible to use the means of an exclusion requirement to force an offender already in the UK not to enter the UK – there is no power of expulsion: *R (on the application of Dragoman) v Camberwell Green Magistrates' Court* [2012] EWHC 4105 (Admin), (2013) 177 JP 372.

(7) *Residence requirement*

B[9.16] This is a requirement that, during a period specified in the relevant order, the offender must reside at a place specified in the order.

If the order makes provision, a residence requirement does not prohibit the offender from residing, with the prior approval of the responsible officer, at a place other than that specified in the order.

Before making a community order containing a residence requirement, the court must consider the home surroundings of the offender.

7A *Foreign Travel Prohibition requirement*

B[9.16A] This means a requirement prohibiting the offender from travelling, on a day or days, or for a period specified in the order:

(a) to any country or territory outside the British Isles specified or described in the order;
(b) to any country or territory outside the British Isles other than a country or territory specified or described in the order; or
(c) to any country or territory outside the British Isles.

The specified days or period cannot fall outside/extend beyond 12 months beginning with the day on which the order was made.

(8) *Mental health treatment requirement*

B[9.17] This requires the offender to submit, during periods specified in the order, to treatment by or under the direction of a registered medical practitioner or a chartered psychologist (or both, for different periods) with a view to the improvement of the offender's mental condition.

The treatment required must be one of the following kinds of treatment as may be specified in the relevant order:

(a) treatment as a resident patient in an independent hospital or care home within the meaning of the Care Standards Act 2000 or a hospital within the meaning of the Mental Health Act 1983, but not in hospital premises where high security psychiatric services within the meaning of that Act are provided;
(b) treatment as a non-resident patient at such institution or place as may be specified in the order;
(c) treatment by or under the direction of such registered medical practitioner or chartered psychologist (or both) as may be so specified;

The nature of the treatment may not be specified in the order except as mentioned in (a), (b) or (c) above.

A court may not by virtue of this section include a mental health treatment requirement in an order unless-

(a) the court is satisfied, that the mental condition of the offender–
  (i) is such as requires and may be susceptible to treatment, but
  (ii) is not such as to warrant the making of a hospital order or guardianship order within the meaning of the Mental Health Act 1983;
(b) the court is also satisfied that arrangements have been or can be made for the treatment intended to be specified in the order (including arrangements for the reception of the offender where he is to be required to submit to treatment as a resident patient); and
(c) the offender has expressed his willingness to comply with such a requirement.

While the offender is under treatment as a resident patient in pursuance of a mental health requirement, his responsible officer shall carry out the supervision of the offender to such extent only as may be necessary for the purpose of the revocation or amendment of the order.

(9) *Mental health treatment at place other than that specified in order*

B[9.18] Where the medical practitioner or chartered psychologist, treating the offender in pursuance of a mental health treatment requirement, is of the opinion that part of the treatment can be better or more conveniently given in or at an institution or place which:

(a) is not specified in the relevant order, and
(b) is one in or at which the treatment of the offender will be given by or under the direction of a registered medical practitioner or chartered psychologist,

he may, with the consent of the offender, make arrangements for him to be treated accordingly.

These arrangements as are mentioned may provide for the offender to receive part of his treatment as a resident patient in an institution or place notwithstanding that the institution or place is not one which could have been specified for that purpose in the relevant order.

Where any such arrangements are made for the treatment of an offender the medical practitioner or chartered psychologist by whom the arrangements are made shall give notice in writing to the offender's responsible officer giving details of the place and the treatment provided.

(10) *Drug rehabilitation requirement*

B[9.19] A drug rehabilitation requirement means a requirement that during a period specified in the order the offender must submit to treatment by or under the direction of a specified person having the necessary qualifications or experience with a view to the reduction or elimination of the offender's dependency on or propensity to misuse drugs.

During that period he must provide samples for the purpose of ascertaining whether he has any drug in his body.

A court may not impose a drug rehabilitation requirement unless–

(a) it is satisfied–
  (i) that the offender is dependent on, or has a propensity to misuse, drugs, and
  (ii) that his dependency or propensity is such as requires and may be susceptible to treatment,
(b) it is also satisfied that arrangements have been or can be made for the treatment intended to be specified in the order (including arrangements for the reception of the offender where he is to be required to submit to treatment as a resident),
(c) the requirement has been recommended to the court as being suitable for the offender either by an officer of a local probation board or by a member of a youth offending team, and
(d) the offender expresses his willingness to comply with the requirement.

The treatment and testing period must be no more than three years and must be treatment as a resident in such institution or place as may be specified in the order, or treatment as a non-resident place, as may be so specified.

The nature of the treatment may not be specified in the order except as mentioned in paragraph (a) or (b) above.

A community order imposing a drug rehabilitation requirement must provide that the results of tests carried out on any samples provided by the offender in pursuance of the requirement to a person other than the responsible officer are to be communicated to the responsible officer.

(10A) Drug rehabilitation requirement: provision for review by court

B[9.20] A community order imposing a drug rehabilitation requirement may (and must if the treatment and testing period is more than 12 months),

(a) provide for the requirement to be reviewed periodically at intervals of not less than one month,
(b) provide for each review of the requirement to be made, at a hearing held for the purpose by the court responsible for the order (a "review hearing"),
(c) require the offender to attend each review hearing,
(d) provide for the responsible officer to make to the court responsible for the order, before each review, a report in writing on the offender's progress under the requirement, and
(e) provide for each such report to include the test results communicated to the responsible officer and the views of the treatment provider as to the treatment and testing of the offender.

References to the court responsible for a community order or suspended sentence order imposing a drug rehabilitation requirement are:

(a) where a court is specified in the order, to that court;
(b) in any other case, to the court by which the order is made.

Where the area specified in a community order is not the area for which the court acts, the court may, if it thinks fit, include in the order provision specifying a magistrates' court which acts for the area specified in the order.

(10B) Periodic review of drug rehabilitation requirement

B[9.21] At a review hearing the court may, after considering the responsible officer's report, amend the community order, so far as it relates to the drug rehabilitation requirement but only if the offender expresses his willingness to comply with the requirement as amended.

Nor may the court amend any requirement or provision of the order while an appeal against the order is pending, except with the consent of the offender.

If the offender fails to express his willingness to comply with the drug rehabilitation requirement as proposed to be amended by the court, the court may, revoke the community order and deal with him, for the offence in respect of which the order was made. If the court decides to re-sentence it must take into account the extent to which the offender has complied with the requirements of the order, and may impose a custodial sentence (where the order was made in respect of an offence punishable with such a sentence) notwithstanding anything in CJA 2003, s 152(2). In the case of a juvenile who has attained the age of 18 the court's powers are to do either or both of the following,

(a) to impose a fine not exceeding £5,000 for the offence in respect of which the order was made;
(b) to deal with the offender for that offence in any way in which the court could deal with him if it had just convicted him of an offence punishable with imprisonment for a term not exceeding twelve months.

If at a review hearing the court, after considering the responsible officer's report, is of the opinion that the offender's progress under the requirement is satisfactory, the court may so amend the order as to provide for each subsequent review to be made by the court without a hearing.

If at a review without a hearing the court, after considering the responsible officer's report, is of the opinion that the offender's progress under the requirement is no longer satisfactory, the court may require the offender to attend a hearing of the court at a specified time and place.

At that hearing the court, after considering that report, may:-

(a) exercise the powers conferred by this section as if the hearing were a review hearing, and
(b) so amend the order as to provide for each subsequent review to be made at a review hearing.

(11) Alcohol treatment requirement

B[9.22] This is a requirement that the offender submits during a specified period to treatment by or under the direction of a specified person having the necessary qualifications or experience with a view to the reduction or elimination of the offender's dependency on alcohol.

The court may not impose an alcohol treatment requirement in respect of an offender unless it is satisfied that he is dependent on alcohol, and his dependency is such as requires and may be susceptible to treatment. Arrangements must be made for the treatment intended to be specified in the order (including arrangements for the reception of the offender where he is to be required to submit to treatment as a resident).

A court may not impose an alcohol treatment requirement unless the offender expresses his willingness to comply with its requirements.

The treatment required by an alcohol treatment requirement for any particular period must be,

(a) treatment as a resident in such institution or place as may be specified in the order,
(b) treatment as a non-resident in or at such institution or place, and at such intervals, as may be so specified, or
(c) treatment by or under the direction of such person having the necessary qualification or experience as may be so specified;

but the nature of the treatment shall not be specified in the order except as mentioned in paragraph (a), (b) or (c) above.

(11A) Alcohol abstinence and monitoring requirement

B[9.22A] Section 76 of the Legal Aid, Sentencing and Punishment of Offenders Act 2012 (LASPOA 2012) inserts new s 212A in the Criminal Justice Act 2003 which adds alcohol abstinence and monitoring to the list of requirements that can be included in a community order. For this purpose, the Legal Aid, Sentencing and Punishment of Offenders Act 2012 (Alcohol Abstinence and Monitoring Requirements) Piloting Order 2014, SI 2014/1777 as amended, brought s 76 into force in the local justice areas of: Central London; East London; North East London; North London; North West London; South London; South East London; South West London; and West London with a current expiry date of 31 March 2017.

(12) In the case of an offender who is aged under 25, an attendance centre requirement

B[B9.22B] The aggregate number of hours must be not less than 12 or more than 26. The court may not impose an attendance centre requirement unless it is satisfied that an attendance centre which is available for persons of the offender's description is reasonably accessible to the offender concerned, having regard to the means of access available to him and any other circumstances. See further B[4], ante.

(13) Electronic monitoring of the offender's whereabouts otherwise than for the purpose of securing compliance with other requirements

B[B9.23] In consequence of the full implementation of s 44 of, and Sch 15 to, the Crime and Courts Act 2013 (by SI 2018/1423) an electronic requirement may be imposed to monitor the offender's whereabouts (CJA 2003, s 215(1)(b)).

However, a court may not include such an electronic monitoring requirement in a relevant order in respect of an offender unless the court:

(a) has been notified by the Secretary of State that electronic monitoring arrangements are available in the local justice area proposed to be specified in the order;
(b) is satisfied that the offender can be fitted with any necessary apparatus under the arrangements currently available and that any other necessary provision can be made under those arrangements; and
(c) is satisfied that arrangements are generally operational throughout England and Wales (even if not always operational everywhere there) under which the offender's whereabouts can be electronically monitored (CJA 2003, s 218(9)).

As to the requirement of consent of another person without whose co-operation it would not be practicable to secure the monitoring, and as to the obligations of an offender to submit to fitting, etc, of the relevant equipment, see B[9.9] ante.

Duration of orders

B[9.23A] A community order must specify a date, not more than three years after the date of the making of the order (subject to specific provision in relation to an unpaid work requirement, where the order continues in force until the requirement has been complied with: CJA 2003, s 200(3)), by which all the requirements contained within the order must be complied with; where two or more different requirements are imposed the court may specify different dates for compliance with any one or more of them: CJA 2003, s 177(5).

A community order exists only as a vehicle for the completion of its requirements; thus where an order contained only an unpaid work requirement, which must be completed within one year (subject to the ability to extend this) the order should not have been made for a period in excess of one year: *R v Khan (Gulan Ahmed)* [2015] EWCA Crim 835, [2015] 2 Cr App R (S) 39.

Breach of a requirement

B[9.24] See also A[17]. Under national standards an offender will be given one warning and then returned to court following a subsequent breach. It is open to probation to allege in the information both the original warning before the breach proceedings and the subsequent breach after the warning: *West Yorkshire Probation Board v Robinson and Tinker* [2009] EWHC 2468 (Admin). The court's powers are contained in Sch 8 Criminal Justice Act 2003. On breach of a requirement the court must deal with the offender by:

(a) making the original order more onerous;
(b) imposing a fine of up to £2,500; or
(c) revoking the order and dealing with the offender for the original offence (in the case of wilful and persistent failure to comply, the court may impose custody for a non-imprisonable offence.

Crown Court orders may contain a direction that breaches are dealt with in the magistrates' court or reserved to itself.

Where the Crown Court has not reserved jurisdiction to itself, the magistrates' court may commit the offender to the Crown Court for sentence.

In dealing with an offender, a magistrates' court must take into account the extent to which the offender has complied with the requirements of the order: CJA 2003, Sch 8, Part 2.

Revocation

B[9.25] The offender or responsible officer may apply to revoke the order and the court if satisfied it is in the interests of justice may revoke and or deal with the original offence, giving credit for any part of the order already completed. For the procedure see Part 44 of the Criminal Procedure Rules 2012.

It would be wrong in principle to resentence the offender where the revocation was on the grounds of ill health (*R v Bishop* [2004] EWCA Crim 2956, [2004] All ER (D) 116 (Dec)).

Where a defendant who was sentenced to a community order and a surcharge of £60 was re-sentenced to custody for breach of the community order he was not liable to pay a second surcharge: *R v George (Martin)* [2015] EWCA Crim 1096, [2015] 2 Cr App R (S) 58, [2015] Crim LR 916.

Conviction of a further offence during the currency of a community order

B[9.26] Where an offender subject to a community order is convicted of an offence, and it appears to be in the interests of justice to do so, the court may revoke the order or both revoke the order and sentence the offender for the original offence for which the order was made but in so doing the court must take into account the extent to which the offender has complied with the requirements of the community order: CJA 2003, Sch 8, Part 5.

Breach of community order by failing to comply with requirements

B[9.27] The court must take into account the extent to which the offender has complied with the requirements of the community order when imposing a penalty.

In assessing the level of compliance with the order the court should consider:

(i) the overall attitude and engagement with the order as well as the proportion of elements completed;
(ii) the impact of any completed or partially completed requirements on the offender's behaviour;
(iii) the proximity of breach to imposition of order; and
(iv) evidence of circumstances or offender characteristics, such as disability, mental health issues or learning difficulties which have impeded offender's compliance with the order.

Overall compliance with order	Penalty
Wilful and persistent non-compliance	Revoke the order and re-sentence imposing custodial sentence (even where the offence seriousness did not originally merit custody)
Low level of compliance	Revoke the order and re-sentence original offence **OR** Add curfew requirement 20 – 30 days* **OR** 30 – 50 hours additional unpaid work/extend length of order/add additional requirement(s) **OR** Band C fine
Medium level of compliance	Revoke the order and resentence original offence **OR** Add curfew requirement 10 – 20 days* **OR** 20 – 30 hours additional unpaid work/extend length of order/add additional requirement(s) **OR** Band B fine
High level of compliance	Add curfew requirement 6 – 10 days* **OR** 10 – 20 hours additional unpaid work/extend length of order/add additional requirement(s) **OR** Band A fine

* curfew days do not have to be consecutive and may be distributed over particular periods, for example at weekends, as the court deems appropriate. The period of the curfew should not exceed the duration of the community order and cannot be for longer than 12 months.

Technical guidance

B[9.28]

(a) If imposing more onerous requirements the length of the order may be extended up to 3 years or six months longer than the previous length, which ever is longer (but only once).
(b) If imposing unpaid work as a more onerous requirement and an unpaid work requirement was not previously included, the minimum number of hours that can be imposed is 20.
(c) The maximum fine that can be imposed is £2,500.
(d) If re-sentencing, a suspended sentence **MUST NOT** be imposed as a more severe alternative to a community order. A suspended sentence may only be imposed if it is fully intended that the offender serve a custodial sentence in accordance with the *Imposition of Community and Custodial Sentences* guideline.
(e) Where the order was imposed by the Crown Court, magistrates should consider their sentencing powers in dealing with a breach. Where the judge imposing the order reserved any breach proceedings commit the breach for sentence.

Powers of the court following a subsequent conviction

A conviction for a further offence does not constitute a breach of a community order. However, in such a situation, the court should consider the following guidance from the *Offences Taken into Consideration and Totality guideline*: (https://www.sentencingcouncil.org.uk/wp-content/uploads/Offences-Taken-into-Consideration-and-Totality-definitive-guideline-Web.pdf, p 14).

Offender convicted of an offence while serving a community order

The power to deal with the offender depends on his being convicted whilst the order is still in force; it does not arise where the order has expired, even if the additional offence was committed whilst it was still current.

If an offender, in respect of whom a community order made by a magistrates' court is in force, is convicted by a magistrates' court of an additional offence, the magistrates' court should ordinarily revoke the previous community order and sentence afresh for both the original and the additional offence.

Where an offender, in respect of whom a community order made by a Crown Court is in force, is convicted by a magistrates' court, the magistrates' court may, and ordinarily should, commit the offender to the Crown Court, in order to allow the Crown Court to re-sentence for the original offence and the additional offence.

The sentencing court should consider the overall seriousness of the offending behaviour taking into account the additional offence and the original offence. The court should consider whether the combination of associated offences is sufficiently serious to justify a custodial sentence.

If the court does not consider that custody is necessary, it should impose a single community order that reflects the overall totality of criminality. The court must take into account the extent to which the offender complied with the requirements of the previous order.

B[10]

Compensation order

(Powers of Criminal Courts (Sentencing) Act 2000, ss 130–138)

B[10.1] **Compensation order.** Either as a sentence in its own right or in addition to another sentence, the court may order the defendant to pay compensation to a person who has suffered as a consequence of the defendant's crime.

A court must consider making a compensation order in any case where this section empowers it do so: s 130(2A) of the PCCSA 2000.

Compensation orders are intended to be used in simple, straightforward cases where no great amount is at stake. A compensation order can only be made when sentence is being passed and, therefore, cannot be made when committing for sentence or deferring sentence. The court shall give its reasons, on passing sentence, if it does not make a compensation order where it is empowered to do so. Examples of such reasons will be the defendant's lack of means, or that the loss is difficult to quantify (see below).

Surcharge. It is normally obligatory for the court to require payment of a surcharge – of an amount determined in accordance with the Criminal Justice Act 2003 (Surcharge) Order 2012, SI 2012/1696 – as part its of its sentence. Where, however, the court considers it would be appropriate to make a compensation order, but the offender has insufficient means to pay both the surcharge and appropriate compensation, the court must reduce the amount of the surcharge (if necessary to nil): Criminal Justice Act 2003, s 161A. See further *R v Beckford* [2018] EWCA Crim 2997, [2019] 1 Cr App R (S) 59.

Note: the term "fine" does not include any road fund or excise offence committed under the Vehicle Excise and Registration Act 1994 (C[47]) because the legislation provides for payment of an "excise penalty".

B[10.2] For what may compensation be ordered? For any personal injury, loss or damage (or to make payments for funeral expenses or bereavement in respect of a death resulting from any such offence, other than a death due to an accident arising out of the presence of a motor vehicle on a road – (ie the only such situation likely to arise in a magistrates' court, death arising from careless driving, not being covered)) resulting from the offence or any offences taken into consideration. Personal injury need not be physical injury, compensation may be ordered for terror or distress caused by the offence *(Bond v Chief Constable of Kent* [1983] 1 All ER 456, [1983] 1 WLR 40).

B[10.3] In the case of an offence under the Theft Act 1968, if the property is recovered but is damaged, a compensation order may be made against the defendant no matter how the damage was caused provided it was caused while the property was out of the owner's possession.

Exceptions

B[10.4] Exceptions include:

(a) Loss caused to the dependants of a victim who has died (except funeral expenses etc in the circumstances referred to above).

(b) Injury, loss or damage due to an accident arising out of the presence of a motor vehicle on a road except compensation may be awarded:
   (i) for damage caused to a motor vehicle stolen or taken without the owner's consent but not damage caused by the vehicle, eg to another car on the road; and
   (ii) in cases where the defendant's use of the vehicle was uninsured and no compensation is payable under the Motor Insurers' Bureau scheme (see C[33.18]–C[33.22]).

The amounts ordered under (i) and (ii) may include payment to cover loss of a 'no claims' bonus.

B[10.5] Proof of loss. As a result of amendments made to the law in 1982 it was considered that the approach to establishing the amount of the loss was not so strict as it was formerly. However, in 1985 the judges of the Divisional Court reaffirmed that (unless the amount was admitted by the accused at the outset) it was the duty of the prosecution to establish the loss and its amount, and make it clear to the defendant by means of evidence. If, after this, there was any real dispute as to the loss suffered by the victim, a compensation order should not be made and the victim should be left to resort to civil remedies to obtain compensation (*R v Horsham Justices, ex p Richards* [1985] 2 All ER 1114, [1985] 1 WLR 986)); followed in *R v Stapylton (Ben)* [2012] EWCA Crim 728, [2012] All ER (D) 84 (Apr). However where the exact loss cannot be ascertained but finding the minimum loss was a simple task that latter sum may be ordered (*R v Brazil* [2004] EWCA Crim 1975, [2004] All ER (D) 348 (Jun)).

Fixing the amount

B[10.6] The following need to be taken into account when fixing the amount:

(a) The amount of the loss should be established after proof or agreement.

(b) Where the loss is not determined the court cannot fix an arbitrary amount at a figure below that which is in dispute. Either the lowest amount admitted should be adopted or no order made at all.

(c) Compensation for personal injury may be ascertained having regard to guidelines issued by the Criminal Injuries Compensation Board (see B[10.19]).

(d) There is no limit on the maximum compensation which can be ordered in respect of an adult offender: Powers of Criminal Courts (Sentencing) Act 2000, s 131(1A).

(e) Having ascertained what the loss is, and what the maximum amount is that can be ordered, the court must have regard to the defendant's ability to pay. He may be allowed to pay by instalments but generally such instalments should not extend beyond two years (*R v Olliver and Olliver* (1989) 11 Cr App Rep (S) 10, 153 JP 369), a case in the Crown Court where a large sum was to be paid) although in the magistrates' courts simple straightforward orders will probably be paid within a shorter period. Judicial guidance suggests that magistrates' court orders should be paid within a short period of time, preferably 13 weeks and 52 weeks should be regarded as the maximum period for repayment. Where the defendant is of limited means and would be unable to pay both compensation and a fine, preference must be given to the award of compensation. Neither *R v Olliver and Olliver* nor *R v Yehou* [1997] 2 Cr App Rep (S) 48 was authority for the proposition that there was an outer limit for the period of repayment of a compensation order. Under s 130(4) of the Powers of Criminal Courts (Sentencing) Act 2000, a court making a compensation order must ask whether it is appropriate. That requires an enquiry into whether the compensation order will be oppressive or an undue burden given the offender's means; whether realistically the offender can be expected to repay in the terms proposed and whether the compensation order accords with the nature of the offence and the nature of the offender. In neither case was the order an undue burden. Under s 133 of the PCCSA 2000, if there was a change in financial circumstances of either of the appellants, they could apply for a variation or discharge of the order: *R v Ganyo (Molly and Prize)* [2011] EWCA Crim 2491, [2012] 1 Cr App Rep (S) 650, 176 JP

396. With respect, *Ganyo* is wrong. The CA overlooked the Sentencing Council guidelines which recommend maximum periods for repayment in comity with *Olliver* and *Yehou* above,

It is not wrong in principle to make an order where the defendant will have to borrow money to satisfy the order, provided the material shows that there are sound prospects of the defendant being able to repay the loan; but if there are grounds to suspect that an offer may be unrealistic further inquiries are apt: *R v Carrington* [2014] EWCA Crim 325, [2014] 1 Cr App Rep (S) 337.

Where an offender is reluctant to disclose means, the court could indicate a provisional figure of compensation and then require the offender to show that his means are such that the figure cannot be met if he wishes to avoid that order: *R v Phillips* (1988) 10 Cr App Rep (S) 419, [1989] Crim LR 160, CA.

NB The offender is under a statutory duty to furnish a statement of his financial circumstances, and he commits an offence punishable with a fine not exceeding level 2 if he fails to do so: Criminal Justice Act 1991, s 20A(1A).

The court is also empowered to make a 'financial circumstances order' in relation to an offender, non-compliance with which constitutes an offence punishable with a fine not exceeding level 3: Criminal Justice Act 2003, s 162.

Where there are several claimants and the offenders' means are insufficient to meet all the claims, the course to be adopted as a general rule is apportionment commensurate with the total liability. But the court has an inherent power to see that justice is done, and it may, if there are strong grounds for doing so, depart from the normal pro rata basis to make such adjustment as is reasonable: *R v Amey* [1983] 1 All ER 865, [1983] 1 WLR 345, CA.

(f) If the defendant cannot afford to pay for the whole amount of the loss, then this lower amount, which he can afford, must be ordered.

(g) The circumstances in which a court may subsequently vary a compensation order are limited. Accordingly, an unrealistically high order for compensation may result in the defendant being committed to prison for default; this is wrong in principle (see B[10.17]–B[10.18] 'appeal and review').

B[10.7] **Making an order.** When deliberating whether to make an order, the court should bear in mind that the wealthy offender should never be allowed to buy his way out of prison by offering compensation. Also, the court should be wary of an accused mitigating for a suspended sentence on the basis of extravagant promises to pay compensation.

B[10.8] On the other hand, when a custodial sentence is imposed, compensation should be ordered only if the offender has the means to pay immediately or out of existing resources. He should not have to face the payment of compensation upon his discharge from a custodial sentence unless it is clear that he will then have the means to pay, eg he has savings or by being able to return to gainful employment immediately.

B[10.9] The court should announce the amount of compensation for each offence and against each defendant. Where there are competing claims for compensation, the court may make an order for one compensatee in preference to another, eg a private individual in preference to a financial institution (*R v Amey* [1983] 1 All ER 865, [1983] 1 WLR 345, CA).

B[10.10]–[10.15] In all cases where a compensation order is contemplated, the legal adviser should be consulted.

B[10.16] **Compensation and deprivation orders.** Where a court makes a deprivation order (see B[18]) in a case where a person has suffered personal injury, loss or damage, but a compensation order for the full loss cannot be made because of the offender's inadequate means, it may direct that the proceeds arising from the disposal of the forfeited goods be paid to the victim to make good the deficiency. The amount to be paid is a sum not exceeding the amount of compensation that the court would have ordered were it not for the offender's lack of means. See also B[11] for confiscation orders.

Appeal and review

B[10.17] The entitlement of the victim is suspended for 21 days to allow the defendant time to appeal if he wishes, or until after the appeal is heard. But the enforcement of the order against the offender is not suspended; the obligation to pay arises immediately. Accordingly, where an appeal is successful, the court will have to repay to the appellant any monies that he has already paid.

B[10.18] At any time before the order has been fully complied with, the court may discharge or reduce the order:

(a) if a civil court determines an amount of damage or loss less than that stated in the order; or
(b) if the property or part of it is subsequently recovered; or
(c) where the defendant's means are insufficient to satisfy in full the compensation order and a confiscation order made in the same proceedings; or
(d) where the defendant has suffered a substantial reduction in his means which was unexpected at the time the compensation order was made, and his means seem unlikely to increase for a considerable period.

The permission of the Crown Court is required where it made the original order, if the magistrates' court contemplates the action at (c) or (d).

Guidelines for compensation for personal injury

B[10.19] The Magistrates' Court Sentencing Guidelines contain the following points regarding compensation for personal injury and the suggested starting points for physical and mental injuries:

Introduction

1. The court *must* consider making a compensation order in any case where personal injury, loss or damage has resulted from the offence. It can either be a sentence in its own right or an ancillary order. The court must give reasons if it decides not to order compensation. (Powers of Criminal Courts (Sentencing) Act 2000, s 130.)

2. There is no statutory limit on the amount of compensation that may be imposed in respect of offences for an offender aged 18 or over. Compensation may also be ordered in respect of offences taken into consideration. (Powers of Criminal Courts (Sentencing) Act 2000, s 131.)

3. Where the personal injury, loss or damage arises from a road accident, a compensation order may be made only if there is a conviction for an offence under the Theft Act 1968, or the offender is uninsured and the Motor Insurers' Bureau will not cover the loss.

4. Subject to consideration of the victim's views (see paragraph 6 below), the court must order compensation wherever possible and should not have regard to the availability of other sources such as civil litigation or the Criminal Injuries Compensation Scheme. Any amount paid by an offender under a compensation order will generally be deducted from a subsequent civil award or payment under the Scheme to avoid double compensation.

5. Compensation may be ordered for such amount as the court considers appropriate having regard to any evidence and any representations made by the offender or prosecutor. The court must also take into account the offender's means (see also paragraphs 9–11 below).

6. Compensation should benefit, not inflict further harm on, the victim. Any financial recompense from the offender may cause distress. A victim may or may not want compensation from the offender and assumptions should not be made either way. The victim's views are properly obtained through sensitive discussion by the police or witness care unit, when it can be explained that the offender's ability to pay will ultimately determine whether, and how much, compensation is ordered and whether the compensation will be paid in one lump sum or by instalments. If the victim does not want compensation, this should be made known to the court and respected.

7. In cases where it is difficult to ascertain the full amount of the loss suffered by the victim, consideration should be given to making a compensation order for an amount

representing the agreed or likely loss. Where relevant information is not immediately available, it may be appropriate to grant an adjournment if it would enable it to be obtained.

8. The court should consider two types of loss:

- financial loss sustained as a result of the offence such as the cost of repairing damage or, in case of injury, any loss of earnings or medical expenses;
- pain and suffering caused by the injury (including terror, shock or distress) and any loss of facility. This should be assessed in light of all factors that appear to the court to be relevant, including any medical evidence, the victim's age and personal circumstances.

9. Once the court has formed a preliminary view of the appropriate level of compensation, it must have regard to the means of the offender so far as they are known. Where the offender has little money, the order may have to be scaled down or additional time allowed to pay; the court may allow compensation to be paid over a period of up to three years in appropriate cases.

10. The fact that a custodial sentence is imposed does not, in itself, make it inappropriate to order compensation; however, it may be relevant to whether the offender has the means to satisfy the order. **Consult your legal adviser in any case where you are considering combining compensation with a custodial sentence.**

11. Where the court considers that it would be appropriate to impose a fine and a compensation order but the offender has insufficient means to pay both, priority should be given to compensation. Compensation also takes priority over the victim surcharge where the offender's means are an issue.

Suggested starting points for physical and mental injuries

12. The table below suggests starting points for compensating physical and mental injuries commonly encountered in a magistrates' court. They have been developed to be consistent with the approach in the Criminal Injuries Compensation Authority (CICA) tariff (revised 2012). The CICA tariff makes no award for minor injuries which result in short term disability; the suggested starting points for these injuries are adapted from an earlier tariff.

Type of injury	Description	Starting point
Graze	Depending on size	£75
Bruise	Depending on size	£100
Cut: no permanent scar	Depending on size and whether stitched	£100–£300
Black eye		£125
Eye	Blurred or double vision lasting up to 6 weeks	£500
	Blurred or double vision lasting for 6 to 13 weeks	£1,000
	Blurred or double vision lasting for more than 13 weeks (recovery expected)	£1,500
Brain	Concussion lasting one week	£1,500
Nose	Undisplaced fracture of nasal bone	£1,000
	Displaced fracture requiring manipulation	£2,000
	Deviated nasal septum requiring septoplasty	£2,000
Loss of non-front tooth	Depending on cosmetic effect	£750 per tooth
Loss of front tooth		£1,500 per tooth
Facial scar	Minor disfigurement (permanent)	£1,000

Type of injury	Description	Starting point
Arm	Fractured humerus, radius, ulna (substantial recovery)	£1,500
Shoulder	Dislocated (substantial recovery)	£900
Wrist	Dislocated/fractured – including scaphoid fracture (substantial recovery)	£2,400
	Fractured – colles type (substantial recovery)	£2,400
Sprained wrist, ankle	Disabling for up to 6 weeks	500
	Disabling for 6 to 13 weeks	£800
	Disabling for more than 13 weeks	£1000
Finger	Fractured finger other than index finger (substantial recovery)	£300
	Fractured index finger (substantial recovery)	£1,200
	Fractured thumb (substantial recovery)	£1,750
Leg	Fractured fibula (substantial recovery)	£1,000
	Fractured femur, tibia (substantial recovery)	£1,800
Abdomen	Injury requiring laparotomy	£1,800
Temporary mental anxiety (including terror, shock, distress), not medically verified		£500
Disabling mental anxiety, lasting more than 6 weeks, medically verified		£1,000
Disability mental illness, lasting up to 28 weeks, confirmed by psychiatric diagnosis*		£1,500

* mental injury is disabling if it has a substantial adverse effect on a person's ability to carry out normal day-to-day activities for the time specified (e.g. impaired work or school performance or effects on social relationships or sexual dysfunction).

13. The following table, which is also based on the Criminal Injuries Compensation Authority tariff, sets out suggested starting points for compensating physical and sexual abuse. It will be rare for cases involving this type of harm to be dealt with in a magistrates' court and it will be important to **consult your legal adviser for guidance in these situations.**

Type of injury	Description	Starting point
Physical abuse of adult	Intermittent physical assaults resulting in accumulation of healed wounds, burns or scalds, but with no appreciable disfigurement	£2,000
Physical abuse of child	Isolated or intermittent assault(s) resulting in weals, hair pulled from scalp etc.	£1,000
	Intermittent physical assaults resulting in accumulation of healed wounds, burns or scalds, but with no appreciable disfigurement	£1,000
Sexual abuse of adult	Non-penetrative indecent physical acts over clothing	£1,000
	Non-penetrative indecent act(s) under clothing	£2,000
Sexual abuse of child (under 18)	Non-penetrative indecent physical act(s) over clothing	£1,000
	Non-penetrative frequent assaults over clothing or non-penetrative indecent act under clothing	£1,500 or £2,000
	Repetitive indecent acts under clothing	£3,300

B[11]
Confiscation orders

B[11.1] The prosecutor may ask the magistrates' court to commit the offender to the Crown Court so that a confiscation order may be made. The court must comply with such a request and may also commit any other offence for which he stands to be sentenced (PCA 2002, s 10).

For case law on the enforcement of confiscation orders, see *R (on the application of Johnson) v Birmingham Magistrates' Court and CPS* [2012] EWHC 596 (Admin), 176 JP 298.

In *R (on the application of Beach) v Folkestone Magistrates' Court* [2018] EWHC 2843 (Admin) the claimants owned farmland that was subject to planning restrictions. As a result of breaches of these restrictions prosecutions were brought and confiscation orders were made. Action to enforce the orders was brought. These were adjourned on up to 17 occasions. The delay was because the only real asset owned by the claimants was the property itself. As agricultural property it was worth enough to discharge the orders, but with planning permission it was worth significantly more. However, the property was in the green belt, and planning permission for residential development was unlikely. In 2016, a developer made an offer, but this was subject to the grant of appropriate planning permission. By the time of the final hearing in February 2018, the option agreement had been varied, but an enforcement receiver had not been appointed and little progress had been made for planning permission. The justices issued the commitment warrants, primarily because of the ages of the orders and the value of the available assets even without planning permission.

These committal orders were quashed on judicial review. The alternative of the appointment of an enforcement receiver under s 50(2) of the Proceeds of Crime Act 2002 had been proposed at a hearing on 15 December 2017, and the court on that date had anticipated that this would be done by the February 2018 hearing. In fact, an application was not made until four weeks after the February hearing. It was not clear why the justices had not considered this option. The written reasons for issuing the warrant of commitment showed the decision was based on excessive delay rather than wilful refusal or culpable neglect, and the clear and obvious alternative method of enforcement was not considered.

B[11.2] Term in default. In the same way as with Crown Court fines, the Crown Court fixes the term in default and enforcement is then dealt with in the magistrates' court.

It was held in *R (Gibson) v Secretary of State for Justice* [2015] EWCA Civ 1148, [2016] 4 All ER 244, [2017] 1 WLR 1115 that where the Crown Court has made an order under s 139(2) of the Powers of Criminal Courts Act 2000 fixing a term of imprisonment or detention in default, enforcement becomes the responsibility of the magistrates' court to impose the term in default. The opening words of s 79(2) of the Magistrates' Courts Act 1980 should be interpreted as if they read 'where before or after a period of imprisonment or other detention has been imposed' so that account may be taken of any payment made between the Crown Court fixing the term in default and the imposition of a term of imprisonment in default of payment by a magistrates' court. See also *R (on the application of Beach) v Folkestone Magistrates' Court* [2018] EWHC 2843 (Admin). See also *R (on the application of Beach) v Folkestone Magistrates' Court* [2018] EWHC 2843 (Admin).

A confiscation order made under the Drug Trafficking Act 1994 or the Proceeds of Crime Act 2002 attracts interest on any balance unpaid. The accrual of interest has an effect on the time spent in custody in that any payment made in reduction of the sum due is to be taken as a proportion of the whole sum due, comprehending both the original order and the accrued interest. The default term fixed by the Crown Court is not increased; when interest is added, the rate of reduction for payment of part of the default term is reduced.

In the subsequent appeal to the Supreme Court in *R (on the application of Gibson) v Secretary of State for Justice* [2018] UKSC 2, [2018] 1 WLR 629, [2018] ALL ER (D) 99 (Jan), (2018) The Times January 30, however, it was held that interest was not to be taken into account when determining the reduction to the default term which should be made for subsequent, part payments:

> 'DOES SECTION 79(2) INCLUDE INTEREST IN ITS STARTING POINT?
>
> [18] That leads one to the issue in the present case. If the court which imposes the default term is, for the purposes of s 79(2), the Crown Court in the case of a confiscation order, which is the correct starting point for the arithmetical giving of proportionate credit for part payment? Is it the sum stated in the order as originally made by the Crown Court, or is it that sum plus any interest which has accrued by the time the exercise is conducted by the magistrates? In the present case, is it £5.4m or is it £8.1m?
>
> [19] For the Secretary of State, (Counsel) powerfully submits that it must be the original sum plus interest. The plain purpose of the various statutory provisions for interest, including s 10 of the Drug Trafficking Act, is, he submits, that interest is treated for any enforcement purpose as added to the confiscation order and is expressly made part of "the amount to be recovered from [the defendant] under the confiscation order". So, it is said, the references in s 79(2) to the term set in default of payment of "any sum adjudged to be paid" must, by what he refers to as a necessary statutory fiction, be references to the sum fixed by the original confiscation order plus interest. That is to do no more, he argues, than is already provided for in s 79(2) for the costs and charges of any distress which has been levied, which are expressly added to the principal sum outstanding. Those also, he submits, will in the case of a Crown Court order, necessarily have been incurred after the default term was fixed by that Court. He points to the plain intention, gathered from s 10(1), that interest is to be paid, and to the fact that in the case of a criminal who is in default of payment of the principal sum, civil means of enforcement of interest are unlikely to be effective. He rightly reminds us that a confiscation order is premised on the proposition that the defendant has the means to pay, so that any default is his election. If circumstances change in a way which reduces his ability to pay, the various confiscation statutes provide a procedure for application for a certificate of inadequacy and consequent downward reduction in the amount of the confiscation order.
>
> [20] Those arguments may well reflect, in a purposive manner, the kind of regime for which the successive statutory referrals might have provided. The difficulty with them lies in the operative words of s 79(2), which are the only ones which provide for the treatment of part payments. They say expressly that the days to be deducted are to be the number which bear the same proportion to the total default term imposed (by the Crown Court) as the part payments bear "to so much of the said sum . . . as was due at the time the period of detention was imposed". If the Secretary of State's argument is to be accepted, the words "at the time the period of detention was imposed" have to be done no little violence. At the time the Crown Court imposed the default term, there was as yet no interest accrued at all.
>
> [21] We have concluded that this straining of the wording of s 79(2) cannot be justified in circumstances where it would adversely impact on the period of imprisonment to which a person would be subject. Penal legislation is construed strictly, particularly where the penalty involves deprivation of liberty. The words

of s 79(2) do not provide clearly for a period of imprisonment calculated on the basis for which the Secretary of State contends; on the contrary, they suggest the natural construction that the starting point for the arithmetical calculation of reduction in days of imprisonment is the sum outstanding at the time of the Crown Court order.

[22] Nor is the Secretary of State's construction warranted by the example of the reference in s 79(2) to the costs and charges of distress, where such have been incurred. Since s 79(2) was plainly not drafted with confiscation, or for that matter Crown Court fines, in mind, the reference is adequately explained by the orthodox case of the magistrates first issuing a warrant for distress and only subsequently fixing the default term for non-payment; in such a case the reference to the sum outstanding at the time the period of detention was imposed makes perfectly good sense. In any event, the addition of such costs and charges is expressly provided; that does not mean that an equivalent provision can be read in as a consequence of a provision in a different statute, namely s 10(1) of the Drug Trafficking Act.

[23] A scheme under which the period of imprisonment served in default of payment in full of the amount specified in the confiscation order is based on the entire amount outstanding, including interest, may or may not be what the framers of the confiscation legislation might have wished for or intended if the point had been considered. However, because the means adopted took the form of statutory reference (and re-reference) to provisions which were drafted for a different purpose and without confiscation in mind, they have not achieved that effect. If it is desired that they should do so, express legislation will be needed.

[24] It is also of some relevance that the practical consequences of the Secretary of State's proposed construction would, without specific machinery, be difficult to work out. Interest accrues daily, so the net amount outstanding would also vary daily. That difficulty may be met by a calculation geared to the particular day (or days) on which any part payment is made. But additionally, this construction would have the effect of progressively reducing the incentive to make part payment, as interest rises, because the days credited for such part payment would progressively reduce. Nor would such a scheme provide any consequences at all for the not uncommon defendant who simply makes no payment whatever.'

(Per Lords Reed and Hughes, giving the judgment of the Court.)

B[12] Costs

B[12.1] The award of costs is the exercise of a judicial discretion and any decision must always be made after taking each case on its merits, hearing each party and taking proper account of the law. As a general rule, the successful party in any proceedings can expect to be reimbursed for the costs he has incurred in conducting the proceedings. In civil proceedings, a successful party can receive his costs from the other party. Under the Litigants in Person (Costs and Expenses, Magistrates' Courts) Order 2001 an individual who has been successful in civil proceedings may also benefit from an order for costs to cover work done by him in connection with the case and any resultant expenses or losses. In criminal proceedings, according to the circumstances of the particular case, it may be possible for costs to be awarded either against the unsuccessful party or from central funds, which are monies provided by Parliament to defray the costs of criminal proceedings.

Criminal proceedings

(Prosecution of Offences Act 1985, ss 16–19)

B[12.2] See Part 45 of the CrimPR 2015. In a criminal case, the court's duty is firstly to consider the appropriate sentence. If that is a fine, the offender's means so far as they are known to the court must be taken into account. It is wrong in principle to reduce a fine in order to accommodate an order for costs. Costs should never be awarded as a disguised penalty and the offender's means should be taken into account as above (*R v Nottingham Magistrates' Court, ex p Fohmann* (1986) 84 Cr App Rep 316, 151 JP 49). The costs awarded should be proportionate to the level of any fine (*Nedic v South Staffordshire Council* [2005] EWHC 1481 (Admin), [2005] All ER (D) 182 (Jun)).

B[12.2A] The following must be read in the light of the *Practice Direction (Costs in Criminal Proceedings) 2015* [2015] EWCA CrimPR 1568.

Prosecution costs

B[12.3] **Central funds.** Almost all criminal prosecutions are conducted by the Crown Prosecution Service or a public authority such as the Trading Standards Department of a local authority. The funding for these prosecutions is provided by national or local revenues, and so there is no power to award the costs of the prosecution to these authorities out of central funds, even where the prosecution is successful. This avoids the wasteful practice of transferring moneys from one public fund to another.

B[12.4] **Private prosecutors.** The court may, in a case where an indictable offence is concerned, order the costs of the prosecutor to be paid out of central funds whether the prosecution is successful or not. An indictable offence includes an offence triable either way and also offences of criminal damage where the damage is under £5,000 and is therefore triable only summarily. This provision does not apply to public authorities such as the CPS and local authorities (POA 1985, s 17(2)).

B[12.5] There is no power to order costs from central funds to a prosecutor for purely summary offences. The costs to be awarded would normally be such amounts as the court considers reasonably sufficient to compensate the prosecutor for any expenses properly incurred by him and can include the costs of compensating a witness for the expense, trouble or loss of time properly incurred in his attendance at court. The amount payable to witnesses in respect of travelling expenses and loss of earnings is fixed by regulations and witnesses' expenses are dealt with in the clerk's office. A witness may be reimbursed even if he did not actually give evidence, if he was properly called to do so. Witnesses may be called, for example, in anticipation of a trial only to find that there is a last minute guilty plea. The cost of investigating offences is not included.

B[12.6] Making an order for the costs of a private prosecutor. The court may fix the amount to be paid to the prosecutor out of central funds at the hearing where the prosecutor is in agreement, or in any other case the amount of the costs can be assessed afterwards by the central taking officer. In relation to assessment of costs, provisions analogous to (but less restrictive than) those for a defendant's costs order apply. The differences between the regimes were noted in *R (on the application of Virgin Media Ltd) v Zinga* [2014] EWCA Crim 1823, [2015] q Cr App R 14, [2015] 1 Cr App R (S) 74. Private prosecutors' legal costs are not limited to legal aid rates. A private prosecutor whose prosecution is taken over by the CPS is eligible for his costs incurred prior to the intervention: Prosecution of Offences Act 1985, s 17(6).

B[12.7] Reducing the amount of the prosecutor's order. Where the court is prepared to order the prosecutor's costs out of central funds but is of the opinion that there are circumstances that make it inappropriate to order the full amount of costs, eg where the defendant is convicted of some offences and acquitted of others, the court can assess what in its opinion would be just and reasonable, and specify that amount.

B[12.8] Ordering the accused to pay the prosecution costs. Where a person has been convicted of an either way or purely summary offence, the court can order the accused to pay to the prosecutor (the Crown Prosecution Service, a public authority or a private prosecutor) such costs as it considers just and reasonable. The amount of the costs is specified by the court at the hearing and cannot be left to be assessed later. In general the principle applied to fines imposition (**B[28.16]**) should be applied and should be in keeping with the level of the fine (*R v Northallerton Magistrates' Court, ex p Dove* [2000] 1 Cr App Rep (S) 136, 163 JP 657). In *R (on the application of Middleton) v Cambridge Magistrates' Court* [2012] EWHC 2122 (Admin), 176 JP 569, it was held that there was no requirement for there to be an arithmetical relationship between a fine and the costs sought. In fact, there might well be situations where the fine and costs imposed differed. However, that did not mean that a prosecution could not be brought because it was too expensive as the requirements of justice had to be kept in mind. That being said, the costs imposed should not be grossly disproportionate to the maximum penalty for the offence committed. The instant court could not ignore the fact that the maximum sentence for the offences M had committed was at the lowest level. Notwithstanding the delays because of M's failure to plead guilty at the earliest opportunity, and the inherent complexities, the costs awarded to the prosecution (£6,871) were grossly disproportionate to the fine imposed and could not be sustained as just and reasonable.

The court must consider a defendant's means and ability to pay prosecution costs at the point of sentence. In the case of a defendant who lacked any immigration status and means to pay, the judge had fallen into error by leaving it to a fines review officer to resolve the issue of payment once the defendant had been released from custody: *R v Olaniregun* [2019] EWCA Crim 1294.

An order for costs can include sums expended as part of the investigation but only where the prosecutor has incurred liability for those costs to a third party e.g. an accountancy report, and where the report formed part of the case presented at court. In such a case the court need only be satisfied that it is just and reasonable for the defendant to pay those costs: *Balshaw v Crown Prosecution Service* [2009] EWCA Crim 470, [2009] 2 Cr App Rep 95, [2009] 2 Cr App Rep (S) 712.

B[12.9] Monetary penalty not exceeding £5. Where, on conviction of an offence, the court orders payment of any sum as a fine, penalty, forfeiture or compensation not exceeding £5, the court shall not order the accused to pay the prosecution costs unless in the particular circumstances of the case it considers it right to do so.

B[12.10]–[12.15] Youths. Where a person aged under 18 years is convicted of an offence before a magistrates' (or youth) court and he is ordered to pay the costs, the amount that is ordered shall not exceed the amount of any fine that is properly imposed on him. This restriction does not apply if a parent is made responsible for paying the fine etc (see **B[28.95]**).

Defence costs on acquittal: ss 16 and 16A of the Prosecution of Offences Act 1985

B[12.16] Defence costs may be awarded from central funds where a charge is not proceeded with or is dismissed. Such an order shall be for payment of such amount as the court considers reasonably sufficient to compensate the defendant for any expenses properly incurred by him in the proceedings: s 16(6). Where the court considers that there are circumstances that make it inappropriate for the accused to recover the full amount mentioned above, an order must be for the payment of such lesser amount as the court considers just and reasonable: s 16(6A). Where a defendant was charged with assault occasioning actual bodily harm, he claimed he was acting in his own defence and in the defence of another, he refused to consider pleading guilty to a lesser offence, on the morning of the trial the complainant refused to give evidence, the prosecution offered a binding over and the defendant acquiesced, but the district judge determined that a bind over was inappropriate owing to the time which had elapsed and the defendant's good character, the judge was wrong to restrict the defendant's costs to those necessarily incurred in relation to the date of the trial on the ground that the defendant had acted unreasonably and had not acted expeditiously through his failure to indicate at any stage before the trial that he would accept a bind over. The decision was not inconsistent with the judge's conclusion that a bind over was inappropriate, but the judge's view that the defendant had acted unreasonably ignored the realities of the prosecution and how it had proceeded. The defendant had maintained his innocence throughout. A bind over was not an acceptance of guilt of any wrongdoing. The prosecution had not previously indicated that a bind over would be acceptable and such a resolution would have been inconceivable in view of the injuries suffered by the complainant. When the defendant acquiesced to a bind over, the fact that the judge considered this was unnecessary and inappropriate showed that the defendant went considerably beyond the reasonable. Thus, there was no possible positive reason for not awarding a full defendant's costs order: *Newcombe v CPS* [2013] EWHC 2160 (Admin), [2013] 6 Costs LO 905.

Legal costs may only be awarded, however, where the defendant is an individual and, in the case of Crown Court trials (but not appeals to the Crown Court), only where the defendant was financially ineligible for legal aid: s 16A.

The Practice Direction (Costs in Criminal Proceedings) 2015 [2015] EWCA Crim 1568 summarises the relevant principles and provides:

> '2.1.1 Where an information laid before a justice of the peace charging a person with an offence is not proceeded with or a magistrates' court dealing summarily with an offence dismisses the information the court may make a defendant's costs order. An order under section 16 of the Act may also be made in relation to breach of bind-over proceedings in a magistrates' court or the Crown Court: regulation 14(4) of the General Regulations. Whether to make such an order is a matter in the discretion of the court in the light of the circumstances of each particular case. A defendant's costs order should normally be made unless there are positive reasons for not doing so, for example, where the defendant's own conduct has brought suspicion on himself and has misled the prosecution into thinking that the case against him was stronger than it was. Where the defendant has been acquitted on some counts but convicted on others the court may make an order that only part of the costs be paid: see paragraphs 2.2.1 and 2.2.2 below. The court when declining to make a costs order should explain, in open court, that the reason for not making an order does not involve any suggestion that the defendant is guilty of any criminal conduct but the order is refused because of the positive reason that should be identified: *Hussain v United Kingdom* (2006) 43 EHRR 437. Where the court considers that it would be inappropriate

that the defendant should recover all of the costs properly incurred, either the amount allowed must be specified in the order or the court may describe to the appropriate authority the reduction required.

2.1.2 In respect of proceedings in a magistrates' court commenced on or after 1 October 2012 legal costs (sums paid for advocacy, litigation services or experts' fees) may only be allowed to a defendant who is an individual. Where legal costs may be allowed, if the court fixes the amount to be paid under section 16(6C) of the Act or under sections 62A(4) or 135A(4) of the Extradition Act 2003 it must calculate any amounts allowed in respect of legal costs in accordance with the rates and scales prescribed by the Lord Chancellor. If the court does not fix the amount of costs to be paid out of central funds, the costs will be determined by the appropriate authority in accordance with the General Regulations and any legal costs allowed will be calculated at the prescribed rates and scales.'

When refusing to make an order or refusing an order for costs the court must give its reason: see *Dowler v Merseyrail* [2009] EWHC 558 (Admin), 173 JP 332. See also *R (on the application of Spiteri (Elliott)) v Basildon Crown Court* [2009] EWHC 665 (Admin), 173 JP 327, [2009] 5 Costs LR 772.

B[12.16A] The Criminal Practice Directions (Costs in Criminal Proceedings) 2015 [2015] EWCA Crim 1568 provides:

'1.4.1 If the court does not fix the amount of costs to be paid out of central funds, the costs will be determined in accordance with the General Regulations by the appropriate authority. The appropriate authority will calculate the amount payable in respect of legal costs at such rates and scales as are prescribed by the Lord Chancellor. Where the court makes a defendant's costs order, or an order in favour of a private prosecutor, but is of the opinion there are circumstances which make it inappropriate that the person in whose favour the order is made should recover the full amount of the costs, the court may assess the lesser amount that would in its opinion be just and reasonable, and specify that amount in the order. If the court is not in a position to specify the amount payable, the judge may make remarks which the appropriate authority will take into account as a relevant circumstance when determining the costs payable.

1.4.2 In respect of proceedings commenced on or after 1 October 2012 legal costs (sums paid for advocacy, litigation services or experts' fees) may only be included in a defendant's costs order to a defendant who is an individual and only in proceedings in a magistrates' court, appeals against conviction or sentence from a magistrates' court to the Crown Court, relevant Crown Court proceedings after 27 January 2014 (as to which see paragraph 1.4.3 below) and appeals to the Court of Appeal (i) against a verdict of not guilty by reason of insanity, (ii) against a finding under the Criminal Procedure (Insanity) Act 1964 that the appellant is under a disability or that he did the act or made the omission charged or (iii) under section 16A of the Criminal Appeal Act 1968 (inserted by section 25 of the Domestic Violence, Crime and Victims Act 2004) (appeals against order made in cases of insanity or unfitness to plead).

1.4.3 After 27 January 2014 legal costs may be included in a defendant's costs order, provided that the defendant is an individual, in relevant proceedings in the Crown Court if the Director of Legal Aid Casework has made a determination of financial ineligibility in relation to that defendant. The relevant proceedings are those in which the accused has been sent by a magistrates' court to the Crown Court for trial, where a bill of indictment has been preferred (under section 2(2)(b) of the Administration of Justice (Miscellaneous Provisions) Act 1933) or following an order for a retrial made by the Court of Appeal or the Supreme Court.

...

1.4.4 Where legal costs may be allowed, if the court fixes the amount to be paid to a defendant under section 16(6C) of the Act (inserted by section 62 of and paragraph 2(2) of Schedule 7 to the Legal Aid, Sentencing and Punishment of Offenders Act 2012) or under sections 62A(4) or 135A(4) of the Extradition Act 2003 (inserted by paragraphs 15 and 18 respectively of Schedule 7 to the 2012 Act) it must calculate any amounts to be allowed in respect of legal costs in accordance with rates and scales prescribed by the Lord Chancellor.

1.4.5 Crim PR r 76.2(6), (7) contains general rules about the amount of an award of costs that apply subject to any statutory limitation.'

B[12.17]–[12.18] A publicly aided defendant can only claim those costs which cannot be covered by the representation order, eg his travelling expenses to court.

In *Re Patel and a defendant's costs order* [2012] EWCA Crim 1508, [2012] All ER (D) 115 (Jul), it was decided that whilst the court had jurisdiction to re-open its decision to make a defendant's costs order, as the court had been unaware that the defendant and his solicitors had agreed to remove a cap on fees, which increased the fees retrospectively, it was appropriate to let the assessment by the determining officer take its course.

Costs unnecessarily or improperly incurred (s 19 of the Prosecution of Offences Act 1985)

B[12.19] Where the court is satisfied that one party to criminal proceedings has incurred costs as a result of an unnecessary or improper act or omission, it may order the party responsible to pay the additional costs thereby incurred whatever the final result of the case. This includes the whole of the defence costs where a private prosecutor instituted proceedings knowing an identical prosecution brought by CPS on the same ground had been dismissed without challenge (*Oddy v Bug Bugs Ltd* [2003] All ER (D) 156 (Nov)). This enables the court to mark its displeasure at the unreasonable behaviour of a party, eg where one party has put the other to unnecessary expense by requiring an adjournment when they should have been ready to proceed. Before making such an order both parties should be invited to make representations to the court and the court should determine the sum to be paid.

For the purposes of s 19 of the Act, no distinction could be drawn between the Crown Prosecution Service and the police. The 'party' on the other side from the defendant in such a case was the Crown. 'Improper' did not necessarily connote some grave impropriety. It was intended to cover an act or omission which would not have occurred if the party concerned had conducted his case properly. If the act giving rise to the application consisted of someone on the prosecution side not conducting the case properly and it caused the defendant to incur additional costs, the discretion arose. A single mistake was enough to trigger the court's discretion to make an order. However, s 19(1) of the Act conferred a discretion and the court was not bound to make an order in every case of a mistake causing costs to be incurred. If there was a satisfactory explanation for the mistake, the court might decide that it would not be just to make any order: *R (on the application of Singh) v Ealing Magistrates Court* [2014] EWHC 1443 (Admin), 178 JP 253. See also *R (on the application of Holloway) v Harrow Crown Court* [2019] EWHC 1731 (Admin), [2019] All ER (D) 155 (Jul).

The threshold for making a wasted costs order under s 19 of the Prosecution Act 1985 is a high one. In *R v Cornish, R v Maidstone and Tunbridge Wells NHS Trust* [2016] EWHC 779 (QB), [2016] Crim LR 561 a patient in the Trust's care died seemingly because of inadequate anaesthetic care. Both the anaesthetist and the Trust were prosecuted, the former for gross negligence manslaughter, the latter for corporate manslaughter. Both defendants were acquitted, however, on the direction of the judge. The Trust subsequently sought a wasted costs order on the basis that the decision to prosecute had been unreasonable. The application was rejected. The bar for making a wasted costs order was high. The test was 'impropriety', not 'unreasonableness'. The conduct of the prosecution had to be starkly improper, such as to stand out without needing great investigation into the facts or the decision-making process. Where a case failed as a matter of law, the prosecution were more vulnerable to a claim of impropriety, but this did not necessarily follow since no one had a monopoly of legal wisdom, and many legal points were properly arguable. Orders under s 19 would be made only exceptionally where the prosecution had made a clear and stark error as a result of which a defendant had incurred costs for which it was appropriate to compensate him. The prosecution had acted in good faith. The case against the Trust was based on the alleged lack of qualification of two doctors for the posts they held and alleged inadequate supervision. The prosecution relied on an expert witness for these matters, and the case collapsed as a result of his evidence, especially under cross examination. However, there was no basis for saying the prosecution should have concluded that the expert's views were untenable. The decision to prosecute was a marginal one, but it could not be described as 'improper'.

The law has to guard against inadvertently discouraging people from bringing private prosecutions out of fear of adverse cost consequences, but private prosecutors are subject to the same obligations as public prosecutors; they would not be liable for costs merely through the failure or withdrawal of a prosecution, but where the decision to start a prosecution was wholly inappropriate and amounted to a clear and stark error it was an improper or unnecessary act within s 19 and the interested parties should be paid their costs at private client rates: *R (on the application of Haigh) v City of Westminster Magistrates' Court* [2017] EWHC 232 (Admin), [2017] 1 Costs LR 175. See also *R (on the application of Holloway) v Harrow Crown Court* [2019] EWHC 1731 (Admin), [2019] All ER (D) 155 (Jul).

The court is not entitled to use s 19 at the end of the trial as a means of impugning the decision to prosecute – if such a decision is to be challenged it must be by way of an application to stay the proceedings as an abuse of process, or, exceptionally, by way of judicial review: *R (on the application of the DPP) v Crown Court at Sheffield* [2014] EWHC 2014 (Admin), 178 CL&J 397.

As to the position where a prosecution fails in law (because the offence charged did not exist), see *Najib & Sons Ltd v CPS* [2018] EWCA Crim 1554, [2018] 4 WLR 144.

In *R (on the application of the DPP) v Bury Magistrates' Court* [2007] All ER (D) 208 (Dec) if was held that a court was entitled to make a costs order against the prosecution where it had failed to comply with a court order that it should serve its witness evidence on the defence by a specified date. As the prosecution had given no explanation for its failure there had been a breach of the Criminal Procedural Rules 2013.

A wasted costs order in favour of a legally aided defendant must be limited to the amount which falls to be paid to the legal representatives under the legal aid scheme. It is not permissible to include an amount by way of compensation for work reasonably done in the case which will otherwise not fall to be remunerated (as in the case of work done by way of preparation for a hearing at which the prosecution offered no evidence, where the decision to offer no evidence should have been made earlier and where the fees payable to the defence under the graduated fee scheme would be the same as if the decision had been made when it should have been, ie at an earlier hearing): *R v Fitzgerald* [2012] 3 Costs LR 437, Central Criminal Court (HH Judge Gordon).

As to procedure, see the Practice Direction (Costs in Criminal Proceedings) 2015, 4.1.

As to the history of, and distinction between, the power to award costs under s 19 and the power to make a 'wasted costs' order against a legal representative under s 19A (see B[12.20], below), see *Evans v Serious Fraud Office (No 2) [2015]* EWHC 263 (QB), [2015] 1 WLR 3595, [2015] All ER (D) 148 (Feb). The contexts of ss 19 and 19A are different and the meaning of the word 'improper' in those contexts is different. Two lines of authority have developed in respect of two entirely discrete powers; the derivation of the provisions is entirely different, s 19A was born out of the inherent jurisdiction of the court over solicitors, and it is concerned with, not the acts and omissions of a party itself, but with those of professional lawyers as legal representatives of a party in litigation which result in wasted costs. Although different from the disciplinary jurisdiction of the court over representatives, it is closely associated with that jurisdiction. The focus of it is upon the duty owed by individual legal representatives, as professional lawyers, to the court: an order can only be made against a specific legal representative. On the other hand, s 19 derives purely from the 1985 Act, and is concerned with costs resulting from the acts and omissions of a party: a representative cannot be liable for costs under s 19, because he is not a party to the proceedings.

The court summarised the principles so far as s 19 applications for costs against public prosecutors are concerned as follows:

(1) When any court is considering a potential costs order against any party to criminal proceedings, it must clearly identify the statutory power(s) upon which it is proposing to act; and thus the relevant threshold and discretionary criteria that will be applicable.
(2) In respect of an application under s 19 of the 1985 Act, a threshold criterion is that there must be 'an unnecessary or improper act or omission' on the part of the paying party, ie an act or omission which would not have occurred if the party concerned had conducted his case properly or which could otherwise have been properly avoided.
(3) In assessing whether this test is met, the court must take a broad view as to whether, in all the circumstances, the acts of the relevant party were unnecessary or improper.
(4) Recourse to cases concerning wasted costs applications under s 19A or its civil equivalent, such as *Ridehalgh*, will not be helpful. Similarly, in wasted costs applications under s 19A, recourse to cases under s 19 will not be helpful.
(5) The s 19 procedure is essentially summary; and so a detailed investigation into (eg) the decision-making process of the prosecution will generally be inappropriate.
(6) Each case will be fact-dependent, but cases in which a s 19 application against a public prosecutor will be appropriate will be very rare, and generally restricted to those exceptional cases where the prosecution has acted in bad faith or made a clear and stark error as a result of which a defendant has incurred costs for which it is appropriate to compensate him. The court will be slow to find that such an error has occurred. Generally, a decision to prosecute or similar prosecutorial decision will only be an improper act by the prosecution for these purposes if, in all the circumstances, no reasonable prosecutor could have come to that decision. 'Improper' in s 19A has to be construed as part of the phrase 'improper, unreasonable or negligent', and, in construing that phrase, the focus is very much on the specific context of the provision of legal services. On the other hand in s 19 it should be construed as part of the phrase 'unnecessary or improper', and, in construing that phrase, the focus is on the fact that an order can only be made against a party to the case in relation to his conduct in that case. In determining what might be 'improper', the context is a vital circumstance. The line of authority commencing with *DPP v Denning* [1991] 2 QB 532, [1991] 3 All ER 439 (as applied in magistrates' courts by *R (Singh) v Ealing Magistrates' Court* [2014] EWHC 1443 (Admin)) on s 19 is not to be applied to applications under s 19A to which the principle in *Ridehalgh v Horsefield* [1994] Ch 205 applies.

Costs against legal representatives: s 19A of the Prosecution of Offences Act 1985

B[12.20] In any criminal proceedings, the magistrates may disallow or order a legal representative to meet the whole or any part of any costs incurred by a party as a result of any improper, unreasonable or negligent act or omission of the representative or, where the conduct occurred after the incurring of the costs, the court considers it is unreasonable for the party to pay. Such orders are not common and the court must follow a detailed procedure before ordering costs against a legal representative. If such an order is contemplated, the legal adviser must be consulted.

It has been held that the words 'in any criminal proceedings' are wide enough to cover proceedings initiated by summons for the attendance of a witness before the Crown Court to produce a document. A party served with a witness summons and who served a notice of application asking the court to declare the summons to be of no effect was thus a party to criminal proceedings whose costs could be the subject of a wasted costs order: Re a Solicitor (Wasted Costs Order) [1996] 3 FCR 365, [1996] 1 FLR 40. Note, however, that while s 2C of the Criminal Procedure (Attendance of Witnesses) Act 1965 makes provision for costs to be awarded where a successful application is made to *set aside* a witness summons, no such provision is made where a party successfully *resists* an application for a witness summons; and it is difficult to see what inherent jurisdiction exists outside s 19A to enable the court to award costs to be paid by the solicitors acting for the applicant to a party who successfully resists the application for a witness summons: *DLA Piper UK LLP v BDO LLP* [2013] EWHC 3970 (Admin), [2014] 1 WLR 4425.

In *Re Soni (Appeal against a wasted costs order)* [2019] EWCA Crim 1304, [2019] All ER (D) 34 (Aug) it was held that a person or entity did not initiate or become a party to 'criminal proceedings' merely by seeking documents or information from the court.

As to procedure, see the Practice Direction (Costs in Criminal Proceedings) 2015, 4.2.

Costs against third parties

B[12.20A] Section 19B of the Prosecution of Offences Act 1985 (inserted by s 98 of the Courts Act 2003) empowers a criminal court to make costs orders against a third party where it has been guilty of serious misconduct. A third party accused of 'serious misconduct' must be allowed an opportunity to counter material put before the court by the interested party: *R v Capital Translation and Interpreting Ltd* [2014] EWCA Crim 3460, (2015) JP 36.

An isolated failure to provide an interpreter when under a contract to do so does not amount to 'serious misconduct'. However, a court is entitled to view successive non-attendance of an individual interpreter or successive failures in system as so amounting: *R v Applied Language Solutions Ltd* [2013] EWCA Crim 326, [2013] 1 WLR 3820, [2013] 2 Cr App R 169.

Miscellaneous provisions

B[12.21] **Medical reports.** In criminal proceedings, where the court has required a medical practitioner to make a report to the court orally or in writing, for the purpose inter alia of determining the most suitable method of dealing with the offender, his costs may be ordered to be paid from central funds.

The view is taken that this power embraces not only reports concerned with final disposal but also reports to assist in determining the appropriate procedural course to that stage, for example, whether a case should proceed to a normal trial, or to a fact finding inquiry with a view to the possible making of a hospital order under the Mental Health Act 1983, s 37.

B[12.22] **Interpreters.** In any criminal proceedings provision is made for the payment of interpreters from central funds.

B[12.23] **Proceedings for breach or revocation of community orders including youth community orders etc.** In appropriate circumstances a magistrates' court may now make an award of costs against the offender in breach proceedings where the breach is admitted or found proved.

Civil proceedings

(Magistrates' Courts Act 1980, s 64)

B[12.24] On hearing a complaint (eg concerning a dangerous dog), the court may order the defendant to pay to the successful complainant such costs as it thinks just and reasonable and, where the complaint is dismissed, the complainant may similarly be ordered to pay the defendant's costs (see the case law and principles discussed in detail in section F[2.20]).

B[12.25]–[12.30] In civil cases, it is not usual to order one party to pay or contribute towards the other's costs if both are publicly funded, but there is no reason why an order for costs should not be paid against a party who is not publicly funded where the successful party is so aided, so that the legal aid fund will receive the benefit of the order.

B[12.31] Applications. There is no power to award costs where proceedings are begun by way of an application (eg an application under the Police (Property) Act 1897).

Costs may be awarded under s 64 in favour of a person who has an interest in premises and appears to oppose the making of a closure order under s 2 of the Anti-social Behaviour Act 2003.

B[13]

Criminal behaviour orders

B[13.1] Anti-social behaviour orders on conviction (CrASBOs) were replaced by criminal behaviour orders (CBOs) by the Anti-social Behaviour, Crime and Policing Act 2014 (ABCPA 2014). The commencement day was 23 March 2015 (see SI 2015/373, art 4(a)). This is subject to saving and transitional provisions, as to which see B[2].

B[13.2] Grounds and pre-conditions for an order – There are two conditions. The first condition is that the court is satisfied, beyond reasonable doubt, that the offender has engaged in behaviour that caused or was likely to cause harassment, alarm or distress to any person (ABCPA, s 22(3)). The second condition is that the court considers that making the order will help in preventing the offender from engaging in such behaviour (ABCPA 2014, s 22(4)).

In deciding whether to make a CBO a court may take account of conduct occurring up to one year before the commencement day.

A CBO can only be made as an order ancillary to a sentence for the offence or an order of conditional discharge (ABCPA 2014, s 22(6)). It cannot, therefore, accompany an absolute discharge or a bind over to keep the peace, or be a sentence in its own right.

Where the offender will be under the age of 18 at the time of the application, the police or local authority must consult the youth offending team (YOT) and inform the prosecutor of the YOT's views (ABCPA 2014, s 22(8)). This does not, however, give the YOT a power of veto over the making of an application. It is no more than an obligation to consult.

B[13.3] Procedure – Procedure is governed by Part 31 of the Criminal Procedure Rules 2015. The respondent must be given an opportunity to consider what order is proposed and the evidence relied upon in support and to make representations at a hearing (r 31.2).

Rule 31.3 provides (so far as is relevant to CBOs):

'Application for behaviour order and notice of terms of proposed order: special rules

(2) . . . the prosecutor must serve a notice of intention to apply for such an order on—

(a) the court officer;

(b) the defendant against whom the prosecutor wants the court to make the order; and

(c) any person on whom the order would be likely to have a significant adverse effect,

as soon as practicable (without waiting for the verdict).

(3) A notice under paragraph (2) must—

(a) summarise the relevant facts;

(b) identify the evidence on which the prosecutor relies in support;

(c) attach any written statement that the prosecutor has not already served; and

(d) specify the order that the prosecutor wants the court to make.

(4) A defendant served with a notice under paragraph (2) must—

(a) serve written notice of any evidence on which the defendant relies on—
(i) the court officer, and
(ii) the prosecutor,

(b) in the notice, identify that evidence and attach any written statement that has not already been served.

(7) Where the prosecutor wants the court to make an anti-social behaviour order or a criminal behaviour order, the rules about special measures directions in Part 29 (Measures to assist a witness or defendant to give evidence) apply, but—

(a) the prosecutor must apply when serving a notice under paragraph (2); and

(b) the time limits in rule 29.3(a) do not apply.'

The court cannot proceed in the offender's absence unless it is satisfied that he has had adequate notice of the time and place of the adjourned hearing, but this does not apply to the making of an interim order (ABCPA 2014, s 23(6), s 26(3)).

B[13.4] **Evidence and publicity** – Section 23 of ABCPA 2014 provides that the court may consider evidence led by both parties and it does not matter whether the evidence would have been admissible in the proceedings in which the offender was convicted.

As to the procedure for admitting hearsay evidence, see CrimPR, rr 31.6–31.8.

Section 31 of ABCPA 2014 applies the special measures directions of the Youth Justice and Criminal Evidence Act 1999 to CBO proceedings.

Section 49 of the Children and Young Persons Act 1933 (restrictions on reports of proceedings in which children and young persons are concerned) is disapplied to CBO proceedings involving youths, but s 39 does apply and this gives the court the discretion to prohibit the publication of certain information which would identity the child or young person. Narrative on s 39 can be found at **D[1B.7]**.

B[13.5] **Requirements, duration, variation and discharge of orders** – A CBO may contain prohibitions and/or requirements. If a CBO includes a requirement it must specify the person responsible for supervising compliance; this may be an individual or an organisation (ABCPA 2014, s 24(1)). The court must receive evidence on the enforceability and suitability of the requirement from the individual or, in the case of an organisation, an individual representing that organisation (ABCPA 2014, s 24(2)). The grounds for making a CBO (see B[8.9]) differ from those which applied to CRASBOs. It should be noted in particular that the second part of the test for the making of a CBO uses the term 'help in preventing' which is clearly wider than the CrASBO condition of 'necessary to protect'. It should also be noted that CBOs may include positive requirements as well as prohibitions; CrASBOs could only contain prohibitions.

The effect of the changes made by the 2014 Act was considered in *DPP v Bulmer* [2015] EWHC 2323 (Admin), 165 NLJ 7666, [2015] WLR (D) 355. Section 22 of ABCPA 2014 did not oblige a CBO to contain a positive requirement which addressed the underlying cause of the offending behaviour; it simply enabled it to do so. The 2014 Act had not changed the emphasis when making such an order from 'necessity and protection', which had been the case for making an anti-social behaviour order (ASBO), to 'help and prevention'; nor had the addition of a power to impose a positive requirement by section 22 of the 2014 Act changed the emphasis. Parliament had replaced one regime, designed to prevent anti-social behaviour, with another more flexible one. That flexibility came from the removal of the requirement that the order be 'necessary' and also from the possibility of having positive requirements in the order to address the underlying cause of the anti-social behaviour as well as prohibitions. The fact that the 2014 Act was concerned with whether the order would 'help' to prevent the proscribed behaviour rather than whether it was 'necessary' to do so had lowered the hurdle to be overcome. However, the lowering of the hurdle had not changed the nature of the exercise to be carried out by the court, which remained one of judgment and evaluation. What had been said in earlier decisions on ASBOs about the process to be carried out remained relevant to criminal behaviour orders.

Exclusion areas provide clarity as compared with prohibitions of certain sorts of behaviour. Where the anti-social behaviour had taken place in a particular locality, if the fact that the person would simply move his/her anti-social behaviour to another locality was seen as an important factor against making an order, the court would in effect be deciding not to protect those in his/her primary area of activity. The court also considered the relevance of failure to respond to past orders and the power to arrest somebody already subject to an ASBO. The former is not in itself a reason for not making an order. It could indeed be a reason for varying the order or imposing a new one with different prohibitions and/or requirements. As to the latter, orders need to empower the police to take action before the anti-social behaviour they are designed to prevent takes place. Relying on the ordinary power to arrest on reasonable suspicion may be insufficient to provide pre-emptive protection from a person with a history of anti-social behaviour to those who are or are likely to be affected by the behaviour.

In *R v Janes* [2016] EWCA Crim 676, [2016] 2 Cr App R (S) 27, [2016] Crim LR 785. the defendant was a self-employed gardener. He committed two offences of fraud in circumstances where he had significantly overcharged an elderly man. In addition to imposing 18 months' imprisonment the judge made a CBO for a period of ten years prohibiting the defendant from:

> '(a) approaching or entering, directly or indirectly, any address in the United Kingdom, whether on his own or on others' behalf, for the purpose of offering his own or others' services for garden or building maintenance or any other business or work whatsoever (this prohibition includes dropping leaflets or flyers advertising his own or others' services through letterboxes); (b) instructing others to do any of the acts specified above, whether on his own behalf, or on behalf of any firm of which he is the owner, or company of which he is a shareholder, director, officer, or company secretary.'

The defendant appealed on the grounds it was a one-off offence by a self-employed gardener who had not committed a similar offence in 20 years of such trade, he was illiterate and innumerate and would not, therefore, easily find alternative work. The Court of Appeal rejected the argument that the CBO was wrong in principle. A sustained course of conduct was unnecessary, and there was no limit in the CBO jurisdiction to the sort of unruly behaviour that had led to the making of ASBOs. The defendant could seek work on his release provided he did not 'tout', and it would 'help to prevent' fraud of the kind involved in the present case if the defendant worked under the control of a supervising employer. The term of the order was, however, excessive and was reduced to three years.

In *R v Brown-Morgan (Samuel)* [2016] EWCA Crim 1903, [2017] 1 WLR 118, [2017] 1 Cr App R (S) 33, the appellant appealed against a CBO made on his conviction of three counts of possession of Class A drugs with intent to supply. All three offences were committed in public areas of Swindon. The order prohibited him from: entering Wiltshire; entering parts of Southwark; being together in a public place with seven named associates; carrying a mobile phone not registered to his own name; and carrying a knife or bladed article in any public place. It was held that the first condition for making an order was satisfied, having regard to the repeated supplies of drugs and their circumstances. As to the second condition:

> '16 There was material before the Judge to indicate that the proscribed area in Southwark may be a source of drugs which Mr Browne-Morgan then supplied. There was material to show that Mr Browne-Morgan was in the company of one of the named individuals when stopped in late 2014 and found to have been in possession of Class B drugs. There was material going to the association of that named individual with the other named individuals, and (as the judge put it) that "all of you are associated together as members of a particular gang".
>
> 17 Moreover there was material to show that that gang was violent, and that one of its members had been found in possession of a 10-inch knife when stopped by police, and these were reasons for prohibition 5 of the CBO. A pre-sentence report of November 2011 assessed Mr Browne-Morgan as posing a high risk of harm to members of the general public. The report expressed the view that Mr Browne-Morgan would need to make a conscious effort to distance himself from the area of London Borough of Southwark and his lifestyle and associates.
>
> 18 There was further material, and the Judge considered all of it. Almost inevitably the material was of varying precision and quality, but taken together it cannot be said that the judge was not entitled to consider that restricting Mr Browne-Morgan's movements in a particular area of London and his association with particular individuals for a period would help in preventing the behaviour to which the CBO was directed. It is not in issue that prohibitions 1 and 4 have a sufficient nexus to future behaviour. In our judgment so do prohibitions 2, 3 and 5.'

(As to the second condition, the Court of Appeal substituted, for reasons of proportionality and clarity, 'not to congregate in a public place in a group or two or more persons in a manner causing or likely to cause any person to fear for their safety'.)

B[13.6] **Judicial guidance.** In *R v Boness, R v Bebbington* [2005] EWCA Crim 2395, [2006] 1 Cr App R (S) 690, [2005] 169 JP 621 the Court of Appeal gave the following guidance in relation to the making and terms of CRASBOs, which, as explained above, continues to have relevance as to the process the court must carry out.

(1) An ASBO had to be precise and capable of being understood by the offender. It followed that the court should ask itself, before making an order, whether the terms of the order were clear so that the defendant would know precisely what it was that he was prohibited from doing (it would be wrong to make an ASBO against an offender who by reason of mental health would not have the capacity to understand or comply with the terms of the order: *R (on the application of Cooke) v Director of Public Prosecutions* [2008] EWHC 2703 (Admin), 172 JP 596).

(2) There must be evidence of anti-social behaviour (see *R (on the application of Mills) v Birmingham Magistrates' Court* [2005] EWHC 2732 (Admin), (2005) 170 JP 237, 170 JPN 473). Evidence of later behaviour showing a propensity to behave in an anti-social manner was capable of being relevant, to the question of whether the defendant acted in an anti-social manner at the times and at places alleged in a section complaint. Post-complaint behaviour was also relevant to whether an order was necessary to protect persons from further anti-social acts: see *Birmingham City Council v Dixon* [2009] EWHC 761(Admin), 173 JP 233, (2009) Times, 13 April. Following a finding that the

defendant had acted in an anti-social manner (whether or not the act constituted a criminal offence), the test for making an order that prohibited the offender from doing something was one of necessity (see *R v W; R v F* [2006] EWCA Crim 686, [2006] 3 All ER 562, 170 JPN 716). (In that context, the prohibition on associating with a named individual, who was not the subject of an ASBO with a reciprocal prohibition on association, was held to be lawful in *Hills v Chief Constable of Essex Police* [2006] EWHC 2633 (Admin), 171 JP 14).

(3) Each separate order prohibiting a person from doing a specified thing had to be necessary to protect persons from further anti-social acts by him. Accordingly, any order had to be tailor-made for the individual defendant, not designed on a word processor for use in every case.

(4) The purpose of an order was preventative, not to punish. The use of an ASBO to punish a defendant was unlawful.

(5) Where the ASBO was being sought as ancillary to a criminal sentence or disposal, the court should not allow itself to be diverted by a defendant's representative at the sentencing stage in the hope that the court might make such an order as an alternative to prison or other sanction. It might be better for the court to decide the substantive sentence and then move on to consider whether an ASBO should be made or not after sentence has been pronounced, albeit at the same hearing [subject to the power of the court to adjourn consideration of an ASBO to a later date (Crime and Disorder Act 1998, s 1C as amended)].

(6) The court should not impose an order which prohibited a defendant from committing a specified criminal offence, if the sentence which could be passed following conviction for the offence should be a sufficient deterrent. It followed that an ASBO should not be used merely to increase the sentence of imprisonment which a defendant was liable to receive. Whilst different considerations might apply where the maximum sentence was a fine, the court had still to go through all the steps to ensure that the order was necessary. [In that context, a prohibition on carrying knives or bladed articles in a public place was held to be lawful in *Hills v Chief Constable of Essex* supra, as the order was intended to cover behaviour not caught by s 139 Criminal Justice Act 1988, namely the carrying of knives or bladed articles with a blade of less than three inches in a public place.]

(7) The corollary to (6) above was that a court should be reluctant to impose an order which prohibited a defendant from committing a specified criminal offence. The aim of an ASBO was to prevent anti-social behaviour, by enabling action to be taken before the anti-social behaviour it was designed to prevent was to take place.

(8) The terms of the order had to be proportionate in the sense that they had to be commensurate with the risk to be guarded against. That was particularly important where an order might interfere with a defendant's right under the European Convention of Human Rights.

Section 25 of ABCPA 2014 governs duration. A CBO takes effect on the day it is made unless the offender is already subject to a CBO, in which case the court can direct that the order will commence on the expiry of the earlier order. If the subject is under 18 years of age the order must be for a fixed period in the range one to three years. In the case of an adult, the order must be for a fixed term of at least two years or of indefinite duration. Section 26 of ABCPA 2014 provides that if the court adjourns the hearing for a CBO it can make an interim order if it thinks it just to do so which will last until the final hearing or until further order.

Section 27 of ABCPA 2014 governs variation or discharge. Either the offender or the prosecution may apply for variation or discharge. Where a previous application has been dismissed, that party cannot make a further application without the consent of the court or the agreement of the other party. The power to vary includes power to include additional prohibitions or requirements.

The Crown Court has no power to amend or vary a Criminal Behaviour Order made by a magistrates' court: *R v Potter* [2019] EWCA Crim 461, [2019] Cr App R (S) 5.

Section 28 of ABCPA 2014 provides for the review of orders every 12 months in the case of under-18 offenders.

B[13.7] Breach – Breach of a CBO is punishable in the same way as breach of an ASBO or CrASBO (ABCPA 2014, s 30).

The sentencing guideline on breach of a criminal behaviour order (which also applies to breach of anti-social behaviour order) is reproduced at B[2.5], ante.

B[14]
Criminal courts charge

Introduction to criminal courts charge

B[14.1] The Criminal Justice and Courts Act 2015 introduced the criminal courts charge by the insertion of ss 21A–21F in the Prosecution of Offences Act 1985 The charge is intended to offset some of the cost of running the criminal courts. It applies only to persons aged at least 18 at the time of the offence (or, in the case of breach proceedings, at the time of the original offence), but it is then obligatory. The court must not take into account its duty to impose the charge or any order so made when dealing with a person for an offence or for failure to comply with any of the orders listed in B[14.2] below: Prosecution of Offences Act 1985, s 21A(1), (2), (4).

When obligatory

B[14.2] A magistrates' court must make an order when dealing with a person for: an offence; failure to comply with a community order, any of the community requirements of a suspended sentence order; a supervision requirement imposed under s 256AA of the Criminal Justice Act 2003: Prosecution of Offences Act 1985, s 21B(1).

No charge is payable if the court grants an order of absolute discharge or makes an order under s 37 of the Mental Health Act 1983: Regulation 2 of the Prosecution of Offences Act 1985 (Criminal Courts Charge) Regulations 2015, SI 2015/796.

Charging levels

B[14.3] The charging levels are set by the Prosecution of Offences Act 1985 (Criminal Courts Charge) Regulations 2015, SI 2015/796. Originally, the charging levels ranged from £100 to £1,200. However, the Prosecution of Offences Act 1985 (Criminal Courts Charge) (Amendment) Regulations 2015, SI 2015/1970, omitted reg 3 of, and the Schedule to, the original instrument with the effect that the amount of the charge would no longer be specified from the commencement date of the amending Regulations, namely 24 December 2015. Consequently, under the current state of the Regulations there is nothing to impose. However, charges imposed prior to 24 December 2015 remain payable and are enforceable as on summary conviction: Administration of Justice Act 1970, Part 1 of Sch 9, para 9A.

Enforcement

B[14.4] A magistrates' court may remit the whole or part of the criminal courts charge, but this is subject to a number of restrictions: Prosecution of Offences Act 1985, s 21E.

It is our view, however, that the court retains the ability, subsequent to conviction (see further the narrative on the (victims') surcharge at **B[50]**) to impose a day's detention in default of payment under s 135 of the Magistrates' Courts Act 1980. It is the view of the Justices' Clerks Society, however, that 'split enforcement' is precluded by the terms of the Magistrates' Courts Act 1980, s 150(3) and that the exercise of the power under s 135 must, therefore, relate to all the sums adjudged to be paid by the conviction or order in question; ie it cannot be exercised solely in relation to the charge where other sums imposed under the conviction or order, eg compensation, are also outstanding.

B[15]
Custodial sentences

B[15.1] There are three main forms of custodial sentence: imprisonment, detention in a young offender institution and detention and training orders. By virtue of the CJA 2003, sentences of custody plus and intermittent custody will be available nationally from a date to be appointed. Assuming the provisions of the CJA 2003 are implemented, the new sentencing disposals will only apply to offences committed on or after the operative date.

B[15.2] **Imprisonment** (at B[34]) is confined to defendants over the age of 21 years (**18 years). The minimum period is 5 days (**14 days) and the maximum is that fixed by statute. There is one other form of imprisonment – the suspended sentence.

B[15.3] **Detention in a young offender institution** (at B[19]) is the equivalent of imprisonment for those under 21. The minimum age is 18 years for both males and females. (**From a date to be appointed sentences of detention in a YOI will be replaced by imprisonment for offences committed on or after the operative date.)

B[15.4] The general minimum for 18–21 year old offenders is 21 days. In the case of detention in a young offender institution imposed for breach of a supervision order made on release from such an institution a term not exceeding 30 days may be imposed. (**B[15.2] will apply to offences committed on or after the appointed date.)

B[15.5] The maximum term is generally the maximum term that an adult could receive for the offence. The maximum is 12 months for two indictable offences.

B[15.6] **Detention and training orders.** are available for 12 to 17 year old offenders inclusive. The court may order a period of 4, 6, 8, 10, 12, 18 or 24 months, half of which will be detention in a training centre and half of which will be supervised in the community. The offence must carry a sentence of four months or more were an adult to be charged with a similar offence. Accordingly, a detention and training order is not available in the case of a youth convicted of an offence of criminal damage where the damage alleged is below £5,000 (*Pye v Leeds Youth Court* [2006] EWHC 2527 (Admin), [2006] All ER (D) 16 (Oct)).

B[15.7] **Presence of the accused.** If the proceedings were instituted by an information followed by summons, or by a written charge, the court shall not in absence impose a custodial sentence or order that a suspended sentence shall take effect; in any other case, where such a sentence or order is imposed or made, the offender must be brought before the court before he begins to serve the sentence and the sentence will not be effective until this happens: Magistrates' Courts Act 1980, s 11(3), (3A) and (5).

B[15.8] **Restrictions on imposing custodial sentences.** A person shall not be sentenced to a custodial sentence (immediate or suspended) unless he is legally represented. The exceptions to this are:

(a) representation was made available to him for the purposes of the proceedings under Part 1 of the Legal Aid, Sentencing and Punishment of Offenders Act 2012 but was withdrawn because of his conduct or because it appeared that his financial resources were such that he was not eligible for such representation;
(b) he applied for such representation and the application was refused because it appeared that his financial resources were such that he was not eligible [for such representation; or
(c) having been informed of his right to apply for such representation and having had the opportunity to do so, he refused or failed to apply: Powers of Criminal Courts (Sentencing) Act 2000, s 83.

B[15.9] A court may not pass a custodial sentence in any form on an offender of any age unless it is satisfied that:

(a) the offence, or the combination of the offence and one or more offences associated with it, was so serious that neither a fine alone nor a community sentence can be justified for the offence; or
(b) the offender fails to express a required willingness to comply with a requirement in a community order; or
(c) the offender fails to comply with an order for pre-sentence drug testing (CJA 2003, s 161(2));
(d) in the case of an offender aged under 18, the court must obtain a pre-sentence report. The pre-sentence report must be in writing and cannot be given orally. (For older offenders, see B[15.22], below. For mentally disordered persons, see B[15.23], below.)

B[15.10]–[15.15] In forming such an opinion a court must take into account all such information about the circumstances of the offence (including any associated offences and any aggravating or mitigating factors) as is available to it, which will almost invariably include information in a pre-sentence report (see below). A court may also take into account any information about the offender which is before it. The court may take into account previous convictions and previous failures to respond to sentences when assessing the seriousness of current offending.

B[15.16] Exceptionally ((b) above) the court may impose a custodial sentence where the defendant refuses to give his consent to a requirement in a community order proposed by the court which requires his consent.

B[15.17] Apart from the exceptional case, the court must state in open court that it is of the opinion that either one or other of the criteria (a), (b) or (c) apply and why it is of that opinion. In any case, the court must explain to the offender in ordinary language why it is imposing a custodial sentence on him.

Even where the custody threshold is reached the court should take into account:

- the clear intention of the threshold test is to reserve custody as a punishment for the most serious offences;
- passing the custody threshold does not mean that a custodial sentence should be deemed inevitable; custody can still be avoided in light of personal mitigation or where there is a suitable intervention in the community which provides sufficient restriction (by way of punishment) while addressing the rehabilitation of the offender to prevent future crime. However, where the offence would otherwise appear to warrant a term of imprisonment within the Crown Court's jurisdiction, it is for the Crown Court to make that judgement;
- the approach to the imposition of a custodial sentence should be as follows:
  (a) Has the custody threshold been passed?
  (b) If so, is it unavoidable that a custodial sentence be imposed?
  (c) If so, can that sentence be suspended? (Sentencers should be clear that they would have imposed a custodial sentence if the power to suspend had not been available.)
  (d) If not, impose a sentence which takes immediate effect for the shortest possible term commensurate with the seriousness of the offence (CJA 2003, s 153(2)).

The Sentencing Council's definitive guideline on the Imposition of Community and Custodial Sentences states:

> 'Passing the custody threshold does not mean that a custodial sentence should be deemed inevitable. Custody should not be imposed where a community order could provide sufficient restriction on an offender's liberty (by way of punishment) while addressing the rehabilitation of the offender to prevent further crime. For offenders on the cusp of custody, imprisonment should not be imposed where there would be an impact on dependants which would make a custodial sentence disproportionate to achieving the aims of sentencing.'

Immediate or suspended?

The above guideline states that factors indicating it would not be appropriate to suspend are:

- offender presents a risk/danger to the public;
- appropriate punishment can only be achieved by immediate custody;
- there is a history of poor compliance with court orders.

Factors indicating it may be appropriate to suspend are:

- there is a realistic prospect of rehabilitation;
- a strong personal mitigation;
- immediate custody will result in significant harmful impact upon others.

In *R v Ebbs* [2019] EWCA Crim 175, [2019] All ER (D) 142 (Feb), while a sentence of 12 months' imprisonment for an offence of affray, which resulted in a serious injury, at a football match, when the offender was under the influence of drink, was justified, the judge was wrong not to order a pre-sentence report and not to suspend the sentence; all three factors set out in the guideline as indicating it may be appropriate to suspend the sentence in fact applied, namely: a realistic prospect of rehabilitation, strong personal mitigation and the fact that immediate custody would result in a significant harmful impact on others.

Length of custodial sentences

B[15.18] A custodial sentence passed by a court shall be for such term (not exceeding the permitted maximum) as in the opinion of the court is commensurate with the seriousness of the offence, or a combination of the offence and other offences associated with it.

B[15.19] In determining sentence the court must have regard to the guidelines set by the Sentencing Guidelines Council and, if it departs from those guidelines, the court must state its opinion and reasons in open court and give an explanation to the offender in ordinary language.

B[15.20] In forming an opinion on the appropriate length of sentence the court must take into account all such information about the circumstances of the offence (including any associated offences and any aggravating or mitigating factors) as is available to it (such as a pre-sentence report).

Section 108 of the Legal Aid, Sentencing and Punishment of Offenders Act 2012 inserted s 240ZA of the Criminal Justice Act 20031 in place of s 240. The effect is to disapply the discretion to withhold credit for time on remand in custody for the offence or a related offence; instead, such time is to be calculated and applied administratively. There are three exceptions, however, where credit for time on remand in custody does not apply, namely:

(a) if, on any day on which the offender was remanded in custody in connection with the offence, the offender was also detained in connection with any other matter, that day is not to count as time served;

(b) a day counts as time served in relation to only one sentence, and only once in relation to that sentence;
(c) a day does not to count as time served as part of any period of 28 days served by the offender before automatic release.

Consecutive and concurrent sentences, where a prisoner has not been released between serving such sentences, are counted as one sentence for the purpose of deducting remand time.

For the purpose of crediting time on remand in custody, a suspended sentence is to be treated as a sentence of imprisonment when it takes effect and is to be treated as imposed by the order under which it takes effect.

The 2003 Act provisions on credit for time on remand apply to any sentence of imprisonment, whether it is: an original sentence of imprisonment; one imposed for breach/revocation of a community order; one imposed by way of activation of a suspended sentence; one imposed in default of payment of a sum adjudged to be paid by way of a conviction; one imposed for want of sufficient distress to satisfy any sum of money; or one imposed for failure to be or abstain from doing anything required to be done or left undone.

It was previously the position that a suspended sentence should not be imposed in a case where the offender had spent time on remand in custody which was equivalent to any immediate term of imprisonment which could be imposed (which is now beyond question), but that the court might nonetheless make a community order. The removal of the discretion to withhold credit when re-sentencing for breach of such an order may result in reconsideration of the latter, though an order for the rehabilitation of the offender may remain open even in a case where the offender has already spent more time on remand in custody than any term of imprisonment which the offence merits.

Sections 21 and 22 of the Criminal Justice and Immigration Act 2008 introduced new provisions which apply to offenders on bail subject to a qualifying curfew condition, defined as a condition to remain at one or more specified places for a total of not less than nine hours in any given day combined with an electronic monitoring condition. In summary, such offenders were entitled, subject to exceptions made by rules, and subject to the court's discretion to withhold credit on interests of justice grounds, to have half the period spent on such curfew count towards any sentence of imprisonment imposed for the offence.

Significant changes were made by the s 109 of the Legal Aid, Sentencing and Punishment of Offenders Act 2012. Principally, the changes were:

(a) a new method of calculating the 'credit period';
(b) the enactment of exceptions;
(c) the removal of the 'interests of justice' discretion to withhold credit.

The credit period is calculated by taking the following, five steps:

(1) Add–
The number of days on which the offender's bail was subject to the relevant conditions, including the first whether the condition applied for the whole of the day or not, but excluding the last if the offender spends the last part of it in custody.
(2) Deduct–
Any of the above days on which the offender was subject to an electronically monitored curfew requirement in connection with any other sentence including on release under home detention curfew) or temporarily released from prison in relation to another sentence.
(3) Deduct–
From the remaining days, the number of days during that remainder on which the offender has broken either or both of the relevant conditions.
(4) Divide–
The result by two.
(5) Round up–

If necessary, to the nearest round number.

A day of the credit period counts as time served in relation to only one sentence and only once in relation to that sentence.

A day of the credit period is not to count as time served as part of any period of 28 days served by the offender before automatic release. (This prevents any shortening of any recall made under s 255B of the 2003 Act where the maximum length of the recall is 28 days.)

If a curfew is not accompanied by an electronic tag the statutory conditions are not met and a court is entitled to refuse to give credit for the curfew period even though it qualified in terms of length and the defendant complied with it; there might, however, be circumstances where some allowance should be made, for example, where there are two defendants for sentence who have been subject to curfews but for some reason only one defendant has been electronically tagged.

The court needs to know the exact number of days of the curfew since it is for the court to work out and announce the number of days to be credited.

In passing a detention and training order on a juvenile offender the [youth] court must also take into account any time spent on secure remand when fixing the length of sentence, and time spent on remand must be calculated and announced at time of sentence in cases of imprisonment.

Pre-sentence report

B[15.21] This means a report in writing which is made by a probation officer (or social worker) with a view to assisting the court in determining the most suitable method of dealing with an offender and contains such information as to such matters as may be prescribed by the Secretary of State.

B[15.22] Before forming an opinion on the necessity for, and appropriate length of, a custodial sentence the court should obtain a pre-sentence report. Although a custodial sentence is not invalidated by the court's failure to obtain such a report, magistrates will no doubt continue to wish to meet the statutory requirement in all cases where an offender is in jeopardy of losing his liberty despite the 'let out' clause 'unless the court is of the opinion that it is unnecessary to obtain a pre-sentence report' (see **B[15.9]**).

As to ordering pre-sentence reports on committal for sentence, see **B[8.16]**, ante.

Post-release supervision

B[15.22A] Significant changes to supervision after release were made by the Offender Rehabilitation Act 2014. The Act applies to offences committed on or after 1 February 2015 (see the Offender Rehabilitation Act 2014 (Commencement No 2) Order 2015, SI 2015/40, art 2).

The Act provides for post-sentence supervision for offenders who receive more than one day but less than two years' imprisonment (amending the duty to release prisoners serving less than 12 months unconditionally at the half way point of the sentence).

The new regime applies to offenders aged at least 18 years at the half way point of the custodial term. (New s 243A(1) and (1A) of the Criminal Justice Act 2003 reduces the duty to release unconditionally to: (a) offenders serving a sentence of a term of one day; (b) offenders serving a term of less than 12 months who are aged under 18 at the half way point of the sentence; and (c) offenders serving a sentence of less than 12 months for an offence committed before the commencement of s 1 of the 2014 Act.)

The effects of the changes are noted in the sections dealing with particular custodial sentences, eg Imprisonment B[34].

Mentally disordered offenders

B[15.23] Where the offender is, or appears to be, mentally disordered, the court must, unless in the circumstances of the case it appears unnecessary to do so, obtain a medical report made orally or in writing by a doctor approved under the Mental Health Act 1983 as having special experience in the diagnosis or treatment of mental disorder.

B[15.24] Where a court is considering a custodial sentence in such circumstances it must consider:

(a) any information before it which relates to his mental condition (whether given in a medical report, a pre-sentence report or otherwise); and
(b) the likely effect of such a sentence on that condition and on any treatment which may be available for it.

B[16]

Deferment of sentence

(Powers of Criminal Courts (Sentencing) Act 2000, ss 1A–1F)

Limitations

B[16.1] The offender must consent, and undertake to comply with any requirements the court considers appropriate to impose during the period of deferment.

B[16.2] Deferment may be used only once in respect of any one offence.

B[16.3] The court must be satisfied that it is in the interests of justice to defer sentence, having regard to the nature of the offence and the character and circumstances of the offender.

B[16.4] There are no limitations as to age or the nature of the offence. The court may have regard to the defendant's conduct after conviction (including if appropriate any reparation made by him) and any change in his circumstances. The court may impose requirements as to the offender's conduct during the deferment and appoint an appropriate supervisor with their consent.

Section 1ZA of the Powers of Criminal Courts (Sentencing) Act 2000 was inserted by the Crime and Courts Act 2013 with the effect that the requirements of a deferred sentence may include restorative justice requirements, defined as a requirement to participate in an activity:

(a) where the participants consist of, or include, the offender and one or more of the victims;
(b) which aims to maximise the offender's awareness of the impact of the offending concerned on the victims; and
(c) which gives an opportunity to a victim or victims to talk about, or by other means express experience of, the offending and its impact.

The imposition of a restorative justice requirement requires, in addition to the offender's consent and undertaking, the consent of every other person who would be a participant in the activity concerned.

Ancillary orders

B[16.5]–[16.7] None, because this is not a final disposal of the case, except that a restitution order may be made.

General considerations of deferment of sentence

B[16.8] This power of the court might be less confusing if it were referred to as deferment of sentencing. There is no question, contrary to what is sometimes believed, that the court decides upon a sentence but postpones announcing it in case it changes its mind.

B[16.9] Only exceptionally may a custodial sentence be imposed after deferment; it is advised that where an offender is liable to be ordered to serve a suspended sentence it will rarely be appropriate to defer sentencing him for the offence which he has committed during the operational period.

B[16.10]–[16.15] Deferment is appropriate when some event may occur in the near future which, according to whether it occurred or not, would influence the court when imposing a sentence. It may be, for example, that the offender has an uncertain chance of employment upon which voluntary compensation depends. There should always be some reason for deferment which can be stated so that the offender knows what is expected of him and may, as he thinks fit, take steps to improve his situation from a sentencing point of view. Great care should be exercised, however, not to use this power as a threat or coercion or to give an offender an opportunity to buy his way out of prison by making compensation (especially if he may do so by resorting to further offences).

B[16.16] The concern of a victim of the offence should be borne in mind when considering deferment; one effect of deferment, for example, may be to postpone the day when compensation is ordered.

B[16.17] The maximum period for which sentencing may be deferred is six months. The defendant cannot be remanded. A summons or warrant may be issued if he fails to appear on the date for sentencing specified by the court.

Sentence after the period of deferral. The deferred sentence did not represent part of the sentence which was imposed at the end of the period of deferment. Section 204(3) of the Criminal Justice Act 2003 provided that the period with regard to curfew requirements runs from the date of the making of the community order. The six-month curfew condition of the deferred sentence was a factor which needed to be taken into account at the point of sentence when determining the community requirements of the order and the length of any requirement: *R v Saeed Ali* [2011] EWCA Crim 2747, 176 JP 1.

B[16.18] The court will obviously wish to be informed at the end of the period of deferment whether the offender has done what it was hoped he would do, or whether the event has taken place which was the reason for the deferment. In many cases it will be convenient to ask the supervising officer to report, but in some cases only the offender or a third party will be able to satisfy the court. It is advised that the court when deferring sentence makes clear arrangements at that time as to how such information is to be provided.

B[16.19] The court might consider that a conditional discharge for six months but imposed immediately would achieve the court's objectives. It is not necessary, but may be desirable, that the same magistrates should impose the sentence as those who deferred sentence. Provided the requirement and reasons for deferment are explicitly stated, the legal adviser will note them and bring them to the attention of the sentencing court.

B[16.20] The offender can be returned to court if the supervisor has reported to the court that the offender has failed to comply with one or more requirements in respect of which an offender gave an undertaking (s 1B(2)(c)). The can issue a summons or warrant for the offender to appear before it (s 1B(3)).

B[16.21] If the offender commits an offence during the period of deferment, the court convicting him of that offence may deal with the deferred case even though the period of deferment has not expired. Section 1C sets out the powers of the Crown Court and magistrates' courts in these cases. If the original sentence was deferred by a Crown Court, it must be a Crown Court that passes sentence for both offences. The power to commit to the Crown Court for sentence under s 3 PCC(S)A 2000 is retained by s 1D(2)(b) PCC(S)A 2000**.

B[17] Deportation

B[17.1]

> . . . a person who is not a British citizen shall be . . . liable to deportation from the United Kingdom if, after he has attained the age of seventeen, he is convicted of an offence for which he is punishable with imprisonment and on his conviction is recommended for deportation by a court

Immigration Act 1971, s 3(6)

B[17.2] **Recommendation.** A magistrates' court cannot order deportation, but it can make a recommendation to the Home Secretary for the deportation of the convicted person. In sentencing the offender the court does not have to take into account what might happen in the offender's own country if he is returned (*R v Ukoh* [2004] EWCA Crim 3270, [2005] Crim LR 314, (2004) Times, 28 December).

B[17.3] **Not a British citizen.** The following categories of citizens cannot be deported:

(a) British citizens;
(b) Commonwealth citizens having a right of abode in the UK;
(c) Commonwealth citizens not included in (b) and citizens of the Republic of Ireland provided in either case they were such citizens at the time of the coming into force of the Immigration Act 1971 and were ordinarily resident in the UK and at the time of conviction had been ordinarily resident in the UK and Islands for the last five years.

B[17.4] The following may be deported:

(a) Commonwealth citizens not included in (b) or (c) above;
(b) aliens;
(c) aliens being citizens of countries which are members of the European Community.

B[17.5] **Age of seventeen.** A person shall be deemed to have obtained the age of 17 at the time of his conviction, if on consideration of any available evidence he appears to have done so to the court.

B[17.6] **Convicted.** Means found to have committed the offence.

B[17.7] **Punishable with imprisonment.** This means punishable with imprisonment in the case of a person over 21 years even though the defendant himself may not be liable to imprisonment.

Criteria for making a recommendation

General considerations

B[17.8] Under s 32 of the UK Borders Act 2007 'foreign criminals' (as defined) are subject to automatic deportation by the Secretary of State if the offender is sentenced to a term of at least 12 months' imprisonment for a single offence, or any term imprisonment for a specified offence; the former may justify structuring the sentence in a way that reduces the individual terms to less than 12 months' imprisonment where deportation is not in the court's contemplation and it is not appropriate owing to the offender's character and lengthy residence in the UK: *R v Farhad Hakimzadeh*

[2009] EWCA Crim 959, [2010] 1 Cr App Rep (S) 49, [2009] Crim LR 676. However, it was held in *R v Mintchev* [2011] EWCA Crim 499, [2011] 2 Cr App Rep (S) 465, [2011] Crim LR 483 that, as a matter of principle, it would not be right to reduce an otherwise appropriate sentence to avoid the automatic deportation provisions. *Hakimzadeh* was concerned with the structure of the sentence, not its overall length, and there was no warrant for widening its ratio. See also *R v Turner* [2010] EWCA Crim 2897, [2011] 2 Cr App R (S) 18.

B[17.8A] There is no rule of law that the deportation of a settled migrant who has lawfully spent all or the major part of his or her childhood and youth in the host country constitutes a disproportionate interference with the migrant's art 8 rights unless the state can show, irrespective of the other factors involved, that there are very serious reasons, connoting very serious offences, for the migrant's deportation: *R (Akpinar) v Upper Tribunal, AV (Democratic Republic of Congo) v Secretary of State for the Home Department* [2014] EWCA Civ 937, 1 WLR 2015. As to the effect of the UK Borders Act 2007(deportation of foreign criminals) and the relevant provisions of the Statement of Changes in Immigration Rules (1994) (HC 395), introduced by paragraphs 111 and 114 of the Statement of Changes in Immigration Rules (2012) (HC 194), see *MF (Nigeria) v Secretary of State for the Home Department* [2014] 1 WLR 544, considered at paras 53 and 54 of *Akpinar*, supra.

B[17.9] The use of the power to recommend deportation following the commencement of the UK Borders Act 2007 was comprehensively reviewed in *R v Kluxen* [2010] EWCA Crim 1081, [2011] 1 Cr App R (S) 249, [2010] Crim LR 657. Since the coming into force of the 2007 Act it is no longer appropriate for courts to recommend the deportation of 'foreign criminals' as defined. It serves no useful purpose. See, for example, *R v Gheorghiu* [2013] EWCA Crim 281, [2013] 2 Cr App Rep (S) 74, where the Court of Appeal quashed a recommendation for deportation in respect of a Romanian sentenced to 14 months' imprisonment for burglary. The Secretary of State must make a deportation order under s 32(5) of the Act unless one or more of the exceptions specified in s 33 apply. The court does not need to explain that it is not recommending deportation because the Act applies, though it may do so.

Where the offender is not a British citizen, but is not caught by the definition of 'foreign criminal', the court must decide whether or not to recommend deportation. The test laid down in *R v Nazari* [1980] 3 All ER 880, [1980] 1 WLR 1366, CA was whether the continued presence of the offender in the UK was to its detriment. In *Nazari* none of the defendants was a citizen of the EU. In C-30/77 *R v Bouchereau* [1978] QB 732, [1981] 2 All ER 924n, ECJ (a decision of the ECJ) the opposite was the case (ie all the defendants were EU citizens) and it was said that the court must consider whether or not the offender's conduct constituted 'a genuine and sufficiently serious threat to the requirements of public policy affecting one of the fundamental interests of society'. This test was based on an EC Directive since replaced by EC Directive 2004/38, the main elements of which were transposed into UK law by the Immigration (European Economic Area) Regulations 2006 (SI 2006/1003). In the court's view the *Bouchereau* test survived the new Directive and, for practical purposes, was substantially the same as the *Nazari* test. Both set a high bar before a recommendation for deportation could be made, and it would be rare that either test would be satisfied in relation to an offender who was not a 'foreign criminal'. An offender who repeatedly committed minor offences could conceivably do so, as could a person who committed a single offence involving the possession or use of false identity documents, but such cases would be rare and the Secretary of State could in any event deport such a person if this was deemed to be conducive to the public good.

B[17.10] For an example of a false identification document case, see *R v Junab* [2012] EWCA Crim 2660, [2013] 2 Cr App R (S) 23, [2013] Crim LR 348. The overall prison term was seven months, but the recommendation for deportation was upheld by the Court of Appeal. Such offences can be of such seriousness, in the sense of the detrimental effect the offender's continued presence can have on society, as to merit a recommendation for deportation and the court is obliged to ignore the consequences of deportation for the offender and the offender's family.

In *R v Mobeen Ul Haq* [2013] EWCA Crim 1478, [2014] 1 Cr App Rep (S) 307 the appellant was convicted of an act of outraging public decency and four offences of sexual assault. He targeted lone women on the public transport system. He was sentenced to a total of 12 months' imprisonment and made the subject of a sexual offences prevention order preventing him from using public transport in a particular area for five years. A recommendation for deportation was made and upheld by the Court of Appeal. The *Nazari* test was met. The sexual offences prevention orders (SOPO) was of limited temporal geographical scope and thus did not reduce the prospect of detriment sufficiently to make the recommendation for deportation inappropriate.

B[17.11] *Matters not to be taken into account* On those rare occasions when deportation is being considered there are five matters that should not be taken into account: (a) Convention rights under the ECHR, for the reasons explained in *R v Carmona* [2006] EWCA Crim 508, [2006] 1 WLR 2264, [2006] 2 Cr App R (S) 662; (b) the effect that a recommendation might have on innocent persons not before the court; (c) the political situation in the country to which the offender might be deported; (d) art 38 of the Directive, since this applies to an 'expulsion decision' and not a recommendation; and (e) the 2006 Regulations, again because they apply only to the decision of the Secretary of State.

Procedure

B[17.12] Where such a recommendation is made a certificate in the form set out in Home Office Circular No 215/1972, should be sent as soon as possible to: The Court Collator, Group 3R, Home Office, Lunar House, 40, Wellesley Road, Croydon, CR9 2BY. With this certificate a copy of any probation officer's report considered by the court should be sent.

B[17.13]–[17.16] Where the court makes a recommendation and the offender is not sentenced to imprisonment or liable to be detained for any other reason, he is liable to be detained under para 2 of Sch 3 to the Immigration Act 1971 (ie until a deportation order is made and until his removal from the UK). Where the court makes a recommendation for deportation of an offender not otherwise liable to be detained and does not direct that he shall not be detained in custody, a copy, certified by the clerk, of the court's certificate of recommendation should be given to the officer whose duty it is to take the offender to prison (or other place of detention), as an authority for his conveyance and detention there. Where a commitment is issued for non-payment of a fine (after time has been allowed) it should be noted thereon that the offender is also subject to a recommendation for deportation. Although the Bail Act 1976 does not apply, it is suggested that courts consider, when deciding whether or not to order the release of a person recommended for deportation, the principal grounds for withholding bail in criminal proceedings. A person who is recommended for deportation may be released subject to such restrictions as to residence and as to reporting to the police as the court may direct; see Sch 3, para 4, below. If the court directs that the offender should not be detained pending consideration of the recommendation, the Secretary of State asks that his attention shall be called to this fact in a separate covering letter when the certificate of recommendation is forwarded. Where an offender who has been recommended for deportation appeals against the recommendation or the related conviction or against sentence, notification should be sent to the Home Office (at the address quoted above) of the appeal. For general guidance as to the appropriate practice when a recommendation for deportation is made, see Home Office Circulars No 215/1972, 113/1978 and 37/1988.

B[18]

Deprivation of property and forfeiture

(Powers of Criminal Courts (Sentencing) Act 2000, s 143)

B[18.1] Any court which has convicted a person of an offence and

(a) is satisfied
  (a) that any property
  (b) which has been lawfully seized from him or was in his possession or under his control at the time when he was apprehended for the offence or when a summons in respect of it was issued
  (c) has been used for the purposes of committing, or facilitating the commission of any offence or was intended to be used for that purpose

or

(b) the offence (or an offence taken into consideration) consists of unlawful possession of property in the circumstances of (ii) above

may make an order to deprive him of that property.

Where the grounds for making an order are in dispute, the court should follow normal adversarial practice and arrive at a determination. Thus, where an offender pleaded guilty to an offence of possession of Class A drugs with intent to supply, and £4,600 in cash had been found in his home, and the defendant had sought to provide a legitimate explanation for the existence of the cash, a forfeiture should not have been made without a proper enquiry, including giving the defendant the opportunity to call evidence: *R v Jones* [2017] EWCA Crim 2192, [2018] 1 Cr App R (S) 35.

B[18.2] **Property.** Does not include land. For applications under the Proceeds of Crime Act 2002 see F[5.47]. It was held under previous legislation that a deprivation order was not available in respect of property which appeared to be the proceeds of earlier offences: *R v Neville* (1987) 9 Cr App R (S) 222, [1987] Crim LR 585, CA; see, however, *R v Farrell* (1988) 10 Cr App R (S) 74 in which an offender's 'working capital' for future drugs dealing was held to be properly forfeited.

B[18.3] **Possession.** Usually means physical possession but can include a legal right to possession. If there is any dispute the legal adviser should be consulted.

B[18.4] **Facilitating.** This includes the taking of any steps after the offence has been committed to dispose of property which is the subject of the crime or to avoid apprehension or detection. The property need not have been used personally by the defendant provided he intended it be used for criminal purposes, even by another.

B[18.5] **The effect of an order.** The accused is deprived of his rights in the property which passes into the possession of the police. Accordingly, the true owner retained the full rights including a right to possession. The owner had a right to bring civil proceedings for conversion. The orders under PCCSA 2000, s 143 made by the magistrates' court provided no defence to the police to that right, unless possibly there was a public policy defence (*Chief Constable of Merseyside Police v Owens*

[2012] EWHC 1515 (Admin), 176 JP 688, 176 CL&J 353 considered): *O'Leary International Ltd v Chief Constable of North Wales and CPS* [2012] EWHC 1516 (Admin), 176 JP 514, 176 CL&J 370.

The provisions of the Police Property Act 1897 (at F[1]) apply and a person may claim the property provided that he satisfies the court that either:

(a) he had not consented to the offender having possession; or
(b) he did not know, and had no reason to suspect, that the property was likely to be used for the purpose of committing an offence.

B[18.6] If no successful claim is made the property will be sold and the proceeds disposed of in the same way as described at F[1].

B[18.7] Sentencing. The court may make an order under this section in respect of the property whether or not it also deals with the offender in respect of the offence in any other way, and may combine the making of the order with an absolute or conditional discharge.

B[18.8] Under previous legislation it was stated that an order depriving a defendant of property should not be made for the purpose of realising assets to pay fines or compensation (*R v Kingston-upon-Hull Stipendiary Magistrates, ex p Hartung* [1981] RTR 262, 72 Cr App Rep 26).

B[18.9] In considering whether to make a deprivation order the court shall have regard:

(a) to the value of the property; and
(b) to the likely financial and other effects on the offender of the making of the order (together with any other order the court is contemplating) (see *Trans Berckx BVBA v North Avon Magistrates' Court* [2011] EWHC 2605 (Admin));
(c) any representations of the parties (*R v Ball* [2002] EWCA Crim 2777, [2003] 2 Cr App Rep (S) 92), [2003] Crim LR 122.

B[18.10] In *R v De Jesus* [2015] EWCA Crim 1118, [2015] 2 Cr App R (S) 44 D and X were driving around Cardiff in D's Mercedes and they confronted two students and robbed them of their wallets and mobile phones. The substantive sentence was 28 months' detention in a young offender institution and a deprivation order in respect of the car which was worth £14,000. The order was quashed on appeal. When viewed in conjunction with the custodial sentence it was a penalty which was excessive in itself and created an unreasonable disparity between D and X.

B[18.11]–[18.15] But where the offence has resulted in a person suffering personal injury, loss or damage and the court has not been able to make a compensation order because of the defendant's lack of means, the proceeds of sale resulting from a deprivation order may be used for compensation.

B[18.16] This order only takes effect after a period of six months in order to allow a person to make a claim under the Police Property Act 1897.

B[18.17] Motor vehicles. Where a person commits an offence under the Road Traffic Act 1988 which is imprisonable, or an offence of manslaughter, or an offence under s 35 of the Offences Against the Person Act 1861 (wanton and furious driving) by driving, attempting to drive, or being in charge of a vehicle, or failing to comply with a requirement under s 7 or 7A of the Road Traffic Act 1988 (failing to provide specimens), or failing to comply with s 170(2) or (3) of the Road Traffic Act 1988 (duty to stop and give information or report accident) the vehicle shall be regarded for the purposes of ss 143 and 144 of the Powers of Criminal Courts (Sentencing) Act 2000 as used for the purpose of committing the offence (or aiding, abetting, etc, its commission: PCC(S)A 2000, s 143(6), (7). The significant use of a motor vehicle (manoeuvring to strike and injure a victim) justified the forfeiture of a motor car in *R v Norman* [2007] EWCA Crim 624, [2007] All ER (D) 523 (Mar).

B[18.18] **Disqualification for any offence:** See C[5.45].

B[18.19] **Other provisions for forfeiture.** Formerly the provisions described here were confined to offences punishable with at least 2 years' imprisonment, but now they are available without regard to maximum penalty and so will overlap with some existing forfeiture powers, eg forfeiture of controlled drugs and firearms and the Customs and Excise Management Act 1979. See for example *Customs and Excise Comrs v Newbury* [2003] EWHC 702 (Admin), [2003] 2 All ER 964, [2003] 1 WLR 2131.

B[19]

Detention and training orders

(Powers of the Criminal Courts (Sentencing) Act 2000, s 100)

B[19.1] Detention and training orders (DTO) are the sole custodial sentence available to the courts which may be imposed on a young person aged under 18. Age is generally determined at the time of conviction rather than at sentence. The order is available in the youth court only and not the adult court. The DTO is a rehabilitative order and not simply a young offender's prison.

B[19.2] Where a DTO is a likely sentence the Youth Offending Team (YOT) will make contact with the Youth Justice Board before the court hearing to establish if accommodation is available.

B[19.3] All the restrictions outlined at **B**[34] and contained in s 152 CJA 2003 apply to the detention and training order because it is defined as a custodial sentence.

B[19.4] Before making an order the court must be satisfied that the following additional circumstances pertain:

(a) the offender is not less than 12 years of age when the offence for which he is to be dealt with is found proved;

(b) where the offender is under the age of 15 years at the time of conviction the courts must be of the opinion that he is a persistent young offender. Note this is 15 years old at the time of conviction (*R v Thomas* (2004) although *R v LM* [2002] EWCA Crim 3047, [2003] 2 Cr App Rep (S) 124, [2003] Crim LR 205 suggests that a non-persistent offender who is under the age of 15 when a non-grave offence is committed cannot receive a DTO even when 15 at date of conviction.

This is not the same definition as a persistent offender for the purposes of monitoring speed of case throughput (*R v Charlton* (2000) 164 JP 685, CA). Where there has been a series of offences on separate occasions the offender may be persistent (*R v Smith* (2000) 164 JP 681, [2000] Crim LR 613, CA). For the purposes of determining whether an offender under the age of 15 at the time of conviction is a 'persistent offender', the court may have regard to earlier offences for which he has been cautioned by the police: *R v D* [2000] Crim LR 867, CA. The court may also have regard to offences committed after the present offence: *R v Cawthorn* [2001] Crim LR 51, (2000) Times, 27 October, CA. Persistent offending does not necessarily involve persistent appearances before a court: *R v Charlton*, above. A series of offences committed over only two days may be sufficient to qualify an offender as persistent, even though he has no previous convictions: *R v Smith (Andrew Benjamin)* (2000) 164 JP 681, CA. However, two reprimands for dissimilar offences and three robberies committed on the same occasion within a minute or so of each other could not be characterised as 'persistent offending': *R v L* [2012] EWCA Crim 1336, [2013] 1 Cr App R (S) 56.

B[19.5] Where the court passes a detention and training order it must state in open court that it is of the opinion that the above conditions are satisfied.

B[19.6] **Length of the order.** The term of a detention and training order (DTO) may only be 4, 6, 8, 10, 12, 18 or 24 months. However the court may not exceed the maximum term the Crown Court could impose for the offence on an offender aged 21. This means that the youth court must be careful when dealing with a case of summary criminal damage (maximum three months' imprisonment) making a DTO unavailable (see *Pye v Leeds Youth Court* [2006] EWHC 2527 (Admin), [2006] All ER (D) 16 (Oct)) and cases involving other summary offences where the maximum sentence for an adult offender will generally be less than six months (see further para B[19.8] below). Note that the offence of absconding under s 6 of the Bail Act 1976 carries only three months' imprisonment in the magistrates' court, but 12 months in the Crown Court. Thus, a DTO may be made.

B[19.6A] **Credit for time on remand.** Time spent on a qualifying remand is not automatically credited, but in determining the term of a detention for an offence the court shall take into account any period of remand in custody and any period on bail subject to a qualifying curfew condition. 'Custody' includes police detention, remands in or committed to custody by an order of a court, remands to youth detention accommodation and remands, admission removal to hospital under certain provisions of the Mental Health Act 1983, but not remands to local authority accommodation: Powers of Criminal Courts (Sentencing) Act 2000, s 101(8), (11), (12).

B[19.7] In assessing the length of sentence the court must give credit for a guilty plea. The level of credit will generally depend on the time the plea of guilty is entered. Sentencing Guideline Council guidance prescribes up to a third for a timely guilty plea, reducing to roughly 10% for a plea entered on the date set for trial: see B[45.46]. In rare circumstances credit for plea can be withheld altogether. The court must also take into account in deciding the overall the length of the DTO any time spent on remand in custody: *R v B* [2000] Crim LR 870. See also *R (on the application of A) v Governor of Huntercombe Young Offender Institution* [2006] EWHC 2544 (Admin), 171 JP 65, 171 JPN 345.

B[19.8] Consecutive orders may be made provided that the overall term does not exceed 24 months. Where the defendant is already serving a DTO and the period of supervision of that order has not begun, the new period may be ordered to run consecutively to the earlier order provide the effect would not be that the offender would be subject to a DTO which exceeds 24 months: PCC(S)A 2000, s 101((3), (4) and (6). Where the term exceeds 24 months, the excess shall be treated as remitted: PCC(S)A 2000. s 101(5). The new order must be for one of the specified terms, but the aggregate period need not be: *R v Norris* (2000) 164 JP 689.

Section 133 of the Magistrates' Courts 1980 limits the total aggregate sentence that can be imposed on an adult offender to six months (unless the court is dealing with two or more offences which are triable either way, where the maximum becomes 12 months). While this provision does not apply to youths, it has been held to be contrary to modern sentencing principles and practice that a youth should be dealt with more severely than an adult. Therefore a sentence of two consecutive terms of four months detention and training in respect of offences where only one offence was triable either way was held to be unlawful in *B v Leeds Crown Court* [2016] EWHC 1230 (Admin), (2016) 180 JP 282 (not following *LCC v DPP* [2001] EWHC Admin 453, (2001) 165 JP 806, sub nom *C v DPP* [2002] 1 Cr App Rep (S) 189, [2001] Crim LR 671).

Period of supervision and breach of supervision requirements

B[19.9] Before the amendments made by the Offender Rehabilitation Act 2014 the position was that half the order would be served in a secure establishment and the offender would then be subject to supervision for the remainder of the DTO. Following the 2014 Act the position is as follows.

(1) Where the term of the DTO is 24 months, or the offender was aged under 18 at the half way point of the term, or the offences were committed before 1 February 2015, the period of supervision of an offender who is subject to a detention and training order:

(a) shall begin with the offender's release, whether at the half-way point of the term of the order or otherwise; and
(b) shall end when the term of the order ends: Powers of Criminal Courts (Sentencing) Act 2000, s 103(1).

(2) Where the term of the DTO is less than 24 months and the offender was aged 18 or over at the half way point of the term, and the offences were committed on or after 1 February 2015 the period of supervision ends 12 months after the half-way point of the DTO. For example, if the DTO was for 10 months, the offender will be released after serving five months and will then be under supervision for 12 months and not five months as before: Criminal Justice Act 2003, s 106B, s 103, as respectively inserted and amended.

Ie where the case falls within (1) above the position is unchanged, but where the case falls with (2) the amendments made by the 2014 apply.

The Secretary of State may by order provide that the period of supervision shall end at such point during the term of a detention and training order as may be specified in the order, but the Secretary of State may not make such provision where the offender was aged 18 or over at the half-way point of the term of the DTO and the order was made for offences committed on or after 1 February 2015: Powers of Criminal Courts (Sentencing) Act 2000, s 103(2), (2A).

During the period of supervision, the offender shall be under the supervision of:

(a) a probation officer; or
(b) a member of a youth offending team;

and the category of person to supervise the offender shall be determined from time to time by the Secretary of State: Powers of Criminal Courts (Sentencing) Act 2000, s 103(3).

The offender must be given a notice from the Secretary of State specifying the category of person for the time being responsible for his supervision and any requirements with which he must for the time being comply. The notice must be given to the offender before the period of supervision commences and before any alteration in the category of person to supervise the offender or in the supervision requirements takes effect: Powers of Criminal Courts (Sentencing) Act 2000, s 103(6), (7).

Where a detention and training order is in force in respect of an offender and it appears on information to a justice of the peace that the offender has failed to comply with the supervision requirements, the justice:

(a) may issue a summons requiring the offender to appear at the place and time specified in the summons; or
(b) if the information is in writing and on oath, may issue a warrant for the offender's arrest: Powers of Criminal Courts (Sentencing) Act 2000, s 104(1).

Any summons or warrant issued as above shall require the offender to appear or to be brought:

(a) before a youth court acting for the local justice area in which the offender resides; or
(b) if it is not known where the offender resides, before a youth court acting for the same local justice area as the justice who issued the summons or warrant: Powers of Criminal Courts (Sentencing) Act 2000, s 104(2).

Where a defendant is sentenced to detention and training orders in respect of a number of offences they constitute a single order for the purpose of breach proceedings and the court record should show a breach of only one order; where, however, there are two separate breaches of the licence, for example – failing to keep in touch with the supervising officer and failing to reside where directed – there is a need to lay separate informations in respect of each of the kinds of breach, though within each kind there is no need to allege each of the instances separately: *Stewart v Doncaster Youth Offending Team* [2003] EWHC 1128 (Admin), (2003) 167 JP 381.

If it is proved to the satisfaction of the youth court before which an offender appears or is brought that he has failed to comply with requirements specified in the notice from the Secretary of State, that court may:

(a) order the offender to be detained, in such youth detention accommodation as the Secretary of State may determine, for such period, not exceeding the maximum period, as the court may specify;
(b) order the offender to be subject to such period of supervision, not exceeding the maximum period, as the court may specify; or
(c) impose on the offender a fine not exceeding level 3 on the standard scale: Powers of Criminal Courts (Sentencing) Act 2000, s 104(3).

As to the application of ss 103–105 of the 2000 Act to supervision orders made under this power, see s 104A. In broad terms, the further period works in the same way as a period of supervision under a DTO. Thus, requirements can be imposed and the order can again be enforced under s 104.

As to the interaction of orders of detention for breach with other sentences, see s 104B of the 2000 Act.

The maximum period referred to in (a) and (b) above is the shorter of:

(i) three months; and
(ii) the period beginning with the date of the offender's failure and ending with the last day of the term of the detention and training order: Powers of Criminal Courts (Sentencing) Act 2000, s 104(3A).

Where the failure if found to have occurred over two or more days, it is to be taken to have occurred on the first of those days: Powers of Criminal Courts (Sentencing) Act 2000, s 104(3B).

A court may order a period of detention or supervision, or impose a fine, before or after the end of the term of the detention and training order: Powers of Criminal Courts (Sentencing) Act 2000, s 104(3C).

A period of detention or supervision imposed under, respectively, (a) and (b) above begins on the day the order is made and may overlap to any extent with the period of supervision under the detention and training order: Powers of Criminal Courts (Sentencing) Act 2000, s 104(3D).

Following the abolition of detention in a young offender institution, where an order of detention is made under (a) above in the case of a person who has attained the age of 18 the order has effect to require the person to be detained in prison for the period specified in the order: Powers of Criminal Courts (Sentencing) Act 2000, s 104(4A).

Detention and training order: offences during currency of order

B[19.10] The power to deal with a person for an offence committed during the currency of a detention and training order arises if that person after his release and before the date on which the term of the order ends, commits an offence punishable with imprisonment in the case of a person aged 21 or over, and before or after that date, he is convicted of that offence ('the new offence'). The court by or before which such a person is convicted of the new offence may, whether or not it passes any other sentence on him, order him to be detained in such youth detention accommodation as the Secretary of State may determine for the whole or any part of the period which:

(a) begins with the date of the court's order; and
(b) is equal in length to the period between the date on which the new offence was committed and the date on which the term of the detention and training order ends: Powers of Criminal Courts (Sentencing) Act 2000, s 105(1), (2).

The period for which a person under these provisions is ordered to be detained in youth detention accommodation:

(a) shall, as the court may direct, either be served before and be followed by, or be served concurrently with, any sentence imposed for the new offence; and
(b) in either case, shall be disregarded in determining the appropriate length of that sentence: Powers of Criminal Courts (Sentencing) Act 2000, s 105(3).

Section 105 must, however, be read together with s 106 of the Act, which provides, in subs (1):

> '(1) Where a court passes a sentence of detention in a young offender institution in the case of an offender who is subject to a detention and training order, the sentence shall take effect as follows—
>
> (a) if the offender has been released by virtue of subsection (2), (3), (4) or (5) of section 102 above, at the beginning of the day on which it is passed;
> (b) if not, either as mentioned in paragraph (a) above or, if the court so orders, at the time when the offender would otherwise be released by virtue of subsection (2), (3), (4) or (5) of section 102.'

As originally enacted, s 106(1)(a) was subject to s 105(3)(a), but this ceased to be the case in consequence of the repeal made by the Criminal Justice Act 2003, Sch 32(1), para 112. Thus, where a term of detention in a young offender institute is imposed upon a person who is in breach of a DTO, the new sentence must have immediate effect: see *R v McGeechan* [2019] EWCA Crim 235, [2019] 2 Cr App R S 12 [2019] Crim LR 554.

Where the new offence is found to have been committed over a period of two or more days, or at some time during a period of two or more days, it shall be taken to have been committed on the last of those days: Powers of Criminal Courts (Sentencing) Act 2000, s 105(4).

Guidance of the Sentencing Council on custodial sentences for children and young people

B[19.11] The following guidance appears in the definitive guideline 'Sentencing Children and Young People Overarching Principles and Offence Specific Guidelines for Sexual Offences and Robbery'.

Custodial sentences

A custodial sentence should always be used as a last resort. If offence specific guidelines for children and young people are available then the court should consult them in the first instance to asses whether custody is the most appropriate disposal. The available custodial sentences for children and young people are:

Youth Court	Crown Court
Detention and training order for the following periods:	Detention and training order (the same periods are available as in the youth court)
4 months;	Long-term detention (under section 91 of the Powers of Criminal Courts (Sentencing) Act 2000)
6 months;	Extended sentence of detention or detention for life (if dangerousness criteria are met)
8 months;	Detention at Her Majesty's pleasure (for offences of murder)
10 months;	
12 months;	
18 months; or	
24 months.	

6.42 Under both domestic and international law, a custodial sentence must only be imposed as a 'measure of last resort;' statute provides that such a sentence may be imposed only where an offence is "so serious that neither a fine alone nor a community sentence can be justified." (Criminal Justice Act 2003, s 152(2).) If a custodial sentence is imposed, a court must state its reasons for being satisfied that the offence is so serious that no other sanction would be appropriate and, in particular, why a YRO with intensive supervision and surveillance or fostering could not be justified.

6.43 The term of a custodial sentence must be the shortest commensurate with the seriousness of the offence; any case that warrants a DTO of less than four months must result in a non-custodial sentence. The court should take account of the circumstances, age and maturity of the child or young person.

6.44 In determining whether an offence has crossed the custody threshold the court will need to assess the seriousness of the offence, in particular the level of harm that was caused, or was likely to have been caused, by the offence. The risk of serious harm in the future must also be assessed. The pre-sentence report will assess this criterion and must be considered before a custodial sentence is imposed. A custodial sentence is most likely to be unavoidable where it is necessary to protect the public from serious harm.

6.45 Only if the court is satisfied that the offence crosses the custody threshold, and that no other sentence is appropriate, the court may, as a preliminary consideration, consult the equivalent adult guideline in order to decide upon the appropriate length of the sentence.

6.46 When considering the relevant adult guideline, the court **may** feel it appropriate to apply a sentence broadly within the region of half to two thirds of the adult sentence for those aged 15–17 and allow a greater reduction for those aged under 15. This is only a rough guide and must not be applied mechanistically. In most cases when considering the appropriate reduction from the adult sentence **the emotional and developmental age and maturity of the child or young person is of at least equal importance as their chronological age.**

6.47 The individual factors relating to the offence and the child or young person are of the greatest importance and may present good reason to impose a sentence outside of this range. The court should bear in mind the negative effects a short custodial sentence can have; short sentences disrupt education and/or training and family relationships and support which are crucial stabilising factors to prevent re-offending.

6.48 There is an expectation that custodial sentences will be particularly rare for a child or young person aged 14 or under. If custody is imposed, it should be for a shorter length of time than that which a young person aged 15–17 would receive if found guilty of the same offence. For a child or young person aged 14 or under the sentence should normally be imposed in a youth court (except in cases of homicide or when the dangerous offender criteria are met).

6.49 The welfare of the child or young person must be considered when imposing any sentence but is especially important when a custodial sentence is being considered. A custodial sentence could have a significant effect on the prospects and opportunities of the child or young person and a child or young person is likely to be more susceptible than an adult to the contaminating influences that can be expected within a custodial setting. There is a high reconviction rate for children and young people that have had custodial sentences and there have been many studies profiling the effect on vulnerable children and young people, particularly the risk of self harm and suicide and so it is of utmost importance that custody is a last resort.

Detention and training order (DTO)

6.50 A court can only impose a DTO if the child or young person is legally represented unless they have refused to apply for legal aid or it has been withdrawn as a result of their conduct.

6.51 If it is determined that the offence is of such seriousness that a custodial sentence is unavoidable then the length of this sentence must be considered on an individual basis. The court must take into account the chronological age of the child or young person, as well as their maturity, emotional and developmental age and other relevant factors, such as their mental health or any learning disabilities.

6.52 A DTO cannot be imposed on any child under the age of 12 at the time of the finding of guilt and is only applicable to children aged 12–14 if they are deemed to be a persistent offender. (See section on persistent offenders on page 22 [of the definitive guideline 'Sentencing Children and Young People Overarching Principles and Offence Specific Guidelines for Sexual Offences and Robbery'].)

6.53 A DTO can be made only for the periods prescribed – 4, 6, 8, 10, 12, 18 or 24 months. Any time spent on remand in custody or on bail subject to a qualifying curfew condition should be taken into account when calculating the length of the order. The accepted approach is to double the time spent on remand before deciding the appropriate period of detention, in order to ensure that the regime is in line with that applied to adult offenders. (*R v Eagles* [2006] EWCA Crim 2368.) After doubling the time spent on remand the court should then adopt the nearest prescribed period available for a DTO.

Long-term detention

6.54 A child or young person may be sentenced by the Crown Court to long-term detention under section 91 of the Powers of Criminal Courts (Sentencing) Act 2000 if found guilty of a grave crime and neither a community order nor a DTO is suitable.

6.55 These cases may be sent for trial to the Crown Court or committed for sentence only (Powers of Criminal Courts (Sentencing) Act 2000, s 3(b) (as amended).) (see section two [of the definitive guideline 'Sentencing Children and Young People Overarching Principles and Offence Specific Guidelines for Sexual Offences and Robbery'] for further information).

6.56 It is possible that, following a guilty plea, a two year detention order may be appropriate as opposed to a sentence of section 91 detention, to account for the reduction.

B[20]

Detention for one day at the court or at a police station

(Magistrates' Courts Act 1980, s 135)

B[20.1] Magistrates may order the detention of a defendant aged 18 years or more in the precincts of the court house or at a police station for any period until 8 pm on the day of the hearing; but the offence must be punishable with imprisonment or alternatively the detention must be an alternative to payment of a fine. The magistrates should announce at what time the defendant can be released, taking into account that the defendant should be given the opportunity of returning home that day.

B[20.2] Section 135 is a useful tool for deeming served financial orders which, for practical or other reasons, cannot or should not be enforced, and the power to impose imprisonment cannot be exercised because of the restrictions imposed by ss 82 and 88 of the Magistrates' Courts Act 1980. These restrictions include the prohibition of imprisonment on the date of conviction for non payment of the criminal courts charge and the (victims') surcharge (the exception that other financial orders on conviction may be so enforced where the defendant is a serving prisoner or is then sentenced to immediate custody is disapplied to the charge and surcharge by s 82((1A)). Consequently, it was thought that s 135 could be invoked as a way round s 82(1A). However, it was held in *Frimpong v Crown Prosecution Service (Secretary of State for Justice intervening)* [2015] EWCA Crim 1933, [2016] 1 Cr App R (S) 59 that the power under s 135 was intended as an alternative to imprisonment and it had no application where imprisonment was imposed. The case was concerned with the criminal courts charge, for which no sums are currently set, but the decision must apply equally to the (victims') surcharge since, as noted above, both are on the same statutory footing.

B[21]

Detention in a young offender institution

(Powers of the Criminal Courts (Sentencing) Act 2000, s 96)

B[21.0] **Section 96 will be repealed by the Criminal Justice and Courts Services Act 2000, Sch 7 from a date to be appointed. Section 96 will, in effect, be replaced by the provisions to be found in Chapter 3 (ss 181–195 inclusive) of the CJA 2003. This will make available prison sentences, and suspended sentences for offenders aged 18 years or more at the date of conviction (not sentence). It is likely the new regime will only apply to offences committed on or after the operative date ie from a date to be appointed. See B[34] onwards.

There are currently transitory provisions making suspended sentence available for offenders aged 18–20 years inclusive. However, see *R v Campbell* [2006] EWCA Crim 726, [2006] 2 Cr App Rep (S) 626.

General matters regarding detention in a young offender institution

B[21.1] Imprisonment is not available for offenders under the age of 21 years. The main custodial provision for these offenders is detention in a young offender institution. This is subject to the criteria restricting the use of custodial sentences imposed by the Powers of the Criminal Courts (Sentencing) Act 2000.

B[21.2] As with all custodial sentences the court must explain:

(a) how long the defendant will spend in custody;
(b) how long after release he will be liable to recall; and
(c) how long after release he will be subject to supervision.

Limitations

B[21.3] **Imprisonable offence.** The offence of which the offender is found guilty must be punishable with imprisonment in the case of a person aged 21 or over.

B[21.4] **Age of offender.** The minimum age for male and female offenders is 18 years. In either case the offender must be under 21 years.

B[21.5] **Criteria for imposing a custodial sentence.** The court must be of the opinion:

(a) that the offence, or the combination of the offence and any other offences associated with it, was so serious that only such a sentence can be justified for the offence;
(b) where the offence is a violent or sexual offence, that only such a sentence would be adequate to protect the public from serious harm from the offender.

B[21.6] **Other circumstances in which custody may be imposed.** Nothing in paragraphs (a) and (b) above prevents the court imposing a custodial sentence on an offender who refuses to consent to a community sentence proposed by the court which requires his willingness to comply with a proposed requirement. A court may also impose custody for a wilful and persistent breach of a community order.

B[21.7] So serious. See B[34.6]. The court must take account of all the information about the circumstances of the offence including any aggravating or mitigating factors as are available to it.

B[21.8] Associated offence. An offence of which the offender has been convicted in the same proceedings or for which he is sentenced at the same time, or an offence taken into consideration.

B[21.9] Violent offence. An offence which leads, or is intended or likely to lead, to a person's death or to physical injury to a person, and includes an offence which is required to be charged as arson.

B[21.10]–[21.15] Sexual offence under the Sexual Offences Act 2003. It does not include offences relating to prostitution. Nor does it include offences in public lavatories.

B[21.16] Protection from serious harm. This refers to protecting members of the public from death or serious personal injury, whether physical or psychological, occasioned by further such offences committed by the offender.

B[21.17] Pre-sentence report. Except where the court considers it unnecessary to do so, the court must obtain and consider a pre-sentence report before forming an opinion on:

(a) whether the offence etc was so serious;
(b) (violent or sexual offence) only custody would be adequate to protect the public etc;
(c) the length of term commensurate with the offence;
(d) (violent or sexual offence) the length of term necessary to protect the public etc.

B[21.18] In all cases where a court is contemplating sentencing a defendant to custody for the first time a report should be obtained: *R v Gillette* (1999) Times, 3 December, CA.

B[21.19] Failure to obtain pre-sentence report. Does not invalidate the sentence but the appeal court must obtain and consider such a report if the court below was not justified in forming an opinion that a report was unnecessary.

B[21.20] Mentally disordered offender. Where an offender is or appears to be mentally disordered, ie suffering from a mental disorder within the meaning of the Mental Health Act 1983, the court must additionally obtain and consider a medical report before passing a custodial sentence unless the court considers it unnecessary to do so. The court must take any such information into account and consider the likely effect of any custodial sentence on his condition and any treatment for it. Failure to obtain a medical report does not invalidate any sentence but one must be obtained and considered by an appeal court.

B[21.21] Legal representation. The offender must first be given the opportunity to be legally represented unless he has failed to take up the offer of legal representation or has been refused legal representation based on financial grounds. Note that the requirement is not that he should be represented, but that he should have an opportunity to be.

B[21.22] Offenders under 18 years. A magistrates' court (as opposed to a youth court) cannot commit defendants aged under 18 years to custody. Such juveniles must be remitted on bail or in local authority accommodation to a youth court which will usually be the youth court for the area in which they reside.

Passing sentence

B[21.23]–[21.24] Maximum length of sentence. Twelve months or the maximum term of imprisonment available for the offence, whichever is the lesser term, six months if suspended.

B[21.25]–[21.30] Minimum length of sentence. 21 days over 18 years of age, 14 days if suspended except for detention imposed where an offender has breached a supervision order made on his release. See B[21.39].

B[21.31] Consecutive terms. Detention in a young offender institution may be ordered to be consecutive to an existing period of detention or, if more than one period of detention is imposed on the same occasion, one period of detention may be ordered to be consecutive to another so, however, that the offender will not be liable to a period of more than 12 months in total. If a longer period is ordered the excess period will be treated as remitted.

B[21.32] Length of custodial sentence. Shall be for a term which is commensurate with the seriousness of the offence or the combination of the offence and other offences associated with it or, in the case of a violent or sexual offence, for such longer term as is necessary to protect the public from serious harm from the offender. The court may suspend the sentence for an operational period of 2 years maximum.

B[21.33] Committal to Crown Court. The longest term of detention available to a magistrates' court in respect of an offender for a single indictable or either way offence is six months. However, in certain circumstances a magistrates' court may commit offenders aged 18 years to the Crown Court for sentence under s 3 Powers of Criminal Courts (Sentencing) Act 2000** (see B[8.2]).

Reasons for decisions

B[21.34] It is the duty of the court to state in open court:

(a) that it is of the opinion that either or both of paragraphs (a) and (b) at B[21.35] apply:
(b) that it is of the opinion that in the case of a violent or sexual offence it is necessary to pass a longer term than is commensurate with the seriousness of the offence to protect the public from serious harm from the offender;
(c) why it is of that opinion;

and in all cases to explain to the offender in open court and in ordinary language why it is passing a custodial sentence on him or such longer term.

How to announce

B[21.35] We have decided to pass a sentence of detention in a young offender institution on the defendant and we are of the opinion that:

(a) **the offence (or the combination of the offence and other associated offence(s) namely [. . . . .]) was so serious that only such a sentence can be justified for the offence; and/or**
(b) **this is a violent/sexual offence and only such a sentence would be adequate to protect the public from serious harm from him**

because [*then explain why either or both of the paragraphs apply*]. (Violent/sexual offence): We are also passing a sentence of detention for a term longer than is commensurate with the seriousness of the offence as this is necessary to protect the public from serious harm from him because [*give reasons*].

Accordingly [*addressing the defendant*] you will be sent to a young offender institution for [*state period*]. On release you will be subject to supervision for [*state how long*] and you will be subject to recall to detention for the next [*state time*] and this is because [*explain in ordinary language why he is receiving a custodial sentence and, where applicable, why he is receiving a term longer than is commensurate with the seriousness of the offence*].

Note – If there is more than one offence it should be clearly stated what the total period of detention is to be.

Ancillary orders

B[21.36] Compensation at B[10]

Costs at B[12]

Disqualification at C[5]

Endorsement at C[5]

Deprivation of property and forfeiture at B[18]

Restitution order at B[42]

Early release and supervision

B[21.37] Persons sentenced to detention under s 96 of the Powers of Criminal Courts (Sentencing) Act 2000 must be released at the half-way point of the sentence: Criminal Justice Act 2003, s 244. As to the length of supervision after release, s 256B of the Criminal Justice Act 2003 was amended by s 4 of the Offender Rehabilitation Act 2014, with the effect that:

(a) if the term was less than 12 months and the sentence was imposed for offences committed before the commencement day, the period of supervision is three months (whether or not the offender is detained for breach of supervision requirements or otherwise);

(b) in all other cases the offender will be on licence for the remainder of the custodial term and then supervised until the end of the period of 12 months immediately after the half-way point of their sentence; for example, an offender sentenced to six months' detention will be released on serving one half of that sentence and will then be on licence for a period of three months followed by a period of supervision of nine months: Criminal Justice Act 2003, s 256AA. (As to the period of licence where the sentence contains terms of imprisonment for offences straddling the commencement of the 2014 Act, see s 264B of the Criminal Justice Act 2003. As to the requirements of the offender which the Secretary of State may specify during the supervision period, see s 256AB of the Criminal Justice Act 2003.)

The commencement day is 1 February 2015.

B[21.38] **Breach of supervision requirements.** For offenders within category (a) above of B[21.37], a magistrates' court may impose detention for up to 30 days or order the offender to pay a fine not exceeding level 3 on the standard scale: Criminal Justice Act 2003, s 256C(4). For offenders in category (b) above of B[21.37], the available sanctions are: committal to prison for a period not exceeding 14 days; a fine not exceeding level 3 on the standard scale; or a 'supervision default order' imposing either an unpaid work requirement or a curfew requirement: Criminal Justice Act 2003, s 256AC.

B[21.39]–[21.45] Failure to comply with requirements as to supervision is punishable by custody of up to 30 days or a fine of up to £1,000.

B[21.46] **Further offences.** Where an offender commits an imprisonable offence before he would (but for his release) have served his sentence in full, the court which deals with him for the later offence may return him to custody for the whole or part of the period which begins with the making of the order of return and is equal in length to the period between the date of commission of the new offence and the date of expiry of the original term.

Sentencing Council's Definitive Guideline

B[21.47] The Sentencing Council has issued a definitive guideline on breach offences. This includes a section on breach of a suspended sentence order and a section on breach of post-sentence supervision. These are reproduced under 'Imprisonment' at B[34.55], post.

B[22]

Discharge (absolute or conditional)

(Powers of Criminal Courts (Sentencing) Act 2000, s 12)

Limitations

B[22.1]

Absolute	–	None.
Conditional	–	minimum period, none,
	–	maximum period, three years.

B[22.2] **Special consideration.** Before making either of these orders the court must be of opinion, having regard to the circumstances including the nature of the offence and the character of the offender, that it is inexpedient to inflict punishment.

Unless there are exceptional circumstances a magistrates' court (which includes a youth court), may not make an order for conditional discharge in respect of an offence committed within two years of a final warning (CDA 1998, s 66(4)).

B[22.3] Before making an order for conditional discharge the court must explain to the offender in ordinary language that if he commits another offence during the period of discharge he will be liable to be sentenced for the offence for which the conditional discharge is given. This is the court's duty and only in the most exceptional circumstances may it be delegated to another person, eg the accused's lawyer.

Ancillary orders

B[22.4]–[22.6] Compensation at B[10]

Costs at B[12]

Disqualification at C[5]

Endorsement at C[5]

Deprivation of property and forfeiture at B[18]

Restitution at B[42]

Legal note

B[22.7] A defendant who is convicted of an offence while subject to a Crown Court conditional discharge may be committed to the Crown Court to be sentenced for the offence for which the conditional discharge was originally ordered, under the Powers of Criminal Courts (Sentencing) Act 2000, s 13(5). He may also be committed to be dealt with for the new offence, under Powers of Criminal Courts (Sentencing) Act 2000, s 6 (*R v Penfold* (1995) 16 Cr App Rep (S) 1016, [1995] Crim LR 666, CA).

General considerations of discharge (absolute or conditional)

B[22.8] It is most important to note that only after the court has decided that it is inexpedient to inflict punishment because of all the circumstances may it make an order for discharge. But magistrates are specifically empowered to make a deprivation order or order for costs and compensation where appropriate: Power of Criminal Courts (Sentencing) Act 2000, s 12(7) as amended. Disqualification and endorsement may be ordered where appropriate.

B[22.9] This is not a conviction for the purposes of the Sex Offenders Act 1997.

B[22.10]–[22.15] No conditions or requirements may be added to either of these orders.

B[22.16] Period of conditional discharge. This must always commence on the pronouncement of sentence. There is no provision to make this period consecutive to any other period.

B[23]

Domestic violence protection notice

Power to issue

B[23.1] Sections 24–30 of the Crime and Security Act 2010 came fully into effect on 8 March 2014. These provisions include the power for an authorising officer to issue a domestic violence protection notice to an alleged perpetrator of domestic violence, and the power for a magistrates' court, on an application made by complaint by a constable, to make a domestic violence protection order.

Contents and service of a domestic violence protection notice

B[23.2] A DVPN must state:

(a) the grounds on which it has been issued,
(b) that a constable may arrest P without warrant if the constable has reasonable grounds for believing that P is in breach of the DVPN,
(c) that an application for a domestic violence protection order under section 27 will be heard within 48 hours of the time of service of the DVPN and a notice of the hearing will be given to P (see **B[24]** below).
(d) that the DVPN continues in effect until that application has been determined, and
(e) the provision that a magistrates' court may include in a domestic violence protection order.

A DVPN must be in writing and must be served on P personally by a constable. On serving P with a DVPN, the constable must ask P for an address for the purposes of being given the notice of the hearing of the application for the domestic violence protection order.

Breach and enforcement of a DVPN

B[23.3] A person arrested for a breach of a DVPN must be held in custody and brought before the magistrates' court which will hear the application for the DVPO under s 27 (see below)—

(a) before the end of the period of 24 hours beginning with the time of the arrest, or
(b) if earlier, at the hearing of that application.

If the person is brought before the court and the hearing is adjourned the court may remand the person.

In calculating when the period of 24 hours mentioned above ends, Christmas Day, Good Friday, any Sunday and any day which is a bank holiday in England and Wales under the Banking and Financial Dealings Act 1971 are to be disregarded.

No penalty is prescribed for breach of an order under the 2010 legislation. Breach of a magistrates' court order (other than for payment of money) is provided for by s 63 of the Magistrates' Courts Act 1980. Where breach of an order is established (to the criminal standard it is submitted) the maximum penalty is:

(a) a fine not exceeding £50 for every day during which P is in default or a sum not exceeding £5,000;
(b) committal to custody until he has remedied his default or for a period not exceeding 2 months.

B[24]

Domestic violence protection order

Application for a domestic violence protection order

B[24.1] Sections 24-30 of the Crime and Security Act 2010 came fully into effect on 8 March 2014. These provisions include the power for an authorising officer to issue a domestic violence protection notice to an alleged perpetrator of domestic violence, and the power for a magistrates' court, on an application made by complaint by a constable, to make a domestic violence protection order.

Conditions for and contents of a DVPO

B[24.2] The court may make a DVPO if two conditions are met.

The first condition is that the court is satisfied on the balance of probabilities that P has been violent towards, or has threatened violence towards, an associated person.

The second condition is that the court thinks that making the DVPO is necessary to protect that person from violence or a threat of violence by P.

Before making a DVPO, the court must, in particular, consider—

(a) the welfare of any person under the age of 18 whose interests the court considers relevant to the making of the DVPO (whether or not that person is an associated person), and
(b) any opinion of which the court is made aware—
  (i) of the person for whose protection the DVPO would be made, and
  (ii) in the case of provision included by virtue of subsection (8), of any other associated person who lives in the premises to which the provision would relate.

But the court may make a DVPO in circumstances where the person for whose protection it is made does not consent to the making of the DVPO.

A DVPO must contain provision to prohibit P from molesting the person for whose protection it is made. Provision required to be included may be expressed so as to refer to molestation in general, to particular acts of molestation, or to both.

If P lives in premises which are also lived in by a person for whose protection the DVPO is made, the DVPO may also contain provision—

(a) to prohibit P from evicting or excluding from the premises the person for whose protection the DVPO is made
(b) to prohibit P from entering the premises,
(c) to require P to leave the premises, or
(d) to prohibit P from coming within such distance of the premises as may be specified in the DVPO.

A DVPO must state that a constable may arrest P without warrant if the constable has reasonable grounds for believing that P is in breach of the DVPO.

A DVPO may be in force for—

(a) no fewer than 14 days beginning with the day on which it is made,
(b) no more than 28 days beginning with that day.

A DVPO must state the period for which it is to be in force.

Breach and Enforcement of a DVPO

B[24.3] A person arrested by virtue of section 28(9) for a breach of a DVPO must be held in custody and brought before a magistrates' court within the period of 24 hours beginning with the time of the arrest.

If the matter is not disposed of when the person is brought before the court, the court may remand the person.

In calculating when the period of 24 hours mentioned in subsection (1) ends, Christmas Day, Good Friday, any Sunday and any day which is a bank holiday in England and Wales under the Banking and Financial Dealings Act 1971 are to be disregarded.

There are further provisions about remand to be found in s 30 of the 2010 Act.

No penalty is prescribed for breach of an order under the 2010 legislation. Breach of a magistrates' court order (other than for payment of money) is provided for by s 63 of the Magistrates' Courts Act 1980. Where breach of an order is established (to the criminal standard it is submitted) the maximum penalty is:

(a) **a fine not exceeding £50 for every day during which P is in default or a sum not exceeding £5,000; or**

(b) **committal to custody until he has remedied his default or for a period not exceeding 2 months.**

B[25]
Drink Banning Orders

B[25.1] The Violent Crime Reduction Act 2006 introduced drink banning orders on conviction and on complaint. These provisions were repealed by the Anti-social Behaviour Crime and Policing Act 2014.

Orders made before the repeal continue to have effect, but they may not be varied to extend the period of the order or any of its provisions: Anti-social Behaviour, Crime and Policing Act 2014, s 21(2), (4) and s 33(2), (3).

At the end of five years beginning with the commencement day, any drink banning orders still in force have effect, with any necessary modifications, as if the provisions of the orders were provisions of injunctions (civil orders) or criminal behaviour orders (orders on conviction): Anti-social Behaviour, Crime and Policing Act 2014, s 21(5) and s 33(4). The commencement day for civil orders is 23 March 2015 (see SI 2015/373, art 4(a)).The commencement day for orders on conviction is 24 October 2014 (see SI 2014/2590, art 3(a)).

B[26]

European protection order

Criminal Justice (European Protection Order) (England and Wales) Regulations 2014

B[26.1] The Criminal Justice (European Protection Order) (England and Wales) Regulations 2014, SI 2014/3300 transpose Directive 2011/99 EU of the European Parliament and of the Council of 3 December 2011 on the European Protection Order.

Orders giving effect elsewhere in the EU to UK protective measures

B[26.2] Where a magistrates' court (and, in certain circumstances, the Crown Court) has made a 'protection measure', ie imposed:

- a prohibition from entering certain localities, places or defined areas where the protected person resides or visits;
- a prohibition or restriction of contact with the protected person by any means (including by telephone, post, facsimile transmission or electronic mail);
- or a prohibition or restriction preventing the individual from approaching the protected person whether at all or to within a particular distance;

the court may, on request where specified conditions are met, in particular that the protected person has decided to reside or stay or is already residing or staying in a Member State other than the UK, make a 'European protection order'. (For the specified conditions, see the Criminal Justice (European Protection Order) (England and Wales) Regulations 2014, reg 4.)

When deciding whether to make an order the court must take into account the length of the period or periods that the protected person intends to reside or stay in the executing State; the seriousness of the need for protection of the protected person while residing or staying in the executing State; and such other matters as it considers appropriate.

A request for a European protection order may be made to the magistrates' court or the competent authority of the executing State. In the latter case the request is transferred to the central authority for England and Wales (the Lord Chancellor) and is treated as a request made to a magistrates' court.

A European protection order must be in the form set out in Annex 1 to the Directive and contain the specified information.

Where a magistrates' court has made a protection measure, it must ensure that the protected person is informed in an appropriate way of the possibility to request a European protection order if the person decides to reside or stay in another Member State and of the basic conditions for making such a request; and advised to submit a request for a European protection order before leaving the UK. If the court refuses to make a European protection order it must inform the protected person of any applicable legal remedy that may be available against the decision.

The court which makes a European protection order must notify the competent authority of the executing State of the European protection order by giving specified documents specified in paragraph to that authority.

Requests from outside the UK

B[26.3] Where a competent authority of a Member State other than the United Kingdom makes a European protection order and makes a request for the recognition of the European protection order, it must send the Annex I form to the central authority for England and Wales which will send it to a magistrates' court. The magistrates' court must decide, without undue delay, whether any of the grounds for refusal to give effect to a European protection order apply. (For the grounds for refusal, see the Criminal Justice (European Protection Order) (England and Wales) Regulations 2014, Sch.)

If the magistrates' court decides that none of the groups for refusal applies, it must give effect to the order. If the magistrates' court decides that one or more of the grounds for refusal applies, it may refuse to recognise the European protection order.

Where the court gives effect to the European protection order the court officer must include in the notice served on the requesting authority the terms of the restraining order made by the court, serve notice of those terms, and of the potential legal consequences of breaching them, on the person restrained by the order made by the court and on the person protected by that order, and serve notice on the Lord Chancellor of any breach of the restraining order which is reported to the court. Where the court refuses to give effect to the European protection order the court officer must include in the notice served on the requesting authority the grounds for the refusal, where appropriate, inform the protected person, or any representative or guardian of that person, of the possibility of applying for a comparable order under the law of England and Wales, and arrange for that person, representative or guardian to be informed of any available avenue of appeal or review against the court's decision. Unless the court otherwise directs, the court officer must omit from any notice served on a person against whom a restraining order may be, or has been, made the address or contact details of the person who is the object of the European protection order: CrimPR 2015, r 31.10.

Means of giving effect within UK

B[26.4] The magistrates' court gives effect to the order by making a restraining order under s 5 of the Protection from Harassment Act 1997.

Provision is made for a magistrates' court to give effect to any modified prohibitions or restrictions made by the issuing state or discharging the order where the competent authority of the issuing State has revoked or withdrawn a European protection order or where the magistrates' court is satisfied the protected person is no longer residing or staying in England and Wales.

B[27]
Exclusion orders

Licensed Premises (Exclusion of Certain Persons) Act 1980

B[27.1] **This Act was to be repealed by the Violent Crime Reduction Act 2006, and replaced by drink banning orders on conviction under ss 6–8 of the latter. However, drink banning orders were implemented only in certain local justice areas and were repealed by the Anti-social Behaviour, Crime and Policing Act 2014 (drink banning orders on conviction and on complaint have been subsumed in, respectively, criminal behaviour orders and injunctions).**

When a person is convicted of an offence (of whatever nature) which was committed on licensed premises and the court which convicts him is satisfied that when he committed the offence he resorted to violence, or offered or threatened violence, the court may make an exclusion order prohibiting him from entering those licensed premises or any other licensed premises which the court may specify in the order. Such an order is made in addition to any sentence imposed, including a discharge.

"Licensed premises" for this purpose means those in respect of which a premises licence under the Licensing Act 2003 has been granted by the relevant local authority authorising the supply of alcohol (within the meaning of s 14 of that Act) for consumption on the premises.

The court must state the period during which the defendant is to be excluded; the minimum period is three months and the maximum is two years. Any person who is subject to such an order and is in the specified premises otherwise than with the express consent of the licensee or one of his staff is guilty of an offence punishable with a fine on level 4 and one months' imprisonment.

Thus, a person convicted of breach of an exclusion order who is also the subject of a suspended sentence (which might be imposed for the offence which gave rise to the exclusion order) will be in jeopardy of having to serve that additional sentence. Courts would probably want to make this point to the defendant both in fairness to him and also perhaps the better to enforce the order. At the time of convicting a person for breach of an exclusion order the court may also determine whether to revoke the order or vary it by deleting the name of any specified premises.

B[27.2] The licensee or his staff may expel from his premises any person whom he reasonably suspects of having entered in breach of an exclusion order and a constable shall at the request of the licensee or his staff, help to expel anyperson whom the constable reasonably suspects of being present in breach of such an order.

B[28]

Fines

For 'Assessment of Fines: Sentencing Process' see B[3] above

Limitations

B[28.1] Offences. The court may fine for any criminal offence.

Surcharge. See B[28.4] below.

B[28.2] Maximum fine. The power of magistrates' courts (unlike that of the Crown Court) to impose a fine is entirely controlled by statute. Therefore the maximum fine for the offence may not be exceeded.

B[28.3] The maximum fine for the vast majority of offences which are only triable by magistrates is expressed as being on one of five levels, each level representing a monetary limit. (The maximum for most offences triable either way is expressed as the 'statutory maximum' or 'prescribed sum'.)

Level 1: maximum fine is £200

Level 2: maximum fine is £500

Level 3: maximum fine is £1,000

Level 4: maximum fine is £2,500

Level 5: maximum fine is £5,000*

(Either way offences: prescribed sum is £5,000*.)

*For offences committed on or after 12 March 2015 an unlimited fine (with some exceptions) replaces the £5,000 limit: see the Legal Aid, Sentencing and Punishment of Offenders Act 2012, ss 85 and 86, and SI 2015/504, art 2.

B[28.4] This is known as the standard scale of fines and it has been devised as an attempt to rationalise the maximum amounts of fines and to provide a simple means of increasing them in inflationary times.

Juveniles

B[28.5] Offender under 14 (a child). Maximum fine is the amount in the statute creating the offence or £250, whichever is less.

B[28.6] Offender 14 to under 18 (young person). Maximum fine is the amount in the statute creating the offence or £1,000, whichever is less.

Parental responsibility for payment

B[28.7] In the case of a person under 16 the court must order the parent or guardian to pay unless either he cannot be found or the court is satisfied that it would be unreasonable to order the parent to pay having regard to the circumstances of the case. Provided the parent has been given the opportunity to attend court, an order for payment may be made against him in his absence. If he is present, he must be given the opportunity of making representations about whether he should be ordered to pay.

B[28.8] Before exercising its power to make an order that a parent should pay a financial order in respect of an offence committed by a child the court must be satisfied that it is reasonable to do so. Before making an order a parent or guardian should be given the opportunity of being heard (PCC(S)A 2000, s 137(4)).

B[28.9] Where the offender is aged 16 or 17, and it would not be unreasonable to do so, the court has a power to make the parent responsible for the financial order.

B[28.10]–[28.15] Where a local authority has parental responsibility for a child in their care or accommodated by them, the local authority is responsible for payment, unless it has done everything reasonably and properly expected of it to protect the public from the young offender (*D (a minor) v DPP* [1995] 16 Cr App Rep (S) 1040, [1995] 3 FCR 725).

Determining the amount of any fine

B[28.16] **Introduction.** The amount of a fine must reflect the **seriousness** of the offence (CJA 2003, s 164(2)). The court must also take into account the **financial circumstances** of the offender; this applies whether it has the effect of increasing or reducing the fine (CJA 2003, s 164(1) and (4)). The **aim** is for the fine to have an equal impact on offenders with different financial circumstances; it should be a hardship but should not force the offender below a reasonable "subsistence" level.

Fine Bands. For the Magistrates' Court Sentencing Guidelines, a fine is normally based on one of three bands, namely A, B or C. The selection of the relevant band and the position of the individual offence within that band, is determined by the seriousness of the offence. In some cases bands D–F may be used even where the community or custody threshold have been passed.

Starting points based on first time offender pleading not guilty

	Starting point	Range
Fine Band A	50% of relevant weekly income	25%–75% of relevant weekly income
Fine Band B	100% of relevant weekly income	75%–125% of relevant weekly income
Fine Band C	150% of relevant weekly income	125%–175% of relevant weekly income
Fine Band D	250% of relevant weekly income	200%–300% of relevant weekly income
Fine Band E	400% of relevant weekly income	300%–500% of relevant weekly income
Fine Band F	600% of relevant weekly income	500%–700% of relevant weekly income

Multiple offences. The starting point and ranges indicated in the individual offence guidelines assume that the offender is being sentenced for a single offence. Where an offender is being sentenced for multiple offences, the overall sentence must be just and appropriate having regard to the totality of the offending; the court should not simply aggregate the sentences considered suitable for the individual offences. The court's assessment of the totality of the offending may result in an overall sentence above the range indicated by the individual offences, including, where permitted, a sentence of a different type (see CJA 2003, ss 148(1) and 152(2)).

Where an offender is to be fined for two or more offences that arise out of the **same incident**, it will often be appropriate to impose on the most serious offence a fine which reflects the totality of the offending where this can be achieved within the maximum for that offence. "no separate penalty" should be imposed for other offences.

Ancillary orders – order of priority. Where **compensation** is being ordered, that will need to be attributed to the relevant offence as will any necessary **ancillary** orders.

Where the offender does not have sufficient means to pay the total financial penalty, the order of priority is compensation, surcharge, fine and then costs.

Offences not included in the SGC guidelines. Where an offence is not included in this or any other SGC guideline, it may assist in determining sentence to consider the starting points and ranges indicated for offences that are of a similar level of seriousness.

B[28.17] Definition of relevant weekly income. The seriousness of an offence determines the choice of fine band and the position of the offence within the range for that band. The offender's *financial circumstances* are taken into account by expressing that position as a proportion of the offender's *relevant weekly income.*

Where and offender's only source of income is state benefit (including where there is relatively low additional income as permitted by the benefit regulations) or the offender is in receipt of income from employment or is self-employed but the amount of income after deduction of tax and national insurance is £120 per week or less the relevant weekly income is deemed to be £120.

In calculating relevant weekly income no account should be taken of tax credits, housing benefit, child benefit or similar.

B[28.18] Determining relevant weekly income – means Information and no reliable information. Under s 95 of the Courts Act 2003 (which amends s 20A of the Criminal Justice Act 1991) it is an offence for a defendant to fail to provide means information to the court when charged. The best way for the court to receive that information is on the standard *Means Form* which should be issued to all defendants so that if they are found guilty the court can impose a fine appropriate to the offender's means and ability to pay.

Where an offender has failed to provide information, or the court is not satisfied that it has been given sufficient reliable information, it is entitled to make such determination as it thinks fit regarding the financial circumstances of the offender (CJA 2003, s 164(5)). Any such determination should be clearly stated on the court records for use in any subsequent variation or enforcement proceedings. A record should also be made of the applicable fine band and the court's assessment of the position of the offence within that band based on the seriousness of the offence.

Where there is *no information* on which a determination can be made, the court should proceed on the basis of an *assumed relevant weekly income of £440*. This is derived from national median pre-tax earnings; a gross figure is used as, in the absence of financial information from the offender, it is not possible to calculate appropriate deductions.

Where there is some information that tends to suggest a significantly lower or higher income than the recommended £440 default sum, the court should make a determination based on that information. A court is empowered to remit a fine in whole or in part if the offender subsequently provides information as to means (CJA 2003, s 165(2)). The assessment of offence seriousness and, therefore, the appropriate fine band and the position of the offence within that band is **not** affected by the provision of this information.

A court is empowered to remit a fine in whole or part if the offender subsequently provides information as to means. The assessment of offence seriousness and, therefore, the appropriate fine band and the position of the offence within that band are not affected by the provision of this information.

B[28.18A] Approach to offenders on low income (including state benefit). An offender whose primary source of income is state benefit will generally receive a base level of benefit (eg job seekers' allowance, a relevant disability benefit or income support) and may also be eligible for the supplementary benefits depending on his or her individual circumstances (such as child tax credits, housing benefit, council tax benefit and similar. If *relevant weekly income* were defined as the amount of benefit received, this would usually result in higher fines being imposed on offenders with a higher level of need; in most circumstances that would not properly balance the seriousness of the offence with the financial circumstances of the offender. While it might be possible to exclude from the calculation any allowance above the basic entitlement of a single person, that could be complicated and time consuming. Similar issues can arise where the offender is in receipt of a low earned income since this may trigger eligibility for means related benefits such as working tax credits and housing benefit depending on the particular circumstances. It will not always be possible with any confidence whether such a person's financial circumstances are significantly different from those of a person whose primary source of income is state benefit.

For those reasons, a simpler and fairer approach to cases involving offenders in receipt of low income (whether primarily earned or as a result of benefit) is to identify an amount that is *deemed* to represent the offender's relevant weekly income. While a precise calculation is neither possible nor desirable, it is considered that an amount that is approximately half-way between the base rate for job seekers' allowance and the net weekly income of an adult earning the minimum wage for 30 hours per week represents a starting point that is both realistic and appropriately; that is *currently £120*. The calculation is based on a 30 hour working week in recognition of the fact that many of those on a minimum wage do not work a full 37 hour week and that lower minimum wage rates apply to younger people. It is expected that this figure will remain in use until 31 March 2011. Future revisions of the guideline will update the amount in accordance with current benefit and minimum wage levels.

B[28.19] **Assessment of financial circumstances.** While the initial consideration for the assessment of a fine is the offender's relevant weekly income, the court is required to take account of the offender's **financial circumstances** more broadly. An offender's financial circumstances may have the effect of increasing or reducing the amount of the fine; however they are **not** relevant to the assessment of offence seriousness. They should be considered separately from the selection of the appropriate fine band and the court's assessment of the position of the offence band within the range for that band.

B[28.20] **Out of the ordinary expenses.** In deciding the proportions of relevant weekly income that are the starting point and ranges for each fine band, account has been taken of reasonable living expenses. Accordingly, no further allowances should normally be made for these. In addition, no allowance should normally be made where the offender has dependants. Outgoings will be relevant to the amount of the fine only where the expenditure is *out of the ordinary* and *substantially* reduces the ability to pay a financial penalty so that the requirement to pay a fine based on the standard approach would lead to undue hardship.

Example: Court determines offence seriousness is a Band A fine. Defendant's relevant weekly income is £600 per week. Defendant pleads guilty at the first availability opportunity. The court determines to take into account out of the ordinary expenditure of £50 per week.

Fine = 50% of £600–£300 less a one-third discount for plea = £200 less £50 for out of the ordinary expenses = a total fine of £150.

Unusually low outgoings

Where the offender's living expenses are substantially lower than would normally be expected, it may be appropriate to adjust the amount of the fine to reflect this. This may apply, for example, where an offender does not make any financial contribution towards his or her own living costs.

B[28.21] **Savings**

Where an offender has savings these will not normally be relevant to the assessment of the amount of a fine although they may influence the decision on time to pay. However, where an offender has substantial savings, the court may consider it appropriate to adjust the amount of the fine to reflect this.

B[28.22] **Household has more than one source of income.** Where the household of which the offender is a part has more than one source of income, the fine should normally be based on the income of the offender alone. However, where the offender's part of the income is very small (or the offender is wholly dependent on the income of another), the court may have regard to the extent of the householder's income and assets which will be available to meet any fine imposed on the offender (*R v Engen* [2004] EWCA Crim 1536, [2004] All ER (D) 117 (Jun)).

B[28.23] **Potential earning capacity.** Where there is reason to believe that an offender's potential earning capacity is greater than his or her current income, the court may wish to adjust the amount of the fine to reflect this (*R v Little* (14 April

1976, unreported), CA. This may apply, for example, where an unemployed offender states an expectation to gain paid employment within a short time. The basis for the calculation of fine should be recorded in order to ensure that there is a clear record for use in variation or enforcement proceedings.

High income offenders. Where the offender is in receipt of a very high income, a fine based on a proportion of relevant weekly income may be disproportionately high when compared with the seriousness of the offence. In such cases, the court should adjust the fine to an appropriate level; as a general indication, in most cases the fine for a first time offender pleading not guilty **should not exceed** 75% of the maximum fine. In the case of unlimited fines, magistrates should seek guidance from the legal adviser.

B[28.24] Offence committed for 'commercial' purposes. Some offences are committed with the intention of gaining a significant commercial benefit. These often occur, where, in order to carry out an activity lawfully, a person has to comply with certain processes which may be expensive. They include, for example, 'taxi-touting' (where unauthorised persons seek to operate as taxi drivers) and 'fly-tipping' (where the cost of lawful disposal is considerable). In some of these cases, a fine based on the standard approach set out above may not reflect the level of financial gain achieved or sought through the offending. Accordingly:

(a) where the offender has generated income or avoided expenditure to a level that can be calculated or estimated, the court may wish to consider that amount when determining the financial penalty;
(b) where it is not possible to calculate or estimate that amount, the court may wish to draw on information from the law enforcing authorities about the general costs of operating within the law.

B[28.24A] Offence committed by an organisation. Where an offence is committed by an organisation, guidance on fines can be found in the environmental offences guideline at p 262 of the Magistrates' Court Sentencing Guidelines. See the Criminal Practice Direction CPD Xiii Listing Annex, reproduced at **A**[80.5]–**A**[80.6], ante, for directions on dealing with cases involving very large fines in magistrates' courts.

B[28.25] Reduction for a guilty plea. Where a guilty plea has been entered, the amount of the fine should be reduced by an appropriate proportion. See **B**[45.46].

B[28.25A] Imposition of fines with custodial sentences. A fine and a custodial sentence may be imposed for the same offence although there will be few circumstances in which this is appropriate, particularly where the custodial sentence is to be served immediately. One example might be where an offender has profited financially from an offence but there is no obvious victim to whom compensation can be awarded. Combining these sentences is most likely to be appropriate only where the custodial sentence is short and/or the offender clearly has, or will have, the means to pay.

Care must be taken to ensure that the overall sentence is proportionate to the seriousness of the offence and that better off offenders are not able to 'buy themselves out of custody'.

Announcing the fine and time to pay

B[28.26] Time to pay. A fine is payable in full on the day on which it is imposed. The offender should always be asked for immediate payment when present in court and some payment on the day should be required wherever possible.

Where that is not possible, the court may, in certain circumstances, require the offender to be detained. More commonly, a court will allow payments to be made over a period set by the court.

(a) If periodic payments are allowed, the fine should normally be payable within a maximum of 12 months.
(b) Compensation should normally be payable within 12 months. However, in exceptional circumstances it may be appropriate to allow it to be paid over a period of up to three years.

Where fine bands D, E and F apply, it may be appropriate for the fine to be of an amount that is larger than can be repaid within 12 months. In such cases, the fine should normally be payable within a maximum of 18 months (band D) or two years (bands E and F). When allowing payment by instalments payments should be set at a realistic rate taking into account the offender's disposable income. The following approach may be useful:

Net weekly income	Suggested starting point for weekly payment
£60	£5
£120	£10
£200	$25
£300	£50
£400	£80

If the offender has dependants or larger than usual commitments, the weekly payment is likely to be decreased.

The payment terms must be included in any collection order made in respect of the amount Imposed.

Collection orders. The Courts Act 2003 created a fines collection scheme which provides for greater administrative enforcement of fines.

Attachment of earnings orders/applications for benefit deductions. Unless it would be impracticable or inappropriate to do so, the court must make an attachment of earnings order (AEO) or application for benefit deductions (ABD) whenever compensation is imposed; or the court concludes that the offender is an existing defaulter and that the existing default cannot be disregarded.

In other cases, the court may make an AEO or ABD with the offender's consent.

The court must make a collection order in every case in which a fine or compensation order is imposed unless this would be impracticable or inappropriate. The collection order must state: the amount of the sum due, including the amount of any fine, compensation order or other sum; whether the court considers the offender to be an existing defaulter; whether an AEO or ABD has been made and information about the effect of the order; if the court has not made an AEO or ABD, the payment terms; and if an AEO or ABD has been made, the reserve terms (ie the payment terms that will apply if the AEO or ABD fails). It will often be appropriate to set a reserve term of payment in full within 14 days.

B[28.27]–[28.29] An immediate committal to prison in default of payment can only be ordered in the four types of cases mentioned below. In other cases the court must announce (and cause to be entered in the register) the time allowed for payment. This may be a fixed period, eg 14 days, or it may be an order that the defendant pays by instalments.

B[28.30] **Limited companies.** In law a company is a person. Therefore a fine imposed against a company can only be enforceable against the company and not against any of its officials. For non-payment of a fine a distress warrant can be issued against the company and its property seized and sold to meet the fine and any costs involved in conducting the sale.

B[28.31] Payment of the fine can sometimes be enforced in the High Court or county court. Consult the legal adviser. In certain circumstances the appropriate officer (the collecting officer, in this case the Area Director) may apply to the High Court to have a company wound up under the Insolvency Act 1986.

B[28.32] **Partnership firm.** The conviction will have been against the partners personally and fines can be enforced against them personally in the usual way.

B[28.33] **Searching.** The court may order the defendant to be searched and any money found used to pay the fine, compensation and costs. If there is a balance this must be returned to the defendant.

B[28.34] Such money must not be taken if the court is satisfied that the money does not belong to the defendant or if the loss of money would be more injurious to his family than his detention.

B[28.35]–[28.37] **Fine supervision order.** Instead of the court fixing the time to pay or ordering fixed instalments, it may decide that the defendant is so incompetent or feckless that he will not put aside the money to meet the fine. In such circumstances the court can make a supervision order placing the defendant under the care of some person (often a probation officer) whose duty is not to collect the fine or decide the rate of payments, but to persuade the offender to pay so as to keep out of prison. When making such an order the rate of payment should be fixed by the court.

Procedure for enforcing fines

B[28.38] **Procedure for enforcing fines.** The following applies on the first occasion on which the payer ('P') is in default on a collection order containing payment terms and there is no pending: application, appeal or reference of a specified kind (ie an application for the variation of the collection order or an attachment of earnings order; an appeal against a decision of the fines officer; or a reference by the fines officer to the court). The fines officer must make an attachment of earnings order or an application for benefit deductions unless it would be impracticable or inappropriate to make such an order or application: Courts Act 2003, Sch 5, para 26(1) and (2).

If a collection order contains reserve terms and the attachment of earnings order or application for benefit deductions fails, the fines officer must deliver to P a notice informing him of the failure and that the reserve terms have come into effect, what he must do to comply with those terms and of his right to apply to the fines officer to vary the reserve terms. P may then apply to the fines officer to vary those terms: Courts Act 2003, Sch 5, para 31(1). (For the relevant criteria, procedure, powers of the fines officer and right of appeal, see paras 31(2)–(4) and 32.)

If P is in default on a collection order, the provisions stated above concerning the making of an attachment of earnings order or application for deduction of benefits on the occasion of the first default on a collection order do not apply, and there is no pending application, appeal of reference of a specified kind (see above), the fines officer must refer P's case to the magistrates' court or deliver to him a 'further steps notice' in writing and dated, describing the further steps he intends to take. Within ten working days of the date of the further steps notice P may appeal against it to the magistrates' court: Courts Act 2003, Sch 5, para 37.

The further steps are:

- the issue of a warrant of control;
- registering the sum in the register of judgements and orders required to be kept under s 98 of the Courts Act 2003;
- making an attachment of earnings order or an application for benefit deductions;
- a clamping order (a vehicle cannot be clamped unless it is registered in P's name under the Vehicle Excise and Registration Act 1994: para 38(3));
- taking proceedings by virtue of the Magistrates' Courts Act 1980, s 87(1) to enforce payment by the High Court or county court, provided that the fines officer has made enquiries into the defaulter's means and it appears to the fines officer that the defaulter has sufficient means to pay the sum forthwith: Magistrates' Courts Act 1980, s 87(3A); and
- issuing a certificate requesting enforcement under the Framework Decision on financial penalties (where the sum is a financial penalty as defined by the Criminal Justice and Immigration Act 2008, s 80, and P normally resides, or has property or income, in another Member State): Courts Act 2003, Sch 5, para 38.

If P does not appeal within ten days, or he does so but the further steps notice is confirmed or varied, any of the step specified in the notice (or the notice as varied) may be taken: Courts Act 2003, Sch 5, para 40.

The fines officer may also refer a case to the magistrates' court at any time while a collection order is in force and the whole or part of the sum due remains outstanding: Courts Act 2003, Sch 5, para 42.

To ensure that P attends the magistrates' court pursuant to either kind of reference described above, the fines officer may issue a summons: Regulation 4 of the Fines Collection Regulations 2006.

If the fines officer clamps a car and wants to sell the vehicle he will have to first seek the permission of the court. The fines officer will have to have the case listed and go before the court to seek permission.

There is a new power for the fines officer to transfer cases for enforcement without referring them back to the court. This can be used where the court receives new information on the whereabouts of the offender and it is necessary to transfer for enforcement purposes.

If the fines officer considers that the above disposals are insufficient to recover payment he will refer the matter back to court, for example, to increase the fine or to impose imprisonment in default.

Immediate enforcement

B[28.39] When a fine is imposed the court can use the following methods to enforce immediate payment, if there is a good reason not to make a collection order.

B[28.40] 1 **Search.** The court can order the defendant to be searched for money to meet the fine. See above.

B[28.41]–[28.45] 2 **Immediate committal to prison.** In the circumstances listed below the court may order imprisonment forthwith for a period determined in accordance with the following scale:

An amount not exceeding £200	7 days
An amount exceeding £200 but not exceeding £500	14 days
An amount exceeding £500 but not exceeding £1,000	28 days
An amount exceeding £1,000 but not exceeding £2,500	45 days
An amount exceeding £2,500 but not exceeding £5,000	3 months
An amount exceeding £5,000 but not exceeding £10,000	6 months
An amount exceeding £10,000	12 months

B[28.46] It must be borne in mind that these are the maximum periods applicable, the court is not obliged to impose the maximum period in default. In other words, the number of days in default should be proportionate to the sum outstanding eg if the sum imposed was £520 and nothing has been paid, pro rata 15 days (rather than 28 days) should be ordered to be served in default of payment.

B[28.47] If part payments have been made then the period of imprisonment is calculated by taking the period of imprisonment considered appropriate for the whole sum and reducing that period by the proportion which the part payment bears to the original sum due. For example, if a defendant is fined £600 and over a period pays £400, the maximum period of imprisonment for that balance is one-third of 28 days in band 4. Where a defendant is fined at one time for several offences, each fine must be calculated separately and the periods of imprisonment may be made consecutive. However, it is not appropriate to fix consecutive terms of imprisonment in respect of fines imposed for several offences arising out of the same incident. In every case where several fines are outstanding the court must look realistically at the total situation.

NB: Where several fines are ordered to run consecutive to each other the total number of days in default should not exceed the statutory maximum. For example, if four separate fines of £240 are ordered to run consecutive to each other the total number of days in default should not exceed the statutory maximum outlined in B[28.40] above ie 28 days.

B[28.48] The above table applies to monetary penalties (ie fines, costs and compensation) and not to civil orders eg arrears of maintenance for which the maximum period is six weeks. Nor does it apply to the community charge for which the maximum period is three months. (It may be convenient to mention here that periods of imprisonment for more than one amount of unpaid community charge may not be made consecutive.)

B[28.49] An immediate committal to prison can only be ordered in the following cases:

(a) if the offence is punishable with imprisonment and the defendant appears to the court to have sufficient means to pay immediately; or
(b) if it appears to the court that the defendant is unlikely to remain at an address in the UK long enough for the fine to be enforced by other methods; or
(c) if the defendant is already serving a prison or detention sentence; or
(d) if the defendant is being sent to prison or detention on the same or another charge.

Note, however, that s 82(1)(c) of the Magistrates' Courts Act 1980 (power to impose imprisonment in default of payment of any sum adjudged to be paid on conviction where the court imposes immediate imprisonment or detention for that or another offence, or the offender is already a serving prisoner) does not apply to the surcharge in consequence of the insertion of s 82(1A) of the MCA 1980 by s 179 of the Anti-social Behaviour, Crime and Policing Act 2014. Section 135 of the MCA 1980 (one day's detention) was not amended, but it was held in *Frimpong v Crown Prosecution Service (Secretary of State for Justice intervening)* [2015] EWCA Crim 1933, [2016] 1 Cr App R (S) 59 that this power was intended as an alternative to imprisonment and it had no application where imprisonment was imposed. This case was concerned with the criminal courts charge, for which no sums are currently set, but the decision must apply equally to the (victims') surcharge since both are on the same statutory footing.

B[28.50] The court should announce its reasons (that is, (a), (b), (c) or (d) above) for making an immediate committal to prison and these reasons should be entered in the court register and on the committal warrant. Failure to comply may result in a challenge to the decision by judicial review (*R v Oldham Justices, ex p Cawley* [1997] QB 1, [1996] 1 All ER 464). If the defendant has second thoughts about paying and tenders payment to the court staff, the police or the prison officials he is entitled to be released. If only part of the fine is paid then he is entitled to a proportionate remission of the prison sentence. This applies even if he offers part payment after he has served a part of the prison sentence. A committal order, forthwith or suspended, will be inappropriate for a single mother with very little income, trying her best to balance her financial obligations (*R (on the application of Stokes) v Gwent Magistrates' Court* [2001] EWHC 569 (Admin), [2001] All ER (D) 125 (Jul)). A defaulter's human rights may be breached if he is not offered legal representation (*Best v UK* (2005) Times, 10 March).

B[28.51] The period of imprisonment for non-payment can be concurrent with or consecutive to another sentence already being served; or if more than one fine is being enforced, the periods of imprisonment for non-payment can be consecutive to each other subject to the overall restrictions on the aggregate length of sentences. Consult the legal adviser.

B[28.52] **3 Suspended committal order.** The court can order a committal to prison under the scale at B[28.40] to be suspended for a definite period of time during which the defendant has to find the money for the fine or it may suspend the prison sentence whilst he pays instalments at a rate decided by the court (usually weekly, fortnightly or monthly). Such a suspended committal order can only be ordered if the case falls into one of the categories listed at **B[28.49]** as (a), (b), (c), or (d). If more than one fine is being enforced in this way, the periods of imprisonment for non-payment can be concurrent with or consecutive to each other subject to the overall restrictions on the aggregate length of sentence (at **B[28.40]**). The defendant may apply subsequently to the court to vary the terms of the postponement. Where the defendant subsequently defaults in payment of the order, the court must give him notice that the warrant of commitment falls to be issued. Magistrates should adjourn hearing a warrant for committal case if they know that the defendant has not been served with proceedings (*R v Doncaster Justices, ex p Hannan* (1998) 163 JP 182, [1998] 32 LS Gaz R 30). He then has an opportunity to make representations orally or in writing as to why the warrant should not issue. Consult the legal adviser.

B[28.53] **4 Detention for one day or overnight at a police station.** The court can order the defendant to be detained for the remainder of the day within the precincts of the court or police station but must be released at a time which will allow him to get home the same day or at the latest by 8 p.m. The release time should be announced by the court. Similarly, overnight detention authorises the police to arrest the defendant and keep him until 8 a.m. on the morning following his arrest or if he is arrested between midnight and 8 o'clock in the morning, until 8 o'clock in the morning of the day on which he is arrested. The effect of this is to wipe out the fine.

B[28.54] **5 Warrant of control.** The magistrates can issue a warrant of control which orders the seizure of the defendant's property to meet the unpaid fine. Such an order may be suspended on terms that the defaulter pays as ordered by the court.

B[28.55]–[28.60] **6 Supervision order.** This means placing the defendant under supervision, usually of the probation officer, see **B[28.34]**.

B[28.61] **7 Fixing a means inquiry.** When imposing a fine etc the court may fix a date on which the offender must appear in court for a means inquiry if at that time any part of the monetary penalty remains unpaid.

Enforcement as a result of a referral by the fines officer

B[28.62] If the defendant fails to pay the fine or other enforcement has failed, the fines officer will arrange for the issuing of a summons or warrant to bring the defendant back before the court who will conduct a means inquiry to investigate the defendant's ability to pay the fine and may demand that the defendant produce documentary evidence of his financial resources, eg pay slips, account books, post office savings book, bank statements etc. The defendant must produce a statement of means either before the inquiry or during the inquiry by a specified date and failure to produce such a statement is punishable with a fine up to level 3 if directed by the court and level 2 if directed by the fines officer.

Additionally the court may discharge a fines collection order and revert to its standard powers following an appeal against a decision of the fines officer to vary terms or take action by the use of alternative sanctions (including wheel clamping).

B[28.63] **Increase in fine.** Where the defendant is in default on a collection order, the sum due consists of or includes a fine, and the fines officer has referred the default to a magistrates' court either as an alternative to the issue of a further steps notice or after taking any of the further steps described in **B[28.38]**, above, if the court is satisfied that the default is due to the defendant's wilful refusal or culpable neglect it may increase the fine (but not any other sum which is due) by 50%: Courts Act 2003, Sch 5, para 42A and the Fines Collection Regulations 2006, SI 2006/501, reg 3.

Remission. A fine (but only a fine) may be remitted in whole or in part if the court thinks it is just to do so having regard to a change in circumstances which has occurred since the conviction. A magistrates' court may not, however, remit the whole or any part of a fine imposed by, or sum due under a recognizance forfeited by, the Crown Court or Court of Appeal or Supreme Court, without the consent of the Crown Court. Where a fine is remitted this automatically remits the surcharge to the level it would have been if the fine had not included the remitted amount.

B[28.64]–[28.65] For compensation see B[10].

B[28.66] At a means inquiry magistrates can enforce payment by the following methods:

B[28.67] **1 Attachment orders.** If the magistrates are satisfied that the defendant is being paid earnings they may make an attachment order directing that the employer make deductions from the defendant's wages and remit them to the court. If the magistrates have this course in mind they should first consult the legal adviser and/or direct that the defendant completes a means form as the court must obtain certain details about the defendant and his employment.

B[28.68] **2 Warrant of control.** See above.

B[28.69] **3 Search.** See B[28.32].

B[28.70]–[28.75] **4 Immediate committal to prison.** The magistrates can order an immediate committal to prison for a specified period according to the scale set out at B[28.40]. For calculation of the term in default see **B[28.47]**. Immediate committal to prison can only be ordered if:

(a) the offence for which he has been fined is also punishable with imprisonment and the defendant appears to the court to have the means to pay immediately; or

(b) the court is satisfied that the default is due to the offender's wilful refusal or culpable neglect and the court has considered or tried all other methods of enforcement and it appears to the court that they are inappropriate or unsuccessful.

Culpable neglect cannot be found where a defaulter has no capital or income to pay a fine. Nor should the assumption be made that someone else will pay the fine (*R (on the application of McDonough) v Wigan Magistrates' Court* [2004] EWHC 3272 (Admin), [2005] All ER (D) 304 (Feb)).

A high threshold has to be crossed before making a finding of *wilful refusal* (*R (on the application of Louis) v Ealing Magistrates' Court* [2009] EWHC 521 (Admin), 173 JP 248).

B[28.76] The test in s 82(4) of the MCA 1980 was that the court had to have regard to other methods of enforcement; it was not obliged to have tried them all: *R (on application of Johnson (Craig Matthew)) v Birmingham Magistrates' Court and CPS* [2012] EWHC 596 (Admin), 176 JP 298.

The other methods referred to are warrants of control, application to the High Court or county court for enforcement, supervision, attachment of earnings and, if under 21, attendance centre.

B[28.77] **5 Detention for one day or overnight at a police station.** See B[28.53].

B[28.78]–[28.79] **6 Suspended committal to prison.** The court can order a suspended committal to prison for a period in accordance with the scale on at B[28.40]. This imprisonment can then be suspended for a definite period of time during which the defendant must pay the fine or alternatively the court may direct that the defendant shall pay at so much per week or month. Such a suspended committal can only be ordered if the offence for which the defendant was fined is punishable with imprisonment and the defendant appears to have sufficient means to pay; or the court is satisfied that the default is due to the offender's wilful refusal or culpable neglect and the court has considered all the other methods of enforcement and it appears that they are inappropriate or unsuccessful. See above.

B[28.80] **8 Deduction from benefit.** After a means inquiry has been made the court may request the Department of Works and Pensions to make payments towards a fine or compensation direct from the offender's benefit, subject to any right of review or appeal he may have.

B[28.81] **9 Transfer to High Court or county court.** If the defendant is a holder of shares or has certain kinds of assets, enforcement can sometimes be transferred to the High Court or county court. Consult the legal adviser.

B[28.82] **Defendant already in prison.** If a defendant, who has not paid part or the whole of a fine, is serving a sentence of imprisonment or is confined in a detention centre a committal warrant can be issued without any means inquiry taking place. The clerk will give notice to the debtor who may appear or make written representations.

B[28.83] **Curfew and community service orders.** Where the court has power to issue a warrant of commitment, it may instead make a community service or curfew order provided it has been notified by the Secretary of State that arrangements for implementing the order are available in the relevant area: Crime (Sentences) Act 1997, s 35. These powers are prospectively repealed and replaced, respectively, by Part 7 of Sch 37 to, and s 300 of, the Criminal Justice Act 2003.

Fines imposed by Central Criminal Court and Crown Court

B[28.84] These fines are payable to and enforceable by magistrates' courts.

B[28.85] The whole fine or part of it can be remitted only with the consent of the higher court.

B[28.85A] With both Crown Court fines and confiscation orders, it is the Crown Court which sets the default term, and responsibility for enforcement then passes to the magistrates' court. As to the effect of part payments on the actual term to be served, see B[11.2], ante.

Defendants aged 18 to 21

B[28.86]–[28.90] The above provisions can also be employed in respect of defendants in this age group except that an order of detention in default of payment should only be ordered if a supervision order has already been tried or the court is satisfied that a supervision order is either undesirable or impracticable. These considerations must be noted on any commitment warrant (*R v Oldham Justices, ex p Cawley* [1997] QB 1, [1996] 1 All ER 464 and *R v Stockport Justices, ex p Conlon* [1997] 2 All ER 204, 161 JP 81).

B[28.91] If the court has available to it an attendance centre for defaulters to the age of 25, the court can send the defendant for up to 36 hours in all in default of payment.

B[28.92] The clerk should be consulted as to the exact number of hours that the defendant should attend at the attendance centre.

Defendants aged 10 to 17

B[28.93] **Maximum fine.** Children under 14, £250; young persons, 14 or over, £1,000, or, in either case the lesser sum applicable in the case of an adult (Powers of the Criminal Courts (Sentencing) Act 2000, s 135).

B[28.94] **Costs.** The costs ordered must not exceed the amount of the fines unless a parent or guardian is ordered to pay.

B[28.95] **Parental liability to pay.** The child's parent or guardian must be ordered to pay the fine and costs unless he cannot be found or the court considers it would be unreasonable to order him to pay. In the case of a young person the court has a power to order the parent to pay. If the parent or guardian does not pay, enforcement takes place in the adult court as described at B[28.7]–B[28.10].

Enforcement

B[28.96] The power to make a fines supervision order or an attachment of earnings order is available in the case of juveniles. In addition, where the court is satisfied that the juvenile has had the money to pay but has refused or neglected to pay it may make an order requiring:

(a) the parent to enter a recognisance to ensure that the defaulter pays the fine or balance; or
(b) the court may transfer the debt to the parent in which case further enforcement, if necessary, would be taken as if the fine has been imposed on that parent.

B[28.97] The parent must, according to the statute, consent before an order may be made for him to enter into a recognisance. The parent's consent is not required for the responsibility for the fine to be transferred to him provided the court is satisfied in all the circumstances that it is reasonable to make the order.

B[28.98] If an attendance centre is available for persons of the debtor's class or description, he may be ordered to attend, up to the age of 25 years.

B[28.99] The powers mentioned under this heading must be exercised after a means inquiry. An order transferring the debt to the parent may be made in his absence provided he has been given adequate notice of the proceedings; if he is present, he must be given the opportunity of speaking to the court before such an order is made.

B[29]

Football banning orders

(Football Spectators Act 1989, ss 14 and 22 and Football (Disorder) Act 2000)

Criminal orders

B[29.1] A banning order means an order made under Part II of the Football Spectators Act 1989 which:

(a) in relation to regulated football matches in the UK, prohibits the person who is subject to the order from entering any premises for the purpose of attending such matches; and
(b) in relation to football matches outside the UK, requires that person to report to a police station in accordance with Part II.

As to (a) a football banning order prevents the subject from attending any regulated football match and there is no power to make a limiting order: *R v Doyle* [2012] EWCA Crim 995, [2013] 1 Cr App R (S) 36, *Commissioner of Police of the Metropolis v Thorpe* [2015] EWHC 3339 (Admin), [2016] 1 Cr App R (S) 46.

B[29.2] A **regulated football match** is an association football match (whether in the UK or elsewhere) which is a prescribed match or a match of a prescribed description.

The Football Spectators (Prescription) Order 2004, SI 2004/2409, as amended, provides:

> '3.(1) An association football match (in England and Wales) described in paragraphs (2) or (3) shall be a regulated football match for the purposes of Part II of the 1989 Act.
>
> (2) A regulated match is an association football match in which one or both of the participating teams represents–
>
> (a) a club which is for the time being a member (whether a full or associate member) of the Football League, the Football Association Premier League, the Football Conference, the Welsh Premier League or the Scottish Professional Football League;
> (b) a club whose home ground is situated outside England and Wales; or
> (c) a country or territory.
>
> (3) A regulated football match is an association football match played in the Football Association Cup (other than in a preliminary or qualifying round).
>
> 4.(1) An association football match (outside England and Wales) described in paragraph (2) shall be a regulated football match for the purposes of Part II of the 1989 Act.
>
> (2) A regulated match is an association football match involving-
>
> (a) a national team appointed by the Football Association to represent England or appointed by the Football Association of Wales to represent Wales;
> (b) a team representing a club which is for the time being a member (whether a full or associate member) of the Football League, the Football Association Premier League, the Football Conference, the Welsh Premier League, the Scottish Professional Football League;
> (c) a team representing any country or territory whose football association is for the time being a member of FIFA, where–

(i) the match is part of a competition or tournament organised by, or under the authority of, FIFA or UEFA, and
(ii) the competition or tournament is one in which a team referred to in sub-paragraph (a) above is eligible to participate or has participated; or

(d) a team representing a club which is for the time being a member (whether a full or associate member) of, or affiliated to, a national football association which is a member of FIFA, where–
(i) (the match is part of a competition or tournament organised by, or under the authority of, FIFA or UEFA, and
(ii) the competition or tournament is one in which a club referred to in sub-paragraph (b) above is eligible to participate or has participated.

B[29.3] Failure to comply with a banning order is a criminal offence triable only by magistrates with a maximum penalty on level 5 and six months' imprisonment.

B[29.4] Relevant offence means:

(1) An offence in the Football Spectators Act 1989, Sch 1 which includes:

(a) an offence under the Sporting Events (Control of Alcohol etc) Act 1985, s 2;
(b) offences under the Public Order Act 1986, s 5 and Part III (racial hatred or sexual orientation);
(c) an offence involving the threat or use of violence to a person or property: this includes an offence under Public Order Act 1986, s 4(1)(a) (*R v O' Keefe* (2004))
(d) offences under the Football (Offences) Act 1991.

See Football Spectators Act 1989, Sch 1 (as amended) for an exhaustive list.

B[29.5] Offences (b)–(d) must be committed during a period relevant to a designated football match at any premises while the accused was at, or was entering or leaving or trying to enter or leave, the premises. Therefore a defendant convicted of a public order offence on a train travelling away from a match he had been refused entry to was on a factual basis not related to a football match (*R v Smith* [2002] EWCA Crim 683, [2003] 1 Cr App Rep 212).

There is, however, no need to prove in a criminal case the civil requirements that the defendants caused or contributed to violence or disorder: s 14B (*R (on the application of Brown) v Inner London Crown Court* [2003] EWHC 3194 (Admin), [2003] All ER (D) 256 (Dec)).

B[29.6] Relevant period. A period beginning 24 hours before the start of the match or, if earlier, 24 hours before the time it is advertised to start or the time at which spectators are first admitted to the premises, and ends 24 hours after the end of the match. Where a match is postponed or cancelled, the period includes the 24 hours before and 24 hours after the advertised start of the event. Regulated football match' for the purposes of these offences and those described below (a)–(d) is described above.

B[29.7] (2) The following offences committed on a journey to or from a designated football match where the court makes a declaration that the offence related to football matches:

(a) offences under (b) and (c) above;
(b) drunkenness;
(c) an offence under the Sporting Events (Control of Alcohol etc) Act 1985, s 1;
(d) driving whilst unfit or over the prescribed limit of alcohol: Road Traffic Act 1988, ss 4 and 5

"Related to a football match" is to be given its ordinary meaning (*DPP v Beaumont* [2008] EWHC 523 (Admin), [2008] 1 WLR 2186, [2008] 2 Cr App Rep (S) 549; *R v Arbery and Mobley* [2008] EWCA Crim 702, 172 JP 291).

In *R v Pakes; R v Cartwright* [2010] EWCA Crim 2803, [2011] 2 Cr App Rep (S) 54, 175 JP 33, it was decided that the spark which caused the violence was related to football, that is a match between two Championship sides. From what occurred it was clear that there was hostility between two sets of rival supporters. It mattered not that one of the appellants did not go to an area of the West Midlands looking for trouble; the fact that he became caught up in the hostility which erupted between two rival sets of fans was sufficient.

Where violence arose out of a racial incident between two sets of football supporters outside a London pub and not in relation to the match or matches, the offences could not be said to be "football-related" and banning orders under s 14A were quashed on appeal (*R v Arbery and Mobley* supra; *R v Mabee (Craig)* [2007] EWCA Crim 3230, [2008] 2 Cr App Rep (S) 143).

For the court to make a 'declaration of related to', an offence of affray had to be committed in the circumstances stipulated by Schedule 1. Further, there had to be reasonable grounds to believe that the making of a banning order would help to prevent violence or disorder at or in connection with any regulated football matches. In the present case, the court did not so determine and the evidence showed only that the affray arose out of the fact that the defendants were drunk, rather than that it had any connection to football: *R v Doyle; R v Wise; R v Wise* [2012] EWCA Crim 995, 176 JP 337, 176 CL&J 322.

B[29.8] The prosecution must normally give five days' notice of its intention to seek a declaration that the offence related to football matches.

B[29.9] (3) Offences under paras (a) and (c) committed on journeys to designated matches played outside the UK.

B[29.10]–[29.17] **Offences committed abroad** Section 22 of the Football Spectators Act 1989 enables an Order in Council to be made specifying 'corresponding offences' under the laws of countries outside England and Wales. A conviction of such an offence may give rise to a banning order. However, Orders made under this section were revoked by SI 2015/212 because s 22 has fallen into disuse owing to the number of alternative routes under the Act to securing a banning order, in particular s 14B (see below).

B[29.18] **Criterion**. The court must make a football banning order in relation to the offender if satisfied that there are reasonable grounds to believe that it would help to prevent violence or disorder at or in connection with regulated football matches. Repetition and propensity are not required for the making of an order under s 14A, and the court is entitled to take into account and to give weight to the question of deterrence: *R (on the application of White) v Crown Court at Blackfriars* [2008] EWHC 510 (Admin), [2008] 2 Cr App Rep (S) 542, (2008) 172 JP 321. See also *R v Lewis Cash Curtis* [2009] EWCA Crim 1225, [2010] 1 Cr App R (S) 193 where a banning order was upheld even though the behaviour was an isolated first incident in the case of the defendant. If it does not make an order the court must state in open court its reasons for not being satisfied an order was required: see r 50.2 of the Criminal Procedure Rules 2013.

It is important that courts who are considering the rather complex provisions of the Football Spectators Act 1989 should have in mind the nature of the regime for which it provides. It should also address its mind to the differences between the consequences of a football banning order on the one hand and a prohibited activities requirement attached either to a suspended sentence or a community order on the other. They are not to be treated as equivalents.

There is some difference between the two kinds of order as to sanction. Disobedience to a football banning order is itself an offence, whereas disobedience to a prohibited activity requirement is not. But there is ample sanction for disobedience to a prohibited activity requirement because if it is attached to a suspended sentence the suspended sentence can be activated for breach, and if it is attached to a community order then on breach the court can re-sentence for the original offence and that may well involve loss of liberty. The principal difference between the two forms of order lies in the regime which exists. There is quite a sophisticated regime for the co-ordination of intelligence relating to those who are subject to football banning orders. Where such an order is in contemplation, courts who are addressing the test of whether making an order would help to prevent violence or disorder ought to have in mind the extent of the regime as well of course as its potentially draconian effect: *R v Boggild* [2011] EWCA Crim 1928, 175 CL&J 502, (2011) Times, 5 September.

B[29.19]–[29.20] **Procedure.** Since 6 April 2007, amendments to the primary legislation have been made to allow a court to remand an offender where proceedings are adjourned under s 14A Football Spectators Act 1989.

May only be made in addition to a sentence (which includes a community rehabilitation order and an order for conditional or absolute discharge) imposed in respect of the offence of which the accused was convicted. The court must:

(a) certify that the offence is a relevant offence where appropriate;
(b) specify the police station in England and Wales at which the person must report initially;
(c) explain to the person the effect of the order in ordinary language;
(d) give a copy of the order to the defendant, and send copies to the Football Banning Orders Authority and the Chief Executive of the Football Association, the specified police station and, if appropriate, the relevant prison governor. The relevant authority is currently based at: UK Football Policing Unit, Football Banning Orders Authority, PO Box 51997, London, SW9 6TN. The Chief Executive of the Football Association is currently based at: Football Association, 25 Soho Square, London, W1D 4FA.

B[29.21] **Duration.** Where the person receives an immediate prison sentence but not other forms of detention the mandatory period is a maximum of 10 years and a minimum of 6 years. In any other football case the maximum is 5 years and the minimum three years. In a non-football-related offence, the period is between two and three years.

B[29.22] **Effect.** The person is under a duty to report initially to the police station specified in the order within five days of the making of the order and thereafter to report to a police station specified when notified by the Banning Orders Authority. Note a banning order is not a punishment for the purposes of ECHR Art 7 (*Gough v Chief Constable of the Derbyshire Constabulary* [2001] EWHC 554 (Admin), [2002] QB 459, [2001] 4 All ER 289; affd sub nom *Gough v Chief Constable of Derbyshire Constabulary* [2002] EWCA Civ 351, [2002] QB 1213, [2002] 2 All ER 985).

B[29.22A] **Further obligatory requirements.** A banning order must require the person subject to the order to give notification within seven day to the enforcing authority of the events listed below within seven days beginning with the day of occurrence:

(a) a change of any of his names;
(b) the first use by him after the making of the order of a name for himself that was not disclosed by him at the time of making the order;
(c) a change of his home address;
(d) his acquisition of a temporary address;
(e) a change of his temporary address or ceasing to have one;
(f) his becoming aware of the loss of his travel authorisation;
(g) receipt by him of a new travel authorisation;
(h) an appeal by him in relation to the order;
(i) an application by for him for the termination of the order;
(j) an appeal against the making of a declaration of relevance in respect of an offence of which he has been convicted.

A banning order must impose a requirement as to the surrender in accordance with Part II of the Football Spectators Act 1989, in connection with regulated football matches outside the UK, of the travel authorisation of the person subject to the order.

Provision is made by s 19 of the Football Spectators Act 1989 for the making of further requirements by the enforcing authority, ie the Football Banning Order

Authority. When a person subject to a banning order reports initially at the police station, the officer responsible for the station may make such requirements of that person as are determined by the enforcing authority to be necessary or expedient for giving effect to the banning order, so far as relating to regulated football matches outside the UK. If, in relation to any such match, the enforcing authority is of the opinion that requiring any person subject to a banning order to report is necessary or expedient to reduce the likelihood of violence or disorder at or in connection with the match, the authority must give that person a written notice to report to the police station specified at the specified time and to surrender his travel authorisation. The notice may also include additional requirements.

The enforcing authority is also empowered by notice to impose additional requirements in the case of any regulated football match.

A notice under s 19 may not require reporting/surrender of travel authorisation except with the control period. The notice must require the recipient to state where he intends to stay or has stayed for one night or more during the control period.

B[29.23] Exemption may be granted from reporting in respect of a particular match either an application to the Banning Orders Authority or in cases of urgency to the police. Exemption might be granted, for example, to cover a stay in hospital or the funeral of a close relative.

B[29.24] **Application to terminate.** The person subject to the order may apply to the court to terminate the order after two-thirds of the period determined has expired.

B[29.25]–[29.30] The court will have regard to the person's character, his conduct since the order was made, the nature of the offence which led to it and any other circumstances of the case.

B[29.31] Further application may not be made within six months of a refusal.

B[29.32] Appeal is to the Crown Court against the making of a banning order or a refusal to award compensation (see below). Prosecutors can now appeal to the Crown Court against the refusal of a magistrates' court to make a banning order on conviction of a "*relevant offence*" (s 14A(5A) Football Spectators Act 1989). These relevant offences are listed in schedule 1 to the Football Spectators Act 1989.

B[29.33] **Civil applications.** In addition to its imposition as a result of a football-related conviction, a banning order may be imposed by a magistrates' court in accordance with a civil procedure, following a complaint by the police. The requirement that applications by complaint could only be made by the Chief Constable of the area where the individual resides was removed by the Violent Crime Reduction Act 2006. Applications can be made by any Chief Constable including the Chief Constable of the British Transport Police and the Director of Public Prosecutions.

The Violent Crime Reduction Act 2006 removed the statutory time limit of 27 August 2007 for making an application on complaint for a football banning order on complaint under s 14B Football Spectators Act 1989. Also, the power of summary detention by a police constable (as distinct from arrest) under s 21A of the 1989 Act has been removed.

The court must be satisfied that the person who is the subject of the complaint has at any time caused or contributed to any violence or disorder in the UK or elsewhere, and that there are reasonable grounds to believe that making a banning order would help to prevent violence or disorder at or in connection with any regulated football matches. This is a civil order and not a sentence (*Gough v Chief Constable of the Derbyshire Constabulary* [2001] EWHC 554 (Admin), [2002] QB 459, [2001] 4 All ER 289; affd sub nom *Gough v Chief Constable of Derbyshire Constabulary* [2002] EWCA Civ 351, [2002] QB 1213, [2002] 2 All ER 985).

B[29.34] If, during a control period when international bans are activated, a police officer has reasonable grounds for suspecting that a person before him or her has caused or contributed to any violence or disorder in the UK or elsewhere, and for believing that imposing a banning order on that person would help to prevent violence or disorder at or in connection with any regulated football matches, the officer may, with the authorisation of an inspector of police, give the person a notice in writing requiring him or her to appear before a magistrates' court within 24 hours and in the meantime not to leave England and Wales. The magistrates' court will then treat the notice as an application for a banning order under the new civil procedure. Section 14B of the 1989 Act was further amended by the Violent Crime Reduction Act 2006 so that magistrates' Courts are now empowered to remand a respondent when adjourning proceedings on complaint.

B[29.35] **Appeal.** The respondent may appeal to the Crown Court against the making by a magistrates' court of a banning order on complaint (s 14D Football Spectators Act 1989).

B[29.36] **Compensation** Where a notice has been issued by a police officer under these powers and a court subsequently refuses to impose a banning order, the court may order compensation up to £5000 to be paid to that person out of central funds if it is satisfied that the notice should not have been given in the first place, that the person has suffered loss as a result of the notice, and that it is appropriate to order the payment of compensation in respect of that loss. There is no statutory definition of the word refuse and so presumably if the police seek to withdraw the proceedings the right to compensation is lost although the right to apply for legal costs remains.

B[29.37] **Length of order** The minimum civil order has been altered by the Violent Crime Reduction Act 2006. The minimum order will last for three years and the maximum five years.

B[30]

Foreign Travel Restriction Order

B[30.1] Schedule 5 of the Counter-Terrorism Act 2008 authorises a chief officer of police to apply by way of *complaint* to a magistrates' court for a foreign travel restriction order. An order can only be sought against a person who is already subject to a notification requirement (see ss 41–45 and Sch 4 of the 2008 Act). The legislation came into force on 1 October 2009.

An order places restrictions on where the person concerned may travel outside the UK. The court may make an order where it is satisfied that the person's behaviour since being dealt with for the original offence makes it necessary for an order to be made to prevent him from taking part in terrorism activity outside the UK (Sch 5, para 2(3)).

A foreign travel restriction order must have effect for a fixed term not exceeding 6 months (Sch 5, para 7(1)). Although proceedings are instituted by way of complaint and therefore the procedures are essentially civil in nature, the imposition of criminal sanctions means that the criminal standard of proof applies to the application: see case law under B[2.4].

There are provisions relating to variation, renewal or discharge: Sch 5, para 8. There is no provision to make an interim order. Failure without reasonable excuse to comply with an order is an offence triable either way carrying an unlimited fine and/or five years' imprisonment on conviction on indictment: Sch 5, para 15(2). On summary conviction the offence carries six months' imprisonment and/or a fine. The magistrates' court may not impose a conditional discharge: Sch 5, para 15(4)(a).

B[31]

Forfeiture or suspension of personal liquor licence

(Licensing Act 2003, s 129)

B[31.1] Where an offender who holds a personal licence to supply alcohol is charged with a "relevant offence", he or she is required to produce the licence to the court, or inform the court of its existence, no later than his or her first court appearance.

"Relevant offences" are listed in Sch 4 of the Licensing Act 2003 and are set out below.

Where the offender is convicted the court may order forfeiture of the licence or suspend it for up to 6 months pursuant to s 129 (2) LA 2003. When deciding whether to order forfeiture or suspension, the court may take account of the offender's previous convictions for "relevant offences" (s 129 (3)).

Whether or not forfeiture or suspension is ordered, the court is required to notify the licensing authority of the offender's conviction and the sentence imposed.

B[31.2] "Relevant offence"

These include:

- An offence under the Licensing Act 2003
- An offence under the Firearms Act 1968
- Theft – s 1 Theft Act 1968
- Burglary – s 9 Theft Act 1968
- Abstracting electricity – s 13 Theft Act 1968
- Handling stolen goods – s 22 Theft Act 1968
- Going equipped for theft etc – s 25 Theft Act 1968
- Production of a controlled drug – s 4(2) Misuse of Drugs Act 1971
- Supply of a controlled drug – s 4(3) Misuse of Drugs Act 1971
- Possession with intent to supply – s 5(3) Misuse of Drugs Act 1971
- Evasion of duty – s 170 Customs and Excise Management Act 1979 (except s 170(1)(a))
- Driving/attempting to drive while unfit through drink or drugs – s 4 RTA 1988
- In charge of a motor vehicle when unfit through drink or drugs – s 4 RTA 1988
- Driving/attempting to drive with excess alcohol – s 5 RTA 1988
- In charge of a vehicle with excess alcohol – s 5 RTA 1988
- Unauthorised use of a trade mark where the goods in question are or include alcohol – ss 92(1) and 92(2) Trade Marks Act 1994
- Sexual assault – s 3 SOA 2003
- Exploitation of prostitution – ss 52 and 53 SOA 2003
- Exposure – s 66 SOA 2003
- Voyeurism – s 67 SOA 2003
- A violent offence, being any offence which leads, or is intended to lead, to death or to physical injury

B[32]

Guardianship order

(Mental Health Act 1983, s 37)

Limitations

B[32.1]–[32.2] The offence must be punishable in the case of an adult with imprisonment. Where a court would have power to make an order on conviction, and the court is satisfied that the accused did the act or made the omission charged, the court may, if it thinks fit, make the order without convicting him: Mental Health Act 1983, s 37(3). It follows that as there is no requirement for a trial, the provisions of s 20 of the Magistrates' Courts Act 1980 (procedure where summary trial appears more suitable for an offence triable either way) do not apply. However, the circumstances in which it will be appropriate to exercise this power will be very rare and will usually require the consent of those acting for the accused if he is under a disability so that he cannot be tried: *R v Lincolnshire (Kesteven) Justices, ex p O'Connor* [1983] 1 All ER 901, [1983] 1 WLR 335. Magistrates may still proceed to act under subsection (3) even where the defendant has elected to go for trial by jury: *R v Ramsgate Justices, ex p Kazmarek* (1984) 80 Cr App Rep 366, (1984) 149 JP 16, DC, but not where the offence is triable only on indictment: *R v Chippenham Magistrates' Court, ex p Thompson* (1995) 160 JP 207.

B[32.3] The minimum age for a guardianship order is ten.

B[32.4]–[32.5] The conditions for the making of an order are that the court is satisfied on the written or oral evidence of two registered medical practitioners, at least one of whom must be approved by the Secretary of State as having special experience in the diagnosis and treatment of mental disorder, that the offender is suffering from mental disorder and, in the case of an offender who has attained the age of 16 years, that the mental disorder is of a nature or degree which warrants his reception into guardianship, and the court is of the opinion, have regard to all the circumstances of the case including the nature of the offence and the character and antecedents of the offender, and to the other available methods of dealing with him, that the most suitable method of disposal is by means of making a guardianship order.

A guardianship order cannot be made unless the relevant authority or person is willing to receive the offender into guardianship: Mental Health Act 1983, s 37(6).

Where a court is minded to make a guardianship order it may request the local social services authority to inform the court whether it or any other person approved by it is willing to receive the offender into guardianship and to give such information as it reasonably can about how it or the other person could be expected to exercise guardianship powers: Mental Health Act 1983, s 39A.

Ancillary orders

B[32.6]–[32.16] Compensation at B[10]

Costs at B[12]

Disqualification at C[5]

Endorsement at C[5]

Deprivation of property and forfeiture at B[18]

Restitution at B[42]

General considerations of guardianship orders

B[32.17] Effect of guardianship order. A guardianship order confers on the authority or person named in it as guardian the same powers as guardianship under Part II of the Mental Health Act 1983. These are set out in s 8 and, in outline, are: to determine place of residence; to require attendance for treatment, occupation, education or training; and to require access to the patient in any place of residence for a doctor, social worker or other person specified.

B[32.18] Normally it will lapse after six months, but the mental specialists can recommend an extension when it will be extended for a further six months. After that the order can be extended for one-year periods or until the mental health authorities consider it safe to grant the defendant a discharge.

B[32.19] As the defendant has now become a patient and not a prisoner his discharge from guardianship can be made on the advice of the mental specialist in charge of his case.

B[32.20] The defendant need not wait for the mental specialist to act, but can apply for his discharge at any time during the first six months of the guardianship order or on any occasion when the order is renewed.

B[32.21] The defendant's nearest relative can make application once a year to the Mental Health Review Tribunal for his release.

B[33]

Hospital order

(Mental Health Act 1983, s 37)

Criteria

B[33.1] The relevant conditions are the same as for the making of a guardianship order (see **B[32.4]**, above) except that the court must also be satisfied that the mental disorder is treatable: Mental Health Act 1983, s 37(2)(a)(i). The court must also be satisfied that on the evidence of the approved clinician who would have responsibility for the offender's case or some other person representing the managers of the hospital that arrangements have been made for his admission to that hospital within the period of 28 days beginning with the date of the making of such an order; the court may, pending his admission within that period, give such directions as it thinks fit for his conveyance to and detention in a place of safety: Mental Health Act 1983, s 37(4).

General considerations of hospital orders

B[33.2]–[33.5] Legal representation should be offered to the defendant, or he should be recommended to consult a solicitor if the court is considering a hospital order.

In limited circumstances it is open to a defendant tried in a magistrates' court to plead **insanity**. There are limits on the availability of this defence. For a review of the authorities and procedures see *R (on the application of Singh) v Stratford Magistrates' Court* [2007] EWHC 1582 (Admin), (2007) Times, 13 August. The judgment also discusses the nature and limitations of the availability of an order under s 37 MHA 1983. It is advisable to consult the legal adviser.

B[33.6] **Effect of a hospital order.** The court does not fix the period that the defendant has to stay in hospital. The date of his release will be decided by the hospital authorities.

B[33.7] Normally the hospital order lapses after six months but it can be renewed for a further six months on the recommendation of the mental specialist in charge of the case, and thereafter the order can be renewed for one-yearly periods. The procedure is that the responsible mental specialist examines the patient and sends a report to the mental health authorities, which can be the hospital managers, who may then act on the recommendation to retain or discharge the patient. Thus the patient can be discharged at any time without reference back to the sentencing court.

B[33.8] The defendant, once a mental patient, can apply for his discharge at any time after the first six months of the order or whenever it is proposed to extend the order. For these reasons the order is in the discretion of the court and custody may still be dictated by public policy considerations (*R v Nafel* (2004)).

B[33.9] The defendant's nearest relative can apply for his discharge once a year to the Mental Health Review Tribunal.

B[33.10]–[33.15] **Including a restriction clause in a hospital order** (Mental Health Act 1983, s 41). If the defendant is 14 or more and was convicted (as opposed to having 'done the act'), and the magistrates consider a court restriction should be imposed on his release, he can be committed to the Crown Court for sentence pursuant to PCC(S)A 2000, s 3. [**It would appear that this power will no longer be available on or after a date to be appointed unless the committal for sentence is made immediately after the entering of a plea or the offence is a specified offence and the defendant is committed for sentence on the basis that he is a dangerous offender: see **B[8]**).

B[33.16] The Crown Court can make a hospital order, and include in it a restriction upon the date of release either for a specified period of time or indefinitely.

B[33.17] The magistrates can commit the defendant to prison pending his appearance at the Crown Court or, if satisfied that a vacancy is available at a mental hospital, can order him to be detained there pending his appearance at the Crown Court.

B[33.18] If the Crown Court includes a restriction clause the defendant cannot be discharged by the mental specialist or allowed out of the specified hospital without the consent of the Home Secretary.

B[33.19] The Home Secretary may at any time refer the case to a Mental Health Review Tribunal for their advice, but does not have to accept the advice if he considers that discharge of the patient is not in the public interest.

B[33.20] If the Home Secretary does decide that the patient should be discharged from the mental hospital, he has powers to impose conditions for the discharge such as the place of residence, a scheme of supervision and the liability to recall if a lapse occurs.

B[33.21] **Remand for report on accused's mental condition (s 35).** Where a doctor satisfies the court that there is reason to suspect that the accused suffers from one or other of several mental disorders and

(a) the accused has been convicted of an offence punishable on summary conviction with imprisonment or 'did the act' or has consented to this course of action; and
(b) it is otherwise impracticable to obtain medical reports; and
(c) arrangements have been made for his reception into a hospital;

the court may remand the accused in a hospital for up to 28 days. There may be further such remands for a total period of up to 12 weeks.

The purpose of an order under s 35 is to inform a court about issues relevant to the defendant's fitness to plead and disposal; it does not permit an order to be made for the purpose of obtaining evidence relevant to an issue at trial, eg the defendant's ability to form the specific intent required by the offence: *R (on the application of M) v Kingston Crown Court* [2014] EWHC 2702 (Admin), [2015] 1 Cr App R 27, 178 JP 438.

Interim hospital order (s 38)

B[33.22] Provision is made by s 38 of the Mental Health Act 1983 for the making of an interim hospital order for the purpose of establishing whether or not a convicted person is suitable to be the subject of a hospital order. The conditions are virtually the same as for the making of a full hospital order. One difference is that one of the reporting doctors must be employed at the hospital where the offender is to be detained.

An interim order can last for up to 12 weeks and can then be renewed for periods of up to 28 days subject to an overall limit of 12 months. The defendant need not be present at renewal hearings provided he is legally represented and his legal representative is given an opportunity of being heard.

B[34]

Imprisonment

(Powers of Criminal Courts (Sentencing) Act 2000, s 78)

Limitations

B[34.1] (a) **Imprisonable offence.**

B[34.2] (b) **Presence of offender.** If the proceedings were instituted by an information followed by a summons, or by a written charge, the court shall not in absence impose a custodial sentence or order that a suspended sentence shall take effect; in any other case, where such a sentence or order is imposed or made, the offender must be brought before the court before he begins to serve the sentence and the sentence will not be effective until this happens: Magistrates' Courts Act 1980, s 11(3), (3A) and (5).

B[34.3] (c) **Age limit.** Defendant must be 21 or over. For offenders under 21 the appropriate custodial sentence would be detention in a young offender institution.

B[34.4] **Criteria for imposing a custodial sentence.** The court must be of the opinion that the offence, or the combination of the offence and any other offence associated with it, is so serious that neither a fine nor a community sentence can be a justified penalty for it.

B[34.5] **Other circumstances in which custody may be imposed.** Nothing in paragraph (a) above prevents the court imposing a custodial sentence on an offender who refuses to consent to a community sentence proposed by the court which requires his consent. A court may also impose custody for a wilful and persistent breach of a community order.

B[34.6] **So serious.** Courts should always bear in mind that criminal sentences were in almost every case intended to protect the public whether by punishing the offender or reforming him, or deterring him and others, or all of those things. The sentence imposed should be no longer than is commensurate with the seriousness of the offence (Criminal Justice Act 2003, s 153). The court must take account of all the information about the circumstances of the offence including any aggravating or mitigating factors as is available to it.

In *R v Mills* [2002] EWCA Crim 26, [2002] 2 Cr App Rep (S) 51, [2002] Crim LR 331, the Lord Chief Justice said that imprisonment was often unnecessary for non-violent crimes of dishonesty committed by mothers caring for young families. In *R v Kefford* [2002] EWCA Crim 519, [2002] Crim LR 432 this principle is extended to those persons with no previous convictions convicted of economic crimes.

B[34.7]–[34.15] **Associated offence.** An offence of which the offender has been convicted in the same proceedings or for which he is sentenced at the same time, or an offence taken into consideration.

B[34.16] **Pre-sentence report.** A magistrates' court, unless it considers it unnecessary to do so, must obtain and consider a pre-sentence report before forming an opinion on:

(a) whether the offence etc was so serious;
(b) the length of term commensurate with the offence.

In all cases where a court is contemplating sentencing a defendant to prison for the first time, other than a very short period, it should be the inevitable practice that a pre-sentence report is obtained (*R v Gillette* (1999) Times, 3 December, CA).

B[34.17] **Failure to obtain pre-sentence report.** Does not invalidate the sentence but the appeal court must obtain and consider such a report if the court below was not justified in forming the opinion that a report was not necessary (Criminal Justice Act 2003, s 156).

B[34.18] **Mentally disordered offender.** Where an offender is or appears to be mentally disordered, ie suffering from a mental disorder within the meaning of the Mental Health Act 1983, the court must additionally obtain and consider a medical report before passing a custodial sentence unless the court considers it unnecessary to do so. The court must take any such information into account and consider the likely effect of any custodial sentence on his condition and any treatment for it. Failure to obtain a medical report does not invalidate any sentence but one must be obtained and considered by an appeal court (Criminal Justice Act 2003, s 157).

B[34.19] **Legal representation.** The offender, who has not previously been imprisoned, must first be given the opportunity to be legally represented unless he has been refused legal aid for financial reasons. Note the requirement is not that he should be represented but that he should have the opportunity to be.

Reasons for decisions

B[34.20] It is the duty of the court to state in open court that it is of the opinion that either or both of paragraph B[34.4] and B[34.2] above apply and why it is of that opinion and in all cases (including where a custodial sentence has been imposed following the offender's refusal to comply with a proposed requirement in a community sentence) explain to the offender in open court and in ordinary language why it is passing a custodial sentence on him or, if applicable, why imprisonment is for a longer term than would normally be commensurate with the seriousness of the offence.

B[34.21] **Suspended sentences.** All these limitations apply equally to suspended sentences.

General considerations of imprisonment

B[34.22] **Consecutive sentences.** If the defendant is sentenced to immediate or suspended imprisonment on each of two or more offences the terms will run concurrently unless the court orders they are to run consecutively. Consecutively means that one term of imprisonment follows another.

B[34.23] When a magistrates' court sentences an offender for two or more offences it may order that one sentence runs consecutively to the other. In addition (when sentencing for one or more offences) the court may order that a term of imprisonment shall be consecutive to a term already being served by the defendant. In such a case the term imposed should be stated to be consecutive to the total period to which the defendant is subject.

B[34.24] The total period of two or more consecutive sentences imposed on the same occasion by a magistrates' court must not exceed 6 months, unless two or more of the offences are triable either way, when the total period may not exceed 12 months. If the defendant is convicted of two offences, the former being an offence triable either way and the latter which is purely summary, the maximum total remains as six months. If the court orders a suspended prison sentence to take effect, it can order that sentence to take effect consecutively to a period of imprisonment for the later offence, even though the total period will exceed the above limits. When a previously suspended sentence is ordered to be served it should normally be made consecutive to a sentence imposed for the later offence. Minimum sentence is 14 days if the sentence is suspended.

There are conflicting authorities as to whether a sentence may exceed six months where the terms imposed for the either way offences are in total less than six months; eg is it permissible under s 133 of the Magistrates' Courts Act 1980 to impose a sentence comprising two months for one either way offence, one month consecutive for another either way offence, and further consecutive terms of two months for each of three summary offences, making a total of nine months' imprisonment? In *R v King's Lynn Magistrates' Court, ex p Hyman* (QB) CO/1320/91 this was precisely the position and it was held that 'the construction of the section is clear beyond argument' (per Tudor Evans J) and permitted such a sentence. The opposite view, however, was reached in *R v Goldie Steadman* [2003] EWCA Crim 2031, 2003 WL 22002214 where it was held 'As we understand (s 133), where consecutive sentences have been passed that total more than six months but less than twelve months, it is required that each of those offences shall have been offences capable of being tried either way' (per Hedley J). In *Steadman* it appears that the court was not referred to the *King's Lynn* case. We are of the opinion that the former authority is correct. Section 133(2), to which s 133(1) is subject, does not contain the proviso that the term or terms which take the sentence above six months must relate to either way offences. If this had been Parliament's intention it could, and in our submission would, have been made explicit in the terms of s 133(2).

B[34.25]–[34.30] Where several offences arise out of one incident consecutive sentences should not be imposed but the incident should be looked at as a whole and one appropriate period fixed. The same principle would apply to a series of offences committed against the same person over a relatively short period, eg an employee who falsifies a weekly claim for expenses.

B[34.31] Consecutive sentences are appropriate where, although there is a single incident, there is more than one offence but they do not arise as a matter of course from the principal offence. For example, the burglar who attacks a householder who discovers him, or an assault on a police officer effecting an arrest for another offence.

Although there may be some cases where it would not be wrong in principle to impose consecutive sentences for offences of affray and possession of an offensive weapon where the latter was the aggravating feature of the former, it was not appropriate to do so where the sentencing judge referred expressly to the principle of totality and it was difficult to ascertain from his sentencing remarks how, if he was imposing a consecutive sentence, he was giving effect to that principle: *R v Birchall (Leevon)* [2018] EWCA Crim 1267, [2018] 2 Crim App R (S) 43.

Offences committed on bail should normally attract a consecutive sentence where imprisonment is appropriate as offending on bail is an aggravating factor.

B[34.32] When consecutive sentences are imposed the court should pay particular regard to the total period and reduce it if it is excessive; this is especially the rule to follow with young offenders and those receiving a first custodial sentence. One method of adjusting the total period in such cases is to consider concurrent rather than consecutive sentences.

B[34.33] **Multiple offences.** When sentencing a defendant for several offences it is best to refer to the nature of each offence and the sentence and to state the total time to be served. To say 'For the first offence you will go to prison for two months, for the second two months consecutive, for the third two months concurrent . . .' can be quite meaningless. Some chairmen prefer to begin with what is perhaps the most important aspect of the sentence first: 'You will go to prison for a total of 6 months. That is made up of two months for stealing the watch, a further two months for stealing the camera . . . etc.'

B[34.34] When consecutive sentences are being considered the total period should be reviewed and reduced if it is excessive.

B[34.35] **Period of imprisonment.** Great care must be exercised in determining the period of imprisonment, especially if it is to be suspended. The length of a custodial sentence must not exceed a term justified by the seriousness of the offence(s) and where there is appropriate mitigation, may be shorter.

B[34.36] Magistrates' courts tend to consider sentences in units of months and the commonest terms are 3, 6 (and where appropriate) 9 and 12 months. It should be remembered that there is a complete discretion within the range available for a particular offence. It may be that for some offenders receiving a custodial sentence for the first time, a sentence of 7 or 14 days would be a salutary lesson, but with no other sentencing objective.

B[34.37] Magistrates should reserve the maximum period available for an offence for those cases which are the worst type of case they would deal with.

B[34.38] Offences of attempt will not usually attract the same period as would the completed offence.

B[34.39] **Credit for time on remand.** Section 108 of the Legal Aid, Sentencing and Punishment of Offenders Act 2012 inserted s 240ZA of the Criminal Justice Act 20031 in place of s 240. The effect is to disapply the discretion to withhold credit for time on remand in custody for the offence or a related offence; instead, such time is to be calculated and applied administratively. There are three exceptions, however, where credit for time on remand in custody does not apply, namely:

(a) if, on any day on which the offender was remanded in custody in connection with the offence, the offender was also detained in connection with any other matter, that day is not to count as time served;
(b) a day counts as time served in relation to only one sentence, and only once in relation to that sentence;
(c) a day is not to count as time served as part of any period of 28 days served by the offender before automatic release. (This prevents remand time from shortening any recall under s 255B of the Criminal Justice Act 2003 where the maximum length of the recall is 28 days.)

Consecutive and concurrent sentences, where a prisoner has not been released between serving such sentences, are counted as one sentence for the purpose of deducting remand time.

For the purpose of crediting time on remand in custody, a suspended sentence is to be treated as a sentence of imprisonment when it takes effect and is to be treated as imposed by the order under which it takes effect.

The 2003 Act provisions on credit for time on remand apply to any sentence of imprisonment, whether it is: an original sentence of imprisonment; one imposed for breach/revocation of a community order; one imposed by way of activation of a suspended sentence; one imposed in default of payment of a sum adjudged to be paid by way of a conviction; one imposed for want of sufficient distress to satisfy any sum of money; or one imposed for failure to be or abstain from doing anything required to be done or left undone.

B[34.39A] **Credit for time spent on qualifying bail curfew.** Sections 21 and 22 of the Criminal Justice and Immigration Act 2008 introduced new provisions which apply to offenders on bail subject to a qualifying curfew condition, defined as a condition to remain at one or more specified places for a total of not less than nine hours in any given day combined with an electronic monitoring condition.

In summary, such offenders were entitled, subject to exceptions made by rules, and subject to the court's discretion to withhold credit on interests of justice grounds, to have half the period spent on such curfew count towards any sentence of imprisonment imposed for the offence.

Significant changes were made by the s 109 of the Legal Aid, Sentencing and Punishment of Offenders Act 2012. Principally, the changes were:

(a) a new method of calculating the 'credit period';
(b) the enactment of exceptions;
(c) the removal of the 'interests of justice' discretion to withhold credit.

The credit period is calculated by taking the following, five steps:

(1) Add–
The number of days on which the offender's bail was subject to the relevant conditions, including the first whether the condition applied for the whole of the day or not, but excluding the last if the offender spends the last part of it in custody.
(2) Deduct–
Any of the above days on which the offender was subject to an electronically monitored curfew requirement in connection with any other sentence (including on release under home detention curfew) or temporarily released from prison in relation to another sentence.

(3) Deduct–
From the remaining days, the number of days during that remainder on which the offender has broken either or both of the relevant conditions.
(4) Divide–
The result by two.
(5) Round up–
If necessary, to the nearest round number.

A day of the credit period counts as time served in relation to only once sentence and only once in relation to that sentence.

A day of the credit period is not to count as time served as part of any period of 28 days served by the offender before automatic release.

If a curfew is not accompanied by an electronic tag, the statutory conditions are not met and a court is entitled to refuse to give credit for the curfew period even though it qualified in terms of length and the defendant complied with it; there might, however, be circumstances where some allowance should be made, for example, where there are two defendants for sentence who have been subject to curfews but for some reason only one defendant has been electronically tagged: *R v Barrett* [2009] EWCA Crim 2213, [2010] 1 Cr App Rep (S) 572, [2010] Crim LR 159. See also *Rv Sherif* [2008] EWCA Crim 2653, , [2009] 2 Cr App Rep (S) 235, and *R v Monaghan (Rudie Aaron)* [2009] EWCA Crim 2699, [2010] 2 Cr App Rep (S) 343, [2010] Crim LR 322.

B[34.40]–[34.45] Suspended sentences (Criminal Justice Act 2003, s 189).

The maximum prison term which can be suspended was increased by the Legal Aid, Sentencing and Punishment of Offenders Act 2012 to two years, though magistrates' courts continue to be subject to the normal limits of six months, or 12 months where the court is dealing with two or more offences triable either way. The minimum term which can be suspended is 14 days or, in the case of offenders aged 18–20, 21 days. For offenders aged 18–20 the form of custody is detention in a young offender institution.

The operational period of a suspended sentence is a minimum of six months and a maximum of two years.

B[34.46] When the court suspends a sentence, it may impose one or more requirements for the offender to undertake in the community. The requirements are identical to those available for community orders.

If the offender *fails* to comply with a community requirement or commits a further offence, the court must *either* activate the suspended sentence in full or in part unless it is unjust to do so; *or* amend the order so as to:

(a) extend the period during which the offender is subject to community requirements;
(b) make the community requirements more onerous;
(c) may order the offender to pay a fine not exceeding £2,500; or
(d) extend the operational period (CJA 2003, Sch 12, para 8).

If the suspended sentence was imposed by the Crown Court, and the offender is found to have breached any of its requirements, and the suspended sentence order includes a direction that any failure to comply with its requirements is to be dealt with by the magistrates' court, the magistrates' court may activate the sentence in full or with a reduced term or impose a fine of up to £2,500, or impose more onerous requirements, or extend either the supervision period or operational period of the sentence; alternatively, the court may commit the breach to the Crown Court and remand the offender on bail or in custody: Criminal Justice Act 2003, Sch 12, paras 6 and 8. If an offender commits an offence during the operational period of a Crown Court suspended sentence, the court may commit the offender to the Crown Court for sentence and, if it does not, it must give written notice of the conviction to the Crown Court. If the former course is taken, there is a bespoke power under PCC(S)A 2000, s 6(4)(e) to commit the offender to the Crown Court for the new offence. If the committal is pursuant to this power, the sentencing powers of the Crown Court in respect of the new offence/s will be the same as those of the magistrates' court: *R v Bateman; R v Doyle* [2012] EWCA Crim 2158, [2013] 1 WLR 1710, [2013] Crim LR 352; *R v Hester-Wox* [2016] EWCA Crim 1397, (2017) 181 JP 180, [2017] Crim LR 154. Therefore, if the magistrates' court considers that the new offence justifies a sentence in excess of its powers, it should commit the offender under s 3 of the PCC(S)A 2000.

Where an offender commits an offence during the operational period of a suspended sentence and is also in breach of its requirements, the sentence can only be activated once: *R v Maunder* [2015] EWCA Crim 778, [2015] 2 Cr App R (S) 26.

If a suspended sentence is activated with a reduced term it is not possible to leave the remaining balance of the suspended sentencing hanging over the defendant: *R v Bostan* [2018] EWCA Crim 494, [2018] 2 Cr App R (S) 15.

NB: In *West Yorkshire Probation Board v Cruickshanks* [2010] EWHC 615 (Admin), 174 JP 305 it was held that the Probation Service could not enforce an unpaid work requirement under a suspended sentence order following expiration of the operational period of the order. This means that the Probation Service should be alive to laying breaches during the currency of the order. Levenson LJ, who gave the judgment of the court was also of the view that there was no power to extend the operational period once it had expired.

B[34.47]–[34.49] There are many similarities between suspended sentences and community orders; requirements can be imposed on the offender and the court can respond to breach by sending him or her to custody. The crucial difference is that a suspended sentence is a custodial sentence; it may be imposed **only** where the court is satisfied that the custodial threshold has been passed and that it is not appropriate to impose a community order, fine or other non-custodial disposal.

A further difference is the approach to any breach; while sentencing for breach of a community order, the primary objective is to ensure that the requirements of the order are complied with. When responding to breach of a suspended sentence, the **statutory presumption** is that the custodial sentence will be activated.

In *R v Levesconte* [2011] EWCA Crim 2754, [2012] 2 Cr App Rep (S) 80, 176 JP 204 it was held that the sentencer was not entitled to treat the fact that the offence was committed during the operational period of the suspended sentence as a factor justifying the increase of the second sentence, not at least in circumstances where the suspended sentence was activated in full. To take that factor into account again was to increase the sentence referable to that fact beyond the maximum for which the defendant had been at risk. The court recognised that the same argument may not apply where the suspended sentence is not fully implemented.

B[34.50]–[34.51] The Sentencing Council's definitive guideline 'Imposition of Community Sentence' emphasises that a suspended sentence must not be imposed as a more severe form of community order. It is a custodial sentence and the court should make clear that it would impose an immediate custodial sentence if the power to suspend were not available.

Where a sentence is suspended, the term of imprisonment should be the same that would have applied if the sentence was to be served immediately.

As to the factors to be weighed in considering whether or not it is possible to suspend the sentence, see **B[15.17]**, ante.

In *R v Finn* [2012] EWCA Crim 881, [2012] 2 Cr App Rep (S) 569 the 29 year old appellant had 36 convictions for 86 different offences. In February 2010 he was sentenced to 9 months' imprisonment, suspended for two years, for one offence of affray and one offence of possession of a bladed article. He was sentenced to an 18-month supervision order with an unpaid work requirement of 140 hours.

In January 2012, he was sentenced to six months' imprisonment for one offence of shop theft committed in November 2011. In addition, on that occasion the Recorder activated the full nine month suspended sentence, making a total sentence of 15 months. He appealed against the activation of all nine months of the suspended sentence. The Court of Appeal held:

> In the circumstances of this particular case, we do not believe that the judge erred in principle in concluding that it was not unjust to impose the suspended sentence in full. We recognise that some judges might have given the appellant modest credit for the unpaid work he had carried out, but that is not the test. A suspended sentence order must be complied with in full; non-compliance risks activation of the suspended sentence in full. In those circumstances, a defendant such as the appellant in the present case, who does not comply with the terms of the suspended sentence order, only has himself to blame if non-compliance leads to activation of the suspended sentence in full.

Similarly, the length of time an offender has been subject to a suspended sentence before committing a further offence does not necessarily require a reduction in the activated term; there is no 'sliding scale' by which a term should be reduced: *R v Wolstenholme* [2016] EWCA Crim 638, [2016] 2 Cr App R (S) 19.

Ancillary orders

B[34.52] Compensation at B[10]

Costs at B[17]

Disqualification at C[5]

Endorsement at C[5]

Deprivation of property and forfeiture at B[18]

Restitution order at B[42]

Post-release supervision

B[34.53] Significant changes to supervision after release were made by the Offender Rehabilitation Act 2014. The Act applies to offences committed on or after 1 February 2015 (See The Offender Rehabilitation Act 2014 (Commencement No 2) Order 2015, SI 2015/40, art 2.)

The Act provides for post-sentence supervision for offenders who receive more than one day but less than two years' imprisonment (amending the duty to release prisoners serving less than 12 months unconditionally at the half way point of the sentence).

The new regime applies to offenders aged at least 18 years at the half way point of the custodial term. (New s 243A(1) and (1A) of the Criminal Justice Act 2003 reduces the duty to release unconditionally to: (a) offenders serving a sentence of a term of one day; (b) offenders serving a term of less than 12 months who are aged under 18 at the half way point of the sentence; and (c) offenders serving a sentence of less than 12 months for an offence committed before the commencement of s 1 of the 2014 Act.)

Such offenders will continue to be released at the half way point, but not unconditionally as before. They will be on licence for the remainder of the custodial term and then supervised until the end of the period of 12 months immediately after the half-way point of their sentence; for example, an offender sentenced to six months' imprisonment will be released on serving one half of that sentence and will then be on licence for a period of three months followed by a period of supervision of nine months: Criminal Justice Act 2003, s 256AA. (As to the period of licence where the sentence contains terms of imprisonment for offences straddling the commencement of the 2014 Act, see s 264B of the Criminal Justice Act 2003. As to the requirements of the offender which the Secretary of State may specify during the supervision period, see s 256AB of the Criminal Justice Act 2003.)

Breach of post-sentence supervision requirements will be dealt with in the magistrates' court, even if the original sentence was imposed by the Crown Court. The available sanctions are: (a) committal to prison for a period not exceeding 14 days; (b) a fine not exceeding level 3 on the standard scale; or a 'supervision default order' imposing either an unpaid work requirement or a curfew requirement Criminal Justice Act 2003, s 256AC.

Early release on home detention curfew

B[34.54] Section 246 of the Criminal Justice Act 2003 provides for the early release on licence of certain fixed term prisoners. The Secretary of State may release a qualifying offenders up to 135 days before the day on which the offender would have served the requisite custodial period. However, such release is not available unless the requisite custodial period is at least six weeks, and the offender has served whichever is the longer of four weeks and one half of that period. Moreover, various categories of prisoners are excluded from early release. Where a prisoner is released under these provisions a curfew condition must be imposed, together with electronic monitoring, and these conditions will continue until the day on which the offender would otherwise (ie without early release) have been released.

Breach of a suspended sentence order

Criminal Justice Act 2003, Sch 12

B[34.55] This text is taken from the Sentencing Council's Breach offences: Definitive guideline, published on 7 June 2018, with effect from 1 October 2018.

Effective from: 1 October 2018

1) Conviction for further offence committed during operational period of order

The court **must activate the custodial sentence** unless it would be unjust in all the circumstances to do so. The predominant factor in determining whether activation is unjust relates to the level of compliance with the suspended sentence order and the facts/nature of any new offence. **These factors are already provided for in the penalties below which are determined by the nature of the new offence and level of compliance, but permit a reduction to the custodial term for relevant completed or partially completed requirements where appropriate.**

The facts/nature of the new offence is the primary consideration in assessing the action to be taken on the breach.

Where the breach is in the second or third category below, the prior level of compliance is also relevant. In assessing the level of compliance with the order the court should consider:

(i) the overall attitude and engagement with the order as well as the proportion of elements completed;
(ii) the impact of any completed or partially completed requirements on the offender's behaviour;
(iii) the proximity of breach to imposition of order; and
(iv) evidence of circumstances or offender characteristics, such as disability, mental health issues or learning difficulties which have impeded offender's compliance with the order.

Breach involves	Penalty
Multiple and/or more serious new offence(s) committed	Full activation of original custodial term
New offence similar in type and gravity to offence for which suspended sentence order imposed and:	

a) No/low level of compliance with suspended sentence order	Full activation of original custodial term
OR	
b) Medium or high level of compliance with suspended sentence order	Activate sentence but apply appropriate reduction* to original custodial term taking into consideration any unpaid work or curfew requirements completed
New offence less serious than original offence but requires a custodial sentence and:	
a) No/low level of compliance with suspended sentence order	Full activation of original custodial term
OR	
b) Medium or high level of compliance with suspended sentence order	Activate sentence but apply appropriate reduction to original custodial term taking into consideration any unpaid work or curfew requirements completed
New offence less serious than original offence but requires a custodial sentence and:	Activate sentence but apply appropriate reduction to original custodial term taking into consideration any unpaid work or curfew requirements completed OR Impose more onerous requirement(s) and/or extend supervision period and/or extend operational period and/or impose fine

* It is for the court dealing with the breach to identify the appropriate proportionate reduction depending on the extent of any compliance with the requirements specified.

Unjust in all the circumstances

The court dealing with the breach should remember that the court imposing the original sentence determined that a custodial sentence was appropriate in the original case.

In determining if there are other factors which would cause activation to be unjust, the court may consider all factors including:

- any strong personal mitigation;
- whether there is a realistic prospect of rehabilitation;
- whether immediate custody will result in significant impact on others.

Only new and exceptional factors/circumstances not present at the time the suspended sentence order was imposed should be taken into account.

In cases where the court considers that it would be unjust to order the custodial sentence to take effect, it must state its reasons and it must deal with the offender in one of the following ways:

(a) impose a fine not exceeding £2,500; OR
(b) extend the operational period (to a maximum of two years from date of original sentence); OR
(c) if the SSO imposes community requirements, do one or more of:
 (i) impose more onerous community requirements;
 (ii) extend the supervision period (to a maximum of two years from date of original sentence);
 (iii) extend the operational period (to a maximum of two years from date of original sentence).

2) Failure to comply with a community requirement during the supervision period of the order

The court must activate the custodial sentence unless it would be unjust in all the circumstances to do so. The predominant factor in determining whether activation is unjust relates to the level of compliance with the suspended sentence order. This **factor is already provided for in the penalties below which are determined by the level of compliance, but permit a reduction to the custodial term for relevant completed or partially completed requirements where appropriate.**

The court must take into account the extent to which the offender has complied with the suspended sentence order when imposing a sentence.

In assessing the level of compliance with the order the court should consider:

(i) the overall attitude and engagement with the order as well as the proportion of elements completed;
(ii) the impact of any completed or partially completed requirements on the offender's behaviour; and
(iii) the proximity of breach to imposition of order; and
(iv) evidence of circumstances or offender characteristics, such as disability, mental health issues or learning difficulties which have impeded offender's compliance with the order.

Breach involves	Penalty
No/low level of compliance	Full activation of original custodial term
Medium level of compliance	Activate sentence but apply appropriate reduction* to original custodial term taking into consideration any unpaid work or curfew requirements completed
High level of compliance	Activate sentence but apply appropriate reduction to original custodial term taking into consideration any unpaid work or curfew requirements completed **OR** Impose more onerous requirement(s) and/or extend supervision period and/or extend operational period and/or impose fine

* It is for the court dealing with the breach to identify the appropriate proportionate reduction depending on the extent of any compliance with the requirements specified.

Unjust in all the circumstances

The court dealing with the breach should remember that the court imposing the original sentence determined that a custodial sentence was appropriate in the original case.

In determining if there are other factors which would cause activation to be unjust, the court may consider all factors including:

- any strong personal mitigation;
- whether there is a realistic prospect of rehabilitation;
- whether immediate custody will result in significant impact on others.

Only new and exceptional factors/circumstances not present at the time the suspended sentence order was imposed should be taken into account.

In cases where the court considers that it would be unjust to order the custodial sentence to take effect, it must state its reasons and it **must** deal with the offender in one of the following ways:

(a) impose a fine not exceeding £2,500; **OR**
(b) extend the operational period (to a maximum of two years from date of original sentence); **OR**
(c) if the SSO imposes community requirements, do one or more of:
 (i) impose more onerous community requirements;

(ii) extend the supervision period (to a maximum of two years from date of original sentence);
(iii) extend the operational period (to a maximum of two years from date of original sentence).

B[35]

Injunctions for gang-related violence

Granting injunctions for gang-related violence

B[35.1] In the case of a person aged at least 14 and under 18 years, a youth court may grant an injunction to prevent gang-related violence: Policing and Crime Act 2009, s 34(1). In relation to persons who have attained 18 years, jurisdiction is that of the High Court or county court. See below for those who attain 18 years during the course of the proceedings or while an injunction is in force.

Meaning of gang-related violence and conditions for granting an injunction

B[35.2] 'Gang-related violence' means violence or a threat of violence which occurs in the course of, or is otherwise related to, the activities of a group that consists of at least three people, uses a name emblem or colour or has any other characteristic that enables its members to be identified by others as a group, and is associated with a particular area: Policing and Crime Act 2009, s 34(5).

The Secretary of State is required to issue guidance relating to such injunctions: Policing and Crime Act 2009, s 47.

A court may only grant such injunction if two conditions are met:

(a) it is satisfied on the balance of probabilities that the respondent has engaged in, or has encouraged or assisted, gang-related violence or gang-related drug-dealing activity;

(b) it is necessary to grant the injunction for either or both of the following purposes:

  (i) to prevent the respondent from engaging in, or encouraging or assisting, gang-related violence or gang-related drug-dealing activity;

  (ii) to protect the respondent from gang-related violence or gang-related drug-dealing activity. (Policing and Crime Act 2009, s 34(2), (3))

It was affirmed in *Jones v Birmingham City Council* [2018] EWCA Civ 1189, [2018] 3 WLR 1693, [2018] 2 Cr App R 23 that proceedings for a gang/drug dealing-related injunction are civil in nature and the 'balance of probabilities' standard of proof is not incompatible with art 6(1) of the ECHR.

Prohibitions and requirements

B[35.3] An injunction may for either of those purposes, impose prohibitions on the respondent from doing anything described in the injunction and or require the respondent to do anything described in the injunction: Policing and Crime Act 2009, s 34(4).

The prohibitions and requirements included in the injunction must, so far as is practicable, be for the purposes of preventing the respondent from engaging in, or encouraging or assisting, gang-related violence or drug-dealing activity or protecting the respondent from gang-related violence or drug-dealing activity.

Prohibitions included in an injunction may, in particular, have the effect of prohibiting the respondent from being in a particular place (which for this purpose includes an area); being with particular persons in a particular place; being in charge of a particular species of animal in a particular place; wearing particular descriptions of articles of clothing in a particular place; using the internet to facilitate or encourage violence. Requirements included in an injunction may, in particular, have the effect of requiring the respondent to: notify the respondent's address and of any change to that address; be at a particular place between particular times on particular days (for up to eight hours in any day); present himself or herself to a particular person at a place where he or she is required to be between particular times on particular days; participate in particular activities between particular times on particular days. The prohibitions and requirements included in the injunction must, so far as practicable, avoid any conflict with the respondent's religious beliefs, and any interference with the times at which the respondent normally works or attends any educational establishment. Any prohibition or requirement in an injunction may not have effect after the end of a period of two years beginning with the day on which the injunction is granted: Policing and Crime Act 2009, s 35(3), (4), (5), (7) and 36(2).

Reviews

B[35.4] The court may order the applicant and the respondent to attend one or more review hearings, ie a hearing held for the purpose of considering whether the injunction should be varied or discharged. A review hearing must generally be held within the last four weeks of the first year where prohibitions or requirements extend beyond that year. In the case of a respondent who was under the age of 18 years when the injunction was granted there is a requirement in any event to hold a review within four weeks of the respondent's 18th birthday where any prohibition or requirement is to extend by at least four weeks beyond that date: Policing and Crime Act 2009, s 36(3), (4), (4A), (5). (See also the Magistrates' Courts (Injunctions: Gang-related Violence) Rules 2015, SI 2015/421, r 15.)

Attaching power of arrest

B[35.5] The court may attach a power of arrest in relation to any prohibition in the injunction, or any requirement in the injunction (other than one which has the effect of requiring the respondent to participate in particular activities) and may specify that the power is to have effect for a shorter period than the prohibition or requirement to which it relates: Policing and Crime Act 2009, s 36(6), (7). (See also the Magistrates' Courts (Injunctions: Gang-related Violence) Rules 2015, SI 2015/421, r 5.)

Applications

B[35.6] An application for a gang-related violence injunction may be made by the police or a local authority: Policing and Crime Act 2009, s 37. An application must be made by way of complaint in writing: Magistrates' Courts (Injunctions: Gang-related Violence) Rules 2015, SI 2015/421, rr 2 and 3.

Except in the case of a without notice application (see below), before applying for an injunction the applicant must consult any local authority, police and any other body or individual that the applicant thinks it appropriate to consult including, where the respondent will be under 18 years when the application is made, the youth offending team for the area in whose area it appears to the applicant that the respondent resides: Policing and Crime Act 2009, s 38.

Applications without notice

B[35.7] An application may be made without the respondent being given notice. In this case there is no requirement for prior consultation. But where an application without notice is made, the court must either dismiss it or adjourn the proceedings, which then triggers the requirement for consultation before the date of the first hearing of which notice has been given to the respondent. An injunction made without notice will not take effect until served on the respondent personally: Policing and Crime Act 2009, s 39(1); Magistrates' Courts (Injunctions: Gang-related Violence) Rules 2015, SI 2015/421, r 4.

Respondent attaining 18 years after commencement or proceedings

B[35.8] Where a respondent attains the age of 18 after the commencement of proceedings, the proceedings must remain in a youth court, but the court may, at the request of the applicant or the respondent or of its own motion direct that the proceedings be transferred to the High Court or county court, having had regard in particular to the stage which the proceedings have reached; the circumstances of the applicant and the respondent; and the need to ensure fairness between the applicant and the respondent, or direct that the proceedings be transferred to a youth court for the local justice area in which the respondent currently resides, in order for that court to consider whether to make such direction: see the Magistrates' Courts (Injunctions: Gang-related Violence) Rules 2015, SI 2015/421, r 16.

Interim injunctions

B[35.9] Where the court adjourns an on notice hearing, the court may grant an interim injunction if it thinks that it is just and convenient to do so: Policing and Crime Act 2009, s 40(1), (2).

An interim injunction granted following an on notice hearing may include any provision which the court has power to include in a full injunction (including a power of arrest): Policing and Crime Act 2009, s 40(3).

Where the adjournment is of a without notice hearing, the court may grant an interim injunction if it thinks that it is necessary to do so: Policing and Crime Act 2009, s 41(1), (2).

An interim injunction granted following a without notice hearing may not have the effect of requiring the respondent to participate in particular activities but may otherwise include any provision which the court has power to include in a full injunction (including a power of arrest): Policing and Crime Act 2009, s 41(4).

Variation and discharge

B[35.10] The court may vary or discharge an injunction if a review hearing is held, or an application to vary or discharge the injunction is made by the person who applied for the injunction or the respondent: Policing and Crime Act 2009, s 42(1), (2). For procedure, see the Magistrates' Courts (Injunctions: Gang-related Violence) Rules 2015, SI 2015/421, r 6.

Where an application to vary or discharge is made by the person who applied for the injunction, the applicant must notify the persons previously consulted: Policing and Crime Act 2009, s 42(5).

The power to vary an injunction includes power to include an additional prohibition or requirement in the injunction; extend the period for which a prohibition or requirement in the injunction has effect (up to a maximum of two years from when the injunction was originally granted); attach a power of arrest or extend the period for which a power of arrest attached to the injunction has effect: Policing and Crime Act 2009, s 42(3).

The requirement to review an injunction after one year does not apply where the injunction was varied in the four weeks preceding the end of the first year: Policing and Crime Act 2009, s 36(4) and 42(4). The intention appears to have been that the requirement to review an injunction within four weeks of a respondent's 18th birthday would not apply where there has been a review of the injunction within the preceding four weeks but it is not clear that the legislation achieves that: see the Explanatory note to the Crime and Security Act 2010, para 128 and the Policing and Crime Act 2009, s 42(4A).

If an application to vary or discharge an injunction is dismissed, no further application may be made without consent of the court: Policing and Crime Act 2009, s 42(6), and the Magistrates' Courts (Injunctions: Gang-related Violence) Rules 2015, SI 2015/421, r 14.

Arrest and remand

B[35.11] Where a power of arrest is attached to a provision of an injunction a constable may arrest without warrant a person whom the constable has reasonable cause to suspect to be in breach of the provision and inform the person who applied for the injunction of the arrest: Policing and Crime Act 2009, s 43(2), (3). A person arrested must be brought before a judge of the youth court which granted the injunction within the period of 24 hours beginning with the time of the arrest: Policing and Crime Act 2009, s 43(4), (7). 'Judge of the court' means a person qualified to sit as a member of the youth court which made the injunction: Policing and Crime Act 2009, s 49(1).

Where the respondent has attained the age of 18 years the respondent will be brought before a judge of the county court: Policing and Crime Act 2009, s 43(7)(a)(b).

If the matter is not disposed of when the person is brought before the judge, the person may be remanded but only on bail: Policing and Crime Act 2009, ss 43(5), 46 and Sch 5. Only persons who have attained 18 years may be remanded in custody and such persons will be brought before a judge of the county court: Policing and Crime Act 2009, Sch 5, para 2(1) and see s 43(7).

If the person who applied for the injunction considers that the respondent is in breach of any of its provisions, the person may apply to the judge of the court for the issue of a warrant for the arrest of the respondent: Policing and Crime Act 2009, s 44(2). The application must be substantiated on oath: Magistrates' Courts (Injunctions: Gang-related Violence) Rules 2015, SI 2015/421, r 7. A warrant may not be issued unless the judge has reasonable grounds for believing that the respondent is in breach of any provision of the injunction: Policing and Crime Act 2009, s 44(3).

A person brought before a court by virtue of a warrant may be remanded on bail where the matter is not disposed of: Policing and Crime Act 2009, s 44(4).

For proceedings following arrest, see the Magistrates' Courts (Injunctions: Gang-related Violence) Rules 2015, SI 2015/421 r 8.

Remand for medical examination and report

B[35.12] Where an arrested person is brought before the relevant judge or the court and there is reason to consider that a medical report will be required, the person may be remanded for the purpose of enabling a medical examination to take place and a report to be made. If the person is remanded on bail for that purpose, the adjournment may not be for more than four weeks at a time. If the judge or the court has reason to suspect that the person is suffering from a mental disorder within the meaning of the Mental Health Act 1983, the judge or the court has the same power to make an order under s 35 of that Act (remand for report on accused's medical condition) as the Crown Court has under that section in the case of an accused person (within the meaning of that section): Policing and Crime Act 2009, s 45(2), (4) and (5).

Injunctions for gang-related violence: appeals

B[35.13] An appeal lies to the Crown Court and on an appeal the Crown Court may make whatever orders are necessary to give effect to its determination of the appeal and whatever incidental or consequential orders appear to it to be just. An order of the Crown Court made on an appeal (other than one directing that an application be re-heard by a youth court) is to be treated as an order of a youth court: Policing and Crime Act 2009, s 46B(1), (2), (3).

Breach of injunction

B[35.14] Where on the application of the person who applied for the injunction, the court is satisfied beyond reasonable doubt that the respondent is in breach of any provision of the injunction, the court may make a supervision order or a detention order for a period not exceeding three months where the person is under 18 years. The court must consider a report from the youth offending team. Before making a detention order, the court must be satisfied, in view of the severity or extent of the breach, that no other order available to the court is appropriate and given reasons for that view in open court: Policing and Crime Act 2009, s 46A and Sch 5A, Pt 1.

Requirements in a supervision order include: keeping appointments with the responsible officer; activity requirements; curfew requirements; and electric monitoring requirements. Where there has been failure to comply with supervision requirements the powers of the court include the making of a detention order: Policing and Crime Act 2009, s 46A and Sch 5A, Pt 2 and the Magistrates' Courts (Injunctions: Gang-related Violence) Rules 2015, SI 2015/421, rr 10–13.

B[36]

Multiplicity of charges

B[36.1] It may be improper to charge or enter a conviction for more than one offence arising from the same facts: *Welton v Taneborne* (1908) 6 LGR 891, 72 JP 419, 21 Cox CC 702, 99 LT 668, 24 TLR 873 (charge of speeding where the question of speed had previously been taken into consideration on a conviction of dangerous driving); *R v Harris* [1969] 2 All ER 599, [1969] 1 WLR 745, CA (buggery and indecent assault – the facts of one offence really merged into a conviction for the graver charge, the two charges arising from one and the same incident); *R v Burnham Justices, ex p Ansorge* [1959] 3 ALL ER 505, [1959] 1 WLR 1041, 133 JP 539 (causing a motor car to stand on a certain road so as to cause unnecessary obstruction and contravention of parking regulations).

Before the magistrates can decide whether to convict or not to convict on the second information they must inquire into the matter to see what are the facts: *R v Burnham Justices, ex p Ansorge* supra. There is no general statutory provision which allows a defendant in the magistrates' court to be convicted of a lesser offence than that with which he is specifically charged. The practice in magistrates' courts is for both the greater and the lesser offence to be charged but if the greater charge is made out, it is not open to the magistrates' court to convict of both offences as the double conviction is of itself unfair. The right course is for the court to adjourn the lesser charge at the end of the trial but before conviction. In the event of a successful appeal relating to the aggravated offence, and that appeal succeeding on the footing that the aggravating element was not made out, a conviction on the lesser offence might thereafter properly be recorded against the defendant: *R (on the application of Dyer) v Watford Magistrates' Court* [2013] EWHC 547 (Admin), 177 JP 265 expressly declining to follow *DPP v Gane* (1991) 155 JP 846, [1991] Crim LR 711 and *R (on the application of the Crown prosecution Service) v Blaydon Youth Court* [2004] EWHC 2296 (Admin), 168 JP 638, [2005] Crim LR 495. See also *R v Akhtar* [2015] EWCA Crim 176, [2015] 1 WLR 3046, [2015] 2 Cr App Rep 81. *Dyer* was followed in *Henderson v CPS* [2016] EWHC 464 (Admin).

B[37] Parenting order

(Crime and Disorder Act 1998, ss 8–10; Anti-social Behaviour Act 2003, ss 19–28)

B[37.1] In any court proceedings where:

(a) a child safety order is made in respect of a child or the court determines on an application under s 12(6) below that a child has failed to comply with any requirement included in such an order;
(b) a parental compensation order is made in relation to a child's behaviour (in force only in certain areas: see SI 2006/1871, art 2);
(c) an injunction is granted under s 1 of the Anti-social Behaviour, Crime and Policing Act 2014, an order is made under s 22 of that Act or a sexual harm prevention order is made in respect of a child or young person;
(d) a child or young person is convicted of an offence; or
(e) a person is convicted of an offence under s 443 (failure to comply with school attendance order) or s 444 (failure to secure regular attendance at school of registered pupil) of the Education Act 1996;

if in the proceedings the court is satisfied that the relevant condition is fulfilled, it may make a parenting order in respect of a person who is a parent or guardian of the child or young person or, as the case may be, the person convicted of the offence under s 443 or 444: Crime and Disorder Act 1998, s 8.

The relevant condition is that the parenting order would be desirable in the interests of preventing: in a case falling within (a), (b) or (c) any repetition of the kind of behaviour which led to the order being made or the injunction granted; in a case falling within (d), the commission of any further offence by the child or young person; in a case falling with (e), the commission of any further such offence: Crime and Disorder Act 1998, s 8(6).

This is subject to two provisos. First, a court shall not make a parenting order unless it has been notified by the Secretary of State that arrangements for implementing such orders are available in the area in which it appears to the court that the parent resides or will reside and the notice has not been withdrawn. Secondly, special provision is made for offenders aged under 16 on conviction and injunctions made against those under 16 (see below).

B[37.2] Offenders/respondents under the age of 16. Where a person under the age of 16 is convicted of an offence, the court by or before which he is so convicted, if it is satisfied that the relevant condition is fulfilled, shall make a parenting order, and if it is not so satisfied, shall state in open court that it is not and why it is not: Crime and Disorder Act 1998, s 9(1). These requirements do not apply where the court makes a referral order: Crime and Disorder Act 1998, s 9(1A). Where the court grants an injunction under s 1 of the Anti-social Behaviour, Crime and Policing Act 2014, or makes a criminal behaviour order under s 22 of that Act, and the person concerned is under the age of 16, the court must make a parenting order if it is satisfied that the relevant condition is fulfilled and, if it is not so satisfied, it must state in open court that it is not and why it is not.

B[37.3] Cases of exclusion or potential exclusion from school. If a school pupil has been excluded on disciplinary grounds from a relevant school for a fixed period or permanently, or has engaged in behaviour which warrant such exclusion, and such conditions as may be prescribed by regulations - see the Education (Parenting Contracts and Parenting Orders) (England) Regulations 2007, SI 2007/1869, as amended, and the Education (Parenting Contracts and Parenting Orders) (Wales) Regulations 2010, SI 2010/2954 - a relevant body may apply to a magistrates' court for a parenting order in respect of the pupil. The court may then make an order if it is satisfied, in the case of potential exclusion, that the pupil has engaged in behaviour which would warrant his exclusion and, in any case, that the making of an order would be desirable in the interests of improving the behaviour of the pupil. In making its decision the court must take into account any refusal by the parent to enter into a parenting contract or, if the parent has entered into such a contract, any failure to comply with its requirements. The court must also take into account any failure by the parent without reasonable excuse to attend a reintegration interview: Anti-social Behaviour Act 2003, s 21(1), (1A). Forms are prescribed for applications and orders: see Magistrates' Courts (Parenting Orders) Rules 2004, SI 2004/247.

B[37.4] **Parenting orders for criminal conduct and anti-social behaviour: youth offending teams.** The Anti-social Behaviour Act 2003 also introduced parenting contracts and parenting orders in respect of criminal conduct and anti-social behaviour, following a reference to a youth offending team. Where a child or young person has been so referred, the team may enter into the contract with a parent or it may apply to the court for a parenting order. The court may make the order if it is satisfied that the child or young person has engaged in criminal conduct or further anti-social behaviour, and that the making of an order would be desirable in the interests of preventing the child or young person from engaging in further criminal conduct or further anti-social behaviour: Anti-social Behaviour Act 2003, s 26. In making its decision the court must take into account any refusal by the parent to enter into a parenting contract or, if the parent has entered into such a contract, any failure to comply with its requirements.

B[37.4A] **Parenting orders for criminal conduct and anti-social behaviour: local authorities, etc.** A local authority may apply for a parenting order in respect of a child or young person where the authority has reason to believe that the child or young person has engaged in anti-social behaviour and is resident, or appears to reside, in the authority's area. Such an application may be made to the magistrates' court or may be added to certain county court proceedings: Anti-social Behaviour Act 2003, s 26A. Like provision in respect of relevant housing providers is made by s 26B where the behaviour in question directly or indirectly affects its management functions. In either case the court may make an order if it is satisfied that the child or young person has engaged in anti-social behaviour and that an order would be desirable in the interests of preventing the child or young person from engaging in further anti-social behaviour: Anti-social Behaviour Act 2003, ss 26A(2), 26B(2).

B[37.5] **Meaning of parenting order.** A parenting order is an order which requires the parent:

(i) to comply, for a period not exceeding 12 months, with such requirements as are specified in the order; and
(ii) to attend, for a concurrent period not exceeding three months and not more than once in any week, such counselling or guidance sessions as may be specified in directions given by the responsible officer: Crime and Disorder Act 1998, s 8(4), Anti-social Behaviour Act 2003, ss 20(4), 26(4), 26A(3), 26B(3).

However, the court need not include the last mentioned requirement in any case where a parenting order has been made in respect of the parent on a previous occasion.

A counselling or guidance session may be or may include a residential course, provided that the court is satisfied as to the likely effectiveness of such a course (as compared with a non-residential course) to prevent repetition of the kind of behaviour or the commission of a further offence and provided that any interference with family life likely to occur from attendance at the course is proportionate in all the circumstances: Crime and Disorder Act 1998, s 8(7A); Anti-social Behaviour Act 2003, s 26(6), (7), (8).

B[37.6] Duty to obtain and consider information. Before making a parenting order in a case within B[37.1] paragraph (a), in a case falling within paragraph (c) or (d) where the person concerned is under the age of 16, or in a case falling within paragraph (e) where the person to whom the offence related is under that age, a court must obtain and consider information about the person's family circumstances and the likely effect of the order on those circumstances. There is like provision in cases brought under the Anti-social Behaviour Act 2003 where the person concerned is aged under 16, see ss 20(2) and 27(2).

B[37.7] Duty to explain. Before making a parenting order, a court must explain to the parent in ordinary language:

(i) the effect of the order and of the requirements proposed to be included in it;
(ii) the consequences which may follow if he fails to comply with any of those requirements; and
(iii) that the court has power to review the order on the application either of the parent or of the responsible officer: Crime and Disorder Act 1998, s 9(7), which is also applied to cases brought under the Anti-social Behaviour Act 2003 (see ss 21(3), 27(3)).

B[37.8] Requirements that may be specified. The requirements that may be specified in a parenting order under s 8(4)(a) of the Crime and Disorder Act 1998 are those which the court considers desirable in the interests of preventing any such repetition or, as the case may be, the commission of any such further offence.

Requirements specified in, and directions given under, a parenting order shall, so far as practicable, be such as to avoid any conflict with the parent's religious beliefs, and any interference with the times, if any, at which he normally works or attends an educational establishment: Crime and Disorder Act 1998, s 9(4).

B[37.9] Discharge and variation. If while a parenting order is in force it appears to the court which made it, on the application of the responsible officer or the parent, that it is appropriate to do so, the court may make an order discharging the parenting order or varying it by cancelling any provision included in it, or by inserting in it any provision that could have been included in the order if the court had then had power to make it and were exercising the power. Where an application for the discharge of a parenting order is dismissed, no further application for its discharge shall be made by any person except with the consent of the court which made the order: Crime and Disorder Act 1998, s 9(5), (6), which is also applied to cases brought under the Anti-social Behaviour Act 2003 (see ss 21(3), 27(3)).

B[37.10] Penalty for non-compliance. If while a parenting order is in force the parent without reasonable excuse fails to comply with any requirement included in the order, or specified in directions given by the responsible officer, he shall be liable on summary conviction to a fine not exceeding level 3 on the standard scale: Crime and Disorder Act 1998, s 9(7), which is also applied to cases brought under the Anti-social Behaviour Act 2003 (see ss 21(3), 27(3)).

B[37.11] Meaning of 'responsible officer'. References above to a responsible officer mean one of the following who is specified in the order, namely a probation officer, a social worker of a local authority social services department, and member of a youth offending team: Crime and Disorder Act 1998, s 8(8). As to the 'responsible officer' in parenting orders in cases brought by local authorities and housing providers under ss 26A and 26B of the Anti-social Behaviour Act 2003, see s 26A(8) and s 26B(9).

B[37.12] Right of appeal. Where an order is made by virtue of B[37.1] (a) (non-compliance with child safety order) an appeal against the making of a parenting order lies to the county court; in the case of an order made under B[37.1] (c) (injunctions, etc), an appeal lies to the Crown Court: Crime and Disorder Act 1998, s 10(1). On such an appeal the county court or the Crown Court may make such orders as may be necessary to give effect to its determination of the appeal; and may also make such incidental or consequential orders as appear to it to be just: Crime and Disorder Act 1998, s 10(2).

In the case of an order made under B[37.1] (d) (on conviction of a child or young person) the person against whom the order was made shall have the same right of appeal against the making of the order as if the offence that led to the making of the order were an offence committed by him; and the order were a sentence passed on him for the offence: Crime and Disorder Act 1998, s 10(4). In the case of an order made under B[37.1] (e) (on conviction of an offence under s 443 or 444 of the Education Act 1996) the person against whom the order was made shall have the same right of appeal against the making of the order as if the order were a sentence passed on him for the offence that led to the making of the order: Crime and Disorder Act 1998, s 10(5).

In the case of orders made under the Anti-social Behaviour Act 2003, appeals lie to the Crown Court which has the same powers as those described above: Anti-social Behaviour Act 2003, ss 22 and 28.

B[38]

Power to review decisions – criminal and civil proceedings

(MCA 1980, s 142)

B[38.1] Section 142 of the Magistrates' Courts Act 1980 empowers magistrates' courts 'to re-open cases to rectify mistakes etc'. It is concerned with criminal cases only (for civil cases see B[38.6], below). It enables the court to:

(a) vary or rescind a sentence or other order imposed or made when dealing with; and

(b) where a person is convicted, to direct that the case should be heard again by different justices,

in either case where it appears to the court that it would be in the interests of justice to do so.

Varying or rescinding sentences or other orders on conviction

B[38.2] Where the court can vary or rescind a sentence or order, the court may exercise its power under this section on application by a party or on its own initiative. The procedure to be followed for variation of a sentence by a party is prescribed by rules of court and an application must be in writing except that the court may allow an application to be made orally and may extend any time limit. The court may not exercise the power in the defendant's absence unless it makes the variation proposed by the defendant or he has had an opportunity to make representations at a hearing (whether or not he in fact attends): see the Criminal Procedure Rules, r 42.2.

A variation of sentence to impose a points disqualification should not be dealt with administratively but in open court: *R v Cox* [2019] EWCA Crim 71, [2019] 2 Cr App R (S) 7.

Note, the Criminal Procedure (Amendment No 2) Rules 2019, SI 2019/1119, amended rule 28.4 to require the announcement in public of a decision to vary a sentence, or of a refusal to do so.

The court has power to vary or rescind a sentence or order and may substitute some other sentence or order (*R v Sheffield City Justices, ex p Foster* (1999) Times, 2 November. If, however, the decision has already been subject to an appeal to a higher court, the power to reopen no longer applies. Likewise, a magistrates' court had no power to quash a conviction and order a rehearing under s 142(2) where the justices had agreed to state a case for the opinion of the High Court: see *R (on the application of Rhodes-Presley) v South Worcestershire Magistrates' Court* [2008] EWHC 2700 (Admin), [2008] All ER (D) 92 (Nov).

It was inappropriate for magistrates to exercise their powers under s 142 to increase a sentence originally imposed some 20 months earlier. There had to be finality of proceedings and a power of rectification had to be exercised speedily after the date of the original sentence: see *R (on the application of Trigger) v Northampton Magistrates' Court (Northamptonshire Probation Trust and Northamptonshire Crown Prosecution Service, Interested Parties)* [2011] EWHC 149 (Admin), (2011) 175 JP 101.

B[38.3] The provisions may operate against a defendant, for example where the court has omitted to impose penalty points or an endorsable road traffic offence.

Note, however, the power does not extend to overturning an acquittal (*R v Gravesend Justices, ex p Dexter* [1977] Crim LR 298). The power is directed towards sentences or other orders; it had no bearing on convictions which had been entered by way of procedural irregularity (*R (on the application of D) v Sheffield Youth Court* [2008] EWHC 601 (Admin), 172 JP 576).

B[38.4] When the court alters a sentence or order under this procedure, and substitutes another, that other sentence or order will take effect from the date of the first sentence or order, unless the court otherwise directs.

Note the power under the Magistrates Courts Act 1980, s 142 does not extend to civil proceedings (*R (on the application of Mathialagan) v Southwark London Borough Council* [2004] EWCA Civ 1689, [2005] RA 43, (2004) Times, 21 December. Nor does s 142 have any bearing on criminal convictions which had been entered by way of procedural irregularity (*R (on the application of D) v Sheffield Youth Court* [2008] EWHC 601 (Admin), 172 JP 576.

Re-opening convictions

B[38.5] Nothing in this section operates to prevent a court acting under its common law powers to amend a plea from 'guilty' to 'not guilty' at any time before final adjudication: see *S (an infant) v Manchester City Recorder* [1971] AC 481, [1969] 3 All ER 1230; to hear and adjudicate upon a (summary) case wrongly committed for trial (*Bannister v Clarke* [1920] 3 KB 598, 85 JP 12); to commit for trial following an acquittal for an offence triable only on indictment (*R v West* [1964] 1 QB 15, [1962] 2 All ER 624, CCA); to re-try a case where some irregularity has vitiated the proceedings (*R v Marsham, ex p Pethick Lawrence* [1912] 2 KB 362, 76 JP 284); or, generally, to deal with a matter when the hearing or sentence was a nullity (*R v Norfolk Justices, ex p DPP* [1950] 2 KB 558, [1950] 2 All ER 42, 114 JP 312; *R v Warwick Quarter Sessions, ex p Patterson* (1971) 115 Sol Jo 484).

The purpose of s 142 is to rectify mistakes. It is generally to be regarded as a slip rule and the power under the section cannot be extended to cover situations beyond those akin to a mistake. It was confirmed in *R (on the application of Williamson) v City of Westminster Magistrates' Court* [2012] EWHC 1444 (Admin), [2012] 2 Cr App Rep 299, [2012] Crim LR 975 that the power to re-open proceedings under s 142 was not to be given a broad interpretation. Section 142 was designed to deal with an obvious mischief: namely the waste of time, energy and resources in correcting clear mistakes made in magistrates' courts by using appellate or review proceedings. It was not a power equivalent to an appeal to the Crown Court or the High Court, nor was it a general power of review. Accordingly, it is wrong to employ s 142(2) as a method by which a defendant can obtain a rehearing in circumstances where he could not appeal to the Crown Court by reason of his unequivocal plea of guilty: *R v Croydon Youth Court, ex p DPP* [1997] 2 Cr App Rep 411. See also *Zykin v CPS* [2009] EWHC 1469 (Admin), (2009) 173 JP 361. This section does not empower a court to re-open a plea of guilty where the court had failed to conduct the mode of trial procedure under s 24 of the Magistrates' Courts Act 1980. Nothing in *S v Recorder of Manchester* (above) suggests that in allowing a change of plea, the court is exercising a power under s 142 or that the power to accept a change of plea extends to a power to re-open, contrary to the wishes of a defendant, a conviction based on an unequivocal plea of guilty previously entered and accepted: *R (D) v Sheffield Youth Court* [2008] EWHC 601 (Admin), 172 JP 576.

There may be circumstances where s 142 can be used to allow an unequivocal plea of guilty to be set aside – eg offence unknown to law or impropriety by the prosecution – but the alleged incompetence of the defendant's own legal adviser, even if established, provides no analogy with prosecution fraud. Nor is s 142 a power equivalent to an appeal or a general review; accordingly, once the court has returned a guilty verdict the defendant is not entitled to make further submissions with a view to persuading the court to change its mind and substitute a not guilty verdict: *DPP v Chajed* [2013] EWHC 188 (Admin), [2013] 2 Cr App Rep 60, (2013) 177 JP 350.

When exercising its discretion as to whether the interests of justice require a rehearing, the court must act on proper judicial grounds; accordingly, the late arrival at court of a defendant was held not to be a proper ground for refusing a rehearing: *R v Camberwell Green Magistrates' Court, ex p Ibrahim* (1984) 148 JP 400. While delay in making an application under s 142 is always likely to be harmful and is a factor to be taken into account, justices should not reject an application on that ground alone and must consider judicially all the relevant circumstances: *R v Ealing Magistrates' Court, ex p Sahota* (1997) 162 JP 73, [1997] 45 LS Gaz R 29. See also *R (on the application of Blick) v Doncaster Magistrates' Court* [2008] EWHC 2698 (Admin), 172 JP 651, where it was held the magistrates' court had been wrong to take the question of whether the accused had acted 'with all due diligence' as the primary test, and that 'the inconvenience of the court can never outweigh the interests of justice' (at para 19). However, in *R v Gwent Magistrates' Court, ex p Carey* (1996) 160 JP 613, DC, it was held that justices were entrusted with a broad discretion and were entitled to take into account the fact that the defendant failed to appear through his own fault and that the witnesses would be inconvenienced by ordering a re-trial. The justices could also properly take into account the fact that the defendant was not being deprived of a fair trial by way of appeal in the Crown Court.

In *R (on the application of Rathor) v Southampton Magistrates' Court* [2018] 3278 (Admin), [2019] Crim LR 431 the judge convicted the defendant in his absence, rejecting a medical certificate because it did not specifically address fitness to attend court. Subsequently, a further sick note was submitted, which stated the defendant had been unfit to attend court. The judge was invited to re-open the proceeding under s 142 of the MCA 1980, but refused on the ground that the power was exercisable only as a slip rule to correct mistakes and, on the information before him at the time of the trial, he had not made such a mistake.

The Administrative Court quashed the conviction. The judge had been wrong to proceed in absence (see **D[16.19A]**). Moreover, the judge should have re-opened the proceedings in consequence of the second medical certificate. He should have asked himself if he would have adjourned the trial if it had been before him at the time, and the proper answer to that was plainly 'yes'.

Civil proceedings

B[38.6] There are three criteria to be satisfied before an order made by a magistrates' court in its civil jurisdiction can be set aside:

(a) there must be a genuine and arguable dispute as to the defendant's liability to the order in question;
(b) the order must be made as a result of a substantial procedural error, defect or mishap; and
(c) the application to the justices for the order to be set aside must be made promptly after the defendant learns that it has been made or has notice that an order may have been made: *R (on the application of Newham London Borough Council) v Stratford Magistrates' Court* [2008] EWHC 125 (Admin), [2008] RA 108, 173 JP 30.

In proceedings for a liability order to recover non-domestic rates, where justices had made an order unaware of an application to adjourn, they had jurisdiction to set aside their order. Although there was no express statutory provision, the justices had not exhausted their jurisdiction where they had failed to exercise a judicial discretion whether to proceed or adjourn: *Liverpool City Council v Pleroma Distribution Ltd* [2002] EWHC 2467 (Admin), [2003] RA 34, [2003] 04 LS Gaz R 33.

Although magistrates of their own motion might correct a clear mistake by the court itself going to the basis of its jurisdiction, or the fairness of the proceedings, they do not have a general power to set aside their own decision merely because of the existence of grounds which might support an application for judicial review. However, it might be sensible, where there had for example been an obvious mistake or where a party had failed to attend through no fault of his own, such as a traffic accident, for all parties to agree to rehear the matter and thereby avoid the expense and delay of judicial review: *R (on the application of Mathialagan) v Southwark London Borough Council* [2004] EWCA Civ 1689, [2005] RA 43, (2004) Times, 21 December.

B[38A]

Premises and prohibition orders – psychoactive substances

B[38A.1] In addition to creating a number of offences concerned with the supply, etc, of psychoactive substances – see A[87] – the Psychoactive Substances Act 2016 introduced prohibition and premises orders. These orders may arise from non compliance with prohibition or premises notices (see infra). The aim of these orders is to prohibit/prevent the carrying on of a 'prohibited activity'.

Meaning of prohibited activity

B[38A.2] Any of the following constitutes a prohibited activity, unless one of the exceptions to offences in s 11 of the PSA 2016 applies: producing a psychoactive substance which is like to be consumed by individuals for its psychoactive effects; supplying, offering to supply, importing or exporting such a substance; or assisting or encouraging any of the aforementioned activities: PSA 2016, s 12.

Prohibition notices

B[38A.3] A senior officer of a police or a local authority may give a prohibition notice if he/it reasonably believes that the person is carrying on or is likely to carry on a prohibited activity and that it is necessary and proportionate to give notice to prevent this. Such a notice requires the person not to carry on any, or any specified, prohibited activity: PSA 2016, s 13. If the recipient is under the age of 18 the notice must be for a fixed period of no longer than three years: PSA 2016, s 13(6). A notice must set out the grounds for its issue and explain the consequences of non compliance, and it may subsequently be withdrawn: PSA 2016, s 15.

Premises notices

B[38A.4] A senior officer of a police or a local authority may give a premises notice if he/it reasonably believes that a prohibited activity is being, or is likely to be, carried on at particular premises, and the person (who must be 18 or older) owns, leases. occupies, controls or operates the premises, and it is necessary and the officer/authority reasonably believes that it is necessary and proportionate to give the person the notice to prevent any prohibited activity from being carried on at those premises: PSA 2016, s 14. A notice must set out the grounds for its issue and explain the consequences of non compliance, and it may subsequently be withdrawn: PSA 2016, s 15.

Prohibition orders

B[38A.5] A prohibition order is an order prohibiting the person concerned from carrying on a prohibited activity or any specified prohibited activity: PSA 2016, s 17(1). Such an order may be made on conviction or on application as described below. As to the making of orders on conviction, see A[87.9], ante.

The appropriate court (a youth court or magistrates' court) may make an order on application if the court is satisfied on a balance of probabilities that the person has failed to comply with a prohibition notice or, where none has been given or it has been withdrawn, the court is satisfied on the balance of probabilities that the person is carrying on, or is likely to carry on, a prohibited activity and the court considers that the person would fail to comply with a prohibition notice if given; and the court considers it necessary and proportionate to make the order to prevent the person from carrying on the prohibited activity: PSA 2016, s 18.

If at the time of making the order the person concerned is aged under 18 the order must be for a fixed period which must not exceed three years.

Premises orders

B[38A.6] A premises order is an order which requires the person concerned to take all reasonable steps to prevent any prohibited activity or specified prohibited activity from being carried on at any specified premises that are owned, leased, occupied, controlled or operated by that person: PSA 2016, s 20(2).

The appropriate court (a magistrates' court) may make an order on application if it is satisfied on the balance of probabilities that the person has failed to comply with a premises notice or, where none has been given or it has been withdrawn, the court is satisfied on a balance of probabilities that a prohibited activity is being, or is likely to be, carried on at particular premises, and the person (who must be 18 or older) owns, leases, occupies, controls or operates the premises, and the court considers that the person would fail to comply with a premises notice if given; and the court considers it necessary and proportionate to make the order for to prevent any prohibited activity from being carried on at any premises owned, leased, occupied, controlled or operated by the person: PSA 2016, s 20.

Applications for prohibition and premises orders

B[38A.7] An application may be made by the chief officer of police for a police area, the Chief Officer of the British Transport Police Force, the Director General of the National Crime Agency, the Secretary of State by whom general customs functions are exercisable, or by a local authority. Where the application is based on non compliance with a notice, it must be made by the same agency which issued it, eg if the notice was given by a constable, by the chief officer of police or chief constable (as the case may be) of the same police force. An application is by way of complaint: PSA 2016, s 21.

As to the availability of special measures for vulnerable and intimated witnesses, see PSA 2016, s 33.

Provision that may be made by prohibition and premises orders

B[38A.8] On the making or variation of a prohibition or premises order the court may impose any prohibitions, restrictions or requirements that the court considers appropriate in addition to the general prohibition and requirement referred to in B[38A.5]–B[38A.6] above. Examples are given in PSA 2016, s 22(3)–(6), but these are not exclusive. They include, for example, in the case of a premises order, restrictions on access to the premises concerned: PSA 2016, s 22(6). Section 23 provides for enforcement of access prohibitions, and provision is made in s 24 for the reimbursement of any costs incurred in clearing, securing or maintaining premises for which an access prohibition is in force, and by s 25 for exemption from civil liability.

Offences of non compliance

B[38A.9] Non compliance with a prohibition order or a premises order constitutes an offence triable either way with a maximum punishment on conviction on indictment of two years' imprisonment and/or a fine. A person does not commit an offence if s/he took all reasonable steps to comply with the order or there is some other reasonable excuse for the failure to comply: PSA 2016, s 26.

It is also an offence without reasonable excuse to remain or enter premises in contravention of an access provision, or to obstruct a person acting under s 23 (enforcement of access provisions). These offences are summary only and carry the maximum punishment on summary conviction (ie 6 months' imprisonment and/or a fine): PSA 2016, s 27.

Variation, appeals, etc

B[38A.10] Provision is made for the variation and discharge of prohibition and premises orders (PSA 2016, s 28), and for appeals against the making of such orders or their variation or discharge (PSA 2016, ss 33, 31).

B[39]

Referral order

(Powers of Criminal Courts (Sentencing) Act 2000, s 16)

Limitations

B[39.1] A referral order may be made by an adult magistrates' court and this is usually encouraged in preference to remitting to the youth court.

B[39.2] Age limits – Person in respect of whom the order is made must be under 18.

B[39.3] Maximum period – 12 months.

B[39.4] Minimum period – 3 months.

B[39.5] Consent – Consent of offender not required.

Ancillary orders

B[39.6] Compensation at B[10]

Costs at B[17]

Disqualification at C[5]

Endorsement at C[5]

Deprivation of property and forfeiture at B[18]

Parenting order B[37]

Restitution at B[42]

General considerations of referral orders

B[39.7] Where a youth aged 10–17 years is before a court for an offence where neither the offence nor a connected offence is one for which the sentence is fixed by law eg murder; the court is not proposing to impose a custodial sentence or make a hospital order (within the meaning of the Mental Health Act 1983); and, the court is not proposing to discharge the youth absolutely or conditionally, if referral is available, the court must, if the compulsory referral conditions are satisfied, or may, if the discretionary referral conditions are satisfied, sentence the youth for the offence by ordering him to be referred to a youth offender panel.

Referral is available within England and Wales following notification from the Secretary of State. The relevant youth offender panel will be located in the area in which the youth resides or will reside.

Connected offence. An offence is connected with another if the youth falls to be dealt with at the same time as he is dealt with for the other offence whether or not he is convicted of the offences at the same time by or before the same court.

Compulsory referral conditions. The offence is punishable with imprisonment and the offender pleaded guilty to the offence and to any connected offence and he has never been convicted by or before a court in the UK of any other than the offence and the connected offence or convicted by or before a court in another member State of any offence: Powers of Criminal Courts (Sentencing) Act 200, s 17(1).

Discretionary referral conditions. The compulsory referral conditions are not satisfied in relation to the offence and the offender pleaded guilty to the offence or, if the offender is being dealt with by the court for the offence and any connected offence, to at least one of those offences: Powers of Criminal Courts (Sentencing) Act 200, s 17(2).

Previous conviction. A conviction resulting in the imposition of a conditional discharge is not a conviction for the purposes of the referral conditions.

Appropriate officer. A member of a youth offending team; an officer of a local probation board; or an officer of a provider of probation services.

Attendance of parent or guardian. On making a referral order, the court may order a parent or guardian (which includes a representative of a local authority where the youth is being looked after by that authority), to attend meetings of the youth offender panel.

Prohibited orders

B[39.8] Where a court makes a referral order in respect of an offence it may not deal with him for the offence in any of the prohibited ways. In respect of a connected offence, the court must either make a referral order or an absolute discharge and may not deal with the offence in any of the prohibited ways.

The prohibited ways are:

(a) a community sentence;
(b) a fine;
(c) an order under s 1(2A) of the Street Offences Act 1959 (order for person convicted of loitering/soliciting for prostitution to attend three meetings);
(d) a reparation order;
(e) a conditional discharge;
(f) a bind over; and
(g) binding over of parent or guardian.

Where the compulsory referral conditions are satisfied the court may not defer sentence but its power of remission to another court, adjournment, committal to the Crown Court or under the mental health legislation are unaffected.

Variation and discharge

B[39.9] Courts have a discretion to discharge referral orders early on application for good behaviour.

Likewise, courts have the option of extending the term of the referral order for up to three months, on application and, at the recommendation of the youth offender panel, eg, in cases of breach. Note the extension cannot exceed the overall maximum of 12 months.

B[39.10] **Breach.** The young offender may be referred back to the court for a revocation of the order if he fails to attend the panel, fails to agree a contract or fails to comply with the terms of the contract.

On receiving a report of a breach the court must summons or issue a warrant for the appearance of the juvenile.

On his appearance they must consider if the panel was right to refer the breach back. If they decide it was not then the order continues.

If a breach is proved, the court may revoke the order and deal with the original offence in any way it could have done, other than making a referral order.

When dealing with the youth, the court must have regard to:

(i) the circumstances of his referral back to the court; and
(ii) the extent of his compliance, if any, with the terms of his referral contract.

If the court does not revoke the referral order, and the failure to comply with it occurred after 13 April 2015, it may impose a fine of up to £2,500 or extend the youth offender contract up to a maximum of five months.

B[39.11] **Appeal.** On a breach, where the court revokes the referral order and deals with the youth for the original offence(s), he may appeal to the Crown Court against the sentence.

B[39.12] **Extension on further conviction.** Where an offender aged under 18 is subject to a referral order and the court (magistrates' or youth) is dealing with him for an offence and neither that offence nor any offence connected with it is one for which the sentence is fixed by law, and the court is not proposing to impose a custodial sentence or hospital order for that offence of any connected offence or to deal with the offender by way of an absolute or conditional discharge, the court may sentence the offender by making an order extending any compliance period up to a maximum of 12 months.

B[39.13] **Revocation on further conviction.** Where an offender is subject to a referral order and the court deals with the offence by making an order other than one extending the compliance period or discharging the offender absolutely or conditionally, the order shall have the effect of revoking the referral order (or orders) and any related extension orders. Where an order is so revoked the court may, if it appears to the court that it would be in the interests of justice to do so, deal with the offender for the offence for which the revoked order was made in any way in which he could have been dealt with by the court which made the order (assuming the duty and power to make a referral order had not applied); in exercising this power the court must take into account the extent of the offender's compliance with any contract that has had effect between the offender and the panel.

B[40]

Remission to another court

B[40.1] If the following conditions are met a magistrates' court may remit an offender to another magistrates' court (Powers of Criminal Courts (Sentencing) Act 2000, s 10). The conditions are:

(a) The court proposing to remit has convicted the offender of an offence which is punishable by either imprisonment or disqualification.
(b) The offender has attained 18 years of age.
(c) The court to which the convicting court proposes to remit has convicted the offender of another such offence but has not sentenced him nor committed him to the crown court to be dealt with.
(d) The receiving court consents to the remission.

B[40.2] The offender may be remitted on bail or in custody. He is not required to consent to the remission nor has he any right of appeal against it.

B[40.3] Juveniles. A magistrates' court which has found a juvenile offender (under 18) guilty of an offence must remit the juvenile to a youth court unless satisfied that it is undesirable to do so (Powers of Criminal Courts (Sentencing) Act 2000, s 8) and must exercise that power unless it is of the opinion that the case is one which can properly be dealt with by means of:

(a) an absolute or conditional discharge;
(b) a fine.

It was held in *R v Dillon* [2017] EWCA Crim 2671, [2019] Crim LR 247 that a Crown Court judge has no power to make a referral order, therefore if such an order is to be made the case must be remitted to the youth court. Given the exclusive competence of the youth court to make a referral order this is not a case where a Crown Court judge can acquire jurisdiction by exercising the general jurisdiction of a district judge pursuant to s 66 of the Courts Act 2003. See also *R v Koffi* [2019] EWCA Crim 300, [2019] 2 Cr App R S 17.

B[40.4] The court to which he is remitted will normally be the youth court for the area in which he resides. If the court finding the juvenile guilty is itself a youth court it may remit to another youth court or deal with him as it thinks fit.

Remittal to an adult court

B[40.5] If a juvenile attains the age of 18 before trial in the youth court or after conviction but before sentence the youth court may remit for trial or sentence to the adult court in the same petty sessions area. The remittal may be on bail or in custody.

There is power for a magistrates' court to remit a youth to the youth court for trial where an adult co-accused pleads guilty: Magistrates' Courts Act 1980, s 29(2). Where a youth is sent to the Crown Court for trial with an adult, similar power is now provided: Crime and Disorder Act 1998, Sch 3, para 13 (overturning the effect of the decision in *R (on the application of W) v Leeds Crown Court* [2011] EWHC 2326 (Admin), [2012] 1 Cr App R 13, (2012) 175 JP 367.

B[41]

Reparation order

(Powers of Criminal Courts (Sentencing) Act 2000, s 73)

Limitations

B[41.1] May only be made in the Youth Court. The offence involved need not be serious enough to merit a community penalty.

B[41.2] A reparation order may not be made if the court proposes to pass a custodial sentence or to make a youth rehabilitation order or a referral order.

Maximum periods

B[41.3] A reparation order may not require the offender to work for more than 24 hours in all, or to make reparation to any person without the consent of that person.

B[41.4] The reparation must be made within three months of the making of the order.

Reports

B[41.5] The order does not require a full pre-sentence report (PSR) but before making a reparation order the court must obtain and consider a report indicating:

(a) the type of work that is suitable for the offender; and
(b) the attitude of the victim or victims to the requirements proposed to be included in the order.

General consideration of a reparation order

B[41.6]–[41.7] A reparation order should be considered in less serious cases where the court wishes to

- take into account the feelings and wishes of the victims of crime; and
- prevent the young offender from committing further offences by confronting him with the consequences of his criminal behaviour, and allowing him to make some amends.

B[41.8] Reparation can be in the form of direct or indirect reparation. The court will require a report setting out the reparation activities appropriate, such as writing a letter of apology or meeting the victim in person to apologise, repairing criminal damage for which the young person has been responsible, cleaning graffiti, and working on an environmental or other community project.

B[41.9]–[41.15] Reparation carried out under a reparation order should be reparation in kind rather than financial reparation. Courts are already able to make a compensation order if they believe that financial reparation is appropriate.

Reasons

B[41.16] The court must give reasons if it does not make an order where it has power to do so.

Breach of the order

B[41.17] The responsible officer will instigate breach proceedings.

B[41.18] The powers available to the court are:

(a) fine up to level 3 or,
(b) revoke and re-sentence for the original offence; or
(c) in the case of an order made by the Crown Court the magistrates can commit the offender on bail or in custody until he can be brought up or appear before the Crown Court.

B[42]

Restitution order

(Powers of Criminal Courts (Sentencing) Act 2000, s 148)

B[42.1] Where goods have been stolen and a person is convicted of any offence with reference to the theft (whether or not the stealing is the gist of his offence) or such an offence is taken into consideration the court may make a restitution order.

B[42.2] **Stolen** includes obtaining by deception or blackmail.

B[42.3] **Restitution.** The court:

(a) may simply order the defendant to restore the goods to the person entitled to them whether or not any application is made for restitution; or
(b) (where an application has been made) order the delivery over of any goods directly or indirectly representing the proceeds of the stolen goods; or
(c) where money was taken from the possession of the accused on his apprehension, order its payment to the aggrieved,

but the beneficiary of the restitution must not receive more than the value of the original goods, a matter particularly to note when a combination of orders under (b) and (c) is made.

B[42.4] **Innocent purchasers.** Sometimes the thief has sold the goods to an innocent purchaser. The goods will be restored to the owner but the court may also order the defendant to pay out of any monies in his possession when apprehended a sum to the innocent third party up to the amount he paid for the goods.

B[42.5] **Making a restitution order.** Can be made on conviction of the offender whether or not sentencing is otherwise deferred.

B[42.6] **Evidence.** In the opinion of the court the relevant facts must sufficiently appear from the evidence at the trial, or available documents (ie witness statements, depositions or other documents which were made for use and would have been admissible as evidence in the proceedings) together with any other admissions made.

B[43]

Sentencing tables

B[43.1] See the following pages for the sentencing tables.

B[43.1A] Table A Available sentences for either way offences punishable with imprisonment on summary conviction are shaded. See Index to sentencing for paragraph references.

Age	10	11	12	13	14	15	16	17	18	19	20	21 & over
Imprisonment												■
Suspended with requirements												■
Detention in young offender institution (can be suspended)									■	■	■	
Detention Training Order*			■ *	■ *	■ *	■	■	■				
Detention (One Day)									■	■	■	■
Community Order with requirements (CJA 2003, s 177)									■	■	■	■
Unpaid work									■	■	■	■
Activity requirement or, for offences commited on or after 1 February 2015, a rehabilitation activity requirement									■	■	■	■
Programme requirement									■	■	■	■
Prohibited Activity requirement									■	■	■	■
Curfew requirement									■	■	■	■
Exclusion requirement									■	■	■	■
Residence requirement									■	■	■	■
Foreign travel prohibition requirement									■	■	■	■
Mental Health Treatment requirement									■	■	■	■
Drug Rehabilitation requirement									■	■	■	■
Alcohol Treatment requirement									■	■	■	■
Alcohol abstinence and monitoring requirement†									■	■	■	■
Supervision requirement or, for offences commited on or after 1 February 2015, a rehabilitation activity requirement									■	■	■	■
Attendance Centre requirement**									■ **	■ **	■ **	■ **
Referral to a Youth Offender Panel	■	■	■	■	■	■	■	■				

Restrictions on custodial sentences: offence 'so serious' etc, pre-sentence report, legal representation

*Under 15-year-old: court must specify the offender is persistent

Community Order
Offence 'serious enough'
pre-sentence report
See **B[9]** onwards

† when in force and initially to be piloted in certain areas

**Offenders aged 18–24 years only

Fine													u-14 max £250, 14–17 £1,000 see **B[10]** and **B[18]**
Compensation/Deprivation Order													
Discharge (Abs/Cond)													
Hospital Order													} Medical recommendation
Guardianship Order													
Committal for Sentence	*	*	*	*	*	*	*	*					
PCC(S)A 2000, s 3 or 4 (adult offenders) PCC(S)A 2000, s 3C (youths)*													*PSR re: dangerousness for youths normally obtained
Deferred Sentence with requirements													Court to give reasons
Reparation Order													
Youth Rehabilitation Order with requirements													
Activity requirement or, for offences commited on or after 1 February 2015, a rehabilitation activity requirement													Youth Rehabilitation Order Offence "serious enough" Pre-sentence report required See **B[49.3]** onwards
Supervision requirement or, for offences commited on or after 1 February 2015, a rehabilitation activity requirement													
Unpaid Work requirement (16-17 year olds only)													
Programme requirement													
Attendance Centre requirement													
Prohibited activity requirement													
Curfew requirement													
Exclusion requirement													
Residence requirement													
Foreign travel prohibition requirement													
Local Authority Residence requirement													
Mental Health Treatment requirement													
Drug Treatment requirement													
Intoxicating Substance Treatment requirement													
Education requirement													

B[43.2] Table B Available sentences for purely summary offences punishable with imprisonment are shaded. See Index to sentencing for paragraph references.

(■ = shaded)

Age	10	11	12	13	14	15	16	17	18	19	20	21 & over	
Imprisonment												■	Restrictions on custodial sentences: offence 'so serious' etc, pre-sentence report, legal representation
Suspended with requirements												■	
Detention in young offender institution (can be suspended)									■	■	■		
Detention Training Order*			■ *	■ *	■ *	■	■	■					*Under 15-year-old: court must specify the offender is persistent
Detention (One Day)									■	■	■	■	
Community Order with requirements (CJA 2003, s 177)									■	■	■	■	
Unpaid work									■	■	■	■	Community Order Offence 'serious enough' pre-sentence report See B[9] onwards
Activity requirement or, for offences commited on or after 1 February 2015, a rehabilitation activity requirement									■	■	■	■	
Programme requirement									■	■	■	■	
Prohibited Activity requirement									■	■	■	■	
Curfew requirement									■	■	■	■	
Exclusion requirement									■	■	■	■	
Residence requirement									■	■	■	■	
Foreign travel prohibition requirement									■	■	■	■	
Mental Health Treatment requirement									■	■	■	■	
Drug Rehabilitation requirement									■	■	■	■	
Alcohol Treatment requirement									■	■	■	■	
Alcohol abstinence and monitoring requirement†									■	■	■	■	† when in force and initially to be piloted in certain areas
Supervision requirement or, for offences commited on or after 1 February 2015, a rehabilitation activity requirement									■	■	■	■	
Attendance Centre requirement**									■ **	■ **	■ **	■ **	**Offenders aged 18–24 years only
Referral to a Youth Offender Panel	■	■	■	■	■	■	■	■					

Fine	u-14 max £250, 14–17 £1,000 see **B[10]** and **B[18]**
Compensation/Deprivation Order	
Discharge (Abs/Cond)	
Hospital Order	Medical recommendation
Guardianship Order	
Committal for Sentence	
PCC(S)A 2000, s 6 (committal for sentence in certain cases where offender committed in respect of another offence	
Deferred Sentence with requirements	Court to give reasons
Reparation Order	
Youth Rehabilitation Order with requirements	
Activity requirement or, for offences commited on or after 1 February 2015, a rehabilitation activity requirement	Youth Rehabilitation Order Offence "serious enough" Pre-sentence report required See **B[49.3]** onwards
Supervision requirement or, for offences commited on or after 1 February 2015, a rehabilitation activity requirement	
Unpaid Work requirement (16–17 year olds only)	
Programme requirement	
Attendance Centre requirement	
Prohibited activity requirement	
Curfew requirement	
Exclusion requirement	
Residence requirement	
Local Authority Residence requirement	
Mental Health Treatment requirement	
Drug Treatment requirement	
Intoxicating Substance Treatment requirement	
Education requirement	

B[43.3] Table C Available sentences for purely summary offences not carrying imprisonment are shaded. See Index to sentencing for paragraph references.

Age	10	11	12	13	14	15	16	17	18	19	20	21 & over
Imprisonment												
Suspended with requirements												
Detention in young offender institution (can be suspended)												
Detention Training Order												
Detention (One Day)												
Community Order with requirements (CJA 2003, s 177)												
Unpaid work												
Activity requirement or, for offences commited on or after 1 February 2015, a rehabilitation activity requirement												
Programme requirement												
Prohibited Activity requirement												
Curfew requirement												
Exclusion requirement												
Residence requirement												
Mental Health Treatment requirement												
Drug Rehabilitation requirement												
Alcohol Treatment requirement												
Supervision requirement or, for offences commited on or after 1 February 2015, a rehabilitation activity requirement												
Attendance Centre requirement**												

Community Order
The power is restricted to imprisonable offences

See **B[9]** onwards

*Offenders aged 18–24 years only

Referral to a Youth Offender Panel	**	**	**	**	**	**	**	**					**Discretionary referral conditions must apply, See B[39] onwards and s 17 PCC(S)A 2000
Fine													u-14 max £250, 14–17 £1,000
Compensation/Deprivation Order													see **B[10]** and **B[18]**
Discharge (Abs/Cond)													
Hospital Order													Medical recommendation
Guardianship Order													
Committal for Sentence													
Deferred Sentence with requirements													Court to give reasons
Reparation Order													
Youth Rehabilitation Order with requirements													
Activity requirement or, for offences commited on or after 1 February 2015, a rehabilitation requirement													Youth Rehabilitation Order The power is restricted to imprisonable offences See **B[49.3]** onwards
Supervision requirement or, for offences commited on or after 1 February 2015, a rehabilitation activity requirement													
Unpaid Work requirement (16–17 year olds only)													
Programme requirement													
Attendance Centre requirement													
Prohibited activity requirement													
Curfew requirement													
Exclusion requirement													
Residence requirement													
Local Authority Residence requirement													
Mental Health Treatment requirement													
Drug Treatment requirement													
Intoxicating Substance Treatment requirement													
Education requirement													

B[43.4] Table D Available sentences according to age of offender are shaded. See Index to sentencing for paragraph references.

Age	10	11	12	13	14	15	16	17	18	19	20	21 & over
Imprisonment												■
Suspended with requirements												■
Detention in young offenders institution (can be suspended)[1]									■	■	■	
Detention Training Order[1, 2] *			■	■	■	■	■	■				
Detention (One Day)[1]									■	■	■	■
Community Order with requirements (CJA 2003, s 177)									■	■	■	■
Unpaid work									■	■	■	■
Activity requirement or, for offences commited on or after 1 February 2015, a rehabilitation activity requirement									■	■	■	■
Programme requirement									■	■	■	■
Prohibited Activity requirement									■	■	■	■
Curfew requirement									■	■	■	■
Exclusion requirement									■	■	■	■
Residence requirement									■	■	■	■
Foreign travel prohibition requirement									■	■	■	■
Mental Health Treatment requirement									■	■	■	■
Drug Rehabilitation requirement									■	■	■	■
Alcohol Treatment requirement									■	■	■	■
Alcohol abstinence and monitoring requirement†									■	■	■	■
Supervision requirement or, for offences commited on or after 1 February 2015, a rehabilitation activity requirement									■	■	■	■
Attendance Centre requirement**									■ **	■ **	■ **	■ **
Fine	■	■	■	■	■	■	■	■	■	■	■	■
Compensation/Deprivation Order[3]	■	■	■	■	■	■	■	■	■	■	■	■

Restrictions on custodial sentences: offence 'so serious' etc, pre-sentence report, legal representation

*Under 15-year-old: court must specify the offender is persistent

Community Order
Offence 'serious enough'
pre-sentence report
See **B[9]** onwards

† when in force and initially to be piloted in certain areas

**Offenders aged 18–24 years only

u-14 max £250, 14–17 £1,000
see **B[10]** and **B[18]**

Discharge (Abs/Cond)	
Hospital Order[1, 2]	Medical recommendation
Guardianship Order[1, 2]	Medical recommendation
Committal for Sentence PCC(S)A 2000, ss 3 and 4	Either way offences
Deferred Sentence with requirements	Court to give reasons
Reparation Order[2]	
Youth Rehabilitation Order with requirements	
Activity requirement or, for offences commited on or after 1 February 2015, a rehabilitation activity requirement	Youth Rehabilitation Order Offence "serious enough" Pre-sentence report required See **B[49.3]** onwards
Supervision requirement or, for offences commited on or after 1 February 2015, a rehabilitation activity requirement	
Unpaid Work requirement (16–17 year olds only)	
Programme requirement	
Attendance Centre requirement	
Prohibited activity requirement	
Curfew requirement	
Exclusion requirement	
Residence requirement	
Local Authority Residence requirement	
Mental Health Treatment requirement	
Drug Treatment requirement	
Intoxicating Substance Treatment requirement	
Education requirement	

(a) Sentences marked with [1] can only be imposed if the offence is punishable with imprisonment when committed by an adult over 21 years.

(b) As far as offenders under 18 are concerned, a magistrates' court (as opposed to a youth court) cannot impose any of the penalties marked with a [2]. The magistrates' court must remit such juveniles on bail or in care to a youth court which will usually be the youth court for the area in which he lives.

(c) [3] Under PCC(S)A 2000, s 143: see **B[34]**

** Available up to the age of 25 in cases of default in payment of money where the court would have the power to commit to prison

B[44]

Sexual harm prevention order

Anti-social Behaviour, Crime and Policing Act 2014

B[44.1] The Anti-social Behaviour, Crime and Policing Act 2014 introduced sexual harm prevention orders (and sexual risk orders), which replace, in England and Wales: sexual offences prevention orders; risk of sexual harm orders; and foreign travel orders.

A sexual harm prevention order may be made conviction or by way of complaint. Where the court could make an order on conviction, the procedure is regulated by Part 31 of the Criminal Procedure Rules 2015.

Orders on conviction

B[44.2] The court can make a sexual harm prevention order (SHPO) if: (a) the offence is one listed in Schs 3 or 5 to the Sexual Offences Act 2013; and (b) the court is satisfied that it is necessary to make a sexual harm prevention order for the purpose of:

(i) protecting the public or any particular members of the public from sexual harm from the defendant; or
(ii) protecting children or vulnerable adults generally, or any particular children or vulnerable adults, from sexual harm from the defendant outside the UK: Sexual Offences Act 2003, s 103A(1), (2).

'Sexual harm' and 'vulnerable adult' are defined in s 103B(1).

The object of the new orders was to rationalise and strengthen the civil orders provided for in the Sexual Offences Act 2003. There are, consequently, a number of differences between the new regime and the old. For example, a sexual offences prevention order (SOPO) could only be made to protect from serious sexual harm. Both SHPOs and SOPOs, and the guidance given by the Court of Appeal on the making and terms of SOPOs, continues to be relevant: *R v NC* [2016] EWCA Crim 1448, [2017] 1 Cr App R (S) 13, [2017] Crim LR 334. In relation to SOPOs it was held that the focus is on the risk of further offences and the court has to conduct a risk assessment and to satisfy itself that it is necessary (which imports a higher threshold than 'desirable') to make an order because of the likelihood of the defendant committing further, relevant offences, not necessarily against the person to be protected by the order but with that person being likely to suffer serious harm, which may be psychological harm, as a result; although there are powers to vary orders under s 108, they may be invoked only by the persons specified in s 108(2) and if the order prevents contact with a family member who is not qualified to invoke s 108 it may contain a provision that the jurisdiction of the family courts can be invoked: *R v D (sexual offences: prevention order)* [2005] EWCA Crim 3660, [2006] 2 All ER 726, [2006] 1 WLR 1088 (where the offences were against the defendant's daughter and the order prohibited any contact or communication not only with her but also with the defendant's psychologically disturbed son; however, the order was amended so that the family jurisdiction could be invoked to lift the prohibition).

The court is entitled to make a sexual offences prevention order for an offence of sexual assault, notwithstanding that it has decided not to impose a sentence of imprisonment for public protection (IPP); there are a number of material differences between the two as to the relevant criteria and other matters: *R v Rampley* [2006] EWCA Crim 2203, [2007] 1 Cr App Rep (S) 542. (The same conclusion was reached, though by a different route, in *R v Richards* [2006] EWCA Crim 2519, [2007] 1 WLR 847, [2007] 1 Cr App Rep (S) 734.)

Repeated indecent exposure towards girls and young women justifies an order due to the psychological harm it causes to the victims: *R v Whitton* [2006] EWCA Crim

3229, [2007] 2 Cr App Rep (S) 67 (though the period was reduced from 10 to 5 years and a prohibition in relation to work and organised activities was removed since all the offences had occurred in streets).

In *R v Jones* [2014] EWCA Crim 1959, [2015] 1 Cr App R (S) 68 a SOPO prohibiting unsupervised contact with children under 16 was quashed since there was no evidence that the defendant's offending (downloading indecent images of children) would escalate into contact offences. See also *R v Sokolowski* [2017] EWCA Crim 1903, [2018] 1 Cr App R (S) 30. Where a defendant was convicted of viewing indecent images of children, an SHPO should only contain provisions preventing contact, or permitting only supervised contact, with children where there was a real risk that the offending would progress to contact offences. A 'safety first' approach was impermissible. In *R v Bingham* [2015] EWCA Crim 1342, [2016] 1 Cr App R (S), however, it was held that, while not every case of distribution of indecent images warrants the making of a SHPO, where the distribution was to a young person, a stranger, for the purpose of persuading that person to expose his penis to the defendant, the test of necessity was met and the making of a SHPO was not wrong in principle.

In *R v Lewis* [2016] EWCA Crim 1020, [2017] 1 Cr App R (S) 2, [2017] Crim LR 147 the Court of Appeal considered both 'necessity' and the relevance of a barring order made under the Safeguarding of Vulnerable Groups Act 2006. The offences were possession of indecent images and extreme pornography. The prohibition on contact with children was quashed in the absence of evidence that it was necessary. A 'safety first' approach was not appropriate. The terms of the barring order which had been made led the court to quash, also, the prohibition in the SHPO on carrying out the role of a coach (which the appellant had been) in any sporting environment with persons under the age of 18. In practice it would not be feasible for L to be a coach without falling foul of the restrictions imposed by the 2006 Act. It was only if there was a real risk that an offender might undertake some activity outside the terms of the order that such a prohibition could be justified.

B[44.3] *Guidance on the making and terms of orders* The following, additional, general guidance on the making and terms of sexual offences prevention orders in criminal cases was given by the Court of Appeal in *R v Smith* [2011] EWCA Crim 1772, [2012] 1 All ER 451, [2012] 1 WLR 1316.

(1) A SOPO must be tailored to the prevention of Sch 3 offences; it might not prohibit unusual or socially disapproved sexual behaviour unless such was likely to lead to the commission of Sch 3 offences.
(2) A convicted person might be subject to at least three other relevant regimes: a notification requirement; disqualification from working with children; and licence on release from prison. A SOPO is unnecessary if it merely duplicates another regime, and a SOPO must not interfere with such a regime.
(3) Following *R v Bolton (Simon David)* [2010] EWCA Crim 1177 and *R v Longman (Mark)* [2010] EWCA Crim 2046, a SOPO is generally inappropriate, because it is unnecessary, if an indefinite sentence is being imposed; by contrast an order might plainly be necessary for determinate or extended sentences, where licence conditions have a defined and limited life, and a SOPO can extend beyond the licence period.
(4) A SOPO must operate in tandem with the notification requirement; it must not conflict with such a requirement, and it is improper to impose a SOPO which amounts in effect to no more than a notification requirement and runs for a longer period.
(5) Subject to the above, there is no reason why a SOPO should not run for longer than a notification requirement if the circumstances so require; conversely, a SOPO for a definite period can be made alongside an indefinite notification requirement.
(6) In the case of offences involving the use of the internet, the court drew these conclusions:
    (a) a blanket prohibition on computer use or internet access is impermissible (affirmed in *R v Parsons, R v Morgan* [2017] EWCA Crim 2163, [2018] 1 Cr App R (S) 43, where the Court of Appeal noted the availability of risk management monitoring software to police use of the internet);

(b) a formulation restricting internet use to job search, study, work, lawful recreation and purchases, while having its attractions, suffers from the same flaw that the legitimate use of the internet extends beyond such spheres of activity;
(c) a prohibition on possession of a computer without notifying the police carries the problem that numerous devices have computer functions and internet access;
(d) there are fewer difficulties about a prohibition from internet access without filtering software, though this can give rise to problems of uncertainty and policing;
(e) of the formulations so far devised the one which is likely to be most effective is to require a readable internet history to be submitted to inspection on request;
(f) where the risk consists of or includes the use of chat lines, etc, to groom young people, it may be appropriate to include a prohibition on communicating via the internet with any young person known or believed to be under the age of 16; prohibitions on contact with children under 18 might be justified for offences committed under ss 16–19 and 25 and 26 of the Sexual Offences Act 2003; and
(g) prohibitions on contact with children must, however, be necessary; multiple prohibitions just in case the offending might progress from, for example, downloading child pornography are not legitimate.

(7) In the case of offences concerning children within the offender's family:
(a) any order should ordinarily be subject to any order made in family proceedings;
(b) where it is necessary to impose a prohibition on contact with children, it is essential to include a saving for incidental contact such as is inherent in everyday life, otherwise, for example, an offender committed an offence if he was dealt with by a 15-year-old at a shop checkout.

(8) Prohibitions from taking part in activities which might bring an offender into contact with children must be justified as required beyond the restrictions placed on the offender by the Independent Safeguarding Authority. The prosecution should be required to justify this.

(9) It was essential that there should be a written draft properly considered in advance of the sentencing hearing. This should normally be served on the court and the defence at least two days in advance.

Note, the guidance provided by *Smith* does not provide a basis for a successful appeal against a SOPO imposed long before *Smith* was decided, and an application to vary the order under s 108 of the Sexual Offences Act 2003 brought on the ground that the order was not '*Smith*-compliant' would be bound to fail. An applicant should set out in detail what has happened since the order was originally made to justify the making of the application: *R v Spencer* [2013] EWCA Crim 2286, [2014] 2 Cr App Rep (S) 127.

Where an offender totally refused to acknowledge his offending behaviour or its causes, and gave no indication he would address those matters, and the risk to children would be a continuing one, a SHPO of indefinite duration was necessary and proportionate; where a serious risk was explicitly identified and explained, it was not for the prosecution to prove that an order lasting for longer than the notification period prescribed for the sentence in question was justified, rather the evidential burden was on the defendant to show that during that period things have materially changed: *R v Al Mahmood* [2019] EWCA crim 788, [2019] 2 Cr App R (S) 23.

It is primarily the responsibility of prosecution counsel to put before the court provisions which go no further than are necessary and proportionate to provide for the protection of children and other vulnerable persons in the future. If there is a question of what are the appropriate provisions that should be included in a particular SOPO, or argument as to the extent to which the prohibitions should be imposed, it is essential that the court is referred to the leading authorities, so that the court is able to judge for itself what is appropriate: *R v Jackson* [2012] EWCA Crim 2602, 177 JP 147 (in which certain of the restrictions were held to be entirely disproportionate to the offences committed and the danger J posed to children in the future). See further *R v Sokolowski* [2017] EWCA Crim 1903, [2018] 1 Cr App R (S) 30.

A blanket ban on access to the internet is impermissible. Prohibitions can be drafted in a way which enables legitimate access while at the same time affording sufficient protection from the risk of abuse: see *R v Connor* [2019] EWCA Crim 234, [2019] 4 WLR 76, [2019] 2 Cr App R (S) 19; see also *R v Hewitt (Richard)* [2018] EWCA Crim 2309, [2019] 1 Cr App R (S) 34.

In *R v Brown (Benjamin Adam)* [2011] EWCA Crim 1223, the final provision of the SOPO made against B read as follows: 'Save where to do so is inadvertent or unavoidable, not to possess any images of a child under the age of 16 years unless the prior permission of that child's parents or guardian has been obtained'. It was decided that the said restriction would, for example, serve to criminalise the continued possession of a daily newspaper which happened to have an inoffensive photograph of a child in it unless it was disposed of straight away upon realisation that such a photograph was in the newspaper. It was not adequate to rely upon the good sense of prosecutors in cases of this type so that very widely drafted prohibitions could be incorporated into such orders. The Court of Appeal regarded that prohibition as being far too widely drafted and proposed to delete it.

A prohibition from undertaking any work likely to bring the offender into contact with boys under the age of 17, save with the written permission of the chief constable, has been quashed on the basis that it would have prevented the offender from having almost any employment without police consent, and it was difficult to think of any job for which he was qualified that he could properly do other than something carried out entirely in his own house; it is undesirable to condemn somebody to spend the rest of his life on benefits: *R v Kimpriktzis* [2013] EWCA Crim 734, [2014] 1 Cr App Rep (S) 23.

See also *R v Gass* [2015] EWCA Crim 579, [2015] 2 Cr App R (S) 20, [2015] Crim LR 733 where G (25) was convicted of eight counts of sexual activity with a child of 14, which involved significant planning and grooming. G was sentenced to seven years' imprisonment and a SOPO. However, a prohibition from 'seeking or undertaking employment including voluntary work, whether for payment or otherwise which is likely at some time to allow him unsupervised access to a child under the age of 16 years (where that contact is more than transient and a child or a young person's parents or guardian is absent)' was held to be too wide and was replaced with the formulation used in *Jackson* (save for the italicised words, which were added because G might seek to minimise the conviction), namely 'having any unsupervised contact of any kind with any female under 16 other than: (i) such as is inadvertent and which [is] not reasonably avoidable in the course of lawful daily life'; or that (ii) 'with the consent of the child's parents or guardian who has knowledge of his conviction *and the terms of this order*', but excepting G's daughter. This rendered unnecessary a further prohibition from 'employing directly or indirectly any female staff under the age of 16 whether for payment or otherwise within any of his business enterprises (either present or future)', and this was quashed.

Where a music teacher and assistant house master at a private school downloaded and viewed, but did not distribute, indecent images between 1999 and 2013 and was made the subject of a community order with requirements, including participation in a 'community sex offenders work group' and supervision, the court was entitled to make a SHPO for a period of five years in the terms:

> 'Having any unsupervised contact with any child under the age of 16 other than:
>
> (a) Such as inadvertent and not reasonably avoidable in the course of lawful daily life.
> (b) With the consent of the child's parent/guardian who has knowledge of his conviction and such contact had previously been assessed and approved by Children's Services for that area.
>
> Using any device capable of accessing the internet unless:
>
> (a) It has the capacity to retain and display the history of the internet use.
> (b) The device is made available on request for inspection by a Police Officer or member of Police Support Staff.
> (c) Deleting such history.'

There was an obvious risk that, living alone and isolated from the school surroundings he was used to, the offender might seek contact with a child, and that unsupervised contact could lead to offending given the offender's admitted attraction to young children. If e-mails were excluded from the second prohibition it would enable offenders to set up e-mail accounts at will to access children, or to receive images as e-mail attachments which would remain undetected by a less invasive prohibition: *R v McDonald* [2015] EWCA Crim 2119, [2016] 1 Cr App R (S) 48.

A prohibition which totally prevents a person from leaving his premises is unlawful, but a person subject to a SOPO may be required to wearing a tag when away from the premises at which he is residing or staying overnight; the only restrictions as to what may be includes in a SOPO are those in s 107(2) and 108(5) of the Sexual Offences Act 2003: *R (on the application of Richards) v Teesside Magistrates Court* [2015] EWCA Civ 7, [2015] 1 WLR 1695, [2015] 1 Cr App Rep (S) 412.

Where there was a discrepancy between the terms of a sexual offences prevention order announced by the court and the order issued by the court administration, the appellant was subject to the order announced in court: *R v P* (2012) May 10, CA.

Sexual harm prevention orders – civil applications

B[44.4] If it appears to a chief officer of police (CPO) or the Director General of the National Crime Agency (DG) that the following conditions are fulfilled, namely:

(a) the person is a qualifying offender (see below); and
(b) the person has since the appropriate date (see below) acted in such a way has to give reasonable cause to believe that it is necessary for such an order to be made;

the CPO/DFG may make an application by way of complaint to a magistrates' court for a sexual harm prevention order (Sexual Offences Act 2003, s 103A(4)).

If it is proved that the defendant:

(a) is a qualifying offender (see below); and
(b) the court is satisfied that the defendant's behaviour since the appropriate date (see below) makes it necessary to make a SHPO for the purpose of:
    (i) protecting the public or any particular members of the public from sexual harm from the defendant; or
    (ii) protecting children or vulnerable adults generally, or any particular children or vulnerable adults, from sexual harm from the defendant outside the UK;

the court may make a SHPO.

It was held in relation to SOPOs, which SHPOs replace, that the standard of proof as to what the defendant actually did is effectively the criminal standard: see *Cleveland Police v Haggas* [2009] EWHC 3231 (Admin), [2010] 3 All ER 506, [2011] 1 WLR 2512.

It was further held in relation to SOPOs that the key words or phrases were 'necessary', 'for the purpose of protecting' and '[serious - now deleted] harm'. The prohibitions should be capable of compliance without unreasonable difficulty or the assistance of a third party and should not be capable of unintended breach. Nor should they have the effect of giving the police powers of search unaccompanied by the usual procedural safeguards: *R v Hemsley* [2010] EWCA Crim 225, [2010] 3 All ER 965, 174 CL&J 172.

Duration of orders

B[44.5] A SHPO prohibits the defendant from doing anything described in the order. A prohibition on foreign travel must be for a fixed period of not more than five years (Sexual Offences Act 2003, s 103D(1)). As to prohibitions on foreign travel, see

Sexual Offences Act 2003, s 103D (2)–(7)). Otherwise, a prohibition has effect for a fixed period specified in the order of at least five years, or until further order (Sexual Offences Act 2003, s 103C(2)). Different periods may be specified for different prohibitions, and some prohibitions may have fixed terms and others may have effect until further order (Sexual Offences Act 2003, s 103C(3)).

Guidance on the duration of SHPOs was given by the Court of Appeal in *R v McLellan; R v Bingley* [2017] EWCA Crim 1464, [2018] Crim LR 92. It was held that there was no requirement that a SHPO should not exceed the duration of the applicable notification requirements, but a SHPO should not be made for longer than was necessary, it should not be made for an indefinite period unless the court was satisfied of the need to do so and all concerned should be alert to the fact that the effect of a SHPO which exceeded those notification requirements was to extend their operation and inadvertent extension was to be avoided. The draft SHPO required to be served by r.31.3(5) of the Crim PR (see further below) should indicate the proposed duration of the SHPO or at least flag the question of duration for consideration.

See further *R v Sokolowski* [2017] EWCA Crim 1903, [2018] 1 Cr App R (S) 30. It is essential that a written draft of the proposed SHPO is both served on the defendant and lodged with the court, preferably in electronic as well as hard-copy form, so that this could be considered by both the defendant and the judge before the sentencing hearing. The normal requirement was two clear days before the hearing. It is not acceptable for a draft to be produced at the hearing itself. The draft should set out the proposed terms, including the proposed duration of the order or, at the very least, flag the latter for consideration by the defendant and the court. The judge should consider the draft before the hearing and, if he/she did not have sufficient time to do so, he/she had the power to put the matter back to another. Where any delay was the fault of one party, or that party's legal representatives, the judge had appropriate powers to make a costs order in relation to any necessary adjournment.

If the respondent appeals against a five-year order and this is dismissed, the Crown Court cannot direct that the period should run from the date of the dismissal of the appeal; it runs from the date of the order appealed against: *R (Grant) v Kingston Crown Court* [2015] EWHC 767 (Admin), [2015] 2 Cr App R (S) 11.

'Qualifying offender' and 'appropriate date'

B[44.6] For these purposes a 'qualifying offender' is a person who at any time has been convicted, found not guilty by reason of insanity or to be under a disability and to have done the act charged, or cautioned in respect of an offence under Sch 3 (other than para 60) or Sch 5 to the Sexual Offences Act 2003 or an equivalent offence under the law of a country outside the UK (Sexual Offences Act 2003, s 103B(2)–(4)). The 'appropriate date' means the date or first date on which the offender was so convicted, found or cautioned (Sexual Offences Act 2003, s 103B(1)). Acts, behaviour, convictions and findings include those occurring before the commencement of these provisions (Sexual Offences Act 2003, s 103B(5)). Where a foreign conviction is relied on, the condition that it would have constituted an offence under Sch 3 (except para 60) or Sch 5 unless the defendant serves a notice challenging this with grounds, or the court permits the defendant to put the applicant to proof without service of such a notice (Sexual Offences Act 2003, s 103B(6), (7)).

SHPOs: variation, renewals and discharges, interim SHPOs, SHPOs and notification requirements, and appeal

B[44.7] Provision is made in respect of these matters: in the case of variation, renewals and discharges by the Sexual Offences Act 2003, s 103E; in the case of interim orders by the Sexual Offences Act 2003, s 103F; in the case of notification requirements by Sexual Offences Act 2003, s 103G; and in the case of appeals by the Sexual Offences Act 2003, s 103H.

Breach of a sexual harm prevention order (also applicable to breach of a sexual offences prevention order and to breach of a foreign travel order)

Sexual Offences Act 2003 (section 103I)

B[44.8] The text of this guideline is taken from the Sentencing Council's Breach offenses: Definitive guideline, published on 7 July 2018, with effect from 1 October 2018.

Effective from: 1 October 2018

Triable either way

Maximum: 5 years' custody

Offence range: Fine–4 years and 6 months' custody

STEP 1

Determining the offence category

The court should determine the offence category with reference only to the factors listed in the tables below. In order to determine the category the court should assess culpability and harm.

Culpability

In assessing culpability, the court should consider the **intention** and **motivation** of the offender in committing any breach.

A	• Very serious or persistent breach
B	• Deliberate breach falling between A and C
C	• Minor breach • Breach just short of reasonable excuse

Harm

The level of **harm** is determined by weighing up all the factors of the case to determine the harm that has been caused or was at risk of being caused.

In assessing any risk of harm posed by the breach, consideration should be given to the original offence(s) or activity for which the order was imposed and the circumstances in which the breach arose.

Category 1	Breach causes very serious harm or distress
Category 2	Cases falling between categories 1 and 3
Category 3	Breach causes little or no harm or distress

STEP 2

Starting point and category range

Having determined the category at step one, the court should use the corresponding starting point to reach a sentence within the category range in the table below. The starting point applies to all offenders irrespective of plea or previous convictions.

	Culpability		
Harm	**A**	**B**	**C**
Category 1	**Starting point** 3 years' custody **Category range** 2 – 4 years 6 months' custody	**Starting point** 2 years' custody **Category range** 36 week – 3 years' custody	**Starting point** 1 years' custody **Category range** High level community order – 2 year's custody

Harm	Culpability A	B	C
Category 2	**Starting point** 2 years' custody **Category range** 36 weeks – 3 years' custody	**Starting point** 1 years' custody **Category range** High level community order – 2 year's custody	**Starting point** High level community order **Category range** Medium level community order – 26 weeks' custody
Category 3	**Starting point** 1 years' custody **Category range** High level community order – 2 year's custody	**Starting point** 26 weeks' custody **Category range** Medium level community order – 36 weeks' custody	**Starting point** Medium level community order **Category range** Band B fine – High level community order

The table below contains a **non-exhaustive** list of additional factual elements providing the context of the offence and factors relating to the offender. Identify whether any combination of these, or other relevant factors, should result in an upward or downward adjustment from the starting point. In some cases, having considered these factors, it may be appropriate to move outside the identified category range.

Factors increasing seriousness

Statutory aggravating factors:
Previous convictions, having regard to a) the **nature** of the offence to which the conviction relates and its **relevance** to the current offence; and b) the **time** that has elapsed since the conviction
Offence committed whilst on bail
Other aggravating factors:
Breach committed shortly after order made
History of disobedience of court orders (where not already taken into account as a previous conviction)
Breach involves a further offence (where not separately prosecuted)
Targeting of particular individual the order was made to protect
Victim or protected subject of order is particularly vulnerable
Offender takes steps to prevent victim or subject harmed by breach from reporting an incident or seeking assistance
Offence committed on licence or while subject to post sentence supervision

Factors reducing seriousness or reflecting personal mitigation

Breach committed after long period of compliance
Prompt voluntary surrender/admission of breach
Age and/or lack of maturity where it affects the responsibility of the offender
Mental disorder or learning disability where linked to the commission of the offence
Sole or primary carer for dependent relatives

STEP 3

Consider any factors which indicate a reduction, such as assistance to the prosecution

The court should take into account sections 73 and 74 of the Serious Organised Crime and Police Act 2005 (assistance by defendants: reduction or review of sentence) and any other rule of law by virtue of which an offender may receive a discounted sentence in consequence of assistance given (or offered) to the prosecutor or investigator.

STEP 4

Reduction for guilty pleas

The court should take account of any potential reduction for a guilty plea in accordance with section 144 of the Criminal Justice Act 2003 and the *Guilty Plea* guideline.

STEP 5

Totality principle

If sentencing an offender for more than one offence, or where the offender is already serving a sentence, consider whether the total sentence is just and proportionate to the overall offending behaviour in accordance with the *Offences Taken into Consideration and Totality* guideline.

STEP 6

Ancillary orders

In all cases, the court should consider whether to make compensation and/or ancillary orders.

STEP 7

Reasons

Section 174 of the Criminal Justice Act 2003 imposes a duty to give reasons for, and explain the effect of, the sentence.

STEP 8

Consideration for time spent on bail

The court must consider whether to give credit for time spent on bail in accordance with section 240A of the Criminal Justice Act 2003.

B[45]

The process of sentencing

Introduction to the process of sentencing

B[45.1] Sentencing is not and never will be an exact science; only rarely could a group of sentencers agree that a particular sentence was exactly right and, even if they did, they would probably be agreeing only that it was right to show a particular level of leniency. The prerogative of saying what is 'right' in terms of sentencing levels belongs to the Sentencing Council who aim to promote consistency in sentencing and guidance in respect of offences or offenders in a particular category.

Sentencing is dominated by sentencing guidelines, and the Lord Chief Justice has said this regarding the citation of authority:

> '21 ... The citation of decisions of the Court of Appeal Criminal Division in the application and interpretation of guidelines is generally of no assistance. There may be cases where the court is asked to say something about a guideline where, in wholly exceptional circumstances – and we wish to emphasise that these are rare – the guideline may be unclear. In such circumstances the court will make observations which may be cited to the court in the future. However, in those circumstances it is highly likely that the Council will revise the guideline and the authority will cease to be of any application.
>
> 22 It is important that practitioners appreciate that our system now proceeds on the basis of guidelines, not case law. It will, therefore, be very rare, where there is an applicable guideline, for any party to cite to this court cases that seek to express how the guideline works, other than in the rare circumstances we have set out. Decisions of this court are of particular importance to the individuals concerned, but they are unlikely to be of any assistance to further appeals where the guidelines are in issue.'
>
> (Per Lord Thomas LCH in *R v Thelwall* [2016] EWCA Crim, [2017] Crim LR 240.)

Sentencing structure

Magistrates' Courts Sentencing Guidance – Definitive Guideline

B[45.2] Section 172 of the Criminal Justice Act 2003 places a statutory obligation on courts to follow Sentencing Council sentencing guidelines. In general, a court's reasons for departing from sentencing guidelines would be specific to the offence and offenders under consideration. A court which had departed from the guidelines essentially because it considered that they needed reconsideration had erred: *R v Heathcote-Smith (Benjamin) and Melton (Christopher Timothy)* [2011] EWCA Crim 2846, [2012] 2 Cr App Rep (S) 133, [2012] Crim LR 304.

Using sentencing guidelines

The following is reproduced from MCSG. It will seen that there are two structures: one for guidelines issued by the former Sentencing Guidelines Council (pre–2010); and one for guidelines issued by the Sentencing Council (2011 onwards).

Using pre-Sentencing Council guidelines

The offence guidelines include two structures: pre-Sentencing Council guidelines (issued by the Sentencing Guidelines Council) before 2010 and Sentencing Council guidelines issued from 2011 onwards.

Using pre-Sentencing Council guidelines (guidelines issued before 2010)

This section explains the key decisions involved in the sentencing process for SGC guidelines.

1. Assess offence seriousness (culpability and harm)

Offence seriousness is the starting point for sentencing under the Criminal Justice Act 2003. The court's assessment of offence seriousness will:

- determine which of the sentencing thresholds has been crossed;
- indicate whether a custodial, community or other sentence is the most appropriate;
- be the key factor in deciding the length of a custodial sentence, the onerousness of requirements to be incorporated in a community sentence and the amount of any fine imposed.

When considering the seriousness of any offence, the court must consider the offender's culpability in committing the offence and any harm which the offence caused, was intended to cause, or might forseeably have caused (Criminal Justice Act 2003, s 143(1)). In using these guidelines, this assessment should be approached in two stages.

2. Offence seriousness (culpability and harm)

A. Identify the appropriate starting point

The guidelines set out examples of the nature of activity which may constitute the offence, progressing from less to more serious conduct, and provide a starting point based on a first time offender pleading not guilty. The guidelines also specify a sentencing range for each example of activity. Within the guidelines, a first time offender is a person who does not have a conviction which, by virtue of section 143(2) of the Criminal Justice Act 2003, must be treated as an aggravating factor.

Sentencers should begin by considering which of the examples of offence activity corresponds most closely to the circumstances of the particular case in order to identify the appropriate starting point:

- where the starting point is a fine, this is indicated as band A, B or C. For more information, see the approach to assessing fines;
- where the community sentence threshold is passed, the guideline sets out whether the starting point should be a low, medium or high level community order. For more information, see community order ranges;
- where the starting point is a custodial sentence, see custodial sentences.

The Council's definitive guideline Overarching Principles: Seriousness, published 16 December 2004, identifies four levels of culpability for sentencing purposes (intention, recklessness, knowledge and negligence). The starting points in the individual offence guidelines assume that culpability is at the highest level applicable to the offence (often, but not always, intention). Where a lower level of culpability is present, this should be taken into account.

2. Offence seriousness (culpability and harm)

B. Consider the effect of aggravating and mitigating factors

Once the starting point has been identified, the court can add to or reduce this to reflect any aggravating or mitigating factors that impact on the culpability of the offender and/or harm caused by the offence to reach a provisional sentence. Any factors contained in the description of the activity used to reach the starting point must not be counted again. The range is the bracket into which the provisional sentence will normally fall after having regard to factors which aggravate or mitigate the seriousness of the offence. However:

- the court is not precluded from going outside the range where the facts justify it;
- previous convictions which aggravate the seriousness of the current offence may take the provisional sentence beyond the range, especially where there are significant other aggravating factors present.

In addition, where an offender is being sentenced for multiple offences, the court's assessment of the totality of the offending may result in a sentence above the range indicated for the individual offences, including a sentence of a different type. See the definitive guideline on Offences Taken into Consideration and Totality for more information. The guidelines identify aggravating and mitigating factors which may be particularly relevant to each individual offence. These include some factors drawn from the general list of aggravating and mitigating factors in the Council's definitive guideline (see 'seriousness' link above). In each case, sentencers should have regard to the full list, which includes the factors that, by statute, make an offence more serious:

- offence committed while on bail for other offences;
- offence was racially or religiously aggravated;
- offence was motivated by, or demonstrates, hostility based on the victim's sexual orientation (or presumed sexual orientation);
- offence was motivated by, or demonstrates, hostility based on the victim being (or being presumed to be) transgender;
- offence was motivated by, or demonstrates, hostility based on the victim's disability (or presumed disability);
- offender has previous convictions that the court considers can reasonably be treated as aggravating factors having regard to their relevance to the current offence and the time that has elapsed since conviction.

While the lists in the offence guidelines and other material referenced above, aim to identify the most common aggravating and mitigating factors, they are not intended to be exhaustive. Sentencers should always consider whether there are any other factors that make the offence more or less serious.

3. Form a preliminary view of the appropriate sentence, then consider offender mitigation

When the court has reached a provisional sentence based on its assessment of offence seriousness, it should take into account matters of offender mitigation. The Council guideline Overarching Principles: Seriousness states that the issue of remorse should be taken into account at this point along with other mitigating features such as admissions to the police in interview.

4. Consider a reduction for a guilty plea

For cases where the first hearing is before 1 June 2017

The Council guideline Reduction in Sentence for a Guilty Plea, revised 2007, states that the punitive elements of the sentence should be reduced to recognise an offender's guilty plea. The reduction has no impact on sentencing decisions in relation to ancillary orders, including disqualification. The level of the reduction should reflect the stage at which the offender indicated a willingness to admit guilt and will be gauged on a sliding scale, ranging from a recommended one third (where the guilty plea was entered at the first reasonable opportunity), reducing to a recommended one quarter (where a trial date has been set) and to a recommended one tenth (for a guilty plea entered at the 'door of the court' or after the trial has begun). There is a presumption that the recommended reduction will be given unless there are good reasons for a lower amount. The application of the reduction may affect the type, as well as the severity, of the sentence. It may also take the sentence below the range in some cases. The court must state that it has reduced a sentence to reflect a guilty plea (Criminal Justice Act 2003, s 174(2)(d)). It should usually indicate what the sentence would have been if there had been no reduction as a result of the plea.

For cases where the first hearing is on or after 1 June 2017

Refer to the new Sentencing Council Reduction in Sentence for a Guilty Plea guideline.

5. Consider ancillary orders, including compensation

Ancillary orders of particular relevance to individual offences are identified in the relevant guidelines. The court must always consider making a compensation order where the offending has resulted in personal injury, loss or damage (Powers of Criminal Courts (Sentencing) Act 2000, s 130(1)). The court is required to give reasons if it decides not to make such an order (Powers of Criminal Courts (Sentencing) Act 2000, s 130(3)).

6. Decide sentence Give reasons

Review the total sentence to ensure that it is proportional to the offending behaviour and properly balanced. Sentencers must state reasons for the sentence passed in every case, including for any ancillary orders imposed (Criminal Justice Act 2003, s 174(1)). It is particularly important to identify any aggravating or mitigating factors, or matters of offender mitigation, that have resulted in a sentence more or less severe than the suggested starting point. If a court imposes a sentence of a different kind or outside the range indicated in the guidelines, it must state its reasons for doing so (Criminal Justice Act 2003, s.174(2)(a)). The court should also give its reasons for not making an order that has been canvassed before it or that it might have been expected to make.

Where there is no guideline for an offence, it may assist in determining sentence to consider the starting points and ranges indicated for offences that are of a similar level of seriousness.

Using Sentencing Council guidelines

The offence guidelines include two structures: pre-Sentencing Council guidelines (issued by the Sentencing Guidelines Council) before 2010 and Sentencing Council guidelines issued from 2011 onwards.

Using Sentencing Council guidelines (guidelines effective from 2011 onwards)

This section of the user guide explains the key decisions involved in the sentencing process for Sentencing Council guidelines.

STEP ONE: Determining the offence category

The decision making process includes a two-step approach to assessing seriousness. The first step is to determine the offence category by means of an assessment of the offender's culpability and the harm caused, or intended, by reference only to the factors set out at step one in each guideline. The contents are tailored for each offence and comprise the principal factual elements of the offence.

STEP TWO: Starting point and category range

The guidelines provide a starting point which applies to all offenders irrespective of plea or previous convictions. The guidelines also specify a category range for each offence category. The guidelines provide non-exhaustive lists of aggravating and mitigating factors relating to the context of the offence and to the offender. Sentencers should identify whether any combination of these, or other relevant factors, should result in an upward or downward adjustment from the starting point. In some cases, it may be appropriate to move outside the identified category range when reaching a provisional sentence.

FURTHER STEPS

Having reached a provisional sentence, there are a number of further steps within the guidelines. These steps are clearly set out within each guideline and are tailored specifically for each offence in order to ensure that only the most appropriate guidance is included within each offence specific guideline. The further steps include:

- reduction for assistance to the prosecution;
- reduction for guilty pleas (courts should refer to the Reduction in Sentence for a Guilty Plea guideline);

- where an offender is being sentenced for multiple offences – the court's assessment of the totality of the offending may result in a sentence above the range indicated for the individual offences, including a sentence of a different type (for more information, refer to the Offences Taken into Consideration and Totality guideline);
- compensation orders and/or ancillary orders appropriate to the case; and
- give reasons for, and explain the effect of, the sentence.

Where there is no guideline for an offence, it may assist in determining sentence to consider the starting points and ranges indicated for offences that are of a similar level of seriousness.

List of aggravating and mitigating factors

B[45.2A] (Taken from the SGC Guideline 'Overarching Principles' (www.sentencingcouncil.org.uk/overarching-guides/magistrates-court/item/general-guideline-overarching-principles/))

Effective from: 1 October 2019:

- For sentencing offences for which there is no offence specific sentencing guideline, and
- For use in conjunction with offence specific sentencing guidelines.

STEP 1
Reaching a provisional sentence

(a) Where there is no definitive sentencing guideline for the offence, to arrive at a provisional sentence the court should take account of all of the following (if they apply):

- the statutory maximum sentence (and if appropriate minimum sentence) for the offence;
- sentencing judgments of the Court of Appeal (Criminal Division) for the offence; and
- definitive sentencing guidelines for analogous offences.

The court will be assisted by the parties in identifying the above.

For the avoidance of doubt the court should not take account of any draft sentencing guidelines.

When considering definitive guidelines for analogous offences the court must apply these carefully, making adjustments for any differences in the statutory maximum sentence and in the elements of the offence. This will not be a merely arithmetical exercise.

(b) Where possible the court should follow the stepped approach of sentencing guidelines to arrive at the sentence.

The seriousness of the offence is assessed by considering:

- the culpability of the offender, and
- the harm caused by the offending.

(c) The initial assessment of harm and culpability should take no account of plea or previous convictions.

The court should consider which of the five purposes of sentencing (below) it is seeking to achieve through the sentence that is imposed. More than one purpose might be relevant and the importance of each must be weighed against the particular offence and offender characteristics when determining sentence.

- The punishment of offenders

- The reduction of crime (including its reduction by deterrence)
- The reform and rehabilitation of offenders
- The protection of the public
- The making of reparation by offenders to persons affected by their offences

STEP 2
Aggravating and mitigating factors

Once a provisional sentence is arrived at the court should take into account factors that may make the offence more serious and factors which may reduce seriousness or reflect personal mitigation.

- Identify whether a combination of these or other relevant factors should result in any upward or downward adjustment from the sentence arrived at so far.
- It is for the sentencing court to determine how much weight should be assigned to the aggravating and mitigating factors taking into account all of the circumstances of the offence and the offender.
- Not all factors that apply will necessarily influence the sentence.
- When sentencing an offence for which a **fixed penalty notice** was available the reason why the offender did not take advantage of the fixed penalty will be a relevant consideration.
- **If considering a fine – see information on fine band ranges below.**
- **If considering a community or custodial sentence refer also to the Imposition of community and custodial sentences definitive guideline – see information on community orders and custodial sentences below.**

Fines

Starting points based on first time offender pleading not guilty

	Starting point	Range
Fine Band A	50% of relevant weekly income	25%–75% of relevant weekly income
Fine Band B	100% of relevant weekly income	75%–125% of relevant weekly income
Fine Band C	150% of relevant weekly income	125%–175% of relevant weekly income
Fine Band D	250% of relevant weekly income	200%–300% of relevant weekly income
Fine Band E	400% of relevant weekly income	300%–500% of relevant weekly income
Fine Band F	600% of relevant weekly income	500%–700% of relevant weekly income

- The court should determine the appropriate level of fine in accordance with this guideline and section 164 of the Criminal Justice Act 2003, which requires that the fine must reflect the seriousness of the offence and that the court must take into account the financial circumstances of the offender.
- Where possible, if a financial penalty is imposed, it should remove any economic benefit the offender has derived through the commission of the offence including:
  - avoided costs;
  - operating savings;
  - any gain made as a direct result of the offence.
- The fine should meet, in a fair and proportionate way, the objectives of punishment, deterrence and the removal of gain derived through the commission of the offence; **it should not be cheaper to offend than to comply with the law.**
- In considering economic benefit, the court should avoid double recovery.
- Where the means of the offender are limited, priority should be given to compensation (where applicable) over payment of any other financial penalty.

- Where it is not possible to calculate or estimate the economic benefit, the court may wish to draw on information from the enforcing authorities about the general costs of operating within the law.
- When sentencing **organisations** the fine must be sufficiently substantial to have a real economic impact which will bring home to both management and shareholders the need to comply with the law.
- The court should ensure that the effect of the fine (particularly if it will result in closure of the business) is proportionate to the gravity of the offence.
- Obtaining financial information: It is for the offender to disclose to the court such data relevant to their financial position as will enable it to assess what they can reasonably afford to pay. If necessary, the court may compel the disclosure of an individual offender's financial circumstances pursuant to section 162 of the Criminal Justice Act 2003. In the absence of such disclosure, or where the court is not satisfied that it has been given sufficient reliable information, the court will be entitled to draw reasonable inferences as to the offender's means from evidence it has heard and from all the circumstances of the case. In setting a fine, the court may conclude that the offender is able to pay any fine imposed unless the offender has supplied financial information to the contrary.

Community orders

For further information see [the Sentencing Council's] 'Imposition of community and custodial sentences' [definitive guideline].

- The seriousness of the offence should be the **initial** factor in determining which requirements to include in a community order. Offence specific guidelines refer to three sentencing levels within the community order band based on offence seriousness (low, medium and high). The culpability and harm present in the offence(s) should be considered to identify which of the three sentencing levels within the community order band is appropriate. See below for non-exhaustive examples of requirements that might be appropriate in each.
- At least one requirement **MUST** be imposed for the purpose of punishment and/or a fine imposed in addition to the community order unless there are exceptional circumstances which relate to the offence or the offender that would make it unjust in all the circumstances to do so.
- A suspended sentence **MUST NOT** be imposed as a more severe form of community order. A suspended sentence is a custodial sentence.
- Community orders can fulfil all of the purposes of sentencing. In particular, they can have the effect of restricting the offender's liberty while providing punishment in the community, rehabilitation for the offender, and/or ensuring that the offender engages in reparative activities.
- A community order must not be imposed unless the offence is 'serious enough to warrant such a sentence'. Where an offender is being sentenced for a non-imprisonable offence, there is no power to make a community order.
- Sentencers must consider all available disposals at the time of sentence; even where the threshold for a community sentence has been passed, a fine or discharge may be an appropriate penalty. In particular, a Band D fine may be an appropriate alternative to a community order.
- The court must ensure that the restriction on the offender's liberty is commensurate with the seriousness of the offence and that the requirements imposed are the most suitable for the offender.
- Sentences should not necessarily escalate from one community order range to the next on each sentencing occasion. The decision as to the appropriate range of community order should be based upon the seriousness of the new offence(s) (which will take into account any previous convictions).
- In many cases, a pre-sentence report will be pivotal in helping the court decide whether to impose a community order and, if so, whether particular requirements or combinations of requirements are suitable for an individual offender. Whenever the court reaches the provisional view that a community order may be appropriate, it should request a pre-sentence report (whether written or verbal) unless the court is of the opinion that a report is unnecessary in all the circumstances of the case.

- It may be helpful to indicate to the National Probation Service the court's preliminary opinion as to which of the three sentencing ranges is relevant and the purpose(s) of sentencing that the package of requirements is expected to fulfil. Ideally a pre-sentence report should be completed on the same day to avoid adjourning the case. If an adjournment cannot be avoided, the information should be provided to the National Probation Service in written form and a copy retained on the court file for the benefit of the sentencing court. However, the court must make clear to the offender that all sentencing options remain open including, in appropriate cases, committal for sentence to the Crown Court.

Low	Medium	High
Offences only just cross community order threshold, where the seriousness of the offence or the nature of the offender's record means that a discharge or fine is inappropriate In general, only one requirement will be appropriate and the length may be curtailed if additional requirements are necessary	Offences that obviously fall within the community order band	Offences only just fall below the custody threshold or the custody threshold is crossed but a community order is more appropriate in the circumstances More intensive sentences which combine two or more requirements may be appropriate
Suitable requirements might include: • Any appropriate rehabilitative requirement(s) • 40–80 hours of unpaid work • Curfew requirement for example up to 16 hours per day for a few weeks • Exclusion requirement, for a few months • Prohibited activity requirement • Attendance centre requirement (where available)	Suitable requirements might include: • Any appropriate rehabilitative requirement(s) • 80–150 hours of unpaid work • Curfew requirement for example up to 16 hours for 2–3 months • Exclusion requirement lasting in the region of 6 months • Prohibited activity requirement	Suitable requirements might include: • Any appropriate rehabilitative requirement(s) • 150–300 hours of unpaid work • Curfew requirement for example up to 16 hours per day for 4–12 months • Exclusion requirement lasting in the region of 12 months
* If order does not contain a punitive requirement, suggested fine levels are indicated below:		
BAND A FINE	BAND B FINE	BAND C FINE

Custodial sentences

Sentencing flowcharts are available at [the Sentencing Council's] 'Imposition of Community and Custodial Sentences' definitive guideline.

The approach to the imposition of a custodial sentence should be as follows:

(1) **Has the custody threshold been passed?**

- A custodial sentence must not be imposed unless the offence or the combination of the offence and one or more offences associated with it was so serious that neither a fine alone nor a community sentence can be justified for the offence.
- There is no general definition of where the custody threshold lies. The circumstances of the individual offence and the factors assessed by offence-specific guidelines will determine whether an offence is so serious that neither

a fine alone nor a community sentence can be justified. Where no offence specific guideline is available to determine seriousness, the harm caused by the offence, the culpability of the offender and any previous convictions will be relevant to the assessment.

- The clear intention of the threshold test is to reserve prison as a punishment for the most serious offences.

(2) **Is it unavoidable that a sentence of imprisonment be imposed?**

- Passing the custody threshold does not mean that a custodial sentence should be deemed inevitable. Custody should not be imposed where a community order could provide sufficient restriction on an offender's liberty (by way of punishment) while addressing the rehabilitation of the offender to prevent future crime.
- For offenders on the cusp of custody, imprisonment should not be imposed where there would be an impact on dependants which would make a custodial sentence disproportionate to achieving the aims of sentencing.

(3) **What is the shortest term commensurate with the seriousness of the offence?**

- In considering this the court must NOT consider any licence or post sentence supervision requirements which may subsequently be imposed upon the offender's release.

(4) **Can the sentence be suspended?**

- A suspended sentence **MUST NOT** be imposed as a more severe form of community order. A suspended sentence is a custodial sentence. **Sentencers should be clear that they would impose an immediate custodial sentence if the power to suspend were not available.** If not, a non-custodial sentence should be imposed.

The following factors should be weighed in considering whether it is possible to suspend the sentence:

Factors indicating that it would <u>not</u> be appropriate to suspend a custodial sentence
Offender presents a risk/danger to the public
Appropriate punishment can only be achieved by immediate custody
History of poor compliance with court orders
Factors indicating that it may be appropriate to suspend a custodial sentence
Realistic prospect of rehabilitation
Strong personal mitigation
Immediate custody will result in significant harmful impact upon others

The imposition of a custodial sentence is both punishment and a deterrent. To ensure that the overall terms of the suspended sentence are commensurate with offence seriousness, care must be taken to ensure requirements imposed are not excessive. A court wishing to impose onerous or intensive requirements should reconsider whether a community sentence might be more appropriate.

Pre-sentence report

Whenever the court reaches the provisional view that:

- the custody threshold has been passed; and, if so
- the length of imprisonment which represents the shortest term commensurate with the seriousness of the offence;

the court should obtain a pre-sentence report, whether verbal or written, unless the court considers a report to be unnecessary. Ideally a pre-sentence report should be completed on the same day to avoid adjourning the case.

Magistrates: Consult your legal adviser before deciding to sentence to custody without a pre-sentence report.

Suspended sentences: general guidance

(i) The guidance regarding pre-sentence reports applies if suspending custody.

(ii) If the court imposes a term of imprisonment of between 14 days and 2 years (subject to magistrates' courts sentencing powers), it may suspend the sentence for between 6 months and 2 years (the 'operational period'). The time for which a sentence is suspended should reflect the length of the sentence; up to 12 months might normally be appropriate for a suspended sentence of up to 6 months.

(iii) Where the court imposes two or more sentences to be served consecutively, the court may suspend the sentence where the aggregate of the terms is between 14 days and 2 years (subject to magistrates' courts sentencing powers).

(iv) When the court suspends a sentence, it may impose one or more requirements for the offender to undertake in the community. The requirements are identical to those available for community orders, see the [Sentencing Council's definitive] guideline on Imposition of Community and Custodial Sentences.

(v) A custodial sentence that is suspended should be for the same term that would have applied if the sentence was to be served immediately.

Factors increasing seriousness
(Factors are not listed in any particular order and are not exhaustive)

Statutory aggravating factors
Previous convictions, having regard to a) the **nature** of the offence to which the conviction relates and its **relevance** to the current offence; and b) the **time** that has elapsed since the conviction
Offence committed whilst on bail
Offence motivated by, or demonstrating hostility based on any of the following characteristics or presumed characteristics of the victim: religion, race, disability, sexual orientation, or transgender identity
Offence was committed against an emergency worker acting in the exercise of functions as such a worker
Other aggravating factors
Commission of offence whilst under the influence of alcohol or drugs
Offence was committed as part of a group
Offence involved use or threat of a weapon
Planning of an offence
Commission of the offence for financial gain
High level of profit from the offence
Abuse of trust or dominant position
Restraint, detention or additional degradation of the victim
Vulnerable victim
Victim was providing a public service or performing a public duty at the time of the offence
Other(s) put at risk of harm by the offending
Offence committed in the presence of other(s) (especially children)
Actions after the event including but not limited to attempts to cover up/conceal evidence
Blame wrongly placed on other(s)

Failure to respond to warnings or concerns expressed by others about the offender's behaviour
Offence committed on licence or while subject to court order(s)
Offence committed in custody
Offences taken into consideration
Offence committed in a domestic context
Offence committed in a terrorist context
Location and/or timing of offence
Established evidence of community/wider impact
Prevalence

Factors reducing seriousness or reflecting personal mitigation
(Factors are not listed in any particular order and are not exhaustive)

No previous convictions or no relevant/recent convictions
Good character and/or exemplary conduct
Remorse
Self-reporting
Cooperation with the investigation/early admissions
Little or no planning
The offender was in a lesser or subordinate role if acting with others/performed limited role under direction
Involved through coercion, intimidation or exploitation
Limited awareness or understanding of the offence
Little or no financial gain
Delay since apprehension
Activity originally legitimate
Age and/or lack of maturity
Sole or primary carer for dependent relatives
Physical disability or serious medical condition requiring urgent, intensive or long-term treatment
Mental disorder or learning disability
Determination and/or demonstration of steps having been taken to address addiction or offending behaviour

STEP 3
Consider any factors which indicate a reduction for assistance to the prosecution

The court should take into account sections 73 and 74 of the Serious Organised Crime and Police Act 2005 (assistance by defendants: reduction or review of sentence) and any other rule of law by virtue of which an offender may receive a discounted sentence in consequence of assistance given (or offered) to the prosecutor or investigator.

STEP 4
Reduction for guilty pleas

The court should take account of any potential reduction for a guilty plea in accordance with section 144 of the Criminal Justice Act 2003 and the guideline for Reduction in Sentence for a Guilty Plea (where first hearing is on or after 1 June 2017, or first hearing before 1 June 2017).

STEP 5
Dangerousness

Where the offence is listed in Schedule 15 and/or Schedule 15B of the Criminal Justice Act 2003

The court should consider whether having regard to the criteria contained in Chapter 5 of Part 12 of the Criminal Justice Act 2003 it would be appropriate to impose a life sentence (section 224A or section 225) or an extended sentence (section 226A). When sentencing offenders to a life sentence under these provisions, the notional determinate sentence should be used as the basis for the setting of a minimum term.

STEP 6
Special custodial sentence for certain offenders of particular concern

Where the offence is listed in Schedule 18A of the Criminal Justice Act 2003 and the court does not impose a sentence of imprisonment for life or an extended sentence, but does impose a period of imprisonment, the term of the sentence must be equal to the aggregate of the appropriate custodial term and a further period of 1 year for which the offender is to be subject to a licence.

STEP 7
Totality principle

If sentencing an offender for more than one offence, or where the offender is already serving a sentence, consider whether the total sentence is just and proportionate to the overall offending behaviour in accordance with the [Sentencing Council's] 'Offences Taken into Consideration' and 'Totality' guidelines.

STEP 8
Compensation and ancillary orders

In all cases the court should consider whether to make compensation and/or other ancillary orders.

Where the offence involves a firearm, an imitation firearm or an offensive weapon the court may consider the criteria in section 19 of the Serious Crime Act 2007 for the imposition of a Serious Crime Prevention Order.

STEP 9
Reasons

Section 174 of the Criminal Justice Act 2003 imposes a duty to give reasons for, and explain the effect of, the sentence.

STEP 10
Consideration for time spent on bail (tagged curfew)

The court must consider whether to give credit for time spent on bail in accordance with section 240A of the Criminal Justice Act 2003.

Aggravation related to race, religion, disability or sexual orientation

B[45.2B] **Racial or religious aggravation – statutory provisions**

(1) Sections 29 to 32 of the Crime and Disorder Act 1998 create specific racially or religiously aggravated offences which have higher maximum penalties than the non-aggravated versions of those offences. The individual offence guidelines (see **Part A**) indicate whether there is a specifically aggravated form of the offence.

(2) An offence is racially or religiously aggravated for the purposes of ss 29–32 of the Act if the offender demonstrates hostility towards the victim based on his or her membership (or presumed membership) of a racial group, or if the offence is racially or religiously motivated: s 28 CDA 1998.

(3) For all other offences, s 145 of the CJA 2003 provides that the court must regard racial or religious aggravation as an aggravating factor.

(4) The court should not treat an offence as racially or religiously aggravated for the purposes of s 145 where a racially or religiously aggravated form of the offence was charged but resulted in an acquittal: *R v McGillivray* [2005] EWCA Crim 604, [2005] 2 Cr App Rep (S) 366, [2005] Crim LR 484. The court should not normally treat an offence as racially or religiously aggravated if a racially or religiously form of the offence was available but was not charged: *R v O'Callaghan* [2005] EWCA Crim 317, [2005] 2 Cr App Rep (S) 514, [2005] Crim LR 486. **Consult your legal adviser for further guidance in these situations.**

Aggravation related to disability, sexual orientation or transgender identity – statutory provisions

(5) Under s 146 of the CJA 2003, the court must treat as an aggravating factor the fact that:
- an offender demonstrated hostility towards the victim based on his or her sexual orientation or disability (or presumed sexual orientation, transgender identity or disability); or
- the offence was motivated by hostility towards persons who are of a particular sexual orientation, transgender or who have a particular disability.

Approach to sentencing

(6) A court should not conclude that offending involved aggravation relating to race, religion, disability, sexual orientation or transgender without first putting the offender on notice and allowing him or her to challenge allegation.

(7) When sentencing any offence where such aggravation is found to be present, the following approach should be followed. This applies both to the specific racially or religiously aggravated offences under the CDA 1998 and to offences which are regarded as aggravated under s 145 or 146 of the CJA 2003 (*R v Kelly and Donnelly* [2001] EWCA Crim 1751, [2002] 1 Cr App Rep (S) 360, [2001] Crim LR 836):
- sentencers should first determine the appropriate sentence, leaving aside the element of aggravation relating to race, religion etc but taking into account al other aggravating and mitigating features;
- the sentence should then be increased to take account of the aggravation related to race, religion, disability or sexual orientation'
- the increase may mean that a more onerous penalty of the same type is appropriate, or that the threshold for a more severe type of sentence is passed;
- the sentencer must state in open court that the offence was aggravated by reason of race, religion, disability or sexual orientation;
- the sentencer should state what the sentence would have been without that element of aggravation.

(8) The extent to which the sentence is increased will depend on the seriousness of the aggravation. The following factors could be taken as indicating a high level of aggravation:

Offender's intention
- The element of aggravation based on race, religion etc was planned
- The offence was part of a pattern of offending by the offender
- The offender was a member of, or was associated with, a group promoting hostility based on race, religion, disability or sexual orientation
- The incident was deliberately set up to be offensive or humiliating to the victim or to the group of which the victim is a member

Impact on the victim or others
- The offence was committed in the victim's home
- The victim was providing a service to the public

- The timing or location of the offence was calculated to maximise the harm or distress it caused
- The expressions of hostility were repeated or prolonged
- The offence caused fear and distress throughout a local community or more widely
- The offence caused particular distress to the victim and/or the victim's family

(9) At the lower end of the scale, the aggravation may be regarded as less serious if:
- It was limited in scope or duration
- The offence was not motivated by hostility on the basis of race, religion, disability or sexual orientation, and the element of hostility or abuse was minor or incidental.

(10) In these guidelines, the specific racially or religiously aggravated offences under the CDA 1998 are addressed on the same page as the "basic offence"; the starting points and ranges indicated on the guidelines (see Part A) relate to the "basic" (ie non-aggravated) offence. The increase for the element of racial or religious aggravation may result in a sentence above the range; this will not constitute a departure from the guideline for which reasons must be given.

1 The offence

B[45.3] An important principle of sentencing is that a sentence should not be more severe than is warranted by the seriousness of the offence and other offences associated with it. When considering the seriousness of the current offence or offences, previous convictions and failures to respond to previous sentences may be taken into account where relevant. Custodial sentences are reserved primarily for offenders who have committed an offence 'so serious' that only a custodial sentence can be justified for it, and community sentences are only available where the offence is 'serious enough' to warrant such a sentence.

The Purposes of Sentencing

B[45.4] In respect of adults, the Criminal Justice Act 2003 sets out the objectives of sentencing as punishment, the reduction of crime (including deterrence), reforms and rehabilitation, protection of the public and reparation.

B[45.5] A custodial sentence may also be imposed where the offender has refused to consent to a drug testing order or certain conditions requiring consent (see B[15.9]).

B[45.6] Otherwise any sentence imposed will generally be commensurate with the seriousness of the offence, although the court, having considered all the mitigation, may take this into account in mitigating an offender's sentence.

Determining seriousness

B[45.7] **Meaning of 'range', 'starting point' and 'first time offender'.** As in previous editions, and consistent with other SC guidelines, these guidelines are for a first time offender convicted after a trial. The guidelines provide a starting point based on an assessment of the seriousness of the offence and a range within which the sentence will normally fall in most cases.

B[45.8] **The facts.** The court must be satisfied that the facts of the offence or offences for which sentence is to be passed have been proved or agreed.

In determining the seriousness of an offence the court must take into account all information about the circumstances of the offence, any aggravating or mitigating factors as are available to it, and information in a pre-sentence report. The court must consider the offender's culpability and any harm or potential harm caused by the offence.

B[45.9] **Associated offence.** In considering whether an offence is 'serious enough' to warrant a community sentence, or 'so serious' that only a custodial sentence can be justified, the court may consider the combination of the offence and other offences associated with it. An 'associated offence' is in essence another offence for which the offender is to be sentenced at that time or is to be taken into consideration. Whether it is appropriate for offences to be TIC'd see *R v Lavery* [2008] EWCA Crim 2499, [2009] 3 All ER 295, 172 JP 561.

B[45.10]–[45.15] Guidance on the seriousness of offences and aggravating and mitigating features is to be found at B[45.2] and B[45.2A].

B[45.16] Parliament also gives broad guidance to the courts by prescribing the maximum penalties available. For example, many minor offences are punishable only by a fine on level 1 (max £200) and level 5 (max £5,000). Other, more serious, offences are also punishable with imprisonment of up to 6 (**12) months.

2 Mitigation

B[45.17] There are two particular objectives of mitigation: to draw to the attention of the court any factors relevant to mitigating the seriousness of the offence, and to highlight mitigation personal to the offender.

B[45.18] The first consideration for the court in determining sentence is the seriousness of the offence. The seriousness of the offence will generally determine whether the court must impose a custodial sentence or if the offence warrants the making of a community sentence, a fine or discharge.

B[45.19] In addressing the seriousness of the offence, the circumstances of the offence should be examined to see whether they disclose any mitigating circumstances. Guidance on what may amount to a mitigating (or aggravating) feature of an offence is given by the Sentencing Guidelines Council (see B[45.2A] and B[45.2] above).

B[45.20] The seriousness of the offence including culpability and harm considerations will broadly determine which range of sentencing options is open to the court: custody, community, financial or a discharge. Where the court is concerned with a violent or sexual offence and is considering a custodial sentence to protect the public, the personal circumstances and history will become relevant. However, personal mitigation is usually more relevant at the second stage when the general level of seriousness has been determined, where mitigation will affect the final choice of sentence and the impact it will have on the offender. While no sentence may be more severe than is justified by the defendant's offence, personal mitigation may serve to reduce the punishment or suggest that a more individualised approach may be appropriate. In forming an opinion, whether a particular community order or orders comprising a community sentence is or are the most suitable for the offender, the court may take into account any information about the offender which is before it. Mitigating factors which have commonly been considered by the courts are referred to under 'Consideration of sentences' at B[45.36]–B[45.48].

3 Availability of sentences

B[45.21] Available sentences are determined by the maximum penalties prescribed by Parliament and by the court's assessment of the gravity of the offence.

As mentioned above the maximum penalty for an offence is fixed by statute as being a fine, or a fine and custody. Some sentences and orders of the court are available only where an offence is punishable in the case of an adult with imprisonment (the defendant himself does not need to be liable to imprisonment). A comparison of Tables A and C at B[43.1] and B[43.3] will make this apparent. Furthermore some sentences are only available to offenders of a certain age – see B[40.5].

B[45.22] By a systematic process of noting whether an offence is punishable with imprisonment and the age of the offender, the sentencing options available to the court can be narrowed progressively.

B[45.23] Criminal Justice Act 2003. This further categorises sentences and orders into four broad divisions: discharges (instead of sentencing), financial, community and custodial. In addition there are orders providing for the medical treatment of mentally disturbed offenders.

B[45.24] Discharges (absolute/conditional). These are available to all offenders and for all offences where the court is satisfied that having regard to the circumstances of the offence and the offender it is inexpedient to inflict punishment. See B[22].

B[45.25]–[45.31] Financial penalties. These include fines (B[28]), compensation (B[10]) and deprivation of property (B[18]) and are available to all offenders and for all offences.

B[45.32] Community orders (adults). The court may only impose a community sentence which consists of one or more requirements where the offence carries imprisonment and the court considers the offence, or a combination of the offence and other 'associated offences' to be 'serious enough' to warrant such a sentence. The fact that an offence is 'serious enough' does not mean that the court must pass a community sentence, only that it may do so.

B[45.33] Custodial sentences (see B[15]). The custodial sentences available to the magistrates are imprisonment and for offenders under 21, detention in a young offender institution (**to be replaced by a sentence of imprisonment from a date to be appointed by virtue of the CJA 2003) and detention and training orders for offenders aged 12 to 17 inclusive. They are only available where statute defines an offence as being punishable with imprisonment.

B[45.34] A custodial sentence may generally only be imposed where the offence or a combination of the offence and 'associated offences' is 'so serious' that neither a community penalty nor a fine cannot be justified for it. The court will usually find it helpful to consider the nature and extent of the defendant's criminal culpability and the nature and extent of any injury or damage caused to the victim (*R v Howells* [1999] 1 All ER 50, [1999] 1 WLR 307, CA). However, although this criterion may be satisfied the court may nevertheless, in the case of a mentally ill defendant, make a hospital or guardianship order.

B[45.35] Exceptionally a custodial sentence may be imposed where the offender has refused to consent to a drug testing order and certain conditions in a community order requiring consent ie a willingness to comply with the requirements.

4 Consideration of sentences

B[45.36] When the court has ascertained the range of sentences appropriate for the seriousness of the offence, it must then proceed to select the particular sentence appropriate for the case. In this task it will be assisted by its appreciation of the seriousness of the offence but also by mitigation personal to the offender, any pre-sentence report and the court's objective in sentencing.

B[45.37] Mitigation. Nothing shall prevent a court from mitigating an offender's sentence by taking into account any such matters as, in the opinion of the court, are relevant in mitigation of sentence. Mitigating factors which have commonly been considered by courts include the following.

B[45.38] 1 Youth of the offender. This may operate as mitigation and will usually indicate a lower level of sentence (eg a smaller fine or shorter period of custody) than would be appropriate otherwise. The mitigating effect of youth, however, may be cancelled out by other factors, such as a record of previous convictions which is serious having regard to the offender's age, or which shows a proclivity for crime beyond what one would expect for his age.

B[45.39] 2 Older offenders who have not previously offended would receive credit for a previously blameless life especially when receiving a more serious penalty such as a community sentence or custody.

B[45.40]–[45.45] 3 Effect of previous convictions. Previous convictions must be taken into account and may make an offence more serious although this will depend upon the nature of the offence and the time elapsed since conviction. Within the range of sentences appropriate to the seriousness of the offence good character is almost always strong mitigation and the worse an offender's previous record is, the less 'discount' he can expect for good character. Occasionally, the record of previous convictions may show a significant gap since the last conviction and might be taken as evidence of a genuine effort to keep out of trouble. The record may also show that the present offence is out of character, for example, when a man with a long record of petty theft appears on a charge of indecent assault.

B[45.46] 4 Plea of guilty. The Sentencing Council issued a new definitive guideline 'Reduction in sentence for a guilty plea' on 7 March 2017. This applies to all adult cases first listed on or after 1 July 2017, whenever the offence occurred. This approach must be followed and it is wrong in principle to give credit simply by suspending a sentence of imprisonment: *R v Hussain* [2018] EWCA Crim 780, [2018] 2 Cr App R (S) 12, [2018] Crim LR 770.

The guideline is reproduced below save as to the sections on applicability, mandatory life sentences for murder and the flowcharts.

'Reduction in Sentence for a Guilty Plea

Section 144 of the Criminal Justice Act 2003 provides:

(1) In determining what sentence to pass on an offender who has pleaded guilty to an offence ("Offence" includes breach of an order where this constitutes a separate criminal offence but not breach of terms of a sentence or licence.) in proceedings before that court or another court, a court must take into account:

(a) the stage in the proceedings for the offence at which the offender indicated his intention to plead guilty, and
(b) the circumstances in which this indication was given.

Nothing in this guideline affects the duty of the parties to progress cases (including the service of material) and identify any issues in dispute in compliance with the Criminal Procedure Rules and Criminal Practice Directions.

...

B. KEY PRINCIPLES

The purpose of this guideline is to encourage those who are going to plead guilty to do so as early in the court process as possible. Nothing in the guideline should be used to put pressure on a defendant to plead guilty.

Although a guilty person is entitled not to admit the offence and to put the prosecution to proof of its case, an acceptance of guilt:
(a) normally reduces the impact of the crime upon victims;
(b) saves victims and witnesses from having to testify; and
(c) is in the public interest in that it saves public time and money on investigations and trials.

A guilty plea produces greater benefits the earlier the plea is indicated. In order to maximise the above benefits and to provide an incentive to those who are guilty to indicate a guilty plea as early as possible, this guideline makes a clear distinction between a reduction in the sentence available at the first stage of the proceedings and a reduction in the sentence available at a later stage of the proceedings.

The purpose of reducing the sentence for a guilty plea is to yield the benefits described above. The guilty plea should be considered by the court to be independent of the offender's personal mitigation.

- Factors such as admissions at interview, co-operation with the investigation and demonstrations of remorse should not be taken into account in determining the level of reduction. Rather, they should be considered separately and prior to any guilty plea reduction, as potential mitigating factors.
- The benefits apply regardless of the strength of the evidence against an offender. The strength of the evidence should not be taken into account when determining the level of reduction.
- The guideline applies only to the punitive elements of the sentence and has no impact on ancillary orders including orders of disqualification from driving.

C. THE APPROACH

Stage 1: Determine the appropriate sentence for the offence(s) in accordance with any offence specific sentencing guideline.

Stage 2: Determine the level of reduction for a guilty plea in accordance with this guideline.

Stage 3: State the amount of that reduction.

Stage 4: Apply the reduction to the appropriate sentence.

Stage 5: Follow any further steps in the offence specific guideline to determine the final sentence.

D. DETERMINING THE LEVEL OF REDUCTION

The maximum level of reduction in sentence for a guilty plea is one-third

D1. Plea indicated at the first stage of the proceedings

Where a guilty plea is indicated at the first stage of proceedings a reduction of one-third should be made (subject to the exceptions in section F). The first stage will normally be the first hearing at which a plea or indication of plea is sought and recorded by the court. (In cases where (in accordance with the Criminal Procedure Rules) a defendant is given the opportunity to enter a guilty plea without attending a court hearing, doing so within the required time limits will constitute a plea at the first stage of proceedings.)

D2. Plea indicated after the first stage of proceedings – maximum one quarter – sliding scale of reduction thereafter

After the first stage of the proceedings the maximum level of reduction is one-quarter (subject to the exceptions in section F).

The reduction should be decreased from one-quarter to a maximum of one-tenth on the first day of trial having regard to the time when the guilty plea is first indicated to the court relative to the progress of the case and the trial date (subject to the exceptions in section F). The reduction should normally be decreased further, even to zero, if the guilty plea is entered during the course of the trial.

For the purposes of this guideline a trial will be deemed to have started when pre-recorded cross-examination has begun.

E. APPLYING THE REDUCTION

E1. Imposing one type of sentence rather than another

The reduction in sentence for a guilty plea can be taken into account by imposing one type of sentence rather than another; for example:

- by reducing a custodial sentence to a community sentence, or
- by reducing a community sentence to a fine.

Where a court has imposed one sentence rather than another to reflect the guilty plea there should normally be no further reduction on account of the guilty plea. Where, however, the less severe type of sentence is justified by other factors, the appropriate reduction for the plea should be applied in the normal way.

E2. More than one summary offence

When dealing with more than one summary offence, the aggregate sentence is limited to a maximum of six months. Allowing for a reduction for each guilty plea, consecutive sentences might result in the imposition of the maximum six month sentence. Where this is the case, the court may make a modest additional reduction to the overall sentence to reflect the benefits derived from the guilty pleas.

E3. Keeping an either way case in the magistrates' court to reflect a guilty plea

Reducing a custodial sentence to reflect a guilty plea may enable a magistrates' court to retain jurisdiction of an either way offence rather than committing the case for sentence to the Crown Court.

In such cases a magistrates' court should apply the appropriate reduction to the sentence for the offence(s) arrived at in accordance with any offence specific sentencing guideline and if the resulting sentence is then within its jurisdiction it should go on to sentence.

F. EXCEPTIONS

F1. Further information, assistance or advice necessary before indicating plea

Where the sentencing court is satisfied that there were particular circumstances which significantly reduced the defendant's ability to understand what was alleged or otherwise made it unreasonable to expect the defendant to indicate a guilty plea sooner than was done, a reduction of one-third should still be made.

In considering whether this exception applies, sentencers should distinguish between cases in which it is necessary to receive advice and/or have sight of evidence in order to understand whether the defendant is in fact and law guilty of the offence(s) charged, and cases in which a defendant merely delays guilty plea(s) in order to assess the strength of the prosecution evidence and the prospects of conviction or acquittal.

F2. Newton Hearings and special reasons hearings

In circumstances where an offender's version of events is rejected at a Newton hearing (A Newton hearing is held when an offender pleads guilty but disputes the case as put forward by the prosecution and the dispute would make a difference to the sentence. The judge will normally hear evidence from witnesses to decide which version of the disputed facts to base the sentence on.) or special reasons hearing, (A special reasons hearing occurs when an offender is convicted of an offence carrying mandatory licence endorsement or disqualification from driving and seeks to persuade the court that there are extenuating circumstances relating to the offence that the court should take into account by reducing or avoiding endorsement or disqualification. This may involve calling witnesses to give evidence.) the reduction which would have been available at the stage of proceedings the plea was indicated should normally be halved. Where witnesses are called during such a hearing, it may be appropriate further to decrease the reduction.

F3. Offender convicted of a lesser or different offence

If an offender is convicted of a lesser or different offence from that originally charged, and has earlier made an unequivocal indication of a guilty plea to this lesser or different offence to the prosecution and the court, the court should give the level of reduction that is appropriate to the stage in the proceedings at which this indication of plea (to the lesser or different offence) was made taking into account any other of these exceptions that apply. In the Crown Court where the offered plea is a permissible alternative on the indictment as charged, the offender will not be treated as having made an unequivocal indication unless the offender has entered that plea.

F4. Minimum sentence under section 51A of the Firearms Act 1968

There can be no reduction for a guilty plea if the effect of doing so would be to reduce the length of sentence below the required minimum term.

F5. Appropriate custodial sentences for persons aged 18 or over when convicted under the Prevention of Crime Act 1953 and Criminal Justice Act 1988 and prescribed custodial sentences under the Power of Criminal Courts (Sentencing) Act 2000

In circumstances where:

- an *appropriate* custodial sentence of at least six months falls to be imposed on a person aged 18 or over who has been convicted under sections 1 or 1A of the Prevention of Crime Act 1953; or sections 139, 139AA or 139A of the Criminal Justice Act 1988 (certain possession of knives or offensive weapon offences) **or**
- a *prescribed* custodial sentence falls to be imposed under section 110 of the Powers of Criminal Courts (Sentencing) Act 2000 (drug trafficking offences) or section 111 of the Powers of Criminal Courts (Sentencing) Act 2000 (burglary offences),

the court may impose any sentence in accordance with this guideline which is not less than 80 per cent of the appropriate or prescribed custodial period. (In accordance with s 144(2) and (3) of the Criminal Justice Act 2003.)'

B[45.46A] The approach prescribed by the SC guideline (see 'C The Approach', ante) must be followed and it is wrong in principle to give credit simply by suspending a sentence of imprisonment: *R v Hussain* [2018] EWCA Crim 780, [2018] 2 Cr App R (S) 12, [2018] Crim LR 770.

B[45.47] **5 Loss of employment etc.** An offender must generally be taken to have foreseen the normal consequences of conviction and so factors such as distress to his family, loss of job, pension, good character, etc will usually have little mitigating value. Where consequences follow which could not reasonably have been foreseen, for example, where the offence was unconnected with the offender's employment but he nevertheless finds himself dismissed, or where the offence was committed on the spur of the moment under provocation with no opportunity to consider the consequences, some allowance may be made if those consequences turn out to be disastrous. The person who is especially vulnerable must be expected to take special care. So, for example, the person whose employment depends upon his having a driving licence must be expected to take particular care not to commit endorsable offences. People such as doctors, nurses and solicitors, from whom a high ethical standard is expected, must expect the consequences of conviction for an offence which amounts to a breach of those standards and cannot claim professional disciplinary action in mitigation.

B[45.48] **Unrepresented defendant.** The court has a duty itself to seek out mitigating factors before finally arriving at a sentence. It should be especially careful not to assume that there are none in the case of the inarticulate unrepresented defendant.

5 The totality of sentencing

B[45.49] The Sentencing Council laid down a definitive guideline ('Totality') which applies to all offenders, whose cases are dealt with on or after **11 June 2012.** The reader is also recommended to consult the section dealing with 'Offences Taken Into Consideration'. The principle of totality comprises two elements:

(1) All courts, when sentencing for more than a single offence, should pass a total sentence which reflects all the offending behaviour before it and is just and proportionate. This is so whether the sentences are structured as concurrent or consecutive. Therefore, concurrent sentences will ordinarily be longer than a single sentence for a single offence.

(2) It is usually impossible to arrive at a just and proportionate sentence for a multiple offending simply by adding together notional single sentences. It is necessary to address the offending behaviour, together with the factors personal to the offender as a whole.

Concurrent/consecutive sentences. There is no inflexible rule governing whether sentences should be structured as concurrent or consecutive components. The overriding principle is that the overall sentence must be just and proportionate. Space precludes some examples which are set out in the SC Guideline. The reader is invited to consult the SC website where necessary.

6 Choice of sentence

B[45.50] The deliberations of the court will have brought into focus more than one form of sentence. For example, it may be that the offence is 'serious enough' to warrant a community sentence. The pre-sentence report may have considered a range of community orders. The probation officer will have considered the seriousness of the offence and have proposed a sentence which is commensurate with the seriousness of the offence and takes into account the circumstances of the offender. The court will need to be clear that the sentence adequately reflects the seriousness of the offence while (in the case of a community penalty) also being the most suitable for the offender. It does not mean that if an offence is serious enough to warrant a community sentence that is the only sentence which may be imposed. If there is mitigation which allows the court to impose a fine then the fine must reflect the seriousness of the offence and the financial circumstances of the offender.

B[45.51] The advice of the legal adviser will be essential to ensure that all the statutory criteria which must be satisfied before sentence can be passed and the correct ancillary orders made.

B[45.52] The good chairman will have noted during the hearing such matters as applications for costs, or forfeiture of drugs. Liability for endorsement and disqualification will also have occupied attention and after the substantive sentence has been agreed by (at least) a majority of the justices, the chairman will deal with each of these matters in turn. Save in the simplest cases, the chairman will make a written note of the total decision so that no error or omission is made.

7 Statement accompanying the sentence

B[45.53] The Criminal Justice Act 2003, s 174 (as amended by s 64 of the Legal Aid, Sentencing and Punishment of Offenders Act 2012, from a date to be appointed) requires a court to give reasons for and explain the effect of its sentence

The requirement of Article 6 of the European Convention on Human Rights means that reasons should be given. Indeed the effect, not to say the benefit, of a sound sentencing decision can sometimes be lost because the defendant does not understand the reasoning behind it, or because the public do not.

B[45.54] When a particular sentence falls within the Sentencing Guidelines Council guidance for the kind of offence and offender – when it is the sort of sentence the defendant probably expected to receive – there will seldom be justification for garnishing the reasons. However, when the court imposes a sentence which might be unexpected the reasons for this departure from normal sentencing habits might be fuller. Likewise, when different types of sentence are imposed on co-accused whose circumstances may appear to be similar. The needs of the public as well as those of the defendant and any victim of his offence should be borne in mind. A structured approach to the sentencing decision, consultation with the clerk and a careful note will assist the chairman when giving reasons

Victim Personal Statement

B[45.55]–[45.60] The Criminal Practice Directions 2015 [2015] EWCA Crim 1567 provide as follows:

'F.1 Victims of crime are invited to make a statement, known as a Victim Personal Statement ("VPS"). The statement gives victims a formal opportunity to say how a crime has affected them. It may help to identify whether they have a particular need for information, support and protection. The court will take the statement into account when determining sentence. In some circumstances, it may be appropriate for relatives of a victim to make a VPS, for example where the victim has died as a result of the relevant criminal conduct. The Code of Practice for Victims of Crime, the revised version of which was published in the summer of 2013 and will come into force shortly, gives further information about victims' entitlements within the criminal justice system, and the duties placed on criminal justice agencies when dealing with victims of crime.

F.2 When a police officer takes a statement from a victim, the victim should be told about the scheme and given the chance to make a VPS. The decision about whether or not to make a VPS is entirely a matter for the victim; no pressure should be brought to bear on their decision, and no conclusion should be drawn if they choose not to make such a statement. A VPS or an updated VPS may be made (in proper s.9 form, see below) at any time prior to the disposal of the case. It will not normally be appropriate for a VPS to be made after the disposal of the case; there may be rare occasions between sentence and appeal when an update to the VPS may be necessary, for example, when the victim was injured and the final prognosis was not available at the date of sentence. However, VPS after disposal should be confined to presenting up to date factual material, such as medical information, and should be used sparingly.

F.3 If the court is presented with a VPS the following approach, subject to the further guidance given by the Court of Appeal in *R v Perkins; Bennett; Hall* [2013] EWCA Crim 323, [2013] Crim L.R. 533, should be adopted:

(a) The VPS and any evidence in support should be considered and taken into account by the court, prior to passing sentence.

(b) Evidence of the effects of an offence on the victim contained in the VPS or other statement must be in proper form, that is a witness statement made under section 9 of the Criminal Justice Act 1967 or an expert's report; and served in good time upon the defendant's solicitor or the defendant, if he is not represented. Except where inferences can properly be drawn from the nature of or circumstances surrounding the offence, a sentencing court must not make assumptions unsupported by evidence about the effects of an offence on the victim.

(c) In all cases it will be appropriate for a VPS to be referred to in the course of the sentencing hearing and/or in the sentencing remarks. Subject to the court's discretion, the contents of the VPS may be summarised and in an appropriate case even read out in open court.

(d) The court must pass what it judges to be the appropriate sentence having regard to the circumstances of the offence and of the offender, taking into account, so far as the court considers it appropriate, the impact on the victim. The opinions of the victim or the victim's close relatives as to what the sentence should be are therefore not relevant, unlike the consequences of the offence on them. Victims should be advised of this. If, despite the advice, opinions as to sentence are included in the statement, the court should pay no attention to them.'

For cases involving sexual offences see also **B[10]** regarding the relevance of the victim's views to any compensation order that may be imposed.

Guidance on victim personal and family impact statements was given in *R v Perkins* [2013] EWCA Crim 323, [2013] Crim LR 533. The following extract from the judgment stresses the fundamental principles.

'[9] Without suggesting any amendments or additions to the current Practice Direction, a number of its aspects need emphasis:

"(a) The decision whether to make a statement must be made by the victims personally. They must be provided with information which makes it clear that they are entitled to make a statement, but, as the Guide to Police Officers and Investigators underlines, no pressure, either way, should be brought to bear on their decision. They are entitled to make statements, and they are equally entitled not to do so. They should be informed of their right, and allowed to exercise it as they wish: in particular the perception should not be allowed to emerge that if they chose not to do so the court may misunderstand or minimise the harm caused by the crime.

(b) When the decision whether or not to make a statement is being made, it should be clearly understood that the victim's opinion about the type and level of sentence should not be included. Again that is entirely consistent with the Guide to Police Officers and Investigators. If necessary, victims must be assisted to appreciate that the court is required to pass the appropriate sentence, in accordance with decisions of this court, and definitive guidelines issued by the Sentencing Guidelines Council or the Sentencing Council, and make a judgment based on all the facts of the case, including both the aggravating and the mitigating features.

(c) The statement constitutes evidence. That is the basis on which it is admitted. It must therefore be treated as evidence. It must be in a formal witness statement, served on the Defendant's legal advisors in time for the Defendant's instructions to be taken, and for any objection to the use of the statement, or part of it, if necessary, to be prepared. In *Perkins*, the statement was handed over far too late in the process, and indeed we are concerned that some of the submissions from counsel in these cases suggest that a somewhat haphazard and slovenly approach to the time when the statement is served may have developed, at any rate in some parts of the country.

(d) Just because the statement is intended to inform the sentencing court of specific features of the consequences of the offence on the victim, responsibility for presenting admissible evidence remains with the prosecution.

(e) It follows that the statement may be challenged, in cross-examination, and it may give rise to disclosure obligations, and indeed as the case of *Hall* underlines, may be used, after conviction, to deploy an argument that the credibility of the victim is open to question."'

Other impact statements

B[45.60A] The Criminal Practice Directions 2015 also make provision for impact statements for businesses, and for the making of a community impact statement by a police officer. These will be found in CPD VII Sentencing I and H, respectively.

Reasons for, and explanation of, sentences

B[45.61] Section 174 of the Criminal Justice Act 2003 requires the following.

The court must state in open court, in ordinary language and in general terms, the court's reasons for deciding on the sentence.

The court must explain to the offender in ordinary language:

(a) the effect of the sentence;
(b) the effects of non-compliance with any order that the offender is required to comply with and that forms part of the sentence;

(c) any power of the court to vary or review any order that forms part of the sentence; and
(d) the effects of failure to pay a fine, if the sentence consists of or includes a fine.

Particular duties of the court in complying with the above are:

(a) To identify any definitive sentencing guidelines relevant to the offender's case and:
  (i) explain how the court discharged any duty imposed on it by s 125 of the Coroners and Justice Act 2009 (duty to follow guidelines unless satisfied it would be contrary to the interests of justice to do so);
  (ii) where the court was satisfied it would be contrary to the interests of justice to follow the guidelines, state why.
(b) Where, as a result of taking into account any matter referred to in s 144(1) (guilty pleas), the court imposes a punishment on the offender which is less severe than the punishment it would otherwise have imposed, the court must state that fact.
(c) Where the offender is under 18 and the court imposes a sentence that may only be imposed in the offender's case if the court is of the opinion mentioned in:
  (i) s 1(4)(a)–(c) of the Criminal Justice and Immigration Act 2008 and s 148(1) of this Act (youth rehabilitation order with intensive supervision and surveillance or with fostering); or
  (ii) s 152(2) of this Act (discretionary custodial sentence), the court must state why it is of that opinion.

Other requirements to give reasons include:

(a) a decision not to activate a suspended sentence on the commission of a further offence;
(b) a finding of special reasons not to endorse or disqualify from driving; and
(c) a decision not to award compensation in a case where the court is empowered to make such an award.

B[45.62] It is generally inadvisable to deliver a lecture or homily or offer any other words of worldly wisdom to a defendant who is being sentenced. Research has shown that most prisoners cannot remember even a short time after sentence much of what the judge said and even whether he said anything at all.

8 Pronouncement of sentence

B[45.63] The chairman should announce the sentence(s) in a way which leaves no one in court in any doubt as to the court's decision. In the following pages each possible sentence is considered and a form of words is provided as a guide to the way in which the sentence may be announced. It is not suggested that the chairman should read the sentence from this book but that a glance at the wording suggested here will assist in ensuring that all the necessary legal points have been covered. Where an offender is to be sentenced for more than one offence it is advised that each sentence is related to each offence by description. It is bad practice to sentence in such terms as, 'For the first offence you will be fined £50. For the second offence you will be fined £100 and your licence endorsed. For the third offence etc.' Bear in mind that the offender has no idea of the order in which offences appear on the list and therefore has no way of relating the penalties to the offences if they are announced in this fashion. The better practice is exemplified as follows: 'For the burglary and theft at Jackson's, the butchers, you will go to prison for 20 days; for using the credit card to obtain a camera from Browns, you will go to prison for 15 days which will be in addition to the first sentence, which means you will go to prison for a total of 35 days.' Whenever there are several sentences to be announced, the chairman should totalise the effect of them, that is, the total amount of a monetary penalty, the total period of imprisonment or of disqualification should be stated. Words such as concurrent or consecutive need not be used if other words are used which make it clear what the total effect of the sentence is, as in the example above.

B[45.64] When offences have been taken into consideration in arriving at a sentence that fact should be stated as a preamble to the sentence.

B[45.65] Where relevant the chairman should announce by how much the sentence has been reduced by virtue of the defendant's guilty plea.

B[46]
Transfer of criminal proceedings

B[46.1] Where a person appears or is brought before a magistrates' court:

(a) to be tried by the court for an offence, or
(b) for the court to inquire into the offence as examining justices,

the court may transfer the matter to another magistrates' court (MCA 1980, s 27A as inserted by Courts Act 2003, s 46).

The court may transfer the matter before or after beginning the trial or inquiry. If the magistrates' court transfers before hearing all of the evidence and the parties the court to whom the case has been transferred must, in effect, hear the evidence and the parties again. The power to transfer must be exercised in accordance with any directions given under Courts Act 2003, s 30(3).

B[46.2] It would appear that the consent of the magistrates' court to which the proceedings are to be transferred is not a legal requirement. Good practice suggests that the court to whom the case has been transferred should be contacted prior to transfer. (See JCS document: 'Guidance on the use of s 27A MCA 1980'; ref 54.004, Intel October 2008.)

B[47]
Violent Offender Order

B[47.1] Part VII of the Criminal Justice & Immigration Act 2008, ie ss 98–117, created the Violent Offender Order (VOO). The legislation came into force on 3 August 2009.

A VOO may be made against an offender aged 18 years or more on the application of a chief officer of police. The application is made by way of complaint to a magistrates' court. The proceedings rank as civil proceedings.

The application may be made against an offender convicted of manslaughter, soliciting, conspiracy or attempted murder, corresponding offences under legislation relating to the armed forces, causing GBH or wounding with intent (s 18 OPA 1861) or offences contrary to s 20 OPA 1861 (inflicting or causing GBH).

A VOO when made contains prohibitions, restrictions and conditions intended to protect the public from serious violent harm. The order must be for a minimum duration of two years and a maximum of five years unless renewed or discharged: s 98(1)(b).

Qualifying Offender (s 99)

B[47.2] A person is a qualifying offender if he is aged 18 years or more, has been convicted of a qualifying offence (see above) and received either a custodial sentence of 12 months or more, a hospital order, a supervision order (within the meaning of the Criminal Procedure (Insanity) Act 1964) or found not guilty by way of insanity.

A person is also a qualifying offender if convicted of an equivalent offence or offences and has been dealt with in an equivalent fashion according to the law of any country outside England and Wales: s 99(4).

Application (ss 100–101)

B[47.3] Application is made by complaint via a chief officer of police. The application should specify that the chief officer believes since the date of conviction or finding of insanity etc that the offender has acted in such a way as to give reasonable cause to believe that it is necessary for a VOO to be made in respect of him.

The court may make the order if satisfied that the conditions are met, but in determining whether an order is **necessary** the court must have regard to whether the offender would, at any time while such an order is in force, be subject under any other enactment to any measures that would operate to protect the public from the risk of serious violent harm caused by him.

A VOO cannot come into force while an offender is serving a custodial sentence, is on licence, subject to a hospital or supervision order (see above); nevertheless the order may be sought and made at any time.

Prohibitions, conditions restrictions (s 102) and notification requirements (ss 107–112)

B[47.4] The order may contain specific terms which prevent an offender from going to specified premises or places at any time or specified times, attending any specified event, or having contact with any specified individual.

A person subject to a VOO or interim order is under a duty to notify the police of his name, address, national insurance number and any plans to travel abroad. An offender must comply with the notification requirement within 3 days of the order coming into force. There is also a periodic duty to notify the police of a change of circumstances, make periodic reports and notify any plans to travel outside the UK.

Variation, discharge and renewal (s 103)

B[47.5] A full order may be varied, discharged or renewed on application by way of complaint to a magistrates' court. An order may not be discharged within the first two years unless both the offender and police consent.

Interim orders (s 104)

B[47.6] An interim order may be made where the court is not in a position to make a final determination but the person concerned is a qualifying offender and the court considers that it would be likely to be make a full order and that it is desirable to act to provide the public with immediate protection. As with full orders the VOO will not come into effect while the offender is serving a custodial sentence etc. An interim order ceases to have effect at the end of the specified period subject to any application to vary or discharge the order. There is no provision to extend an interim order. A fresh application would have to be made.

Notice provisions and appeals (ss 105–106)

B[47.7] An application for a full or interim order, discharge, variation or renewal may not be heard unless the court is satisfied that the person concerned has been given reasonable notice of the application. An appeal lies to the Crown Court against the making of an order, interim order, renewal or variation, or a refusal to make or the discharge of an order.

Breach of a VOO (s 113)

B[47.8] Section 113 makes it an offence to fail without reasonable excuse to comply with the terms of the order or with the notification requirements, or notifying false information. The offences are triable either way and punishable summarily to a £5,000 fine, 6 months custody or both. On indictment the offence carries an unlimited fine and/or five years' imprisonment. Unlike ASBOs there is nothing to prevent a court from imposing a conditional discharge for a breach of the order.

Jurisdiction for breach proceedings to be commenced lies with the court in the area where the offender resides or is found: s 113(8).

B[48]

Youth injunctions

Introduction to youth injunctions

B[48.1] Anti-social behaviour orders in free-standing proceedings or on conviction of a criminal offence (known as ASBOs and CrASBOs) were repealed by the Anti-social Behaviour, Crime and Policing Act 2014 and replaced, respectively, with injunctions and criminal behaviour orders.

Narrative on criminal behaviour orders (which also replaced drink banning orders on conviction) will be found at paragraph **B[8]**.

Injunctions in respect of youths are governed by PART 1 of, and Schs 1 and 2 to, the Anti-social, Crime and Policing Act 2014.

Proceedings for an injunction are civil in nature and the 'balance of probabilities' standard of proof is not incompatible with art 6(1) of the ECHR: *Jones v Birmingham City Council* [2018] EWCA Civ 1189, [2018] 2 Cr App R 23.

Jurisdiction to grant injunctions in respect of youths (which also replace drink banning orders on application, intervention orders and individual support orders) is vested in the youth court; adult jurisdiction has been transferred from the magistrates' court to the county court and High Court, though the youth court may grant permission for an application for an injunction against a person aged 18 or over to be made to the youth court if such an application has been made against a person under the age of 18 and it is in the interests of justice for the applications to be heard together: Magistrates' Courts (Injunctions: Anti-social Behaviour) Rules 2015, r 15. Where a respondent attains the age of 18 after the commencement of proceedings, the proceedings must remain in the youth court, though the court may direct that the proceedings be transferred to the county court or the High Court: r 16.

Where the injunction was granted by the youth court, any subsequent action upon it – arrest for breach, variation, etc – will be undertaken by the county court if the respondent has attained the age of 18 years by the relevant date: See Anti-social Behaviour, Crime and Policing Act 2014, ss 9(3) and 10(2).

Power to grant injunctions

B[48.2] An injunction may be granted against a person aged 10 or over if two conditions are met:

(a) the court is satisfied, on the balance of probabilities, that the respondent has engaged or threatens to engage in anti-social behaviour; and
(b) the court considers it just and convenient to grant the injunction for the purpose of preventing the respondent from engaging in anti-social behaviour: Anti-social Behaviour, Crime and Policing Act 2014, s 1(1)–(3).

'Anti-social behaviour' means conduct that has caused, or is likely to cause, harassment, alarm or distress to any person; or conduct capable of causing housing-related nuisance or annoyance to any person. Where, but only where, the applicant is a housing provider, a local authority or a chief officer of police, anti-social behaviour also means conduct capable of causing nuisance or annoyance to a person in relation to that person's occupation of residential premises: Anti-social Behaviour, Crime and Policing Act 2014, s 2(1)(a), (b) and (c). 'Housing related' means directly or indirectly relating to the housing management functions of a housing provider or a local authority: Anti-social Behaviour, Crime and Policing Act 2014, s 2(3).

Applications for injunction may be made by a wide range of organisations: see Anti-social Behaviour, Crime and Policing Act 2014, s 5. (As to the requirement to consult before making an application if the respondent will be under the age of 18 when the application is made, see s 14.)

Prohibitions and requirements in injunctions – duration of orders

B[48.3] Injunctions may for the purpose of preventing the respondent from engaging in anti-social behaviour include prohibitions or requirements: Anti-social Behaviour, Crime and Policing Act 2014, s 1(4). Note, however, that an injunction may not have the effect of excluding the respondent from the place where he or she normally lives if he or she is under the age of 18: Anti-social Behaviour, Crime and Policing Act 2014, s 13(1).

Prohibitions or requirements must, so far as is practicable, be such as to avoid interference with work or educational commitments or any conflict with the requirements of any other court order the respondent faces: Anti-social Behaviour, Crime and Policing Act 2014, s 1(5). Compliance with requirements must be supervised by a specified person or organisation and before a requirement can be included the court must receive evidence from the person or organisation to be specified about its suitability and enforceability: Anti-social Behaviour, Crime and Policing Act 2014, s 3(1), (2). The respondent must keep in touch with the supervisor as the latter instructs and notify any change of address; these obligations have effect as requirements of the injunction: Anti-social Behaviour, Crime and Policing Act 2014, s 3(6).

Where the respondent is an adult, an injunction may be made for any fixed period or until further order; where, however, the respondent is under the age of 18 when the injunction is granted the period must be specified and must not exceed 12 months. Subject to this, the court may specify different periods for which particular prohibitions or requirements have effect: Anti-social Behaviour, Crime and Policing Act 2014, s 1(6), (7).

Power of arrest

(a) Arrest without warrant

B[48.4] A power of arrest may be attached to a prohibition or requirement if the anti-social behaviour in which the respondent has engaged or threatens to engage consists of or includes the use or threatened use of violence against other persons, or there is a significant risk of harm to other persons from the respondent, but a power of arrest may not be attached to a requirement to participate in particular activities: Anti-social Behaviour, Crime and Policing Act 2014, s 4(1). A power of arrest may be for a shorter period than that of the prohibition or requirement to which it relates: Anti-social Behaviour, Crime and Policing Act 2014, s 4(2). A power of arrest enables a constable to arrest the respondent without warrant if the constable has reasonable cause to suspect that the respondent in breach of the provision and the constable must then inform the person who applied for the injunction; the respondent if still aged under 18 must then be brought before a justice of the peace within 24 hours of the time of the arrest (disregarding Christmas Day, Good Friday or any Sunday) or, if aged 18 or over, the respondent must be brought before a judge of the county court: Anti-social Behaviour, Crime and Policing Act 2014, s 9(1)–(4). The respondent must then be remanded if the matter is not disposed of straight away: Anti-social Behaviour, Crime and Policing Act 2014, s 9(5), (6). Remands are governed by Sch 1 to the Act, see below.

(b) Issue of arrest warrant

B[48.5] If the person who applied for an injunction thinks that the respondent is in breach of any of its provisions, the person may apply for the issue of a warrant for the respondent's arrest. If the respondent is under the age of 18 the application must be made to a justice of the peace and the warrant must require the respondent to appear before the youth court; if the respondent has attained the age of 18 since the injunction was granted the application any subsequent proceedings will be in the county court: Anti-social Behaviour, Crime and Policing Act 2014, s 10(1), (2), (5), (6). An application for a warrant of arrest under s 10(1) must be substantiated on oath; such an application may be made without notice: the Magistrates' Courts (Injunctions: Antisocial Behaviour) Rules 2015, r 7. As to the need for an application to be supported by evidence of the breach and to include a statement that the requisite prior consultation has taken place, see the Magistrates' Courts (Injunctions: Anti-social Behaviour) Rules 2015, r 10.

A warrant may only be issued if the justice or judge has reasonable grounds for believing that the respondent is in breach of a provision of the injunction: Anti-social Behaviour, Crime and Policing Act 2014, s 10(3). A constable who arrests a person under such a warrant must inform the person who applied for the injunction: Anti-social Behaviour, Crime and Policing Act 2014, s 10(7). If the respondent is brought before the court under such a warrant but the matter is not disposed of straight away, the court may remand the respondent: Anti-social Behaviour, Crime and Policing Act 2014, s 10(8). Remands are governed by Sch 1 to the Act, see below.

Applications without notice, interim injunctions and variation or discharge of injunctions

(a) Applications without notice

B[48.6] An application for an injunction may be made without notice; where this occurs the court must either adjourn the proceedings with or without granting an interim injunction, or dismiss the application: Anti-social Behaviour, Crime and Policing Act 2014, s 6. There is no requirement of prior consultation before a without notice application, but such a requirement arises if the court adjourns the application: Anti-social Behaviour, Crime and Policing Act 2014, see s 14(1), (2).

(b) Interim injunctions

B[48.7] Where the court adjourns the hearing of the application for an injunction, it may grant an interim injunction lasting until the final hearing of the application or until further order if the court thinks it just to do so: Anti-social Behaviour, Crime and Policing Act 2014, s 7(1), (2). If the hearing was without notice the interim junction may not have the effect of requiring the respondent to participate in particular activities; otherwise the court has the same powers, including the power to attach a power of arrest, as it has in relation to a final order: Anti-social Behaviour, Crime and Policing Act 2014, s 7(3), (4). An interim injunction made on an application made without notice is not effective until served: the Magistrates' Courts (Injunctions: Anti-social Behaviour) Rules 2015, r 4.

(c) Variation or discharge of injunctions

B[48.8] The court may vary or discharge the injunction on the application of the person who applied for it or the respondent: Anti-social Behaviour, Crime and Policing Act 2014, s 8(1). As to the requirement of prior consultation, see s 14(3). As to the court to which the application must be made and the particulars to be stated in the application, see the Magistrates' Courts (Injunctions: Anti-social Behaviour) Rules 2015, r 6.

The court having jurisdiction will be the youth court if the respondent remains under the age of 18, otherwise it will be the county court: Anti-social Behaviour, Crime and Policing Act 2014, s 8(2). The power to vary includes power to include an additional prohibition or requirement, or to extend the period for which a prohibition or requirement has effect, or to attach a power of arrest or to extend the period for which a power of arrest has effect: Anti-social Behaviour, Crime and Policing Act 2014, s 8(3).

Remands in breach proceedings

B[48.9] A remand following arrest with or without a warrant may be on bail or in custody, but if the respondent is under the age of 18 the remand must not be in custody unless the court is satisfied on the written or oral evidence of a medical practitioner that there is reason to suspect that the respondent is suffering from mental disorder and is of the opinion that it would be impracticable for a report on the respondent's mental condition to be made if he or she were remanded on bail: Anti-social Behaviour, Crime and Policing Act 2014, Sch 1, paras 2, 6. The maximum period of such a remand is three weeks at a time: see para 5.

A remand on bail is by means of taking a personal recognisance from the respondent, which may be with or without sureties; the court may fix the amount of the recognisances with a view to their being taken subsequently and, in the meantime, commit the respondent to custody: Anti-social Behaviour, Crime and Policing Act 2014, Sch 1, para 2(3). As to who may take such a recognisance, see the Magistrates' Courts (Injunctions: Anti-social Behaviour) Rules 2015, r 9.

A surety may be conditioned for the respondent's appearance on a fixed date or it may be continuous: Anti-social Behaviour, Crime and Policing Act 2014, Sch 1, para 3.

A remand for a medical report may be for a maximum of three weeks at a time if in custody or four weeks at a time if on bail: Anti-social Behaviour, Crime and Policing Act 2014, Sch 1, para 5. Otherwise, the respondent may not be remanded for a period exceeding eight clear days unless the remand is on bail and the applicant for the injunction consents: Anti-social Behaviour, Crime and Policing Act 2014, Sch 1, para 4. (As to further remands and the enlargement of recognizances and sureties in absence, see para 7.) But the matter must be dealt with within 28 days of the date on which the arrested person appears in court and the arrested person must be given at least two days' notice of the hearing: the Magistrates' Courts (Injunctions: Anti-social Behaviour) Rules 2015, r 8(3).

A person remanded on bail may be required to comply, before release or later, with any requirements that appear to the court to be necessary to secure that the person does not interfere with witnesses or otherwise obstruct the course of justice: Anti-social Behaviour, Crime and Policing Act 2014, Sch 1, para 9.

Breach of injunctions: powers of court in respect of under-18s

B[48.10] Breach of an injunction by an adult will be a contempt of court and punishable in the usual way by the county court by imprisonment of up to two years or an unlimited fine. In the case of persons under the age of 18, the powers on breach are prescribed by Sch 2 to the Anti-social Behaviour, Crime and Policing Act 2014.

A youth court may, if satisfied beyond reasonable doubt that a person is in breach of a provision of an injunction, impose a supervision order or a detention order, but such an order may only be made on the application of the person who applied for the injunction: Anti-social Behaviour, Crime and Policing Act 2014, Sch 2, para 1(1), (2). The applicant must first consult the youth offending team and inform any other body the applicant thinks appropriate, and the youth court must consider any representations made by the youth offending in considering whether and how to exercise its powers: Anti-social Behaviour, Crime and Policing Act 2014, Sch 2, para 1(3), (4).

A detention order cannot be made unless the respondent is aged at least 14 and the court is satisfied that, in view of the severity or extent of the breach, no other power available to the court is appropriate and the court must state in open court why it is so satisfied: Anti-social Behaviour, Crime and Policing Act 2014, Sch 2 para 1(5), (6). The period of detention must not exceed three months (not counting the day on which the order is made) and this will be served in whatever youth detention accommodation – a secure training centre, a young offender institution or secure accommodation – the Secretary of State decides: Anti-social Behaviour, Crime and Policing Act 2014, Sch 2, para 14(1). There is power to revoke a detention order on the applications of the original applicant or the defaulter: Anti-social Behaviour, Crime and Policing Act 2014, Sch 2, para 15.

A supervision order is an order imposing one or more of the following requirements: a supervision requirement; an activity requirement; and a curfew requirement: Anti-social Behaviour, Crime and Policing Act 2014, Sch 2 para 2(1). The order must specify the maximum period for the operation of any requirement and this must not exceed six months (not counting the day on which the order is made); the order must also specify the youth offending team in whose area it appears that the respondent will live during the operational period of any requirements: Anti-social Behaviour, Crime and Policing Act 2014, Sch 2 para 2(5)–(7).

'Supervision requirements', activity requirements' and curfew requirements' are defined by the Anti-social Behaviour, Crime and Policing Act 2014, Sch 2, paras 3,

4 and 5, respectively. A curfew requirement may be accompanied by an electronic monitoring requirement: Anti-social Behaviour, Crime and Policing Act 2014, Sch 2, para 6.

An order may be amended on the application of the original applicant to substitute a different operational period of any requirement (with the same maximum period of six months), or to make any other amendment to a requirement as the court thinks appropriate, or to substitute a different youth offending team on a change of address: Anti-social Behaviour, Crime and Policing Act 2014, Sch 2, paras 8 and 9. As to amending activity requirements, see also para 4(12), (13).

An order may also be revoked or amended to remove a requirement on the application of the original applicant or the defaulter, but if such an application is dismissed no further application may be made by that applicant without the consent of the court or the agreement of the other party: Anti-social Behaviour, Crime and Policing Act 2014, Sch 2, para 10.

It is the task of the 'responsible officer' to inform the original applicant if the officer considers that the defaulter has failed to comply with a requirement of a supervision order, and on being so informed the original applicant may apply to a youth court: Anti-social Behaviour, Crime and Policing Act 2014, Sch 2, para 12. 'Responsible officer' is defined by para 7 and will be a member of Youth Offending Team (YOT) unless the sole requirement of the injunction is a curfew with electronic monitoring. As to prior consultation before an application can be made, see para 12(3). As to the need to provide supporting evidence of the breach of a supervision order and a statement that the required consultation has been undertaken, see the Magistrates' Courts (Injunctions: Anti-social Behaviour) Rules 2015, r 11.

If the court is satisfied beyond reasonable doubt that the defaulter has without reasonable excuse failed to comply with a requirement of an injunction it may evoke the order and make a new one, or revoke the order and make a detention order; before exercising its powers the court must consider any representations made by the youth offending team: Anti-social Behaviour, Crime and Policing Act 2014, Sch 2, para 12(4), (6). The court cannot exercise its powers if the defaulter has attained the age of 18, but where this is not the case the powers are in addition to any other power of the court in relation to the breach of the supervision order: Anti-social Behaviour, Crime and Policing Act 2014, Sch 2, para 12(5).

Rights of appeal, etc

B[48.11] A right of appeal from a decision of a youth court lies to the Crown Court: Anti-social Behaviour, Crime and Policing Act 2014, s 15.

Provision is made for the making of special measures directions: Anti-social Behaviour, Crime and Policing Act 2014, s 16.

The automatic reporting restrictions of s 49 of the Children and Young Persons Act 1933 do not apply, but s 39 of that Act does apply and gives the court the discretion to restrict the publication of certain information to protect the identity of the child or young person: Anti-social Behaviour, Crime and Policing Act 2014, s 17.

Saving and transitional provisions

B[48.12] Provision is made to preserve existing ASBOs, etc, and to enable the continuation of proceedings commenced before the commencement of Part 1 of the Anti-social Behaviour, Crime and Policing Act 2014, but post-commencement there may be no variation of any existing order which extends its term or the period of any of its provisions; at the end of five years beginning with the commencement day any of these order or injunctions still in force will automatically be treated as an injunction: Anti-social Behaviour, Crime and Policing Act 2014, s 21.

B[49]
Youth Rehabilitation Order

B[49.1] The youth rehabilitation order (YRO) was introduced by the Criminal Justice and Immigration Act 2008 for offenders aged under 18. It is a single generic community sentence. It replaced action plan, supervision, intensive supervision, curfew and exclusion orders, and prospectively replaces attendance centre orders. It also replaced community orders in relation to 16 and 17-year-olds (for which provision was made by the Criminal Justice Act 2003, but was never implemented).

YROs are also subject to the restrictions that apply to the making of community sentences generally.

The definitive guideline of the Sentencing Guidelines Council 'Overarching Principles – Sentencing Youths' contains guidance at paragraph 10 on the availability, making and treatment of breach of YROs.

Requirements which may be included: CJ & IA 2008, s 1

B[49.2] When imposing a YRO the court is able to choose one or more requirements from the following 'menu':

- an activity requirement (B[49.6]);
- a supervision requirement (B[49.7]);
- if the offender is aged 16 or 17, an unpaid work requirement (B[49.8]);
- a programme requirement (B[49.9]);
- an attendance centre requirement (B[49.10]);
- a prohibited activity requirement (B[49.11]);
- a curfew requirement (B[49.12]);
- an exclusion requirement (B[49.13]);
- a residence requirement (B[49.14]);
- a local authority residence requirement (B[49.15]);
- a mental health treatment requirement (B[49.17]);
- a drug treatment requirement (B[49.19]);
- an intoxicating substance treatment requirement (B[49.20]);
- an education requirement ([B[49.21]).

Electronic monitoring: CJ & IA 2008, Sch 1, Pt 1, para 2

B[49.3] A YRO may also impose an electronic monitoring requirement and must do so if the YRO imposes a curfew or exclusion requirement unless, in the circumstances of the particular case, the court is satisfied that it would be inappropriate to do so, or it is not practicable to do so either because a third party whose co-operation would be required does not consent or the relevant arrangements for electronic monitoring are not available in the relevant local justice area.

Intensive supervision and fostering: CJ & IA 2008, s 1(3), (4)

B[49.4] A YRO may include intensive supervision and surveillance ('an extended activity requirement', where the number of days exceeds the normal limit of 90 up to a maximum of 180) or a fostering requirement, subject to certain sentencing threshold and other conditions, namely:

(a) the offence or offences are punishable with imprisonment;
(b) the offence or the combination of the offence and offences associated with it is so serious that, but for these provisions, a custodial sentence would be appropriate or, if the offender is aged under 12 at the time of conviction, would have been appropriate if he had been aged 12 or older; and
(c) if the offender is aged 12–15 years, he is a persistent offender.

These restrictions do not, however, prevent the making of a YRO with intensive supervision and surveillance if the offender has failed to comply with an order under s 161(2) of the Criminal Justice Act 2003 (pre-sentence drug testing).

In the case of a fostering requirement, the court must additionally be satisfied that the behaviour which constituted the offence was due to a significant extent to the circumstances in which the offender was living and that the imposition of a fostering requirement would assist in the offender's rehabilitation: CJ & IA 2008, Sch 1, Pt 1, para 4. See further **B[49.16]**, below.

An extended activity requirement must be accompanied by a supervision requirement and a curfew requirement (and accordingly an electronic monitoring requirement, as above): CJ & IA 2008, Sch 1, Pt 1, para 3. It cannot, however, be accompanied by a fostering requirement: CJ & IA 2008, Sch 1, Pt 1, para 4. Subject to this, before a court makes a YRO containing two or more requirements, or two or more YROs in relation to associated offences, it must consider whether the requirements to be imposed are mutually compatible: CJ & IA 2008, Sch 1, Pt 1, para 29.

The court must also ensure, as far as practicable, that any requirement avoids any conflict with the offender's religious beliefs, or interference with his work or education, or any conflict with the requirements of any other YRO to which he may be subject: CJ & IA 2008, Sch 1, Pt 1, para 29.

Duration: CJ & IA 2008, Sch 1, Pt 1, paras 30, 32

B[49.4A] A YRO takes effect on the day after the day on which it was made, unless the offender is subject to a detention and training order in which case the court may direct that the YRO will take effect when the period of supervision under the DTO begins or on the expiry of the term of the DTO.

A youth rehabilitation order must specify a date, 'the end date', not more than three years after the date on which the order takes effect, by which all the requirements in it must have been complied with. If a youth rehabilitation order imposes two or more different requirements, the order may also specify a date by which each of those requirements must have been complied with; and the last of those dates must be the same as the end date. In the case of a youth rehabilitation order with intensive supervision and surveillance, the end date must not be earlier than six months after the date on which the order takes effect. Unless revoked, a youth rehabilitation order imposing an unpaid work requirement remains in force until the offender has worked under it for the number of hours specified in it.

B[49.4B] There are provisions dealing with specifying the local justice area in which the offender resides or will reside, providing copies of the order and empowering the Secretary of State by order, inter alia, to enable or require courts to provide for periodic review of the order.

(1) Intensive supervision and surveillance requirement

B[49.5] The order may be used for juveniles where the following criteria apply:

(a) the offence or offences are punishable with imprisonment;
(b) the offence or the combination of the offences associate with it are so serious that, but for these provisions, a custodial sentence would be appropriate, or if the offender is under 12 at the time of conviction, would have been appropriate if he had been aged 12 or more); and
(c) if the offender was aged 12–15 years, he is a persistent offender.

The restrictions outlined above do not apply if the offender has failed to comply with an order for pre-sentence drug testing pursuant to s 161(2) of the CJA 2003.

The court may include one or more of the other requirements (with the exception of fostering) set out below subject to the caveat that the requirements must be proportionate to the seriousness of the offence or offences.

The court may in addition make an extended activity requirement of up to 180 days. If it does so it *must* also impose a supervision requirement with electronic monitoring.

Copies of the order must be served on the offender ant other person involved with the order: CJ & IA 2008, Sch 2, para 24.

(2) Activity requirement

B[49.6] The offender must do any or all of the following:

(a) participate, on such days as may be specified, in activities at the place or places specified by presenting himself at the place specified or to a specified person in accordance with instructions given by the responsible officer and comply with such instructions given by, or under the authority of, the person in charge of that activity;
(b) participate in activity, or activities, specified in the order on such number of days so specified;
(c) participate in one or more residential exercises for a continuous period or periods compromising such number of days as specified;
(d) engage in activities in accordance with instructions of the responsible officer on such number of days as may be specified.

As far as requirement (c) above is concerned, the *consent* of a parent or guardian of the offender must be obtained.

Specified activities may include *reparation*, direct or indirect, or as directed by the responsible officer.

Before making an order the court should consult either an officer of the local probation board or a member of a youth offending team. The court must be satisfied that the activities to be specified can be made under arrangements that exist in the local justice area in which the offender resides and that it is feasible to secure compliance with those requirements. Where compliance with an activity involves the co-operation of a person other than the offender and/or the responsible officer, that person's consent must be obtained.

The aggregate number of days upon which a juvenile may be required to comply with directions must not exceed 90 unless the 'custody' criteria are satisfied (see B[49.3]) when the total number of days permitted is 180: CJ & IA 2008, s 1(4)(a)–(c).

(3) Supervision requirement

B[49.7] When a youth court makes a supervision requirement the effect is to place the juvenile under the supervision of the responsible officer or another person determined by him for the relevant period. The "relevant period" for these purposes means the period for which the order remains in force ie for up to three years. The purpose of the requirement is to promote the offender's rehabilitation.

(4) Unpaid work requirement (16 and 17 year old offenders only)

B[49.8] This is a requirement that the offender must perform unpaid work in accordance for the number of hours specified in the order, at such times as he may be instructed by the responsible officer. Unless revoked, an unpaid work requirement remains in force until the offender has completed the number of hours specified.

The number of hours which a person may be required to work under an unpaid work requirement must be specified in the relevant order and must be in the aggregate:

(a) not less than 40, and
(b) not more than 240.

The court may not impose an unpaid work requirement in respect of an offender unless after hearing (if the court thinks necessary) from an appropriate officer, the court is satisfied that the offender is a suitable person to perform work under such a requirement.

Where the court makes orders in respect of two or more offences of which the offender has been convicted on the same occasion and includes unpaid work requirements in each of them, the court may direct that the hours of work specified in any of those requirements is to be concurrent or consecutive. However the total number of hours must not exceed the maximum of 240 hours.

(5) Programme requirement

B[49.9] This requirement involves the offender's participation in a systematic set of activities specified in the order, on such number of days as may be specified. The court may not include a programme requirement unless:

(a) the proposed programme has been recommended to the court as being suitable for the offender by an officer of a local probation board or a youth offending team or a provider of probation services; and
(b) the programme is available at the specified place.

Where compliance with an activity involves the co-operation of a person other than the offender and/or the responsible officer, that person's consent must be obtained.

The programme requirement means the offender must:

(a) in accordance with instructions given by the responsible officer, participate in the programme at the place specified in the order on the number of days specified in the order; and
(b) while at that place, comply with instructions given by, or under the authority of, the person in charge of the programme.

(6) Attendance centre requirement

B[49.10] This is a requirement to attend at an attendance centre for any period on any occasion at the beginning of the period and, during that period, to engage in occupations, or receive instruction, under the supervision of and in accordance with instructions given by, or under the authority of the officer in charge of the centre. The aggregate number of hours will depend on the age of the offender:

(a) offender aged 16 or over at the time of conviction: not less than 12 and not more than 36 hours.
(b) offender aged 14 or over but under 16 at the time of conviction: not less than 12 and not more than 24 hours
(c) offender aged under 14 at the time of conviction: not more than 12 hours.

The court must have been notified of the availability of a centre for persons of the offender's age and sex. Regard must be paid to the accessibility of the centre to the offender.

(7) Prohibited activity requirement

B[49.11] This requires the offender to refrain from participating in activities specified in the order on a day or days so specified *or* during a period so specified.

The court must first consult either a provider of probation services such as an officer of a local probation board or a member of a youth offending team. One requirement which may be included in an order is that the offender is not to possess, use or carry a firearm within the meaning of the Firearms Act 1968. It is recommended that the court should consult first with its legal adviser before including such a requirement.

(8) Curfew requirement

B[49.12] A curfew requirement is a requirement that the offender must remain, for periods specified in the relevant order, at a place so specified. It may specify different places or different periods for different days, but may not specify periods which amount to less than two hours or more than sixteen hours in any one day.

The order may not exceed a period of 12 months beginning with the day on which it first takes effect. The court must also make an electronic monitoring requirement unless the court considers it inappropriate to do so in the particular circumstances of the case or the court is prevented from doing so eg it is not practicable to secure the co-operation of a person other than the offender: see CJ & IA 2008, Sch 1, para 26.

Before making a relevant order imposing a curfew requirement, the court must obtain and consider information about the place proposed to be specified in the order (including information as to the attitude of persons likely to be affected by the enforced presence there of the offender).

(9) Exclusion requirement

B[49.13] An exclusion requirement is a provision prohibiting the offender from entering a place named in the order for a specified period of not more than three months.

An exclusion requirement:

(a) may provide for the prohibition to operate only during the periods specified in the order; and
(b) may specify different places or areas for different periods or days.

The court must also make an electronic monitoring requirement unless the court considers it inappropriate to do so in the particular circumstances of the case or the court is prevented from doing so eg it is not practicable to secure the co-operation of a person other than the offender: see CJ & IA 2008, Sch 1, para 26.

(10) Residence requirement

B[49.14] **This requirement is only applicable to offenders aged 16 or over at the time of conviction.**

Residence means that, during a period specified in the relevant order, the offender must reside with an individual *or* at a place specified in the order. If the court proposes to specify residence with a named individual, that person's consent must first be obtained.

If the order makes specific provision, a residence requirement does not prohibit the offender from residing, with the prior approval of the responsible officer, at a place other than that specified in the order.

Before making a YRO containing a residence requirement, the court must consider the home surroundings of the offender.

A court may not specify a hostel or other institution as the place where an offender must reside, except on the recommendation of an officer of a local probation board, or a provider of probation services, a local authority social worker or a member of a youth offending team.

(11) Local authority residence requirement

B[49.15] Local authority residence means that, during a period specified in the relevant order, the offender must reside in accommodation provided by or on behalf of a local authority specified in the order.

The court must be satisfied that the behaviour which constituted the offence was due to a significant extent to the circumstances in which the offender was living, and that the imposition of such a requirement will assist in his rehabilitation.

The court must first consult with the local authority and a parent or guardian of the offender (unless it is not practicable to do so) and the local authority that is to receive the offender (if different). The order may stipulate that the offender is not to reside with a person specified in the order.

The order must specify the local authority in whose area the offender resides or is to reside.

Any period specified in the order as a period for which the offender must reside in accommodation provided by or on behalf of a local authority must not exceed six months, and it must not include any period after the offender attains 18 years of age.

A youth court may not include a *local authority residence requirement* in a YRO unless the offender is legally represented or funding by the Legal Services Commission has been withdrawn because of the offender's conduct; or, having been informed of his right to apply for such representation, has refused or failed to apply.

A local authority has power to place an offender with a local authority foster patent where a local authority residence requirement is imposed: CJ & IA 2008, Sch 2, Pt 2, para 18.

(12) Fostering requirement

B[49.16] During a period specified in the relevant order, the offender must reside with a local authority foster parent.

The specified period of fostering must end no later 12 months beginning with the date on which the requirement takes effect but must not include any period after the offender has attained 18 years of age. An 18-month period may be substituted following breach proceedings: CJ & IA 2008, Sch 2, paras 8 and 16.

The requirement must specify the local authority that is to place the offender with a local authority foster parent under s 23(2)(a) of the Children Act 1989. The authority so specified must be the local authority in whose area the offender resides or is to reside.

If at any time during that period the responsible officer notifies the offender that no suitable local authority foster parent is available, and that he proposes or has applied for the revocation or amendment of the YRO, the fostering requirement is, until the determination of that application, to be taken as requiring the offender to reside in accommodation provided by or on behalf of the a local authority.

Such a requirement cannot be made unless the court has been notified by the Secretary of State that arrangements for placing the offender with a local authority foster parent are available in the relevant local authority area.

(13) Mental health treatment requirement

B[49.17] This requires the offender to submit, during periods specified in the order, to treatment by or under the direction of a registered medical practitioner or a chartered psychologist (or both, for different periods) with a view to the improvement of the offender's mental condition.

The treatment required must be one of the following kinds of treatment as may be specified in the relevant order:

(a) treatment as a resident patient in an independent hospital or care home within the meaning of the Care Standards Act 2000 or a hospital within the meaning of the Mental Health Act 1983, but not in hospital premises where high security psychiatric services within the meaning of that Act are provided;
(b) treatment as a non-resident patient at such institution or place as may be specified in the order;
(c) treatment by or under the direction of such registered medical practitioner or chartered psychologist (or both) as may be so specified;

The nature of the treatment may not be specified in the order except as mentioned in (a), (b) or (c) above.

A court may not by virtue of this section include a mental health treatment requirement in an order unless:

(a) the court is satisfied, that the mental condition of the offender:

(i) is such as requires and may be susceptible to treatment, but
(ii) is not such as to warrant the making of a hospital order or guardianship order within the meaning of the Mental Health Act 1983;

(b) the court is also satisfied that arrangements have been or can be made for the treatment intended to be specified in the order (including arrangements for the reception of the offender where he is to be required to submit to treatment as a resident patient); and

(c) the offender has expressed his willingness to comply with such a requirement.

While the offender is under treatment as a resident patient in pursuance of a mental health requirement, his responsible officer shall carry out the supervision of the offender to such extent only as may be necessary for the purpose of the revocation or amendment of the order.

B[49.18] **Mental health treatment at place other than that specified in order** Where the medical practitioner or chartered psychologist, treating the offender in pursuance of a mental health treatment requirement, is of the opinion that part of the treatment can be better or more conveniently given in or at an institution or place which:

(a) is not specified in the relevant order, and
(b) is one in or at which the treatment of the offender will be given by or under the direction of a registered medical practitioner or chartered psychologist,

he may, with the consent of the offender, make arrangements for him to be treated accordingly.

These arrangements as are mentioned may provide for the offender to receive part of his treatment as a resident patient in an institution or place notwithstanding that the institution or place is not one which could have been specified for that purpose in the relevant order.

Where any such arrangements are made for the treatment of an offender the medical practitioner or chartered psychologist by whom the arrangements are made shall give notice in writing to the offender's responsible officer giving details of the place and the treatment provided.

(14) Drug treatment/drug testing requirement

B[49.19] A drug rehabilitation requirement means a requirement that during a period specified in the order the offender must submit to treatment by or under the direction of a specified person having the necessary qualifications or experience with a view to the reduction or elimination of the offender's dependency on or propensity to misuse drugs.

During that period he must provide samples for the purpose of ascertaining whether he has any drug in his body (a drug testing requirement).

A drug testing requirement may not be made unless the court has been notified that arrangements for implementing drug-testing are in force in the local justice area where the offender resides. The offender must also express his willingness to comply with the order.

Where a requirement is imposed the court must specify for each month the minimum number of occasions on which samples are to be provided. The court may also specify at which, and the circumstances in which, the responsible officer or treatment provider may require samples and descriptions of the samples that may be required.

A court may not impose a drug rehabilitation requirement unless:

(a) it is satisfied:
(i) that the offender is dependent on, or has a propensity to misuse, drugs, and
(ii) that his dependency or propensity is such as requires and may be susceptible to treatment;

(b) it is also satisfied that arrangements have been or can be made for the treatment intended to be specified in the order (including arrangements for the reception of the offender where he is to be required to submit to treatment as a resident);
(c) the requirement has been recommended to the court as being suitable for the offender either by an officer of a local probation board (or provider of probation services) or by a member of a youth offending team; and
(d) the offender expresses his willingness to comply with the requirement.

The treatment and testing period is the period specified in the YRO and will be treatment either as a resident in such institution or place as may be specified in the order, or treatment as a non-resident place, as may be so specified.

A YRO imposing a drug rehabilitation requirement must provide that the results of tests carried out on any samples provided by the offender in pursuance of the requirement to a person other than the responsible officer are to be communicated to the responsible officer.

(15) Intoxicating substance treatment requirement

B[49.20] This is a requirement that the offender submits during a specified period or periods to treatment by or under the direction of a specified person having the necessary qualifications or experience with a view to the reduction or elimination of the offender's dependency on or propensity to misuse intoxicating substances.

Intoxicating substances are defined as alcohol or other substance or product (other than a drug) which is, of the fumes of which are, capable of being inhaled or otherwise used for the purpose of causing intoxication.

The court may not impose an alcohol treatment requirement in respect of an offender unless it is satisfied that he is dependent on or has a tendency to misuse intoxicating substances, and his dependency is such as requires and may be susceptible to treatment. Arrangements must be made for the treatment intended to be specified in the order (including arrangements for the reception of the offender where he is to be required to submit to treatment as a resident).

The court must be satisfied that arrangements have been or can be made for the treatment intended and the requirement must have been recommended to the court as suitable for the offender by a member of the youth offending team, an officer of the local probation service or a provider of probation services.

A court may not impose an alcohol treatment requirement unless the offender expresses his willingness to comply with its requirements.

The treatment required by an intoxicating substance treatment requirement for any particular period must be:

(a) treatment as a resident in such institution or place as may be specified in the order; or
(b) treatment as a non-resident in or at such institution or place, and at such intervals, as may be so specified;

but the nature of the treatment shall not be specified in the order except as mentioned in paragraph (a) or (b) above.

(16) Education requirement

B[49.21] The offender must comply during a period or periods specified in the order with approved education arrangements. These may be arrangements made for the offender's education n by his parent or guardian and approved by the local education authority specified in the order. The authority should be the local education authority for the area in which the offender resides.

The court must consult with the local education authority and be satisfied that arrangements exist for the offender to receive sufficient full-time education suitable for his age, ability, aptitude and special education needs (if any).

The court must be satisfied that the requirement is necessary for securing the good conduct of the offender or for preventing the commission of further offences. Any period specified in the YRO cannot include a period once the offender has ceased to be of compulsory school age.

(17) Electronic monitoring requirement

B[49.22] This requirement must normally be added to a curfew or exclusion requirement and may be added to other requirements.

Before making the order arrangements for electronic monitoring must be available in the local justice area proposed to be specified in the order and the order must make provision for making a person responsible for the monitoring of the offender.

The period for monitoring the offender's compliance with other requirements will be specified in the order or determined by the responsible officer in accordance with the relevant requirement. Accordingly, where the responsible officer is to determine when an electronic monitoring is to take effect, he must notify the offender, the monitoring person and any other person whose co-operation is required to ensure that monitoring takes place. The consent of any such person is required and the requirement may not be included in the order without that consent.

Guidance of the Sentencing Council on requirements in YROs

B[49.22A] The following guidance appears in the definitive guideline 'Sentencing Children and Young People Overarching Principles and Offence Specific Guidelines for Sexual Offences and Robbery'.

6.28 When determining the nature and extent of the requirements the court should primarily consider the likelihood of the child or young person re-offending and the risk of the child or young person causing serious harm. A higher risk of re-offending does not in itself justify a greater restriction on liberty than is warranted by the seriousness of the offence; any requirements should still be commensurate with the seriousness of the offence and regard must still be had for the welfare of the child or young person.

6.29 The YOT will assess this as part of their report and recommend an intervention level to the court for consideration. It is possible for the court to ask the YOT to consider a particular requirement.

	Child or young person profile	Requirements of order[33]
Standard	Low likelihood of re-offending and a low risk of serious harm	Primarily seek to repair harm caused through, for example: • reparation; • unpaid work; • supervision; and/or • attendance centre.
Enhanced	Medium likelihood of re-offending or a medium risk of serious harm	Seek to repair harm caused and to enable help or change through, for example: • supervision; • reparation; • requirement to address behaviour e.g. drug treatment, offending behaviour programme, education programme; and/or • a combination of the above.

Intensive	High likelihood of re-offending or a very high risk of serious harm	Seek to ensure the control of and enable help or change for the child or young person through, for example: • supervision; • reparation; • requirement to address behaviour; • requirement to monitor or restrict movement, e.g. prohibited activity, curfew, exclusion or electronic monitoring; and/or • a combination of the above.
[33] The examples provided here are not exclusive; the YOT will make recommendations based upon their assessment of the young offender which may vary from some of the examples given.		

6.30 If a child or young person is assessed as presenting a high risk of re-offending or of causing serious harm but the offence that was committed is of relatively low seriousness then the appropriate requirements are likely to be primarily rehabilitative or for the protection of the public.

6.31 Likewise if a child or young person is assessed as presenting a low risk of re-offending or of causing serious harm but the offence was of relatively high seriousness then the appropriate requirements are likely to be primarily punitive.

Breach of a requirement or order (Sch 2, CJIA 2008)

B[49.23] If at any time while a relevant order is in force in respect of an offender it appears on information to a justice of the peace acting for the local justice area concerned that the offender has failed to comply with any of the requirements, the justice may:

(a) issue a summons requiring the offender to appear at the place and time specified in it; or
(b) if the information is in writing and on oath, issue a warrant for his arrest.

If the offender is aged 18 or over breach proceedings will normally commence in an adult magistrates' court. Offenders aged under 18 will appear before a youth court (see *R v Uxbridge Youth Court, ex p Howard* (1998) 162 JP 327).

If it is proved that the offender has failed without reasonable excuse to comply with any of the requirements, the court may deal with the offender in respect of the failure in one of the following ways (the legislation prescribes **must** deal with him in one of the following ways if the relevant order is in force):

(a) a fine not exceeding £2,500;
(b) by amending the YRO requirements so as to add to or substitute any requirement imposed by the order. However, this may not include an extended activity requirement or fostering requirement if the original order did not already contain such a requirement. Where the original requirement included a fostering and this is substituted by a new fostering requirement the order may run for 18 months (as opposed to the original 12) beginning with the date on which the original requirement first took effect;
(c) except where the order was made by the Crown Court without a direction (see infra), revoke the order and re-sentence the offender in any way in which the court could have dealt with the offender for that offence (had the offender been before that court to be dealt with for it).

The following guidance appears in the definitive guideline 'Sentencing Children and Young People Overarching Principles and Offence Specific Guidelines for Sexual Offences and Robbery'. In relation to breaches and the commission of further offences during the period of an order at para 6.12: 'If a child or young person is found guilty of breaching an order, the court will have various options available depending on the nature of the order ... [t]he primary aim of the court should be to encourage compliance and seek to support the rehabilitation of the child or young person'.

Where the court amends the order to impose a new requirement, any such requirement must be capable of being complied with before the end date. However, the court may substitute a later date as the end date of up to six months from the original end date provided this power has not been exercised previously.

Where the original order did not contain an unpaid work requirement and the court imposes such a requirement, the minimum number of hours that may be imposed is reduced from 40 to 20.

When dealing with the original offence(s) under (c) above, the court shall take into account the extent to which the offender has complied with the requirements of the relevant order. A person so sentenced may appeal to the Crown Court against that sentence.

In the case of an offender who has wilfully and persistently failed to comply with the requirement(s) of a YRO, and the court is dealing with him under (c) above, the court may impose an intensive supervision and surveillance requirement without regard to the fact that the court is not dealing with the offender for an offence that is punishable with imprisonment nor need it form the opinion that the offence is so serious that it would (but for the statutory restrictions) merit a custodial sentence. Where the court does revoke and re-sentence on breach for any offence not punishable with imprisonment, the court is deemed to have power to deal with the offender for the offence by imposing a detention and training order for a term not exceeding four months: CJIA 2008, Sch 2, paras 12–14.

Where the Crown Court makes a YRO it may include in the order a direction that further proceedings relating to the order be in a youth court or other magistrates' court: CJ & IA 2008, Sch 1, para 36. This gives the youth court or magistrates' court all the powers on breach set out above. However, the court may instead commit the offender in custody or on bail to the Crown Court to be dealt with: CJ & IA 2008, Sch 2, para 7.

Commission of further offence

B[49.24] An offender who is convicted and sentenced of a further offence while subject to a YRO, a youth court may revoke that order and re-sentence the offender for the original offence. That power extends to a YRO made in the Crown Court where the Crown Court has directed that breaches may be dealt with in a youth court. If the court revokes the order and re-sentences, it must take into account the extent to which the offender has complied with the order.

The court must not revoke and re-sentence unless it is in the interests of justice to do so, having regard to the circumstances that have arisen since the YRO was made.

Where a youth court is authorised to deal with a Crown Court order, it may nonetheless commit the offender back to the Crown Court in custody or on bail. **Section 6 of the Powers of Criminal Courts Act 2000 will require amendment to enable a youth court to be able to commit for sentence any summary offence committed during the currency of a YRO requirement.

Application to revoke (Sch 2, Pt 5)

B[49.25] Where a relevant order made by a youth court or adult magistrates' court is in force and, and on the application of the responsible officer, it appears to the court that, having regard to circumstances that have arisen since the order was made, it would be in the interests of justice for the order to be revoked, or for the offence to be dealt with in some other way for the original offence, the court may:

(a) revoke the order; or
(b) revoke the order, and deal with the offender for the offence in respect of which the order was made, in any way in which he could have been dealt with for the original offence.

An application to revoke may be based on the offender making good progress or responding satisfactorily to a supervision requirement as the case may be.

If the offender is over 18 the application will be heard in the adult magistrates' court; if under 18, in a youth court.

If an application to revoke is refused (dismissed), no further application may be brought within three months except with the consent of the appropriate court: CJIA 2008, Sch 2, Part 3, para 11(7).

In dealing with an offender for the original offence, the court shall take into account the extent to which the offender has complied with the requirements of a YRO. A person so dealt with may appeal to the Crown Court against that sentence.

Unless the application is made by the offender, the court shall summons the offender to appear before the court, and if he does not appear, may issue a warrant for his arrest.

Amendment

B[49.26] Where an offender has or proposes to change residence from one local justice area to another, at any time while the order is in force, a youth or an adult magistrates' court for the local justice area named in the order, may transfer the relevant order.

On the application of an eligible person, the same court may amend an order by cancelling or inserting any of the requirements in the order (either in addition to or in substitution for any of its requirements) that the court could include if it were then making the order (although see treatment requirements below).

As with breach or revocation applications, the procedural requirements for the issue of summonses or warrant are required to be followed unless the application is to cancel a requirement of an order, reducing the period of an order, reducing the period of any one requirement, or transferring the order to a new local justice area. Natural justice dictates that notice of the amendment should be given to the offender.

In either case where the original order contains a specific area requirement (for example, a curfew requirement), or a programme requirement, the court must not make an amendment that would prevent the offender from complying with that requirement. In such circumstances, the court must substitute a similar requirement within the new area.

Where the court amends by including a new requirement, the new requirement must be capable of being complied with before the end of the order. In the case of a fostering requirement that substitutes a new fostering requirement it may run for a period of 18 months beginning with the date on which the original requirement first had effect.

An order containing an unpaid work requirement may, on the application of the offender or the responsible officer, be amended by extending the period of 12 months during which the order must be complied with. Such an order should only be extended if it is in the interests of justice to do so having regard to circumstances that have arisen since the order was made.

Treatment requirements. The court may not impose a treatment requirement such as mental health treatment, drug treatment or drug testing *by way of amendment* unless the offender has expressed his willingness to comply with the requirement.

B[50]
The victim surcharge

B[50.1] The Criminal Justice Act 2003 (Surcharge) Order 2012, SI 2012/1696, as amended, has effect. This provides for the adding of a surcharge to sentences including non-financial penalties.

While not officially entitled the victims' surcharge (hence our use of parenthesis) this is said to be its purpose and it is entitled the 'Victim Surcharge' in the Magistrates' Court Sentencing Guidelines.

B[50.2] The levels of the surcharge. In summary, the position is this: for a single offence committed on or after 28 June 2019, or for multiple offences all of which were committed on or after 8 April 2016, the surcharge levels are (the former figures, which continue to apply to earlier offences, are in parenthesis):

(a) for fines the amount of the surcharge, rounded up or down to the nearest pound, rises to 10% of the value of the fine subject to a minimum of £32 (£30) and a maximum of £181 (£170)

(b) for other disposals, the surcharge ranges from £21 (£20) (conditional discharge), to £90 (£85) (community order) and to £122 (£115) (custodial sentences of up to six months – higher figures apply to longer terms). Note that the surcharge applies to custodial sentences imposed in the magistrates' court only if the offence or all of the offences with which the court is dealing was committed after 31 August 2014: see the Criminal Justice Act 2003 (Surcharge) (Amendment) Order 2014, SI 2014/2120.

The Criminal Justice Act 2003 (Surcharge) Order 2012 does not include its own definition of 'fine'. In practice, courts follow the definition of 'fine' in paragraph 2 of Part 1 of Schedule 5 to the Courts Act 2003 with the result that excise penalties imposed under the Vehicle Excise and Registration Act 1994, though they refer to the standard scale, are not 'fines' for surcharge purposes.

Where the court imposes two or more different disposals for which the levels of surcharge vary, the amount is the highest of the relevant surcharges.

Where the offence, or any of the offences, was committed before 1 October 2012, the surcharge is payable only if the sentence is or includes a fine, and the amount is then fixed at £15: see art 7 of the Criminal Justice Act 2003 (Surcharge) Order 2012, which disapplies the revocation of the Criminal Justice Act 2003 (Surcharge) (No 2) Order in such a case.

Where a defendant is sentenced for breach of an order made for an offence committed prior to the commencement (on 1 October 2012) of the Criminal Justice Act 2003 (Surcharge) Order 2012, the surcharge prescribed by that Order does not apply even though the breach occurred after its commencement. The court is still 'dealing' with the original offence: *R v Bailey* [2013] EWCA Crim 1551, [2013] 1 Cr App Rep (S) 376. Where a defendant who was sentenced to a community order and a surcharge of £60 was re-sentenced to custody for breach of the community order, he was not liable to pay a second surcharge: *R v George (Martin)* [2015] EWCA Crim 1096, [2015] 2 Cr App R (S) 58, [2015] Crim LR 916.

For offenders aged under 18 at the time of the offence or any other the offences, the levels of surcharge are:

(a) £16 (£15) (conditional discharge);
(b) £32 (£30) (custody, including suspended sentences); and

(c) £21 (£20) (for any intermediate disposal including a referral order).

As with adults, the figures in parenthesis apply if the offence, or any of the offences, was committed before 8 April, 2016.

For offences committed by persons who are not individuals, the levels of surcharge for conditional discharges and fines are as for adult offenders.

B[50.3] **Compensation has priority.** In any case where the court considers it would be appropriate to make a compensation order, but the offender has insufficient means to pay both the surcharge and appropriate compensation, the court must reduce the amount of the surcharge (if necessary to nil): Criminal Justice Act 2003, s 161A.

B[50.4] **Enforcement.** A surcharge is enforced as a fine imposed on summary conviction: see the Administration of Justice Act 1970, Sch 9, para 13. Note, however, that s 82(1)(c) of the Magistrates' Courts Act 1980 (power to impose imprisonment in default of payment of any sum adjudged to be paid on conviction where the court imposes immediate imprisonment or detention for that or another offence, or the offender is already a serving prisoner) does not apply to the surcharge in consequence of the insertion of s 82(1A) of the Magistrates' Courts Act 1980 by s 179 of the Anti-social, Crime and Policing Act 2014. Section 135 of the Magistrates' Courts Act 1980 (see **B[24]**, ante) was not, however, amended.

In *Frimpong v Crown Prosecution Service (Secretary of State for Justice intervening)* [2015] EWCA Crim 1933, [2016] 1 Cr App R (S) 59 a Circuit Judge imposed a prison sentence of six months for an offence and then ordered payment of the criminal courts charge of £900 (varying her earlier ruling that it be 'deemed served' by the sentence of imprisonment). One of the issues in the appeal was whether or not the judge was entitled to exercise the enforcement powers of a District Judge (Magistrates' Courts) and to impose one day's detention in default of payment under s 135 of the Magistrates' Courts Act 1980. Reliance was placed on s 66 of the Courts Act 2003 (under which a Circuit judge can exercise the powers of a District Judge (Magistrates' Courts)). It was held that as a matter of construction s 66 did not permit the Circuit judge to specify herself as a magistrates' court under s 41(1)(b) of the Administration of Justice Act 1970 for the purpose of enforcement. As to s 135 of the Magistrates' Courts Act 1980, '36 It is not arguable that the court had "a power to commit to prison" for failing to pay the charge since, as we have already explained, the appellant had been given time to pay. Even if it might be argued that the power to impose a sentence of imprisonment was a separate "power to commit to prison" the power under s 135 is an alternative to a prison sentence. Where, as here, a sentence of imprisonment is imposed s 135 is of no application' (per Fulford LJ).

Since the surcharge is on the same legislative footing in this respect as the criminal courts charge the same reasoning must apply. Note the case was concerned with enforcement at the time of conviction, not subsequently. In the latter case we see no reason why s 135 should not be available as an alternative to imprisonment in default.

Section 179 of the Anti-social Behaviour, Crime and Policing Act 2014 also amended s 85 of the Magistrates' Courts Act 1980 and s 165 of the Criminal Justice Act 2003, which are concerned with the remission of fines. The effect is to remit the surcharge to the level it would have been if the fine had not included the remitted amount. Note also that one day's detention can be imposed as a sentence in its own right where the offence is punishable with imprisonment. Where this is the case (and no other sentence is imposed for any other offence) there is no surcharge at all.

Note the restrictions on the ability of the court to remit the criminal courts charge – Prosecution of Offences Act 1985, s 21E – apply only to that charge. Accordingly, remission of the surcharge is available in the same way as it applies to other sums adjudged to be paid under a conviction: see Magistrates' Courts Act 1980, ss 85 and 150(1).

Section C

Road traffic offences

C[1]

Index and penalties for road traffic offences

Maximum fines and the standard scale

C[1.1]

MCA 1980, s 32(9); Interpretation Act 1978, s 32, Sch 1	The statutory maximum fine on summary conviction of an offence triable either way, being the prescribed sum under the Magistrates' Court Act 1980,	£5,000*
CJA 1982, s 37(2)	The standard scale giving maximum fines on an adult on conviction for a summary offence:	
	level 1	£200
	level 2	£500
	level 3	£1,000
	level 4	£2,500
	level 5	£5,000*

* Section 85 of the Legal Aid, Sentencing and Punishment of Offenders Act 2012 provides that where a relevant offence would on commencement day be punishable on summary conviction by a fine or maximum fine of £5,000, however expressed, and the offence was committed on or after that date, the court may impose a fine of any amount, The commencement date is 12 March 2015: see the Legal Aid, Sentencing and Punishment of Offenders Act 2012 (Commencement No 11) Order 2015, SI 2015/504. Note however that this is disapplied to certain offences by the Legal Aid, Sentencing and Punishment of Offenders Act 2012 (Fines on Summary Conviction) Regulations 2015, SI 2015/664.

C[1.2] The following table contains an alphabetical list of the road traffic offences dealt with in this book, together with some others included to provide the maximum penalty. Readers will wish to note the penalties recommended in the Magistrates' Association National Sentencing Guidelines.

C[1.3] Speed/distance chart. See C[2]

C[1.4] Stopping distances. See C[3]

C[1.5] Endorsement codes. See C[6]

C[1.6]

Offences and endorsement code	*Standard scale*	*Licence and penalty points*	*para*
Abandoning a motor vehicle	level 4+3 months		
Accident, failing to give particulars AC 20	level 5+6 months	E 5–10	C[32]
Report AC 20	level 5+6 months	E 5–10	C[32]
stop after AC 10	level 5+6 months	E 5–10	C[31]
Bicycle			
defective brakes riding	level 3		
Careless	level 3		
Dangerous	level 4		
Inconsiderate	level 3		
two persons on	level 1		
when unfit through drink	level 3		
Brakes, defective			
on private vehicle CU 10 §	level 4	E*3	C[9]
on goods vehicle CU 10 §	level 5	E*3	C[9]
on bicycle	level 3		
Breath test, refusing DR 70	level 3	E 3–11	C[24]
Car door, opening to cause			
injury or danger §	level 3		C[37]
Car dumping	level 4 + 3 months	104	A[60]
Careless driving CD 10	level 5	E 3–9	C[25]
Common land, driving on §	level 3		
Dangerous condition			
using private vehicle in CU 20 §	level 4	E*3 (D) – see C[10]	C[10]
using goods vehicle in CU 20 §	level 5	E*3 (D) – see C[10]	C[10]
Dangerous load			
on private vehicle CU 50 §	level 4	E*3	
on goods vehicle CU 50 §	level 5	E*3	
Dangerous position, leaving			
motor vehicle in MS 10 §	level 3	E 3	
Date of birth, failing to give	level 3		
Defective tyre			
private vehicle CU 30 §	level 4	E*3	C[53]
goods vehicle CU 30 §	level 5	E*3	C[53]
Driver, failing to give particulars of date of birth	level 3		
Driving			
Careless CD 10	level 5	E 3–9	C[25]

Offences and endorsement code	*Standard scale*	*Licence and penalty points*	*para*
causing death by careless or inconsiderate driving †(from 18/8/08)	level 5 + 12 months	E 3–11	C[16A]
dangerous†DD 40	level 5 + 6 months	D 3–11	C[16]
causing death by driving while disqualified BA 40	level 5 + 6 months	D 3–11	C[16B]
causing death by driving: unlicensed or uninsured† (from 18/8/08)	level 5 + 12 months	D 3–11	C[16B]
causing serious injury by disqualified driving BA 60		D 3–11	C[16C]
causing serious injury by dangerous driving DD 10	level 5 + 12 months	D 3–11	C[16C]
disqualified BA 10	level 5 + 12 months	E 6	C[19]
drink, under influence of DR 20	level 5 + 6 months	D 3–11	C[20]
Driving without due care and attention	level 3		
Without			
due care and attention CD 10	level 4 5 for offences on or after 24/9/07	E 3–9	C[25]
licence (excise)	£1,000 or 5 times duty		C[47]
Driving without reasonable consideration	level 5 for offences on or after 24/9/07	E 3–9	C[46]
Drug: driving when unfit DR80	level 5 + 6 months	D 3-11	C[20]
Drug: in charge when unfit DR 90	level 4 + 3 months	E 10	C[21]
Drug: driving above specified limit DG10	level 5 + 6 months	D 3-11	C[22A]
Drug: in charge above specified limit DG40	level 5 + 3 months	E 10	C[22A]
Drunk in charge DR 50	level 4 + 3 months	E 10	C[21]
Excess alcohol			
driving DR 10	level 5 + 6 months	D 3–11	C[20]
in charge DR 40	level 5 + 3 months	E 10	C[21]
Excise licence			
making false statement to obtain	level 5		
using/keeping vehicle without	level 3 or 5 times duty		C[47]
Eyesight, driving with defective MS 70	level 3	E 3	
Failing to comply with traffic sign §	level 3	+ 3	C[52]
(constable or traffic warden on traffic duty) TS 40 §	level 3	E 3	
Fail to provide specimen of			

Offences and endorsement code	*Standard scale*	*Licence and penalty points*	*para*
breath DR 70	level 3	E 4	C[24]
blood/urine/breath			
driving or attempting DR 30	level 5 + 6 months	D 3–11	C[24]
in charge DR 60	level 4 + 3 months	E 10	C[24]
Failing to provide information as to identity of driver	level 3	E 6	C[32A]
False declaration to obtain excise licence †	level 5		
False statement to obtain			
driving licence	level 4		
Insurance	level 4		
Footpath, driving on			
(Highways Act 1835, s 72)	level 2		
Forging, etc			
insurance certificate	level 5		
test certificate †	level 5		
Front seat, carrying child in §	level 3		C[48]
Getting on to vehicle to	level 1		
be carried			
Heavy goods vehicle			
driving without LGV licence	level 3		
overloading §	level 5		C[38]
parking on verge, etc §	level 3		
using without plating certificate	level 3		
using without test certificate	level 4		
Holding on to vehicle to be towed or carried	level 1		
Hours, driving for excessive number	level 4		
Insecure load			
private vehicle CU 50 §	level 4	E*3	
goods vehicle CU 50 §	level 5	E*3	
Insurance			
using without, causing or			
permitting IN 10 §	level 5	E 6–8	C[33]
failing to produce certificate	level 3		C[17]
false statement to obtain	level 4		
Jay walking	level 3		
Licence			
driving otherwise than in accordance with LC 10 §	level 3	E 3–6	C[18]
excise, keeping/using vehicle without	level 3 or 5 times duty		C[47]
failing to produce for endorsement	level 3		

Offences and endorsement code	*Standard scale*	*Licence and penalty points*	*para*
failing to produce to constable	level 3		C[17]
LGV, driving otherwise than in accordance with	10 units		C[19]
obtaining while disqualified	level 3		
Lights, driving or parking			
without §	level 4 (goods vehicle etc) level 3 (other)		C[34]
(Breach of requirements as to control of vehicle, Mobile Telephone etc)	level 4 if committed in respect of a good vehicle or a vehicle adapted to carry more than 8 persons, otherwise level 3	For a mobile telephone offence committed on or after 1/3/17 and prosecuted under RTA 1988, s 41D(b) E 6. Otherwise, E 3.	
Motor cyclists not wearing helmet §	level 2		C[35]
Neglecting policeman's directions			
driver TS 40 §	level 3	E 3	
Pedestrian	level 3		
Obstruction, causing			
unnecessary §	level 4 (goods vehicle etc) level 3 (other)		C[36]
Opening door to cause danger or injury §	level 4 (goods vehicle) level 3 (other)		C[37]
One way street, driving in wrong direction §	level 3	E 3	C[52]
Overloading §	level 5		C[38]
Owner failing to identify driver	level 3	E 6	
Parking			
heavy vehicle on footpath,	level 3		
on offside at night §	level 4 (goods vehicle etc)		
on yellow lines §	level 3		
breach of regulations for			
on street parking places §	level 2		

Offences and endorsement code	*Standard scale*	*Licence and penalty points*	*para*
(abuse of parking for the disabled) §	level 3		
off street parking places	level 2		
(abuse of parking for the disabled)	level 3		
failure to pay initial or excess charge	level 2 + amount unpaid		
interfering with meter with intent to defraud	level 3		
Pedal cycle, *see* Bicycle			
Pedestrian			
failing to comply with direction of constable on traffic duty	level 3		
Pedestrian crossing			
not giving precedence PC 20 §	level 3	E 3	C[39]
overtaking within limits PC 20 §	level 3	E 3	C[39.10]
Stopping within limits PC 30 §	level 3	E 3	C[40]
Provisional licence holder			
Reasonable consideration			
driving without CD 20	level 5	E 3–9	C[46]
Record of hours, failing to keep	level 4		
Riding bicycle, *see* Bicycle			
Seat belt, failure to wear (front §)	level 2		C[48]
(rear §)	level 2 (child in rear seat)		
School crossing, fail to stop			
at TS 60	level 3	E 3	
Silencer, defective §	level 4 (goods vehicle etc) level 3 (other)		
Speeding SP 30 §	level 3	E 3–6(FP3) [2–6 under the Road Safety Act 2006]	C[49]
motorway SP 50 §	level 4	E 3–6(FP3) [2–6 under the Road Safety Act 2006]	C[49]

Offences and endorsement code	*Standard scale*	*Licence and penalty points*	*para*
Speed assessment equipment detection devices	level 4 if committed on a special road, otherwise level 3	E 3–6 (FP3) from a date to be appointed under the Road Safety Act 2006	C[38A]
Stealing (or attempt) vehicle †			
NE 99	level 5 + 6 months	D (discretionary)	A[57], A[65]
Steering, defective			
private vehicle CU 40 §	level 4	E*3	C[50]
goods vehicle CU 40 §	level 5	E*3	
Taking motor vehicle without consent			
NE 99	level 5	D (discretionary)	A[57], A[65]
(Theft Act 1968, s 12) Aggravated Vehicle Taking UT 50	6 months Level 5	D	A[3]
(Theft Act 1968, s 12A)	6 months		
Tampering with motor vehicle	level 3 + 3 months		A[63]
Test certificate §			
using etc vehicle without	level 3		C[51]
using goods vehicle without	level 4		C[51]
failing to produce	level 3		C[17]
Traffic sign, non compliance with §	level 3	E 3	C[52]
Tyre, defective			
private vehicle CU 30 §	level 4	E*3	C[53]
goods vehicle CU 30 §	level 5	E*3	C[53]
Waiting on yellow lines §	level 3		

D means that the offence attracts an obligatory disqualification.

E means that the offence attracts an obligatory endorsement; in all such cases disqualification is discretionary.

* The defendant in cases thus marked is not liable to an endorsement if he satisfies the court that he did not know of the defect and had no reasonable cause to suspect that it was present.

\+ Endorsable only if the sign is a traffic light (TS 10), double white lines (TS 20), Stop (TS 30), no entry sign or failure to comply with a green arrow traffic sign, abnormal load failing to observe procedure at railway crossing (TS 50), or vehicle contravening height restriction (TS 50).

† Triable either way.

§ The prosecution may offer a fixed penalty instead of prosecuting in the normal way. See C[8].

C[2]

Speed and distance chart

C[2.1] An approximate guide to the distance covered by a vehicle moving at a constant speed is that half the number of miles per hour is roughly the number of yards per second, eg 30 mph = 15 yds per second. The following table is more accurate than that and the distances are expressed in feet. But it must be borne in mind that the distance given will be covered only by a vehicle travelling at the speed given for the whole of the distance, ie at a constant speed. The table cannot therefore be used in the case of a vehicle slowing down or accelerating.

Miles per hour	*Feet per second*
20	29
30	44
40	59
50	73
60	88
70	103
80	117
90	132
100	146

C[3]

Braking distances

(Taken, with permission, from the Highway Code)

C[3.1] The following braking table appears in the Highway Code. It must be taken as a guide only since no information is given with it as to whether a vehicle with disc or servo assisted brakes, or any particular tyres could improve upon these figures. It is submitted that the court can take judicial notice of the table and may form part of the cross-examination of a witness including the defendant. Moreover, the table, like any other part of the Highway Code, is embraced by the Road Traffic Act 1988, s 38(7) which states:

> A failure on the part of a person to observe a provision of the Highway Code shall not of itself render that person liable to criminal proceedings of any kind, but any such failure may in any proceedings (whether civil or criminal and including proceedings under the Traffic Acts . . .) be relied upon by any party to the proceedings as tending to establish or negative any liability which is in question in those proceedings.

C[4]

Shortest stopping distances – in feet

[4.1]

On a dry road, a good car with good brakes and tyres and an alert driver will stop in the distances shown. Remember these are shortest stopping distances. Stopping distances increase greatly with wet and slippery roads, poor brakes and tyres and tired drivers.

Mph	*Thinking distance*		*Braking distance*		*Overall stopping distance*	
	m	ft	m	ft	m	ft
20	6	20	6	20	12	40
30	9	30	14	45	23	75
40	12	40	24	80	36	120
50	15	50	38	125	53	175
60	18	60	55	180	73	240
70	21	70	75	245	96	315

C[5]
Endorsement and disqualification

C[5.1] The Traffic legislation imposes on the courts an obligation to endorse the licence of any person convicted of certain offences. In the case of a convicted person who does not hold a driving licence this acts as an order to endorse any licence which he may obtain during the period when the endorsement is effective. An endorsement means that particulars of the offence and sentence will be recorded in code (as to which see C[6]) on the defendant's licence, unless it is a foreign licence. In the case of a foreign licence, the order for endorsement should be made (subject to there being special reasons for not making it, see below) and the clerk will notify the DVLA. The court must order endorsement unless it decides after hearing sworn evidence (which may be no more than the evidence given during the trial of the offence) that there are special reasons for not doing so.

C[5.2] **Special reasons.** This has become a term of art; it has a significance which is determined by law rather than by the ordinary meaning of the words. In order to avoid endorsement or compulsory disqualification the defendant must give to the court at least one specific reason why he should not be penalised by endorsement (or disqualification in cases where that is mandatory) and that reason must meet all of the following criteria:

(a) it must be a mitigating or extenuating circumstance;
(b) it must not amount to a legal defence to the charge;
(c) it must be directly connected with the circumstances in which the offence was committed, and not relate solely to the circumstances of the offender;
(d) it should be a factor which the court ought properly to take into consideration when deciding the sentence (*R v Wickins* (1958) 42 Cr App Rep 236, 122 JP 518, CCA).

C[5.3] Case law has provided very many examples of circumstances under (c) above which may, and other circumstances which may not, be accepted as special reasons and some circumstances (eg the distance driven by the defendant) may be accepted or rejected according to the offence with which he is charged. For this reason examples are not set out here since they may confuse rather than clarify the position. Magistrates are recommended always to consult the legal adviser before reaching any final decision on this question.

C[5.4] **Disqualification.** Disqualification is mandatory for certain offences. In every case where the court can order an endorsement it has the discretion also to disqualify. Thus it can be seen how important it may be for a defendant to persuade the court that there are special reasons for not endorsing, because if he is successful and the court does not order endorsement, it may not disqualify. In cases where disqualification is mandatory, eg dangerous driving and drinking and driving offences, the defendant may submit special reasons for not disqualifying while conceding the endorsement.

C[5.5] For offences of theft of vehicles, going equipped to steal vehicles and taking vehicles without consent, the court may disqualify even though there is no power to impose penalty points. Disqualification may also be imposed for offences of assault involving a motor vehicle and, indeed, where following a motoring incident one driver follows another and assaults him the power to disqualify will arise (*R v Rajesh Patel* (1994) 16 Cr App Rep (S) 756, [1995] Crim LR 440, CA). A discretionary disqualification may not be imposed where the defendant is also liable to be disqualified under the penalty points provisions (see below).

There is a discretionary power to disqualify for any offence under PCC(S) Act 2000, s 146. See C[5.45].

Length of disqualification

C[5.6] Where an offence carries obligatory disqualification, the minimum period the court must impose is 12 months: RTOA 1988, s 34(1). This is subject to RTOA 1988, s 34(3) & (4) (see below).

Where the offence carries discretionary disqualification, and the offender is not liable to be disqualified under the penalty points system, the court may disqualify for a shorter period or not at all: RTOA 1988, s 34(2).

The RTOA 1988, S 34(3) & (4) prescribe longer, minimum periods of obligatory disqualification in the following cases:

(3) Where a person convicted of an offence under any of the following provisions of the Road Traffic Act 1988, that is—

- (aa) section 3A (causing death by careless driving when under the influence of drink or drugs),
- (a) section 4(1) (driving or attempting to drive while unfit),
- (b) section 5(1)(a) (driving or attempting to drive with excess alcohol),
- (ba) section 5A(1)(a) and (2) (driving or attempting to drive with concentration of specified controlled drug above specified limit),
- (c) section 7(6) (failing to provide a specimen) where that is an offence involving obligatory disqualification,
- (d) section 7A(6) (failing to allow a specimen to be subjected to laboratory test) where that is an offence involving obligatory disqualification,

has within the ten years immediately preceding the commission of the offence been convicted of any such offence, subsection (1) above shall apply in relation to him as if the reference to twelve months were a reference to three years.

(4) Subject to subsection (3) above, subsection (1) above shall apply as if the reference to twelve months were a reference to two years—

(a) in relation to a person convicted of—

- (i) manslaughter, or in Scotland culpable homicide, or
- (ii) an offence under section 1 of the Road Traffic Act 1988 (causing death by dangerous driving), or
- (iia) an offence under section 1A of that Act (causing serious injury by dangerous driving), or]
- (iib) an offence under section 3ZC of that Act (causing death by driving: disqualified drivers), or
- (iic) an offence under section 3ZD of that Act (causing serious injury by driving: disqualified drivers), or
- (iii) an offence under section 3A of that Act (causing death by careless driving while under the influence of drink or drugs), and

(b) in relation to a person on whom more than one disqualification for a fixed period of 56 days or more has been imposed within the three years immediately preceding the commission of the offence.'

For the purposes of (4)(b), interim disqualifications and bans imposed under: PCC(S)A 2000, s 26 or s 147; or for theft of a motor vehicle; or for an offence under s 12 or 25 of the Theft Act 1968; or for an offence under s 178 of the RTA 1988; or for an offence of attempting to commit any of these offences, shall be disregarded: RTOA 1988, s 34(4A).

Disqualification combined with custodial sentences

C[5.7] Section 137 of and Sch 2 to the Coroners and Justice Act 2009, as amended by s 30 of the Criminal Justice and Courts Act 2015, introduced into the RTOA 1988, ss 35A and 35B. The 2015 Act also introduced mirror provisions, namely ss 147(A) and 147(B), into the PCC(S)A 2000.

The intention in all cases is that periods of disqualification should be served by offenders while they are at liberty, but different mechanisms are employed and the inter-relationship of ss 35A and 35B of the RTOA is by no means straightforward.

All aspects of the legislation were considered by the Court of Appeal in *R v Needham and others* [2016] EWCA Crim 455. We summarise the Court of Appeal's conclusions.

(1) *Commencement.*This is 15 April 2015 (SI 2015/819). If an offence straddles this date the new provisions will not apply. This will be the case where a 'relevant event', being 'any act or other event (including any consequence of an act) proof of which is required for conviction of the offence' (Coroners and Justice Act 2009, Sch 22, para 29) occurs before the commencement. In the case of driving whilst disqualified, this does not require the order of disqualification to post date commencement. All elements of the offence are committed on the occasion that the offender drives while disqualified.

(2) *Section 35A person convicted of an offence for which custody and disqualification, under s 34 or s 35 of the RTOA, are imposed.* The extension period is the part of the sentence which must be served in custody (generally half but in some cases longer), disregarding the possibility of early release.

(3) *Additional custodial sentences.* Section 35A refers only to motoring offences for which custody is imposed and not to any other custodial sentences imposed at the same time. In relation to the other offences, section 35B will come into play.

(4) *Section 35B.* Effect of custodial sentence in other cases Section 35B applies where the court proposes to disqualify under s 34 or s 35 of the RTOA 1988 and (a) the court proposes to impose a custodial sentence for another offence, or (b) the offender is still serving a custodial sentence imposed for earlier offence. In this case the court 'must have regard . . . if and to the extent that it is appropriate to do so' to the diminished effect as a distinct punishment on a person who is also detained under a custodial sentence.

(5) *Interrelationship between ss 35A and s 35B.* The latter complements the former. Thus, in case of mixed motoring and non-motoring custodial sentences, s 35A will apply to the former and not the global term. Section 35B will apply to the latter and this will be added to the s 35A period. The following example is given in the judgment (In para 28). D is convicted of dangerous driving and wounding. The court proposes to disqualify D for 12 months for the former offence. As the substantive sentence, the court imposes to impose terms of 12 months the dangerous driving offence and 36 months consecutive for the wounding offence. The s 35A extension period will be six months. The s 35B uplift to the s 34 disqualification will be 18 months, making the three years. This means D will serve 12 months' disqualification following his release (after 24 months) from prison.

(6) *The exercise of discretion under s 35B.* The legislation uses the terms 'must have regard' and 'if and to the extent it is appropriate', but in 'the ordinary run of cases' there should be an adjustment to the length of disqualification to ensure that it is fully served outside custody'.

(7) *Minimum periods of obligatory disqualification.* The extension period under s 35A does not form part of any minimum period prescribed for s 34 or 35 of the RTOA 1988.

(8) *Time spent on remand in custody.* This does not fall to be deducted but in a s 35A case it might be taken into account in relation to the length of a discretionary period of disqualification.*

(9) *Time on remand subject to an electronically monitored curfew.* Since the offender remains able to drive while subject to such a curfew there is no justification for making any reduction to a discretionary disqualification on this account.

(10) *Reduced disqualification for attendance on course.* As s 34A of the RTOA 1988 currently stands, any reduction in the disqualification period comes of the entire disqualification, including the extension period under s 35A. If the amendments made by the 2009 Act are fully implemented, this will change and the reduction will apply only to the discretionary part of the disqualification.

(11) *Interim disqualification for offenders in custody.* It will be generally be inappropriate to impose this in view of the policy of the legislation.

(12) *Sentencing guidelines* In relation to the Sentencing Council's guidelines for causing death by dangerous driving on the length of disqualification where imprisonment is imposed (para [31]), courts should now focus on the legislation to avoid the risk of 'double counting'.

* The imposition of a discretionary disqualification period which does not take account of time spent in custody on remand would lead to a defendant so remanded being disqualified for longer than a defendant remanded on bail: see *R v Oliver* [2016] EWCA Crim 2017.

C[5.8] Disqualification starts on the day on which the order is made and that day counts as one full day of the disqualification.

C[5.9] **Disqualification for life.** Such a disqualification will be rare. Only where there are exceptional circumstances should a disqualification for life be imposed (*R v Rivano* (1993) 14 Cr App Rep (S) 578, 158 JP 288, CA), for example, where there is psychiatric evidence that the driver would indefinitely be a danger to the public if allowed to drive (*R v King* [1993] RTR 245, 13 Cr App Rep (S) 668, CA) or evidence of many previous convictions which indicated the same possibility (*R v Buckley* (1994) 15 Cr App Rep (S) 695, [1994] Crim LR 387, CA).

The penalty points system

C[5.10]–[5.15] Persons convicted of certain offences must be disqualified from driving, eg for driving with excess alcohol. A court has a discretion to disqualify any person who has been convicted of an endorsable offence and will do so where the particular offence with which it is dealing is serious. The person who persistently commits minor endorsable offences may therefore escape these mandatory or discretionary disqualifications but will be caught by the disqualification imposed under the penalty points system. This provides in essence that where a person accumulates 12 or more penalty points over a three-year period, he must generally be disqualified for a minimum period.

C[5.16] **Penalty points.** Every endorsable offence attracts a number of penalty points varying from 2 to 11. Some offences (including careless driving, uninsured use of a vehicle and failing to stop or report after an accident) give the court a discretion to attach a number of penalty points within a range, so indicating the court's view of the relative gravity of the offence. The choice of the number of penalty points in these cases will on occasion determine whether a disqualification must be imposed. For example, Brian A Driver has already accumulated 8 penalty points and is convicted of careless driving for which anything from 3 to 9 penalty points may be awarded. If the court imposes 3 points, Driver escapes disqualification because he does not reach a total of 12; but if the court imposes more than 3 then he must be disqualified, subject to his proving mitigating circumstances amounting to exceptional hardship.

C[5.17] When a driver is convicted of a single endorsable offence his licence will be endorsed with the number of penalty points appropriate to that offence, or with a number within the appropriate range. However, where he is convicted of a number of offences committed on the same occasion (which is not the same as saying on the same day) the number of points to be endorsed will usually be the number for the offence attracting the highest number. For example, if in addition to his careless driving conviction (3–9 penalty points) Brian A Driver is also convicted of driving whilst disqualified (6 penalty points) and driving in a play street (2 penalty points) then his endorsement will show at least 6 penalty points, that being the highest figure. If the court decides to endorse 8 penalty points for the careless driving (that being a number within the range for that offence) then the endorsement would show 8 penalty points. It is these 8 penalty points which count towards disqualification, not the total number for the three offences.

C[5.18] Two things will be evident from this in the normal situation:

(a) although every endorsable offence has a penalty points value, the endorsement relating to that offence may show a higher number; and

(b) when a conviction relates to a number of offences committed on the same occasion the number of penalty points which count towards disqualification is the number relating to the offence with the highest number of penalty points.

C[5.19] However, the court may if it thinks fit decide to accumulate the points for offences committed on the same occasion. If it does so it must state its reasons in open court and enter them in the register.

Note that the court should not order penalty points to be endorsed if it orders the offender to be disqualified in respect of any offence of which he has been convicted on that occasion (*Martin v DPP* [2000] RTR 188, [2000] 2 Cr App Rep (S) 18, 164 JP 405, [2000] Crim LR 320).

Penalty points to be taken into account

C[5.20] There is a general misconception as to the law and practice following the decision in *Jones v Chief Constable of West Mercia Police Authority* (2000) 165 JP 6. A totting ban is usually for not less than 6, 12 or 24 months which is substantially longer than the majority of discretionary bans. Accordingly, the starting point is to calculate the number of points to be taken into account and to determine whether the offender tots. As the court in *Jones* indicated the usual practice is to impose a totting ban without reference to the seriousness or triviality of the offence (as provided for by s 35 of the Offenders Act). Only in an exceptional case will the court first consider if it wishes to impose a discretionary disqualification bearing in mind the seriousness of the offence and previous offences. If a discretionary disqualification is imposed any existing points remain on the licence. If discretionary disqualification is not appropriate the court imposes points and goes on to consider the totting-up procedure.

The effect of the decision in *Jones* above was nullified by the introduction of the Magistrates' Courts Sentencing Guidelines – see page 185, para 12 which clearly states that if the court is considering discretionary disqualification but D would be liable to totting up if further points were imposed the court should go down the totting up route not the discretionary ban route. This plugged the *Jones* 'gap' whereby some courts were being persuaded to impose short discretionary bans in the absence of exceptional hardship thus circumventing the totting up.

Subject to there being grounds for mitigation, disqualification is incurred when the number of penalty points to be taken into account reaches or exceeds 12. The following penalty points are to be taken into account at the time of conviction:

(a) those endorsed at the time of that conviction. Where a person is made the subject of a mandatory or discretionary disqualification no penalty points for the offence for which he was disqualified will be taken into account, for the purpose of imposing an additional disqualification under the penalty points provisions;

(b) those endorsed previously in respect of any offence committed within three years of the present offence, except where a disqualification under the penalty points provisions has been ordered, in which case the court is only concerned with the penalty points incurred since that disqualification.

C[5.21] Therefore, only a disqualification under the penalty points provisions will have the effect of 'wiping clean' any points previously incurred.

Period of disqualification

C[5.22] Once a defendant becomes liable for disqualification under this scheme he may be disqualified for any period at the court's discretion, but this discretion is limited by the fixing of minimum periods. These minimum periods are as follows:

(a) six months if no previous disqualification is to be taken into account;

(b) one year if one previous disqualification is to be taken into account; and
(c) two years if there is more than one such disqualification.

C[5.23] For a prior disqualification to be taken into account it must have been imposed within three years of the latest offence which has brought the offender's total of penalty points up to 12. Such disqualification may have been imposed:

(a) for an offence for which it was obligatory (eg driving with excess alcohol); or
(b) for an offence for which it was optional (eg a bad case of careless driving); or
(c) for 12 or more penalty points;

and must have been for a period of 56 days or more and was not imposed for stealing a motor vehicle, taking without consent or going equipped for theft.

Mitigating grounds

C[5.24] When a defendant becomes liable to disqualification under this procedure he may claim that there are grounds for mitigating the normal consequences of conviction and if the court finds such grounds it may reduce the minimum period to which the offender is liable or it may decide not to disqualify. In either event it must state its reasons which will be recorded. The court's discretion, however, is limited. It may not take into account:

(a) any circumstances which are alleged to make the offence (or any of them) not a serious offence;
(b) the fact that disqualification would cause hardship (but it may take account of exceptional hardship);
(c) any circumstances which have been taken into account during the previous three years so as to avoid or reduce disqualification.

The case of *Miller v DPP* [2004] EWHC 595 (Admin), [2004] 17 LS Gaz R 30, [2004] All ER (D) 477 (Mar) suggests that where there has been excessive delay (over 2 years) in sentencing the defendant this is a proper ground for reducing the length of a disqualification under RTOA 1988, s 35(1).

C[5.25]–[5.30] So, for example, Mr Zimmer is liable to disqualification but successfully avoids it by pleading that being disabled a disqualification would cause exceptional hardship because his specially adapted vehicle is his only means of getting to work. If he is convicted and attracts a totting disqualification again within three years he is unable to put forward that ground for avoiding disqualification but once three years have passed, that ground is resurrected and may be used again.

C[5.31] Under the penalty points scheme only one disqualification is imposed irrespective of the number of offences. In the event of an appeal against any one or more of the offences, the disqualification will be treated as having been imposed on each offence and in any event the Crown Court has the power to alter sentences imposed by the magistrates' court for several offences even if there is only an appeal against the sentence on one offence.

C[5.32] Summary. Upon conviction of certain offences the court must order endorsement unless either there are special reasons (although the Road Traffic Offenders Act 1988 uses the plural it has always been treated as the singular) for not doing so, or in the case of some offences under the Road Vehicles (Construction and Use) Regulations 1986, the defendant did not know of and had no reason to suspect the condition of the vehicle. These offences are noted in the table at C[1.6].

C[5.33] No disqualification may be ordered unless it is for an endorsable offence (except for offences of theft, going equipped to steal vehicles and taking vehicles without consent). Some few offences carry a compulsory order for disqualification and this must be imposed by the court unless there are special reasons for not doing so.

C[5.34] The term 'special reasons' has a very narrow meaning, in particular, hardship to the defendant is excluded from consideration.

C[5.35] A period of disqualification takes effect immediately. This includes disqualification for 12 or more penalty points. Only one period of disqualification is ordered under the penalty points scheme irrespective of the number of offences. The three year period during which penalty points are to be counted runs between dates of offence, not conviction. The three year period during which, the circumstances once used as mitigating grounds for not disqualifying under the penalty points system may not be used again, is measured between dates of their original use and the present conviction.

C[5.36] Where appeal against sentence is lodged, the court may suspend the effect of disqualification until the appeal is *heard*. This should not be done automatically but only after careful consideration.

Disqualification until passes a test

C[5.37] The court *must* disqualify an offender until he passes an extended driving test where:

(a) he is convicted of an offence of dangerous driving; or
(b) in the Crown Court, the offences of manslaughter, causing death by dangerous driving or causing death by careless driving whilst under the influence of drink or drugs; or
(c) the court orders him to be disqualified until a test of competence is passed, having convicted him of an offence involving obligatory disqualification under s 34 or he is disqualified under s 35 of the RTOA 1988.

C[5.38] The court has a *discretion* to disqualify until an ordinary test of competence is passed where the offender has been convicted of any offence involving obligatory endorsement. The defendant is entitled to drive but must display L plates and be supervised. In cases where the court is exercising its discretion it must have regard to the safety of road users and an order is inappropriate as a punishment, but is suitable for the following cases:

(a) for people who are growing aged or infirm, or show some incompetence in the offence which needs looking into. In addition a licence may be revoked by the Secretary of State on medical grounds and a provisional licence issued for the sole purpose of a road reassessment;
(b) where the defendant is disqualified for a long period for the offence and there is doubt about his ability to drive at the expiry of the disqualification period;
(c) where the manner of the defendant's driving suggests a threat to the safety of other road users (*R v Miller* (1993) 15 Cr App Rep (S) 505, [1994] Crim LR 231, CA). See the Road Traffic Offenders Act 1988, s 36;
(d) it is not usually appropriate in the cases of passengers in vehicles taken without the owner's consent (*R v Wiggins* [2001] RTR 37, CA). It is not the case that the court would never order a passenger to take an extended driving test at the end of a period of disqualification. In *R v Beech and others* [2016] EWCA Crim 1746, [2016] 4 WLR 182, [2017] Crim L R 238 the three defendants were disturbed by the police when attempting to steal from an ATM and they tried to escape with the driver, at one point, reaching a speed of 150 mph. While the passengers were less culpable than the driver, their culpability was nonetheless extremely high because they had participated fully in the car being driven very dangerously. The orders to take extended driving tests were, therefore, upheld.

The onus is on the defendant charged with driving whilst disqualified when not having completed a retest to show he held a provisional licence and was complying with the conditions of that licence (*DPP v Barker* (2004) 168 JP 617, [2004] All ER (D) 246 (Oct), DC).

Interim disqualification

C[5.39] A magistrates' court may impose an interim disqualification on a person where:

(a) it commits him to the Crown Court for sentence or remits his case to another magistrates' court; or

(b) it defers or adjourns his case before passing sentence (including a transfer to another magistrates' court post conviction). An interim order of disqualification may continue until the defendant is finally dealt with subject to a limit of six months and any subsequent order of disqualification will be reduced by the period of the interim order.

Disqualification by the Crown Court

C[5.40]–[5.44] Where the Crown Court either convicts or sentences a person who was convicted by a magistrates' court of an offence punishable with at least two years' imprisonment it may disqualify the defendant for an unlimited period if it is satisfied that a motor vehicle was used (whether by him or by an accomplice) to commit or to facilitate the commission of the offence.

Where a vehicle is used for the fraudulent evasion of duty chargeable on cigarettes, disqualification under this section is appropriate and may be imposed whether or not any particular defendant was actually involved in the driving: *R v Skitt* [2004] EWCA Crim 3141, [2005] 2 Cr App R (S) 122. In *R v Ketteridge* [2014] EWCA Crim 1962, [2015] RTR 40, [2015] 1 Cr App Rep (S) 89, the defendant committed two offences of indecent exposure by masturbating while driving his vehicle which he was steering with his other hand. No offence of bad driving was before the court, but the offences created an obvious risk of danger to other road users. If this had been the sole reason for the ban it would have been wrong in principle, but on both occasions the offences were facilitated by the defendant's driving of a motor vehicle and the judge had not been bound to ignore the undeniable circumstances of the driving; 12 months' disqualification was, therefore, upheld.

C[5.45] Disqualification for any offence. This is a power to disqualify a person from driving instead of or as an addition to dealing with him in any other way and it applies to any criminal offence (PCC(S)A 2000, s 146). Certain non endorsable offences recommend themselves for such a penalty including kerb crawling, unlawful tipping and driving off road unlawfully. It is not necessary for the offence for which the defendant is being sentenced to be connected to the use of a motor car, though there must be sufficient reason for the disqualification: *R v Cliff* [2004] EWCA Crim 3139, [2005] RTR 147, [2005] 2 Cr App Rep (S) 118.

Authorities regarding the public protection function of a disqualification from driving are probably not apt, in respect of the use of the power in s 146 of the Powers of Criminal Courts (Sentencing) Act 2000, to disqualify an offender from driving, as there is no requirement under that section that the offences were connected with a motor vehicle; the power conferred by the section is an additional punitive power: *R v Griffin* [2019] EWCA Crim 563, [2019] 2 Cr App R (S) 32.

The effect of endorsement on new drivers

C[5.46] Drivers within the first two years of first passing a driving test are in a probationary period. If, during that period, such a driver accumulates 6 or more penalty points on his licence the DVLA will automatically revoke his driving licence when it is sent to them or they are notified by the court.

C[5.47] This is not a disqualification but the new driver will only be entitled to hold a provisional licence until he passes a retest, which will restore his previous entitlements. Revocation will occur whether the penalty points are added following a conviction by a court or following a fixed penalty.

C[5.48] Points accumulated before the test was taken will count, unless they were committed more than three years before the current offence (*R (on the application of Adebowale) v Secretary of State for Transport* [2004] EWHC 1741 (Admin), [2004] All ER (D) 335 (Jun)). Points accumulated after the test is passed will count if the *offence* is within two years of the date on which the test was passed. In *R v Damien Joseph Edmunds* [2000] 2 Cr App Rep (S) 62, CA the Court of Appeal reduced the points imposed from 6 to 5 to avoid the defendant from losing his full licence on the grounds that he lived in a rural area without public transport. It is submitted that the Court's basis for so doing was not what Parliament intended when introducing changes to the law on endorsement for new drivers.

C[5.49] If in any proceedings for an offence committed in respect of a motor vehicle it appears to the court that the accused may be suffering from any relevant disability or prospective disability (within the meaning of Part III of the Road Traffic Act 1988), the court **must** notify the Secretary of State.

There must be sufficient material before the court, even if only by way of something said in mitigation, suggesting that the defendant is suffering from a relevant disability or a prospective disability, before the court can properly refer the matter to the Secretary of State. A good example is alcoholism or epilepsy (see *R v Chichester JJ, ex p Crouch* (1981) 146 JP 26). Note that the court has no discretion in the matter. It is advisable to consult the legal adviser.

C[6]
Driving licence codes

C[6.1] Offences and the sentences imposed therefor are recorded on driving licences in code. The codes are reproduced below by permission of the Department of the Environment.

Endorsement code

C[6.2] **Aiding, abetting, counselling or procuring**

Aiding, etc

Offence as coded below, but with zero changed to 2, eg LC10 becomes LC12.

Causing or permitting offences

Offence as coded below, but with zero changed to 4, eg IN10 becomes IN14.

Inciting

Offences as coded below, but with zero changed to 6, eg DD 30 becomes DD 36.

Periods of time

Periods of time are signified as follows: D = days; M = months; Y = years.

Code	**Accident offences**
AC 10	Failing to stop after an accident.
AC 20	Failing to give particulars or to report an accident within 24 hours.
AC 30	Undefined accident offence.
	Disqualified driver
BA 10	Driving whilst disqualified by order of court.
BA 20	Driving whilst disqualified by reason of age (obsolete).
BA 30	Attempting to drive whilst disqualified by order of court.
BA 40	Causing death by driving while disqualified
BA 60	Causing serious injury by driving while disqualified
	Careless driving
CD 10	Driving without due care and attention.
CD 20	Driving without reasonable consideration for other road users.
CD 30	Driving without due care and attention or without reasonable consideration for other road users (primarily for use by Scottish courts).
CD 40	Causing death by careless driving when unfit through drink.
CD 50	Causing death by careless driving when unfit through drugs.
CD 60	Causing death by careless driving with alcohol level above the limit.
CD 70	Causing death by careless driving, then failing to supply specimen for analysis.
CD 71	Causing death by careless driving, then failing to supply a specimen for drug analysis.
CD 80	Causing death by careless or inconsiderate driving.

Code	Accident offences
CD 90	Causing death by driving: unlicensed, disqualified or uninsured drivers.
	Construction and use offences
CU 10	Using a vehicle with defective brakes.
CU 20	Causing or likely to cause danger by reason of use of unsuitable vehicle or using a vehicle with parts or accessories (excluding brakes, steering or tyres) in a dangerous condition.
CU 30	Using a vehicle with defective tyres.
CU 40	Using a vehicle with defective steering.
CU 50	Causing or likely to cause danger by reason of load or passengers.
CU 60	Undefined failure to comply with Road Vehicles (Construction and Use) Regulations 1986.
CU 80	Breach of requirements as to control of vehicle, mobile telephones etc
	Reckless driving
DD 10	Causing serious injury by dangerous driving
DD 30	Reckless driving (obsolete).
DD 40	Dangerous driving.
DD 60	Manslaughter or culpable homicide while driving a vehicle.
DD 70	Causing death by reckless driving (obsolete).
DD 80	Causing death by dangerous driving.
DD 90	Furious driving
	Drink or drugs
DR 10	Driving or attempting to drive with alcohol concentration above limit.
DR 20	Driving or attempting to drive while unfit through drink.
DR 30	Driving or attempting to drive then refusing to supply a specimen for laboratory testing.
DR 40	In charge of a vehicle with alcohol concentration above limit.
DR 50	In charge of a vehicle when unfit through drink.
DR 60	In charge of a vehicle then refusing to supply a specimen for laboratory testing.
DR 61	In charge of a vehicle then refusing to supply a specimen for drug analysis.
DR 70	Failing to provide specimen for breath test (roadside).
DG 10	Driving or attempting to drive with drug level above the specified limit
DG 60	Causing death by careless driving with drug level above the limit
DR 80	Driving or attempting to drive when unfit through drugs.
DG 40	In charge of a vehicle while drug level above specified limit
DR 90	In charge of a vehicle when unfit through drugs.
	Insurance offences
IN 10	Using a vehicle uninsured against third party risks.
	Licence offences
LC 10	Driving without a licence (obsolete).
LC 20	Driving otherwise than in accordance with a licence.

Code	Accident offences
LC 30	Driving after making a false declaration about fitness when applying for a licence.
LC 40	Driving a vehicle having failed to notify a disability.
LC 50	Driving after a licence has been revoked or refused on medical grounds.
	Miscellaneous offences
MS 10	Leaving a vehicle in a dangerous position.
MS 20	Unlawful pillion riding.
MS 30	Playstreet offences.
MS 40	Driving with uncorrected defective eyesight or refusing to submit to a test. (Obsolete code, see now MS 70 and MS 80.)
MS 50	Motor racing on the highway.
MS 60	Offences not covered by other codes.
MS 70	Driving with uncorrected defective eyesight.
MS 80	Refusing to submit to eyesight test.
MS 90	Failure to give information as to identity of driver in certain cases.
	Motorway offences
MW 10	Contravention of Special Road Regulations (excluding speed limits).
	Road Traffic Regulation Act 1984
	Non-endorsable offences
NE 98	Disqualification under Powers of Criminal Courts (Sentencing) Act 2000, s 146
NE 99	Disqualification under Criminal Justice Act 1972, s 24 and Powers of Criminal Courts (Sentencing) Act 2000, s 147 (and for offences of unauthorised taking see A[77]).
	Pedestrian crossings
PC 10	Undefined contravention of Zebra, Pelican and Puffin Pedestrian Crossing Regulations and General Directions 1997 (primarily for use by Scottish courts).
PC 20	Contravention of Zebra, Pelican and Puffin Pedestrian Crossing Regulations and General Directions 1997 with moving vehicle.
PC 30	Contravention of Zebra, Pelican and Puffin Pedestrian Crossing Regulations and General Directions 1997 with stationary vehicle.
	Provisional licence offences (obsolete, see now LC 20)
PL 10	Driving without 'L' plates.
PL 20	Not accompanied by a qualified person.
PL 30	Carrying a person not qualified.
PL 40	Drawing an unauthorised trailer.
PL 50	Undefined failure to comply with conditions of a provisional licence.
	Speed limits
SP 10	Exceeding goods vehicle speed limit.
SP 20	Exceeding speed limit for type of vehicle (excluding goods or passenger vehicles).
SP 30	Exceeding statutory speed limit on a public road.
SP 40	Exceeding passenger vehicle speed limit.

Code	Accident offences
SP 50	Exceeding speed limit on a motorway.
SP 60	Undefined speed limit offence.
	Traffic directions and signs
TS 10	Failing to comply with traffic light signals.
TS 20	Failing to comply with double white lines.
TS 30	Failing to comply with a 'stop' sign.
TS 40	Failing to comply with directions of a constable or traffic warden.
TS 50	Failing to comply with a traffic sign (excluding 'stop' signs, traffic lights or double white lines).
TS 60	Failing to comply with a school crossing patrol sign.
TS 70	Undefined failure to comply with a traffic direction or sign.
	Theft or unauthorised taking (obsolete (except UT 50), see now NE 99)
UT 10	Taking and driving away a vehicle without consent or an attempt thereat (primarily for use by Scottish courts).
UT 20	Stealing or attempting to steal a vehicle.
UT 30	Going equipped for stealing or taking a vehicle.
UT 40	Taking or attempting to take a vehicle without consent; driving or attempting to drive a vehicle knowing it to have been taken without consent, allowing oneself to be carried in or on a vehicle knowing it to have been taken without consent.
UT 50	Aggravated taking of a vehicle.
	Special codes
TT 99	Disqualification for accumulating 12 or more penalty points.
NSP	(No separate penalty.) Where court does not impose penalty points for minor offences committed at the same time as a more serious one.

C[7]
Sentence code

C[7.1] The sentence is represented by four characters, eg G 02 Y (community rehabilitation order two years). The first letter indicates the nature of the sentence, the middle two numbers (0 always precedes what would otherwise be a single figure) and the final letter indicate the period of the sentence, if any, as hours (H), days (D), months (M), or years (Y). Apart from the special code TT 99 which indicates a disqualification under the penalty points procedure there is no code to represent disqualification because this appears in a special column on the licence. In the case of an absolute discharge there is no period so the code J 000 is used.

C[7.2] The first letter of the code indicates the sentence as follows:

A	imprisonment
B	detention in a place approved by the Secretary of State
C	suspended sentence of imprisonment
E	conditional discharge
F	bound over
G	community rehabilitation
H	supervision order (youth court)
I	no separate penalty
J	absolute discharge
K	attendance centre
M	community punishment order
P	young offender institution
S	compensation
T	hospital or guardianship order
W	care order

C[8]

Fixed penalties

C[8.1] For some time it has been possible to avoid the expense of court proceedings for some criminal and motoring offences by the expedient of the prosecution offering the defendant a 'fixed penalty ticket'. If he accepts the offer he pays the required sum and the matter is settled, otherwise he is summoned to court and the matter proceeds in the usual way.

C[8.2] In the interests of relieving the burden on the courts of having to deal with many minor motoring cases, the fixed penalty system (formerly almost exclusively confined to motoring offences) has been greatly extended to cover a wide range of offences. These are noted in the index at C[1.6] and include a number of offences which carry an endorsement.

C[8.3] A summary of the procedure is as follows:

Offering the fixed penalty

C[8.4] When a constable observes that a 'fixed penalty' offence has been committed, he must decide whether it is endorsable or not.

C[8.5] **Non-endorsable offences.** He may give the fixed penalty ticket to the driver or affix it to the vehicle if the driver is not present. In the case of criminal offences the offender must be present and at least 18 years old.

C[8.6] **Endorsable offences.** The driver must be present and the officer will require him to produce his driving licence for examination. If the driver is not liable to disqualification because he will not have accumulated 12 or more penalty points, the officer may offer him the option of a fixed penalty and invite him to surrender his licence in exchange for a receipt which he may use as evidence that he is a licence holder. It is then for the driver to decide whether to accept the offer of a fixed penalty.

C[8.7] If the driver does not have his driving licence with him, the procedure is modified in that he may be required to produce his driving licence within seven days at a chosen police station where it will be inspected and, if appropriate, a fixed penalty offered.

Where the offence carries obligatory endorsement and the offender is not the holder of a driving licence, a fixed penalty may only be given if the officer is satisfied, on accessing the offender's driving record, that he would not be liable to points disqualification for the offence.

C[8.8] **Note.** There are no fixed penalties for endorsable offences when the driver is not present (but see 'Conditional offer of fixed penalty', below), nor where he is present but declines the offer. Also the police have a discretion whether to offer a fixed penalty so that, for example, a constable might decline to offer it for an isolated offence which is serious in nature.

From a date to be appointed s 3 of the **Road Safety Act 2006**, will amend s 53 of the Road Traffic Offenders Act 1988, to cater for the introduction of graduated fixed penalties. Similarly s 4 of the **Road Safety Act 2006** will likewise introduce a graduated fixed penalty points scheme.

Paying the fixed penalty

C[8.9] The defendant has to pay the fixed penalty within 21 days (or such longer period as is allowed by the ticket) to the court responsible for fixed penalties.

Offences	*Fixed penalty*
A fixed penalty offence under section 3 of the Road Traffic Act 1988	£100
A fixed penalty offence under s 41D(b) of the RRA 1988	£200
A fixed penalty offence under s 143 of the RTA 1988	£300
A fixed penalty offence under s 172 of the RTA 1988	£200
Any other fixed penalty offence involving obligatory endorsement	£100
A fixed penalty parking offence committed in Greater London on a red route	£60
Any other fixed penalty parking offence committed in Greater London	£40
A fixed penalty offence under s 14 (seat belts: adults) of the RTA 1988	£100
A fixed penalty offence under s 15(2) or 15(4) of the RTA 1988 (restrictions on carrying children not wearing seat belts in motor vehicles)	£100
A fixed penalty offence under s 47 of the RTA 1988	£100
A fixed penalty offence under s 42(1) of the Vehicle Excise and Registration Act 1994 (driving or keeping a vehicle without required registration mark)	£100
A fixed penalty offence under s 43(1) of the Vehicle Excise and Registration Act 1994 (driving or keeping a vehicle with registration mark obscured etc)	£100
A fixed penalty offence under s 59 of VERA 1994 (failure to fit prescribed registration mark to a vehicle in accordance with regulations made under s 23(4)(a) of that Act)	£100
A fixed penalty offence under s 98(4) of the TA 1968	£300
A fixed penalty offence under s 99(4) of the TA 1968	£300
A fixed penalty offence under s 99ZD(1) of the TA 1968	£300
A fixed penalty offence under s 99C of the TA 1968	£300
A fixed penalty offence under s 3(1) of the Road Traffic (Foreign Vehicles) Act 1972	£300
A fixed penalty offence under s 12(5) of the Public Passenger Vehicles Act, 1981	£300
A fixed penalty offence under s 71(1) of the RTA 1988	£300
A fixed penalty offence under s 90D(6) of the RTOA 1988	£300
A fixed penalty offence under s 2(5) of the Goods Vehicles (Licensing of Operators) Act 1995	£300
A fixed penalty offence under reg 3 of the Goods Vehicles (Community Authorisations) Regulations 1992	£100
A fixed penalty offence under reg 3 of the Public Service Vehicles (Community Licences) Regulations 1999	£100
A fixed penalty offence under reg 3(1) of the Road Transport (Passenger Vehicles Cabotage) Regulations 1999	£100
A fixed penalty offence under reg 4(1) of the Road Transport (Passenger Vehicle Cabotage) Regulations 1999	£100

Offences	*Fixed penalty*
An offence under s 144A of the Road Traffic Act 1988 of keeping a motor vehicle which does not meet insurance requirements	£100, or £50 if the penalty is paid within 21 days
A fixed penalty offence under s 11 of the HGV Road User Levy Act 2013	£300
A fixed penalty offence under regulation 4 of the Goods Vehicles (Community Licences) Regulations 2011	£100
A fixed penalty offence under section 8(1) of the Haulage Permits and Trailer Registration Act 2018	£300
A fixed penalty offence under section 8(2) of the Haulage Permits and Trailer Registration Act 2018	£300
A fixed penalty offence under section 8(3) of the Haulage Permits and Trailer Registration Act 2018	£300
A fixed penalty offence under section 8(4)(a) of the Haulage Permits and Trailer Registration Act 2018	£300
A fixed penalty offence under regulation 5 of the Trailer Registration Regulations 2018	£100
A fixed penalty offence under regulation 19(1)(a) of the Trailer Registration Regulations 2018	£100
A fixed penalty offence under regulation 19(1)(f) of the Trailer Registration Regulations	£100
A fixed penalty offence under regulation 19(1)(g) of the Trailer Registration Regulations 2018	£100
A fixed penalty offence under regulation 19(1)(h) of the Trailer Registration Regulations 2018	£100
A fixed penalty offence under regulation 20 of the Trailer Registration Regulations 2018	£100
A fixed penalty offence under regulation 21 of the Trailer Registration Regulations 2018	£100
A fixed penalty offence under regulation 22(a) of the Trailer Registration Regulations 2018	£300
Any other fixed penalty offence except for a fixed penalty parking offence	£50
Any other fixed penalty parking offence	£30

C[8.10]–[8.15] For the purpose of the higher parking penalties, London is regarded as the Metropolitan Police District. The licence that was surrendered to the police is sent to the fixed penalty clerk who places the endorsement on it and returns it to the defendant when the penalty has been paid.

Instituting proceedings

C[8.16] In any case where a fixed penalty has been offered the defendant can at any time before the time for payment has expired, request a hearing before the magistrates and plead guilty or not guilty as he thinks fit.

Where the fixed penalty is not paid

C[8.17] In the case of an endorsable offence, the defendant's licence will already be in the possession of the police who will have forwarded it to the clerk responsible for fixed penalties. If the penalty is unpaid at the end of the required period, the police will register the penalty at the court for the area in which the defendant lives and the clerk who already holds the licence will endorse it and return it to the defendant. Unfortunately for him the penalty is registered as a fine 50% above the fixed penalty.

Similar provisions apply to non-endorsable offences where the ticket is given to the driver.

C[8.18] Where the offence is non-endorsable and the ticket was affixed to the vehicle, the police send a notice to the person they believe to be the owner requesting him either to pay the penalty or to inform them who is the actual owner. If he fails to co-operate by not replying at all, he will have the enhanced penalty registered against him. He is similarly liable if he replies and admits he was the owner unless either (a) he pays the penalty, or (b) persuades the actual driver to pay it for him, or (c) he returns a form signed by the person who was actually driving and who requests a court hearing.

Enforcement of payment

C[8.19] Once a penalty has been registered, it is regarded as a fine. Non-payment of the registered penalty will result in enforcement proceedings being taken in the manner described at **B[28.96]**.

Penalty points

C[8.20] If the accused has committed several endorsable offences on the *same occasion*, and one is dealt with under the fixed penalty procedure and his licence is to be endorsed, the penalty points for those offences dealt with at a court hearing are to be treated as being reduced by those points to be endorsed under the fixed penalty procedure.

Conditional offer of fixed penalty

C[8.21] The Road Traffic Act 1988, s 172 provides for the police to issue a notice to the keeper of the vehicle requiring information as to the identity of the driver. If the keeper fails to give the information he will be guilty of an endorsable offence deemed to have taken place in the place to where the reply ought to have been sent (*Kennet District Council v Young* [1999] RTR 235, 163 JP 622). Any reply must be in writing and signed (*DPP v Broomfield* [2002] EWHC 1962 (Admin), [2003] RTR 108). A telephone call will not be sufficient compliance with the section but a letter accompanying the form and disclosing the required information will be (*Jones v DPP* [2004] EWHC 236 (Admin), [2004] All ER (D) 319 (Jan)) but not if it is left unsigned (*Francis v DPP* [2004] EWHC 591 (Admin), [2004] All ER (D) 443 (Mar)). In *R (on the application of Flegg) v Southampton and New Forest Justices* [2006] EWHC 396 (Admin), 170 JP 373 the defendant returned a section 172 request with a covering note stating that he could not say who the driver was. The conviction was upheld on the basis that the information given was both misleading and inaccurate. The defendant as the owner or keeper of the vehicle has a duty to name potential drivers not just actual drivers.

Where the driver is identified, a conditional offer of a fixed penalty is sent to him and if he wishes to accept the offer he will send his driving licence and payment to the fixed penalty office within 28 days of the issue of the offer. The fixed penalty will be accepted unless the details of the licence disclose that the offender is liable to be disqualified under the penalty points provisions. In this case the police will be notified and a summons issued in the normal way.

In *DPP v Holden* [2006] All ER (D) 363 (Feb), the notice sent to the defendant stated that the response to the police had to be returned within 28 days but failed to specify the period during which a speeding offence could be commenced (see s 75(7)(c) RTOA 1988). In the absence of bad faith this was not a matter which directly affected the fairness of the trial; further, the delay in instituting proceedings was not so exceptional as to warrant a stay of proceedings on the ground of delay.

In *Thomson (Procurator Fiscal) v Jackson* [2010] HCJAC 96, [2011] RTR 210, the High Court of Justiciary dissented from the opinion in *Wilkinson's Road Traffic Offences* (24th edn, 2009), to the effect that there could be more than one valid requirement addressed to the same person, and in relation to the same incident under RTA 1988, s 172. There is nothing in the legislation to suggest that there can only be one requirement. The relevance of the argument goes to questions of statutory time limits and/or issues of abuse of process based on delay. The above decision is of *persuasive* authority only and it is open to question whether it would be followed in England and Wales.

Note, where a defendant is convicted of an offence under s 172, the penalty has been increased to allow for an endorsement with 6 penalty points for offences committed on or after 24 September 2007 (Road Safety Act 2006 (Commencement No 2) Order 2007 (SI 2007/2472 (C 91)).

C[8.22] This procedure would appear not to breach the rule against self-incrimination contained in Art 6 of the ECHR: see *Tora Tolinos v Spain* (No 23816/94) (17 May 1995, unreported), ECtHR, *Brown v Stott* [2001] 2 All ER 97, [2001] 2 WLR 817, PC and *Hayes v DPP* [2004] EWHC 277 (Admin), [2004] All ER (D) 55 (Feb). In *O'Halloran v United Kingdom* [2007] All ER (D) 7 (Jul), [2007] ECHR 15809/02 it was decided:

> The right to remain silent and the right not to incriminate oneself were not absolute rights and the right to require an actual or potential suspect to provide information which contributed or might contribute to his conviction by direct compulsion would not cumulatively result in a violation of article 6 of the Convention. While the right to a fair trial was an unqualified right, what constituted a fair trial could not be the subject of a single unvarying rule, but had to depend on the circumstances of the particular case. In order to determine whether the essence of the applicant's right to remain silent and privilege against self-incrimination had been infringed, it was necessary to focus on the nature and degree of compulsion used to obtain the evidence, the existence of any relevant safeguards in the procedure, and the use to which any material so obtained was put.

Looking at s 172(2)(a) the ECHR noted that it was not an offence of strict liability; certain defences were still available. The essence of the applicant's right to remain silent and the privilege against self-incrimination had not been destroyed. Hence, it decided there was no violation of Art 6.

The prosecution should annex to s 9 statements proving service, a notice of intended prosecution and the requirement to provide details. If the defence fail to raise the issue, that the requirement was not lawfully made, before the end of the prosecution case the court should permit the prosecution to re open their case to prove the point (*Mohindra v DPP* [2004] EWHC 490 (Admin), [2004] All ER (D) 269 (Mar)).

C[9]
Brakes defective

Charge (Brakes defective)

C[9.1] **Using, causing or permitting to be used on a road a motor vehicle or trailer with defective brakes**

Road Vehicles (Construction and Use) Regulations 1986, reg 18; Road Traffic Act 1988, s 41A(b)

Maximum penalty – For goods vehicles fine level 5*. Other motor vehicles or trailers fine level 4 (for fines see para B[28]). For endorsement and disqualification-see below, and under 'Sentencing'.

'Goods vehicles' for this purpose includes vehicles adapted to carry more than eight passengers; as to whether this includes the driver, consult the clerk.

If the defendant can satisfy the court that he did not know and had no reasonable cause to suspect the deficiency of the brakes then disqualification and endorsement cannot be ordered. The defendant does not have to establish this point beyond reasonable doubt but merely that it is true on the balance of probabilities.

Penalty points – 3.

Fixed penalty – £60.

* Section 85 of the Legal Aid, Sentencing and Punishment of Offenders Act 2012 provides that where a relevant offence would on commencement day be punishable on summary conviction by a fine or maximum fine of £5,000, however expressed, and the offence was committed on or after that date, the court may impose a fine of any amount. The commencement date is 12 March 2015: see the Legal Aid, Sentencing and Punishment of Offenders Act 2012 (Commencement No 11) Order 2015, SI 2015/504.

Legal notes and definitions

C[9.2] **Goods vehicle.** Means a motor vehicle or trailer constructed or adapted for the carrying or hauling of goods or burden.

C[9.3] The law requires that every part of every braking system and of the means of operating the braking system must be maintained in good and efficient working order and must be properly adjusted. The offence is an absolute one and the vehicle must have proper brakes at all times. If the charge is using the prosecution need not prove that the defendant knew of the defect. If the vehicle had no brakes at all then he will be charged under a different regulation.

C[9.4] **Using.** This does not mean only driving along a road; mere presence on a road, even in a useless condition, may constitute using (*Pumbien v Vines* [1996] RTR 37, [1996] Crim LR 124). The term means 'to have the use of the vehicle on the road'. The test to be applied is whether or not such steps had been taken as would make it impossible for anyone to use the car. 'Use' involves an element of control, management or operation as a vehicle. Therefore, an accused who was in the driving seat of a 'vehicle' where the steering was locked, there was no ignition key, the brakes were seized on and the engine could not be started was not 'using' it when it was being towed along the road. It was an inanimate hunk of metal. It would be different if there was a possibility of control, ie its steering could be operated and its brakes were working, even if its engine were not working. In doubtful cases the legal adviser should be consulted. A person, limited company or corporate body which owns a vehicle that is being driven in the course of the owner's business is using the vehicle (*West Yorkshire Trading Standards Service v Lex Vehicle Leasing Ltd* [1996] RTR 70). Knowledge of the facts which constitute the offence is not necessary. For a recent judgment where the High Court were unable to agree on whether knowledge on the part of the employer company was required (s 5 RTRA 1984) see *Cambridgeshire County Council v Associated Lead Mills Ltd* [2005] EWHC 1627 (Admin), [2006] RTR 82.

A passenger in a car knowing the driver to be uninsured and allowing himself to be carried in it in pursuance of a joint enterprise is a person using the vehicle for insurance purposes (*Stinton v Stinton* [1995] RTR 167, [1995] 01 LS Gaz R 37, sub nom Stinton v Motor Insurers Bureau 159 JP 656, [1999] Lloyd's Rep IR 305, CA).

C[9.5] **Causing.** This implies some express or positive mandate from the person causing the vehicle to be used or some authority from him and knowledge of the *fact* which constitutes the offence (but there need be no *intention* to commit an offence). Acquiescence could amount to permission (see below) but falls short of a positive mandate (*Redhead Freight Ltd v Shulman* [1989] RTR 1, [1988] Crim LR 696).

C[9.6] **Permitting.** This includes express permission and also circumstances in which permission may be inferred. If the defendant is a limited company or corporate body it must be proved that some person for whose criminal act the company is responsible permitted the offence. A defendant charged with permitting must be shown to have known that the vehicle was being used or it must be shown that he shut his eyes to something that made it obvious to him that the vehicle was being used on a road (*Roper v Taylor's Central Garages Ltd* [1951] 2 TLR 284). In other road traffic offences permitting in the case of an employer may mean failing to take reasonable steps to prevent a contravention of the transport regulations (*Vehicle Inspectorate v Nuttall (t/a Redline Coaches)* [1999] 3 All ER 833, [1999] 1 WLR 629, HL).

C[9.7] **Motor vehicle.** Means a mechanically propelled vehicle intended or adapted for use on roads. The test of whether a vehicle is 'intended or adapted for use on roads' is whether a reasonable person, looking at the vehicle, and forming a view as to its general user, would say the vehicle might well be used on the road: *Chief Constable of Avon and Somerset v Fleming* [1987] 1 All ER 318, [1987] RTR 378. The burden of proving that a vehicle is intended or adapted for use on roads is on the prosecution: *Reader v Bunyard* [1987] RTR 406, [1987] Crim LR 274. In *Macdonald v Carmichael* 1941 JC 27, 106 JP Jo 53 (considered in *McCrone v J & L Rigby (Wigan) Ltd* [1951] 2 TLR 911), it was held that in the circumstances of the case a diesel 'dumper' was not intended or adapted for use on roads and was therefore not a 'motor vehicle'. It has been held in the absence of evidence supporting the contrary view, that a 'dumper' used in the manner described in the case was not 'intended to be used on a road': *Daley v Hargreaves* [1961] 1 All ER 552, 125 JP 193. However, a 30-ton earth mover which because of its size was not transportable and had to move from site to site under its own power was held to be intended to be used on roads: *Childs v Coghlan* (1968) 112 Sol Jo 175. See also *Lewington v Motor Insurers' Bureau* [2017] EWHC 2848 (Comm) [2018] RTR 18, in which a dumper was held to be 'intended or adapted for use on roads'. The case was concerned with the compulsory insurance requirements of Part VI of the RTA 1988, where a purposive approach is required to ensure compatibility with EU law. See further *Percy v Smith* [1986] RTR 252 in which a fork lift truck was in the circumstances of the case 'intended for use on roads', despite its licensing as a works truck.

In *Burns v Currell* [1963] 2 QB 433, [1963] 2 All ER 297, 127 JP 397, it was held that a Go-Kart was not 'intended or adapted for use on roads'. The roadworthiness of a conveyance, however, is not decisive. Thus, a 'Go-ped' has been held to fall within the definition: *Chief Constable of North Yorkshire Police v Saddington* (2000) 165 JP 122, [2001] RTR 15. This decision was followed in *DPP v King* [2008] EWHC 447 (Admin), 172 JP 401, where a City Mantis electric scooter with a maximum speed of 10 mph was held to be a 'motor vehicle'. The same conclusion was reached about the 'Segway' in *Coates v Crown Prosecution Service* [2011] EWHC 2032 (Admin), 175 JP 401.

The definition of 'motor vehicle' in s 185 of the RTA 1988 is expressly subject to the provisions of s 20 of the Chronically Sick and Disabled Persons Act 1970. Consequently, where an invalid carriage complies with the prescribed requirements and is being used in accordance with the prescribed requirements the driver cannot be guilty of driving a motor vehicle with excess alcohol, contrary to s 5 of the RTA 1988: *Croitoru v Crown Prosecution Service* [2016] EWHC 1645 (Admin), (2016) 180 JP 451, [2017] RTR 17.

C[9.8] For 'mechanically propelled' see the note at C[47.9].

C[9.9] A trailer. Means any vehicle being drawn by a motor vehicle.

C[9.10]–[9.15] A road. Means any highway (including footpaths and bridleways) and any other road to which the public has access and includes bridges but not a car park the purpose of which is to enable cars to stand and wait rather than move along it to a destination (*Cutter v Eagle Star Insurance Co Ltd* [1998] 4 All ER 417, [1998] 1 WLR 1647, HL).

Sentencing
SC Guideline – Brakes defective

C[9.16] Starting point – Band B fine (driver); Band B fine (owner-driver but consider an uplift of 25% of at least 25% on the driver's fine); Band C fine (owner-company)

C[9.16A] If the defendant proves that he did not know, and had no reasonable cause to suspect, that the brakes were deficient, endorsement and disqualification cannot be ordered. The defendant only has to prove that it is more probable than not that this was the case. Otherwise he can be disqualified and the licence **must** be endorsed unless there are 'special reasons'; see C[5.2].

C[9.17] It may sometimes be appropriate to grant a conditional or absolute discharge but if this course is adopted then a disqualification can still be imposed. Endorsement must still be ordered unless 'special reasons' exist.

C[9.18] If it appears to the court that the accused suffers from some disease or physical disability likely to cause his driving to be a source of danger to the public then the court shall notify the licensing authority (see C[5.49]).

C[9.19] When the vehicle concerned is a goods vehicle the fine will reflect the potential danger to the public and to the driver of the vehicle, and the gross weight and nature of the load may well be relevant.

C[9.20] For fines see B[28].

C[10]–C[15]

Dangerous condition/bodywork

Charge (Dangerous condition/bodywork)

C[10.1] **Using, causing or permitting to be used a motor vehicle or trailer on a road when**

[the condition of the motor vehicle or trailer, or of its accessories or equipment]

[the purpose for which it is used]

[the number of passengers carried by it, or the manner in which they are carried]

[the weight, position or distribution of its load, or the manner in which it is secured]

is such that the use of the motor vehicle or trailer involves a danger of injury to another person

Road Traffic Act 1988, s 40A

Maximum penalty-For goods vehicle or vehicle adapted to carry more than eight passengers fine level 5*. For other vehicles or trailers fine level 4 (for fines see B[28]).

Licence must be endorsed unless special reasons exist. *May be disqualified for any period and/or until he passes a driving test. Endorsement and disqualification cannot be ordered if defendant can satisfy the court that he did not know of, and he had no reasonable cause to suspect, the dangerous condition. The defendant does not have to prove this beyond reasonable doubt. He need only prove that on the balance of probabilities it is true.

Must disqualify for at least 6 months where the offence under s 40A has been committed within three years of a previous conviction of the offender under the same section; otherwise, disqualification is discretionary: Road Safety Act 2006 (Commencement No 2) Order 2007 (SI 2007/2472 (C 91)).

Penalty points – 3.

Fixed penalty – £60.

---

* Section 85 of the Legal Aid, Sentencing and Punishment of Offenders Act 2012 provides that where a relevant offence would on commencement day be punishable on summary conviction by a fine or maximum fine of £5,000, however expressed, and the offence was committed on or after that date, the court may impose a fine of any amount. The commencement date is 12 March 2015: see the Legal Aid, Sentencing and Punishment of Offenders Act 2012 (Commencement No 11) Order 2015, SI 2015/504.

Legal notes and definitions

C[10.2] **Goods vehicle.** Means a motor vehicle or trailer constructed or adapted for the carriage of goods or burden. The clerk should be consulted if there is a question whether a vehicle is a goods vehicle.

C[10.3] **Using, causing, permitting.** See the notes under these headings for the offence of defective brakes at C[9.4]–C[9.6].

C[10.4] Road. Means any highway (including footpaths and bridleways) and any other road to which the public has access and includes bridges.

Motor vehicle. See C[9.7].

C[10.5] The offence is an absolute one. It is no defence that the defect was latent, and only became apparent during the journey. The section requires that the vehicle (or trailer) and all its parts and accessories are both in good repair and efficient working order.

C[10.6] The wording of the summons or charge should specify the exact part or accessory which is said to be dangerous. The court can allow the prosecution to amend the wording to remedy such an omission and to offer the defence an adjournment if it needs further time to prepare its case.

Sentencing

SC Guideline – Dangerous condition/bodywork

C[10.7] Starting point – Band B fine (driver); Band B fine (owner-driver but consider an uplift of 25% of at least 25% on the driver's fine); Band C fine (owner-company)

C[10.7A] If the defendant can establish that he did not know and he had no reason to suspect the dangerous condition, in this case endorsement and disqualification cannot be ordered. The defendant does not have to prove this beyond reasonable doubt. He need only prove that on the balance of probabilities it is true.

C[10.8] If it appears to the court that the accused suffers from some disease or physical disability likely to cause his driving to be a source of danger to the public then the court shall notify the licensing authority (see C[5.49]).

C[10.9] For fines see B[28].

C[16]
Dangerous driving

Charge (Dangerous driving)

C[16.1] **Driving a mechanically propelled vehicle dangerously on a road or other public place**

Road Traffic Act 1988, s 2 (as substituted by the Road Traffic Act 1991)

Maximum penalty – Fine level 5* and 6 months (for fines see **B[28]**). Triable either way. Must disqualify for at least one year unless special reasons. The disqualification may be for any period exceeding a year. If disqualified he *must* also be ordered to pass an extended driving test. Must endorse licence unless special reasons exist.

Crown Court – 2 years' imprisonment and unlimited fine.

Penalty points – 3–11.

---

* Section 85 of the Legal Aid, Sentencing and Punishment of Offenders Act 2012 provides that where a relevant offence would on commencement day be punishable on summary conviction by a fine or maximum fine of £5,000, however expressed, and the offence was committed on or after that date, the court may impose a fine of any amount. The commencement date is 12 March 2015: see the Legal Aid, Sentencing and Punishment of Offenders Act 2012 (Commencement No 11) Order 2015, SI 2015/504.

Mode of trial

C[16.2] Consider the SC guideline at C[16.7] below.

Legal notes and definitions

C[16.3] **Driving.** See the note under the offence of no driving licence at C[18.8].

C[16.4] **Mechanically propelled vehicle.** See C[47.9].

C[16.5] **Dangerously.** Means that the defendant's driving falls far below what would be expected of a competent and careful driver *and* it would be obvious to a competent and careful driver that driving in that way would be dangerous.

A person is also to be regarded as driving dangerously if it would be obvious to a competent and careful driver that driving the vehicle in its current state would be dangerous. The unintentional pressing of the wrong pedal is not a defence to dangerous driving (*A-G's Reference (No 4 of 2000)* (2001)).

C[16.6] **Aid and Abet.** In *R v Webster* [2006] EWCA Crim 415, (2005) Times, 15 March, the defendant allowed a friend to drive his vehicle while drunk. It was held that whilst the condition of the driver could be relevant to the manner in which the vehicle was driven on the facts this had not been established by the Crown. In this case there was no evidence that the defendant had been given the opportunity to intervene once he became aware the defendant was driving in a dangerous manner.

In *Clark v Farley* [2018] EWHC 1007 (QB) [2019 RTR 21, [2018] Lloyd's Rep IR 645 the court considered dangerous driving and joint enterprise in the context of a claim for damages by the pillion passenger of a motorcyclist who was driving dangerously. It was held that it was necessary to find that the claimant intended to encourage or assist the motorcyclists to ride dangerously, mere foreseeability was not enough. While, given their speed at the time of the collision and their condition, the riding of the motorbikes was dangerous, there was no evidence of a history of deliberate or reckless thrill seeking or risk taking on the park path in question, which was popular with bikers and was locally known as the 'mad mile', or that the claimant had been there for such a purpose. On the evidence, it could not be inferred that the claimant intended the motorbike to be ridden dangerously or knew that it was in a dangerous condition, or that he encouraged or intended to encourage the third defendant to drive dangerously.

C[16.7] Dangerous refers to danger either of injury to any person or of serious damage to property.

C[16.8] In determining what would be expected of, or obvious to, a competent and careful driver in a particular case, regard shall be had not only to the circumstances of which he could be expected to be aware but also to any circumstances shown to have been within the knowledge of the accused. The effect of s 2A(3) of the 1988 Act was not to offend against the rule that the test for dangerous driving was objective; it simply refined the objective test by reference to existing circumstances. By enacting s 2A(3) Parliament directed the court to have regard to any circumstances shown to have been within the knowledge of the accused. Subjective considerations, such as what the driver thought about the situation were irrelevant, but in so far as circumstances relevant to the issue of dangerousness was capable of being established as being within the knowledge of the accused, the fact finder had to have regard to it.

In *Milton v DPP* [2007] EWHC 532 (Admin), [2007] All ER (D) 285 (Mar), it was decided the fact that the defendant was an advanced police driver was a circumstance to which regard had to be had pursuant to s 2A(3). *Milton v DPP* has recently been overruled by *R v Bannister* [2009] EWCA Crim 1571, (2009) Times, 24 August. In the latter case the Court of Appeal reconsidered the position of a police officer who claimed specialist driving skills should be taken into account when judging the standard of driving. The Court of Appeal held: ' . . . the special skill (or indeed lack of skill) of a driver is an irrelevant circumstance when considering whether the driving is dangerous'.

C[16.9] In determining the state of the vehicle regard may be had to anything attached to or carried on or in it and to the manner in which it is attached or carried.

C[16.10]–[16.14] **Road.** See C[10.4] and C[22.5].

C[16.15] **Public place.** See C[20.7]–C[20.8].

C[16.16] **Warning of proceedings.** If the defence claim that notice should have been given within 14 days of intention to prosecute, consult the legal adviser.

Defences

C[16.17] It was held in *Loake v Crown Prosecution Service* [2017] EWHC 2855 (Admin), [2018] 2 WLR 1159 that insanity is available to offences of strict liability (not following *DPP v H* [1998] RTR 200 (DC).

The defence of automatism may be relied upon by a defendant charged with dangerous driving. If it is shown that a defendant suffered a sudden mischance for which he/she was in no way to blame and which rendered him/her unconscious or otherwise prevented the defendant from controlling the vehicle, then the defendant will not be held to have been 'driving': *Hill v Baxter* [1958] 1 QB 277, [1958] 1 All ER 193, DC. There must, however, be a complete loss of consciousness; continuing to drive after suffering disabling symptoms is, in itself, negligent: *Roberts v Ramsbottom* [1980] 1 All ER 7, [2980] RTR 261. Moreover, the loss of consciousness must not arise from any deliberate act or conduct of the defendant and it must arise from a cause which a reasonable man had no reason to think, and which the defendant did not think, might occur: *R v Sibbles* [1959] Crim L R 660.

Necessity can be a defence, but only where the facts establish 'duress of circumstances', ie where the defendant was constrained by circumstances to drive as he/she did to avoid serious bodily harm to him/herself or to another person: *R v Conway* [1989] QB 290, [1988] 3 ALL ER 1025, [1989] RTR 35. The defence is available, however, only where, viewed objectively, the driver could be said to have been acting reasonably and proportionately in driving as he/she did; the test is whether a sober person of reasonable firmness, sharing the characteristics of the defendant, might have responded to the situation as the defendant did: *R v Martin* [1989] 1 All ER 65, [1989] RTR 63. The manner of driving must also have been causally linked to the duress: *R v Denton* [1987] RTR 129, 85 Cr App Rep 246, CA.

Self defence is capable of arising with regard to a count of dangerous driving, but it is likely to be a rare case where it can even be raised. The distinctions between this defence and duress of circumstances are that the latter normally requires a threat of death or serious injury and gives rise to a requirement of reasonableness as to the relevant belief held, while in self defence, though the response of the defendant must be reasonable and proportionate, this is to be decided by reference to the circumstances in which, subjectively, even if mistakenly and even if unreasonably, the defendant believed he or she was in: *R v Riddell* [2017] EWHC Crim 413, [2018] 1 All ER 62, [2017] 1 WLR 3593, [2017] 2 Cr App R 3.

The defence under s 3(1) of the Criminal Law Act 1967 of reasonable force for the purpose of assisting in the arrest of an offender is also available to this charge, but this applies to the prevention of a crime and does not apply where the crime is no longer being committed: *R v Attwater* [2010] EWCA Crim 2399, [2011] RTR 12. See further *R v Morris* [2013] EWCA Crim 436, [2013] RTR 22.

Sentencing

SC Guideline – Dangerous Driving

C[16.18] Must endorse and disqualify for at least 12 months

Must disqualify for **at least** 2 years if offender has had two or more disqualifications for periods of 56 days or more in preceding 3 years – consult your legal adviser for further guidance

If there is a delay in sentencing after conviction, consider interim disqualification

OFFENCE SERIOUSNESS (CULPABILITY AND HARM) A. IDENTIFY THE APPROPRIATE STARTING POINT Starting points based on first time offender pleading not guilty		
Examples of nature of activity	**Starting point**	**Range**
Single incident where little or no damage or risk of personal injury	Medium level community penalty	Low level community order to high level community order Disqualify 12 – 15 months
Incident(s) involving excessive speed or showing off, especially on busy roads or in built-up area; OR Single incident where little or no damage or risk of personal injury but offender was disqualified driver	12 weeks custody	High level community order to 26 weeks custody Disqualify 15 – 24 months

Prolonged bad driving involving deliberate disregard for safety of others; OR Incident(s) involving excessive speed or showing off, especially on busy roads or in built-up area, by disqualified driver; OR Driving as described in box above while being pursued by the police	Crown Court	Crown Court* *Consider interim disqualification

OFFENCE SERIOUSNESS (CULPABILITY AND HARM) **B. CONSIDER THE EFFECT OF AGGRAVATING AND MITIGATING FACTORS (OTHER THAN THOSE WITHIN EXAMPLES ABOVE)** Common aggravating and mitigating factors are identified at **B[45.2A]**. The following may be particularly relevant but **these lists are not exhaustive**	
Factors indicating higher culpability	*Factors indicating lower culpability*
1. Disregarding warnings of others 2. Evidence of alcohol or drugs 3. Carrying out other tasks while driving 4. Carrying passengers or heavy load 5. Tiredness 6. Aggressive driving, such as driving much too close to vehicle in front, racing, inappropriate attempts to overtake, or cutting in after overtaking 7.Driving when knowingly suffering from a medical condition which significantly impairs the offender's driving skills 8. Driving a poorly maintained or dangerously loaded vehicle, especially where motivated by commercial concerns	1. Genuine emergency 2. Speed not excessive 3. Offence due to inexperience rather than irresponsibility of driver
Factors indicating greater degree of harm 1. Injury to others 2. Damage to other vehicles or property	
FORM A PRELIMINARY VIEW OF THE APPROPRIATE SENTENCE, THEN CONSIDER OFFENDER MITIGATION Common factors are identified at B[45.2A]	
CONSIDER A REDUCTION FOR A GUILTY PLEA	
CONSIDER ANCILLARY ORDERS, INCLUDING COMPENSATION AND DEPRIVATION OF PROPERTY Refer to B[10] for guidance on compensation and Part B for available ancillary orders	
DECIDE SENTENCE **GIVE REASONS**	

C[16.19] See Table A at B[43.1A] for available sentences.

C[16.20] If the prosecution have not brought an alternative charge of careless driving and the court finds the defendant not guilty of dangerous driving but the allegations amount to an offence of careless driving or inconsiderate driving, he may be convicted of one of these offences. For the procedure see *R v Gloucester Magistrates' Court, ex p Chung* (1989) 153 JP 75.

C[16.21] If convicted of dangerous driving the defendant's licence must be endorsed and he must be disqualified from holding a licence for at least one year (two years if the defendant has had two or more disqualifications of 56 days or more imposed three years immediately preceding the commission of the latest offence). If special reasons are found (at C[5.2]) he may avoid endorsement or a disqualification. If he is not disqualified the court must determine the number of penalty points to be recorded on any endorsement.

C[16.22]–[16.30] Forfeiture of vehicle. See B[18].

C[16A]

Causing death by careless, or inconsiderate driving

Charge (Causing death by driving: careless etc)

C[16A.1] Being the driver of a mechanically propelled motor vehicle on a road or other public place did cause the death of another person by driving the said vehicle without due care and attention, or without reasonable consideration for other persons using the road or place.

Road Traffic Act 1988, s 2B (as inserted by the Road Safety Act 2006 from 18 August 2008 by virtue of the Road Safety Act (Commencement No 4) Order 2008, SI 2008/1918)

Maximum penalty – Fine level 5* and 12 months (for fines see **B[28]**). Triable either way. Must disqualify for at least 12 months unless special reasons. The disqualification may be for any period exceeding one year. If disqualified he *must* also be ordered to pass an extended driving test. Must endorse licence unless special reasons exist.

Crown Court – 5 years' imprisonment and unlimited fine.

Penalty points – 3–11.

---

* Section 85 of the Legal Aid, Sentencing and Punishment of Offenders Act 2012 provides that where a relevant offence would on commencement day be punishable on summary conviction by a fine or maximum fine of £5,000, however expressed, and the offence was committed on or after that date, the court may impose a fine of any amount. The commencement date is 12 March 2015: see the Legal Aid, Sentencing and Punishment of Offenders Act 2012 (Commencement No 11) Order 2015, SI 2015/504.

Mode of trial

C[16A.2] Consider the SC Guideline at **C[16A.10]** below. In general, offences of causing death by careless or inconsiderate driving should be tried summarily except for the presence of one or more of the aggravating factors (a)–(e), outlined under 'Sentencing' at **C[16.18]**.

Legal notes and definitions

C[16A.3] Driving. See the note under the offence of no driving licence at C[18.8].

Mechanically propelled vehicle. See C[47.9].

C[16A.4] Road. See C[22.5].

C[16A.5] Public Place. See C[20.7]-C[20.8]. The car park of a dealership has been found to be a public place (*May v DPP* [2005] EWHC 1280 (Admin), [2005] All ER (D) 182 (Apr)).

C[16A.6] Cause. The contribution of the driving to the death must be more than minute: *R v Hennigan* [1971] 3 All ER 133, 55 Cr App Rep 262, 135 JP 504. The term 'substantial cause' may imply a larger meaning whilst reference to more than a 'slight or trifling' link is a useful way to avoid the term 'de minimis': *R v Kimsey*

[1996] Crim LR 35. The driving does not need to be coterminous with the impact causing death. The question is simply whether the driving played a part in causing death, and not simply creating the occasion of the fatality: also *R v Skelton* [1995] Crim LR 635, CA. See also *R v Jenkins* [2012] EWCA Crim 2909, [2013] RTR 21.

Due care and attention. See the detailed notes at C[25]-C[30].

Reasonable consideration. See the detailed notes at C[46] onwards.

C[16A.7] Where magistrates see fit, they may allow separate informations for an offence under s 2B and s 3 to be heard together. In this event, if the defendant is convicted of one offence, the second information may be adjourned *sine die* or the justices may make "*no adjudication*". Should the driver successfully appeal against conviction, he can later be tried on the second information.

C[16A.8] Alternatively, where there is a single information alleging causing death by careless driving or causing death by inconsiderate driving and the magistrates do not find this proved, they may convict of careless or inconsiderate driving in the alternative (s 24 RTOA 1988 as amended by s 20 of the Road Safety Act 2006).

C[16A.9] **Warning of proceedings.** If the defence claim that notice should have been given within 14 days of intention to prosecute, consult the legal adviser.

Sentencing
SC Guideline – Causing death by careless or inconsiderate driving

C[16A.10] This guideline applies only to offenders aged 18 or over. The advice and full guideline are available on sentencingcouncil.judiciary.gov.uk.

Road Traffic Act 1988 (s 2B)

Maximum penalty. 5 years' imprisonment; minimum disqualification of 12 months, discretionary re-test

This guideline and accompanying notes are taken from the SGC's definitive guideline *Causing Death by Driving*, published 15 July 2008 and coming into force on 18 August 2008.

Key factors

(a) It is unavoidable that some cases will be on the borderline between *dangerous* and *careless* driving, or may involve a number of factors that significantly increase the seriousness of the offence. As a result, the guideline for this offence identifies three levels of seriousness, the range for the highest of which overlaps with ranges for the lower levels of seriousness for *causing death by dangerous driving*.

(b) The three levels of seriousness are defined by the degree of carelessness involved in the standard of driving:
- the most serious level for this offence is where the offender's driving fell not that far short of dangerous;
- the least serious group of offences relates to those cases where the level of culpability is low – for example in a case involving an offender who misjudges the speed of another vehicle, or turns without seeing an oncoming vehicle because of restricted visibility;
- other cases will fall into the intermediate level.

(c) Where the level of carelessness is low and there are no aggravating factors, even the fact that death was caused is not sufficient to justify a prison sentence.

(d) A fine is unlikely to be an appropriate sentence for this offence; where a non-custodial sentence is considered appropriate, this should be a community order. The nature of the requirements will be determined by the **purpose** (CJA

2003, s 142(1)) identified by the court as of primary importance. Requirements most likely to be relevant include unpaid work requirement, programme requirement and curfew requirement.

(e) Offender mitigation particularly relevant to this offence includes conduct after the offence such as where the offender gave direct, positive, assistance at the scene of a collision to victim(s). It may also include remorse – whilst it can be expected that anyone who has caused a death by driving would be remorseful, this cannot undermine its importance for sentencing purposes. It is for the court to determine whether an expression of remorse is genuine.

(f) Where an offender has a good driving record, this is not a factor that automatically should be treated as mitigation, especially now that the presence of previous convictions is a statutory aggravating factor. However, any evidence to show that an offender has previously been an exemplary driver, for example, having driven an ambulance, police vehicle, bus, taxi or similar vehicle conscientiously and without incident for many years, is a fact that the courts may well wish to take into account by way of offender mitigation. This is likely to have even greater effect where the offender is driving on public duty (for example, on ambulance, fire services or police duties) and was responding to an emergency.

(g) Disqualification of the offender from driving and endorsement of the offender's driving licence are mandatory, and the offence carries between 3 and 11 points when the court finds special reasons for not imposing disqualification. There is a discretionary power to order an extended driving test/re-test where a person is convicted of an offence: s 36(4) of the Road Traffic Offenders Act 1988.

NB: In *R v Campbell* [2009] EWCA Crim 2459 a case which could be described as a single incident of misjudgement (as opposed to momentary inattention) fell into category 2 of the guidelines as opposed to category 1.

OFFENCE SERIOUSNESS (CULPABILITY AND HARM) **A. IDENTIFY THE APPROPRIATE STARTING POINT** Starting points based on first time offender pleading not guilty		
Nature of offence	**Starting point**	**Sentencing range**
Careless or inconsiderate driving arising from momentary inattention with no aggravating factors	Medium level community order	Low level community order to high level community order
Other cases of careless or inconsiderate driving	Crown Court	High level community order to Crown Court
Careless or inconsiderate driving falling not far short of dangerous driving	Crown Court	Crown Court

OFFENCE SERIOUSNESS (CULPABILITY AND HARM) **B. CONSIDER THE EFFECT OF AGGRAVATING AND MITIGATING FACTORS (OTHER THAN THOSE WITHIN EXAMPLES ABOVE)** Common aggravating and mitigating factors are identified at B[45.2A]. The following may be particularly relevant but **these lists are not exhaustive**	
Factors indicating higher culpability	*Factors indicating lower culpability*

1. Other offences committed at the same time, such as driving other than in accordance with the terms of a valid licence; driving while disqualified; driving without insurance; taking a motor vehicle without consent; driving a stolen vehicle	1. Offender seriously injured in collision
2. Previous convictions for motoring offences, particularly offences that involve bad driving	2. The victim was a close friend or relative
3. Irresponsible behaviour, such as failing to stop or falsely claiming that one of the victims was responsible for the collision	3. The actions of the victim or a third party contributed to the commission of the offence 4. The offender's lack of driving experience contributed significantly to the likelihood of a collision occurring and/or death resulting 5. The driving was in response to a proven and genuine emergency falling short of a defence
Factors indicating greater degree of harm 1. More than one person was killed as a result of the offence 2. Serious injury to one or more persons in addition to death(s)	
FORM A PRELIMINARY VIEW OF THE APPROPRIATE SENTENCE, THEN CONSIDER OFFENDER MITIGATION Common factors are identified at B[45.2A]	
CONSIDER A REDUCTION FOR A GUILTY PLEA	
CONSIDER ANCILLARY ORDERS, INCLUDING COMPENSATION AND DEPRIVATION OF PROPERTY Refer to B[10] for guidance on compensation and **Part B** for available ancillary orders	
DECIDE SENTENCE GIVE REASONS	

C[16A.11] Forfeiture of vehicle. See B[34].

C[16B]

Causing death by driving: unlicensed or uninsured drivers

C[16B.1] With effect from 13 April 2015, causing death by driving when disqualified from driving is an offence contrary to s 3ZC of the Road Traffic Act 1988 and is punishable only on indictment.

Did cause the death of another person by driving a motor vehicle on a road, and at the time when he was driving, the circumstances are such that he was committing an offence under – s 87(1) of the Road Traffic Act 1988 (driving otherwise than in accordance with a licence), s 103(1)(b) of the Road Traffic Act 1988 (driving while disqualified), or s 143 of the said Act (driving while uninsured or unsecured against third party risks).

Road Traffic Act 1988, s 3ZB (as inserted by the Road Safety Act 2006 from 18 August 2008 by virtue of the Road Safety Act (Commencement No 4) Order 2008, SI 2008/1918).

Maximum penalty – Fine level 5* and 12 months (6 months in Scotland). For fines see B[28]. Triable either way. Must disqualify for at least one year unless special reasons. The disqualification may be for any period exceeding one year. If disqualified he *may* be ordered to pass an extended driving test. Must endorse licence unless special reasons exist.

Crown Court – 2 years' imprisonment and unlimited fine.

Penalty points – 3–11.

* Section 85 of the Legal Aid, Sentencing and Punishment of Offenders Act 2012 provides that where a relevant offence would on commencement day be punishable on summary conviction by a fine or maximum fine of £5,000, however expressed, and the offence was committed on or after that date, the court may impose a fine of any amount. The commencement date is 12 March 2015: see the Legal Aid, Sentencing and Punishment of Offenders Act 2012 (Commencement No 11) Order 2015, SI 2015/504.

Mode of trial

C[16B.2] Consider first the guidance notes at D[4]. In general, offences of causing death by unlicensed, disqualified or uninsured drivers should be tried summarily except for the presence of one or more of the aggravating factors (a)–(e), outlined under 'Sentencing' at C[16.8].

C[16B.3] **Driving.** See the note under the offence of no driving licence at C[18.8].

C[16B.4] **Motor vehicle.** See the definition at A[60.4].

C[16B.5] **Driving otherwise than in accordance with the conditions of a driving licence.** See the notes at C[18] onwards.

Driving while uninsured. See the notes at C[33] onwards.

C[16B.5A] Cause. It was held in *R v Williams* [2010] EWCA Crim 2552, [2011] 3 All ER 969, [2011] 1 WLR 588, 174 JP 606, [2011] Crim LR 471, 174 CL&J 75 that no fault or blameworthy conduct on the part of the defendant was required to commit an offence under s 3ZB; it was sufficient that driving was a cause. *Williams* was followed in *Prosecution Appeal; R v H* [2011] EWCA Crim 1508, [2011] 4 All ER 761, but the decision of the Court of Appeal was reversed by the Supreme Court on further appeal in *R v Hughes* [2013] UKSC 56, [2013] 1 WLR 2461.

> '[33] Juries should thus be directed that it is not necessary for the Crown to prove careless or inconsiderate driving, but that there must be something open to proper criticism in the driving of the Defendant, beyond the mere presence of the vehicle on the road, and which contributed in some more than minimal way to the death. How much this offence will in practice add to the other offences of causing death by driving will have to be worked out as factual scenarios present themselves . . .
>
> [36] For the reasons set out, enquiry into apportionment of liability in civil terms is not appropriate to a criminal trial. But it must follow from the use of the expression "causes ... death ... by driving" that s 3ZB requires at least some act or omission in the control of the car, which involves some element of fault, whether amounting to careless/inconsiderate driving or not, and which contributes in some more than minimal way to the death. It is not necessary that such act or omission be the principal cause of the death. In which circumstances the offence under s 3ZB will then add to the other offences of causing death by driving must remain to be worked out as factual scenarios are presented to the courts . . . ' (per Lords Hughes and Toulson)

Causation is to be considered in the context of causing death, and not causing the accident which led to death. The accident may have been unavoidable, but if the bad driving contributed more than minimally to the fatal outcome by increasing the risk of that consequence, the test of causation will have been satisfied: *R v Wilson* [2018] EWCA Crim 1184, [2019] 1 WLR 3916, [2019] RTR 24.

Sentencing

SC Guideline – Causing death by driving: unlicensed, disqualified or uninsured drivers

C[16B.6] This guideline applies only to offenders aged 18 or over. The advice and full guideline are available on sentencingcouncil.judiciary.gov.uk.

Road Traffic Act 1988 (s 3ZB)

Maximum penalty. 2 years' imprisonment; minimum disqualification of 12 months, discretionary re-test

This guideline and accompanying notes are taken from the SGC's definitive guideline *Causing Death by Driving*, published 15 July 2008 and coming into force on 18 August 2008.

Key factors

(a) Culpability arises from the offender driving a vehicle on a road or other public place when, by law, not allowed to do so; the offence does not involve any fault in the standard of driving.

(b) Since driving while disqualified is more culpable that driving while unlicensed or uninsured, a higher starting point is proposed when the offender.

(c) Being uninsured, unlicensed or disqualified are the only determinants of the seriousness for this offence, as there are no factors relating to th standard of driving. The list of aggravating factors identified is slightly different as the emphasis is on the decision to drive by an offender who is not permitted by the law to do so.

(d) A fine is unlikely to be an appropriate sentence for this offence; where a non-custodial sentence is considered appropriate, this should be a community order.

(e) Where the decision to drive was brought about by a genuine and proven emergency, that may mitigate offence seriousness and so it is included as an additional mitigating factor.

(f) Offender mitigation particularly relevant to this offence includes conduct after the offence such as where the offender gave direct, positive, assistance at the scene of a collision to victim(s). It may also include remorse – whilst it can be expected that anyone who has caused a death by driving would be remorseful, this cannot undermine its importance for sentencing purposes. It is for the court to determine whether an expression of remorse is genuine.

(g) Where an offender has a good driving record, this is not a factor that automatically should be treated as mitigation, especially now that the presence of previous convictions is a statutory aggravating factor. However, any evidence to show that an offender has previously been an exemplary driver, for example, having driven an ambulance, police vehicle, bus, taxi or similar vehicle conscientiously and without incident for many years, is a fact that the courts may well wish to take into account by way of offender mitigation. This is likely to have even greater effect where the offender is driving on public duty (for example, on ambulance, fire services or police duties) and was responding to an emergency.

(h) Disqualification of the offender from driving and endorsement of the offender's driving licence are mandatory, and the offence carries between 3 and 11 points when the court finds special reasons for not imposing disqualification. There is a discretionary power to order an extended driving test/re-test where a person is convicted of an offence: s 36 (4) Road Traffic Offenders Act 1988.

OFFENCE SERIOUSNESS (CULPABILITY AND HARM)

A. IDENTIFY THE APPROPRIATE STARTING POINT

Starting points based on first time offender pleading not guilty

Nature of offence	Starting point	Sentencing range
The offender was disqualified from driving OR	12 months custody	36 weeks – 2 years custody
The offender was unlicensed or uninsured plus 2 or more aggravating factors from the list below		
The offender was unlicensed or uninsured plus at least 1 aggravating factor from the list below	26 weeks custody	High level community order to 36 weeks custody
The offender was unlicensed or uninsured – no aggravating factors	Medium level community order	Low level community order to High level community order

Additional aggravating factors	*Additional mitigating factors*
Previous convictions for motoring offences, whether involving bad driving or involving an offence of the same kind that forms part of the present conviction (i.e. unlicensed, disqualified or uninsured driving)	The decision to drive was brought about by a proven and genuine emergency falling short of a defence

More than one person was killed as a result of the offence	The offender genuinely believed that he or she was insured or licensed to drive
Serious injury to one or more persons in addition to the death(s)	The offender was seriously injured as a result of the collision
Irresponsible behaviour such as failing to stop or falsely claiming that someone else was driving	The victim was a close friend or relative

C[16B.7] Forfeiture. See B[18].

C[16C]
Causing serious injury by dangerous driving

Charge (Causing serious injury by dangerous driving)

C[16C.1] **Being the driver of a mechanically propelled vehicle on a road or other public place, did cause serious injury to another person by driving the said vehicle dangerously**

Road Traffic Act 1988, s 1A

Maximum penalty – Fine level 5* and 12 months (for fines see **B[28]**). Triable either way. Must disqualify for at least 12 months unless special reasons. The disqualification may be for any period exceeding one year. If disqualified he must also be ordered to pass an extended driving test. Must endorse licence unless special reasons exist.

Crown Court – 5 years' imprisonment and unlimited fine.

Penalty points – 3–11.

---

* Section 85 of the Legal Aid, Sentencing and Punishment of Offenders Act 2012 provides that where a relevant offence would on commencement day be punishable on summary conviction by a fine or maximum fine of £5,000, however expressed, and the offence was committed on or after that date, the court may impose a fine of any amount. The commencement date is 12 March 2015: see the Legal Aid, Sentencing and Punishment of Offenders Act 2012 (Commencement No 11) Order 2015, SI 2015/504.

Mode of trial

C[16C.2] No SC guidance at the time of writing.

Legal notes and definitions

C[16C.3] The offence differs from the offence of dangerous driving only by the added element of causing serious injury.

'Serious injury' means, in England and Wales, physical harm which amounts to grievous bodily harm for the purposes of the Offences Against the Person Act 1861, and, in Scotland, severe physical injury. 'Grievous bodily harm' has been interpreted to mean no more than 'serious bodily harm': *DPP v Smith* [1961] AC 290, HL. The totality of the injuries may be taken into consideration: *R v Grundy* [1977] Crim LR 543, CA. The injury does not need to be permanent or life threatening. 'Grievous' is a matter of objective assessment, but the characteristics of the victim may be relevant. For example, what is grievous bodily harm to a child might not be for an adult: *R v Bollom* [2003] EWCA Crim 2846, [2004] 2 Cr App R 50, (2003) Times, 15 December.

The Crown Prosecution Service has drawn up guidance on what might amount to grievous bodily harm for the purposes of the Offences Act the Person Act 1861.

Sentencing
SC Guideline – causing serious injury by dangerous driving: unlicensed

C[16C.4] No SC guideline has been published at the time of writing.

On a charge of causing serious injury by dangerous driving, where several people were injured in consequence of the driving but only one of them seriously, and the case fell within level 1 of the sentencing guidelines for dangerous driving, because the offender had shown '... an apparent disregard to the great danger being caused to others', the court was entitled to take all the injuries into account when determining the appropriate sentence: *R v Aziz* [2016] EWCA Crim 1945, [2017] 1 Cr App R (S) 28, [2017] Crim L R 414.

C[16D]

Causing serious injury by driving: disqualified drivers

Charge (Causing serious injury by driving)

C[16D.1] **Did cause serious injury to another person by driving a motor vehicle on a road and at the time when he was driving he was committing an offence under s 103(1)(b) of the Road Traffic Act 1988 (driving while disqualified)**

Road Traffic Act 1988, s 3ZC, as inserted by the Criminal Justice and Courts Act 2015, s 29, with effect from 13 April 2015

Maximum penalty — Fine level 5 (ie an unlimited fine since any offence will post-date the commencement of s 85 of the Legal Aid, Sentencing and Punishment of Offenders Act 2012) and 12 months (6 months in Scotland). Triable either way, with a maximum penalty of four years' imprisonment or a fine on indictment. Must disqualify for at least unless special reasons exist. If disqualified he must be ordered to pass an extended driving test. Must endorse licence unless special reasons exist.

Crown Court – 4 years' imprisonment and unlimited fine

Mode of trial

C[16D.2] See generally **D[4]**. There are currently no sentencing guidelines for this offence.

The offence of causing serious injury by driving whilst disqualified was inserted by the Courts and Criminal Justice Act 2015. 'Serious injury' is defined by Road Traffic Act 1988, s 3ZD(2) in the same terms as it is defined in the offence of causing serious injury by dangerous driving: see **C[16C.3]**.

A person acquitted of this offence may in the alternative be convicted of the basic offence of driving whilst disqualified.

The purpose of this offence is to bridge the gap between the offence of causing death by driving when disqualified – which now carries a maximum penalty of 10 years' imprisonment – and the basic offence of driving whilst disqualified (which is summary only).

C[17]

Failing to produce driving licence, insurance certificate or test certificate

Charge (Failing to produce driving licence)

C[17.1] **1 Being the driver of a motor vehicle on a road,**

OR

C[17.2] **2 Being a person whom a police constable reasonably believed to have driven a motor vehicle when an accident occurred owing to its presence on a road, or other public place.**

OR

C[17.3] **3 Being a person whom a police constable reasonably believed had committed an offence in relation to the use on a road or other public place of a motor vehicle, failed on being so required by a police constable to produce (his driving licence) (the relevant certificate of insurance) (the relevant test certificate) for examination.**

Road Traffic Act 1988, s 164 (driving licence); s 165 (insurance and test certificates)

Maximum penalty– Fine level 3 (for fines see B[28]). No power to disqualify or endorse.

Legal notes and definitions

C[17.4] **Right to demand production.** Before the police officer is entitled to require the defendant to produce his driving licence or certificate of insurance the defendant must:

(a) be driving a motor vehicle on a road or other public place; or
(b) have been reasonably believed by the police to be the driver of a motor vehicle which was on a road or other public place and involved in an accident; or
(c) have been reasonably believed by the police to have committed a motor vehicle offence on a road or other public place;

in addition, where a requirement is made to produce a test certificate, the vehicle must require a test certificate.

C[17.5] **Purpose of production.** In the case of a driving licence, to enable the constable to ascertain inter alia the holder's name and address; in the case of test and insurance certificates the person must give his name and address and those of the owner where required. Additionally, if a driver fails to produce his insurance/licence when required and the constable has reasonable grounds to believe that he doesn't have a licence/insurance, or he fails to stop for long enough for enquiries to be made, and the constable believes that he has no licence or insurance, the constable may seize and remove the vehicle, and may enter premises by force to do so (but not a private dwelling). The constable must first warn the driver unless it is impracticable to do so.

C[17.6] **Driver.** See the notes under the heading 'driving' for the offence of driving without a licence C[18.8].

C[17.7] **Person supervising a learner driver.** In the circumstances (a)–(c) outlined above the supervisor may be required to produce his driving licence.

C[17.8] **Motor vehicle.** See C[9.7].

C[17.9] **Road.** Means any highway (including footpaths and bridleways) and any other road to which the public has access and includes bridges.

Other public place. Will exclude private property but will normally include such places as car parks.

C[17.10]–[17.15] Constable. Includes a police constable of any rank. Traffic wardens also have power to require production of a driving licence and the giving of a name and address in certain, very limited, circumstances. Certain vehicle examiners may also require production of documents.

C[17.16] Insurance certificate. The law requires that the insurance certificate be produced and not the policy or a premium receipt, unless the vehicle is covered by a certificate of security instead of a conventional insurance policy. Instead of an insurance policy the compulsory insurance of a motor vehicle can be covered by depositing £500,000 with the Accountant-General of the Supreme Court and a duplicate copy of this certificate will suffice instead of an insurance certificate. It will also be acceptable to produce a certificate in the prescribed form signed by the vehicle's owner (or by an agent on his behalf) stating that he has £500,000 on deposit with the Accountant-General of the Supreme Court.

C[17.17] If the vehicle is subject to a hire-purchase agreement either party to that agreement can be the 'owner'.

C[17.18] If the motor vehicle is owned by a local authority or a police authority then that authority may issue a 'Certificate of Ownership' in a prescribed form which makes an insurance certificate unnecessary.

Defences

C[17.19] There are several defences that the defendant can use:

(a) If the defendant is unable to produce his documents at the time, he can elect to produce them at some police station of his own choosing within seven days. Although it is not compulsory, the constable will issue the defendant with a special form (HORT1) requiring him to produce the documents. A driving licence has to be produced in *person*; insurance and test certificates merely have to be *produced*.

(b) If the documents were not produced within the seven days it is a defence if they were produced (in person for a driving licence) at the specified police station as soon as was reasonably practicable.

Or

(c) It is also a defence if it was not reasonably practicable for the documents to be produced in the required manner before the day on which the proceedings for non-production were commenced by the laying of an information. A defendant may instead produce a *current* receipt for a licence surrendered for a fixed penalty.

C[17.20] The burden of proof to establish any of these defences rests with the defendant, however he does not have to prove his point beyond reasonable doubt but only on the balance of probabilities.

Sentencing

SC Guideline – failing to produce documents

C[17.21] Starting point – Band A fine (special considerations: fine per offence, not per document).

C[17.22] For fines see B[28].

C[18]

Driving licence offences

Charges (Driving licence offences)

C[18.1] Driving on a road a motor vehicle otherwise than in accordance with a licence to drive a vehicle of that class

Road Traffic Act 1988, s 87

Maximum penalty-Fine level 3. May disqualify for any period and must endorse, unless special reasons exist (except where the driving of the accused was in accordance with any licence that could have been granted to him).

Penalty points – 3–6 (fixed penalty 3).

Fixed penalty – £60.

Legal notes and definitions

C[18.2] On an appropriate application the Secretary of State may grant a provisional licence with a view to the applicant passing a test of competence to drive. A provisional licence is subject to conditions and restrictions such as to class of vehicle which may be driven, or, in the case of motor cycles, the power of the engine. Breach of any of these conditions or restrictions is an offence (Road Traffic Act 1988, s 87 and the Motor Vehicles (Driving Licences) Regulations 1987).

C[18.3] For driving a motor car a provisional licence holder must comply with the following conditions:

(a) *Learner plates*. He must clearly display front and rear in a conspicuous position a red letter 'L' of regulation size (102mm x 89mm x 38mm) on a white background (178mm × 178mm; the corners may be rounded off).

(b) *Supervision*. He must be supervised by a qualified driver. This offence applies to three-wheeled cars.

C[18.4] From July 1999 all driving licence applications are in the form of the new photocard type licence.

C[18.5] Supervised. Means that the supervisor must have been in a suitable part of the vehicle for supervising. For example, if the supervisor was in a rear seat from which it was difficult to supervise, the court may decide the defendant was not supervised. If a supervised driver is convicted of an offence, eg driving without due care, the supervisor can be convicted of aiding and abetting.

C[18.6] Qualified driver. Means that the supervisor must have held a full licence to drive the same type of vehicle for at least three years and be at least 21 years of age (exemption is provided for the military).

C[18.7] Motor cyclists who are learners must not drive or ride a motorcycle to which a sidecar is not attached and carry a passenger. A motor cycle which has a bare chassis or framework attached to its side does not have a side car.

C[18.8] Driving. A person steering a car whilst another person pushes the vehicle is driving. A person who walks alongside his car, pushing it and steering it with one hand is not driving it. A motor cyclist sitting on his machine and propelling it along with his feet is driving but he is not driving it if he walks beside it pushing it [but he may be "riding" the vehicle] (*Gunnell v DPP* [1993] Crim LR 619). A person sitting in the driver's seat of a car, stationary but with the engine running, was found to be driving. (*Planton v DPP* [2001] EWHC 450 (Admin), (2001) 166 JP 324). In *DPP v Alderton* [2003] EWHC 2917 (Admin), [2003] All ER (D) 360 (Nov) the defendant was driving even though the car was stationary on the verge as the wheels were spinning and he was exercising control over the vehicle by use of the handbrake. In *R (on the application of Traves) v DPP* [2005] EWHC 1482 (Admin), 169 JP 421, applying the brakes to a vehicle being towed was held to be "driving".

C[18.9] A person pushed a motor cycle along a road, its lights were on and he had used the brakes. At some point he had turned the ignition on for long enough to warm up the exhaust pipe. When apprehended he was astride the machine and was wearing a crash helmet. It was held to be within the magistrates' discretion to find that he was driving (*McKoen v Ellis* [1987] RTR 26, 151 JP 60, [1987] Crim LR 54). A person is driving who steers and brakes a vehicle being towed by a rope or chain. The position with regard to a vehicle drawn by a rigid tow bar has not been authoritatively decided but a case decided in 1985 implies that a person in the driving seat of the towed vehicle in such a case is not driving. The nature of the force used to put or keep a vehicle in motion is irrelevant in determining whether a person is driving. The essence of driving is the use of the driver's controls in order to direct the movement, however that movement is produced (*Traves v DPP* [2005] EWHC 1482 (Admin), 169 JP 421, sub nom Traves v DPP [2005] All ER (D) 381 (Jun)). An important test in deciding whether a person is driving is whether he was in a substantial sense controlling the movement and direction of the vehicle. If he is, then the question has to be answered whether his actions fall within the ordinary meaning of the word 'driving'. It is also helpful to consider whether the defendant himself deliberately set the vehicle in motion and also the length of time that he was handling the controls. A person who knelt on the driving seat of a vehicle, released the handbrake and thereafter attempted to reapply the handbrake to stop the movement of the vehicle was held to be driving the vehicle. However a momentary seizing of the steering wheel causing the vehicle to swerve cannot properly be said to be driving (*DPP v Hastings* [1993] RTR 205, 158 JP 118). In *Cawthorn v DPP* [2000] RTR 45, sub nom Cawthorn v Newcastle upon Tyne Crown Court (1994) 164 JP 527 a man who had left his vehicle briefly to post a letter, leaving the hazard warning lights on, was held to be the driver responsible for reporting an accident when the vehicle rolled down a hill and into a wall.

C[18.10]–[18.15] Motor vehicle. See C[9.7].

C[18.16] **A road.** Is any highway (including footpaths and bridleways) and any other road to which the public has access and includes bridges. However it will not normally include a car park (*Clarke v Kato* [1998] 4 All ER 417, [1998] 1 WLR 1647, sub nom Clarke v General Accident Fire and Life Assurance Corpn plc [1999] RTR 153, 163 JP 502, HL).

C[18.17] **Burden of proof.** Proof that the driver held the appropriate driving licence rests with the defendant. The prosecution does not have to prove that the defendant did not hold a licence. As with all document offences there is not statutory requirement that the prosecution issue the defendant with a production notice; it is sufficient that they show he drove the vehicle on a road (*DPP v Hay* [2005] EWHC 1395 (Admin), [2005] All ER (D) 90 (Jun)).

C[18.18] The driver does not have to prove this beyond reasonable doubt. He need only prove that on the balance of probabilities he did hold a licence.

C[18.19] **Employers.** No employer shall let an employee drive unless the employee holds the appropriate driving licence, and it is his responsibility to make the necessary check that the employee has such a licence. Thus the employer is liable for permitting unless he can prove that his employee was licensed. Being misled by the employee is probably not a defence though the court might consider it a mitigating circumstance.

C[18.20] A partner is neither the employee nor employer of another partner in the same firm.

Sentencing

SC Guideline – No driving licence

C[18.21] Starting point – Band A fine (Special considerations: Aggravating factor if no licence ever held).

C[18.22] If it appears to the court that the accused suffers from some disease or physical disability likely to cause his driving to be a source of danger to the public, then the court shall notify the licensing authority. Even if the accused has never obtained a licence, the court may consider it appropriate to bring the disease or disability to the attention of the licensing authority in case the accused should apply for a licence at some future date (see C[5.49]).

C[18.23] A defendant will generally not have a licence because he has not passed a test. Therefore, the case is serious and may attract a high fine and compulsory endorsement.

C[18.24] For fines see B[28].

Large goods vehicles

C[18.24A] It is an offence to drive a large goods vehicle (or to employ a person to do so) unless the driver holds a large goods vehicle driving licence authorising him to drive large goods vehicles of that class. The LGV licence is an additional entitlement to the ordinary licence.

C[18.25]–[18.30] **Penalty.** Same as for an ordinary licence. For definition of large goods vehicle consult the legal adviser.

C[18.31] Under the provisions of the Road Traffic (Driver Licensing and Information Systems) Act 1989 existing Heavy Goods Vehicle Licences will be phased out. Instead a driver who passes an appropriate test of competency and who satisfies the Secretary of State that he is a fit person may be granted a 'large goods vehicle licence' which is in effect an ordinary driving licence which authorises the holder to drive vehicles of the classes formerly covered by a Heavy Goods Vehicle Licence. The penalty for driving without a licence is the same as for an ordinary licence.

C[18.32] The new style licences were issued from 1 October 1990 for licences commencing on or after 1 January 1991 and as existing HGV licences become due for renewal.

C[19]

Driving whilst disqualified

Charge (Driving whilst disqualified)

C[19.1] Driving a motor vehicle on a road when disqualified for holding or obtaining a driving licence

Road Traffic Act 1988, s 103

Maximum penalty-Fine level 5* and 6 months' imprisonment (for fines see B[28]). May disqualify for any period and/or until a driving test has been passed. Must endorse unless special reasons. Triable only by magistrates.

Penalty points – 6.

* Section 85 of the Legal Aid, Sentencing and Punishment of Offenders Act 2012 provides that where a relevant offence would on commencement day be punishable on summary conviction by a fine or maximum fine of £5,000, however expressed, and the offence was committed on or after that date, the court may impose a fine of any amount. The commencement date is 12 March 2015: see the Legal Aid, Sentencing and Punishment of Offenders Act 2012 (Commencement No 11) Order 2015, SI 2015/504.

Legal notes and definitions

C[19.2] **Time limit.** Subject to overall maximum of three years, proceedings may be brought within six months from when, in the prosecutor's opinion, he had sufficient evidence to warrant proceedings. A certificate signed by or on behalf of the prosecutor, as to when that date was, is conclusive evidence on that point.

C[19.3] **Driving.** See the notes under the offence of driving without a licence at C[18.8]–C[18.9]. Once it is established that a person was driving, he may continue to be the driver of a vehicle although his conduct has changed and he no longer fulfils the test mentioned on that page.

C[19.4] **Motor vehicle.** See C[9.7].

C[19.5] **Road.** Means any highway (including footpaths and bridleways) and any other road to which the public has access and includes bridges.

C[19.6] **Disqualified.** The prosecution must prove the defendant was driving and that the record of disqualification relates to that defendant, although there are a number of ways in which this can be done (*R v Derwentside Magistrates' Court, ex p Swift* [1997] RTR 89, 160 JP 468). It is the prosecution's task to prove all the elements of the offence and it is therefore not for the court to consult its own records to show that the defendant was in fact a disqualified driver (*Kingsnorth v DPP* [2003] All ER (D) 235 (Mar)). In *R (on the application of Howe) v South Durham Justices* [2004] EWHC 362 (Admin), 168 JP 424, [2004] All ER (D) 226 (Feb) a court permitted the defendant's solicitor to be a witness summoned for the purposes of identifying the disqualified person. A defendant disqualified in his absence and subsequently arrested for driving whilst disqualified may make a statutory declaration to the effect that he did not know of the proceedings. However this will make the earlier proceedings void but not void ab initio leaving the disqualification as valid at the time he was driving (*Singh v DPP* [1999] RTR 424, 164 JP 82, [1999] Crim LR 914).

In *Pattison v DPP* [2005] EWHC 2938 (Admin), [2006] 2 All ER 317, it was held that evidence of identity could be proved by admission (formal or otherwise), fingerprints, a witness who was present in court, or a match between the personal details of the accused and a certificate of conviction. Even where the personal details were not uncommon eg the name, address and date of birth of the accused, that might be sufficient to found a prima facie case. See also *Mills v DPP* [2008] EWHC 3304 (Admin), [2009] RTR 143.

C[19.7] Knowledge. It is not necessary to prove that the defendant knew he was disqualified, nor that he knew he was on a road. When disqualified until a test is passed the onus is on the defendant to show that he held a provisional licence and was complying with the conditions of that licence at the time he was driving (*DPP v Baker* (2004) 168 JP 140, [2004] All ER (D) 28 (Nov), DC).

Sentencing
SC Guideline – Driving whilst Disqualified

Drive whilst disqualified (Revised 2017)

C[19.8]

Road Traffic Act 1988, s 103

Effective from: 24 April 2017

Triable only summarily:

Maximum: Unlimited fine and/or 6 months

Offence range: Band C fine–26 weeks' custody

Step 1 — Determining the offence category

The Court should determine the offence category using the table below.

Category 1	Higher culpability **and** greater harm
Category 2	Higher culpability **and** lesser harm **or** lower culpability **and** greater harm
Category 3	Lower culpability **and** lesser harm

The court should determine the offender's culpability and the harm caused with reference **only** to the factors below. Where an offence does not fall squarely into a category, individual factors may require a degree of weighting before making an overall assessment and determining the appropriate offence category.

CULPABILITY demonstrated by one or more of the following:

Factors indicating higher culpability

- Driving shortly after disqualification imposed
- Vehicle obtained during disqualification period
- Driving for reward

Factors indicating lower culpability

- All other cases

HARM demonstrated by one or more of the following:

Factors indicating greater harm

- Significant distance driven
- Evidence of associated bad driving

Factors indicating lesser harm

- All other cases

Step 2 — Starting point and category range

Having determined the category at step one, the court should use the appropriate starting point to reach a sentence within the category range in the table below. The starting point applies to all offenders irrespective of plea or previous convictions.

Level of seriousness	Starting Point	Range	Penalty points/disqualification
Category 1	12 weeks' custody	High Level community order–26 weeks' custody	Disqualify for 12–18 months beyond expiry of current ban (Extend if imposing immediate custody)
Category 2	High level community order	Medium level community order–12 weeks' custody	Disqualify for 6–12 months beyond expiry of current ban (Extend if imposing immediate custody)
Category 3	Low level community order	Band C fine–Medium level community order	Disqualify for 3–6 months beyond expiry of current ban OR 6 points

- **Must endorse and may disqualify. If no disqualification impose 6 points**
- **Extend disqualification if imposing immediate custody**

The court should then consider further adjustment for any aggravating or mitigating factors. The following is a **non-exhaustive** list of additional factual elements providing the context of the offence and factors relating to the offender. Identify whether any combination of these, or other relevant factors, should result in an upward or downward adjustment from the sentence arrived at so far.

Factors increasing seriousness

Statutory aggravating factors:

- Previous convictions, having regard to a) the **nature** of the offence to which the conviction relates and its **relevance** to the current offence; and b) the **time** that has elapsed since the conviction
  Note
  An offender convicted of this offence will always have at least one relevant previous conviction for the offence that resulted in disqualification. The starting points and ranges take this into account; any other previous convictions should be considered in the usual way.
- Offence committed whilst on bail

Other aggravating factors:

- Failure to comply with current court orders (not including the current order for disqualification)
- Offence committed on licence or post sentence supervision
- Carrying passengers
- Giving false details

Factors reducing seriousness or reflecting personal mitigation

- No previous convictions **or** no relevant/recent convictions
- Good character and/or exemplary conduct
- Remorse
- Genuine emergency established
- Age and/or lack of maturity where it affects the responsibility of the offender

- Serious medical condition requiring urgent, intensive or long-term treatment
- Sole or primary carer for dependent relatives

Step 3 — Consider any factors which indicate a reduction, such as assistance to the prosecution

The court should take into account sections 73 and 74 of the Serious Organised Crime and Police Act 2005 (assistance by defendants: reduction or review of sentence) and any other rule of law by virtue of which an offender may receive a discounted sentence in consequence of assistance given (or offered) to the prosecutor or investigator.

Step 4 — Reduction for guilty pleas

The court should take account of any potential reduction for a guilty plea in accordance with section 144 of the Criminal Justice Act 2003 and the *Guilty Plea* guideline.

Step 5 — Totality principle

If sentencing an offender for more than one offence, or where the offender is already serving a sentence, consider whether the total sentence is just and proportionate to the overall offending behaviour in accordance with the *Offences Taken into Consideration and Totality* guideline.

Step 6 — Compensation and ancillary orders

In all cases, the court should consider whether to make compensation and/or other ancillary orders including disqualification from driving.

Step 7 — Reasons

Section 174 of the Criminal Justice Act 2003 imposes a duty to give reasons for, and explain the effect of, the sentence.

Step 8 — Consideration for time spent on bail

The court must consider whether to give credit for time spent on bail in accordance with section 240A of the Criminal Justice Act 2003.

C[19.9] See Table B at B[43.2] for available sentences.

C[19.10] If it appears to the magistrates that the accused suffers from a disease or physical disability likely to cause his driving to be a source of danger to the public, they must notify the licensing authority in case the accused applies for a licence at some future date (see C[5.49]).

C[19.11]–[19.17] The offence does not apply to offenders who are driving under age. They are guilty of driving otherwise than in accordance with a licence, see C[18].

C[20]

'Unfit through drink or drugs' (drive/attempt drive)

Charge ('Unfit through drink or drugs' (drive/attempt))

C[20.1] **Driving or attempting to drive a mechanically propelled vehicle on a road (or public place) when unfit through drink or drugs**

Road Traffic Act 1988, s 4(1), as amended

Maximum penalty – Fine level 5* and 6 months' imprisonment (for fines see B[28]). Must disqualify for at least one year unless special reasons. The disqualification may be for any period exceeding a year. He may also be ordered to pass a driving test. Must endorse licence unless special reasons exist.

Where a person has been convicted within the ten years immediately preceding the present offence of any of the following offences, the minimum period of disqualification increases to three years. The offences are:

- s 3A (causing death by careless driving when under the influence of drink or drugs);
- s 4(1) (driving or attempting to drive while unfit);
- s 5(1)(a) (driving or attempting to drive with excess alcohol);
- s 5A(1)(a) and (2) (driving or attempting to drive with concentration of specified controlled drug above specified limit);
- s 7(6) (failing to provide a specimen) where that is an offence involving obligatory disqualification; and
- s 7A(6) (failing to allow a specimen to be subjected to laboratory test) where that is an offence involving obligatory disqualification.

Penalty points – 3–11.

---

* Section 85 of the Legal Aid, Sentencing and Punishment of Offenders Act 2012 provides that where a relevant offence would on commencement day be punishable on summary conviction by a fine or maximum fine of £5,000, however expressed, and the offence was committed on or after that date, the court may impose a fine of any amount. The commencement date is 12 March 2015: see the Legal Aid, Sentencing and Punishment of Offenders Act 2012 (Commencement No 11) Order 2015, SI 2015/504.

Legal notes and definitions

C[20.2] The charge may allege either driving or attempting to drive. It must not allege both.

C[20.3] The court must be satisfied that the defendant drove (or attempted to drive) a mechanically propelled vehicle on a road or public place when his ability to drive properly was impaired by drink or drugs. The offence is one of strict liability and therefore the defence of insanity is not available (*DPP v H* [1997] 1 WLR 1406, [1998] RTR 200, sub nom DPP v Harper (1997) 161 JP 697).

C[20.4] **Driving.** See the notes under this heading for the offence of driving without a licence at C[18.9].

C[20.5] **Mechanically propelled vehicle.** See C[47.9].

C[20.6] **Road.** Means any highway (including footpaths and bridleways) and any other road to which the public has access and includes bridges.

C[20.7] Public place. Need not be a road. A field or enclosure at the rear of licensed premises for parking cars has been held to be a public place. In *Lewis v DPP* [2004] EWHC 3081 (Admin), [2005] All ER (D) 66 (Jan), it was decided that magistrates were entitled to infer that a public house car park was a public place and that the prosecution did not need to adduce evidence of public utilisation. See also *May v DPP* [2005] EWHC 1280 (Admin), [2005] All ER (D) 182 (Apr).

Car parks may or may not be 'other public places', depending on the extent, purpose and legality of public accessibility. In *Richardson v DPP* [2019] EWHC 428 (Admin), [2019] Crim LR 733, [2019] All ER (D) 39 (Mar) the justices rejected a submission of no case to answer and ultimately convicted the defendant on the basis that the car park in question was a public place because:

(a) it had no physical restrictions on access;
(b) there were a number of different signs for different parking spaces; and
(c) the defendant was parked as a member of the public.

The Administrative Court quashed the conviction. The submission of no case to answer should have succeeded. The photographic evidence showed that the car park comprised several different parking areas, for use by different groups, and some were unquestionably private. This alone was fatal to the conviction. Secondly, there was an absence of evidence of any use by the public, as opposed to members of the public who happened to have business at the premises served by the car park. Thirdly, there was an absence of evidence that, even if the public did in fact use the car park, they had lawful permission to do so. This, again, would on its own be fatal to the conviction

C[20.8] Whether the scene of the charge is a road or public place is a question of fact for the court to decide (such as a car park in (*R v Spence* [1999] RTR 353, 163 JP 754, [1999] Crim LR 975, CA; or the parking area of a privately owned tyre and exhaust centre: *Filmer v DPP* [2006] EWHC 3450 (Admin), [2006] All ER (D) 08 (Nov)). See *Hallett v DPP* [2011] EWHC 488 (Admin) in which the key question was whether there was before the justices evidence of public use of an unmade service road. Any road might be regarded as open to which the public had access if the public was there without overcoming physical obstruction or in defiance of a prohibition. Whether a place was public would generally be a question of fact and degree. Help might also be derived from asking whether access was only for a special class of members of the public, including guests of residents, postmen and milkmen. A sign or barrier lent weight to restriction of the area to a special class and thus to it being private, but the absence of a sign or barrier was not determinative.

In *Cowan v DPP* [2013] EWHC 192 (Admin), (2013) 177 JP 474 the appellant was driving on an internal roadway at the Kingston Hill Campus of Kingston University when the car left the road. He was later breathalysed and found to be over the limit. The justices convicted the appellant. However, they did not identify which members of the public had access to the site and for what purpose. This resulted in the quashing of the conviction. There were no doubt university campuses which provided a means of passage for ordinary members of the public. However, in the present case, there was simply no evidence of such use. What was required was a finding that the public did use the roadway on the campus as members of the public. Students were not to be treated as members of the public; they had a right to occupy their rooms and make use of the facilities not as members of the public, but in their status as students. As to their visitors, in gaining access to the site, they were not doing so as ordinary members of the public, but for the purposes of the occupier of the site. However, the court emphasised that it would not have taken much additional evidence to establish that members of the public did have access to the site and the result did not mean that anyone could drive against the law on the scores of university campuses in the United Kingdom.

C[20.9] Unfit. A person is taken to be unfit to drive if his ability to drive properly is for the time being impaired. It need not be proved that the defendant was *incapable* of driving.

C[20.10] The court may take note of such evidence as, for example, where there is evidence of drink or drugs:

(a) driving erratically;
(b) colliding with a stationary object for no apparent reason;
(c) the defendant's condition-slurred speech, staggering, mental confusion. Also account may be taken of evidence of an analyst's certificate where the accused has given a sample of blood/breath/urine.

C[20.11]–[20.15] Even where the defendant has taken a drink subsequent to the incident the certificate may be evidence of the amount of alcohol consumed at the time of the incident unless the accused proves on the balance of probabilities that had he not consumed the subsequent drink his ability to drive would not have been impaired.

C[20.16] A witness who is not an expert can give his impressions as to whether an accused had taken drink but he may not give evidence whether the accused was fit to drive.

C[20.17] **Drink or drugs.** Drink means an alcoholic drink. Drugs can refer to medicine, ie something given to cure, alleviate or assist an ailing body, or it can be something which, when consumed, affected the control of the body. Accordingly, 'glue sniffing' would come within the ambit of this offence.

C[20.18] **Alternative verdict.** If the allegation is 'driving' the court may convict on the basis of attempting to drive. Where the defendant is found not guilty of an offence under s 4(1) but the allegations amount to or include an offence under the Road Traffic Act 1988, s 4(2) (being in charge when unfit to drive through drink or drugs) the court may convict him of that offence (Road Traffic Offenders Act 1988, s 24 as substituted by the Road Traffic Act 1991, s 24).

Sentencing

SC Guideline – Unfit through drink or drugs (drive/attempt to drive)

Unfit through drink or drugs (drive/ attempt to drive) (Revised 2017)

C[20.19]

Road Traffic Act 1988, s 4(1)

Effective from: 24 April 2017

Triable only summarily:

Maximum: Unlimited fine and/or 6 months

Offence range: Band B fine–26 weeks' custody

Step 1 — Determining the offence category

The Court should determine the offence category using the table below.

Category 1	Higher culpability and greater harm
Category 2	Higher culpability and lesser harm or lower culpability and greater harm
Category 3	Lower culpability and lesser harm

The court should determine the offender's culpability and the harm caused with reference only to the factors below. Where an offence does not fall squarely into a category, individual factors may require a degree of weighting before making an overall assessment and determining the appropriate offence category.

CULPABILITY demonstrated by one or more of the following:

Factors indicating higher culpability

- Driving LGV, HGV or PSV etc.
- Driving for hire or reward

Factors indicating lower culpability

- All other cases

HARM demonstrated by one or more of the following:

Factors indicating greater harm

- High level of impairment

Factors indicating lesser harm

- All other cases

Step 2 — Starting point and category range

Having determined the category at step one, the court should use the appropriate starting point to reach a sentence within the category range in the table below.

- **Must endorse and disqualify for at least 12 months**
- **Must disqualify for at least 2 years if offender has had two or more disqualifications for periods of 56 days or more in preceding 3 years – refer to the disqualification guidance and consult your legal adviser for further guidance**
- **Must disqualify for at least 3 years if offender has been convicted of a relevant offence in preceding 10 years -consult your legal adviser for further guidance**
- **Extend disqualification if imposing immediate custody**

If there is a delay in sentencing after conviction, consider interim disqualification.

The starting point applies to all offenders irrespective of plea or previous convictions.

Level of seriousness	Starting point	Range	Disqualification	Disqual. 2nd offence in 10 years
Category 1	12 weeks' custody	High level community order–26 weeks' custody	29–36 months (Extend if imposing immediate custody)	36–60 months (Extend if imposing immediate custody
Category 2	Medium level community order	Low level community order–High level community order	17–28 months	36–52 months
Category 3	Band C fine	Band B fine–Low level community order	12–16 months	36–40 months

Note: when considering the guidance regarding the length of disqualification in the case of a second offence, the period to be imposed in any individual case will depend on an assessment of all the relevant circumstances, including the length of time since the earlier ban was imposed and the gravity of the current offence but disqualification must be for at least three years.

The court should then consider further adjustment for any aggravating or mitigating factors. The following is a **non-exhaustive** list of additional factual elements providing the context of the offence and factors relating to the offender. Identify whether any combination of these, or other relevant factors, should result in an upward or downward adjustment from the sentence arrived at so far.

Factors increasing seriousness

Statutory aggravating factors:

- Previous convictions, having regard to a) the nature of the offence to which the conviction relates and its relevance to the current offence; and b) the time that has elapsed since the conviction
- Offence committed whilst on bail

Other aggravating factors:

- Failure to comply with current court orders
- Offence committed on licence or post sentence supervision
- Poor road or weather conditions
- Evidence of unacceptable standard of driving
- Involved in accident
- Carrying passengers
- High level of traffic or pedestrians in the vicinity

Factors reducing seriousness or reflecting personal mitigation

- No previous convictions or no relevant/recent convictions
- Remorse
- Good character and/or exemplary conduct
- Serious medical condition requiring urgent, intensive or long-term treatment
- Age and/or lack of maturity where it affects the responsibility of the offender
- Mental disorder or learning disability
- Sole or primary carer for dependent relatives

Step 3 — Consider any factors which indicate a reduction, such as assistance to the prosecution

The court should take into account sections 73 and 74 of the Serious Organised Crime and Police Act 2005 (assistance by defendants: reduction or review of sentence) and any other rule of law by virtue of which an offender may receive a discounted sentence in consequence of assistance given (or offered) to the prosecutor or investigator.

Step 4 — Reduction for guilty pleas

The court should take account of any potential reduction for a guilty plea in accordance with section 144 of the Criminal Justice Act 2003 and the *Guilty Plea* guideline.

Step 5 — Totality principle

If sentencing an offender for more than one offence, or where the offender is already serving a sentence, consider whether the total sentence is just and proportionate to the overall offending behaviour in accordance with the *Offences Taken into Consideration and Totality* guideline.

Step 6 — Compensation and ancillary orders

In all cases, the court should consider whether to make compensation and/or other ancillary orders including offering a drink/drive rehabilitation course, deprivation, and /or forfeiture or suspension of personal liquor licence.

Step 7 — Reasons

Section 174 of the Criminal Justice Act 2003 imposes a duty to give reasons for, and explain the effect of, the sentence.

Step 8 — Consideration for time spent on bail

The court must consider whether to give credit for time spent on bail in accordance with section 240A of the Criminal Justice Act 2003.

C[20.20] See Table B at B[43.2] for available sentences and the notes to the offence of 'Alcohol over the prescribed limit' at C[22.2] and C[22.56] for rehabilitation courses and their effect upon disqualifications.

C[21]

'Unfit through drink or drugs (in charge)'

Charge ('Unfit through drink or drugs (in charge)')

C[21.1] **Being in charge of a mechanically propelled vehicle on a road (or public place) when unfit through drink or drugs**

Road Traffic Act 1988, s 4(2), as amended

Maximum penalty – Fine level 4 and 3 months' imprisonment (for fines see B[28]). May disqualify for any period and/or until a driving test has been passed. Must endorse unless there are special reasons.

Penalty points – 10.

Legal notes and definitions

C[21.2] See the notes for the offence of 'drunken driving' at C[20.2].

C[21.3] **In charge.** This is a potentially wide concept. There must be proof of some connection, which can be less than attempting to drive, between the defendant and a motor vehicle on a road or public place. The owner or a person who had recently driven the vehicle would be 'in charge' unless he put the vehicle in someone else's charge or unless there was no realistic possibility of his resuming actual control, eg where he was at home in bed or a great distance from the car (*DPP v Watkins* [1989] QB 821, [1989] 1 All ER 1126 where there is further guidance in respect of defendants who are not the owner or have not recently driven the vehicle). A qualified driver supervising a provisional licence holder is 'in charge'.

C[21.4] A person is deemed not to be in charge if he can demonstrate from the evidence that at the material time the circumstances were such that there was no likelihood of his driving the vehicle so long as he remained unfit to drive through drink or drugs but in determining whether there was such a likelihood the court may disregard any injury to him and any damage to the vehicle. A supervisor of a learner driver is in charge and may need to take over at any time (*DPP v Janman* [2004] EWHC 101 (Admin), [2004] Crim LR 478, [2004] All ER (D) 171 (Jan)).

C[21.4A] **ECHR.** The House of Lords held that this was a reasonable and legitimate burden on the defendant (*Sheldrake v DPP* [2003] EWHC 273 (Admin), [2004] QB 487; revsd [2004] UKHL 43, [2004] 3 WLR 976).

Sentencing

SC Guideline – Unfit through drink or drugs (in charge)

Unfit through drink or drugs (in charge)
(Revised 2017)

C[21.5]

Road Traffic Act, 1988, s 4(2)

Effective from: 24 April 2017

Triable only summarily:

Maximum: Level 4 fine and/ or 3 months

Offence range: Band B fine–12 weeks' custody

Step 1 — Determining the offence category

The Court should determine the offence category using the table below.

Category 1	Higher culpability and greater harm
Category 2	Higher culpability and lesser harm or lower culpability and greater harm
Category 3	Lower culpability and lesser harm

The court should determine the offender's culpability and the harm caused with reference only to the factors below. Where an offence does not fall squarely into a category, individual factors may require a degree of weighting before making an overall assessment and determining the appropriate offence category.

CULPABILITY demonstrated by one or more of the following:

Factors indicating higher culpability

- High likelihood of driving
- In charge of LGV, HGV or PSV etc.
- Offering to drive for hire or reward

Factors indicating lower culpability

- All other cases

HARM demonstrated by one or more of the following:

Factors indicating greater harm

- High level of impairment

Factors indicating lesser harm

- All other cases

Step 2 — Starting point and category range

Having determined the category at step one, the court should use the appropriate starting point to reach a sentence within the category range in the table below.

- **Must endorse and may disqualify. If no disqualification impose 10 points**
- **Extend disqualification if imposing immediate custody**

The starting point applies to all offenders irrespective of plea or previous convictions.

Level of seriousness	Starting Point	Range	Disqualification/points
Category 1	High level community order	Medium level community order–12 weeks' custody	Consider disqualification (extend if imposing immediate custody) OR 10 points
Category 2	Band C fine	Band B fine–Medium level community order	Consider disqualification OR 10 points
Category 3	Band B fine	Band B fine	10 points

The court should then consider further adjustment for any aggravating or mitigating factors. The following is a **non-exhaustive** list of additional factual elements providing the context of the offence and factors relating to the offender. Identify whether any combination of these, or other relevant factors, should result in an upward or downward adjustment from the sentence arrived at so far.

Factors increasing seriousness

Statutory aggravating factors:

- Previous convictions, having regard to a) the **nature** of the offence to which the conviction relates and its **relevance** to the current offence; and b) the **time** that has elapsed since the conviction
- Offence committed whilst on bail

Other aggravating factors:

- Failure to comply with current court orders
- Offence committed on licence or post sentence supervision

Factors reducing seriousness or reflecting personal mitigation

- No previous convictions **or** no relevant/recent convictions
- Remorse
- Good character and/or exemplary conduct
- Serious medical condition requiring urgent, intensive or long-term treatment
- Age and/or lack of maturity where it affects the responsibility of the offender
- Mental disorder or learning disability
- Sole or primary carer for dependent relatives

Step 3 — Consider any factors which indicate a reduction, such as assistance to the prosecution

The court should take into account sections 73 and 74 of the Serious Organised Crime and Police Act 2005 (assistance by defendants: reduction or review of sentence) and any other rule of law by virtue of which an offender may receive a discounted sentence in consequence of assistance given (or offered) to the prosecutor or investigator.

Step 4 — Reduction for guilty pleas

The court should take account of any potential reduction for a guilty plea in accordance with section 144 of the Criminal Justice Act 2003 and the *Guilty Plea* guideline.

Step 5 — Totality principle

If sentencing an offender for more than one offence, or where the offender is already serving a sentence, consider whether the total sentence is just and proportionate to the overall offending behaviour in accordance with the *Offences Taken into Consideration and Totality* guideline.

Step 6 — Compensation and ancillary orders

In all cases, the court should consider whether to make compensation and/or other ancillary orders including offering a drink/drive rehabilitation course, deprivation, and /or forfeiture or suspension of personal liquor licence.

Step 7 — Reasons

Section 174 of the Criminal Justice Act 2003 imposes a duty to give reasons for, and explain the effect of, the sentence.

Step 8 — Consideration for time spent on bail

The court must consider whether to give credit for time spent on bail in accordance with section 240A of the Criminal Justice Act 2003.

C[21.6] See Table B at B[43.2] for available sentences and the notes to the offence of 'Alcohol over the prescribed limit' at C[22.2].

C[22]

Excess alcohol (drive/attempt to drive or in charge)

Charge 1 (Excess alcohol (drive/attempt or in charge))

C[22.1] Driving (or attempting to drive) a motor vehicle on a road (or public place) with alcohol above the prescribed limit

Road Traffic Act 1988, s 5(1)(a)

Maximum penalty-Fine level 5* and 6 months' imprisonment (for fines see B[28]). Must disqualify for at least one year unless special reasons. The disqualification may be for any period exceeding a year. The defendant may also be ordered to take a test again. Must endorse licence unless special reasons.

It is not a special reason that the defendant's driving was not impaired.

Where a person has been convicted within the ten years immediately preceding the present offence of any of the following offences, the minimum period of disqualification increases to three years. The offences are:

- s 3A (causing death by careless driving when under the influence of drink or drugs);
- s 4(1) (driving or attempting to drive while unfit);
- s 5(1)(a) (driving or attempting to drive with excess alcohol);
- s 5A(1)(a) and (2) (driving or attempting to drive with concentration of specified controlled drug above specified limit);
- s 7(6) (failing to provide a specimen) where that is an offence involving obligatory disqualification; and
- s 7A(6) (failing to allow a specimen to be subjected to laboratory test) where that is an offence involving obligatory disqualification.

Penalty points – 3–11.

---

* Section 85 of the Legal Aid, Sentencing and Punishment of Offenders Act 2012 provides that where a relevant offence would on commencement day be punishable on summary conviction by a fine or maximum fine of £5,000, however expressed, and the offence was committed on or after that date, the court may impose a fine of any amount. The commencement date is 12 March 2015: see the Legal Aid, Sentencing and Punishment of Offenders Act 2012 (Commencement No 11) Order 2015, SI 2015/504.

Legal notes and definitions

C[22.2] The charge may allege either driving or attempting to drive. It is important to note that it must not allege both. The prosecution need not prove that the defendant's ability to drive was impaired.

C[22.3] **Driving.** See the notes under the offence of no driving licence at C[18.2].

C[22.4] **Motor vehicle.** See C[9.7].

C[22.5] **Road.** Means any highway (including footpaths and bridleways) and any other road to which the public has access and includes bridges. The information may read 'road or other public place', but if it does not the specific allegation must be proved (*Plunkett v DPP* [2004] EWHC 1937 (Admin), [2004] All ER (D) 82 (Jul)).

C[22.6] Public place. Need not be a road. A field or enclosure at the rear of licensed premises for parking cars has been held to be a public place (see C[20.7]).

C[22.7] Whether the scene of the charge is a road or public place is a question of fact for the court to decide. It is basically a question of whether at the relevant time the public enjoyed access to the place where the offence was committed.

C[22.8] Prescribed limit. If a blood specimen was provided by the defendant the prescribed limit is 80 mg of alcohol in 100 ml of blood; if a urine specimen, 107 mg of alcohol in 100 ml of urine; if breath, 35 µg of alcohol in 100 ml of breath. Comparison of these levels is achieved by multiplying a breath/alcohol level by 2.3 and rounding up to convert to blood alcohol. The following conversion table relates blood, urine and breath levels.

C[22.9]

Blood	*Urine*	*Breath*	*Blood*	*Urine*	*Breath*
80	107	35	110	147	48
83	110	36	113	150	49
85	113	37	115	153	50
87	116	38	117	156	51
90	119	39	120	159	52
92	122	40	122	162	53
94	125	41	124	165	54
97	129	42	126	168	55
99	132	43	129	171	56
101	135	44	131	174	57
103	138	45	133	177	58
106	141	46	136	181	59
108	144	47	138	184	60
140	187	61	163	217	71
143	190	62	166	220	72
145	193	63	168	223	73
147	196	64	170	226	74
147	199	65	172	230	75
152	154	205	175	233	76
154	205	67	178	236	77
156	208	68	180	239	78
159	211	69	182	242	79
161	214	70	184	245	80

C[22.10]–[22.15] Breath tests. A constable in uniform may require a person to submit to a breath test if the constable reasonably suspects him to have alcohol in his body or to have committed a traffic offence while the vehicle was in motion. The test may also be required in these circumstances after a person has ceased to be a driver. If the test indicates the presence of alcohol the driver need not, but may be, arrested and taken to a police station where he will be required to offer a specimen of blood, urine or breath at the choice of the police. The roadside breath test may be taken by blowing into a bag or into a machine, but these devices are a preliminary test and the sample of breath used in these tests is not the one which is analysed to determine its alcohol content.

Once a negative breath test has been given, the police lose the power of arrest under the Road Traffic Act 1988, s 6, but may in appropriate circumstances arrest under s 4 of the Act (*DPP v Robertson* [2002] 15 LS Gaz R 33).

Breath is not confined to deep lung air but includes all that is exhaled (*Zafar v DPP* (2004) Times, 1 November).

C[22.16] Approved device. If the police require a breath sample for analysis it will be analysed in a machine approved by the Secretary of State such as a Lion Intoxilyzer 6000 UK. It works by, analysing the level of alcohol in the breath by the absorption of infra red radiation and giving a printed record of the result of two samples of breath given within a short time. The lower reading is the one which will be used to determine whether a prosecution will follow. Each machine works with a simulator, a device enabling the machine to check itself for accuracy. If for any reason the police decide not to use the machine they may ask for a sample of blood or urine.

The modification of a device, which did not affect its operation, did not take it out of the approved category (*Breckon v DPP* [2007] EWHC 2013 (Admin)); whether a modification to an intoxyliser machine took it out of a type approved under the Breath Analysis Devices Approval Order 2005 required a common sense consideration of whether the function of the modified device still had the character, essence and identity of the device with type approval: *R (on the application of Coxon v Manchester City Magistrates' Court* [2010] EWHC 712 (Admin), 174 CL&J 221.

Where the contention is that the device which was originally type approved has been altered without the Secretary of State's written consent in such a way as to take it out of type approval, and disclosure is sought to further that contention, the court will require more than the asserted fact of unapproved modification to justify disclosure. There will have to be some material which explains how the alteration could go to loss of type approval in the Schedule and how disclosure could advance that point. A change to a parameter in the software which was still described as UK5.23 would not be such a change. Where the edited printouts still showed that the software was UK5.23, the unedited ones would still show that the software was UK.5.23. Where there was nothing to suggest a change to the gas delivery system which took it out of type approval it would be difficult to see how allegedly defective maintenance practices could cause a device to lose its type approval, but they would have to be potentially of that gravity before becoming relevant to a loss of type approval argument. The material of which disclosure is sought must have some potential for bearing on the issue in respect of which it is raised. The nature and degree of an alleged unreliability has to be such that it might be able to throw doubt on the excess in the reading to such an extent that the level of alcohol in the breath might have been below the level at which a prosecution would have been instituted. If on any view there would still be an excess leading to prosecution it is difficult to see how that could justify disclosure of the material sought to make an irrelevant point about reliability. The nature of the defence claims as to what alcohol had been consumed, and when, may matter. In considering disclosure applications based on a claim about a particular machine's unreliability, and its possible basis for a defence, the court needs explicitly to consider the effect of the safeguards provided by the taking of two specimens, the intervening clearances of the device and the evidential use of the lower specimen of the two, together with the opportunity to give specimens of blood or urine and the fact that there is leeway above the breath limit before prosecution takes place. They are relevant to whether the alleged unreliability could possibly advance the stated defence. Similarly, the nature and extent of the possible changes to type had to be so fundamental that it could no longer be said that this was a type approved machine; that was the issue to which the disclosure material had to be addressed: *DPP v Wood* [2006] EWHC 32 (Admin), 170 JP 177.

C[22.17] The form of print-out from the machine will give the subject's name and the time and date of the test. They will show the results of each of two samples given by the subject and the results of each of two checks which the machine carries out to prove its accuracy. These calibration checks must show a reading within a range of 32–38 µg; figures outside this range on either check will render the test void.

C[22.18] The print-out will be signed by the operator and by the subject and a machine-produced copy will be handed to the driver, the other copy being retained by the police. It is unlikely that a prosecution will follow if the lowest reading is less than 40. In the absence of any suggestion that the machine was not used properly and providing the calibration checks show readings within the parameters mentioned above, the print-out from the machine is evidence of the level of alcohol in the breath without further proof provided that a print-out was handed to the accused at the time it was produced, or served on him more than seven days before the hearing, either personally or by registered or recorded post.

C[22.19] Evidence by certificate. A certificate signed by an authorised analyst stating the proportion of alcohol in the specimen is admissible without the analyst being called as a witness: the same applies to a certificate signed by a doctor who took a blood specimen from the defendant.

C[22.20]–[22.21] The defendant is entitled to insist on the attendance at court of the analyst or doctor. As the police were bound to provide the defendant with specimens of blood or urine taken at the same time, it is possible that sometimes a defendant may call his own analyst to give evidence as to the proportion of alcohol.

C[22.22] The High Court has quashed a conviction because a pathologist declared the blood specimen handed to the defendant to be inadequate for examination: *Earl v Roy* [1969] 2 All ER 684, 133 JP 520.

C[22.23] **Challenging the reliability of the device**

(a) Reliability of an individual machine – burden of proof on prosecution

Any challenge to admission of evidence which is based upon the reliability of the intoximeter machine needs to be considered in the light of *Cracknell v Willis* [1988] AC 450, [1987] 3 All ER 801, [1987] 3 WLR 1082, HL. The presumption is that the proportion of alcohol in the relevant specimen is no less that the proportion of alcohol in the breath at the time of the offence (Road Traffic Offenders Act 1988, s 15(2)). In the event of that assumption being challenged by the defendant, the justices have to be satisfied on relevant evidence that the reading provided by the machine is one on which they can rely, the burden being on the prosecution.

(b) Challenging reliability

The functioning of the device may be challenged by relevant evidence. It is not necessary in all cases in order to rebut the presumption of reliability of the intoximeter to adduce expert or technical evidence. It is the function of justices in each case to weigh the facts critically in each case and determine whether such evidence is necessary. In such cases, the justices should bear in mind the following factors:

- discrepancy between claimed consumption and a reading: consider the reliability of the defendant's evidence while having in mind the presumption of reliability of the device.
- minimal claimed consumption, a high reading and little other evidence: the discrepancy will be solely derived from the defendant's claimed consumption, which means it has to be weighed against the presumption that the machine is reliable. Rebutting the presumption in such circumstances is likely to be difficult.
- no observable signs of alcohol save on the breath: certain people can develop a high tolerance to alcohol and have high levels of alcohol without there being observable signs; expert evidence may be necessary.
- claims of lower consumption: signs of surprise by the defendant at the reading, or the very fact of a positive test, would be expected.
- no notice given of claim the device was defective: prosecution may apply for an adjournment:
  - within the justices' discretion to order the defendant to pay the costs of the adjournment;
  - as a matter of general rule, there is no reason why a defendant should not be taken to be required to give notice in advance of trial that he intended to rely on the fact that the device was defective;
  - having regard to the presumption of reliability, the efficient administration of justice requires the prosecution to know that the defendant intended to rebut the presumption.

DPP v Spurrier [2000] RTR 60, sub nom *R v Crown Prosecution Service, ex p Spurrier* 164 JP 369, DC.

Where a challenge is made to the reliability of the substantive breath testing device used at the police station, the court is entitled to rely upon the result of the roadside, screening test as evidence tending to support the reliability of the police station procedure: *Director of Public Prosecutions v Vince, Kang v Director of Public Prosecutions* [2016] EWHC 3014 (Admin), [2017] 4 WLR 3, [2017] Crim L R 307.

Where the 'ambient fail' message is recorded, it is not necessarily the case that the machine is not working properly and the result of a subsequent test on the same machine will be admissible if the court finds as fact that the accused caused the message to appear and for the first test to abort by his failure to breathe properly into the device, the machine was working properly and its readings are reliable: *DPP v Vince*, supra.

We reproduce in the paragraph below some of the early cases on reliability, but with the caveat that there have been significant advances and improvements in the reliability and accuracy of substantive breath testing devices and there will very rarely now be any genuine basis for questioning the results of the analysis.

Where there is evidence that the device was not, or might not have been, working properly it is essential for the prosecution to prove that the device was properly calibrated, either by production of the printout or by oral evidence of readings on the display panel: see *Mayon v DPP* [1988] RTR 281. Where, however, there is no such evidence it may reasonably be assumed that the device was correctly calibrating itself: *Haggis v DPP* [2003] EWHC 2481 (Admin), [2004] 2 All ER 382.

Provided a Lion Intoximeter 3000 device is demonstrated to be calibrating properly, justices are entitled to infer that it was operating efficiently, despite evidence of substantial differences between readings: *Maharaj v Solomon* [1987] RTR 295 – 20.9% difference did not prevent conviction.

Justices may not regard a device as reliable if it is operating in any way outside its area of tolerance, eg 0.1° above the maximum permissible temperature: *Waite v Smith* [1986] Crim LR 405). The mere fact that the device was defective does not however render evidence from it incapable of founding a conviction *Wright v Taplin* [1986] RTR 388n (readings too low) applied in *Fawcett v Gasparics* [1986] RTR 375, [1987] Crim LR 53 (printout stating correct numerical date but wrong day) and see *DPP v McKeown* [1997] 1 All ER 737, [1997] 1 WLR 295, [1997] 2 Cr App Rep 155, HL, (the fact that the wrong time was displayed on the intoximeter was not relevant to the proper functioning of the computer (Lion Intoximeter)); applied in *DPP v Barber* (1998) 163 JP 457 (printout with letters missing – held evidence of the printout and of a service engineer who remedied a fault on the printer was admissible). Where the two readings produced a difference of 16 microgrammes, but nevertheless expert evidence showed that the defendant must have exceeded the permitted level and there was no other evidence to suggest that the machine was not working correctly, the court should convict: *Gordon v Thorpe* [1986] RTR 358. Where a device was found to be unreliable at the time breath specimens were provided, justices were entitled to conclude, in the absence of further evidence, that the device was not reliable 100 minutes later: *Oxford v Baxendale* [1987] RTR 247).

When an intoximeter device is all observable respects complying with its type approval and when supplied should have had the approved version of the operating software installed, and there is no evidence of any changes to the software, the court is entitled to assume that the device is functioning correctly: *Skinner v DPP* [2004] EWHC 2914 (Admin), [2005] RTR 17.

As to challenges to type approval and applications by the defence for disclosure, see C[22.16], ante.

(c) Applications for disclosure of machine logs, etc

In *R (DPP) v Manchester and Salford Magistrates' Court* [2017] EWHC 1708 (Admin), challenges were brought by the prosecution to orders of disclosure made by the District Judge. Although these were interlocutory case management decisions, the Administrative Court held that it had jurisdiction to entertain the application for judicial review.

Both defendants claimed the alcohol they had consumed was far below the level indicated by the device. They served defence case statements and persuaded the District Judge to make wide ranging order for disclosure. These were quashed by the Divisional Court. Sir Brian Leveson, giving the judgment of the Court, held:

> '49. It is not enough for the purposes of s 8(3)(a) or (b) (of the CPIA 1996) that the material is in the prosecutor's possession or has been inspected by him. Subsection (4) is an addition to the definition of "prosecution material" found in s 3.
>
> 50. For these purposes, (Counsel for the CPS) accepted that the metrological record of service to the machine, kept with it in the custody suite, the records of the 300 tests in the memory of the device, and the calibration certificates, were in the possession of the police. [It should be noted that this concession was not made in the grounds for judicial review.]
>
> 51. However, we accept his submission that none of the material was "prosecution material" within s 8(3)(a) or (b) since none of it came into the prosecutor's possession in connection with the case against the accused nor had it been inspected in connection with that case either. The service certificates and engineer logs were not in the possession of the prosecutor at all, but were obtained by request of Lion Laboratories Ltd., the manufacturer of the device.
>
> 52. Section 8(4) provided the only other route for statutory disclosure. There was no obligation on Lion Laboratories to provide the service certificates and engineer logs to the prosecutor, if asked, or to make them available for inspection. The subsection focuses on the obligation to supply, not on any obligation to make a request. So those items fall outside s 8(4).
>
> 53. The documents in the custody suite, including for these purposes the memory within the device, could only come within s 8(4) if they were held by the Investigating Officer or by the Disclosure Officer; see the reasoning in *DPP v Wood and McGillicuddy* [2006] EWHC 32 (Admin), [50 and 55]. Once it is accepted, as it was here, that they are in the possession of the police, it was not suggested that they would fall outside s 8(4) upon a request being made by the prosecutor pursuant to an operative code. The relevant Code is the March 2015 CPIA s 23(1) Code of Practice issued by the Ministry of Justice. Paragraphs 3.5–3.6 in the section headed "General Responsibilities" require the investigator to "pursue all reasonable lines of enquiry whether these points towards or away from the suspect." If there is an obligation on the prosecutor to ask for the material under that provision, s 8(4) would be satisfied. But there would still be no obligation under either s 3, or under the continuing obligation in s 7A, to disclose such material unless it was reasonably capable of undermining the prosecution case or assisting the defence. And, of course, if it were known that that was the position, it would not be a reasonable line of enquiry to pursue either. We therefore turn to the second issue.
>
> *Could the District Judge rationally conclude on the evidence that these materials were reasonably capable of undermining the prosecution or advancing the defence cases?*
>
> 54. In our judgment, the answer to that is no, and disclosure should not have been ordered here. There was no basis upon which they could reasonably have been thought capable of undermining the prosecution or advancing the defence case.
>
> 55. First, those seeking and those making disclosure orders in excess alcohol cases must bear in mind the risks to which Lord Goff spoke, as set out above in *Cracknell v Willis*, above. These have been brought home recently by the decision of the Divisional Court in *R (Hassani) v West London Magistrates' Court* [2017] EWHC 1270 (Admin), and the appended extracts from the judgment of Senior District Judge Riddle in *CPS v Cipriani*. This means that there must be a proper

evidential basis for concluding that the material sought is reasonably capable of undermining the prosecution or of assisting the defence, or that it represents a reasonable line of enquiry to pursue ...

56. Second, it is not enough for one or more experts to say that the material is necessary to verify that the device was reliable ... Nor does the written application for s 8 disclosure provide any evidential basis for it. It is not enough to say that the defence case is that the amount drunk would not put the defendant over the limit or anywhere near it, and therefore the machine must be unreliable. What the evidence needed to do, in order to provide a basis for such a disclosure order was to address two critical features.

57. The first requirement is the basis for contending how the device might produce a printout which, on its face, demonstrated that it was operating in proper fashion, but which could generate a very significantly false positive reading, where, on the defence case, the true reading would have been well below the prosecution limit. The second requirement is to identify how the material which was sought could assist to demonstrate how that might have happened. Those are the two issues which arise and which the expert evidence in support of disclosure should address. Unless that evidence is provided, the disclosure is irrelevant.

58. But (both defence experts) ignored the printout, and the way in which the device is designed and operates. They provide no explanation as to how the device could have malfunctioned in the way they say it must have done and still have produced a positive reading so far from the true reading which they say it would have produced. No explanation of any sort is offered for the four blank readings and the two simulator readings all designed to demonstrate that the machine is operating correctly. Their generalised assertions that the machine could be unreliable and that its reliability needed to be verified was accompanied by no evidence that the disclosure sought could cast any light on its reliability in that way.

59. Third, this is not to say that the machine must be taken to be infallible. *Cracknell v Willis* permits evidence to be given that the defendant had not been drinking anything like enough to produce a positive reading, even if he cannot demonstrate how the machine might have malfunctioned. But these disclosure applications go further and are addressed to identifying how that might have happened. However, unless the disclosure application addresses the two questions which we have identified, this extensive disclosure would have to be given in every case in which a defendant alleged that his alcohol consumption had been too low to sustain a positive reading, and in effect proof of reliability would always be required and the presumption of accuracy would be displaced.

...

61. Finally, if the DJs required disclosure of material in the hands of Lion Laboratories Ltd, a third party, the appropriate procedure should have been invoked. Orders cannot be made requiring the CPS to obtain what it has no right to obtain, on pain perhaps of the prosecution being dismissed. It is not to the point that the third party may prove quite co-operative.

See also *Beattie v CPS* [2018] EWHC 787 (Admin), a drug driving case in which the blood sample taken from the appellant was divided into two, he did not take his part of the specimen (there was a dispute, resolved eventually in favour of the prosecution as to whether he had been offered it) but later sought that specimen through the disclosure regime so that he could arrange his own analysis. The application was rejected and this was upheld on appeal. There was no basis for the dispute as to the accuracy of the analysis other than the appellant's assertion that he was not under the influence of cannabis at the time he was arrested. There was nothing which might reasonably be considered capable of undermining the prosecution's case or assisting that for the accused. None of the requests provided any basis for suggesting that the sample had not been correctly analysed.

C[22.23A] Criticism of negative defence tactics

The courts have expressed trenchant criticism of defence lawyers who take 'every imaginable point' in drink driving cases, and have urged increased rigour and firmness in case management. It is the professional obligation of those with the conduct of drink driving cases to cite the judgment in *R (Hassani) v West London Magistrates' Court* [2017] EWHC 1270 (Admin), (2017] 181 JP 253, [2017] Crim L R 720 when issues of adjournment or case management arise. We reproduce below some extracts from the judgment which demonstrate the extent and strength of the Court's criticisms.

> '6. The trial was marred by an excessive number of technical points being raised on Mr Hassani's behalf. There were complaints about disclosure. There were attempts to lengthen the trial without advance notice being given ...
>
> 8. Not only was every imaginable point taken below, but (defence counsel) settled grounds of appeal with seven grounds. Upon a reading of the papers, it appears to me that they are, and were, all without foundation.
>
> 9. The criminal law is not a game to be played in the hope of a lucky outcome, a game to be played as long and in as involved a fashion as the paying client is able or prepared to afford.
>
> 10. ... Other courts faced with this kind of approach ... (however constituted) must consider the Criminal Procedure Rules, which are there to be employed actively so as to preclude game-playing and ensure that the courts only have to address real issues with some substance.
>
> 11. The Criminal Procedure Rules provisions most in question might be thought to be as follows. Each participant in a criminal case, that is to say lawyers as well as parties, must prepare and conduct their care in accordance with the rules: see CPR 1.2(1)(a) and (b). The key objective under the rules is to deal fairly with the case, and that includes dealing with the case efficiently and expeditiously: CPR 1.1(2)(e). Time wasting, extension of hearings and taking hopeless points in the hope of wearing down an opponent or the court are neither proper nor legitimate ways in which to conduct a case, for a party or for a party's lawyers. Courts must be aware of such behaviour and employ firm case management to prevent it.
>
> 12. Each participant in a case has the obligation set out in CPR 1.2(1)(c):
>
> "At once inform the court and all parties of any significant failure (whether or not that participant is responsible for that failure) to take any procedural step required by these Rules, any practice direction or any direction of the court. A failure is significant if it might hinder the court in furthering the overriding objective."
>
> That means, for example, that if defence lawyers consider that a document is missing or service of a document has not taken place, their obligation is to say so early. Not to say so early may hinder the overriding objective because it is likely to cause an adjournment which could be avoided, and thus prevent the case being decided "efficiently and expeditiously". If the defence are going to suggest that some document or some piece of service is missing, they must do so early. If they do not, then it is open to the court to find that the point was raised late, and any direction then sought to produce a document or to apply for an adjournment may properly be refused.
>
> 13. Critical rules affecting all parties, including defendants and their representatives, are rr.3.2, 3.3 and 3.11. It is not necessary for me to quote them in full, but the attention of a court dealing with such cases should be drawn to those

rules and perhaps in particular to 3.2(2)(a) – active case management includes the early identification of the real issues; 3.3(1) – each party must (a) actively assist the court in fulfilling its duty under rule 3.2, with, or if necessary without, a direction and (b) apply for a direction if needed to further the overriding objective; 3.3(2) active assistance for the purposes of this rule includes (a) at the beginning of the case communication between the prosecutor and the defendant at the first available opportunity; (c)(ii) what is agreed and what is likely to be disputed (in other words, what is agreed and what is likely to be disputed should be the subject of active assistance and early communication); (c)(iii) likewise, what information or other material is required by one party of another and why; and (iv) what is to be done, by whom and when. CPR 3.11: in order to manage a trial or an appeal, the court (a) must establish with the active assistance of the parties what are the disputed issues; and (d) may limit (i) the examination, cross-examination or re-examination of a witness and (ii) the duration of any stage of the hearing.

14. In the absence of some specific evidence which indicates that there is a problem with the Intoximeter EC/IR machine, approved in 1998 and, with approval, reissued in 2005, extensive exploration of technicalities will normally be a waste of time.

15. It is perfectly open to a court to ask if a defendant intends to give evidence to the effect that he or she had not been drinking or had drunk so little that the excess alcohol reading cannot properly be explained. If the answer is no, then the court can properly question what may be the evidential basis for a challenge to the reading produced by the testing equipment, provided the proper procedures have been followed.

16. Lawyers advising defendants on the conduct of such a case as this should routinely remind clients that these cases are criminal proceedings, that their evidence will be given on oath or following affirmation, and that lying in such evidence will be perjury.' (Per Irwin LJ.)

See also *Crown Prosecution Service v C* [2017] Crim L R 62, in which the then Senior District Judge gave an extensive judgment which was described in Hassani as 'dealing authoritatively with many aspects of such litigation as this'.

The police follow and complete a pro forma, known as MD DD/A, during the substantive breath test procedure. The admissibility of the form and its use by the officer as an aide memoir were considered in *DPP v Sugden* [2018] EWHC 544 (Admin), where the original form was not in court, the prosecution sought to rely on a copy of it and the defence objected on 'best evidence' grounds. Refreshing memory is now governed by s 139 of the Criminal Justice Act 2009. It was held as follows:

'38. In my judgment, the combined effect of the common law and section 139(1) is that the position can be summarised as follows:

(1) A document containing a record of relevant factual evidence is generally admissible in the ordinary way, because the content of the document is relevant to an issue in the case.

(2) If the document is a copy or other form of secondary evidence, it is not thereby made inadmissible. However, the absence of the original calls for an explanation if one is one is sought by the opposing party.

(3) If the original is not produced, the court may, not must, refuse to admit in evidence a copy or other secondary evidence and will consider the likely accuracy or otherwise of the copy or other secondary evidence.

(4) In criminal proceedings, the court will also consider any explanation for its absence, its probative value and any prejudicial effect on the defence (cf. section 78 of the Police and Criminal Evidence Act 1984).

(5) Where there is no reason to doubt that the document is a true copy of the original (e.g. where it is a straightforward photocopy of a missing original) and its content is within the knowledge of the defendant so that its accuracy can be challenged in cross-examination, there will generally be no prejudice to the defence in admitting the copy document in evidence.

(6) Whether or not the document or copy or other secondary evidence of its content is admitted, a party may refresh his or her memory from the document if the requirements of section 139(1) of the 2003 Act are met.

(7) The witness may refresh his or her memory from either the original document or from a secondary document – i.e. a copy, or other document derived from the original – if the secondary document is likely to be an accurate reflection of the content of the original, provided that the witness verified either the original or the secondary document at a time when his or her recall was better than at the time of giving oral evidence.

(8) Where a witness is permitted to refresh his or her memory from a document and the document is not adduced as evidence by the party relying on it, the content of that document may or may not become evidence in the case, depending on the nature and extent of cross-examination on its content.

Whether or not the document becomes evidence in the case, the court will always consider and give appropriate weight to any discrepancy or risk of discrepancy between its content and an original or source document of which it is a copy or from which it is derived.' (per Kerr J.)

C[22.24] **Special reasons.** It is not a defence to the charge that unknown to him the defendant's drink had been laced. If this is put forward as a reason for not disqualifying the question must be answered whether the extra drink by itself is what took the level of alcohol in the blood over the limit and the defendant, if there is any doubt, should be invited to call expert evidence. Note that even if special reasons are proved this only gives the justices a discretion not to disqualify. They may still do so depending on the circumstances of the case (*R v Crown Court at St Albans, ex p O'Donovan* [2000] 1 Cr App Rep (S) 344).

A motorist drove 350 metres to his home address fearing the loss of valuable work tools in his van. Held, not special reasons: *DPP v Oram* [2005] EWHC 964 (Admin), [2005] All ER (D) 57 (May).

C[22.25]–[22.29] Driving in an emergency may amount to a special reason not to disqualify, but only where a sober, reasonable and responsible friend of the defendant present at the time, but unable to drive, would have advised the defendant to drive (*DPP v Bristow* [1998] RTR 100, 161 JP 35). Shortness of distance driven may be a special reason but not where the defendant's intention was to drive a longer distance than he in fact managed (*DPP v Humphries* [2000] RTR 52, sub nom Crown Prosecution Service v Humphries [2000] 2 Cr App Rep (S) 1, 164 JP 502). No specific reasons could be argued by a defendant who assumed without enquiry that a drink he consumed contained no alcohol (*Lloyd Robinson v DPP* [2003] EWHC 2718 (Admin), (2004) 168 JP 522, [2004] Crim LR 670, [2003] All ER (D) 05 (Nov)); nor where the defendant drove to the scene of an accident involving his son, having failed to wake his wife who could have legally driven (*Khan v DPP* [2004] EWHC 2505 (Admin), sub nom Khan v DPP [2004] All ER (D) 134 (Oct)).

In *Ng v DPP* [2007] EWHC 36 (Admin), the defendant contended that his breath reading had been affected by eructation (belching) during the procedure. It was decided that the evidence on which the defendant had sought to rely went directly to the commission of the offence. If accepted it could provide an explanation as to why the level of alcohol exceeded the prescribed limit. It was capable therefore of amounting a special reason.

Driving a short distance to avoid car park charges was held not to be a special reason because, on the facts, there was danger of the defendant coming into contact with other road users (*DPP v Cove* [2008] EWHC 441 (Admin), [2008] All ER (D) 199 (Feb).

C[22.30] **Drinking after driving.** If the accused claims that the alcohol level was increased because he had taken drink after ceasing to drive then he must prove on the balance of probabilities that the post-driving drink took him over the limit and that he was not over the limit while he was driving. This is because the law requires the court to assume that the alcohol level at the time of the driving was not less than that at the time of the test (*Griffiths v DPP* [2002] EWHC 792 (Admin), 166 JP 629, [2002] All ER (D) 132 (Apr)). If an accused wishes to raise this defence he will almost certainly have to call medical or scientific evidence.

C[22.31] **Alternative verdict.** If the allegation is 'driving' the court may convict him on the basis of attempting to drive. Where the defendant is found not guilty of an offence under the Road Traffic Act 1988, s 5(1)(a) but the allegations amount to or include an offence under s 5(1)(b) (being in charge of a vehicle with excess alcohol in breath, blood or urine) the court may convict him of that offence (RTOA 1988, s 24).

Sentencing

SC Guideline – Excess Alcohol (drive/attempt to drive)

Excess Alcohol (drive/attempt to drive)
(Revised 2017)

C[22.32]

Road Traffic Act 1988, s 5(1)(a)

Effective from: 24 April 2017

Triable only summarily:

Maximum: Unlimited fine and/or 6 months

Offence range: Band B fine–26 weeks' custody

Steps 1 and 2 — Determining the offence seriousness

- **Must endorse and disqualify for at least 12 months**
- **Must disqualify for at least 2 years if offender has had two or more disqualifications for periods of 56 days or more in preceding 3 years — refer to disqualification guidance and consult your legal adviser for further guidance**
- **Must disqualify for at least 3 years if offender has been convicted of a relevant offence in preceding 10 years — consult your legal adviser for further guidance**
- **Extend disqualification if imposing immediate custody**

If there is a delay in sentencing after conviction, consider interim disqualification

The starting point applies to all offenders irrespective of plea or previous convictions.

Level of alcohol			Starting point	Range	Disqualification	Disqual. 2nd offence in 10 years – see note above
Breath (ug)	Blood (mg)	Urine (mg)				
120–150 and above	276–345 and above	367–459 and above	12 weeks' custody	High level community order–26 weeks' custody	29–36 months (Extend if imposing immediate custody)	36–60 months
90–119	207–275	275–366	Medium level community order	Low level community order–High level community order	23–28 months	36–52 months
60–89	138–206	184–274	Band C Fine	Band C Fine–Low level community order	17–22 months	36–46 months
36–59	81–137	108–183	Band C Fine	Band B Fine–Band C fine	12–16 months	36–40 months

Note: when considering the guidance regarding the length of disqualification in the case of a second offence, the period to be imposed in any individual case will depend on an assessment of all the relevant circumstances, including the length of time since the earlier ban was imposed and the gravity of the current offence but disqualification must be for at least three years.

The court should then consider further adjustment for any aggravating or mitigating factors. The following is a **non-exhaustive** list of additional factual elements providing the context of the offence and factors relating to the offender. Identify whether any combination of these, or other relevant factors, should result in an upward or downward adjustment from the sentence arrived at so far.

Factors increasing seriousness

Statutory aggravating factors:

- Previous convictions, having regard to a) the **nature** of the offence to which the conviction relates and its **relevance** to the current offence; and b) the **time** that has elapsed since the conviction
- Offence committed whilst on bail

Other aggravating factors:

- Failure to comply with current court orders
- Offence committed on licence or post sentence supervision
- LGV, HGV, PSV etc
- Poor road or weather conditions
- Carrying passengers
- Driving for hire or reward

- Evidence of unacceptable standard of driving
- Involved in accident
- High level of traffic or pedestrians in the vicinity

Factors reducing seriousness or reflecting personal mitigation

- No previous convictions or no relevant/recent convictions
- Genuine emergency established*
- Spiked drinks *
- Very short distance driven *
- Remorse
- Good character and/or exemplary conduct
- Serious medical condition requiring urgent, intensive or long-term treatment
- Age and/or lack of maturity where it affects the responsibility of the offender
- Mental disorder or learning disability
- Sole or primary carer for dependent relatives

Step 3 — Consider any factors which indicate a reduction, such as assistance to the prosecution

The court should take into account sections 73 and 74 of the Serious Organised Crime and Police Act 2005 (assistance by defendants: reduction or review of sentence) and any other rule of law by virtue of which an offender may receive a discounted sentence in consequence of assistance given (or offered) to the prosecutor or investigator.

Step 4 — Reduction for guilty pleas

The court should take account of any potential reduction for a guilty plea in accordance with section 144 of the Criminal Justice Act 2003 and the *Guilty Plea* guideline.

Step 5 — Totality principle

If sentencing an offender for more than one offence, or where the offender is already serving a sentence, consider whether the total sentence is just and proportionate to the overall offending behaviour in accordance with the *Offences Taken into Consideration and Totality* guideline.

Step 6 — Compensation and ancillary orders

In all cases, the court should consider whether to make compensation and/or other ancillary orders including offering a drink/drive rehabilitation course, deprivation, and /or forfeiture or suspension of personal liquor licence.

Step 7 — Reasons

Section 174 of the Criminal Justice Act 2003 imposes a duty to give reasons for, and explain the effect of, the sentence.

Step 8 — Consideration for time spent on bail

The court must consider whether to give credit for time spent on bail in accordance with section 240A of the Criminal Justice Act 2003.

---

* even where not amounting to special reasons

C[22.33] Structure of the sentencing decision. See B[9.7].

C[22.34] Available sentences. See Table B at B[43.2].

C[22.35]–[22.40] Custodial sentence. See B[15].

C[22.41] Community sentence. See B[9].

C[22.42] Fine. See B[28].

C[22.43] Forfeiture of vehicle. See B[18].

C[22.44] Disqualification. See C[5].

C[22.45] High risk offenders. An offender is a 'high risk offender' if he falls within any of the following categories, which are prescribed by reg 74 of the Motor Vehicles (Driving Licences) Regulations 1999, SI 1999/286, namely he:

(a) has been disqualified by an order of a court by reason that the proportion of alcohol in his body equalled or exceeded—
  (i) 87.5 microgrammes per 100 millilitres of breath, or
  (ii) 200 milligrammes per 100 millilitres of blood, or
  (iii) 267.5 milligrammes per 100 millilitres of urine;

(b) has been disqualified by order of a court by reason that he has failed, without reasonable excuse, to provide a specimen when required to do so pursuant to section 7 of the Traffic Act; ...

(bb) has been disqualified by order of a court by reason of failure, without reasonable excuse, to give permission for a laboratory test of a specimen of blood taken pursuant to section 7A of the Traffic Act; or

(c) has been disqualified by order of a court on two or more occasions within any period of 10 years by reason that—
  (i) the proportion of alcohol in his breath, blood or urine exceeded the limit prescribed by virtue of section 5 of the Traffic Act, or
  (ii) he was unfit to drive through drink contrary to section 4 of that Act.

For the purposes of paragraph (a) and (b) a court order shall not be taken into account unless it was made on or after 1 June 1990 and paragraph (c) shall not apply to a person unless the last such order was made on or after 1 June 1990.

For the purposes of paragraph (bb) a court order shall not be taken into account unless it was made on or after 1 June 2013.

C[22.46] The DVLA will write to a high risk offender and explain that the disqualification is considered to be an indication of a drink problem. Shortly before the expiry of the disqualification, a further letter will be sent explaining what must be done to apply for the return of the licence. The applicant will have to submit to a medical examination and pay an administration fee and medical fees to the examining doctor.

C[22.47] If it appears to the court that the accused suffers from a disease or physical disability likely to cause his driving to be a source of danger to the public, it must notify the licensing authority (see C[5.49]).

C[22.48] The fact that the amount of alcohol is only slightly over the statutory limit is not a special reason for avoiding imposing disqualification and endorsement.

C[22.49] The 12 months' mandatory disqualification is to be regarded as a minimum and not as a tariff and should be increased in appropriate cases. The national sentencing guidelines suggest an increased disqualification for cases between 56mg and 70mg.

C[22.50]–[22.55] If the defendant submits as a special reason for not disqualifying him that he was obliged to drive by some sudden crisis or emergency he must show that he acted responsibly and that the crisis or emergency was not one which arose through his own irresponsibility or lack of reasonable foresight. The driving must have been only to the extent occasioned by the emergency.

C[22.56] **Reduced disqualification for attendance on courses.** Reduced disqualification for attendance on a course may be offered to an offender convicted of a 'relevant drink offence' (or, when s 35 of the Road Safety Act 2006 is brought fully into force, a 'specified offence') who is disqualified by the court under s 34 of the RTOA 1988 for at least 12 months.

C[22.57] A 'relevant drink offence' means:

(a) an offence under s 3A(1)(a) of the RTA1988 (causing death by careless driving when unfit to drive through drink) committed when unfit to drive through drink,
(b) an offence under paragraph (b) of that subsection (causing death by careless driving with excess alcohol),
(c) an offence under paragraph (c) of that subsection (failing to provide a specimen) where the specimen is required in connection with drink or consumption of alcohol,
(d) an offence under s 4 of that Act (driving or being in charge when under influence of drink) committed by reason of unfitness through drink,
(e) an offence under s 5(1) of that Act (driving or being in charge with excess alcohol),
(f) an offence under s 7(6) of that Act (failing to provide a specimen) committed in the course of an investigation into an offence within any of the preceding paragraphs, or
(g) an offence under s 7A(6) of that Act (failing to allow a specimen to be subjected to a laboratory test) in the course of an investigation into an offence within any of the preceding paragraphs.

RTA 1988, s 34A(3).

Offenders who come within the criteria for High Risk Offenders (HRO) may be referred to a rehabilitation scheme, but will still have to meet the requirements of the HRO scheme before their licence will be returned to them by the Secretary of State. Although referral to a rehabilitation scheme is not precluded, training courses for drink-drive offenders as a condition of a community order may be more appropriate for offenders where a higher degree of intervention is necessary to match the seriousness of the offence (DETR Guide issued in respect of the former scheme).

C[22.58] The court must have made an order for disqualification for not less than 12 months.

C[22.59] The reduction specified must be not less than three months and not more than one quarter of the original period (ie 9 months' disqualification must remain where the original unreduced period was 12 months). The reduction should be announced in open court.

C[22.60] Criteria. The court should decide whether or not to offer the offender an opportunity to participate. It must then check that:

(a) a place on the course is available;
(b) the offender is aged 17 years or more;
(c) the court has explained the effect of the order in ordinary language, the amount of fees payable and that they must be paid before beginning the course;
(d) the offender consents.

The course must be completed at least two months before the end of the reduced period of disqualification. The scheme is voluntary after referral. There is no additional penalty if the offender fails to attend the course but the full period of disqualification applies.

C[22.61] On completion, the organiser of the course will give the offender a certificate for presentation to the court.

Charge 2 (Excess alcohol (drive/attempt or in charge))

C[22.62] **Being in charge of a motor vehicle on a road (or public place) having consumed alcohol over the prescribed limit**

Road Traffic Act 1988, s 5(1)(b)

Maximum penalty-Fine on level 4 and 3 months' imprisonment (for fines see B[28]). May disqualify for any period and/or until a driving test has been passed. Must endorse unless there are special reasons.

Penalty points – 10.

Legal notes and definitions

C[22.63] In charge. See notes at C[21.3].

C[22.64] ECHR. The defendant is entitled to be acquitted if he can establish from the evidence that there was no likelihood of his driving whilst he probably had an excessive proportion of alcohol in his blood. He only has to prove this on the balance of probabilities and the House of Lords held that the burden on the defendant was both reasonable and legitimate (*Sheldrake v DPP* [2003] EWHC 273 (Admin), [2004] QB 487; revsd [2004] UKHL 43, [2004] 3 WLR 976). Note that a passenger supervising a learner driver who has been drinking may be in charge for the purposes of this section (*DPP v Janman* [2004] EWHC 101 (Admin), [2004] All ER (D) 171 (Jan)).

See also the legal and sentencing notes for the previous offence, at C[21.2].

Sentencing
SC Guideline – Excess Alcohol (in charge)

Excess Alcohol (in charge) (Revised 2017)

C[22.65]

Road Traffic Act 1988, s 5(1)(b)

Effective from: 24 April 2017

Triable only summarily:

Maximum: Level 4 fine and/ or 3 months

Offence range: Band A fine–6 weeks' custody

Steps 1 and 2 — Determining the offence seriousness

- **Must endorse and may disqualify. If no disqualification impose 10 points**
- **Extend any disqualification if imposing immediate custody**

The starting point applies to all offenders irrespective of plea or previous convictions.

Level of alcohol			Starting point	Range	Disqualification/ Points
Breath (Ug)	Blood (mg)	Urine (mg)			
120–150 and above	276–345 and above	367–459 and above	Medium level community order	Low level community order–6 weeks' custody	Disqualify 6–12 months (Extend if imposing immediate custody)
90–119	207–275	275–366	Band C fine	Band C Fine–Medium level community order	Consider disqualification up to 6 months OR 10 points

Level of alcohol			Starting point	Range	Disqualification/ Points
60–89	138–206	184–274	Band B fine	Band B fine–Band C fine	Consider disqualification OR 10 points
36–59	81–137	108–183	Band B fine	Band A fine–Band B fine	10 points

The court should then consider further adjustment for any aggravating or mitigating factors. The following is a **non-exhaustive** list of additional factual elements providing the context of the offence and factors relating to the offender. Identify whether any combination of these, or other relevant factors, should result in an upward or downward adjustment from the sentence arrived at so far.

Factors increasing seriousness

Statutory aggravating factors:

- Previous convictions, having regard to a) the **nature** of the offence to which the conviction relates and its **relevance** to the current offence; and b) the **time** that has elapsed since the conviction
- Offence committed whilst on bail

Other aggravating factors:

- Failure to comply with current court orders
- Offence committed on licence or post sentence supervision
- In charge of LGV, HGV, PSV etc
- High likelihood of driving
- Offering to drive for hire or reward

Factors reducing seriousness or reflecting personal mitigation

- No previous convictions **or** no relevant/recent convictions
- Low likelihood of driving
- Spiked drinks
- Remorse
- Good character and/or exemplary conduct
- Serious medical condition requiring urgent, intensive or long-term treatment
- Age and/or lack of maturity where it affects the responsibility of the offender
- Mental disorder or learning disability
- Sole or primary carer for dependent relatives

* even when not amounting to special reasons

Step 3 — Consider any factors which indicate a reduction, such as assistance to the prosecution

The court should take into account sections 73 and 74 of the Serious Organised Crime and Police Act 2005 (assistance by defendants: reduction or review of sentence) and any other rule of law by virtue of which an offender may receive a discounted sentence in consequence of assistance given (or offered) to the prosecutor or investigator.

Step 4 — Reduction for guilty pleas

The court should take account of any potential reduction for a guilty plea in accordance with section 144 of the Criminal Justice Act 2003 and the *Guilty Plea* guideline.

Step 5 — Totality principle

If sentencing an offender for more than one offence, or where the offender is already serving a sentence, consider whether the total sentence is just and proportionate to the overall offending behaviour in accordance with the *Offences Taken into Consideration and Totality* guideline.

Step 6 — Compensation and ancillary orders

In all cases, the court should consider whether to make compensation and/or other ancillary orders including offering a drink/drive rehabilitation course, deprivation, and /or forfeiture or suspension of personal liquor licence.

Step 7 — Reasons

Section 174 of the Criminal Justice Act 2003 imposes a duty to give reasons for, and explain the effect of, the sentence.

Step 8 — Consideration for time spent on bail

The court must consider whether to give credit for time spent on bail in accordance with section 240A of the Criminal Justice Act 2003.

C[22.66]–[22.71] See Table B at B[43.2] for available sentences and the notes for the previous offence.

C[22A]

Driving or being in charge of a motor vehicle with a concentration of a specified controlled drug in excess of the specified limit

These offences took effect on March 2015.

Charge (Driving or being in charge of a motor vehicle etc)

C[22A.1] **When [driving or attempting to drive] or [being in charge of] a motor vehicle [specify] on a road or other public place [specify] you had in your body a specified controlled drug and the proportion of that drug in your blood or urine exceeded the specified limit for that drug, contrary to s 5A of the Road Traffic Act 1988**

The penalties for these offences are the same as for the offences of driving and being in charge of a vehicle while unfit though drink or drugs. See C[**22.1**], above, with the same increase in the minimum period of disqualification where the defendant has within the ten years immediately preceding the commission of the present offence been convicted of any of the following offences:

- s 3A (causing death by careless driving when under the influence of drink or drugs);
- s 4(1) (driving or attempting to drive while unfit);
- s 5(1)(a) (driving or attempting to drive with excess alcohol);
- s 5A(1)(a) and (2) (driving or attempting to drive with concentration of specified controlled drug above specified limit);
- s 7(6) (failing to provide a specimen) where that is an offence involving obligatory disqualification; and
- s 7A(6) (failing to allow a specimen to be subjected to laboratory test) where that is an offence involving obligatory disqualification.

C[22A.2] Section 56 of the Crime and Courts Act 2013 introduced these new offences, and various consequential changes to other offences and procedures – preliminary tests, detention, etc – are made by Sch 22. These provisions came into force on 2nd March 2015.

Section 56 inserted new s 5A in the Road Traffic Act 1988. We reproduce this in full because it contains many elements.

> **'5A Driving or being in charge of a motor vehicle with concentration of specified controlled drug above specified limit**
>
> (1) This section applies where a person ("D")—
>
> (a) drives or attempts to drive a motor vehicle on a road or other public place, or
>
> (b) is in charge of a motor vehicle on a road or other public place,
>
> and there is in D's body a specified controlled drug.
>
> (2) D is guilty of an offence if the proportion of the drug in D's blood or urine exceeds the specified limit for that drug.
>
> (3) It is a defence for a person ("D") charged with an offence under this section to show that—
>
> (a) the specified controlled drug had been prescribed or supplied to D for medical or dental purposes,
>
> (b) D took the drug in accordance with any directions given by the person by whom the drug was prescribed or supplied, and with any accompanying instructions (so far as consistent with any such directions) given by the manufacturer or distributor of the drug, and

(c) D's possession of the drug immediately before taking it was not unlawful under section 5(1) of the Misuse of Drugs Act 1971 (restriction of possession of controlled drugs) because of an exemption in regulations made under section 7 of that Act (authorisation of activities otherwise unlawful under foregoing provisions).

(4) The defence in subsection (3) is not available if D's actions were—

(a) contrary to any advice, given by the person by whom the drug was prescribed or supplied, about the amount of time that should elapse between taking the drug and driving a motor vehicle, or

(b) contrary to any accompanying instructions about that matter (so far as consistent with any such advice) given by the manufacturer or distributor of the drug.

(5) If evidence is adduced that is sufficient to raise an issue with respect to the defence in subsection (3), the court must assume that the defence is satisfied unless the prosecution proves beyond reasonable doubt that it is not.

(6) It is a defence for a person ("D") charged with an offence by virtue of subsection (1)(b) to prove that at the time D is alleged to have committed the offence the circumstances were such that there was no likelihood of D driving the vehicle whilst the proportion of the specified controlled drug in D's blood or urine remained likely to exceed the specified limit for that drug.

(7) The court may, in determining whether there was such a likelihood, disregard any injury to D and any damage to the vehicle.

(8) In this section, and in sections 3A, 6C(1), 6D and 10, "specified" means specified in regulations made—

(a) by the Secretary of State, in relation to driving or attempting to drive, or being in charge of a vehicle, in England and Wales;

(b) by the Scottish Ministers, in relation to driving or attempting to drive, or being in charge of a vehicle, in Scotland.

(9) A limit specified under subsection (2) may be zero.'

C[22A.3] Specified controlled drugs and limits. The Drug Driving (Specified Limits) (England and Wales) Regulations 2014, SI 2014/2868 specify the following controlled drugs and limits. The limits are for microgrammes of the drug per litre of blood.

Controlled drug	Limit
Benzoylecgonine	50
Clonazepam	50
Cocaine	10
Delta-9-Tetrahydrocannabinol	2
Diazepam	550
Flunitrazepam	300
Ketamine	20
Lorazepam	100
Lysergic Acid Diethylamide	1
Methadone	500
Methylamphetamine	10
Methylenedioxymethamphetamine . . . 10	10
6-Monoacetylmorphine	5
Morphine	80
Oxazepam	300

Controlled drug	Limit
Temazepam	1000
Amphetamine	250

C[22A.4] **Consequential amendments.** Schedule 22 to the Crime and Courts Act 2013 makes a number of amendments in consequence of these new offences. These are:

(a) The offence in s 3A of the Road Traffic Act 1988 of causing death by careless driving when under the influence of drink or drugs is extended (by the insertion of s 3A(1)(ba)) to include having an excess in blood or urine of the specified limit of a specified controlled drug.

(b) Section 6C of the 1988 Act (preliminary drug test) is amended to add use of the preliminary drug test procedure to establish whether the drug is a specified controlled drug and, if so, whether the proportion of it in blood or urine is likely to exceed the specified limit for that drug. Up to three preliminary drug tests may be administered.

(c) Section 6D (arrest) is amended to include reasonable suspicion that the person has a specified controlled drug in his body and the proportion of it in his blood or urine exceeds the prescribed limit for that drug.

(d) Section 7(1A) is inserted to enable a constable to require a sample of blood or urine in the course of an investigation into a possible s 5A offence.

(e) Section 15 of the Road Traffic Offenders Act 1988 is amended to include the new offence and to apply the statutory assumption to the proportion of a specified controlled drug found in a person's blood or urine (rebuttable in the same way as with alcohol). Also, where drugs are concerned, the defence of post driving/being in charge consumption of drugs is extended to the offences under ss 3A, 4 and the new 5A.

(f) Section 24 of the Road Traffic Offenders Act 1988 is amended to bring the new offences within the alternative verdict framework, ie a person of acquitted of driving may be found guilty of the in charge offence where the information amounts to or includes an allegation of the latter.

(g) Sections 45 and 45A of, and Sch 2 to, the Road Traffic Offenders Act 1988 are amended to provide for the same penalties to be available as those already available in relation to similar alcohol related road traffic offences.

Defences

C[22A.5] Section 5A(6) is in the same terms as the defences at s 4(3) and 5(2) with the same ability to disregard any injury to the defendant or any damage to the vehicle.

The defence prescribed by s 5A(3) and (4) is unique to this offence. Note that the burden on the defendant here is merely an evidential burden (see subsection (5)). Even if the defence is made out, however, it will be possible (if such an alternative information has been laid) to convict of the unfit to drive offence, which is not subject to this prescribed drugs defence, though such a consequence seems rather harsh and could give rise to a submission of 'special reasons' for not disqualifying.

Statutory assumption

C[22A.6] As noted above, s 15 of the Road Traffic Offenders Act 1988 has been amended to extend the statutory assumption to the proportion of the specified controlled drug found in the suspect's blood or urine. The relevant provisions state:

'(2) ...

(b) it is to be assumed, subject to subsection (3A) below, that the proportion of a drug in the accused's blood or urine at the time of the alleged offence was not less than in the specimen . . .

(3A) The assumption is subsection (2)(b) above is not to be made if the accused proves –

(a) that he took the drug before he provided the specimen or had the specimen taken from him and–

(i) in relation to an offence under s 3A, after the time of the alleged offence, and

(ii) otherwise, after he had ceased to drive, attempt to drive or be in charge of a vehicle on a road or other public place, and

(b) had he not done so the proportion of the drug in his blood or urine–

(i) in the case of a specified controlled drug, would not have exceeded the specified limit for that drug, and

(ii) if it is alleged that he was unfit to drive through drugs, would not have been such as to impair his ability to drive properly.'

Again, as with alcohol, it is open to the prosecution to prove by back calculation that the proportion of the specified controlled drug was *higher* at the relevant time.

Sentencing (Driving or being in charge of a motor vehicle etc)

C[22A.7] The following interim guidance has been given by the Sentencing Council.

'**Introduction**

Since the new offence came into force in March 2015 the Sentencing Council has received a large number of requests for a sentencing guideline. It has been brought to our attention that there are concerns with sentencing in this area and a risk of inconsistent practices developing.

The new offence is a strict liability offence, which is committed once the specified limit for any of 17 specified controlled drugs is exceeded. The 17 drugs include both illegal drugs and drugs that may be medically prescribed. The limits for illegal drugs are set in line with a zero tolerance approach but ruling out accidental exposure.

The limits for drugs that may be medically prescribed are set in line with a road safety risk-based approach, at levels above the normal concentrations found with therapeutic use. This is different from the approach taken when setting the limit for alcohol, where the limit was set at a level where the effect of the alcohol would be expected to have impaired a person's driving ability. **For these reasons it would be wrong to rely on the Driving with Excess Alcohol guideline when sentencing an offence under this legislation.**

Guidance Only

At present there is insufficient reliable data available from the Department for Transport upon which the Sentencing Council can devise a full guideline. For that reason, and given the number of requests for guidance that have been received, the Sentencing Council has devised the attached guidance to assist sentencers.

It is important to note that this guidance does not carry the same authority as a sentencing guideline, and sentencers are not obliged to follow it. However, it is hoped that the majority of sentencers will find it useful in assisting them to deal with these cases.

The Sentencing Council will, in due course produce a guideline with the assistance of evidence and data gathered by the Department for Transport. Any new guideline will be made subject to public consultation before it is finalised.

Drug Driving Guidance

Background

The Crime and Courts Act 2013 inserted a new section 5A into the Road Traffic Act 1988 (RTA), which makes it an offence to drive, attempt to drive, or be in charge of a motor vehicle with a concentration of a specified controlled drug in the body above the specified limit. The offence came into force on 2 March 2015.

Driving or Attempting to Drive

Triable only summarily:

Maximum: Unlimited fine and/or 6 months

- Must endorse and disqualify for at least 12 months
- Must disqualify for at least 2 years if offender has had two or more disqualifications for periods of 56 days or more in preceding 3 years – refer to disqualification guidance and consult your legal adviser for further guidance
- Must disqualify for at least 3 years if offender has been convicted of a relevant offence in preceding 10 years – consult your legal adviser for further guidance

If there is a delay in sentencing after conviction, consider interim disqualification.

- As a guide, where an offence of driving or attempting to drive has been committed and there are no factors that increase seriousness the Court should consider a starting point of a **B and C fine**, and a disqualification in the region of 12–22 months. The list of factors that increase seriousness appears at page 3. Please note this is an exhaustive list and only factors that appear in the list should be considered.
- Where there are factors that increase seriousness the Court should consider increasing the sentence on the basis of the level of seriousness.
- The **community order** threshold is likely to be crossed where there is evidence of one or more factors that increase seriousness. The Court should also consider imposing a disqualification in the region of 23–28 months.
- The **custody** threshold is likely to be crossed where there is evidence of one or more factors that increase seriousness and one or more aggravating factors (see below). The Court should also consider imposing a disqualification in the region of 29–36 months.
- Having determined a starting point, the Court should consider additional factors that may make the offence more or less serious. A non-exhaustive list of aggravating and mitigating factors is set out below.

Factors that increase seriousness (this is an exhaustive list)

- Evidence of another specified drug[1] or of alcohol in the body
- Evidence of an unacceptable standard of driving
- Driving (or in charge of) an LGV, HGV or PSV
- Driving (or in charge of) a vehicle driven for hire or reward

Aggravating and mitigating factors (these are non-exhaustive lists)

Aggravating Factors

- Previous convictions having regard to a) the **nature** of the offence to which the conviction relates and its **relevance** to the current offence; and b) the **time** that has elapsed since the conviction
- Location e.g. near school
- Carrying passengers
- High level of traffic or pedestrians in the vicinity
- Poor road or weather conditions

Mitigating Factors

- No previous convictions or no relevant/recent convictions

- Remorse
- Good character and/or exemplary conduct
- Age and/or lack of maturity where it affects the responsibility of the offender
- Mental disorder or learning disability
- Sole or primary carer for dependent relatives
- Very short distance driven
- Genuine emergency established

[1]For these purposes, cocaine and benzoylecgonine (BZE) shall be treated as one drug as they both occur in the body as a result of cocaine use rather than poly-drug use. Similarly 6-Monoacteylmorphine and Morphine shall be treated as one drug as they both occur in the body as a result of heroin use. Finally, Diazepam and Temazepam shall be treated as one drug as they also both occur in the body as a result of Temazepam use.

In Charge

Triable only summarily:

Maximum: Level 4 fine and/or 3 months

Must endorse and may disqualify. If no disqualification, impose 10 points

- As a guide, where an offence of being in charge has been committed but there are no factors that increase seriousness the Court should consider a starting point of a **B and B fine**, and endorsing the licence with 10 penalty points. The list of factors that increase seriousness appears below. Please note this is an exhaustive list and only factors that appear in the list should be considered.
- Where there are factors that increase seriousness the Court should consider increasing the sentence on the basis of the level of seriousness.
- The **community order** threshold is likely to be crossed where there is evidence of one or more factors that increase seriousness and one or more aggravating factors (see below). The Court should also consider imposing a disqualification.
- Where there is evidence of one or more factors that increase seriousness and a greater number of aggravating factors (see below) the Court may consider it appropriate to impose a short **custodial** sentence of up to 12 weeks. The Court should also consider imposing a disqualification.
- Having determined a starting point, the Court should consider additional factors that may make the offence more or less serious. A non-exhaustive list of aggravating and mitigating factors is set out below.

Factors that increase seriousness – (this is an exhaustive list)

- Evidence of another specified drug[2] or of alcohol in the body
- Evidence of an unacceptable standard of driving
- Driving (or in charge of) an LGV, HGV or PSV
- Driving (or in charge of) a vehicle driven for hire or reward

Aggravating and mitigating factors (these are non-exhaustive lists)

Aggravating Factors

- Previous convictions having regard to a) the **nature** of the offence to which the conviction relates and its **relevance** to the current offence; and b) the **time** that has elapsed since the conviction
- Location e.g. near school
- Carrying passengers
- High level of traffic or pedestrians in the vicinity
- Poor road or weather conditions

Mitigating Factors

- No previous convictions **or** no relevant/recent convictions
- Remorse

- Good character and/or exemplary conduct
- Age and/or lack of maturity where it affects the responsibility of the offender
- Mental disorder or learning disability
- Sole or primary carer for dependent relatives
- Very short distance driven
- Genuine emergency established

[2]For these purposes, cocaine and benzoylecgonine (BZE) shall be treated as one drug as they both occur in the body as a result of cocaine use rather than poly-drug use. Similarly 6-Monoacteylmorphine and Morphine shall be treated as one drug as they both occur in the body as a result of heroin use. Finally, Diazepam and Temazepam shall be treated as one drug as they also both occur in the body as a result of Temazepam use.'

C[23]

Fail to provide specimen for analysis (drive/attempt to drive)

Charge (Fail to provide specimen for analysis)

C[23.1] **Failing, without reasonable excuse, to provide a specimen of blood, urine or breath for analysis –**

Road Traffic Act 1988, s 7(6) and s 7A

Maximum penalty – This varies according to whether it is alleged the defendant was driving or in charge. Accordingly the summons should make clear which of the alternative offences at C[21] and C[22], is alleged.

(a) If the defendant drove or attempted to drive a motor vehicle on a road or public place fine on level 5* and 6 months' imprisonment. Must disqualify for at least one year (the guideline penalty is two years) unless special reasons. The disqualification may be for any period exceeding a year. The defendant may also be ordered to take a test again. Must endorse licence unless special reasons.

Where a person has been convicted within the ten years immediately preceding the present offence of any of the following offences, the minimum period of disqualification increases to three years. The offences are:

- s 3A (causing death by careless driving when under the influence of drink or drugs);
- s 4(1) (driving or attempting to drive while unfit);
- s 5(1)(a) (driving or attempting to drive with excess alcohol);
- s 5A(1)(a) and (2) (driving or attempting to drive with concentration of specified controlled drug above specified limit);
- s 7(6) (failing to provide a specimen) where that is an offence involving obligatory disqualification; and
- s 7A(6) (failing to allow a specimen to be subjected to laboratory test) where that is an offence involving obligatory disqualification.

Penalty points – 3–11.

(g) If the defendant was in charge of a motor vehicle on a road or a public place fine level 4 and 3 months' imprisonment. May disqualify for any period and/or until a driving test has been passed. Must endorse unless there are special reasons.

Penalty points – 10.

---

* Section 85 of the Legal Aid, Sentencing and Punishment of Offenders Act 2012 provides that where a relevant offence would on commencement day be punishable on summary conviction by a fine or maximum fine of £5,000, however expressed, and the offence was committed on or after that date, the court may impose a fine of any amount. The commencement date is 12 March 2015: see the Legal Aid, Sentencing and Punishment of Offenders Act 2012 (Commencement No 11) Order 2015, SI 2015/504.

Legal notes and definitions

C[23.2] A constable, in the course of an investigation into whether a person has committed an offence under the Road Traffic Act 1988, s 3A (causing death by careless driving where under the influence of drink or drugs) the Road Traffic Act 1988, s 4 or s 5, may require him to provide two specimens of breath or a specimen of blood or urine for analysis.

C[23.3] **Fails to provide.** If the case concerns a refusal to provide a blood specimen, an offence is committed if the defendant would only allow blood to be taken from an inappropriate part of the body (toe, penis, etc). In one case a woman refused to provide a blood or urine specimen and claimed embarrassment, there being no doctor or policewoman present. The High Court ruled this amounted to refusal. An agreement to provide a specimen which is conditional will generally be treated as a refusal. In the case of a sample of breath being required for analysis it must be provided in such a way as to make that analysis possible, that is, the required quantity at the required pressure. If a driver has a phobia/medical condition he must inform the police officer so that the police officer can require an alternative specimen (*Martiner v DPP* [2004] EWHC 2484 (Admin), [2004] All ER (D) 122 (Oct)).

In *DPP v Karamouzis* [2006] All ER (D) 109 (Oct), the defendant provided a positive roadside breath test. She was arrested and taken to a police station where she was required to provide specimens of breath for analysis. She argued that she had already been required to provide an evidential breath test under s 7 and accordingly there was no power to arrest and convey her to a police station. It was held that the roadside test was a preliminary test under s 6 and that the defendant had failed to provide specimens as required under s 7.

There must be sufficient breath to enable a test to be carried out although deep lung breath is not a legal requirement. Where an officer had requested a specimen from a Lion Intoxilyser device and requested the defendant blow into the machine and the defendant had removed the mouthpiece on eight occasions, where the device registered there was an insufficient specimen an offence under s 7(6) was made out (*DPP v Darwin* [2007] EWHC 337 (Admin). See also *DPP v Heywood* [1997] RTR 1; *Zafar v DPP* [2004] All ER (D) 6 (Nov)).

In *Rweikiza v DPP* [2008] EWHC 396 (Admin), [2008] All ER (D) 259 (Jan) the defendant's conviction was upheld because he had been properly instructed on how to use the intoxilyser and had deliberately failed to comply with those instructions and had deliberately frustrated the objectives of the test. In those circumstances the court had been correct to find that the specimen was not sufficient to enable the test or analysis to be carried out or the objective to be satisfactorily achieved.

C[23.4] **Reasonable excuse.** The Court of Appeal has said: 'In our judgment no excuse can be adjudged a reasonable one unless the person from whom the specimen is required is physically or mentally unable to provide it, or the provision of the specimen would entail a substantial risk to health.' The fact that a driver has not consumed alcohol at all, or that he has consumed alcohol since being involved in an accident, does not amount to a reasonable excuse for not providing a specimen. Nor can he demand to see a law book before complying (*DPP v Noe* [2000] RTR 351, [2000] 20 LS Gaz R 43), or refuse to take a test until legal advice has been received (*Kirkup v DPP* [2003] EWHC 2354 (Admin), [2003] All ER (D) 53 (Oct)).

The defendant must adduce sufficient evidence, including cross-examination where appropriate: once the defence is so raised, the onus is on the prosecution to negative it: *Parker v Smith* [1974] Crim LR 426; *McKeon v DPP* [2007] EWHC 3216, [2008] RTR 165.

Merely asserting needle phobia at the police station, as a reason for not providing a blood sample, without providing any evidence to the magistrates' court in support of the claim, does not constitute a basis requiring the prosecution to disprove it: *R (Cuns) v Hammersmith Magistrates' Court* [2016] EWHC 748 (Admin), (2017) 181 JP 111, [2017] Crim L R 580.

Defendant must have been warned of consequences of refusing a specimen

C[23.5] The Act expressly directs a policeman requesting a specimen to warn the defendant that a failure to provide such a specimen may make the defendant liable to prosecution. If this warning has not been given, the magistrates can dismiss the charge. If the driver is incapable of understanding the warning (for example, because he does not understand English sufficiently) he may not be convicted if he refuses to provide a sample. Separate procedures apply under s 7A where the defendant is unable to give consent due to a medical condition following an accident. In such circumstances the police surgeon may take a sample of blood. The defendant must be told that the sample has been taken when he is conscious and his permission for a lab test has been obtained. Failure to give consent is an offence with the same penalties as failure to supply a sample.

Inability to provide breath specimens owing to intoxication does not constitute a reasonable excuse. The court must recognise the object and purpose of the 1988 Act and must gauge whether, in that light, the excuse can properly be regarded as 'reasonable'. This is an objective exercise in the light of the evidence. It is unattractive that a motorist who is too intoxicated to understand the requirement to provide breath specimens, or to be able to provide them, should be able to take advantage of a statutory defence not available to a less intoxicated motorist: *DPP v Cramp* [2017] EWHC 3119 (Admin), [2018] All ER (D) 45 (Jan).

C[23.6] There are three possible ways of providing a specimen: breath, blood or urine. The current law places the choice entirely in the hands of the police who will use the breath-analysis machine, only offering the defendant blood or urine if the machine is broken or unavailable, or where there are medical reasons for not requiring a sample of breath. Where the police require a specimen of blood for analysis they are not required to offer the motorist a preference but must ask whether there are any reasons why a specimen cannot or should not be taken by a medical practitioner (*DPP v Warren* [1993] AC 319, [1992] 4 All ER 865, HL). The officer must act reasonably in his choice and not ignore for example a defendant's assertions that he could not give blood due to religious reasons (*Joseph v DPP* [2003] EWHC 3078 (Admin), [2003] All ER (D) 326 (Nov)).

There was nothing in the legislation to state that where a driver failed to provide a specimen of breath and the custody sergeant sought a blood test it was not possible to abandon the blood testing procedure and prosecute the driver under s 7 (6) (*Longstaff v DPP* [2008 EWHC 303 (Admin), [2008] All ER (D) 276 (Jan)); see also *McNeil v DPP* [2008] EWHC 1254 (Admin), [2008] All ER (D) 375 (Apr).

C[23.6A] **Right to legal advice.** Section 58(1) of PACE provides that '[a] person arrested and held in custody in a police station or other premises shall be entitled, if he so requests, to consult a solicitor privately at any time'. There is no statutory exception in relation to the breathalyser procedure. The police will want, however, to conduct the procedure expeditiously before any significant elimination of alcohol from the motorist's body has occurred. This tension has given rise to a significant body of case law, but it is submitted that the following propositions, derived from the judgment of Kennedy LJ in *Kennedy v DPP* [2002] EWHC 2297 (Admin), [2004] RTR 6 accurately summarise the law: (a) a person arrested and in custody in a police station is entitled under s 58 of PACE to consult a solicitor if he or she asks (prompted or unprompted) to do so; (b) if such a request is made, such consultation must be permitted 'as soon as is practicable' and the custody officer 'must act without delay' to secure the provision of legal advice; (c) that does not mean, however, that the custody officer must at once suspend procedures and ring the solicitors' call centre pursuant to the detainee's request; (d) the public interest requires that the obtaining of breath specimens in a drink/driving investigation cannot be delayed to any significant extent to enable a suspect to obtain legal advice; (e) this means that if there is a solicitor immediately available in the charge office or on the telephone that the detainee wishes to consult for a couple of minutes he or she must be allowed to do so; (f) where, however, the suspect does no more than indicate a general desire to have legal advice the custody officer can continue to take details and alert the call centre at the first convenient opportunity.

Referring to the case of Kennedy Latham LJ stated in *Gearing v DPP* [2008] EWHC 1695, [2009] RTR 72: 'If it is apparent that the advice can be readily made available, as indicated by Kennedy LJ, in a couple of minutes or so, it would be appropriate to balance the rights and obligations in question by requiring the police to delay the breath test for that short time. If it is anything greater than that, it does not seem to me that it is a requirement that the police should delay the giving of the breath test for that reason.' While the police should have called the call centre when first requested to, it was inevitable to the court in *Gearing* from the material that had been presented that there would have been significant – and in the context of the breath testing procedure, unacceptable – delay (a total of 23 minutes elapsed between the police attempting to contact the duty solicitor and the latter speaking to the police following a conversation with the suspect), and that the police would, thus, have been entitled to continue with the breathalyser procedure.

In *Chalupa v Crown Prosecution Service* [2009] EWHC 3082 (Admin), (2010) 174 JP 111 the appellant provided a positive roadside test and was kept in detention at the police station. The custody record recorded him as confirming he required legal advice 01.35. The police did not, however, call the duty solicitor until about 20 minutes later. Meanwhile, the breath test procedure had been initiated. The appellant was asking questions about his options, but the operator formed the view he was procrastinating and in practice refusing to take part in the test. It was made plain that he would not be allowed to delay the procedure pending obtaining advice. He was told the solicitor would tell him the same. He would still not provide breath and was charged with refusing to provide a specimen. Meanwhile, when the duty solicitor was called he returned the call within two minutes. He was told, wrongly, that the appellant was currently on the Intoxilyser machine, and to call back in about 20 minutes to discover the readings. The appellant was convicted, he then appealed unsuccessfully, first to the Crown Court and then to the Administrative court.

Lord Justice Elias gave the judgment of the court. The passages cited below encapsulate the key issue.

> '14. ... Fourth, although Lord Justice Kennedy indicated that a suspect should be allowed access to a solicitor in the exceptional circumstances where the solicitor is immediately available, he did not spell out the consequences if that access were not in fact permitted. I do not infer that his Lordship is intending to say that it would be a reasonable excuse to refuse to provide a specimen under the circumstances, nor that the court would be obliged to exclude the evidence under section 78.
>
> ...
>
> 19. As I read Lord Justice Latham's judgment (in *Gearing v DPP*) he is limiting any argument about whether the evidence should be excluded under section 78 to the specific case where a solicitor is immediately available, but where the police nevertheless insist on carrying on with the breathalyser procedure. Even then it will, of course, be a matter of discretion on the facts of each case whether evidence should be excluded.'

His Lordship concluded:

> '26. In my judgment, there are two answers to this appeal. The first is that this is not in my view one of those exceptional cases where a solicitor was immediately available, such that it could be said that any delay would necessarily have been minimal. I do not accept that the exception identified in *Kennedy* applies here. The appellant submits that it does on the basis that fortuitously, as it happens, the duty solicitor did respond within two minutes of being contacted. That may be true in this case, but there is plainly no guarantee under the duty solicitor scheme that there will always be such a speedy response. Moreover, he would not necessarily have been in a position to respond so promptly had he been contacted earlier. In my judgment, this was not one of those cases therefore which falls within that exceptional category.
>
> 27. It follows that we are not in the territory where s.78 is properly engaged in the sense that there is no arguable basis at all for excluding the evidence. The authorities establish that the right to prompt legal advice and any breach of that right will, in general, have no bearing whatsoever upon the obligation to provide a specimen of breath. It is not a reasonable excuse to refuse to provide a specimen

until advice has been received ... Accordingly, there is nothing unfair or improper with the police insisting on a specimen being provided before advice is obtained. To use the language of s.78, there is nothing about the particular circumstance in which the evidence is obtained which might even arguably render it unfair to admit the evidence. Nor can the general circumstance that s.58 is infringed as a result of a short, albeit unjustified, delay in contacting the solicitor, begin to constitute such a justification. It could not possibly be said that to admit this evidence would have an adverse affect on the fairness of the trial. It would simply punish the prosecution in a manner wholly disproportionate to the nature of the wrongdoing, given in particular the public interest in the test being promptly conducted, and the importance of bringing to book those who are suspected of breaking this law.'

Sentencing (Fail to provide specimen for analysis)

C[23.7] Where either the defendant was driving or attempting to drive or where he was in charge see Table B at B[43.2] and see the notes to the offence of 'Alcohol over the prescribed limit' at C[22].

SC Guideline – Failure to Provide Evidential Specimen (drive/attempt to drive)

See C[23.9] for SC Guideline (in charge)

Fail to provide specimen for analysis (drive/attempt to drive) (Revised 2017)

C[23.8]

Road Traffic Act 1988, s 7(6)

Effective from: 24 April 2017

Triable only summarily:

Maximum: Unlimited fine and/ or 6 months

Offence range: Band B fine–26 weeks' custody

Step 1 — Determining the offence category

The Court should determine the offence category using the table below.

Category 1	Higher culpability and greater harm
Category 2	Higher culpability and lesser harm or lower culpability and greater harm
Category 3	Lower culpability and lesser harm

The court should determine the offender's culpability and the harm caused with reference only to the factors below. Where an offence does not fall squarely into a category, individual factors may require a degree of weighting before making an overall assessment and determining the appropriate offence category.

CULPABILITY demonstrated by one or more of the following:

Factors indicating higher culpability

- Deliberate refusal/ failure

Factors indicating lower culpability

- All other cases

HARM demonstrated by one or more of the following:

Factors indicating greater harm

- High level of impairment

Factors indicating lesser harm

- All other cases

Step 2 — Starting point and category range

Having determined the category at step one, the court should use the appropriate starting point to reach a sentence within the category range in the table below.

- **Must endorse and disqualify for at least 12 months**
- **Must disqualify for at least 2 years if offender has had two or more disqualifications for periods of 56 days or more in preceding 3 years — refer to the disqualification guidance and consult your legal adviser for further guidance**
- **Must disqualify for at least 3 years if offender has been convicted of a relevant offence in preceding 10 years -consult your legal adviser for further guidance**
- **Extend disqualification if imposing immediate custody**

If there is a delay in sentencing after conviction, consider interim disqualification.

The starting point applies to all offenders irrespective of plea or previous convictions.

Level of seriousness	Starting point	Range	Disqualification	Disqual. 2_{nd} offence in 10 years
Category 1	12 weeks' custody	High level community order–26 weeks' custody	29–36 months (Extend if imposing immediate custody)	36–60 months (Extend if imposing immediate custody
Category 2	Medium level community order	Low level community order–High level community order	17–28 months	36–52 months
Category 3	Band C fine	Band B fine–Low level community order	12–16 months	36–40 months

Note: when considering the guidance regarding the length of disqualification in the case of a second offence, the period to be imposed in any individual case will depend on an assessment of all the relevant circumstances, including the length of time since the earlier ban was imposed and the gravity of the current offence but disqualification must be for at least three years.

The court should then consider further adjustment for any aggravating or mitigating factors. The following is a **non-exhaustive** list of additional factual elements providing the context of the offence and factors relating to the offender. Identify whether any combination of these, or other relevant factors, should result in an upward or downward adjustment from the sentence arrived at so far.

Factors increasing seriousness

Statutory aggravating factors:

- Previous convictions, having regard to a) the **nature** of the offence to which the conviction relates and its **relevance** to the current offence; and b) the **time** that has elapsed since the conviction

- Offence committed whilst on bail

Other aggravating factors:

- Failure to comply with current court orders
- Offence committed on licence or post sentence supervision
- LGV, HGV PSV etc.
- Poor road or weather conditions
- Carrying passengers
- Driving for hire or reward
- Evidence of unacceptable standard of driving
- Involved in accident
- High level of traffic or pedestrians in the vicinity

Factors reducing seriousness or reflecting personal mitigation

- No previous convictions or no relevant/recent convictions
- Remorse
- Good character and/or exemplary conduct
- Serious medical condition requiring urgent, intensive or long-term treatment
- Age and/or lack of maturity where it affects the responsibility of the offender
- Mental disorder or learning disability
- Sole or primary carer for dependent relatives

Step 3 — Consider any factors which indicate a reduction, such as assistance to the prosecution

The court should take into account sections 73 and 74 of the Serious Organised Crime and Police Act 2005 (assistance by defendants: reduction or review of sentence) and any other rule of law by virtue of which an offender may receive a discounted sentence in consequence of assistance given (or offered) to the prosecutor or investigator.

Step 4 — Reduction for guilty pleas

The court should take account of any potential reduction for a guilty plea in accordance with section 144 of the Criminal Justice Act 2003 and the *Guilty Plea* guideline.

Step 5 — Totality principle

If sentencing an offender for more than one offence, or where the offender is already serving a sentence, consider whether the total sentence is just and proportionate to the overall offending behaviour in accordance with the *Offences Taken into Consideration and Totality* guideline.

Step 6 — Consider ancillary orders

In all cases, the court should consider whether to make compensation and/or other ancillary orders including offering a drink/drive rehabilitation course.

Step 7 — Reasons

Section 174 of the Criminal Justice Act 2003 imposes a duty to give reasons for, and explain the effect of, the sentence.

Step 8 — Consideration for time spent on bail

The court must consider whether to give credit for time spent on bail in accordance with section 240A of the Criminal Justice Act 2003.

SC Guideline – Failure to Provide Evidential Specimen (in charge)

See C[23.8] for SC Guideline (drive/attempt to drive)

Fail to provide specimen for analysis (in charge) (Revised 2017)

C[23.9]

Road Traffic Act 1988, s 7(6)

Effective from: 24 April 2017

Triable only summarily:

Maximum: Level 4 fine and/or 3 months

Offence range: Band B fine–6 weeks' custody

Step 1 — Determining the offence category

The Court should determine the offence category using the table below.

Category 1	Higher culpability and greater harm
Category 2	Higher culpability and lesser harm or lower culpability and greater harm
Category 3	Lower culpability and lesser harm

The court should determine the offender's culpability and the harm caused with reference only to the factors below. Where an offence does not fall squarely into a category, individual factors may require a degree of weighting before making an overall assessment and determining the appropriate offence category.

CULPABILITY demonstrated by one or more of the following:

Factors indicating higher culpability

- Deliberate refusal/ failure

Factors indicating lower culpability

- Honestly held belief but unreasonable excuse
- Genuine attempt to comply
- All other cases

HARM demonstrated by one or more of the following:

Factors indicating greater harm

- High level of impairment

Factors indicating lesser harm

- All other cases

Step 2 — Starting point and category range

Having determined the category at step one, the court should use the corresponding starting point to reach a sentence within the category range below.

- **Must endorse and may disqualify. If no disqualification impose 10 points**
- **Extend any disqualification if imposing immediate custody**

The starting point applies to all offenders irrespective of plea or previous convictions.

Level of seriousness	Starting Point	Range	Disqualification/ points
Category 1	Medium level community order	Low level community order–6 weeks' custody	Disqualify 6–12 months (Extend if imposing immediate custody)

Level of seriousness	Starting Point	Range	Disqualification/ points
Category 2	Band C fine	Band C fine–Medium level community order	Disqualify up to 6 months **OR** 10 points
Category 3	Band B fine	Band B fine	10 points

The court should then consider further adjustment for any aggravating or mitigating factors. The following is a **non-exhaustive** list of additional factual elements providing the context of the offence and factors relating to the offender. Identify whether any combination of these, or other relevant factors, should result in an upward or downward adjustment from the sentence arrived at so far.

Factors increasing seriousness

Statutory aggravating factors:

- Previous convictions, having regard to a) the **nature** of the offence to which the conviction relates and its **relevance** to the current offence; and b) the **time** that has elapsed since the conviction
- Offence committed whilst on bail

Other aggravating factors:

- High likelihood of driving
- Failure to comply with current court orders
- Offence committed on licence or post sentence supervision
- In charge of LGV, HGV, PSV etc.
- Offering to drive for hire or reward

Factors reducing seriousness or reflecting personal mitigation

- No previous convictions **or** no relevant/recent convictions
- Remorse
- Good character and/or exemplary conduct
- Serious medical condition requiring urgent, intensive or long-term treatment
- Age and/or lack of maturity where it affects the responsibility of the offender
- Mental disorder or learning disability
- Sole or primary carer for dependent relatives

Step 3 — Consider any factors which indicate a reduction, such as assistance to the prosecution

The court should take into account sections 73 and 74 of the Serious Organised Crime and Police Act 2005 (assistance by defendants: reduction or review of sentence) and any other rule of law by virtue of which an offender may receive a discounted sentence in consequence of assistance given (or offered) to the prosecutor or investigator.

Step 4 — Reduction for guilty pleas

The court should take account of any potential reduction for a guilty plea in accordance with section 144 of the Criminal Justice Act 2003 and the *Guilty Plea* guideline.

Step 5 — Totality principle

If sentencing an offender for more than one offence, or where the offender is already serving a sentence, consider whether the total sentence is just and proportionate to the overall offending behaviour in accordance with the *Offences Taken into Consideration and Totality* guideline.

Step 6 — Compensation and ancillary orders

In all cases, the court should consider whether to make compensation and/or other ancillary orders including offering a drink/drive rehabilitation course, deprivation, and /or forfeiture or suspension of personal liquor licence.

Step 7 — Reasons

Section 174 of the Criminal Justice Act 2003 imposes a duty to give reasons for, and explain the effect of, the sentence.

Step 8 — Consideration for time spent on bail

The court must consider whether to give credit for time spent on bail in accordance with section 240A of the Criminal Justice Act 2003.

C[24]

Failure to co-operate with roadside breath test

Charge (Failure to co-operate with roadside breath test)

C[24.1] Failing, without reasonable excuse, to co-operate with a preliminary test when required to do so by a constable in uniform

Road Traffic Act 1988, s 6(6)

Maximum penalty-Fine of level 3. Must endorse unless special reasons. Disqualification is discretionary.

Penalty points – 4.

Legal notes and definitions

C[24.2] A constable may require a person to co-operate with any one or more preliminary tests administered to the person by that constable or another constable. There are three kinds of preliminary tests: preliminary breath tests; preliminary impairment tests; and preliminary drug tests. These are defined, respectively, by ss 6A, 6B and 6C. Preliminary breath and drug tests must be carried out by means of devices approved by the Secretary of State. Preliminary impairment tests are conducted in accordance with a code of practice issued by the Secretary of State.

C[24.3] A defendant can only be required to take this test by a constable in uniform who has reasonable cause for suspecting:

(a) the defendant *is* driving or attempting to drive a motor vehicle on a road or other public place and has alcohol or a drug in his body or has committed a traffic offence whilst the vehicle was in motion; or
(b) he *has been* driving or attempting to drive on a road or other public place with alcohol or a drug in his body and he still has alcohol or a drug in his body; or
(c) he *has been* driving or attempting to drive a motor vehicle on a road or other public place and has committed a traffic offence as defined whilst the vehicle was in motion.

For these purposes 'driving' includes being 'in charge'.

C[24.4] In addition, where there has been an accident, a constable (whether in uniform or not) may require any person who he has reasonable cause to believe was driving or attempting to drive or in charge of the vehicle at the time of the accident to provide a breath test.

C[24.5] The instructions on the breath test device need not be strictly observed. If the constable had no reason to suspect that the motorist had drunk alcohol in the previous 20 minutes he can be required to take the test immediately.

See also C[23.3].

C[24.6] Motorist in hospital. If a motorist is in a hospital as a patient, he can still be required to take a breath test, provided that the doctor in immediate charge of him is notified and does not object.

C[24.7] Reasonable excuse. If the defendant satisfies the magistrates that he had a reasonable excuse for failing to take a breath test he is entitled to be acquitted. Such a defendant will probably be rare. One example may be that the defendant was hurrying to get a doctor to deal with an emergency. The degree of proof required of the defendant is to prove that this point is probably true. He does not have to establish it beyond reasonable doubt.

C[24.8] The legal adviser should be consulted if the defence raise this point.

Sentencing
SC Guideline – Failing to co-operate with roadside breath test

C[24.9] Starting point – Band B fine.

Since 'reasonable excuse' is a defence (see above) a conviction implies that the defendant had no excuse and therefore this is not a trivial offence and carries an endorsement.

C[25]–C[30]

Careless driving (drive without due care and attention)

Charge (Careless driving (without due care and attention))

C[25.1] Driving a mechanically propelled vehicle on a road or other public place without due care and attention

Road Traffic Act 1988, s 3, as amended

Maximum penalty – Fine level 5* for offences committed on or after 24/9/07. For fines see B[28]). May disqualify for any period and/or until a driving test has been passed. Must endorse unless special reasons.

Penalty points – 3–9.

Fixed penalty – £100/3 penalty points. The police are also able to offer educational training as an alternative to endorsement.

ACPO has given the following guidance:

Fixed penalty. Fixed penalty and/or educational training can be offered in situations of officer-observed, low level careless, aggressive and inconsiderate driving where other drivers are not unduly affected such as:

- driving too close to the vehicle in front;
- failing to give way at a junction (no evasive action by another driver);
- overtaking and forcing into a queue of traffic;
- wrong lane at a roundabout;
- ignoring a lane closed sign and forcing into an orderly queue;
- lane discipline such as remaining in lane two or three when lane one is empty and there is no other vehicle to overtake;
- inappropriate speed;
- wheel spins and hand brake turns.

Summons. A summons will continue to be issued in situations of aggressive driving where other drivers are endangered. These may be officer observed, witnessed or involve collisions and include:

- fast overtakes and lane hopping/weaving with other drivers having to evade;
- pulling out in front of other moving vehicle that needs to brake;
- overtaking and causing the approaching vehicle to brake or take evading action or pulling in causing the overtaken vehicle to brake or swerve;
- wrong lane at roundabout causing another vehicle on the roundabout to brake or swerve;
- staying in lane two or three with vehicles behind being held up or forced to pass on nearside.

* Section 85 of the Legal Aid, Sentencing and Punishment of Offenders Act 2012 provides that where a relevant offence would on commencement day be punishable on summary conviction by a fine or maximum fine of £5,000, however expressed, and the offence was committed on or after that date, the court may impose a fine of any amount. The commencement date is 12 March 2015: see the Legal Aid, Sentencing and Punishment of Offenders Act 2012 (Commencement No 11) Order 2015, SI 2015/504.

Legal notes and definitions

C[25.2] Mechanically propelled vehicle. See C[47.9].

C[25.3] Road. See C[22.5].

C[25.4] **Public place.** See C[20.7]–C[20.8]. The car park of a dealership has been found to be a public place (*May v DPP* [2005] EWHC 1280 (Admin), [2005] All ER (D) 182 (Apr)).

C[25.5] **Due care and attention.** The standard of driving expected by the law is that of the degree of care and attention to be exercised by a reasonable and prudent driver in the circumstances. The standard of careful driving expected in law from a motorist is the same for all, even the holder of a provisional licence.

Definition: For offences committed or after 24 September 2007 the **Road Safety Act** 2006 inserts after s 3 of the Road Traffic Act 1988, a new s 3ZA which provides a statutory meaning of careless, or inconsiderate, driving as follows:

(1) This section has effect for the purposes of sections 2B and 3 above and section 3A below.

(2) A person is to be regarded as driving without due care and attention if (and only if) the way he drives falls below what would be expected of a competent and careful driver.

(3) In determining for the purposes of subsection (2) above what would be expected of a competent and careful driver in a particular case, regard shall be had not only to the circumstances of which he could be expected to be aware but also to any circumstances shown to have been within the knowledge of the accused.

(4) A person is to be regarded as driving without reasonable consideration for other persons only if those persons are inconvenienced by his driving.

C[25.6] A skid may or may not be due to lack of care, but being overcome by sleep is not a defence.

C[25.7] Where a motorist is confronted by an emergency during the course of driving, he should be judged by the test of whether it was reasonable for him to have acted as he did and not according to the standard of perfection yielded by hindsight.

C[25.8] If the driving complained of was due to a mechanical defect in the vehicle, that is a defence unless the defendant knew of the defect, or he could have discovered it by exercising prudence; but the burden of proof remains on the prosecution to establish beyond reasonable doubt a lack of due care and attention.

C[25.9] Observance or non-observance of the Highway Code can be used to establish or disprove guilt. General impressions formed by a witness as to the speed of a vehicle may be admitted (*Blake v DPP* [2002] EWHC 2014 (Admin), [2002] All ER (D) 125 (Sep)).

C[25.10] **Warning of proceedings.** If the defence claim that notice should have been given within 14 days of intention to prosecute, consult the clerk.

Evidence will not be excluded because of the failure of a police officer to issue a caution before asking a driver if he was driving a particular vehicle involved in an accident (*Kemsley v DPP* [2005] 169 JP 148).

C[25.11]–[25.15] **Death.** As a matter of practice justices should not proceed with a summary trial until the inquest has been held (*Smith v DPP* [2000] RTR 36, 164 JP 96).

C[25.16] **Careless or inconsiderate driving (Road Traffic Act 1988, s 3) and dangerous driving (s 2).** Where the magistrates see fit, they may allow information for an offence under s 3 and s 2 to be heard together. In this event, if the defendant is convicted of one offence, the second information may be adjourned *sine die* or the justices may make "*no adjudication*". Should the driver successfully appeal against conviction, he can later be tried on the second information.

C[25.17] Alternatively, where there is a single information alleging dangerous driving and the magistrates do not find this proved, they may convict of careless driving in the alternative (s 24 RTOA 1988).

C[25.18] **Emergency vehicles.** The same standard of care and attention is required of the drivers of fire engines, ambulances, coastguard and police vehicles as of any other driver. That standard is that the driver takes 'due' care and pays 'due' attention.

C[25.19] **Driving.** See the note under the offence of no driving licence at C[18.2].

Sentencing

SC Guideline – Careless driving (drive without due care and attention)

Careless Driving (drive without due care and attention) (Revised 2017)

C[25.20]

Road Traffic Act 1988, s 3

Effective from: 24 April 2017

Triable only summarily:

Maximum: Unlimited fine

Offence range: Band A fine–Band C fine

Step 1 — Determining the offence category

The Court should determine the offence category using the table below.

Category 1	Higher culpability and greater harm
Category 2	Higher culpability and lesser harm or lower culpability and greater harm
Category3	Lower culpability and lesser harm

The court should determine the offender's culpability and the harm caused with reference only to the factors below. Where an offence does not fall squarely into a category, individual factors may require a degree of weighting before making an overall assessment and determining the appropriate offence category.

CULPABILITY demonstrated by one or more of the following:

Factors indicating higher culpability

- Excessive speed or aggressive driving
- Carrying out other tasks while driving
- Vehicle used for the carriage of heavy goods or for the carriage of passengers for reward
- Tiredness or driving whilst unwell
- Driving contrary to medical advice (including written advice from the drug manufacturer not to drive when taking any medicine)

Factors indicating lower culpability

- All other cases

HARM demonstrated by one or more of the following:

Factors indicating greater harm

- Injury to others
- Damage to other vehicles or property
- High level of traffic or pedestrians in vicinity

Factors indicating lesser harm

- All other cases

Step 2 — Starting point and category range

Having determined the category at step one, the court should use the appropriate starting point to reach a sentence within the category range in the table below. The starting point applies to all offenders irrespective of plea or previous convictions.

Level of seriousness	Starting Point	Range	Disqualification/points
Category 1	Band C fine	Band C fine	Consider disqualification OR 7–9 points
Category 2	Band B fine	Band B fine	5–6 points
Category 3	Band A fine	Band A fine	3–4 points

- **Must endorse and may disqualify. If no disqualification impose 3–9 points**

The court should then consider further adjustment for any aggravating or mitigating factors. The following is a **non-exhaustive** list of additional factual elements providing the context of the offence and factors relating to the offender. Identify whether any combination of these, or other relevant factors, should result in an upward or downward adjustment from the sentence arrived at so far.

Factors increasing seriousness

Statutory aggravating factors:

- Previous convictions, having regard to a) the **nature** of the offence to which the conviction relates and its **relevance** to the current offence; and b) the **time** that has elapsed since the conviction
- Offence committed whilst on bail

Other aggravating factors:

- Failure to comply with current court orders
- Offence committed on licence or post sentence supervision
- Contravening a red signal at a level crossing

Factors reducing seriousness or reflecting personal mitigation

- No previous convictions **or** no relevant/recent convictions
- Remorse
- Good character and/or exemplary conduct

Step 3 — Consider any factors which indicate a reduction, such as assistance to the prosecution

The court should take into account sections 73 and 74 of the Serious Organised Crime and Police Act 2005 (assistance by defendants: reduction or review of sentence) and any other rule of law by virtue of which an offender may receive a discounted sentence in consequence of assistance given (or offered) to the prosecutor or investigator.

Step 4 — Reduction for guilty pleas

The court should take account of any potential reduction for a guilty plea in accordance with section 144 of the Criminal Justice Act 2003 and the *Guilty Plea* guideline.

Step 5 — Totality principle

If sentencing an offender for more than one offence, or where the offender is already serving a sentence, consider whether the total sentence is just and proportionate to the overall offending behaviour in accordance with the *Offences Taken into Consideration and Totality* guideline.

Step 6 — Compensation and ancillary orders

In all cases, the court should consider whether to make compensation and/or other ancillary orders, including disqualification from driving.

Step 7 — Reasons

Section 174 of the Criminal Justice Act 2003 imposes a duty to give reasons for, and explain the effect of, the sentence.

C[25.21] If it appears to the court that the offender suffers from a disease or physical disability likely to cause his driving to be a source of danger to the public, then the court shall notify the licensing authority who may take steps to withdraw the driving licence (see C[5.49]).

C[31]

Failing to stop and give details after accident

Charge (Failing to stop and give details after accident)

C[31.1] **As a driver of a mechanically propelled vehicle, owing to the presence of which on a road or other public place, an accident occurred whereby injury was caused to another person (or damage caused to another vehicle or to roadside property or injury to an animal)**

[failed to stop]

[upon being reasonably required to give his name and address, the name and address of the owner of the vehicle and the number of the vehicle, failing to do so]

Road Traffic Act 1988, s 170 (4), as amended

Maximum penalty-Fine level 5* and 6 months' imprisonment. May disqualify for any period and/or until a driving test has been passed. Must endorse unless there are special reasons.

Penalty points – 5–10.

---

* Section 85 of the Legal Aid, Sentencing and Punishment of Offenders Act 2012 provides that where a relevant offence would on commencement day be punishable on summary conviction by a fine or maximum fine of £5,000, however expressed, and the offence was committed on or after that date, the court may impose a fine of any amount. The commencement date is 12 March 2015: see the Legal Aid, Sentencing and Punishment of Offenders Act 2012 (Commencement No 11) Order 2015, SI 2015/504.

Legal notes and definitions

C[31.2] **Charge.** The one charge may include both factual situations without offending the rule against duplicity (*DPP v Bennett* [1993] RTR 175, 157 JP 493).

C[31.3] **Relationship between the offences of failing to stop and give details and failing to report an accident.** Where an accident has occurred in the circumstances described above, there is an obligation on the driver to stop at the scene of the accident. If he does not do so immediately and as soon as he could safely and conveniently, he commits the offence described here (*Hallinan v DPP* [1998] Crim LR 754). Having stopped at the scene of the accident, he has a duty to give his name and address, the name and address of the owner of the vehicle and the identification marks of the vehicle to any person having reasonable grounds for such a request. If he fails to do so, he has also committed the offence described here. Unless he has actually given his particulars to such other person, he must report the accident at a police station or to a police constable *as soon as reasonably practicable*, and in any case within 24 hours of the accident, otherwise he commits the offence at C[32.18].

C[31.4] **Mechanically propelled vehicle.** See C[47.9].

C[31.5] **A road or other public place.** See C[22.5].

C[31.6] **An animal.** Means any horse, cattle, ass, mule, sheep, pig, goat or dog.

C[31.7] **Roadside property.** Means any property constructed on, fixed to, growing in or otherwise forming part of the land on which the road in question is situated, or land adjacent thereto.

C[31.8] The law requires the driver to give the appropriate particulars upon being reasonably required to do so. It is acceptable to give a business address or a lawyer's office where one can be contacted *(DPP v McCarthy* [1999] RTR 323, 163 JP 585). It is not sufficient to report the incident to the police within 24 hours. Where the defendant was the driver of the vehicle involved in the accident, there is a rebuttable presumption that the defendant knew that he had been involved in the accident. If the defendant can satisfy the court that he was unaware of any accident he must be acquitted (*Selby v Chief Constable of Avon and Somerset* [1988] RTR 216). Where, however, the defendant's ignorance of the accident was the result of voluntary intoxication, this cannot be prayed in aid to negate the inference of knowledge: *Magee v CPS* [2014] EWHC 4089 (Admin), 179 JP 261.

C[31.9] The degree of proof required of the defendant is to satisfy the court that this was probably true; he does not have to prove this beyond reasonable doubt.

C[31.10]–[31.15] **Driver.** The notes under the heading 'driving' for the offence of driving without a licence at C[18.2] may be of assistance. A person may continue to be the driver of a motor vehicle if having fulfilled the requirements mentioned on that page he ceases to do so by reason of a change of activity.

C[31.16] **Accidents involving personal injury (to a person other than the driver).** The driver must at the time produce his certificate of insurance to a constable or other person having reasonable cause to require it. If he does not do so, he must report the accident as described above and produce his insurance certificate. Otherwise he commits an offence under the Road Traffic Act 1988, s 170(7)- maximum penalty a fine of up to level 3. There is a defence if the certificate is produced within seven days of the accident at a police station specified by him at the time when the accident was reported. This provision does not apply to the driver of an invalid carriage.

Sentencing

SC Guideline – Failing to stop/report accident

Fail to stop/report road accident (Revised 2017)

C[31.17]

Road Traffic Act 1988, s 170(4)

Effective from: 24 April 2017

Triable only summarily:

Maximum: Unlimited fine and/or 6 months

Offence range: Band A fine–26 weeks' custody

Step 1 — Determining the offence category

The Court should determine the offence category using the table below.

Category 1	Higher culpability and greater harm
Category 2	Higher culpability and lesser harm or lower culpability and greater harm
Category 3	Lower culpability and lesser harm

The court should determine the offender's culpability and the harm caused with reference only to the factors below. Where an offence does not fall squarely into a category, individual factors may require a degree of weighting before making an overall assessment and determining the appropriate offence category.

CULPABILITY demonstrated by one or more of the following:

Factors indicating higher culpability

- Offence committed in circumstances where a request for a sample of breath, blood or urine would have been made had the offender stopped
- Offence committed by offender seeking to avoid arrest for another offence
- Offender knew or suspected that personal injury caused and/or left injured party at scene
- Giving false details

Factors indicating lower culpability

- All other cases

HARM demonstrated by one or more of the following:

Factors indicating greater harm

- Injury caused
- Significant damage

Factors indicating lesser harm

- All other cases

Step 2 — Starting point and category range

Having determined the category at step one, the court should use the appropriate starting point to reach a sentence within the category range in the table below. The starting point applies to all offenders irrespective of plea or previous convictions.

Level of seriousness	Starting Point	Range	Disqualification/ points
Category 1	High level community order	Low level community order–26 weeks' custody	Disqualify 6–12 months **OR** 9–10 points (Extend if imposing immediate custody)
Category 2	Band C fine	Band B fine–Medium level community order	Disqualify up to 6 months **OR** 7–8 points
Category 3	Band B fine	Band A fine–Band C fine	5–6 points

- **Must endorse and may disqualify. If no disqualification impose 5–10 points**
- **Extend disqualification if imposing immediate custody**

The court should then consider further adjustment for any aggravating or mitigating factors. The following is a **non-exhaustive** list of additional factual elements providing the context of the offence and factors relating to the offender. Identify whether any combination of these, or other relevant factors, should result in an upward or downward adjustment from the sentence arrived at so far.

Factors increasing seriousness

Statutory aggravating factors:

- Previous convictions, having regard to a) the **nature** of the offence to which the conviction relates and its **relevance** to the current offence; and b) the **time** that has elapsed since the conviction
- Offence committed whilst on bail

Other aggravating factors:

- Little or no attempt made to comply with duty
- Evidence of bad driving
- Failure to comply with current court orders
- Offence committed on licence or post sentence supervision

Factors reducing seriousness or reflecting personal mitigation

- No previous convictions or no relevant/recent convictions
- Remorse
- Good character and/or exemplary conduct
- Reasonably believed identity known
- Genuine fear of retribution
- Significant attempt made to comply with duty
- Serious medical condition requiring urgent, intensive or long-term treatment
- Age and/or lack of maturity where it affects the responsibility of the offender
- Mental disorder or learning disability
- Sole or primary carer for dependent relatives

Step 3 — Consider any factors which indicate a reduction, such as assistance to the prosecution

The court should take into account sections 73 and 74 of the Serious Organised Crime and Police Act 2005 (assistance by defendants: reduction or review of sentence) and any other rule of law by virtue of which an offender may receive a discounted sentence in consequence of assistance given (or offered) to the prosecutor or investigator.

Step 4 — Reduction for guilty pleas

The court should take account of any potential reduction for a guilty plea in accordance with section 144 of the Criminal Justice Act 2003 and the *Guilty Plea* guideline.

Step 5 — Totality principle

If sentencing an offender for more than one offence, or where the offender is already serving a sentence, consider whether the total sentence is just and proportionate to the overall offending behaviour in accordance with the *Offences Taken into Consideration and Totality* guideline.

Step 6 — Compensation and ancillary orders

In all cases, the court should consider whether to make compensation and/or other ancillary orders, including disqualification from driving and deprivation of a vehicle.

Step 7 — Reasons

Section 174 of the Criminal Justice Act 2003 imposes a duty to give reasons for, and explain the effect of, the sentence.

Step 8 — Consideration for time spent on bail

The court must consider whether to give credit for time spent on bail in accordance with section 240A of the Criminal Justice Act 2003.

C[31.18] If it appears to the court that the accused suffers from a disease or physical disability likely to cause his driving to be a source of danger to the public, then the court shall notify the licensing authority who may take steps to withdraw the driving licence (see C[5.49]).

C[31.19] For fines see B[28].

C[32]

Failing to report after accident

Charge (Failing to report after accident)

C[32.1] **As a driver of a mechanically propelled vehicle, owing to the presence of which on a road or other public place an accident occurred whereby injury was caused to another person (or damage caused to another vehicle or to roadside property or to an animal), not giving his name and address to any person having reasonable grounds for requiring this information, failing to report to the police as soon as reasonably practicable and in any case within 24 hours**

Road Traffic Act 1988, s 170(4), as amended

Maximum penalty – Fine level 5 and 6 months' imprisonment. May disqualify for any period and/or until a driving test has been passed. Must endorse unless there are special reasons.

Penalty points – 5–10.

* Section 85 of the Legal Aid, Sentencing and Punishment of Offenders Act 2012 provides that where a relevant offence would on commencement day be punishable on summary conviction by a fine or maximum fine of £5,000, however expressed, and the offence was committed on or after that date, the court may impose a fine of any amount. The commencement date is 12 March 2015: see the Legal Aid, Sentencing and Punishment of Offenders Act 2012 (Commencement No 11) Order 2015, SI 2015/504.

Legal notes and definitions

C[32.2] **Relationship between the offences of failing to stop and give details and failing to report an accident.** See C[31].

C[32.3] **Mechanically propelled vehicle.** See C[47.9].

C[32.4] **A road or other public place.** See C[22.5].

C[32.5] **An animal.** Means any horse, cattle, ass, mule, sheep, pig, goat or dog.

C[32.6]–[32.15] If he has given his name and address and other particulars to the other driver he need not report to the police under this subsection: *Green v Dunn* [1953] 1 All ER 550, DC.

The onus is on the prosecution to establish a prima facie case that the accident has occurred whereby a statutory duty was upon the defendant to stop and that he had failed to do so: if the defendant then satisfies the court (and the evidential burden is upon him) that he was unaware that an accident had occurred, he is entitled to be acquitted: *Harding v Price* [1948] 1 KB 695, [1948] 1 All ER 283, 112 JP 189, an appeal from a magistrates' court which had found as a fact that the driver of a 'mechanical horse' to which a large trailer was attached was not aware that the trailer had collided with a stationary motor car. In this case Lord Goddard CJ, commented, 'It must not be thought that this decision provides an easy defence to motorists who fail to report an accident'. Where, however, the defendant's ignorance of the accident was the result of voluntary intoxication, this cannot be prayed in aid to negate the inference of knowledge: *Magee v CPS* [2014] EWHC 4089 (Admin), 179 JP 261. A driver who is not aware of an accident at the time it occurred, but subsequently becomes aware of it, has a duty to report the accident provided that he becomes so aware within 24 hours of the occurrence of the accident: *DPP v Drury* [1989] RTR 165, (1988) 153 JP 417, DC, .

The obligation to report is not confined to where the driver has been required to give his name and address, and has not done so, but extends to every case where he has not, in fact, given his name and address, eg where no one is present at the scene of the accident: *Peek v Towle* [1945] KB 458, [1945] 2 All ER 611, DC. It makes no difference for this purpose that the accident was observed by a police officer but he made no request for information; the obligation to report still exists: *DPP v Hay* [2005] EWHC (Admin) 1395, [2006] RTR 32, (2005) 169 JP 429.

In *Wisdom v Macdonald* [1983] RTR 186, [1982] Crim LR 758, DC, on the facts of that case, it was held that reporting the accident by telephone did not avoid commission of an offence. When reporting an accident the driver is obliged to make clear to the police officer, whether at a police station or elsewhere, that the report is being made for the purposes of the obligation to report an accident, to identify the accident, giving the place, time, date, and to be prepared to give his name and address, and those of the owner of the vehicle and its identification marks; see *Wisdom v Macdonald* above.

C[32.16] **Roadside property.** Means any property constructed on, fixed to, growing in or otherwise forming part of the land on which the road in question is situated or land adjacent thereto.

C[32.17] **Driver.** See note under the offence of no driving licence at C[18.8]. A person does not necessarily cease to be a driver if having met the requirements mentioned on that page, he ceased to do so by reason of a change of activity.

C[32.18] **Reasonably practicable.** A driver is not saved from conviction because he reported the accident within 24 hours if he could reasonably have reported it sooner. If, for example, he continued his journey after the accident and drove past a police station he would need a very strong reason for not reporting at that station. It appears that he is not obliged to go in search of a public telephone in order to telephone the police. It is for the court to decide what is 'reasonably practicable' in the particular circumstances of each case and the test is not 'Is it reasonable for the defendant to have reported the accident earlier?' but 'Did he report it as soon as practicable?'

In *DPP v Hay* [2005] EWHC 1395 (Admin), (2005) Times, 13 July, it was decided that, after discharging himself from hospital, a driver was still under an obligation to report an accident despite the fact that the police had seen the motorist at the hospital and despite the fact that the police did not issue the driver with an HORT 1 notice to produce the relevant documents such as insurance within 7 days.

Sentencing (Failing to report after accident)

C[32.19] See the definitive guideline at C[31.17], ante.

C[32A] Failing to provide information as to identity of driver

Charge

C[32A.1] **Keeper. Being the keeper of a vehicle the driver of which is alleged to have been guilty of an offence specified in the Road Traffic Act 1988, s 172, namely [specify] did fail to give such information as to the identity of the driver as you were required to give by [or on behalf of] a chief officer of police, or the Chief Constable of the British Transport Police.**

Road Traffic Act 1988, s 172(2)(a) and (3)

Person other than keeper. Did fail when required by [or on behalf of] a chief officer of police, or the Chief Constable of the British Transport Police, to give information which it was in your power to give which might have led to the identification of the driver of a vehicle who was alleged to have been guilty of an offence specified in the Road Traffic Act 1988, s 172.

Road Traffic Act 1988, s 172(2)(b) and (3)

Note. The above precedents should be used where it is definitely known whether or not the defendant is the actual keeper. However, s 172 creates a single offence and all the information needs to state is:

Did on [date] fail to give information relating to the driver of a motor vehicle [specify] who was alleged to have been guilty of an offence, contrary to s 172(3) of the Road traffic Act 1988, and Schedule 2 to the Road Traffic Offenders Act 1988 (per Moses J in *Mohindra v DPP, Browne v Chief Constable of Greater Manchester Police* [2004] EWHC 490 (Admin), [2005] RTR 95, 168 JP 448, at para 18.)

The police are not required to specify the nature of the alleged offence when they require information from an owner or other person: *Pulton v Leader* [1949] 2 All ER 747, 113 JP 637.

Maximum penalty – Fine level 3. Must endorse unless special reasons. Disqualification is discretionary.

Penalty points – 6.

Legal notes and definitions

C[32A.2] **Trigger offences.** Section 192(1) sets out the offences which can trigger a requirement to give information. These include: most offences under the RTA 1988; offences under ss 25, 26 or 27 of the RTOA 1988; any offence against any other enactment relating to the use of vehicles on roads; and manslaughter by the driver of a motor vehicle.

C[32A.3] **Persons who may be required to give information.** The person keeping the vehicle shall give such information as to the identity of the driver as he or she may be required to give by or on behalf of a chief officer of police or the Chief Constable of the British Transport Police: s 172(2)(a). 'The person' includes the plural. A vehicle may be registered in more than one name and in such a case they are jointly responsible and they can all commit the offence of failing to respond, though it remains an open question whether a response by one of them discharges the obligations under s 172 of the others: *Lynes v DPP* [2012] EWHC 1300 (Admin), [2013] RTR 13, [2013] Crim L R 333.

Any other person shall if required as stated above give any information which it is in his/her power to give and may lead to the identification of the driver. This includes the driver him/herself: *Bingham v Bruce* [1962] 1q All ER 136, 126 JP 81, and a doctor who, under this section, may be required to give information about a patient which may lead to the identification of the driver: *Hunter v Mann* [1974] QB 767, [1974] 2 All ER 414, 138 JP 473.

The essential difference is that where the request is made to the keeper he/she must prove that he or she neither knew who the driver was and that he/she could not, with all reasonable diligence, have ascertained who the driver was, whereas if the request is made to any other person the prosecution must prove that he/she has not given all the information in his/her power to give about who was the driver. The reason for this variation in the standard of proof is that one who keeps a vehicle is presumed to know the information required unless he/she can prove otherwise: *Mohindra v DPP, Browne v Chief Constable of Greater Manchester Police*, supra. Where the registered keeper is not the actual keeper the higher, 'any other person' standard of proof will apply. To deal with the problem where the prosecution does not know whether or not the registered keeper was the actual keeper, the defendant must before the close of the prosecution case raise the issue that he/she is not the actual keeper: *Mohindra v DPP, Browne v Chief Constable of Greater Manchester Police*, supra.

C[32A.4] **Service of the notice.** A requirement under subsection (2) may be made by written notice served by post; and where it is so made: (a) it shall have effect as a requirement to give the information within the period of 28 days beginning with the day on which the notice is served, and (b) the person on whom the notice is served shall not be guilty of an offence under this section if he/she shows either that he/she gave the information as soon as reasonably practicable after the end of that period or that it has not been reasonably practicable for him to give it: RTA 1988, s 172(7).

No offence can be committed until the expiry of the 28 day period: *Foster v DPP* [2013] EWHC 2039 (Admin), (2014) 178 JP 15.

Where a notice is sent to a company address or the last known address of an individual, service is deemed to have been effected when the notice would have arrived in the ordinary course of the post: Interpretation Act 1978, s 7.

A notice may be properly served whether it is received by the addressee or not: CrimPR r 4.4(2)(a). The obligation to provide information does not arise, however, until the notice is properly served (and arises from that moment and not the moment when it is actually seen or received by the defendant), and cannot be triggered by receipt of a reminder since only the notice itself can give rise to the obligation. Therefore, if the presumption of proper service is rebutted by the defendant no offence can have been committed and it is unnecessary for the court to consider any defence under s 172(7): *Krishevsky v DPP* [2014] EWHC 1755 (Admin), 178 JP 369. Section 172 does not impose a duty on a registered keeper to be available at the registered address to receive communications, such as notices of intended prosecution. A failure to be so available, however, is a factor which may make it very difficult, if not impossible, for the registered keeper to discharge the burden of establishing the defence under s 172(7)(b): *R (on the application of Purnell) v Snaresbrook Crown Court, Crown Prosecution Service (Interested Party)* [2011] EWHC 934, 175 JP 233. See further, [C32A.8], infra.

C[32A.5] **Challenging the validity of a request.** Where there is a challenge to the validity of a request, provided justices exercise great care, test the notice and have regard to its authenticity, in the absence of any evidence to doubt that the document came into existence other than in an official way, they may rely on its appearance, its official nature and whether or not it could have other uses: *Pamplin v Gorman* [1980] RTR 54, [1980] Crim LR 52. Provided the justices are satisfied that the sender of the notice was acting 'on behalf of a chief officer of police', it is not necessary that the specially authorised person should sign every notice that is issued and justices were upheld in finding that there was a valid request where the computerised notice emanated from the central ticket office and was sent from a person 'for the Chief Constable' and was not signed: *Arnold v DPP* [1999] RTR 99. There should be annexed to s 9 statements a copy of the notice of intended prosecution to identify the alleged offence by the driver and a copy of the requirement to provide details so that it is clear that the latter has been made by or on behalf of the chief officer of police: *Mohindra v DPP*, supra.

C[32A.6] Form in which information must be given. Where the notice specifies how the information is to be given and the manner that it specifies is reasonable, the information must be given in that way: *DPP v Broomfield* [2002] EWHC 1962 (Admin), (2002) 166 JP 736, [2003] RTR 108).

It was held in *Mawdesley v Chief Constable of Cheshire Constabulary, Yorke v DPP* [2003] EWHC 1586 (Admin), [2004] 1 All ER 58, [2004] 1 WLR 1035, [2004] RTR 13 that the insertion of a name in block capitals on the form, but with the space for the signature left blank, did not amount to a statement in writing purporting to be signed by the accused such as to be admissible under s 12 of the Road Traffic Offenders Act 1988 (but an unsigned form sent in response to a s 172 requirement to name the person driving at the time of the alleged offence (though not if completed and returned by a person acting as agent for the addressee) could amount to a confession under s 82 of PACE and could be proved under s 27 of the Criminal Justice Act 1988 and could give rise to a case to answer). In *Jones v DPP* [2004] Admin 236, (2004) 168 JP 393, the defendant responded to a s 172 notice by returning it almost blank but enclosing a signed letter stating that he was the owner of the vehicle (one of six in a medical practice fleet), but could not state who was driving on the relevant occasion. This was held to be a proper compliance with s 172(2); it answered all the questions asked by the police and gave a reason why he could not identify the driver (though there remained the question of whether this made out the defence under s 172(4), infra). In *R (Flegg) v Southampton and New Forest Justices* [2006] EWHC 396 (Admin), 170 JP 373, however,where the defendant had submitted a letter in response stating that he could not be sure which of two persons had been driving but gave no further details, it was held that in so doing he was in breach of s 172(2)(a) as he did not give the name of the driver or information in his power which would lead to the driver's identification and to avoid conviction he had to make good a defence under s 172(4). In considering such a defence, a request calls for an accurate response and statement of reasons. The provision of an inaccurate and misleading response does not constitute compliance with the requirements of the notice.

All the above cases were considered in *Francis v DPP* [2004] EWHC Admin 591, 168 JP 492, in which it was held that the chief officer of police was entitled to require the addressee of the s 172 notice to sign it.

In *Lord Howard of Lympe v DPP* [2018] EWHC 100, [2018] Crim L R 489 the appellant filled in Part 1 of the form, apart from the driver licence number, but struck through the words 'I was the driver at the time shown overleaf', adding in manuscript 'The driver was my wife or myself. We don't know which.' The District Judge convicted the appellant on the basis that, though he had made reference to his wife, he had not given the required information as to her full name and address, which he could have given in Part 2 of the form. In the light of this failure the Judge did not proceed the defence of reasonable diligence (see below). The appeal was brought on the ground that the appellant had complied with the form. The choice it presented was to fill in Part 1 if the keeper was the driver, or Part 2 if the driver was somebody else. In the present case the appellant did not know who the driver was.

The Administrative Court agreed that the offence was not committed by failing to fill out the form correctly. The form required him to name the driver and not, in the alternative, to provide any other information which may have led to the identification of the driver (the accompanying letter referred to this, but the form provided no space for this). By not naming the driver the appellant had committed an offence under s 172(3), but this was subject to the reasonable diligence defence under s 172(4), which the District Judge had wrongly failed to consider.

C[32A.7] The duty is upon the recipient personally. Where that person leaves the notice in a post room at his place of work and it then goes astray, he or she does not discharge this duty, which is to ensure that this personal post was posted in the appropriate manner: *Phiri v DPP* [2017] EWHC 2546 (Admin), [2017] All ER (D) 118 (Nov).

C[32A.8] Ignorance is no defence. The elements of the offence were considered in *Whiteside v Director of Public Prosecutions* [2011] EWHC 3471 (Admin), 176 JP 103, where the defendant accepted that the notice had arrived at his address but disputed personally receiving it or being made aware of it. Questions arose as to: (a) whether the offence included a mental element; (b) whether a notice is 'served' in such circumstances; and (c) whether the justices had been right to conclude that the defendant had not satisfied the defence under s 172(7)(b) because he should have ensured that systems were in place to deal with the receipt of such important documents.

It was held:

(1) The offence created by s 172(3) of the Act did not require knowledge on the defendant's part that he or she was under an obligation to provide the specified information. The presumption of mens rea did not apply to cases where the offence was not criminal in any real sense, but concerned acts which in the public interest were prohibited under penalty. The offence created by s 172(3) fell into the latter category. Further, it was not a strict liability offence imposing criminal penalties without any culpability. Defences were provided under s 172(4) and (7)(b) to exonerate a defendant who for one reason or another was unable to comply and should not be held culpable.

(2) It was plain that service could be effected by post whether the notice was in fact received by the defendant or not. Rule 4.4(2)(a) of the Criminal Procedure Rules was clear on that point. The notice had been properly served on the defendant notwithstanding that he had not actually received it.

(3) In an appropriate case, a defendant might be able to show that it was not reasonably practicable for him or her to have been aware of the notice, in which case the defence under s 172(7)(b) of the Act would apply. However, the defendant did not have a defence under s 172(7)(b) merely by virtue of lack of knowledge that the notice had been sent. The justices had properly considered whether the defendant had satisfied them that it was not reasonably practicable to respond to the notice on the ground that he had never been aware of them, and they had concluded that he had not discharged that burden. They had held that it had been reasonably practicable to him to have become aware of it and that had been a conclusion open to them on the evidence.

As to the offence under s 172(2)(b) in cases of non-receipt, see further *R (on the application of Purnell) v Snaresbrook Crown Court, Crown Prosecution Service (Interested Party)*, supra.

C[32A.9] **The reasonable diligence defence.** Section 172(4) provides: 'A person shall not be guilty of an offence by virtue of paragraph (a) of subsection (2) above if he shows that he did not know and could not with reasonable diligence have ascertained who the driver of the vehicle'.

Where this defence is raised the court must give adequate reasons for rejecting it: *Weightman v DPP* [2007] EWHC 634 (Admin), [2007] RTR 565.

Reasonable diligence falls to be assessed at the time the request for information was received: *Atkinson v DPP* [2011] EWHC 3363 (Admin), [2012] RTR 171, 176, CL&J 274. The defendant had let somebody test drive her motor scooter which was for sale. He returned the scooter and did not get in further contact. The justices' decision that due diligence began when the defendant allowed her scooter to be driven was wrong in law, and if there had been no duty to know who had been driving, at the time of that driving, then it became more difficult to identify the undertaking or task in respect of which diligence could be assessed.

In *Marshall v Crown Prosecution Service* [2015] EWHC 2333 (Admin), (2016) 180 JP 33 a husband and wife were stated to be the persons who regularly drove a car and the wife was its registered keeper. The car was caught speeding by a speed camera and the husband received a notice under s 172(2). He replied stating that either he or his wife had been the driver and he gave her details. Six weeks after the incident the wife then received a notice under s 17(2) to which she replied 'I do not know for sure who the driver was, either me or my husband'. She was charged with failing to provide information. At the trial the husband testified that he had not noticed a flash camera on his journey home, and the wife stated that she had given her temporary cleaner a lift home, after which her husband had driven the car to their home in Richmond. Both journeys involved passing the speed camera. She also stated that both she and her husband had driven the car within 25 minutes of each other. She did not explain what she had done, if anything, to ascertain who had been driving when the camera was activated. The justices found on this evidence that the statutory test had not been made out and the wife appealed by way of case stated. The two, connected grounds of appeal were: (a) the justices had asked themselves the wrong question – the issue is not whether or not the defendant exercised reasonable diligence, but whether or not 'he did not know and could not with reasonable diligence have ascertained who the driver was'; and (b) if the justices had asked themselves the right question, the evidence pointed to only one rational conclusion, namely even with reasonable diligence the identity of the driver could not have been ascertained.

The appeal was dismissed. The common shared use of motor vehicles potentially gives scope for avoiding sanctions for moving traffic offences:

> '34. In that context I would wish to emphasise that Langstaff J at para 22 of *Atkinson v DPP* [2011] EWHC 3363 (Admin), [2012] RTR 14, an appeal in which I participated, was giving no more than a hypothetical example on one particular factual scenario. He was not providing a blueprint for successful evasion of liability under s.172(3) of the Act.
>
> 35. With that background, it is in my view understandable and indeed commendable that a magistrates' court trying an alleged offence under s.172(3) of the Act should examine with the utmost care and rigour whether the alleged offender himself or herself did in fact exercise reasonable diligence with a view to ascertaining the identity of the driver at the time of the alleged traffic offence. If the alleged offender himself or herself has not exercised such reasonable diligence it is likely, to put the matter at its lowest, to be extremely difficult to persuade the court that even if reasonable diligence had been deployed the exercise would have been futile and would have led nowhere in the search for the driver. This is fully supported by Langstaff J's analysis in *Atkinson* at para 28 (per Parker J).'

The justices had a rational basis for concluding that if the defendant had taken steps and actions to resolve who had been driving at the relevant time it would have been possible to have identified whether that had been herself or her husband.

Sentencing

SC Guideline – Failure to give information of driver's identity as required

C[32A.10] Starting point. Fine Band C.

C[33]

No insurance (using, causing, or permitting)

Charge (No insurance)

C[33.1] **Using (or causing or permitting to be used) a motor vehicle on a road or other public place when there is not in force a policy of insurance or security against third party risks**

Road Traffic Act 1988, s 143

Maximum penalty – Fine level 5*. May disqualify for any period and/or until defendant has passed a driving test. Must endorse unless special reasons.

Penalty points – 6–8.

Fixed penalty – £300/6 points

* Section 85 of the Legal Aid, Sentencing and Punishment of Offenders Act 2012 provides that where a relevant offence would on commencement day be punishable on summary conviction by a fine or maximum fine of £5,000, however expressed, and the offence was committed on or after that date, the court may impose a fine of any amount. The commencement date is 12 March 2015: see the Legal Aid, Sentencing and Punishment of Offenders Act 2012 (Commencement No 11) Order 2015, SI 2015/504.

Legal notes and definitions

C[33.2] **Motor vehicle.** See C[9.7].

Other public place. Not private property but can include such places as car parks.

C[33.3] **A road.** Means any highway (including footpaths and bridleways) and any other road to which the public has access and includes bridges.

C[33.4] **Security in respect of third party risks.** The requirement to have insurance or a security does not apply to a vehicle owned by a person who has deposited with the Accountant General of the Supreme Court the sum of £500,000, at a time when the vehicle is being driven under the owner's control. Nor does it apply to vehicles owned by bodies such as local authorities or the police. Certain other undertakings may have instead of insurance a security given by an insurer that the undertaking will meet any liability it may incur.

Note: The Motor Vehicles (Compulsory Insurance) (Miscellaneous Amendments) Regulations 2019, SI 2019/1047 remove, by regs 2–4, the ability to deposit a prescribed sum or take out a security with a security giver as alternatives to conventional motor insurance. Regulations 2, 3 and 4 will come into force on 1 November 2019. Regulation 5 provides for a transitional period of up to two years (until 1 November 2021) for existing securities and deposits. After this time (or earlier if the security or deposit holder so chooses) compulsory motor insurance will be required.

C[33.5] **Time limit.** Subject to an overall maximum of three years, proceedings may be brought within 6 months from when, in the prosecutor's opinion, he had sufficient evidence to warrant proceedings. A certificate signed by or on behalf of the prosecutor as to when that date was constitutes conclusive evidence on that point.

C[33.6] **Burden of proof.** Once the prosecution have proved use, etc, of a motor vehicle on a road or public place it is for the defendant to prove that he held insurance. If the defendant discharges this burden, the onus reverts to the prosecution to prove that the policy did not cover the particular use.

In *DPP v Whittaker* [2015] EWHC 1850 (Admin), (2015) 179 JP 321 a police officer stopped the respondent who was driving a van. On inspection, the officer found that the van contained a lot of DVDs and the way in which they were arranged indicated that it looked like a mobile library. The respondent was charged with using a motor vehicle on the road when there was not in force, in relation to that use, a policy or insurance that complied with s 143 of the Road Traffic Act 1988. That was on the basis that the certificate of insurance did not cover business use of the vehicle on the road. At the end of the prosecution case, the respondent made a submission of no case to answer. The justices found that the burden of proof had been on the prosecution to prove beyond reasonable doubt that the respondent had been using the vehicle for business. It then found that there was no case to answer because the essential element necessary to show that the respondent had been trading at the time he had been stopped was missing. Accordingly, they dismissed the summons and their decision was upheld by the High Court. Once a defendant had produced a valid certificate of insurance, but the prosecution was maintained on the basis he had been using the vehicle in a way not permitted by the insurance certificate, proof of the user in question reverted to the prosecution. The fact that the police might not be in position to rebut an exculpatory account whose accuracy was questionable did not justify requiring a defendant to assume a legal burden.

C[33.7] **Insurance certificate.** This is in law the main item of proof of insurance and until it has been delivered to the insured he is held not to be insured. Mere proof that he has paid the premium or holds an actual policy is not sufficient.

C[33.8] **Using on a road or other public place.** This expression does not in law only mean driving the vehicle along the road; its mere presence on a road, jacked up and without a battery, may constitute using on a road (*Pumbien v Vines* [1996] RTR 37, [1996] Crim LR 124). A vehicle which is being towed is being used. In any given case where doubt exists consult the legal adviser. See also at C[9] (Brakes).

C[33.9] Use. In *UK Insurance v Holden* [2017] EWCA Civ 259, [2017] 4 All ER 199, [2017] 3 WLR 450, [2017] RTR 25 it was held at first instance that 'use' suggests an activity performed by the vehicle on a public road and, as it is not a normal use of a vehicle to undergo repair, a welding repair carried out negligently and causing a fire did not amount to a 'use'; nor did the fire arise from any use of the vehicle but was caused by the negligence of the welder. The Court of Appeal reversed this decision, but this was also reversed by the Supreme Court in *R&S Pilling (T/A Phoenix Engineering) v UK Insurance Ltd* [2019] UKSC 16, [2019] 2 WLR 1015, [2019] 3 All ER 917, [2019] RTR 28.

> '45 In summary, section 145(3) of the RTA must be interpreted as mandating third party motor insurance against liability in respect of death or bodily injury of a person or damage to property which is caused by or arises out of the use of the vehicle on a road or other public place. The relevant use occurs where a person uses or has the use of a vehicle on a road or public place, including where he or she parks an immobilised vehicle in such a place (as the English case law requires), and the relevant damage has to have arisen out of that use.' (per Lord Hodge JSC)

It was not for a domestic court adjudicating in an action between private parties to 'read down' s 145(3) to comply with Directive 2009/103, which extends insurance obligations to private land.

The terms of the policy had to be construed so as to meet the requirements of RTA 1988, s 145, but the alternation which the Court of Appeal favoured was much radical. It expanded the cover significantly beyond the requirements of s 145(3)(a) by removing the statutory causal link between the use of the vehicle on a road or other public place and the accident; the appropriate correction to give effect to the requirements of RTA 1988 was to read it as providing cover for accidents arising out of the use of the vehicle as above.

The repairs that were carried out on private property did not entail the use of the vehicle within s 145(3)(a). While they might be said to have arisen from the use of the vehicle, since this had caused the disrepair, it did not follow that the property damage had been 'caused by, or arisen out of, the use of the vehicle'. It was the alleged negligence of the welder which caused the fire, and not the prior use of the car as a means of transport

Policies must cover liabilities for death, injury or damage 'arising out of the use' of vehicles on roads or other public places: RTA 1988, s 145(3)(a).

While the term 'arising out of' covers more remote consequences than 'caused by', it does not extend to extraneous conduct, such as sedation and sexual abuse of women by a taxi driver in his cab: *1 AXN v Worboys* [2012] EWHC 1730, [2013] Lloyds Rep L R 207.

In *Wastell v Woodward (Deceased)* [2017] Lloyds Rep L R a hamburger van was parked in a lay. It was held that the qualification 'use of the vehicle as a motor vehicle on a road', while simple to apply and reflecting the principal purpose of any motor vehicle, put certainty of outcome over the breadth and flexibility the statute required. The authorities favoured an examination of the particular use of the vehicle, which might be an ice cream van, an ambulance, a car, etc. The use on the road of such diverse vehicles varied greatly. The court had to determine the relevant use and then ask whether the accident arose out of it. In the present case, the accident (the claimant collided with the owner of the van who had stepped into the road after displaying a sign for his business) arose out of the use of the hamburger van as a hamburger van, and the accident was closely linked to that use.

Permitting an uninsured driver to drive a hire car does not constitute 'use of' the vehicle for the purposes of s 145(3)(a); therefore the liability of somebody giving such permission does not need to be covered by a policy of insurance: *Sahin v Havard and another* [2016] EWCA Civ 1202, [2017] 1 WLR 1853.

Where a vehicle was insured for 'business purposes including the carriage of passengers for hire or reward under a public hire licence', the hackney carriage licence held by the driver entitled the vehicle to be plied for hire only within the area of the local authority which issues it, and the driver plied for hire outside that authority area, the reference to the area restriction was rendered ineffective by s 148(2)(e) and the policy was to be read as if it were not there; accordingly, the court was right to acquit the driver of using a vehicle without insurance: *Oldham Borough Council v Sajjad* [2016] EWHC 3597 (Admin), [2018] RTR 4.

C[33.10]–[33.15] **Causing** involves an express or positive mandate from the defendant to the driver.

C[33.16] **Permitting.** Permission must be given by someone able to permit or withhold permissions but may be express or inferred. See further the note under this heading at C[9.6] in the section on Brakes.

C[33.17] **Defence open to employed drivers.** An employed driver cannot be convicted if he can prove that:

(a) the vehicle did not belong to him; and
(b) it was not in his possession under a hiring contract or on loan to him; and
(c) he was using it in the course of his employment; and
(d) he did not know and had no reason to believe he was not insured. The degree of proof required from the defendant is to prove that this defence is probably true; he does not have to prove beyond reasonable doubt.

C[33.18] **The Motor Insurers' Bureau** is a company funded by insurers transacting compulsory motor insurance. Under an agreement with the Secretary of State for Transport the Bureau, subject to certain limitations and exceptions, will compensate the victims of uninsured motorists. A brief outline of the scheme is given here (for the full details see the text of the agreement which is published by HMSO).

C[33.19] To obtain compensation the victim must obtain judgment in a civil court against the uninsured driver, having given the MIB notice within seven days of starting the proceedings. If the judgment is not met within seven days the victim will be entitled to be compensated by the MIB.

C[33.20] Compensation is payable for personal injury or for damage to property (except for the first £300 of the claim in respect of property damage and this figure will be the relevant limit of a compensation order made against an uninsured driver in the magistrates' court).

C[33.21] There are exceptions to claims against the MIB such as claims in relation to Crown vehicles but more particularly where damage is to the claimant's own vehicle which he himself has failed to insure as required by the Road Traffic Act or where the claimant is the passenger in a vehicle which he knew had been stolen or unlawfully taken or was being used without insurance. (However, the crime exception has been held to be incompatible with EU law in *Delaney v Secretary of State for Transport* [2015] 3 All ER 329, [2015] 2 CMLR 914,

C[33.22] A separate agreement covers the case of victims of untraced drivers.

Sentencing

SC Guideline – No insurance

No insurance (Revised 2017)

C[33.23]

Road Traffic Act 1988, s 143

Effective from: 24 April 2017

Triable only summarily:

Maximum: Unlimited fine

Offence range: Band B–Band C fine

Step 1 — Determining the offence category

The Court should determine the offence category using the table below.

Category 1	Higher culpability and greater harm
Category 2	Higher culpability and lesser harm or lower culpability and greater harm
Category 3	Lower culpability and lesser harm

The court should determine the offender's culpability and the harm caused with reference **only** to the factors below. Where an offence does not fall squarely into a category, individual factors may require a degree of weighting before making an overall assessment and determining the appropriate offence category.

CULPABILITY demonstrated by one or more of the following:

Factors indicating higher culpability

- Never passed test
- Gave false details
- Driving LGV, HGV, PSV etc
- Driving for hire or reward
- Evidence of sustained uninsured use

Factors indicating lower culpability

- All other cases

HARM demonstrated by one or more of the following:

Factors indicating greater harm

- Involved in accident where injury caused
- Involved in accident where damage caused

Factors indicating lesser harm

- All other cases

Step 2 — Starting point and category range

Having determined the category at step one, the court should use the appropriate starting point to reach a sentence within the category range in the table below. The starting point applies to all offenders irrespective of plea or previous convictions.

Level of seriousness	Starting Point	Range	Disqualification/ points
Category 1	Band C fine	Band C fine	Disqualify 6–12 months
Category 2	Band C fine	Band C fine	Consider disqualification for up to 6 months **OR** 8 points
Category 3	Band C fine	Band B fine–Band C fine	6–8 points

- **Must endorse and may disqualify. If no disqualification impose 6–8 points**

The court should then consider further adjustment for any aggravating or mitigating factors. The following is a **non-exhaustive** list of additional factual elements providing the context of the offence and factors relating to the offender. Identify whether any combination of these, or other relevant factors, should result in an upward or downward adjustment from the sentence arrived at so far.

Factors increasing seriousness

Statutory aggravating factors:

- Previous convictions, having regard to a) the **nature** of the offence to which the conviction relates and its **relevance** to the current offence; and b) the **time** that has elapsed since the conviction
- Offence committed whilst on bail

Other aggravating factors:

- Failure to comply with current court orders
- Offence committed on licence or post sentence supervision

Factors reducing seriousness or reflecting personal mitigation

- No previous convictions **or** no relevant/recent convictions
- Remorse
- Good character and/or exemplary conduct
- Responsibility for providing insurance rests with another (where not amounting to a defence)
- Genuine misunderstanding
- Recent failure to renew or failure to transfer vehicle details where insurance was in existence
- Vehicle not being driven

Step 3 — Consider any factors which indicate a reduction, such as assistance to the prosecution

The court should take into account sections 73 and 74 of the Serious Organised Crime and Police Act 2005 (assistance by defendants: reduction or review of

sentence) and any other rule of law by virtue of which an offender may receive a discounted sentence in consequence of assistance given (or offered) to the prosecutor or investigator.

Step 4 — Reduction for guilty pleas

The court should take account of any potential reduction for a guilty plea in accordance with section 144 of the Criminal Justice Act 2003 and the *Guilty Plea* guideline.

Step 5 — Totality principle

If sentencing an offender for more than one offence, or where the offender is already serving a sentence, consider whether the total sentence is just and proportionate to the overall offending behaviour in accordance with the *Offences Taken into Consideration and Totality* guideline.

Step 6 — Compensation and ancillary orders

In all cases, the court should consider whether to make compensation and/or other ancillary orders.

Step 7 — Reasons

Section 174 of the Criminal Justice Act 2003 imposes a duty to give reasons for, and explain the effect of, the sentence.

C[33.23A] Endorsement must be ordered unless special reasons exist. A short distance driven can amount to a special reason. In *DPP v Heritage* [2002] EWHC 2139 (Admin), 166 JP 772 a car was pushed onto the road to be cleaned and a vehicle collided with it.

C[33.24] If it appears to the court that the accused suffers from some disease or physical disability likely to cause his driving to be a source of danger to the public, then the court shall notify the licensing authority who may take steps to withdraw the driving licence (see C[5.49]).

C[33.25]–[33.30] Clearly a lower level of fine may be appropriate for the vehicle sitting unused outside the owner's house, whereas deliberate driving around without insurance cover aggravates the seriousness considerably.

C[33.31] For fines see B[28].

C[34]

Lights defective

Charge (Lights defective)

C[34.1] **1 Using or causing or permitting to be used on a road a vehicle without every front position lamp, rear position lamp, headlamp, rear registration plate lamp, side marker lamp, end-outline marker lamp, rear fog lamp, retro reflector and rear marking with which it is required to be fitted by the Regulations, and every stop lamp and direction indicator, running lamp, dim- dip device, headlamp levelling device and hazard warning signal device with which it is fitted in good working order and, in the case of a lamp, clean**

C[34.2] **2 Using, causing or permitting to be used on a road any vehicle with a headlamp, front fog lamp, or rear fog lamp so as to cause undue dazzle or discomfort to other persons using the road**

C[34.3] **3 Using or causing or permitting to be used on a road a vehicle which is in motion between sunset and sunrise (or between sunrise and sunset in seriously reduced visibility), (or allowing to remain at rest, or causing or permitting to be allowed to remain at rest, on a road any vehicle between sunset and sunrise) unless every front position lamp, rear position lamp, rear registration plate lamp, side marker lamp and end-outline marker lamp with which the vehicle is required by the Regulations to be fitted is kept lit and unobscured**

C[34.4] **4 Using, or causing or permitting to be used on a road a vehicle which is fitted with obligatory dipped beam headlamps without such lamps being lit during the hours of darkness (or in seriously reduced visibility)**

Road Vehicles Lighting Regulations 1989, reg 23(1) (charge 1); reg 27 (charge 2); reg 24(1) (charge 3); reg 25(1) (charge 4);

Road Traffic Act 1988, s 42

Maximum penalty – Fine level 4 (goods vehicles etc), level 3 (private vehicles) (for fines see **B[28]**). No power to disqualify or endorse.

Fixed penalty – £50.

Legal notes and definitions

C[34.5] **Using, causing or permitting.** The charge should allege only one of these. For 'using', 'causing' and 'permitting' see **C[9.4]–C[9.6]**.

C[34.6] The obligatory minimum requirements for an ordinary motor car are two front position lights, two headlights (with a dipped beam facility), direction indicators, hazard warning lights, two rear position lamps, one rear fog lamp (vehicles first used after 1 April 1980), two stop lamps, a rear registration plate lamp and two rear reflex reflectors.

C[34.7] These requirements vary according to the category of vehicle concerned. If the matter is in dispute the legal adviser will be able to provide a list of the requirements.

C[34.8] **Vehicle.** Means a vehicle of any description and includes a machine or implement of any kind drawn or propelled along roads whether by animal or mechanical power.

C[34.9] **Road.** Means any road or highway to which the public has access and includes bridges and footways.

C[34.10]–[34.15] **Front position lamp.** Means a lamp used to indicate the presence and width of a vehicle when viewed from the front.

C[34.16] **Hours of darkness.** Means the time between half an hour after sunset and half an hour before sunrise. An almanac can be produced to establish this period if it is in dispute.

C[34.17] **Exempted vehicles include:**

(a) Pedal cycles and hand drawn vehicles are not required to be fitted with lamps between sunrise and sunset.
(b) Vehicles temporarily imported or proceeding to port for export provided they comply with international Conventions.
(c) Military vehicles which comply with certain requirements.
(d) Vehicles drawn or propelled by hand which have an overall width (including load) not exceeding 800 millimetres are not required to be fitted with lamps and reflectors except when they are used on a carriageway between sunset and sunrise (unless they are close to the near side or are crossing the road).

Possible defences include:

C[34.18] Offence 1 where a defective lamp or reflector is fitted to the vehicle which is in use between sunrise and sunset if the lamp etc becomes defective during the journey or if arrangements have been made to remedy the defect with all reasonable expedition.

C[34.19] Offence 3 where the vehicle is a car or does not exceed 1,525 kilograms and is parked on a road with a speed limit of 30 miles per hour or less in force and the vehicle is parked in a designated parking place or lay-by or is parked parallel to the kerb, close to it and facing the direction of traffic and is not less than 10 metres from a junction.

C[34.20] **Offence 4.** Except where there is seriously reduced visibility, the car is on a road restricted to 30 miles per hour by virtue of a system of street lighting which is lit at the time of the alleged offence.

Sentencing
SC Guideline – Lights defective

C[34.21] Starting point – Band A fine (driver); Band A fine (owner-driver but consider an uplift of at least 25% on the driver's fine); Band B fine (owner-company).

C[34.22] For fines see B[28].

C[35]

Motor cyclist not wearing helmet

Charge (Motor cyclist not wearing helmet)

C[35.1] Being a person driving (or riding on) a motor cycle on a road, did not wear protective headgear

Motor Cycles (Protective Helmets) Regulations 1980, reg 4; Road Traffic Act 1988, s 16(4)

Maximum penalty – Fine level 3 (for fines see B[28]). There is no power to endorse or disqualify.

Fixed penalty – £50.

Legal notes and definitions

C[35.2] Where the person actually in breach of the regulations by not wearing a helmet is over 16, there can be no prosecution of another person for aiding and abetting. However, aiders and abettors of defendants under 16 can be prosecuted.

C[35.3] **Riding on.** This includes a pillion rider but not a passenger in a side-car.

C[35.4] **Protective headgear** is defined in the regulations as being that which complies with a certain British Standard. Headgear manufactured for use by persons on motorcycles which appears to afford the same or a greater degree of protection than laid down by the Standard is also included. But before any helmet satisfies the definition it must also be securely fastened to the head of the wearer by the straps or fastenings provided on the helmet. An unfastened helmet, therefore, would not suffice.

C[35.5] **Driving.** See the notes under this heading for the offence of driving without a licence at C[18.8]–C[18.9] but bear in mind the exemption mentioned at (b) below.

C[35.6] **Exemptions.** There is no requirement to wear a helmet:

(a) if the motor cycle is a mowing machine;
(b) if the motor cycle is being propelled by a person on foot;
(c) if the driver is a Sikh and is wearing a turban.

Sentencing (Motor cyclist not wearing helmet)

C[35.7] No SC Guideline.

Starting point – Band A fine suggested.

C[35.8] For fines see B[28].

C[36]
Obstruction

Charge 1 (Obstruction)

C[36.1] Causing unnecessary obstruction of a road by a person in charge of a motor vehicle or trailer

Road Vehicles (Construction and Use) Regulations 1986, reg 103; Road Traffic Act 1988, s 42

Maximum penalty – Fine level 4 (goods vehicle etc), level 3 (otherwise) (for fines see B[28]). No power to disqualify or endorse.

Fixed penalty – £50.

Charge 2 (Obstruction)

C[36.1A] Did without lawful authority or excuse wilfully obstruct the free passage along a highway.

Highways Act 1980, s 137

Maximum penalty – Fine level 3

Legal notes and definitions

C[36.2] **Unnecessary obstruction.** There need be no notice or sign displayed as is the case where a driver is charged in parking offences. This offence can be committed on a road to which local parking regulations are applicable.

Wilful. If anyone does something by exercise of their free will which causes an obstruction, an offence is committed (*Arrowsmith v Jenkins* [1963] 2 QB 561, [1963] 2 All ER 210). See further A[85]

C[36.3] If the vehicle is parked in a lawfully designated parking place then there can be no charge of obstruction.

C[36.4] The High Court has ruled that a motorist who left his car on a road 24 ft wide for 75 minutes did not commit this offence (*Evans v Barker* [1971] RTR 453). An obstruction was not committed by a reasonable protest taking up 2 ft of an 11ft-wide path (*Westminster City Council v Haw* [2002] All ER (D) 59 (Oct)).

C[36.5] A taxi-driver was held by the High Court to have committed this offence in waiting in the road to turn right, thereby holding up heavy traffic.

C[36.6] The question is one for the justices to decide on the facts of each case. An obstruction caused by a doctor answering an emergency call may, for example, be necessary.

C[36.7] **A road.** Means any highway (including footpaths and bridleways) and any other road to which the public has access and includes bridges. A road is provided as a means of transit from one place to another and not as a place to park motor vehicles.

C[36.8] **Trailer.** Means any vehicle drawn by a motor vehicle.

C[36.9] **A motor vehicle.** See C[9.7]. If left on a road for an unreasonable time may constitute an unnecessary obstruction.

Power to order the removal of the obstruction rests with the magistrates when recording a conviction under the Highways Act 1980, s 137. Failure to comply with the order without reasonable excuse is an offence punishable by a fine not exceeding level 5 and a daily fine thereafter.

Sentencing (Obstruction)

C[36.10]–[36.15] No SC Guideline.

Starting point – Band A fine suggested.

An average case will not usually attract more than a small fine; where there is a complete disregard for the convenience or safety of others (eg access of fire appliances or ambulances) a heavier fine is called for.

C[36.16] For fines see B[28].

C[37]
Opening door

Charge (Opening door)

C[37.1] Opening a door of a motor vehicle or trailer on a road so as to cause injury or danger

Road Vehicles (Construction and Use) Regulations 1986, reg 105; Road Traffic Act 1988, s 42

Maximum penalty – Fine level 4 (goods vehicle etc), level 3 (otherwise) (for fines see B[28]). No power to disqualify or endorse.

Fixed penalty – £50.

Legal notes and definitions

C[37.2] **Motor vehicle.** See C[9.7].

C[37.3] **Trailer.** Means any vehicle drawn by a motor vehicle.

C[37.4] **Road.** Means any highway (including footpaths and bridleways) and any other road to which the public has access and includes bridges.

C[37.5] **The offence.** Consists of opening or causing or permitting a door to be opened so as to cause injury or danger to any person. The offence can be committed by a passenger as well as the driver. If a child opened the door and his parent was present and knew the child was about to open the door, then the parent could be charged with permitting. If the child opened the door on the instructions of a parent then the latter could be guilty of causing the offence. Door opening, permitting or causing are all identical offences for the purpose of the penalties that may be inflicted. Only one of the offences should be alleged.

C[37.6] The prosecution does not have to prove carelessness; nor that someone was actually struck or injured. It is enough if the act caused danger.

Sentencing (Opening door)

C[37.7] No SC Guideline.

Starting point – Band A fine suggested.

The amount of the fine will vary according to the circumstances. It will rarely be appropriate to impose a fine less than the fixed penalty. When the offence is very dangerous, eg where it causes a motor cyclist to swerve to the offside of a busy main road, this will aggravate the seriousness. Where actual injury is caused a similar level of penalty should apply.

C[37.8] If it appears to the court that a driver suffers from some disease or physical disability likely to cause his driving to be a source of danger to the public, then the court shall notify the licensing authority who may take steps to withdraw his driving licence (see C[5.49]).

C[37.9] For fines see B[28].

C[38]

Overloading/exceeding axle weight

Charge (Overloading/exceeding axle weight)

C[38.1] **Using, causing or permitting to be used on a road a vehicle which equals or exceeds* the maximum (gross weight) (train weight) (weight for specified axle) shown on the (plating certificate) (manufacturer's plate fitted to the vehicle)**

Road Vehicles (Construction and Use) Regulations 1986, reg 80; Road Traffic Act 1988, s 41B

Maximum penalty – Fine level 5* (for fines see B[28]). Not endorsable.

Fixed penalty – £100.

* Note the Road Vehicles (Construction and Use) (Amendment) Regulations 2014, SI 2014/264, amended reg 80 of the Construction and Use Regulations 1986 as to the way in which weight band limits are expressed. The purpose was to remove an historic difference in terminology between Directive 1999/62/EC and the Regulations, which affects vehicles on those limits. This has been achieved by inserting 'equalled or' or 'equal or' before, respectively, 'exceeded' and 'exceed'. The subsequent text should be read accordingly.

---

* Section 85 of the Legal Aid, Sentencing and Punishment of Offenders Act 2012 provides that where a relevant offence would on commencement day be punishable on summary conviction by a fine or maximum fine of £5,000, however expressed, and the offence was committed on or after that date, the court may impose a fine of any amount. The commencement date is 12 March 2015: see the Legal Aid, Sentencing and Punishment of Offenders Act 2012 (Commencement No 11) Order 2015, SI 2015/504.

Legal notes and definitions

C[38.2] Certain vehicles specified in the Road Vehicles (Construction and Use) Regulations 1986, reg 66 must be fitted with a plate which contains information prescribed in Sch 8 or the relevant EC Directives. In particular the plate must show the maximum gross weight, train weight and weight for each axle. The weights may be specified by the manufacturer and are the limits at or below which the vehicle is considered fit for use, having regard to its design, construction and equipment and the stresses to which it is likely to be subjected in use. Further, the weights must also be specified at which the use of the vehicle will be legal in the UK having regard, inter alia, to the maximum weights set out in regs 75–79. This is a 'manufacturer's plate'.

C[38.3] In addition, goods vehicles are now covered by the compulsory 'type approval' system whereby the Secretary of State issues a certificate that a type of vehicle conforms with the appropriate requirements and the manufacturer issues a Certificate of Conformity that the vehicle conforms with the approved type. This certificate is *treated* as a 'plating certificate' and a plate (which is in fact a piece of paper) is affixed to the vehicle, which is *deemed* to be a 'ministry plate' (for this and 'plating certificate' see below).

C[38.4] After one year and annually thereafter goods vehicles must be submitted for a goods vehicle test and at the *first* test the vehicle will also be examined for the purpose of issuing a 'plating certificate'. The examiner will issue a certificate containing information similar to that on the plate previously affixed to the vehicle. If the vehicle passes its goods vehicle test the ministry plate will remain affixed in a conspicuous and readily accessible position on the vehicle and in the cab. Only one plating certificate is issued, but it will be amended where there has been a 'notifiable alteration' to the vehicle.

C[38.5] **Using; causing; permitting.** See C[9.4]–C[9.6].

C[38.6] **Road.** See C[9.10].

C[38.7] **Vehicle.** The provisions concerning manufacturers' plates cover such vehicles as non-agricultural tractors of various weights which do not carry loads, buses and various trailers. This article is concerned with offences committed by goods vehicles, being the most commonly encountered in the magistrates' court.

C[38.8] **Maximum gross weight.** The sum of the weights to be transmitted to the road surface by all the wheels of the motor vehicle (including any load imposed by a trailer on the vehicle).

C[38.9] **Maximum train weight.** The maximum gross weight and the weight transmitted to the road surface by any trailer drawn.

C[38.10]–[38.15] **Maximum axle weight.** The sum of the weights to be transmitted to the road surface by all the wheels of that axle.

C[38.16] **Multiple charges.** Under the former regulations 'gross', 'train' or 'axle' weight were the subject of separate charges and not combined into one. It was not oppressive for there to be a charge in respect of each axle that was overweight and for exceeding the gross weight. The new regulations are worded slightly differently but it is still permissible to prefer several charges where appropriate (*Travel-Gas (Midlands) Ltd v Reynolds* [1989] RTR 75).

C[38.17] **Evidence.** Unless proved to the contrary the weight indicated on a ministry plate is presumed to be the weight recorded on the relevant plating certificate.

C[38.18] **Defences.** In the case of a goods vehicle it is a defence for the accused to prove:

(a) that at the time when the vehicle was being used on the road it was proceeding to a weighbridge which was the nearest available one to the place where the loading of the vehicle was completed for the purpose of being weighed, or was proceeding from a weighbridge after being weighed to the nearest point at which it was reasonably practicable to reduce the weight to the relevant limit without causing an obstruction on any road; or

(b) in a case where the limit of that weight was not exceeded by more than 5%, that limit was not exceeded at the time the loading of the vehicle was originally completed and that since that time no person has made any addition to the load (eg a load which becomes wet owing to falling rain).

C[38.18A] **'Nearest available weighbridge'** means the nearest available weighbridge that was actually available as a matter of objective fact regardless of the knowledge of the driver (*Vehicle and Operator Services Agency v F & S Gibbs Transport Services Ltd* [2006] EWHC 1109 (Admin), 170 JP 586.

C[38.19] The degree of proof required from the defendant is to prove that the defence is probably true; he does not have to prove beyond reasonable doubt.

Sentencing

SC Guideline – Overloading/exceeding axle weight

C[38.20] Starting point – Mechanically propelled vehicle-Band A fine (driver); Band A fine (owner-driver but consider an uplift of at least 25% on the driver's fine); Band B fine (owner-company). The starting point presumes an excess overload etc of no more than 10%. A further uplift of 1% for every 1% more than 10% is permissible but the total fine must not be out of proportion to the offence and the means of the defendant may be relevant.

Starting point – HGV, LGV or PSV – Band B fine (driver); Band B fine (owner-driver but consider an uplift of at least 25% on the driver's fine); Band C fine (owner-company). A further uplift of 1% for every 1% more than 10% is permissible but the total fine must not be out of proportion to the offence and the means of the defendant may be relevant.

C[38.21] For fines see B[28].

C[38A]

Breach of requirement as to speed assessment equipment detection devices

Charge (Breach of requirement as to speed detection devices)

C[38A.1] A person who –

(a) **contravenes or fails to comply with a construction or use requirement as to speed assessment equipment detection devices, or**
(b) **uses on a road a motor vehicle or trailer which does not comply with such a requirement, or causes or permits a motor vehicle or trailer to be so used, is guilty of an offence.**

Road Traffic Act 1988, s 41C as inserted (from a date to be appointed) by s 18 **Road Safety Act 2006.**

Maximum penalty – Fine level 4 if committed on a special road otherwise level 3. Must endorse unless special reasons.

Penalty points – 3–6 (fixed penalty 3).

Fixed penalty– £100.

Legal notes and definitions

C[38A.2] **Motor vehicle.** See C[9.7] for definition.

Trailer. See C[9.9] for definition.

Road. See C[9.10]–C[9.15] for definition.

Sentencing (Breach of requirement as to speed detection devices)

C[38A.3] Awaiting SC Guidance.

C[39]

Pelican/zebra crossing contravention

Charge (Pelican/zebra crossing contravention)

C[39.1] **Failure of a driver of any vehicle to accord precedence to a pedestrian within the limits of an uncontrolled pedestrian crossing**

The Traffic Signs Regulations and General Directions 2016, SI 2016/362 came into effect on 22 April 2016 with the transitional and savings provisions specified in reg 14. The regulations consolidate, with substantial amendments, the:

(a) Zebra, Pelican and Puffin Pedestrian Crossings Regulations and General Directions 1997;
(b) Traffic Signs (Temporary Obstructions) Regulations 1997;
(c) Traffic Signs Regulations and General Directions 2002;
(d) School Crossing Patrol Sign (England and Wales) Regulations 2006.

The transitional provisions provide as follows in relation to pelican crossings:

'Transitional and savings provisions

14 . . .

(5) The Zebra, Pelican and Puffin Pedestrian Crossings Regulations 1997(a) ("the 1997 Regulations") are to be treated as remaining in force in relation to Pelican crossings (within the meaning of those Regulations) established—
(a) before the coming into force of these Regulations; or
(b) within a period of six months beginning with the day on which these Regulations come into force.

(6) In their application to Pelican crossings for the purposes of paragraph (5), the 1997 Regulations are modified in accordance with paragraphs (7) and (8).

(7) The exceptions to the prohibition imposed by regulation 12(1)(c) and (d) of the 1997 Regulations (about proceeding beyond a stop line when a steady amber or red signal is showing) are those at paragraph 5(4) to (6) of Part 1 of Schedule 14 to this Instrument and not those at regulation 12(1)(e) to (ec) of the 1997 Regulations (with the reference in paragraph 5(4) to the prohibition in sub-paragraph (3) treated as being instead a reference to the prohibition in paragraph (c) or (d) in regulation 12(1)).

(8) The exceptions to the prohibition imposed by regulation 20 of the 1997 Regulations (about stopping in a controlled area) in regulation 21(c) to (e) of those Regulations do not apply and instead the exceptions set out in paragraph 4(2)(d) of Part 5 of Schedule 14 to this Instrument apply.'

The modified exceptions concern vehicles being used for fire brigade, ambulance, national blood service, police, National Crime Agency and special forces purposes. Since the Regulations are otherwise the same in their application, and it will be some time after their commencement (on 22 April 2016) before signs constructed under the 2016 Regulations will begin to appear, the narrative in the remainder of this Part L continues to refer to the 1997 Regulations.

Maximum penalty – Fine of level 3 (for fines see B[28]). If the offence was committed in a motor vehicle, the court may disqualify for any period and/or until a driving test has been passed. Must endorse unless special reasons exist.

Penalty points – 3.

Fixed penalty – £100 (3PP)

Legal notes and definitions

C[39.2] Vehicle. A bicycle is a vehicle (but not in the case of offences of stopping in an area *adjacent* to a zebra crossing, see C[40.7]–C[40.9]).

C[39.3] Zebra crossing. A driver should approach such a crossing in a manner that enables him to stop before reaching it, unless he can see there is no pedestrian on the crossing.

C[39.4] The law imposes a very strict duty on the driver and the prosecution has the advantage of not having to prove any negligence or want of care. It would, however, be a sufficient defence to satisfy the magistrates that the failure to accord precedence was due to circumstances over which the defendant had no control (eg being attacked by a swarm of bees, or a sudden brake failure).

C[39.5] The High Court in Scotland has held that where a woman was pushing her child in a pram and the pram was on the crossing but she herself had not actually stepped on to the crossing, the mother had the right of way.

C[39.6] The limits of the crossing are marked by studs bordering the striped lines. The broken white line along the striped crossing is to indicate where vehicles should give way.

C[39.7] The sections of pedestrian crossings on each side of a dual carriageway, central street refuge or reservation are considered to be two separate crossings.

C[39.8] A crossing may still legally remain a crossing even if one or more of its stripes are missing, discoloured or imperfect, or if a globe or one of its lights is missing, or even if some of the studs have disappeared. The magistrates should consult the legal adviser if a submission is made on any of these matters.

C[39.9] The regulations require pedestrians to cross 'with reasonable dispatch'.

C[39.10]–[39.15] On each side of crossings are zigzag lines parallel to the carriageway. These indicate the 'area controlled by the crossing'. On the approach side of the crossing it is an offence for a vehicle to overtake another vehicle in that area if that vehicle is either the only other vehicle in the area or is the nearest vehicle of several to the crossing. 'Overtaking' includes allowing part of the rearmost vehicle to pass the front of the overtaken vehicle, a complete passing is not necessary. The prohibition on overtaking does not apply if the overtaken vehicle is stationary otherwise than to allow pedestrians to cross (eg if it is waiting to turn left or right) or if the crossing is for the time being controlled by a policeman or traffic warden, but it applies where a vehicle has stopped to wait for pedestrians to step on to the crossing, for example as a courtesy. It also applies when the pedestrians have passed the stationary vehicle which is overtaken.

Vehicles which are waiting to proceed are not, by definition, 'proceeding'. The only circumstances in which overtaking a stationary vehicle in an approach to a crossing can amount to an offence are those set out in reg 24(1)(b), namely passing ahead of a vehicle which is stationary because: (a) of a red light; (b) it has stopped to give precedence to a pedestrian at a zebra crossing; or (c) it has stopped to give precedence to a pedestrian at a pedestrian crossing: *Brooks v Blackpool Borough Council* [2013] EWHC 3735 (Admin), (2014) 178 JP 79.

C[39.16] Pelican crossings. Similar provisions apply. A vehicle approaching such a crossing shall proceed with due regard to the safety of other users of the road. When a red light shows the vehicle must stop, similarly where a constant amber light shows, a vehicle must stop except where the vehicle cannot safely be stopped in line with the signal. Where there is a flashing amber light, a vehicle must accord precedence to pedestrians already on the crossing. Failure to comply with any of the regulations is an offence with a maximum penalty of a fine on level 3.

C[39.17] Pedestrian. A person walking and pushing a bicycle is a pedestrian. He ceases to be a pedestrian if he uses the bicycle to carry him, for example, by placing one foot on a pedal and pushing himself along with the other.

C[39.18] Precedence means allowing the pedestrian to go before the vehicle. Once the pedestrian has safely passed the vehicle's line of travel the vehicle may proceed even though the pedestrian is still on the crossing.

Sentencing

SC Guideline – Pelican/zebra crossing contravention

C[39.19] Starting point – Band A fine.

C[39.20] If it appears to the court that the defendant driver of a motor vehicle suffers from some disease or physical disability likely to cause his driving to be a source of danger to the public, then the court shall notify the licensing authority who may take steps to withdraw the driving licence (see C[5.49]).

C[39.21] For fines see B[28].

C[40]–[45]

Stopping on pedestrian crossing

Charge (Stopping on pedestrian crossing)

C[40.1] **That a driver of a vehicle caused it or any part of it to stop within the limits of zebra crossing**

Zebra, Pelican etc Pedestrian Crossing Regulations 1997, reg 18

The Traffic Signs Regulations and General Directions 2016 came into effect on 22 April 2016 with the transitional and savings provisions specified in reg 14. These provisions keep the 1997 Regulations in force for existing crossings and those established within six months of the commencement. See further C[39.1], ante.

Maximum penalty – Fine level 3 (for fines see B[28]). If the offence was committed in a motor vehicle, the court may disqualify for any period and/or until the defendant has passed a driving test. Must endorse unless special reasons exist.

Penalty points – 3.

Fixed penalty – £100 (3PP).

Legal notes and definitions

C[40.2] The defendant must be acquitted if he establishes any of the following:

(a) that circumstances beyond his control compelled him to stop;
(b) that he had to stop to avoid an accident (see C[40.9]).

C[40.3] The degree of proof required from the defendant is to prove that one of these is probably true; he does not have to prove one of them beyond reasonable doubt.

C[40.4] The term 'vehicle' includes a pedal cycle.

C[40.5] This charge does not apply to a push-button controlled crossing which is subject to special regulations.

C[40.6] A crossing may still legally remain a crossing even if one or more stripes are missing, discoloured or imperfect, or if a globe or its light is missing or even if some of the studs have disappeared. Consult the legal adviser.

C[40.7] **Stopping in area adjacent to zebra crossing.** It is also an offence to stop in a zebra-controlled area, ie the part of a road indicated by zig-zag lines at either side of the crossing (Zebra, Pelican etc Pedestrian Crossing Regulations 1997, reg 20).

C[40.8] For the purposes of this regulation 'vehicle' does *not* include a pedal cycle.

C[40.9] Defences are:

(a) that circumstances beyond his control compelled him to stop;
(b) that he had to stop to avoid an accident;
(c) that the stopping was for the purpose of allowing free passage to pedestrians on the crossing;
(d) that he had to stop for fire brigade, ambulance or police purposes, because of demolitions, repairs to road, gas, water, electricity services etc;
(e) that he stopped for the purpose of making a left or right turn;
(f) a stage carriage or express carriage vehicle (not on a trip or excursion) in the controlled area beyond the zebra crossing for the purposes of picking up or setting down passengers.

Sentencing
SC Guideline – Pelican/zebra crossing contravention

C[40.10]–[40.15] Starting point – Band A fine.

C[40.16] If it appears to the court that the defendant driver of a motor vehicle suffers from some disease or physical disability likely to cause his driving to be a source of danger to the public, then the court shall notify the licensing authority who may take steps to withdraw the driving licence (see C[5.49]).

C[40.17] For fines see B[28].

C[46] Reasonable consideration

Charge (Reasonable consideration)

C[46.1] Driving a mechanically propelled vehicle on a road or other public place without reasonable consideration for other persons using the road or place

Road Traffic Act 1988, s 3, as amended

Maximum penalty – Fine level 4 [level 5* for offences committed on or after 24/9/07] (for fines see B[28]). May disqualify for any period and/or until a driving test has been passed. Must endorse unless special reasons exist.

Penalty points – 3–9.

Fixed penalty – £100/3 penalty points. The police are also able to offer educational training as an alternative to endorsement. See further C[25.1], above.

---

* Section 85 of the Legal Aid, Sentencing and Punishment of Offenders Act 2012 provides that where a relevant offence would on commencement day be punishable on summary conviction by a fine or maximum fine of £5,000, however expressed, and the offence was committed on or after that date, the court may impose a fine of any amount. The commencement date is 12 March 2015: see the Legal Aid, Sentencing and Punishment of Offenders Act 2012 (Commencement No 11) Order 2015, SI 2015/504.

Legal notes and definitions

C[46.2] Reasonable consideration. At the time of the offence there must have been other people also using the road. They could be passengers in the defendant's vehicle. Another example of this offence is driving the vehicle through a muddy puddle and splashing pedestrians.

Definition: See C[25.5] for a new statutory definition which has been added to s 3ZA of the Road Traffic Act 1988 by the Road Safety Act 2006.

C[46.3] If no other person but the driver is using the road then this charge fails.

C[46.4] Observance or non-observance of the Highway Code can be used to establish or disprove liability.

C[46.5] The driver alleged to have committed this offence must give his name and address on request to any person having reasonable grounds for requiring it, otherwise he commits an offence under the Road Traffic Act 1988, s 168, maximum penalty fine on level 3.

C[46.6] Mechanically propelled vehicle. See C[47.9].

C[46.7] Road. See C[22.5].

C[46.8] Public place. See C[20.7]–C[20.8].

C[46.9] Warning of prosecution. If the defence claim that notice should have been given within 14 days of intention to prosecute, consult the legal adviser.

C[46.10]–[46.15] Other persons using the road. May include passengers in the defendant's vehicle. There must be evidence that another road user was inconvenienced by the manner of driving adopted by the accused.

C[46.16] Careless or inconsiderate driving (Road Traffic Act 1988, s 3) and dangerous driving (s 2). Where the magistrates see fit, they may allow informations for an offence under s 3 and s 2 to be heard together. In this event, if the defendant is convicted of one offence, the second information can either be adjourned *sine die* or the justices may make "*no adjudication*". Should the driver successfully appeal against conviction for dangerous driving, he can later be tried on the second information.

C[46.17] Alternatively, where there is a single information alleging dangerous driving and the magistrates do not find this proved, they may convict of driving without reasonable consideration in the alternative (s 24 RTOA 1988).

C[46.18] Driving. See the note under the offence of no driving licence at C[18.8]–C[18.9].

Sentencing (Reasonable consideration)

C[46.19] SC Guideline – Careless (or inconsiderate) driving – see C[25.20].

C[46.20] In rare cases it may be appropriate to grant an absolute discharge; if this course is adopted disqualification can be imposed but this would be an unusual course to take. Endorsement must be ordered unless special reasons exist.

C[46.21] If it appears to the court that the accused suffers from some disease or physical disability likely to cause his driving to be a source of danger to the public then the court shall notify the licensing authority who may take steps to withdraw the driving licence (see C[5.49]).

C[46.22] It is the lack of consideration rather than the consequences of it which normally determines the punishment.

C[46.23] For fines see B[28].

C[47]
No excise licence

Charge 1 (No excise licence)

C[47.1] Using or keeping on a public road a mechanically propelled vehicle when no excise licence is in force and doing so when a SORN is in force

Vehicle Excise and Registration Act 1994, s 29 and s 29(3A)

C[47.2] **Maximum penalty**-A fine of level 3 (s 29(3)) or level 4 (s 29(3A)) or 5 times the value of the licence, whichever is the greater. No power to disqualify or endorse.

Charge 2 (No excise licence)

Keeping an unlicensed vehicle while the registered keeper

Vehicle Excise and Registration Act 1994, s 31A

Maximum penalty –A fine of level 3 or 5 times the annual duty. Additional penalty of a least £1,000 if the vehicle remains unlicensed from the date of offence to the start of proceedings.

C[47.3] In addition to a fine the court is compelled, in certain cases, to order the defendant to pay loss of duty. See C[47.18] under 'Sentencing'.

Legal notes and definitions

C[47.4] The charge must stipulate whether the defendant is being charged with using or keeping. One charge cannot allege both.

C[47.5] **Prosecutor and time limit.** Only the Secretary of State, the police acting with his approval, or a person or authority authorised by that Secretary of State can conduct the prosecution. Proceedings must start within 6 months of their receiving sufficient evidence to warrant proceedings; subject to an overall limit of three years from the offence.

C[47.6] **Using.** In law means not only driving the vehicle but can also include the vehicle's mere presence on the road. The owner is not liable to be charged with using the vehicle if he allowed some other person to have the vehicle and who used it outside the scope of the authority given by the owner.

C[47.7] **Keeping.** Means causing the vehicle to be on a public road for any period, however short, when the vehicle is not in use. See *Secretary of State for the Environment, Transport and the Regions v Holt* [2000] RTR 309, where the High Court ruled that proof that the defendant was the registered keeper together with the adverse inference drawn from his failure to give information as to the identity of the driver was sufficient to prove he was the keeper on the day in question.

C[47.8] **Public road.** Refers to a road repairable at the public expense. This is different from the more usual definition of a road which means any highway (including footpaths and bridleways) and any other road to which the public has access and includes bridges.

C[47.9] **Mechanically propelled vehicle.** Means a vehicle with some form of engine; thus even a motor assisted pedal cycle comes within the legal definition even if the rider is just pedalling the machine without the use of the engine. A car does not cease to be a mechanically propelled vehicle after removal of its engine, nor if there is some temporary defect which prevents the engine working. If the condition of the vehicle is such that there is no reasonable prospect of it ever being made mobile again, then it ceases to be a mechanically propelled vehicle.

C[47.10]–[47.15] **Employees, drivers, chauffeurs.** It has been decided that it is oppressive to prosecute an employee who was not responsible for licensing the vehicle.

C[47.16] **A dishonoured cheque.** If offered in payment of the licensing fee renders the licence void. The licensing authority will send a notice requiring the excise licence to be delivered up within seven days of the posting of the notice. Failure to comply is an offence punishable with a maximum fine of level 3 or 5 times the annual rate of duty applicable (Customs and Excise Management Act 1979, s 102). For liability for back duty see below.

C[47.17] **Exempted vehicles.** Certain vehicles are exempt from duty and the clerk can supply a list: ambulances, fire engines, military vehicles, some agricultural vehicles; vehicles going for a *pre-arranged* test and some vehicles acquired by overseas residents, vehicles more than 25 years old, calculated from the 31 December of the year of first registration. This latter class of vehicles must still be licensed annually and display a VED disc. See Sch 2 of the 1994 Act. A vehicle kept off the public road may be subject to a Statutory Off-Road Notification (SORN). A SORN declaration is valid for 12 months. Failure to make or renew a SORN may be subject to a level 3 fine.

Sentencing

SC Guideline – No excise licence

C[47.18] Starting point – Band A fine (1–3 months unpaid); Band B fine (4–6 months unpaid); Band C fine (7–12 months lost).

(Special considerations: in all cases add duty lost).

The fine and the arrears of duty should be announced as separate items; we do not recommend the practice of some courts of announcing a single sum and stipulating that it includes the back duty.

Liability for back duty

C[47.19] If the defendant was the person who *kept* the vehicle at the time of the offence the court must order him to pay an amount to cover the loss of duty. Such order is in addition to a fine and the chairman of the court must announce two amounts, namely the amount of the fine and the amount of the lost duty.

C[47.20] If the court decides not to impose a fine but to grant an absolute or conditional discharge the court must still order the payment of the lost duty as well and this must be announced. It must be stressed that this provision applies only if the defendant is the person who *kept* the vehicle at the time of the offence. Thus this provision would not apply to an employed lorry driver but would apply to a private motorist who kept and used his own vehicle. It would also apply to a company which kept and used its own vehicles.

C[47.21] **Dishonoured cheques.** In relation to licences taken out on or after 27 July 1989 the court must, in addition to any penalty it may impose under the Customs and Excise Management Act 1979, s 102, order the defendant to pay an amount to cover the loss of duty incurred for the period for which he had the benefit of the licence.

C[47.22] **Calculating back duty.** This period will usually commence with the date of the expiry of the expired licence, or when the defendant notified his acquisition of the vehicle to the appropriate authority. It will terminate with the date of offence. If there is doubt about the length of the 'relevant period' consult the legal adviser. Back duty is calculated for each month or part thereof. Use on one day in a month will render him liable for back duty for the whole month.

C[47.23] Previous convictions. If the defendant has a previous conviction in respect of the same vehicle for a similar offence for which the court made an order for lost revenue then in the present proceedings the relevant period will commence with the day after the date of the previous offence.

C[47.24] Costs can be ordered as well as a fine and back duty.

C[47.25]–[47.30] Defence against back duty. If the defendant can prove any one of the following in respect of any part of the relevant period back duty cannot be ordered against him for that part of the relevant period:

(a) the vehicle was not kept by him; or

(b) he paid duty in respect of the vehicle for any month or part of a month (where relevant) whether or not on a licence. The defendant does not have to establish this beyond reasonable doubt but only that his contention is probably true.

Defences for a registered keeper (s 31B). The burden is on the defendant to show either:

(i) he is no longer the keeper and has complied with the requirements under the Act;

(ii) the vehicle was not kept on a public road and the requirements have been complied with;

(iii) the vehicle was stolen and not recovered and the notification requirements complied with.

Note that it is an offence to use a vehicle in public if it is not properly registered; defence of no reasonable opportunity or reasonable grounds for believing that registration details were correct – level 3 fine (fixed penalty offence). A constable or authorised person may require production of vehicle registration certificate – level 2 fine for failure to do so.

C[47.31] A person is liable for all the periods when he kept a vehicle without a current tax whether it was on a public road or not. It is not obligatory for a person to tax a car that is kept off the road for the whole of that period. However since 31 January 1998 keepers of vehicles which become unlicensed and are to be kept off the public road are required to provide a declaration to the DVLA. If he ventures onto the road without tax he may find himself with a liability extending back over the time when it was not taxed or to the date when he notified his acquisition of the vehicle.

C[48]

Seat belt offences

Charge (Seat belt offences)

C[48.1] **Unlawfully did drive or ride in a motor vehicle of a class specified in the Motor Vehicles (Wearing of Seat Belts) Regulations 1993 otherwise than in accordance with the provisions of those Regulations**

Road Traffic Act 1988, s 14

Maximum penalty – Fine level 2 (for fines see B[28]). No power to endorse or disqualify.

Fixed penalty – £100

C[48.2] **Unlawfully did drive a motor vehicle with a child in the front seat not wearing a seat belt**

OR

C[48.3] **Unlawfully did drive a motor vehicle with a child in the rear seat not wearing a seat belt**

Motor Vehicles (Wearing of Seat Belts by Children in Front Seats) Regulations 1993

Road Traffic Act, s 15

Maximum penalty	—	(Front seat) level 2
	—	(Rear seat) level 2 for offence (child)

No endorsement or disqualification.

Fixed penalty – £100.

Legal notes and definitions

C[48.4] **Criminal liability.** Only the person actually committing the contravention can be prosecuted. There are no provisions for another person to be prosecuted for aiding and abetting etc and causing or permitting.

C[48.5] **Specified passenger's seat** is the front seat alongside the driver's seat, or, if there is more than one such seat, the one furthest from the driver's seat. If there is no seat alongside the driver's seat, then the specified passenger's seat is the foremost forward facing seat furthest from the driver's seat, unless there is a fixed partition separating it from the space in front of it and alongside the driver's seat as, for example, in a London type taxi cab.

C[48.6] **Class of vehicle.** Every motor car registered on or after 1 January 1965, every three-wheeled vehicle not weighing more than 225 kg manufactured on or after 1 March 1970 and first used on or after 1 September 1970 and heavy motor cars first used on or after 1 October 1988, eg goods vehicles and minibuses.

C[48.7] **Seat belt.** The seat belt must comply with the requirements of the relevant regulations, about which the legal adviser will clarify.

C[48.8] **Exemptions.** Every driver and every person occupying the specified passenger's seat, as defined above, must wear a seat belt when in the vehicle, even when the vehicle is stationary, except a person who is:

(a) using a vehicle constructed or adapted for the delivery or collection of goods or mail to consumers or addressees, as the case may be, whilst engaged in making local rounds of deliveries or collections;
(b) driving the vehicle while performing a manoeuvre which includes reversing;
(c) a qualified driver, and is supervising a provisional licence holder while that person is performing a manoeuvre which includes reversing;
(d) the holder of a valid certificate in a form supplied by the Secretary of State, containing the information required by it, and signed by a registered medical practitioner to the effect that it is inadvisable on medical grounds for him to wear a seat belt;
(e) a constable protecting or escorting another person;
(f) not a constable, but is protecting or escorting another person by virtue of powers the same as or similar to those of a constable for that person;
(g) in the service of a fire brigade and is donning operational clothing or equipment;
(h) the driver of:
    (i) a taxi which is being used for seeking hire, or answering a call for hire, or carrying a passenger for hire; or
    (ii) a private hire vehicle which is being so used to carry a passenger for hire;
(i) a person by whom a test of competence to drive is being conducted and his wearing a seat belt would endanger himself or any other person;
(j) occupying a seat for which the seat belt either:
    (i) does not comply with the relevant standards; or
    (ii) has an inertia reel mechanism which is locked as a result of the vehicle being, or having been, on a steep incline;
(k) riding in a vehicle being used under a trade licence, for the purpose of investigating or remedying a mechanical fault in the vehicle.

C[48.9] Children under 14 years. The above regulations do not apply but it is an offence under the Road Traffic Act 1988, s 15(2) punishable with a maximum fine on level 2 for a person without reasonable excuse to drive on a road with a child under 14 years in the front of a motor vehicle who is not wearing a seat belt.

C[48.10]–[48.15] The seat belt must conform to the Motor Vehicles (Wearing of Seat Belts by Children in Front Seats) Regulations 1993 which provide for the use of special child restraining devices, or, according to age, adult seat belts for use in the front passenger seat.

C[48.16] Exemptions similar to those at (d) and (j) apply. Generally it is now unlawful to drive a vehicle with a small child in the front unless he is wearing a suitable restraint.

C[48.17] Rear seat belts. It is also compulsory for both adults and children in the rear seats of a vehicle fitted with seat belts to wear them. If a child (ie a person under 14 years) on the rear seat is not wearing a seat belt (with a booster cushion where necessary, or a child restraint), the driver of the vehicle will incur liability (maximum penalty a fine on level 1) [level 2 for offences committed on or after 24/9/07]. In the case of a passenger aged 14 years or more, only he will be liable (maximum penalty a fine on level 2), there are no provisions for the driver to be guilty of aiding and abetting the offence. There is no liability where all available seat belts are in use.

C[48.18] The following table summarises the main legal requirements for wearing seat belts.

	Front seat	*Rear seat*	*Whose responsibility*
Driver	Must be worn if fitted	—	Driver
child under 3 years of age	Appropriate child restraint must be worn	Appropriate child restraint must be worn	Driver

	Front seat	*Rear seat*	*Whose responsibility*
child aged 3–11 and under 1.5 metres (about 5 feet) in height	Appropriate child restraint must be worn if available. If not an adult seat belt must be worn	Appropriate child restraint must be worn if available. If not an adult seat belt must be worn	Driver
child aged 12 or 13 or younger 1.5 metres or more in height	Adult seat belt must be worn if available	Adult seat belt must be worn if available	Driver
adult passengers	Must be worn if available	Must be worn if available	Passenger

Sentencing

SC Guideline – Seat belt offences

C[48.19] Starting point – Band A fine.

C[49] Speeding

Charge (Speeding)

C[49.1] **Driving a motor vehicle on a road at a speed exceeding a statutory limit**

Road Traffic Regulation Act 1984, ss 81 (84 or 86) and 89

Maximum penalty – Fine level 3 (for fines see **B[28]**). May disqualify for any period and/or until a driving test has been passed. Must endorse unless there are special reasons.

Note – Speeding on a motorway may be charged under the Road Traffic Regulation Act 1984, s 17 in which case the maximum penalty is a fine on level 4.

Penalty points – 3–6. [from a date to be appointed 2–6 under the **Road Safety Act** 2006] (Fixed penalty – 3.)

Fixed penalty – £100

Legal notes and definitions

C[49.2] Speeding can be considered under five main headings:

(A) Speeding on restricted roads (Road Traffic Regulation Act 1984, s 16).
(B) Speeding on motorways (s 17).
(C) Breaking the speed limit imposed by the Secretary of State for the Environment or highway authorities on roads other than restricted roads (s 84).
(D) Driving a vehicle at a speed in excess of that permitted for that class of vehicle (s 86).
(E) Breaking a temporary or experimental speed limit imposed by the Secretary of State for the Environment on certain specified roads (s 88), or by the highway authority because of road works, etc (s 14).

These classes of speeding are dealt with in the above order on the following pages.

C[49.3] Warning of prosecution must have been given to the defendant except in circumstances prescribed in the Road Traffic Offenders Act 1988, s 2, as amended (eg following an 'accident'). Section 2 required only that there was a sufficiently causal link between the relevant offence and the offender, so that the driver need not be warned of the risk of prosecution (*R v Myers* [2007] All ER [D] 241 (Feb)). The word 'accident' in s 2 had to be given a common sense meaning and was not restricted to untoward or unintended consequences having an adverse physical effect (*R v Currie* [2007] EWCA Crim 926).

C[49.4] **Evidence.** The Road Traffic Offenders Act 1988, s 20 (as substituted by the Road Traffic Act 1991) provides that it will be sufficient for evidence of an offence of speeding or contravening a red traffic light to be obtained by approved devices, such as a Gatso camera, which also records speeds and times as appropriate. The record must be signed by a constable or by a person authorised by or on behalf of the chief officer of police for the relevant area. It was held in *Crader v Chief Constable of Hampshire Constabulary* [2015] EWHC 3553 (Admin), (2016) 180 JP 199 that the certificate does not need to state on its face that it is signed either by a constable or a person who is authorised by or on behalf of the chief officer of police; there need only be sufficient indications on its face that it purports to be a s 20 certificate made with the authority of the chief officer. The accused may require the attendance of the person who signed the document not less than three days before the trial.

In *DPP v Thornley* [2006] EWHC 312 (Admin), [2006] 09 LS Gaz R 32, it was held that s 20(8) of the RTOA 1988 was permissive in its terms and therefore the prosecution were entitled to admit the record of speeding as a species of "real evidence". *DPP v Thornley* has since been applied and followed in *Griffiths v DPP* [2007] EWHC 619 (Admin).

A police officer was entitled to corroborate his opinion that a motorist had travelled at an excessive speed by reference to the speed reading given by a speed measuring device that was a prescribed device but which was not of an approved type. Section 20 of the Road Traffic Offenders Act 1988 was a self-contained code which did not apply to a prosecution brought under s 89 of the Road Traffic Regulation Act 1984: *Connell v DPP* [2011] EWHC 158 (Admin), 175 JP 151.

See 'Conditional offer of fixed penalty' at C[8.21]–C[8.22].

C[49.5] If the evidence merely consists of one witness's opinion that the defendant was exceeding the speed limit there cannot be a conviction. If the single witness is supported by a speedometer, stop watch, radar meter or Vascar, then there can be a conviction.

C[49.6] The evidence of two witnesses estimating the speed at the same time can result in a conviction, but if their estimates refer to speeds at different parts of the road then that will not suffice.

C[49.7] If a vehicle was being used for the purpose of the fire brigade, the police, or the ambulance services, and the driver can establish that observing the speed limit would have hindered him in the execution of his official duties, then that could be accepted as a successful line of defence by the court. It is for the court to decide this issue as there is no inherent right for all such vehicles to exceed the speed limit, for instance an empty ambulance merely returning to its garage or a fire engine out on routine test carry no exemption from a speed limit. The defence of necessity is also available to a private person and is not confined to circumstances where there is a risk to life: *Pipe v DPP* [2012] EWHC 1821 (Admin), [2012] All ER (D) 238 (May). A police officer using a vehicle to 'hone' his skills may be guilty of speeding (see C[16] and *DPP v Milton* [2006] EWHC 242 (Admin), (2006) 170 JP 319).

C[49.8] The defendant merely has to prove that this defence is probably true; he need not prove it beyond reasonable doubt.

C[49.9] Although the driver must be identified, the fact that he was driving when stopped is prima facie evidence that he drove over the whole distance for which he was timed.

C[49.10]–[49.14] The Traffic Signs Regulations and General Directions 2016, SI 2016/362 came into effect on 22 April 2016 with the transitional and savings provisions specified in reg 14 (see below). The regulations consolidate, with substantial amendments, the:

(a) Zebra, Pelican and Puffin Pedestrian Crossings Regulations and General Directions 1997;
(b) Traffic Signs (Temporary Obstructions) Regulations 1997;
(c) Traffic Signs Regulations and General Directions 2002;
(d) School Crossing Patrol Sign (England and Wales) Regulations 2006.

Regulation 14(2) provides:

> '(2) A sign to which this paragraph applies and which is of a size, colour and type prescribed, or treated as prescribed, by the Traffic Signs Regulations 2002(b) ("the 2002 Regulations") is to be treated as being of a size, colour and type prescribed by these Regulations.'

Therefore, signs made under and compliant with the 2002 Regulations are treated as complying with the 2016 Regulations. This covers the sign, but not the nature of the prohibition or obligation to comply. The latter will be as per the 2016 Regulations and prosecutions for post-commencement offences will need to be framed accordingly. Speed limit signs are now governed by Sch 10 to the Regulations.

Signs erected under, and in conformity with, the 2002 are treated as being of the colour, size and type prescribed by the 2016 Regulations. Where an offence postdates the commencement of the 2016 Regulations and concerns a sign erected under the 2002 Regulations, it is our view that the new, 'relaxed' requirements may, if necessary, be relied on by the prosecution, and the narrative which follows needs to be read accordingly. For example, a repeater sign is no longer a requirement and the absence of such a sign would not, therefore, be fatal to such a prosecution. Subject to this, old case law on signage continues, in our view, to be relevant.

DfT Circular 01/2016 contains, in Annexes A and B, an overview of the changes made by the 2016 Regulations, with cross references showing where the new requirements will be found. As to speed limit signs, the changes are described at paras 13.2–13.7.

C[49.15] **Speed limit signs.** The ordinary meaning of the words in s 85(4) of the Road Traffic Regulation Act 1984 meant that two tests had to be satisfied before the defendant could be convicted. The first was that at the time the offence was being committed there were such signs as were mentioned in s 85(1) or (2). The second was that those signs indicated the relevant speed limit. Accordingly, no offence was committed where speed signs were obscured by hedgerows (*Coombe v DPP* [2006] EWHC 3263 (Admin), [2007] RTR 383); further, in *DPP v Butler* (unreported) 4/3/10, DC, it was held that a magistrates' court was entitled to find that a terminal speed limit located within 50 metres of a street lamp did not comply with the Traffic Signs Directions and Regulations 2002, Sch 17, item 10, as it was not illuminated in darkness. Accordingly, on the facts found no offence of speeding was made out. However, see *Peake v DPP* immediately below.

In *Peake v DPP* [2010] EWHC 286 (Admin) the High Court adopted a **purposive approach** and rejected the argument that the enforcement of a speed limit was dependent upon every sign within a 40 mph area having to be compliant with the Traffic Signs Directions and Regulations 2002. On the facts found the argument was rejected because there were no deficiencies in the road along which the defendant had driven or they were de minimis (minor).

If the defendant submits that the speed sign was unlawful because of its size, composition, character or colour, etc, the legal adviser should be consulted.

On a natural reading of the relevant primary and secondary legislation and adopting a purposive approach to interpretation to the relevant provisions, if at the point of enforcement there are signs complying with the directions of the Secretary of State which in fact provide adequate guidance of the speed limit at that point, this satisfies the requirements of s 85(4) of the Road Traffic Regulation Act 1984. If the prosecution can establish the route taken by the defendant, it will only have to show that compliant signs provide adequate guidance at the point of enforcement for a motorist taking that route. If the prosecution cannot establish the route, they would have to show compliant signs on all routes the driver may have taken (*Coombes v DPP* and *Peake v DPP* considered): *Jones v DPP* [2011] EWHC 50 (Admin), 175 JP 129.

Category A – speeding on restricted roads (Road Traffic Regulation Act 1984, s 81)

Legal notes and definitions

C[49.16] **Restricted road.** A road becomes a restricted road in one of two ways:

(a) it has a system of street lamps placed not more than two hundred yards apart, in which case the speed limit is 30 miles per hour; or
(b) it is directed by the relevant authority that it becomes a restricted road, in which case the speed limit is again 30 miles per hour.

A road restricted by (a) above need not display 'repeater' signs but a road in category (b) does have to display the repeater '30' signs.

C[49.17] The relevant authority may direct that an (a) category road may be derestricted. 'Restricted road' is a term of art referring to a road having a 30 mile per hour limit because of the above provisions. Confusingly, restricted road is commonly, but erroneously, used to refer to any road having a speed limit less than the overall maxima of 70 miles per hour for motorways and dual carriageways and 60 miles per hour for single carriageways.

C[49.18] The limit on a restricted road of 30 mph can be altered by the Secretary of State for the Environment and the Home Secretary acting jointly.

C[49.19] A vehicle which is limited to a lower speed than the limit for the road must always conform to its own scheduled speed limit, for example, a lorry drawing more than one trailer is limited to 20 mph and must keep to that limit even on a restricted road where a 30 mph limit is in force.

Category B – speeding on motorways (Road Traffic Regulation Act 1984, s 17)

C[49.20] Motorway. The legal adviser can provide a detailed definition if it should be necessary. The motorway includes the hard shoulder and access and exit roads.

C[49.21] The general speed limit on a motorway is 70 miles per hour although there are lower speed limits on certain stretches of motorway.

C[49.22] Contraventions of certain temporary restrictions on motorways (eg for roadworks) are offences under s 16 and also carry an endorsement.

Category C – driving a motor vehicle at a speed in excess of a limit imposed on a road, other than a restricted road, by the highway authority (Road Traffic Regulation Act 1984, s 84)

Legal notes and definitions

C[49.23] For the purposes of this offence the appropriate highway authority for trunk roads is the Secretary of State for the Environment. For non-trunk roads the appropriate authority is either the Secretary of State for the Environment or the local authority (for instance a county council or, in London, the relevant London borough) but the local authority has to have his consent.

C[49.24] These speed limits can be ordered to be in general use or merely during specified periods.

C[49.25]–[49.30] This is the provision which enables a 40 or 50 (or whatever) miles per hour limit to be imposed on a specified road. If the road would otherwise be a 'restricted' (ie having a limit of 30 miles per hour) road, eg because of having lamp posts not more than 200 yards apart, it ceases to be a 'restricted' road when an order is made imposing a limit under this provision.

Category D – driving a motor vehicle at a speed exceeding the limit prescribed for that class of vehicle (Road Traffic Regulation Act 1984, s 86)

Legal notes and definitions

C[49.31] Permitted speed limits for restricted classes of vehicles include:

	Motor-way	*Dual car-riageway*	*Other road*
Coach or motor caravan having an unladen weight exceeding 3.05 tonnes or adapted to carry more than 8 passengers			
(a) if not exceeding 12 metres in overall length	70	60	50
(b) if exceeding 12 metres in overall length	60	60	50
Car, motor caravan, car-derived van drawing one trailer, eg a caravan	60	60	50
Goods vehicle maximum laden weight not exceeding 7.5 tonnes (except car-derived van and articulated vehicles)	70	60	50
Goods vehicle maximum laden weight exceeding 7.5 tonnes	60	50	40
Articulated goods vehicles			
(a) maximum laden weight not exceeding 7.5 tonnes	60	50	50
(b) maximum laden weight exceeding 7.5 tonnes	60	50	40

Category E – where temporary or experimental speed limits have been imposed by the Ministry of Transport (Road Traffic Regulation Act 1984, s 88) or by the Highway Authority during road works, etc (RTRA 1984, s 14)

Legal notes and definitions

C[49.32] The Secretary of State for the Environment may, for a period of up to 18 months, impose a speed limit on all roads or on certain specified roads in the interests of safety or traffic flow. The limit may be general or apply only at specified times.

C[49.33] Unless such an order directs otherwise, it will not interfere with existing speed limits on restricted roads or roads which are already the subject of an order. It is an order under this provision which has imposed a general speed limit of 70 miles per hour on dual carriageways and 60 miles per hour on single carriageways. Originally of a temporary nature, the order has now been made indefinite.

C[49.34] A speed limit may be imposed on a stretch of road for a temporary period to prevent danger from works on or near the highway.

C[49.35] These provisions do not apply to motorways.

C[49.35A] The RTRA 1984, s 14 provides that if the traffic authority for a road are satisfied that traffic on the road should be restricted or prohibited—

(a) because works are being or are proposed to be executed on or near the road; or

(b) because of the likelihood of danger to the public, or of serious damage to the road, which is not attributable to such works; or

(c) for the purpose of enabling the duty imposed by section 89(1)(a) or (2) of the Environmental Protection Act 1990 (litter clearing and cleaning) to be discharged,

the authority may by order restrict or prohibit temporarily the use of that road, or of any part of it, by vehicles, or vehicles of any class, or by pedestrians, to such extent and subject to such conditions or exceptions as they may consider necessary.

It is an offence under s 16 to use or permitting the use of a vehicle in contravention of an order made under s 14.

In *Castle v Wakefield and Pontefract Magistrates' Court* [2014] EWHC 587 (Admin), [2014] RTR 268, 178 JP 285 the appellant challenged the *vires* of an order which provided for speed limits of 60 or 50 mph on certain designated stretches of road, during such times and to such extent as would from time to time be indicated by traffic signs. It was contended that this fell outside the scope of the enabling legislation. There were further *vires* arguments as to the legality of the order being signed by a team leader in the Highways Agency and as to the ability to delegate to the Agency whether the limit should be 60 or 50 mph.

The Divisional Court rejected all the challenges. Section 14 conferred wide powers and enabled the imposition of variable speed limits. The Secretary of State was accountable to Parliament for the Agency. Therefore, the signing of the order and setting of speed restrictions were acts lawfully performed by the Agency acting on behalf of the Secretary of State.

Sentencing
SC Guideline – Speeding

Speeding (Revised 2017)

C[49.36]

Road Traffic Regulation Act 1984, s 89(1)

Effective from: 24 April 2017

Triable only summarily:

Maximum: Level 3 fine (level 4 if motorway)

Offence range: Band A fine–Band C fine

Steps 1 and 2 — Determining the offence seriousness

The starting point applies to all offenders irrespective of plea or previous convictions.

Speed limit (mph)	Recorded speed (mph)		
20	41 and above	31–40	21–30
30	51 and above	41–50	31–40
40	66 and above	56–65	41–55
50	76 and above	66–75	51–65
60	91 and above	81–90	61–80
70	101 and above	91–100	71–90
Sentencing range	**Band C fine**	**Band B fine**	**Band A fine**
Points/ disqualification	Disqualify 7–56 days **OR** 6 points	Disqualify 7–28 days **OR** 4–6 points	3 points

- **Must endorse and may disqualify. If no disqualification impose 3–6 points**
- **Where an offender is driving grossly in excess of the speed limit the court should consider a disqualification in excess of 56 days.**

The court should then consider further adjustment for any aggravating or mitigating factors. The following is a **non-exhaustive** list of additional factual elements providing the context of the offence and factors relating to the offender. Identify whether any combination of these, or other relevant factors, should result in an upward or downward adjustment from the sentence arrived at so far.

Factors increasing seriousness

Statutory aggravating factors:

- Previous convictions, having regard to a) the **nature** of the offence to which the conviction relates and its **relevance** to the current offence; and b) the **time** that has elapsed since the conviction
- Offence committed whilst on bail

Other aggravating factors:

- Offence committed on licence or post sentence supervision
- Poor road or weather conditions
- Driving LGV, HGV, PSV etc.
- Towing caravan/trailer
- Carrying passengers or heavy load
- Driving for hire or reward
- Evidence of unacceptable standard of driving over and above speed
- Location e.g. near school
- High level of traffic or pedestrians in the vicinity

Factors reducing seriousness or reflecting personal mitigation

- No previous convictions or no relevant/recent convictions
- Good character and/or exemplary conduct
- Genuine emergency established

Step 3 — Consider any factors which indicate a reduction, such as assistance to the prosecution

The court should take into account sections 73 and 74 of the Serious Organised Crime and Police Act 2005 (assistance by defendants: reduction or review of sentence) and any other rule of law by virtue of which an offender may receive a discounted sentence in consequence of assistance given (or offered) to the prosecutor or investigator.

Step 4 — Reduction for guilty pleas

The court should take account of any potential reduction for a guilty plea in accordance with section 144 of the Criminal Justice Act 2003 and the *Guilty Plea* guideline.

Step 5 — Totality principle

If sentencing an offender for more than one offence, or where the offender is already serving a sentence, consider whether the total sentence is just and proportionate to the overall offending behaviour in accordance with the *Offences Taken into Consideration and Totality* guideline.

Step 6 — Compensation and ancillary orders

In all cases, the court should consider whether to make compensation and/or other ancillary orders.

Step 7 — Reasons

Section 174 of the Criminal Justice Act 2003 imposes a duty to give reasons for, and explain the effect of, the sentence.

C[49.37] If it appears to the court that the accused suffers from some disease or physical disability likely to cause his driving to be a source of danger to the public, then the court shall notify the licensing authority who may take steps to withdraw the driving licence (see C[5.49]).

C[50]

Steering defective

Charge (Steering defective)

C[50.1] **Using, causing or permitting to be used on a road a motor vehicle with defective steering**

Road Vehicles (Construction and Use) Regulations 1986, reg 29; Road Traffic Act 1988, s 41A(b)

Maximum penalty – For a goods vehicle, fine on level 5, otherwise level 4 (for fines see B[28]).

Penalty points – 3.

Fixed penalty – £100 (3PP).

Legal notes and definitions

C[50.2] All the details as to maximum penalty, legal notes, exemption from endorsement and disqualification, and definitions and sentencing set out at C[9] for defective brakes apply to this charge of defective steering.

C[50.3] As with brakes, the law demands that the steering fitted to a motor vehicle on a road shall at all times be maintained in good and efficient working order and properly adjusted.

Sentencing
SGC Guideline – Steering defective

C[50.4] Starting point – either mechanically propelled vehicle or HGV, LGV or PSV – Band B fine (driver); Band B fine (owner-driver but consider an uplift of at least 25% on the driver's fine); Band C fine (owner-company)

C[51]

No test certificate

Charge (No test certificate)

C[51.1] **Using, causing or permitting a motor vehicle to be on the road first registered 3 or more years previously without having a test certificate in force**

Road Traffic Act 1988, s 47(1)

Maximum penalty – Fine level 3. Vehicles adapted to carry more than eight passengers, level 4 (for fines see **B**[28]). No power to endorse or disqualify.

Fixed penalty – £100

Legal notes and definitions

C[51.2] **Passenger vehicles carrying more than eight passengers.** These vehicles and some taxis and ambulances must be tested after one year.

C[51.3] **Motor vehicle.** See C[9.7].

C[51.4] **Road.** Means any highway (including footpaths and bridleways) and any other road to which the public has access and includes bridges.

C[51.5] **Using.** This does not in law only mean driving a vehicle along a road; its mere presence on a road, even in a useless condition may constitute using (*Pumbien v Vines* [1996] RTR 37, [1996] Crim LR 124). The test is whether steps had been taken to make it impossible for a driver to drive the vehicle. Where doubt exists consult the legal adviser. A person, limited company, a corporate body which owns a vehicle that is driven in the course of the owner's business is using the vehicle. See C[9.4].

C[51.6] **Causing.** This implies some express or positive mandate from the person causing the vehicle to be used; or some authority from him and knowledge of the facts which constitute the offence.

C[51.7] **Permitting.** This includes express permission and also circumstances in which permission may be inferred.

C[51.8] If the defendant is a limited company, it must be proved that some person for whose criminal act the company is responsible permitted the offence. A defendant charged with permitting must be shown to have known the vehicle was being used or that he shut his eyes to something that would have made the use obvious to him.

C[51.9] Examples of exempted vehicles include:

Goods vehicles the design gross weight of which exceeds 3,500 kg.

Motor tractors.

Articulated vehicles, and their several parts.

Works trucks.

Pedestrian-controlled vehicles.

Invalid vehicles.

Some taxis.

Certain vehicles from abroad and Northern Ireland only here temporarily.

Vehicles en route for export.

Agricultural motor vehicles.

C[51.10]–[51.15] Examples of exempted uses include:

(a) that by a previous arrangement the vehicle was being used for the purpose of taking it for a test or for bringing it back from a test (*Williams v Richards* (1997) Times, 29 July);

(b) that the examiner or a person under his personal direction was using the vehicle in the course of or in connection with a test;

(c) that following an unsuccessful test the vehicle was being used by being towed to a place where it could be broken up; or

(d) that by a previous arrangement the vehicle was being taken to or from a place where it was to be or had been taken to remedy defects on the ground of which a test certificate had been refused.

C[51.16] The defendant need not prove either kind of exemption (ie exempted vehicle or exempted use) beyond reasonable doubt; he need only prove this defence is probably true.

C[51.17] Renewal of certificate. A certificate lasts for one year. Within one month from the expiry of the certificate, the vehicle may be retested and a further certificate issued to commence on the expiry of the existing certificate.

Sentencing

SC Guideline – (1) No test certificate (2) No goods vehicle test certificate

C[51.18] Starting point – mechanically propelled vehicle – Band A fine (driver); Band A fine (owner-driver but consider an uplift of at least 25% on the driver's fine); Band B fine (owner-company).

Starting point – goods vehicle – Band B fine (driver); Band B fine (owner-driver but consider an uplift of at least 25% on the driver's fine); Band C fine (owner-company).

C[52] Traffic signs

Charge (Traffic signs)

C[52.1] **Failing to comply with the indication given by a traffic sign**

Road Traffic Act 1988, s 36.

Maximum penalty – Fine level 3. Non-compliance with certain traffic signs where the vehicle was a motor vehicle carries endorsement of three penalty points: see C[52.16], post.

Fixed penalty – £100 for endorsable offences, £50 otherwise

Traffic Signs Regulations and General Directions 2016 Traffic signs are defined by the RTRA 1984, s 64, and are prescribed by the Traffic Signs Regulations and General Directions 2016, with the transitional and savings provisions specified in regulation 14 (see infra). The 2016 regulations consolidate, with substantial amendments, the:

(a) Zebra, Pelican and Puffin Pedestrian Crossings Regulations and General Directions 1997;
(b) Traffic Signs (Temporary Obstructions) Regulations 1997;
(c) Traffic Signs Regulations and General Directions 2002;
(d) School Crossing Patrol Sign (England and Wales) Regulations 2006.

The offence creating provision of the RTA 1988, s 36, is applied in the regulations to certain signs, but the style which has been adopted is different from that which appeared in the Traffic Signs Regulations and General Directions 2002. There is no equivalent of the list which appeared in reg 10 of the 2002 regulations (as to this and as to the application of endorsement and discretionary disqualification under the RTOA 1988, Sch 2). The application of these provisions is, instead, stated within the schedules, which set out the requirements that apply to particular signs. Each schedule covers a different class of sign.

The Department for Transport has issued DfT Circular 01/2016 to provide guidance to practitioners. Very helpfully, Annexes A and B to the circular provides an overview of the changes between the 2002 and the 2016 Regulations, with cross references.

Regulation 14 contains the transitional provisions. Signs made under and compliant with the Traffic Signs Regulations and General Directions 2002 are treated as complying with the 2016 Regulations. This covers the sign, but not the nature of the prohibition or obligation to comply. The latter will be as per the 2016 Regulations and prosecutions for post-commencement offences will need to be framed accordingly.

In our opinion, the principles stated below continue to apply.

Legal notes and definitions

C[52.2] It is not a defence that the sign was not seen.

C[52.3] The defendant can only be convicted if at the time of the offence he was warned of possible prosecution, or a summons or a notice of intended prosecution was served within 14 days upon the registered owner of the vehicle. It will be presumed that this requirement was complied with unless the contrary is proved by the defendant on the balance of probabilities.

C[52.4] The offence applies to all vehicles including pedal cycles and is not limited to mechanically propelled vehicles.

C[52.5] Even wheeling a pedal cycle in contravention of the sign is an offence.

C[52.6] A traffic sign. This is presumed to be of correct size, colour and type unless proved to the contrary by the defence.

C[52.7] Automatic traffic lights are presumed to be in proper working order unless the contrary is proved by the defence.

C[52.8] Traffic lights. It is an offence if any part of the vehicle crosses the 'stop' line when the light is red, for example, if the front part of the vehicle is already over the line and the light turns red an offence is committed if the rear part of the vehicle then crosses the line with the light still at red.

C[52.9] Double white lines. It is an offence to overtake or park in contravention of double white lines in the middle of the road. There are certain exceptions, however, such as passing a slow moving road sweeper or a taxi stopping to allow a passenger to alight or board. Ask the legal adviser for details.

C[52.10]–[52.15] A road. Means any highway (including footpaths and bridleways) and any other road to which the public has access and includes bridges.

C[52.16] Signs to which the offence applies. These include:

Emergency traffic signs placed by a constable on the instructions of a chief officer of police.

Stop at major road ahead.[1]

Give way at major road ahead.

Stop one way working.

No entry.[1]

Arrow indicating direction to be followed.

Arrow indicating keep left or right.

Red light including portable light signals and at automatic level crossings.[1]

Double white lines.[1]

Keep left dual carriageway.

Turn left at dual carriageway.

Drivers of 'abnormal loads' at railway level crossings.[1]

Prohibition on vehicles exceeding specified height.[1]

Green arrow traffic signals.[1]

No 'U' turn.

Mini roundabout sign.

---

1 Only these offences qualify for endorsement and disqualification.

Sentencing

SC Guideline – Failing to comply with traffic sign

C[52.17] Starting point – Band A fine (Endorsement and disqualification can only be ordered if the vehicle was a motor vehicle and the traffic sign was one of those mentioned under 'Maximum penalty').

C[52.18] If it appears to the court that the accused suffers from some disease or physical disability likely to cause his driving to be a source of danger to the public, then the court shall notify the licensing authority who may take steps to withdraw the driving licence (see C[5.49]).

C[53]

Tyres defective

Charge (Tyres defective)

C[53.1] Using, causing or permitting to be used on a road a motor vehicle or trailer with defective tyres

Road Vehicles (Construction and Use) Regulations 1986, reg 27; Road Traffic Act 1988, s 41A(b)

Maximum penalty – For a goods vehicle, fine level 5, otherwise level 4 (for fines see B[28]). May disqualify for any period and/or until a driving test has been passed. Must endorse unless special reasons exist.

For 'special reasons', see **C**[5.2].

Penalty points – 3

Fixed penalty – £100 (3PP)

Legal notes and definitions

C[53.2] All the details as to legal notes, exemption from endorsement and disqualification, definitions and sentencing set out on at C[9] for defective brakes also apply to these charges.

C[53.3] It is an offence for a tyre on a car or light van (gross weight not exceeding 3,500 kg) and their trailers to be in any of the following conditions:

(a) tyre being unsuitable having regard to the use to which the vehicle is put;
(b) tyre being unsuitable having regard to types of tyres on other wheels;
(c) tyre not so inflated as to make it fit for use to which vehicle is being put;
(d) break in fabric of tyre;
(e) ply or cord structure exposed;
(f) the grooves of the tread pattern of the tyre do not have a depth of at least 1 millimetre throughout a continuous band comprising the central three-quarters of the breadth of the tread and round the entire outer circumference of the tyre;
(g) tyre must be free from any defect which might damage the road surface or cause danger to persons in the vehicle or on the road.

Consult the legal adviser for the complete list.

C[53.4] The law requires all tyres of a motor vehicle or trailer on a road to be free from any defect which might in any way cause damage to the road surface or cause danger to persons in or on a vehicle or to other persons using the road.

C[53.5] If no tyre is fitted at all the offence will be brought under a different regulation.

C[53.6] Two or more defective tyres. If a vehicle has two or more defective tyres, a separate charge should be alleged for each.

Sentencing

SC Guideline – Tyres defective

C[53.7] Starting point – mechanically propelled vehicle – Band A fine (driver); Band A fine (owner-driver but consider an uplift of at least 25% on the driver's fine); Band B fine (owner-company).

Starting point – goods vehicle – Band B fine (driver); Band B fine (owner-driver but consider an uplift of at least 25% on the driver's fine); Band C fine (owner-company).

C[53.8] As for 'brakes' see C[9.16]. A vehicle with two defective tyres is much more dangerous than a vehicle with only one defective tyre. Where the means of the offender permit the penalty should usually ensure that it is cheaper to keep the vehicle in good condition than to risk a fine. A short disqualification can also be considered.

Section D

Procedure

D[1]
The Human Rights Act

D[1.1] The purpose of the Human Rights Act 1998 is to allow citizens of the United Kingdom to enforce their rights under the Human Rights Convention in the domestic courts.

The Act requires all courts and tribunals to give effect to Convention rights by interpreting existing legislation and laws, where possible, compatibly with the Convention.

D[1.2] With regard to statute (primary legislation) the courts are required to interpret the legislation so as to uphold the Convention rights unless legislation is so clearly incompatible with the Convention that it is impossible to do so. If a Convention right is contravened by a provision in primary legislation which the court is unable to interpret compatibly it must give effect to the will of Parliament. However, in such circumstances an appeal may be made to the High Court for a *declaration of incompatibility* which leads to a fast track procedure in Parliament for the passing of a *remedial order* to cure the apparent incompatibility.

In the case of secondary legislation or precedent the court's duty is to give effect to Convention rights; firstly through the medium of interpretation or secondly through disapplying the relevant domestic law.

D[1.3] Additionally, courts must take into account judgments, decisions and opinions of the European Court of Human Rights and the Commission. All public authorities have a positive obligation to act compatibly with the Convention. This includes magistrates' courts, local authorities, the Probation Service and justices' clerks.

D[1.4] Advocates wishing to raise a Convention point in magistrates' courts should be prepared to identify the article of the Convention which it is suggested may be breached, the reason for the breach and the remedy required of the courts. Court may give directions requiring the parties to file skeleton arguments in support of any Convention arguments.

Procedural steps

D[1.5] **Step 1 Ask if a Convention right is engaged.**

If no Convention right is engaged, the case must be decided on the basis of domestic law.

If the Convention is engaged move to step 2

Step 2 Identify the relevant article and its class

- Absolute Rights:
  Article 3: prohibition of torture, inhuman or degrading treatment
  Article 4(1): prohibition of slavery or servitude

Article 7: prohibition of punishment without law

- Limited Rights:
  Article 2: right to life
  Article 4(2): prohibition of forced or compulsory labour
  Article 5: right to liberty
  Article 6: right to a fair trial
- Qualified Rights:
  Article 8: right to respect for private and family life
  Article 9: freedom of thought, conscience and religion
  Article 10: freedom of expression
  Article 11: freedom of assembly
- Parts of Article 6 such as art 6(1) confer limited rights. Other parts, such as art 6(3) confer qualified rights.

D[1.6] The threshold is high for breach of an *absolute right* but once breached for any reason, a violation is established.

Limited rights contain definitive statements of the circumstances which *permit* a breach of the right. If the restrictions are not complied with, there has been a violation of the Article.

Qualified Rights *may* be breached if:

- the breach is prescribed by domestic law
- the law is clear and accessible
- the breach pursues a legitimate aim which is set out in the Article
- the measure is a proportional response

If these provisions do not apply there is likely to be a violation of the convention.

D[1.7] A magistrates' court which finds a breach or potential breach of the Convention may grant such relief or remedy, or make that order within its powers and it considers just and appropriate. In essence this may mean a simple adjournment to provide more time to prepare for a trial or it may involve the exclusion of evidence which would have had an unfair effect on the trial itself.

In *R (Laporte) v Chief Constable of Gloucestershire* [2004] EWCA Civ 1639, [2005] 1 All ER 473 the High Court found that the police acted reasonably in stopping a coach party, in apprehension of a breach of the peace and did not violate their Article 10 rights. However their actions in forcibly returning the coach to London breached Article 5.

D[1.8] **Burden of Proof.** Where a statutory provision imposes a burden of proof on a defendant the court must first ascertain if it is an evidential or a legal burden. An evidential burden can be discharged by some evidence which could result in a decision in the defendant's favour. A legal burden on the other hand may breach the presumption of innocence in Article 6 (*R v Johnstone* [2003] UKHL 28, [2003] All ER (D) 323 (May), HL and *A-G's Reference No 1* (2004)).

D[1A]

Reasons for decision

D[1A.1] There are many statutory requirements to give reasons in court. Examples are the imposition of imprisonment or where a court orders the removal of press restriction normally applicable in court. Such requirements are outlined in the text of this work. Article 6(1) states: '. . . everyone is entitled to a fair and public hearing within a reasonable time by an independent and impartial tribunal established by law. Judgment shall be pronounced publicly . . . '.

D[1A.2] The giving of reasons enables an aggrieved person to understand the decision and make an informed decision on the right to appeal. It also provides an explanation for the public at large and those observing the proceedings in court. Reasons need not be elaborate (*McKerry v Teesdale and Wear Valley Justices* (2000) 164 JP 355, [2000] Crim LR 594, CA).

D[1A.3] However, a reasoned judgment at the end of a trial should cover the major issues in dispute, and any legal submissions, together with the findings of fact. In *Ruiz Torija v Spain* (1994) 19 EHRR 542, ECtHR the European Court stated: 'The court reiterates that Article 6(1) obliges the courts to give reasons for their judgments, but cannot be understood as requiring a detailed answer to every argument. The extent to which this duty to give reasons applies may vary according to the nature of the decision'. One area where it is clear the court will have to give reasons is where there is any suggestion that an inference from the exercise of the right to silence is to be drawn: see *Condron v United Kingdom* [2000] Crim LR 679, 8 BHRC 290, ECtHR.

D[1A.4] One other area that would appear to be clear is that the courts must not resort to formatted or standard reasons. In *Yagci and Sargin v Turkey* (1995) 20 EHRR 505, ECtHR the European Court disapproved of the use of stereotyped reasons by a court when refusing bail.

D[1A.5] The court, like all other tribunals and public authorities, must act compatibly with the European Convention. In general a rigorous approach to giving reasons for a decision will normally alert the court to any human rights issues. A structured approach to those issues should lead to a successful resolution of human rights problems in court.

D[1B]

Proceedings to be in open court

D[1B.1] Magistrates conducting a summary trial must generally sit in open court (Magistrates' Courts Act 1980, s 121) and comply with the provisions of Art 6 of the ECHR that everyone is entitled to a fair and public hearing. See Part 24 of the Criminal Procedure Rules 2015 (Trial and Sentence in a Magistrates' Court).

D[1B.2] Exceptions. A magistrates' court, may in the exercise of its inherent power to control the conduct of proceedings exclude the public where it becomes necessary in order to administer justice, but there must be compelling reasons for the court to sit in camera: *R v Malvern Justices, ex parte Evans and another; R v Evesham Justices, ex parte McDonagh and another* [1988] QB 540, [1988] 1 All ER 371, 152 JP 74. Usually, except for statutory exceptions, the court should only exclude the public if the administration of justice would be rendered impracticable by their presence, whether because the case could not be effectively tried, or the parties entitled to justice would be reasonably deterred from seeking it at the hands of the court.

In the exercise of its inherent jurisdiction to restrict access in the interests of the administration of justice, the court is entitled to take into account such matters as security, public order, decency, safety and the protection of minors: *Re L* (1990) 155 JP 273, [1991] Crim LR 633. Even in a case involving national security, however, no departure from the principle of open justice should be greater than necessary, and it is difficult to conceive of a situation where both holding a trial in camera and granting anonymity to the defendants could be justified: *Guardian News and Media Ltd v Incedal* [2014] EWCA Crim 1861, [2015] 1 Cr App Rep 36, (2014) Times, 29 October.

In *R (on the application of O'Connor and Jerrard) v Aldershot Magistrates' Court* [2016] EWHC 2792, [2017] 181 JP 117 a decision had been taken administratively to bar anyone associated with a defendant from entering the court building, because the court administration had been informed by the police that a protest had been planned to take place that day. Questions arose as to whether the exclusion of those people had been lawful and, if not, whether it had the consequence that the hearing was not a public hearing. The Administrative Court considered the power to exclude under s 53 of the Courts Act 2003. This power can be exercised without reference to the judiciary, and in plain cases, eg the person is drunk or violent, there is no reason to consult. But where there is room for dispute about whether a person has the right to enter, the question should be decided by the court concerned at the time the question arises. In the present case, the decision to exclude anyone associated with a particular campaign group was bound to be controversial and was a paradigm example of a situation where reference to the court was essential. The magistrates' decision to deny admission to the proceedings was taken without them being advised that it was for them to judge whether this was reasonably necessary for one or more of the statutory purposes and in the mistaken belief that the issue was an administrative matter. If the magistrates had inquired properly into the facts they would have found that the decision was also defective because it had not been based on any evidence. The magistrates' decision was, therefore, flawed and, consequently, unlawful. The nature and extent of the exclusion, which had no valid reason, were such as to deprive the hearing of its open and public character and to create a strong and understandable sense of grievance that justice could not be seen to done; consequently, the proceedings that day had not been valid.

D[1B.3] **Power to clear court while child or young person is giving evidence in certain cases.** Where, in any proceedings in relation to an offence against or any conduct contrary to decency or morality, a juvenile is called as a witness, the court may be cleared of persons other than members or officers of the court, parties to the case, their counsel or solicitors, and persons otherwise directly concerned with the case, but bona fide representatives of the press may not be excluded (Children and Young Persons Act 1933, s 37).

D[1B.4] Apart from the statutory exceptions evidence must be given in open court except where it may be necessary to depart from this principle where the nature or circumstances of the particular proceedings are such that the application of the general rule in its entirety would frustrate or render impracticable the administration of justice (*A-G v Leveller Magazines Ltd* [1979] AC 440, [1979] 1 All ER 745, HL).

D[1B.5] The High Court has commented on the magistrates' decision to hear mitigation in camera because embarrassing and intimate details of the defendant's personal life would have to be given by her and she had an overwhelming fear of revealing them publicly. The judges felt the magistrates' exercise of their discretion was unsustainable and out of accord with principle (*R v Malvern Justices, ex p Evans* [1988] QB 553, [1988] 1 All ER 371).

D[1B.6] **Non-disclosure of evidence given in open court.** Sometimes where the court decides not to sit in camera there is a request that a witness may write down his name on a piece of paper or use a pseudonym. In criminal cases at least this should only be done where the criteria for sitting in camera are met and such a device is normally only encountered in blackmail cases. Such a power is not designed for the benefit of the comfort and feelings of defendants such as where publication of a defendant's address might cause him to be harassed by his former wife (*R v Evesham Justices, ex p McDonagh* [1988] QB 553, [1988] 1 All ER 371).

Reporting of court proceedings

D[1B.7] Apart from the special provisions governing the youth and family proceedings courts referred to above, the press may report all legal proceedings held in public (Contempt of Court Act 1981, s 4(1)). There are certain exceptions to the general rule:

(a) *Children and young persons* By a combination of the commencement of s 45 of the Youth Justice and Criminal Evidence Act 1999 and amendments made by ss 78–79 of the Criminal Justice and Courts Act 2015, which inserted new s 45A of, and Sch 2A to, the 1999 Act and amended s 39 of, and inserted new Sch 1A to, the Children and Young Persons Act 1933 the position now is this:

  (i) In criminal proceedings other than in youth courts, the governing provision is s 45 of the 1999 Act. The court may direct that no matter relating to any person concerned in the proceedings shall while he is under the age of 18 be included in any publication if it is likely to lead members to identify him as a person concerned in the proceedings. The reference here to 'a person concerned in the proceedings' is to a person against or in respect of whom the proceedings were taken, or to a witness in the proceedings: s 45(7). As to the matters which may not be published, see s 45(8): they particularly include the person's name, address, the identity of any school or other educational establishment the person attends, the identity of any place of work and any still or moving picture of the person. Section 45(4)–(6) makes provision for excepting directions on interests of justice/public interest grounds and require the court when deciding whether or not to make directions or excepting directions to have regard to the welfare of the person concerned.

  (ii) In proceedings in or on appeal from youth courts, or in the magistrates' court for breach, etc, of a youth rehabilitation order, the governing provision is s 49 of the 1933 Act. The exception to this is proceedings for an injunction in the youth court, to which s 39 of the 1933 Act applies

(iii) In civil proceedings other than in youth courts, and in proceedings for an injunction in the youth court, the governing provision is s 39 of the 1933 Act. Section 39 was amended by s 79 of the 2015 Act to expand the scope of reporting restrictions to cover any communication to the public at large or any section of the public.

(iv) New s 45A of the 1999 Act gives courts the ability to impose lifetime reporting restrictions for victims and witnesses under the age of 18 involved in criminal proceedings in any court.

New Sch 1A to the 1933 Act and new Sch 2A to the 1999 Act set out provisions applicable to providers of information society services where a breach of a reporting restriction made under s 39 of the 1933 Act, or where an offence under s 49 of the 1999 Act, has occurred.

The following principles were established in relation to s 39 of the Children and Young Persons Act 1933 when it applied to both criminal and civil proceedings.

This legislation seeks to capture, in wide language, at least the central participants in proceedings whether civil or criminal. It is therefore wide enough to include a child who is the 'victim' of an offence of a person being drunk in a public place whilst having the charge of a child under the age of seven years (Licensing Act 1902, s 2(1)): *R (on the application of A) v Lowestoft Magistrates' Court* [2013] EWHC 659 (Admin), (2013) 177 JP 377, [2013] Crim L R 763. Note, however, there is a clear distinction between the position in the youth court, where under the CYPA 1933, s 49 publication of the identity of the child or young person is prohibited subject to certain exceptions, and s 39 where the court has to exercise a discretion whether or not to make an order restricting publicity.

An order under s 39 must be clear as to precisely what is prohibited: *Briffet v DPP* [2001] EWHC Admin 841, 166 JP 66, [2002] EMLR 203 (sub nom *Briffett and Bradshaw v Crown Prosecution Service*), and should be in writing: *Re BBC Litigation Department* [2002] All ER (D) 69 (Apr), CA.

Great care should be taken by magistrates' courts when making an order under s 39. Before making such an order the court should generally ask members of the press whether they had any submissions so the court fully understood the issues, given the great importance of making these orders. Orders are not to be made as a matter of routine, and require a careful balance of matters relating to the public interest, after submissions have been made: *C v CPS* [2008] EWHC 854 (Admin), 172 JP 273, (2008) Times, 20 February (any embarrassment that might flow to the children was an unfortunate consequence of a parent being convicted of a crime). Unless there were exceptional circumstances the balance between arts 8 and 10 of the ECHR fell firmly in favour of removing the s 39 prohibition: *C v CPS*, above; *Re Trinity Mirror plc* [2008] EWCA Crim 50, [2008] 2 All ER 1159.

It has been doubted whether an order under s 39 can embrace reporting in digitised or other form not in existence when s 39 was enacted: *MXB v East Sussex Hospitals NHS Trust* [2012] EWHC 32769, (2012) 177 JP 177.

An order made under s 39 cannot extend to reports of proceedings after the subject of the order has attained the age of 18: *R (on the application of JC and another) v Central Criminal Court* [2014] EWHC (Admin), (2014) 178 JP 188.

A decision to vary reporting restrictions in relation to a young offender pursuant to the Children and Young Persons Act 1933, s 39 was quashed as the proper test had not been applied and inadequate reasons had been given to justify the variation. In deciding whether to impose reporting restrictions under s 39, a court had to balance the welfare of the child, the public interest and the requirements of the ECHR, art 10, and to restrict publication if the factors were evenly balanced. Prior to conviction, the former is likely to prevail. After conviction, the defendant's age and the gravity of the crime are likely to be particularly relevant: *R (on the application of Y) v Aylesbury Crown Court, Crown Prosecution Service and Newsquest*.

(b) After an allegation of rape and other sexual offences (eg see **A**[53]) has been made the general statutory rule is that no material likely to lead to the identification by the public of the complainant may be published or broadcast (Sexual Offences (Amendment) Act 1992).

(c) *Publication of matters exempted from disclosure in court:* Where a court has allowed a name or other matter to be withheld from the public in proceedings before the court, the court may give such directions prohibiting the publication of that name or matter in connection with the proceedings as appear to the court to be necessary for the purpose for which it was so withheld (Contempt of Court Act 1981, s 11). The order must be in writing and must state with precision its exact terms, extent and purpose. For the court to exercise the power under s 11 the court must first have allowed the matter to have been withheld from the public and have had the power to allow that matter to have been withheld; directions made under s 11 need therefore to be linked the purpose for which the 'matter' was withheld in the first place: *Times Newspapers, RE sub nom R v Abdulaziz (Elisan)* [2016] EWCA Crim 887, [2016] 1 WLR 4399, [2016] 1 Cr App R 28.
There has to be a very compelling reason to withhold the addresses of serving police officers charged with criminal offences: see *R (on the application of Harper) v Aldershot Magistrates' Court* [2010] EWHC 1319 (Admin), 174 JP 410, 174 CL&J 383.

(d) *Power to postpone publication of reports of court proceedings:* Where it appears to be necessary for avoiding a substantial risk of prejudice to the administration of justice in those proceedings or in any other proceedings pending or imminent the court may order that the publication of any report of the proceedings or any part of the proceedings be postponed for such period as the court thinks necessary for that purpose (Contempt of Court Act 1981, s 4(2)). The order should be no wider than is necessary for the prevention of prejudice to the administration of justice (*R v Horsham Justices, ex p Farquharson* [1982] QB 762, [1982] 2 All ER 269, CA) and must be in writing and must state with precision its exact terms, extent and purpose.
Comprehensive guidance as to procedure and the exercise of the power to postpone the reporting of proceedings was given by Lord Burnett CJ in *R v Sarker* [2018] EWCA Crim 1341, [2018] 4 All ER 694, [2018] 1 WLR 6023.

> '30 A clear articulation of the approach to be adopted is to be found in the judgment of Longmore LJ in *R v Sherwood (ex parte Telegraph Group)* [2001] 1 WLR 1983, para 22 (which was approved by the Privy Council in *Independent Publishing Co Ltd* [2005] 1 AC 190, para 69).
>
> (i) The first question is whether reporting would give rise to a substantial risk of prejudice to the administration of justice in the relevant proceedings: see para 32 below. If not, that will be the end of the matter.
>
> (ii) If such a risk is perceived to exist, then the second question arises: would a section 4(2) order eliminate it? If not, there could be no necessity to impose such a ban. On the other hand, even if the judge is satisfied that an order would achieve the objective, he or she would still have to consider whether the risk could satisfactorily be overcome by some less restrictive means. If so, it could not be said to be "necessary" to take the more drastic approach: *Ex p Central Television plc* [1991] 1 WLR 4, 8d–g, per Lord Lane CJ.
>
> (iii) If the judge is satisfied that there is indeed no other way of eliminating the perceived risk of prejudice, it still does not necessarily follow that an order has to be made. The judge may still have to ask whether the degree of risk contemplated should be regarded as tolerable in the sense of being "the lesser of two evils". It is at this stage that value judgments may have to be made as to the priority between the competing public interests; fair trial and freedom of expression/open justice: *Ex p The Telegraph plc* [1993] 1 WLR 980, 986b–c.'

(e) Under s 46 of the Youth Justice and Criminal Evidence Act 1999 the court may prevent publication of any matter which may lead to the identification of an adult witness for the duration of that person's life, if it is satisfied that the quality of their evidence or their participation would be diminished by fear or distress related to public information.

(f) Note, that by virtue of the Coroners and Justice Act 2009, Chapter 2, Part 3, witness anonymity is available in criminal proceedings including summary proceedings. As to the making of witness anonymity orders, see rr 18-8–18.22 of the Criminal Procedure Rules 2015.

Procedure for imposing restriction on access to hearing or reporting

D[1B.7A] Where the court can: impose, vary or remove, a restriction on reporting what takes place at a public hearing, or public access to what otherwise would be a public hearing; withhold information from the public during a public hearing; order a trial in private; allow there to take place during a hearing a sound recording, or communication by electronic means (apart from arrangements required by legislation, or directed by the court, in connection with sound recording during a hearing, or the transcription of such a recording; or measures to assist a witness or defendant to give evidence), procedure is regulated by Part 6 of the Criminal Procedure Rules. The rules prescribe the matters to which the court is to have regard when considering whether to exercise its powers; the right of each party and a person directly affected to be present or make representations; and the procedure for considering such matters. Particular provision is made with regard to reporting and access restrictions and trials in private and the making of representations; sound recording and electronic communication.

D[1B.8] **Twitter and other live, text-based communication.** The Criminal Practice Directions 2015 [2015] EWCA Crim 1567 make the following provision.

The new guidance makes clear that:

'CPD I General matters 6C: USE OF LIVE TEXT-BASED FORMS OF COMMUNICATION (INCLUDING TWITTER) FROM COURT FOR THE PURPOSES OF FAIR AND ACCURATE REPORTING

6C.1 This part clarifies the use which may be made of live text-based communications, such as mobile email, social media (including Twitter) and internet-enabled laptops in and from courts throughout England and Wales. For the purpose of this part these means of communication are referred to, compendiously, as 'live text-based communications'. It is consistent with the legislative structure which:

(a) prohibits:
  (i) the taking of photographs in court (section 41 of the Criminal Justice Act 1925);
  (ii) the use of sound recording equipment in court unless the leave of the judge has first been obtained (section 9 of the Contempt of Court Act 1981); and

(b) requires compliance with the strict prohibition rules created by sections 1, 2 and 4 of the Contempt of Court Act 1981 in relation to the reporting of court proceedings.

General Principles

6C.2 The judge has an overriding responsibility to ensure that proceedings are conducted consistently, with the proper administration of justice, and to avoid any improper interference with its processes.

6C.3 A fundamental aspect of the proper administration of justice is the principle of open justice. Fair and accurate reporting of court proceedings forms part of that principle. The principle is, however, subject to well-known statutory and discretionary exceptions. Two such exceptions are the prohibitions, set out in paragraph 6C.1(a), on photography in court and on making sound recordings of court proceedings.

6C.4 The statutory prohibition on photography in court, by any means, is absolute. There is no judicial discretion to suspend or dispense with it. Any equipment which has photographic capability must not have that function activated.

6C.5 Sound recordings are also prohibited unless, in the exercise of its discretion, the court permits such equipment to be used. In criminal proceedings, some of the factors relevant to the exercise of that discretion are contained in 6A.2. The same factors are likely to be relevant when consideration is being given to the exercise of this discretion in civil or family proceedings.

Use of Live Text-based Communications: General Considerations

6C.6 The normal, indeed almost invariable, rule has been that mobile phones must be turned off in court. There is however no statutory prohibition on the use of live text-based communications in open court.

6C.7 Where a member of the public, who is in court, wishes to use live text-based communications during court proceedings an application for permission to activate and use, in silent mode, a mobile phone, small laptop or similar piece of equipment, solely in order to make live text-based communications of the proceedings will need to be made. The application may be made formally or informally (for instance by communicating a request to the judge through court staff).

6C.8 It is presumed that a representative of the media or a legal commentator using live text-based communications from court does not pose a danger of interference to the proper administration of justice in the individual case. This is because the most obvious purpose of permitting the use of live text-based communications would be to enable the media to produce fair and accurate reports of the proceedings. As such, a representative of the media or a legal commentator who wishes to use live text-based communications from court may do so without making an application to the court.

6C.9 When considering, either generally on its own motion, or following a formal application or informal request by a member of the public, whether to permit live text-based communications, and if so by whom, the paramount question for the judge will be whether the application may interfere with the proper administration of justice.

6C.10 In considering the question of permission, the factors listed in paragraph 6A.2 are likely to be relevant.

6C.11 Without being exhaustive, the danger to the administration of justice is likely to be at its most acute in the context of criminal trials e.g., where witnesses who are out of court may be informed of what has already happened in court and so coached or briefed before they then give evidence, or where information posted on, for instance, Twitter about inadmissible evidence may influence members of the jury. However, the danger is not confined to criminal proceedings; in civil and sometimes family proceedings, simultaneous reporting from the courtroom may create pressure on witnesses, by distracting or worrying them.

6C.12 It may be necessary for the judge to limit live text-based communications to representatives of the media for journalistic purposes but to disallow its use by the wider public in court. That may arise if it is necessary, for example, to limit the number of mobile electronic devices in use at any given time because of the potential for electronic interference with the court's own sound recording equipment, or because the widespread use of such devices in court may cause a distraction in the proceedings.

6C.13 Subject to these considerations, the use of an unobtrusive, hand-held, silent piece of modern equipment, for the purposes of simultaneous reporting of proceedings to the outside world as they unfold in court, is generally unlikely to interfere with the proper administration of justice.

6C.14 Permission to use live text-based communications from court may be withdrawn by the court at any time.'

See further the Criminal Procedure Rules 2015, rule 6(9).

D[1B.9] **Photographs and sketches in court.** No person shall take or attempt to take a photograph, or make or attempt to make any portrait or sketch of a justice or party or witness to proceedings, in a court room or in a court building or precincts or entering or leaving them (Criminal Justice Act 1925, s 41).

The fact that taking pictures in court and publishing them constitute summary offences under s 41 of the Criminal Justice Act 1925 does not prevent those acts from being punished as contempts of court: *Solicitor General v Cox* [2016] EWHC 1241 (QB), [2016] 2 Cr App R 15.

D[1B.10] **Tape recorders.** It is a contempt of court to use a tape recorder (other than for the purpose of making an official transcript) in a court without the leave of the court (Contempt of Court Act 1981, s 9). The Criminal Practice Directions 2015 make the following provision.

'CPD I General matters 6A: UNOFFICIAL SOUND RECORDING OF PROCEEDINGS

6A.1 Section 9 of the Contempt of Court Act 1981 contains provisions governing the unofficial use of equipment for recording sound in court.

Section 9(1) provides that it is a contempt of court:

(a) to use in court, or bring into court for use, any tape recorder or other instrument for recording sound, except with the permission of the court;

(b) to publish a recording of legal proceedings made by means of any such instrument, or any recording derived directly or indirectly from it, by playing it in the hearing of the public or any section of the public, or to dispose of it or any recording so derived, with a view to such publication;

(c) to use any such recording in contravention of any conditions of leave granted under paragraph (a).

These provisions do not apply to the making or use of sound recordings for purposes of official transcripts of the proceedings, upon which the Act imposes no restriction whatever.

6A.2 The discretion given to the court to grant, withhold or withdraw leave to use equipment for recording sound or to impose conditions as to the use of the recording is unlimited, but the following factors may be relevant to its exercise:

(a) the existence of any reasonable need on the part of the applicant for leave, whether a litigant or a person connected with the press or broadcasting, for the recording to be made;

(b) the risk that the recording could be used for the purpose of briefing witnesses out of court;

(c) any possibility that the use of the recorder would disturb the proceedings or distract or worry any witnesses or other participants.

6A.3 Consideration should always be given whether conditions as to the use of a recording made pursuant to leave should be imposed. The identity and role of the applicant for leave and the nature of the subject matter of the proceedings may be relevant to this.

6A.4 The particular restriction imposed by section 9(1)(b) applies in every case, but may not be present in the mind of every applicant to whom leave is given. It may therefore be desirable on occasion for this provision to be drawn to the attention of those to whom leave is given.

6A.5 The transcript of a permitted recording is intended for the use of the person given leave to make it and is not intended to be used as, or to compete with, the official transcript mentioned in section 9(4).

6A.6 Where a contravention of section 9(1) is alleged, the procedure in section 2 of Part 48 of the Rules should be followed. Section 9(3) of the 1981 Act permits the court to "order the instrument, or any recording made with it, or both, to be forfeited". The procedure at CrimPR 6.10 should be followed.

See further the Criminal Procedure Rules 2015, rule 6.9.

D[1B.11] Abuse of the process. Courts have the power and the duty to secure fairness for those who appear before them and can stay proceedings where the conclusion is reached that the accused cannot receive a fair trial, or that it would be unfair for the accused to be tried owing to manipulation or misuse of the process of the court so as to deprive the defendant of a protection afforded by the law or to take unfair advantage of a technicality or action by the executive that threatens either basic human rights or the rule of law.

The jurisdiction exercised by justices to protect the court's process from abuse does not extend to the wider supervisory jurisdiction for upholding the rule of law which is vested in the High Court: *R v Horseferry Road Magistrates' Court, ex p Bennett* [1994] AC 42, [1993] 3 All ER 138, [1993] 3 WLR 90. It must not be used, therefore, to exercise a disciplinary function over eg executive decisions made by a prosecuting authority.

Whilst a magistrate's court lacks jurisdiction to determine an application for a stay of a prosecution made on the basis that it would be unfair for the accused to be tried, in such circumstances, the summary trial should proceed to a conclusion after the necessary findings of fact have been made on the evidence presented to it. The High Court, on an appeal by way of case stated, then has jurisdiction to stay a prosecution in situations where there had been a promise not to prosecute an accused, or a legitimate expectation had arisen that the accused would not be prosecuted, or where there had been an abuse of executive power: *Woolls v North Somerset Council* [2016] EWHC 1410 (Admin), [2016] Crim LR 765.

The parameters of this power are narrowly drawn. Justices may only stay proceedings where it would be unfair to try the defendant or where the defendant cannot receive a fair trial. It may be an abuse of process if either (a) the prosecution have manipulated or misused the process of the court so as to deprive the defendant of a protection provided by the law or to take unfair advantage of a technicality, or (b) the defendant has been, or will be, prejudiced in the preparation or conduct of his defence by delay on the part of the prosecution which is unjustifiable.

The defence should give advance notice of such application. Where notice is not given magistrates should look favourably on an adjournment application by the prosecution. In addition, the court should give directions for the filing of skeleton arguments by the parties. A skeleton argument should focus on the issues arising in the case and the relevant principles. An excessive citation of authorities is to be deprecated.

D[1B.12] Principles. May be summarised as follows:

(1) The discretionary decision as to whether or not to grant a stay as an abuse is an exercise in judicial assessment dependent on judgement, rather than on any conclusion as to fact based on evidence. Accordingly, in cases of delay it is potentially misleading to apply to the exercise of that discretion the language of burden and standard of proof, which is more apt to an evidence-based, fact-finding process (*R v S* [2006] EWCA Crim 756, (2006) 170 JP 434).

(2) The applicant must identify the ground or grounds upon which he relies eg delay, manipulation of the proceedings or destruction of evidence.
(3) Where there is no fault attributable to, or the prosecution have acted in good faith, it will be very rare for a stay to be granted.
(4) Is there serious prejudice to the accused? No stay should be granted in the absence of serious prejudice to the accused. When assessing possible serious prejudice, the court should consider its powers to regulate the admissibility of evidence, and that the trial process itself should ensure that all relevant factual issues arising from eg delay or the destruction of evidence, are placed before the court for its consideration.
(5) When assessing possible serious prejudice, the court can take into account its powers in relation to sentence, assuming there is a conviction or a guilty plea.
(6) A permanent stay should be the exception rather than the rule.
(7) If having considered all the relevant factors, the court's assessment is that a fair trial will be possible, a stay should not be granted.

The legal principles relating to abuse are the same whether the case involves a public prosecution or a private prosecution: *D Ltd v A* [2017] EWCA Crim 1172, [2018] Crim LR 993.

As to (3) above (fault), it has been stated that in abuse submissions founded upon loss of evidence, the question whether the defendant can have a fair trial does not logically depend upon whether anyone was at fault for the exigency which created the loss of the evidence; if vital evidence has been lost to the defendant, whether through fault or otherwise, the issue is whether the disadvantage to the defendant can be accommodated so as to ensure a fair trial: *Clay v Cambridgeshire Justices* [2014] EWHC 321 (Admin), [2015] RTR 1.

Abuse of the process – long delay – relevant principles: *R v F* [2011] EWCA Crim 726, [2011] 2 Cr App Rep 145, 175 CL&J 213.

The Court of Appeal derived from a review of authority five propositions concerning the treatment of criminal proceedings brought after a long delay. Those propositions were:

- Proceedings should be stayed only if the court was satisfied that delay precluded a fair trial.
- An application for a stay should *normally* be made at trial after all the evidence has been heard.
- In assessing [serious] prejudice to the defendant, the court had to balance evidence that had survived the delay against missing evidence and critically examine the importance of the missing evidence.
- Having identified [serious] prejudice, the court had to consider whether it could come compensate for the prejudice by special [jury] directions.
- Unjustified delay by a complainant in coming forward was relevant to whether a fair trial could be achieved, but it had to be firmly borne in mind that sexual abuse victims were often unwilling to talk about their experiences for some time and for good reason.

Disclosure – delay – abuse of the process – test to be applied: *Brants v DPP* [2011] EWHC 754 (Admin), 175 JP 246.

A positive decision not to disclose relevant material culminating in delay may amount to an abuse of the process. In the case of *Brants*, the appellant, a driver of a heavy goods vehicle, was stopped by a police constable and required to produce his digital driver card. The officer downloaded the material held on the card onto his laptop. From this he produced reports and a list of offences under the Transport Act 1968, s 96. An information was laid alleging four contraventions relating to drivers' hours and rest periods. On 16 March 2009, solicitors for the appellant requested disclosure of the digital material downloaded by the police officer. It was first directed by the magistrates' court to be handed over on 14 May 2009. The material was not disclosed until 26 July 2009. At a later date, and as a preliminary issue, it was submitted that the proceedings were an abuse of the process by reason of delay. The justices ruled against the appellant and he changed his plea to guilty.

It was held not to be an abuse of process where the defence sought CCTV of the breathalyser procedure (it was claimed the police had not given the statutory warning), but the footage brought to court was not in a format that could be played on any of the equipment available at the court; there was no basis for concluding that the footage, if playable, might, still less would, have assisted the defendant; the defendant could properly have made play of the fact that the footage was unavailable through no fault of his own and, in this way, the trial process could safely and fairly dealt with the 'hole' in the case arising from the prosecution failure. Generally, on CCTV, the court added that if the prosecution does not intend to use CCTV footage as part of its case it is 'unused material'. The prosecution must, therefore, consider whether it satisfies the test for disclosure. To do this properly, the prosecution must view the CCTV (which will focus minds on ensuring that that the footage, if disclosable, is in a suitable format to be played in court): *DPP v Petrie* [2015] EWHC 48 (Admin), (2015) 179 JP 251.

It is submitted that the justices in *Brants* could have inferred a deliberate decision not to disclose the relevant material, having regard to the lapse of time and the number of adjourned hearings after a direction to disclose the material was given.

It was affirmed in *DPP v Gowing* [2013] EWHC 4614 (Admin), (2014) 178 JP 181 that the jurisdiction to stay proceedings as an abuse of process is exceptional and there must be a firm basis for its exercise, either bad faith or inability to hold a fair trial. The power to stay should not be used to punish prosecution inefficiency where a fair trial was still possible, Courts have a duty to investigate carefully any claims of prejudice or unfairness arising from non-compliance with disclosure duties.

It was not an abuse of process to prosecute historic sexual offences committed by an Anglican priest against children in a care home. Contemporaneous records, principally the children's home records, had gone missing, but they would not necessarily have cast doubt on the complainant's evidence. It had not been demonstrated that irredeemable prejudice had been done to the defendant's case: *R v Halahan* [2014] EWCA Crim 2079, [2014] All ER (D) 284 (Oct).

A stay would have brought the criminal justice system into disrepute where a defendant found in possession of a revolver and a round of ammunition had 'inexplicably' been charged under s 1(1)(a) of the Firearms Act 1968, for which he was sentenced to four months' detention, and was then charged under s 5(1)(a)(aba) of the Act – the 'obvious' charge – which carries a prescribed minimum sentence of five years' imprisonment: *R v Antoine* [2014] EWCA Crim 1971, [2014] All ER (D) 172 (Oct).

D[2]
Misbehaviour in court

D[2.1] Misbehaviour by members of the public:

(a) Where persons misbehave in court the first approach should be to attempt to calm down offenders by an appeal to reason and good manners. A court can also consider putting the case back for a 'cooling off' period and the chairman may also make mention in very general terms of the court's powers to maintain order.

(b) If this is not successful a court has power to order persons disrupting the court to leave the court room. If they refuse, and their removal is necessary to enable justice to be administered properly, the court may order a court security officer or the police to remove such persons using reasonable force if necessary.

(c) Where persons are misbehaving in court the magistrates should not exercise their power to **bind over**). For procedure on binding over, see B[5.20]–B[5.21].

D[3]

Contempt of court

Charges (Contempt of court)

D[3.1]–[3.3] Contempt of court

(a) **Wilfully did insult AB being a justice of the peace (or a witness before the court, or an officer of the court, or a solicitor or counsel having business before the court) during his sitting or attendance in court or when he was going to or returning from the court; or**
(b) **wilfully interrupted the proceedings of a magistrates' court; or**
(c) **wilfully misbehaved in a magistrates' court.**

Contempt of Court Act 1981, s 12.

D[3.4] **Maximum penalty.** Fine of level 4 and one month. Proceedings under s 12: offender may be ordered to be taken into custody by an officer of the court or a constable and detained until the rising of the court in addition to or instead of the penalty mentioned above. A person under 18 years may not be committed for contempt. A substantial prison sentence (12 months) was upheld in *R v D (contempt of court: illegal photography)* (2004) Times, 13 May where the defendant had photographed the interior of the Crown Court (see **D[1B.8]**).

Legal notes

D[3.5] **Wilfully insult.** The word 'insult' has to be given its ordinary English meaning. A person who had *threatened* a defendant had not 'insulted' him and was not in breach of s 12 (*R v Havant Justices, ex p Palmer* (1985) 149 JP 609, [1985] Crim LR 658).

D[3.6] **Officer of the court.** This term is not defined in the Act. It will apply to the justices' clerk and his staff, presumably whether or not they are concerned in the particular proceedings in which the insult occurs. If there is any doubt, the matter could certainly be resolved by simply alleging misbehaviour in court.

D[3.7] **Procedure.** This is governed by the Criminal Procedure Rules 2015, Part 48. The provisions relevant to magistrates' court are set out below

> 'CONTEMPT OF COURT BY OBSTRUCTION, DISRUPTION, ETC.
>
> Initial procedure on obstruction, disruption, etc.
>
> 48.5
>
> (1) This rule applies where the court observes, or someone reports to the court—
> > (c) in a magistrates' court, a contravention of—
> > > (i) section 97(4) of the Magistrates' Courts Act 1980 (refusing to give evidence), or
> > > (ii) section 12 of the Contempt of Court Act 1981 (insulting or interrupting the court, etc);
> >
> > (d) a contravention of section 9 of the Contempt of Court Act 1981 (without the court's permission, recording the proceedings, etc);
> > (e) any other conduct with which the court can deal as, or as if it were, a criminal contempt of court, except failure to surrender to bail under section 6 of the Bail Act 1976.
>
> (2) Unless the respondent's behaviour makes it impracticable to do so, the court must—
> > (a) explain, in terms the respondent can understand (with help, if necessary)—

(i) the conduct that is in question,
(ii) that the court can impose imprisonment, or a fine, or both, for such conduct,
(iii) (where relevant) that the court has power to order the respondent's immediate temporary detention, if in the court's opinion that is required,
(iv) that the respondent may explain the conduct,
(v) that the respondent may apologise, if he or she so wishes, and that this may persuade the court to take no further action, and
(vi) that the respondent may take legal advice; and

(b) allow the respondent a reasonable opportunity to reflect, take advice, explain and, if he or she so wishes, apologise.

(3) The court may then—
(a) take no further action in respect of that conduct;
(b) enquire into the conduct there and then; or
(c) postpone that enquiry (if a magistrates' court, only until later the same day).

[Note The conduct to which this rule applies is sometimes described as 'criminal' contempt of court.]

...

Under section 97(4) of the Magistrates' Courts Act 1980, and under sections 12 and 14 of the Contempt of Court Act 1981, a magistrates' court can imprison (for a maximum of 1 month), or fine (to a maximum of £2,500), or both, a respondent who contravenes a provision listed in paragraph (1)(c) or (d). Section 12(1) of the 1981 Act allows the court to deal with any person who—

(a) wilfully insults the justice or justices, any witness before or officer of the court or any solicitor or counsel having business in the court, during his or their sitting or attendance in court or in going to or returning from the court; or

(b) wilfully interrupts the proceedings of the court or otherwise misbehaves in court. Under section 89 of the Powers of Criminal Courts (Sentencing) Act 2000, no respondent who is under 21 may be imprisoned for contempt of court. Under section 108 of that Act, a respondent who is at least 18 but under 21 may be detained if the court is of the opinion that no other method of dealing with him or her is appropriate. Under section 14(2A) of the Contempt of Court Act 1981, a respondent who is under 17 may not be ordered to attend an attendance centre.

Under section 258 of the Criminal Justice Act 2003, a respondent who is imprisoned for contempt of court must be released unconditionally after serving half the term.

Under sections 14, 15 and 16 of the Legal Aid, Sentencing and Punishment of Offenders Act 2012, the respondent may receive advice and representation in "proceedings for contempt committed, or alleged to have been committed, by an individual in the face of the court".

. . . a magistrates' court can temporarily detain a respondent until later the same day on a contravention of that section.

Part 14 contains rules about bail.]

48.6. Review after temporary detention

(1) This rule applies in a case in which the court has ordered the respondent's immediate temporary detention for conduct to which rule 48.5 applies.

(2) The court must review the case—
   (a) if a magistrates' court, later the same day . . .

(3) On the review, the court must—
   (a) unless the respondent is absent, repeat the explanations required by rule 48.5(2)(a); and
   (b) allow the respondent a reasonable opportunity to reflect, take advice, explain and, if he or she so wishes, apologise.

(4) The court may then—
   (a) take no further action in respect of the conduct;
   (b) if a magistrates' court, enquire into the conduct there and then . . .'

See further *Practice Direction: Committal for Contempt* [2015] 2 All ER 541.

D[3.8] **Unauthorised use of disclosed prosecution material under s 17 of the CPIA 1996** The Criminal Procedure Rules 2015, r 48.9-48.17 (not reproduced) deal with the procedure for such contempt, which is punishable in the magistrates' court by imprisonment for six months, or a fine of £5,000, or both.

D[3.9] **Witnesses.** In addition to the powers outlined above, where a witness refuses to take the oath or to answer a question, he may be committed to prison for a period of up to one month (and ordered to pay a fine on level 4). He may be released immediately he changes his mind and decides to co-operate with the court. This advice may ensure his compliance.

D[3.10]–[3.14] **Defendants.** Disorderly defendants may be dealt with as outlined above. However, a court is naturally reluctant to deal with the case in the absence of a defendant. Accordingly, if the defendant has to be ejected the court should carefully consider adjourning the case for a 'cooling off' period. The more serious the case the less appropriate it will be to proceed in the defendant's absence. The defendant should be informed that he will be readmitted to the court any time he is prepared to conduct himself properly.

D[3.15] Taking a photograph in court with a mobile phone is a contempt of court and has resulted in immediate prison sentences in the Crown Court (*R v D* (2004) Times, 13 May). See **D[1B.8]**.

D[3.16] **Appeal.** An appeal against conviction and/or sentence under s 108 Magistrates' Courts Act 1980 lies to the Crown Court pursuant to s 12(5) of the 1981 Act (*Haw and Tucker v City of Westminster Magistrates' Court* [2007] EWHC 2960 (Admin), [2008] 2 All ER 326). Procedure on appeals is governed by Part 63 of the Criminal Procedure Rules 2014.

D[4]

Allocation and sending

D[4.1] The mode of trial and committal for sentence provisions of Sch 3 to the Criminal Justice Act 2003 were brought into force on 28 May 2013. These provisions are intricate and often complicated.

Order of consideration – adult offenders charged with offences triable either way (except certain low value either way offences)

D[4.2] The court must first proceed in accordance with s 50A of the Crime and Disorder Act 1998, as follows.

If notice is given in respect of the either way offence under s 51B (notices in serious or complex fraud cases) or s 51C (notices in certain cases involving children) of the 1998 Act, the court must send deal with the offence by sending it to the Crown Court under s 51 of the 1998 Act.

Otherwise:

(a) (Offences relating to a purely indictable or notice sending)

(i) if the adult (or another adult with whom the adult is jointly charged with the relevant offence) is sent for trial for an indictable offence or in consequence of a notice issued under s 51B or 51C and the either way offence appears to be a 'related' offence, the court must also send forthwith the either way offence (and any summary offence related to the sent offence or to the either way offence, provided the summary offence carries imprisonment or obligatory/discretionary disqualification) to the Crown Court;

(ii) if the adult (or another adult with whom the adult is jointly charged with the relevant offence) has previously been sent for trial for an indictable offence or in consequence of a notice issued under s 51B or 51C and the either way offence appears to be a 'related' offence, the power to send as above (together with any summary offence as described above) is discretionary, not mandatory. If the court does not send the adult for trial it shall proceed to deal with the relevant offence in accordance with ss 17A–23 of the Magistrates' Courts Act 1980. An either way offence is related to an indictable offence 'if the charge for the either way offence could be joined in the same indictment as the charge for the indictable offence'; a summary offence is 'related' to an indictable offence 'if it arises out of circumstances which are the same as or connected with those giving rise to the indictable offence': Crime and Disorder Act 1998, s 51E(c), (d). Note, Bail Act offences are not 'related' and must be tried in the magistrates' court. If the defendant is convicted, he/she can be committed to the Crown Court for sentence under s 6(6) of the Bail Act 1976. See further D[5.1], post: *R v Osman* [2017] EWCA Crim 2178. See further D[4.9A] (low-value shoplifting) and D[5.1] (sending for trial – indictable only offences: procedure), post.

(b) In all other cases:

(i) the court must first consider the relevant offence under ss 17A–20 of the Magistrates' Courts Act 1980 (excluding s 20(8) and (9))*;

(ii) if a guilty plea is indicated under s 17A(6), (17(B)(2) or 20(7), the court shall proceed as consequently required by the relevant provision;

(iii) in any other case the court shall consider the relevant offence under the sending provisions of ss 51 and 51A of the Crime and Disorder Act 1998 and, if the adult is not then sent to the Crown Court for trial the court shall ask the adult if he consents to summary trial and proceed thereafter in accordance with the adult's election.

(*The excluded provisions provide for the case where an accused has not indicated a guilty plea, the court determines summary trial to be suitable and the defendant does not thereafter indicate that he wishes to plead guilty. The accused must then be asked whether or not he consents to summary trial and the case must thereafter proceed in accordance with the election the accused makes. The reason for the exclusion is to ensure that, if a co-accused has elected Crown Court trial, it will no longer be the case that the other accused must be tried summarily if that is his wish. The other accused must now to be sent to the Crown Court if the two accused are appearing together, or may be sent if he appears on a subsequent occasion.)

Multiple defendant cases involving youths and adults are considered subsequently.

Offences triable either way: plea before venue

D[4.3] The court must then explain to the accused in ordinary language that he may indicate whether, if the offence were to proceed to trial, he would plead guilty or not guilty. The court must further explain to the accused that if he indicates he would plead guilty:

(a) the court will proceed as if he had pleaded guilty to an information which was being tried summarily; and
(b) that he may be committed for sentence to the Crown Court if the court is of opinion that greater punishment should be inflicted for the offence than the court has power to impose, or that the offender meets the criteria for the imposition of a dangerous offender sentence.

The court shall then ask the accused whether (if the offence were to proceed to trial) he would plead guilty or not guilty. If the accused indicates a guilty plea the court will then hear the prosecution case against him, listen to his mitigation and either determine sentence or commit to the Crown Court for sentence. If the accused indicates he would plead not guilty, or if he fails to indicate how he would plead, he shall be taken to indicate he would plead not guilty, and the procedure described below (mode of trial) will apply. Compliance with these procedures is obligatory. Accordingly, where defendants indicated their guilty pleas through their barrister and the case was committed to the Crown Court for sentence and for confiscation proceedings, the failure to comply with s 17A of the Magistrates' Courts Act 1980 meant the magistrates' court had acted without jurisdiction and the committal for sentence was consequently invalid thus fatally undermining the Crown Court proceedings: *Westminster City Council v Owadally* [2017] EWHC 1092 (Admin), [2017] 2 Cr App R 18, (2017) Times, 22 June. See also *R (on the application of Bahbahani) v Ealing Magistrates' Court* [2019] EWHC 1385 (Admin), [2019] All ER (D) 85 (Jun). Compliance with the requirements set out in ss 17A and 20 of the Magistrates' Court Act 1980 is a precondition of a magistrates' court having jurisdiction to try an either-way offence; in the absence of clear evidence that the accused was himself a party to deliberate misleading of the court as to the identity of the person appearing before it, there was non-compliance where he had been impersonated by an agent.

Committal to the Crown Court for sentence is dealt with in Section B.

Offences triable either way (except where a notice is received under ss 51B or 51C of the Crime and Disorder Act 1998): mode of trial

D[4.4] The following procedure applies where an adult is charged with an either way offence and either he or his representative indicates that if the offence were to proceed to trial he would plead not guilty.

The court shall decide whether the offence appears to it more suitable for summary trial or for trial on indictment. Before making this decision the court:

(a) shall give the prosecution an opportunity to inform the court of the accused's previous convictions (if any) (defined to include foreign convictions which would constitute an offence in the UK if committed here and service convictions); and
(b) shall give the prosecution and the accused an opportunity to make representations as to whether summary trial or trial on indictment would be more suitable.

In making its decision the court shall consider:

(a) whether the sentence which a magistrates' court would have power to impose for the offence would be adequate; and
(b) any representations made by the prosecution or the accused under subsection (2)(b) above,

and shall have regard to any allocation guidelines (or revised allocation guidelines) issued as definitive guidelines under s 122 of the Coroners and Justice Act 2009.

Where:

(a) the accused is charged with two or more offences; and
(b) it appears to the court that the charges for the offences could be joined in the same indictment or that the offences arise out of the same or connected circumstances,

references to the sentence which a magistrates' court would have power to impose refer to the maximum aggregate sentence which a magistrates' court would have power to impose for all of the offences taken together.

Procedure where summary trial appears more suitable

D[4.5] The court shall explain to the accused in ordinary language:

(a) that it appears to the court more suitable for him to be tried summarily for the offence;
(b) that he can either consent to be so tried or, if he wishes, be tried on indictment; and
(c) that if he is tried summarily and is convicted by the court, he may be committed for sentence to the Crown Court under s 3 or (if applicable) s 3A of the Powers of Criminal Courts (Sentencing) Act 2000 if the court is of such opinion as is mentioned in subsection (2) of the applicable section.

The accused may then request an indication ('an indication of sentence') of whether a custodial sentence or non-custodial sentence would be more likely to be imposed if he were to be tried summarily for the offence and to plead guilty.

If the accused requests an indication of sentence, the court may, but need not, give such an indication. If the accused requests and the court gives an indication of sentence, the court shall ask the accused whether he wishes, on the basis of the indication, to reconsider the indication of plea which he previously gave, and if the accused indicates that he wishes to reconsider that indication, the court shall ask the accused whether (if the offence were to proceed to trial) he would plead guilty or not guilty.

If the accused indicates that he would plead guilty the court shall proceed to deal with the case as a summary trial in which the accused has pleaded guilty.

If no indication is sought, or, if sought, no indication is given by the court, or the defendant does not indicate following an indication that he would plead guilty, the court shall ask the accused whether he consents to be tried summarily or wishes to be tried on indictment. If the defendant consents to be tried summarily, the court shall proceed to the summary trial of the information; and if he does not so consent, shall proceed in relation to the offence in accordance with s 51(1) of the Crime and Disorder Act 1998 (ie by sending the case to the Crown Court.

Absence of legally represented accused

D[4.6] Where:

(a) the accused is represented by a legal representative who in his absence signifies to the court the accused's consent to the proceedings for determining how he is to be tried for the offence being conducted in his absence; and

(b) the court is satisfied that there is good reason for proceeding in the absence of the accused,

the following procedure shall apply.

The court may proceed in the absence of the accused in accordance with such of the provisions of ss 19 to 22 of the Magistrates' Court Act 1980 as are applicable in the circumstances.

If the offence is one of those listed in Sch 2 to the Magistrates' Courts Act 1980 (certain either way offences where the value involved is relevant to mode of trial), and it is unclear to the court whether or not the value exceeds the relevant sum (currently £5,000), if the accused's consent to be tried summarily has been or is signified by the person representing him, the court shall proceed as if the offence were triable only summarily in accordance with subsection (2) of that section as if that subsection applied. If such consent is not signified, the court shall deal with mode of trial in the normal way.

If the court decides that the offence appears to be more suitable for summary trial, then:

(a) if the accused's consent to be tried summarily has been or is signified by the person representing him, the court shall proceed without further ado to the summary trial of the information; or
(b) if that consent has not been and is not so signified, the court shall proceed, again without further ado, in accordance with the sending provisions of s 51(1) of the Crime and Disorder Act 1998.

If the court decides under s 19 that the offence appears to it more suitable for trial on indictment, the court shall proceed, again without further ado, in accordance with the sending provisions of s 51(1) of the Crime and Disorder Act 1998.

Joint adult defendants

D[4.7] For cases where two or more adults are charged together, see para D[4.2], above. One of the key purposes of the changes made by the allocation and mode of trial provisions of Sch 3 to the Criminal Justice Act 2003 was to bring to an end the requirement to hold separate trials in the Crown Court and the magistrates' courts where two or more defendants made conflicting choices on venue.

Adults jointly charged with youths

D[4.8] This topic is considered in detail at para E[3.18A], above, and the following is a summary only.

The legislative policy is that youths should be tried summarily wherever possible. Certain offences must, however, be sent to the Crown Court. Where this applies and an adult offender, jointly charged with an either way offence or charged with a related either way offence, appears before the court he *must* if it is the same occasion, or *may* if he appears on a subsequent occasion, be sent forthwith to the Crown Court, unless a guilty plea has been indicated by or on behalf of the adult.

Offences of criminal damage where the value is low

D[4.9] If the offence charged is criminal damage, excluding arson, or aggravated vehicle-taking (where only damage is alleged), the court will as a preliminary ask the prosecutor and the accused the value of the damage; if it appears to be £5,000 or under, the court will proceed to summary trial. If it is unclear whether the value is £5,000 or under, the court will read the charge to the accused and then say to him:

> 'If you consent now to be tried by this court, you will be so tried, and the maximum imprisonment and fine this court will inflict if it finds you guilty will be

three months and £2,500 (or 6 months and/or £5,000 in a case of aggravated vehicle-taking); nor will you be liable to be sent to the Crown court for a heavier sentence. Do you consent to be tried by this court?'

If the accused refuses, the court will proceed to the plea before venue procedure described in D[4.3] and, if the accused then indicates a plea of not guilty or gives no indication as to plea, the court will proceed to the mode of trial procedure described in D[4.4].

These provisions relating to such an offence where the value is small create an absolute obligation on the court to deal with the matter as a summary offence and the procedures for plea before venue and mode of trial do not apply: *R v Kelly* [2001] RTR 45, CA. The court's task is to identify the value of the damage itself and it is not concerned with determining what, if any, consequential losses may have been sustained as a result of the damage; thus, where genetically modified crops were damaged, the farmer valued the damage at £750 but there were also wasted research costs making the overall loss somewhere between £3,250 and £14,650, it was impossible to criticise the justices for concluding that the value for mode of trial purposes was clearly less than £5,000: *R v Colchester Magistrates' Court, ex p Abbott* (2001)165 JP 386, [2001] Crim LR 564, DC. The difficulty of assessing the value in respect of damaged crops is that there is no open market for sale of damaged genetically modified crops grown for research not sale. In the circumstances of the case a court was justified in concluding that, as the crops in question had a value for research purposes, it was more than the market value of ordinary maize, but as there was no realistic way of putting a price on it, it was justified in holding that it was not clear whether the value was above or below £5,000: *R (DPP) v Prestatyn Magistrates' Court* [2002] EWHC 1177 (Admin), [2002] Crim LR 924.

Low value shoplifting

D[4.9A] Section 176 of the Anti-social Behaviour, Crime and Policing Act 2014 inserted new s 22A of the Magistrates' Court Act 1980 to make 'low value shoplifting' triable only summarily, but where the accused is an adult and appears before the court before the summary trial of the offence begins, the court must give him the opportunity to elect Crown Court trial and, if he so elects, he must be sent to the Crown Court for trial. The preservation of the right to elect may lead one to question the administrative benefits of this reform; only in very rare circumstances would magistrates decline jurisdiction. The answer, however, appears to be this. The right to elect applies only where the accused appears before the summary trial begins. Otherwise, the offence is summary for all purposes (save those mentioned below). Thus, the written plea of guilty procedure under the Magistrates' Courts Act 1980, s 12, can be invoked; or the court can proceed to try the defendant in his absence without a prior mode of trial procedure (thereby avoiding the need to issue an arrest warrant before conviction).

Where an offence of low-value shoplifting 'appears to be related' to an indictable offence which is sent for trial, it may be sent to the Crown Court pursuant to s 51(3)(b) of the Crime and Disorder Act 1998. See *R v Maxwell* [2017] EWCA Crim 1233, [2018] 1 Cr App R 5, [2018] Crim LR 60. See further D[4.2], ante, and D[5.1], post.

'Low-value shoplifting' is defined as theft of goods where the value does not exceed £200, the goods were being offered for sale in shop or any other premises, stall, vehicle or place from which there is carried on a trade or business, and at the time the accused was or was purporting to be a customer or potential customer of the person offering the goods for sale.

The value of the goods is defined as the price at which they were being offered for sale at the time. (In our view this requires a clear verbal or written representation as to the price.) Where a person is charged on the same occasion with two or more offences of low-value shoplifting the reference to the value is a reference to the aggregate of the values involved.

A person convicted of low-value shoplifting may not appeal against conviction to the Crown Court on the ground that the convicting court was mistaken as to whether the offence was one of low-value shoplifting.

These provisions apply to secondary parties as well as principal offenders.

Amendments to the Criminal Attempts Act 1981 and the Police and Criminal Evidence Act 1984 preserve, respectively, the ability to charge an offence of attempt and the inclusion of low-value shoplifting in any reference to an 'indictable offence'.

Power to change from summary trial to sending for trial

D[4.10] Where an adult defendant has proceeded to summary trial, the prosecution may, before the trial begins and before any other issue has been determined, apply for the offence to be tried on indictment instead. The court may grant this application, but only if it is satisfied that its sentencing powers, or aggregate sentencing powers, would be inadequate: Magistrates' Courts Act 1980, s 25..

Abuse of process

D[4.11] Prior to sending an indictable offence to the Crown Court under the Crime and Disorder Act 1998, s 51, a magistrates' court has jurisdiction to stay criminal proceedings as an abuse of the process: *R (on the application of Craik, Chief Constable of Northumbria Police) v Newcastle Upon Tyne Magistrates' Court (Price, interested party)* [2010] EWHC 935 (Admin), 174 CL&J 334, [2010] 5 Archbold Review, 2. However, it will rarely be appropriate to do so. The rule seems analogous to committal proceedings, ie such matters should normally be left to the Crown Court Judge to determine. See *R v Belmarsh Magistrates' Court, ex p Watts* [1999] 2 Cr App Rep 188.

Allocation guideline

D[4.12] The Sentencing Council has issued the following definitive guideline.

Allocation guideline
Determining whether cases should be dealt with by a magistrates' court or the Crown Court

Applicability of guideline

In accordance with section 122(2) of the Coroners and Justice Act 2009, the Sentencing Council issues this definitive guideline. It applies to all defendants in the magistrates' court (including youths jointly charged with adults) whose cases are dealt with on or after 1 March 2016.

It also applies to allocation decisions made in the Crown Court pursuant to Schedule 3 of the Crime and Disorder Act 1998. It will not be applicable in the youth court where a separate statutory procedure applies.

Venue for trial

It is important to ensure that all cases are tried at the appropriate level.

1. **In general, either way offences should be tried summarily unless:**

- the outcome would clearly be a sentence in excess of the court's powers for the offence(s) concerned after taking into account personal mitigation and any potential reduction for a guilty plea; or
- for reasons of unusual legal, procedural or factual complexity, the case should be tried in the Crown Court. This exception may apply in cases where a very substantial fine is the likely sentence. Other circumstances where this exception will apply are likely to be rare and case specific; the court will rely on the submissions of the parties to identify relevant cases.

2. In cases with no factual or legal complications the court should bear in mind **its power to commit for sentence after a trial** and may **retain jurisdiction** notwithstanding that the likely sentence might exceed its powers.

3. Cases may be tried summarily even where the defendant is subject to a Crown Court Suspended Sentence Order or Community Order.

4. All parties should be asked by the court to make representations as to whether the case is suitable for summary trial. The court should refer to definitive guidelines (if any) to assess the likely sentence for the offence in the light of the facts alleged by the prosecution case, taking into account all aspects of the case including those advanced by the defence, including any personal mitigation to which the defence wish to refer.

Where the court decides that the case is suitable to be dealt with in the magistrates' court, it must warn the defendant that all sentencing options remain open and, if the defendant consents to summary trial and is convicted by the court or pleads guilty, the defendant may be committed to the Crown Court for sentence.

Committal for sentence

There is ordinarily no statutory restriction on committing an either way case for sentence following conviction. The general power of the magistrates' court to commit to the Crown Court for sentence after a finding that a case is suitable for summary trial and/or conviction continues to be available where the court is of the opinion 'that the offence or the combination of the offence and one or more offences associated with it was so serious that the Crown Court should, in the court's opinion, have the power to deal with the offender in any way it could deal with him if he had been convicted on indictment.

However, where the court proceeds to the summary trial of certain offences relating to criminal damage, upon conviction there is no power to commit to the Crown Court for sentence. The court should refer to any definitive guideline to arrive at the appropriate sentence taking into account all of the circumstances of the case including personal mitigation and the appropriate guilty plea reduction.

In borderline cases the court should consider obtaining a pre-sentence report before deciding whether to commit it to the Crown Court for sentence.

Where the offending is so serious that the court is of the opinion that the Crown Court should have the power to deal with the offender, the case should be committed to the Crown Court for sentence even if a community order may be the appropriate sentence (this will allow the Crown Court to deal with any breach of a community order, if that is the sentence passed).

Youths jointly charged with adults – interests of justice test

The proper venue for the trial of any youth is normally the youth court. Subject to statutory restrictions, that remains the case where a youth is charged jointly with an adult.

This guideline does not provide information on the complex statutory framework for dealing with a youth jointly charged with an adult: consult your legal adviser for advice.

The court should refer to any definitive guideline to arrive at the appropriate sentence taking into account all of the circumstances of the case including personal mitigation and the appropriate guilty plea reduction.

The following guidance must be applied in those cases where the interests of justice test falls to be considered:

1. If the adult is sent for trial to the Crown Court, the court should conclude that the youth must be tried separately in the youth court unless it is in the interests of justice for the youth and the adult to be tried jointly.

2. Examples of factors that should be considered when deciding whether it is in the interests of justice to send the youth to the Crown Court (rather than having a trial in the youth court) include:
   - whether separate trials will cause injustice to witnesses or to the case as a whole (consideration should be given to the provisions of sections 27 and 28 of the Youth Justice and Criminal Evidence Act 1999);
   - the age of the youth: the younger the youth, the greater the desirability that the youth be tried in the youth court;
   - the age gap between the youth and the adult: a substantial gap in age militates in favour of the youth being tried in the youth court;
   - the lack of maturity of the youth;
   - the relative culpability of the youth compared with the adult and whether the alleged role played by the youth was minor;
   - the lack of previous convictions on the part of the youth.

3. The court should bear in mind that the youth court now has a general power to commit for sentence following conviction pursuant to Section 3B of the Powers of Criminal Courts (Sentencing) Act 2000 (as amended). In appropriate cases this will permit the same court to sentence adults and youths who have been tried separately.

D[5]

Sending for trial – indictable only offences: Procedure

D[5.1] Section 52 of the Crime and Disorder Act 1998 provides (subject as therein stated) for the remand in custody or on bail of a person sent to the Crown Court under ss 51 or 51A of that Act. It further provides (in subsection (5)) that the court may adjourn proceedings under ss 51 and 51A and, if it does so, it shall remand the accused.

Section 51D of the Crime and Disorder Act 1998 deals with the notices which the court must serve on the accused and the Crown Court as to the offences which have been sent under s 51 or, in the case of a youth, s 51A. Where more than one offence has been sent, the notice must specify the relevant subsection under which each offence has been sent. If it is a 'related offence', the offence to which it is related must also be specified. The power to send 'related' offences is conferred by s 51(3). Section 51E defines 'related' in different terms for either way offences and summary offences, the test for the latter being narrower (see D[4.2], ante). This is consistent with an intention that only those summary offences which have a close link to more serious offences sent to the Crown Court should trouble that court. See further *R v Maxwell* [2017] EWCA Crim 1233, [2018] 1 Cr App R 5, [2018] Crim LR 60, mentioned at D[4.9A], ante.

'Appears' provides some leeway, and an apparent connection is something less than a determination that the offences are in fact 'related': *R v Maxwell*, supra.

Where a defendant commits a Bail Act offence before being sent for trial, the only means by which that offence can end up in the Crown Court is by committal for sentence under s 6(6)(b) of the Bail Act 1976: *R v Osman* [2017] EWCA Crim 2178, [2018] 1 Cr App R (S) 23.

Where the court selects the place of trial, s 51D specifies the matters to which the court shall have regard.

Schedule 3 to the Crime and Disorder Act makes further provision as to persons sent to the Crown Court under ss 51 or 51A of the Act. The key features are these:

- Copies of the prosecution evidence must be served on the accused and the court within prescribed time limits.
- Prior to arraignment, the accused may apply for the dismissal of the charge or any of the charges on the ground that the evidence is insufficient for the accused to be properly convicted of that charge, and if the charged is so dismissed by the judge no further proceedings may be brought on that charge except by the preferment of a voluntary bill of indictment.
- Reporting restrictions apply to applications for dismissal.
- There is provision for a justice to take a deposition from a person who is likely to be able to give or to produce material evidence on a sent charge, and for the issue of a summons or warrant to require that person's attendance before the justice for that purpose.
- Provision is made, following conviction on indictment, for the Crown Court to deal with any summary offences which were included in the sending provided they are related and the defendant pleads guilty or the prosecution offers no evidence.
- Provision is made to cover the case where no 'main offence' (ie the offence which caused the defendant to be sent) remains before arraignment. If the defendant is an adult, the Crown Court must follow procedures which mirror those for mode of trial in the magistrates' court. If the defendant is a youth, he must be remitted to the magistrates' court.

Joinder of certain summary offences in an indictment

D[5.2] Section 40 of the Criminal Justice Act 1988 enables certain offences – for example, common assault and driving while disqualified – to be included in an indictment where the offence is founded on the same facts or evidence as a count charging an indictable offence, or is part of a series of offences of the same or similar character as such a count. The offence will then be tried in the same manner as an indictable offence, but the powers of the Crown Court on conviction will be limited to those of the magistrates' court.

D[6]
Summary proceedings

1 Criminal Procedure Rules (CrimPR)

D[6.1] The Criminal Procedure Rules 2015, supplemented by the Criminal Practice Directions 2015, regulate the conduct of criminal litigation. Their purpose is to promote efficiency and consistency and it is incumbent on the parties to comply with the rules and for the courts to police this.

The practice of republishing the rules every year ended in 2015, when significant changes were made. Subsequent amendments have been comparatively minor owing to the stability and maturity which the rules have now attained.

CrimPR 2015, Part 1

D[6.2] This part sets out the 'mission statement' of the rules and the fundamental obligations of the participants in criminal cases. Its importance is such that we reproduce it in full:

'**The overriding objective**

(1) The overriding objective of this procedural code is that criminal cases be dealt with justly.

(2) Dealing with a criminal case justly includes—
  (a) acquitting the innocent and convicting the guilty;
  (b) dealing with the prosecution and the defence fairly;
  (c) recognising the rights of a defendant, particularly those under Article 6 of the European Convention on Human Rights;
  (d) respecting the interests of witnesses, victims and jurors and keeping them informed of the progress of the case;
  (e) dealing with the case efficiently and expeditiously;
  (f) ensuring that appropriate information is available to the court when bail and sentence are considered; and
  (g) dealing with the case in ways that take into account—
    (i) the gravity of the offence alleged,
    (ii) the complexity of what is in issue,
    (iii) the severity of the consequences for the defendant and others affected, and
    (iv) the needs of other cases.

The duty of the participants in a criminal case

(1) Each participant, in the conduct of each case, must—
  (a) prepare and conduct the case in accordance with the overriding objective;
  (b) comply with these Rules, practice directions and directions made by the court; and
  (c) at once inform the court and all parties of any significant failure (whether or not that participant is responsible for that failure) to take any procedural step required by these Rules, any practice direction or any direction of the court. A failure is significant if it might hinder the court in furthering the overriding objective.

(2) Anyone involved in any way with a criminal case is a participant in its conduct for the purposes of this rule.

The application by the court of the overriding objective

(a) exercising any power given to it by legislation (including these Rules);

(b) applying any practice direction; or
(c) interpreting any rule or practice direction.'

The Criminal Practice Directions 2015

D[6.3] The Criminal Practice Directions 2015 [2015] EWCA Crim 1567 give further effect to the CrimPR 2015. They are nearly as important as the CrimPR itself and we reproduce below the provisions on case management which are relevant to magistrates' courts:

'CrimPR Part 3 Case management

CPD I General matters 3A: CASE MANAGEMENT

3A.1 CrimPR 1.1(2)(e) requires that cases be dealt with efficiently and expeditiously. CrimPR 3.2 requires the court to further the overriding objective by actively managing the case, for example:

(a) When dealing with an offence which is triable only on indictment the court must ask the defendant whether he or she intends to plead guilty at the Crown Court (CrimPR 9.7(5));
(b) On a guilty plea, the court must pass sentence at the earliest opportunity, in accordance with CrimPR 24.11(9)(a) (magistrates' courts) and 25.16(7)(a) (the Crown Court).

3A.2 Given these duties, magistrates' courts and the Crown Court therefore will proceed as described in paragraphs 3A.3 to 3A.28 below. The parties will be expected to have prepared in accordance with CrimPR 3.3(1) to avoid unnecessary and wasted hearings. They will be expected to have communicated with each other by the time of the first hearing; to report to the court on that communication at the first hearing; and to continue thereafter to communicate with each other and with the court officer, in accordance with CrimPR 3.3(2).

3A.3 There is a Preparation for Effective Trial form for use in the magistrates' courts, and a Plea and Trial Preparation Hearing form for use in the Crown Court, each of which must be used as appropriate in connection with CrimPR Part 3: see paragraph 5A.2 of these Practice Directions. Versions of those forms in pdf and Word, together with guidance notes, are available on the Criminal Procedure Rules pages of the Ministry of Justice website.

Case progression and trial preparation in magistrates' courts

3A.4 CrimPR 8.3 applies in all cases and requires the prosecutor to serve:

(i) a summary of the circumstances of the offence;
(ii) any account given by the defendant in interview, whether contained in that summary or in another document;
(iii) any written witness statement or exhibit that the prosecutor then has available and considers material to plea or to the allocation of the case for trial or sentence; iv. a list of the defendant's criminal record, if any; and
(iv) a list of the defendant's criminal record, if any; and
(v) any available statement of the effect of the offence on a victim, a victim's family or others.

The details must include sufficient information to allow the defendant and the court at the first hearing to take an informed view:

(i) on plea;
(ii) on venue for trial (if applicable);

(iii) for the purposes of case management; or
(iv) for the purposes of sentencing (including committal for sentence, if applicable).

Defendant in custody

3A.5 If the defendant has been detained in custody after being charged with an offence which is indictable only or triable either way, at the first hearing a magistrates' court will proceed at once with the allocation of the case for trial, where appropriate, and, if so required, with the sending of the defendant to the Crown Court for trial. The court will be expected to ask for and record any indication of plea and issues for trial to assist the Crown Court.

3A.6 If the offence charged is triable only summarily, or if at that hearing the case is allocated for summary trial, the court will forthwith give such directions as are necessary, either (on a guilty plea) to prepare for sentencing, or for a trial.

Defendant on bail

3A.7 If the defendant has been released on bail after being charged, the case must be listed for the first hearing 14 days after charge, or the next available court date thereafter when the prosecutor anticipates a guilty plea which is likely to be sentenced in the magistrates' court. In cases where there is an anticipated not guilty plea or the case is likely to be sent or committed to the Crown Court for either trial or sentence, then it must be listed for the first hearing 28 days after charge or the next available court date thereafter.

Guilty plea in the magistrates' courts

3A.8 Where a defendant pleads guilty or indicates a guilty plea in a magistrates' court the court should consider whether a pre-sentence report – a stand down report if possible – is necessary.

Guilty plea in the Crown Court

3A.9 Where a magistrates' court is considering committal for sentence or the defendant has indicated an intention to plead guilty in a matter which is to be sent to the Crown Court, the magistrates' court should request the preparation of a pre-sentence report for the Crown Court's use if the magistrates' court considers that:
(a) there is a realistic alternative to a custodial sentence; or
(b) the defendant may satisfy the criteria for classification as a dangerous offender; or
(c) there is some other appropriate reason for doing so.

3A.10 When a magistrates' court sends a case to the Crown Court for trial and the defendant indicates an intention to plead guilty at the Crown Court, then that magistrates' court must set a date for a Plea and Trial Preparation Hearing at the Crown Court, in accordance with CrimPR 9.7(5)(a)(i).

Case sent for Crown Court trial: no indication of guilty plea

3A.11 In any case sent to the Crown Court for trial, other than one in which the defendant indicates an intention to plead guilty, the magistrates' court must set a date for a Plea and Trial Preparation Hearing, in accordance with CrimPR 9.7(5)(a)(ii). The Plea and Trial Preparation Hearing must be held within 28 days of sending, unless the standard directions of the Presiding Judges of the circuit direct otherwise. Paragraph 3A.16 below additionally applies to the arrangements for such hearings. A magistrates' court may give other directions appropriate to the needs of the case, in accordance with CrimPR 3.5(3), and in accordance with any standard directions issued by the Presiding Judges of the circuit.

Defendant on bail: anticipated not guilty plea

3A.12 Where the defendant has been released on bail after being charged, and where the prosecutor does not anticipate a guilty plea at the first hearing in a magistrates' court, then it is essential that the initial details of the prosecution case that are provided for that first hearing are sufficient to assist the court, in order to identify the real issues and to give appropriate directions for an effective trial (regardless of whether the trial is to be heard in the magistrates' court or the Crown Court). In these circumstances, unless there is good reason not to do so, the prosecution should make available the following material in advance of the first hearing in the magistrates' court:

(a) A summary of the circumstances of the offence(s) including a summary of any account given by the defendant in interview;

(b) Statements and exhibits that the prosecution has identified as being of importance for the purpose of plea or initial case management, including any relevant CCTV that would be relied upon at trial and any Streamlined Forensic Report;

(c) Details of witness availability, as far as they are known at that hearing;

(d) Defendant's criminal record;

(e) Victim Personal Statements if provided;

(f) An indication of any medical or other expert evidence that the prosecution is likely to adduce in relation to a victim or the defendant;

(g) Any information as to special measures, bad character or hearsay, where applicable.

3A.13 In addition to the material required by CrimPR Part 8, the information required by the Preparation for Effective Trial form must be available to be submitted at the first hearing, and the parties must complete that form, in accordance with the guidance published with it. Where there is to be a contested trial in a magistrates' court, that form includes directions and a timetable that will apply in every case unless the court otherwise orders.

3A.14 Nothing in paragraph 3A.12-3A.13 shall preclude the court from taking a plea pursuant to CrimPR 3.9(2)(b) at the first hearing and for the court to case manage as far as practicable under Part 3 CrimPR.

Exercise of magistrates' court's powers

3A.15 In accordance with CrimPR 9.1, sections 49, 51(13) and 51A(11) of the Crime and Disorder Act 1998, and sections 17E, 18(5) and 24D of the Magistrates' Courts Act 1980 a single justice can:

(a) allocate and send for trial;

(b) take an indication of a guilty plea (but not pass sentence);

(c) take a not guilty plea and give directions for the preparation of trial including:

- (i) timetable for the proceedings;
- (ii) the attendance of the parties;
- (iii) the service of documents;
- (iv) the manner in which evidence is to be given.'

Pre-trial hearings in a magistrates' court – general rules

D[6.4A] The Criminal Procedure (Amendment No 4) Rules 2017, SI 2017/915, added the following provisions to Part 3:

'3.27.—(1) A magistrates' court—

(a) must conduct a preparation for trial hearing unless—
  (i) the court sends the defendant for trial in the Crown Court, or
  (ii) the case is one to which rule 24.8 or rule 24.9 applies (Written guilty plea: special rules; Single justice procedure: special rules);
(b) may conduct a further pre-trial case management hearing (and if necessary more than one such hearing) only where—
  (i) the court anticipates a guilty plea,
  (ii) it is necessary to conduct such a hearing in order to give directions for an effective trial, or
  (iii) such a hearing is required to set ground rules for the conduct of the questioning of a witness or defendant.

(2) At a preparation for trial hearing the court must give directions for an effective trial.

(3) At a preparation for trial hearing, if the defendant is present the court must—

(a) satisfy itself that there has been explained to the defendant, in terms the defendant can understand (with help, if necessary), that the defendant will receive credit for a guilty plea;
(b) take the defendant's plea or if no plea can be taken then find out whether the defendant is likely to plead guilty or not guilty; and
(c) unless the defendant pleads guilty, satisfy itself that there has been explained to the defendant, in terms the defendant can understand (with help, if necessary), that at the trial—
  (i) the defendant will have the right to give evidence after the court has heard the prosecution case,
  (ii) if the defendant does not attend, the trial is likely to take place in the defendant's absence, and
  (iii) where the defendant is released on bail, failure to attend court when required is an offence for which the defendant may be arrested and punished and bail may be withdrawn.

(4) A pre-trial case management hearing must be in public, as a general rule, but all or part of the hearing may be in private if the court so directs.

(5) The court—

(a) at the first hearing in the case must require a defendant who is present to provide, in writing or orally, his or her name, date of birth and nationality; and
(b) at any subsequent hearing may require such a defendant to provide that information by those means.'

Not guilty pleas – first hearing

D[6.4AA] There have been a number of reviews and initiatives aimed at enhancing efficiency and reducing adjournments. The aim in contested cases is to avoid intermediate hearings between the initial hearing and the trial itself. The purpose of the initial hearing is to case-manage to the fullest possible extent, which is achieved by clearly identifying what is in dispute and why, reducing to the minimum the need for 'live' evidence, and where a witness must be called explaining why this is so and setting realistic estimates for examination in chief and cross examination. If it is impossible to take any necessary step at the initial hearing because, for example, the relevant material has not been served, the court should proceed as far as it can and make directions as to the further steps the parties must take.

There may be cases where it is appropriate to conduct an unscheduled trial, but there must be compliance with Part 24 the Criminal Procedure Rules 2015 – Trial and Sentence in a Magistrates' court – and this was not the position where the prosecutor was an associate prosecutor and did not have the opportunity to resist a submission of no case to answer based on the evidence disclosed in the prosecution witness statements: *DPP v Berry* [2019] EWCA 825 (Admin), [2019] Crim L R 798.

The defendant must give details of any witness he proposes to call: Criminal Procedure and Investigations Act 1996, s 6C. If the defendant does not intend to run a 'positive' defence, but merely 'to put the prosecution to proof' this will prevent the defence from making positive assertions at the trial and will severely restrict the challenges which may be made to prosecution evidence. Unless the defence provides good reason for a witness to be called the court could decide to admit the statement under s 114 of the Criminal Justice Act 2003, turning the case, in effect, to a trial on the papers.

Detailed provision is made in the *Adult Criminal Case Management (Magistrates' Courts)* for what is expected of a first hearing.

Effective case management is a prerequisite of accurate trial scheduling, the importance of which was emphasised by Sir Anthony May P in *R (Drinkwater) v Solihull Magistrates' Court* [2012 EWHC 765 (Admin), [2012] All ER (D) 206 (Mar):

> 'In setting the timetable, the court should scrutinise the reasons why it is said a witness is necessary and the time examination and cross-examination would take. It is also important in setting a timetable to have regard to the nature of the issues and the fact that the trial is a summary trial; any estimate of more than a day in the Magistrates' Courts should be scrutinised with the utmost rigour. Parties must realise that a summary trial requires a proportionate approach. If a timetable for the trial is not set, it is difficult to have any real confidence that the estimate is accurate. At the commencement of the trial, the Magistrates' Court should check with the parties that the timetable and the estimates remain valid. If there is any variation which lengthens the estimate, the court should make every effort to see if the trial can still be accommodated that day by sitting late or otherwise. Once the trial has started, the court must actively manage the trial, keeping an eye on progress in relation to the timetable...'

Defence duty to assist in the identification of the issues

D[6.4AB] The Criminal Practice Directions Amendment No 1 [2016] EWCA Crim 9 contains a new practice direction on the defence indications of the issues in magistrates' courts and the Crown Court. As to magistrates' courts, CPD VI Trial 24B.4 provides:

> '24B.4 The identification of issues at the case management stage will have been made without the risk that they would be used at trial as statements of the defendant admissible in evidence against the defendant, provided the advocate follows the letter and the spirit of the Criminal Procedure Rules. The court may take the view that a party is not acting in the spirit of the Criminal Procedure Rules in seeking to ambush the other party or raising late and technical legal arguments that were not previously raised as issues. No party that seeks to ambush the other at trial should derive an advantage from such a course of action. The court may also take the view that a defendant is not acting in the spirit of the Criminal Procedure Rules if he or she refuses to identify the issues and puts the prosecutor to proof at the case management stage. In both such circumstances the court may limit the proceedings on the day of trial in accordance with CrimPR 3.11(d). In addition any significant divergence from the issues identified at case management at this late stage may well result in the exercise of the court's powers under CrimPR 3.5(6), the powers to impose sanctions.'

Other issues that may be capable of determination at the first hearing

D[6.4B] The existence of 'post plea' time limits for making/responding to applications, or furnishing material, does not necessarily prevent the court from raising these issues and seeking to resolve them at the plea and case management hearing.

Witness summonses, special measures and prohibition of cross examination by defendant in person See Parts 17, 18 and 23 of CrimPR 2015. Section 97 of the Magistrates' Courts Act 1980 no longer requires the court to be satisfied that a witness would be unlikely to attend. The criteria are: ability to give/produce material evidence; and that it is in the interests of justice to issue a summons to secure the attendance of the witness. There are many cases where the court can reach the conclusions at the first hearing, eg cases of domestic violence, where experience shows that complainants often fail to attend without giving any prior indication of a change of heart.

There are conditions for making special measures directions: see ss 16 and 17 of the Youth Justice and Criminal Evidence Act 1999 (YJCEA 1999). Ideally, the views of the witness will be canvassed at the time the statement is taken, but this does not always happen. Nevertheless, enough may be known of the nature and circumstances of the offence to enable the court to make a judgment on the relevant matters. Where this is the case, directions should be made, eg for the use of screens. The decision can always be reconsidered on the day of trial. By dealing with the matter at the case management hearing the trial can be listed in a courtroom with the appropriate facilities.

Sections 36 and 38 of the YJCEA 1999 empower the court, respectively, to direct that the defendant be prohibited from cross examining particular witnesses in person and to appoint a qualified legal representative to undertake such cross examination on behalf of the defendant if he does appoint his own representative. There are criteria for a direction under s 36, but, again it is often possible for the court to reach the required conclusion from the circumstances of the offence. In practice, many defendants are represented at the first hearing by the duty solicitor and do not, by that stage, have legal aid. By making these directions at the first hearing a 'fall back' position is established in case the defendant does not apply for, or receive, legal and is unable or unwilling to pay privately.

CCTV If all or part of the incident was captured on CCTV the prosecution may wish to include it in the evidence. In this case, if it has not already been served on the defence, the court should direct that this be done. If the CCTV is not part of the prosecution case it will be unused material and subject to the usual disclosure test. The court should not, therefore, make any direction as to service. See further D[6.12], below.

Hearsay evidence and evidence bad character See, respectively, Parts 20 and 21 of CrimPR 2015. While there are time limits for making/responding to applications they can be varied and the court can allow an application to be made orally at the first hearing and should do so where the material in the case establishes sufficiently clearly what the outcome should be, one way or the other, eg the defendant makes a clear attack on the character of a prosecution witness in his police interview, or his record plainly shows a propensity to commit offences of the kind he is now charged with, or a key prosecution witness has previously convictions which plainly go to the credibility of his evidence.

Interpreters It is important to establish at the first hearing whether or not an interpreter is required for the defendant or any witness. This will ensure that an interpreter is booked well in advance and that the court makes due allowance in the trial listing for any lengthening of the trial likely to result therefrom.

Examination of a number of decisions of the superior courts suggests that the judges in those courts will be prepared to uphold pre-trial decisions of magistrates including applications for adjournments (whether pre-trial or on the day of hearing), provided the magistrates, through their reasons, can demonstrate that they have properly identified and taken into account the relevant factors and exercised their discretion appropriately: see for example, *R (on the application of Khan) v Waltham Forest Magistrates' Court* [2007] EWHC 1801 (Admin), [2007] All ER (D) 29 (Jul).

D[6.4C] *Case management where the defendant may be suffering from mental ill health* Unlike the Crown Court, where the Criminal Procedure (Insanity) Act 1964 applies, there is no statutory scheme in the magistrates' court for determining fitness to stand trial. However, the mental health of the defendant may bear on whether or not he/she can raise a defence of lack of mens rea or insanity. Mental disorder can also result in the making of a hospital or guardianship order on conviction, or without a conviction where the court is satisfied that the defendant did the act or made the omission charged (see the Mental Health Act 1983, s 37).

It is, accordingly, important to identify as early as possible the appropriate course to take where there are grounds to believe the defendant may be suffering from mental disorder. Consequently, r 3.28 has been added to the Criminal Procedure Rules 2015. This imposes detailed procedural requirements for commissioning a medical report about a defendant's mental health other than for sentencing purposes. (Reports for sentencing purposes are covered by new r 28.8.)

As to payment, the view is taken that section 19(3B)(b)(i) of the Prosecution of Offences Act 1985 embraces not only reports concerned with final disposal but also reports to assist in determining the appropriate procedural course to that stage.

Adjournment applications

D[6.5] Examination of a number of decisions of the superior courts suggests that the judges in those courts will be prepared to uphold pre-trial decisions of magistrates including applications for adjournments (whether pre-trial or on the day of hearing), provided the magistrates, through their reasons, can demonstrate that they have properly identified and taken into account the relevant factors and exercised their discretion appropriately: see for example, *R (on the application of Khan) v Waltham Forest Magistrates' Court* [2007] EWHC 1801 (Admin), [2007] All ER (D) 29 (Jul).

This topic has attracted considerable case law. See D[6.17]–D[6.17E], post. This has been codified in CPD VI Trial 24C: Trial adjournment in magistrates' courts, which was added to the Criminal Practice Directions 2015 by [2019] EWCA Crim 495.

Adjournment applications – checklist

D[6.6] The following checklist applies to adjournment applications:

- CPR 2015, Part 1: Overriding duty on court to ensure criminal cases are dealt with justly
- ECHR, Article 6: The accused is entitled to a trial within a reasonable period of time
- ECHR, Article 6: The accused is entitled to a reasonable period of time in order to prepare his case

The 'overriding duty' does not mean that the court must adjourn on application, even where both parties seek an adjournment.

Broad approach to adjournment applications

D[6.7]–[6.9] The following broad approach should be taken to adjournment applications:

- What is the full (or relevant) history of the case?
- Has there been any pre-trial correspondence? – What was the court's response?
- Is it just or fair to depart from that pre-trial decision (reasons needed)? (see *Robinson v Abergavenny Magistrates' Court* [2007] EWHC 2005 (Admin)).

Legal Aid

D[6.10] Has the defendant submitted an application? When? Why any delay in submission? – If defendant in receipt of benefits or paid employment stand back in the list for a decision by the court administration.

If the defendant is self-employed, has he attached accounts to the legal aid application? If not, why not? Put back to clarify the position with the court administration.

Seek clarification as to when a decision as to legal representation can be made. If necessary to adjourn, list on the earliest practicable date.

Prosecution Evidence (initial disclosure)

See D[6.3] above where the relevant part of the Criminal Practice Directions 2015 is set out.

D[6.11] The Criminal Procedure Rules 2015 provide:

'Providing initial details of the prosecution case

8.2. —

(1) The prosecutor must serve initial details of the prosecution case on the court officer—
  (a) as soon as practicable; and
  (b) in any event, no later than the beginning of the day of the first hearing.

(2) Where a defendant requests those details, the prosecutor must serve them on the defendant—
  (a) as soon as practicable; and
  (b) in any event, no later than the beginning of the day of the first hearing.

(3) Where a defendant does not request those details, the prosecutor must make them available to the defendant at, or before, the beginning of the day of the first hearing.

Content of initial details

8.3. Initial details of the prosecution case must include—

(a) where, immediately before the first hearing in the magistrates' court, the defendant was in police custody for the offence charged—
  (i) a summary of the circumstances of the offence, and
  (ii) the defendant's criminal record, if any;

(b) where paragraph (a) does not apply—
  (i) a summary of the circumstances of the offence,
  (ii) any account given by the defendant in interview, whether contained in that summary or in another document,
  (iii) any written witness statement or exhibit that the prosecutor then has available and considers material to plea, or to the allocation of the case for trial, or to sentence,
  (iv) the defendant's criminal record, if any, and
  (v) any available statement of the effect of the offence on a victim, a victim's family or others.'

D[6.12] **Disclosure of unused prosecution material.**See generally: s 3 of the Criminal Procedure and Investigations Act 1996; Part 15 of the Criminal Procedure Rules; Part IV of the Criminal Practice Directions Part IV; the Attorney General's Guidelines on Disclosure; and the Judicial Protocol in the Disclosure of Unused Material in Criminal Cases.

The duty on the prosecutor arises *only* after a not guilty plea has been entered. As to the particulars that a defence statement must contain, see Criminal Procedure and Investigations Act 1996, s 6A. This provision post-dates the decision in *DPP v Wood* [2006] EWHC 32 (Admin), (2006) 177 JP 170, [2006] NLJR 146, where it was stated that there were real dangers of injustice in treating deficient defence statements as so wholly ineffective as to be non-existent in reality and thus to remove the court's jurisdiction to make an order under s 8 of the Criminal Procedure and Investigations Act 1996, and this may now require reconsideration.

Unused material: Any prosecution material which might reasonably be considered capable of undermining the case for the prosecution against the accused or of assisting the case for the accused.

Has the CPS fully complied with its legal duties (see below)?

Has the defence filed a voluntary defence statement? If not, the accused *cannot* make an application for disclosure of unused material.

Any voluntary defence statement should normally be served *within 14 days* of the date upon which the prosecution has complied with its duty to provide initial disclosure.

Has the accused in his defence statement set out particulars of the matters of fact on which he intends to rely for the purposes of his defence?

Any defence application to extend the timeframe must be in writing and must be made *before* the time limit expires.

The late service of a defence statement does not formally preclude the court from considering a proper application.

Where there is late service of a defence statement, any application to adjourn for further disclosure or to adjourn the trial, must be scrutinised closely (see immediately below).

If it is just to adjourn the case, the court should immediately consider the question of wasted costs (see ss 19, 19A and 19B Prosecution of Offences Act 1985 and regulations made thereunder); or, where the defendant is publicly funded, to notify the Legal Services Commission. The court must give *reasons* for its decision.

Pre-trial Issues

D[6.13] Power to make, vary or discharge pre-trial rulings. Section 8A of the Magistrates' Courts Act 1980 authorises a magistrates' court to make binding pre-trial rulings. That ruling remains binding upon the parties and the court unless a party applies to the court to discharge or vary that ruling on the grounds that there has been a material change of circumstances since the ruling was made (MCA 1980, s 8B).

The scope of the power to make preliminary rulings under s 8A was one of the issues which arose in *Riley v CPS* [2016] EWHC 2531 (Admin), [2017] 1WLR 505, [2017] 181 JP 77, [2017] Crim L R 222. It was held that, in the exercise of its discretion, the court is entitled to refuse to make a ruling which effectively stops the proceedings, but case management powers can be exercised to require the prosecution to clarify its case on the core facts alleged against a defendant within a short period.

It is open to a court of its own motion to vary or discharge a previous ruling of the magistrates' court but not solely on the basis that it would have reached a different conclusion; there must be a compelling reason such as changed circumstances or fresh evidence (*R (on the application of the CPS) v Gloucester Justices* [2008] EWHC 1488 (Admin), 172 JP 406).

In *Jones v South East Surrey Local Justice Area* [2010] EWHC 916 (Admin), 174 JP 342 it was recognised at common law that a lower court had limited power to reverse and to revoke a previously made order. It could so in the interests of justice, in particular, in changed circumstances. However, the parameters of the interests of justice test were to be measured not simply by reference to a "change of circumstances" but by reference to ss 8A and 8B of the Magistrates' Courts Act 1980 and the overriding objective of the Criminal Procedure Rules. As a result each case had to be decided in the light of it own particular circumstances. In the instant case, the justices had been right to grant the adjournment sought. There had been a "change of circumstances". For one it was clear on the day of trial, unlike the previous day, that the error for the delay lay with the police and not the Crown Prosecution Service. That may have influenced the decision that the magistrates made to refuse the adjournment.

Per Cranston J: "None of what I have said is to give encouragement to poor initial applications, which have to be supplemented later by applications to remedy the defect".

A magistrates' court does have the power to revisit a decision to vacate a trial if the court has been materially misled. Accordingly, where a court has been misled or given incorrect information about the basis for an application to vacate a trial (namely, whether or not a witness is required to attend) and grants the application, the court is entitled to revisit that decision (and hear renewed submissions) when the correct information is provided: *DPP v Woods* [2017] EWHC 1070 (Admin), 181 JP 395.

Special measures for vulnerable and intimidated witnesses

D[6.13A] Definition: In the case of certain witnesses in criminal proceedings (other than the accused), a magistrates' court may make a 'special measures direction' for the purpose of improving the quality of a witness's evidence. The statutory test or emphasis is designed to improve 'the quality of a witness's evidence'.

Special measures can take one of a number of forms:

- Screening the witness from the accused
- The giving of evidence by live link
- The giving of evidence in private
- Removal of wigs and gowns (arises normally only in the Crown Court)
- Video recorded evidence in chief
- Video recorded cross-examination and re-examination
- Examination of a witness through an intermediary
- Aids to communication

Other protection afforded to a witness can include:

- Protection from cross-examination by the accused in person
- Restrictions on evidence and questions about the complainant's bad character and more important (in a sexual case), sexual behaviour
- Restrictions on reporting

Inherent powers to protect a witness (as well as the accused) continue to apply:

— Provision of an interpreter (including an intermediary): see *R (on the application of AS) v Great Yarmouth Youth Court* [2011] EWHC 2059 (Admin), [2012] Crim LR 478; and *R (on the application of OP) v Secretary of State for Justice, Cheltenham Magistrates' Court, CPS (Interested Parties) and Just for Kids (Intervener)* [2014] EWHC 1944 (Admin), [2015] 1 Cr App Rep 70, (2014) 178 JP 377 where the court dealt with the distinction between giving general support during a trial to a defendant – normally readily achievable by an adult of appropriate experience – and giving skill support and intervention associated with the defendant giving evidence, which requires developed skills of the sort contemplated by inclusion within the Witness Intermediary Scheme.
— Use of screens

Expediting proceedings where the witness is aged under 10 years

Protocol has been agreed detailing the working arrangements between the police, the CPS and Her Majesty's Courts and Tribunals Service (HMCTS) to expedite cases involving very young witnesses to:

(a) maximise the opportunity for them to provide their best evidence; and

(b) minimise the stress and emotional impact of the Criminal Justices process.

The Protocol applies to cases charged on or after 1 April 2015 where:

(a) a witness is under the age of 10 at the time the incident is reported to the police; and
(b) the witness under 10 has provided an evidential statement or achieving best evidence (ABE) interview in relation to the incident, either in support of the prosecution or defence.

Witnesses eligible for assistance on grounds of age or incapacity

See Youth Justice and Criminal Evidence Act 1999, s 16. Under this provision a witness is eligible for assistance if:

(a) he/she is aged under 18 at the time of the hearing; or
(b) the court considers that the quality of evidence given by the witness is likely to be diminished by reason of any of the following circumstances, namely that the witness:
    (i) suffers from mental disorder within the meaning of the Mental Health Act 1983, or
    (ii) otherwise has a significant impairment of intelligence and social functioning; or
    (iii) has a physical disability or is suffering from a physical disorder.

References to the quality of a witness's evidence are to its quality in terms of completeness, coherence and accuracy; and for this purpose 'coherence' refers to a witness's ability in giving evidence to give answers which address the questions put to the witness and can be understood both individually and collectively.

Witness eligible for assistance on grounds of fear or distress about testifying

See Youth Justice and Criminal Evidence Act 1999, s 17. Under this provision a witness is eligible for assistance if the court is satisfied that the quality of evidence given by the witness is likely to be diminished by reason of fear or distress on the part of the witness in testifying in the proceedings. The court must take into account in particular:

(a) the nature and alleged circumstances of the offence to which the proceedings relate;
(b) the age of the witness;
(c) such of the following matters as appear to the court to be relevant:
    (i) the social and cultural background and ethnic origins of the witness;
    (ii) the domestic and employment circumstances of the witness;
    (iii) any religious beliefs or political opinions of the witness;
(d) any behaviour towards the witness on the part of:
    (i) the accused;
    (ii) members of the family or associates of the accused; or
    (iii) any other person who is likely to be an accused or a witness in the proceedings.

The court must in addition consider any views expressed by the witness.

Eligibility is, however, automatic:

(a) where the complainant in respect of a sexual offence or an offence under s 4 of the Asylum and Immigration (Treatment of Claimants, etc) Act 2004 (trafficking people for exploitation) is a witness in proceedings relating to that offence (or to that offence and any other offences);
(b) the witness is a witness to a 'relevant offence', ie an offence specified in Sch 1A to the Youth Justice and Criminal Evidence Act 1999;

unless, in either case, the witness has informed the court of the witness's wish not to be so eligible.

The Coroners and Justice Act 2009 removed the special category of child witnesses who are "in need of special protection". The effect is to place all child witnesses on the same footing, regardless of the offence to which the proceedings relate. There are further provisions allowing the child witness to opt out of giving evidence by a combination of video recorded and live link. The provisions are quite involved and magistrates should consult their legal adviser before giving further directions as to the conduct of the trial.

Evidence by live link: The court is able to give a direction allowing a witness to give evidence by live link. The court can also direct that a person specified by the court can accompany the witness when he/she is giving evidence by live link. The court must take the witness's wishes into account when it determines who is to accompany the witness.

Protected witness: Section 35 of the 1999 Act prevents the cross-examination of a "protected witness" by an accused in person. The definition of a protected witness includes a child. The definition of "child" has been amended to mean a person under the age of 18 years (as opposed to 17 years).

Quality of evidence: Special measures may only be authorised where the court considers that they would improve the quality of a witness's evidence, ie in terms of completeness, coherence and accuracy. Coherence refers to a witness's ability in giving evidence to give answers which address the questions put to the witness and can be understood both individually and collectively.

Procedure: The Criminal Procedure Rules 2015 govern the process. In broad terms the application for special measures must normally be made within a specific time frame and address the matters canvassed above; notably, the application must identify what sort of measures are sought and how those measures will improve the quality of the witness's evidence. It is good practice for the prosecution to attach a statement from the witness where it is being asserted that he/she is in fear or distress (not necessarily of the accused but of the court process).

If another party (usually the defence) object to the application they should normally object in writing within a given time frame. The notice of objection should address the points raised in the application for special measures.

Decision: It is for the court to determine and weigh the application in the light of the representations or evidence put before it. Be careful not to attach too much weight to assertions unsupported by evidence. The fact that there is some suggestion from the defence that there has been contact between the witness and defence during the court proceedings is not in itself sufficient to rebut the application. If there is a statement from a witness saying that he/she is in fear of giving evidence in front of the defendant without special measures, the court should attach some weight to this evidence when assessing whether it would be likely to improve the quality of the witness's evidence.

The Criminal Law Review (Issue No 7, 2012) reported two cases which may be of substantial benefit to the work of the court: *R v Edwards* [2011] EWCA Crim 3028, [2012] Crim LR 563 and *R v Wills* [2011] EWCA Crim 1938, [2012] 1 Cr App Rep 16, [2012] Crim LR 565.

If you read the judgments you will see in the Commentaries that the Judicial College accepted the invitation of the Court of Appeal in *Wills* and subsequently issued a Bench Checklist for Young Witness cases now available at: www.judiciary.gov.uk/publications-and-reports/guidance/2012/jc-bench-checklist-young-wit-cases.

This guidance, inter alia, instructs both advocates at 'ground rules' discussions to adapt their questions to a child's developmental stage enabling the child to give his/her best evidence. Consistent with the CrimPR it will also enable the court to control the conduct of the case and the manner in which the advocates conduct their cases, notably, the defence advocate's cross-examination of the witness.

Judging by the observation in the Commentary to *R v E* it seems to me there may be merit in the court directing the appointment of an intermediary who can be of real value in privately advising the prosecution or defence on how to formulate particular questions for a very young witness or one with learning difficulties

D[6.14] CrimPR, Part 21 - **bad character – defendant.** Has the prosecutor complied with the notice requirements? – If not, is there an acceptable reason for not complying with the rules?

Applications made very late or on the date of trial without good reason should be dealt with robustly, including a refusal of the application if its primary effect is to prejudice the fair trial of the accused.

Check that the application is not caught by s 98 of the CJA 2003 (definition of the term 'bad character'). [See *R v Chopra* [2006] EWCA Crim 2133, [2006] All ER (D) 44 (Dec); *R v Wallace* [2007] EWCA Crim 1760, 171 JP 543.]

Under which gateway or gateways is the application made (see s 101 CJA 2003)? The application should identify the gateway and its relevance.

In some cases, the court is entitled to exclude the bad character evidence on the grounds that its prejudicial effect outweighs its probative value (s 101(1)(d), (g) CJA 2003).

Reasons needed.

Case law: see *R v Hanson* [2005] EWCA Crim 824, (2005) 1 WLR 3169.

D[6.15] CrimPR, Part 21 – **bad character – non-defendant (witness).** Have the notice requirements been complied with? If not, is there an acceptable reason for not complying with the rules?

Has a certificate of readiness for trial already been filed by the party seeking to make the application?

Applications made very late or on the day of trial without good reason should be dealt with robustly, including a refusal of the application, having regard to the statutory assumption (see below) and if its primary effect is to prejudice a fair trial.

What is the relevance of the non-defendant's bad character? Assume the evidence is not admissible unless under s 100 of the CJA 2003 it is–

(a) important explanatory evidence,
(b) it has substantial probative value in relation to a matter which –
 (i) is a matter in issue in the proceedings, and
 (ii) is of substantial importance in the context of the case as a whole, or
(c) all the parties to the proceedings agree to the evidence being admissible.
 - Ask the parties to define 'important explanatory evidence'.
 - Ask the parties to define 'substantial probative value'.
 - Except where paragraph (c) above applies, evidence of the bad character of a witness may not be given without the leave of the court.
 - Court must give reasons for its decision.

D[6.16] CrimPR, Part 20 - **hearsay evidence.** Have the notice requirements been complied with? If not, is there an acceptable reason for not complying with the rules?

Has a certificate of readiness for trial already been filed by the party seeking to make the application?

Applications made very late or on the day of trial without good reason should be dealt with robustly, including a refusal of the application, if its primary affect is to prejudice a fair trial.

Does the application identify the nature and type of hearsay evidence to be adduced (see s 114 CJA 2003 onwards)?

How important is the hearsay evidence in the context of the case a whole?

Weigh the relevant factors and other considerations prescribed by s 114(2) CJA 2003 (see *R v Cole* [2007] EWCA Crim 1924).

Court to reach a determination and give reasons for its decision.

Trial

Applications to adjourn

D[6.17] CPD VI Trial 24C: Trial adjournment in magistrates' courts was added to the Criminal Practice Directions 2015 by [2019] EWCA Crim 495. This codifies the considerable case law on this subject. Applications to adjourn on the day of trial are dealt with under the headings:

- General Principles 24C.5–9;
- The Relevance of Fault 24C.10–13;
- Length of Adjournment 24C.14–15;
- Absence of Defendant 24C.17–19;
- Absence of Witness 24C.20;
- Failure to Serve Evidence in Time 24C.21–22;
- Failure to Comply with Disclosure Obligations 24C.23-26

General factors

D[6.17A] The court is empowered to adjourn proceedings at any time: Magistrates' Courts Act 1980, s 10(1). Factors to which the court will have consideration include:

(a) the need for expedition in the prosecution of criminal proceedings (summary justice should be speedy justice which is not a matter of administrative convenience although efficient administration and economy are in themselves desirable ends but delays deprive other defendants of the opportunity of speedy trials when recollections are fresh: *R v Hereford Magistrates' Court, ex p Rowlands* [1988] QB 110);

(b) the interests of justice as they affect both sides, eg the interest of the defendant in concluding a matter hanging over him and the interest of the prosecution, representing the public, that a charge properly preferred against the defendant should be the subject of proper adjudication: *R v Aberdare Justices, ex p DPP* (1990) JP 324, DC;

(c) also the particular interest of those people who may be personally affected by the alleged offence to whom the proper prosecution and, if appropriate, conviction of an offender might be a very significant event: *DPP v Shuttleworth* [2002] EWHC 621 (Admin), 166 JP 417;

(d) whether the prosecution has been at fault: *R v Aberdare Justices*, above;

(e) whether the defendant has been denied a full opportunity to present his case (but a defendant is not to be permitted to frustrate a speedy trial without substantial grounds and a defendant who deliberately seeks to postpone a trial without good reason has no cause for complaint if an adjournment is refused): *R v Hereford Magistrates' Court*, above.

Justices must fully examine the circumstances leading to applications, the reasons for such applications and the consequences both to the prosecution and the defence. These factors were summarised by Jack J in *DPP v Picton* [2006] EWHC 1108 (Admin), 170 JP 707, 170 JPN 954:

> 'A decision whether to adjourn is a decision within the discretion of the trial court. An appellate court will interfere only if very clear grounds for doing so are shown. Magistrates should pay great attention to the need for expedition in the prosecution of criminal proceedings; delays are scandalous; they bring the law into disrepute; summary justice should be speedy justice; an application for an adjournment should be rigorously scrutinized.

> Where an adjournment is sought by the prosecution, magistrates must consider both the interest of the defendant in getting the matter dealt with, and the interest of the public that criminal charges should be adjudicated upon, and the guilty convicted as well as the innocent acquitted. With a more serious charge the public interest that there be a trial will carry greater weight.
>
> Where an adjournment is sought by the accused, the magistrates must consider whether, if it is not granted, he will be able fully to present his defence and, if he will not be able to do so, the degree to which his ability to do so is compromised. In considering the competing interests of the parties the magistrates should examine the likely consequences of the proposed adjournment, in particular its likely length, and the need to decide the facts while recollections are fresh.
>
> The reason that the adjournment is required should be examined and, if it arises through the fault of the party asking for the adjournment, that is a factor against granting the adjournment, carrying weight in accordance with the gravity of the fault. If that party was not at fault, that may favour an adjournment. Likewise if the party opposing the adjournment has been at fault, that will favour an adjournment. The magistrates should take appropriate account of the history of the case, and whether there have been earlier adjournments and at whose request and why.
>
> Lastly, of course the factors to be considered cannot be comprehensively stated but depend upon the particular circumstances of each case, and they will often overlap. The court's duty is to do justice between the parties in the circumstances as they have arisen.'

That guidance given in *Picton* was somewhat qualified in the case of *R (on the application of Drinkwater) v Solihull Magistrates Court and CPS* [2012] EWHC 765 (Admin), 170 JPN 954. The court also had some particularly robust comments to make about the importance of accurate time estimates for trials, and appropriate case management thereafter.

In *Drinkwater* the decision to continue a part-heard trial in the absence of the ill (depressed) defendant, which effectively prevented her defence of self defence from being properly advanced, was quashed. The court had this to say about *Picton*:

> 'I also accept (counsel's) submission that the magistrates did not consider the principles to be applied to the trial of a defendant in his or her absence as set out by the Court of Appeal and the House of Lords in the case of (*R v Jones* [2003] 1 AC 1, [2002] 2 All ER 113) ... Apart from the contrast between the formulation of the principles in Jones and others and the guidance in *Picton's* case, which may in part be explained because the Divisional Court did not consider the earlier case, it is important not to lose sight of the context in which *Picton's* case was decided. The factors identified in it remain important. But it is noteworthy that some of the authorities reviewed were decided at a time when the delays in the Magistrates' Courts were far greater than they have been more recently as a result of CJSSS ("simple, speedy and summary justice") and other initiatives. The case management techniques now available under the Criminal Procedure Rules also mean that the context in which applications to adjourn are now decided is, or should generally be different.' (per Beatson J at [39], [41])

(In *Drinkwater* no reference was made to s 11 of the Magistrates' Courts Act 1980. It is submitted, however, that this would not have affected the outcome since the court found, in effect, it was contrary to the interests of justice to proceed in the absence of the defendant.)

As to absent defendants and medical certificates, see **D[16.19A]**, post.

In *R (Parashar) v Sunderland Magistrates' Court* [2019] EWHC 514 (Admin), [2019] 2 Cr App R 3, [2019] Crim LR 627 the Administrative Court quashed a decision not to vacate a trial date when the defence expert was unable to attend that and earlier delays had been the fault of the prosecution.

Failures by the prosecution – disclosure, etc

D[6.17B] The CPS Disclosure Manual (2018) (www.cps.gov.uk) states at pages 5–6 that ' . . . it is essential to ensure that the duties imposed by the CPIA 1996 and t he Codes of Practice are scrupulously observed. If the prosecutor is satisfied that a fair trial cannot take place because of a failure to disclose that which cannot or will not remedied . . . he or she must not continue with the case'. The court has no power, however, to prevent a prosecution from proceeding on the ground of non-compliance with disclosure requirements other than by means of the exceptional course of staying the proceedings as an abuse of process.

If it is necessary to adjourn the case to enable justice to be done following a failure by the prosecution to disclose matters which ought to be disclosed, then the adjournment must be granted, unless the court is satisfied that no prejudice would be caused to the defendant by proceeding: *S v DPP* [2006] EWHC 1207 (Admin), (2006) 170 JP 707, 171 JPN 161 (failure to disclose a case of affray pending against the victim where his credibility was crucial to the present case and the details might well have damaged his credibility). Similarly, if the party seeking the adjournment will suffer a clear risk of prejudice if the trial proceeds such that he might not have a fair trial, and he was in no way responsible for causing the problems leading to that risk, the adjournment should be granted: *R (on the application of Costello) v North East Essex Magistrates' Court* [2006] EWHC 3145 (Admin), (2007) 171 JP 153, 171 JPN 393.

There must, however, be a proper basis for concluding that a fair trial cannot take place. In *DPP v Petrie* [2015] EWHC 48 (Admin), (2015) 179 JP 251 the defendant was charged with driving with excess alcohol. He pleaded not guilty and his representative stated that there were disputed issues including the procedure which had been carried out at the police station; in particular that the statutory warning had not been given and that questions had not been put in accordance with the standard form. There was CCTV covering the procedure and, while the court had not been asked to make a direction as to service, the defence put the Crown on notice at an early stage that the relevant footage was required. This was supplied on the day of trial, but it was not in a form that could be played on any equipment in the court. The prosecution sought an adjournment with a view to making enquiries about possibly obtaining the original footage from the police station that day. This was opposed and the court refused the application on case management principles, holding that the prosecution 'had been lax' and that it had been clear from the outset that CCTV had been required. The defence then submitted abuse of process. The prosecution countered this by submitting that the trial could proceed simply by hearing the evidence of the police officer who carried out the breathalyser procedure. The justices ruled that it would be unfair to proceed and the defendant would not have a fair trial if the case proceeded that day, which the court had directed that it should.

The Administrative Court agreed that the justices had been entitled to refuse the adjournment. This was a 'robust case management decision', but it was none the worse for that. However, it was held that the proceedings should not have been stayed. The prosecution had been at fault, but there was no question of this amounting to such grave misconduct as to justify a stay on the ground that it was unfair to proceed with the trial. The decision that a fair trial was not possible was also unsustainable. This was purely speculative. It was not known whether the CCTV covered the relevant part of the procedure or, if it did, whether it captured the precise detail of what was said. The justices had no basis, therefore, for concluding that the footage, if playable, might, still less would, have assisted the defence. The trial could and should have proceeded on the available evidence.

See also *R (Imbeah) v Willesden Magistrates' Court* [2016] EWHC 1760 (Admin), [2017] 1 Cr App R 3, another excess alcohol case where the issue was disclosure of custody suit CCTV. It was held that the district judge was right not to have ordered disclosure following service of a defence case statement at the conclusion of the evidence of the prosecution's witness. The CCTV was identified as disclosable in the schedule of unused material but had not been viewed by either the prosecution or defence and was not relied on by the defence as a reason for seeking an adjournment at the time. In relation to the application to adjourn, the district judge was plainly right to regard the suggestion that the CCTV footage might undermine the prosecution case or assist the case for the defence as wholly speculative.

Adjournments will, however, be likely to be granted to avoid 'unmeritorious' acquittals, even where there has been fault on the part of the prosecution. In *R (on the application of Robinson) v Abergavenny Magistrates' Court* [2007] EWHC 2005 (Admin), (2007) 171 JP 683, 172 JPN 188, though the prosecution had been at fault in failing to serve certificates under s 20 of the Road Traffic Offenders 1988 in two cases of speeding (the apparent identification of other issues having deflected their attention elsewhere), it was held that the justices had been entitled to grant adjournments at the request of the prosecution. There had been dramatic changes in the conduct of litigation in magistrates' courts since the decision in *DPP v Cheshire Justices* [2002] EWHC 466 (Admin), [2002] All ER (D) 93 (Mar):

> 'The overriding objective of the Criminal Procedure Rules is that criminal cases be dealt with justly . . . Each participant in the conduct of the case must prepare and conduct the case in accordance with the overriding objectives. That includes at once informing the court and all parties of any significant failure by another party to take any procedural step. It includes responsibility for early identification of the real issues in the case and the obligation actively to assist the court in fulfilling its duties, including early identification of the real issues and co-operating with the progress of the case . . . Nothing in this judgment is to be taken as a licence for the CPS to fail to attend to the necessity of proving its case or for the need for justices to subject applications to close scrutiny. But the mere fact of CPS failure cannot be determinative of an application to adjourn.'

Fault on the part of the party making the application is, however, is a factor against granting the application and the weight it carries increases with the gravity of the fault.

> 'The prosecution must not think that they are always allowed at least one application to adjourn the case. If that idea were to gain currency, no trial would ever start on the first date set for trial. . . . I have no doubt that there is a high public interest in trials taking place on the date set for trial, and that trials should not be adjourned unless there is a good and compelling reason to do so. The sooner the prosecution understand this - that they cannot rely on their own failures properly to warn witnesses - the sooner the efficiency in the magistrates' court system improves.' (per Elias J in *R (on the application of Visvaratnam) v Brent Magistrates' Court* [2009] EWHC 3017 (Admin), (2010) 174 JP 61)

As to the failure of witnesses to attend, see **D[6.17C]** below.

In *R (Taylor) v Southampton Magistrates' Court* [2008] 3006 (Admin), (2009) 173 JP 17 a district judge was acting within the scope of his discretion to invite the prosecution, which had closed its case, to apply for an adjournment to ensure that a highly technical point as to service was fully and properly dealt with on the evidence.

Failure of witnesses to attend

D[6.17C] In *Cherpion v DPP* [2013] EWHC 615 (Admin), 177 CL&J 225, in October 2011, the claimant was driving a van and was involved in an accident. He was taken to hospital, where a specimen of blood was taken which was found to contain alcohol levels exceeding the legal limit. The case was first listed for trial in November 2011. However, the trial was subsequently adjourned on more than one occasion. The respondent indicated, amongst other things, that K, a doctor at the hospital, would be called to give evidence at trial. On 12 July 2012, at the adjourned trial, the respondent was unable to begin on time as not all of its witnesses had appeared. The claimant opposed the respondent's request for further time, but it subsequently became clear that the witnesses in question would be available. Then, the claimant applied for an adjournment, as K had not been requested to attend notwithstanding the indication that she would be. The justices refused to grant the adjournment on the basis, amongst other things: (i) of the already lengthy history; (ii) that the other witnesses were ready; (iii) that the claimant had already requested that the case continue; and (iv) that the claimant could have called K. The key issues in the trial included whether K had been the medical practitioner in immediate charge in the claimant's case and, accordingly, whether the procedure by which the claimant's blood had been taken had been lawful. The justices found, on the evidence, that K had been the medical practitioner in immediate charge of the claimant and the claimant was subsequently convicted of a road traffic offence. The Administrative Court held that, on the facts, the justices had not been wrong to refuse the adjournment. Whilst the respondent had been wrong in not calling K to give evidence, there was no doubt that the justices had been entitled to refuse to adjourn the trial. It had been a matter entirely for their discretion.

Having considered all the relevant factors, magistrates were correct to refuse the prosecutor an adjournment where the witnesses had been wrongly notified to attend at 2pm, and had considered that any trial would not have been concluded that day owing to the listing of another case for trial in the afternoon and that there would be significant delay if the case were part heard: *DPP v Picton*, above. On the other hand, where a trial had been listed after a pre-trial review but no prosecution witnesses had appeared and the CPS conceded that no attempt to warn the witnesses the justices were wrong to grant an adjournment on the basis of the seriousness of the allegation and that it was the first listing for trial: *R (on the application of Walden) v Highbury Corner Magistrates Court* [2003] EWHC 708 (Admin), [2003] All ER (D) 285 (Mar). In *R (on the application of DPP) v Ipswich Magistrates' Court* [2013] EWHC 1388 (Admin), 177 CL&J 397 the claimant challenged the defendant magistrates' court's decision to refuse to adjourn a trial because of the non-attendance of prosecution witnesses. In February 2012, the interested party had been charged with an offence of domestic violence under s 39 of the Criminal Justice Act 1988. The trial was listed for April 2012 but was adjourned on the application of the interested party and re-listed for September 2012. The April trial was due to take place in the afternoon. The new trial date was for a morning start. On the date, it transpired that the Crown Prosecution Service (CPS) had failed to fully update the file and witnesses had been advised to attend in the afternoon as originally listed. Once the reason for their non-attendance had been discovered, the CPS requested an adjournment. The justices, having taken advice from their legal advisor, decided to refuse an adjournment. The claimant missed the opportunity to appeal by way of case stated and so issued judicial review proceedings. The Administrative Court dismissed the application. The justices had fully had in mind the extent of the eight-month delay already incurred and the further five-month delay that would occur if the trial was to be adjourned for a second time. The justices had been entitled to take into account that considerable delay in deciding to refuse to adjourn the trial. Moreover, because of the CPS error, it would not have been possible to fulfil the overriding objective set out in the Criminal Procedure Rules. The previous adjournment was a neutral factor, but the justices were entitled to take into account that an old case would become increasingly stale as a result of a further adjournment.

See also *Decani v City of London Magistrates' Court* [2017] EWHC 3422 (Admin), in which it was held that magistrates had been wrong to adjourn a drink-driving trial where the prosecution had failed to warn a relevant witness who did not appear and the defendant was ready to proceed. The witness had been legitimately required and there was no suggestion the defence were 'playing games'; the defendant was pursuing a legitimate defence, supported by evidence. In *R (DPP) v Birmingham Magistrates' Court* [2017] EWHC 3444 (Admin), however, the Administrative Court held that an adjournment should have been granted where the complainant in an allegation of sexual assault notified the court through here fiancé that five members of her family had been killed overnight in an accident in the Yemen and she was willing to attend any date to which the trial might be adjourned. The refusal to adjourn had been 'plainly wrong'. In particular, there was no reason to believe that the fatal events in relation to family members had not occurred; it was an unrealistically high standard to expect A and her fiancé to attend at court; and the judge made clear that if they had attended the information would have been accepted. In addition, there was the fact that the explanation had been volunteered at the earliest moment on the day of the trial, rather than needing to be sought after non-appearance. There was also the absence of consideration of the various balancing factors in the doing of justice between the parties that (prosecuting counsel) had underlined – including the seriousness of the offence; the public interest (including that of the complainant); the fact that the prosecution had done no wrong hitherto; and the lack of prejudice to the interested party via some additional delay (per Sweeney J at para 26).

In *Smith v RSPCA* [2017] EWHC 3536 Admin it was held that the District Judge had been entitled to refuse to adjourn a part-heard trial on the basis of evidence from a GP as to the continuing impact on them of the suicide of a co-defendant. The judge had ruled:

> 'I am not satisfied on the evidence I have heard from Dr R that these two defendants are unfit to attend court, given (a) the dates when they were last examined by a medical practitioner; (b) the nature of the ailment described as "depression"; (c) it is not self-evident why the condition of depression and distress renders them unfit to attend court and defend themselves; (d) there is no clear indication as to when either of these defendants might be considered fit to be able to attend court. For all the above reasons I do not agree to adjourn this hearing any further.'

Parties must be allowed to present their case where adjournments are refused

D[6.17D] Where they have refused an application by the prosecution to adjourn a trial, justices have no power to dismiss an information without hearing any evidence, even though they may be of the view that it would be unjust or prejudicial to the defendant to continue: *R v Birmingham Justices, ex p Lamb* [1983] 3 All ER 23, [1983] 1 WLR 339. If justices dismiss an information without hearing the evidence which the parties properly wish to lay before them, they act without jurisdiction and a quashing order will issue: *Re Harrington* [1984] AC 473, [1984] 2 All ER 474, HL. Accordingly, if the prosecutor is present and has evidence available which he desires to call, the justices must, if they refuse an application for an adjournment, give the prosecutor the opportunity of calling that evidence if he so wishes, hear that evidence and hear the parties and then adjudicate on all the evidence.

Absence of the prosecutor or prosecution file

D[6.17E] It is a breach of the rules of natural justice and unlawful for justices to refuse an adjournment of a case and to go on to dismiss informations for want of prosecution where the justices know that the case has been wrongly listed and that the arrival of the prosecutor is imminent: *R v Dudley Magistrates' Court, ex p DPP* (1992) 157 JP 177, DC.

Where a prosecutor did not have a file in court for a particular case, although the case was on the court agenda which had been supplied to the CPS the previous day, justices were wrong to dismiss the matter for want of prosecution without enquiring whether a plea could be taken. A prosecutor 'does not appear' for the purposes of s 15(1) of the Magistrates' Courts Act 1980 when, though physically present in court, he is unable to proceed with the particular part of the case which is before the court. If there is enough information before the court to allow the plea of the defendant to be taken and the plea is not guilty, the matter will be put off for a trial. If the plea is guilty, the court will have to decide whether it is in a position to proceed to sentence. If it is, it is at the stage of opening the case that the prosecutor will be in difficulties. The appropriate course will then be to adjourn the case and the court may consider an order for costs: *R v Aberdare Justices*, above.

Guilty plea entered

D[6.18] Where possible proceed to sentence.

- How serious is the offence?
- What is the guideline or starting point?
- Does the court need a psychiatric report? Would it materially affect the sentence?
- Does the court need more information? Would it materially affect the sentence?
- How long would it take to obtain a psychiatric report?
- Is a full pre-sentence report necessary? Would an oral or fast-delivery report suffice?

2 Not guilty plea

D[6.19] See section 1 above and in particular issues associated with pre-trial disclosure and pre-trial issues eg bad character applications.

At the commencement of the trial, the Magistrates' Court should check with the parties that the timetable and the estimates remain valid. If there is any variation which lengthens the estimate, the court should make every effort to see if the trial can still be accommodated that day by sitting late or otherwise. Once the trial has started, the court must actively manage the trial, keeping an eye on progress in relation to the timetable: *R (on the application of Drinkwater) v Solihull Magistrates Court and CPS* [2012] EWHC 765 (Admin), 170 JP 567, 170 JPN 954.

Trial in absence. Subject to the qualifications set out below, where at the time and place appointed for the trial or adjourned trial of an information the prosecutor appears but the accused does not:

(a) if the accused is under 18 years of age, the court *may* proceed in his absence: and

(b) if the accused has attained the age of 18 years, the court *shall* proceed in his absence unless it appears to the court to be contrary to the interests of justice to do so, and if the court decides not to proceed in an adult case it must state its reasons and cause those reasons to be entered in the court register.

Magistrates' Courts Act 1980, s 11(1) and (7).

The qualifications referred to above are these:

(a) where a summons has been issued it must be proved in the prescribed manner to the satisfaction of the court that the summons was served within a reasonable time of the trial or adjourned trial or the accused appeared on a previous occasion to answer the information: Magistrates' Courts Act 1980 (MCA 1980), s 11(2);

(b) the court shall not proceed if it considers that there is an acceptable reason for the failure to appear: MCA 1980, s 11(2A);

(c) if the proceedings were instituted by an information followed by summons, or by a written charge, the court shall not in absence impose a custodial sentence or order that a suspended sentence shall take effect; in any other case, where such a sentence or order is imposed or made, the offender must be brought before the court before he begins to serve the sentence and the sentence will not be effective until this happens: MCA 1980, s 11(3), (3A) and (5);

(d) if the proceedings were instituted by laying an information followed by a summons, or by a written charge, the court shall not in absence impose any disqualification on the accused except following an adjournment the notice of which must include the reason for the adjournment: MCA 1980, s 11(5).

Nothing in the above requires the court to inquire into the reasons for the accused's failure to appear before deciding whether or not to proceed in his absence: MCA 1980, s 11(6).

When bailing an accused to a trial date, it should be made clear that if he fails to attend the trial will proceed in his absence: *R v O'Hare* [2006] EWCA Crim 471, [2006] Crim LR 950.

Proceedings not covered by the above

The above narrative states the position relating to summary, adult criminal proceedings only. In the case of trial on indictment, the relevant considerations were set out in *R v Jones* [2002] UKHL 5, [2003] AC 1, [2002] 2 All ER 113, [2002] 2 WLR 524. The same principles are relevant to summary proceedings where the presumption of proceeding does not apply (see *R (Moresby) v Tower Bridge Magistrates' Court* [2007] EWHC 2766, (2008) 172 JP 155) and to civil proceedings in magistrates' courts, especially those which involve allegations of misbehaviour (eg ASBO – now injunction – applications) (see *R (on the application of M) v Burnley, Pendle & Rossendale Magistrates' Court* [2009] EWHC 2874, (2010) 174 JP 102).

Absent defendants and medical certificates

D[6.19A] See generally Part 5C of the Criminal Practice Directions 2015. The court is not absolutely bound by a medical certificate; it may require the medical practitioner to give evidence, or it may disregard a certificate which it finds unsatisfactory: *R v Ealing Magistrates' Court* [2001] 165 JP 82. Reasons for which a court might find a certificate to be unsatisfactory include: reference to the defendant being unfit to attend work rather than to attend court; the nature of the ailment does not appear to be capable of preventing attendance at court; and the defendant is certified as suffering from stress, anxiety or depression and there is no indication of the defendant recovering within a realistic timescale.

However, a careful and fair approach is always required. In *R (on the application of Rathor) v Southampton Magistrates' Court* [2018] 3278 (Admin), [2019] Crim LR 431 the defendant had attended three previous trial listings, and the failure to proceed on those occasions was the result either of prosecution applications to adjourn or lack of court time. The defendant failed to attend the fourth trial hearing owing to food poisoning. A sick note was sent, but this did not address whether the defendant was well enough to attend court. The judge decided to proceed in absence and the defendant was convicted. Subsequently, a further sick note was submitted, which stated the defendant had been unfit to attend court. The judge was invited to re-open the proceeding under s 142 of the MCA 1980, but refused.

The Administrative Court quashed the conviction. The judge should have taken the medical certificate into account. If the judge regarded it as spurious, this should have been made clear and not left to inference. The judge had also been obliged to consider whether to refuse an application to adjourn was contrary to the interests of justice. Moreover, the judge should have re-opened the proceedings in consequence of the second medical certificate. He should have asked himself if he would have adjourned the trial if it had been before him at the time, and the proper answer to that was plainly 'yes'.

D[6.20] In a trial all the facts relevant to the proof of guilt are said to be 'in issue' which means that the prosecutor must either prove those facts beyond reasonable doubt or (in some few cases) must establish facts which then place the burden of proving his innocence on the accused. An example of this last situation occurs where the police allege the uninsured use of a motor vehicle. Once they establish that the accused used a motor vehicle on a road the burden switches to the accused to show that he had a policy of insurance (if he does so, the burden reverts to the prosecution to prove it does not cover the use in question where this is in contention). The prosecutor will establish his facts by the oral testimony of witnesses who may then be cross-examined, and/or by the production of witness statements of which the accused will have had prior notice in order to object to them if he wishes, and/or by formal admissions from the accused which should be written down and signed by him. If the accused wishes to give evidence he may use all or any of these methods of doing so.

D[6.21] **No case to answer.** There must be a sufficient case for the defendant to answer by the end of the prosecution case. If the prosecution have failed to prove an essential ingredient of the offence or the evidence adduced has been so discredited by cross- examination or is shown to be manifestly unreliable then if no reasonable tribunal could convict at that stage the case should be dismissed (*R v Galbraith* [1981] 2 All ER 1060, [1981] 1 WLR 1039 CA).

Where the court dismisses the case it must give reasons for its decision. The converse does not normally apply ie the court is not usually required to give reasons if it finds a case to answer (*Moran v DPP* [2002] EWHC 89 (Admin), (2002) 166 JP 467).

For a recent decision where it was held that the justices' decision that the case could not proceed beyond the half-way stage, in the light of weaknesses and inconsistencies in the accounts of prosecution witnesses, was perverse see *DPP v S* [2007] All ER (D) 148 (Dec).

A submission of no case to answer may not be made and/or considered prior to the close of the prosecution case (*Prosecution Appeal (No 32 of 2007; R v N Ltd* [2008] EWCA Crim 1223).

In *R (on the application of the Crown Prosecution Service) v Norwich Magistrates' Court* [2011] EWHC 82 (Admin), the High Court ruled that the justices erred by not permitting the Crown to re-open or to call additional evidence after the closure of its case. The prosecution had not appreciated there was any issue over identification until it had closed its case. The justices' refusal to exercise their discretion ran contrary to the overriding objective of the Criminal Procedure Rules 2010, was plainly contrary to the interests of justice and lacked any reasonable basis.

D[6.22] Inferences from silence.

(a) *Accused's failure to mention facts when questioned or charged*

(1) Are there legal proceedings against the accused for an offence?
(2) Did the alleged failure to mention a fact or facts occur before the accused was charged?
(3) Did the alleged failure to mention a fact or facts occur while under caution by a constable or other investigating officer?
(4) Was the constable's or other officer's questioning directed towards trying to discover whether or by whom the alleged offence had been committed?
(5) Was the alleged fact or facts (not mentioned before charge) relied upon by the accused in his defence in these proceedings?
(6) Was the accused's failure to mention the alleged fact or facts something which he/she could reasonably have been expected to mention when so questioned?
(7) Can the accused's failure to mention the alleged fact or facts only be sensibly explained in that he had no answer at the time of his interview or none that would stand up to scrutiny?
(8) Apart from the failure to mention that fact or facts is the prosecution's case sufficiently strong to amount to a case to answer against the accused?

Only if the court is sure as to 1–8 above may it draw an inference. The court may draw such inference as it deems appropriate. The inference itself may be one solely as to credit, credibility or an inference as to guilt. However, the court may not convict solely on the basis of the inferences it has drawn (see *R v Argent* (1996) 161 JP 190; *Condron v UK* (2001) 21 EHRR 1; *R v Beckles* [2005] 1 All ER 705).

In *R v Hackett* [2011] EWCA Crim 380, [2011] 2 Cr App Rep 35, the Court of Appeal held that it was wrong to give both a s 34 and a *Lucas* direction (lies as corroboration): *R v Rana* [2007] EWCA Crim 2261 applied. The Judge should have confined his directions to a s 34 direction whilst reminding the jury that unless they rejected H's explanation for not revealing his trip to the petrol station and its purpose at the first interview then no adverse inference could be drawn.

R v Rana did not decide that a s 34 direction should always be given in place of a *Lucas* direction. *Rana* decided that it had been appropriate for the trial judge to modify his directions under s 34 to take account of lies allegedly given by R in his account to the police. The principle flowing from the judgment applies equally to magistrates' courts; that is, a suitably modified direction under s 34 should be given in any advice to the justices, or, they should be invited to focus solely on whether the lies support the prosecution case in accordance with the principles laid down in *R v Lucas*.

(b) *Accused's failure or refusal to account for objects, substances or marks (s 36 Criminal Justice and Public Order Act 1994)*

(1) When the accused was arrested by a police constable did the accused have with him, or in or on his clothing, or on his footwear (delete as appropriate); or was there at the place he was arrested an object, substance or mark concerned (delete as appropriate)?
(2) Did the constable reasonably believe, for example, that the accused may have eg used the object to commit the crime for which he is being tried?
(3) Did the officer inform the accused of his reasonable belief and ask him/her to account for the presence of eg the object/substance/mark (delete as appropriate)?
(4) Did the officer warn the accused that if he did not account eg for the presence of the object, a court may later ask why?
(5) Did the accused fail or refuse to account eg for the presence of the object?
(6) Was the accused's failure or refusal to account eg for the presence of the object, one which he/she could reasonably have been expected to mention when arrested?
(7) Was the accused's failure or refusal to account eg for the presence of an object, because he/she had no innocent explanation to give or none that would stand up to scrutiny?
(8) Apart from the failure or refusal to account for eg the presence of an object, is the prosecution's case sufficiently strong to amount to a case to answer against the accused?

Only if the court is sure as to 1–8 above may it draw an inference. The court may draw such inference as it deems appropriate. The inference itself may be one solely as to credit, credibility or an inference as to guilt. However, the court may not convict solely on the basis of the inferences it has drawn.

(c) *Accused's failure or refusal to account for presence at a particular place (s 37 Criminal Justice and Public Order Act 1994)*

(1) When the accused was arrested by a police constable (or Revenue and Customs officer) was he found at or near the place (at or about the time the offence for which he was arrested was alleged to have been committed)?
(2) Was the 'place' any building or part of a building, any vehicle, vessel, aircraft, hovercraft or any other place whatsoever?
(3) Did the officer or an officer investigating the offence reasonably believe that the accused was participating in the crime for which he was arrested?
(4) Did the officer tell the accused of his belief and ask him to account for his presence?
(5) Did the accused fail or refuse to account for his presence?
(6) Was the accused's failure or refusal one which he could reasonably have been expected to account for?
(7) Was the accused's failure or refusal because he/she had no innocent explanation to give or none that would stand up to scrutiny?
(8) Apart from the failure or refusal to account for presence at a particular place, is the prosecution's case sufficiently strong to amount to a case to answer against the accused?

Only if the court is sure as to 1–8 above may it draw an inference. The court may draw such inference as it deems appropriate. The inference itself may be one solely as to credit, credibility or an inference as to guilt. However, the court may not convict solely on the basis of the inferences it has drawn.

(d) *Accused's silence at trial (s 35 Criminal Justice and Public Order Act 1994)*

If the accused is **legally represented**, at the conclusion of the evidence for the prosecution (assuming there is a case to answer), if the court is informed that the accused does not intend to give evidence, the legal adviser should, in the presence of the magistrates, inquire of the representative in these terms:

> Have you advised your client that the stage has now been reached at which he may give evidence and, if he chooses not to do so, or having been sworn, without good cause refuses to answer any question, the court may draw such inferences as appear proper from his failure to do so?

If the reply is that the accused has been so advised the trial may proceed. If the answer is in the negative the court must direct the representative to advise his client and the consequences of such a failure.

If the accused is **not legally represented,** at the conclusion of the evidence for the prosecution (assuming there is a case to answer), the legal adviser should, in the presence of the magistrates, say to the accused:

> You have heard the evidence against you. Now is the time to make your defence. You may give evidence on oath, and be cross-examined like any other witness. If you do not give evidence, or having been sworn, without good cause refuse to answer any question, the court may draw such inferences as appear proper. That means they may hold it against you. You may also call any witness or witnesses whom you have arranged to attend court [today]. Afterwards, you may also, if you wish, address the court by arguing your case from the dock. But you cannot at that stage give evidence. Do you now intend to give evidence?

The Court of Appeal has held that the following must be highlighted when directing a jury on the application of s 35:

(i) The burden of proof remains on the prosecution throughout, and the prosecution must prove guilt beyond reasonable doubt.
(ii) The defendant is entitled to remain silent. That is his right and his choice. The right of silence remains.
(iii) An inference from failure to give evidence cannot on its own prove guilt; that is expressly stated in s 38(3) of the 1994 Act.
(iv) The court must be satisfied that the prosecution has established a case to answer before drawing any inferences from silence.
(v) If an accused person gives as a reason for not answering questions that he had been advised by his solicitor not to do so, that advice does not amount to a waiver of privilege, but that bare assertion is not likely of itself to be regarded as a sufficient reason for not mentioning matters relevant to the defence.
(vi) If, despite any evidence relied on to explain his silence or in the absence of any such evidence, the court concludes the silence can only sensibly be attributed to the defendant's having no answer, or none that would stand up to cross-examination, the court may draw an adverse inference: *R v Cowan* [1996] QB 373, [1995] 4 All ER 939, CA.

Subject to the above, the court may draw such inference as it deems appropriate.

The inference itself may be one solely as to credit, credibility or an inference as to guilt. However, the court may not convict solely on the basis of the inferences it has drawn (*R v Cowan* [1996] QB 373, [1995] 4 All ER 939, (1996) 160 JP 165; *R v Condron and Condron* [1997] 1 WLR 827, [1997] 1 Cr App Rep 185, CA; *Radford v Kent County Council* (1998) 162 JP 697; *R v Gough* (2001) 165 JPN 895; *R v Becouarn* [2005] UKHL 55, [2005] 1 WLR 2589).

A magistrates' court may not draw an inference from the defendant's failure to give evidence under s 35 of the CJPOA 1994 on account of his absence. However, a magistrates' court may draw an inference under s 35 from the defendant's failure to give evidence where he is present but a co-accused is not. There may be occasions where, in the interests of being seen to be even-handed to both defendants, the court will decline to draw an inference: *R v Hamidi* [2010] EWCA Crim 66, [2010] Crim LR 578.

D[6.23] Amendment of charge or information. Justices have a discretion to allow the amendment of a charge or information under the Magistrates' Courts Act 1980, s 123. This may even allege a different summary offence after the 6 month limitation period and even as late as the close of the prosecution case, but only where they are satisfied the allegation arises out of the same facts and it is in the interests of justice to allow the amendment (see *DPP v Everest* [2005] EWHC 1124 (Admin), [2005] All ER (D) 363 (May)).

In *DPP v Hammerton* [2009] EWHC 921 (Admin), [2009] 2 Cr App Rep 322, the Administrative Court stated that the CPS could not assume that they would be permitted to substitute or amend charges as a matter of course. The court retained a discretion to permit such a course of action but the overriding objective of the CPR 2005 (now CPR 2014), that a criminal case is dealt with justly, must be also be borne in mind. See also *Williams v DPP* [2009] EWHC 2354 (Admin), [2009] All ER (D) 292 (Jul)).

It is impermissible to amend an information by substituting a different defendant where the six-month statutory time limit has expired (*R (on the application of Sainsbury's Supermarkets Ltd) v Plymouth Magistrates' Court and R (on the application of J Sainsbury's Supermarkets Ltd) v Plymouth Magistrates' Court* [2006] EWHC 1749 (Admin), [2006] All ER (D) 137 (Jun)).

It is permissible to amend an information for an indictable offence to a summary only offence outside the six-month time limit provided the original information was laid within that time limit: *Dougall v Crown Prosecution Service* [2018] EWHC 1367 (Admin), [2018] Crim L R 763 (the original charge of assault occasioning actual bodily harm, which was sought to be amended to assault by beating, was laid eight months after the alleged offence; the proposed substitution was, consequently, time-barred by s 127 of the MCA 1980).

There are limitations on the power to amend an information. In *Shaw v DPP* [2007] EWHC 207 (Admin), a new charge was introduced in the defendant's absence after the expiry of the six-month time limit under s 127 MCA 1980, rendering him liable to imprisonment when he had not been before. In the circumstances it was not an appropriate course to take. Even if the justices had been justified in allowing the amendment, the term 'misled' in s 123(2) bore a very wide meaning and they should have adjourned to give the defendant a further opportunity to attend.

In *R (on the application of Thornhill) v Uxbridge Magistrates' Court* [2008] EWHC 508 (Admin), 172 JP 297, 172 JPN 580 the Divisional Court held that magistrates were wrong to allow the prosecution to amend an information alleging a failure to provide a specimen of breath to one of failure to provide a specimen of urine pursuant to s 7(6) of the Road Traffic Act 1988. The Divisional Court said that there was a distinct difference between the two offences and accordingly there was no need to consider if the amendment was 'in the interests of justice'. The procedures may be different but s 7(6) creates one offence of 'failing to provide a specimen'. This judgment does not sit well with previous judgments and by analogy *DPP v Butterworth* [1995] 1 AC 381, HL.

3 Guilty plea

D[6.24]–[6.25] A guilty plea must be unequivocal; when an accused purports to admit an offence but then adds words or offers an explanation redolent of a defence the legal adviser should normally be left to clarify the plea. If the defendant is unrepresented it might be advisable for the case to be stood back for the accused to seek independent legal advice from a solicitor. If the court concludes that the plea is equivocal it has no discretion but to substitute a plea of not guilty.

A guilty plea, however, is an admission of the offence charged and not necessarily of every fact which the prosecutor may allege as a circumstance of it. A guilty plea to assault, for example, would not indicate an acceptance of the prosecution's allegations of the number of blows struck or their severity. Where there is a dispute about an important circumstance of the offence either side may call evidence notwithstanding the guilty plea. The court can also decline to sentence until the matter has been resolved by evidence. This procedure is known as a **Newton hearing**. There are one or two exceptions. Evidence may also be called if there is a dispute relating to an ancillary matter, such as the amount of compensation or liability for back duty. The evidence should be confined solely to deciding the issue in question and, if the prosecution cannot establish its version of the facts beyond a reasonable doubt, the defence version must be accepted.

Where there is a dispute as to whether an offence is aggravated under section 146 of the CJA 2003, it is difficult to envisage circumstances in which the statutory aggravation would be immaterial. A Newton hearing is, therefore, necessary; protecting the victim from giving evidence is not a reason for not holding a Newton hearing: *DPP v Giles* [2019] EWHC 2015 (Admin), [2019] All ER (D) 175 (Jul).

See generally The Criminal Practice Directions 2015 Sentencing B: Determining the factual basis of sentence.

The other aspect of the question is that the court must sentence only on the basis of the case put forward by the prosecution and not on the basis of conclusions it might draw that the case is in reality more serious. For example, if a person is accused of two cases of theft from his employer the court must not infer that in fact this was a common occurrence and sentence accordingly. Sometimes the inference might be inescapable. The important thing is that it does not affect the sentence for the offence charged. There are exceptions to the above rule eg in the case of sample or specimen charges or offences admitted and taken into consideration. Magistrates should clarify the legal principles with their legal adviser.

D[6.26] **Application to change a plea of guilty to not guilty.** A magistrates' court may allow a defendant to withdrawn his plea of guilty at any time up to sentence being passed (*S (an infant) v Manchester City Recorder* [1971] AC 481, HL). The onus lies on a party seeking to vacate a guilty plea to demonstrate that justice requires that this should be permitted.

Where the defendant pleads guilty by post under s 12 of the MCA 1980 and the plea is accepted by the court, at an adjourned hearing the accused would have to seek leave to change his plea, in accordance with the CPR outlined immediately below: see *Rymer v DPP* [2010] EWHC 1848 (Admin), 174 CL&J 526.

For the principles and procedures governing the exercise of the discretion see *R v South Tameside Magistrates' Court, ex p Rowland* (1984) 148 JP 202. For a more recent authority see *DPP v Revitt* [2006] EWHC 2266 (Admin), [2006] NLJR 1476, (2006) 170 JP 729.

D[6.27] **Application to withdraw a guilty plea.** CrimPR, r 24.10 provides:

(2) The defendant must apply to do so –
  (a) as soon as practicable after becoming aware of the reasons for doing so; and
  (b) before sentence.

(3) Unless the court otherwise directs, the application must be in writing and the defendant must serve it on –
  (a) the court officer; and
  (b) the prosecutor.

(4) The application must –
  (a) explain why it would be unjust not to allow the defendant to withdraw the guilty plea;
  (b) identify –
    (i) any witness that the defendant wishes to call, and
    (ii) any other proposed witness; and
  (c) say whether the defendant waives legal professional privilege, giving any relevant name and date.

4 Legal Advice

D[6.28] The legal adviser has a duty to advise on matters of law and matters of mixed law and fact. Justices who refuse to act on his advice in a straightforward matter (eg a driver's liability to disqualification) may run the risk of being ordered to pay the costs of a consequent appeal. The justices are entitled to invite the legal adviser to retire with them if they think that a matter may arise on which they will seek his advice. In a case of any complexity it is wise to invite the legal adviser to retire at an early stage in order that he can give such advice as the occasion may require during the justices' discussions. If the legal adviser has taken a full note of the evidence he may be called upon to refresh the justices' memory from it. However, so far as it is practical to do so, the legal adviser should be asked to give his advice openly in court. This will not always be a practical way to give advice, especially in complicated matters, or where reference to books may be necessary, or where a discussion with one or more of the justices may be involved. The justices' clerk has the right to advise the justices even though he is not sitting with them in court so that, if he is available, he may always be sent for if necessary. It should be noted, however, where representations have been made to the court which the justices' clerk has not heard they should be repeated in the presence of the justices' clerk before he gives his advice to the bench. It is especially useful to bear this in mind when sitting with an inexperienced legal adviser. Equally, where the legal adviser finds it necessary to give advice in the retiring room on a point not canvassed with the advocates then the legal adviser should return to court telling them of the advice given and allowing them to address the bench if they have anything additional to contribute.

D[6.29] For a fuller account of the role of the justices' clerk and his staff see **Section F**.

5 *Consideration of guilt*

D[6.30] The question for justices to ask themselves at this stage is, 'Has the prosecutor satisfied the majority of us beyond reasonable doubt that the accused committed the offence with which he has been charged?' A reasonable doubt must not be a fanciful doubt nurtured by prejudice. The burden of proof, that is the degree to which a court should be convinced of guilt, is a matter of law and one on which the legal adviser can assist.

D[6.31] When announcing the decision in court it is generally better to avoid using a reference to 'the case'. It is better to say, 'We find you guilty of theft' or as the case may be, rather than, 'We find the case proved'. The accused feels he has 'a case' too, and the latter expression of the decision sometimes creates the impression that 'the case' which the court has been concerned with has been the prosecution case. The former method of announcing the decision leaves nothing to doubt or prejudice and is especially to be recommended when there has been more than one charge or accused.

6 *Reports etc*

D[6.32] Irrespective the plea, once the guilt of the accused has been established the court may hear further information about him relevant to sentence. The prosecutor will give information about previous convictions or the fact that there are none. He will also indicate if the accused has admitted other similar offences which he wishes the court to take into consideration when determining the sentence. These will have been written down and should be put one by one by the clerk and the accused should be asked to signify his admission of each such offence separately. This is important because offences admitted and taken into consideration ('TICs' as these offences are usually known) may be significant in the sentencing decision and because (especially if there is a long list) it is very easy for the police to include in a list of outstanding offences some which a prisoner will admit through not giving the matter proper thought. Compensation may be ordered in respect of offences taken into consideration and this is another reason for being procedurally correct when dealing with them. The maximum amount of compensation depends on the number of substantive charges eg a plea of guilty to two charges of theft and 24 TICs means that the magistrates' powers to award compensation are limited to £10,000 (£5,000 per offence).

D[6.33] Also at this stage the prosecutor will ask for any appropriate ancillary orders such as costs or the forfeiture of a weapon or drugs, etc. The chairman should make a written note of such matters so that they are not overlooked when the final sentencing decision is made. See *Nicholas v Chester Magistrates' Court* [2009] EWHC 1504 (Admin). As a general proposition, magistrates adjourning for a full pre-sentence report cannot bind the sentencing court as to the general level of sentence, unless the same magistrates return to deal with the offender. Magistrates must also have regard to the SC Magistrates' Courts Sentencing Guidelines under s 172(1)(b) of the Criminal Justice Act 2003 when giving an indication as to the level of sentence proposed: see *Thornton v CPS* [2010] EWHC 346 (Admin), 174 JP 121.

D[6.34] **Pre-sentence report.** The court may at this stage consider a pre-sentence report and if one is not available the question of an adjournment in order to obtain one should not be overlooked. Although they need not do so if they are of the opinion that it is unnecessary, it is still a statutory requirement for a magistrates' court to consider a pre-sentence report before imposing any custodial sentence or a community sentence (except a probation order with no additional requirements, although the obtaining of a pre-sentence report is nevertheless still strongly advised).

D[6.35] The pre-sentence report is to assist the court in determining the most suitable method of dealing with an offender. The responsibility for determining the seriousness of an offence remains solely with the magistrates. However, the pre-sentence report will contain impartial advice and information and will balance the aggravating and mitigating factors in the case and report on the nature of the defendants offending: *R v Salisbury Magistrates' Court, ex p Gray* [2000] 1 Cr App Rep (S) 267, 163 JP 732. The report may give advice in support of a particular sentence although it will bear in mind the ultimate responsibility of the sentencer. The Crown prosecutor may make representations on matters contained in the pre-sentence report.

D[6.36] **Short or fast-delivery reports.** It is now common for the probation service to offer either to interview the defendant at court that day, or on a date in the near future, with the report being given either orally or in writing shortly after the interview. 'Fast delivery' reports are not offered, however, in cases of domestic violence or where more detailed investigation is necessary, eg as to a mental health or a substance abuse problems.

Suitability for a curfew or unpaid work can often be assessed by way of a stand down and short interview.

D[6.37] **Medical report.** Where the offender is, or appears to be, mentally disordered, the court must, if it is considering a custodial sentence, obtain a medical report. Such a report is made orally or in writing by a doctor approved under the Mental Health Act 1983 as having experience in the diagnosis or treatment of mental disorder. As to directions for commissioning medical reports for sentencing purposes, see Crim PR r 28.8, which was inserted by SI 2018/847.

D[6.38] Reports from other sources may be available, for example, a reference from an offender's employer or educational establishment etc. In any case where the court thinks fit it may adjourn and call upon the maker of a report to attend for questioning upon its contents.

D[6.39] The court must give the accused or his solicitor and the Crown Prosecutor a copy of the pre-sentence report. In the youth court the report will be given to a parent or guardian. It is very important, however, that the accused is aware of the contents of any written report submitted to the court. It is not considered entirely satisfactory simply to hand a written report to an unrepresented defendant in court. He may have difficulty in reading, especially in the stressful situation of court proceedings, so that he may not absorb the contents of the report at all, or he may not have finished reading it by the time he is invited to comment on it. Furthermore, he may not understand the meaning of everything he reads and he almost certainly will have had inadequate time to gather his thoughts and to express a useful opinion about anything contained in the report. The better practice, therefore, is that the probation officer (or youth offending officer) has discussed the contents of the pre-sentence report and especially the implications of any proposal therein, with the offender before the case is dealt with in court.

7 Guilty plea by post procedure

D[6.40] This is a quick and effective procedure for dealing with summary cases, in the absence of the accused (specified proceedings). The procedures outlined below only apply to offences dealt with in the adult court and those offences which do not carry a term of imprisonment of more than three months.

D[6.41] A summons is served on the defendant along with a witness statement of evidence. The defendant may plead guilty in absence on the basis of the evidence supplied and the clerk to the court reads the statement (or if directed by the court a summary) in open court before the court decides to accept the plea.

D[6.42] The legal adviser will then read any statement in mitigation from the defendant and any statement of means is considered along with the driving licence, in endorsable cases. The court may then pass sentence or adjourn if it requires the defendant's attendance, for example if it is considering a disqualification. This may be done in the absence of a prosecutor.

D[6.43] Failure to respond. If the summons and statements are properly served but the defendant fails to respond the proceedings become non-specified and the prosecution may use the evidence in the statements to prove the case against the defendant at the first hearing.

D[6.44] Not guilty plea. Where the defendant indicates in writing that he wishes to plead not guilty but attends court to give evidence the statement may be used at an adjourned trial date unless the defendant has indicated he wishes any of the prosecution witnesses to attend court. Note that the police will be able to ask for costs in writing against a defendant who has either pleaded guilty or been convicted on the statements served. There is also a hybrid procedure of serving the defendant with a statement of facts, upon which he may enter a guilty plea, and witness statements which will be used if he fails to enter a plea.

D[6.44A] Trial by single justice on the papers. The Criminal Justice and Courts Act 2015 introduced trial by a single justice on the papers by the insertion of new ss 16A–16E in the Magistrates' Courts Act 1980. The main features of the new procedure are as follows.

(1) Where a relevant prosecutor issues a written charge it must (but see infra) at the same time issue a requisition *or* a single justice procedure notice: Criminal Justice Act 2003, s 29(2). The latter course may be taken in respect of any summary offence not punishable with imprisonment where the defendant is an adult. For the conditions of trial by a single justice on the papers, see Magistrates' Courts Act 1980, s 16A.

(2) Service of the notice must be accompanied by service of such documents as are prescribed by the criminal Procedure Rules: Magistrates' Courts Act 1980, s 16A(2), Criminal Justice Act 2003, s 29(3B).

(3) The notice is a document which requires the recipient to indicate his plea to the charge and, if guilty, whether or not he wishes the case to be tried in accordance with the single justice procedure: Criminal Justice Act 2003, s 29(2B).

(4) If the recipient indicates a not guilty plea or a desire not to be dealt with under the single justice procedure the case will proceed before a full court in the normal way: Magistrates' Courts Act 1980, s 16A(1)(d). The court must then issue a summons to the accused: Magistrates' Courts Act 1980, s 16B(3).Otherwise, provided the court is satisfied as to service of the notice and accompanying documents, the case may proceed under the single justice procedure.

(5) Only the documents which have been served and any written mitigation from the defendant may be considered; oral evidence is not permitted: Magistrates' Courts Act 1980, s 16A(3). The proceedings may be held in private and in the absence of the parties: Magistrates' Courts Act 1980, s 16A(6)–(7). If the court decides that it is not appropriate to convict the accused under the single justice procedure it may not try or continue to try the charge in that way; the trial must be adjourned, if has begun, and a summons must be issued requiring the accused to appear before the court for trial: Magistrates' Courts Act 1980, s 16B(3).

(6) The court may also decide after conviction that it is not appropriate to try the matter under the single justice procedure, or the court may propose to disqualify the defendant under ss 34 or 35 of the Road Traffic Offenders Act 1988 and thus be obliged to give the defendant the opportunity to make representations. In the first case the court must adjourn the trial and issue a summons, and the same applies in the second case if the defendant indicates a wish to make representations: Magistrates' Courts Act 1980, s 16C.

(7) Provision is made for the making of a statutory declaration where the defendant was not aware of the single justice procedure notice: Magistrates' Courts Act 1980, s 16E.

(8) The powers of the single justice on conviction are restricted to orders of discharge, fines, ancillary financial orders and orders of endorsement and disqualification: Magistrates' Courts Act 1980, s 121(5A).

A failure to issue a requisition or single justice procedure notice at the same time as the charge may be a procedural error but it does not render the proceedings a nullity: *DPP v McFarlane* [2019] EWHC 1895.

See further the Criminal Procedure Rules 2015, r 24.9.

8 Appeals

D[6.45] There are three common forms of appeal from the Magistrates' Courts.

D[6.46] **Appeal against conviction and or sentence to the Crown Court.** Notice for such an appeal must be lodged within 21 days of the date of sentence. This time limit may be extended with the consent of the Crown Court (s 108 MCA 1980).

D[6.47] **Appeal by way of case stated to the High Court on a point of law.** The justices may be asked to state a case within 21 days of their decision. There is no power to extend this period. Once an application for a case stated is made the right to appeal to the Crown Court normally ceases (s 111 MCA 1980) (confirmed in *Mishra v Colchester Magistrates' Court, Colquhoun v Stratford Magistrates' Court* [2017] EWHC 2869 (Admin), (2018) 182 JP 89, [2018] Crim L R 245).

D[6.48] **Application for judicial review.** This application must be lodged with the High Court as soon as practicable and in any event within 3 months of the grounds for the appeal arising (Senior Courts Act 1981, ss 29, 31; Civil Procedure Rules 1998, Part 54). If successful the High Court may make quashing, prohibiting and mandatory orders to correct or prevent an error in law or a failure to exercise jurisdiction. See for example *R (on the application of Durham County Council) v North Durham Justices* [2004] EWHC 1073 (Admin), [2004] All ER (D) 260 (Apr).

Sections 84 and 85 of the Criminal Justice and Courts Act 2015 amended the Senior Courts Act 1981 to provide that the court must refuse to grant leave or a remedy where it considers that it is highly likely that the outcome for the applicant would not have been substantially different if the conduct complained of had not occurred.

Where justices (or the Crown Court on appeal) refuse to state a case, the aggrieved should apply without delay for permission to bring judicial review, either to compel the justices to state a case and/or to quash the order sought to be appealed. Where the court below has already given a reasoned judgment containing all the necessary findings of fact and/or explained its refusal to state a case in terms which clearly raise the true point of law in issue, the correct course is for the single judge, if the point is properly arguable, to grant permission for judicial review which directly challenges the order complained of and thereby avoids the need for a case stated at all: *Sunworld Ltd v Hammersmith and Fulham London Borough Council* [2000] 2 All ER 837, [2000] 1 WLR 2102, followed in *R (Arthur) v Crown Court at Blackfriars* [2017] EWHC 3416 (Admin), [2018] 2 Cr App R 4.

D[7]

Publicly funded representation

Introduction and civil legal aid

D[7.1] Part 1 of the Legal Aid, Sentencing and Punishment of Offenders Act 2012 (LASPOA 2012) established an entirely new framework for the provision of publicly funded legal services.

The Act abolished the Legal Services Commission and established a Director of Legal Aid Casework who leads an executive agency within the Ministry of Justice which administers the delivery of legal aid services in England and Wales. The Lord Chancellor has broad powers to issue directions and guidance, but may not do so in individual cases.

The Act fundamentally changed the nature of civil legal aid by making it available only for those areas of law which are expressly included, which are listed in Sch 1 (provision for exceptional cases is made by s 10).

The Civil Legal Aid (Procedure) Regulations 2012, SI 2012/3098, have been made about the making and withdrawal of determinations that an individual qualifies for civil legal services under the Act.

The Civil Legal Aid (Merits Criteria) Regulations 2013, SI 2013/104 have also been made to prescribe the criteria the Director of Legal Aid Casework must apply when determining whether or not an individual or legal person qualifies for such services.

Criminal legal aid

D[7.2] The scheme for criminal legal aid (other than as to the administrative framework) remains substantially the same, though there are two changes of note. The first is that provision is made (by LASPOA 2012, s 20) for the Director or a court to make a provisional determination that an individual qualifies for representation in criminal proceedings where the individual is involved in an investigation which may result in such proceedings. The second is that Sch 3 to the Act enables the grant of legal aid to 'legal persons' other than individuals.

D[7.3] The Criminal Legal Aid (General) Regulations 2013, SI 2013/9, have been made to deal with the scope, making and withdrawal of applications, appeals, etc. The principal features are described below.

Scope of publicly funded representation

D[7.4] Advice and assistance is provided for people under arrest and held in custody. The application for initial advice and assistance must be made to the Defence Solicitor Call Centre and in accordance with the requirements set out in the 2010 Standard Crime Contract for the Unit of Work which is the subject of the application (LASPOA 2012, s 13 and The Criminal Legal Aid (General) Regulations 2013, Pt 2). Police station work is not means tested.

'Criminal proceedings' includes: proceedings in magistrates' courts for failure to pay a sum due or to obey an order of the court where such failure carries a risk of imprisonment; and proceedings in relation to various kinds of behaviour orders, eg ASBOs, football banning orders, restraining orders on acquittal (LASPOA 2012, s 14 and the Criminal Legal Aid (General) Regulations 2013, reg 9).

Prescribed advice and assistance is made available to individuals falling within certain categories where one of the prescribed conditions (listed in the Criminal Legal Aid (General) Regulations 2013, reg 12) is met and the Director has determined that the individual qualifies for advice and assistance having regard to the interests of justice and subject to financial eligibility. The latter is governed by the Criminal Legal Aid (Financial Resources) Regulations 2013, SI 2013/471. The client must pass both the income and capital tests, but persons in receipt of certain kinds of benefits automatically qualify. Income from certain sources is excepted, eg disability living allowance, but the income and capital of any partner are taken into account. Capital includes all assets and resources, but, where the client owns property, disregarding the first £100,000 of any equity.

The application must be made in accordance with the requirements of the 2010 Standard Crime Contract for the Unit of Work which is the subject of the application. If the Director determines not to grant the application on interests of justice grounds or because the qualifying criteria of the 2010 Contract are not met, an appeal may be made to the Independent Funding Adjudicator.

Advice and assistance covers all necessary work, other than police station work up to the point of charge or summons. Costs are limited to £300, though this can be extended on application.

Qualification for representation post charge or summons – representation orders

D[7.5] Qualification for representation in criminal proceedings is determined in accordance with the financial resources of the individual and the interests of justice (LASPOA 2012, s 17(1)).

In determining what the interests of justice consist of certain factors (LASPOA 2012, s 17(2) must be taken into account, namely:

(a) whether the applicant would be likely to lose his or her liberty or livelihood or to suffer serious damage to his or her reputation;
(b) whether consideration may need to be given to a substantial question of law;
(c) whether the applicant may be unable to understand the proceedings or to state his or her own case;
(d) whether the proceedings may involve the tracing, interviewing or expert cross examination of witnesses on behalf of the applicant; and
(e) whether it is in the interests of another person that the applicant be represented.

Guidance on the merits test will be found at www.gov.uk/guidance/work-out-who-qualifies-for-criminal-legal-aid.

D[7.6] The Criminal Legal Aid (General) Regulations 2013 further provide as follows. Proceedings (other than appeals) in the Crown Court, High Court, Court of Appeal and the Supreme Court automatically meet the interest of justice test. A determination in relation to proceedings before the magistrates' court automatically includes representation in the Crown Court following sending or committal for trial or sentence, but not in relation to appeals.

Where legal aid has been refused on interest of justice grounds, or withdrawn on those grounds, an appeal lies to the magistrates' court (which for this purpose includes a single justice or District Judge (magistrates' courts)), which must either affirm the determination or decide that the interests of justice require representation to be available or to continue to be available. If an appeal succeeds, legal aid must be granted if the individual's financial circumstances have not changed so as to make him financially ineligible.

As to the application of the regulations to 'legal persons' other than individuals, see Part 6 of the Regulations.

Financial eligibility

D[7.7] Representation orders (ROs) are means tested. Applications are made to the administrative centre for the court where the case is to be heard, which will apply the means test. (Complex financial cases are referred to the Legal Aid Agency's National Courts Team.)

Details of the test and eligibility limits will be found in the Criminal Legal Aid (Financial Resources) Regulations 2013, SI 2013/471.

Certain benefits are 'passported', ie confer automatic eligibility, namely:

- income support;
- income-based jobseeker's allowance;
- guarantee state pension credit;
- income related employment and support allowance; and
- universal credit.

This includes being a dependant in another person's claim to such a benefit.

If the applicant's gross income (defined below) is below the initial threshold, currently £12,475 pa, eligibility is again automatic. If gross income is over £22,325 pa the converse applies. Between these figures, a full means test to determine disposable income will be necessary. If this is found to be less than £3,398 pa the applicant will be eligible.

Assistance for assessing financial eligibility can be found at: www.justice.gov.uk/legal-aid/assess-your-clients-eligibility/criminal-eligibility-calculator.

'Gross income' is income from all sources, excluding certain benefits. It includes income received by the applicant's partner, unless the partner has a 'contrary interest' in the proceedings, eg is a prosecution witness. It also includes financial resources and maintenance received from another person.

Allowance is made for the applicant's partner and children by giving each such family member a weighting, adding these to 1 and then dividing the gross income by the resultant total. For example, the weighting for a partner is 0.64 and, for a child 2-4 years, 0.3. Thus, if the applicant has a partner and two such children the divider will be 1 + 0.64 + 0.3 + 0.3 = 2.24.

'Disposable income' is gross income minus:

- tax and NI;
- council tax;
- rent, mortgage, etc;
- childcare costs;
- maintenance payments; and
- living expenses allowance.

Living expenses allowance is increased using the same weighting scale for family members. The current base figure is £5.676. So, using the above example of an applicant with a partner and two small children, this will be multiplied by 2.24 = £12,714.

Proof of means is always necessary unless the applicant is in custody, in which case a statement of truth must be signed instead.

D[7.8] An RO is deemed to be granted on the date that a proper application was received. As a general rule, there can be no claim for prior work, but an order can be back-dated where urgent work was necessary (defined as a hearing within ten working days of taking initial instructions), and there was no undue delay in making the application (it was submitted no more than five days after taking initial instructions).

Where legal aid is refused on means an 'early cover' fixed fee of £75 may be claimed if certain conditions are met. Where legal aid is refused on the merits a 'pre-order cover' claim, limited to one hour's preparation at preparation rates, may be made if a qualified solicitor states on the file why it was believed the interests of justice test was passed, and not claim for early cover is made.

D[7.9] Where an individual is not financially eligible, but can demonstrate that to pay privately would cause hardship, an application can be made for hardship funding. The application is made to the Legal Aid Authority rather than the courts.

Choice of legal representative

D[7.10] The Criminal Legal Aid (Determinations by a Court and Choice of Representative) Regulations 2013, SI 2013/614, deal in Part 3 with the selection of representatives, changes of representation and level of representation. The position in the magistrates' court is summarised below.

Where there is a co-defendant, the same provider must be selected unless the relevant court or the Director determines that there is or is likely to be a conflict of interest.

There is no right to change providers unless there has been a breakdown in the relationship between the defendant and the original provider, or there is some other compelling reason why the latter cannot continue to act, or the latter considers that he is professionally obliged to withdraw or can no longer represent the defendant for reasons beyond the provider's control and the court has been provided with the relevant details. It has been held that, if it is the litigator's view that there has been no breakdown, the defendant cannot rely on the absence of details of the nature of the breakdown for the purpose of contending 'some other compelling reason': *R v Iqbal (Naseem)* [2011] EWCA Crim 1294, [2011] 2 Cr App Rep 250, (2011) Times, 21 April.

Where representation has been withdrawn and there is a subsequent determination that the defendant qualifies for representation, the original provider must be selected unless the relevant court determines there are good reasons why a different provider should be selected.

Representation may not include an advocate unless the proceedings relate to an extradition hearing under the Extradition Act 2003 or an indictable offence, and the relevant court determines that because there are circumstances which make the proceedings unusually grave or difficult, representation by an advocate would be desirable. Where these criteria are met in an extradition case, the court may determine that representation may consist of Queen's counsel or more than one advocate if the relevant court determines that the defendant could not otherwise be adequately represented.

Contribution orders

D[7.11] The Criminal Legal Aid (Contribution Orders) Regulations 2013, I 2013/483 make provision for the liability of individuals to make a payment in connection with the provision of representation, based on an assessment of the financial resources of the individual. The Regulations apply to Crown Court trials (Part 2) and appeals to the Crown Court (Part 3). Part 4 of the Regulations deals with the enforcement of contribution orders. Overdue sums payable under the Regulations are recoverable summarily as a civil debt.

Duty solicitor work

D[7.12] A solicitor who has passed both the Police Station Qualification and the Magistrates' Court Qualification and has registered as a duty solicitor with the LAA is entitled to apply to join the duty solicitor rota of his/her local court.

Duty solicitors advise and assist persons who would otherwise be unrepresented.

Court duty advice is available to those who qualify for assistance without regard to means. The duty solicitor scheme covers a wide area of representation, but excludes conducting trials or acting in cases where the client has had the services of a duty solicitor at a previous hearing.

A duty solicitor may, with the client's permission, apply for a representation order, but this should not be done where the case concludes on the day of the duty.

D[8]

Remands in custody and on bail

'Remand'

D[8.1] When a case is adjourned to a fresh date the defendant may be remanded to ensure his attendance at the next hearing. The accused may be remanded in custody or released on bail.

Bail and the Human Rights Act 1998

D[8.2] Some sections of the Bail Act 1976 have been subject to challenge under the ECHR, for example the power to remove bail based solely on a police officer's belief that a defendant will breach a bail condition (Sch 1, Part 1, para 6). It is now established that while there is no need for a full inquiry following an arrest for breach of bail conditions, Art 5 does apply to any remand in custody (*R v Havering Magistrates' Court, ex p DPP* [2001] 3 All ER 997, [2000] All ER (D) 2307).

However, the Bail Act as outlined before should comply with Convention requirements if the overall concepts of fairness and proportionality are borne in mind. For example, a defendant may be remanded in custody on substantial grounds that he will commit a further offence, but that must relate to a serious offence based solely on the facts of the individual case. See *HB v Switzerland* (Application No 26899/95) (2001) 37 EHRR 1000, [2001] ECHR 26899/95, ECtHR for the application of Article 5 to the defendant's rights on arrest and production before a court.

D[8.3] **Remand on unconditional bail.** The accused is released with an obligation to surrender to the custody of the court on a certain day at a specified time. If he fails to do so, there are two consequences: the court can immediately issue a warrant for his arrest and he may be prosecuted for the criminal offence of failing to answer his bail.

D[8.4] **Remand on conditional bail.** The accused is on bail but with conditions attached to that bail, to ensure that he appears at court on the appointed day at the appropriate time or does not commit offences in the meantime or does not interfere with the witnesses in the case.

D[8.5] **Remand in custody.** Where bail is refused, the defendant is detained in prison or in police cells until his next appearance in court.

D[8.6] **Youths.** For the remands of children and young persons aged under 18, see E[3.3]–[3.18].

When must the court remand?

D[8.7] Where the court is acting with a view to committal for trial or sending an accused to the Crown Court for trial the accused must always be remanded on bail or in custody.

D[8.8] If the offence is triable either way, the court must always remand where the accused was initially arrested by the police and brought to court in custody or bailed for his appearance, or he has previously been remanded in the proceedings.

D[8.9] Where the offence is purely summary, the court always has a discretion whether to remand or simply adjourn the case.

D[8.10]–[8.15] In the case of juveniles (under 18) the court may remand if it thinks it is necessary to do so in those cases where it must do so when the defendant is 18 or over.

Length of the remand – before conviction

D[8.16] **In custody.** A remand in custody is not normally for longer than 8 clear days, ie the day when the decision to remand is made and the day when the defendant is next due to appear in court, are excluded. Therefore a remand in custody may be from the Monday of one week to the Wednesday of the next.

D[8.17] There are three major exceptions:

(a) If the defendant is to be kept in police cells, the maximum period is 3 clear days or 24 hours in the case of a juvenile.
(b) Where the accused is already serving a custodial sentence and will not be released in the intervening period, he may be remanded for up to 28 days.
(c) The court may remand a defendant present before the court who has previously been remanded in custody for a period not exceeding when the next stage of the proceedings is reached or 28 days, whichever is the less. In exercising this power the court will have to have regard to the total length of time which the accused would spend in custody if it were to exercise the power. This would not affect the right of the defendant to apply for bail during this period.

D[8.18] **On bail.** Unless the accused consents, a remand on bail cannot be for more than 8 clear days. However, defendants always do consent to longer remands and that is why, as mentioned above, it is important for the magistrates to exercise control over the granting of adjournments. It should be remembered that bail is always granted to a fixed date and so it is not possible to adjourn a case *sine die* where the accused is remanded. An exception to this rule is a send to the Crown Court although a plea and directions hearing may be specified.

Length of remand – after conviction

D[8.19] A remand after conviction (for further inquiries and pre-sentence reports) cannot be for longer than 3 weeks if in custody, or should not be for longer than 4 weeks on bail.

Send to the Crown Court

D[8.20] When a magistrates' court commit or sends proceedings to the Crown Court for trial (or commits for sentence) the court may order the accused to be kept in custody until his trial (or sentence) or it may grant him bail.

Remands in the absence of the accused

D[8.21] An application for a remand for not more than 8 clear days may in prescribed circumstances be heard in the absence of the accused. The conditions to be complied with before this is possible are as follows:

(a) the court is adjourning a case before conviction; and
(b) the accused is present before the court;
(c) he is legally represented before the court (although his solicitor need not necessarily be present in court).

D[8.22] The accused must be asked whether he consents to future remands being determined in his absence. If he does, the court may remand him for up to three occasions in his absence. This means that the defendant must be brought before the court every four weeks. If the accused withdraws his consent or for any reason ceases to be legally represented, arrangements will be made by the justices' clerk to bring him before the court at the earliest opportunity, even though the period of his remand has not expired.

D[8.22A] **Video remands.** The Crime and Disorder Act 1998, s 57 provides for the use of video conferencing between the prison and the court for defendants previously refused bail in person. No consent is required and the defendant's next physical appearance before either the magistrates' court or the Crown Court will be for trial or plea and sentence.

Section 57 has had new sections added by s 45 of the Police and Justice Act 2006. The 2006 Act has extended a video remand hearing to include eg youths remanded to local authority accommodation or youth detention accommodation; and live video links are available for the sentencing hearing of adult and youths remanded to local authority accommodation or youth detention accommodation where the defendant consents. The new provisions came into force on **15 January 2007**. Further amendments have since been made by the Coroners and Justice Act 2009 from **14 December 2009**.

Justices are advised to consult their legal adviser before making an order.

D[8.22B] **Vulnerable accused – live video links.** From **15 January 2007** the Youth Justice and Criminal Evidence Act 1999 was amended to permit a direction for a vulnerable accused to give evidence by a live link. A court may give a direction on the application of the accused for the accused to give evidence via live video link where –

(1) the accused is aged *under 18*; his ability to participate effectively is compromised by his level of intellectual ability or social functioning; and the live link would enable him to participate more effectively in proceedings; or

(2) the accused has *attained the age of 18*; is suffering from a mental disorder and for that reason is unable to participate effectively; and that the live link would enable more effective participation.

D[8.22C] **Live links in criminal proceedings – witnesses.** From **26 April 2010** the Criminal Justice Act 2003, s 51, provides that if a magistrates' court so directs, a witness may give evidence through a live link at suitable premises other than court premises. The direction may be given in relation either to a trial or where the accused has pleaded guilty eg a "Newton hearing". A direction may be given on the application by a party to the proceedings or of the court's own motion. A direction may not be given unless the court is satisfied that it is in the interests of the efficient or effective administration of justice for the person concerned to give evidence in the proceedings through a live link. There is provision for the court to review and rescind a live video link direction: CJA 2003, s 52.

D[8.23] If the defendant has been remanded on bail or in custody and cannot appear because of accident or illness, the court may further remand him in absence. A court can always further remand in absence an accused who is on bail. *R (on the application of Grimshaw) v Leeds Magistrates' Court* [2001] EWHC Admin 880, [2001] All ER (D) 350 (Oct) is authority for a remand in the absence of the accused where he has not been produced due to a mistake.

The decision whether to remand in custody or on bail

D[8.24] **Presumption of liberty.** The general principle is that an accused man has a right to be released on bail where he has not been convicted of the charge or where his case has been adjourned for pre-sentence reports. This means that the accused never has to apply for bail, it is up to the prosecution to object to his right to bail (although in practice the defence are referred to as making an application for bail). Therefore, it is no reason for remanding an accused in custody that he has not applied for bail. However this right to bail does not apply to a committal to the Crown Court for sentence.

D[8.25] **Grant of opposed bail.** Where the court grants bail following a prosecution objection to bail the court must state its reasons for doing so.

Exceptions to the right to bail

Disapplication of exceptions to the right to bail where there is no real prospect that the defendant will be sentenced to a custodial sentence

D[8.26] The Legal Aid, Sentencing and Punishment of Offenders Act 2012 made significant amendments to the Bail Act 1976 with the aim of increasing the availability of bail. Of particular note, *certain* exceptions to the right to bail do not apply to bail in non extradition proceedings where:

(a) the defendant has attained the age of 18;
(b) the defendant has not been convicted of an offence in those proceedings; and
(c) it appears to the court that there is no real prospect that the defendant will be sentenced to a custodial sentence in the proceedings.

The exceptions in the narrative below which are not disapplied are marked ***.

Imprisonable offences other than summary only offences and low value criminal damage, etc

D[8.27] The defendant need not be granted bail in the following cases (which are listed in the order in which they appear in Part 1 of Schedule 1 to the Bail Act 1976).

(1) The court is satisfied that there are substantial grounds for believing that the defendant, if released on bail (whether subject to conditions or not) would:
 (a) fail to surrender to custody; or
 (b) commit an offence while on bail; or
 (c) interfere with witnesses or otherwise obstruct the course of justice, whether in relation to himself or any other person.

 In taking the decisions required by this exception the court shall have regard to such of the following considerations as appear to it to be relevant, namely:
 (i) the nature and seriousness of the offence or default (and the probable method of dealing with the defendant for it);
 (ii) the character, antecedents, associations and community ties of the defendant;
 (iii) the defendant's record as respects the fulfilment of his obligations under previous grants of bail in criminal proceedings;
 (iv) except in the case of a defendant whose case is adjourned for inquiries or a report, the strength of the evidence of his having committed the offence or having defaulted;
 (v) if the court is satisfied that there are substantial grounds for believing that the defendant, if released on bail (whether subject to conditions or not), would commit an offence while on bail, the risk that the defendant may do so by engaging in conduct that would, or would be likely to, cause physical or mental injury to any person other than the defendant,

 as well as to any others which appear to be relevant.

(2) The court is satisfied that there are substantial grounds for believing that the defendant, if released on bail conditionally or unconditionally, would commit an offence on bail by engaging in conduct that would, or would be likely to, cause:
 (a) physical or mental injury to an associated person (this means a person who is associated with the defendant within the meaning of s 62 of the Family Law Act 1996); or
 (b) an associated person to fear physical or mental injury.***

(3) Where:
 (a) the offence is an indictable offence or an offence triable either way; and
 (b) it appears to the court that the defendant was on bail in criminal proceedings on the date of the offence.

(4) The court is satisfied that the defendant should be kept in custody for his own protection or, if he is a child or young person, for his own welfare.***

(5) The defendant is serving a custodial sentence.***

(6) The court is satisfied that it has not been practicable to obtain sufficient information for the purpose of taking the decisions required by this Part of this Schedule for want of time since the institution of the proceedings against him.***

(7) Where, having previously been released on bail in, or in connection with, the proceedings, the defendant has been arrested in pursuance of s 7 of the Bail Act 1976 (absconding or breaking bail conditions).

(8) (This relates to defendants charged with murder, but in such cases bail decisions must be made by a Crown Court judge.)***

(9) In relation only to a defendant whose case is adjourned for inquires or a report, the defendant need not be granted bail if it appears to the court that it would be impracticable to complete the inquiries or make the report without keeping the defendant in custody.***

*** This exception is not subject to the 'no real prospect of a custodial sentence' qualification: see para D[8.26], above.

Exceptions to the right to bail: summary-only imprisonable offences and low value criminal damage, etc

The no real prospect of a custodial sentence disapplication (see D[8.26], above) applies to the exceptions listed below other than those marked***.

D[8.28] The defendant need not be granted bail in the following cases (which are listed in the order in which they appear in Part 1A of Schedule 1 to the Bail Act 1976):

(1) Where:
  (a) it appears to the court that, having been previously granted bail in criminal proceedings, he has failed to surrender to custody in accordance with his obligations under the grant of bail; and
  (b) the court believes, in view of that failure, that the defendant, if released on bail (whether subject to conditions or not) would fail to surrender to custody.

(2) Where:
  (a) it appears to the court that the defendant was on bail in criminal proceedings on the date of the offence; and
  (b) the court is satisfied that there are substantial grounds for believing that the defendant, if released on bail (whether subject to conditions or not) would commit an offence while on bail.

(3) If the court is satisfied that there are substantial grounds for believing that the defendant, if released on bail (whether subject to conditions or not), would commit an offence while on bail by engaging in conduct that would, or would be likely to, cause:
  (a) physical or mental injury to an associated person (within the meaning of s 62 of the Family Law Act 1996); or
  (b) an associated person to fear physical or mental injury.***

(4) If the court is satisfied that the defendant should be kept in custody for his own protection or, if he is a child or young person, for his own welfare.***

(5) Where the defendant is a serving prisoner.***

(6) Where:
  (a) having previously been released on bail in, or in connection with, the proceedings, the defendant has been arrested in pursuance of s 7 of the Bail Act 1976 (absconding or breaking bail conditions); and
  (b) the court is satisfied that there are substantial grounds for believing that the defendant, if released on bail (whether subject to conditions or not) would fail to surrender to custody, commit an offence while on bail or interfere with witnesses or otherwise obstruct the course of justice (whether in relation to himself or any other person).

(7) The defendant need not be granted bail where the court is satisfied that it has not been practicable to obtain sufficient information for the purpose of taking the decisions required by this Part of this Schedule for want of time since the institution of the proceedings against him.***

Exceptions to the right to bail: non-imprisonable offences

D[8.29] The defendant need not be granted bail in the following cases (which are listed in the order in which they appear in Part II of Schedule 1 to the Bail Act 1976).

(1) Where defendant is a child or young person or has been convicted in the proceedings of an offence and:
  (a) it appears to the court that, having been previously granted bail in criminal proceedings, he has failed to surrender to custody in accordance with his obligations under the grant of bail; and

(b) the court believes, in view of that failure, that the defendant, if released on bail (whether subject to conditions or not) would fail to surrender to custody.

(2) If the court is satisfied that the defendant should be kept in custody for his own protection or, if he is a child or young person, for his own welfare.

(3) Where the defendant is a serving prisoner.

(4) Where the defendant is a child or young person or has been convicted in the proceedings of an offence and:

(a) having been released on bail in or in connection with the proceedings for the offence, he has been arrested in pursuance of s 7 of this Act (absconding or breaking bail conditions); and

(b) the court is satisfied that there are substantial grounds for believing that the defendant, if released on bail (whether subject to conditions or not) would fail to surrender to custody, commit an offence on bail or interfere with witnesses or otherwise obstruct the course of justice (whether in relation to himself or any other person).

(5) Where:

(a) having been released on bail in, or in connection with, the proceedings for the offence, the defendant has been arrested in pursuance of s 7 (absconding or breaking bail conditions), and

(b) the court is satisfied that there are substantial grounds for believing that the defendant, if released on bail (whether subject to conditions or not), would commit an offence while on bail by engaging in conduct that would, or would be likely to, cause:

(i) physical or mental injury to an associated person (within the meaning of s 62 of the Family Law Act 1996); or

(ii) an associated person to fear physical or mental injury.

Special provision for drug users

D[8.30] Subject to the proviso stated below, a defendant who meets the following conditions may not be granted bail unless the court is of the opinion that that there is no significant risk of his committing an offence while on bail (whether subject to conditions or not). This exception does not apply to non-imprisonable offences, but applies in all other cases.

The conditions are:

(a) the defendant is aged 18 or over;

(b) a sample taken:

(i) under s 63B of the Police and Criminal Evidence Act 1984 (testing for presence of Class A drugs) in connection with the offence; or

(ii) under s 161 of the Criminal Justice Act 2003 (drug testing after conviction of an offence but before sentence),

has revealed the presence in his body of a specified Class A drug;

(c) either the offence is one under s 5(2) or (3) of the Misuse of Drugs Act 1971 and relates to a specified Class A drug, or the court is satisfied that there are substantial grounds for believing:

(i) that misuse by him of any specified Class A drug caused or contributed to the offence; or

(ii) (even if it did not) that the offence was motivated wholly or partly by his intended misuse of such a drug; and

(d) the condition set out in (e) below is satisfied or (if the court is considering on a second or subsequent occasion whether or not to grant bail) has been, and continues to be, satisfied;

(e) the condition referred to above is that after the taking and analysis of the sample:

(i) a relevant assessment has been offered to the defendant but he does not agree to undergo it; or

(ii) he has undergone a relevant assessment, and relevant follow-up has been proposed to him, but he does not agree to participate in it.

The proviso referred to above is the court has been notified by the Secretary of State that arrangements for conducting a relevant assessment or, as the case may be, providing relevant follow-up have been made for the local justice area in which it appears to the court that the defendant would reside if granted bail and the notice has not been withdrawn.

Conditions to be imposed where bail is granted

D[8.31] This is subject to the proviso set out above as to arrangements for conducting assessments, etc, where the defendant:

(a) after analysis of the sample referred to in paragraph (b)above, has been offered a relevant assessment or, if a relevant assessment has been carried out, the defendant has had relevant follow-up proposed to him; and
(b) the defendant has agreed to undergo the relevant assessment or, as the case may be, to participate in the relevant follow-up,

the court, if it grants bail, must impose as a condition of bail that the defendant both undergo the relevant assessment and participate in any relevant follow-up proposed to him or, if a relevant assessment has been carried out, that the defendant participate in the relevant follow-up.

Bail in cases of homicide or rape after a previous conviction of such offences

D[8.32] A person who in any proceedings has been charged with or convicted of an offence to which s 25 of the Criminal Justice and Public Order Act 1994 applies, in circumstances to which it applies, shall be granted bail in those proceedings only if the court considering the grant of bail is satisfied that there are exceptional circumstances which justify it.

The offences to which s 25 of the 1994 Act applies are as follows:

(a) murder;
(b) attempted murder;
(c) manslaughter;
(d) rape and other serious sexual offences and attempts.

Section 25 applies to a person charged with or convicted of any of the above offences only if he has been previously convicted by or before a court in any part of the United Kingdom of any such offence or of culpable homicide, or of a comparable offence or culpable homicide within a Member State of the EU, and, in the case of a previous conviction of manslaughter or of culpable homicide, if he was then sentenced to imprisonment or detention (detention in the case of an EU conviction) or, if he was then a child or young person, to long-term detention (in the case of an EU conviction, to a term of detention of at least two years.

Prosecution right of appeal

D[8.33]–[8.50] The Bail Amendment Act 1993 enables the prosecution to appeal against the grant of bail, subject to the conditions stated below.

Where a magistrates' court grants bail to a person who is charged with, or convicted of, an offence punishable by imprisonment the prosecution may appeal to a judge of the Crown Court against the granting of bail. Such an appeal may be made only where the prosecution is conducted by the Director of Public Prosecutions or other person falling within a class prescribed by order of the Secretary of State and it may be made only if the prosecution made representations that bail should not be granted, and the representations were made before it was granted.

In the event of the prosecution wishing to exercise this right of appeal, oral notice of appeal must be given to the magistrates' court at the conclusion of the proceedings in which bail has been granted and before the release from custody of the person concerned. Written notice of appeal must then be served on the magistrates' court and the person concerned within two hours of the conclusion of the proceedings.

The hearing of an appeal against a decision to grant bail must be commenced within 48 hours, excluding weekends and any public holiday (ie Christmas Day, Good Friday or a bank holiday) from the date on which oral notice of appeal is given. The appeal shall be by way of re-hearing and the judge may remand the person concerned in custody or may grant bail subject to such conditions, if any, as he thinks fit. While the provisions of ss 128 and 128A of the Magistrates' Courts Act 1980 do not apply to the Crown Court, if that Court upholds a prosecution appeal it should remand in custody consonantly with those provisions.

This right of appeal applies to a child or young person as if for the reference above to a remand in custody there were substituted a reference to a remand to local authority accommodation.

General considerations of remands in custody and on bail

D[8.51] Custody time limits. The Prosecution of Offences Act 1985, s 22 provides for restrictions on the period for which a person charged with an either way, indictable or summary offence may be remanded in custody. The maximum period of a custodial remand is 70 days between his first appearance and the start of a summary trial or committal proceedings, as appropriate. Where, in the case of an either way offence, summary trial is decided upon within 56 days the summary trial must commence within 56 days of the first appearance. Time limits also apply to proceedings before the Crown Court.

NB: An offence 'triable either way' includes an offence which, although triable only on indictment in the case of an adult, is in the case of a juvenile person under 18 years of age triable summarily or on indictment under s 24 of the Magistrates' Courts Act 1980 (grave crimes procedure) (*R v Stratford Youth Court, ex p S* (1998) 162 JP 552).

D[8.52] The court may extend the custody time limits on receipt of an application either orally or in writing but the court must not grant an extension *unless* satisfied that the need for it is justified by virtue of one of three criteria:

(a) illness or absence of the accused, a necessary witness, a judge or magistrate; or
(b) a postponement occasioned by the ordering by the court of separate trials in the case of two or more accused or two or more offences; or
(c) some other good and sufficient cause.

The procedure for an application to extend time limits may be informal but the prosecution must still satisfy the court and the defendant be given an opportunity to test the application (*Wildman v DPP* [2001] EWHC 14 (Admin), (2001) 165 JP 453).

The unavailability of a suitable judge or a suitable courtroom within the maximum period specified in the CTL regulations may, in special cases and on appropriate facts, amount to good and sufficient cause for granting an extension of custody time limits. However, the CPS must provide evidence to support an extension. The court was reliant on information provided by HMCTS staff. That was wholly inadequate. The case was not given that intense level of scrutiny required. If the court had been provided with the correct information he would not have extended the CTL. The President of the Queen's Bench Division then proceeded to lay down guidance on the approach the Crown Court should take in a routine case where an extension to the CTL is sought because of a lack of resources: *R (on the application of McAuley (Clarke)) v Coventry Magistrates' Court and CPS* [2012] EWHC 680 (Admin), [2012] 3 All ER 519, [2012] 1 WLR 2766.

A successful application to vacate the trial by the defence is relevant to a reconsideration of a refusal to extend custody limits (*R (on the application of the DPP) v Blackfriars Crown Court* [2001] EWHC Admin 56, [2001] All ER (D) 205).

However, custody time limits were not extended when the defence requested an adjournment to consider disclosure which was two months late as the fault was that of the prosecution (*R (on the application of Holland) v Leeds Crown Court* [2002] EWHC 1862 (Admin), [2003] Crim LR 272).

D[8.53] The court must also be satisfied the prosecution has acted with all due diligence as well as expedition. See *R v Central Criminal Court, ex p Johnson* [1999] 2 Cr App Rep 51. The fact that a trial could not proceed because of the illness of a victim is irrelevant if the prosecution have failed otherwise to act with due diligence (*R v Central Criminal Court, ex p Bennett* (1999) Times, 25 January). This approach was rejected by the High Court in *R v Leeds Crown Court, ex p Bagoutie* (1999) Times, 31 May as leading to absurd results so that it does not matter that the prosecution has not acted with all due diligence if there is good and sufficient cause in the eyes of the court. However, in complex matters where the defendant is asking for extensive disclosure the prosecution could expect reasonable notice of such enquiries to enable it to comply (*R (on the application of Smith) v Crown Court at Woolwich* [2002] EWHC 995 (Admin), [2002] All ER (D) 05 (May)).

D[8.54] Where a custody time limit has expired the accused must be released on bail with or without conditions. However, a new charge will attract its own custody time limit (*R v Leeds Crown Court, ex p Wardle* [2001] UKHL 12, [2002] 1 AC 754, [2001] 2 All ER 1).

Conditional bail

Bail granted by the police

Police street bail

D[8.55] Section 30A of PACE (inserted by the CJA 2003) gave the police power to release on bail an arrested person at 'any time before he arrives at a police station'. From April 1, 2007 the Police and Justice Act 2006 amended PACE to allow conditions to be imposed by a constable where they are necessary:

(a) to secure that person's surrender to custody;
(b) to secure that person does not commit an offence;
(c) to secure that person does not interfere with witnesses or otherwise obstruct the course of justice;
(d) for the person's protection/welfare.

Those conditions, however, cannot include:

(a) a recognisance;
(b) a security;
(c) a surety;
(d) residence at a bail hostel.

A bail notice given to the arrested person must specify:

(i) the requirements imposed by the condition;
(ii) the process for applying to vary those conditions.

Application to vary can be made either to the police or to a magistrates' court. A magistrates' court may consider an application to vary police street bail conditions where:

(a) the street conditions have previously been varied by the police,
(b) a request for variation by the police has been made and refused, or
(c) a request was made and more than 48 hours has elapsed and the application has neither been withdrawn nor granted (PACE, s 30CB as inserted by Police and Justice Act 2006, s 6 and Sch 10).

A constable may arrest without warrant a person released on conditional bail granted on the street if he has reasonable grounds for suspecting the person has broken any of the conditions imposed by the police. A person arrested for breach of street bail conditions must be taken to a police station as soon as is practicable after the arrest.

Police bail before charge

D[8.56] Any grant of bail before charge may now have attached to it the full range of conditions similar to those outlined at D[8.55]. Applications to vary these conditions are dealt with under s 47(1E) of PACE and in accordance with r 14.6 of the Criminal Procedure Rules 2015. For variation of court bail see D[8.80].

Significant changes to pre-charge police bail were made by the Policing and Crime Act 2017. These include creating a presumption in favour of release without bail, and statutory time limits and judicial oversight of extensions of bail beyond three months. As to the procedure for the extension of police bail before charge, see rr 14.20 and 14.21 of the Criminal Procedure Rules 2015.

Police bail after charge

D[8.57]–[8.60] A custody sergeant at the police station may grant an accused conditional bail and may do so for the same reasons as a bench of magistrates who may decide that the defendant cannot be released on unconditional bail. It is only if conditional bail would be inadequate that custody should be contemplated.

Court bail

D[8.61] Conditions are only to be attached to bail where it appears to the bench necessary to do so for the purpose of preventing the accused:

(a) failing to surrender to custody; or
(b) committing an offence while on bail; or
(c) interfering with witnesses or obstructing the course of justice; or
(d) from being harmed, ie for his own protection or in the case of a juvenile for his welfare.

D[8.62] Conditions may also be imposed to enable a pre-sentence report to be prepared, or requiring a defendant to attend an interview with a legal representative before the next court hearing. The court must give its reasons for imposing conditions on the bail.

See para D[8.29] as to special provision for drug users.

D[8.63] Commonly imposed conditions are:

- residence (absconding);
- curfew (fresh offences);
- reporting to a police station (absconding);
- non-association with specified people (interference with the course of justice);
- a security or surety (absconding).

Other conditions may be imposed provided they are reasonable and are enforceable, including a 'doorstep' condition for those on a curfew condition (*R v Chorley Justices* [2002] EWHC 2162 (Admin), 166 JP 764, sub nom *R (DPP) v Chorley Justices* [2002] 43 LS Gaz R 34).

See r 19.11 of the CPR 2014. The defendant should give notice of any proposed address at which he/she would reside if granted bail to enable the court to assess its suitability.

D[8.64] It must be emphasised that conditions are not to be imposed as a matter of course; they can only be imposed to prevent one of the occurrences mentioned above. If a condition is imposed it must relate to the mischief which is feared (a *guide* is given by the words in brackets above). Conditions must not be imposed which have no relevance to the reason given by the court, eg a surety because the bench fears fresh offences.

D[8.65] Conditions may also be imposed to require defendants to comply with hostel rules where residing at a bail or probation hostel on remand or for assessment. Electronic monitoring of defendants on bail to enforce a curfew is also permitted. Electronic monitoring of children over the age of 12 is also permitted subject to the same restrictions imposed on the use of secure accommodation: s 3AA of the Bail Act 1976 (see D[8.6])*.

*When LASPOA 2012, s 151(1) is brought into force, the criteria for remanding children on bail with an electronic monitoring condition will be modified.

D[8.66] **Sureties.** With one exception, mentioned below, no one has to deposit money or valuables to secure a person's release in remand proceedings. However, a third party may agree to stand as surety for an accused. A surety is a person who agrees to forfeit a sum of money fixed by the court (called a recognisance and pronounced 'reconnaissance') if the accused fails to surrender to custody. A surety's obligations are to ensure that the accused surrenders to custody; he is not there to ensure that the accused complies with the conditions of his bail. The court should specify that the person standing surety is to secure the accused's attendance at the next hearing or for each occasion to which the case may, from time to time, be adjourned.

A surety cannot be required for the purpose of ensuring compliance with a bail condition designed to prevent further offending: *R (on the application of Shea) v Winchester Crown Court* [2013] EWHC 1050, DC.

D[8.67] In deciding whether to accept a person as a surety, the court should in particular have regard to:

(a) the surety's financial resources;
(b) his character and any previous convictions of his;
(c) his proximity (whether in point of kinship, place or otherwise) to the person for whom he is to be surety.

D[8.68] **Forfeiting the recognisance of a surety.** If the accused fails to answer to his bail, the surety should be informed by the court that it is considering forfeiting his recognisance. Standing surety is a solemn obligation. The court will start from the basis that the whole amount is to be forfeited. The culpability of the surety will be investigated to see what steps he took to ensure the defendant's attendance. However, a surety should not forfeit his recognisance if he is not to blame for the defendant's failure to surrender when required to do so. When forfeiting a recognisance the court must take into account the surety's ability to pay.

D[8.69] **Depositing a security.** An exception to the rule that an accused does not have to deposit money or valuables is where the court believes a security is necessary to ensure the defendant surrenders to custody. The usual security is money, but it could be a valuable item such as motor car, provided it is readily convertible into money.

In the case of a security the law presumes that the sum deposited by way of security should be forfeited and it is for the person who deposited the security – on receipt of a court notice – to show cause why the sum should not remain forfeited.

D[8.70]–[8.75] **The effectiveness of conditions.** The usefulness of some conditions is questionable. A condition of reporting to the police at anything longer than 24-hour intervals is generally of little value and such a condition should be not imposed to make the accused more readily available for questioning. Nor should a condition be imposed for its nuisance value to the accused. A condition of depositing a passport is of little value, especially where the accused can travel within the EU without a passport.

European supervision order

D[8.76] Provision is made by Council Framework Decision 2009/829JHA of 23rd October 2009 and the Framework Decision, Criminal Justice and Data Protection (Protocol No 26) Regulations 2014, SI 2014/3141 for the UK to make requests to other Member States for monitoring 'supervision measures', and vice versa. 'Supervision measures' are bail conditions imposed under s 3(6) of the Bail Act 1996. This arise where a defendant is lawfully and ordinarily resident in another Member State (the 'executing state') and consents to return there with a view to the supervision measures being monitored there under the Framework Decision.

Where bail is refused

D[8.77] **Making a further application.** At the first hearing after that at which the court decided not to grant the defendant bail (which normally would have been the first time the case was remanded) he is entitled to apply for bail as of right. At any subsequent hearings the court need not hear any arguments as to fact or law which it has heard previously: see *R (on the application of B) v Brent Youth Court* [2010] All ER (D) 76 (Jul).

D[8.78] The court must, however, always consider the matter of bail on each occasion on which the case is remanded. As the liberty of the accused is at stake, it is suggested that any doubt whether to allow a fresh application should be resolved in the accused's favour.

D[8.79] **Appeals.** The defendant may appeal to the Crown Court against the imposition of bail conditions relating to residence (other than to a bail hostel), sureties and securities, curfew and contact with other persons. Such an application may only be made following the determination of an application to vary the bail conditions made in the magistrates' court. There is no concurrent power to appeal to the High Court.

Application to a Crown Court Judge in chambers. Where the magistrates have heard a full application and refused bail, their legal adviser will supply the accused with a certificate to that effect. He then has a right to make a bail application to a Crown Court Judge in chambers.

Application to vary bail conditions imposed by the court

D[8.80]–[8.81] Advance notice (24 hours minimum) must be given by the defence of an application to vary conditions of bail, including a change of address. A new rule 19.11 has been added to the Criminal Procedure Rules 2013 whereby the defence must give notice of the address at which the defendant would reside if the court granted or varied bail, to enable the court to assess the suitability of the address proposed.

Prosecution for failing to surrender to custody

D[8.82] The law is that the accused is released on bail with a duty to turn up at court on the appointed day at the appointed time. If he fails to do so the first consequence is that a warrant may be issued for his arrest. Second, he may be prosecuted for the criminal offence of failing to surrender to custody. See D[8.85] below.

D[8.83] Where bail has been granted by a police officer for an accused to surrender either to a police station or a magistrates' court, any failure to surrender to custody should be initiated by charging the accused or laying an information. On the other hand, an accused who fails to answer to bail granted by the magistrates themselves should be brought before the court following his arrest. The court will then initiate proceedings following an express invitation by the prosecutor. The prosecutor will conduct the proceedings and, where the matter is contested, call the evidence. Any trial should normally take place immediately. In the meantime the defendant can expect to have bail revoked. In cases which cannot or are unlikely to result in custodial sentences a trial in the absence of the defendant may be a pragmatic solution. The bail offence should be dealt with immediately in normal circumstances (Criminal Practice Directions 2015, 14C.5).

D[8.84] Section 6 of the Bail Act 1976 creates two offences. The first offence is failing without reasonable cause to surrender to custody: Bail Act 1976, s 6(1); the second offence arises where there was reasonable cause for the failure to surrender, but the accused then failed to surrender to custody at the appointed place as soon after the appointed time as was reasonably practicable: Bail Act 1976, s 6(2).

The offences are triable only summarily, but s 127 of the Magistrates' Courts Act 1980 (time limits) does not apply to court bail; where the bail was granted by a constable the information must be laid within six months of the failure to appear or within three months of the person's surrender to custody or arrest/attendance at a police/coming before the court for the failure to answer bail: Bail Act 1976, s 6(10)–(14).

D[8.85]–[8.90] **Defence.** It is a defence to such a charge if he proves (that it is more probable than not) that he had a reasonable cause for not answering his bail, or that having a reasonable cause for failing to surrender to custody at the appointed time and place, he surrendered to custody at the appointed place as soon after the appointed time as was reasonably practicable. It is not a defence that the accused was not given a copy of the decision to grant him bail.

'Surrender to custody' means 'at the appointed time and place' and the mere fact that the defendant is eg half an hour late cannot afford him a defence (*R v Scott (Casim)* [2007] EWCA Crim 2757, 172 JP 149).

It has been held that: 'if a court provides a procedure which, by some form of direction, by notice or orally, instructs a person surrendering to bail to report to a particular office or to a particular official, when he complies with that direction he surrenders to his bail. Thereafter, albeit he may not be physically restrained, albeit he may be allowed to sit in the court concourse and visit the court canteen, he is in the custody of the court. I have already suggested that he is under an implied, if not an express obligation, not to leave the building without consent until the case is called on. The argument that section 7(2) would have no meaning if that were not the correct construction is one which seems to me to be correct. I emphasise that if a person simply goes to the courthouse and does not report to anybody he has not surrendered to his bail. That is not enough. He has to report to somebody and do whatever he is directed to do, but when he does comply with the procedure which he is directed to follow by the court, then I emphasise that he has surrendered' (per Glidewell LJ in *DPP v Richards* [1988] QB 701). As to the position in the Crown Court, see *R v Evans* [2011] EWCA Crim 2842, [2012] 1 WLR 1192, [2012] 2 Cr App Rep 279, 176 JP 139. In the absence of special arrangements either particular to the court or to the individual case, surrender is accomplished when the defendant presents himself to the custody officers by entering the dock.

It is suggested that, when granting bail, the court should state and record that surrender to custody requires the defendant to arrive at court by the appointed time, to report his arrival in accordance with the practice of the court, to remain in court until his case is called and then to present himself to the custody officers by entering the dock (or such other part of the court as accords with its practice).

D[8.91] **Penalty.** A maximum penalty of 3 months' imprisonment and a fine on level 5 in the magistrates' court or the accused may be committed for sentence to the Crown Court, where the maximum penalty is 12 months' imprisonment and an unlimited fine. In *R v Clarke* [2000] 1 Cr App Rep (S) 224, CA the Court of Appeal upheld a prison sentence for the offence. Any such sentence will normally be consecutive to the sentence for the substantive offence (*R v White* (2002) Times, 9 December).

D[8.92] **Failing to comply with a condition.** Failing to comply with a condition of bail is not an offence (see *R v Ashley* [2003] EWCA Crim 2571, [2003] All ER (D) 106 (Aug)). It does mean, however, that a police officer can arrest the accused forthwith and bring him before the court. His failure to comply with the condition may in itself constitute an exception to the general 'right to bail'. If a defendant is arrested in breach of a bail condition the court should ask if he admits or denies the breach. If a denial is recorded the magistrates should hear evidence or a statement of the arresting officer's 'reasonable grounds' for arrest.

In determining whether the accused has broken a condition of his bail, the court is entitled to apply the civil standard of proof i.e. a balance of probabilities. The court is entitled to receive written hearsay evidence eg the statement of the arresting officer; the court's duty is to then weigh the evidence having regard to the hearsay nature of the evidence and the fact that the evidence cannot be tested by cross-examination: see *R (on the application of Thomas) v Greenwich Magistrates' Court* [2009] EWHC 1180 (Admin), 173 JP 345).

If the court is of the opinion that the defendant was in breach of his bail conditions he may be further remanded either in custody or on bail. If there is no breach of condition there is an entitlement to bail on the same conditions. Only after a finding of breach does the consideration of the reasons for breach become relevant (*R (Vickers) v West London Magistrates Court* [2003] EWHC 1809 (Admin), [2003] All ER (D) 211 (Jul)).

Note that the breach of bail exception to the right to bail is subject to the real prospect of a custodial sentence qualification (see D[8.26]); ie, unless there is such a prospect the defendant must be re-bailed.

Such hearing must be within 24 hours of arrest although there is power for the case to be put back in the list during that time period *(R (Hussain) v Derby Magistrates' Court* [2001] EWHC 507 (Admin), [2001] 1 WLR 2454). In *R (on the application of Culley) v Dorchester Crown Court* [2007] EWHC 109 (Admin), 172 JP 373, it was decided that:

(1) Following the arrest of a person for breach of a bail condition, under s 7(4) Bail Act 1976 that person must be brought before a magistrates' court as soon as practicable and in any case within 24 hours of the arrest.
(2) After the arrest of that person the court is required to complete the investigation and make a decision on whether there has been a breach of bail and, if there is a breach to remand in custody or to re-admit that person to bail.
(3) Once 24 hours has elapsed after the arrest of that person, a magistrates' court no longer has jurisdiction under s 7(5) to deal with the breach of bail.

Bail pending appeal

D[8.93] The policy of the Court of Appeal has for long been against the granting of bail pending the hearing of an appeal against a custodial sentence, unless there are exceptional circumstances. The appellant's remedy is to apply for an expedited appeal. It is generally felt to be unsatisfactory that a person sentenced to custody is released in the hope of a successful appeal and is subsequently required to return to prison to serve his sentence. Therefore, only exceptional circumstances will lead to the granting of bail (*R v Watton* (1978) 68 Cr App Rep 293, [1979] Crim LR 246, CA). The court considering the application is not concerned with whether it would have imposed the same sentence, but only whether the sentence was reasonable. Where the sentence is clearly appropriate for the offence, then personal matters which are the basis for an appeal for clemency should not influence the court considering the bail application.

D[9]
The justices' clerk

D[9.1] Some justices' clerks continue to hold independent public office. They may not be dismissed without the approval of the Lord Chancellor, who must in turn consider any representations made to him by the magistrates for the local justice area concerned. Although more recently some justices' clerks are appointed on a fixed-term contract they are still the holder of an independent public office.

D[9.2] The justices' clerk must be distinguished from those of his assistants ('legal advisers') who on his behalf give advice to justices in court when the justices' clerk is not personally in attendance. Both however are obliged to act compatibly with the ECHR.

Functions of the justices' clerk

D[9.3] Some of the functions of the justices' clerk will be seen from the following extract from the Courts Act 2003, which is not an exhaustive statement:

> The functions of a justices' clerk include giving advice to any or all of the justices to whom he is clerk about matters of law (including procedure or practice) on questions arising in connection with the discharge of their functions, including questions arising when the clerk is not personally attending on them . . . The powers of a justices' clerk include, at any time when he thinks he should do so, bringing to the attention of any or all of the justices of the peace to whom he is clerk any point of law (including procedure or practice) that is or may be involved in any question so arising.

D[9.4] The Courts Act 2003 uses the titles 'justices' clerk' and 'assistant clerk ', the latter as shorthand for 'assistant to a justices' clerk'. The latter is not subject to the direction of any person other than a justices' clerk: Courts Act 2003, s 29.

The Courts Service and Structure

D[9.5] The office of justices' chief executive was abolished by the Courts Act 2003. The Courts Act 2003 unified the court structure by abolishing magistrates' courts committees and bringing magistrates' courts within the Courts Service ('Her Majesty's Courts Service'). The Head of the Courts Service responsible for administration locally is the cluster manager but the head of the Service for the relevant region is the Delivery Director. The Delivery Director line manages both the cluster manager and the justices' clerk, although the judicial independence of the magistracy and justices' clerks (including legal advisers, whose advice in individual cases the justices' clerk is responsible for) is preserved by s 29 of the Courts Act 2003.

Advice in court

D[9.6] Although the extract from the Courts Act 2003 above refers solely to the justices' clerk himself, it is recognised that in practice he may delegate his advisory functions to legal advisers who are either professionally qualified as barristers or solicitors or are qualified under the Justices' Clerks (Qualification of Assistants) Rules 1979 as amended. Part 24A of the Criminal Practice Directions 2015 [2015] EWCA Crim 1567 deals with the duties and responsibilities of bench legal advisers.

> 'CPD Trial 24A: ROLE OF THE JUSTICES' CLERK/LEGAL ADVISER
>
> 24A.1 The role of the justices' clerk/legal adviser is a unique one, which carries with it independence from direction when undertaking a judicial function and when advising magistrates. These functions must be carried out in accordance with the Bangalore Principles of Judicial Conduct (judicial independence, impar-

tiality, integrity, propriety, ensuring fair treatment and competence and diligence). More specifically, duties must be discharged in accordance with the relevant professional Code of Conduct and the Legal Adviser Competence Framework.

24A.2 A justices' clerk is responsible for:

(a) the legal advice tendered to the justices within the area;
(b) the performance of any of the functions set out below by any member of his staff acting as justices' legal adviser;
(c) ensuring that competent advice is available to justices when the justices' clerk is not personally present in court; and
(d) ensuring that advice given at all stages of proceedings and powers exercised (including those delegated to justices' legal advisers) take into account the court's duty to deal with cases justly and actively to manage the case.

24A.3 Where a person other than the justices' clerk (a justices' legal adviser), who is authorised to do so, performs any of the functions referred to in this direction, he or she will have the same duties, powers and responsibilities as the justices' clerk. The justices' legal adviser may consult the justices' clerk, or other person authorised by the justices' clerk for that purpose, before tendering advice to the bench. If the justices' clerk or that person gives any advice directly to the bench, he or she should give the parties or their advocates an opportunity of repeating any relevant submissions, prior to the advice being given.

24A.4 When exercising judicial powers, a justices' clerk or legal adviser is acting in exactly the same capacity as a magistrate. The justices' clerk may delegate powers to a justices' legal adviser in accordance with the relevant statutory authority. The scheme of delegation must be clear and in writing, so that all justices' legal advisers are certain of the extent of their powers. Once a power is delegated, judicial discretion in an individual case lies with the justices' legal adviser exercising the power. When exercise of a power does not require the consent of the parties, a justices' clerk or legal adviser may deal with and decide a contested issue or may refer that issue to the court.

24A.5 It shall be the responsibility of the justices' clerk or legal adviser to provide the justices with any advice they require to perform their functions justly, whether or not the advice has been requested, on:

(a) questions of law;
(b) questions of mixed law and fact;
(c) matters of practice and procedure;
(d) the process to be followed at sentence and the matters to be taken into account, together with the range of penalties and ancillary orders available, in accordance with the relevant sentencing guidelines;
(e) any relevant decisions of the superior courts or other guidelines;
(f) the appropriate decision-making structure to be applied in any given case; and
(g) other issues relevant to the matter before the court.

24A.6 In addition to advising the justices, it shall be the justices' legal adviser's responsibility to assist the court, where appropriate, as to the formulation of reasons and the recording of those reasons.

24A.7 The justices' legal adviser has a duty to assist an unrepresented defendant, see CrimPR 9.4(3)(a), 14.3(2)(a) and 24.15(3)(a), in particular when the court is making a decision on allocation, bail, at trial and on sentence.

24A.8 Where the court must determine allocation, the legal adviser may deal with any aspect of the allocation hearing save for the decision on allocation, indication of sentence and sentence.

24A.9 When a defendant acting in person indicates a guilty plea, the legal adviser must explain the procedure and inform the defendant of their right to address the court on the facts and to provide details of their personal circumstances in order that the court can decide the appropriate sentence.

24A.10 When a defendant indicates a not guilty plea but has not completed the relevant sections of the Magistrates' Courts Trial Preparation Form, the legal adviser must either ensure that the Form is completed or, in appropriate cases, assist the court to obtain and record the essential information on the form.

24A.11 Immediately prior to the commencement of a trial, the legal adviser must summarise for the court the agreed and disputed issues, together with the way in which the parties propose to present their cases. If this is done by way of pre-court briefing, it should be confirmed in court or agreed with the parties.

24A.12A justices' clerk or legal adviser must not play any part in making findings of fact, but may assist the bench by reminding them of the evidence, using any notes of the proceedings for this purpose, and clarifying the issues which are agreed and those which are to be determined.

24A.13A justices' clerk or legal adviser may ask questions of witnesses and the parties in order to clarify the evidence and any issues in the case. A legal adviser has a duty to ensure that every case is conducted justly.

24A.14 When advising the justices, the justices' clerk or legal adviser, whether or not previously in court, should:

(a) ensure that he is aware of the relevant facts; and
(b) provide the parties with an opportunity to respond to any advice given.

24A.15 At any time, justices are entitled to receive advice to assist them in discharging their responsibilities. If they are in any doubt as to the evidence which has been given, they should seek the aid of their legal adviser, referring to his notes as appropriate. This should ordinarily be done in open court. Where the justices request their adviser to join them in the retiring room, this request should be made in the presence of the parties in court. Any legal advice given to the justices other than in open court should be clearly stated to be provisional; and the adviser should subsequently repeat the substance of the advice in open court and give the parties the opportunity to make any representations they wish on that provisional advice. The legal adviser should then state in open court whether the provisional advice is confirmed or, if it is varied, the nature of the variation.

24A.16 The legal adviser is under a duty to assist unrepresented parties, whether defendants or not, to present their case, but must do so without appearing to become an advocate for the party concerned. The legal adviser should also ensure that members of the court are aware of obligations under the Victims' Code.

24A.17 The role of legal advisers in fine default proceedings, or any other proceedings for the enforcement of financial orders, obligations or penalties, is to assist the court. They must not act in an adversarial or partisan manner, such as by attempting to establish wilful refusal or neglect or any other type of culpable behaviour, to offer an opinion on the facts, or to urge a particular course of action upon the justices. The expectation is that a legal adviser will ask questions of the defaulter to elicit information which the justices will require to make an adjudication, such as the explanation for the default. A legal adviser may also advise the justices as to the options open to them in dealing with the case.

24A.18 The performance of a legal adviser is subject to regular appraisal. For that purpose the appraiser may be present in the justices' retiring room. The content of the appraisal is confidential, but the fact that an appraisal has taken place, and the presence of the appraiser in the retiring room, should be briefly explained in open court.'

D[9.7] In court the legal adviser's duties are both advisory and executive. He may, if the justices so desire, perform those many tasks which ensure the smooth progress of the court's business. For example, he may decide the order in which cases are called, identify, caution and charge defendants, take their pleas and put to them other offences for the court to take into consideration. He may deal with the swearing of witnesses, he may deal with such matters as the explanation of a sentence such as a supervision requirement and confirm the defendant's consent to the requirement. He is empowered to take recognisances which have been fixed by the court, dealing with the arrangements for paying monetary penalties and the questioning of witnesses or defendants on the justices' behalf, including the conduct of a means inquiry. When the justices' clerk (or one of his legal advisers) performs these or any other similar tasks, he carries out those functions on behalf of the justices. There are at least three good reasons why he should carry out most, if not all of these executive functions: his legal knowledge, experience and professional ethics will usually mean that he can perform these functions more effectively than a justice can; there will be more uniformity of procedure if these functions are left to the legal adviser; the less the chairman has to worry about procedural tasks, the more of his attention he can give to listening and decision making.

D[9.8] The extent to which the legal adviser exercises these tasks, however, varies from court to court and even in the same place it may change according to which chairman is sitting or whether the justices' clerk himself or one of his staff is in court. Whatever the legal adviser does he should be careful to avoid giving to the general public the impression that he and not the chairman is in charge of the court's affairs. The conduct of the court is always the responsibility of the chairman in consultation with his colleagues on the bench; but a wise chairman will usually leave the general conduct of business in court to the legal adviser.

D[9.9] The Lord Chief Justice has warned that justices who fail to take the clerk's advice on a legal point may be ordered to pay the costs of any resulting appeal. This warning arose in a case where justices insisted on finding 'special reasons' in spite of advice given to them in court by the clerk and later in writing.

D[9.10]–[9.15] If the justices retire the legal adviser should not retire with them as a matter of course: either the chairman should specifically and audibly invite him to join the justices or the legal adviser should remain in court and be seen to have been sent for. NB: There is not the same prohibition on the legal adviser retiring immediately to join the justices in family proceedings eg in order to assist in the drawing up of the justices' reasons.

D[9.16] If the justices retire the legal adviser may join them. All too often justices are themselves unaware that a point has arisen in their discussion upon which they need advice, and unless the legal adviser is with them to hear their discussion he too will be unaware that they need advice. Moreover, if he is present during their discussion the legal adviser may be able to help by reminding them of parts of the evidence they may have overlooked, or by explaining the legal significance of particular evidence, or by correcting errors of recollection. In the event that the justices are later asked to state a case the clerk will find it a considerable advantage to have listened to the justices' discussion in the retiring room. Once the legal adviser is satisfied that he can be of no further assistance to the justices he should return to his place in court.

D[9.17] If the justices do not send for the clerk when they retire, he is entitled to go to advise them if he considers it necessary to do so, but will inform the parties as to what he is going to say to the justices, giving them an opportunity of making representations before that [provisional] advice is given. See *Clark (Procurator Fiscal, Kirkcaldy) v Kelly* [2003] UKPC D1, [2004] 1 AC 681, [2003] 1 All ER 1106 on the legality of the justices' clerk's advice and its compatibility with Article 6 of the ECHR.

Delegation

D[9.18] Apart from his duty to provide justices with advice when they sit in court, the justices' clerk may perform those judicial functions of a single justice which are prescribed by the Justices' Clerks Rules 2005. Amongst the more important judicial functions which a justices' clerk can perform are: the issue of a summons, a witness summons, a distress warrant or a warrant for arrest following a defendant's failure to appear at court so long as no objection is raised on behalf of the accused. The justices' clerk may adjourn a case and grant bail to an accused in his absence with the consent of the prosecution and in the same terms as previously imposed.

When acting as the nominated case manager, a justices' clerk or assistant may exercise all the case management powers conferred by the Criminal Procedure Rules, r 3.5, including the determination of a contested application to adjourn, and is not limited to the powers in the Justices' Clerks Rules: *Bourne v Scarborough Magistrates' Court* [2017] EWHC 2828 (Admin), 182 JP 49, [2018] Crim LR 258.

D[9.19] The justices' clerk may take a plea and fix a trial date where the defendant is on bail. He may authorise a legal adviser to exercise these functions and under the Children Act 1989 to conduct directions appointments and appoint guardians ad litem. Delegation should be by specific authorisation and in writing.

Delegation in relation to the grant of legal representation in criminal proceedings is currently governed by the Access to Justice Act 1999 and regulations made thereunder. The Criminal Defence Service Act 2006, from a date to be appointed, envisages that responsibility for the grant of representation will ultimately shift to the Legal Services Commission. However, in the first instance it is anticipated that magistrates' courts will retain the power to grant or refuse representation. The Act and regulations envisage that those functions are administrative in nature and will be delegated to court staff via the Area Director.

D[9.20] The justices' clerk and those of his assistants with delegated powers have case management powers which can be exercised as if by a single justice. Often referred to as 'Narey Courts' the justices' clerk may sit alone in an early first hearing court where simple cases can be listed and a guilty plea is anticipated. Where the case is more complex or a not guilty plea is anticipated the case can be listed for an early administrative hearing where the justices' clerk can deal with trial listing, conditional bail variation (with the consent of the prosecution and the defence) and warrants of arrest in the event of a non-appearance by the accused.

Section E

The youth court

E[1]

Juveniles

(Children and Young Persons Acts 1933, 1963 and 1969)

E[1.1] Children (10–13) and young persons (14–17) are juveniles. Cases involving juveniles are heard in the youth court apart from exceptional cases in criminal proceedings where the juvenile appears before the adult magistrates' court charged with an adult defendant. The adult court may also remand a juvenile, when no youth court is sitting.

Determining the age of the defendant

E[1.2] Where anyone is brought before any court except as a witness and it appears that he is a child or young person, the court must make enquiry as to his age, and the age presumed or declared by the court is deemed to be his true age: Children and Young Persons Act 1933, s 99. This applies generally to determining whether a person appearing before any court is an adult or young person, and to establishing an age for the purposes of the proceedings. The statutory provisions for sentencing also make express reference to the age of the defendant. The effect of these is that the age of the offender will be deemed to be that which it appears to the court to be after considering any available evidence: see Powers of Criminal Courts (Sentencing) Act 2000, s 164(1). An order will be made on this basis. Where it is subsequently established that the defendant is of an age which precludes the sentence imposed on him, the sentence is not invalidated: *R v Brown* (1989) 11 Cr App Rep (S) 263, [1989] Crim LR 750, CA.

Where there is a dispute as to age which is material, it is better for the court to adjourn for more detailed inquiries if there is any doubt about the matter: *R v Steed* [1990] Crim LR 816.

When making an order in respect of young offenders it is generally the date of the finding of guilt that is relevant when determining the age of the offender for the purpose of the availability of orders: *R v Danga* (1991) 13 Cr App Rep (S) 408; *R v Hahn* [2003] EWCA Crim 825, [2003] 2 Cr App R (S) 106. See, however, *Aldis v DPP* [2002] EWHC 403 (Admin), [2002] 2 Cr App Rep (S) 400, [2002] Crim LR 434 where it was held, in relation to a defendant aged 17 at the time of mode of trial, at which hearing it must have been plain to all present that the possibility of a two-year detention and training order was a factor in the court's decision to try the case summarily, that the attainment of 18 before the trial and conviction did not prevent the justices from imposing a detention and training order; Parliament's intention must have been that s 100 of the Powers of Criminal Courts (Sentencing) Act 2000 should be interpreted as subject to s 29 of the Children and Young Persons Act 1963. The latter provides that where a young person attains 18 before the conclusion of the proceedings the court may deal with the case and make any order it could have made if he had not attained that age.

The youth court retains its jurisdiction concurrently with the adult court to deal with a breach of a conditional discharge where the defendant has attained 18 years: Children and Young Persons Act 1933, s 48(2). Proceedings for breach of a supervision order where a person has attained 18 years are heard in the adult magistrates' court: Powers of Criminal Courts (Sentencing) Act 2000, Sch 7, para 1.

In *R v Ghafoor* [2002] EWCA Crim 1857, [2003] Cr App R (S) 428 it was held that the starting point for sentencing was the age of the defendant at the date of the offence.

Children and young persons generally to be tried in the youth court

E[1.3] The basic principle is that a charge against a child or young person must be heard by a youth court: Children and Young Persons Act 1933, s 46. In some circumstances, however, proceedings must be commenced in an adult magistrates' court and certain cases must be sent for trial to the Crown Court.

The exceptions to the basic principle are:

(a) the child or young person is jointly charged with an adult: CYPA 1933, s 46(1); or
(b) the child or young person is charged with an offence arising out of circumstances which are the same as, or connected with, those giving rise to an offence with which a person who had attained the age of 18 is charged at the same time: CYPA 1963, s 18; or
(c) an adult is charged with aiding, abetting, counselling, procuring, allowing or permitting the offence by the child or young person: CYPA 1933, s 46(1); or
(d) the child or young person is charged with aiding and abetting, counselling, procuring, allowing, or permitting the offence by the adult: CYPA 1963, s 18; or
(e) proceedings against the child or young person are started in the adult court and it only becomes apparent later that the defendant is a child or young person: CYPA 1933, s 46(1) (and see *R v Tottenham Youth Court, ex p Fawzy* [1998] 1 All ER 365, [1999] 1 WLR 1350); or
(f) a written plea of guilty has been received and the court has no reason to believe that the accused is a child or young person. If it then transpires that the accused is a child or young person he shall nonetheless be deemed to have attained the age of 18;
(g) the court is conducting remand proceedings: CYPA 1933, s 46(1).

Where exception (a) (joint charge with adult) applies the case shall be heard in the adult magistrates' court, but where any of the other exceptions (b)–(d) apply the decision is discretionary. Exception (g) enables an adult court, where necessary, to hear a remand of a child or young person: CYPA 1933, s 46(2).

Whether an adult and a youth are jointly charged depends on a present state of affairs and it is not sufficient to embrace the situation where an adult was originally charged with the youth but has subsequently dropped out of the case.

As to sending youths to the Crown Court for trial and committing youths to the Crown Court for sentence, see E[3], below.

See also the Sentencing Council's allocation guideline at D[4.12], ante.

E[2]
The youth court

E[2.1] Under s 50 of the Courts Act 2003, responsibility for the selection and authorisation of magistrates to sit in youth courts passed to the Lord Chief Justice. Through rules of court he has delegated that function to Bench Training and Development Committees (BTDC). From 13 September 2007, authorisation for winger and chairmanship selection is undertaken by BTDCs for the relevant local justice area (see the Justices of the Peace (Training and Development Committee) Rules 2007 (SI 2007/1609) and the Youth Courts (Constitution of Committees and Right to Preside) Rules 2007 (SI 2007/1611 (L9)). Copies of these rules can be viewed and downloaded from www.opsi.gov.uk.

E[2.2] Each youth court should (except in unforeseen circumstances) consist of three such magistrates, at least one of whom should be male and one female and the court should be presided over by the chairman or a deputy chairman of the panel. In *R v Birmingham Justices, ex p F* (2000) 164 JP 523, [2000] Crim LR 588 it was made clear that the court should consider representations before proceeding with a single sex bench. A district judge may sit alone in the youth court.

E[2.3] Persons present during the hearing. Only the following are allowed to be present:

- members and officers of the court;
- parties to the case before the court, their solicitors and counsel, and witnesses and other persons directly concerned with that case;
- bona fide representatives of newspapers or news agencies;
- such other persons as the court may specially authorise to be present.

E[2.4] Restrictions on reporting. The press may not report details of the name, address or school of a juvenile who is a defendant or witness in any proceedings before the youth court or any other details including the printing of a photograph which would identify him. An exception to this is when the court is dealing with an anti-social behaviour order. In such case the court may make an order under s 39 Children and Young Persons Act 1933 and give its reasons. For the principles governing a s 39 order see **D[1B.7]**.

E[2.5] These restrictions may be lifted:

- in order to avoid an injustice to a juvenile or in certain circumstances where a juvenile is unlawfully at large on application of the Director of Public Prosecutions; or
- the juvenile is convicted and the court, having listened to representations of the parties, believes it is in the public interest to do so.

Publication leading to the identification of an adult witness may also be prohibited under s 49 Youth Justice and Criminal Evidence Act 1999: see **D[1B.7]**.

E[3] Criminal proceedings

E[3.1] It shall be the principal aim of the youth justice system to prevent offending by children and young persons. Youth courts must have regard to this aim.

Age of criminal responsibility

E[3.2] A child under the age of ten cannot be guilty of any offence (Children and Young Persons Act 1933, s 50).

In relation to offenders aged 10–14 years, the presumption and the defence of 'doli incapax' (mischievous discretion) was abolished by s 34 of the Crime and Disorder Act 1998 (*R v T* [2008] EWCA Crim 815, [2008] 3 WLR 923; affd sub nom R v JTB [2009] UKHL 20, [2009] 3 All ER 1).

Attendance of parent

E[3.3] Unless the court considers it unreasonable to do so, it must insist on the attendance of the parent or guardian of a child or young person under 16 years. In respect of those who are 16 and 17 years' old, the court has a discretion. 'Parent' will include a local authority where the juvenile is in their care. At all stages of the proceedings, if a parent refuses to attend a warrant can be issued against him or her.

Remands of children and young persons

E[3.4] When proceedings are adjourned the court may adjourn the case or remand the accused. A child (defined for these purposes as any person aged under 18) may be remanded on bail, or to local authority accommodation, or to youth detention accommodation. Remand hearings may take place in the adult court or the youth court: Children and Young Persons Act 1933, s 46.

The Bail Act 1976 applies, with some differences from the exceptions to the right to bail and the power to impose bail conditions which apply to adult offenders.

Where bail is refused, a child or young person will usually be remanded to local authority accommodation. The exceptions are:

(a) in certain circumstances the remand may be to the custody of a constable for a period of up to 24 hours: Magistrates' Courts Act 1980, s 128(7);
(b) where either of the prescribed sets of conditions is met, the remand may be to youth detention accommodation (see below).

Where a child is remanded to local authority accommodation, the court can impose conditions with which the child must comply and can impose requirements on the local authority to secure compliance with those conditions.

A child charged with murder cannot be granted bail by a magistrates' court and must be committed to the Crown Court either in local authority accommodation or youth detention accommodation: Coroners and Justice Act 2009, s 115. The relevant provisions are to be applied as they would be in any other case: *R (A) v Lewisham Crown Court* [2011] EWHC 1193 (Admin), (2011) 175 JP 321.

Remands and committals to local authority accommodation

E[3.5] Chapter 3 of Part 3 of the Legal Aid, Sentencing and Punishment of Offenders Act 2012 makes provision for remands and committal to local authority accommodation. Section 91 provides that where a child (ie a person aged under 18) is charged or convicted of an offence and the court remands the child, including where the court sends the child for trial or commits the child for sentence, and the child is not released on bail, the court must generally remand the child to local authority accommodation in accordance with s 92, subject to the exceptions stated in E[3.4] above (remands to police detention or to youth detention accommodation).

Section 92 provides that a remand to local authority accommodation is a remand to accommodation provided by or on behalf of a local authority. The court must designate the local authority concerned. In the case a looked after child, this will be the local authority which is looking after the child; in any other case, it will the local authority in whose area it appears to the court that the child habitually resides, or in whose area the offence or one of the offence was committed.

Section 93 provides that a court remanding a child to local authority accommodation may require the child to comply with any conditions that could be imposed if the court were granting conditional bail under s 3(6) of the Bail Act 1976. Subject to s 94 (requirements for electronic monitoring), the court may also require the child to comply with any conditions imposed for electronic monitoring for the purpose of securing compliance with the conditions imposed as above. The court may also impose on the designated local authority requirements for the purpose of securing compliance with either of the types of conditions described above. None of the above mentioned conditions or requirements can be imposed without prior consultation with the designated authority. This refers to such consultation (if any) as is reasonably practicable in all the circumstances of the case. There is provision for a relevant court to add any of the above mentioned conditions or requirements where a child has been remanded to local authority accommodation on the application of the designated authority. A relevant court may also vary or revoke any of the conditions or requirements on the application of the designated authority or the child.

Section 97 provides for liability to arrest for breaking remand conditions. Where a constable has reasonable grounds for suspecting such a breach, he may arrest the child and the child must then be brought before a court as soon as is reasonably practicable and in any event within 24 hours. If the court is of the opinion that the child has broken any of the remand conditions, it must remand him either to local authority accommodation or, if either set of conditions of remand to youth detention accommodation is met, to youth detention accommodation. If the court is not of this opinion, it must remand the child on the same conditions as before.

Remands to youth detention accommodation

E[3.6] The *first set of conditions* of the Legal Aid, Sentencing and Punishment of Offenders Act 2012, s 98:

(a) the child must have reached the age of 12;
(b) the offence must be a 'violent' or 'sexual offence' (defined in the Legal Aid, Sentencing and Punishment of Offenders Act 2012, s 94(8)) or an offence punishable in the case of an adult with imprisonment for a term of at least 14 years;
(c) the court must be of the opinion, after considering all of the remand options, that only a remand to youth detention accommodation would be adequate:
  (i) to protect the public form death or serious personal injury (whether physical or psychological) occasioned by further offences committed by the child; or
  (ii) to prevent the commission by the child of imprisonable offences; and
(d) the child is legal represented, or such representation has been withdrawn because of the child's conduct or financial ineligibility, or an application for such representation has been refused owing to financial ineligibility, or the child has refused or failed to take up the opportunity to apply for such representation despite being informed of his right to do so.

The *second set of conditions* of the Legal Aid, Sentencing and Punishment of Offenders Act 2012, s 99:

(a) the child must have reached the age of 12;
(b) it must appear to the court that there is a real prospect that the child will be sentenced to a custodial sentence for the offence or any one of them;
(c) the offence or any one of them is an imprisonable offence;
(d) either of the following 'history' conditions must be met:
  (i) the child has a recent history of absconding while subject to a custodial remand, and the offence or any one of them is alleged to be or has been found to have been committed while the child was remanded to local authority accommodation; or
  (ii) the offence or any one of them, together with any other imprisonable offences of which the child has been convicted in any proceedings, amount or would, if the child were convicted of that offence or offences, amount to a recent history of committing imprisonable offences while on bail or subject to a custodial remand;
(e) the court must be of the opinion, after considering all of the remand options, that only a remand to youth detention accommodation would be adequate:
  (i) to protect the public form death or serious personal injury (whether physical or psychological) occasioned by further offences committed by the child; or
  (ii) to prevent the commission by the child of imprisonable offences; and
(f) the child is legally represented, or such representation has been withdrawn because of the child's or financial ineligibility, or an application for such representation has been refused owing to financial ineligibility, or the child has refused or failed to take up the opportunity to apply for such representation despite being informed of his right to do so.

A remand to youth detention accommodation is a remand to such accommodation of one of the kinds listed below as the Secretary of State, after consultation with the designated local authority, directs in the child's case:

(a) a secure children's home;
(b) a secure training centre;
(c) a young offender institution; and
(d) youth detention accommodation for the purposes of the detention and training order provisions.

The designated local authority, which the court must specify, will be either:
(a) in the case of a child looked after by a local authority, that authority; or
(b) in any other case, the local authority in whose area it appears to the court that the child habitually resides or the offence or one of the offence was committed.

Secure accommodation

E[3.7] A local authority may not use secure accommodation, ie accommodation provided for the purpose of restricting liberty, for a period of more than 72 hours whether consecutively or in aggregate, in any period of 28 consecutive days without an order of the court authorising the use of secure accommodation. There are exemptions for public holidays and Sundays and for disregarding periods prior to a court authorisation. These provisions apply to all children accommodated by a local authority by virtue of a warrant under the Children and Young Persons Act 1969.

The primary statutory provision, s 25 of the Children Act 1989, which is supplemented by the Secure Accommodation Regulations 1991 and the Secure Accommodation (No 2) Regulations 1991, relates to both the family and criminal jurisdictions. The terminology of the family courts is used, ie the subject of any application is a 'child' defined by the Children Act 1989, s 105(1) as a person under 18.

It is the restriction of liberty which is the essential factor in determining what is secure accommodation; accordingly, a hospital ward may be 'secure accommodation': *A Metropolitan Borough Council v DB* [1997] 1 FLR 767.

In determining an application for a secure accommodation order the 'welfare principle' and the 'no order' principles of the Children Act 1989 do not apply. Where the court has found any of the criteria in the Children Act or the regulations is satisfied, it is bound to make a secure accommodation order: *Re M (a minor) (secure accommodation order)* [1995] 3 All ER 407, [1995] 2 FCR 373, [1995] 2 WLR 302, [1995] 1 FLR 418, CA and the Children Act 1989, s 25(4).

Secure accommodation – criteria

E[3.8]–[3.16] The criteria for placing/keeping a child in secure accommodation are modified in relation to children who are being looked after by a local authority and are aged 12 or over but under 17 and are being detained by the police under the Police and Criminal Evidence Act 1984, s 38(6). In such a case it must appear to the court that any other accommodation is inappropriate because:

(a) the child is likely to abscond from such other accommodation; or
(b) the child is likely to injure himself or other people if he is kept in any such other accommodation: Regulation 6 of the Children (Secure Accommodation) Regulations 1991, SI 1991/1505, reg 16.

In all other cases, the criteria are those applicable to family cases, namely:
(a) the child has a history of absconding and is likely to abscond form any other description of accommodation; and
(b) if he absconds, he is likely to suffer significant harm: Children Act 1989, s 25(1).

No court shall exercise its powers relating to secure accommodation in respect of a child who is not legally represented unless, having been informed of his right to apply for legal aid and having had the opportunity to do so, he refused or failed to apply: Children Act 1989, s 25(6).

The welfare of the child is relevant, but not paramount, in a remand situation: *Re M (a minor) (secure accommodation)* [1995] Fam 108, [1995] 3 All ER 407, CA.

The procedure is prescribed by the Magistrates' Courts (Children and Young Person) Rules 1992, SI 1992/2071.

E[3.17] The maximum period for which a court may from time to time authorise a child who has been remanded to local authority accommodation under s 91(3) of the Legal Aid, Sentencing and Punishment of Offenders Act 2012 is the period of the remand, subject to maximum of 28 days without further authorisation.

Youths and sending for trial – Crime and Disorder Act 1998, ss 51A–51E

E[3.18] The legislative policy is that youths should be tried summarily wherever possible. Certain offences must, however, be sent forthwith to the Crown Court. These are listed below. In the case of b), sending is subject to ss 24A and 24B of the Magistrates' Courts 1980 (indication of plea to be sought prior to making the relevant determination).

(a) The offence is an offence of homicide, or each of the requirements of s 51A(1) of the Firearms Act 1968 would be satisfied with respect to the offence and the person charged with it if he were convicted of the offence, or s 29(3) of the Violent Crime Reduction Act 2006 (minimum sentences in certain cases of using someone to mind a weapon) would apply if her were convicted of the offence.
(b) The offence is one of the serious offences mentioned in s 91 of the Powers of Criminal Courts (Sentencing) Act 2000 (other than one mentioned in d) below which appears to meet the criteria for the imposition of a dangerous offender sentence on conviction) and the court considers that if the offender is found guilty it ought to be possible to sentence him in accordance with subsection (3) of that section.
(c) Notice is given in respect of an either way offence under s 51B (notices in serious or complex fraud cases) or s 51C (notices in certain cases involving children) of the 1998 Act.

(d) The offence is a specified offence within the meaning of s 224 of the Criminal Justice Act 2003 and it appears to the court that if the offender is found guilty of the offence the criteria for a sentence under s 226B of that Act (extended sentence for certain violent or sexual offences) would be met.

Sending further offences on the same or on a subsequent occasion

E[3.18A] Where a youth is sent as per the above the court may at the same time send him to the Crown Court for trial for any indictable offence which is related to the sent offence, or for any summary offence which is imprisonable in the case of an adult or carries obligatory or discretionary disqualification and which appears to be related to the sent offence or to the indictable offence (subject, again, to indication of plea, unless the sent offence is one within s 51A(12) of the Crime and Disorder Act 1998 (ie homicide, etc, see (a) above) – s 24A of the Magistrates' Courts Act 1980 excepts this case from the indication of plea provisions the section proceeds to prescribe). (The term 'related' is defined by s 51E of the Crime and Disorder Act 1998.) There is like power to send forthwith where the youth has been sent as per the above and subsequently appears before the court charged with such a related indictable offence or summary offence (subject again to indication of plea, except where the sent offence was one within s 51A(12) of the Crime and Disorder Act 1998 as above).

Youths jointly charged with adults

E[3.18B] Where an *adult* is sent to the Crown Court and a youth is brought before the court on the same or on a subsequent occasion charged jointly with the adult with any indictable offence for which the adult is sent for trial, or an indictable offence which appears to be related to that offence, the court shall, *if it considers it necessary in the interest of justice (see below) to do so*, send the youth forthwith to the Crown Court for trial in respect of the indictable offence together with any indictable offence related to it, and any summary offence related to the sent offence or to the indictable offence which is imprisonable or carries obligatory or discretionary carrying disqualification. This is, again, subject to indication of plea under s 24A or s 24B of the Magistrates' Courts Act 1980, unless the sent offence is one within s 51A(12) of the Crime and Disorder Act 1998 – s 24A of the Magistrates' Courts Act 1980 excepts this case from the indication of plea provisions the section proceeds to prescribe.

This power to send the youth arises only after consideration has been to such of the sending conditions mentioned in E[13.18] above as may apply to the case. For example, if the adult and youth are jointly charged with robbery, the adult must be sent, consideration must then be given in the case of the youth to 'dangerousness' (indication of plea does not apply) and then, if the dangerousness criteria are not met, to the punishment of grave crimes, prior to the determination of which an indication of plea must be sought. It is only where the indication is 'not guilty' and the court determines that its powers are sufficient that the 'interests of justice' test will be considered. If the court determines that it is not in the interests of justice to send the youth to the Crown Court for trial it will remit the youth to the youth court.

Where a *youth* is sent to the Crown Court and an adult offender, jointly charged with an either way offence or charged with a related either way offence, appears before the court he *must* if it is the same occasion, or *may* if he appears on a subsequent occasion, be sent forthwith to the Crown Court, unless a guilty plea has been indicated by or on behalf of the adult. If the adult is so sent, the court shall at the time send him to the Crown Court for trial for any related either way offence (again, unless a guilty plea has been indicated), and any summary offence which is related to either of the former and which is punishable with imprisonment or carries obligatory or discretionary disqualification.

'Jointly charged' does not acquire a restricted meaning, but must be given its natural meaning. The phrase 'jointly charged' normally means two persons named in the same charge or series of charges; thus, while only one person can drive a vehicle, where two persons were charged with driving and allowing themselves to be carried in a vehicle taken without the owner's consent, they were properly considered to be 'jointly charged': *R v Peterborough Magistrates' Court, ex p Allgood* (1995) 159 JP 627, [1996] RTR 26.

See further the Sentencing Council's allocation guideline at D[4.12], ante.

Dangerous offenders and offenders accused of grave crimes

E[3.18C] **Dangerous offenders.** Where the offence is a specified offence within the meaning of s 224 of the Criminal Justice Act 2003 and it appears to the court that if the youth is found guilty of the offence the criteria for a sentence under s 226B of that Act (extended sentence for certain violent or sexual offences) would be met, the youth must be sent for trial. The words 'if the offender is found guilty' preclude committal in a case where it is clear the defendant is unfit to stand trial: *R (on the application of P) v Derby Youth Court* [2015] EWHC 573 (Admin), (2015) 179 JP 139. *Indication of plea before venue does not apply to this case.* The criteria for the imposition of an extended sentence are:

(a) the offence is a specified offence;
(b) the court considers that there is a significant risk to members of the public of serious harm occasioned by the commission by the offender of further specified offences;
(c) the court is not required by s 226(2) to impose a sentence of detention for life under s 91 of the PCVC(S)A 2000; and
(d) if the court were to impose an extended sentence, the term that it would specify as the appropriate custodial term would be at least four years.

In practice, the magistrates' court will rarely be in a position, at the stage of considering venue for the trial of the youth, to make the relevant determination on dangerousness owing to lack of reports, etc. Such cases are likely, therefore, to come before the Crown Court by sending under another power or on committal for sentence under s 3C of the Powers of Criminal Courts (Sentencing) Act 2000.

Offenders liable to be sentenced to long-term detention. If the offence is one of the serious offences mentioned in s 91 Powers of Criminal Courts (Sentencing) Act 2000, other than one which appears to meet the criteria for the imposition of a dangerous offender sentence on conviction, and the court considers that if the offender is found guilty it ought to be possible to sentence him in accordance with subsection (3) of that section, the youth must be sent for trial, *but in this case only if he indicates a not guilty plea.*

The offences to which s 91(3) applies are:

(a) an offence punishable in the case of an adult with imprisonment for 14 years or more, not being an offence the sentence for which is fixed by law;
(b) an offence under s 3, 13, 25 or 26 of the Sexual Offences Act 2003;
(c) certain offences under the Firearms Act 1968 which carry a minimum sentence, but the court is of the opinion that there are exceptional circumstances which justify its not imposing the required custodial sentence;
(d) offences under s 28 of the Violent Crime Reduction Act 2006, which attract a minimum sentence under s 29, but the court is of the opinion that there are exceptional circumstances which justify its not imposing the required custodial sentence.

The power to commit youths for trial for 'grave crimes' was formerly exercisable under s 24 of the Magistrates' Courts Act 1980 and a substantial body of case law arose from challenges to decisions to commit for trial. The principles which have evolved are set out below. The most significant development has been the amendment of s 3B of the Powers of Criminal Courts (Sentencing) Act 2000 to enable committal for sentence following a trial in the youth court.

The proper approach for the magistrates' court is to ask itself whether it would be proper for the Crown Court sentencing the defendant for the offence of which he is charged to exercise its powers under s 91 of the Powers of Criminal Courts (Sentencing) Act 2000: *R v Inner London Youth Court, ex p DPP* (1996) 161 JP 178, [1996] Crim LR 834. Magistrates should not decline jurisdiction unless the offence and the circumstances surrounding it and the offender are such as to make it 'more than a vague or theoretical possibility', a 'real possibility' or a 'real prospect' that a sentence of at least two years will be imposed: see *R (CPS) v Redbridge Youth Court* [2005] EWHC 1390 (Admin), 169 JP 393.

The Divisional Court has been concerned at the number of inappropriate committals for trial of juveniles who have not attained 15 years and has emphasised that such committals should be rare in *R (on the application of D) v Manchester City Youth Court* [2001] EWHC 860 (Admin), 166 JP 15 and in a number of authorities cited below. In *R (on the application of H) v Southampton Youth Court* [2004] EWHC 2912 (Admin), 169 JP 37, [2005] Crim LR 395 Leveson J, with the approval of the Vice President of the Court of Appeal (Criminal Division) summarised the position for the assistance of magistrates:

> '[33] 1. The general policy of the legislature is that those who are under 18 years of age and in particular children under 15 years of age should, wherever possible, be tried in the youth court. It is that court which is best designed to meet their specific needs. A trial in the Crown Court with the inevitably greater formality and greatly increased number of people involved (including a jury and the public) should be reserved for the most serious cases.
>
> [34] 2. It is further policy of the legislature that, generally speaking, first-time offenders aged 12 to 14 and all offenders under 12 should not be detained in custody and decisions as to jurisdiction should have regard to the fact that the exceptional power to detain for grave offences should not be used to water down the general principle. Those under '15 will rarely attract a period of detention and, even more rarely, those who are under 12.
>
> [35] 3. In each case the court should ask itself whether there is a real prospect, having regard to his or her age, that this defendant whose case they are considering might require a sentence of, or in excess of, two years or, alternatively, whether although the sentence might be less than two years, there is some unusual feature of the case which justifies declining jurisdiction, bearing in mind that the absence of a power to impose a detention and training order because the defendant is under 15 is not an unusual feature.'

The effect of the amendment to the youth court's power to commit for sentence (see above) was considered by Leveson P in the *R (on the application of DPP) v South Tyneside Youth Court* [2015] EWHC 1455 (Admin), [2015] 2 Cr App R (S) 411, [2015] Crim L R 746.

> 'On its face, s 3B of the 2000 Act as amended means that a youth court can commit a defendant for sentence after conviction in that court if it is of the opinion that the Crown Court should have the power to impose detention under Section 91(3) of the 2000 Act. However, the question of whether it "ought to be possible" to impose (or whether, in *Southampton Youth Court* terms there is a real prospect of) such a sentence, already will have been considered at the point of allocation. If the prosecution case is taken at its highest and given the mandatory nature of the requirement to commit for trial in such circumstances, it is difficult to see the circumstances in which a case could be accepted as fit for trial in the youth court and then require committal for sentence.
>
> If that analysis is correct, s 3B of the 2000 Act and s 51A of the 1998 Act might appear to be in conflict. However, it is reasonable to assume that legislation has been enacted for a purpose and that its purpose should not be rendered of no practical effect by existing legislation. Against that background, it is necessary to consider whether it is appropriate to consider whether an approach can properly be adopted within the boundaries of the statutory wording so as to give proper force to s 3B of the 2000 Act while at the same time ensuring that it is consistent with s 51A of the 1998 Act.
>
> I have set out the approach prescribed in *Southampton Youth Court* and start by emphasising the first principle that the general policy of the legislature that children and young persons should, wherever possible, be tried in the youth

court, a court best designed to meet their specific needs, avoiding the greater formality and public involvement of the Crown Court. Since that decision, public concern over the propriety of trials in the Crown Court for those under the age of 18 has increased rather than diminished. In 2014 Lord Carlile QC chaired a parliamentary inquiry in the Youth Court in England and Wales. He reported that "an overwhelming majority of the respondents" to the inquiry considered that the Crown Court was not an appropriate venue for the trial of defendants eligible by age to be tried in the Youth Court. On its face the amendment to Section 3B of the 2000 Act would enable full effect to be given to the first principle which I have again summarised.

The test set out in *Southampton Youth Court*, (whether there was a "real prospect" that the defendant might require a sentence in excess of the powers of the youth court) has been recognised and followed as a sensible interpretation of the requirements of s 51A of the 1998 Act. When formulated, however, it had to be applied in the context of an irrevocable allocation decision. If the youth court retained jurisdiction for trial and it emerged in the course of the trial that the circumstances were more serious than had been understood at the allocation hearing, the court remained restricted in its sentencing powers. That factor justified the requirement in *Oldham Youth Court* to take the prosecution case at its highest.

In practical terms, however, the youth court often would have only limited material at the allocation hearing with the result that the "real prospect" test would be met for want of information and in the knowledge that further material emerging later in the proceedings could not permit any change in venue. For my part, I have no doubt in recognising that this will have resulted in an understandable caution in respect of allocation decisions by youth Courts and I am aware that it has been the experience of Resident and other judges in Crown Courts in different parts of England and Wales that cases have been sent from the youth court for trial where, after fuller investigation, it has become apparent that the sentencing powers of the youth court were sufficient to meet the justice of the case. This case is a good example. Without considerably more information, it is quite impossible to determine whether B requires condign punishment, education or psychological therapy.

Because s 3B (as amended) of the 2000 Act means that the youth court is not making a once and for all decision at the point of allocation, the "real prospect" assessment requires a different emphasis and taking the prosecution case at its highest is no longer necessary; to that extent, the observations of Langstaff J in *Oldham Youth Court* no longer apply. For the future, there will, of course, be cases in which the alleged offending is so grave that a sentence of or excess of two years will be a "real prospect" irrespective of particular considerations in relation either to the offence or the offender's role in it: such cases are, however, likely to be rare. As the time of allocation and determination of venue, the court will doubtless take the views of the prosecution and defence into account; these views could include representations as the value of privacy of the proceedings or, alternatively, the desire for a jury trial. Subject to such submissions, however, in most cases whether there is such a "real prospect" will generally be apparent only when the court has determined the full circumstances of the offence and has a far greater understanding of the position of the offender. Since the youth court now has the option of committing a defendant for sentence after conviction if the court considers that the Crown Court should have the power to impose a sentence of detention pursuant to s 91(3) of the 2000 Act, it will generally be at that point when the assessment can and should be made. In that way, the observations in Southampton Youth Court (at para 33) that Crown Court trial for a youth "should be reserved for the most serious cases" remain entirely apposite. It is worth observing that this approach is entirely consistent with the intended purpose of the amendment as explained by the Parliamentary Under-Secretary of State for Justice during the Report and Third Reading of the Bill: see Hansard, Vol 580, Col 464.

For the sake of completeness, I add only that cases of homicide and offences subject to minimum terms under the Firearms Act 1968 are dealt with separately within s 51A of the 1998 Act. Offences of that kind do not fall within the "real prospect" test.'

It was previously held that if the conditions laid down (now for sending) were met, the court must send the accused for trial; the suitability of the Crown Court for the trial of a young person is not a separate consideration to take into account by the youth court in making this decision: *R (on the application of C and D) v Sheffield Youth Court* [2003] EWHC 35 (Admin), 167 JP 159, [2003] 12 LS Gaz R 29 – not following *R (on the application of R) v Balham Youth Court Justices* [2002] EWHC 2426 (Admin), [2002] All ER (D) 73 (Sep) on this point; see also *R v Devizes Youth Court, ex p A* (2000) 164 JP 330. This must now be read in the light of the *South Tyneside* case

The appropriate way to challenge a decision to commit (now send) to the Crown Court for trial is to apply for judicial review and not to apply to the Crown to stay the proceedings as an abuse of process: *R v AH* [2002] EWCA Crim 2938, (2003) 167 JP 30. If the Director of Public Prosecutions is concerned about a decision of a youth court to retain jurisdiction he can either seek judicial review or apply for a voluntary bill of indictment; but the defendant's rights are better safeguarded in judicial review and that is the course which should normally be followed: *R (on the application of DPP) v Camberwell Youth Court* and *R (on the application of H) v Camberwell Youth Court* [2004] EWHC Admin 1805, [2005] 1 All ER 999, [2005] 1 WLR 810, (2005) 169 JP 105, [2005] Crim LR 165.

Plea before venue procedure

E[3.18D] Where the power to send a youth to the Crown Court for trial arises from one of the following cases the youth must be sent forthwith.

(a) it is an offence of homicide, or each of the requirements of s 51A(1) of the Firearms Act 1968 would be satisfied with respect to the offence and the person charged with it if he were convicted of the offence, or s 29(3) of the Violent Crime Reduction Act 2006 (minimum sentences in certain cases of using someone to mind a weapon) would apply if he were convicted of the offence;
(b) notice is given in respect of an either way offence under s 51B (notices in serious or complex fraud cases) or s 51C (notices in certain cases involving children) of the 1998 Act;
(c) the offence is a specified offence within the meaning of s 224 of the Criminal Justice Act 20031 and it appears to the court that if the offender is found guilty of the offence the criteria for a sentence under s 226B of that Act (extended sentence for certain violent or sexual offences) would be met.

In all other cases where the court would be required to determine, in relation to the offence, whether to send the youth to the Crown Court, or to determine any matter the effect of which would be to determine whether the youth is sent for trial, the indication of plea provisions of ss 24A and 24B of the Magistrates' Courts Act 1980 apply.

Procedure where the accused is present

E[3.18E] The procedure is as follows.

(a) The court shall cause the charge to be written down, if this has not already been done, and to be read to the accused.
(b) The court shall then explain to the accused in ordinary language that he may indicate whether (if the offence were to proceed to trial) he would plead guilty or not guilty, and that if he indicates that he would plead guilty:

(i) the court must proceed as mentioned in subsection (d) below; and
(ii) in cases where the offence is one mentioned in s 91(1) of the Powers of Criminal Courts (Sentencing) Act 2000) he may be sent to the Crown Court for sentencing under section 3B or (if applicable) 3C of that Act if the court is of such opinion as is mentioned in subsection (2) of the applicable section.

(c) The court shall then ask the accused whether (if the offence were to proceed to trial) he would plead guilty or not guilty.
(d) If the accused indicates that he would plead guilty, the court shall proceed as if:
(i) the proceedings constituted from the beginning the summary trial of the information; and
(ii) s 9(1) above was complied with and he pleaded guilty under it,

and, accordingly, the court shall not (and shall not be required to) proceed to make the relevant determination or to proceed further under s 51 or (as the case may be) s 51A of the 1998 Act in relation to the offence.
(e) If the accused indicates that he would plead not guilty, the court shall proceed to make the relevant determination and this section shall cease to apply.
(f) If the accused in fact fails to indicate how he would plead, for the purposes of this section he shall be taken to indicate that he would plead not guilty.
(g) Subject to subsection (d) above, the following shall not for any purpose be taken to constitute the taking of a plea:
(i) asking the accused under this section whether (if the offence were to proceed to trial) he would plead guilty or not guilty;
(ii) an indication by the accused under this section of how he would plead.

Procedure where the youth is absent

E[3.18F] Section 24B of the Magistrates' Courts Act 1980 has effect where the indication of plea provisions of s 24A apply, the youth is represented by a legal representative, and the court considers that by reason of the youth's disorderly conduct before the court it is not practicable for proceedings under s 24A to be conducted in the youth's presence and that it should proceed in the youth's absence. In such a case:

(a) the court shall cause the charge to be written down, if this has not already been done, and to be read to the representative;
(b) the court shall ask the representative whether (if the offence were to proceed to trial) the accused would plead guilty or not guilty;
(c) if the representative indicates that the accused would plead guilty the court shall proceed as if the proceedings constituted from the beginning the summary trial of the information, and as if s 9(1) of the Magistrates' Courts Act 1980 was complied with and the accused pleaded guilty under it;
(d) if the representative indicates that the accused would plead not guilty the court shall proceed to make the relevant determination and this section shall cease to apply;
(e) if the representative in fact fails to indicate how the accused would plead, for the purposes of this section he shall be taken to indicate that the accused would plead not guilty;
(f) subject to (c) above, the following shall not for any purpose be taken to constitute the taking of a plea:
(i) asking the representative under this section whether (if the offence were to proceed to trial) the accused would plead guilty or not guilty;
(ii) an indication by the representative under this section of how the accused would plead.

Crown Court sitting as a youth court to deal with summary only matters

E[3.18G] The following observations were made by Walker J in *R v Iles* [2012] EWCA Crim 1610, (2012) 176 JP 601:

'3. Second, the complexities are such that there appears to have developed a practice under which the magistrates' courts adjourn summary-only matters, knowing the offender is due to appear at a Crown Court on other matters, and invite the Crown Court to enable the summary cases to be dealt with at the same time by the expedient of arranging for a Circuit Judge to sit as a District Judge. Such a practice has advantages, but there are dangers. Therefore, before this practice is followed, the magistrates' court must carefully consider whether this is in the interests of justice and ensure that there is power to do so. A Crown Court Judge who is invited to deal with two sets of proceedings in this way must decide whether it is appropriate in the light of submissions from both the prosecution and the defence. For this purpose it must be kept firmly in mind that, when sentencing as a District Judge, the sentence is imposed by the magistrates' court, and consideration must be given not only to advantages but also to dangers that may arise because (1) the Judge would, as regards the magistrates' court matters, be limited to the powers of a magistrates' court, powers which must be carefully checked by counsel and the court; and (2) sentences that the Judge imposes when sitting as a magistrates' court would have a different route of appeal from that applicable to sentences imposed by the Judge when sitting in the Crown Court. If the invitation is accepted, then consideration must again be given to these dangers at the stage of deciding what sentence should be imposed by the Judge when sitting as a magistrates' court.'

Committal to the Crown Court for sentence

E[3.18H]–[3.19] There are three powers of committal for sentence:

(a) where a guilty plea has been indicated to an offence which is one of those listed in s 91(1) of the PCC(S)A 2000, or, in consequence of the amendment of s 3B of the PCC(S)A 2000 by s 53 of the Criminal Justice and Courts Act 2015, where a person under the age of 18 has been convicted of such an offence (ie a decision to accept jurisdiction following a 'not guilty' is no longer a complete bar to committal to the Crown Court – see *R (on the application of DPP) v South Tyneside Youth Court* [2015] EWHC 1455 (Admin), [2015] 2 Cr App Rep (S) 411, [2015] Crim LR 746), and the court is of the opinion that the offence, or the combination of the offence and one or more offences associated with it, is such that the sentencing powers of s 91 of the PCC(S)A 2000 should be available: PCC(S)A 2000, s 3B (see **E[3.18C]**);

(b) where the offence is a specified offence and the court forms the opinion (subsequent to mode of trial) that the criteria for the imposition of an extended sentence are met (see **E[3.18C]**): PCC(S)A 2000, s 3C; and

(c) where the offence is one of those listed in s 91(1) of the PCC(S)A 2000, a guilty plea has been indicated and the court has sent the offender for trial for one or more related offences (ie if both the offences were prosecuted in the Crown Court they could be joined in the same indictment): PCC(S)A 2000, s 4A.

Where any of the above powers is used, the court may additionally commit for sentence any other offence under PCC(S)A 2000, s 6.

In case(a) and (b) above the Crown Court has the same sentencing powers as if the offender had just been of the offence on indictment before the court: PCC(S)A 2000, s 5A. In case (c), however, if the court does not state that, in its opinion, it has the power to commit under either (a) or (b), and the offender is not convicted in the Crown Court of the or any of the related offences sent there for trial, the Crown Court's powers of sentencing are limited to those of the youth court: PCC(S)A 2000, ss 4A(4) and (5), 5A(2). Only youth court powers are available for offences committed for sentence under s 6: PCC(S)A 2000, s 7.

Procedure

E[3.20] The court has to consider two general duties, the welfare of the child and the principal aim of the youth justice system to prevent offending by juveniles.

E[3.21] The court must take care to ensure that he understands the proceedings and the charge should be explained in simple terms appropriate to his age and understanding. If not represented, his parents should be allowed to assist him in his defence.

E[3.22] Oath. In the youth court, the evidence of children under 14 years must be given unsworn, otherwise the defendant and all the witnesses use a modified form of oath which commences 'I promise before Almighty God to tell the truth' etc. This oath is also used by a juvenile who gives evidence in the adult court (Children and Young Persons Act 1963, s 28).

Evidence from a witness in need of special protection (a child victim of a violent or sexual offence) will give evidence via a live video link (*R v Camberwell Green Youth Court, ex p G* [2005] UKHL 4, [2005] All ER (D) 259 (Jan)). For vulnerable accused see D[8.22B]. For witnesses other than the accused see **D[8.22C]**.

E[3.23] Remission to a local court. Where the court before which a juvenile appears is not the youth court for the area in which he resides it may (and if it is an adult magistrates' court, it must unless it exercises its limited powers of sentence) remit him to be dealt with by his local youth court. This would normally be done, for example, where reports are required and the case has to be adjourned in order to obtain them. The court may give directions as to whether the defendant should be bailed or kept in custody until he appears before the local court.

E[3.24] Remission to the adult court. Where a juvenile attains the age of 18 before conviction or after conviction but before sentencing he may be remitted on bail or in custody to be dealt with in the adult court, but not for an indictable offence (*R (on the application of Denny) v Acton Youth Court* (2004) Independent, 24 May).

E[3.25] Abuse of Process – for general principles consult **D[1B.11]–D[1B.12]**.

Abuse of Process – youth incapable of following proceedings. Guidance was given in *DPP v P* [2007] EWHC 946 (Admin) as follows:

(1) Although the youth court had an inherent jurisdiction to stay proceedings as an abuse of the process, the jurisdiction was limited directly to matters affecting the fairness of the trial of the particular defendant concerned, and should only be exercised in exceptional circumstances, on the ground of one or more of the capacity issues, before any evidence was heard.

(2) The fact that a higher authority had previously held that a person was unfit to plead did not make it an abuse to try that person for subsequent criminal acts. The issue of the child's capacity to participate effectively had to be decided afresh.

(3) A child in early adolescence might well develop significantly over a relatively short period. However, where the medical evidence suggested that the child's condition had not changed since his appearance before that higher court, the decisions of that previous court would be relevant matters to be considered, although not determinative or binding.

(4) Medical evidence should be considered as part of the evidence in the case and not as the sole evidence in a [preliminary] application. It was the court's opinion of the child's level of understanding which had to determine whether a trial was to proceed.

(5) Although the medical evidence might be of great importance, it had always to be set in the context of other evidence relating to the child, which might bear upon the issues of his understanding, mental capacity and ability to participate effectively in a trial. Medical evidence on its own might appear quite strong, but when other matters were considered the court might conclude that the defendant's understanding and ability to take part in the trial were greater than was suggested by the doctors and that, with proper assistance from his legal adviser and suitable adjustments to the procedure of the court, the trial could properly proceed to a conclusion.

(6) Other factors might also be relevant to the decision that the court had to take. If a trial began, the court would wish to ensure that the child understood each stage of the process. That might involve some direct exchanges between the bench and the child (engagement). The child's responses might assist the court in deciding the child's level of understanding. Further, it might become apparent from the way in which the trial was conducted that the child's representative did not have adequate instructions on which to cross-examine witnesses.

(7) The court had a duty to keep under continuing review the question of whether the criminal trial ought to continue. If at any stage the court concluded that the child was unable to participate effectively in the trial, it might decide to

call a halt. Nevertheless, the court might consider that it was in the best interests of the child that the trial should continue. If the prosecution evidence was weak, there might be no case to answer. It might be that the defendant's representative would invite the court to acquit on the ground that the child did not know that what he had done was seriously wrong: *R (on the application of P) v West London Youth Court* [2005] EWHC 2583 (Admin), [2006] 1 All ER 447 applied.

(8) If the court decided it should call a halt to the criminal trial on the ground that the child could not take an effective part in the proceedings, it should then consider whether to switch to a consideration of whether the child had done the acts alleged. That decision was one for the discretion of the court, but the proceedings should be stayed as an abuse of process before fact finding only if no useful purpose could be served by finding the facts. The court would wish to consider the possibility that it might be appropriate to make a hospital [or guardianship] order, but even if such an order appeared unlikely, there might be other advantages in continuing to complete the fact finding process. If the court found that the child had done the acts alleged, it might be appropriate to alert the local authority to the position with a view to the consideration of care proceedings. If the court found that the child had not done the acts alleged, the proceedings would be brought to an end by a finding of not guilty: *R (on the application of P) v Barking Youth Court* [2002] All ER (D) 93 (Apr) applied.

(9) It would be right for a court to stay proceedings at the outset if the child was so severely impaired as to be unable to participate in the trial and where there would be no useful purpose in finding the facts.

Vulnerable accused. Where it is said that the accused is vulnerable and may not be able to participate effectively in the proceedings the court should bear in mind that it has the power to direct that the accused can give evidence via a live video link. See **D[8.22B]**.

Abuse of Process – delay. A stay of proceedings even on the grounds of unjustifiable delay will not normally be acceptable in a Youth Court (*R (on the application of DPP) v Croydon Youth Court* (2001) 165 JP 181, 165 JPN 34) but see *R (on the application of Knight) v West Dorset Magistrates' Court* [2002] EWHC 2152 (Admin), 166 JP 705. See **D[1B.11]**.

E[4]
Possible orders for juveniles

E[4.1] See the Process of sentencing at B[45], and also the notes on each type of sentence in the 'Sentencing' section at B[2]–B[31].

E[4.2] In the following list of orders available to courts in dealing with a minor (age 10–17 inclusive), only those marked with an asterisk * may be used by a magistrates' court that is not a youth court: Powers of Criminal Courts (Sentencing) Act 2000, s 8(6).

- *Referral order: Powers of Criminal Courts (Sentencing) Act 2000, s 16;
- *Absolute and conditional discharge: Powers of Criminal Courts (Sentencing) Act 2000, ss 12–15;
- Compensation: Powers of Criminal Courts (Sentencing) Act 2000, ss 130–134;
- Order made under s 1C of the Crime and Disorder Act 1998 (Anti-social Behaviour): Crime and Disorder Act 1998, s 1C;
- *Fine: Powers of Criminal Courts (Sentencing) Act 2000, s 135;
- *Binding over parent or guardian: Powers of Criminal Courts (Sentencing) Act 2000, s 150;
- Reparation order: Powers of Criminal Courts (Sentencing) Act 2000, ss 73–75, Sch 8;
- Attendance centre: Powers of Criminal Courts (Sentencing) Act 2000, ss 60–62, Sch 5;
- Youth rehabilitation order: Criminal Justice and Immigration Act 2008, ss 1–7 and Schs 1–4.
- Detention and training order: Powers of Criminal Courts (Sentencing) Act 2000, s 89;
- Punishment of certain grave crimes (Crown Court only): Powers of Criminal Courts (Sentencing) Act 2000, ss 90, 91;
- Committal for sentence of dangerous young offenders: Powers of Criminal Courts (Sentencing) Act 2000, s 3C.

These disposals are considered in detail in Section B Sentencing, except for punishment of grave crimes and committal for sentence of dangerous offences, which are dealt with in the immediately preceding part of this section.

Before finally disposing of the case or before remitting the case to another court, unless it considers it undesirable to do so, the court shall inform the child or young person and his parent or guardian if present, or any person assisting him in his defence, of the manner in which it proposes to deal with the case, and allow any of those persons so informed to make representations: Criminal Procedure Rules 2013, Pt 44.

E[5]

Sentencing children and young people

(Overarching principles and offence specific guidelines for sexual offences and robbery)

Overarching Principles and Offence Specific Guidelines for Sexual Offences and Robbery Definitive Guideline

E[5.1] This guideline applies to all children or young people where the first hearing takes place on or after 1 June 2017, regardless of the date of the offence.

Section one: General approach

Sentencing principles

1.1 When sentencing children or young people (those aged under 18 at the date of the finding of guilt) a court must (This section does not apply when imposing a mandatory life sentence, when imposing a statutory minimum custodial sentence, when imposing detention for life under the dangerous offender provisions or when making certain orders under the Mental Health Act 1983.) have regard to:

- the principal aim of the youth justice system (to prevent offending by children and young people) (Crime and Disorder Act 1998, s 37(1)); and
- the welfare of the child or young person (Children and Young Persons Act 1933, s 44(1)).

1.2 While the seriousness of the offence will be the starting point, the approach to sentencing should be individualistic and focused on the child or young person, as opposed to offence focused. For a child or young person the sentence should focus on rehabilitation where possible. A court should also consider the effect the sentence is likely to have on the child or young person (both positive and negative) as well as any underlying factors contributing to the offending behaviour.

1.3 Domestic and international laws dictate that a custodial sentence should always be a measure of last resort for children and young people and statute provides that a custodial sentence may only be imposed when the offence is so serious that no other sanction is appropriate (see section six for more information on custodial sentences).

1.4 It is important to avoid 'criminalising' children and young people unnecessarily; the primary purpose of the youth justice system is to encourage children and young people to take responsibility for their own actions and promote re-integration into society rather than to punish. Restorative justice disposals may be of particular value for children and young people as they can encourage them to take responsibility for their actions and understand the impact their offence may have had on others.

1.5 It is important to bear in mind any factors that may diminish the culpability of a child or young person. Children and young people are not fully developed and they have not attained full maturity. As such, this can impact on their decision making and risk taking behaviour. It is important to consider the extent to which the child or young person has been acting impulsively and whether their conduct has been affected by inexperience, emotional volatility or negative influences. They may not fully appreciate the effect their actions can have on other people and may not be capable of fully understanding the distress and pain they cause to the victims of their crimes. Children and young people are also likely to be susceptible to peer pressure and other external influences and changes taking place during adolescence can lead to experimentation, resulting in criminal behaviour. When considering a child or young person's age their emotional and developmental age is of at least equal importance to their chronological age (if not greater).

1.6 For these reasons, children and young people are likely to benefit from being given an opportunity to address their behaviour and may be receptive to changing their conduct. They should, if possible, be given the opportunity to learn from their mistakes without undue penalisation or stigma, especially as a court sanction might have a significant effect on the prospects and opportunities of the child or young person and hinder their re-integration into society.

1.7 Offending by a child or young person is often a phase which passes fairly rapidly and so the sentence should not result in the alienation of the child or young person from society if that can be avoided.

1.8 The impact of punishment is likely to be felt more heavily by a child or young person in comparison to an adult as any sentence will seem longer due to their young age. In addition penal interventions may interfere with a child or young person's education and this should be considered by a court at sentencing.

1.9 Any restriction on liberty must be commensurate with the seriousness of the offence. In considering the seriousness of any offence, the court must consider the child or young person's culpability in committing the offence and any harm which the offence caused, was intended to cause or might foreseeably have caused (Criminal Justice Act 2003, s 143(1)).

1.10 Section 142 of the Criminal Justice Act 2003 sets out the purposes of sentencing for offenders who are over 18 on the date of conviction. That Act was amended in 2008 to add section 142A which sets out the purposes of sentencing for children and young people, subject to a commencement order being made. The difference between the purposes of sentencing for those under and over 18 is that section 142A does not include as a purpose of sentencing 'the reduction of crime (including its reduction by deterrence)'. Section 142A has not been brought into effect. Unless and until that happens, deterrence can be a factor in sentencing children and young people although normally it should be restricted to serious offences and can, and often will, be outweighed by considerations of the child or young person's welfare.

For more information on assessing the seriousness of the offence see section four.

Welfare

1.11 The statutory obligation to have regard to the welfare of a child or young person includes the obligation to secure proper provision for education and training (Children and Young Persons Act 1933, s 44), to remove the child or young person from undesirable surroundings where appropriate (Children and Young Persons Act 1933, s 44) and the need to choose the best option for the child or young person taking account of the circumstances of the offence.

1.12 **In having regard to the welfare of the child or young person, a court should ensure that it is alert to:**

- **any mental health problems or learning difficulties/disabilities;**
- **any experiences of brain injury or traumatic life experience (including exposure to drug and alcohol abuse) and the developmental impact this may have had;**
- **any speech and language difficulties and the effect this may have on the ability of the child or young person (or any accompanying adult) to communicate with the court, to understand the sanction imposed or to fulfil the obligations resulting from that sanction;**
- **the vulnerability of children and young people to self harm, particularly within a custodial environment; and**
- **the effect on children and young people of experiences of loss and neglect and/or abuse.**

1.13 Factors regularly present in the background of children and young people that come before the court include deprived homes, poor parental employment records, low educational attainment, early experience of offending by other family members, experience of abuse and/or neglect, negative influences from peer associates and the misuse of drugs and/or alcohol.

1.14 The court should always seek to ensure that it has access to information about how best to identify and respond to these factors and, where necessary, that a proper assessment has taken place in order to enable the most appropriate sentence to be imposed.

1.15 The court should consider the reasons why, on some occasions, a child or young person may conduct themselves inappropriately in court (e.g. due to nervousness, a lack of understanding of the system, a belief that they will be discriminated against, peer pressure to behave in a certain way because of others present, a lack of maturity etc) and take this into account.

1.16 Evidence shows that looked after children and young people are over-represented in the criminal justice system. (Department for Education (2014) Outcomes for Children Looked After by Local Authorities in England, as at 31 March 2014. Statistical First Release 49/2014 [accessed via: https://www.gov.uk/government/statistics/outcomes-for-children-looked-after-by-local-authorities].) When dealing with a child or young person who is looked after the court should also bear in mind the additional complex vulnerabilities that are likely to be present in their background. For example, looked after children and young people may have no or little contact with their family and/or friends, they may have special educational needs and/or emotional and behavioural problems, they may be heavily exposed to peers who have committed crime and they are likely to have accessed the care system as a result of abuse, neglect or parental absence due to bereavement, imprisonment or desertion. The court should also bear in mind that the level of parental-type support that a looked after child or young person receives throughout the criminal justice process may vary, and may be limited. For example, while parents are required to attend court hearings, this is not the case for social workers responsible for looked after children and young people. In some instances a looked after child or young person (including those placed in foster homes and independent accommodation, as well as in care homes) may be before the court for a low level offence that the police would not have been involved in, if it had occurred in an ordinary family setting.

1.17 For looked after children and young people who have committed an offence that crosses the custody threshold sentencers will need to consider any impact a custodial sentence may have on their leaving care rights and whether this impact is proportionate to the seriousness of the offence. For other young people who are in the process of leaving care or have recently left care then sentencers should bear in mind any effect this often difficult transition may have had on the young person's behaviour.

1.18 There is also evidence to suggest that black and minority ethnic children and young people are over-represented in the youth justice system (https://www.gov.uk/government/uploads/system/uploads/attachment_data/file/568680/bame-disproportionality-in-the-cjs.pdf). The factors contributing to this are complex. One factor is that a significant proportion of looked after children and young people are from a black and minority ethnic background (https://www.gov.uk/government/statistics/children-looked-after-in-england-including-adoption-2015-to-2016 (National table, figure B1)). A further factor may be the experience of such children and young people in terms of discrimination and negative experiences of authority. When having regard to the welfare of the child or young person to be sentenced, the particular factors which arise in the case of black and minority ethnic children and young people need to be taken into account.

1.19 The requirement to have regard to the welfare of a child or young person is subject to the obligation to impose only those restrictions on liberty that are commensurate with the seriousness of the offence; accordingly, a court should not impose greater restrictions because of other factors in the child or young person's life.

1.20 When considering a child or young person who may be particularly vulnerable, sentencers should consider which available disposal is best able to support the child or young person and which disposals could potentially exacerbate any underlying issues. This is particularly important when considering custodial sentences as there are concerns about the effect on vulnerable children and young people of being in closed conditions, with significant risks of self harm, including suicide.

1.21 The vulnerability factors that are often present in the background of children and young people should also be considered in light of the offending behaviour itself.

Although they do not alone cause offending behaviour – there are many children and young people who have experienced these circumstances but do not commit crime – there is a correlation and any response to criminal activity amongst children and young people will need to recognise the presence of such factors in order to be effective.

These principles do not undermine the fact that the sentence should reflect the seriousness of the offence. Further guidance on assessing the seriousness of an offence can be found at section four.

Section two: Allocation

(See also the allocation charts at pages 11–13 [of this Definitive Guideline] when reading this section.)

2.1 **Subject to the exceptions noted below, cases involving children and young people should be tried in the youth court.** It is the court which is best designed to meet their specific needs. A trial in the Crown Court with the inevitably greater formality and greatly increased number of people involved (including a jury and the public) should be reserved for the most serious cases (*R on the application of H, A and O v Southampton Youth Court* [2004] EWHC 2912 Admin). The welfare principles in this guideline apply to all cases, including those tried or sentenced in the Crown Court.

This section covers the exceptions to this requirement (Magistrates' Courts Act 1980, s 24).

2.2 A child or young person must always appear in the Crown Court for trial if:

- charged with homicide;
- charged with a firearms offence subject to a mandatory minimum sentence of three years (and is over 16 years of age at the time of the offence); or
- notice has been given to the court (under section 51B or 51C of the Crime and Disorder Act 1998) in a serious or complex fraud or child case.

Dangerousness

2.3 A case should be sent to the Crown Court for trial if the offence charged is a specified offence (As listed in the Criminal Justice Act 2003, Sch 15) **and** it seems to the court that if found guilty the child or young person would meet the criteria for a sentence under the dangerous offender provisions.

2.4 A sentence under the dangerous offender provisions can only be imposed if:

- the child or young person is found guilty of a specified violent or sexual offence; **and**
- the court is of the opinion that there is a significant risk to the public of serious harm caused by the child or young person committing further specified offences; **and**
- a custodial term of at least four years would be imposed for the offence.

2.5 A 'significant risk' is more than a mere possibility of occurrence. The assessment of dangerousness should take into account all the available information relating to the circumstances of the offence and **may** also take into account any information regarding previous patterns of behaviour relating to this offence and any other relevant information relating to the child or young person. In making this assessment it will be essential to obtain a pre-sentence report.

2.6 Children and young people may change and develop within a shorter time than adults and this factor, along with their level of maturity, may be highly relevant when assessing probable future conduct and whether it may cause a significant risk of serious harm (*R v Lang* [2005] EWCA Crim 2864, [2006] 1 WLR 2509).

2.7 In anything but the most serious cases it may be impossible for the court to form a view as to whether the child or young person would meet the criteria of the dangerous offender provisions without greater knowledge of the circumstances of the offence and the child or young person. In those circumstances jurisdiction for the case should be retained in the youth court. If, following a guilty plea or a finding of guilt, the dangerousness criteria appear to be met then the child or young person should be committed **for sentence.**

Grave crimes

2.8 Where a child or young person is before the court for an offence to which section 91(1) of the Powers of Criminal Courts (Sentencing) Act 2000 applies and the court considers that it ought to be possible to sentence them to more than two years' detention if found guilty of the offence, then they should be sent to the Crown Court. The test to be applied by the court is whether there is a **real prospect** that a sentence in excess of two years' detention will be imposed.

2.9 An offence comes within section 91 where:

- it is punishable with 14 years imprisonment or more for an adult (but is not a sentence fixed by law);
- it is an offence of sexual assault, a child sex offence committed by a child or young person, sexual activity with a child family member or inciting a child family member to engage in sexual activity; or
- it is one of a number of specified offences in relation to firearms, ammunition and weapons which are subject to a minimum term but, in respect of which, a court has found exceptional circumstances justifying a lesser sentence.

2.10 Before deciding whether to send the case to the Crown Court or retain jurisdiction in the youth court, the court should hear submissions from the prosecution and defence. As there is now a power to commit grave crimes for sentence (Powers of Criminal Courts (Sentencing) Act 2000, s 3(b) (as amended)) the court should no longer take the prosecution case at its highest when deciding whether to retain jurisdiction (*R (DPP) v South Tyneside Youth Court* [2015] EWHC 1455 (Admin)). In most cases it is likely to be impossible to decide whether there is a real prospect that a sentence in excess of two years' detention will be imposed without knowing more about the facts of the case and the circumstances of the child or young person. In those circumstances the youth court should retain jurisdiction and commit for sentence if it is of the view, having heard more about the facts and the circumstances of the child or young person, that its powers of sentence are insufficient.

Where the court decides that the case is suitable to be dealt with in the youth court it must warn the child or young person that all available sentencing options remain open and, if found guilty, the child or young person may be committed to the Crown Court for sentence.

Children and young people should only be sent for trial or committed for sentence to the Crown Court when charged with or found guilty of an offence of such gravity that a custodial sentence substantially exceeding two years is a realistic possibility. For children aged 10 or 11, and children/young people aged 12–14 who are not persistent offenders, the court should take into account the normal prohibition on imposing custodial sentences.

Charged alongside an adult

2.11 The proper venue for the trial of any child or young person is normally the youth court. Subject to statutory restrictions, that remains the case where a child or young person is jointly charged with an adult. If the adult is sent for trial to the Crown Court, the court should conclude that the child or young person must be tried separately in the youth court unless it is in the interests of justice for the child or young person and the adult to be tried jointly.

2.12 Examples of factors that should be considered when deciding whether to send the child or young person to the Crown Court (rather than having a trial in the youth court) include:

- whether separate trials will cause injustice to witnesses or to the case as a whole (consideration should be given to the provisions of sections 27 and 28 of the Youth Justice and Criminal Evidence Act 1999);
- the age of the child or young person; the younger the child or young person, the greater the desirability that the child or young person be tried in the youth court;
- the age gap between the child or young person and the adult; a substantial gap in age militates in favour of the child or young person being tried in the youth court;
- the lack of maturity of the child or young person;
- the relative culpability of the child or young person compared with the adult and whether the alleged role played by the child or young person was minor; and/or
- the lack of previous findings of guilt on the part of the child or young person.

2.13 The court should bear in mind that the youth court now has a general power to commit for sentence (as discussed at paragraph 2.9); in appropriate cases this will permit a sentence to be imposed by the same court on adults and children and young people who have been tried separately.

2.14 The court should follow the plea before venue procedure (see flowcharts on pages 11–13) prior to considering whether it is in the interests of justice for the child or young person and the adult to be tried jointly.

Remittal from the Crown Court for sentence

2.15 If a child or young person is found guilty before the Crown Court of an offence other than homicide the court must remit the case to the youth court, unless it would be undesirable to do so (Powers of Criminal Courts (Sentencing) Act 2000, s 8). In considering whether remittal is undesirable a court should balance the need for expertise in the sentencing of children and young people with the benefits of the sentence being imposed by the court which determined guilt.

2.16 Particular attention should be given to children and young people who are appearing before the Crown Court only because they have been charged with an adult offender; referral orders are generally not available in the Crown Court but may be the most appropriate sentence.

Child or young person charged alone or with other children and young people

[This section ends with flowcharts dealing with: a 'Child or young person charged alone or with other children and young people'; a 'Child or young person and adult charged as co-defendants where the adult is charged with an indictable only offence (or an offence where notice is given to the court under Crime and Disorder Act 1998, s 51B or 51C)'; and a 'Child or young person and adult charged as co-defendants where the adult is charged with either way offence'. These flowcharts are not reproduced in this work.]

Section three: Parental responsibilities

3.1 For any child or young person aged under 16 appearing before court there is a statutory requirement that parents/guardians attend during all stages of proceedings, unless the court is satisfied that this would be unreasonable having regard to the circumstances of the case (Children and Young Persons Act 1933, s 34A). The court may also enforce this requirement for a young person aged 16 and above if it deems it desirable to do so.

3.2 Although this requirement can cause a delay in the case before the court it is important it is adhered to. If a court does find exception to proceed in the absence of a responsible adult then extra care must be taken to ensure the outcomes are clearly communicated to and understood by the child or young person.

3.3 In addition to this responsibility there are also orders that can be imposed on parents. If the child or young person is aged under 16 then the court has a duty to make a **parental bind over** or impose a **parenting order**, if it would be desirable in the interest of preventing the commission of further offences (Powers of Criminal Courts (Sentencing) Act 2000, s 150 and Crime and Disorder Act 1998, s 8). There is a discretionary power to make these orders where the young person is aged 16 or 17. If the court chooses not to impose a parental bind over or parenting order it must state its reasons for not doing so in open court. In most circumstances a parenting order is likely to be more appropriate than a parental bind over.

3.4 A court cannot make a bind over alongside a referral order. If the court makes a referral order the duty on the court to impose a parenting order in respect of a child or young person under 16 years old is replaced by a discretion (Crime and Disorder Act 1998, s 9(1A)).

Section four: Determining the sentence

4.1 In determining the sentence, the key elements to consider are:

- the principal aim of the youth justice system (to prevent re-offending by children and young people);
- the welfare of the child or young person;
- the age of the child or young person (chronological, developmental and emotional);
- the seriousness of the offence;
- the likelihood of further offences being committed; and
- the extent of harm likely to result from those further offences.

The seriousness of the offence

(This applies to all offences; when offence specific guidance for children and young people is available this should be referred to.)

4.2 The seriousness of the offence is the starting point for determining the appropriate sentence; the sentence imposed and any restriction on liberty must be commensurate with the seriousness of the offence.

4.3 The approach to sentencing children and young people should always be individualistic and the court should always have in mind the principal aims of the youth justice system.

4.4 In order to determine the seriousness of the offence the court should assess the culpability of the child or young person and the harm that was caused, intended to be caused or could foreseeably have been caused.

4.5 In assessing **culpability** the court will wish to consider the extent to which the offence was planned, the role of the child or young person (if the offence was committed as part of a group), the level of force that was used in the commission of the offence and the awareness that the child or young person had of their actions and its possible consequences. There is an expectation that in general a child or young person will be dealt with less severely than an adult offender. In part, this is because children and young people are unlikely to have the same experience and capacity as an adult to understand the effect of their actions on other people or to appreciate the pain and distress caused and because a child or young person may be less able to resist temptation, especially where peer pressure is exerted. Children and young people are inherently more vulnerable than adults due to their age and the court will need to consider any mental health problems and/or learning disabilities they may have, as well as their emotional and developmental age. Any external factors that may have affected the child or young person's behaviour should be taken into account.

4.6 In assessing **harm** the court should consider the level of physical and psychological harm caused to the victim, the degree of any loss caused to the victim and the extent of any damage caused to property. (This assessment should also include a consideration of any harm that was intended to be caused or could foreseeably have been caused in the committal of the offence.)

4.7 The court should also consider any aggravating or mitigating factors that may increase or reduce the overall seriousness of the offence. **If any of these factors are included in the definition of the committed offence they should not be taken into account when considering the relative seriousness of the offence before the court.**

Aggravating factors
Statutory aggravating factors:
Previous findings of guilt, having regard to a) the **nature** of the offence to which the finding of guilt relates and its **relevance** to the current offence; and b) the **time** that has elapsed since the finding of guilt
Offence committed whilst on bail
Offence motivated by, or demonstrating hostility based on any of the following characteristics or presumed characteristics of the victim: religion, race, disability, sexual orientation or transgender identity
Other aggravating factors (non-exhaustive):
Steps taken to prevent the victim reporting or obtaining assistance
Steps taken to prevent the victim from assisting or supporting the prosecution
Victim is particularly vulnerable due to factors including but not limited to age, mental or physical disability
Restraint, detention or additional degradation of the victim
Prolonged nature of offence
Attempts to conceal/dispose of evidence
Established evidence of community/wider impact
Failure to comply with current court orders
Attempt to conceal identity
Involvement of others through peer pressure, bullying, coercion or manipulation
Commission of offence whilst under the influence of alcohol or drugs
History of antagonising or bullying the victim
Deliberate humiliation of victim, including but not limited to filming of the offence, deliberately committing the offence before a group of peers with the intention of causing additional distress or circulating details/photos/videos etc of the offence on social media or within peer groups

Factors reducing seriousness or reflecting personal mitigation (non-exhaustive)
No previous findings of guilt or no relevant/recent findings of guilt
Remorse, particularly where evidenced by voluntary reparation to the victim
Good character and/or exemplary conduct
Unstable upbringing including but not limited to: • time spent looked after • lack of familial presence or support • disrupted experiences in accommodation or education • exposure to drug/alcohol abuse, familial criminal behaviour or domestic abuse • victim of neglect or abuse, or exposure to neglect or abuse of others • experiences of trauma or loss
Participated in offence due to bullying, peer pressure, coercion or manipulation
Limited understanding of effect on victim
Serious medical condition requiring urgent, intensive or long-term treatment
Communication or learning disabilities or mental health concerns
In education, work or training
Particularly young or immature child or young person (where it affects their responsibility)

Determination and/or demonstration of steps taken to address addiction or offending behaviour

Age and maturity of the child or young person

4.8 There is a statutory presumption that no child under the age of 10 can be guilty of an offence (Children and Young Persons Act 1933, s 50).

4.9 With a child or young person, the consideration of age requires a different approach to that which would be adopted in relation to the age of an adult. Even within the category of child or young person the response of a court to an offence is likely to be very different depending on whether the child or young person is at the lower end of the age bracket, in the middle or towards the top end.

4.10 Although chronological age dictates in some instances what sentence can be imposed (see section six for more information) the developmental and emotional age of the child or young person should always be considered and it is of at least equal importance as their chronological age. It is important to consider whether the child or young person has the necessary maturity to appreciate fully the consequences of their conduct, the extent to which the child or young person has been acting on an impulsive basis and whether their conduct has been affected by inexperience, emotional volatility or negative influences.

Section five: Guilty plea

This section of the guideline applies regardless of the date of the offence to all children or young people where the **first hearing** is on or after 1 June 2017. It applies equally in youth courts, magistrates' courts and the Crown Court.

Key principles

5.1 The purpose of this section of the guideline is to encourage those who are going to plead guilty to do so as early in the court process as possible. Nothing in this section should be used to put pressure on a child or young person to plead guilty.

5.2 Although a guilty person is entitled not to admit the offence and to put the prosecution to proof of its case, an acceptance of guilt:

(a) normally reduces the impact of the crime upon victims;
(b) saves victims and witnesses from having to testify; and
(c) is in the public interest in that it saves public time and money on investigations and trials.

5.3 A guilty plea produces greater benefits the earlier the plea is made. In order to maximise the above benefits and to provide an incentive to those who are guilty to indicate a guilty plea as early as possible, this section of the guideline makes a clear distinction between a reduction in the sentence available at the first stage of the proceedings and a reduction in the sentence available at a later stage of the proceedings.

5.4 The purpose of reducing the sentence for a guilty plea is to yield the benefits described above and the guilty plea should be considered by the court to be independent of the child or young person's mitigation.

- Factors such as admissions at interview, co-operation with the investigation and demonstrations of remorse should **not** be taken into account in determining the level of reduction. Rather, they should be considered separately and prior to any guilty plea reduction, as potential mitigating factors.
- The benefits apply regardless of the strength of the evidence against a child or young person. The strength of the evidence should **not** be taken into account when determining the level of reduction.
- This section applies only to the punitive elements of the sentence and has no impact on ancillary orders including orders of disqualification from driving.

The approach

Stage 1: Determine the appropriate sentence for the offence(s) in accordance with any offence specific sentencing guideline or using this Overarching Principles guideline.

Stage 2: Determine the level of reduction for a guilty plea in accordance with this guideline.

Stage 3: State the amount of that reduction.

Stage 4: Apply the reduction to the appropriate sentence.

Stage 5: Follow any further steps in the offence specific guideline to determine the final sentence.

Nothing in this guideline affects the duty of the parties to progress cases (including the service of material) and identify any issues in dispute in compliance with the Criminal Procedure Rules and Criminal Practice Directions.

Determining the level of reduction

The maximum level of reduction for a guilty plea is one-third.

5.5 Plea indicated at the first stage of the proceedings

Where a guilty plea is indicated at the first stage of proceedings a reduction of **one-third** should be made (subject to the exceptions below). The first stage will normally be the first hearing in the magistrates' or youth court at which a plea is sought and recorded by the court. (In cases where (in accordance with the Criminal Procedure Rules) a child/young person is given the opportunity to enter a guilty plea without attending a court hearing, doing so within the required time limits will constitute a plea at the first stage of proceedings.)

5.6 Plea indicated after the first stage of proceedings – maximum one quarter – sliding scale of reduction thereafter

After the first stage of the proceedings the maximum level of reduction is **one-quarter** (subject to the exceptions below).

5.7 The reduction should be decreased from **one-quarter** to a maximum of **one-tenth** on the first day of trial having regard to the time when the guilty plea is first indicated relative to the progress of the case and the trial date (subject to the exceptions below). The reduction should normally be decreased further, even to zero, if the guilty plea is entered during the course of the trial.

5.8 For the purposes of this guideline a trial will be deemed to have started when pre-recorded cross-examination has begun.

Applying the reduction

Detention and training orders

5.9 A detention and training order (DTO) can only be imposed for the periods prescribed – 4, 6, 8, 10, 12, 18 or 24 months. If the reduction in sentence for a guilty plea results in a sentence that falls between two prescribed periods the court must impose the lesser of those two periods. This may result in a reduction greater than a third, in order that the full reduction is given and a lawful sentence imposed.

Imposing one type of sentence rather than another

5.10 The reduction in sentence for a guilty plea can be taken into account by imposing one type of sentence rather than another, for example:

- by reducing a custodial sentence to a community sentence; or
- by reducing a community sentence to a different means of disposal.

Alternatively the court could reduce the length or severity of any punitive requirements attached to a community sentence.

5.11 The court must always have regard to the principal aim of the youth justice system, which is to prevent offending by children and young people. It is, therefore, important that the court ensures that any sentence imposed is an effective disposal.

5.12 Where a court has imposed one sentence rather than another to reflect the guilty plea there should normally be no further reduction on account of the guilty plea. Where, however, the less severe type of sentence is justified by other factors, the appropriate reduction for the plea should be applied in the normal way.

More than one summary offence

5.13 When dealing with more than one summary offence, the aggregate sentence is limited to a maximum of six months. Allowing for a reduction for each guilty plea, consecutive sentences might result in the imposition of the maximum six month sentence. Where this is the case, the court **may** make a modest *additional* reduction to the overall sentence to reflect the benefits derived from the guilty plea.

Sentencing up to 24 months DTO for offences committed by children and young people

5.14 A DTO of up to 24 months may be imposed on a child or young person if the offence is one which, but for the plea, would have attracted a sentence of detention in excess of 24 months under section 91 of the Powers of Criminal Courts (Sentencing) Act 2000.

Exceptions

Referral order

5.15 As a referral order is a sentence that is only available upon pleading guilty there should be no further reduction of the sentence to reflect the guilty plea.

Further information, assistance or advice necessary before indicating plea

5.16 Where the sentencing court is satisfied that there were particular circumstances which significantly reduced the child or young person's ability to understand what was alleged, or otherwise made it unreasonable to expect the child or young person to indicate a guilty plea **sooner than was done**, a reduction of one-third should still be made.

5.17 In considering whether this exception applies, sentencers should distinguish between cases in which it is necessary to receive advice and/or have sight of evidence in order to understand whether the child or young person is, in fact and law, guilty of the offence(s) charged, and cases in which a child or young person merely delays guilty plea(s) in order to assess the strength of the prosecution evidence and the prospects of a finding of guilt or acquittal.

Newton hearings and special reasons hearings

5.18 In circumstances where a child or young person's version of events is rejected at a Newton hearing (A Newton hearing is held when a child/young person pleads guilty but disputes the case as put forward by the prosecution and the dispute would make a difference to the sentence. The judge will normally hear evidence from witnesses to decide which version of the disputed facts to base the sentence on.) or special reasons hearing (A special reasons hearing occurs when a child/young person is found guilty of an offence carrying a mandatory licence endorsement or disqualification from driving and seeks to persuade the court that there are extenuating circumstances relating to the offence that the court should take into account by reducing or avoiding endorsement or disqualification. This may involve calling witnesses to give evidence.), the reduction which would have been available at the stage of proceedings the plea was indicated should normally be halved. Where witnesses are called during such a hearing, it may be appropriate further to decrease the reduction.

Child or young person found guilty of a lesser or different offence

5.19 If a child or young person is found guilty of a lesser or different offence from that originally charged, and has earlier made an unequivocal indication of a guilty plea to this lesser or different offence to the prosecution and the court, the court should give the level of reduction that is appropriate to the stage in the proceedings at which this indication of plea (to the lesser or different offence) was made taking into account any other of these exceptions that apply. In the Crown Court where the offered plea is a permissible alternative on the indictment as charged, the child or young person will not be treated as having made an unequivocal indication unless the defendant has entered that plea.

Minimum sentence under section 51A of the Firearms Act 1968

5.20 There can be no reduction for a guilty plea if the effect of doing so would be to reduce the length of sentence below the required minimum term.

Appropriate custodial sentences for young persons aged at least 16 but under 18 when found guilty under the Prevention of Crime Act 1953 and Criminal Justice Act 1988

5.21 In circumstances where an appropriate custodial sentence of a DTO of at least four months falls to be imposed on a young person who is aged at least 16 but under 18, who has been found guilty under sections 1 or 1A of the Prevention of Crime Act 1953; or section 139, 139AA or 139A of the Criminal Justice Act 1988 (certain possession of knives or offensive weapon offences) the court may impose any sentence that it considers appropriate, having taken into consideration the general principles set out above.

Mandatory life sentences for murder

5.22 Murder is the most serious criminal offence and the sentence prescribed is different from all other sentences. By law, the sentence for murder is detention for life and the child or young person will remain subject to the sentence for the rest of their life.

5.23 Given the special characteristic of the offence of murder and the unique statutory provision in Schedule 21 of the Criminal Justice Act 2003 of starting points for the minimum term to be served by a child or young person, careful consideration has to be given to the extent of any reduction for a guilty plea and to the need to ensure that the minimum term properly reflects the seriousness of the offence.

5.24 Whilst the general principles continue to apply (both that a guilty plea should be encouraged and that the extent of any reduction should reduce if the indication of plea is later than the first stage of the proceedings) the process of determining the level of reduction will be different.

Determining the level of reduction

5.25 In other circumstances:

- the court will weigh carefully the overall length of the minimum term taking into account other reductions for which the child or young person may be eligible so as to avoid a combination leading to an inappropriately short sentence;
- where it is appropriate to reduce the minimum term having regard to a plea of guilty, the reduction will not exceed one-sixth and will never exceed five years; and
- the maximum reduction of one-sixth or five years (whichever is less) should only be given when a guilty plea has been indicated at the first stage of the proceedings. Lesser reductions should be given for guilty pleas after that point, with a maximum of one-twentieth being given for a guilty plea on the day of trial.

The exceptions outlined at 5.16–5.18 apply to murder cases.

Section six: Available sentences

Crossing a significant age threshold between commission of offence and sentence

6.1 There will be occasions when an increase in the age of a child or young person will result in the maximum sentence on the date of the *finding of guilt* being greater than that available on the date on which the offence was *committed* (primarily turning 12, 15 or 18 years old).

6.2 In such situations the court should take as its starting point the sentence likely to have been imposed on the date at which the offence was committed. This includes young people who attain the age of 18 between the *commission* and the *the finding of guilt* of the offence (*R v Ghafoor [2002] EWCA Crim 1857, [2003] 1 Cr App R (S) 428*) but when this occurs the purpose of sentencing adult offenders (Criminal Justice Act 2003, s 142) has to be taken into account, which is:

- the punishment of offenders;
- the reduction of crime (including its reduction by deterrence);
- the reform and rehabilitation of offenders;
- the protection of the public; and
- the making of reparation by offenders to persons affected by their offences.

6.3 When any significant age threshold is passed it will rarely be appropriate that a more severe sentence than the maximum that the court could have imposed at the time the offence was committed should be imposed. However, a sentence at or close to that maximum may be appropriate.

Persistent offenders

6.4 Some sentences can only be imposed on children and young people if they are deemed a persistent offender. A child or young person **must** be classed as such for one of the following to be imposed:

- a youth rehabilitation order (YRO) with intensive supervision and surveillance when aged under 15;
- a YRO with fostering when aged under 15; and
- a detention and training order (DTO) when aged 12–14.

6.5 The term persistent offender is not defined in statute but has been considered by the Court of Appeal. In general it is expected that the child or young person would have had previous contact with authority as a result of criminal behaviour. This includes previous findings of guilt as well as admissions of guilt such as restorative justice disposals and conditional cautions.

6.6 A child or young person who has committed one previous offence cannot reasonably be classed as a persistent offender, and a child or young person who has committed two or more previous offences should not necessarily be assumed to be one. To determine if the behaviour is persistent the nature of the previous offences and the lapse of time between the offences would need to be considered (*R v M [2008] EWCA Crim 3329*).

6.7 If there have been three findings of guilt in the past 12 months for imprisonable offences of a comparable nature (or the child or young person has been made the subject of orders as detailed above in relation to an imprisonable offence) then the court could certainly justify classing the child or young person as a persistent offender.

6.8 When a child or young person is being sentenced in a single appearance for a series of separate, comparable offences committed over a short space of time then the court could justifiably consider the child or young person to be a persistent offender, despite the fact that there may be no previous findings of guilt (*R v S* [2000] 1 Cr App

R (S)18). In these cases the court should consider whether the child or young person has had prior opportunity to address their offending behaviour before imposing one of the optional sentences available for persistent offenders only; if the court determines that the child or young person has not had an opportunity to address their behaviour and believes that an alternative sentence has a reasonable prospect of preventing re-offending then this alternative sentence should be imposed.

6.9 The court may also wish to consider any evidence of a reduction in the level of offending when taking into account previous offending behaviour. Children and young people may be unlikely to desist from committing crime in a clear cut manner but there may be changes in patterns of criminal behaviour (e.g. committing fewer and/or less serious offences or there being longer lengths of time between offences) that indicate that the child or young person is attempting to desist from crime.

6.10 Even where a child or young person is found to be a persistent offender, a court is not obliged to impose one of the optional sentences. The approach should still be individualistic and all other considerations still apply. **Custodial sentences must be a last resort for all children and young people** and there is an expectation that they will be particularly rare for children and young people aged 14 or under.

[This section continues with: a table listing sentences available by age; narrative on these sentences; narrative on breaches and the commission of further offences during the period of any order (see also Appendix one); and narrative on different orders. These parts are not reproduced in this work since these topics are covered fully in Part B.]

Appendix one: Breach of orders

Breach of a conditional discharge

7.1 If a child or young person commits an offence during the period of conditional discharge then the court has the power to re-sentence the original offence. The child or young person should be dealt with on the basis of their current age and not the age at the time of the finding of guilt and the court can deal with the original offence(s) in any way which it could have if the child or young person had just been found guilty.

7.2 There is no requirement to re-sentence; if a court deems it appropriate to do so they can sentence the child or young person for the new offence and leave the conditional discharge in place. If the order was made by the Crown Court then the youth court can commit the child or young person in custody or release them on bail until they can be brought or appear before the Crown Court. The court shall also send to the Crown Court a memorandum of conviction.

7.3 If the offender is convicted of committing a new offence after attaining the age of 18 but during the period of a conditional discharge made by a youth court then they may be re-sentenced for the original offence by the convicting adult magistrates' court. If the adult magistrates' court decides to take no action then the youth court that imposed the conditional discharge may summon the offender for the breach to be dealt with.

Breach of a reparation order

7.4 If it is proved to the appropriate court that the child or young person has failed to comply with any requirement of a reparation order that is currently in force then the court can:

- order the child or young person to pay a fine not exceeding £1,000; or
- revoke the order and re-sentence the child or young person in any way which they could have been dealt with for that offence.

If re-sentencing the child or young person the court must take into account the extent to which the child or young person has complied with the requirements of this order.

7.5 If the order was made by the Crown Court then the youth court can commit the child or young person in custody or release them on bail until they can be brought or appear before the Crown Court.

7.6 The child or young person or a Youth Offending Team (YOT) officer can also apply for the order to be revoked or amended but any new provisions must be ones that the court would have been able to include when the original reparation order was given. There is no power to re-sentence in this situation as the child or young person has not been found to be in breach of requirements.

Even when an offender has attained the age of 18 breach of a reparation order must be dealt with in the youth court.

Breach of a referral order (referral back to court)

7.7 If a child or young person is found to have breached the conditions of their referral order the court can revoke the referral order and re-sentence the child or young person using the range of sentencing options (other than a referral order) that would have been available to the court that originally sentenced them. If the court chooses not to revoke the referral order then it is possible to:

- allow the referral order to continue with the existing contract;
- extend the length of the referral order up to a maximum of 12 months (in total); or
- impose a fine up to a maximum of £2,500.

7.8 If an offender has attained the age of 18 by the first court hearing then breach proceedings must be dealt with by the adult magistrates' court. If the court chooses to revoke the order then its powers are limited to those available to the court at the time of the original sentence.

Commission of further offences whilst on a referral order

7.9 The court has the power to extend a referral order in respect of additional or further offences. This applies to not only a first referral order but also to any subsequent referral orders. Any period of extension must not exceed the total 12 month limit for a referral order.

7.10 If the court chooses not to extend the existing referral order or impose a discharge they have the power to impose a new referral order (where the discretionary referral order conditions are satisfied) in respect of the new offences only. This order can remain or run alongside the new order or the court may direct that the contract under the new order is not to take effect until the earlier order is revoked or discharged. Alternatively, the court may impose an absolute or conditional discharge.

7.11 If the court sentences in any other way they have a discretionary power to revoke the referral order. Where an order is revoked, if it appears to be in the interests of justice, the court may deal with the original offence(s) in any way that the original court could have done, but may not make a new referral order. Where the referral contract has taken effect, the court shall have regard to the extent of the child or young person's compliance with the terms of the contract.

Breach of a youth rehabilitation order (YRO)

7.12 Where a child or young person is in breach of a YRO the following options are available to the court:

- take no action and allow the order to continue in its original form;
- impose a fine (up to £2,500)(and allow the order to continue in its original form);
- amend the terms of the order; or
- revoke the order and re-sentence the child or young person.

7.13 If the terms of the order are amended the new requirements must be capable of being complied with before the expiry of the overall period. The court may impose any requirement that it could have imposed when making the order and this may be in addition to, or in substitution for, any requirements contained in the order. If the YRO did not contain an unpaid work requirement and the court includes such a requirement using this power, the minimum period of unpaid work is 20 hours; this will give greater flexibility when responding to less serious breaches or where there are significant other requirements to be complied with.

7.14 A court may not amend the terms of a YRO that did not include an extended activity requirement or a fostering requirement by inserting them at this stage; should these requirements be considered appropriate following breach, the child or young person must be re-sentenced and the original YRO revoked.

7.15 A court must ensure that it has sufficient information to enable it to understand why the order has been breached and should be satisfied that the YOT and other local authority services have taken all steps necessary to ensure that the child or young person has been given appropriate opportunity and the support necessary for compliance. This is particularly important if the court is considering imposing a custodial sentence as a result of the breach.

7.16 Where the failure arises primarily from non-compliance with reporting or other similar obligations and a sanction is necessary, the most appropriate response is likely to be the inclusion of (or increase in) a primarily punitive requirement such as the curfew requirement, unpaid work, the exclusion requirement and the prohibited activity requirement or the imposition of a fine. However, continuing failure to comply with the order is likely to lead to revocation of the order and re-sentencing for the original offence.

7.17 Where the child or young person has 'wilfully and persistently' failed to comply with the order, and the court proposes to sentence again for the offence(s) in respect of which the order was made, additional powers are available.

A child or young person will almost certainly be considered to have 'wilfully and persistently' breached a YRO where there have been three breaches that have demonstrated a lack of willingness to comply with the order that have resulted in an appearance before court.

7.18 The additional powers available to the court when re-sentencing a child or young person who has 'wilfully and persistently' breached their order are:

- the making of a YRO with intensive supervision and surveillance even though the offence is non-imprisonable;
- a custodial sentence if the YRO that is breached is one with an intensive supervision and surveillance requirement, which was imposed for an offence that was imprisonable; and
- the imposition of a DTO for four months for breach of a YRO with intensive supervision and surveillance which was imposed following wilful and persistent breach of an order made for a non-imprisonable offence.

The primary objective when sentencing for breach of a YRO is to ensure that the child or young person completes the requirements imposed by the court.

7.19 If an offender has attained the age of 18 by the first court hearing then breach proceedings must be dealt with by the adult magistrates' court. If the court chooses to revoke the order then its powers are limited to those available to the court at the time of the original sentence.

Commission of further offences during a YRO

7.20 If a child or young person commits an offence whilst subject to a YRO the court can impose any sentence for the new matter, but can only impose a new YRO if they revoke the existing order. Where the court revokes the original order they may re-sentence that matter at the same time as sentencing the new offence.

Breach of a detention and training order (DTO)

7.21 If a child or young person is found to have breached a supervision requirement after release from custody then the court may:

- impose a further period of custody of up to three months or the length of time from the date the breach was committed until the end of the order, **whichever is shorter;**
- impose a further period of supervision of up to three months or the length of time from the date the breach was committed until the end of the order, **whichever is shorter;**
- impose a fine of up to £1,000; or
- take no action.

Even if the offender has attained the age of 18 proceedings for breach of the supervision requirements must be dealt with in the youth court.

Commission of further offences during a DTO

7.22 If a child or young person is found guilty of a further imprisonable offence committed during the currency of the order then the court can impose a further period of detention. This period of detention cannot exceed the period between the date of the new offence and the date of when the original order would have expired.

7.23 This period can be served consecutively or concurrently with any sentence imposed for the new offence and this period should not be taken into account when determining the appropriate length of the sentence for the new offence.

Sexual Offences Guideline

Sentencing a child or young person for sexual offences involves a number of different considerations from adults. The primary difference is the age and level of maturity. Children and young people are less emotionally developed than adults; offending can arise through inappropriate sexual experimentation; gang or peer group pressure to engage in sexual activity; or a lack of understanding regarding consent, exploitation, coercion and appropriate sexual behaviour.

Below is a non-exhaustive list of factors that illustrate the type of background factors that may have played a part in leading a child or young person to commit an offence of this kind.

- Victim of neglect or abuse (sexual, physical or emotional) or has witnessed the neglect or abuse of another.
- Exposure to pornography or materials which are age inappropriate.
- Involvement in gangs.
- Associated with child sexual exploitation.
- Unstable living or educational arrangements.
- Communication or learning disabilities or mental health concerns.
- Part of a peer group, school or neighbourhood where harmful sexual norms and attitudes go unchallenged.
- A trigger event such as the death of a close relative or a family breakdown.

This guideline should be read alongside the *Overarching Principles – Sentencing Children and Young People* definitive guideline which provides comprehensive guidance on the sentencing principles and welfare considerations that the court should have in mind when sentencing children and young people.

The first step in determining the sentence is to assess the seriousness of the offence. This assessment is made by considering the nature of the offence and any aggravating and mitigating factors relating to the offence itself. **The fact that a sentence threshold is crossed does not necessarily mean that that sentence should be imposed.**

STEP ONE
Offence Seriousness – Nature of the offence

The boxes below give **examples** of the type of culpability and harm factors that may indicate that a particular threshold of sentence has been crossed.

A non-custodial sentence* may be the most suitable disposal where one or more of the following factors apply:

Any form of non-penetrative sexual activity
Any form of sexual activity (including penetration) without coercion, exploitation or pressure except where there is a significant disparity in age or maturity
Minimal psychological or physical harm caused to the victim

A custodial sentence or youth rehabilitation order with intensive supervision and surveillance* or fostering* may be justified where one or more of the following factors apply:
Any penetrative activity involving coercion, exploitation or pressure
Use or threats of violence against the victim or someone known to the victim
Prolonged detention/sustained incident
Severe psychological or physical harm caused to the victim

* Where the child or young person appears in the magistrates' court, and the conditions for a compulsory referral order apply, a referral order must be imposed unless the court is considering imposing a discharge, hospital order or custody.

STEP TWO
Offence Seriousness – Aggravating and mitigating factors

To complete the assessment of seriousness the court should consider the aggravating and mitigating factors relevant to the offence.

Aggravating factors
Statutory aggravating factors:
Previous findings of guilt, having regard to a) the **nature** of the offence to which the finding of guilt relates and its **relevance** to the current offence; and b) the **time** that has elapsed since the finding of guilt
Offence committed whilst on bail
Offence motivated by, or demonstrating hostility based on any of the following characteristics or presumed characteristics of the victim: religion, race, disability, sexual orientation or transgender identity
Other aggravating factors (non-exhaustive):
Significant degree of planning
Child or young person acts together with others to commit the offence
Use of alcohol/drugs on victim to facilitate the offence
Abuse of trust
Deliberate humiliation of victim, including but not limited to filming of the offence, deliberately committing the offence before a group of peers with the intention of causing additional distress or circulating details/photos/videos etc of the offence on social media or within peer groups
Grooming
Significant disparity of age between the child or young person and the victim (measured chronologically or with reference to level of maturity) (where not taken into account at step one)
Victim is particularly vulnerable due to factors including but not limited to age, mental or physical disability
Any steps taken to prevent reporting the incident/seeking assistance
Pregnancy or STI as a consequence of offence
Blackmail
Use of weapon

Mitigating factors (non-exhaustive)
No previous findings of guilt or no relevant/recent findings of guilt
Good character and/or exemplary conduct
Participated in offence due to bullying, peer pressure, coercion or manipulation
Genuine belief that activity was lawful

STEP THREE
Personal mitigation

Having assessed the offence seriousness, the court should then consider the mitigation personal to the child or young person to determine whether a custodial sentence or a community sentence is necessary. The effect of personal mitigation may reduce what would otherwise be a custodial sentence to a non-custodial one, or a community sentence to a different means of disposal.

Personal mitigating factors (non-exhaustive)
Particularly young or immature child or young person (where it affects their responsibility)
Communication or learning disabilities or mental health concerns
Unstable upbringing including but not limited to:- • time spent looked after • lack of familial presence or support • disrupted experiences in accommodation or education • exposure to drug/alcohol abuse, familial criminal behaviour or domestic abuse • exposure by others to pornography or sexually explicit materials • victim of neglect or abuse, or exposure to neglect or abuse of others • experiences of trauma or loss
Determination and/or demonstration of steps taken to address offending behaviour
Strong prospect of rehabilitation
Child or young person in education, training or employment

STEP FOUR
Reduction for guilty plea

The court should take account of any potential reduction for a guilty plea in accordance with section 144 of the Criminal Justice Act 2003 and part one, section five of the *Overarching Principles – Sentencing Children and Young People* definitive guideline. The reduction in sentence for a guilty plea can be taken into account by imposing one type of sentence rather than another; for example:

- by reducing a custodial sentence to a community sentence; or
- by reducing a community sentence to a different means of disposal.

Alternatively the court could reduce the length or severity of any punitive requirements attached to a community sentence.

See the *Overarching Principles – Sentencing Children and Young People* definitive guideline for details of other available sentences including Referral Orders and Reparation Orders.

STEP FIVE
Review the sentence

The court must now review the sentence to ensure it is the most appropriate one for the child or young person. This will include an assessment of the likelihood of reoffending and the risk of causing serious harm. A report from the Youth Offending Team may assist.

See the *Overarching Principles – Sentencing Children and Young People* definitive guideline for comprehensive guidance on the sentencing principles and welfare considerations that the court should have in mind when sentencing children and young people, and for the full range of the sentences available to the court.

Referral Orders

In cases where children or young people have offended for the first time and have pleaded guilty to committing an offence which is on the cusp of the custody threshold, YOTs should be encouraged to convene a Youth Offender Panel prior to sentence (sometimes referred to as a'pseudo-panel' or 'pre-panel') where the child or young person is asked to attend before a panel and agree an intensive contract. If that contract is placed before the sentencing youth court, the court can then decide whether it is sufficient to move below custody on this occasion. The proposed contract is not something the court can alter in any way; the court will still have to make a decision between referral order and custody but can do so on the basis that if it makes a referral order it can have confidence in what that will entail in the particular case.

The court determines the length of the order but a Referral Order Panel determines the requirements of the order.

Offence seriousness	Suggested length of referral order
Low	• 3–5 months
Medium	• 5–7 months
High	• 7–9 months
Very high	• 10–12 months

The YOT may propose certain requirements and the length of these requirements may not correspond to the above table; if the court feels these requirements will best achieve the aims of the youth justice system then they may still be imposed.

Youth Rehabilitation Order (YRO)

The following table sets out the different levels of intensity that are available under a Youth Rehabilitation Order. The level of intensity and the content of the order will depend upon the court's assessment of seriousness.

		Requirements of order
Standard	Low likelihood of re--offending and a low risk of serious harm	Primarily seek to repair harm caused through, for example: • reparation; • unpaid work; • supervision; and/or • attendance centre.
Enhanced	Medium likelihood of re-offending or a medium risk of serious harm	Seek to repair harm caused and to enable help or change through, for example: • supervision; • reparation; • requirement to address behaviour e.g. drug treatment, offending behaviour programme, education programme; and/or • a combination of the above.

Intensive	High likelihood of re-offending or a very high risk of serious harm	Seek to ensure the control of and enable help or change for the child or young person through, for example: • supervision; • reparation; • requirement to address behaviour; • requirement to monitor or restrict movement, e.g. prohibited activity, curfew, exclusion or electronic monitoring; and/or • a combination of the above.

YRO with Intensive Supervision and Surveillance (ISS) or YRO with Fostering

YRO with an ISS or fostering requirement can only be imposed where the court is of the opinion that the offence has crossed the custody threshold and custody is merited. The YRO with ISS includes an extended activity requirement, a supervision requirement and curfew.

The YRO with fostering requires the child or young person to reside with a local authority foster parent for a specified period of up to 12 months.

Custodial Sentences

If a custodial sentence is imposed, the court must state its reasons for being satisfied that the offence is so serious that no other sanction would be appropriate and, in particular, why a YRO with ISS or fostering could not be justified.

Where a custodial sentence is **unavoidable** the length of custody imposed must be the shortest commensurate with the seriousness of the offence. The court may want to consider the equivalent adult guideline in order to determine the appropriate length of the sentence.

If considering the adult guideline, the court may feel it appropriate to apply a sentence broadly within the region of half to two thirds of the appropriate adult sentence for those aged 15–17 and allow a greater reduction for those aged under 15. This is only a rough guide and must not be applied mechanistically. The individual factors relating to the offence and the child or young person are of the greatest importance and may present good reason to impose a sentence outside of this range.

Robbery Guideline

This guideline should be read alongside the *Overarching Principles – Sentencing Children and Young People* definitive guideline which provides comprehensive guidance on the sentencing principles and welfare considerations that the court should have in mind when sentencing children and young people.

The first step in determining the sentence is to assess the seriousness of the offence. This assessment is made by considering the nature of the offence and any aggravating and mitigating factors relating to the offence itself. **The fact that a sentence threshold is crossed does not necessarily mean that that sentence should be imposed.**

STEP ONE
Offence Seriousness – Nature of the offence

The boxes below give **examples** of the type of culpability and harm factors that may indicate that a particular threshold of sentence has been crossed.

A non-custodial sentence* may be the most suitable disposal where one or more of the following factors apply:

Threat or use of minimal force
Little or no physical or psychological harm caused to the victim
Involved through coercion, intimidation or exploitation

A custodial sentence or youth rehabilitation order with intensive supervision and surveillance* or fostering* may be justified where one or more of the following factors apply:
Use of very significant force
Threat or use of a bladed article, firearm or imitation firearm (where produced)
Significant physical or psychological harm caused to the victim

* Where the child or young person appears in the magistrates' court, and the conditions for a compulsory referral order apply, a referral order must be imposed unless the court is considering imposing a discharge, hospital order or custody.

STEP TWO
Offence Seriousness – Aggravating and mitigating factors

To complete the assessment of seriousness the court should consider the aggravating and mitigating factors relevant to the offence.

Aggravating factors
Statutory aggravating factors:
Previous findings of guilt, having regard to a) the **nature** of the offence to which the finding of guilt relates and its **relevance** to the current offence; and b) the **time** that has elapsed since the finding of guilt
Offence committed whilst on bail
Offence motivated by, or demonstrating hostility based on any of the following characteristics or presumed characteristics of the victim: religion, race, disability, sexual orientation or transgender identity
Other aggravating factors (non-exhaustive):
Significant degree of planning
Deliberate humiliation of victim, including but not limited to filming of the offence, deliberately committing the offence before a group of peers with the intention of causing additional distress or circulating details/photos/videos etc of the offence on social media or within peer groups
Threat or use of a weapon other than a bladed article, firearm or imitation firearm (whether produced or not)
Threat to use a bladed article, firearm or imitation firearm (not produced)
Victim is particularly vulnerable due to factors including but not limited to age, mental or physical disability
A leading role where offending is part of a group
Attempt to conceal identity (for example, wearing a balaclava or hood)
Any steps taken to prevent reporting the incident/seeking assistance
High value goods or sums targeted or obtained (includes economic, personal or sentimental)
Restraint, detention or additional degradation of the victim

Mitigating factors (non-exhaustive)
No previous findings of guilt or no relevant/recent findings of guilt
Good character and/or exemplary conduct
Participated in offence due to bullying, peer pressure, coercion or manipulation

Remorse, particularly where evidenced by voluntary reparation to the victim
Little or no planning

STEP THREE
Personal mitigation

Having assessed the offence seriousness, the court should then consider the mitigation personal to the child or young person to determine whether a custodial sentence or a community sentence is necessary. The effect of personal mitigation may reduce what would otherwise be a custodial sentence to a non-custodial one, or a community sentence to a different means of disposal.

Personal mitigating factors (non-exhaustive)
Particularly young or immature child or young person (where it affects their responsibility)
Communication or learning disabilities or mental health concerns
Unstable upbringing including but not limited to: • time spent looked after • lack of familial presence or support • disrupted experiences in accommodation or education • exposure to drug/alcohol abuse, familial criminal behaviour or domestic abuse • victim of neglect or abuse, or exposure to neglect or abuse of others • experiences of trauma or loss
Determination and/or demonstration of steps taken to address offending behaviour
Child or young person in education, training or employment

STEP FOUR
Reduction for guilty plea

The court should take account of any potential reduction for a guilty plea in accordance with section 144 of the Criminal Justice Act 2003 and part one, section five of the *Overarching Principles – Sentencing Children and Young People* definitive guideline.

The reduction in sentence for a guilty plea can be taken into account by imposing one type of sentence rather than another; for example:

- by reducing a custodial sentence to a community sentence; or
- by reducing a community sentence to a different means of disposal.

Alternatively the court could reduce the length or severity of any punitive requirements attached to a community sentence.

See the *Overarching Principles – Sentencing Children and Young People* definitive guideline for details of other available sentences including Referral Orders and Reparation Orders.

STEP FIVE
Review the sentence

The court must now review the sentence to ensure it is the most appropriate one for the child or young person. This will include an assessment of the likelihood of reoffending and the risk of causing serious harm. A report from the Youth Offending Team may assist.

See the *Overarching Principles – Sentencing Children and Young People* definitive guideline for comprehensive guidance on the sentencing principles and welfare considerations that the court should have in mind when sentencing children and young people, and for the full range of the sentences available to the court.

Referral Orders

In cases where children or young people have offended for the first time and have pleaded guilty to committing an offence which is on the cusp of the custody threshold, YOTs should be encouraged to convene a Youth Offender Panel prior to sentence (sometimes referred to as a 'pseudo-panel' or 'pre-panel') where the child or young person is asked to attend before a panel and agree an intensive contract. If that contract is placed before the sentencing youth court, the court can then decide whether it is sufficient to move below custody on this occasion. The proposed contract is not something the court can alter in any way; the court will still have to make a decision between referral order and custody but can do so on the basis that if it makes a referral order it can have confidence in what that will entail in the particular case.

The court determines the length of the order but a Referral Order Panel determines the requirements of the order.

Offence seriousness	Suggested length of referral order
Low	• 3–5 months
Medium	• 5–7 months
High	• 7–9 months
Very high	• 10–12 months

The YOT may propose certain requirements and the length of these requirements may not correspond to the above table; if the court feels these requirements will best achieve the aims of the youth justice system then they may still be imposed.

Youth Rehabilitation Order (YRO)

The following table sets out the different levels of intensity that are available under a YRO. The level of intensity and the content of the order will depend upon the court's assessment of seriousness.

		Requirements of order
Standard	Low likelihood of re--offending and a low risk of serious harm	Primarily seek to repair harm caused through, for example: • reparation; • unpaid work; • supervision; and/or • attendance centre.
Enhanced	Medium likelihood of re-offending or a medium risk of serious harm	Seek to repair harm caused and to enable help or change through, for example: • supervision; • reparation; • requirement to address behaviour e.g. drug treatment, offending behaviour programme, education programme; and/or • a combination of the above.
Intensive	High likelihood of re-offending or a very high risk of serious harm	Seek to ensure the control of and enable help or change for the child or young person through, for example: • supervision; • reparation; • requirement to address behaviour; • requirement to monitor or restrict movement, e.g. prohibited activity, curfew, exclusion or electronic monitoring; and/or • a combination of the above.

YRO with Intensive Supervision and Surveillance (ISS) or YRO with fostering

A YRO with an ISS or fostering requirement can only be imposed where the court is of the opinion that the offence has crossed the custody threshold, and custody is merited. The YRO with ISS includes an extended activity requirement, a supervision requirement and curfew. The YRO with fostering requires the child or young person to reside with a local authority foster parent for a specified period of up to 12 months.

Custodial Sentences

If a custodial sentence is imposed, the court must state its reasons for being satisfied that the offence is so serious that no other sanction would be appropriate and, in particular, why a YRO with ISS or fostering could not be justified.

Where a custodial sentence is **unavoidable** the length of custody imposed must be the shortest commensurate with the seriousness of the offence. The court may want to consider the equivalent adult guideline in order to determine the appropriate length of the sentence.

If considering the adult guideline, the court may feel it appropriate to apply a sentence broadly within the region of half to two thirds of the appropriate adult sentence for those aged 15–17 and allow a greater reduction for those aged under 15. This is only a rough guide and must not be applied mechanistically. The individual factors relating to the offence and the child or young person are of the greatest importance and may present good reason to impose a sentence outside of this range.

Bladed Articles and Offensive Weapons (Possession and Threats) – Children and Young People Guideline

This guideline should be read alongside the *Overarching Principles – Sentencing Children and Young People* definitive guideline which provides comprehensive guidance on the sentencing principles and welfare considerations that the court should have in mind when sentencing children and young people.

This offence is subject to statutory minimum sentencing provisions.See STEP FIVE for further details.

The first step in determining the sentence is to assess the seriousness of the offence. This assessment is made by considering the nature of the offence and any aggravating and mitigating factors relating to the offence itself. **The fact that a sentence threshold is crossed does not necessarily mean that that sentence should be imposed.**

STEP ONE
Offence Seriousness – Nature of the offence

The [lists] below give **examples** of the type of culpability and harm factors that may indicate that a particular threshold of sentence has been crossed.

A non-custodial sentence* may be the most suitable disposal where one or more of the following factors apply:

- Possession of weapon falls just short of reasonable excuse
- No/minimal risk of weapon being used to threaten or cause harm
- Fleeting incident and no/minimal distress

(* Where the child or young person appears in the magistrates' court, and the conditions for a compulsory referral order apply, a referral order must be imposed unless the court is considering imposing a discharge, hospital order or custody.)

A custodial sentence or youth rehabilitation order with intensive supervision and surveillance* or fostering* may be justified where one or more of the following factors apply:

- Possession of a bladed article whether produced or not
- Possession of a highly dangerous weapon+ whether produced or not
- Offence motivated by, or demonstrating hostility based on any of the following characteristics or presumed characteristics of the victim: religion, race, disability, sexual orientation or transgender identity
- Prolonged incident and serious alarm/distress
- Offence committed at a school or other place where vulnerable people may be present

(* Where the child or young person appears in the magistrates' court, and the conditions for a compulsory referral order apply, a referral order must be imposed unless the court is considering imposing a discharge, hospital order or custody.)

(+ NB an offensive weapon is defined in legislation as 'any article made or adapted for use for causing injury, or is intended by the person having it with him for such use'. A highly dangerous weapon is, therefore, a weapon, including a corrosive substance (such as acid), whose dangerous nature must be substantially above and beyond this. The court must determine whether the weapon is highly dangerous on the facts and circumstances of the case.)

STEP TWO
Offence Seriousness – Aggravating and mitigating factors

To complete the assessment of seriousness the court should consider the aggravating and mitigating factors relevant to the offence.

Aggravating factors

Statutory aggravating factors:
Previous findings of guilt, having regard to a) the **nature** of the offence to which the finding of guilt relates and its **relevance** to the current offence; and b) the **time** that has elapsed since the finding of guilt (unless the convictions will be relevant for the purposes of the statutory minimum sentencing provisions – see step five)
Offence committed whilst on bail
Other aggravating factors (non-exhaustive):
Significant degree of planning/premeditation
Deliberate humiliation of victim, including but not limited to filming of the offence, deliberately committing the offence before a group of peers with the intent of causing additional distress or circulating details/photos/videos etc of the offence on social media or within peer groups
Victim is particularly vulnerable due to factors including but not limited to age, mental or physical disability
Offence was committed as part of a group or gang
Attempts to conceal identity
Steps taken to prevent reporting the incident/seeking assistance
Commission of offence whilst under the influence of alcohol or drugs
Offence committed against those working in the public sector or providing a service to the public

Mitigating factors (non-exhaustive)

No findings of guilt or no relevant/recent findings of guilt
Good character and/or exemplary conduct
Participated in offence due to bullying, peer pressure, coercion or manipulation
Little or no planning

Co-operation with the police

STEP THREE
Personal Mitigation

Having assessed the offence seriousness the court should then consider the mitigation personal to the child or young person to determine whether a custodial sentence or a community sentence is necessary. The effect of personal mitigation may reduce what would otherwise be a custodial sentence to a non-custodial one or a community sentence to a different means of disposal.

Personal mitigating factors (non-exhaustive)

Particularly young or immature child or young person (where it affects their responsibility)
Communication or learning disabilities or mental health concerns
Unstable upbringing including but not limited to:- • time spent looked after • lack of familial presence or support • disrupted experiences in accommodation or education • exposure to drug/alcohol abuse, familial criminal behaviour or domestic abuse • victim of neglect or abuse, or exposure to neglect or abuse of others • experiences of trauma or loss
Determination and/or demonstration of steps taken to address offending behaviour
Child or young person in education, training or employment

STEP FOUR
Reduction for guilty pleas

The court should take account of any potential reduction for a guilty plea in accordance with section 144 of the Criminal Justice Act 2003 and part one, section five of the *Overarching Principles Sentencing Children and Young People* definitive guideline.

The reduction in sentence for a guilty plea can be taken into account by imposing one type of sentence rather than another; for example:

- by reducing a custodial sentence to a community sentence, or
- by reducing a community sentence to a different means of disposal.

Alternatively the court could reduce the length or severity of any punitive requirements attached to a community sentence.

See the *Overarching Principles – Sentencing Children and Young People* definitive guideline for details of other available sentences including Referral Orders and Reparation Orders.

STEP FIVE
Statutory minimum sentencing provisions

The following provisions apply to those young people who were aged 16 or over on the date of the offence[1]

Threatening with Bladed Articles or Offensive Weapons

When sentencing these offences a court must impose a sentence of at least 4 months Detention and Training Order **unless the court is of the opinion that there are particular circumstances relating to the offence, the previous offence or the young person which make it unjust to do so in all the circumstances.**

Possession of Bladed Articles or Offensive Weapons

When sentencing the offences of:

- possession of an offensive weapon in a public place;
- possession of an article with a blade/point in a public place;
- possession of an offensive weapon on school premises; and
- possession of an article with blade/point on school premises

a court must impose a sentence of at least 4 months' Detention and Training Order where this is **a second or further** relevant offence **unless the court is of the opinion that there are particular circumstances relating to the offence, any previous relevant offence or the young person which make it unjust to do so in all the circumstances.**

A 'relevant offence' includes those offences listed above and the following offences:

- threatening with an offensive weapon in a public place;
- threatening with an article with a blade/point in a public place;
- threatening with an article with a blade/point on school premises; and
- threatening with an offensive weapon on school premises.

Unjust in all of the circumstances

In considering whether a statutory minimum sentence would be 'unjust in all of the circumstances' the court must have regard to the particular circumstances of the offence, any relevant previous offence and the young person. If the circumstances make it unjust to impose the statutory minimum sentence then the court **must impose an alternative sentence.**

The offence:

Having reached this stage of the guideline the court should have made a provisional assessment of the seriousness of the offence. Where the court has determined that the offence seriousness falls far below the custody threshold the court may consider it unjust to impose the statutory minimum sentence.

Where the court is considering a statutory minimum sentence as a result of a second or further relevant offence, consideration should be given to the seriousness of the previous offence(s) and the period of time that has elapsed between offending. Where the seriousness of the combined offences is such that it falls far below the custody threshold, or where there has been a significant period of time between the offences, the court may consider it unjust to impose the statutory minimum sentence.

The young person:

The statutory obligation to have regard to the welfare of a young person includes the obligation to secure proper provision for education and training, to remove the young person from undesirable surroundings where appropriate, and the need to choose the best option for the young person taking account of the circumstances of the offence.

In having regard to the welfare of the young person, a court should ensure that it considers:

- any mental health problems or learning difficulties/disabilities;
- any experiences of brain injury or traumatic life experience (including exposure to drug and alcohol abuse) and the developmental impact this mav have had;
- any speech and language difficulties and the effect this may have on the ability of the young person (or any accompanying adult) to communicate with the court, to understand the sanction imposed or to fulfil the obligations resulting from that sanction;
- the vulnerability of young people to self harm, particularly within a custodial environment; and

- the effect on young people of experiences of loss and neglect and/or abuse.

In certain cases the concerns about the welfare of the young person may be so significant that the court considers it unjust to impose the statutory minimum sentence.

STEP SIX
Review the sentence

The court must now review the sentence to ensure it is the most appropriate one for the child or young person. This will include an assessment of the likelihood of reoffending and the risk of causing serious harm. A report from the Youth Offending Team may assist.

See the *Overarching Principles – Sentencing Children and Young People* definitive guideline for comprehensive guidance on the sentencing principles and welfare considerations that the court should have in mind when sentencing children and young people, and for the full range of sentences available to the court.

Referral Orders

In cases where children oryoung people have offended for the first time and have pleaded guilty to committing an offence which is on the cusp of the custody threshold, youth offending teams (YOT) should be encouraged to convene a Youth Offender Panel prior to sentence (sometimes referred to as a "pseudo-panel" or "pre-panel") where the child or young person is asked to attend before a panel and agree an intensive contract. If that contract is placed before the sentencing youth court, the court can then decide whether it is sufficient to move below custody on this occasion. The proposed contract is not something the court can alter in any way; the court will still have to make a decision between referral order and custody but can do so on the basis that if it makes a referral order it can have confidence in what that will entail in the particular case.

The court determines the length of the order but a Referral Order Panel determines the requirements of the order.

Offence seriousness	Suggested length of referral order
Low	3–5 months
Medium	5–7 months
High	7–9 months
Very high	10–12 months

The YOT may propose certain requirements and the length of these requirements may not correspond to the above table; if the court feels these requirements will best achieve the aims of the youth justice system then they may still be imposed.

Youth Rehabilitation Order (YRO)

The following table sets out the different levels of intensity that are available under a Youth Rehabilitation Order. The level of intensity and the content of the order will depend upon the court's assessment of seriousness.

Requirements of Order

Standard	Low likelihood of re-offending and a low risk of serious harm.	Primarily seek to repair harm caused through, for example: • reparation; • unpaid work; • supervision; and/or • attendance centre.

Enhanced	Medium likelihood of re-offending or a medium risk of serious harm	Seek to repair harm caused and to enable help or change through, for example: • supervision; • reparation; • requirement to address behaviour e.g. drug treatment, offending behaviour programme, education programme; and/or • a combination of the above.
Intensive	High likelihood of re-offending or a very high risk of serious harm	Seek to ensure the control of and enable help or change for the child or young person through, for example: • supervision; • reparation; • requirement to address behaviour • requirement to monitor or restrict movement, e.g. prohibited activity, curfew, exclusion or electronic monitoring; and/or • a combination of the above.

YRO with Intensive Supervision and Surveillance (ISS) or YRO with fostering

A YRO with an 155 or fostering requirement can only be imposed where the court is of the opinion that the offence has crossed the custody threshold and custody is merited.

The YRO with 155 includes an extended activity requirement, a supervision requirement and curfew. The YRO with fostering requires the child or young person to reside with a local authority foster parent for a specified period of up to 12 months.

Custodial Sentences

If a custodial sentence is imposed, the court must state its reasons for being satisfied that the offence is so serious that no other sanction would be appropriate and, in particular, why a YRO with 155 or fostering could not be justified.

Where a custodial sentence is **unavoidable** the length of custody imposed must be the shortest commensurate with the seriousness of the offence. The court may want to consider the equivalent adult guideline in order to determine the appropriate length of the sentence.

If considering the adult guideline, the court may feel it appropriate to apply a sentence broadly within the region of half to two thirds of the appropriate adult sentence for those aged 15–17 and allow a greater reduction for those aged under 15. This is only a rough guide and must not be applied mechanistically. The individual factors relating to the offence and the child or young person are of the greatest importance and may present good reason to impose a sentence outside of this range.

Section F

Civil and miscellaneous matters

F[1]

Property in possession of police

Police (Property) Act 1897

F[1.1] Application for an order for the delivery of property in possession of the police in connection with their investigation of a suspected offence under s 1 of the Act.

Legal notes and definitions

F[1.2] While this proceeding is a civil case of a kind that is more usually dealt with at a county court, nevertheless it can be dealt with at a magistrates' court. Clearly it will be cheaper and more expeditious if a magistrates' court deals with the matter fairly soon after the hearing of a criminal charge, thus saving a hearing in the county court or High Court. Sufficient notice of the date of hearing should be given to each claimant of the property to enable him to prepare for the hearing before the magistrates.

F[1.3] **When applicable.** This procedure applies when the police have in their possession property which has come into their hands during investigation into a suspected offence. It is not necessary that the person has been charged with any offence.

The powers of the executive to seize and retain goods were carefully circumscribed both at common law and by statute. As a matter of principle the police must not keep an article, or prevent its removal, for any longer than is reasonably necessary to complete their investigations or preserve it for evidence. If a copy will suffice, it should be made and the original returned. As soon as the case is over, or it is decided not to go on with it, the article should be returned. The terms of s 22(2)–(4) of PACE were directed to the retention of the article for use as evidence at trial or for investigation in connection with an offence. There was nothing in s 22 which suggested that the power of retention can be for any purpose other than a purpose for which it was originally seized: *Chief Constable of Merseyside Police v Owens* [2012] EWHC 1515 (Admin), 176 JP 688, 176 CL&J 353).

F[1.4] Often there is no such difficulty as stolen property can be restored direct to the rightful owner. In other cases where the defendant has been convicted for several offences eg theft, at the end of the case the police may be in possession of a large sum of money taken from the defendant. The various losers may each claim part or all of this money as being stolen from them or arising from the sale by the thief of the stolen property.

F[1.5] The police, any claimant or even the defendant can lay a complaint or make an application asking the magistrates to decide the ownership of property and/or to whom the property should be delivered.

F[1.6] At the hearing the police or a claimant has the right to call witnesses, cross-examine the other party's witnesses and to address the magistrates. The hearing can be expedited by the filing of written evidence which can include hearsay evidence.

F[1.7] **Powers of the magistrates.** Having heard all the parties the magistrates may make an order for delivery of the property to the person who appears to the court to be the owner or if he cannot be ascertained they may make such order as they think fit. The court could only decline to return the property to its owner where it was satisfied that the use of its process would in fact indirectly assist in or encourage a crime: *Chief Constable of Merseyside Police v Owens* [2012] EWHC 1515 (Admin), 176 JP 688, 176 CL&J 353).

F[1.8] This gives the magistrates wide powers of discretion. If, for instance, the magistrates are not impressed by any of the claims then they can order the money or the monies the police obtain from selling the stolen property (eg a stolen motor vehicle) to be paid to the Police Property Act Fund which is administered by the Police Authority. The money is invested and the income is used (a) to defray the expenses in handling and storing such property; (b) for compensating the persons who deliver such property to the police; (c) for charitable purposes.

F[1.9] If there are several claimants, magistrates might find in favour of one claimant and order his claim to be paid and find against the other claimants and then order the balance of the money to be delivered to the fund.

F[1.10]–[1.16] **Deliver.** It is to be noted that the word used in disposing of the property is 'delivered'. This means that an unsuccessful claimant can sue in the county court the authority or person to whom the magistrates order delivery, but must do so within six months from the date of the hearing, or his/her right ceases.

F[1.17] **Case unsuitable for magistrates' courts.** The High Court has ruled that magistrates should hesitate to deal with a claim of a similar kind if the value of the property is substantial or if difficult matters of law are likely to arise. For example, a motor car which was stolen whilst subject to a hire-purchase agreement led to there being several claimants. See *Gough v Chief Constable of West Midlands* [2004] EWCA Civ 206, [2004] All ER (D) 45 (Mar) for the interaction with civil proceedings.

F[1.18] If the magistrates decide that if either of the above points arise the best course is to adjourn the hearing *sine die* and to invite the claimant or claimants to commence proceedings in the county court or the High Court. Alternatively, the magistrates can decline to exercise their jurisdiction. A magistrates' court is not obliged to make an order.

F[1.19] **Criminal Damage Act 1971.** The above provisions also apply if the police have possession of property following the execution of a search warrant granted under the Criminal Damage Act 1971, s 6.

F[1.20] **Costs.** Proceedings should be commenced by way of complaint because in magistrates' courts there is no power to award costs where proceedings have been commenced by way of "application" (see for example, *R v Salisbury and Tisbury and Mere Combined Juvenile Court, ex p Ball* (1985) 149 JP 346. Where proceedings have begun by way of a complaint it is inappropriate to order costs against the police where they do not object to the order sought (*R v Uxbridge Justices, ex p Metropolitan Police Comr* [1981] 1 All ER 940, [1981] 1 WLR 112; affd [1981] QB 829, [1981] 3 All ER 129, CA).

Modification of the 1897 Act following the making of a deprivation order

F[1.21] Section 144(1) of the Powers of Criminal Courts (Sentencing) Act 2000 provides that:

(a) no application shall be made under s 1(1) of the 1897 Act by any claimant of the property after the end of six months from the date on which the order in respect of the property was made under s 143 above; and

(b) no such application shall succeed unless the claimant satisfies the court either:
  - (i) that he had not consented to the offender having possession of the property; or
  - (ii) where an order is made under subsection (1) of s 143 (property used for the purpose of committing, etc, an offence) above, that he did not know, and had no reason to suspect, that the property was likely to be used for the purpose mentioned in that subsection.

In *O'Leary International Ltd v Chief Constable of North Wales Police and Crown Prosecution Service (interested party)* [2012] EWHC 1516 (Admin), 176 JP 514, 176 CL&J 370, the appellant company owned a fleet of lorries. As a result of offences committed by drivers employed by the company four lorries and trailers were seized by the police, and in subsequent criminal proceedings against the drivers, deprivation orders were made under s 143. The company sought the return of the lorries and trailers under s 1(1) of the Police (property) Act 1897, but, applying s 144(1)(b), and despite the substantial loss to the company, the magistrates' court declined to order the return of the vehicles to the company. On appeal by way of case stated the view was expressed that the orders under s 143 would probably not have been made if the attention of the magistrates had been drawn to the relevant case law (which is set out in para 14 of the judgment). Since, however, the Divisional Court had no power to set those orders aside in the current appeal their Lordships had to proceed on the basis that the orders were extant.

It was held that s 144 did not provide exclusive statutory machinery for the owner to recover the goods. The appellant retained the full rights of the true owner, including the right to possession. The orders provided no defence to the police to that right, unless there was a public policy defence, the continued availability of which had been considered in *Chief Constable of Merseyside Police v Owens* [2012] EWHC 1515 (Admin), 176 JP 688, 176 CL&J 353. No such defence could have advanced by the police and the Court ordered the return of the lorries.

Though this disposed of the appeal, the Court proceeded to consider whether s 144 should be 'read down' by adding as a ground for return that 'deprivation would be disproportionate' (which was factually conceded). Case law concerning art 1 of the First Protocol to the ECHR was considered. It was held that it would be disproportionate for a court to have no power to consider the value of the property, the degree of culpability of the owner and the financial effect on the owner of deprivation of his goods. In considering whether or not to make an order of deprivation against the offender the court was entitled to take into account the value of the goods and the financial effect on the offender. It was, therefore, necessary to 'read down' s 144(1)(b), so that it contained the additional exception 'or (iii) deprivation would be disproportionate'.

F[2]

Liquor licensing

Appeals under the Licensing Act 2003

Background

F[2.1] The Licensing Act 2003 makes provision for the grant of both personal and premises licences by local authorities.

F[2.2] A personal licence is granted under section 111 to an individual and authorises that person to supply alcohol for a period of ten years.

NB: The Licensing Act 2003 (Premises licences and club premises certificates) (Amendment) Regulations 2012 (SI 2012/955) came into force on 25 April 2012. These Regulations amend the Licensing Act 2003 (Premises licences and club premises certificates) Regulations 2005 to give effect to certain amendments made to the Licensing Act 2003 by the Police Reform and Social Responsibility Act 2011. For example, the category of 'interested party' is removed from the 2003 Act to enable any person to participate in the various processes set out in that Act, regardless of their physical proximity to the premises concerned. Moreover, the Secretary of State must by regulations require licensing authorities to advertise certain applications in a prescribed form and in a prescribed manner which is likely to bring the application to the attention of persons likely to be affected by it.

F[2.3] A premises licence under section 11 and may be granted in respect of any premises and authorises the premises to be used for one or more licensable activities.

F[2.4] The licensable activities are defined in section 1 as,

(a) sale by retail of alcohol
(b) supply of alcohol by club
(c) provision of regulated entertainment and
(d) provision of late-night refreshment.

F[2.5] The local authority will determine the application or licence under section 120 and must grant where the applicant is 18 all over, possesses a described licensing qualification, has not forfeited his personal licence within the previous five-year period nor been convicted of any relevant offence. In the case of the first three criteria the local authority must reject the application where they are not met.

Appeals

F[2.6] In respect of any of the local authority's functions outlined above or variation or imposition of conditions the applicant has a right to appeal to a magistrates' court. Schedule 5 of the Licensing Act 2003 set out in detail the decisions against which an appeal from the local authority may be made.

F[2.7]–[2.11] When the appellant considers the local authorities licensing policy to be incompatible or 'ultra vires' the provisions of the statute, an appeal to the High Court by way of judicial review may be appropriate

Notices

F[2.12] An appeal is commenced by way of written notice being given to a magistrates' court, in the case of a personal licence to the court for the area in which the local authority concerned is situated and in the case of a premises licence, the magistrates' court for the area in which premises are situated.

Period of notice

F[2.13] Notice of appeal must be lodged within the period of 21 days beginning with the date on which the appellant is notified of the local authority's decision. It is the appellant's responsibility to serve notice on all respondents and prove to the court that such notice has been given.

The hearing

F[2.14] Whilst any justice of a local magistrates' court may hear and determine an appeal most courts will have appointed an appeals panel in accordance with guidance issued by the Justices' Clerk's Society. In potentially complex appeals the court may hold a pre-hearing review to identify the issues, the numbers of witnesses and a time estimate for the hearing together with other preliminary matters. At such a hearing the justices may make directions regarding disclosure by the parties to each other (*Rushmoor Borough Council v Richards* (1996) 160 LG Rev 460). The proceedings are civil proceedings and therefore hearsay evidence may be admitted. To shorten proceedings justices or their legal adviser may give directions as to the conduct of the case – including the filing of evidence and any skeleton legal arguments.

F[2.15] The court's powers (section 181). On hearing the application the court may:

(i) dismiss the appeal; or
(ii) uphold the appeal and make any other decision which could have been made by the licensing authority; or
(iii) remit the case to the licensing authority to dispose of in accordance with the direction of the court, if, for example, the local authority has simply failed to process an application.

Procedure

F[2.16] The appellant's case may be presented in person or by a representative qualified under the provisions of the Courts and Legal Services Act 1990. The appeal is by way of a rehearing on the merits of the case and is neither a review of the local authority's decision nor an appeal on a point of law. The court is, therefore, able to hear all the evidence that was before the local authority committee and any relevant evidence, which has arisen subsequent to the local authority's decision.

Order of speeches

F[2.17] As the appeal is commenced by way of a complaint the order of proceedings is governed by the Magistrates' Courts Rules 1981 (rule 14). This means that the appellant will open the case and call evidence in support of the appeal. Any respondent will be permitted to cross-examine witnesses called by the appellant and the appellant may re-examine any of those witnesses.

F[2.18] Subject to any questions the justices may have, at the end of the appellant's case the respondent will outline his case and call witnesses in support. Such witnesses may be cross-examined and re-examined and the respondent may make a closing speech leaving the appellant with the final address to the court.

The Magistrates' Courts Rules 1981, r 34 provides that where a statutory appeal lies to a magistrates' court against a decision of a local authority the appeal shall be made by way of complaint, the procedure for which involves calling evidence. Such an appeal takes the form of a fresh hearing at which the parties are free to adduce whatever evidence they think fit, subject to the control of the court. Section 181(2)(b) does not restrict the evidence which may be laid before the justices but simply makes clear that the justices have the power to make any order of the kind that the licensing authority could have made, without saying anything about the grounds on which such an order might be made. The justices' function is to consider the application by reference to the statutory licensing objectives untrammelled by any of the regulations that govern the procedure for a review under s 51. The justices are therefore entitled to consider evidence of events occurring before the application to the licensing authority as well as evidence of events occurring since its decision. Whilst it is right that a person whose licence is under threat ought to have notice of the nature of the case against him so that he has a fair chance of meeting it, this can be achieved without limiting the hearing before the magistrates to the allegations that were made before the licensing authority. The magistrates, therefore, are not limited to considering only those grounds of complaint that were raised in the notice of application or the representations before the licensing authority: *R (on the application of Khan) v Coventry Magistrates' Court* [2011] EWCA Civ 751.

The decision

F[2.19] In *R (on the application of Raphael trading as Orleans) v Highbury Corner Magistrates Court* [2011] EWCA Civ 462, the Court of Appeal decided that at a Licensing Committee's meeting, a resolution was passed establishing and empowering sub-committees for the future discharge of licensing functions. That resolution was passed after ss 7 and 10 of the Licensing Act 2003 came into force. Accordingly, the sub-committee had jurisdiction to amend the conditions of the appellant's nightclub licence and the justices (on appeal from the local authority) had been correct to reject that ground of appeal.

The court will have regard to the licensing authority's statement of licensing policy and any guidance issued by the Secretary of State under s 182 of the Act. The court will also make its decision with the aim of promoting the licensing objectives set out in the Act namely:

(i) the prevention of crime and disorder,
(ii) public safety,
(iii) the prevention of public nuisance, and
(iv) the protection of children from harm.

The licensing objective for the prevention of crime does not require that a crime be committed, let alone prosecuted: *East Lindsey DC v Hanif (t/a Zaraf Restaurant and Takeaway)* [2016] EWHC 1265 (Admin), [2016] CTLC 81.

The court will give reasons for its decision and if the court departs from either the statutory guidance or the licensing statement it will give reasons for doing so. Justices hearing an appeal should not consider or engage in planning matters which fell properly within the jurisdiction of the licensing authority (*R (on the application of Blackwood) v Birmingham Magistrates' Court* [2006] All ER (D) 324 (Jun)). Except in the case of a closure order there is no further statutory entitlement to appeal the decision of the magistrates' court.

For more up to date guidance on the relevance of the Licensing Act's objectives when justices are hearing an appeal see (*R (on the application of Daniel Thwaites plc) v Wirral Borough Magistrates' Court* [2008] EWHC 838 (Admin), 172 JP 301).

When dealing with an appeal against a decision of a local licensing authority, the magistrates' court had to pay careful attention to the licensing committee's reasons and exercise its own judgement as to how much weight to accord to them. The fuller and clearer the reasons, the more force they were likely to carry. The appellant bore the burden of persuading the appellate court that the committee ought to have exercised its discretion differently, rather than the court being required to exercise the discretion afresh: *Stepney Borough Council v Joffe* [1949] 1 KB 599, [1949] 1 All ER 256, DC considered; *Sagnata Investments Ltd v Norwich Corporation* [1971] 2 QB 614, [1971] 2 All ER 1441, CA applied: *R (on the application of Hope and Glory Public House) v City of Westminster Magistrates' Court (Lord Mayor and Citizens of the City of Westminster, interested party)* [2011] EWCA Civ 31, [2011] 3 All ER 579, [2011] PTSR 868.

In *R (on the application of Developing Retail Ltd) v East Hampshire Magistrates' Court* [2011] EWHC 618 (Admin), on an appeal against the grant of a provisional premises licence, in accordance with s 29 of the LA 2003, the justices had sought to impose two conditions. Analogous to bail conditions, the High Court stressed the need for conditions to be clear, precise and enforceable.

The first condition modified an original condition to ensure that an external seating area was vacated by customers at 11pm. That condition was directed at late night noise emanating from the premises. The justices added to the condition by including a balcony on the premises. It was held that the justices had been entitled to regard the condition as preventative rather than reactive like the regulatory conditions preventing noise. The condition was clear and proportionate and was tailored to the activities intended to take place at the premises.

However, the justices had imposed a second condition, namely that all noise from regulated entertainment at the premises should be inaudible one metre outside any noise sensitive premises. Although a condition was justified by reference to a decibel level to protect local residents, the condition was quashed and the matter remitted to the justices to consider an alternative condition. The original condition was so vague as to be unenforceable. There was no clarity as to the premises or location intended to be protected and the meaning of 'inaudible', in that context, was unclear.

Costs

F[2.20] The court may make such order for costs as it thinks fit under s 181 of the Licensing Act 2003. Case law such as *Bradford Metropolitan District Council v Booth* (2002) suggests that public authorities need to be able to make honest, reasonable and sound administrative decisions in the public interest without fear of exposure to undue financial prejudice if they are successfully appealed.

In *Crawley Borough Council v Attenborough* [2006] EWHC 1278 (Admin), (2006) 170 JP 593, the justices varied conditions imposed by the Borough Council in relation to licensed premises run by the respondent. The justices ordered the local authority to pay all of the costs of the respondent. On appeal it was agreed that there was no practical distinction between the terms of s 64 of the MCA 1980 (civil proceedings) and s 181 of the Licensing Act 2003. The Divisional Court upheld the justices' decision to award costs having regard to the fact that they had considered all of the circumstances including the facts and the history of the case and bearing in mind the order was varied on appeal by the justices.

Just over one week later, in *Cambridge City Council v Alex Nestling Ltd* [2006] EWHC 1374 (Admin), (2006) 170 JP 539, 170 JPN 975 it was decided that although as a matter of strict law the power of the appellate court in such circumstances to award costs is not confined to cases where the local authority acted unreasonably or in bad faith, the fact that the local authority has acted reasonably and in good faith in the discharge of its public function is plainly a most important factor. In ordinary civil litigation the principle that costs follow the event does not apply in this type of case. Therefore, an award of costs should not routinely follow in favour of a successful appellant in this type of case, if anything, quite the contrary.

It is submitted that if there is a perceived conflict between the two authorities above, there was fuller argument in the latter case and therefore the approach adopted in *Alex Nesting Ltd* is to be preferred.

Note that the principles outlined in *Bradford Metropolitan District Council v Booth* above, apply equally to costs sought in forfeiture proceedings brought under s 298(2) of the Proceeds of Crime Act 2002. See **F[5.47]**.

Closure Orders: police powers

F[2.21] Power. On licensed premises only

- closure for a period not exceeding 24 hours
- no entry to members of the public during closure
- purchases or supplies prohibited during closure
- contravention without reasonable excuse is liable to a fine not exceeding £20,000 or to imprisonment for a term not exceeding 3 months, or to both.

F[2.22] Grounds. Requires authorisation by a senior police officer who believes that:

- likely to be disorder in or near premises and that closure is necessary in the interests of public safety, or
- disorder already taking place and that closure is necessary in the interests of public safety, or
- public nuisance is being caused by noise from the premises and that closure is necessary to prevent nuisance.

F[2.23] Duration.

- up to 24 hours (notice must be given in writing);

- may be cancelled by police at any time after the order has been made (notice must be given in writing);
- order may be extended by responsible senior police officer if he/she believes grounds continue to apply and that magistrates will not have considered the order by end of closure period;
- no such extension shall come into force unless notice is given by end of previous closure period.

F[2.24] Consideration hearing by magistrates (ss 164–165).

- as soon as reasonably practicable (must have written notice);
- must be in 'open court';
- powers may be exercised by a magistrates' court (which can be exercised by a single justice);
- evidence given must be on oath.

F[2.25] Powers. The court may:

- revoke the order and any extension of it if the order or extension is still in force; or
- order the relevant premises to remain, or to be, closed until the matter is dealt with by the licensing authority. In considering whether to exercise this power the magistrates will have regard to s 161 in determining whether the grounds for making the order are continuing, or are likely to continue;
- order the premises to remain or be closed until dealt with by the licensing authority under s 167 but subject to specified exceptions;
- order the premises to remain or be closed until determination by the licensing authority unless conditions specified in the order are satisfied.

F[2.26] Appeal from the Justices. Any person aggrieved by the decision of the magistrates may appeal to the Crown Court (Licensing Act 2003, s 166).

F[2.27] Closure notices for persistently selling alcohol to children under s 147A Licensing Act 2003.

Power. Applies to any premises:

- prohibition for a period not exceeding 48 hours of sales of alcohol;
- offers the opportunity to discharge all criminal liability.

For more detail see s 169A of the Licensing Act 2003 as added by s 24 of the Violent Crime Reduction Act 2006. This legislation came into force on 6 April 2007.

The Licensing Act 2003 (Persistent Selling of Alcohol to Children) (Prescribed Form of Closure Notice) Regulations 2012 (SI 2012/963) came into force on 25 April 2012.

These Regulations revoke the Licensing Act 2003 (Persistent Selling of Alcohol to Children) (Prescribed Form of Closure Notice) Regulations 2007 and prescribe the form of a closure notice given under s 169A of the Licensing Act 2003 ('the 2003 Act') to give effect to certain amendments made to that Act by the Police Reform and Social Responsibility Act 2011.

A closure notice represents an alternative to prosecution under s 147A of the 2003 Act for the offence of persistently selling alcohol to children. The offence may be committed by the holder of a premises licence if on two or more occasions within three consecutive months alcohol is sold unlawfully to an individual aged under 18 on the premises to which the licence relates.

Previously, the effect of a closure notice was that alcohol sales at the licensed premises to which it relates could be prohibited for a period of up to 48 hours. Following the amendment to the 2003 Act, a closure notice may prohibit alcohol sales from the premises to which it relates for a period of between 48 and 336 hours. These Regulations prescribe the form of a closure notice which contains reference to the period for which premises may be prohibited from making sales of alcohol in accordance with the amendment to the 2003 Act.

Offence of fraudulently receiving programmes (Copyright, Designs and Patents Act 1988, s 297)

F[2.28] Prosecution of designated premises supervisors and premises licence holders. The Federation Against Copyright Theft is engaged in the private prosecution of designated premises supervisors and premises licence holders throughout England and Wales for offences contrary to s 297(1). This is a relevant offence for *personal licence holders* as defined by Sch 4 to the Licensing Act 2003 and magistrates have certain powers and obligations when dealing with personal licence holders, namely:

- The requirement for a personal licence holder to produce his licence on his first appearance in court (s 128(1)).
- The power to order forfeiture or suspension of the personal licence (s 129).
- The notification of a conviction for a relevant offence to the licensing authority that issued the personal licence (s 131(2)(a)).

F[3]

Betting and gaming licensing

Gambling Act 2005

F[3.1] **The Gambling Act 2005** contains a new regulatory system to govern the provision of all forms of gambling in Great Britain, other than the National lottery and spread betting. From **1 September** 2007 the Act repealed the Betting, Gaming and Lotteries Act 1963, the Gaming Act 1968 and the Lotteries and Amusements Act 1976 respectively (see the Gambling Act 2005 (Commencement No 6 and Transitional) Provisions Order 2006 (2006/3272) (C119) as modified by several amending orders.

The following is a brief summary of the changes in procedure and jurisdiction.

General changes

F[3.2] The following general changes have been made:

- Creation of a Gambling Commission.
- A two-tier jurisdiction with local authorities dealing with premises.
- The Act removes all responsibility from licensing, betting and gaming justices for granting betting and gaming permissions, which they exercised previously.
- Decisions of the licensing authority, ie the relevant local authority, may be the subject of an appeal to the local magistrates' court. Decisions of the Gambling Commission may be the subject of an appeal to the Gambling Appeals Tribunal (but not a magistrates' court).

Appeals under the Gambling Act 2005 from local authorities

Background

F[3.3] Operating and personal licences fall under the jurisdiction of the Gambling Commission by virtue of Part 7 (s 140 onwards) of the Gambling Act 2005. Appeals lie to the Gambling Appeal Tribunal.

Premises licences fall under the licensing authority's jurisdiction ie the relevant local authority under Part 8 (s 153 onwards).

Appeals in respect of premises licences are governed by ss 206 and 207 of the Gambling Act 2005.

Appeals

F[3.4] Section 206 stipulates who is entitled to appeal.

Section 207 states that an appeal under s 206 in relation to premises must be instituted:

(a) in the magistrates' court for a local justice area in which the premises are wholly or mainly situated
(b) by notice of appeal given to the designated officer; and
(c) within the period of 21 days beginning with the day on which the appellant receives notice of the decision against which the appeal is brought (**NB**: there does not appear to be a power to extend the 21 day period);
(d) a fee will be payable to the magistrates' court hearing the appeal.

Section 207 prescribes who the respondent is.

Section 207(3) states that on hearing the appeal the **magistrates may**:

(a) dismiss the appeal;

(b) substitute for the decision appealed against any decision that the licensing authority could have made;
(c) remit the case to the local authority to decide in accordance with the direction of the court;
(d) make an order about costs.

Section 208 permits a stay of the order pending appeal.

There is no appeal from the decision of the magistrates' court to the Crown Court. An aggrieved party may appeal on a point of law to the High Court.

NB: As these are essentially civil proceedings, the hearing, procedure, order of speeches and the discretion to award costs are to all intents and purposes the same as in licensing appeals, see F[2] above.

F[4]
Council tax

Background to council tax

F[4.1] The administration and enforcement of the council tax is regulated by the Council Tax (Administration and Enforcement) Regulations 1992.

Recovery and enforcement

F[4.2] The first action the courts are involved in is the issue of a summons by a single justice or a justices' clerk against the alleged debtor following a complaint by a local authority of non-payment. Section 127(1) of the Magistrates' Courts Act 1980 (time limit for instituting proceedings) is disapplied by the regulations; the application may be made up to six years from the date that the sum became due, which is the date when the demand was served and not when the amount of tax was set by the billing authority: *Regentford Ltd v Thanet District Council* [2004] EWHC 246 (Admin), [2004] RA 113, [2004] 11 LS Gaz R 35. Prior to this the local authority will have served a demand notice on the liable person and when payment has not been forthcoming the authority must serve a reminder notice. If payment is not made within seven days of the issue of the reminder notice the whole amount outstanding becomes due after a further seven-day period. The final step the local authority takes before making a complaint for a liability order is the issue of a final notice. Such notice will state the sum outstanding and the amount of any costs reasonably incurred in obtaining the liability order. The court will fix a date when the applications for the liability order will be heard.

F[4.3] A summons may be served on a person by delivering it to him; leaving it in his usual or last known place of abode; sending it to him by post to that address or leaving it or sending it by post to an address given by the person as an address at which the service of the summons will be accepted (eg a solicitor's office). In the case of a company service can be effected at the company's registered office.

The court hearing

F[4.4] The court hearing is conducted as a complaint and the complainant council may make out their case for a liability order on the balance of probabilities, whether or not the non-payer appears in court. In order to be successful the council must satisfy the court that:

(a) council tax has been set by resolution of the authority;
(b) a sum due has been demanded in accordance with the regulations as set out above; and
(c) a summons has been served.

F[4.5] It follows that if the amount has not been demanded in accordance with the regulations or has been duly paid then this will amount to a defence.

F[4.6] Reopening

It is noteworthy that the power to reopen and rehear a case under s 142 of the Magistrates' Courts Act 1980 does not apply to this type of civil proceedings (*R (on the application of Mathialagan) v Southwark London Borough Council* [2004] EWCA Civ 1689, [2004] All ER (D) 179 (Dec)).

Nor can the power be used when a case has been dismissed (*Verderers of the New Forest v Young* [2004] EWHC 2954 (Admin), [2004] All ER (D) 14 (Dec)). However, reg 36A of the Council Tax (Administration and Enforcement) Regulations 1992 permits a liability order to be rescinded on the application of the local authority; further, there does appear to be a limited power to review civil orders in exceptional circumstances: see case law under B[38.5].

Evidential requirements

F[4.7] Much of the evidence may be produced by way of certificate, for example, a certified copy signed by the appropriate officer showing the council's resolution setting the amount of the council tax for the given local authority area. In addition:

(a) computer generated documents are admissible under the Civil Evidence Act 1995 so long as the document constitutes or forms part of a record compiled by the authority;
(b) direct oral evidence of any facts stated would have been admissible; and
(c) where the document has been produced by a computer it is accompanied by a certificate which:
   (i) must identify the document and the computer by which it was produced;
   (ii) give appropriate explanations to the contents of the document; and
   (iii) be signed by a person occupying a responsible position in relation to the operation of the computer.

F[4.8] The only legitimate defences against the making of the liability order are outlined above and such matters as pending appeals at the valuation tribunal as to the correct banding, or disputes as to the amount owed, will not amount to a reason for the court to decline to issue a liability order. The justices are obliged to prevent the claimant from putting forward irrelevant matters such as whether the defendant should have received council tax benefit (*R (on application of Williams) v Pontefract Magistrates' Court* [2002] All ER (D) 465 (May)).

The liability order

F[4.9] Where magistrates are satisfied that the local authority has made out its case then they have no further discretion but to issue a liability order. This order will include an order for reasonable costs. A liability order gives the local authority the power to take enforcement action such as an attachment of earnings order, distress or deductions from income support. Matters which may be raised at a valuation tribunal are not relevant in liability order proceedings.

Costs of obtaining a liability order

F[4.9A] Local authorities bring many thousands of applications before magistrates' courts. The vast majority of applications proceed swiftly to the granting of orders. Courts have agreed procedures for the bulk handling of such orders. One of the aspects of these procedures is that local authorities make routine applications for costs in a set amount under reg 34(7)(b) of the Council Tax (Administration and Enforcement) Regulations 1992, SI 1992/613. Unlike the position in Wales there is no statutory prescription about the amount of costs. The court has to be satisfied:

(a) that the local authority has actually incurred those costs;
(b) that the costs in question were incurred in obtaining the liability order; and
(c) that it was reasonable for the local authority to incur them.

Whether the requirements are satisfied is an issue of mixed fact and law, not a matter of discretion. Once the court is satisfied that the costs have been reasonably incurred, it has no discretion but to award costs in that amount, and the ability of a particular respondent to pay those costs is not a relevant consideration. On the other hand, a defendant is entitled to know how the court is able to satisfy itself that the costs claimed do represent the costs reasonably incurred in obtaining the liability order, in the absence of any information as to how that figure was computed. Guidance to local councils on good practice in the collection of Council Tax arrears was issued in 2013 that they are only permitted to charge reasonable costs for the court summons and liability order. They should be able to provide a breakdown, on request, showing how these costs are calculated.

The provisions in reg 34(7) were considered in *R (Nicholson) v Tottenham Magistrates' Court* [2015] EWHC 1252 (Admin), (2015) PTSR 1045, (2015) 179 JP

421. It was held it was insufficient for the court to rely on general and vague assertions with no supporting particulars. The focus must be not on whether the costs claimed was a reasonable amount but whether those costs were reasonably incurred in obtaining the liability order. Given the large number of summonses issued, it will not be practical for the local authority to carry out and provide a detailed calculation of the actual costs incurred in each and every case, therefore it may be a legitimate approach for a local authority to calculate an average figure which could be levied across the board in 'standard' cases. The next question is whether the costs claimed have been 'reasonably' incurred which is not the same thing as establishing that the costs are reasonable in amount. Given the absence of any independent assessment, the scope for abuse of the system is self-evident, and that makes it all the more important that due process is observed. Therefore, it is incumbent upon the magistrates to reach a proper judicial determination of the amount of costs reasonably incurred by the applicant Council, in obtaining the liability order. They need to have sufficient information as to how the figure was arrived at and that the costs were incurred in obtaining the order and not, for example, in sending out council tax bills to all the taxpayers in the Borough. See also *Ewing v Highbury Corner Magistrates' Court* [2015] EWHC 3788 (Admin), [2016] R.V.R. 174, where an order for costs was quashed. The court had not had sufficient relevant information to reach a proper determination of whether the costs claimed represented costs reasonably incurred by the local authority in obtaining the liability order. See also *Nicolson v Grant Thornton UK LLP* [2016] EWHC 710 (Admin), [2016] 2 Costs L.R. 211.

There is nothing to prevent a summons from stating on its face the amount of costs claimed by the local authority in connection with the complaint: *Williams v East Northamptonshire DC* [2016] EWHC 470 (Admin), [2016] R.A. 191.

Committal proceedings

F[4.10] Following the failure of liability or other enforcement methods the local authority may apply to the court for a means inquiry to be held with a view to a committal to prison in default of payment of the outstanding council tax. A warrant of commitment may only be applied for if the local authority has first attempted to levy distress and have received a report that the bailiffs were unable to find sufficient goods on which to levy the amount outstanding. In order to secure the debtor's attendance the court may issue a summons or a warrant for his arrest. At the committal hearing the court will inquire into the defaulter's means and may impose a period of three months maximum to be served in imprisonment where they are satisfied that failure to pay is due to the person's wilful refusal or culpable neglect. Justices using this power should be satisfied of the criteria on a criminal standard of proof or a high civil standard (*R v South Tyneside Justices, ex p Martin* (1995) Independent, 20 September). The defaulter must be present before the court and although local authorities are not under a statutory obligation to exhaust all other remedies before making an application for committal, it may well be advisable for them to do so. Courts will therefore be keen to see such action being tried as clearer evidence that the defendant is culpable in his neglect to pay and not just unable to pay through impecuniosity or mismanagement.

F[4.11] When dealing with a committal application then the magistrates may:

(a) issue a warrant for commitment;
(b) fix a term of imprisonment and postpone the issue of the warrant until such time and on such conditions as the court thinks fit; note that where a warrant is issued after postponement and, since the term of imprisonment was fixed, part-payments have been made, these payments will reduce the imprisonment in a proportion to the full amount outstanding;
(c) adjourn the application;
(d) dismiss the application;
(e) remit all or part of the sum owing. As a guideline payments should be able to be made within a three-year period (*R (on the application of Broadhurst) v Sheffield Justices* (2000) 164 JP 870). Previous case law points to the fact that, as with rates enforcement, this may only be appropriate if the debtor cannot afford to pay; remission remains an option only up to the point at which a term of imprisonment has been fixed (*Harrogate Borough Council v Barker* (1995) 159 LG Rev 889, 159 JP 809);

(f) theoretically the court might find wilful refusal or culpable neglect but not issue a commitment warrant as the matter does rest within its discretion: once a warrant of commitment has been issued or a term of imprisonment fixed, a charging authority may not take further steps to recover the debt under the liability order (Council Tax (Administration and Enforcement) Regulations 1992, reg 52).

F[4.12] The Council Tax (Administration and Enforcement) Regulations 1992, regulation 47(2) makes it clear that on an application for commitment to prison being made the court shall, in the debtor's presence, inquire into his means and inquire whether the failure to pay which has led to *the application* is due to his wilful refusal or culpable neglect. In other words, the court's inquiries concern the period of time after the issue of the liability order but before the application for a commitment to prison. This in fact makes it even more important that local authorities pursue all available options to them under the authority's liability order before coming into court to ask for a commitment warrant to be issued.

There must be a separate enquiry by the magistrates into the circumstances relevant under reg 47 of the Council Tax (Administration and Enforcement) Regulations 1992, SI 1992/613, for each of the separate years of liability. Otherwise this will be fatal to the decision of the magistrates: *R v Leeds Justices, ex p Kennett* [1996] RVR 53.

In *R (on the application of Aldous) v Dartford Magistrates' Court* [2011] EWHC 1919 (Admin), it was held that the form of enquiry as to means was hopelessly inadequate and did not meet the requirements of reg 47. The claimant was invited to fill in a standard means form, but it was deficient in terms of discovering how the claimant could meet her liability for payment in excess of £7,000. There did not appear to have been anything like an adequate number of questions posed to discover what the claimant's means were. Accordingly, there was nothing which could properly be called an enquiry. Further, the period of any imprisonment imposed under reg 47(3) must vary according to the culpability of the person in question. It was less serious to fail to pay rates through culpable neglect rather than through wilful refusal. In order to fix the amount of any term of committal it was necessary to determine whether it was due to wilful refusal or culpable neglect which had led to the failure to pay. The magistrates in the present case failed to distinguish between the two statutory criteria and failed to make a finding which was a necessary precondition to fixing a term of imprisonment in default: *R v Highbury Corner Magistrates' Court, ex p Uchendu* (1994) 158 LGR 481, [1994] RA 51, (1994) 158 JP 409 considered.

F[4.13] Although the council may only deduct 5% of debtors' benefit payments direct from income support a magistrates' court may order a payment in excess of this figure in appropriate circumstances (*R v Felixstowe, Ipswich and Woodbridge Magistrates' Court and Ipswich Borough Council, ex p Herridge* [1993] RA 83, 158 JP 307).

Suspended commitments

F[4.14] Where a commitment to prison is issued but postponed on terms it appears that the court must hold a further inquiry before the commitment warrant is issued to take the defaulter to prison. This was considered in *R v Faversham and Sittingbourne Justices, ex p Ursell* [1992] RA 99, 156 JP 765. The court considered that a further inquiry into a commitment warrant postponed on terms was necessary before that warrant could be issued. This was a further opportunity to enable the court to be satisfied that the conditions had not been met by the debtor as well as giving the debtor a further opportunity to explain his default.

F[4.15] The role of a defaulter was considered in *R v Wolverhampton Stipendiary Magistrate, ex p Mould* (1992) Times, 16 November. This was a case under the community charge legislation. The role of the defaulter was defined as going beyond the mere giving of evidence. He could also:

(a) challenge the evidence given by the charging authority as to indebtedness and any steps to levy distress;

(b) challenge the information given about his means;
(c) submit that failure to pay was not due to wilful refusal or culpable neglect; and
(d) even if it was, that a warrant of commitment postponed on suitable conditions was to be preferred to immediate custody.

F[4.16] Where the defaulter fails to attend the magistrates must be satisfied that he has received notice of the hearing and must carry out an appropriate inquiry to make sure that the notice must have come into his hands. Accordingly the notice should be sent by recorded delivery: see *R v Newcastle upon Tyne Justices, ex p Devine* (1998) 162 JP 602, DC (a case decided under the similarly worded reg 41 of the Community Charge (Administration and Enforcement) Regulations 1989, SI 1989/712).

F[4.17] A number of cases have emphasised that before committing a debtor to prison the court must have considered all available alternatives to attempt recovery of the sum due (*R v Newcastle under Lyme Justices, ex p Massey* [1995] 1 All ER 120, 158 JP 1037, [1994] NLJR 1444, sub nom R v Stoke-on-Trent Justices, ex p Knight [1994] 1 WLR 1684).

F[5]

Applications to a justice

Warrants to enter premises

F[5.1] See generally the Criminal Procedure Rules 2015, Part 47 and Criminal Practice Directions 2015, Division XI Other proceedings, 47A Investigation orders and warrants.

1 *The applicant*

Usually such applications are made by a police officer. If not, the magistrate should check whether any authority is needed by the applicant, eg in the case of an official from a supplier of Gas or Electricity (see F[5.31]). As a sensible precaution, a police officer should be asked to produce his warrant card, and anyone else evidence of his identity, and where appropriate, his authority to bring proceedings.

The obligation on an applicant is the same as that imposed on any person making a 'without notice' application, namely one of full and frank disclosure. The applicant should, for example, disclose that a private prosecution is expected to follow the issue of the warrant: *R v Zinga* [2012] EWCA Crim 2357, [2013] Crim L R 226, and ordinarily the fact that the occupant of the premises is a solicitor, especially if he is a duty solicitor and will thus be likely to keep work based devices at his home: (*R (on the application of AB) v Huddersfield Magistrates' Court* [2014] EWHC 1089 (Admin), [2014] 4 All ER 500, [2014] 2 Cr App Rep 409. The disclosure must be as full and frank as the circumstances of each case requires. For a summary of the relevant principles, see *R (on the application of Rawlinson and Hunter Trustees) v Central Criminal Court* [2012] EWHC 2254 (Admin), [2013] 1 WLR 1634. See also *R (Golfrate Property Management Ltd and Another) v Southwark Crown Court and Others* [2014] EWHC 840 (Admin), [2014] 2 Cr App R 12; and *R (on the application of S,F and L) v Chief Constable of the British Transport Police* [2013] EWHC 2189 (Admin), [2014] 1 All ER 268, [2014] 1 WLR 1647.

2 *Authority for issuing a warrant*

F[5.2] A warrant of entry may only be issued where a statute gives authority to do so. When considering an application the magistrate should ask the applicant under what Act and section he is applying for a warrant. The warrant and supporting paperwork should indicate the Act and section. Note that the Justices' Clerks' Society has produced a checklist (dated October 2011) and any magistrate who may be asked to deal with search warrant applications should be afforded access to that checklist.

F[5.3] **Applications by the police** generally fall into one of two categories:

F[5.4] **Search for unlawful articles.** These are powers of search for goods which generally it is an offence knowingly to possess, eg warrants to enter and search for:

- stolen goods – Theft Act 1968, s 26;
- drugs – Misuse of Drugs Act 1971, s 23;
- obscene articles – Obscene Publications Act 1959, s 3;
- firearm or ammunition – Firearms Act 1968, s 46.

Under the MDA 1971, s 23(4), a forcible search may be justified where the suspect refuses to submit to a request to spit out drugs which he was concealing in his mouth: see *James v DPP* [2012] EWHC 1317 (Admin), 176 JP 346, 176 CL&J 291.

F[5.5] **Search for evidence.** Until the Police and Criminal Evidence Act 1984, there was no power to issue a warrant to search for *evidence*, eg of a murder, unless the object of the search was also an 'unlawful article' so that a warrant could be issued under the powers described above. The Police and Criminal Evidence Act 1984, s 8 (as amended by the Serious Organised Crime and Police Act 2005) now provides a general power to search for evidence of an offence. However since the Police and Criminal Evidence Act 1984 also gives the police considerable powers of search without a warrant in connection with the arrest of a defendant, an application for a warrant to search for evidence will very often entail the power to enter the premises of a possibly innocent third party to look for evidence implicating the accused.

In certain cases, investigators may have to decide whether to use the search warrant procedure or their post-arrest powers. The statutory provisions relating to both procedures reveal no indication of priority or preference between them. They are distinct powers with distinct criteria. Where the criteria for both processes could be fulfilled, the investigator has a choice, although different considerations would arise if there was an element of bad faith or improper motive in making the choice: *R (Singh) v National Crime Agency* [2018] EWHC 1119 (Admin), [2018] 1 WLR 5093, [2019] 1 Cr App R 11.

Issuing a warrant to search for evidence of an indictable offence (Police and Criminal Evidence Act 1984, s 8)

F[5.6] The application must be made by the police and the magistrate must have reasonable grounds for believing:

(a) that an indictable offence has been committed; and
(b) that there is material on premises specified in the application which is likely to be of substantial value (whether by itself or together with other material) to the investigation of the offence; and
(c) that the material is likely to be relevant evidence; and
(d) that it does not consist of or include items subject to legal privilege, excluded material or special procedure material; and
(e) that any of the following applies:
  (i) that it is not practicable to communicate with any person entitled to grant entry to the premises;
  (ii) that it is practicable to communicate with a person entitled to grant access to the premises but it is not practicable to communicate with any person entitled to grant access to the evidence;
  (iii) that entry to the premises will not be granted unless a warrant is produced;
  (iv) that the purpose of a search may be frustrated or seriously prejudiced unless a constable arriving at the premises can secure immediate entry to them.

In *R (on the application of Wood) v North Avon Magistrates' Court* [2009] EWHC 3614 (Admin), 174 JP 157 the High Court suggested that, save in exceptional circumstances, the officer applying for the warrant and giving evidence on oath must be an officer directly involved in the investigation.

F[5.7] Reasonable grounds for believing. The magistrate himself must have reasonable grounds for believing etc and his judgment will be based on the information supplied by the officer. It is advisable for a short note to be kept by the magistrate of the reasons for granting or refusing a warrant (which can be attached to the application). In the Code of Practice issued for guidance to the police, the officer must take reasonable steps to check that the information is accurate, recent and has not been provided maliciously or irresponsibly. An application may not be made on the basis of information from an anonymous source unless corroboration is sought. The identity of an informant need not be disclosed but the officer should be prepared to deal with any questions from the magistrate about the accuracy of previous information provided by that source or other related matters. 'Belief' is something more than suspicion and implies an acceptance that something is true even though formal, admissible evidence may be lacking. It may be helpful to consider the reference to this matter made when considering the offence of handling stolen goods at A[49].

There was nothing in the 1984 Act which required the court to give reasons why it was satisfied that there were reasonable grounds for believing the matters set out in s 8(1)(a)–(e) was satisfied. In some cases it might be unnecessary to do so, such as where the written information was compelling as to the grounds for a belief and clearly addressed the specific matters in s 8(1)(a)–(d): *Glenn & Co (Essex) Ltd v Her Majesty's Commissioners for Revenues and Customs and East Berkshire Magistrates' Court* [2011] EWHC 2998 (Admin), [2012] 1 Cr App Rep 291, 176 JP 65.

Reasonable suspicion. Some legislation requires only 'reasonable suspicion' as opposed to 'reasonable grounds for belief'. In *R (on the application of Eastenders Barking Ltd) v South Western Magistrates' Court* 22 March 2011, QBD, it was held that the grant of a search warrant under s 46 of the Firearms Act 1968 required only reasonable suspicion that an offence had or might have been committed under the Act as opposed to the higher threshold of reasonable belief (see *R v Central Criminal Court, ex p Bright* [2001] 2 All ER 244, [2001]1 WLR 662, DC; *R v Windsor* [2011] EWCA Crim 143, [2011] 2 Cr App Rep 71, 175 CL&J 110.

The test for establishing reasonable suspicion was a two-fold test which comprised a subjective and objective element The issue was whether (a) the Judge or magistrate was satisfied that there were reasonable grounds for suspecting an offence had been committed under the Act; and (b) if he/she was, whether there was material before him/her on which he/she was entitled to be satisfied.

In the present case there were reasonable grounds to satisfy the objective test because intelligence existed which was reliable. The source of the evidence had been given to the Judge. The fact that more information could have been elicited did not mean there was insufficient evidence to give rise to reasonable suspicion, the threshold of which was relatively low.

F[5.8] **Indictable offence** means an offence which, if committed by an adult, is triable on indictment, whether it is exclusively so or triable either way. The definition also includes a 'relevant offence' as defined in s 28D(4) of the Immigration Act 1971: s 8(5) PACE 1984.

F[5.9] **Relevant evidence** means anything that would be admissible in evidence at a trial for the offence. The application (information) and the warrant should identify, so far as is practicable, the articles or persons to be sought: see s 15(6)(b) of PACE and *Power-Hynes v Norwich Magistrates' Court* [2009] EWHC 1512 (Admin), (2009) 173 JP 573.

F[5.10] **Premises.** The premises referred to above are:

- one or more sets of premises specified in the application (a '*specific premises warrant*'); or
- any premises occupied or controlled by a person specified in the application, including such sets of premises as are so specified (an '*all premises warrant*').

If the application is for an '*all premises warrant*', the magistrate must also be satisfied:

- that because of the particulars of the offence referred to in the application, there are reasonable grounds for believing that it is necessary to search premises occupied or controlled by the person in question which are not specified in the application in order to find the material referred to in the application; and
- that it is not reasonably practicable to specify in the application all the premises which he occupies or controls and which might need to be searched.

The warrant may authorise entry to and search of premises on more than one occasion if, on the application, the magistrate is satisfied that it is necessary to authorise multiple entries in order to achieve for which he issues the warrant.

A copy of the search warrant issued under PACE, s 8 had, on its face, to record the address being searched so that when the occupier was served with a copy he would know for certain that the warrant as issued did indeed cover his premises: *R (on the application of Bhatti) v Croydon Magistrates' Court* [2010] EWHC 522 (Admin)., [2010] 3 All ER 671, [2011] 1 WLR 948.

F[5.11]–[5.15] **Legal privilege** means in essence communications between a legal adviser and his client or communications between them and a third party in contemplation of legal proceedings. The legal adviser can supply a full definition.

F[5.16] **Excluded and special procedure material.** This includes material held in confidence such as personal or business records, human tissues or fluids taken for the purpose of diagnosis or treatment and journalistic material.

One of the criteria for the issue of a search warrant under s 8 of PACE 1984 is that the material sought 'does not consist of or include items subject to legal privilege, excluded material or special procedure material': s 8(1)(d). In *Bates Chief Constable of Avon and Somerset Police and Bristol Magistrates' Court* [2009] EWHC 942 (Admin), it was held that the justices had had no jurisdiction to issue the warrant in the form that they had because the occupier of the premises had been an expert witness for many years and neither the court nor the police could have been satisfied that his computers did not contain items subject to legal privilege or which amounted to special procedure material. *Bates* was distinguished in *R (on the application of Sharer) v City of London and Westminster Magistrates' Court* [2016] EWHC 1412 (Admin), 181 JP 48, where the claimant (suspected of evading income tax for a number of years) was not a lawyer or an accountant and, while the application acknowledged that it was possible that special procedure would be found, no such material was sought within the scope of the application and if it was not reasonably practicable to determine the contents of an item it might be seized under s 50 of the Criminal Justice and Police Act 2001 and dealt with in line with that legislation and HMRC procedures.

See further *R(A) v Central Criminal Court* [2017] EWHC 70 (Admin), [2017] 1 WLR 3567. Computers which may contain LPP material can properly be the subject of a search warrant, provided the warrant is properly drafted to exclude LPP material from its scope (in the present case the warrant did so in express terms, and it was stated that this was desirable where the search was of the premises of a professional man where items subject to LPP might be encountered).

F[5.17] **May issue.** Even where all the criteria have been fulfilled, the magistrate still has a discretion.

3 *Procedure for search warrants issued to the police for evidence under the Police and Criminal Evidence Act 1954, s 8 and other statutes*

F[5.17A] Procedural rules in relation to search warrants have been in place since 2013 and were initially renumbered as Part 47 in the Crim PR 2015. The 2016 amending rules have replaced Part 47 with comprehensive provisions bringing together all investigation orders as well as warrants. This is supplemented by the Criminal Practice Directions 2015 *47A Investigation orders and warrants*. These requirements apply to justices of the peace where they can issue a warrant under s 8 of the Police and Criminal Evidence Act 1984, s 2 of the Criminal Justice Act 1987 or where a justice can issue a warrant to search for and seize articles or persons under another power.

Before making the application, the constable must:

- take reasonable steps to check the information he has received is accurate, recent and not provided maliciously or irresponsibly. Corroboration should be sought for anonymous information;
- ascertain as specifically as possible the nature of the articles concerned and their location;
- make reasonable inquiries to establish if anything is known about the likely occupier of and the nature of the premises;
- obtain any other relevant information;
- support the application by a signed written authority from an officer of inspector rank or above (or next most senior officer in urgent cases); and
- consult the local police/community liaison officer (urgent cases as soon as practicable thereafter) where there is reason to believe a search might have an adverse effect on relations between the police and the community.

(Police and Criminal Evidence Act 1984 Code B, para 3)

F[5.18] (1) The application may be made by a constable but it must have been authorised by an inspector or more senior officer, or in a case of urgency, the senior officer on duty. Where application is made by a member of the Serious and Organised Crime Agency authorisation by a Grade 3 Officer or above is sufficient. Where the officer is not known to the magistrate, a warrant card may be produced to establish identity.

F[5.19] (2) Except in a case of emergency, if there is reason to believe that a search might have an adverse effect on relations between the police and the community, the local Police Community Liaison Officer should have been consulted.

F[5.20] (3) The application must be supported by an information in writing stating:

(a) the ground on which he makes the application;
(b) the enactment under which the warrant would be issued; and
(c) if the application is for a warrant authorising entry and search on more than one occasion, the ground on which he applies for such a warrant, and whether he seeks a warrant authorising an unlimited number of entries, or (if not) the maximum number of entries desired;
(d) to identify, so far as is practicable, the articles or persons to be sought; and
(e) to specify the matters set out in F[5.20A] below.

F[5.20A] The matters which must be specified as in (d) above are:

(a) if the application relates to one or more sets of premises specified in the application, each set of premises which it is desired to search and enter;
(b) if the application relates to any premises occupied or controlled by a person specified in the application:
  (i) as many sets of premises which it is desired to enter and search as it is reasonable practicable to specify;
  (ii) the person who is in occupation or control of those premises and any others which it is desired to enter and search;
  (iii) why it is necessary to search more premises than those specified under (i) above; and
  (iv) why it is not reasonably practicable to specify all the premises which it is desired to enter and search.

In *Redknapp v Comr of the City of London Police Department* [2008] EWHC 1177 (Admin) it was stressed that all the necessary material to justify the grant of a search warrant should be contained in the information provided in the relevant pro forma. If the magistrate, on an application under s 8 requires any further information in order to satisfy himself that the warrant was justified, a note should be made of the additional information so that there was a proper record of the full basis upon which the warrant has been granted.

The obligation 'to identify, so far as is practicable, the articles or persons to be sought' (s 15(6)(b)) is a reference to articles which the justice concluded to be within s 8(1) (see F[F.6], above) and in relation to the search for which the warrant was issued. It is necessary, therefore, to look back to the information before the justice to identify what the articles must have been. Where a warrant is in vague and general terms in contrast to the information supplied to the justice there is non-compliance with s 15(6)(b). Its purpose is to protect the occupier of the premises in question, who is entitled to know from the warrant the extent of the powers of search and seizure available to the officers: *R (on the application of Lees) v Solihull Magistrates' Court* [2013] EWHC 3779 (Admin), [2014] Lloyd's Rep FC 233. See also *R (on the application of AB) v Huddersfield Magistrates' Court* [2014] EWHC 1089 (Admin), [2014] 4 All ER 500, [2014] 2 Cr App Rep 409, where the occupiers were suspected of assisting a relation (S) to evade justice, but the use of forward slashes between the categories of items sought supported the conclusion that the categories were separate and discrete and not collectively governed by the preceding words 'supporting the finance of [S]'.

R (Cabot Global Ltd and Others) v Barkingside Magistrates' Court and Another [2015] EWHC 1458 (Admin), [2015] Cr App R 355, [2015] Crim L R 821, as part of an investigation into allegations that the claimants were selling motor vehicles whose mileage odometers had been illegally altered, a detective constable applied to the magistrates' court for search warrants in respect of four properties. The magistrates' court granted the search warrants, which authorised the police to enter the premises to search for 'computer equipment, mobile phones . . . and cash representing the proceeds of criminal activity'. The search warrants were executed and the police removed a number of items. The claimants brought an application for judicial review against the magistrates' court and the Commissioner, on the grounds that: (i) the warrants failed to identify, so far as was practicable, the articles sought and that, therefore, the entries, searches and seizures of property were unlawful; (ii) alternatively, so far as the computers and mobile phones were concerned, the police should have relied on ss 19 or 20 of the 1984 Act or on s 50 of the Criminal Justice and Police Act 2001 and, therefore, should not have sought to remove the computers or mobile phones but instead should have requested copies of particular documents or other information contained within them.

The application was dismissed. 'Material' in s 8(1)(b) had been accorded a broad meaning and could include a computer and its hard disk. As a result, a warrant could properly authorise the seizure of computers or hard disks, if there were reasonable grounds to believe that they contained incriminating material, even though they might also contain irrelevant material. (Contrast *R (F, J and K) v Blackfriars Crown Court* [2014] EWHC 1541 (Admin) in which the Commissioner conceded that the reference in a warrant to 'any computer hard-drive or other information storage device capable of storing the above information' (emphasis added) was too wide.)

It would not have been 'practicable' in the present case to specify the items within the computers and mobile telephones to which the search related since the investigating authorities would have been interested not only in any records relating to the alleged offences but in establishing the timings, pattern and content of any communications between the suspects. Permitting the police to seize 'cash representing the proceeds of criminal activity' was a precise and reasonable description of the extent to which the police could, under s 8, seize monies. As to the second ground, ss 19 and 20 of the 1984 Act and s 50 of the 2001 Act were concerned with powers of seizure, not search, and there was no sustainable basis for suggesting that the police were obliged to resort to those provisions, rather than rely on s 8 of the 1984 Act. It was unrealistic of the claimants to suggest that the police should have taken away relevant material from computers or mobile phones in paper form or on memory sticks since the computers and mobile phones were likely to contain a very considerable amount of information and it would have taken a significant length of time to identify any relevant documents.

F[5.21] (4) The constable must answer on oath any questions which the magistrate may ask him. Apart from questions designed to ensure that the grounds for the application have been made out, eg under the Theft Act 1968, s 26, the magistrate might usefully inquire whether the officer has had the same application previously refused by another magistrate. The police cannot 'shop around' for a magistrate willing to sign the warrant. A second application can only be made where it is based on additional grounds. Finally, there is a discretion whether to issue a warrant.

F[5.22] (5) The police will usually have prepared a warrant and two copies beforehand. If he is prepared to issue the warrant, the magistrate should read it carefully and check that it covers the matters referred to in (3) above.

F[5.23] (6) The justices' clerk should retain the information and the police must forward to him, after three months at the latest, the warrant either unexecuted or endorsed as to whether the articles or persons sought were found; and whether any articles were seized, other than the articles which were sought.

F[5.24] (7) A note of reasons for grant or refusal should be retained

Subsequent applications for disclosure of material used to obtain warrant

F[5.24A] In *Metropolitan Police Comr v B* [2014] EWHC 546 (Admin), (2014) 178 JP 158 a person aggrieved by the issue of a search warrant (under s 23 of the

Misuse of Drugs 1971) sought disclosure of the Information and supporting evidence laid before the court. The appellant objected on the ground of public interest immunity. The Administrative Court dealt with a number of procedural matters. These have now been effectively codified in Part 5 of the Criminal Procedure Rules 2015. As to the correct tests to apply and balancing the competing interests where PII is claimed, see paragraphs 36 to 58 of the judgment.

The common law right to obtain information justifying the issue of search warrant must, however, be seen in the context of the statutory scheme under the 1984 Act, which was one of ex parte proceedings in which some material presented to the court cannot be disclosed to the subject of a warrant. A magistrate or judge needed to consider both whether the search warrant or the retention of the property seized was justified and what information could be disclosed to the party affected by the warrant. The result might be that because of the information withheld that party would not be able to see how the warrant or retention was justified, but that was the balance which Parliament had struck. It would be at odds with the public interest in the investigation and prosecution of crime if, when a search warrant was based on information from a single but reliable source, the police if challenged would have to disclose that person's identity or return the material seized, even if on the material presented to the court the issue of the warrant was unimpeachable: *R (Haralambous) v Crown Court at St Albans and another (Secretary of State for the Home Department intervening)* [2018] UKSC 1, [2018] 2 WLR 357, [2018] ALL ER (D) 96 (Jan).

4 *Procedure for warrants issued to persons other than police officers*

F[5.25] The provisions outlined above might usefully be taken into account where relevant. For non-police warrants the information is laid on oath. The applicant will usually produce a prepared information and swear to it in the following words: 'I swear by Almighty God that this is my information and that the contents thereof are true to the best of my knowledge and belief.' If he prefers it, he may substitute for the words, 'I swear by Almighty God . . . ' the words, 'I solemnly and sincerely declare and affirm . . . '. If the wording on the information is not sufficient a further written statement should be appended to the information.

F[5.26] As a matter of practice the informant signs the information and the magistrate should retain this and forward it to the justices' clerk.

Search warrants under section 161A Customs and Excise Management Act 1979

F[5.27]–[5.30] The Justices' Clerks' Society was contacted by HM Revenue and Customs with regard to the above. There is a concern that the police are applying for search warrants when it should be an officer of HM Revenue and Customs.

The section states:

161A Power to search premises: search warrant

(1) If a justice of the peace is satisfied by information upon oath given by an officer that there are reasonable grounds to suspect that anything liable to forfeiture under the customs and excise Acts is kept or concealed in any building or place, he may by warrant under his hand authorise any officer, and any person accompanying an officer, to enter and search the building or place named in the warrant.

(2) An officer or other person so authorised has power—

(a) to enter the building or place at any time, whether by day or night, on any day, and search for, seize, and detain or remove any such thing, and

(b) so far as is necessary for the purpose of such entry, search, seizure, detention or removal, to break open any door, window or container and force and remove any other impediment or obstruction.

(3) Where there are reasonable grounds to suspect that any still, vessel, utensil, spirits or materials for the manufacture of spirits is or are unlawfully kept or deposited in any building or place, subsections (1) and (2) above apply in relation to any constable as they would apply in relation to an officer.

(4) The powers conferred by a warrant under this section are exercisable until the end of the period of one month beginning with the day on which the warrant is issued.

(5) A person other than a constable shall not exercise the power of entry conferred by this section by night unless accompanied by a constable

Section 161A(1) allows an 'Officer' to make the application. 'Officer" is defined in s 1(1) of the Act as 'a person commissioned by the Commissioners' for Revenue and Customs. Section 8(2) qualifies this to allow other persons to act as and be given the powers of 'officers' when 'engaged by the orders or with the concurrence of the Commissioners'. Section 161A(3) gives powers to a police constable to make the application for a search warrant under this section but only where there are reasonable grounds to suspect that any 'still, vessel, utensil, spirits or materials for the manufacture of spirits is or are unlawfully kept or deposited in any building or place'.

There is a concern that the police are applying for search warrants where articles not listed in s 161A(3) are being searched for. The JCS believes the legislation is clear that the power is only available to the police where the conditions of sub-section (3) are satisfied; ie that an alcohol still or vessel etc is being searched for (dated 10 February 2012).

Warrants of entry for gas and electricity suppliers

F[5.31] The provisions are complex and are summarised below. It is good practice for all such applications to be considered at a courthouse in the presence of a legal adviser from whom advice may be obtained. Those subject to the application should receive notification of the date and venue of the application.

F[5.32] Applications may be made, for example, for entry to read a meter or to cut off the supply following non-payment of a bill. An electricity supplier may cut off the supply where the customer has not paid within 20 working days of a demand in writing and after two working days' notice of the supplier's intention to do so. However this power is not available where there is a genuine dispute about the amount owed. (Note – this procedure only applies to a bill for electricity supplied and would not include monies owed on an article supplied by way of a credit sale such as a cooker. Nor is it relevant that there is a genuine dispute about the quality of service since the customer may use a separate procedure to obtain compensation.) The relevant periods where a gas supply is concerned are 28 days after the demand in writing and seven days' notice of intent to cut off the supply.

F[5.33] **Right of entry.** An officer of the supplier after one working day's notice (electricity) 24 hours' notice (gas) may at all reasonable times, on production of some duly authenticated document showing his authority, enter the premises for the purpose of cutting off the supply. No notice is required for entry to read a meter except where a warrant is to be applied for.

F[5.34] **Warrant of entry.** No right of entry may be exercised except with the consent of the occupier of the premises or under the authority of a justice's warrant (except in cases of emergency).

F[5.35] **Requirements.** There must be a sworn information in writing and the applicant must satisfy the justice:

(a) that admission to the premises is reasonably required for the specified purpose;
(b) the applicant has a right of entry to the premises;
(c) the requirements of any relevant enactment have been complied with; and in particular

(d) the relevant notices have been given, including notice of the hearing.

F[5.36] The justice might also ensure that:

(e) there is no genuine dispute about the amount owed; and
(f) the amount owed is in respect of the supply of gas or electricity.

F[5.37] **Code of practice.** Gas and electricity suppliers operate a Code of Practice (of which the clerk of the justices may be able to supply a copy) under which it is undertaken to provide assistance to domestic customers to meet their bills and the suppliers may refrain from cutting off the supply from those who are particularly vulnerable during the winter months; nevertheless where default has occurred, the suppliers may resort to the procedure outlined above.

F[5.38] **Duty to repair damage etc.** Where a right of entry has been exercised the supplier must ensure that the premises concerned are left no less secure by reason of the entry and must make good or pay compensation for any damage caused in entering the premises or making them secure.

5 The warrant

F[5.39] If the magistrate is satisfied with the application he will sign the warrant (which will normally have been prepared in advance by the applicant). This is handed back to the applicant and is his authority to enter and search etc. A magistrate who has issued a search warrant should say nothing to anyone about it, not even to a member of his own family. This is so that no suspicion falls on him in the event that it may appear that the occupier of the premises was expecting a search.

6 Who may sign

F[5.40]–[5.45] Any magistrate may sign a search warrant provided he is not on the Supplemental List (ie retired from active work on the bench).

Warrants of arrest

F[5.46] Magistrates will frequently have encountered these during sittings at court, eg for failing to answer bail. The procedure is very similar to that for issuing warrants of entry. However, it is virtually inconceivable that it should be necessary to approach a magistrate at home. The Police and Criminal Evidence Act 1984 provides wide powers of arrest without warrant even for minor offences where there is doubt about the identity of the arrested person or an arrest is necessary to prevent harm to him or the public. Accordingly, a magistrate would be unwise to issue such a warrant unless he has the advice of his justices' clerk or a legal adviser. Such applications should, as a matter of practice, be heard at the courthouse.

Proceeds of Crime Act 2002 (POCA 2002)

F[5.46A] **Introduction.** This Act was enacted to enable the enable the recovery of the proceeds of crime, and to tackle money laundering. Chapter 2 of Part V of the Act vests jurisdiction in respect of recovery orders in the High Court; Chapter 3 of Part 5 provides for the recovery of cash (as defined – see infra) in summary proceedings

The Criminal Finances Act 2017 (CFA 2017) makes significant changes to POCA 2002. Of particular note in relation to magistrates' courts:

- Jurisdiction is conferred to make 'further information orders' arising from a disclosure under Part 7 of POCA 2002 (or a corresponding foreign requirement). These are orders authorising a law enforcement officer to require anyone that they think has relevant information to an investigation to answer questions, provide information or produce documents. The purpose is to gather information to assist in a money laundering investigation or to determine whether such an investigation should be started. Failure to comply is punishable by a monetary penalty of up to £5,000, which is enforceable as a fine.

- 'Unlawful conduct' is extended to certain gross human rights abuses or violations (as defined) which occur outside the UK.
- 'Cash' is extended to include gaming vouchers; fixed-value casino tokens; and betting receipts.
- A new Chapter 3A (inserted by s 15 of CFA 2017) makes provision for the seizure and recovery of listed types of personal and moveable property. These provisions build upon the cash seizure and recovery provisions in Chapter 3 and work broadly in the same way, except that prior judicial authority must usually be obtained before the search powers can be used and there are a number of provisions dealing with 'associated property' and 'joint property'.
- Forfeiture of money held in bank and building society accounts was formerly a matter for the High Court (as part of its jurisdiction as to the recovery of property other than cash), but s 16 of CFA 2017 inserts ss 303Z1–303Z19 in POCA 2002 to transfer this jurisdiction to the magistrates' court. The process begins with an account freezing order. A senior officer may then (mirroring the position with cash forfeiture) issue an account forfeiture notice. If no objection is received, at the end of the notice period the amount of money stated in the account forfeiture notice will be forfeited. (A senior officer does not have to issue an account forfeiture notice if he/she wishes to seek forfeiture under a court order.)
- New offences are inserted in POCA 2002 dealing with assault and obstruction of officers.
- A number of powers – for example, disclosure orders and seizure and forfeiture powers for bank accounts and moveable items of store – are extended to apply to anti-terrorist legislation.
- New offences are created of corporate failure to prevent tax evasion.

F[5.47] **Minimum amount.** Section 294 of the 2002 Act allows a customs officer or constable to seize and apply for forfeiture of cash which is not less than £1,000 and is obtained through or intended to be used in unlawful conduct (see the Proceeds of Crime Act 2002 (Recovery of Cash in Summary Proceedings: Minimum amount) Order 2006, SI 2006/1699).

In appropriate circumstances, different sums taken from different individuals can be aggregated for the purpose of meeting the minimum amount requirement: *Commissioners of Customs and Excise v Duffy, Gunning and Attawia* [2002] EWHC 425 (Admin). The case concerned the minimum amount of £10,000 prescribed by s 42 of the Drug Trafficking Act 1994. Three men were stopped at Gatwick Airport. They were travelling together to Malaga. Cash was seized from each man. The total was £20,000, but none of the individual seizures exceeded £10,000. The justices concluded it was necessary for each man to be carrying a sum of at least the prescribed amount. The Administrative Court, however, disagreed.

> '17. In my judgment the words of the statute are silent as to where the cash is before it is seized; it may be with one individual, it may be with more than one individual, or it may be with no individual at all ... What matters is whether it is identifiably cash which is being exported which can be regarded as a single item in order to, first of all, to examine its totality (see section 42(1)(a)), and, secondly, consider its origin or purpose (see section 42(1)(b). So if the evidence shows only that there are various sums held by individuals who are apparently unconnected, those sums cannot be aggregated, but if it can be shown that the money comes from a common source or has a common destination, that may readily lead to the conclusion that in reality it is a single exportation of cash. The court asked to exercise its powers under section 42(2) is then entitled, in my judgment, to look at the reality.' (per Kennedy LJ giving the judgment of the court).

Search power. The police or customs may search a person or premises for tainted cash. An authorisation may be given by a single justice ex parte. A search warrant under this provision does not authorise entry to premises.

Detention of seized cash. Application may be made to any magistrate in England and Wales who may extend the officers right to detain cash for 48 hours, for up to three months. In calculating the 48 hours for which seized cash may initially be held, Saturdays, Sundays, Christmas Day, Good Friday and bank holidays should be ignored. The applicant must serve notice on anyone from whom the cash was seized, sent to or by. Service of the notice need not be proved.

Grounds for detention order. A magistrate may make the order for six months detention if he is satisfied that there are reasonable grounds for the officer's suspicion and the continued detention is justified for the purposes of investigation of its origins or use. Further extensions which may be for a total period of two years, must be made by a full court. Application for the release of detained money may also be made.

Forfeiture. The police or customs may apply for detained cash to be forfeited and a magistrates' court can make an order if it is satisfied that the cash is recoverable property or intended for use in unlawful conduct: s 298(2). At this stage, the court is not concerned with the legality of the original seizure, and there is no requirement that the basis of the seizure, detention and forfeiture should have remained the same throughout; the respondent can mount any relevant challenge to the case for forfeiture if it is pertinent to the factual matters that need to be established under s 298(2), but not with a view to challenging the legality of earlier stages in the process; the only purpose of s 298(1) is to impose a temporal limit upon the ability of the constable to seek a forfeiture order: *Campbell v Bromley Magistrates' Court* [2017] EWCA Civ 1161, [2017] Crim L R 987 (approving *Secretary of State for the Home Department v Tuncel* [2012] EWHC 402 (Admin), [2012] 1 WLR 3355).

A costs order may be made under s 64(1) of the Magistrates' Courts Act 1980. This includes the situation where the complaint is not proceeded with by virtue of s 52 of the Courts Act 1971 (see *Chief Constable of Cleveland Police v Vaughan* [2009] EWHC 2831 (Admin)). As to the principles, see **F[2.20]**. In *R (on the application of Stone) v Camberwell Magistrates' Court* [2010] EWHC 2333 (Admin), the High Court declined to consider whether there was jurisdiction to award costs in forfeiture proceedings pursuant to either s 52 (3) of the Courts Act 1971 or s 64 of the Magistrates' Courts Act 1980 describing the legal position as 'difficult'.

Legal notes

F[5.47A] Cash. Means notes and coins, postal orders, cheques or traveller's cheques, bankers drafts and bearer bonds and shares.

Minimum amount. Cash is only subject to the act if it is a minimum sum of £1,000, singly or as part of a larger sum. The amount may be estimated to preserve evidence.

As to the aggregation of different sums taken from different individuals, see F[5.47], ante

Notice of forfeiture proceedings. In *R (on the application of Harrison) v Birmingham Magistrates' Court* [2011] EWCA Civ 332, [2011] 14 LS Gaz R 21, a forfeiture order made in respect of cash confiscated by the police when searching the house of a person arrested on suspicion of fraud was quashed where her unchallenged evidence was that she had not received a notice of the forfeiture hearing. The appellant had appealed to the Crown Court against the forfeiture order which held that by virtue of s 299(2) it had no jurisdiction to hear the appeal out of time. The Court invited the Lord Chief Justice to consider an amendment to the Magistrates' Courts (Detention and Forfeiture of Cash) Rules 2002 to permit a person to show that, notwithstanding ostensible service, the purported recipient had not in fact received notice.

The guidance handed down was that pending any amendment to the 2002 Rules, magistrates should be particularly prudent about continuing with an application for a forfeiture order in the absence of a person with a claim to the money. If criminal proceedings were still ongoing, it might be worthwhile to give notice of the hearing to the solicitors dealing with the criminal case; albeit, those solicitors had not been instructed in the civil proceedings for forfeiture.

Following that judgment, the Magistrates' Courts (Detention and Forfeiture of Cash) (Amendment) Rules 2012, SI 2012/1275 have been made. These Rules amend the

2002 Rules to allow for effective service of documents to be assumed unless the contrary is shown. The amended rules came into force on 2 July 2012.

Unlawful conduct. Includes conduct which is unlawful under the criminal law in the UK and conduct which occurs outside the UK if it would have been unlawful in the UK.

In *Angus v United Kingdom Border Agency* [2011] EWHC 461 (Admin), the appellant had been stopped at a British airport and £40,000 was found to be in her handbag, some of it wrapped in casino wrappings. She claimed that the monies represented repayment of a loan to her uncle. She later revised her story and said that the sums represented the repayment of loans made by her mother to two other individuals, repaid through their winnings obtained at casinos. An application for forfeiture was made pursuant to s 298 of the Proceeds of Crime Act 2002. The magistrates' court and on appeal, the Crown Court, found that the cash seized may well have been the proceeds of money laundering and that there was an irresistible inference that it was obtained through unlawful conduct. The appellant challenged the Crown Court's decision by way of case stated.

The Administrative Court held that irrespective of whether the litigation was High Court civil recovery proceedings or magistrates' court or Crown Court forfeiture proceedings, the test was the same. Applying the provisions of s 242(2)(b) of the PCA 2002, although it was not necessary to allege the commission of any specific offence, the matters that were alleged to constitute the particular kind or kinds of unlawful conduct by or in return for which the property was obtained had to be set out: *Director of Assets Recovery Agency v Green* [2005] EWHC 3168 (Admin), (2006) Times, 27 February considered. Accordingly, the answer to the question posed was that, in a case of cash forfeiture, a customs officer did have to show that the property seized was obtained through conduct of one of a number of kinds each of which would have been unlawful conduct.

In *Christopher Hendrik Weise v UK Border Agency* (2012) 29th June, CA, a forfeiture order made under the Proceeds of Crime Act 2002, s 298 was revoked as the Judge had not given adequate reasons for concluding that forfeited money which had been carried by a South African businessman in hand luggage and in the hold of an aeroplane constituted the proceeds of money laundering. Further, in *Begum v West Midlands Police* [2012] EWHC 2304 (Admin), it was held that a magistrates' court had erred in ordering the forfeiture of cash under s 298(2) by an offender who had failed to declare the extent of her savings in order to obtain benefits, since the undeclared cash had not been intended for use in unlawful conduct.

Legal aid. A criminal legal representation order is not available. Civil legal aid may apply subject to means.

Recoverable property. The police are not required to show that the apparent criminality of a company rendered the whole of its business unlawful. The police as claimant only had to show that there were 'reasonable grounds to suspect' that the property [cash] was in the company's hands because illegal labour had made a contribution to its acquisition *R (on the application of the Chief Constable of Greater Manchester Police) v City of Salford Magistrates' Court*, [2008] EWHC 1651 (Admin), [2009] 1 WLR 1023, [2008] EWHC 1651 (Admin), 172 JP 497.

Right of Appeal. May be made against the decision of a magistrates' court ordering forfeiture of cash by either party whether the application is dismissed or approved. In this case an appeal lies to the Crown Court: s 299.

European Investigation Orders

F[5.47B] A European Investigation Order is an order specifying one or more investigative measures that are to be carried out in a participating State of the European Union for the purpose of obtaining evidence for use either in the investigation or the proceedings in question or both. Procedure is governed by the Criminal Justice (European Investigation Order) Regulations 2017, SI 2017/730. An application is made to 'a Judicial Authority', ie any judge or justice of the peace, and the following conditions must be satisfied: that an offence has been committed or that there are reasonable grounds for suspecting that an offence has been committed; proceedings in respect of the offence have been instituted or it is being investigated; such order is necessary and proportionate for the purposes of the investigation or proceedings in question; and the investigative measures to be specified could lawfully have been ordered a similar domestic case. Procedure for the making of applications and for hearing such applications is prescribed by the Criminal Procedure Rules.

Miscellaneous matters regarding applications to a justice

Recognisance

F[5.48] A recognisance of a surety for bail should not be taken unless the proposed surety produces a certificate stating the amount and conditions of bail. The surety should be questioned so as to satisfy the magistrate that he has, or can easily obtain, the sum mentioned in the certificate. If the certificate states that a specific person is to be surety, evidence of identity should be required. The clerk or an officer in charge of a police station may take a recognisance and, in any case of doubt, the surety should be referred to one of these persons.

Certificate of good repute

F[5.49] A magistrate should not sign a certificate of good reputation or good character. If approached to do so he should refer the applicant to a legal adviser.

Passports and driving licences

F[5.50] A magistrate should neither endorse an application for a passport, nor sign the photograph therewith unless he knows the applicant sufficiently well to meet the criteria on the form. Similar considerations apply to applications for a photocard licence.

Removal to suitable premises of persons in need of care and attention (National Assistance Act 1948, s 47 and National Assistance (Amendment) Act 1951, s 1)

F[5.51] The following provisions are for the purposes of securing the necessary care and attention for persons who:

(a) are suffering from grave chronic disease or, being aged, infirm or physically incapacitated, are living in insanitary conditions; and
(b) are unable to devote to themselves, and are not receiving from other persons, proper care and attention.

F[5.52] Where the proper officer (formerly the medical officer of health) certifies in writing to the local authority that he is satisfied after thorough inquiry and consideration that in the interests of any such person residing in the local authority's area or for preventing injury to the health of, or serious nuisance to other persons, it is necessary to remove him from his residence, the local authority may apply to a court for an order of removal.

F[5.53] If the proper officer and another registered medical practitioner certify that in their opinion it is necessary in the interests of that person to remove him without delay, the local authority or the proper officer where duly authorised may make an application to a single justice having jurisdiction for the place where the person resides. The justice being satisfied on oral evidence under oath of the allegations in the certificate and that it is expedient so to do, may order his removal to a hospital where one is available or to some other place in, or within convenient distance of, the local authority area. If the justice thinks it necessary, the order can be made without notifying or hearing the person concerned.

F[5.54] **Duration of the order.** The order may be for a period of up to three weeks. After it has expired the local authority would have to make a full application to a court.

F[5.55] It should be noted, however, that as an emergency ex parte application can also be made to a magistrate sitting in a courthouse; accordingly, applications should normally be considered there except where circumstances dictate otherwise.

Statutory declarations

F[5.56] It is necessary to make sure that the clause at the end of the form is properly completed and dated. It is not necessary to read the document, nor need the magistrate be concerned to establish in his own mind the truth of the contents of it. His signature on the document simply attests that he was present and heard the maker of the document declare that the contents are true.

F[5.57]–[5.62] The words for a statutory declaration are:

> **I, AB, do solemnly and sincerely declare and affirm that the contents of this declaration are true to the best of my knowledge and belief, and I make this solemn declaration conscientiously believing the same to be true and by virtue of the provisions of the Statutory Declarations Act 1835.**

F[5.63] A Holy Book is not required for a statutory declaration.

F[5.64] Any magistrate, including those on the Supplemental List, may sign a statutory declaration. Part 24, rule 24.17 of the Criminal Procedure Rules was amended by SI 2019/1119 to enable a justice' legal adviser, or a person nominated by such an adviser, to take a statutory declaration.

Warrants to search for and remove mental patients

(Mental Health Act 1983, s 135)

F[5.65] A justice to whom it appears that there is reasonable cause to suspect that a person believed to be suffering from mental disorder:

(a) has been, or is being, ill-treated, neglected or kept otherwise than under proper control in any place within the jurisdiction of the justice; or

(b) being unable to care for himself, is living alone in any such place;

may issue a warrant authorising his removal to a place of safety with a view to making an application under the Mental Health Act 1983 or other arrangements for his treatment or care.

F[5.66] **Application** is by way of an information laid on oath by a social worker specially approved by the local authority for the purposes of the Mental Health Act 1983. The patient need not be named in the information.

F[5.67] **Warrant** authorises a constable to enter (if need be by force) any premises specified in the warrant and if thought fit to remove him to a place of safety.

F[5.68] **Place of safety** means residential accommodation provided by a local authority or a hospital, police station, mental nursing home, or residential home for mentally disturbed persons or any other suitable place where the occupier is willing to receive the patient.

F[5.69] **Duration.** The detention in a place of safety may not be for more than 72 hours.

Administration of oaths etc in certain probate business

F[5.70] Justices of the peace are empowered by the Courts and Legal Services Act 1990, s 56 to administer oaths and take affidavits in non-contentious probate matters. The Judicial Studies Board has issued the following guidance for the assistance of magistrates' courts:

(a) The oaths envisaged in this Act are those which are non-contentious and of a probate nature, ie, civil proceedings, and should not therefore be of great urgency requiring their administration out of court hours. Each court should therefore publish set hours during which these oaths will be administered.

(b) Justices should be discouraged from administering these oaths outside court hours and away from supervision by suitably qualified court staff.

(c) Justices should not administer oaths for documents which are to be used in court proceedings [including civil proceedings], and court staff should look at document headings with great care, to ensure that there is no court name or reference number thereon which might indicate a current court action.

(d) The wording of the oath to be taken is different from a court witness oath and is 'I swear by Almighty God that the contents of this my [affidavit] [and the exhibits annexed thereto] are true'.

(e) Be prepared for the oath to be sworn by members of all religions in the appropriate form – another reason why 'out of hours oaths' should be discouraged.

(f) An interpreter may be needed and he should be sworn first, taking the appropriate oath.

(g) A deponent may wish to affirm, in which case he will do so in the appropriate form – again a reason for oaths to be administered in the court setting, as justices will not necessarily know the correct wording.

(h) Every alteration to the document has to be initialled by the administering justice.

(i) Any exhibit has to be dated and signed and must clearly indicate that it is the exhibit annexed to the affidavit produced and sworn by the deponent on that same occasion.

(j) The jurat or attestation shall state the date and place the oath or affidavit is taken or made [Courts and Legal Services Act 1990, s 56(2)].

(k) No justice shall exercise the powers conferred in any proceedings in which he is interested [Courts and Legal Services Act 1990, s 56(3)].

(l) In the event of any person being sufficiently handicapped to make it impossible for him or her to attend court to swear a document, arrangement could be made by the clerk to the justices for a justice and member of the court staff to attend upon that person at their home, or a mutually convenient place. This should not occur frequently, but should be provided for by courts.

Index

A

Abandoning a child
generally A19.18–A19.20
Abatement notices
appeal against A84.9
contravention/failure to comply A84.10
generally A74.9
statutory nuisance A84.8
Abatement orders
generally A84.22
Absconding
see Failure to surrender to custody
Absolute discharge
availability B45.24
generally B22Z
sexual assault A53.9
sexual offences against children A52.14
Abstracting electricity without authority
charge A1.1
definitions A1.3
dishonestly A1.3
generally A1.1
maximum penalty A1.1
mode of trial A1.2
notes A1.3
sentencing A1.4
Abuse of position
fraud, and
abuse A36.9
dishonesty A36.9
generally A36.9
mode of trial A36.5
penalty A36.4
Abuse of position – *cont.*
fraud, and – *cont.*
'position' A36.9
statutory wording A36.3
Abuse of process
generally D1B.11
principles D1B.12
sending for trial D4.11
youth courts E3.25
Accidents
failing to report after accident C31.3, C32
failing to stop and give details C31
personal injury, and C31.16
Action plan orders
see now Youth rehabilitation orders
generally B1.1
Actual bodily harm
alternative verdict A8.25
'assault' A8.5
assault occasioning A8
charge A8.1
consent A8.22
defences A8.17–A8.25
definition A8.9
disability, and A8.10–A8.16
domestic violence, and A8.34
exclusion order A8.33
grievous bodily harm distinguished A8.9, A70.6
householder defence A8.20
inference A8.9
intent A8.7–A8.8
licensed premises exclusion orders A8.33
maximum penalty A8.1

Actual bodily harm – *cont.*
misadventure A8.21
mode of trial A8.3
notes A8.5–A8.23
provocation A8.17
psychological damage A8.9
racial aggravation, and A8.10–A8.16
reasonable chastisement A8.22
reasonable force defence A8.18–A8.20
reduction of charge A8.25
religious aggravation, and A8.10–A8.16
self-defence A8.18–A8.20
sentencing A8.31–A8.32
sexual orientation, and A8.10–A8.16
sport A8.23
transgender identity, and A8.10–A8.16
unconsciousness, and A8.9

Adjournment applications
approach D6.7
bad character D6.14–D6.15
checklist D6.6
discharge of pre-trial rulings D6.13A
disclosure of unused material D6.12
first/subsequent hearing D6.12
hearsay evidence D6.16
initial disclosure D6.11
introduction D6.5
legal aid D6.10
plea D6.9
power to make, vary or discharge pre-trial rulings D6.13
pre-trial issues D6.13–D6.16
prosecution evidence D6.11
special measures for vulnerable and intimidated witnesses D6.13A
subsequent hearing D6.12
trials, and D6.17–D6.17E
variation of pre-trial rulings D6.13

Advertisements
application for personal licence/premises licence F2.2

Advice and assistance
see also **Criminal legal aid**
generally D7.4

Affray
charge A2.1
definitions A2.3–A2.10
domestic violence A2.16
generally A2.1
intent A2.9
intoxication A2.10
maximum penalty A2.2
notes A2.3–A2.10
person of reasonable firmness A2.6
sentencing A2.15
threats A2.5
using or threatening violence A2.4
violence A2.7
weapons A2.5

Age of criminal responsibility
generally E3.2

Aggravated vehicle-taking
generally A66

Aggressive commercial practices
generally A75

Aid and abet
dangerous driving C16.6

Air guns
adult supervision A71.5
'air weapon' A71.3
age limit A71.5
charge A71.1
clubs and shooting galleries A71.6
definitions A71.2–A71.6
failing to prevent possession by person under 18
charge A71A.1
definitions A71A.2
general note A71A.2
sentencing A71A.3
fines A71.8
forfeiture A33.13, A71.1

Air guns – *cont.*
general note A71.2–A71.6
generally A76.7
'possession' A71.2
private premises A71.5
'public place' A71.4–A71.6
sentencing A71.7–A71.8
trespassing in a building or on land A77.9
Air weapons
definition A33.7, A71.3
trespassing in a building or on land A77.9
Alcohol
see also **Breath tests**
blood or urine, in
analyst's certificate C22.19–C22.22
drinking after driving C22.30
driving when 'unfit through drink or drugs' C20
excess alcohol offences C22
fail to provide specimen for analysis C23
in charge of vehicle when 'unfit through drink or drugs' C21
laced drink defence C22.24
offences C20–C23
sentencing of high risk offenders C22.45–C22.46
special reasons C22.24–C22.25, C22.50
closure notices, and F2.27
driving when 'unfit through drink or drugs'
alternative charge C20.18
alternative verdict C20.18
car parks C20.7
'drink/drugs' C20.17
driving C20.4
emergency, in C22.25
generally C20.2–C20.3
introduction C20.1
maximum sentence C20.1
mechanically propelled vehicle C20.5
Alcohol – *cont.*
driving when 'unfit through drink or drugs' – *cont.*
public place C20.7–C20.8
road C20.6
sentencing C20.19–C20.20
'unfit' C20.9–C20.16
excess alcohol
disqualification reduced for attendance on course C22.56–C22.61
drive/attempt to drive or in charge C22
sentencing C22.32–C22.61, C22.65
sentencing of high risk offenders C22.45–C22.46
football-related offences
charges A35.1–A35.2
designated grounds and sporting events A35.5
'designated sports ground' A35.10
exceptions A35.7
general note A35.3–A35.10
period of the event A35.6
prohibited articles A35.8–A35.9
public service vehicle A35.4
prohibited articles A35.8–A35.9
sentencing A35.16–A35.17
fraudulent evasion of duty
appeals A4.19
attempt A4.6
charge A4.1–A4.2
death of informant A4.9
definitions A4.4–A4.11
duplicity A4.7
financial reporting orders A4.18
fraudulent evasion A4.6
intent to defraud A4.4
knowingly A4.4–A4.5
mistake A4.11
mode of trial A4.3
notes A4.4–A4.11

Alcohol – *cont.*
fraudulent evasion of duty – *cont.*
presumptions against defendant A4.10
prosecution A4.8
sentencing A4.16–A4.18
value of goods A4.17
persistently sale to children F2.27
sale offences
allowing sale to children A3.3
charge A3.1–A3.3
definitions A3.4
maximum penalty A3.3
notes A3.4
sale to children A3.2
sale to person who is drunk A3.1
sentencing A3.5
sporting events
charges A35.1–A35.2
designated grounds and sporting events A35.5
'designated sports ground' A35.10
exceptions A35.7
general note A35.3–A35.10
period of the event A35.6
prohibited articles A35.8–A35.9
public service vehicle A35.4
prohibited articles A35.8–A35.9
sentencing A35.16–A35.17
urine, in
analyst's certificate C22.19–C22.22
drinking after driving C22.30
driving when 'unfit through drink or drugs' C20
excess alcohol offences C22
fail to provide specimen for analysis C23
in charge of vehicle when 'unfit through drink or drugs' C21
laced drink defence C22.24

Alcohol – *cont.*
urine, in – *cont.*
offences C20–C23
sentencing of high risk offenders C22.45–C22.46
special reasons C22.24–C22.25, C22.50

Alcohol abstinence and monitoring requirement
generally B9.22A
introduction B9.9

Aliens
deportation B17.4

Allocation and sending for trial
absence of legally represented accused D4.6
abuse of process D4.11
adults jointly charged with youths
generally E3.18B
introduction D4.8
criminal damage D4.9
guideline D4.12
indictable only offences
generally D5.1
joinder of summary offences D5.2
introduction D4.1
joinder of summary offences in indictment D5.2
joint adult defendants D4.7
judicial review E3.18C
low value offences
criminal damage D4.9
shoplifting D4.9A
offences triable either way
adult offenders D4.2
mode of trial D4.4
plea before venue D4.3
order of consideration D4.2
power to change from summary trial to sending for trial D4.10
shoplifting D4.9A
summary trial appears more suitable, where D4.5

Allocation and sending for trial –
cont.
young offenders
further offences E3.18A
generally E3.18
youths jointly charged with adults
generally E3.18B
introduction D4.8
Alternative verdicts
actual bodily harm A8.25
Ammunition
carrying a firearm in a public place A33.10
excessive A76.4
forfeiture A76.23, A86.32
meaning A76.8
police permits A76.10
purchasing or possessing without certificate A76
seizure A86.31
shooting galleries A71.6
Animal cruelty
'animal, A5.2
'animal fight' A5.2
charges A5.1
'cruelty' and 'welfare' offence distinguished A5.2
definitions A5.2
deprivation of ownership A5.4
destruction of animal A5.4
disqualification A5.4
docking of tails A5.2
generally A5.1
knowledge A5.2
maximum penalty A5.1
mutilation A5.2
notes A5.2
number of different animals on same occasion A5.2
person responsible for an animal A5.2
previous convictions A5.4
protected animal A5.2
sentencing A5.3–A5.4
time limits for prosecution A5.2
unnecessary suffering A5.2
Animal cruelty – *cont.*
'welfare' offence, and A5.2
Animal rights protestors
harassment A41.5
Animals
see also **Animal cruelty**
definition A5.2
deprivation of ownership A5.4
destruction ordered by court A5.4
disqualification from keeping
generally A5.4
sentencing A5.5
docking of tails A5.2
game A86.6, A86.17
litter and A83.31
meaning C31.6, C32.5
mutilation A5.2
person responsible A5.2
poaching
day-time offence A86.1–A86.8A
forfeiture of equipment A86.32
'game' A86.6, A86.17
hunting with hounds A86.8
night-time offences A86.9–A86.22A
seizure of equipment/game/rabbits A86.31
sentencing A86.31–A86.32A
three or more together A86.22
road traffic offences C31.6, C32.5
wild creatures
property, as A18.21
theft A57.21
Anti-social behaviour orders (ASBOs)
see also **Criminal behaviour orders**
ancillary order, as A82.4
breach of
collateral attack on validity of order or its terms B2.4
commission of criminal offence B2.4

Anti-social behaviour orders (ASBOs) – *cont.*
breach of – *cont.*
conditional discharge, and B2.9
generally B2.4
key factors B2.7
lesser degree of harm caused or intended B2.7
no harm caused or intended B2.7
previous convictions B2.6
reasonable excuse B2.4
sentencing guideline B2.5–B2.6
serious harm caused or intended B2.7
young offenders, and B2.4
conviction, on
discharge B2.3
generally B2.1
variation B2.3
discharge B2.2
introduction B2.1
previous convictions B2.6
reporting restrictions, and E2.4
variation B2.2
young offenders, and B2.4
Antique firearms
generally A76.17
Appeals
against conviction and or sentence D6.46
bail
against conditions D8.79
prosecution right D8.33
betting and gambling licensing
background F3.3
generally F3.4
case stated, by way of D6.47
closure orders
generally F2.26
introduction A26.16
compensation orders B10.17
contempt of court D3.16
Crown Court, to D6.46

Appeals – *cont.*
dangerous dogs
Dogs Act 1871 orders, and A72.38
generally A72.19
football banning orders
civil orders B29.35
generally B29.32
fraudulent evasion of duty A4.10
gaming licences
background F3.3
generally F3.4
gang-related violence injunctions B35.13
High Court, to D6.47
judicial review applications D6.48
liquor licensing
background F2.1–F2.5
costs F2.20
decision F2.19
generally F2.6–F2.7
hearing F2.14–F2.15
judicial review F2.7
notices F2.12
order of speeches F2.17–F2.18
period of notice F2.13
procedure F2.16
right to appeal F2.6
parenting orders B37.12
possession of drugs with intent to supply to another A26.16
procedure
against conviction and or sentence D6.46
case stated, by way of D6.47
Crown Court, to D6.46
High Court, to D6.47
introduction D6.45
judicial review applications D6.48
proceeds of crime F5.47A
psychoactive substances B38A.10
youth injunctions B48.11

Appropriation
theft A57.8–A57.16
Arrest
assault with intent to resist
charge A7.1
definitions A7.3
generally A7.1
maximum penalty A7.1
mode of trial A7.1
notes A7.2
sentencing A7.4
gang-related violence injunctions
attaching power B35.5
generally B35.11
youth injunctions
arrest warrants B48.5
without warrant B48.4
Arrest warrants
bailed person failing to surrender D8.82
generally F5.46
immigration offences A81.7
youth injunctions B48.5
Arson
maximum penalty A18.2
venue for trial A18.2
Articles for fraud
possession
computer programs A38.3
generally A38.1
mode of trial A38.2
sentencing A38.4
Articles with blade
see also **Bladed articles/offensive weapons**
possession
charge A11.1
meaning A11.9
mode of trial A11.2
notes A11.3–A11.13
sentencing A11.15
Assault
actual bodily harm, causing
see also **Actual bodily harm**
generally A8.1–A8.34
common assault
see also **Common assault**

Assault – *cont.*
common assault – *cont.*
charges A15.1–A15.2
domestic violence A15.34
maximum penalty A15.2
notes A15.3–A15.32
sentencing A15.33
constable in the execution of his duty, on
alternative verdict A9.9
burden of proof A9.7
charge A9.1
constable A9.3
definitions A9.2–A9.9
execution of his duty A9.5–A9.8
licensed premises, and A9.11
maximum penalty A9.1
notes A9.2–A9.9
plain clothes officers carrying out drugs search A9.8
reduction of charge A9.9
search of defendant A9.8
sentencing A9.10
court security officer in the execution of his duty, on
alternative verdict A9.9
burden of proof A9.7
charge A9.2
court security officer A9.4
definitions A9.2–A9.9
execution of his duty A9.5–A9.8
licensed premises, and A9.11
maximum penalty A9.1
notes A9.2–A9.9
plain clothes officers carrying out drugs search A9.8
reduction of charge A9.9
search of defendant A9.8
sentencing A9.10
definition A15.5–A15.6
emergency workers
aggravating seriousness of other offences A9A.5
charge A9A.1
definition A9A.3

Assault – *cont.*
emergency workers – *cont.*
generally A9A.2–A9A.4
sentencing A9A.6
exclusion orders A8.33
indecent assault
absolute discharge A53.9
anonymity of victim A52.11
clearing the court A52.10
conditional discharge A53.9
consent A53.5
defences A53.5
generally A53
juvenile offenders A53.9
notification requirements following conviction A52.14, A53.9
reporting restrictions D1B.7
sentencing A52.12–A52.16
sexual harm prevention order A53.10
touching A52.4, A53.4, A53.5
intent to resist arrest, with
charge A7.1
definitions A7.3
generally A7.1
maximum penalty A7.1
mode of trial A7.1
notes A7.2
sentencing A7.4
meaning A15.5–A15.6
motor vehicles, and C5.5
occasioning actual bodily harm
see also **Actual bodily harm**
generally A8.1–A8.34
on licensed premises
exclusion orders A8.33
police constable, on
alternative verdict A9.9
burden of proof A9.7
charge A9.1
constable A9.3
court security officer A9.4
definitions A9.2–A9.9
execution of his duty A9.5–A9.8

Assault – *cont.*
police constable, on – *cont.*
licensed premises, and A9.11
maximum penalty A9.1
notes A9.2–A9.9
sentencing A9.10
racially or religiously aggravated assault
common assault A15.1–A15.33
meaning A15.7
occasioning actual bodily harm A8.1–A8.34
reasonable chastisement A15.16, A19.5
recklessness A8.7, A15.4, A15.5, A70.5
sentencing
actual bodily harm A8.31–A8.32
assault on constable or court security officer A9.10–A9.11
assault with intent to resist arrest A7.4
common assault A15.33
sexual assault
absolute discharge A53.9
anonymity of victim A52.11
clearing the court A52.10
conditional discharge A53.9
consent A53.5
defences A53.5
generally A53
juvenile offenders A53.9
notification requirements following conviction A52.14, A53.9
reporting restrictions D1B.7
sentencing A52.12–A52.16
sexual harm prevention order A53.10
touching A52.4, A53.4, A53.5
unconsciousness, causing A8.9
Asylum seekers
see also **Immigration offences**
assisting entry A81

Asylum seekers – *cont.*
bail applications A81.17
refugee status A81.8A
Attachment of earnings orders
see also **Deductions from benefits orders; Deductions from earnings orders**
payment of fines B28.26, B28.67, B28.76, B28.96
Attempts
assault A15.6
fraudulent evasion of duty A4.6
imprisonment B34.38
theft A57.19
Attendance centre
youth rehabilitation order requirement B49.10
Attendance centre orders
accessibility of centre B4.6
age limits B4.2
aims B4.16
ancillary orders B4.9
announcement B4.10
availability B4.5
community sentences, and B4.8
details B4.17
duration, B4.17
general considerations B4.16
jurisdiction B4.1
juveniles, and B4.7
maximum period B4.3
minimum period B4.4
Attendance centre requirement
generally B9.22BB

B

Bad character
defendants D6.14
witnesses D6.15
Badger traps
destruction A18.19
Bail
see also **Remand in custody**
absence of accused, in D8.21–D8.23
Bail – *cont.*
adjournment of hearing, where D8.1, D8.18
after conviction D8.19
appeals
against conditions D8.79
prosecution right D8.33
asylum see kers facing criminal charges A81.17
before conviction D8.18
children and young persons E3.4
circumstances D8.7–D8.10
conditional bail
appeals D8.79
application to vary bail conditions D8.80
common conditions D8.63
court bail D8.61–D8.70
effectiveness of conditions D8.70
electronic monitoring D8.65
failure to comply with condition D8.92
generally D8.31
hostel rules, compliance with D8.65
introduction D8.4
police bail D8.55–D8.60
pre-sentence report D8.62
recognisance of surety D8.66–D8.68, F5.48
decision whether to D8.24–D8.25
depositing a security D8.69
drug users D8.30
duration
after conviction D8.19
before conviction D8.18
ECHR, challenges under D8.2
electronic monitoring D8.65
European supervision orders D8.76
exceptions to right
conditions to be imposed where bail granted D8.31

Bail – *cont.*
exceptions to right – *cont.*
custody time limits D8.51–D8.54
drug users D8.30
generally D8.26
homicide/rape after previous conviction D8.32
imprisonable offences D8.27–D8.28, D8.32
no real prospect of custodial sentence D8.26
non-imprisonable offences D8.29
prosecution right of appeal D8.33
failure to comply with condition D8.92
failure to surrender to custody
burden of proof A10.2
charge A10.1
committal to Crown Court A10.2
defence D8.85
definitions A10.2
'fails without reasonable cause' A10.2
generally A10.1
maximum penalty A10.1
notes A10.2
penalty D8.91
procedure A10.2
prosecution for A10.2, D8.82–D8.91
sentencing A10.3
'surrender to custody' A10.2
further offences on bail D8.2
homicide cases D8.32
Human Rights Act, and D8.2–D8.96
immigration offences A81.17
imprisonable offences
generally D8.27
homicide or rape D8.32
summary only D8.28
introduction D8.1

Bail – *cont.*
length of remand on
after conviction D8.19
before conviction D8.18
live video links
generally D8.22A
vulnerable accused D8.22B
non-imprisonable offences D8.29
opposed bail, grant of D8.25
pending appeal D8.93
plea before venue B8.13
police bail
after charge D8.57–D8.60
before charge D8.56
street bail D8.55
presumption of liberty D8.24
prosecution right of appeal D8.33
rape cases D8.32
recognisance of surety D8.66–D8.68, F5.48
refusal
appeals D8.79
application to Crown Court judge in chambers D8.79
further application after D8.77–D8.78
relevant circumstances D8.7–D8.10
remission to another court on B40.2
residence conditions, appeals D8.79
security deposit D8.69
sending to Crown Court, when D8.20
street bail D8.55
sureties D8.66–D8.68, F5.48
unconditional bail D8.3
video remands
generally D8.22A
vulnerable accused D8.22B
young offenders D8.6, D8.32
Banned commercial practices
generally A75
Banning orders
see also **Football banning orders**

Banning orders – *cont.*
drinking banning orders B25.1
Battery
see also **Assault**
assault, and A15.5–A15.6
children A15.16, A19.5
Bench Training and Development Committees (BTDCs)
generally E2.1
Benefit deduction orders
payment of fines B28.26, B28.80
Betting licensing
appeals
background F3.3
generally F3.4
Gambling Commission F3.2
general statutory changes F3.2
introduction F3.1
operating licences F3.3
personal licences F3.3
premises licences F3.3
statutory basis F3.1
Bicycle
taking without consent A65
Binding over
age limits B5.5
ancillary orders B5.4
announcement B5.5
antecedents B5.20
breach of order B5.17
burden of proof B5.20
come up for judgment, to B5.20
consent, and B5.6
Consolidated Criminal Practice Direction
introduction B5.1
text (2015) B5.20
costs B5.4
disorderly behaviour A20.20
evidence B5.20
general considerations B5.6–B5.17
guardian, of B5.18–B5.19
intentional harassment A21.18
introduction B5.1–B5.3
Binding over – *cont.*
keep the peace, to B5.20
maximum period B5.2
minimum period B5.3
misbehaviour in court D2.1
parent, of B5.18–B5.19
recognisance
complainant, by B5.8
forfeiture B5.17
parent or guardian, by B5.18–B5.19
refusal to enter into B5.6, B5.20
witness, by B5.8
security for good behaviour B5.20
sureties B5.6
threatening behaviour A21.18
written order B5.20
Bladed articles, possession of
see also **Offensive weapons**
charge A11.1
meaning A11.9
mode of trial A11.2
notes A11.3–A11.13
sentencing A11.15
Blood
alcohol in *see* Alcohol
Borrowing
theft and A57.33
Brakes
braking distances C3
defective
generally C9
sentencing C9.16–C9.20
shortest stopping distances C4
Breath tests
approved device C22.16–C22.18
eructation (belching) during C22.25
failure to co-operate with roadside breath test
charge C24.1
definitions C24.2–C24.8
general note C24.2–C24.8
legal advice C24.8

Breath tests – *cont.*
failure to co-operate with roadside breath test – *cont.*
motorist in hospital C24.6
reasonable excuse C24.7–C24.8
sentencing C24.9
failure to provide specimen for analysis
charge C23.1
definitions C23.2–C23.4
'fails to provide' C23.3
general note C23.2–C23.6A
legal advice C23.6A
reasonable excuse C23.4
sentencing C23.7–C23.9
warning as to consequences C23.5–C23.6
generally C22.10–C22.15
modification of device C22.16
motorist in hospital C24.6
power of arrest, and C22.10
reasonable excuse
failure to co-operate with roadside breath test C24.7–C24.8
failure to provide specimen for analysis C23.4
right to legal advice
failure to co-operate with roadside breath test C24.8
failure to provide specimen for analysis C23.6A
timing C22.10, C24.3–C24.4
Bribery offences
being bribed A89.2, A89.6
bribery of foreign public official A89.2, A89.10
bribing another person A89.2, A89.5
expectation test A89.9
function/activity to which bribe relates A89.7
generally A89
improper performance A89.9
Brothels
assisting in the management A44.3
definition A44.3
keeping a brothel used for prostitution A44
sentencing A44.4
Bullying
generally A19.16
Burglary
aggravated A13.2
'building' A13.7
caravan, of A13.7
domestic
'aggravated burglary' A12.2
'building' A12.10
caravan, of A12.15
charge A12.1
committal to Crown Court A12.4, A12.18
definitions A12.7–A12.18
'dwelling' A12.14
'entering' A12.7
generally A12.1
grievous bodily harm, and A12.3
inhabited vehicle or vessel A12.15
maximum penalty A12.1
mode of trial A12.2–A12.6
notes A12.7–A12.18
rape, and A12.3
sentencing A12.20
'stealing' A12.16
third conviction A12.4, A12.18
third offence becoming indictable only A12.4
threatening or using violence A12.5
trespass A12.10, A12.17
entering A13.6
going equipped for A58
grievous bodily harm, and A13.3

Burglary – *cont.*
inhabited vehicle or vessel A13.7
mode of trial A13.2–A13.5
non-domestic A13
rape, and A13.3
sentencing A13.19
stealing A13.16
threatening violence A13.4
trespass A13.7, A13.17
Butterfly knives
generally A11.13

C

Cameras
see also **Photographs**
concealed A20.9
Cannabis and cannabis resin
cultivation A27
meaning A25.11
possession
common law defence of necessity A25.8A
medical condition A25.8A
produce/be concerned in production A27.3A
Car parks
driving when unfit through drink or drugs C20.7
Cars
see **Motor vehicles**
Caravans
burglary A12.15, A13.7
threatening behaviour A21.9
Careless driving
see also **Dangerous driving**
causing death by careless or inconsiderate driving C16A
dangerous driving and C25.16
definition C25.5
drive without due care and attention
death C25.11
emergencies C25.7
emergency vehicles C25.18
Careless driving – *cont.*
drive without due care and attention – *cont.*
generally C25.1
mechanical defect C25.8
sentencing C25.20–C25.21
warning of proceedings C25.10
endorsement code C6.2
generally C25.16–C25.17
reasonable consideration, driving without C46
reduced disqualification for attendance on course C22.56–C22.61
Cattle
see **Animals; Livestock**
Causing serious injury by dangerous driving
charge C16C.1
definitions C16C.3
legal notices C16C.3
maximum penalty C16C.1
mode of trial C16C.2
sentencing C16C.4
Causing serious injury by driving (disqualified drivers)
charge C16D.1
maximum penalty C16D.1
mode of trial C16D.2
CCTV evidence
generally D6.9
Certificate of good repute
generally F5.49
Change of plea
guilty plea D6.26
not guilty plea D6.20
Chastisement
actual bodily harm A8.22
assault A15.16–A15.18, A19.5
Child cruelty
abandoning A19.18–A19.20
age of offender A19.4
assaulting A19.9
bullying A19.16
'child' A19.6
dealing with A19.24–A19.31

Child cruelty – *cont.*
definitions A19.6–A19.22
exposing
generally A19.21
in a manner likely to cause unnecessary suffering or injury to health A19.22
frightening A19.16
generally A19.1
ill-treating A19.16
maximum penalty A19.1
mode of trial A19.2–A19.31
neglecting A19.17, A19.23
presumption of guilt A19.23
reasonable punishment A19.5
sentencing
generally A19.1
guidelines A19.32–A19.34
'wilfully' A19.8
'young person' A19.7
Child pornography
see also **Indecent photographs of children**
charges A14.1
definitions A14.3–A14.5
maximum penalty A14.1
mode of trial A14.2
notes A14.3–A14.5
'payment' A14.5
'pornography' A14.3
possession of extreme pornographic images, and A14.1A
'prostitute' A14.4
sentencing A14.6
Child prostitution
see also **Indecent photographs of children**
charges A14.1
definitions A14.3–A14.5
maximum penalty A14.1
mode of trial A14.2
notes A14.3–A14.5
'payment' A14.5
'pornography' A14.3
'prostitute' A14.4
sentencing A14.6
Children
see also **Cruelty to a child**
abandoning A19.18–A19.20
age of defendant E1.2
assault A15.16–A15.18, A19.5
binding over parent or guardian
Consolidated Criminal Practice Direction B5.20
generally B5.18–B5.19
bullying A19.16
chastisement by parents A15.16–A15.18, A19.5
committal to Crown Court for sentence
generally E3.18H
procedure E3.20–E3.25
dangerous offenders E3.18C
definition A19.6
dealing with A19.24–A19.31
determining age of defendant E1.2
electronic monitoring D8.65
evidence *see* Evidence
exposing to cruelty A19.21
fines
generally B28.5–B28.6
parental responsibility for payment B28.7–B28.10
grave crimes E3.18C
homicide D8.32
'ill-treating' A19.16
indecent photographs
age of child A43.4
defences A43.8
deletion of computer files A43.3, A43.7
distribution A43.6
downloading indecent images A43.3
evidence A43.5
forfeiture A43.1
introduction A43.1
knowledge A43.7
mode of trial A43.2
notification requirements A43.12
'photograph' A43.3

Children – *cont.*
indecent photographs – *cont.*
'possession' A43.3
'pop-up' cases A43.3
prohibited images A43.4A
pseudo-photographs A43.3, A43.4
sentencing A43.9
stored on computer A43.3
live video link
evidence via E3.22
vulnerable accused D8.22B
neglect
meaning A19.17
presumption of guilt A19.23
oath E3.22
persistently selling alcohol to children F2.27
pornography
charges A14.1
definitions A14.3–A14.5
maximum penalty A14.1
mode of trial A14.2
notes A14.3–A14.5
'payment' A14.5
'pornography' A14.3
'prostitute' A14.4
sentencing A14.6
possible orders E4
prostitution
charges A14.1
definitions A14.3–A14.5
maximum penalty A14.1
mode of trial A14.2
notes A14.3–A14.5
payment' A14.5
'pornography' A14.3
'prostitute' A14.4
sentencing A14.6
punishment by parents A15.16–A15.18, A19.5
reasonable chastisement A15.16–A15.18
reasonable punishment A19.5
remand on bail E3.4

Children – *cont.*
remand in custody
generally E3.4
local authority accommodation E3.5, E3.17
secure accommodation E3.7–E3.8
youth detention accommodation E3.6
remission to local court E3.23
reporting restrictions
generally E2.4–E2.5
human rights D1B.7
seat belts C48.9–C48.16
sexual offences against
absolute discharge A52.14
anonymity of victim A52.11
clearing the court A52.10
competence A52.8
conditional discharge A52.14
defences A52.7
evidence A52.8
introduction A52.1
mistake as to age A52.7
notification requirements following conviction A52.14, A53.9
privacy A52.10
reporting restrictions A52.11
risk of sexual harm order A52.16
sentencing A52.12–A52.16
sexual activity A52.4
sexual offences prevention order A52.16
touching A52.4
youth court trials E1.3, E2
Civil legal aid
generally D7.1
Civil proceedings
power to review decisions B38.6
Closure notices
persistently selling alcohol to children F2.27
Closure orders
appeals
generally F2.26
introduction A26.16

Closure orders – *cont.*
crack houses A26.12
consideration hearings F2.24
court's powers F2.25
disorder, and
enforcement B6.3
generally B6.1–B6.2
drug production or supply A26.12
duration F2.23
extension F2.25
general power F2.21
grounds F2.22
hearings F2.24
nuisance, and
enforcement B6.3
generally B6.1–B6.2
prostitution offences, and
appeals B7.5
compensation B7.6
costs B7.6
criteria B7.2
discharge B7.4
enforcement B7.3
extension B7.4
generally B7.1
offences B7.3
variation B7.4
revocation F2.25
Clubs
gun clubs A71.6
Coercive behaviour in intimate or family relationship
charge A17A.1
defences A17A.3
definitions A17A.2
general note A17A.2
'ought to know' A17A.2
'personally connected' A17A.2
'same family' A17A.2
sentencing A17A.4
Commercial practices
aggressive practice A75
banned commercial practices A75
contrary to professional diligence A75
Commercial practices – *cont.*
definition A75.6
misleading A75
misleading omission A75
sentencing A75.7–A75.10
unfair or prohibited A75
Committal proceedings
see **Allocation and sending for trial**
Committal for sentence
acceptance of summary trial, after B8.6–B8.7
bail, and, B8.13
conditionally discharged person convicted of further offence B8.14
dangerous adult offenders, of B8.1
generally B8.2–B8.4
guidance B8.5
introduction B8.1
mistake in recording basis B8.10
mistaken view of the facts, on B8.11
operational period of suspended sentence, during B8.14
other errors in committal B8.12
other powers B8.14
other than as a dangerous offender B8.2–B8.4
plea and plea before venue B8.13
pre-sentence reports B8.16
related offences, for
generally B8.8
'related' B8.9
suspended sentences, and B8.14–B8.15
triable either way offences, for B8.14
Common assault
see also **Assault**
accidental jostling A15.9
aggravation of offence A15.7
'assault' A15.5–A15.6
certificate of dismissal A15.31
charge A15.1

Common assault – *cont.*
chastisement A15.16–A15.18
consent A15.11
defences A15.8–A15.32
definitions A15.3–A15.32
disability of victim A15.7
domestic violence A15.34
execution of legal process A15.20
games and sports A15.18
generally A15.1
horseplay A15.17
hostile intent A15.10
intent A15.4
jostling A15.9
justification A15.21
lawful sport A15.18
maximum penalty A15.1
misadventure A15.8
notes A15.3–A15.32
officer of court, by A15.20
provocation A15.32
racially or religiously aggravated
charge A15.2
maximum penalty A15.2
meaning A15.7
reasonable chastisement A15.16–A15.18, A19.5
recklessness A15.4
sado-masochistic activities A15.11
self-defence
generally A15.19
onus of proof A15.19
sentencing
domestic violence A15.34
generally A15.33
sexual orientation of victim A15.7
sports and games A15.18
transgender identity of victim A15.7
triviality A15.21
two offences tried together A15.3

Commonwealth citizens
deportation B17.3–B17.4

Communications network offences
elements of offence A16.2
generally A16.1
sentencing A16.7
threats A16.2

Community orders
activity requirement B9.11
age of offender B9.1, B43.1
alcohol abstinence and monitoring requirement
generally B9.22A
introduction B9.9
alcohol treatment requirement B9.22
amending terms to impose more onerous requirements A17.3
attendance centre requirement B9.22B
availability
generally B9.1–B9.2
process of sentencing, and B45.31–B45.32
breach by failure to comply
amending terms to impose more onerous requirements A17.3
approach to proceedings A17.3
burden of proof A17.2
charge A17.1
costs in proceedings B12.23
failed to keep in touch A17.2
generally A17.1
options in proceedings A17.3
reasonable excuse A17.2
revocation and re-sentence A17.3
sentencing approach A17.3
sentencing guideline B9.27
standard of proof A17.2
breach of a requirement B9.24
conviction of further offence during currency B9.26
curfew requirement B9.14

Community orders – *cont.*
drug rehabilitation requirement
generally B9.19
periodic review B9.21
provision for review by court B9.20
duration B9.23A
electronic monitoring
generally B9.23
introduction B9.9
exclusion requirement B9.15
failed to keep in touch A17.2
foreign travel prohibition requirement B9.16A
introduction B9.1–B9.4
mental health treatment requirement
generally B9.17
treatment at place other than that specified in order B9.18
permissible requirements B9.10–B9.26
power to impose B9.8–B9.9
pre-sentence reports B9.5–B9.6, B45.50
previous convictions, and B9.3
programme requirement B9.12
prohibited activity requirement B9.13
refusal to consent to conditions in B15.16, B45.35
rehabilitation activity requirement B9.11A
requirements imposed B9.10–B9.25
residence requirement B9.16
revocation B9.25
revocation and resentence A17.3
sentencing
approach and options A17.3
guideline B9.27
power to impose sentence B9.8–B9.9
setting date for completion of requirements B9.1

Community orders – *cont.*
short or fast-delivery reports D6.36
suspended sentence compared B34.47
technical guidance B9.28
unpaid work requirement B9.10

Community protection notices
generally B8A.2–B8A.5
introduction B8A.1

Compensation
deferment of sentence, and B16.10–B16.16

Compensation orders
amount B10.6
appeals B10.17
availability of sentence B45.25
criminal damage, and B10.3
criteria B10.6
defendant's lack of means B18.10
deprivation orders, and B10.16
discharge B10.18
disposal of forfeited goods B10.16
dog worrying livestock A73.7
exceptions B10.4
fines, and B10.1
fixing the amount B10.6
football banning order B29.36
forgery A78.17
funeral expenses, and B10.2
introduction B10.1–B10.3
legal adviser B10.10
making good deficiency B10.16
personal injuries, and
generally B10.2
guidelines B10.19
procedure B10.7–B10.10
proof of loss B10.5
reduction B10.18
review B10.17
social security benefit, false statement/representation to obtain A54.6
surcharge, and B10.1
theft, for A57.39, B10.3

Compensation orders – *cont.*
victims of uninsured motorists, for C33.18–C33.22
Computer 'hackers'
criminal damage A18.22
Computer program
article possessed for fraud A38.3
erasure of, as criminal damage A18.22
Concealed cameras
generally A20.9
Concentration of specified controlled drug in excess of specified limit, driving with a
charge C22A.1
consequential amendments C22A.4
controlled drugs C22A.3
defences C22A.5
elements C22A.2
limits C22A.3
penalties C22A.1
sentencing C22A.7
specified drugs C22A.3
statutory assumption C22A.6
Conditional discharge
availability B45.24
breach E1.2
Consolidated Criminal Practice Direction
introduction B5.1
text (2015) B5.20
deferment of sentence and B16.19
generally B22Z
juveniles E1.2
security for good behaviour B5.20
sexual assault A53.9
sexual offences against children A52.14
youth court E1.2
Confiscation orders
drug-trafficking offences A26.20
generally B11.1
term in default B11.2
Consent
actual bodily harm A8.22
Constables
see **Police constables**
Contempt of court
appeals D3.16
defendants, by D3.10–D3.11
interruptions D3.1
introduction D3.1
maximum penalty D3.4
meaning D3.1
misbehaviour in court D3.1
officers of the court D3.6
overwhelming disorder in court D3.8
penalties D3.4
photographs in court
generally D1B.9
penalties D3.4
mobile phone, by D3.15
procedure D3.7
reporting restrictions D1B.7
sketches in court D1B.9
tape recorders D1B.10
unauthorised use of disclosed prosecution material D3.8
wilfully insult
generally D3.5
introduction D3.1
witnesses, by D3.9
Contingent destruction orders
dangerous dogs A72.15
Contribution orders
publicly funded representation D7.11
Controlled drugs
driving with a concentration of specified drug in excess of specified limit
charge C22A.1
consequential amendments C22A.4
controlled drugs C22A.3
defences C22A.5
elements C22A.2
limits C22A.3
penalties C22A.1

Controlled drugs – *cont.*
driving with a concentration of specified drug in excess of specified limit – *cont.*
sentencing C22A.7
specified drugs C22A.3
statutory assumption C22A.6
Controlling behaviour in intimate or family relationship
charge A17A.1
defences A17A.3
definitions A17A.2
general note A17A.2
'ought to know' A17A.2
'personally connected' A17A.2
'same family' A17A.2
sentencing A17A.4
Conviction
anti-social behaviour orders (CrASBOs), and
discharge B2.3
generally B2.1
variation B2.3
Costs
advice of justices' clerk
failure to take D6.28, D9.9
binding over orders B5.4
civil proceedings, in
generally B12.24–B12.31
litigants in person B12.1
proceedings begun by way of application B12.31
public funding B12.25
criminal proceedings, in
defence costs on acquittal B12.16–B12.17
introduction B12.2–B12.2A
legal representatives, against B12.20
miscellaneous provisions B12.21–B12.23
prosecution costs B12.3–B12.10
third parties, against B12.20A
unnecessarily or improperly incurred B12.19
defence costs on acquittal
generally B12.16–B12.16A
Costs – *cont.*
defence costs on acquittal – *cont.*
publicly aided defendant B12.17
failure to take advice of justices' clerk D6.28, D9.9
interpreters B12.22
introduction B12.1
legal representatives, against B12.20
liquor licensing appeals F2.20
litigants in person B12.1
maintenance orders, complaints concerning B12.24
medical reports B12.21
possessing a controlled drug with intent to supply A26.17
prosecution costs
central funds B12.3
breach or revocation of community orders, and B12.23
generally B12.3–B12.10
health and safety at work A80.21
introduction B12.3
monetary penalty not exceeding £5 B12.9
ordering accused to pay B12.8
private prosecutors B12.4–B12.6
proportionate to maximum penalty B12.8
reducing amount of prosecutor's order B12.7
youths B12.10
statutory nuisance, complaint by person aggrieved A84.31
third parties, against B12.20A
unnecessarily or improperly incurred B12.19
wasted costs orders A84.31, B12.19, D6.12
Council tax
background F4.1

Council tax – *cont.*
committal proceedings F4.10–F4.13
court hearing
generally F4.4–F4.5
reopening F4.6
evidential requirements F4.7–F4.8
fraud by failing to disclose information A36.8
liability orders
costs of obtaining F4.9A
generally F4.9
recovery and enforcement F4.2–F4.3
reopening and rehearing F4.6
suspended commitments F4.14–F4.17
Counterfeit money
import or export A4.2
Court security officers
assault
alternative verdict A9.9
burden of proof A9.7
charge A9.2
court security officer A9.4
definitions A9.2–A9.9
execution of his duty A9.5–A9.8
licensed premises, and A9.11
maximum penalty A9.1
notes A9.2–A9.9
plain clothes officers carrying out drugs search A9.8
reduction of charge A9.9
search of defendant A9.8
sentencing A9.10
definition A9.4
identifiability A9.6
obstructing or resisting in execution of duty A47
Courtroom procedure
abuse of process
generally D1B.11
principles D1B.12
sending for trial D4.11
youth courts E3.25
Courtroom procedure – *cont.*
appeals
against conviction and or sentence D6.46
case stated, by way of D6.47
Crown Court, to D6.46
High Court, to D6.47
introduction D6.45
judicial review applications D6.48
misbehaviour in court D3.1
open court proceedings
abuse of process D1B.11–D1B.12
exceptions D1B.2
introduction D1B.1
non-disclosure of evidence D1B.6
power to clear court D1B.3
reporting of court proceedings D1B.7–D1B.10
plea before venue
offences triable either way D4.3
youth court E3.18D–E3.18F
reasons for decisions
generally D1A.1–D1A.5
reparation order B41.16
young offender institution B21.34
stay of proceedings
abuse of process D1B.11–D1B.12
sending for trial D4.11
youth court E3.25
Courts Service
generally D9.5
Cows
see **Animals; Livestock**
Crack houses
closure orders A26.12
Credit for time on remand
custodial sentences B34.39
detention and training orders B19.6A–B19.8
Credit for time spent on qualifying bail curfew
generally B34.39A

Criminal anti-social behaviour orders (CrASBOs)
see also Criminal behaviour orders
generally B2.1
Criminal behaviour orders (CBOs)
breach
collateral attack on validity of order or its terms B2.4
commission of criminal offence B2.4
conditional discharge, and B2.9
generally B2.4
introduction B13.7
key factors B2.7
lesser degree of harm caused or intended B2.7
no harm caused or intended B2.7
previous convictions B2.6
reasonable excuse B2.4
sentencing guideline B2.5–B2.6
serious harm caused or intended B2.7
young offenders, and B2.4
discharge B13.5
duration B13.5
evidence B13.4
generally B13.1
grounds B13.2
introduction B13.1
judicial guidance B13.6
pre-conditions B13.2
procedure B13.3
publicity B13.4
requirements B13.5
variation B13.5
Criminal courts charge
enforcement B14.4
introduction B14.1
levels B14.3
relevant circumstances B14.2
Criminal damage
see also Damage to property
Criminal damage – *cont.*
arson A18
assessing value of damage A18.6–A18.8
'belonging to another person' A18.23–A18.24
compensation orders, and B10.3
computer 'hackers' A18.22
computer program, erasure of A18.22
'damage' A18.22
destroy or damage A18.20
destruction of badger traps A18.19
detention and training order B15.6
endangerment of life A18.2
graffiti as A18.22
intention A18.25
Iraq War protesters A18.19
low value D4.9, D8.27
maximum penalty A18.2–A18.5
multiple offences A18.9
new allocation and sending provisions D4.9
possessing anything with intent to destroy or damage property A18B
'property' A18.21
racially or religiously aggravated A18.16–A18.18
reasonable force to prevent commission of crime A18.19
recklessness A18.31
reparation orders B41.8
sentencing A18.3, A18.32, B15.6
temporary functional derangement A18.22
threatening to destroy or damage property A18A
trust property A18.24
venue for trial A18.2–A18.5
wheel clamp removal A18.19
without lawful excuse A18.19

Criminal Injuries Compensation Authority
compensation orders, and B10.19
Criminal legal aid
advice and assistance D7.4
choice of legal representative D7.10
contribution orders D7.11
duty solicitor D7.12
financial eligibility D7.7–D7.9
generally D7.2–D7.3
qualification D7.5–D7.6
scope D7.4
Crossbows
generally A11.3
Crown Court
see also **Allocation and sending for trial**
committal for sentence
acceptance of summary trial, after B8.6–B8.7
bail, and, B8.13
conditionally discharged person convicted of further offence B8.14
dangerous adult offenders B8.1
guidance B8.5
mistake in recording basis B8.10
mistaken view of the facts, on B8.11
operational period of suspended sentence, during B8.14
other errors in committal B8.12
other powers B8.14
other than as a dangerous offender B8.2–B8.4
plea and plea before venue B8.13
pre-sentence reports B8.16
related offences, for B8.8–B8.9
suspended sentences, and B8.14–B8.15
Crown Court – *cont.*
committal for sentence – *cont.*
triable either way offences, for B8.14
disqualification from driving C5.40
press reports D1B.7
sentencing
committal B8.1–B8.16
young offenders, of B21.33
sitting as youth court to deal with summary-only matters E3.18G
young offenders B21.33
Cruelty to animals
see **Animal cruelty**
Cruelty to a child
abandoning A19.18–A19.20
age of offender A19.4
assaulting A19.9
bullying A19.16
'child' A19.6
dealing with A19.24–A19.31
definitions A19.6–A19.22
exposing
generally A19.21
in a manner likely to cause unnecessary suffering or injury to health A19.22
frightening A19.16
generally A19.1
ill-treating A19.16
maximum penalty A19.1
mode of trial A19.2–A19.31
neglecting A19.17, A19.23
presumption of guilt A19.23
reasonable punishment A19.5
sentencing
generally A19.1
guidelines A19.32–A19.34
'wilfully' A19.8
'young person' A19.7
Curfew
community order requirement B9.1, B9.14
credit for time spent on qualifying bail curfew B34.39A

Curfew – *cont.*
fines and B28.83
YRO requirement B49.3, B49.12
Curfew orders
see also Community orders
Custodial sentences
see also Imprisonment; Sentencing; Young offender institutions
aggravating or mitigating factors B15.10
availability B45.33–B45.35
consecutive sentences B34.22–B34.32
credit for time on remand B34.39
credit for time spent on qualifying bail curfew B34.39A
custody plus B15.1
early release
further offences B34.54–B34.55
generally B34.53
enforcement of fine B28.41–B28.51, B28.70
immediate sentence for shortest time B15.17
intermittent custody B15.1, B21.0, B21.1
legal representation
defendant's right to, young offenders B15.8, B21.21
right to B15.8, B33.2, B34.19
length B15.18–B15.20, B34.35–B34.39
mentally disordered defendant B15.23–B15.24, B34.18
post-release supervision B15.22A
pre-sentence reports B15.21–B15.22
previous convictions, taking into account B15.10
proportionality B45.49
Custodial sentences – *cont.*
restrictions on imposing B15.8–B15.9
seriousness of offence
determining B45.7–B45.16
'first time offender' B45.7
generally B45.3
'range' B45.7
'starting point' B45.7
Custody
see Custodial sentences; Remand in custody
Custody plus
generally B15.1
Custody time limits
application to extend D8.52
expiry D8.54
generally D8.51–D8.54
Customs and excise duty
see Revenue and Customs

D

Damage to property
see also Criminal damage
arson A18
criminal damage A18
possessing anything with intent to destroy or damage property A18B
threatening to destroy or damage property A18A
Dangerous adult offenders
committal to Crown Court for sentence B8.1
Dangerous dogs
additional powers A72.16
age of owner A72.2
appeals
Dogs Act 1871 orders, and A72.38
generally A72.19
'assistance dog' A72.5
available sentences A72.9
contingent destruction order A72.15

Dangerous dogs – *cont.*
control or destruction orders (Dogs Act 1871)
appeals A72.38
applications A72.22–A72.24
change of ownership A72.25
disqualification A72.34–A72.37
generally A72.21
measures to be taken A72.32–A72.33
procedure at hearing A72.31
dangerously out of control A72.5
destruction orders
appeals A72.19
contingent orders A72.15
Dogs Act 1871, under A72.21–A72.38
fighting dogs A72.20
generally A72.10
disqualification orders
appeals A72.19
contravention A72.18
Dogs Act 1871, under A72.34–A72.37
fighting dogs A72.20
generally A72.17
escape from enclosed area A72.3
fighting dogs A72.20
householder defence A72.4
introduction A72.1
Japanese Tosas A72.20
maximum penalty A72.1
omission of defendant A72.3
owner A72.2
physical control of dog A72.3
pit bull terriers A72.20
public place, in A72.3–A72.4
sentencing
available sentences A72.9
Guideline A72.8–A72.8A
introduction A72.6
standard of liability A72.3
strict liability A72.3
temporary transfer of control A72.3

Dangerous driving
see also **Careless driving; Driving**
aggravated vehicle taking, after A66
aid and abet C16.6
careless or inconsiderate driving and C25.16
causing death by C9.5
causing serious injury by
charge C16C.1
definitions C16C.3
legal notices C16C.3
maximum penalty C16C.1
mode of trial C16C.2
sentencing C16C.4
charge C16.1
dangerous C16.7–C16.9
dangerously C16.5
defences C16.17
definitions A66.8, C16.3–C16.16
disqualification C16.21
driving C16.3
endorsement of licence C16.21
forfeiture of vehicle B18.17
general note C16.3–C16.16
mechanically propelled vehicle C16.4
mode of trial C16.2
objective test C16.8
public place C16.15
road C16.10
sentencing C16.18–C16.22
warning of proceedings C16.16

Dangerous drugs
see **Drugs**

Declarations
see **Statutory declarations**

Deductions from benefits orders
payment of fines B28.26, B28.80
Deductions from earnings orders
payment of fines B28.26, B28.67, B28.76, B28.96

Defective lights, driving with
charge C34.1–C34.4

Defective lights, driving with – *cont.*
defences C34.18–C34.20
exempted vehicles C34.17
front position lamp C34.10
'hours of darkness' C34.16
maximum penalty C34.4
road C34.9
sentencing C34.21–C34.22
using, causing or permitting C34.5–C34.7
vehicle C34.8
Defective tyres
generally C53
Defence of property
reasonable force A8.18–A8.20
Deferment of sentence
ancillary orders B16.5
compensation provisions B16.10, B16.16
conditional discharge B16.19
consent B16.1
failure to comply with requirements B16.20
limitations B16.1–B16.4
maximum period B16.17
offence during B16.21
reasons B16.10
requirements as to conduct B16.4
sentence after period of deferral B16.2
undertaking to comply with requirements B16.1
victim's concerns B16.16
when appropriate B16.10
Deportation
age of seventeen B17.5
aliens B17.4
citizens who cannot be deported B17.3
Commonwealth citizens B17.3–B17.4
'convicted' B17.6
criteria for making recommendation
generally B17.8–B17.11
introduction A81.17
Deportation – *cont.*
effect of recommendation B17.31
EU Nationals B17.4
Home Secretary's considerations B17.9–B17.16
introduction B17.1
persons who may be deported B17.4
procedure B17.12–B17.16
recommendation B17.2
Deprivation orders
see also **Forfeiture**
availability of sentence B45.25
compensation orders, and B10.16
conversion proceedings B18.5
effect of order B18.5
motor vehicles B18.17
personal loss or injury B18.10–B18.16
property in possession of police, and F1.21
Destruction orders
dangerous dogs
appeals A72.19
contingent orders A72.15
Dogs Act 1871, under A72.21–A72.38
fighting dogs A72.20
generally A72.10
dangerous dogs (Dogs Act 1871)
appeals A72.38
applications A72.22–A72.24
change of ownership A72.25
disqualification A72.34–A72.37
generally A72.21
measures to be taken A72.32–A72.33
procedure at hearing A72.31
Detention
for one day at court or police station B20Z, B28.53
young offender institution *see* Young offender institution
Detention of seized cash
warrants of arrest F5.46

Detention and training orders
availability B45.33
breach of supervision B19.10
conditions B19.3–B19.4
consecutive orders B19.8
credit for time on remand B19.6A–B19.8
determination of age of offender B19.1
duration
credit for time on remand B19.6A–B19.8
generally B19.6
time spent on bail subject to condition B15.20
time spent on remand B15.20
generally B19.1–B19.5
introduction B15.6
offences during currency B19.10
persistent offender B19.4
restrictions B19.3
sentencing guidance B19.11
statement conditions met B19.5
supervision B19.9
time on remand B19.6A–B19.8
Disability
actual bodily harm A8.10–A8.16
aggravation B45.2B
Discharge
absolute discharge
availability B45.24
generally B22Z
sexual assault A53.9
sexual offences against children A52.14
conditional discharge
availability B45.24
breach E1.2
Consolidated Criminal Practice Direction B5.1
deferment of sentence and B16.19
generally B22Z
juveniles E1.2
security for good behaviour B5.20
sexual assault A53.9
Discharge – *cont.*
conditional discharge – *cont.*
sexual offences against children A52.14
youth court E1.2
Disclosing private sexual images
charge A19A.1
'consent' A19A.2
defences A19A.3
definitions A19A.2
'discloses' A19A.2
'filming' A19A.2
general note A19A.2
'photograph or film' A19A.2
'private' A19A.2
sentencing A19A.4
'sexual' A19A.2
Dishonestly
abstracting electricity without authority A1.3
Disorder
see also **Violent disorder**
closure orders
enforcement B6.3
generally B6.1–B6.2
Disorderly behaviour
see also **Football banning orders; Football-related offences**
abusive speech A20.5
another person A20.8
arrest powers A20.18
binding over A20.20
charges A20.1–A20.2
concealed camera A20.9
defences A20.17
defendant's behaviour A20.8
definitions A20.3–A20.18
disorderly A20.5A
drunkenness A20.16
dwelling A20.3B
dwelling-house, in A20.16
freedom of expression A20.5
generally A20.1–A20.2
harassment, alarm or distress
generally A20.3A

Disorderly behaviour – *cont.*
harassment, alarm or distress – *cont.*
intent to cause, with A21.1–A21.18
insulting speech A20.5
intent A20.10
intoxication A20.16
maximum penalty A20.2
misbehaviour in court D2.1
notes A20.3–A2.18
power of arrest A20.18
racially or religiously aggravated
charges A21.1–A21.4
definitions A21.5–A21.10
introduction A20.6
notes A21.5–A21.10
sentencing A21.16–A21.18
sentencing
general A20.19
racially or religiously aggravated A21.17
threatening, abusive, insulting speech A20.5
visible representation A20.11
within hearing or sight of another person A20.8
Disqualification
dangerous dogs
appeals A72.19
contravention A72.18
Dogs Act 1871, under A72.34–A72.37
fighting dogs A72.20
generally A72.17
driving, from
for any offence C5.45
vehicle taking without consent A65.20
keeping animals, from
generally A5.4
sentencing A5.5
Disqualified drivers
causing serious injury by driving
charge C16D.1
maximum penalty C16D.1
mode of trial C16D.2
Disqualified drivers – *cont.*
for any offence C5.45
vehicle taking without consent A65.20
Distance
speed and distance chart C2
Distress warrant
fine, enforcement of B28.54, B28.76
Dogs
see also **Animals; Dangerous dogs**
disqualification from keeping
appeals A72.19
contravention A72.18
Dogs Act 1871, under A72.34–A72.37
fighting dogs A72.20
generally A72.17
fighting dogs A72.20
hunting with A86.8
threat to harm A41.7
worrying livestock A73
Domestic abuse
actual bodily harm A8.34
introduction A2.16
sentencing A15.34
Domestic burglary
'aggravated burglary' A12.2
'building' A12.10
caravan, of A12.15
charge A12.1
committal to Crown Court A12.4, A12.18
definitions A12.7–A12.18
'dwelling' A12.14
'entering' A12.7
generally A12.1
grievous bodily harm, and A12.3
inhabited vehicle or vessel A12.15
maximum penalty A12.1
mode of trial A12.2–A12.6
notes A12.7–A12.18
rape, and A12.3
sentencing A12.20

Domestic burglary – *cont.*
'stealing' A12.16
third conviction A12.4, A12.18
third offence becoming indictable only A12.4
threatening or using violence A12.5
trespass A12.10, A12.17
Domestic football banning orders *see* **Football banning orders**
Domestic violence
actual bodily harm A8.34
introduction A2.16
sentencing A15.34
Domestic violence protection notice (DVPN)
generally B23Z
Domestic violence protection order (DVPO)
generally B24Z
Drawings of court proceedings
general prohibition D1B.9
Drinking banning orders
generally B25.1
Driving
careless
causing death by C16A
dangerous driving, and C25.16
definition C25.5
endorsement code C6.2
generally C25.16–C25.17
causing death by
careless driving C16A
disqualified drivers C16D
inconsiderate driving C16A
unlicensed, disqualified or uninsured drivers C16B
causing serious injury by dangerous driving
charge C16C.1
definitions C16C.3
legal notices C16C.3
maximum penalty C16C.1
mode of trial C16C.2
sentencing C16C.4
causing serious injury by driving (disqualified drivers)
Driving – *cont.*
causing serious injury by driving (disqualified drivers) – *cont.*
charge C16D.1
maximum penalty C16D.1
mode of trial C16D.2
concentration of specified controlled drug in excess of specified limit, with a
charge C22A.1
consequential amendments C22A.4
controlled drugs C22A.3
defences C22A.5
elements C22A.2
limits C22A.3
penalties C22A.1
sentencing C22A.7
specified drugs C22A.3
statutory assumption C22A.6
dangerous
aggravated vehicle taking, after A66
aid and abet C16.6
careless or inconsiderate driving and C25.16
causing death by C9.5
charge C16.1
dangerous C16.7–C16.9
dangerously C16.5
defences C16.17
definitions A66.8, C16.3–C16.16
disqualification C16.21
driving C16.3
endorsement of licence C16.21
forfeiture of vehicle B18.17
general note C16.3–C16.16
mechanically propelled vehicle C16.4
mode of trial C16.2
objective test C16.8
public place C16.15
road C16.10
sentencing C16.18–C16.22
warning of proceedings C16.16

Driving – *cont.*
defective lights, with
charge C34.1–C34.4
defences C34.18–C34.20
exempted vehicles C34.17
front position lamp C34.10
'hours of darkness' C34.16
maximum penalty C34.4
road C34.9
sentencing C34.21–C34.22
using, causing or permitting C34.5–C34.7
vehicle C34.8
disqualification
for any offence C5.45
vehicle taking without consent A65.20
disqualified, whilst C5.38, C19
causing death C16B
sentencing C19.8–C19.17
drugs, while unfit through C20
due care or attention, without
death C25.11
emergencies C25.7
emergency vehicles C25.18
generally C25.1
mechanical defect C25.8
sentencing C25.20–C25.21
warning of proceedings C25.10
excess alcohol, drive/attempt to drive or in charge C22
emergency, in C22.50
high risk offenders C22.45–C22.46
inconsiderate
causing death by C16A
driving without reasonable consideration C46
meaning C25.5
learner drivers, provisions as to C18.3–C18.5
meaning C18.8
no insurance
burden of proof C33.6
causing C33.10
employed drivers C33.17

Driving – *cont.*
no insurance – *cont.*
insurance certificate C33.7
introduction C33.1
maximum penalty C33.1
Motor Insurers' Bureau C33.18–C33.22
motor vehicle C33.2
other public place C33.2
permitting C33.16
proof of insurance C33.7
road C33.2
security in respect of third party risks C33.4
sentencing C33.23–C33.31
time limit C33.5
use C33.9
using on a road or other public place C33.8
probationary period, endorsement during C5.46–C5.48
reasonable consideration, without C46
stationary vehicle C18.8
towed vehicle C18.9
'unfit through drink or drugs', when
alternative charge C20.18
alternative verdict C20.18
car parks C20.7
'drink/drugs' C20.17
driving C20.4
emergency, in C22.25
generally C20.2–C20.3
introduction C20.1
maximum sentence C20.1
mechanically propelled vehicle C20.5
public place C20.7–C20.8
road C20.6
sentencing C20.19–C20.20
'unfit' C20.9–C20.16
without appropriate licence C18
without due care and attention
death C25.11
emergencies C25.7
emergency vehicles C25.18

Driving – *cont.*
without due care and attention – *cont.*
generally C25.1
mechanical defect C25.8
sentencing C25.20–C25.21
warning of proceedings C25.10
without insurance
burden of proof C33.6
causing C33.10
employed drivers C33.17
insurance certificate C33.7
introduction C33.1
maximum penalty C33.1
Motor Insurers' Bureau C33.18–C33.22
motor vehicle C33.2
other public place C33.2
permitting C33.16
proof of insurance C33.7
road C33.2
security in respect of third party risks C33.4
sentencing C33.23–C33.31
time limit C33.5
use C33.9
using on a road or other public place C33.8
Driving licences
appropriate, driving without C18
codes C6
disqualification *see* Driving; Road traffic offences
driving whilst disqualified C19
endorsement *see* Road traffic offences
failure to produce C17
defences C17.19–C17.20
sentencing C17.21–C17.22
large goods vehicle licence C18.24A–C18.32
offences
driving whilst disqualified C19
generally C18
photocard licences C18.4
Driving licences – *cont.*
provisional
failure to display 'L' plates C18.3
offences C18.3–C18.5
supervision C18.3, C18.5
signature of application by magistrate F5.50
unlicensed drivers causing death by driving C16B
Driving test
disqualification until passes C5.37–C5.38
Drug assessment
failure to attend initial/remain for initial assessment A23
follow-up assessment A23.2
Drug treatment and testing order
refusal to consent B45.5, B45.35
see also Community orders
Drugs
see also **Possession of a controlled drug**
charge of vehicle when 'unfit through drink or drugs', in
driving or attempting to drive when C20
generally C21
Class A
fail/refuse to provide sample A24
generally A23
closure orders A26.12
controlled drug
fraudulent evasion of prohibition by bringing into/taking out of UK A27B
Revenue and Customs offences A4.2
sentencing A25.16
supply *see* Supplying or offering to supply a controlled drug
crack houses
closure orders A26.12

Drugs – *cont.*
driving when 'unfit through drink or drugs'
alternative charge C20.18
alternative verdict C20.18
car parks C20.7
'drink/drugs' C20.17
driving C20.4
emergency, in C22.25
generally C20.2–C20.3
introduction C20.1
maximum sentence C20.1
mechanically propelled vehicle C20.5
public place C20.7–C20.8
road C20.6
sentencing C20.19–C20.20
'unfit' C20.9–C20.16
driving with a concentration of specified controlled drug in excess of specified limit
charge C22A.1
consequential amendments C22A.4
controlled drugs C22A.3
defences C22A.5
elements C22A.2
limits C22A.3
penalties C22A.1
sentencing C22A.7
specified drugs C22A.3
statutory assumption C22A.6
drug-trafficking
confiscation order A26.20
minimum sentence A25.3
failure to attend initial/remain for initial drug assessment A23
forfeiture A25.18, B45.52, B18.19, D6.33
misuse
generally A22.1–A22.2
psychoactive substances A22.3
permitting premises to be used A27A
psychoactive substances A22.3
sample, failure to give A24

Drugs – *cont.*
'unfit through drink or drugs' C20, C21

Drunkenness
affray, and A2.10
arrest without warrant A28.4
disorderly behaviour A20.16
driving when 'unfit through drink or drugs' C20
drunk and disorderly A28
arrest without warrant A28.4
meaning A28.5
evidence A28.4
football-related offences
charges A35.1–A35.2
designated grounds and sporting events A35.5
'designated sports ground' A35.10
exceptions A35.7
general note A35.3–A35.10
period of the event A35.6
prohibited articles A35.8–A35.9
public service vehicle A35.4
prohibited articles A35.8–A35.9
sentencing A35.16–A35.17
'found' drunk A28.3
glue sniffing A28.4
highways A28
lawfulness of arrest A28.3
licensed premises A28, A28.7
motoring, in relation to
see also **Alcohol; Breath test**
driving when 'unfit through drink or drugs' C20
excess alcohol offences C22
failure to provide specimen for analysis C23
high risk offenders C22.45–C22.46
'unfit through drink and drugs', in charge of vehicle when C21
public place
generally A28
meaning A28.6

Drunkenness – *cont.*
public service vehicle carrying passengers to sporting event A35
sentencing A28.8–A28.9
sporting events A35
symptoms A28.4
violent disorder A67.8
Due care and attention
see Careless driving
Dumping
litter A83
consent of owner A83.25
public open place, meaning A83.21
sentencing A83.31–A83.34
time limit for proceedings A83.23
motor vehicles A83
burden of proof A83.5
part of A83.3, A83.11
sentencing A83.7–A83.9
Duplicity
fraudulent evasion of duty A4.7
Dwelling house
domestic burglary A12.14
found on enclosed premises A79
police cell, and A21.9
threatening behaviour, and A21.9

E

Early release
further offences B34.54–B34.55
generally B34.53
young offender institution B21.37–B21.46
Electricity
abstraction without authority
charge A1.1
definitions A1.3
dishonestly A1.3
generally A1.1
maximum penalty A1.1
mode of trial A1.2
Electricity – *cont.*
abstraction without authority – *cont.*
notes A1.3
sentencing A1.4
Electricity meters
'black boxes' A39.3
Electricity suppliers
warrants of entry
Code of Practice F5.37
consent of occupier F5.34
generally F5.31–F5.32
repair of damage F5.38
requirements F5.35–F5.36
right of entry F5.33
Electronic communications
see Communications network offences
Electronic monitoring
community orders
curfew requirement B9.14
generally B9.23
introduction B9.9
conditional bail D8.65
length of custodial sentence and B15.20
remand/committal to local authority accommodation E3.5
youth rehabilitation orders
curfew requirement B49.12
duration B49.5
exclusion requirement B49.13
generally B49.3
intensive supervision and fostering B49.4
requirement B49.22
Email
see Communications network offences
Emergency workers
aggravating seriousness of other offences A9A.5
charge A9A.1
definition A9A.3
generally A9A.2–A9A.4
sentencing A9A.6

Enclosed premises
found on A79
Endorsement of driving licence
see **Road traffic offences**
Enforcement
criminal courts charge B14.4
Entry warrants
applicants F5.1
applications by police F5.3
authority to issue
applications by police F5.3
forcible search F5.4
introduction F5.2
search for evidence F5.5
search for unlawful articles F5.4
forcible search F5.4
gas and electricity suppliers, for
Code of Practice F5.37
consent of occupier F5.34
generally F5.31–F5.32
repair of damage F5.38
requirements F5.35–F5.36
right of entry F5.33
immigration offences A81.7
issued to persons other than police officers
customs and excise officers F5.27
generally F5.25–F5.26
search for evidence of indictable offence, to
customs and excise offences F5.27
disclosure of material used to obtain warrant F5.24A
discretion to issue F5.17
excluded material F5.16
generally F5.6
indictable offence F5.8
introduction F5.5
legal privilege F5.11
premises F5.10
procedure F5.17A–F5.24A
reasonable grounds for believing F5.7
reasonable suspicion F5.7
Entry warrants – *cont.*
search for evidence of indictable offence, to – *cont.*
relevant evidence F5.9
special procedure material F5.16
search for unlawful articles, to F5.4
signature F5.39–F5.40
EU citizens
deportation B17.4
European Convention on Human Rights (ECHR)
absolute rights D1.5–D1.6
bail, and D8.2
breach D1.5–D1.8
burden of proof
firearm, carrying in a public place A33.5
firearms certificates A76.16
generally D1.8
health and safety at work A80.19
possession of a controlled drug A25.10
possession of a controlled drug with intent to supply to another A26.4D
shotgun certificate exemption A88.7
witness intimidation A69.7
decision and opinions D1.3
declaration of incompatibility D1.2
engagement of convention rights D1.5
freedom of expression
disorderly behaviour A20.5
racially aggravated behaviour A21.5A
harassment A41.10
introduction D1.1–D1.4
justices' clerks, and D9.2
legal advisers, and D9.2
limited rights D1.5–D1.6
presumption of innocence D1.8

European Convention on Human Rights (ECHR) – *cont.*
privilege against self-incrimination C8.22
procedural steps D1.5–D1.8
qualified rights D1.5–D1.6
reasons for decisions
generally D1A.1–D1A.5
reparation order B41.16
young offender institution B21.34
reasons for sentence B45.53
remands in custody and on bail D8.2
remedial orders D1.2
reporting restrictions D1B.7
restraining orders A41.13
self-incrimination C8.22
sentencing B45.53
silence C8.22
threatening behaviour
general A20.5
racially or religiously aggravated A21.5A
European investigation orders
generally F5.47B
European protection orders
giving effect elsewhere in the EU to UK protective measures B26.2
giving effect within UK B26.4
introduction B26.1
protection measures B26.2
requests from outside the UK B26.3
European supervision orders
generally D8.76
Evidence
CCTV D6.9
children and young persons, by
Bench Checklist for Young Witness cases D6.13A
clearing the court A52.10, D1B.3–D1B.5
competence A52.8
live video link E3.22, D8.22B
Evidence – *cont.*
children and young persons, by – *cont.*
reporting restrictions E2.4–E2.5, D1B.7
sexual offences, as to A52.8–A52.9, D1B.7
unsworn evidence A52.6, E3.22
youth court D1B.7
council tax recovery and enforcement F4.7–F4.8
hearsay *see* Hearsay evidence
inference drawn from failure to give D6.22
live video link *see* Live video link
open court, in
non-disclosure D1B.6
restitution orders B42.6
Excessive noise
see **Noise**
Excise licence
keeping of unlicensed vehicle C47.3–C47.17
liability for back duty C47.19–47.31
payment by dishonoured cheque C47.16
Statutory Off Road Notification (SORN) C47.17
using vehicle without C47
Exclusion orders
see also **Community orders; Drinking banning order**
actual bodily harm A8.33
licensed premises
assault A8.33
assaulting a constable A9.11
expelling persons from B27.2
generally B27.1
wounding/grievous bodily harm A70.20
period B27.1
Exclusion from school
parenting orders B37.3

Exposure
generally A30
Extended sentences
dangerous adult offenders, and B8.1

F

Failure to co-operate with roadside breath test
charge C24.1
definitions C24.2–C24.8
general note C24.2–C24.8
legal advice C24.8
motorist in hospital C24.6
reasonable excuse C24.7–C24.8
sentencing C24.9
Failure to disclose information
dishonesty A36.8
gain and loss A36.8
generally A36.8
legal duty A36.8
liability to pay council tax A36.8
mode of trial A36.5
penalty A36.4
statutory wording A36.2
Failure to produce documents
road traffic offences C17.21–17.22
Failure to produce test certificate
road traffic offences C17
Failure to provide information as to identity of driver
challenging validity of request C32A.5
charge C32A.1
defence C32A.9
definitions C32A.2–C32A.9
duty of recipient personally C32A.7
form of information C32A.6
general note C32A.2–C32A.9
ignorance is no defence C32A.8
persons required to give in formation C32A.3
Failure to provide information as to identity of driver – *cont.*
reasonable diligence C32A.9
sentencing C32A.10
service of notice C32A.4
trigger offences C32A.2
Failure to provide specimen for analysis
charge C23.1
definitions C23.2–C23.4
'fails to provide' C23.3
general note C23.2–C23.6A
legal advice C23.6A
reasonable excuse C23.4
sentencing
drive/attempt to drive C23.8
general C23.7
in charge C23.9
warning as to consequences C23.5–C23.6
Failure to report after accident
animal C32.5
charge C32.1
definitions, C32.3–C32.6
driver C32.17
failing to stop and give details after accident, and C31.3
generally C32
introduction C31.3
maximum penalty C32.1
reasonably practicable C32.18
report C32.6
roadside property C32.16
sentencing guideline C32.19
Failure to stop and give details after accident
animal C31.6
charge C31.1–C31.2
definitions C31.4–C31.16
driver C31.10
failing to report after accident, and C31.3
personal injury (to a person other then the driver) C31.16
roadside property C31.7–C31.9
sentencing guideline C31.17–C31.19

Failure to stop and give details after accident
road traffic offences C31
Failure to surrender to custody
burden of proof A10.2
charge A10.1
committal to Crown Court A10.2
defence D8.85
definitions A10.2
'fails without reasonable cause' A10.2
generally A10.1
maximum penalty A10.1
notes A10.2
penalty D8.91
procedure A10.2
prosecution A10.2, D8.82–D8.91
sentencing A10.3
'surrender to custody' A10.2
Failure to wear a helmet on a motor cycle
charge C35.1
driving C35.5
exemptions C35.6
generally C35.2
maximum penalty C35.1
protective headgear C35.4
riding on C35.3
sentencing C35.7–C5.8
False accounting
generally A31
False identity documents
generally A32
False representation
fraud, and
dishonesty A36.7
gain and loss A36.7
generally A36.6–A36.7
mode of trial A36.5
penalty A36.4
representation A36.7
statutory wording A36.1
Family relationships
controlling or coercive behaviour
Family relationships – *cont.*
controlling or coercive behaviour – *cont.*
charge A17A.1
defences A17A.3
definitions A17A.2
general note A17A.2
'ought to know' A17A.2
'personally connected' A17A.2
'same family' A17A.2
sentencing A17A.4
Fare evasion
railway fare A48
Fast-delivery or short reports
summary proceedings D6.36
Fighting dogs
generally A72.20
Financial reporting orders
fraudulent evasion of duty, and A4.18
Fines
announcement B28.26
applications for benefit deductions B28.26
assessment
sentencing process B3.1
attachment of earnings orders B28.26, B28.67, B28.76, B28.96
availability of sentence B45.25
benefit deduction orders B28.26, B28.80
Central Criminal Court, imposed by B28.84–B28.85A
collection orders
discharge by court B28.62
generally B28.26, B28.38, B28.39
community service orders and B28.83
companies B28.30–B28.31
contempt of court D3.4
Crown Courts, imposed by B28.84–B28.85A
curfew orders, and B28.83

Fines – *cont.*
custodial sentences, and B28.25A
deductions from benefits orders B28.26, B28.80
deductions from earnings orders B28.26
default of payment
culpable neglect B28.70, B28.78
generally B28.27
wilful refusal B28.70, B28.78
default sentence calculation
interest included B28.85A
determining amount
ancillary orders, order of priority B28.16
assessment of financial circumstances B28.19
compensation order and B28.16
custodial sentences, and B28.25A
expenses out of the ordinary B28.20
financial circumstances of offender B28.16
fine bands B28.16
generally B28.16–B28.25A
guilty plea, and B28.25
high income offenders B28.23
household having more than one source of income B28.22
low income/state benefits B28.18A
multiple offences B28.16
offence committed by organisation B28.24A
offence committed for 'commercial' purposes B28.24
offences outside SGC guidelines B28.16
potential earning capacity B28.23
range of fine band B28.16
reduction for guilty plea B28.25

Fines – *cont.*
determining amount – *cont.*
relevant weekly income B28.17–B28.18
savings B28.21
seriousness of offence B28.16
starting point of fine band B28.16
unusually low outgoings B28.20
enforcement
attachment of earnings orders B28.26, B28.67, B28.76, B28.96
attendance centre orders B28.76, B28.98
clamping of offender's car B28.38, B28.62
committal to prison B28.41–B28.51
county court, in B28.31
deductions from benefits orders B28.26, B28.80
deductions from earnings orders B28.26
defendant already in prison, when B28.82
detention for one day or overnight B20Z, B28.53
distress warrant B28.54, B28.76
High Court, in B28.31
immediate committal to prison B28.70
immediate enforcement B28.39–B28.61
imprisonment, by B28.41–B28.51, B28.70
means enquiry, fixing B28.61
part payments B28.38, B28.47
procedure B28.38
recognisance by parent B28.96–B28.97
referral by fines officer, as result of B28.62–B28.83
search B28.33, B28.40

Fines – *cont.*
enforcement – *cont.*
supervision orders B28.35, B28.55
suspended committal orders B28.52
suspended committal to prison B28.78
transfer for enforcement without reference back to court B28.38
transfer to High Court or county court B28.81
young offenders B28.96–B28.99
guilty plea
reduction of amount B28.25
health and safety prosecutions A80.22–A80.24
imprisonment, enforcement by B28.41–B28.51, B28.70
imprisonment for default of payment B28.27
increase in B28.63
levels B28.3
limitations B28.1–B28.18
limited companies B28.30–B28.31
maximum fine B28.2
parental responsibility for payment B28.7–B28.10, B28.95
part payments B28.38, B28.47
partnership firms B28.33
reduction for guilty plea B28.25
remission in whole or part B28.63, B28.85
reserve payment orders B28.38
road traffic offences, for
maximum C1.1
standard scale C1.1
searching for money to pay B28.33, B28.40
sentencing process B3Z
standard scale
generally B28.3–B28.4, B28.41

Fines – *cont.*
standard scale – *cont.*
road traffic offences C1.1
supervision orders B28.35, B28.55, B28.96
surcharge B10.1
suspended committal orders B28.52, B28.78
time to pay B28.26
young offenders
aged 10 to 17 B28.93–B28.95
aged 18 to 21 B28.86–B28.92
generally B28.5–B28.6
parental responsibility for payment B28.7–B28.10, B28.95
recognisance by parent B28.96–B28.97
Fines payment work
generally B28.83
Firearms
acquiring A76
air guns *see* Air guns
air weapon *see* Air weapon
ammunition *see* Ammunition
antique firearms A76.17
carrying in a public place A33
ammunition A33.10
forfeiture A33.13
sentencing A33.11–A33.13
certificates
cancellation A76.24, A77.18
exemptions A76.10
generally A76.5
purchasing etc without A76
clubs A71.6
control by more than one person A76.3
control of arms traffic A76A
forfeiture A33.13, A76.23, A77.17, A86.32, A88.10, B18.19, D6.33
gun clubs A71.6
imitation
carrying in a public place A33

Firearms – *cont.*
imitation – *cont.*
forfeiture A33.13
meaning A33.9A, A77.9A
readily convertible into firearm A33.9, A76.6, A77.8
trespassing in a building or on land and A77
lethal weapon, meaning A33.8, A76.6
meaning A33.8, A76.6–A76.7, A77.8
mental element A76.8A
police permit A76.10
possession A76
prohibition of certain weapons A76A
proprietary control A76.3
purchasing etc without certificate
forfeiture A76.23
generally A76
sentencing A76.18–A76.24
sentencing
carrying in a public place A33.11–A33.13
purchasing etc without certificate, sentencing A76.18–A76.24
trespassing in a building or on land A77.10–A77.18
shooting galleries A71.6
shotguns *see* Shotguns
starting pistols A33.9, A76.6, A77.8
stun guns A11.4
trespassing in a building or on land A77
cancellation of certificate A77.18
forfeiture A77.17
reasonable excuse A77.7
sentencing A77.10–A77.18
visitor's permit A76.10, A88.6
wrongly possessing A76.3
Fixed penalties
see **Road traffic offences**
Flick knives
generallyA11.4–A11.5
Foetus
threats to kill A59.4
Football banning orders
see also **Football-related offences**
appeals
civil orders B29.35
generally B29.32
application to terminate B29.24–B29.32
civil orders
appeals B29.35
compensation B29.36
duration B29.37
generally B29.33–B29.34
compensation B29.36
criminal orders B29.1–B29.32
criterion B29.18
declaration of relevance B29.8, B29.18
disobedience B29.18
duration
civil orders B29.37
generally B29.21
effect
further obligatory requirements B29.22A
generally A34.17, B29.22
exemption B29.23
journey to or from match B29.7
length of order B29.37
notification requirements B29.22A
offences committed abroad B29.17
police notice B29.34
procedure B29.19
prohibited activity requirement B29.18
regulated football match, meaning B29.2
relevant offence B29.4–B29.5
relevant period B29.6
remanding offenders
civil orders B29.34
generally B29.19

Football banning orders – *cont.*
repetition and propensity B29.18
reporting to police station B29.22–B29.22A
Football-related offences
see also **Football banning orders**
being or taking part at match A34.8
charges A34.1–A34.4
control of alcohol
charges A35.1–A35.2
designated grounds and sporting events A35.5
'designated sports ground' A35.10
exceptions A35.7
general note A35.3–A35.10
period of the event A35.6
prohibited articles A35.8–A35.9
public service vehicle A35.4
prohibited articles A35.8–A35.9
sentencing A35.16–A35.17
definitions A34.5–A34.11
designated football matches A34.6–A34.7
'designated sports ground' A35.10
general note A34.5–A34.11
indecent chanting A34.11
prohibited articles A35.8–A35.9
racialist chanting A34.11
sentencing A34.15–A34.17
throwing an object A34.10
ticket touting A34.6A
without lawful authority or lawful excuse A34.9
Foreign public officials
bribery of A89.2, A89.10
Foreign travel prohibition
community order requirement B9.16A
Foreign travel restriction orders
breach B44.8
generally B30.1
Forfeiture
see also **Deprivation orders**
ammunition A76.23, A86.32
compensation orders, and B10.16
deprivation orders
compensation B10.16
generally B18Z
drugs A25.18, B45.52, B18.19, D6.33
firearms A33.13, A76.23, A77.17, A88.10, B18.19, D6.33
generally B18
indecent photographs of children A43.11
motor vehicle B18.17
noise, equipment related to A84.35
personal loss or injury B18.10–B18.16
poaching, equipment for A86.32
recognisances B5.17, D8.68
sentencing B45.52, B18.7, D6.33
subject of offence, of B18Z
consideration by magistrates D6.33
drugs A25.18, B45.52, D6.33
equipment for poaching A86.32
firearms A33.13, A76.23, A77.17, A88.10, D6.33
noise, equipment related to A84.35
Forgery
compensation A78.17
false instrument
intention A78.8
making A78.7
meaning of 'false' A78.6
meaning of 'instrument' A78.5
prejudice A78.9
intention A78.8
mode of trial A78.4
prejudice A78.9

Forgery – *cont.*
sentencing A78.10–A78.17
vehicle licence/registration A64.3
Found on enclosed premises
generally A79
Fraud
abuse of position
abuse A36.9
dishonesty A36.9
generally A36.9
mode of trial A36.5
penalty A36.4
'position' A36.9
statutory wording A36.3
dishonesty A36.7
failing to disclose information
dishonesty A36.8
gain and loss A36.8
generally A36.8
legal duty A36.8
liability to pay council tax A36.8
mode of trial A36.5
penalty A36.4
statutory wording A36.2
false representation
dishonesty A36.7
gain and loss A36.7
generally A36.6–A36.7
mode of trial A36.5
penalty A36.4
representation A36.7
statutory wording A36.1
fraudulently evade duty on alcohol/tobacco A4.1
fraudulently receiving programmes F2.28
gain and loss A36.7
income tax evasion A42
making, adapting, supplying or offering to supply articles for
'black boxes' A39.3
generally A39.1
mode of trial A39.2
mode of trial A36.5
Fraud – *cont.*
obtaining services dishonestly
generally A37.1
mode of trial A37.2
sentencing A37.4
penalty A36.4
possession of articles for
computer programs A38.3
generally A38.1
mode of trial A38.2
sentencing A38.4
tax credit fraud
charge A55.1
definitions A55.3
generallyA55.1
maximum penalty A55.1
mode of trial A55.2
notes A55.3
sentencing A55.4
vehicle registration/trade plate fraud A64

G

Gambling Commission
generally F3.2
Game
see **Poaching**
Gaming licences
appeals
background F3.3
generally F3.4
Gambling Commission F3.2
general statutory changes F3.2
introduction F3.1
operating licences F3.3
personal licences F3.3
premises licences F3.3
statutory basis F3.1
Gang-related violence injunctions
appeals B35.13
applications
generally B35.6
without notice B35.7
arrest B35.11

Gang-related violence injunctions – *cont.*
attaching power of arrest B35.5
attaining 18 years after commencement of proceedings B35.8
breach B35.14
conditions B35.2
discharge B35.10
examination and report B35.12
interim injunctions B35.9
introduction B35.1
meaning B35.2
medical examination and report B35.12
power of arrest B35.5
prohibitions B35.3
remand
generally B35.11
medical examination and report, for B35.12
requirements B35.3
reviews B35.4
variation B35.10
without notice applications B35.7
Gas suppliers
warrants of entry
Code of Practice F5.37
consent of occupier F5.34
generally F5.31–F5.32
repair of damage F5.38
requirements F5.35–F5.36
right of entry F5.33
Glue sniffing
symptoms A28.4
Going equipped for theft
see also **Theft**
disqualification C5.5
generally A58
motor vehicles A58.1, C5.5, C5.33
sentencing A58.8
Goods vehicle
brakes, defective C9
dangerous condition/bodywork C10
Goods vehicle – *cont.*
definition C10.2
large, driving without appropriate licence C18.24A–C18.32
no test certificate C51
overloading/exceeding axle weight C38
Graffiti
criminal damage, as A18.22
reparation orders B41.8
Grievous bodily harm
actual bodily harm distinguished A8.9, A70.6
alternative verdict A70.19
burglary and
domestic burglary A12.3
non-domestic burglary A13.3
intent A70.5
meaning A70.6
provocation A70.7
racially or religiously aggravated A70
reduction of charge A70.19
sentencing A70.7, A70.20
sexual disease, infection through consensual sex A70.5
Guardians
binding over
Consolidated Criminal Practice Direction B5.20
generally B5.18–B5.19
Guardianship order
ancillary orders B32.6
availability of B45.34
conditions for making B32.4
effect B32.17
generally B32
minimum age B32.3
Guilty pleas
application to change D6.26
application to withdraw D6.27
fine reduction B28.25
generally D6.18
introduction D6.24
mitigating factor, as
after 'Newton' hearing B45.46

Guilty pleas – *cont.*
mitigating factor, as – *cont.*
first available opportunity B45.46
generally B45.65
introduction D6.20
overwhelming strong case B45.46
residual flexibility B45.46
revised SGC definitive guidance B45.46
nature D6.24
Newton hearing D6.24
post, by D6.40–D6.43
reduction of amount of fine B28.25
Gun clubs
generally A71.6
Guns
see **Firearms**

H

Hackers
see **Computer 'hackers'**
Handling stolen goods
consideration paid A40.11
generally A40
'goods' A40.7
handling
forms A40.6
meaning A40.4
knowledge or belief A40.8–A40.11
otherwise than in the course of stealing A40.5
sentencing A40.12
Harassment
aggravated offence A41.8B
alternative verdict A41.6
animal rights protestors A41.5
basic offence A41.8A
charges A41.1–A41.4
consultation with complainant, A41.14
Harassment – *cont.*
course of conduct A41.7–A41.8B
defences
generally A41.10–A41.11
introduction A41.8C
definitions A41.7–A41.9
disorderly behaviour A20.3A
home, in his A41.5
ECHR and A41.10
general note A41.7-A41.11
insanity, and A41.8
knows or ought to have known A41.8
mode of trial A41.6
number of incidents A41.7
person in his home, of A41.5
presumed knowledge A41.8
'purpose' A41.10
racially or religiously aggravated
charges A41.2, A41.4
generally A21.1–A21.18
introduction A41.9
restraining orders
see also **Restraining orders**
generally A41.13–A41.14
sentencing A41.11A–A41.12
stalking
aggravated offence A41.8B
defences A41.8C
generally A41.8A
telephone calls A41.7
terms of order A46.3
two or more complainants A41.7
Health and safety at work
costs of investigation A80.21
defences A80.19
fines A80.22–A80.24
mode of trial A80.5–A80.6
offences by bodies corporate A80.9
prosecution by inspectors A80.10
remedial action, power to order A80.16

Health and safety at work – *cont.*
sentencing
costs of investigation A80.21
fines A80.22–A80.24
generally A80.20
Hearsay evidence
adjournment applications D6.16
Helmet
failure to wear on motor cycle
charge C35.1
driving C35.5
exemptions C35.6
generally C35.2
maximum penalty C35.1
protective headgear C35.4
riding on C35.3
sentencing C35.7–C35.8
Highway
drunkenness on A28
meaning A85.4
obstructing A85, C36
Hospital orders
application for discharge B33.8–B33.9
availability of B45.34
conditions for making B33.1
effect B33.6
insanity plea B33.2
interim order B33.22
legal representation B33.2
public policy considerations B33.8
remand for report B33.21
renewal B33.7
restriction clause B33.10–B33.16, B33.18
Hospitals
noise or disturbance on NHS premises A74.1
Hounds
hunting with A86.8
Hours of darkness
meaning C34.16
Householder defence
actual bodily harm A8.20
dangerous dogs A72.4
Human Rights Act 1998
absolute rights D1.5–D1.6
bail, and D8.2
breach D1.5–D1.8
burden of proof
firearm, carrying in a public place A33.5
firearms certificates A76.16
generally D1.8
health and safety at work A80.19
possession of a controlled drug A25.10
possession of a controlled drug with intent to supply to another A26.4D
shotgun certificate exemption A88.7
witness intimidation A69.7
decision and opinions D1.3
declaration of incompatibility D1.2
engagement of convention rights D1.5
freedom of expression
disorderly behaviour A20.5
racially or religiously aggravated behaviour A21.5A
harassment A41.10
introduction D1.1–D1.4
justices' clerks, and D9.2
legal advisers, and D9.2
limited rights D1.5–D1.6
presumption of innocence D1.8
privilege against self-incrimination C8.22
procedural steps D1.5–D1.8
qualified rights D1.5–D1.6
reasons for decisions
generally D1A.1–D1A.5
reparation order B41.16
young offender institution B21.34
reasons for sentence B45.53
remands in custody and on bail D8.2

Human Rights Act 1998 – *cont.*
remedial orders D1.2
reporting restrictions
generally D1B.7
procedure for imposition D1B.7A
restraining orders A41.13
restrictions on access to hearing D1B.7A
self-incrimination C8.22
sentencing B45.53
silence C8.22
threatening behaviour
general A20.5
racially or religiously aggravated A21.5A
Hunting with hounds
see also **Poaching**
generally A86.8
Husband and wife
assault as consensual activity A15.16
domestic violence protection notices B23Z
domestic violence protection orders B24Z

I

Identity documents
false A32
Illegal entry
see also **Immigration offences**
generally A81.1, A81.7
Imitation firearms
carrying in a public place A33
forfeiture A33.13
meaning A33.9A, A77.9A
readily convertible into firearm A33.9, A76.6, A77.8
trespassing in a building or on land and A77
Immigration offences
arrest without warrant A81.7
asylum seekers
see Asylum seekers
Immigration offences – *cont.*
bail applications A81.17
defence based on art 31 of UN Refugee Convention A81.8A
extended time limits for prosecution A81.6
facilitating entry A81.8
illegal entrants A81.8
illegal entry A81.1, A81.7
immigration officer, definition A81.8
knowingly remaining beyond time limit A81.5
mode of trial A81.4
possession of false documents A81.3
search warrants A81.7
sentencing A81.9–A81.17
Immigration officers
generally A81.8
Imprisonment
see also **Custodial sentences; Sentencing**
age limit B34.3
ancillary orders B34.52
associated offence B34.7
attempted crimes, for B34.38
availability of B45.33
consecutive sentences B34.22–B34.32
credit for time on remand B34.39
credit for time spent on qualifying bail curfew B34.39A
criteria for imposing custodial sentence B34.4
early release
generally B34.53–37.55
young offender institution B21.37–B21.46
female defendants with children B34.6
fine enforced by B28.41–B28.51, B28.70
fines, default of payment B28.27

Imprisonment – *cont.*
immediate sentence for shortest time B15.17
intermittent custody B15.1, B21.0, B21.1
legal representation
defendant's right to B15.8, B34.19
young offenders B15.8, B21.21
length of sentence
generally B15.18–B15.20
time on remand B15.20
time spent on bail subject to condition B15.20
limitations B34.1–B34.19
mentally disturbed offenders B34.18
multiple offences B34.33–B34.34
period of imprisonment
determination B34.35–B34.39
generally B15.2
persons with no previous convictions B34.6
pre-sentence reports *see* Pre-sentence reports
presence of offender B34.2
reasons for decision B34.20
sentence, presence of accused, required B15.7
seriousness of offence B34.6
suspended sentences *see* Suspended sentences
young offender *see* Young offender
Income tax evasion
generally A42
Inconsiderate driving
causing death by C16A
driving without reasonable consideration C46
meaning C25.5
Indecency with a child
see **Sexual offences against children**
Indecent assault
see **Sexual assault**
Indecent chanting
at football match A34.11
Indecent photographs of children
age of child A43.4
defences A43.8
deletion of computer files A43.3, A43.7
distribution A43.6
downloading indecent images A43.3
evidence A43.5
forfeiture A43.1
introduction A43.1
knowledge A43.7
mode of trial A43.2
notification requirements A43.12
'photograph' A43.3
'possession' A43.3
'pop-up' cases A43.3
prohibited images A43.4A
pseudo-photographs A43.3, A43.4
sentencing A43.9
stored on computer A43.3
Individual relationships
controlling or coercive behaviour
charge A17A.1
defences A17A.3
definitions A17A.2
general note A17A.2
'ought to know' A17A.2
'personally connected' A17A.2
'same family' A17A.2
sentencing A17A.4
Injunctions
gang-related violence, for
appeals B35.13
applications B35.6–B35.7
arrest B35.11
attaching power of arrest B35.5
attaining 18 years after commencement of proceedings B35.8
breach B35.14

Injunctions – *cont.*
gang-related violence, for – *cont.*
conditions B35.2
discharge B35.10
examination and report B35.12
interim injunctions B35.9
introduction B35.1
meaning B35.2
medical examination and report B35.12
power of arrest B35.5
prohibitions B35.3
remand B35.11–B35.12
requirements B35.3
reviews B35.4
variation B35.10
without notice applications B35.7
youth injunctions
appeals B48.11
applications B48.6
arrest warrants B48.5
arrest without warrant B48.4
breach B48.9–B48.10
discharge B48.8
duration B48.3
interim injunctions B48.7
introduction B48.1
power of arrest B48.4–B48.4
power to grant B48.2
remand on breach B48.9
transitional provisions B48.12
variation B48.8
without notice applications B48.6
Insanity plea
generally B33.2
Installation or use of television receiver without licence
charge A61.1
concessions A61.8
definitions A61.2–A61.9
duration A61.7–A61.8
exemptions A61.8
generally A61.1
licence A61.5–A61.6
Installation or use of television receiver without licence – *cont.*
maximum penalty A61.1
notes A61.2–A61.9
sentencing A61.15
using A61.3–A61.4
Insulting words or behaviour *see* **Disorderly behaviour**
Insurance
causing death by driving
uninsured drivers C16B
failure to produce certificate
defences C17.19–C17.20
sentencing C17.21–C17.22
seven-day rule C17.19
driving without insurance
burden of proof C33.6
causing C33.10
employed drivers C33.17
insurance certificate C33.7
introduction C33.1
maximum penalty C33.1
Motor Insurers' Bureau C33.18–C33.22
motor vehicle C33.2
other public place C33.2
permitting C33.16
proof of insurance C33.7
road C33.2
security in respect of third party risks C33.4
sentencing C33.23–C33.31
time limit C33.5
use C33.9
using on a road or other public place C33.8
Intention
actual bodily harm A8.7–A8.8
assault with intent to resist arrest
charge A7.1
definitions A7.3
generally A7.1
maximum penalty A7.1
mode of trial A7.1
notes A7.2

Intention – *cont.*
assault with intent to resist arrest – *cont.*
sentencing A7.4
fraudulent evasion of duty A4.4
possession of offensive weapons A11.5
Interim injunctions
gang-related violence injunctions B35.9
youth injunctions B48.7
Intermittent custody
generally B15.1, B21.0, B21.1
Internet
downloading indecent images A43.3
Interpreters
costs B12.22
Intimidation of witness
generally A69
Intoxication
see also **Drunkenness**
affray A2.10
Iraq War protesters
criminal damage A18.19

J

Japanese Tosas
generally A72.20
Judicial review
application D6.48
liquor licensing policy F2.7
sending for trial E3.18C
sentencing and B38.6, B28.50
Justices' chief executive
abolition D9.5
Justices' clerk
advice in court D9.6–D9.17
case management powers D9.20
delegation D9.18–D9.20
dismissal D9.1
functions D9.3–D9.4
grant of legal representation D9.19
judicial functions D9.18
Justices' clerk – *cont.*
legal adviser distinguished D9.2
Narey Courts D9.20
role D9.3
Juvenile court
see **Youth court**
Juveniles
see also **Child; Young offender; Young person**
definition E1.1
possible orders E4

K

Keeping a brothel used for prostitution
generally A44
Kerb crawling
see also **Soliciting for prostitution**
disqualification for C5.45
Knives
see also **Bladed articles**
butterfly knife A11.13
disguised A11.5
flick knife A11.4–A11.5
folding pocket knife A11.9
stealth knife A11.4
Knowingly/knowledge
fraudulent evasion of duty A4.4–A4.5
possession of offensive weapons A11.7
Knuckle dusters
possession of offensive weapons A11.5

L

Larceny
see **Theft**
Large goods vehicle
driving without appropriate licence C18.24A–C18.32

Lavatory
  see **Public lavatory**
Lawful authority
  possession of offensive weapons A11.12–A11.13
Legal adviser
  see also **Justices' clerks**
  certificates of good repute F5.49
  compensation orders B10.10
  failure to take advice D6.28
  generally D9.2
  responsibilities D6.28
  retiring with justices D6.28
  role D6.28
Legal aid
  see also **Representation orders**
  adjournment applications D6.10
  advice and assistance D7.4
  civil legal aid D7.1
  criminal legal aid
    choice of legal representative D7.10
    contribution orders D7.11
    duty solicitor D7.12
    financial eligibility D7.7–D7.9
    generally D7.2–D7.3
    qualification D7.5–D7.6
    scope D7.4
  introduction D7.1
Legal privilege
  warrants of entry F5.11
Legal representation
  see also **Representation orders**
  costs orders B12.20
  defendant's rights B15.8, B34.19
  hospital orders B33.2
  young offenders B15.8, B21.21
Legal Services Commission
  abolition D7.1
Lending
  theft and A57.33
Licences
  see **Driving licence; Excise licence; Liquor licensing; TV licence payment evasion**
Licensed premises
  see also **Liquor licensing**
  actual bodily harm A8.33
  closure notices
    persistently selling alcohol to children F2.27
  closure orders
    appeals F2.26
    consideration hearings F2.24
    court's powers F2.25
    duration F2.23
    extension F2.25
    general power F2.21
    grounds F2.22
    hearings F2.24
    revocation F2.25
  drunkenness A28.7
  exclusion orders
    assault A8.33
    assaulting a constable A9.11
    expelling persons B27.2
    generally B27.1
Lights
  driving with defective lights
    charge C34.1– C34.4
    defences C34.18– C34.20
    exempted vehicles C34.17
    front position lamp C34.10
    'hours of darkness' C34.16
    maximum penalty C34.4
    road C34.9
    sentencing C34.21–C34.22
    using, causing or permitting C34.5– C34.7
    vehicle C34.8
Limited companies
  fines B28.30–B28.31
Liquor licensing
  see also **Licensed premises; Personal licence; Premises licence**
  appeals under Licensing Act 2003
    background F2.1–F2.5
    costs F2.20
    decision F2.19
    generally F2.6–F2.7

Liquor licensing – *cont.*
appeals under Licensing Act 2003 – *cont.*
hearing F2.14–F2.15
judicial review F2.7
notices F2.12
order of speeches F2.17–F2.18
period of notice F2.13
procedure F2.16
right to appeal F2.6
determination of application or licence F2.5
licensable activities F2.3–F2.4
Litigants in person
costs recovery B12.1
Litter
car dumping A83
consent of owner A83.25
defence A83.24
'public open place' A83.21
sentencing A83.31–A83.34
time limit for proceedings A83.23
Live video link
children and young persons E3.22, D8.22B
vulnerable accused D8.22B
vulnerable and intimidated witnesses D6.13A
witnesses in criminal proceedings D8.22C
Livestock
worrying by dogs A73
Local authority
accommodation of children/young persons in remand E3.5, E3.17
liquor licensing *see* Liquor licensing
motor vehicle 'Certificate of Ownership' C17.18
proceedings by, statutory nuisance A84.7–A84.18
YRO residence requirement B49.15
Loudspeaker in a street
*see also*Noise
Loudspeaker in a street – *cont.*
day time charge A74.6–A74.9
excessive noise A74
night time charge A74.2–A74.5

M

Magistrates
administration of oaths etc in certain probate business F5.70
certificate of good repute F5.49
driving licence applications F5.50
passport applications F5.50
recognisance F5.48
removal to suitable premises of persons in need of care and attention F5.51–F5.55
statutory declarations F5.56–F5.64
warrant to search for and remove mental patients F5.65–F5.69
Magistrates' court
committal to Crown Court for sentence
acceptance of summary trial, after B8.6–B8.7
bail, and, B8.13
conditionally discharged person convicted of further offence B8.14
dangerous adult offenders B8.1
generally B21.33
guidance B8.5
mistake in recording basis B8.10
mistaken view of the facts, on B8.11
operational period of suspended sentence, during B8.14
other errors in committal B8.12
other powers B8.14

Magistrates' court – *cont.*
committal to Crown Court for sentence – *cont.*
other than as a dangerous offender B8.2–B8.4
plea and plea before venue B8.13
pre-sentence reports B8.16
related offences, for B8.8–B8.9
suspended sentences, and B8.14–B8.15
triable either way offences, for B8.14
legal adviser D6.28, K2.1
remission to youth court B40.3–B40.4
transfer of criminal proceedings B46.1
Magistrates' Courts Committee
abolition D9.5
Making off without payment
dishonesty A45.4, A45.5
generally A45
intent to avoid payment of amount due, with A45.7
meaning of 'making off' A45.7
payment on the spot A45.6
sentencing A45.8
Malicious wounding
see **Wounding**
Married couple
see **Husband and wife**
Martial arts' weapons
generally A11.4, A11.12
Mechanically propelled vehicle
definition A66.5
Medical examination and reports
costs B12.21
custodial sentence B34.18
gang-related violence injunctions B35.12
mentally disordered offenders B15.23, B21.20, B34.18, D6.37
Mental patients
warrant to search for and remove
Mental patients – *cont.*
warrant to search for and remove – *cont.*
applications F5.66
content F5.67
duration F5.69
introduction F5.65
place of safety F5.68
Mentally disordered offenders
custodial sentence B15.23–B15.24, B34.18
guardianship order *see* Guardianship order
hospital order *see* Hospital order
insanity plea B33.2
medical reports B15.23, B21.20, B34.18, D6.37
pre-sentence reports B15.24, B21.20, B34.18
sentencing B15.23–B15.24, B32Z, B34.18, D6.37
young offender B21.20
Misadventure
actual bodily harm A8.21
Misbehaviour in court
contempt of court, and D3.1
generally D2.1
Miscarriage
threats to cause A59.4
Misleading commercial practice
generally A75
Misleading omission in commercial practice
generally A75
Mistake
fraudulent evasion of duty A4.11
getting property by A57.25
Misuse of drugs
generally A22.1–A22.2
psychoactive substances A22.3
Mobile phones
taking photographs in court D3.15
Molestation
see **Non molestation orders**

Motor cycle
driving without appropriate licence C18
failure to wear a helmet
charge C35.1
driving C35.5
exemptions C35.6
generally C35.2
maximum penalty C35.1
protective headgear C35.4
riding on C35.3
sentencing C35.7–C35.8
Motor Insurers' Bureau
compensation scheme C33.18–C33.22
Motor vehicles
aggravated vehicle-taking A66
assault involving, disqualification for C5.5
bodywork in dangerous condition C10
brakes, defective C9
braking distances C3
dangerous condition, using in C10
defective lights C34
defective steering C50
defective tyres C53
definition A63.5, A65.6, A83.4, C9.7
dumping A83
burden of proof A83.5
part of motor vehicle A83.3, A83.11
sentencing A83.7–A83.9
excise licence *see* Excise licence
forfeiture B18.17
Go-Ped C9.7
goods vehicle *see* Goods vehicle
insurance *see* Insurance
intended for use on road, meaning C9.7
interference A63
kerb crawling C5.45
lights, defective C34
no insurance C33
no test certificate C51
noise A84.3
Motor vehicles – *cont.*
obstructing the highway A85, C36
opening door C37
overloading/exceeding axle weight C38
part of, dumping A83.3
registration/trade plate fraud A64
road traffic offences *see* Road traffic offences
seat belt offences C48
shortest stopping distances C4
speed assessment equipment detection devices, breach of requirement C38A
speed and distance chart C2
speeding *see* Speeding
steering, defective C50
stopping distances C4
taking without consent A65
aggravated A66
reduction of charge from theft A57.34, A65.10
sentencing A65.18
successful defence A65.16
time limits A65.11
test certificate *see* Test certificate
theft of
disqualification for A57.40
going equipped for A58, C5.5, C5.33
reduction of charge from A65.10
trade plate fraud A64
traffic noise A84.3
tyres, defective C53
use
causing to be used, meaning C9.5
with defective brakes C9
meaning C9.4
no test certificate C51
offences C51, C53
permitting C9.6
Motoring offences
see Road traffic offences

Motorway
speeding on C49.20–C49.22
Multiplicity of charges
generally B36.1
Mutilation of animals
generally A5.2

N

Narey Courts
generally D9.20
National Health Service Premises
noise or disturbance on A74.1
Necessity defence
possession of cannabis A25.8A
Neglect of child
meaning A19.17
presumption of guilt A19.23
Newton hearing
generally A26.4, D6.24
No case to answer
generally D6.21
Noise
abatement notice A74.9
closure of premises A84.7
defence A84.34
excessive noise A74
forfeiture of equipment A84.35
National Health Service Premises A74.1
nuisance A74.9, A84.2, A84.33–A84.36
on-licensed premises F2
day time charge A74.6–A74.9
licence condition F2.19
night time charge A74.2–A74.5
operating a loudspeaker in a street A74
prejudicial to health A83.3
reasonable excuse A84.34
statutory nuisance A74.9, A84.2, A84.3, A84.33–A84.36
traffic noise A84.3
vibration A84.4
Noise – *cont.*
see also Nuisance
Non-attendance at school
generallyA49
Non-domestic burglary
see also **Domestic burglary**
aggravated A13.2
'building' A13.7
caravan, of A13.7
entering A13.6
going equipped for A58
grievous bodily harm, and A13.3
inhabited vehicle or vessel A13.7
mode of trial A13.2–A13.5
non-domestic A13
rape, and A13.3
sentencing A13.19
stealing, meaning A13.16
threatening violence A13.4
trespass A13.7, A13.17
Non molestation orders
breach
charges A46.1
definitions A46.3
duplicity A46.3
general note A46.3
mode of trial A46.2
sentencing A46.4
Not guilty pleas
absent defendants D6.19A
amendment of charge or information D6.23
application to change to D6.26
change of D6.20
inferences from silence D6.22
introduction D6.19
medical certificates D6.19A
no case to answer D6.21
post, by D6.44
silence D6.22
trial in absence D6.19
writing, in D6.44
Nuisance
see also Statutory nuisance
abatement notice A74.9, A84.8

Nuisance – *cont.*
closure orders
enforcement B6.3
generally B6.1–B6.2
generally A84

O

Oath
administration in certain probate business F5.70
witness refusing to take D3.9
youth court E3.22
see also Statutory declarations
Obstructing a court officer in execution of his duty
generally A47
Obstructing the highway
generally A85, C36
Obstructing or resisting a constable in execution of his duty
generally A47
Obtaining services dishonestly
generally A37.1
mode of trial A37.2
sentencing A37.4
Offensive conduct
see **Disorderly behaviour**
Offensive weapons, possession of
affray and A2.5
aggravated burglary
domestic A12.2
non-domestic A13.2
bladed article A11.9
butterfly knife A11.13
'carrying' A11.6
charge A11.1
controls A11.4
crossbows A11.3
curved blades A11.3
defences A11.11–A11.13
definition A11.5
disguised knives A11.5
Offensive weapons, possession of – *cont.*
flick knives A11.4, A11.5
folding pocket knife A11.9
forgetfulness as to possession A11.12–A11.13
good reason A11.12–A11.13
'have with him' A11.6
in a public place A11.8
intention A11.5
knowledge of possession A11.7
knuckle dusters A11.5
lawful authority A11.12–A11.13
martial arts' weapons A11.4, A11.12
maximum penalty A11.1
mode of trial A11.2
notes A11.3–A11.13
petrol bomb A11.5
pool cue A11.5
public place A11.8
samurai swords A11.3
school premises A11.10
'serious physical harm' A11.11
stealth knife A11.4
stun guns A11.4
threats A2.5, A11.11
unintended possession A11.13
without lawful authority A11.12–A11.13
Open court
abuse of process D1B.11–D1B.12
exceptions D1B.2
introduction D1B.1
non-disclosure of evidence D1B.6
power to clear court D1B.3
reporting of court proceedings D1B.7–D1B.10
Operating licences
betting and gambling F3.3
Overloading/exceeding axle weight
generally C38

P

Parental responsibility
fines, for B28.7–B28.10, B28.95
Parenting contracts for criminal conduct/anti-social behaviour
generally B37.4
Parenting orders
appeal right B37.12
criteria B37.1
discharge B37.9
duty to explain B37.7
duty to obtain and consider information B37.6
exclusion from school B37.3
offenders under 16 B37.2
penalty for non-compliance B37.10
'relevant condition' B37.5
requirements B37.8
responsible officer B37.11
truancy B37.3
variation B37.9
Parents
binding over
Consolidated Criminal Practice Direction B5.20
generally B5.18–B5.19
recognisance
binding over B5.18–B5.19
fines B28.96–B28.97
responsibility for fines of child B28.7–B28.10, B28.95
Parking
lights C34
obstruction C36
Partnerships
enforcement of fines B28.33
theft of partnership property A57.36
Passenger
seat belt offences C48
Passport
see also **Immigration offences**
possession of false passport A81.3
Passport – *cont.*
signature of application by magistrate F5.50
Pedal cycles
taking without consent A65
Pedestrian crossings
pelican/zebra crossing contravention C39
stopping on C40
Penalty points
fixed penalties C8
generally C5.10–C5.38, C8.20
mitigating
grounds C5.24–C5.31
period of disqualification C5.22–C5.23
points to be taken into account C5.20–C5.21
totting ban C5.20
see also Road traffic offences
Personal injuries
compensation orders, and
generally B10.2
guidelines B10.19
Personal licences
betting and gambling F3.3
liquor licensing
advertising of applications F2.2
duration F2.2
grant F2.5
forfeiture or suspension B31Z
Persons in need of care and attention
order for removal to suitable premises
duration F5.54–F5.55
generally F5.51–F5.53
Petrol bombs
possession of offensive weapons A11.5
Photographs
see also **Indecent photographs**
concealed cameras A20.9
court proceedings, in
generally D1B.9
penalties D3.4
mobile phone, by D3.15

Pit bull terriers
generally A72.20
Pleas
see **Guilty plea; Not guilty plea**
Poaching
day-time offence A86.1–A86.8A
forfeiture of equipment A86.32
'game' A86.6, A86.17
generally A86
hunting with hounds A86.8
night-time offences A86.9–A86.22A
seizure of equipment/game/rabbits A86.31
sentencing A86.31–A86.32A
three or more together A86.22
Pointed articles
see **Bladed article; Knives**
Police
see also **Police constables**
closure orders F2
forfeiture of articles to B18.5
property in possession of
application of provisions F1.3–F1.6
case unsuitable for magistrates' courts F1.17–F1.18
costs F1.20
'delivered' F1.10
deprivation orders, and F1.21
execution of search warrant, after F1.19
generally F1.2–F1.20
hearing F1.6
introduction F1.1
powers of magistrates F1.7–F1.9
risk of sexual harm order A52.16
sex offenders' notifications to A52.14, A53.9
Police bail
after charge D8.57–D8.60
before charge D8.56
street bail D8.55
Police constables
assault in the execution of his duty
alternative verdict A9.9
burden of proof A9.7
charge A9.1
constable A9.3
definitions A9.2–A9.9
execution of his duty A9.5–A9.8
licensed premises, and A9.11
maximum penalty A9.1
notes A9.2–A9.9
plain clothes officers carrying out drugs search A9.8
reasonable expectation of breach of the peace A9.5
reduction of charge A9.9
search of defendant A9.8
sentencing A9.10
obstructing a person assisting A47
obstructing or resisting in the execution of his duty
burden of proof A47.13
private premises A47.12
rank A47.10
special constable A47.10
unlawful arrest A47.11
Police station
detention for one day or overnight at B20Z, B28.53
Pornography
see also **Child pornography**
meaning A14.3
Possession of articles for fraud
computer programs A38.3
generally A38.1
mode of trial A38.2
sentencing A38.4
Possession of a controlled drug
see also **Drugs**
burden of proof
ECHR and A25.10
generally A25.9
cannabis A25.11

Possession of a controlled drug – *cont.*
defences
burden of proof A25.9–A25.10
common law defence of necessity A25.8A
generally A25.8
medical condition A25.8A
expert examination A25.6
factual element A25.7
forfeiture A25.18, B45.52, D6.33
identification of substance A25.7A
intent to supply to another, with
aggravation of offence A26.4C
appeal A26.16
'being concerned in supplying' A26.4A
closure orders A26.12
costs A26.17
crack houses A26.12
defences A26.4D
drug-trafficking A26.20
ECHR and A26.4D
generally A26
intention A26.4
involuntary keeper of drugs A26.4
offer to supply A26.4B
sentencing A26.5–A26.20
'supply' A26.4A
lack of knowledge A25.7
maximum penalty A25.1
mental element A25.7
possession A25.7
quantity A25.5
sentencing A25.16–A25.18

Possession of air guns by person under 18
adult supervision A71.5
'air weapon' A71.3
age limit A71.5
charge A71.1
clubs and shooting galleries A71.6
definitions A71.2–A71.6
failing to prevent
charge A71A.1
definitions A71A.2
general note A71A.2
sentencing A71A.3
fines A71.8
forfeiture A33.13, A71.1
general note A71.2–A71.6
generally A76.7
'possession' A71.2
private premises A71.5
'public place' A71.4–A71.6
sentencing A71.7–A71.8
trespassing in a building or on land A77.9

Possession of extreme pornographic images
see also **Child pornography**
defences A14.1A
'extreme images' A14.1A
generally A14.1A
'image' A14.1A
maximum penalty A14.1A
'pornographic' A14.1A
'relevant act' A14.1A

Possession of offensive weapons
affray and A2.5
aggravated burglary
domestic A12.2
non-domestic A13.2
bladed article A11.9
butterfly knife A11.13
'carrying' A11.6
charge A11.1
controls A11.4
crossbows A11.3
curved blades A11.3
defences A11.11–A11.13
definition A11.5
disguised knives A11.5
flick knives A11.4, A11.5
folding pocket knife A11.9
forgetfulness as to possession A11.12–A11.13

Possession of offensive weapons – *cont.*
good reason A11.12–A11.13
'have with him' A11.6
in a public place A11.8
intention A11.5
knowledge of possession A11.7
knuckle dusters A11.5
lawful authority A11.12–A11.13
martial arts' weapons A11.4, A11.12
maximum penalty A11.1
mode of trial A11.2
notes A11.3–A11.13
petrol bomb A11.5
pool cue A11.5
public place A11.8
samurai swords A11.3
school premises A11.10
'serious physical harm' A11.11
stealth knife A11.4
stun guns A11.4
threats A2.5, A11.11
unintended possession A11.13
without lawful authority A11.12–A11.13
Post-release supervision
custodial sentences B15.22A
Powers of attorney
theft of land A57.18
Pre-sentence reports
adjournment to obtain D6.34
committal to Crown Court for sentence B8.16
community orders B45.50
conditional bail and D8.62
custodial sentences B15.21–B15.22, B34.16–B34.18
failure to obtain B21.19, B34.17
generally D6.34–D6.35
imprisonment B34.16–B34.18
mentally disordered offenders B15.24, B21.20, B34.18
purpose D6.35
Pre-sentence reports – *cont.*
young offenders institution B21.17–B21.19
youth court D6.39
Premises closure orders
see **Closure orders**
Premises licences
betting and gambling licensing F3.3
fraudulently receiving programmes F2.28
liquor licensing
advertising of applications F2.2
appeals under Licensing Act 2003 F2.1
licensable activities F2.3–F2.4
Premises notices
psychoactive substances B38A.4
Premises orders
psychoactive substances
appeals B38A.10
applications B38A.7
content B38A.8
generally B38A.6
introduction B38A.1
non compliance offences B38A.9
prohibited activity B38A.2
variation B38A.10
Press restrictions
see **Reporting restrictions**
Previous convictions
animal cruelty A5.4
anti-social behaviour orders B2.6
sentencing B45.3, B45.40, D6.32
Prison
see **Imprisonment**
Private sexual images
disclosure with intent to cause distress
charge A19A.1
'consent' A19A.2
defences A19A.3
definitions A19A.2
'discloses' A19A.2

Private sexual images – *cont.*
disclosure with intent to cause distress – *cont.*
'filming' A19A.2
general note A19A.2
'photograph or film' A19A.2
'private' A19A.2
sentencing A19A.4
'sexual' A19A.2
Probate business
administration of oath F5.70
Proceeds of crime
appeals F5.47A
assault of officers F5.46A
cash
generally F5.47
legislative changes F5.46A
confiscation A26.20
confiscation orders
generally B11.1
term in default B11.2
detention of seized cash F5.47
European investigation orders F5.47B
forfeiture of money
generally F5.47
legislative changes F5.46A
further information orders F5.46A
grounds for detention order F5.47
introduction F5.46A
legal aid F5.47A
legislative changes F5.46A
minimum amount F5.47
notice of forfeiture proceedings F5.47A
obstruction of officers F5.46A
recoverable property F5.47A
search power F5.47
seizure and recovery of property F5.46A
unlawful conduct
generally F5.47A
legislative changes F5.46A
Professional diligence
commercial practices contrary to A75
Prohibited commercial practices
generally A75
Prohibition notices
psychoactive substances B38A.3
Prohibition orders
generally A84.22
psychoactive substances
appeals B38A.10
applications B38A.7
content B38A.8
generally B38A.5
introduction B38A.1
overview A87.9
non compliance offences B38A.9
prohibited activity B38A.2
variation B38A.10
sentencing A87.6–A87.10
Property
arson A18
'belonging to another person' A18.23–A18.24
criminal damage A18
definition A18.21
deprivation orders B18Z
destroying or damaging
arson A18
criminal damage A18
possessing anything with intent to destroy or damage property A18B
threatening to destroy or damage property A18A
forfeiture *see* Forfeiture
mistake, by A57.25
possession of police, in
application of provisions F1.3–F1.6
case unsuitable for magistrates' courts F1.17–F1.18
costs F1.20
'delivered' F1.10

Property – *cont.*
possession of police, in – *cont.*
deprivation orders, and F1.21
execution of search warrant, after F1.19
generally F1.2–F1.20
hearing F1.6
introduction F1.1
powers of magistrates F1.7–F1.9
reasonable force defence A8.18–A8.20
roadside *see* Roadside property
stolen *see* Stolen goods
trust property
generally A18.24
theft A57.23
wild creatures as A18.21
Property in possession of police
application for order for delivery
application of provisions F1.3–F1.6
case unsuitable for magistrates' courts F1.17–F1.18
costs F1.20
'delivered' F1.10
deprivation orders, and F1.21
execution of search warrant, after F1.19
generally F1.2–F1.20
hearing F1.6
introduction F1.1
powers of magistrates F1.7–F1.9
conversion proceedings B18.5
deprivation orders, and F1.21
execution of search warrant, after F1.19
Prosecution costs
central funds B12.3
breach or revocation of community orders, and B12.23
generally B12.3–B12.15
health and safety at work A80.21
Prosecution costs – *cont.*
introduction B12.3
monetary penalty not exceeding £5 B12.9
ordering accused to pay B12.8
private prosecutors B12.4–B12.6
proportionate to maximum penalty B12.8
reducing amount of prosecutor's order B12.7
youths B12.10
Prostitution
child prostitution
charges A14.1
definitions A14.3–A14.5
maximum penalty A14.1
mode of trial A14.2
notes A14.3–A14.5
'payment' A14.5
'pornography' A14.3
'prostitute' A14.4
sentencing A14.6
closure orders, and
appeals B7.5
compensation B7.6
costs B7.6
criteria B7.2
discharge B7.4
enforcement B7.3
extension B7.4
generally B7.1
offences B7.3
variation B7.4
exploitation A29
keeping a brothel used for A44
kerb crawling C5.45
paying for services of prostitute subjected to force A29.2–A29.2A, A82.1
'prostitute' A14.4, A82.2
soliciting A29.1, A82
Protective orders
breach
charges A46.1
definitions A46.3

Protective orders – *cont.*
breach – *cont.*
duplicity A46.3
general note A46.3
mode of trial A46.2
sentencing A46.4
variation A46.5
Provisional driving licence
learner plates, display C18.3
supervision C18.3, C18.5
Provocation
actual bodily harm A8.17
assault A15.32
grievous bodily harm A70.7
Psychoactive substances
aggravation of offences A87.5
charges A87.2
definitions A87.4
forfeiture A87.8
introduction A87.1
legal notes A87.4
misuse of drugs A22.3
mode of trial A87.3
premises notices B38A.4
premises orders
appeals B38A.10
applications B38A.7
content B38A.8
generally B38A.6
introduction B38A.1
non compliance offences B38A.9
prohibited activity B38A.2
variation B38A.10
prohibition notices B38A.3
prohibition orders
appeals B38A.10
applications B38A.7
content B38A.8
generally B38A.5
introduction B38A.1
overview A87.9
non compliance offences B38A.9
prohibited activity B38A.2
variation B38A.10
sentencing A87.6–A87.10
Psychological damage
actual bodily harm A8.9
Public electronic communications
see **Communications network offences**
Public lavatories
sexual activity in
charge A51.1
definitions A51.2
maximum penalty A51.1
notes A51.2
sentencing A51.3
Public order
affray A2
disorderly behaviour A20
harassment *see* Harassment
threatening behaviour A21
violent disorder A67
Public place
car park of dealership C25.4
dangerous dogs A72.3–A72.4
drunkenness A28
firearms
air guns A33, A71.4
carrying A33
litter in A83.21
possession of offensive weapons
generally A11.8
school premises A11.10
sexual activity in a public lavatory
charge A51.1
definitions A51.2
maximum penalty A51.1
notes A51.2
sentencing A51.3
soliciting for prostitution A29.1, A82
telephone kiosk A83.21
Public service vehicles
carrying passengers to sporting event, control of alcohol on A35
meaning A35.4
Public spaces protection orders
generally B8A.6–B8A.12
introduction B8A.1

Publicly funded representation
adjournment applications D6.10
advice and assistance D7.4
civil legal aid D7.1
criminal legal aid
choice of legal representative D7.10
contribution orders D7.11
duty solicitor D7.12
financial eligibility D7.7–D7.9
generally D7.2–D7.3
qualification D7.5–D7.6
scope D7.4
introduction D7.1
Punishment of child
reasonable chastisement A15.16–A15.18, A19.5

R

Racialist chanting
at football match A34.11
Racially aggravated crimes
actual bodily harm A8.1–A8.34
common assault
see also **Common assault**
charge A15.2
maximum penalty A15.2
meaning A15.7
sentencing A15.33–A15.34
criminal damage A18.16–A18.18
disorderly behaviour A21.1–A21.18
'foreigners' as racial group A18.17, A21.10
grievous bodily harm and malicious wounding A70
harassment
generally A41
intent to cause A21.1–A21.18
'racial or religious aggravation' A15.7, A18.17–A18.18, A20.6
Racially aggravated crimes – *cont.*
sentencing A15.33, A20.19, A21.16–A21.17, B45.2B
threatening behaviour A21.1–A21.18
words used
generally A18.17, A20.6, A21.10
victim's perception of A8.16, A18.18
Railway fare evasion
generally A48
Rape
bail in cases of D8.32
burglary and
domestic A12.3
non-domestic A13.3
reporting restrictions D1B.7
Reasonable chastisement
actual bodily harm A8.22
generally A15.16–A15.18
Reasonable diligence
failure to provide information as to identity of driver C32A.9
Reasonable excuse
breach of anti-social behaviour orders B2.4
breach of community order by failure to comply A17.2
breach of criminal behaviour orders B2.4
failure to co-operate with roadside breath test C24.7–C24.8
failure to provide specimen for analysis C23.4
noise A84.34
statutory nuisance A84.17
trespassing in a building or on land A77.7
Reasonable force
actual bodily harm A8.18–A8.20
Reasonable punishment
generally A19.5
Reasons for decisions
generally D1A.1–D1A.5

Reasons for decisions – *cont.*
reparation order B41.16
young offender institution B21.34
Receiving
see **Stolen goods**
Recklessness
assault A8.7, , A70.5
common assault A15.4
criminal damage A18.31
driving, reckless *see* Dangerous driving
meaning A18.31
wounding A70.5
Recognisance
binding over
complainant, by B5.8
forfeiture B5.17
parent or guardian, by B5.18–B5.19
refusal to enter into B5.6, B5.20
witness, by B5.8
conditional bail, and D8.66–D8.68
forfeiture B5.17, D8.68
generally F5.48
parent or guardian, by
binding over B5.18–B5.19
ensure payment of fine, to B28.96–B28.97
Referral order
ancillary orders B39.6
appropriate officer B39.7
attendance of parent or guardian B39.7
breach B39.10
compulsory referral conditions B39.7
connected offence B39.7
discharge B39.9
discretionary referral conditions B39.7
extension B39.9
previous conviction B39.7
prohibited orders B39.8
variation B39.9
Refugees
see **Asylum seekers**
Registration cards
see also **Immigration offences**
possession of false A81.3
Religiously aggravated crimes
see also **Racially aggravated crimes**
actual bodily harm A8.1–A8.34
common assault
see also **Common assault**
charge A15.2
maximum penalty A15.2
meaning A15.7
sentencing A15.33– A15.34
criminal damage A18.16–A18.18
disorderly behaviour A20, A21
'foreigners' as racial group A18.17, A21.10
grievous bodily harm and malicious wounding A70
harassment
generally A41
intent to cause A21.1–A21.18
'racial or religious aggravation' A15.7, A18.17–A18.18, A20.6
sentencing A15.33, A20.19, A21.16, A21.17, B45.2B
threatening behaviour A21.1–A21.18
words used
generally A18.17, A20.6, A21.10
victim's perception of A8.16, A18.18
Remand
see also **Remand on bail**
gang-related violence injunctions
generally B35.11
medical examination and report, for B35.12
introduction D8.1
Remand in custody
absence of accused, in D8.21–D8.23

Remand in custody – *cont.*
adjournment of hearing, where D8.1
children E3.4
local authority accommodation E3.5, E3.17
secure accommodation E3.7–E3.8
youth detention accommodation E3.6
custody time limits
application to extend D8.52
expiry D8.54
generally D8.51–D8.54
decision whether to D8.24–D8.25
ECHR and D8.2
exceptions to right to bail D8.26–D8.33
Human Rights Act, and D8.5
introduction D8.1
length
after conviction D8.19
before conviction D8.16–D8.18
deduction from sentence B34.39
time limits D8.51–D8.54
pending appeal D8.93
required, where D8.7–D8.10
secure accommodation E3.7–E3.8
send to Crown Court D8.20
time limits
application to extend D8.52
expiry D8.54
generally D8.51–D8.54
young persons
generally E3.4
local authority accommodation E3.5, E3.17
secure accommodation E3.7–E3.8
youth detention accommodation E3.6
Remand on bail
see also Remand in custody

Remand on bail – *cont.*
absence of accused, in D8.21–D8.23
adjournment of hearing, where D8.1, D8.18
after conviction D8.19
appeals
against conditions D8.79
prosecution right D8.33
asylum seekers facing criminal charges A81.17
before conviction D8.18
children and young persons E3.4
circumstances D8.7–D8.10
conditional bail
appeals D8.79
application to vary bail conditions D8.80
common conditions D8.63
court bail D8.61–D8.70
effectiveness of conditions D8.70
electronic monitoring D8.65
failure to comply with condition D8.92
generally D8.31
hostel rules, compliance with D8.65
introduction D8.4
police bail D8.55–D8.60
pre-sentence report D8.62
recognisance of surety D8.66–D8.68, F5.48
decision whether to D8.24–D8.25
depositing a security D8.69
drug users D8.30
duration
after conviction D8.19
before conviction D8.18
ECHR, challenges under D8.2
electronic monitoring D8.65
exceptions to right
conditions to be imposed where bail granted D8.31

Remand on bail – *cont.*
exceptions to right – *cont.*
custody time limits D8.51–D8.54
drug users D8.30
generally D8.26
homicide/rape after previous conviction D8.32
imprisonable offences D8.27–D8.28, D8.32
no real prospect of custodial sentence D8.26
non-imprisonable offences D8.29
prosecution right of appeal D8.33
failure to comply with condition D8.92
failure to surrender to custody
burden of proof A10.2
charge A10.1
committal to Crown Court A10.2
defence D8.85
definitions A10.2
'fails without reasonable cause' A10.2
generally A10.1
maximum penalty A10.1
notes A10.2
penalty D8.91
procedure A10.2
prosecution for A10.2, D8.82–D8.91
sentencing A10.3
'surrender to custody' A10.2
further offences on bail D8.2
homicide cases D8.32
Human Rights Act, and D8.2–D8.96
immigration offences A81.17
imprisonable offences
generally D8.27
homicide or rape D8.32
summary only D8.28
introduction D8.1

Remand on bail – *cont.*
length of remand on
after conviction D8.19
before conviction D8.18
live video links
generally D8.22A
vulnerable accused D8.22B
non-imprisonable offences D8.29
opposed bail, grant of D8.25
pending appeal D8.93
plea before venue B8.13
police bail
after charge D8.57–D8.60
before charge D8.56
street bail D8.55
presumption of liberty D8.24
prosecution right of appeal D8.33
rape cases D8.32
recognisance of surety D8.66–D8.68, F5.48
refusal
appeals D8.79
application to Crown Court judge in chambers D8.79
further application after D8.77–D8.78
relevant circumstances D8.7–D8.10
remission to another court on B40.2
residence conditions, appeals D8.79
security deposit D8.69
sending to Crown Court, when D8.20
street bail D8.55
sureties D8.66–D8.68, F5.48
unconditional bail D8.3
video remands
generally D8.22A
vulnerable accused D8.22B
young offenders D8.6, D8.32
Remedial orders
human rights, and D1.2
Remission
bail or in custody B40.2

Removal to suitable premises of persons in need of care and attention
duration F5.54–F5.55
generally F5.51–F5.53
Reparation order
breach B41.17–B41.18
direct or indirect reparation B41.8
generally B38
limitations B41.1–B41.2
maximum periods B41.3–B41.4
reasons, giving B41.16
reparation in kind B41.9
reports B41.5, B41.8
Reporting restrictions
address of service police officer D1B.7
anonymity of witness D1B.7
anti-social behaviour orders, and E2.4
children and young persons D1B.7
identification of witnesses D1B.7
live, text-based communications D1B.8
matters exempted from disclosure in court D1B.7
photographs and sketches of court D1B.9
postponing publication of reports of court proceedings D1B.7
procedure for imposition D1B.7A
rape and sexual offences D1B.7
sexual offences against children A52.11
social media D1B.8
Twitter D1B.8
youth court D1B.2
Representation orders
choice of legal representative D7.10
contribution orders D7.11
duty solicitor D7.12
Representation orders – *cont.*
financial eligibility D7.7–D7.9
generally D7.2–D7.3
qualification D7.5–D7.6
scope D7.4
Reserve payment orders
generally B28.38
Resist arrest
assault with intent to A7
Resisting a constable
execution of duty, in A47
Restitution orders
evidence B42.6
generally B39
innocent purchasers B42.4
Restraining orders
see also **Harassment**
acquittal, on A41.13
breach of
charges A46.1
definitions A46.3
duplicity A46.3
general note A46.3
mode of trial A46.2
sentencing A46.4
conviction, on A41.13
ECHR and A41.13
generally A41.13–A41.14
human rights issues A41.13
terms of order A46.3
variation A46.5
Restriction clause
included in hospital order B33.10–B33.16
Restriction orders
see **Football banning orders**
Revenue and Customs
alcohol/tobacco, fraudulently evade duty A4
income tax evasion A42
search warrants F5.27
VAT evasion A62
Review of decisions
civil proceedings B38.6

Review of decisions – *cont.*
criminal proceedings B38.1–B38.5
Risk of sexual harm orders
sexual offences against children A52.16
Road fund licences
see Excise licences
Road traffic offences
see also Alcohol; Drunkenness
brakes, as to C9
careless driving
see Careless driving
causing death by driving
careless or inconsiderate driving C16A
disqualified drivers C16D
unlicensed, disqualified or uninsured drivers C16B
causing serious injury by dangerous driving
charge C16C.1
definitions C16C.3
legal notices C16C.3
maximum penalty C16C.1
mode of trial C16C.2
sentencing C16C.4
causing serious injury by driving (disqualified drivers)
charge C16D.1
maximum penalty C16D.1
mode of trial C16D.2
dangerous condition/bodywork, using in C10
dangerous driving
see Dangerous driving
defective brakes C9
defective lights C34
defective steering C50
defective tyres C53
driving licence
see Driving licence
driving when 'unfit through drink or drugs'
*see also*Drunkenness
generally C20
driving whilst disqualified C19
Road traffic offences – *cont.*
drugs, in connection with *see* Drugs
due care and attention, driving without
see Careless driving
endorsement and disqualification B45.52, C5
appeal against C5.36
assault involving motor vehicle C5.5
combined disqualification and custodial sentence C5.7–C5.8
commencement of disqualification C5.8
compulsory endorsement C5.1, C5.32
Crown Court, disqualification by C5.40
dangerous driving C16.21
defective brakes C9.16A
disability C5.49
discretionary C5.20, C5.38
discretionary disqualification C5.20, C5.38
disqualification for any offence C5.45
disqualification for life C5.9
disqualification pending sentence C5.39
driving licence codes C6.1
driving off road unlawfully C5.45
driving test, order to take C5.37–C5.38
driving whilst disqualified C19
endorsement code C6.2
foreign licence C5.1
immediate effect C5.35
interim disqualification C5.39
length of disqualification C5.6, C5.22–C5.23
mandatory disqualification C5.4, C5.10, C5.33, C5.37
mitigating grounds C5.24–C5.31

Road traffic offences – *cont.*
endorsement and disqualification – *cont.*
new drivers, effect of endorsement on C5.46–C5.48
offences for which imposed C6.2
penalty points system C5.10–C5.38
period of disqualification C5.6, C5.22–C5.23
reduced for attendance on course C22.56–C22.61
sentence code C7
special reasons C5.2–C5.3, C5.33, C5.34, C9.16A, C9.17, C22.24–C22.25, C22.50
theft of vehicle and A57.40
exceeding axle weight C38
excess alcohol, drive/attempt to drive or in charge C22
excise licence
keeping of unlicensed vehicle C47.3–C47.17
liability for back duty C47.19–47.31
no excise licence C47
failing to produce documents C17.21–17.22
failure to produce test certificate C17
failure to provide specimen for analysis
drive/attempt to drive C23.8
in charge C23.9
introduction C23.7
failing to report after accident C31.3, C32
failing to stop and give details after accident C31
fines
maximum C1.1
standard scale C1.1
fixed penalties C8
conditional offer C8.21–C8.22

Road traffic offences – *cont.*
fixed penalties – *cont.*
endorsable offences C8.6–C8.8
enforcement of payment C8.19
graduated C8.8
instituting proceedings C8.16
non-endorsable offences C8.5
not paid, where C8.17–C8.18
offering C8.4–C8.8
payment C8.9–C8.10, C8.19
penalty points C8.20
index C1
insurance *see* Insurance
large goods vehicles, driving without appropriate licence C18.24A–C18.32
lights, defective C34
mitigating grounds C5.2–C5.3, C5.24–C5.31
motor cycle offences
driving without licence C18
not wearing helmet C35
name and address, duty to give C31
no test certificate C51
non-endorsable C8.5
obstruction A85, C36
opening door C37
overloading/exceeding axle weight C38
pedestrian crossing
see **Pedestrian crossing**
penalties C1
penalty points system C5.10–C5.38
fixed penalties C8.20
graduated fixed penalty points scheme C8.8
provisional licences, as to C18
reasonable consideration, driving without C46
recklessness
see **Dangerous driving**
seat belt offences C48
sentence code C7

Road traffic offences – *cont.*
sentencing
careless driving C25.20–C25.21
causing death by careless or inconsiderate driving C16A.10
dangerous condition/bodywork C10.7–C10.9
dangerous driving C16.18–C16.22
death by inconsiderate driving, causing C16A.10
defective brakes C9.16–C9.20
defective lights C34.21–C34.22
disqualification pending C5.39
driving licence offences C17.21–C17.22, C18.21–C18.32
driving when 'unfit through drink or drugs' C20.19–C20.20
driving whilst disqualified C19.8–C19.17
excess alcohol, drive/attempt to drive or in charge C22.32–22.61, C22.65
failing to produce documents C17.21–17.22
failing to stop/report accident C31.17–C31.19
failure to co-operate with roadside breath test C24.9
failure to provide specimen for analysis C23.7–C23.9
insurance certificate, failure to produce C17.21–C17.22
motor cyclist not wearing helmet C35.7–C35.8
no excise licence C47.18
no insurance C33.23–C33.31
no test certificate C51
obstruction C36.10–C36.16
opening door C37.7–C37.9

Road traffic offences – *cont.*
sentencing – *cont.*
overloading/exceeding axle weight C38.20–C38.21
pelican/zebra crossing contravention C39.20–C39.21
penalty points system C5.10–C5.38
reasonable consideration, driving without C46.19–C46.23
seat belt offences C48.19
speeding C49.36–C49.37
steering, defective C50.4
stopping on pedestrian crossing C40.10–C40.17
traffic signs, failing to comply with C52.17–C52.18
tyres, defective C53.7–C53.8
'unfit through drink or drugs', driving when C20.19–C20.20
unlicensed, disqualified or uninsured drivers, causing death by driving C16B.6
speed and distance chart C2
speeding
see **Speeding**
steering, defective C50
test certificates
failure to produce C17
no test certificate C51
traffic sign, failure to comply with C52
tyres, defective C53
Roadside property
damage to
failure to report C31.3, C32
failure to stop and give details after C31
meaning C31.7, C32.16

S

Sado-masochistic activities
assault A15.11

Safety at work
see Health and safety at work
Sale of alcohol
allowing sale to children A3.3
charge A3.1–A3.3
children, to A3.2
definitions A3.4
maximum penalty A3.3
notes A3.4
person who is drunk, to A3.1
sentencing A3.5
Samurai swords
possession of offensive weaponsA11.3
Sawn-off shotgun
possession A76.18
School exclusion
parenting orders B37.3
School non-attendance
generallyA49
School premises
possession of offensive weapons A11.10
Search
bladed articles/offensive weapons on school premises A11.10
enforcement of fines B28.33, B28.40
Search warrants
applicants F5.1
applications by police F5.3
authority to issue
applications by police F5.3
forcible search F5.4
introduction F5.2
search for evidence F5.5
search for unlawful articles F5.4
customs and excise officers F5.27
evidence of indictable offence, for
customs and excise offences F5.27
disclosure of material used to obtain warrant F5.24A
discretion to issue F5.17
Search warrants – *cont.*
evidence of indictable offence, for – *cont.*
excluded material F5.16
generally F5.6
indictable offence F5.8
introduction F5.5
legal privilege F5.11
premises F5.10
procedure F5.17A–F5.24A
reasonable grounds for believing F5.7
reasonable suspicion F5.7
relevant evidence F5.9
special procedure material F5.16
forcible search F5.4
gas and electricity suppliers, for
Code of Practice F5.37
consent of occupier F5.34
generally F5.31–F5.32
repair of damage F5.38
requirements F5.35–F5.36
right of entry F5.33
immigration offences A81.7
issued to persons other than police officers
customs and excise officers F5.27
generally F5.25–F5.26
Proceeds of Crime 2002, and F5.47
signature F5.39–F5.40
unlawful articles, for F5.4
Seat belt offences
generallyC48
Security
deposit as condition of bail D8.69
Security for good behaviour
conditional discharge B5.20
Self-defence
actual bodily harm A8.18–A8.20
assault
causing actual bodily harm A8.18–A8.20
onus of proof A15.19

Self-defence – *cont.*
attempt to retreat or call off fight A8.18
bladed articles/offensive weapons
possession A11.12–A11.13
reasonable force A8.18–A8.20
threats to kill A59.3
Self-incrimination
privilege against C8.22
Sending for trial
see **Allocation and sending for trial**
Sentencing
absolute discharge
availability B45.24
generally B22Z
sexual assault A53.9
sexual offences against children A52.14
abstracting electricity without authority A1.4
actual bodily harm A8.31–A8.32
affray A2.15
age of offender as mitigating factor B45.38, B45.39
aggravating factors
disability B45.2B
generally B15.10
list B45.2A
race B45.2B
religion B45.2B
sexual orientation B45.2B
transgender identity B45.2B
alcohol sale offences A3.5
alcohol
fraudulent evasion of duty A4.16–A4.18
ancillary orders D6.33
animals
cruelty A5.3–A5.4
disqualification from keeping A5.5
announcement of sentence D6.31
ASBO B2Z

Sentencing – *cont.*
assault
actual bodily harm A8.31–A8.32
common assault A15.33–A15.34
constable in execution of duty, on A9.10
court security officers in execution of duty, on A9.10
emergency workers, on A9A.6
intent to resist arrest, with A7.4
racially or religiously aggravated A15.33
associated offence B45.9
attendance centre orders B4Z
availability of sentences B45.21–B45.35
bail
failure to surrender A10.3
binding over B5Z
bladed articles
possession A11.15
brothel-keeping A44.4
breach of community orders
approach and options A17.3
guideline B9.27
burglary
domestic A12.20
non-domestic A13.19
causing serious injury
dangerous driving, by C16C.4
driving by disqualified drivers, by C16D.1
child cruelty A19.32–A19.34
child pornography A14.6
child prostitution A14.6
choice of sentence B45.50–B45.52
coercive behaviour in intimate or family relationship A17A.4
commercial practices
unfair or prohibited A75.7–A75.10

Sentencing – *cont.*
committal to Crown Court
acceptance of summary trial, after B8.6–B8.7
bail, and, B8.13
conditionally discharged person convicted of further offence B8.14
dangerous adult offenders B8.1
guidance B8.5
mistake in recording basis B8.10
mistaken view of the facts, on B8.11
operational period of suspended sentence, during B8.14
other errors in committal B8.12
other powers B8.14
other than as a dangerous offender B8.2–B8.4
plea and plea before venue B8.13
pre-sentence reports B8.16
related offences, for B8.8–B8.9
suspended sentences, and B8.14–B8.15
triable either way offences, for B8.14
communications network offences A16.7
compensation orders B10Z
concurrent sentences
totality principle B45.49
conditional discharge
availability B45.24
breach E1.2
Consolidated Criminal Practice Direction B5.1
deferment of sentence and B16.19
generally B22Z
juveniles E1.2
security for good behaviour B5.20

Sentencing – *cont.*
conditional discharge – *cont.*
sexual assault A53.9
sexual offences against children A52.14
youth court E1.2
consecutive sentences
imprisonment B34.22–B34.32
totality principle B45.49
consideration of sentences B45.36–B45.48
considerations to be taken into account B45.3–B45.6, B34.22–B34.55
control of arms traffic A76A.5–A76A.7
controlled drugs
cultivation of cannabis A27.4
fail/refuse to provide sample A24.2
fraudulent evasion of prohibition by bringing into/taking out of UK A27B.4
generally A25.16
permitting premises to be used A27A.4
possessing with intent to supply to another A26.5–A26.20
possession A25.16–A25.18
supplying or offering to supply a controlled drug A26.5–A26.20
trafficking A25.3, A26.20
controlling behaviour in intimate or family relationship A17A.4
costs
defence costs on acquittal B12.16–B12.17
introduction B12.2–B12.2A
legal representatives, against B12.20
miscellaneous provisions B12.21–B12.23
prosecution costs B12.3–B12.15
third parties, against B12.20A

Sentencing – *cont.*
costs – *cont.*
unnecessarily or improperly incurred B12.19
criminal damage A18.3, A18.32, B15.6
Crown Court
committal for sentencing B8.1–B8.16
young offenders, of B21.33
cruelty to a child A19.32–A19.34
custodial sentences
see **Custodial sentences**
dangerous adult offenders B8.1
dangerous dogs
available sentences A72.9
Guideline A72.8–A72.8A
introduction A72.6
dangerous offenders E3.18C
decision B43.1, B43.2, B43.3, B43.4
deferment of sentence
ancillary orders B16.5
compensation provisions B16.10, B16.16
conditional discharge B16.19
consent B16.1
failure to comply with requirements B16.20
limitations B16.1–B16.4
maximum period B16.17
offence during B16.21
reasons B16.10
requirements as to conduct B16.4
sentence after period of deferral B16.2
undertaking to comply with requirements B16.1
victim's concerns B16.16
when appropriate B16.10
deportation B17Z
deprivation order B18.7
detention and training order
see **Detention and training orders**

Sentencing – *cont.*
discharge
see **Absolute discharge; Conditional discharge**
availability B45.24
generally B22Z
sexual assault A53.9
sexual offences against children A52.14
youth court E1.2
disclosing private sexual images A19A.4
disorderly behaviour A20.19
disqualification from keeping animals A5.5
domestic burglary A12.20
domestic violence A15.34
driving with a concentration of specified controlled drug in excess of specified limit C22A.7
drug assessment
failure to attend initial/remain for initial assessment A23.3
drugs
cultivation of cannabis A27.4
fail/refuse to provide sample A24.2
fraudulent evasion of prohibition by bringing into/taking out of UK A27B.4
generally A25.16
permitting premises to be used A27A.4
possessing with intent to supply to another A26.5–A26.20
possession A25.16–A25.18
supplying or offering to supply a controlled drug A26.5–A26.20
trafficking A25.3, A26.20
drunk and disorderly in a public place A28.8–A28.9
dumping a motor vehicle A83.7–A83.9

Sentencing – *cont.*
early release
see **Early release**
electricity abstraction/use without authority A1.4
explanation of sentence B45.61
exploitation of prostitution A29.4
exposure A30.3
extended sentences for dangerous adult offenders B8.1
failure to comply with community orders
approach and options A17.3
guideline B9.27
failure to co-operate with roadside breath test C24.9
failure to provide information as to identity of driver C32A.10
failure to provide specimen for analysis C23.7–C23.9
failure to surrender to custody A10.3
false accounting A31
false identity documents A32.3
female defendants with children B34.6
financial reporting order A4.18
fines
see **Fines**
firearms
carrying in a public place A33.11–A33.13
purchasing etc without certificate A76.18–A76.24
trespassing in a building or on land A77.10–A77.18
football related offences A34.15–A34.17
forfeiture, consideration of B45.52, B18.7, D6.33
forgery A78.10–A78.17
found on enclosed premises A79.6–A79.9

Sentencing – *cont.*
fraud
obtaining services dishonestly A37.4
possession of articles for A38.4
fraudulent evasion of duty A4.16–A4.18
grave crimes E3.18C
grievous bodily harm A70.7, A70.20
guardianship order B32Z
handling stolen goods A40.12
harassment A41.11A–A41.13
health and safety at work
costs of investigation A80.21
fines A80.22–A80.24
generally A80.20
hospital order B33Z
immigration offences A81.9–A81.17
imprisonment B15.2, B34Z
inarticulate unrepresented defendant, mitigation and B45.48
indecent photographs of children A43.9
intimidation of witness A69.11
keeping a brothel used for prostitution A44.4
littering A83.31–A83.34
loss of employment etc, mitigating effects of B45.47
Magistrates' Courts Sentencing Guidance - Definitive Guideline B45.2
making off without payment A45.8
medical reports, consideration of D6.37
mentally disordered offenders B32Z, B15.23–B15.24, B34.18, D6.37
mitigation
custodial sentences B15.10
generally B45.37–B45.48

Sentencing – *cont.*
mitigation – *cont.*
guilty plea B45.37, B45.46, B45.65, D6.20
health and safety offences A80.20
list of mitigating factors B45.2A
loss of employment etc B45.47
offender mitigation B45.2A
older offenders B45.39
previous convictions B45.40
seriousness of offence and B45.6, B45.17–B45.20
unrepresented defendant B45.48
youth of offender B45.38
motor vehicle
dumping A83.7–A83.9
interference A63.6
taking without consent A65.18–A65.20
vehicle registration/trade plate fraud A64.5
no previous convictions B34.6
non-domestic burglary A13.19
non-molestation orders
breach A46.4
objectives of sentencing B45.4–B45.6
obstructing or resisting a constable in the execution of his duty A47.15
obtaining services dishonestly A37.4
offensive weapons
possession A11.15
older offenders B45.39
options available B45.21–B45.35
poaching A86.31–A86.32A
powers
tables B43.1–B43.3
pre-sentence reports
adjournment to obtain D6.34

Sentencing – *cont.*
pre-sentence reports – *cont.*
committal to Crown Court for sentence B8.16
community orders B45.50
conditional bail and D8.62
custodial sentences B15.21–B15.22, B34.16–B34.18
failure to obtain B21.19, B34.17
generally D6.34–D6.35
imprisonment B34.16–B34.18
mentally disordered offenders B15.24, B21.20, B34.18
purpose D6.35
young offenders institution B21.17–B21.19
youth court D6.39
previous convictions
effect B45.3, B45.40, D6.32
private sexual images
disclosure with intent to cause distress A19A.4
probation officer recommendations B45.50
process of B5
prohibited commercial practices A75.7–A75.10
pronouncement of sentence D6.31
proportionality B45.49
prostitution
child prostitution A14.6
exploitation A29.4
keeping a brothel A44.4
protection of public B45.4, B21.16
protective orders
breach A46.4
purposes of sentencing B45.4–B45.6
racially or religiously aggravated assault
common assault A15.33
general A20.19, A21.16, A21.17, B45.2B

Sentencing – *cont.*
railway fare evasion A48.9
re-opening convictions B38.5
reasons for sentence, giving
generally B45.53, B45.61, B34.20
young offenders, in case of B21.34
remission to another court B1
reparation order B38
reports, consideration of D6.32–D6.39
rescinding sentences/orders on conviction B38.2
restitution order B39
restraining orders
breach A46.4
restriction clauses B33.10–B33.16
road traffic offences
careless driving C25.20–C25.21
causing death by careless or inconsiderate driving C16A.10
dangerous condition/bodywork C10.7–C10.9
dangerous driving C16.18–C16.22
death by inconsiderate driving, causing C16A.10
defective brakes C9.16–C9.20
defective lights C34.21–C34.22
disqualification pending C5.39
driving licence offences C17.21–C17.22, C18.21–C18.32
driving when 'unfit through drink or drugs' C20.19–C20.20
driving whilst disqualified C19.8–C19.17
excess alcohol, drive/attempt to drive or in charge C22.32–22.61, C22.65

Sentencing – *cont.*
road traffic offences – *cont.*
failing to produce documents C17.21–17.22
failing to stop/report accident C31.17–C31.19
failure to co-operate with roadside breath test C24.9
failure to provide specimen for analysis C23.7–C23.9
insurance certificate, failure to produce C17.21–C17.22
motor cyclist not wearing helmet C35.7–C35.8
no excise licence C47.18
no insurance C33.23–C33.31
no test certificate C51
obstruction C36.10–C36.16
opening door C37.7–C37.9
overloading/exceeding axle weight C38.20–C38.21
pelican/zebra crossing contravention C39.20–C39.21
penalty points system C5.10–C5.38
reasonable consideration, driving without C46.19–C46.23
seat belt offences C48.19
speeding C49.36–C49.37
steering, defective C50.4
stopping on pedestrian crossing C40.10–C40.17
traffic signs, failing to comply with C52.17–C52.18
tyres, defective C53.7–C53.8
'unfit through drink or drugs', driving when C20.19–C20.20
unlicensed, disqualified or uninsured drivers, causing death by driving C16B.6
school non-attendance A49.4
seriousness of offence
associated offence B45.9
determining B45.7–B45.16
generally B45.3, B45.6

Sentencing – *cont.*
seriousness of offence – *cont.*
mitigation and B45.6, B45.17–B45.20
services, obtaining dishonestly A37.4
sex offenders register
failure to comply with notification requirements A50.4
sexual activity in a public lavatory A51.3
sexual assault
child under 13 A52.12–A52.16
notification requirements A52.14, A53.9
sexual images
disclosure with intent to cause distress A19A.4
short or fast-delivery reports D6.36
social security benefits
false statement/representation to obtain A54.6
soliciting for hire A56.3
statement accompanying
generally B45.53–B45.54
victim personal statement B45.55
structure
Magistrates' Courts Sentencing Guidance - Definitive Guideline B45.2
supervision order
see Supervision order
suspended sentence
see Suspended sentence
tax credit fraud A55.4
taxi-touting A56.3
theft
compensation A57.39
general offences A57.37
going equipped for A58.8
motor vehicles A57.37
shop or stall, from A57.37A
structure of decision A57.38

Sentencing – *cont.*
threatening behaviour A21.16
threats to kill A59.5
totality principle B45.49
trade marks
unauthorised use A60.5
transfer of criminal proceedings B46.1
TV licence payment evasion A61.15
unauthorised use of trade marks, A60.5
unfair commercial practices A75.7–A75.10
unrepresented defendants
mitigation B45.48
varying sentences/orders on conviction B38.2–7.B74
vehicle interference A63.6
vehicle registration/trade plate fraud A64.5
vehicle taking
aggravated A66.16–A66.17
without consent A65.18–A65.20
victim personal statement B45.55
violent disorder A67.10
voyeurism A68.5–A68.6
witness intimidation A69.11
wounding A70.20
young offenders
detention and training order B15.6
generally B40.3–B40.5, B43.1, B43.2, B43.3, B43.4
remission to another court B40.3–B40.5
young offender institution, committal to B15.3–B15.5, B21Z
youth of offender as mitigating factor B45.38
youth court B40.3–B40.5, B43.1, B43.2, B43.3, B43.4, E4

Services
obtaining dishonestly A37
Sex offenders register
failure to comply with notification requirements A50
Sexual activity in a public lavatory
charge A51.1
definitions A51.2
generally A51.1
maximum penalty A51.1
notes A51.2
sentencing A51.3
Sexual assault
absolute discharge A53.9
anonymity of victim A52.11
clearing the court A52.10
conditional discharge A53.9
consent A53.5
defences A53.5
generally A53
juvenile offenders A53.9
notification requirements following conviction A52.14, A53.9
reporting restrictions D1B.7
sentencing A52.12–A52.16
sexual harm prevention order A53.10
touching A52.4, A53.4, A53.5
Sexual disease
infection through consensual sex A70.5
Sexual harm prevention orders
'appropriate date' B44.6
breach B44.8
conviction, on B44.2
criteria B44.4
discharge B44.7
duration B44.5
guidance B44.3
interim orders B44.7
introduction B44.1
notification requirements B44.7
'qualifying offender' B44.6
renewal B44.7
sexual assault, and A53.10
Sexual harm prevention orders – *cont.*
variation B44.7
Sexual images
disclosure with intent to cause distress
charge A19A.1
'consent' A19A.2
defences A19A.3
definitions A19A.2
'discloses' A19A.2
'filming' A19A.2
general note A19A.2
'photograph or film' A19A.2
'private' A19A.2
sentencing A19A.4
'sexual' A19A.2
Sexual offences against children
see also **Child prostitution and pornography; Indecent photographs of children**
absolute discharge A52.14
anonymity of victim A52.11
clearing the court A52.10
competence A52.8
conditional discharge A52.14
defences A52.7
evidence A52.8
introduction A52.1
mistake as to age A52.7
notification requirements following conviction A52.14, A53.9
privacy A52.10
reporting restrictions A52.11
risk of sexual harm order A52.16
sentencing A52.12–A52.16
sexual activity A52.4
sexual offences prevention order A52.16
touching A52.4
Sexual offences prevention orders
breach B44.8
generally A52.16
Sexual orientation
actual bodily harm A8.10–A8.16

Sexual orientation – *cont.*
aggravation of offence B45.2B
common assault A15.7
Sheep
see **Animals; Livestock**
Shooting galleries
generally A71.6
Short or fast-delivery reports
generally D6.36
Shotguns
see also **Firearms**
carrying in a public place A33
certificate
cancellation A76.24, A77.18, A88.11
exemptions A88.6
generally A88.5
forfeiture A33.13, A88.10, D6.33
generally A11.3, A76.7
meaning A33.6, A88.4
purchasing etc without certificate A88
sawn-off shotgun A76.18
smooth-bore gun A76.7
trespassing in a building or on land A77.9
visitor's permit A76.10, A88.6
Silence
inferences D6.22
right to remain silent C8.22
Sketches of court
general prohibition D1B.9
Social media
see also **Twitter**
reporting restrictions D1B.8
Social security benefit
false statement/representation to obtain
causes or allows A54.5
change of circumstances A54.3
sentencing A54.6
time limits A54.4
Soliciting for hire
charge A56.1
definitions A56.2
Soliciting for hire – *cont.*
generally A56.1
maximum penalty A56.1
notes A56.2
sentencing A56.3
Soliciting for prostitution
generally A29.1, A82
Solicitor
right to consult B33.2
SORN (Statutory Off Road Notification)
generally C47.17
Special constable
assault during execution of duty A9
Special measures directions
vulnerable and intimidated witnesses D6.13A
Speed assessment equipment detection devices
breach of requirement as to C38A
Speeding
evidence C49.4–C49.9
limit prescribed for class of vehicle C49.31
motorways, on C49.20–C49.22
necessity defence C49.7
restricted roads, on C49.16–C49.19
sentencing C49.36–C49.37
speed and distance chart C2
speed limit signs C49.15
temporary or experimental limits C49.32–C49.35A
traffic signs
generally C49.10
speed limits C49.15
unrestricted road, in C49.23–C49.25
warning of prosecution C49.3
Sporting activities
assault A15.18
Sporting events
see also **Football-related offences**
actual bodily harm A8.23
control of alcohol A35

Spouse
see **Husband and wife**
Stalking
aggravated offence A41.8B
alternative verdict A41.6
animal rights protestors A41.5
basic offence A41.8A
charges A41.1–A41.4
consultation with complainant, A41.14
course of conduct A41.7–A41.8B
defences
generally A41.10–A41.11
introduction A41.8C
definitions A41.7–A41.9
disorderly behaviour A20.3A
home, in his A41.5
ECHR and A41.10
general note A41.7-A41.11
insanity, and A41.8
knows or ought to have known A41.8
mode of trial A41.6
number of incidents A41.7
person in his home, of A41.5
presumed knowledge A41.8
'purpose' A41.10
racially or religiously aggravated
charges A41.2, A41.4
generally A21.1–A21.18
introduction A41.9
restraining orders
see also **Restraining orders**
generally A41.13–A41.14
sentencing A41.11A–A41.12
stalking
aggravated offence A41.8B
defences A41.8C
generally A41.8A
telephone calls A41.7
terms of order A46.3
two or more complainants A41.7
Starting pistols
generally A33.9, A76.6, A77.8
Statutory declarations
see also **Oaths**
generally F5.56–F5.64
Statutory nuisance
abatement notice
appeal against A84.9
contravention/failure to comply A84.10
generally A84.8
introduction A74.9
abatement order A84.22
appeal A84.18
complaint by person aggrieved
costs A84.31
generally A84.19–A84.32
defence A84.16–A84.17, A84.25
exceptions A84.5
local authority
court direction to A84.32
proceedings by A84.7–A84.18
magistrate's order A84.22
noise A74.1, A74.9, A84.2, A84.33–A84.36
prejudicial to health, meaning A84.3
prohibition order A84.22
reasonable excuse A84.17
traffic noise A84.3
Statutory Off Road Notification (SORN)
generally C47.17
Stay of proceedings
abuse of process
generally D1B.11–D1B.12
sending for trial D4.11
youth court E3.25
Stealing
see also **Burglary; Theft**
domestic burglary A12.16
meaning A57.3
non-domestic burglary A13.16
Stealth knife
generally A11.4
Steering
defective C50

Stolen goods
see also **Property in possession of police**
consideration paid in respect of A40.11
handling *see* Handling stolen goods
restitution order B39
Stun guns
possession of offensive weapons A11.4
Summary proceedings
absence defendant of accused, in D6.19
active case management D6.3
adjournment applications
approach D6.7
bad character D6.14–D6.15
checklist D6.6
discharge of pre-trial rulings D6.13A
disclosure of unused material D6.12
first/subsequent hearing D6.12
hearsay evidence D6.16
initial disclosure D6.11
introduction D6.5
legal aid D6.10
plea D6.9
power to make, vary or discharge pre-trial rulings D6.13
pre-trial issues D6.13–D6.16
prosecution evidence D6.11
special measures for vulnerable and intimidated witnesses D6.13A
subsequent hearing D6.12
trials, and D6.17–D6.17E
variation of pre-trial rulings D6.13
amendment of charge or information D6.23
appeals
against conviction and or sentence D6.46
Summary proceedings – *cont.*
appeals – *cont.*
case stated, by way of D6.47
Crown Court, to D6.46
High Court, to D6.47
introduction D6.45
judicial review applications D6.48
bad character
defendant D6.14
non-defendant D6.15
case management D6.3
consideration of guilt D6.30–D6.31
Criminal Practice Directions D6.3
Criminal Procedure Rules (CPR) D6.1
duty of the court D6.3
duty of the parties
generally D6.2
identification of the issues D6.4AB
fast-delivery reports D6.36
first hearing
not guilty plea D6.4AA
other issues D6.4B–D6.4C
guilty plea
application to change D6.26
application to withdraw D6.27
generally D6.18
introduction D6.24
mitigating factor, as D6.20
nature D6.24
Newton hearing D6.24
post, by D6.40–D6.43
identification of the issues D6.4AB
issues capable of determination at first hearing
generally D6.4B–D6.4C
identification D6.4AB
judicial review applications D6.48
legal advice D6.28–D6.29
medical reports D6.37–D6.39
no case to answer D6.21

Summary proceedings – *cont.*
not guilty plea
amendment of charge or information D6.23
application to change to D6.26
change of D6.20
first hearing D6.4AA
inferences from silence D6.22
introduction D6.19
no case to answer D6.21
post, by D6.44
silence D6.22
trial in absence D6.19
notification of intention to call defence witnesses D6.2
overriding objective D6.2
pre-sentence reports D6.34–D6.35
pre-trial hearings in magistrates' court D6.4A
reports
introduction D6.32–D6.33
medical reports D6.37–D6.39
pre-sentence reports D6.34–D6.35
short or fast-delivery reports D6.36
timetable D6.3, D6.19
trial in absence D6.19
Supervision
custodial sentences B15.22A
detention and training orders B19.9
Supervision orders
breach
detention in young offender institution B15.4
generally E1.2
payment of fines B28.35, B28.55, B28.96
Supplying or offering to supply a controlled drug
aggravation of offence A26.4A
'being concerned in supplying' A26.4A
defences A26.4D
ECHR and A26.4D
Supplying or offering to supply a controlled drug – *cont.*
generally A26
intent to supply A26.4
sentencing A26.5–A26.20
'supply' A26.4A
Surcharge
see also **Victim surcharge**
compensation orders B10.1
Surety
see also **Recognisance**
conditional bail and D8.66–D8.68
Suspended sentence orders
breach
introduction B34.47
sentencing B34.55
community orders, and B34.47
community requirement B34.46
generally B34.40–B34.50
introduction B15.2, B28.52, B34.21
sentencing guidelines B34.50
unpaid work requirement B34.46
young offender institution B21.32

T

Taking without consent
see **Motor vehicle**
Tape recorders
use in court D1B.10
Tax credit fraud
charge A55.1
definitions A55.3
generally A55.1
maximum penalty A55.1
mode of trial A55.2
notes A55.3
sentencing A55.4
Taxi-touting/soliciting for hire
charge A56.1
definitions A56.2
generally A56.1

Taxi-touting/soliciting for hire – *cont.*
maximum penalty A56.1
notes A56.2
sentencing A56.3
Telephone kiosk
as public place A83.21
Television
fraudulently receiving programmes F2.28
licence payment evasion A61
Temporary event notice
closure due to noise A84.7
Tent
threatening behaviour in A21.9
Test certificate
failure to produce C17
no test certificate C51
renewal C51.17
Theft
acquiring in good faith A57.16
appropriates A57.8–A57.16
attempting the impossible A57.19
being entrusted with property A57.24
belonging to another A57.22–A57.31
borrowing or lending A57.33
breach of trust A57
burglary
see **Burglary**
charity shop donations A57.22
compensation orders, and A57.39, B10.3
completion of offence A57.10
definition A57.3
dishonestly A57.5–A57.7
dwelling, from A57
generally A57
going equipped for
disqualification C5.5
generally A58
motor vehicles A58.1, C5.5, C5.33
sentencing A58.8
Theft – *cont.*
intention of permanently depriving A57.32–A57.36
land, of A57.18
lending or borrowing A57.33
mistake, getting property by A57.25
motor vehicle, of
disqualification A57.40
going equipped for A58.1, C5.5, C5.33
reduction of charge A57.34, A65.10
partnership property A57.36
person, from A57
power of attorney, and A57.18
proof of stealing one article enough A57.35
property A57.17–A57.21
repentance A57.10
sentencing
compensation A57.39
general offences A57.37
going equipped for A58.8
motor vehicles A57.37
shop or stall, from A57.37A
structure of decision A57.38
shop, from A57
things growing wild A57.20
trust property A57.23
wild creatures A57.21
Threatening behaviour
see also **Disorderly behaviour**
binding over A21.18
dwelling-house, in A21.9
ECHR and A20.5, A21.5A
freedom of expression A20.5, A21.5A
intent A21.5, A21.7
police officers, towards A21.10
private premises A21.9
public place A21.9
racially or religiously aggravated A21.10
sentencing A21.16
threatening, abusive, insulting words/behaviour A21.5
violence A21.6

Threatening to destroy or damage property
generally A18A
Threats
affray A2.5
burglary A13.4
carrying of weapons A2.5
communications network offences A16.2
possession of offensive weapons A11.11
witness intimidation A69
Threats to kill
foetus A59.4
generally A59
lawful excuse A59.3
sentencing A59.5
Ticket touting
football matches A34.6A
Tobacco
fraudulent evasion of duty
appeals A4.19
attempt A4.6
charge A4.1–A4.2
death of informant A4.9
definitions A4.4–A4.11
duplicity A4.7
financial reporting orders A4.18
fraudulent evasion A4.6
intent to defraud A4.4
knowingly A4.4–A4.5
mistake A4.11
mode of trial A4.3
notes A4.4–A4.11
presumptions against defendant A4.10
prosecution A4.8
sentencing A4.16–A4.18
value of goods A4.17
Trade marks
unauthorised use of etc
burden of proof A60.3
charge A60.1
companies, and A60.4
defences A60.3
definitions A60.3
Trade marks – *cont.*
unauthorised use of etc – *cont.*
generally A60.1
'grey goods' A60.3
mode of trial A60.3
notes A60.3
reasonable belief A60.3
sentencing A60.5
validity of registration A60.3
Traffic signs
failure to comply with C52
generally C49.10
speed limits C49.15
Trafficking drugs
see also **Drugs**
confiscation orders A26.20
minimum sentence A25.3
Trailer
dangerous condition/bodywork, using in C10
defective brakes C9
defective tyres C53
definition C9.9
interference A63.2
opening door C37
speed assessment equipment detection devices C38A
Transfer of criminal proceedings
generally B46.1
Transgender identity
actual bodily harm A8.10–A8.16
aggravation of offence related to B45.2B
common assault A15.7
Trespass
aggravated A18.19
burglary
domestic A12.10, A12.17
non-domestic A13.7, A13.17
firearm in a building or on land, with A77
Truancy
parenting order B37.3
Trust property
criminal damage A18.24
theft A57.23

TV licence payment evasion
  charge A61.1
  concessions A61.8
  definitions A61.2–A61.9
  duration A61.7–A61.8
  exemptions A61.8
  generally A61.1
  licence A61.5–A61.6
  maximum penalty A61.1
  notes A61.2–A61.9
  sentencing A61.15
  using A61.3–A61.4
Twitter
  offences A16.2
  reporting restrictions D1B.8
Tyres
  defective C53

U

Unauthorised use of trade marks
  burden of proof A60.3
  charge A60.1
  companies, and A60.4
  defences A60.3
  definitions A60.3
  generally A60.1
  'grey goods' A60.3
  mode of trial A60.3
  notes A60.3
  reasonable belief A60.3
  sentencing A60.5
  validity of registration A60.3
Unconditional bail
  generally D8.3
Unfair commercial practices
  generally A75
Unlicensed, disqualified or uninsured drivers
  causing death by driving C16B
Unpaid work
  community orders B9.10
  suspended sentences B34.46
  youth rehabilitation order B49.8
Urine, alcohol in
  see Alcohol
Using electricity without authority
  charge A1.1
  definitions A1.3
  dishonestly A1.3
  generally A1.1
  maximum penalty A1.1
  mode of trial A1.2
  notes A1.3
  sentencing A1.4

V

VAT evasion
  generally A62
Vehicles
  burglary
    domestic A12.15
    non-domestic A13.7
  interference A63
  registration plate fraud A64
  taking
    aggravated A66
    without consent A65
  threatening behaviour in A21.9
  trade plate fraud A64
Vessel
  burglary
    domestic A12.15
    non-domestic A13.7
  threatening behaviour in A21.9
Vibration
  as noise A84.4
Victim personal statement
  generally B45.55
Victim surcharge
  compensation, and B50.3
  enforcement B50.4
  generally B50.1
  levels B50.2
Video link
  see Live video link
Video remands
  generally D8.22A

Violence
see also Actual bodily harm; Affray; Assault; Disorder; Disorderly behaviour; Grievous bodily harm; Harassment; Threatening behaviour; Violent disorder
affray A2.7
arson A18.2
burglary A13.4
endangerment of life A18.2
harassment A41
meaning A2.7–A2.8, A67.5
putting people in fear A41
threatened A21.6
witness intimidation A69.4
Violent disorder
generally A67
intent A67.7
intoxication A67.8
person of reasonable firmness A67.6
sentencing A67.10
three or more persons A67.4
violence, meaning A67.5
Violent offender orders
appeals B47.7
application B47.3
breach B47.8
conditions B47.4
discharge B47.5
generally B47Z
interim orders B47.6
notice provisions B47.7
notification requirements B47.4
prohibitions B47.4
qualifying offender B47.2
renewal B47.5
restrictions B47.4
variation B47.5
Voluntary restitution
electricity abstraction/use without authority A1.4
Voyeurism
generally A68

W

Warrants
arrest, of
bailed person failing to surrender D8.82
immigration offences A81.7
entry, of
see also Warrants of entry
applicants F5.1
authority to issue F5.2–F5.5
gas and electricity suppliers F5.31–F5.38
immigration offences A81.7
issued to persons other than police officers F5.25–F5.30
search for evidence F5.6–F5.24A
signature F5.39–F5.40
search for and remove mental patients
applications F5.66
content F5.67
duration F5.69
introduction F5.65
place of safety F5.68
Warrants of arrest
bailed person failing to surrender D8.82
generally F5.46
immigration offences A81.7
youth injunctions B48.5
Warrants of entry
applicants F5.1
applications by police F5.3
authority to issue
applications by police F5.3
forcible search F5.4
introduction F5.2
search for evidence F5.5
search for unlawful articles F5.4
customs and excise officers F5.27
forcible search F5.4
gas and electricity suppliers, for
Code of Practice F5.37

Warrants of entry – *cont.*
gas and electricity suppliers, for – *cont.*
consent of occupier F5.34
generally F5.31–F5.32
repair of damage F5.38
requirements F5.35–F5.36
right of entry F5.33
immigration offences A81.7
issued to persons other than police officers
customs and excise officers F5.27
generally F5.25–F5.26
search for evidence of indictable offence, to
customs and excise offences F5.27
disclosure of material used to obtain warrant F5.24A
discretion to issue F5.17
excluded material F5.16
generally F5.6
indictable offence F5.8
introduction F5.5
legal privilege F5.11
premises F5.10
procedure F5.17A–F5.24A
reasonable grounds for believing F5.7
reasonable suspicion F5.7
relevant evidence F5.9
special procedure material F5.16
search for unlawful articles, to F5.4
signature F5.39–F5.40
Warrants to search for and remove mental patients
applications F5.66
content F5.67
duration F5.69
introduction F5.65
place of safety F5.68
Wasted costs orders
generally A84.31, B12.19, D6.12
Weapons
see also **Offensive weapons**
affray A2.5
Wheel clamping
fine defaulters B28.38, B28.62
removal of clamp A18.19
Wife
see **Husband and wife**
Wild creatures
appropriating A57.21
property, as A18.21
theft A57.21
Witnesses
anonymity D1B.7
contempt of court D3.9
intimidation A69
live video link in criminal proceedings D6.13A, D8.22C
notification of intention to call defence witnesses D6.2
preventing publication of matter leading to identification D1B.7
recognisance B5.8
refusal to take oath or answer question D3.9
special measures *see* Special measures direction
Work permit
see also **Immigration offences**
possession of false permits A81.3
Wounding
generally A70
intent A70.5
racially or religiously aggravated A70
recklessness A70.5
sentencing A70.20

Y

Young offender institutions
age limits B15.3, B15.4, B21.4, B21.22
ancillary orders B21.36

Young offender institutions – *cont.*
announcement of sentence B21.35
associated offence B21.8
breach offences B21.47
consecutive terms B21.31
criteria for imposing sentence B21.5–B21.6
Crown Court, committal to B21.33
detention in
generally B15.3–B15.5, B45.33, B21Z
replacement by imprisonment B15.3, B45.33
early release
further offences B21.46
generally B21.37–B21.46
supervision following B21.38
'imprisonable offence' B21.3
legal representation B15.8, B21.21
length of sentence B15.5, B21.23–B21.32
maximum length of sentence B21.23
mentally disturbed offenders B21.20
minimum length of sentence B21.25
offences for which appropriate B21.7–B21.10
offenders under 18 B21.22
passing sentence B21.23–B21.34
period of detention B15.5
pre-sentence reports
failure to obtain B21.19
generally B21.17–B21.18
protection of public B21.16
reasons for decisions B21.34
seriousness of offence B21.7
sexual offences B21.10
suspended sentence B21.32
violent offence B21.9
Young offenders
adult courts
remittal B40.5

Young offenders – *cont.*
age
determining age of defendant E1.2
aged between 18 and 21
see also **Young offender institution**
attendance centre, committal to B4Z, B28.98
detention *see* Young offender institution
imprisonable offence, meaning B21.3
legal representation B15.8, B21.21
local court, remission to B40.4, E3.23
sentencing B15.3–B15.5, B43.1, B43.2, B43.3, B43.4
aged under 15
see **Child**
anti-social behaviour orders, and B2.4
attendance centre orders B4Z
bail, remand on D8.6
committal to Crown Court for sentence
generally E3.18H
procedure E3.20–E3.25
criminal proceedings
see also **Young offender institution**
attendance centre orders B4Z
fines B28.5–B28.6, B28.86–B28.99
guardianship order B32Z
hospital order B33Z
legal representation B15.8
local court, remission to B40.4, E3.23
oath E3.22
remission to adult court E3.24
secure accommodation E3.7–E3.8
sending for trial E3.18

Young offenders – *cont.*
criminal proceedings – *cont.*
sentencing B43.1, B43.2, B43.3, B43.4
supervision order *see* Supervision order
time limits E3.25
dangerous offenders E3.18C
detention and training orders
availability B45.33
breach of supervision B19.10
conditions B19.3–B19.4
consecutive orders B19.8
credit for time on remand B19.6A–B19.8
duration B19.6
generally B19.1–B19.5
introduction B15.6
offences during currency B19.10
persistent offender B19.4
restrictions B19.3
sentencing guidance B19.11
statement conditions met B19.5
supervision B19.9
time spent on bail and remand B15.20
determining age of defendant E1.2
electronic monitoring
see **Electronic monitoring**
fines B28.5–B28.6
aged 10 to 17 B28.93–B28.95
aged 18 to 21 B28.86–B28.92
parental responsibility for payment B28.7–B28.10, B28.95
grave crimes E3.18C
homicide D8.32
incapable of following proceedings
abuse of process E3.25
jointly charged with adult
further offences E3.18A
generally E3.18
legal representation
see also **Representation orders**

Young offenders – *cont.*
legal representation – *cont.*
generally B15.8, B21.21
mental illness
powers of court B33Z
possible orders E4
pre-sentence reports B21.17–B21.19
rape D8.32
referral order
see **Referral order**
rehabilitation order
see **Youth rehabilitation order**
remand in custody
see **Remand in custody**
remission to adult court E3.24
secure accommodation, remand in E3.7–E3.8
sending for trial
further offences E3.18A
generally E3.18
jointly charged with adults E3.18B
sentencing
detention and training order B15.6
generally B40.3–B40.5, B43.1, B43.2, B43.3, B43.4
remission to another court B40.3–B40.5
young offender institution, committal to B15.3–B15.5, B21Z
youth of offender as mitigating factor B45.38
sexual assault A53.9
trial, committal for E3.18
Young person
see also **Young offenders**
air guns
failing to prevent possession A71A.1–A71A.3
possession A71.1–A71.8
binding over parent or guardian
Consolidated Criminal Practice Direction B5.20
generally B5.18–B5.19

Young person – *cont.*
definition A19.7
definition of 'juveniles' E1.1
determining age of defendant E1.2
guardianship order B32Z
hospital order B33Z
parenting order B37.1
possession of air guns
failing to prevent A71A.1–A71A.3
general A71.1–A71.8
reporting restrictions D1B.7
Youth court
abuse of process, and E3.25
adult court remission
generally B40.5
introduction E3.24
age of criminal responsibility E3.2
anti-social behaviour orders, and
generally B2.4
reporting restrictions E2.4
attendance of parent E3.3
bail, and E3.4
capacity of youth to following proceedings E3.25
committal to Crown Court for sentence
abuse of process E3.25
generally E3.18H
oath E3.22
procedure E3.20–E3.25
remission to adult court E3.24
remission to local court E3.23
composition E2.1–E2.2
conditional discharge
breach E1.2
criminal proceedings
age of criminal responsibility E3.2
attendance of parent E3.3
introduction E3.1
remand E3.4
Crown Court sitting as E3.18G
Youth court – *cont.*
dangerous offenders E3.18C
delay E3.25
detention and training orders B15.6
fines B28.5–B28.6, B28.86–B28.99
generally E1.3, E2
grave crimes E3.18C
hearings E2.3
hospital orders B33Z
interim hospital orders B33.22
local authority accommodation, and
generally E3.5
secure accommodation, and E3.7–E3.17
local court remission
generally B40.4
introduction E3.23
magistrates' court remissions B40.3, B40.4, E3.23
murder charge D8.32
oath E3.22
persons present during hearing E2.3
plea before venue procedure
accused is present E3.18E
generally E3.18D
youth is absent E3.18F
possible orders E4
pre-sentence reports D6.39
remand
bail, on E3.4
generally E3.4
local authority accommodation, to E3.5
secure accommodation, and E3.7–E3.17
youth detention accommodation, to E3.6
remission from
adult court, to E3.24
generally B40.4–B40.5
local court, to E3.23
reparation orders B38

Youth court – *cont.*
reporting restrictions E2.4–E2.5
representation orders
choice of legal representative D7.10
contribution orders D7.11
duty solicitor D7.12
financial eligibility D7.7–D7.9
generally D7.2–D7.3
qualification D7.5–D7.6
scope D7.4
secure accommodation, and
criteria E3.8–E3.17
generally E3.7
sending for trial
further offences, and E3.18A
generally E3.18
jointly charged with adult E3.18B
sentencing
committal to Crown Court for sentence E3.18H, E3.20–E3.25
generally B40.3–B40.5, B43.1, B43.2, B43.3, B43.4
introduction E4.1–E4.2
overarching principles E5.1
specific guidelines E5.1
stay of proceedings E3.25
supervision orders
breach E1.2
detention in young offender institution B15.4
payment of fines B28.35, B28.55, B28.96
time limits E3.25
vulnerable accused E3.25
youth detention accommodation, to E3.6
youth incapable of following proceedings E3.25
Youth injunctions
appeals B48.11
applications B48.6
arrest warrants B48.5
arrest without warrant B48.4
breach B48.9–B48.10
Youth injunctions – *cont.*
discharge B48.8
duration B48.3
interim injunctions B48.7
introduction B48.1
power of arrest B48.4
power to grant B48.2
remand on breach B48.9
transitional provisions B48.12
variation B48.8
warrants of arrest B48.5
without notice applications B48.6
Youth offender panels
generally B42.11
Youth rehabilitation orders (YRO)
activity requirement B49.6
attendance centre requirement B49.10
amendment B49.26
application to revoke B49.25
breach B49.23
commission of further offence B49.24
curfew requirement B49.12
drug treatment/drug testing requirement B49.19
duration B49.4A–B49.4B
education requirement B49.21
electronic monitoring
curfew requirement B49.12
duration B49.5
exclusion requirement B49.13
generally B49.3
intensive supervision and fostering B49.4
requirement B49.22
exclusion requirement B49.13
extended activity requirement B49.4
fostering requirement
generally B49.16
intensive supervision B49.4
generally B49.1
guidance B49.22A
intensive supervision and fostering B49.4

Youth rehabilitation orders (YRO) – *cont.*
intoxicating substance treatment requirement B49.20
local authority residence requirement B49.15
mental health treatment requirement B49.17–B49.18
programme requirement B49.9
prohibited activity requirement B49.11
requirements B49.2
activity B49.6
attendance centre B49.10
breach B49.23
curfew B49.3, B49.12
drug treatment/drug testing B49.19
education B49.21
electronic monitoring B49.22
exclusion B49.13
extended activity B49.4
fostering B49.4, B49.16
intensive supervision and surveillance B49.4–B49.4A, B49.5
intoxicating substance treatment B49.20

Youth rehabilitation orders (YRO) – *cont.*
requirements – *cont.*
introduction B49.2
local authority residence B49.15
mental health treatment B49.17–B49.18
programme B49.9
prohibited activity B49.11
residence B49.14
supervision B49.7
unpaid work B49.8
residence requirement B49.14
revocation B49.25
Sentencing Council guidance B49.22A
supervision requirement B49.7
unpaid work requirement B49.8

Z

Zebra crossings
contravention C39
stopping on C40